Federal Land Series

Federal Land Series

A CALENDAR OF ARCHIVAL MATERIALS ON THE LAND PATENTS ISSUED BY THE UNITED STATES GOVERNMENT, WITH SUBJECT, TRACT, AND NAME INDEXES

Volume 2 • 1799–1835

FEDERAL BOUNTY-LAND WARRANTS OF THE AMERICAN REVOLUTION

Clifford Neal Smith

AMERICAN LIBRARY ASSOCIATION · CHICAGO 1973

Library of Congress Cataloging in Publication Data

Smith, Clifford Neal.
Federal bounty-land warrants of the American Revolution, 1799-1835.

(His Federal land series, v. 2)
Includes bibliographical references.
1. Bounties, Military--United States. 2. United States--Genealogy. I. Title. II. Series.
KF5675.A73S6 vol. 2 343'.73'025 73-4767
ISBN 0-8389-0144-1

Printed in the United States of America

Contents

Maps

Introduction

This second volume of the *Federal Land Series* begins what might be called a subseries--volumes dealing with land patents arising from grants of land made as a result of military service in the American Revolution. Such a subseries becomes necessary because, upon investigation, it has been determined that the amount of material now becoming available to the researcher is too large to be compressed into one volume. For historians, this volume is a summary of transactions detailing speculation in federal bounty-land warrants and in the lands of the United States Military District of Ohio; for title searchers in the Ohio counties of Coshocton, Delaware, Franklin, Guernsey, Holmes, Knox, Licking, Marion, Morrow, Muskingum, and Tuscarawas, the volume provides definitive information on the patenting of some, or most, of the land therein; for genealogical researchers, proof of Revolutionary War service antedating the better-known pension files is made accessible.

At the outset, it should be pointed out that this volume includes only those federal bounty-land warrants used in the patenting of land in the United States Military District of Ohio, plus warrants later exchanged for scrip. Not included are the transactions of thousands of veterans who obtained bounty land from the states in whose military units they had served, rather than from the federal government. Likewise excluded are the transactions of some veterans who exchanged their federal bounty-land warrants for land purchased from the Ohio Company or from

John Cleves Symmes.[1] All these transactions await indexing in further volumes of this Series.

The first promise of land in payment for military service in one of the 88 battalions of the Continental Line was made by the Continental Congress on 16 September 1776.[2] The amount of land offered was as follows:

Enlisted men and non-commissioned officers	100 acres
Ensigns	150
Lieutenants	200
Captains	300
Majors	400
Lieutenant Colonels	450
Lieutenant Colonels, when commanding military units[3]	500
Colonels	500

Officers of the medical corps were also to be issued bounty-land warrants--usually for 300 or 400 acres--but chaplains were to receive none. A later enactment promised 850 acres to brigadier generals and 1100 acres to major generals.

The states of New York, Pennsylvania, Virginia, North Carolina, and Georgia--having vast extents of vacant land to their westward--also offered land for service in the Continental Line or in state military units. Their bounties were much more generous than those of the federal government. The schedule of Virginia bounties, for example, ran as high as 15,000 acres for some general officers; that of North Carolina to 12,000 acres. It is no wonder, then, that confusion exists as to the grants actually made, for one must search the records of these five "land states," as well as the records of the federal government, for comprehensive coverage.[4]

By a resolution of 9 July 1788 the Confederation Congress authorized the Secretary of War to issue bounty-land warrants to all eligible veterans upon application. Under this resolution warrants numbered from 1 to 14,220 were issued and recorded in two registers at the War Department. The first of the two registers, containing notations on warrants 1 through 6912, was lost in an early fire. Recently, however, the documents underlying some of these warrants have come to light and have been microfilmed by the National Archives.[5]

There was also a second series of bounty-land warrants, as follows:

Warrant Numbers	*Congressional Authority*
1 - 272	Act of 3 March 1803
273 - 2119	Act of 15 April 1806

Eighteen additional warrants were issued at later dates. These special warrants are described in the introduction to National Archives Microcopy Publication M-829.

In a future volume of the *Federal Land Series*--after having indexed most of the known transactions flowing from Revolutionary War service--this writer intends to prepare a serial listing of the warrants, because it is not known with certainty whether all the warrant numbers were actually issued, and, if so, which of these warrants may have disappeared entirely from our view. Such an inventory of missing warrant numbers should, then, give incentive to further search and, one may hope, to their eventual discovery or reconstruction through other sources.[6]

The modern researcher is also confronted with another difficulty: War Department procedure called first for the issuance of a certificate of military service to the veteran. These certificates were assignable, and many veterans sold them to speculators. Upon presentation of the certificates, properly assigned by endorsement, the War Department then issued bounty-land warrants in the names of assignees, rather than in the names of the veterans. A large number of the warrants listed in this volume of the *Federal Land Series* show only the names of these assignees. This poses a serious problem for the genealogical researcher; fortunately, comparison of warrant numbers with other source materials has identified many of these unnamed veterans.

Actual patenting of land in exchange for bounty-land warrants was not begun until about 1800. By the act of 1 June 1796,[7] Congress authorized the locating of land in a 4000-square-mile tract in Northwest Territory, which became known as the United States Military District. The act required that the land be distributed in quarter-townships of 4000 acres. This meant that a would-be landowner, or an agent, had to accumulate bounty-land warrants in the amount of 4000 acres before presenting them to the Treasury Department for a patent to a quarter-township. Thus, it took the warrants of forty enlisted men to qualify for land in the District. Congress apparently intended that agents would put together the requisite amount of bounty-land warrants, obtain a patent to a 4000-acre quarter-township, and then issue deeds to the original warrantees for their portions thereof. Thus, a private was to assign his 100-acre warrant to an agent who, having accumulated a sufficient amount in warrants, would take title to a quarter-township and then issue a deed to the private for his 100 acres therein. This researcher has found little evidence that the procedure was followed, in fact. Major entrepreneurs, such as Jonathan Dayton, collected large quantities of bounty-land warrants through purchase from veterans or their assignees, and were issued patents to the corresponding number of quarter-townships in the United States Military District of Ohio. Rather than issuing deeds to the original warrantees or their assignees, the entrepreneurs sold the land to all comers, usually actual settlers. Although this seems not to have been the intent of Congress, it was more practical, for most veterans were in their fifties and sixties by the time that land became available in the Military District, and such persons could hardly be expected to leave settled homes and occupations for uncleared lands so close to uncontrolled Indian country. Therefore, the use of bounty-land warrants for the patenting of land in the United States Military District of Ohio cannot be taken as evidence *per se* that the original warrantees settled in the region.

The cumbersome nature of this method of distributing land in the United States Military District, as well as numerous accusations of fraud, soon convinced Congress that the remaining quarter-townships should be surveyed in 100-acre lots and patented directly to warrantees and their heirs. This volume of the *Federal Land Series* contains many examples of such individual land entries. In such cases, the veterans or their heirs are more likely to have settled on the land, but, again, this should not be inferred from federal records alone. Researchers will want to search for the first *deed* to the lot in question--a county, rather than a federal, record--for further evidence of possible settlement thereon by the original patentee.

Finally, it should be mentioned that, as locations within the United States Military District of Ohio became scarcer, Congress permitted, by the act of 30 May 1830,[8] outstanding bounty-land warrants to be exchanged for scrip. With scrip in hand, would-be landowners could locate land in Ohio, Indiana, or Illinois; later, the right was extended to lands anywhere within the public domain open to settlement. The federal government was still honoring its Revolutionary War scrip into the twentieth century.[9]

Sources Indexed in This Volume

The material indexed in this volume of the *Federal Land Series* covers a period from 1799 to about 1835, although final transactions based upon the scrip entries listed herein may have taken place at much later dates.

Source	Serial Entries	Title and Description
A	1 - 420	National Archives Record Group 49, "Records of the Bureau of Land Management," *United States Revolutionary War Bounty Land Warrants Used in the United States Military District of Ohio, and Related Papers (Acts of 1788, 1803, 1806)* (National Archives Microcopy Publication M-829, roll 1) "Register of Army Land Warrants, per Acts of 1796 and 1799." (This register previously appeared as National Archives Microcopy Publication T-1008, but without the index provided in Microcopy Publication M-829.) This register was maintained by the United States Treasury Department in

Source	Serial Entries	Title and Description
		Washington. Recorded therein are land entries from 1799 to 1805, including all the 4000-acre quarter-townships patented, as well as the individual patents to enlisted men and officers after the 1802 change in patenting requirements. As mentioned above, an index to the register has lately been discovered and microfilmed in the new M-829 publication (published in 1971 but first available to the public in the fall of 1972). This index is a partial one including only the names of the warrantees (many of whom were merely assignees and not the original veterans) prepared as a transactional finding aid. Patentees, heirs, devisees, agents, and tract designations are not indexed therein. As a consequence, this writer has re-indexed the entire register to include every name, tract description, and warrant number occurring.
B	421 - 1694	______, "Register of Military Land Warrants Presented to the Treasury for Locating and Patenting, 1804-1835." This register has only recently become known to researchers and is published for the first time in National Archives Microcopy Publication M-829, roll 1.

Source	Serial Entries	Title and Description

The register is a continuation of Source A and, during the first years thereof, includes a number of entries duplicating similar ones in Source A. Occasionally, however, these otherwise duplicative entries contain information or spelling variations not to be found in the corresponding Source A entries, so that the duplications are, in themselves, of considerable value, particularly to genealogical researchers.

Source B also has a partial index. Since this index does not include all names which occur in the register, or the tract descriptions, this writer has re-indexed the register entirely.

Attention is called to the many entries in which warrantees have used the services of their Congressmen to obtain patents. Having determined the state represented by the Congressman, one has almost certain evidence that this is the state in which a warrantee resided at the time he made his application for a patent.[10] This information can be of value to the genealogical researcher tracing a lineage back to the Atlantic seaboard. Evidence of Congressional intercession will also be of use to the

Source	Serial Entries	Title and Description
		historian and biographer interested in the activities of specific legislators. Beginning with serial entry 1619, conversions of bounty-land warrants to scrip are listed. Scrip holders and original warrantees are given, providing valuable clues as to heirs and devisees. Serial entry 1691 is of some interest. It is a list of "caveats," or warnings, listed by the Treasury Department and General Land Office clerks, setting forth certain cases of fraudulent warrants or irregular occurrences in specified land transactions.
C	1695 - 1792	Urbana, Illinois. University of Illinois. Illinois Historical Survey. Richard Clough Anderson Collection. Ledger 11, entitled "Benj. Hough's Book." (Certain unrelated material from Source C is calendared in serial entries 2537 through 2543 of volume 1 of the *Federal Land Series*.) Benjamin Hough was an early surveyor of the United States Military District of Ohio. As such, he maintained a list of all lots located in the District. His list is numerical and seriatim, affording a valuable check on the tract descriptions given in Sources A and B.

Source	Serial Entries	Title and Description
		The most valuable feature of Source C is the fact that Hough usually recorded the name of the original warrantee, whereas Sources A and B may have shown only the corresponding assignee's name. As a consequence, Source C often provides information not to be found in any other extant record.
		A further usefulness of Source C is to be found in the location dates recorded therein. Although these dates cannot be taken as the dates on which the lots were actually settled, further research may determine that they are indicators of some usefulness, inasmuch as unpatented tracts probably remained unsettled--even by squatters--whereas land upon which a patent had been obtained would be attractive to settlers who may then have purchased the tract from the patentee. In this event, the first deed should be sought in county records as more conclusive evidence of settlement date.

How to Use This Volume

The writer suggests the following procedure in order to obtain full use of the information in this volume:

¶ Title searchers should refer directly to the Tract Index, noting all citations listed under the tract description of interest. In addition, they should check the Tract Index to volume 1 of the *Federal Land Series*, in which miscellaneous official correspondence regarding the tract may be calendared.

¶ Genealogical and historical researchers should refer, first, to the Name Index. Since this index contains the names of all assignees, heirs, and devisees--male and female--the search should not be limited to Revolutionary War veterans.

Having found a name of interest, note the information in all citations, particularly the bounty-land warrant numbers. Because the three source registers indexed in this volume give no indication as to the states in whose military units the veterans served--almost a prerequisite for establishing the identities of persons with common names--it has been impossible to list each veteran separately in the Name Index. (For example, the citations in the Name Index under John Smith obviously refer to several individuals of this name and from a number of states.) The identities of the veterans can usually be determined by checking the warrant numbers shown in volume 2 of this Series against those listed under the same names in the National Genealogical Society's *Index of Revolutionary War Pension Applications*.[11] The Society's index shows the states from which the veterans served.

Indeed, it should be said that, in order to get the most use from volume 2 of this Series, researchers will want to have the *Index of Revolutionary War Pension Applications* at hand, as the two publications complement each other. Where the pension application index states that no bounty-land papers are to be found in the pension files, volume 2 of the *Federal Land Series* is likely to supply the missing information. Likewise, it occasionally occurs that volume 2 will show a bounty-land warrant number under the name of a veteran for whom no such information was noted in his pension file.

¶ Having determined the individual of interest to the researcher by the above procedure, all tract descriptions associated with him should be noted.

¶ Enter the Tract Index to determine whether there are further citations shown under the corresponding tract description, for there may be supplemental information as to assignments, errors, devisees, etc., which will be of interest to the researcher.

¶ Check both the name and tract indexes to volume 1 of the *Federal Land Series*. Many land transactions summarized in volume 2 were the occasion of correspondence between the Treasury Department and the district land offices, as calendared in volume 1.

¶ If the warrantee or his assignee has used the services of his Congressman to obtain a patent, it is possible that a search of the Congressman's official papers--if still extant--would uncover original correspondence between him and the warrantee, a matter of considerable interest to genealogical researchers. The *National Union Catalog of Manuscript Collections*, in particular, should be checked for the unpublished official papers of Congressmen.

¶ For further transfers of tracts patented, check the map herein to establish the modern county in which the tract is located. Write to the county recorder of deeds for further information, as chain-of-title information is not to be found in federal records.

Internal Arrangement of This Volume

No subject index has been provided for volume 2, because the source registers indexed herein are summary ones with little, if any, supplemental data not accessible through name and tract indexes.

In general, the headings and abbreviations used herein are those established in volume 1 of the *Federal Land Series*. Volume 2 headings are as follows:

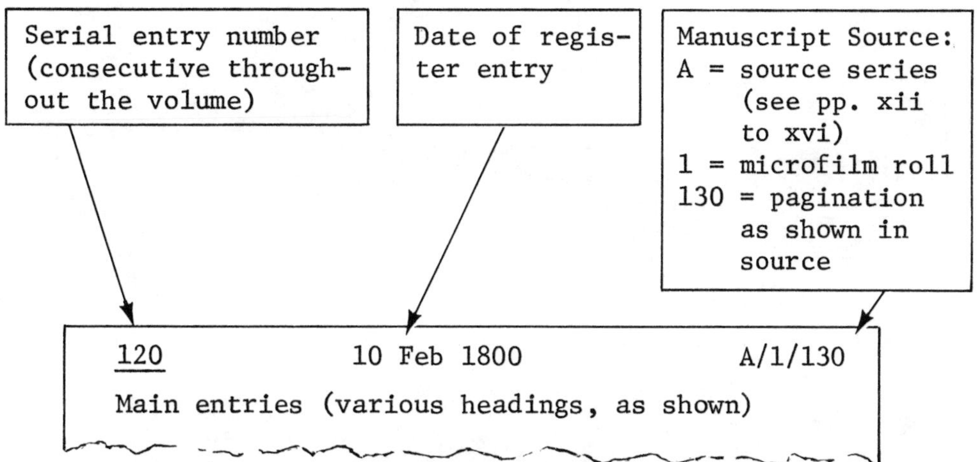

All land entries in this volume pertain to the United States Military District of Ohio and are designated as *Mil*, in accordance with the list of abbreviations set forth in volume 1 of the *Federal Land Series*, pages xxv through xxvii (not reproduced herein because so few of these abbreviations were needed). Thus, a tract description herein might read as follows:

Mil - 3 10 1 23

The description is to be read as Range 3, Township 10, Quarter-township 1, Lot 23, and can be approximately located on the plat map provided in this volume.

Orientation map of Ohio, showing the United States Military District in relation to the rest of the state. A township map of the district is on page 353 in the Tract Index.

Townships within the United States Military District were five miles square (rather than the six-mile square later to become standard throughout states further westward) and were divided into quarter-townships theoretically of 4000 acres each. Not all the quarter-townships were exactly of this size, however, as will be noted from some of the entries herein. Whenever the quarter-township was larger than 4000 acres, the grantee was required to submit bounty-land warrants to make up the difference; when smaller, the district land office issued a certificate in the amount of the difference, entitling the grantee to locate land elsewhere.

The quarter-townships within a township were numbered as follows:

2	1
3	4

They were subdivided privately at the pleasure of the patentees, so that lot lines are irregular. Maps 1 and 2 in volume 1 of the *Federal Land Series* indicate many, but not all, the internal numbering of lots. For further details, the researcher must consult old plat maps for the county in question.

Notes

1. Payson Jackson Treat, *The National Land System 1785-1820* (New York: E. B. Treat & Co., 1910; reprint ed., New York: Russell & Russell, 1967), p. 237. This work, despite its age, remains the authority on the early land history of the United States. It has been supplemented more recently by other works,

principally Malcolm J. Rohrbough, *The Land Office Business: The Settlement and Administration of American Public Lands, 1789-1837* (New York: Oxford University Press, 1968).

2. U.S., Library of Congress, *Journals of the Continental Congress* (Washington, D.C.: Government Printing Office, 1906) 5:763.

3. This quantity is not stated in the original resolution but was later allowed in practice when grants were made.

4. Connecticut also had western lands in Ohio but, so far, this writer has found no references to land grants made to Connecticut veterans specifically compensating them for military service in the American Revolution. Grants to the Connecticut "Sufferers" for property damage during the Revolution has been detailed in volume 1, serial entries 2528 through 2536, of the *Federal Land Series*. South Carolina also held western lands but ceded some or all of them in 1787. So far, no references have been found to western land grants made by this state for military service in the Revolution.

5. National Archives Record Group 49, "Records of the Bureau of Land Management," *United States Revolutionary War Bounty Land Warrants Used in the United States Military District of Ohio, and Related Papers (Acts of 1788, 1803, 1806)* (National Archives Microcopy Publication M-829, in 16 microfilm reels).

6. Reconstructing some information regarding missing warrants seems possible because the pension files, indexed by the National Genealogical Society in its extremely valuable *Index of*

Revolutionary War Pension Applications, contains bounty-land warrant numbers. However, this index may not list all bounty-land warrants, because many veterans who received warrants died before the first pensions were authorized, so that no notations would have been occasioned.

7. 1 Stat. 490.

8. 4 Stat. 423.

9. Treat, *National Land System*, p. 244.

10. For definitive information on the service of Senators and Representatives see: U.S., Congress, Senate, *Biographical Dictionary of the American Congress, 1774-1971*, 92d Cong., 1st sess., Senate doc. 92-B (Washington, D.C.: Government Printing Office, 1971). The first section of this reference work lists congressional districts from whence Representatives came, a valuable indicator as to the area of residence of constituent warrant holders. In the earliest Congresses, which would be in the purview of researchers, Representatives seem to have served at large, however, so that researchers must fall back upon the indexed 1790 federal censuses to establish residence of warrant holders in whom they are interested.

11. Sadye Giller, William H. Dumont, and Louise Dumont, *Index of Revolutionary War Pension Applications, Revised.* National Genealogical Society Publication No. 32 (Washington, D.C.: The Society, n.d.). This publication, now out of print, is being further revised and is to be republished by the Society.

CALENDAR OF ARCHIVAL MATERIAL

1 11 Apr 1799 A/1/ *
By Whom Registered: Elijah Backus
For Whom Registered: Elijah Backus
Location: (4000 acres) Mil - 6 5 - 2
Based upon the following Army land warrants:

Issued to	*No.*	*Date*	*Acres*
Watrous, Daniel	6086	3 Dec 1789	100
Watrous, Daniel	6243	3 Dec 1789	100
Barker, Ephraim, Sgt	3774	3 Dec 1789	100
Hall, William, Pvt	13203	3 Dec 1789	100
Wheeler, Daniel, Sgt	660	1 Sep 1790	100
Flemming, Michael	13468	22 Jan 1790	100
Chappel, Roswell, Pvt	5643	11 Aug 1790	100
McNeely, Simeon, Pvt	8543	- Mar 1790	100
Totten, James? Pvt	8784	- Mar 1790	100
Edwards, Perry, Pvt	3098	31 Dec 1789	100
Limas, Mary	3293	27 Mar 1790	100
Champlin, Nathan, Pvt	3985	31 Dec 1789	100
Potter, John, Pvt	3409	31 Dec 1789	100
Harvey, Edward, Pvt	3229	31 Dec 1789	100
Hills, Ebenezer, Capt	974	14 Jun 1790	300
Lemon, Samuel, Pvt	12307	10 Mar 1790	100
Watrous, Daniel	5494	3 Dec 1789	100
Barker, Moses? W.	5017	3 Dec 1789	100
Watrous, Daniel	1943	3 Dec 1789	400
Boswell, William, Cpl	3793	3 Dec 1789	100
Watrous, Daniel	5236	3 Dec 1789	100
Watrous, Daniel	5764	3 Dec 1789	100
Hendricks, Daniel, Pvt	5922	3 Dec 1789	100
Barker, Moses W.	5253	3 Dec 1789	100
Barker, Moses W.	5352	3 Dec 1789	100
Barker, Moses W.	3840	3 Dec 1789	100
Barker, Moses W.	4040	3 Dec 1789	100
Quay? Lebb, Pvt	6355	3 Dec 1789	100
Bowers, Ephraim, Cpl	5405	3 Dec 1789	100
Noyes, Jonathan, Sgt	4771	3 Dec 1789	100
Barker, Moses W.	4382	3 Dec 1789	100
P---? Benjamin, Pvt	3755	3 Dec 1789	100
Wa---? John	5278	3 Dec 1789	100
[Barker?] Moses W.	4582	3 Dec 1789	100
---? William	4685	-	100

*Microfilm exposures 1 and 2 are reversed on film.

2 11 Apr 1799 A/1/ *
By Whom Registered: Elijah Backus
For Whom Registered: Elijah Backus
Location: (4000 acres) Mil - 14 6 - ?
Based upon the following Army land warrants:

Issued to	*No.*	*Date*	*Acres*
Smith, Richard	12683	13 Jul 1792	100
Means, Richard	13962	2 Nov 1792	100
Ponsonby, George	11256	8 Jan 1796	100
Ponsonby, George	11257	8 Jan 1796	100
Ponsonby, George	11303	8 Jan 1796	100
Haskell, Benjamin	3208	- May 1792	100
Olrie? Loran, Capt	1622	7 Mar 1794	300
Tudor, George, Major	2197	19 May 1790	400
Neal, James I?	2902	26 Jan 1796	100
Neal, James I?	3241	26 Jan 1796	100
Neal, James I?	5351	26 Jan 1796	100
Neal, James I?	2925	26 Jan 1796	100
Smith, Isaiah, Soldier	6506	15 Nov 1792	100
Graves, Francis	11955	9 Dec 1793	100
Means, Robert	11902	18 Feb 1793	100
Pickering, Joshua	4873	25 Apr 1798	100
Fuller, Sylvester	6607	11 Jan 1799	100
---? ---?	10130	10 Jan 1799	100
---? ---? Lt	817	22 Feb 179?	200
---? ---? Pvt	8971	31 Jul 179?	100
---? ---?	5822	11 Jan 17-?	100
Bannister, Seth, Capt	100	31 Dec 1795	300
Ball, Abraham	8684	13 Mar 1799	100
Ripton? William	11318	18 Jul 1793	100
de Baufre, James	11360	27 Feb 1799	100
Thomas, Abisha	11968	6 Mar 1799	100
Taylor, George, Jr	9344	5 Mar 1799	100
Fitch? Elnathan	5378	21 Mar 1799	100
Hamilton, George, Capt	1046	4 Aug 1789	300
Garrison, William	8613	27 Mar 1799	100

*Microfilm exposures 1 and 5. These loose pages have been reproduced in improper order on the film.

3 11 Apr 1799 A/1/ *
By Whom Registered: Elijah Backus
For Whom Registered: Elijah Backus
Location: (4000 acres) Mil - 19 1 - 4
Based upon the following Army land warrants:

Issued to	*No.*	*Date*	*Acres*
Bell, Abraham	9368	27 Mar 1799	100
McElready? Hugh, Pvt	10041	11 Mar 1799	100
Bowen? Thomas? Bartholomew, Capt	198	20 Apr 1796	300
Milligan, James, Lt	1430	25 May 1796	200
Nice, John, Capt	1590	3 Apr 1799	300
Garrison, William	8769	5 Apr 1799	100
Moody? Benjamin, Pvt	10841	3 Apr 1799	100
Kerr, William, Pvt	5638	19 Nov 1789	100
Henshaw, Joshua	1959	18 Dec 1789	200
Lachman? Charles, Surgeon's mate	1323	2 Mar 1791	300
Springer, Sylvester, Surgeon's mate	2107	2 Mar 1791	300
Gilman, Benjamin Ives	4934	24 Aug 1790	100
Gilman, Benjamin Ives	4859	24 Aug 1790	100
Gilman, Benjamin Ives	3705	24 Aug 1790	100
Gilman, Benjamin Ives	4805	24 Aug 1790	100
Gilman, Benjamin Ives	4950	24 Aug 1790	100
Gilman, Benjamin Ives	4861	24 Aug 1790	100
Gilman, Benjamin Ives	10244	24 Aug 1790	100
Gilman, Benjamin Ives	3108	24 Aug 1790	100
Gilman, Benjamin Ives	3553	24 Aug 1790	100
Gilman, Benjamin Ives	3560	24 Aug 1790	100
Gilman, Benjamin Ives	3580	24 Aug 1790	100
Gilman, Benjamin Ives	3264	24 Aug 1790	100
Gilman, Benjamin Ives	507	24 Aug 1790	500
Gilman, Benjamin Ives	75	24 Aug 1790	200

*Microfilm exposures 5 and 6.

4 11 Apr 1799 A/1/ *
By Whom Registered: Elijah Backus
For Whom Registered: Elijah Backus
Location: (4050 acres) Mil - 14 1 - 1
Based upon the following Army land warrants:

Issued to	*No.*	*Date*	*Acres*
Davis, Isaac, Pvt	3064	22 Jul 1790	100
Hull, Jeremiah, Sgt	4300	22 Jul 1790	100
Ferriole, Alexander, Pvt	13072	26 Jul 1790	100
Cady, Samuel, Pvt	5571	20 Aug 1790	100
Fowler, Edward, Pvt	5798	17 Aug 1790	100
Roberts, Reuben, Pvt	3461	31 Dec 1789	100
Luther, John, Drummer	13334	31 Dec 1789	100
Babcock, Primus, Pvt	2974	31 Dec 1789	100
Chadsey, Timothy, Jr., Pvt	3042	31 Dec 1789	100
Carty, Isaac, Pvt	8174	14 Jun 1791	100
Hooper? Robert, Lt	1034	27 May 1791	200
Durkee, John, Capt	533	7 Jul 1791	300
Clark, Augustus, Pvt	5620	11 Jul 1790	100
McCarty, Dennis, Pvt	10067	28 Jul 1791	100

4 [continued]

Issued to	No.	Date	Acres
McGlaughlin, Patrick	12802	26 Jul 1791	100
Powell, Lloyd	13628	11 Sep 1789	100
Backus, Elijah	6329	20 Mar 1795	100
Perkins, Erastus	5419	22 Sep ?	100
Hubbard, Hezekiah	964	19 Nov ?	200
McGonnigle, John, Pvt	10845	2 Sep ?	100
Johnson, Jonathan, LtCol	1136	19 Nov ?	450
Bell, Abraham	8328	10 Apr ?	100
Foster, John, Pvt	5775	19 Nov ?	100
Moncks, Daniel, Pvt	3341	31 Dec 1789	100
Eldridge, Jeremiah, Pvt	4106	31 Dec 1789	100
Thomas, William, Pvt	3531	31 Dec 1789	100
Bramin? Silas, Cpl?	2972	31 Dec 1789	100
Yoder? William, Capt?	1631	31 Dec 1789	300
Holden, John	904	31 Dec 1789	300

*Microfilm exposures 3 and 6.

5 — 16 Apr 1799 — A/1/ *

By Whom Registered: Jonathan Rhea & William Barton

For Whom Registered: Jonathan Rhea & William Barton

Location: (4000 acres) Mil - 11 7 - 1

Based upon the following Army land warrants:

Issued to	*No.*	*Date*	*Acres*
Walker, George, Lt	2376	12 Sep 1789	200
Job, Richard, Drummer	8431	10 Nov 1795	100
Barton, William	8437	7 Sep 1790	100
Pope, John	8561	7 Oct 1789	100
Pope, John	8599	17 Oct 1789	100
Pope, John	8167	9 Sep 1790	100
Pope, John	13741	17 Oct 1789	100
Pope, John	8328	28 Dec 1789	100
Barton, William	8598	7 Sep 1790	100
Barton, William	8076	7 Sep 1790	100
Pope, John	8176	9 Sep 1790	100
Barton, William	8796	7 Sep 1790	100
Barton, William	8587	4 May 1791	100
Barton, William	10139	16 Apr 1796	100
Rhea, Jonathan	2657	21 Dec 1795	450
Barton, William	17--	7 Sep 1790	300
Henzey? Joseph	962-	6 May 1793	100
Ball, Abraham?	91--	6 May 1793	[100]
Barton, William	8284	7 Sep 1790	[100]
Barton, William	8807	25 Apr 1792	[100]
Lyons, William, Pvt	8507	7 Dec 1797	[100]
Clark, William, Pvt	8211	4 Oct 1796	[100]
Neil, Thomas, Sgt	6235	8 Jul 1789	[100]
Tumey, Samuel, Pvt	8794	6 Sep 1798	[100]
Amey, David, Pvt	8072	29 Jun 1789	[100]
Simpson, John, Pvt	8759	25 Jul 1796	[100]
Longstreet, R., & Vorheese, H.	2633	7 Jul 1793	[300]
Hilsey, Joseph, Pvt	8377	28 May 1790	[100]
Sproul, Oliver, & Sproul, Elizabeth	2707	15 Apr 1799	150
Tumey, Samuel "John"	8798	6 Sep 1798	100
Rose, John, Pvt	8659	10 Aug 1792	100

*Microfilm exposures 3 and 4.

6 — 22 Apr 1799 — A/1/ *

By Whom Registered: Godfrey Haga

For Whom Registered: Godfrey Haga

Location: (4000 acres) Mil - 2 8 - 1

Based upon the following Army land warrants:

Issued to	*No.*	*Date*	*Acres*
Alexander, William, Maj	41	16 Jul 1787	400
Campfield, Naptali, Pvt	4530	24 May 1790	100
Drakley, Ebenezer	5632	16 Sep 1790	100
Drakley, Ebenezer	7033	16 Sep 1790	100
Drakley, Ebenezer	5804	16 Sep 1790	100
Smith, John, Cpl	8763	19 Nov 1789	100
Stoy, John	8960	4 Oct 1796	100
Carner, Abraham, Pvt	8169	7 Oct 1796	100
Walsworth, William, Pvt	5376	3 Aug 1795	100
Walsworth, William, Pvt	3406	3 Aug 1795	100
Hubbert, Christian	13799	29 Jul ?	[100]
Hubbert, Christian	10514	29 Jul ?	[100]
Fitzgerald, John, Pvt	9397	? Jul ?	[100]
[one line missing]	-		[100]
Cannon, John	11976	11 Oct 1796	100
Branhom? [Brankom?] William, Pvt	11929	11 Oct 1796	100
Cannon, John	12119	11 Oct 1796	100
McClean, Thomas, Pvt	9931	11 Jun 1795	100
Sutherland, John, Pvt	10342	11 Jun 1795	100
Van Horn, Abraham, Pvt	10547	11 Jun 1795	100
Lands, Thomas, Pvt	10381	11 Jun 1795	100
Murphy, Thomas, Pvt	10042	11 Jun 1795	100
Thompson, George, Pvt	10499	11 Jun 1795	100
Peck, John, Lt	1659	25 Jan 1791	200
Buck, Joseph, Lt	184	7 Jul 1789	200
Hake? [Stake?] Jacob, Capt	2018	14 Mar 1794	300
Dorsey, Richard, Capt	584	19 Jan 1793	300
Power, Alexander	9638	5 May 1794	100
Hanna, John, Pvt	10790	2 Sep 1789	100
Hubbard, Christian	10092	7 May 1794	100
Palatine, Cash, Pvt	6331	7 Aug 1789	100

*Microfilm exposures 4 and 7.

7 — 22 Apr 1799 — A/1/007

By Whom Registered: Godfrey Haga

For Whom Registered: Godfrey Haga

Location: (4000 acres) Mil - 2 6 - 2

Based upon the following Army land warrants:

Issued to	*No.*	*Date*	*Acres*
Lee? [See?] Noah, Capt	1329	25 Apr 1794	300
Ripton, William	2537	19 May 1794	100
Means, Robert	-749	18 Feb 1793	300
Graves, Francis	-519	18 Feb 1793	300
Graves, Francis	--50	7 May 1793	300
Power, Alexander	--63	5 May 1794	100
Lunborn? [Sanborn?] Richard, Pvt	---7	7 Apr 1795	100
Ward, John B., Pvt	----	12 Feb 1794	100
Dowdney, Samuel, Sgt	----	31 May 1790	100
Hubbard, Christian	----	31 May 1799	100
Campbell, Thomas*	435	7 Jul 1789	200
Campbell, Thomas, Capt	413	7 Jul 1789	300
Campbell, Thomas	14076	23 Apr 1794	100
Sample, James	12569	14 Sep 1796	100
Cavennaugh, John, Cpl	9129	25 Sep 1789	100
Traverse, Andrew, Pvt	10492	2 Sep 1796	100
Hogekeys, Samuel, Pvt	12254	14 Sep 1796	100
Craig, David	8073	27 Aug 1796	100
Young, John	12097	28 Sep 1796	100
Dougherty, James, Pvt	9270	29 Nov 1792	100
Young, John	12290	28 Sep 1796	100
Young, John	12253	28 Sep 1796	100
Verdier, Benedict, Lt	2276	29 Aug 1794	200
McLachlin, Colin, Sgt	13435	10 Sep 1796	100
Whitton, Joseph	5790	27 Aug 1796	100
Hertzberg, George, Cpl	13159	9 Aug 1796	100
Knowles, James, Pvt	13301	16 Mar 1796	100
Galbreath, Alexander, Drummer	9414	- Jul 1789	100

*Marginal notation: "The war office says Arch[ibald] Campbell."

8 22 Apr 1799 A/1/008
By Whom Registered: Godfrey Haga
For Whom Registered: Godfrey Haga
Location: (4000 acres) Mil - 1 10 - 3
Based upon the following Army land warrants:

Issued to	*No.*	*Date*	*Acres*
Drakley, Ebenezer	7064	-- 1796	100
Collins, Joseph	6943	-- Sep 1796	100
Benton, Elijah, Pvt	5533	-- Oct 1796	100
Chapple, Curtis, Pvt	5633	-- Oct 1796	100
Hunter, Robert	9189	-- Mar 1795	100
Pitkin, Timothy, Junior	5363	-- Nov 1795	100
Angell, Israel	--41	-- May 1792	100
Angell, Israel	1750	-- May 1792	100
Angell, Israel	-370	-- May 1792	100
Atkinson, Samuel	3490	15 Apr 1796	100
Atkinson, Samuel	4124	15 Apr 1796	100
Atkinson, Samuel	2921	15 Apr 1796	100
Merkle, Gideon	9884	12 Feb 1794	100
Fletcher, Robert	3401	26 Apr 1796	100
Ruggles, Nathan	5802	15 Apr 1796	100
Craddock, Robert, Lt	463	15 Jul 1789	200
Ladd, Elip[hale]t & Cass, Jon[atha]n	1773	21 Jul 1789	400
Thomas, Joseph	644	2 Jun 1796	300
Dayle, London, Pvt	3065	27 Oct 1792	100
Thomas, Joseph	3695	23 Aug 1796	100
Thomas, Joseph	3887	23 Aug 1796	100
Cass, Jonathan	3626	21 Jul 1789	100
Norvel, Lipscomb	1599	26 Oct 1795	200
Henderson, William	7031	23 Apr 1796	300
Bell, Jabez, Lt	111	24 May 1790	200
Thayer, Paul, Pvt	5134	24 May 1790	100
Gay, Jonathan	4274	24 May 1790	100
Buckman, Benjamin, Sgt	3693	24 May 1790	100
Robertson, John, Lt	1861	12 Oct 1792	200

9 22 Apr 1799 A/1/009
By Whom Registered: Godfrey Haga
For Whom Registered: John Heckewelder
Location: (4000 acres) Mil - 2 8 - 2
Based upon the following Army land warrants:

Issued to	*No.*	*Date*	*Acres*
Moore, George	10033	17 Jan 1792	100
Moore, George	10058	17 Jan 1792	100
Cragan, Dennis, Pvt	11120	24 Sep 1792	100
Bennett, John, Pvt	11012	-- May 1790	100
Moore, George	10624	-- Jan 1792	100
Moore, George	9033	-- Mar 1792	100
Moore, George	9600	-- Jan 1792	100
Moore, George	10603	17 Jan 1792	100
Moore, George	10637	19 Mar 1792	100
Moore, George	9180	17 Jan 1792	100
Duncan, James	13740	22 Sep 1789	100
Moore, George	10586	19 Mar 1792	100
Moore, George	12899	24 Mar 1792	100
Johnson, Joseph, Pvt	11377	28 Feb 1795	100
Jones, William, Pvt	11372	24 Sep 1792	100
Moore, George	9763	19 Mar 1792	100
Moore, George	9307	17 Jan 1792	100
Moore, George	9065	17 Jan 1792	100
Pope, John	8315	17 Oct 1789	100
White, Anthony Walton, Col	2420	18 Sep 1789	500
Pope, John	8327	17 Oct 1789	100
Pall, Joseph	10589	27 Nov 1794	100
Hopkins, Francis, Pvt	11304	11 Mar 1791	100
Challand? [Chatland?] William, Pvt	11071	28 Apr 1791	100
Mann, William, Pvt	11481	17 Jul 179-	100
Broom, Thomas, Sgt	12854	20 Oct 1789	100
Onions, John, Pvt	11578	2- Aug 1792	100
Sullivan, William, Pvt	11683	24 Sep 1792	100
Chester, Edward, Pvt	8165	30 May 1793	100
Newton, Moses, Pvt	12440	26 May 1793	100
Willet, Christopher, Pvt	109--	2 Sep 1789	100
King, Samuel	--	-- May 1794	100
Graves, Francis	--	-- May 1793	100
Farnham, Ebenezer	--	2 May 1793	100
Farnham, Ebenezer	5709	22 May 1793	100
Cannon, John	14072	28 Mar 1794	100

10 22 Apr 1799 A/1/011
By Whom Registered: Godfrey Haga
For Whom Registered: John Heckewelder
Location: (4000 acres) Mil - 1 7 - 3
Based upon the following Army land warrants:

Issued to	*No.*	*Date*	*Acres*
Colver, Charles	13871	25 Feb 1791	100
Colver, Charles	9469	25 Feb 1791	100
Colver, Charles	9191	25 Feb 1791	100
Colver, Charles	13064	26 Apr 1791	100
Brookhouse, Rudolph, Pvt	8933	13 Apr 1791	100
Killon, Edward, Pvt	9734	11 Apr 1791	100
Colver, Charles	13112	25 Feb 1791	100
Colver, Charles	13713	25 Feb 1791	100
Gray, Elizabeth	856	29 May 1794	300
Stratton, Annanias	8715	1 Feb 1790	100
Elbert, John L., Surgeon's Mate	2593	22 Sep 1791	300
Taylor, Susannah	1019	7 Dec 1791	200
Dyer, Walter, Lt	587	14 Nov 1791	200
McClelland, John	2596	4 Nov 1791	300
Dougherty, Mary	10749	2 Sep 1789	100
Hart, Martin	9550	10 Mar 1790	100
Ferrell, John	8324	26 May 1790	100
Coleman, Nicholas, Lt	436	8 Dec 1792	200
Power, William, Capt	1713	7 Sep 1789	300
Richards, John Henton	1002	30 Jul 1793	400
Dorrance, Samuel	2639	27 Mar 1794	300
McConnell, Matthew	2122	28 Oct 1789	300

11 22 Apr 1799 A/1/012
By Whom Registered: Godfrey Haga
For Whom Registered: John C. Reich, John Shropp, & Christian Lauge? [Lange?]
Location: (4000 acres) Mil - 2 9 - 4
Based upon the following Army land warrants:

Issued to	*No.*	*Date*	*Acres*
Denniston, Thomas, Pvt	7030	16 Nov 1791	100
Bartle, George, Pvt	9005	29 Mar 1791	100
Merkle, Gideon	9507	9 Jun 1794	100
Hubbard, Christian	9894	1 May 1792	100
Shepherd, Sarah	8941	15 Nov 1791	100
Wright, Henderson	8939	12 Mar 1792	100
Sharpe, Thomas	13732	8 Nov 1791	100
Shepperd, Sarah	8935	12 Jan 1792	100
Cole, Elias	13509	29 Nov 1791	100
Williams, William, Pvt	10567	16 Jul 1792	100
Lewis, Curtis	9650	5 Mar 1792	100
Lane, William	11716	13 Jan 1792	100
Fricklan, Robert, Pvt	8298	21 Nov 1791	100
Carnine, Jeremiah, Pvt	12010	27 Dec 1794	100
Heiner, Jasper	10268	31 Oct 1791	100
Merkle, Gideon	9752	9 Jun 1794	100
Smith, Charlotte	13729	17 Jan 1794	100
Creaton, John, Pvt	12890	25 Feb 1792	100
Roche, Thomas, Pvt	14090	31 Dec 1794	100
Murphy, James, Sgt	10832	2 Sep 1794	100
McConnell, Matthew	215	29 Jun 1789	300

11 [continued]

Budd, Samuel, Capt	296	10 Mar 1790	300
Phillips, John	10184	3 Apr 1794	100
Stever, Daniel	9964	10 Jun 1794	100
Stever, Daniel	10003	19 May 1794	100
Stever, Daniel	9689	10 Jun 1794	100
Jennings, Edward, Pvt	9657	16 May 1793	100
Martin, William, Capt	1450	20 Dec 1797	300
Matthews, James, Pvt	9895	27 Apr 1792	100
Woodin, John, Pvt	10654	11 May 1792	100
Buchanan, James, Pvt	11977	2 May 1794	100
Burrowes, Eden, Lt	181	11 May 1795	200
Batten, John, Pvt	12803	17 Jan 1794	100

12 — 29 Apr 1799 — A/1/013

By Whom Registered: George Stevenson
For Whom Registered: George Stevenson
Location: (4000 acres) Mil - 18 1 - 4
Based upon the following Army land warrants:

Issued to	*No.*	*Date*	*Acres*
Shoemaker, Henry	13810	20 Dec 1791	100
Way, John, Pvt	7992	19 Mar 1792	100
Scott, Charles, Pvt	11692	16 Nov 1796	100
Redman, John, Pvt	13694	16 Nov 1796	100
Holmes, William, Pvt	14141	21 Mar 1796	100
Simpson, John, Surgeon	1942	2 Sep 1789	400
de Beaulieu, Lewis, Lt	640	15 Jun 1793	200
Camp, Robert	269	27 Feb 1796	300
Stevenson, George, Hospital Mate	2118	16 Jul 1789	300
Robb, John, Capt	1830	24 Oct 1789	300
Curtis, Marmaduke	2375	18 Apr 1796	300
Leland, Patrick, Pvt	13316	5 Nov 1789	100
Johnson, Hugh, Pvt	9698	16 Jul 1789	100
Hoadley, Ebenezer, Pvt	5967	10 Feb 1797	100
Hubbard, Christian	10000	17 Dec 1795	100
Phelps, Noah Amherst	12915	10 Feb 1797	100
Stockdell, John	12681	13 Jan 1795	100
Pall, Joseph	9155	27 Nov 1794	100
Driskill, Joseph, Lt	529	30 May 1789	200
Poll? [Pall?] Joseph	10549	27 Nov 1794	100
Stever, Daniel	3905	10 -- 1794	100
Merkle, Gideon	9839	9 -- 1794	100
Mershemer, Boston	10037	23 Aug 1791	100
Hutchins, John, Lt	1004	17 Mar 1791	200
Rogers, Timothy, Pvt	4919	14 Jun 1790	100
Stockdell, John	12675	30 Jan 1795	100

13 — 29 Apr 1799 — A/1/014

By Whom Registered: Cairnoan Medowell
For Whom Registered: Cairnoan Medowell
Location: (4000 acres)* Mil - 9 6 - 3
Based upon the following Army land warrants:

Issued to	*No.*	*Date*	*Acres*
Parsons, William Walter	5570	26 Feb 1794	100
Baldwin, Caleb, Capt	134	8 May 1792	300
King, Daniel	2940	12 Dec 1792	100
Stannard, Seth	6499	18 Mar 1790	100
Robertson, Henry, Pvt	14126	5 Aug 1795	100
Emery, Samuel	5268	2 Jun 1795	100
Grant, Edward, Sgt	4270	2 Mar 1790	100
Nimmough, Neil, Pvt	8597	25 Jul 1789	100
Coleman, Noah, Surgeon	369	1 Mar 1797	400
Power, Alexander	10265	29 Apr 1793	100
Stockdell, John	12502	26 Oct 1795	100
Harris, Benjamin	8875	16 Oct 1789	100
Neal, James A.	4175	6 Nov 1795	100
Graves, Francis	12029	29 May 1792	100
Graves, Francis	12298	29 May 1792	100
Graves, Francis	12470	26 Mar 1792	100
Graves, Francis	12500	12 Apr 1792	100
Graves, Francis	12085	12 Apr 1792	100
Graves, Francis	12364	26 Mar 1792	100
Snell, John	10441	17 Feb 1792	100
Graves, Francis	12201	29 May 1792	100
King, Daniel	-950	12 Dec 1792	100
King, Daniel	4025	12 Dec 1792	100
Muzzy, Amos	954	8 May 1792	300
Sloan, Hugh, Pvt	7789	10 Feb 1792	100
Cook, Richard, Pvt	5557	12 Mar 1792	100
Glover, Lemuel, Pvt	5892	13 Jan 1792	100
Wheeler, Edward, Pvt	5212	21 Nov 1791	100
Sill, Moses	6160	28 Jan 1792	100
Waldron, Resolve	3900	19 Jan 1792	100
Mead, Shadrach	6444	2 Mar 1792	100
Esperance, Joseph L., Fifer	13366	4 Feb 1790	100
Larrabe, Richard	4555	21 Nov 1791	100

*Marginal notation states that lot contains 4050-8/10ths acres. The difference made up by additional certificate, as follows:

Alexander McGlaughlin	31	10 Mar 1800	50

[See also serial entry 273]

14 — 29 Apr 1799 — A/1/015

By Whom Registered: Cairnoan Medowell
For Whom Registered: Cairnoan Medowell
Location: (4000 acres) Mil - 8 6 - 3
Based upon the following Army land warrants:

Issued to	*No.*	*Date*	*Acres*
Mooers? [Movers?] Benj.	13818	22 Jan 1790	100
Nick, Eve	14065	5 Mar 1794	100
Burrows, John	8107	11 Mar 1791	100
Clark, John, Pvt	8164	31 May 1790	100
Rarity, John, Cpl	8685	1 Feb 1790	100
Jones, Alexander, Pvt	8432	10 Mar 1790	100
Woodman, John, Pvt	12652	12 Aug 1791	100
Hedley, Moses, Pvt	8411	31 May 1790	100
Ward, John	11174	11 Jan 1796	100
Thayer, William, Pvt	12613	18 Apr 1794	100
Hulet, John, Pvt	11313	11 Apr 1794	100
Hancock, Stephen, Pvt	11332	5 Oct 1792	100
de Baufre, James	11137	9 Aug 1797	100
de Baufre, James	10950	16 Aug 1797	100
de Baufre, James	11186	9 Aug 1797	100
de Baufre, James	11095	8 Aug 1797	100
de Baufre, James	11516	14 Aug 1797	100
de Baufre, James	11195	14 Aug 1797	100
de Baufre, James	12918	16 Aug 1797	100
de Baufre, James	13535	16 Aug 1797	100
Heth, James, Lt	1081	22 Aug 1789	200
Prior, Abner, Maj	1666	20 May 1791	400
Sherrard, Francis	10991	14 Aug 1795	100
Brown, Joseph	4752	1 Mar 1792	100
Platt, Richard	8038	14 Jul 1790	100
Tarbell, Nathan, Pvt	8783	7 Jul 1789	100
Wyllys, Samuel, Col	2341	12 Oct 1789	500
de Witt, Peter	5958	9 Feb 1793	100
Munson, Eneas	5597	7 Mar 1792	100
de Witt, Peter	3682	9 Feb 1793	100
Chapman, Thomas	13969	3 Mar 1792	100
Beagley, James	10181	2 Aug 1793	100

15 — 2 May 1799 — A/1/016

By Whom Registered: James Miller
For Whom Registered; John Wilkins, Junior
Location: (4000 acres) Mil - 11 2 - 2
Based upon the following Army land warrants:

Issued to	*No.*	*Date*	*Acres*
Shute, Samuel M., Lt	1998	17 Jul 1789	200
Kent, Isaac, Pvt	11425	4 Aug 1789	100

15 [continued]

Ward, Joshua	11651	11 Jan 1796	100
Merkle, Bernard	12426	31 Oct 1795	100
Ward, Joshua	11505	11 Jan 1796	100
Davis, Henry	11264	14 Oct 1795	100
Davis, Henry	11225	14 Oct 1795	100
Ward, Joshua	11537	11 Jan 1790	100
Tannehill, Josiah	2219	9 Jun 1789	200
Smith, William L., LtCol	1991	9 Aug --	450
Van Ness, Cornelius	7907	27 Oct --	100
Wiesenfels, Frederick, Col	2361	29 Jan --	500
Organ, John, Pvt	10176	5 Dec --	100
Wilkins, John, Surgeon's Mate	2390	22 Dec 1790	300
Scott, Charles, BrigGen	2055	25 Apr 1794	850
Ward, Joshua	11712	11 Jan 1796	100
Claiborne, Richard, Lt	470	4 Dec 1794	200
Tannehill, Adamson, Capt	2209	9 Jun 1789	300

16 2 May 1799 A/1/017

By Whom Registered: James Miller
For Whom Registered: John Wilkins, Junior
Location: (4000 acres) Mil - 14 1 - 3
Based upon the following Army land warrants:

Issued to	*No.*	*Date*	*Acres*
Heard, John, Capt	1023	11 Jun 1789	300
Steel, Francis, Pvt	10445	26 Apr 1792	100
Hollingshead, John	8582	28 Dec 1789	100
Richards, William	5861	12 Dec 1794	100
Fuller, James, Pvt	13103	11 Sep 1792	100
Reed, James, Pvt	6949	11 Sep 1792	100
German, William	14048	27 Jun 1793	100
Read, Thomas, Surgeon	1807	15 Dec 1791	400
Hughes, Peter	7442	17 Jun 1790	100
Combs, Lawrence, Pvt	8192	28 Oct 1791	100
Halsey, Luther, Lt	999	11 Jun 1789	200
Walker, Matthias, Pvt	7966	1 Jun 1792	100
Rumbels, Thomas, Pvt	7718	22 Dec 1791	100
Van Woert, Henry, Lt	2252	25 Aug 1790	200
Brown, Joseph	531	20 Dec 1792	300
Organ, Matthew, Pvt	10168	23 Jan 1796	100
Clarke, Oliver, Capt	2631	18 Apr 1793	300
McCarthy, Owen	9681	24 Oct 1792	100
White, William, Pvt	6690	30 Mar 1793	100
Emes, Worsley, Capt	669	5 Apr 1791	300
Ferguson, Hannah	8293	1 Nov 1792	100
Murthwaite, Jane	9119	30 Oct 1792	100
Stephenson, Margaret	13582	24 Oct 1792	100
Libo, Paul	9678	8 Oct 1792	100
Cummins, Ebenezer, Pvt	6934	4 May 1791	100
Hoge, John	9688	23 Sep 1791	100
Nothstone, John	10282	4 Oct 1792	100

17 5 Jun 1799 A/1/018

By Whom Registered: George Skinner
For Whom Registered: George Skinner
Location: (4050 acres) Mil - 7 6 - 2
Based upon the following Army land warrants:

Issued to	*No.*	*Date*	*Acres*
Keith, Japheth, Pvt	4511	6 May 1793	100
Quance, Joshua, Pvt	4820	6 May 1793	100
Champney, Nathan, Sgt	3891	18 Feb 1796	100
Carigan, John, Pvt	12920	20 Dec 1798	100
Irvine, William, BrigGen	1146	18 May 1789	850
von Heer, Barth[olome]w, Capt	2275	13 Jul 1789	300
McConnell, Matthew	13821	29 Jun 1789	100
White, David, Pvt	5220	6 May 1793	100
McCoy, Samuel	8352	28 Dec 1791	100
Harper, John	9017	26 Nov 1791	100
Orcutt, Seth, Pvt	4799	8 Sep 1792	100
Richards, John, Pvt	4959	4 May 1793	100
Wheeler, Hezekiah, Pvt	6685	13 May 1789	100
Talbot, Jeremiah, Maj	2198	13 May 1789	400
Lands, Andrew, Sgt	10367	9 Jul 1789	100
Weare, Nathan, Lt	2281	25 Apr 1798	200
McConnell, Matthew	10281	16 Jul 1789	100
Stringer, Conrad	9301	19 Jan 1791	100
Gray, William, Sgt	9433	6 Apr 1790	100
Phillips, John	8867	24 Oct 1792	100
Nicholson, Samuel	835	7 Feb 1792	300
Springer, Abr[aham]	14030	30 Jan 1792	100
McColgen, John	13457	19 Aug 1791	100
Lafferty, Edward, Pvt	9800	9 Jul 1789	100
Schaffer, George	12720	14 Nov 1792	100

18 8 Jun 1799 A/1/019

By Whom Registered: Benjamin Morgan
For Whom Registered: David Morgan
Location: (4000 acres) Mil - 2 1 - 3
Based upon the following Army land warrants:

Issued to	*No.*	*Date*	*Acres*
Gookin, Daniel, Lt	785	4 Jan 1793	200
Gookin, Daniel	3196	25 Apr 1798	100
Gookin, Daniel	2936	25 Apr 1798	100
Gookin, Daniel	1625	24 Apr 1798	200
Gookin, Daniel	3193	24 Apr 1798	100
Gookin, Daniel	3052	25 Apr 1798	100
Griggs, Jacob	3934	24 May 1797	100
Lewis, Stephen, Pvt	13329	14 Mar 1792	100
Benedict, Timothy	7118	27 Apr 1792	100
Benedict, Timothy	7089	27 Apr 1792	100
Bell, Abraham	8248	23 Apr 1798	100
Bell, Abraham	8456	23 Apr 1798	100
Bell, Abraham	8378	23 Apr 1798	100
Bell, Abraham	8170	23 Apr 1798	100
Gookin, Daniel	5164	25 Apr 1798	100
Irvine, William, Junior	2423	30 Apr 1792	400
Reasoner, John	12489	2 Dec 1793	100
Worsham, Richard, Lt	2438	19 Mar 1794	200
Jefferies, William, Pvt	12266	8 Apr 1794	100
Deacons, William, Pvt	13009	8 Apr 1794	100
Murthwaite, Jane	13027	19 Apr 1792	100
Power, Alexander	13632	11 Apr 1792	100
Richardson, Isabella	10290	11 May 1792	100
McDo--od, John	10057	8 May 1792	100
Smith, John, Pvt	10421	12 Sep 1789	100
Rose, Peter	10763	21 Mar 1792	100
Dixon, John	11134	14 Feb 1797	100
Fennell, Stephen, Pvt	11200	11 Mar 1791	100
Gray, Benjamin, Pvt	12252	4 Jun 1790	100
Davis, William, Pvt	5710	19 Mar 1794	100
Steinmetz, George	9261	19 Mar 1792	100
Thomy, Morton, Pvt	10509	11 Mar 1791	100
Garrisham, James, Pvt	9489	2 May 1798	100
McCortley, Michael, Pvt	9902	26 Apr 1792	100

19 26 Jul 1799 A/1/020

By Whom Registered: John Brown
For Whom Registered: James Taylor
Location: (4000 acres) Mil - 19 5 - 3
Based upon the following Army land warrants:

Issued to	*No.*	*Date*	*Acres*
Stevens, William J., Lt	2076	19 May 1797	200
Jeffries, R[ichar]d & Jeffries, A.	2073	29 Jan 1799	150
Wallace, William B.	2425	27 Mar 1794	400
Dade, William, *et al*	606	5 Jul 1799	200

19 [continued]

Mercer, W. J. H., & Mercer, George	1527	5 Jul 1799	850
Taylor, James	2477	5 Jul 1799	200
Taylor, James	1166	5 Jul 1799	300
Taylor, James	462	5 Jul 1799	200
Taylor, James	1508	5 Jul 1799	300
Taylor, James	870	5 Jul 1799	300
Taylor, James	2428	5 Jul 1799	300
Taylor, James	452	5 Jul 1799	300
Taylor, James	2478	5 Jul 1799	300

20 29 Jul 1799 A/1/021

By Whom Registered: Robert Underwood
For Whom Registered: Isaac Craig "of Pittsburg"
Location: (4000 acres) Mil - 14 6 - 1
Based upon the following Army land warrants:

Issued to	*No.*	*Date*	*Acres*
Swier, Peter	5021	30 Mar 1796	100
Swier, Peter	5148	26 Mar 1796	100
Reynolds, Martin, Pvt	10279	16 Jan 1790	100
Duvall, Richard, Pvt	11148	18 Aug 1792	100
Swier, Peter	4094	26 Mar 1796	100
Swier, Peter	4095	30 Mar 1796	100
Swier, Peter	4337	26 Mar 1796	100
Swier, Peter	4342	26 Mar 1796	100
Swier, Peter	4380	26 Mar 1796	100
Swier, Peter	4395	30 Mar 1796	100
Swier, Peter	3163	26 Mar 1796	100
Swier, Peter	3206	26 Mar 1796	100
Thom, William L.	3475	19 Feb 1796	100
Swier, Peter	4041	26 Mar 1796	100
Swier, Peter	4088	30 Mar 1796	100
Root, Ephraim	329	16 Jan 1790	450
Swier, Peter	361	26 Mar 1796	300
Craig, Isaac, Maj	424	28 Jan 1791	400
Dean, Samuel, Capt	576	27 May 1791	300
Fenwick, Joseph	1083	2 Apr 1796	150
Thom, William L.	1220	19 Feb 1796	300
Guion, Isaac	1990	18 May 1790	200
Swier, Peter	2329	26 Mar 1796	200
Thom, William L.	3008	19 Feb 1796	100
Swier, Peter	3132	26 Mar 1796	100

21 29 Jul 1799 A/1/022

By Whom Registered: Robert Underwood
For Whom Registered: John Matthews & Co.
Location: (4000 acres) Mil - 15 3 - 1
Based upon the following Army land warrants:

Issued to	*No.*	*Date*	*Acres*
Sizer, Daniel, Pvt	6478	19 Nov 1789	100
Goodrich, Bethael, Pvt	5833	19 Apr 1790	100
Cotton, Thaddeus, Pvt	5671	19 Apr 1790	100
Meigs, John, Lt	1383	19 Nov 1789	200
Starr, David, Capt	1949	19 Nov 1789	300
Brainard, Othniel, Pvt	5504	19 Nov 1789	100
Pratt, Allen, Pvt	6277	19 Nov 1789	100
Bowers, Joab, Pvt	5248	19 Apr 1790	100
Hazen, Moses, Col	1118	27 Dec 1798	500
Bell, Abraham	8124	16 Mar 1799	100
Sumner, Elizabeth	1939	9 Apr 1790	450
Thompson, Joseph	2139	11 Oct 1791	450
Holmes, Babriel	12248	18 May 1797	100
Whitaker, Abel	13948	1 Feb 1790	100
Ripton, William	9274	18 Jul 1793	100
Lewis, John	1283	2 Mar 1799	200
Kelly, Edward	1755	27 Feb 1796	150
Campbell, J. J. R[ichar]d & Campbell, John	2500	22 Feb 1799	450
Savage, Samuel P.	1908	12 Sep 1789	200
Goff, Gideon, *et al*	6243	19 Apr 1790	100

22 29 Jul 1799 A/1/022

By Whom Registered: Thomas McEwen & Co.
For Whom Registered: General Edward Hand
Location: (4000 acres) Mil - 16 1 - 3
Based upon the following Army land warrants:

Issued to	*No.*	*Date*	*Acres*
Cyphers, Andrew, Pvt	12033	4 Mar 1796	100
Turner, Malbry, Pvt	3818	22 Jun 1799	100
Lamb, George, Pvt	13354	29 Mar 1790	100
Phillips, Moses, Pvt	6938	28 Dec 1791	100
Phillips, Moses, Pvt	6859	28 Dec 1791	100
Phillips, Moses	6914	28 Dec 1791	100
Vandyck, Cornelius	7175	28 Dec 1791	100
Hart, John, Surgeon	937	22 Apr 1797	400
Burr, Elijah, & Burr, Calvin	128	22 Jun 1799	300
Bell, Abraham	9296	28 Jun 1799	100
Bell, Abraham	13548	28 Jun 1799	100
Bell, Abraham	8654	28 Jun 1799	100
Bell, Abraham	10070	28 Jun 1799	100
Cole, Isaac	11882	1 Jul 1799	100
Hand, Edward, BrigGen	1005	5 May 1789	850
Crocker, Joseph	2458	27 Oct 1789	450
Johnson, Amos	612	2 Feb 1797	200
Daves, John	610	31 Dec 1798	300
Cole, Isaac	479	1 Jul 1799	300

23 12 Aug 1799 A/1/023

By Whom Registered: Abraham Baldwin
For Whom Registered: Abraham Baldwin
Location: (4000 acres) Mil - 18 5 - 3
Based upon the following Army land warrants:

Issued to	*No.*	*Date*	*Acres*
Graves, Francis	11916	26 Mar 1792	100
Graves, Francis	12312	29 May 1792	100
Graves, Francis	12325	11 May 1792	100
Thornton, John	10518	24 Jul 1792	100
Humphrys, James	9703	11 Jan 1793	100
Hessler, Andrew	9415	11 Jan 1792	100
Wildey, Edward	7993	24 Sep 1791	100
Kirkpatrick, Francis	9105	24 Jun 1793	100
Stockdale, John	12686	31 Jan 1793	100
Godfrey, John W.	9034	22 Jun 1792	100
Kirkpatrick, Francis	9919	17 Jun 1793	100
Maus, Samuel	9685	7 Jul 1792	100
Graves, Francis	12469	26 Mar 1792	100
Graves, Francis	11910	29 May 1792	100
Graves, Francis	11867	29 May 1792	100
Graves, Francis	12240	29 May 1792	100
Rhea, James	9365	13 Jun 1792	100
Power, Alexander	10517	27 Apr 1793	100
Dixon, James	5695	26 Feb 1793	100
Workman, Samuel	8863	9 May 1792	100
Hill, Jacob	9523	3 May 1792	100
Snider, Peter	9340	30 Oct 1792	100
Waters, Joseph	6699	11 Apr 1792	100
Hubbart, Christian	9493	17 Jun 1793	100
Steward, John	9243	10 Mar 1795	100
Newkirk, Charles	7114	23 Aug 1790	100
Nicholson, John	9382	7 Apr 1795	100
Nicholson, John	13502	7 Apr 1795	100
Smyth, Richard	12261	30 Jul 1792	100
Graves, Francis	12558	7 Mar 1793	100
Means, Robert	11863	7 Jan 1793	100
Yates, Christopher, executors of [estate]	7825	28 Aug 1790	100

23 [continued]

Bolton? [Botton?] Joseph	8108	27 Dec 1791	100
McLaughlin, Hugh	8573	27 Dec 1791	100
O'Flaherty, John	8618	20 Apr 1792	100
Kelly, William	9776	19 Apr 1792	100
McDonald, James	8584	27 Dec 1791	100
Snell, John	13018	19 Mar 1792	100
Molineaux, Frederick	13379	13 Dec 1792	100
McKenzie, Alexander	12358	26 Nov 1792	100

24 29 Jul 1799 A/1/024

By Whom Registered: Joseph Asheton
For Whom Registered: Joseph Asheton
Location: (4000 acres) Mil - 12 5 - 1
Based upon the following Army land warrants:

Issued to	*No.*	*Date*	*Acres*
Irvin, John, Capt	1148	--	300
Byerly, Frederick	9038	20 Jun 1789	100
Reed, William, Cpl	10276	20 Jun 1789	100
Mitchell, William	9946	20 Jun 1789	100
Messersmith, Peter	10029	20 Jun 1789	100
Stanley, George, Sgt	5104	20 Jun 1789	100
Morris, David	9982	20 Jun 1789	100
Patterson, Robert	10229	20 Jun 1789	100
Ashton, Joseph, CapLt	46	17 Oct 1789	200
Denny, Ebenezer, Lt	565	17 Oct 1789	200
Ashton, Joseph	8975	7 Sep 1790	100
Ashton, Joseph	13575	7 Sep 1790	100
Ashton, Joseph	10642	7 Sep 1790	100
Dempsey, Thomas	9326	20 Jun 1789	100
Smith, Thomas	10354	20 Jun 1789	100
McDonald, William	9869	20 Jun 1789	100
Norton, Patrick	10141	20 Jun 1789	100
White, John	6710	20 Jun 1789	100
Stubbs, Robert	10474	20 Jun 1789	100
Sutton, David	10472	18 Apr 1796	100
Ferguson, William, Capt	748	4 Jun 1789	300
Beatty, Erkuries? Lt	206	17 Oct 1789	200
Duffy, James	12995	20 Jun 1789	100
Brown, Thomas	8921	20 Jun 1789	100
Butler, William, Col Com[mandant?]	189	5 Nov 1789	500
Bowers, George	10995	5 Nov 1789	100
Fletcher, Simon	9410	5 Nov 1789	100
McKinney, Peter	9778	5 Nov 1789	100
Wilson, Galbreath	12654	5 Nov 1789	100

25 12 Aug 1799 A/1/025

By Whom Registered: Abraham Baldwin
For Whom Registered: Abraham Baldwin
Location: (4000 acres) Mil - 13 4 - 3
Based upon the following Army land warrants:

Issued to	*No.*	*Date*	*Acres*
Johnson, Mary	8990	9 Nov 1792	100
Stevenson, John	5223	27 Feb 1793	100
Greaves, Francis	12276	13 Dec 1791	100
Pulford, Elisha	6295	15 Jan 1796	100
Oakly, John	6250	10 Oct 1791	100
Stevens, Theodore	7846	22 May 1793	100
Wiggon, James	8851	5 Jan 1792	100
McDonald, Archibald	12427	7 Oct 1795	100
Hawley, Nathan	5959	15 Mar 1790	100
Case, Benjamin	8490	24 Mar 1790	100
Aymand, John	12715	28 Apr 1795	100
Mix? [Alix?] Rufus	6233	23 Dec 1795	100
Ponsonby, George	11483	8 Jan 1796	100
Salter? [Saller?] John	8771	20 Jul 1795	100
Lines, Ebenezer	6100	12 Oct 1789	100
Catlin, Alexander	13222	5 Apr 1792	100
Blodget, Ezra	4118	8 May 1792	100
Tate, Eleanor	13444	6 Feb 1792	100
Wade, Henry	8836	20 Apr 1793	100
Scriver, Jacob	7784	7 Mar 1792	100
Carson, Thomas	9157	22 Apr 1792	100
Boyd, Thomas	9010	6 Apr 1790	100
Merkle, Gideon	9744	6 Aug 1792	100
Walker, Thomas	13193	15 Jun 1792	100
Mapes, John	13529	26 Apr 1792	100
Curray, Samuel	7158	20 Jul 1790	100
Yates, Tellis	6925	28 Aug 1790	100
Yates, Christopher, executors of [estate]	6749	28 Aug 1790	100
Bennet, James	9313	7 Jun 1793	100
Johnson, Mary	10209	9 Nov 1792	100
McEvoy, Michael	9898	22 Apr 1793	100
Sanders, John	8717	20 Dec 1792	100
Lane, William	9234	22 Jun 1792	100
Lane, William	9257	29 Sep 1792	100
Means, Robert	11922	14 Jul 1792	100
Means, Robert	12669	14 Jul 1792	100
Means, Robert	12531	7 Jul 1792	100
Eddens, Samuel, Capt	683	10 Aug 1795	300

26 12 Aug 1799 A/1/027

By Whom Registered: Abraham Baldwin
For Whom Registered: Abraham Baldwin
Location: (4000 acres) Mil - 13 5 - 3
Based upon the following Army land warrants:

Issued to	*No.*	*Date*	*Acres*
Holmes, David, Surgeon	1084	14 Mar 1796	400
Stockdell, John	12684	30 Jun 1795	100
Deming, Jonathan	5688	13 Sep 1796	100
Dorey, James	12980	21 Jan 1792	100
Jones, John	13253	4 Nov 1791	100
Carr, Matthew	9116	11 Sep 1789	100
Blackmore, George	11978	18 Aug 1795	100
McClean, Isabella	10489	18 May 1795	100
Stanwood, William, Lt	1931	12 Apr 1790	200
Steel, John	5698	8 Apr 1797	100
Packard, John	6328	22 Feb 1799	100
Poor, John, Lt	1933	22 Feb 1799	200
Harrod, Anna, & Davis, Elizabeth (capt)	2702	27 Jul 1798	300
Crocker, Allen	5194	10 May 1799	100
Crocker, Allen	4141	10 May 1799	100
Turner, Marlbry, Lt	2168	10 May 1799	200
Thorp, Thomas	5169	12 Jan 1799	100
Park, Matthew	3711	21 Mar 1792	100
Park, Matthew	4940	21 Mar 1792	100
Bowles, Ralph H., Lt	115	12 Jan 1799	200
Duncan, John	3709	7 Feb 1799	100
Duncan, John	6155	7 Feb 1799	100
Duncan, John	5883	7 Feb 1799	100
Duncan, John	4946	7 Feb 1799	100
Duncan, John	3666	7 Feb 1799	100
Duncan, John	13432	5 Jan 1799	100
Milbourn, Nicholas	11478	20 Oct 1789	100
Keeler, Frederick	7345	7 May 1795	100
Power, Tobias	13596	5 Dec 1791	100
Clay, Matthew, Lt	456	20 May 1797	200

27 21 Aug 1799 A/1/028

By Whom Registered: Jacob D. Hart
For Whom Registered: Thomas McKean Thompson
Location: (4000 acres)* Mil - 13 3 - 3
Based upon the following Army land warrants:

27 [continued]

Issued to	No.	Date	Acres
McKennan, Will., Capt	1471	30 May 1789	300
Anderson, Thomas, Lt	39	30 May 1789	200
Campbell, James, Lt	405	30 May 1789	200
Bennett, Caleb P., Lt	227	30 May 1789	200
Jaquett, Peter, Capt	1160	30 May 1789	300
Patten, John, Maj	1725	30 May 1789	400
Jones, James, Surgeon	1153	30 May 1789	400
Monroe, George, Surgeon	1523	30 May 1789	400
Killen, William, Col	1041	2 Sep 1789	500
Fopless, John	10766	2 Sep 1789	100
Ireland, Samuel	10826	2 Sep 1789	100
Crawford, Charles	12000	20 Aug 1791	100
Gibson, Thomas	8345	29 Jan 1793	100
Davis, James	10743	2 Sep 1789	100
Hanson, John	13242	2 Sep 1789	100
Ferrel, Robert, Sgt	13108	6 Mar 1790	100
McGauhy, Will.	10830	2 Sep 1789	100
Cole, Benjamin	5561	26 Apr 1792	100
Clarke, Benjamin	5553	13 Dec 1791	100
Smith, Martin	6448	22 Sep 1791	100

*Marginal notation:

"Acres rec. per this statement 4000
Tract? rec. & entered 31 Dec 1801 1100
5100
Amount of location 5040
Register's cert. issued for over[age?] 60"

[See also serial entry 278]

28 21 Aug 1799 A/1/029

By Whom Registered: The Reverend Samuel Jones
For Whom Registered: The Reverend Samuel Jones
Location: (4000 acres) Mil - 20 6 - 4
Based upon the following Army land warrants:

Issued to	No.	Date	Acres
Mason, Issacher	11401	8 May 1790	100
Manly, William	11505	24 Sep 1792	100
Cleary, William	11035	24 Sep 1792	100
Robeson, Charles	11202	8 Aug 1792	100
Sullivan, Philip	11745	11 Jun 1790	100
Fitzgerald, John	11239	1 May 1792	100
Buckley, Mary	10966	16 Jul 1792	100
Barber, James Noyes, Ens	154	7 Aug 1789	150
Jameson, Adam, Lt	1162	25 May 1789	200
Reilly, William, Capt	1839	18 Jul 1789	300
Muret, Charles	11546	11 May 1790	100
Trumbull, Jonathan, LtCol	2169	7 Aug 1789	450
Francis, John	11214	8 May 1790	100
Smith, Joseph, Capt	2041	19 Jun 1789	300
Fluhart, Stephen, Sgt	11220	11 Jun 1790	100
de Baufre, James	11701	14 Aug 1797	100
Justice, Jessee	13243	18 Jun 1799	100
Gaine, Jacob	11268	9 Jul 1799	100
Graves, Francis, Capt	1739	26 Mar 1792	300
Thompson, John	7148	25 Sep 1790	100
Means, Robert, Capt	1851	29 May 1792	300
Lord, Levin	11438	9 Jul 1799	100
Windows, Henry	11828	9 Jul 1799	100
Conolly, Charles	10719	2 Sep 1789	100
Wells, Benjamin, Surgeon	2622	17 Jan 1793	300

29 25 Nov 1799 A/1/030

By Whom Registered: George Gillaspy
For Whom Registered: James Taylor & Gillaspy & Strong
Location: (4000 acres) Mil - 9 6 - 2
Based upon the following Army land warrants:

Issued to	No.	Date	Acres
Kettle, Thomas	6060	11 Sep 1792	100
Munson, Eneas	5918	24 Feb 1795	100
Bracket, Hezekiah	5520	19 Apr 1792	100
Albertson, William	3123	1 Dec 1789	100
Dunscomb, Andrew, Lt	1856	4 Sep 1792	200
Dunscomb, Andrew, Capt	1598	4 Sep 1792	300
Bell, Thomas, Capt	256	1 Mar 1796	300
Muth, Jacob	13408	4 Sep 1795	100
Means, Robert	12512	2 Nov 1792	100
Stockdale, John	12473	26 Oct 1795	100
Purdy, Henry	11150	7 Aug 1794	100
Yost, John	10680	21 Mar 1792	100
Shaw, John	10364	19 Sep 1795	100
Holman, George	9606	29 Jul 1794	100
Shaw, John	9042	26 Nov 1795	100
Savage, Edward	7537	14 Feb 1791	100
Sacket, Augustus	7408	21 Feb 1792	100
Patchon, Woolcot	6297	6 Sep 1792	100
Clifton, Whittington	10735	2 Sep 1789	100
Waldron, Resolve	6661	19 Jan 1792	100
Beckman, Bernard, Col	301	7 Jun 1796	500
Means, Robert	14017	2 Nov 1792	100
Wilhelm, Balzer	13872	3 Mar 1791	100
Nicholson, John	13568	7 Apr 1795	100
Moers, Benjamin	13430	21 Sep 1790	100
Walker, Francis	14056	3 Apr 1794	100
Bostman, Frederick	12811	11 Sep 1792	100
de Baufre, James	11838	1 May 1797	100
de Baufre, James	11528	1 May 1797	100
Lynch, William	11465	1 May 1797	100
de Baufre, James	10882	4 May 1797	100

30 7 Dec 1799 A/1/031

By Whom Registered: William Simmons
For Whom Registered: Edward D. Turner
Location: (4000 acres) Mil - 11 7 - 4
Based upon the following Army land warrants:

Issued to	No.	Date	Acres
Tenny, Samuel	5318	27 Aug 1792	100
Bass, Samuel	10703	11 May 1796	100
Connor, John	10729	2 Sep 1789	100
McGuire, Thomas	13941	2 Sep 1789	100
Foster, Abraham	4367	11 Apr 1796	100
Dana, Benjamin	4773	24 Aug 1796	100
Dana, Benjamin	4814	23 Aug 1796	100
Blanchard, William	5184	13 Jul 1796	100
Pool, Abijah, Lt	1663	12 Apr 1790	200
Turner, Thomas, Capt	2147	27 Sep 1796	300
McMullen, Archibald	2923	2 Sep 1789	100
Foster, Abraham	360	11 Apr 1796	450
Dana, Benjamin	348	1 Aug 1796	200
Tenney, Samuel	333	24 Aug 1796	400
Crocker, Joseph, & Crocker, Allen	102	31 Dec 1793	300
Gibson, John, Col	865	24 Oct 1789	500
Hobby, John, Capt	913	16 Apr 1792	300
Newhall, Ezra, LtCol	1574	18 May 1790	450

31 7 Dec 1799 A/1/032

By Whom Registered: William Simmons
For Whom Registered: William Simmons
Location: (4000 acres)* Mil - 8 6 - 4
Based upon the following Army land warrants:

Issued to	No.	Date	Acres
de Baufre, James	11823	4 May 1797	100
Holbrook, Abijah	13332	1 May 1799	100
Bell, Abraham	13633	21 May 1799	100
Moore, Benjamin	13667	20 Feb 1792	100
Russell, Thomas	13803	30 Mar 1793	100

31 [continued]

Ward, Joshua	11238	11 Jan 1796	100
de Baufre, James	11319	31 Jul 1797	100
Ward, Joshua	11461	11 Jan 1796	100
de Baufre, James	11468	31 Jul 1797	100
de Baufre, James	11532	26 Jul 1797	100
Beggs, Moore, Sgt	8977	6 Apr 1790	100
Dixon, Jacob, Pvt	9299	5 Nov 1789	100
Russell, Thomas	9701	24 Jun 1793	100
Hitchins, Major, Pvt	10777	15 Apr 1799	100
Hitchins, Caleb, Pvt	10780	15 Apr 1799	100
Bacon, George	10859	26 May 1790	100
de Baufre, James	10890	1 May 1797	100
Kershaw, Mitchell	10913	15 Apr 1799	100
de Baufre, James	10989	31 Jul 1797	100
Ward, Joshua	11235	11 Jan 1796	100
Bell, Abraham	8162	27 Apr 1799	100
Bell, Abraham	8202	21 May 1799	100
Bell, Abraham	8242	27 Apr 1799	100
Bell, Abraham	8435	21 May 1789	100
Bell, Abraham	8503	27 Apr 1799	100
Wier, Charles	1203	21 May 1799	200
Sawyer, James, Ens	1921	28 Oct 1791	150
Tucker, Thomas Tudor, Surgeon	2240	15 Jun 1789	450
Holbrook, Abijah	3668	1 May 1799	100
Quinton, David	4543	30 Jul 1792	100
Holbrook, Abijah	5196	1 May 1799	100
Allen, Samuel	6459	15 Aug 1792	100
Russell, Thomas	6847	14 May 1793	100
Russell, Thomas	7512	24 Jun 1793	100
Russell, Thomas	8013	14 May 1793	100

*Marginal notation:

"Location made [per above tract citation]	4237 2/10
Warrants recd. by this State for	4000
Since received:	
Johnson, James, Reg[ister's] cert. dated 10 Mar 1800	50
Brevard, Joseph, Warr. 299, dated 12 Jan 1799	200
	4250
Amount of location	4237 2/10
	12 8/10"

[See also serial entry 265]

32 18 Dec 1799 A/1/033

By Whom Registered: James Miller
For Whom Registered: John F. Hamtramick
Location: (4000 acres) Mil - 13 6 - 1
Based upon the following Army land warrants:

Issued to	*No.*	*Date*	*Acres*
Edwards, John, Lt	650	26 Oct 1789	200
Perkins, William, Maj	1639	7 Feb 1794	400
Lillie, John, Capt	1240	13 May 1796	300
Mills, John, Capt	1354	20 Apr 1790	300
Shute, Daniel, Surgeon	1894	26 Oct 1789	400
Allen, Nathaniel C., Capt	13	24 Apr 1794	300
Turner, Malbray	943	23 Mar 1797	200
Dana, Benjamin	4352	31 Jan 1797	100
Dana, Benjamin	312	5 Jan 1797	200
Dana, Benjamin	4050	31 Jan 1797	100
Kettell, Andrew	4528	9 May 1797	100
Dana, Benjamin	3323	3 Nov 1796	100
Dana, Benjamin	3714	23 Feb 1797	100
Mountfort, Benjamin, Pvt	4646	12 Jul 1797	100
Creesy, Benjamin, Pvt	3942	24 May 1797	100
Abbott, Joel	3389	30 Dec 1796	100
Parker, Elias, Lt	1647	16 Jul 1790	200
King, Ezra	4532	3 Apr 1797	100
King, Ezra	4806	20 Jul 1797	100
King, Ezra	4857	20 Jul 1797	100
King, Ezra	3932	3 Apr 1797	100
King, Ezra	5292	3 Apr 1797	100
King, Ezra	3971	3 Apr 1797	100
King, Ezra	4254	3 Apr 1797	100

33 2 Jan 1800 A/1/034

By Whom Registered: Daniel Marsh
For Whom Registered: Daniel Marsh
Location: (4000 acres) Mil - 15 2 - 1
Based upon the following Army land warrants:

Issued to	*No.*	*Date*	*Acres*
Lowell, Ebenezer	1250	21 Aug 1789	150
Moores, Benjamin	13434	22 Jan 1790	100
Moores, Benjamin	13425	22 Jan 1790	100
Moores, Benjamin	13420	22 Jan 1790	100
Moores, Benjamin	52921*	22 Jan 1790	100
Bullard, Asa	6725	1 Nov 1791	100
Sacket, Augustus	7882	1 Nov 1791	100
Platt, Richard	9981	11 Jul 1790	100
Platt, Richard	9960	7 Aug 1789	100
Power, Alexander	4760	9 Jan 1794	100
Wright, John	11347	27 Mar 1794	100
Wright, John	11123	28 Jan 1793	100
Wright, John	11131	22 Jan 1793	100
Wright, John	11019	17 Jan 1793	100
Means, Robert	12125	29 May 1792	100
Platt, Richard	9906	27 Jul 1789	100
Glentworth, George	2584	9 May 1791	450
Moores, Benjamin	13428	22 Jan 1790	100
Cusack, Christopher	11495	8 Aug 1794	100
Needer? [Veeder?] Simon	13687	30 Aug 1790	100
Emery, Samuel	5586	11 Jan 1794	100
Wright, John	11179	12 Sep 1792	100
Wright, John	11592	9 Nov 1792	100
Landsden, William	12315	22 Apr 1794	100
Wright, John	11090	6 Oct 1794	100
Platt, Richard	9930	7 Aug 1789	100
Platt, Richard	9794	7 Aug 1789	100
McConnell, Matthew	9311	29 Jun 1789	100
Stephenson, John	6304	11 Jan 1794	100
Bleecker, John N.	7068	4 Aug 1790	100
Bronson, Isaac	2607	8 May 1792	200
Benedict, Timothy	732	3 Mar 1794	200
Platt, Richard	9799	7 Aug 1789	100
Means, Robert	11904	29 May 1792	100

*So shown in register. This number probably is incorrect.

34 2 Jan 1800 A/1/035

By Whom Registered: Baum & Schenck
For Whom Registered: Jesse Baldwin
Location: (4000 acres) Mil - 11 5 - 1
Based upon the following Army land warrants:

Issued to	*No.*	*Date*	*Acres*
Cumming, William	6761	20 Aug 1790	100
Smith, Whitfield*	3728	19 Apr 1792	100
Blanchard, John	906	18 May 1792	200
Rawlings, Aaron	11626	11 Mar 1791	100
Garnett, Elisha	5844	7 Sep 1790	100
Martin, Joseph	13431	4 Feb 1790	100
Smith, Whitfield	4764	19 Apr 1792	100
Muzzy, Amos	4999	8 May 1792	100
Muzzy, Amos	1578	8 May 1792	200
Blanchard, John	5130	18 May 1792	100
Sullivan, Thomas	10400	19 Dec 1789	100
Ross, Robert	9913	12 Mar 1792	100
Dunbar, Nehemiah, Pvt	4008	1 Jun 1792	100

34 [continued]

Chaps, John, Pvt	5609	13 Jan 1792	100
Verlie, Francis	13860	4 Feb 1790	100
Poulier, Joseph	13605	4 Feb 1790	100
Butler, Zebulon, Col	132	15 Sep 1791	500
Blanchard, Peter, Pvt	12271	4 Feb 1790	100
Dayton, William	8583	10 Feb 1790	100
Platt, Richard	3876	12 Oct 1790	100
de Hart, Cyrus	557	9 Jul 1790	300
Blanchard, John	4263	2 Dec 1791	100
Smith, Platt	7744	15 Sep 1790	100
Green, Pierson	8332	27 Mar 1797	100
Bell, Abraham	8391	2 Jun 1797	100
Bell, Abraham	8137	2 Jun 1797	100
Bell, Abraham	8574	2 Jun 1797	100
Bell, Abraham	8423	2 Jun 1797	100
Bell, Abraham	8776	2 Jun 1797	100
Means, Robert	12042	14 Jul 1792	100
Blair, Robert, Pvt	8110	5 Nov 1789	100
Johnson, Ithamar, Pvt	4459	30 Aug 1790	100

*Marginal notation: "Swift."

35 2 Jan 1800 A/1/037

By Whom Registered: Abraham Baldwin
For Whom Registered: Abraham Baldwin
Location: (4000 acres) Mil - 19 5 - 4
Based upon the following Army land warrants:

Issued to	*No.*	*Date*	*Acres*
Dempsey, Charles	9246	9 Jul 1789	100
Anspach, Peter	8302	9 Jul 1790	100
Roads, Joseph	7295	26 Aug 1790	100
Eells, Samuel	5747	25 Jan 1790	100
Fry, Windsor	3126	31 Dec 1789	100
Perry, John	8641	1 Mar 1790	100
Tennant, William	8789	26 May 1790	100
June? [Tune?] Abraham	12877	4 Oct 1789	100
Platner, John	6279	13 Dec 1791	100
Preston, Stephen	11586	1 Feb 1790	100
Alexander, Nath[anie]l, Surgeon's Mate	70	7 Jun 1798	300
Fairlie, James, Lt	733	13 Jan 1791	200
Pauling, Henry, Capt	1682	14 Feb 1791	300
Matthews, George, Lt	1080	19 May 1797	200
Pine, John, Pvt	10228	7 Feb 1792	100
Merkle, Gideon	10214	13 Dec 1791	100
Bradford, Robert, Capt	103	28 Nov 1789	300
Stewart, Walter	11934	29 May 1792	100
Stewart, Walter, Capt	1504	29 May 1792	300
Stewart, Walter	12310	29 May 1792	100
Flahavan, --, & Wilcox, --, Lt	1434	11 Oct 1792	200
Flahavan, Thomas, Capt	1470	11 Oct 1792	300
Gordon, Peter	13124	23 Jan 1796	100
Duncan, John	9124	12 Apr 1799	100
Christie, John, Capt	418	26 Jun 1792	300

36 6 Jan 1800 A/1/038

By Whom Registered: John Terrell
For Whom Registered: John Terrell "of New Jersey"
Location: (4000 acres) Mil - 9 2 - 3
Based upon the following Army land warrants:

Issued to	*No.*	*Date*	*Acres*
Sherrard, Francis, Pvt	10919	12 Aug 1795	100
Sherrard, Francis	14118	1 May 1795	100
Sherrard, Francis	10924	21 Aug 1795	100
Cooley, Owen, Pvt	12893	27 Sep 1790	100
Sherrard, Francis	10964	14 Aug 1795	100
Thom, William S.	3383	17 Dec 1795	100
Mills, Morgan	8550	9 May 1792	100
Tennell, John	14125	3 Aug 1795	100
Rawlingson, David	12525	13 Jul 1795	100
Kelly, Timothy	9718	9 Nov 1791	100
Power, Alexander	10323	10 Mar 1790	100
Sherrard, Francis	14134	14 Aug 1795	100
Power, Alexander	9796	10 Mar 1790	100
Sherrard, Francis	10926	12 Aug 1795	100
Mason, Jere? [Tere?]	4037	18 Apr 1796	100
Hyde, Azel	5900	30 Mar 1793	100
Davis, Henry	11383	14 Oct 1795	100
Davis, Henry	11067	14 Oct 1795	100
Sherrard, Francis	10930	12 Aug 1795	100
Sherrard, Francis	10931	12 Aug 1795	100
Sherrard, Francis	10972	14 Aug 1795	100
Zerban, Wendell	12428	27 Aug 1795	100
Cornwell, William	11116	22 Sep 1795	100
Thom, William S.	3283	17 Dec 1795	100
Thom, William S.	3488	17 Dec 1795	100
Thom, William S.	3376	17 Dec 1795	100
Mitchell, Amasa	4647	13 Jan 1799	100
Bush, Charles	4409	10 Sep 1789	100
Bush, Charles	13110	10 Sep 1789	100
Bush, Charles	13167	10 Sep 1789	100
Wates, Robert	8844	6 Jun 1791	100
Gardner, Peregrine, Pvt	13114	18 Jul 1791	100
Gibbs, Samuel	6461	27 Jul 1789	100
Means, Robert	12274	2 Nov 1792	100
Mason, Jere? [Tere?]	5282	18 Apr 1796	100
Mason, Jeremiah, Ens	1787	18 Apr 1796	150
Russell, Thomas	1777	31 Aug 1791	150
Davis, Hervey, Pvt	11212	14 Oct 1795	100
Welch, James	12783	23 May 1795	100

37 6 Jan 1800 A/1/039

By Whom Registered: William Wells
For Whom Registered: Jonathan Cass
Location: (4000 acres) Mil - 7 3 - 2
Based upon the following Army land warrants:

Issued to	*No.*	*Date*	*Acres*
Pall, Joseph	10285	27 Nov 1794	100
Stever, Daniel	10011	10 Jun 1794	100
McEwen, James	9973	28 Jan 1795	100
Pall, Joseph	10415	27 Nov 1794	100
de Benneville, Dan[ie]l, Surgeon	2649	21 Jan 1795	400
Bradford, William, Junior, Maj	84	9 May 1796	400
Carey, Lewis, Pvt	3987	27 Dec 1796	100
Fosdick, Joseph, Pvt	4164	12 Jan 1797	100
King, Patrick, Pvt	4521	12 Jun 1797	100
Dana, Benjamin	4234	23 Feb 1797	100
Fosdick, Joseph	4661	16 Mar 1797	100
Dana, Benjamin, Lt	809	23 Mar 1797	200
Garrison, Benjamin	8336	27 Dec 1798	100
Gray, James, Lt	810	27 Jan 1798	200
McGregor, David, Capt	1339	4 Jan 1799	300
Mayberry, Richard, Capt	1371	12 Apr 1799	300
Danford, Joshua, Pvt	3053	24 Feb 1791	100
Mason, Edward, SgtMaj	3329	21 Dec 1790	100
Carter, Peter, Pvt	3890	29 Nov 1796	100
Dana, Benjamin	4035	28 Jun 1797	100
Cass, Jonathan	3579	27 Jan 1798	100
Thompson, Robert	9001	12 Mar 1792	100
Thomson, Robert	10601	15 Apr 1796	100
Stever, Daniel	10619	10 Jun 1794	100
Crafordly, William	10493	29 Jul 1796	100
May, John	4701	16 May 1796	100
Cass, Jonathan	3199	24 Dec 1799	100
Ogen, Thomas	12444	1 Mar 1794	100

38 6 Jan 1800 A/1/040

By Whom Registered: Martin Baum

For Whom Registered: Martin Baum

Location: (4000 acres)* Mil - 12 6 - 3

Based upon the following Army land warrants:

Issued to	*No.*	*Date*	*Acres*
Goldsmith, James	5838	23 Sep 1789	100
McCleland, John	8932	2 Nov 1791	100
Page, Luther	6261	9 Apr 1791	100
Turkentine, Manly	13827	20 Jun 1789	100
Denean, William	8272	12 Sep 1789	100
Brown, Jedediah	5430	28 Jan 1790	100
Sherrard, Francis	10942	14 Aug 1795	100
Sherrard, Francis	10921	14 Aug 1795	100
Holden, Samuel	4378	28 Jan 1790	100
Willis, Zacharias	5241	22 Dec 1791	100
Austin, Holmes	6723	24 Feb 1791	100
Neal, James A.	3269	12 Oct 1795	100
Brown, Benjamin	7829	11 Dec 1789	100
Thomas, Obishai	11969	10 Jun 1791	100
Thomas, Obishai	12411	10 Jun 1791	100
Thomas, Obishai	12698	1 Jun 1790	100
Oakly, John	7578	10 Oct 1791	100
Beard, Moses	3796	29 Feb 1792	100
Graves, Francis	12656	26 Mar 1792	100
Neal, James A.	3541	26 Jan 1796	100
Uffoot? [Usfoot?] Job	6600	12 Dec 1792	100
Lawrence, Nathan, Lt	1315	28 Dec 1791	200
Lamb, Abner, Lt	1314	25 May 1792	200
Brewster, John, Pvt	3820	25 Oct 1792	100
Davis, Jacob	5680	25 Feb 1790	100
Lamb, Abner, LtCol	1310	25 May 1792	500
Rasster, Godfrey J., Pvt	13646	23 Sep 1791	100
Wynn, Webster	10665	21 Jun 1792	100
Henry, John	13177	23 Sep 1791	100
Smith, James	10376	28 Jan 1792	100
Thomas, Abishai	12421	10 Jun 1791	100
Ely, William	6950	4 Nov 1792	100
Foote, Ebenezer	7497	7 Jul 1791	100
Pardy, Nathaniel	6327	7 Sep 1790	100

*Marginal notation:

"Location made . . . 4381-9/10 acres
Warr. recd. this State 4000
Since recd.:
No. 4 Reg[ister's] Cert. dated 10 Mar 1800 in favor of Martin Baum 317-8/10 acres
No. 6903 Warr. dated 23 Aug 1790 in favor of Charles Newkirk for 100 acres
4417-8/10
Amount of location 4381-9/10 acres
35-9/10 acres"

[See also serial entry 266]

39 6 Jan 1800 A/1/041

By Whom Registered: William Wells

For Whom Registered: John Armstrong

Location: (4000 acres) Mil - 13 7 - 2

Based upon the following Army land warrants:

Issued to	*No.*	*Date*	*Acres*
Armstrong, John, Lt	42	20 Jun 1789	200
Golden, William	9462	20 Jun 1789	100
O'Bryan, William	10173	28 Jan 1791	100
Larner, Edward	9804	20 Jun 1789	100
Gibson, John, Junior	874	24 Oct 1789	150
Cabell, Samuel J., LtCol	446	21 Jan 1796	450
Miller, Gavin	10046	20 Jun 1789	100
Power, Alexander	9092	22 Mar 1791	100
Power, Alexander	9612	17 Mar 1791	100
Sprague, Abel	5099	20 Jun 1789	100
Power, Alex[ander]	9126	22 Mar 1791	100
Roberts, Joseph	10257	20 Jun 1789	100
Power, Alex[ande]r	9160	17 Mar 1791	100
Kilby, John	9741	20 Jun 1789	100
Vicker, Robert	10546	20 Jun 1789	100
Cotter, Edward	9198	20 Jun 1789	100
Morey, Jonathan	4673	20 Jun 1789	100
Skinner, William	10877	17 Jan 1791	100
Collins, John	12895	20 Jun 1789	100
Turner, George, Capt	2228	15 Oct 1789	300
Reese, Joshua	13697	20 Jun 1789	100
Power, Alex[ande]r, Lt	578	19 Apr 1791	200
Witham, James	3013	6 Jul 1792	100
Power, Alex[ande]r	10657	17 Mar 1791	100
Shoeman, Charles	13706	20 Jun 1789	100
Witham, James	4789	6 Jul 1792	100
Power, Alex[ande]r	9958	17 Mar 1791	100
Witham, James	5267	6 Jul 1792	100
Thompson, Price	8788	31 Jul 1789	100
Gibbons, James	9437	20 Jun 1789	100
Fisher, Henry	9395	20 Jun 1789	100
Keyser, George	9768	20 Jun 1789	100

40 6 Jan 1800 A/1/042

By Whom Registered: Caleb Swan

For Whom Registered: Caleb Swan

Location: (4000 acres) Mil - 5 5 - 2

Based upon the following Army land warrants:

Issued to	*No.*	*Date*	*Acres*
Frye, Frederick, Ens	708	1 Jul 1796	150
Frye, Nathaniel, Lt	707	13 Nov 1789	200
Laverswyler? [Saverswyler?] Mary, Ens	1284	10 Mar 1790	150
Catlin, Putnam, Fife Maj	5619	8 Jul 1790	100
Rix, Adam, Sgt	10248	10 Mar 1790	100
McLean, Arch[ibal]d, Pvt	9945	8 Jun 1790	100
Platt, Samuel, Surgeon's Mate	1721	30 May 1789	200
Footman, Peter, Pvt	8403	22 Jul 1796	100
Kellog, Solomon	6055	27 Aug 1792	100
Adkins, Jabez	5368	10 May 1798	100
Bailey, Louden, Sgt Maj	5481	7 Jul 1798	100
Allison, Richard, Surgeon's Mate	44	20 Jun 1789	300
Allison, Richard, Lt	1429	20 Jun 1789	200
Strong, David, Capt	1951	17 Oct 1789	300
Dunn, Abner M., Lt	564	7 Sep 1790	200
Kearsey, John, Pvt	9765	20 Jun 1789	100
Redhair, Frederick, Pvt	10310	20 Jun 1789	100
Fennell? [Tennell?] Patrick, Pvt	9371	20 Jun 1789	100
Kingsbury, Jacob, Ens	1190	12 Sep 1789	150
Wood, Joseph M., Pvt	6150	20 Jun 1789	100
Orr, John, Sgt	10179	20 Jun 1789	100
Dixon, John, Pvt	9302	20 Jun 1789	100
Nace, George, Cpl	10143	20 Jun 1789	100
Dougherty, George, Fifer	9318	20 Jun 1789	100
Lattimore, Rich[ar]d, Pvt	9848	20 Jun 1789	100
Ford, Mahlon, Lt	2526	4 Aug 1790	200
Kellog, Josiah, Pvt	6056	27 Aug 1792	100
Swan, Caleb, Ens	1923	13 Nov 1789	150
Kellog, William, Pvt	6060	27 Aug 1792	100

41 6 Jan 1800 A/1/043

By Whom Registered: George Jackson

For Whom Registered: George Jackson

Location: (4000 acres) Mil - 12 2 - 2

Based upon the following Army land warrants:

41 [continued]

Issued to	*No.*	*Date*	*Acres*
Mouser, Jacob, Capt	1462	25 Jul 1796	300
McDonald, Charles, Pvt	6164	6 Jan 1797	100
Parks, John, Pvt	6260	6 Jan 1797	100
Rogers, Heman, Pvt	6375	6 Jan 1797	100
Tomlinson, Joseph	6540	24 Dec 1796	100
Soper, Richard	6523	30 Dec 1796	100
Atkins, Josiah	5372	24 Dec 1796	100
Ashur, Gad	5377	6 Jan 1797	100
Graham, Jesse	5836	30 Dec 1796	100
Ford, Martin	5813	24 Dec 1796	100
Shields, James	6421	6 Jan 1797	100
Ward, Daniel	6674	6 Jan 1797	100
Smith, Ballard, Capt	2075	20 Mar 1792	300
Franklin, Jesse, Lt	613	14 Jan 1797	200
Thorn, William S., Pvt	3489	17 Feb 1797	100
Allyn, John, Pvt	5384	24 Dec 1796	100
Betts, David, Pvt	5496	30 Dec 1796	100
Wheedon, Roswell, Pvt	6624	30 Dec 1796	100
Hull, David, Pvt	5972	5 Dec 1796	100
Rogers, David, Pvt	6371	5 Dec 1796	100
Ticker, Jared, Pvt	6543	24 Dec 1796	100
Keys, Daniel, Pvt	4522	6 Jan 1797	100
Dyer, Joseph, Pvt	4028	6 Jan 1797	100
Freeman, Frank, Pvt	5793	24 Dec 1796	100
Robinson, James, Pvt	10299	29 Jun 1796	100
de Baufre, James, Pvt	10731	13 Nov 1797	100
de Baufre, James, Pvt	11141	16 Aug 1797	100
de Baufre, James, Pvt	11589	13 Nov 1797	100
Nixon, Robert, Pvt	14131	11 Aug 1795	100
Langsden, Charles, Pvt	12314	22 Mar 1796	100
Harper, Nathan, Pvt	11314	13 Jun 1796	100
Brewer, Paul, Pvt	8138	15 Feb 1796	100
Rosier? Abraham	8687	27 May 1793	100
Turner, John	10894	6 Mar 1790	100
Foster, Alex[ande]r W.	10359	7 Dec 1791	100

42 16 Jan 1800 A/1/045

By Whom Registered: John E. Howard
For Whom Registered: John E. Howard
Location: (4000 acres)* Mil - 12 7 - 4
Based upon the following Army land warrants:

Issued to	*No.*	*Date*	*Acres*
Howard, John E., Col	1043	18 Oct 1796	500
Watkins, Rob[ert] & Watkins, Jo[seph?] Capt	451	19 Jun 1799	300
Bernard, William R., Lt	1744	22 Feb 1799	200
Phelps, Asahel, Pvt	10772	10 Oct 1799	100
Clements, Henry, Lt	441	10 Mar 1790	200
Bankson, John, Capt	199	19 May 1789	300
Swan, John, Maj	2058	11 May 1790	400
Mason, Thomas, Capt	1482	24 May 1790	300
Skerritt, Clement, Lt	2047	14 Jul 1789	200
Ramsay, Nath[anie]l, Col	1836	11 Feb 1791	500
Phile, Charles, Capt	1723	14 Feb 1791	300
Phelps, Asahel, Pvt	10785	10 Oct 1799	100
Hall, Josias C., Col	1044	14 Apr 1795	500
Thompson, Corn[elius] Pvt	11754	11 May 1790	100

*Marginal notation: "See vol. 1, page 110."

43 16 Jan 1800 A/1/045

By Whom Registered: Andrew Porter
For Whom Registered: Andrew Porter
Location: (4000 acres) Mil - 19 5 - 2
Based upon the following Army land warrants: .

Issued to	*No.*	*Date*	*Acres*
Porter, Andrew, Pvt	9037	18 Jul 1791	100
Porter, Andrew, Pvt	8596	30 Jul 1791	100
Porter, Andrew, Pvt	10077	18 Jul 1791	100
Porter, Andrew, Pvt	10080	18 Jul 1791	100
Porter, Andrew, LtCol	1699	20 Aug 1789	500
Porter, Andrew, Pvt	13520	3 May 1791	100
Banghman? [Baughman?] George, Pvt	9062	11 Feb 1791	100
Dutall, John, Pvt	9317	6 Jun 1791	100
McCartney, Dennis, Pvt	10047	9 May 1791	100
Kelly, Henry, Pvt	13574	2 Sep 1789	100
Pardo, Joseph, Pvt	10233	14 Feb 1791	100
Wayne, Abraham, & Justice, James, Pvt	13367	1 Aug 1791	100
Homingway, Jon[athan?] Pvt	4320	17 Jan 1791	100
Tureman, John, Lt	2211	1 Sep 1789	200
Mitchell, Robert, Pvt	9996	9 May 1791	100
Ferguson, William, Pvt	9390	9 May 1791	100
Moore, Joseph, Pvt	8540	24 Nov 1791	100
Manifold, Peter, Lt	840	25 May 1792	200
Kantner, John, Pvt	13736	18 Apr 1792	100
Larner, Robert, Pvt	9829	12 Jul 1792	100
Ryan, John, Pvt	13670	14 Feb 1791	100
Baldwine, Waterman, Pvt	5431	8 Feb 1791	100
Horton, Samuel, Pvt	13057	21 Mar 1791	100
Martin, Sarah, Lt	1477	20 Jan 1791	200
Christie, James, Pvt	8228	28 Jan 1791	100
Lounsberry, Walter, Pvt	8484	17 Mar 1791	100
Lane, James, Pvt	9846	3 May 1791	100
Read, Charles, Pvt	10300	13 Apr 1791	100
Lochman, John, Surgeon's Mate	2582	2 Mar 1791	300
Palmer, Andrew, Pvt	10219	16 May 1791	100
Gable, Henry, Pvt	9501	20 Sep 1791	100

44 16 Jan 1800 A/1/046

By Whom Registered: James Johnston
For Whom Registered: James Johnston
Location: (4000 acres) Mil - 14 3 - 1
Based upon the following Army land warrants:

Issued to	*No.*	*Date*	*Acres*
Johnston, Francis, Col	1148	3 Jul 1789	500
Hicks, Gershom, Pvt	9570	20 Apr 1796	100
Lecat, Mitchel, Cpl	10806	26 May 1790	100
White, Jon[athan] Pvt	14033	2 Mar 1792	100
Montgomery, John, Pvt	10071	21 Mar 1792	100
Power, Alexander, Pvt	9770	10 Oct 1792	100
Bigham, Alexander, Lt	2014	4 Oct 1792	200
Cahill, John, Pvt	10050	27 Oct 1792	100
Gibbons, James, Pvt	9458	25 Oct 1792	100
Molineux, Frederick, Pvt	10555	27 Oct 1792	100
Cahill, John, Pvt	10541	27 Oct 1792	100
Freemonet? [Freemouet?] Eliza[beth] Pvt	13099	30 Aug 1792	100
Campbell, Robert, Pvt	8181	28 Aug 1792	100
Thompson, Thomas, Pvt	10891	24 May 1791	100
McMurry, Sarah, Pvt	13499	10 Mar 1790	100
Moore, James, Capt	1472	26 May 1790	300
Warnick, Albert, Pvt	12982	9 Oct 1792	100
Johnston, James, Capt	2011	24 Dec 1799	300
Sork? [Lork?] Valentine, Pvt	8765	6 Jun 1797	100
Coulter, Andrew, Pvt	9162	7 Oct 1792	100
Duffey, James, Pvt	12064	5 Nov 1789	100
Halfpenny, Isaac, Pvt	12191	5 Nov 1789	100
Winghart, Adam, Pvt	10584	20 Jun 1789	100
Leonard, Patrick, Pvt	9843	5 Nov 1789	100
Garvin, Thomas, Pvt	9481	5 Nov 1789	100
Davis, Henry, Pvt	11140	14 Oct 1795	100
Galbreath, Josiah, Cpl	9440	20 Jun 1789	100

44 [continued]

Issued to	No.	Date	Acres
Spear, Edward, Lt	2023	7 Sep 1790	200
Cassaday, William, Pvt	9202	5 Nov 1789	100
Lorden, George, Pvt	9815	20 Jun 1789	100

45 17 Jan 1800 A/1/048

By Whom Registered: Robert Porter
For Whom Registered: Robert Porter
Location: (4000 acres) Mil - 16 5 - 3
Based upon the following Army land warrants:

Issued to	*No.*	*Date*	*Acres*
de Baufre, James, Pvt	11350	4 May 1797	100
de Baufre, James, Pvt	10741	12 May 1797	100
de Baufre, James, Pvt	11084	4 May 1797	100
de Baufre, James, Pvt	11263	12 May 1797	100
Armstrong, James, Capt	1042	2 Sep 1789	300
Howell, Ezekiel, Lt	1025	19 Aug 1789	200
Murray, Francis, Maj	1418	12 Apr 1791	400
Porter, Robert, Lt	1715	20 Aug 1789	200
North, Caleb, LtCol	1589	19 Aug 1789	450
Sproat, William, Capt	2019	14 Aug 1789	300
Davis, John, Surgeon	2589	23 Jul 1791	450
Miles, Benjamin, Capt	2670	1 Dec 1796	300
Manwell, James, Pvt	3138	6 Dec 1799	100
Brooks, Almarine, Ens	186	7 Jul 1789	150
Davis, John, Capt	561	19 Aug 1789	300
Davis, Lewellyn, Lt	569	19 Aug 1789	200
Dietrick, David, Ens	595	22 Jul 1791	150
Manwell, James, Pvt	3684	6 Dec 1799	100

46 17 Jan 1800 A/1/048

By Whom Registered: James Johnston
For Whom Registered: Hugh Holmes & Robert Rainey
Location: (4000 acres) Mil - 16 5 - 4
Based upon the following Army land warrants:

Issued to	*No.*	*Date*	*Acres*
Moore, Benjamin, Pvt	12909	20 Feb 1792	100
Moore, Benjamin, Pvt	12889	20 Feb 1792	100
Moore, Benjamin, Pvt	13250	20 Feb 1792	100
Moore, Benjamin, Pvt	13356	14 Aug 1792	100
Moore, Benjamin, Pvt	13367	20 Feb 1792	100
Moore, Benjamin, Pvt	13589	14 Aug 1792	100
Moore, Benjamin, Pvt	13422	25 Feb 1793	100
Powers, Alex[ande]r, Pvt	10186	11 Dec 1793	100
Iserloan, Caspar, Pvt	9574	16 Dec 1793	100
Iserloan, Caspar, Pvt	9595	16 Dec 1793	100
Iserloan, Caspar, Pvt	9597	16 Dec 1793	100
Iserloan, Caspar, Pvt	8937	5 Feb 1794	100
Iserloan, Caspar, Pvt	8957	5 Feb 1794	100
Thomas, Matthew, Pvt	8801	21 May 1791	100
Connolly, Timothy, Pvt	1115	14 Jun 1796	100
Pilken, Timothy, Junior, Pvt	6254	9 Jun 1796	100
Pilken, Timothy, Junior, Pvt	5905	9 Jun 1796	100
Smith, John, Pvt	3015	13 Apr 1796	100
Hughes, Greenberry, Lt	1033	1 Jun 1796	200
Stever, Michael, Pvt	9687	26 May 1794	100
Stever, Michael, Pvt	9013	26 May 1794	100
Witter, Josiah, Pvt	11052	28 Feb 1794	100
Stever, Michael, Pvt	10374	26 May 1794	100
Stever, Michael, Pvt	10197	26 May 1794	100
Hubbert, Christian, Pvt	10454	25 Nov 1793	100
Ditman, Godfrey, Pvt	13012	19 Nov 1793	100
Moore, Benjamin, Pvt	13000	14 Aug 1792	100
Sellers, Jacob, Pvt	8901	13 May 1794	100
Kirkpatrick, Francis, Pvt	9359	29 Apr 1794	100
Kirkpatrick, Francis, Pvt	10573	20 Mar 1794	100
Kirkpatrick, Francis, Pvt	9836	26 Nov 1793	100
Stever, Michael, Pvt	9745	26 May 1794	100
Kirkpatrick, Francis, Pvt	9904	9 Dec 1793	100
Powers, Alexander, Pvt	13874	9 Dec 1793	100
Iserloan, Caspar, Pvt	9249	25 Nov 1793	100
Moore, Benjamin, Pvt	13342	25 Feb 1793	100
Merkle, Gideon, Pvt	10286	7 Mar 1794	100
Hart, Silas, Pvt	9966	30 Jun 1794	100
Kirkpatrick, Francis, Pvt	8907	26 Nov 1793	100

47 20 Jan 1800 A/1/050

By Whom Registered: George Baer, Junior
For Whom Registered: David Lynn
Location: (4000 acres) Mil - 5 6 - 1
Based upon the following Army land warrants:

Issued to	*No.*	*Date*	*Acres*
Thornton, John, Pvt	11521	29 Nov 1790	100
Currer, James, Pvt	11094	29 Nov 1790	100
McKinsey, Moses, Pvt	11514	8 Apr 1796	100
Jenkins, Edward, Pvt	11060	29 Nov 1790	100
Loyd, Michael, Pvt	11093	29 Nov 1790	100
Knott, James, Pvt	11419	1 Feb 1790	100
Clancy, John, Pvt	11028	1 Feb 1790	100
McCann, Michael, Pvt	11482	1 Feb 1790	100
McManus, Thomas, Pvt	11191	29 Nov 1790	100
Shaw, Bazil, Pvt	11101	29 Nov 1790	100
Blair, John, Pvt	11843	12 Jan 1792	100
Magraw, Christ[opher] Pvt	11475	1 Feb 1790	100
Brannon, Lawrence, Pvt	11162	29 Nov 1790	100
Robins, John, Pvt	11278	29 Nov 1790	100
Smith, John, Pvt	11344	29 Nov 1790	100
Ryon, James, Pvt	11230	29 Nov 1790	100
Boss, Christian, Pvt	11342	29 Nov 1790	100
Jones, John, Pvt	11380	29 Nov 1790	100
Bruff, William, Pvt	11536	29 Nov 1790	100
Bulger, Daniel, Pvt	11569	29 Nov 1790	100
Hardry, Elias, Pvt	11580	29 Nov 1790	100
Cochran, Joshua, Pvt	11654	29 Nov 1790	100
Mudd, Jeremiah, Pvt	11726	29 Nov 1790	100
Moore, James, Pvt	11721	29 Nov 1790	100
Hall, Frederick, Pvt	11718	29 Nov 1790	100
Wilson, Barney, Pvt	11831	29 Nov 1790	100
Fannier, John, Pvt	11836	29 Nov 1790	100
Campbell, Collin, Pvt	11833	29 Nov 1790	100
Wade, Edward, Pvt	11792	1 Feb 1790	100
Fields, George, Pvt	11613	29 Nov 1790	100
Smith, James, Pvt	11671	1 Feb 1790	100
Hope, William, Pvt	11346	1 Feb 1790	100
Jarvins? Daniel, Pvt	11387	1 Feb 1790	100
Dunning, Dennis, Pvt	11132	1 Feb 1790	100
Butt, Thomas, Pvt	10982	1 Feb 1790	100
Lynn, John, Lt	1298	1 May 1792	200
Lynn, David, Capt	1295	1 Feb 1790	300

48 21 Jan 1800 A/1/051

By Whom Registered: Peter Curtenius
For Whom Registered: The Reverend John Dunlap "of Cambridge in the State of New York"
Location: (4000 acres) Mil - 18 2 - 3
Based upon the following Army land warrants:

Issued to	*No.*	*Date*	*Acres*
Bleecker, John N., Pvt	7808	4 Aug 1790	100
Hesum, John, Pvt	7236	6 Jun 1791	100
Hageman, John, Pvt	7945	21 Feb 1791	100
Doughty, John, Capt	551	10 Jun 1791	300
Pierpoint, John, Pvt	7648	23 Oct 1790	100
Robertson, Alex[ande]r, Pvt	7908	28 Sep 1789	100

48 [continued]

Colwell, Clayton, Pvt	11369	26 Nov 1792	100
Means, Robert, Pvt	12075	14 Jul 1792	100
Means, Robert	11875	29 May 1792	100
Neal, James A., Pvt	3070	12 Oct 1795	100
Lucas, Samuel, Pvt	6093	6 Jul 1791	100
Clairey, Daniel, Pvt	5658	19 Jul 1791	100
Pickering, Joshua, Pvt	3254	26 Aug 1796	100
Davis, Henry, Pvt	11307	14 Oct 1795	100
Maxwell, Anthony, Pvt	7300	4 Dec 1790	100
Power, Alex[ande]r, Pvt	9707	4 Feb 1793	100
Campbell, Thomas, Pvt	10128	2 Mar 1792	100
Hart, Silas, Pvt	10149	10 Jun 1794	100
Means, Robert, Pvt	12255	7 Jul 1792	100
Glasser, Silas, Pvt	5879	20 Sep 1790	100
Emery, Samuel, Pvt	3127	18 Jun 1795	100
Greaves, Francis, Pvt	12293	13 Dec 1791	100
Means, Robert, Pvt	13996	2 Nov 1792	100
McLean, Thomas, Pvt	13459	5 Jan 1796	100
Van Wagenen, Teunis, Lt	2256	23 Aug 1790	200
Wheeler, Phineas, Pvt	5283	16 Mar 1792	100
Stockwell, Levi, Lt	2616	31 Mar 1796	200
Mitchell, Isaac, Pvt	3303	16 Mar 1796	100
Bleecker, John N., Pvt	6748	4 Aug 1790	100
Robertson, Alex[ande]r, Pvt	6911	28 Sep 1790	100
Frank, Michael, Pvt	7115	15 Dec 1790	100
Vreedenburgh, William I? [J?] Pvt	7029	12 Jan 1791	100
Lawrence, Thomas, Pvt	6990	24 Sep 1790	100
Lawrence, Thomas, Pvt	7008	24 Sep 1790	100
Dayton, Bennet, Pvt	12978	5 Dec 1789	100
Trimmens, Abner, Pvt	7863	15 Dec 1790	100

49 — 22 Jan 1800 — A/1/052

By Whom Registered: William McCluney
For Whom Registered: William McCluney
Location: (4000 acres) Mil - 3 2 - 4
Based upon the following Army land warrants:

Issued to	*No.*	*Date*	*Acres*
Lloyd, Richard, Capt	1328	2 Aug 1790	300
McCurdy, William, Capt	1421	7 Jul 1789	300
Cross, Patrick, Pvt	9106	20 Jun 1789	100
McIlvaine, Thomas, Pvt	9886	20 Jun 1789	100
Olds, Horace, Pvt	5596	3 Jan 1799	100
Lot, Jeremiah, Pvt	9834	24 Apr 1799	100
McMullen, Mich[ae]l, Pvt	9888	9 Mar 1799	100
Abbott, Reuben, Pvt	11862	20 Aug 1791	100
Guest, Albion, Pvt	9428	6 Apr 1795	100
Detter, Mich[ae]l, Pvt	13021	12 Aug 1789	100
Shoeman, Adam, Pvt	10426	22 Sep 1791	100
Dickison, Isaac, Pvt	8260	24 Apr 1795	100
Compton, George, Pvt	8189	24 Apr 1795	100
Johnston, Lewis, Pvt	8417	11 Apr 1792	100
Phelps, George, Pvt	12449	29 Jun 1789	100
Young, Davis, Pvt	11858	11 Mar 1791	100
Palmer, James, Pvt	7415	3 May 1791	100
Greene, Cato, Pvt	3159	31 Dec 1789	100
Potter, John, Pvt	8360	5 Apr 1793	100
Cook, Thomas, Capt	2652	10 Jul 1797	300
Carson, Samuel, Pvt	9086	31 Mar 1796	100
Hodge, John, & Addison, Alex[ande]r, CaptLt	1279	29 Jan 1790	200
Collins, Thomas, Pvt	10721	18 Oct 1791	100
Anderson, Samuel, Pvt	8078	13 Jan 1792	100
Breese, Timothy, Pvt	8116	10 Feb 1796	100
McClerron, Thomas, Pvt	10049	21 Dec 1791	100
Phelps, Asahel, Pvt	11213	10 Oct 1799	100
Evans, Jenkin, Pvt	10759	6 Dec 1797	100
Ramsey, Henry, Pvt	11629	11 May 1790	100
Black, Samuel, Pvt	9223	23 Sep 1791	100
Black, Samuel, Pvt	13661	21 Feb 1798	100
Hillmen? [Hillmin?] William, Pvt	11323	27 Aug 1789	100
Niblet, William, Pvt	11566	10 Jun 1789	100

50 — 23 Jan 1800 — A/1/054

By Whom Registered: Robert Underwood
For Whom Registered: Robert Underwood
Location: (4000 acres) Mil - 7 1 - 3
Based upon the following Army land warrants:

Issued to	*No.*	*Date*	*Acres*
Hays, Robert, Lt	1098	12 Feb 1795	200
Brown, William D., Lt	1039	6 Jun 1794	200
Harper, John, Lt	1015	24 Apr 1794	200
Faulkner, Peter, Ens	740	28 Jul 1790	150
Forde, Standish, Lt	617	14 Apr 1794	200
Cay, David, Capt	615	4 Jun 1792	300
Campbell, John, Lt	397	3 Feb 1792	200
Baxter, William, Ens	225	14 May 1793	150
Stephenson, John, Ens	1607	14 Sep 1792	150
Cay, David, MajGen	1538	4 Jun 1792	1100
Power, Alex[ande]r, Lt	1442	31 Aug 1792	200
McKinney, John, Lt	1438	4 Feb 1795	200
Cay, David, Lt	1319	4 Jun 1792	200
Lynch, John, Maj	1292	24 May 1794	400
Stephenson, John, Ens	1134	24 Sep 1792	150

51 — 23 Jan 1800 — A/1/054

By Whom Registered: Robert Underwood
For Whom Registered: Robert Underwood
Location: (4000 acres) Mil - 6 6 - 3
Based upon the following Army land warrants:

Issued to	*No.*	*Date*	*Acres*
Thomas, Peter, Pvt	14127	6 Aug 1795	100
Hogg, Ebenezer, Pvt	8471	27 Aug 1792	100
Christie, James, Pvt	8476	18 Jun 1795	100
McQuay, John, Pvt	8529	9 Nov 1792	100
Walters, John, Pvt	8876	24 Jul 1790	100
Molineux, Fred[eric]k, Pvt	8994	27 Oct 1792	100
Power, Alex]ande]r, Pvt	9088	17 Sep 1792	100
Coakley, Robert, Pvt	9186	19 Sep 1791	100
Dorsey, Matthew, Pvt	9251	20 Jul 1791	100
Keenon, John, Pvt	9253	16 Aug 1792	100
Kean, John, Pvt	9289	22 Dec 1791	100
Hutchins, John, Pvt	9535	7 Dec 1790	100
Hoskins, Isaac, Pvt	9610	25 Sep 1792	100
Hopkins, William, Pvt	9617	20 Jun 1789	100
Kain, Manus? Pvt	9740	6 Aug 1792	100
Keenon, John, Pvt	9760	15 Aug 1792	100
Powers, Alexander, Pvt	9781	3 Sep 1792	100
Walker, Slphia, Pvt	9819	12 Jul 1792	100
Mentger? [Metzger?] Christian, Pvt	9892	13 Dec 1791	100
Power, Alex[ande]r, Pvt	9939	4 Oct 1792	100
Peak, James, Pvt	10193	27 Aug 1792	100
Ryan, Michael, Pvt	10308	26 Jun 1792	100
Peters, John, Pvt	10408	12 Oct 1792	100
Delabar, John, Pvt	10432	20 Jun 1792	100
Alexander, Samuel, Pvt	10561	28 Jun 1792	100
Hart, Silas, Pvt	10591	10 Jul 1791	100
Merkle, Gideon, Pvt	10658	16 Jul 1792	100
Humphreys, Ashton, Pvt	10727	28 Dec 1791	100
Harman, Edward, Pvt	10779	2 Sep 1789	100
Teazor, Aaron, Pvt	10889	2 Sep 1789	100
Bell, Alex[ande]r, Pvt	11466	31 Aug 1792	100
McDowell, Thomas, Pvt	11539	26 Sep 1792	100

51 [continued]

Issued to	No.	Date	Acres
Power, Alex[ande]r, Pvt	12794	31 Aug 1792	100
Gates, Ezra, Pvt	13128	8 Mar 1796	100
Cushing, Elmer, Pvt	13132	6 Aug 1792	100
Hess, George, & Hess, Marg[aret?] Pvt	13270	29 May 1792	100
McDonald, Godfrey, Pvt	13491	3 Oct 1791	100
Shindleblower, George, Pvt	13748	8 Mar 1792	100
Wort, Peter, Pvt	13923	21 Jun 1792	100
Reynolds, James, Pvt	14039	28 Aug 1792	100

52 — 23 Jan 1800 — A/1/056

By Whom Registered: Robert Underwood
For Whom Registered: Robert Underwood
Location: (4000 acres) Mil 0 7 1 - 2
Based upon the following Army land warrants:

Issued to	*No.*	*Date*	*Acres*
Keen, Hannah, Pvt	8468	30 Mar 1796	100
Hacket, Joshua, Pvt	8406	9 Jun 1795	100
Muzzy, Amos, Pvt	4707	27 Aug 1792	100
Roderfield, William, Pvt	4960	22 Sep 1789	100
Wrightington, Rob[ert] Pvt	5317	16 Jul 1792	100
Beardsley, William, Pvt	5507	14 Sep 1792	100
Allen, Samuel, Pvt	6403	15 Aug 1792	100
Christie, James, Pvt	8179	27 Jul 1795	100
Christie, James, Pvt	8182	27 Jul 1795	100
Derky? [Desky?] Leaman, Pvt	8241	24 Jul 1790	100
Christie, James, Pvt	8245	18 Jun 1795	100
Fletcher, William, Pvt	8325	26 May 1790	100
Ridgway, Henry, Pvt	8365	16 Mar 1796	100
Cay, David, Surgeon's Mate	1698	4 Jun 1792	300
Cay, David, Capt	1761	4 Jun 1792	300
Brown, William D., Lt	2038	6 Jun 1794	200
Cay, David, Capt	2103	4 Jun 1792	300
Cay, David, Lt	2229	4 Jun 1792	200
Brown, William D., Lt	2269	6 Jun 1794	200
Wigton, John, Lt	2388	19 Aug 1789	200
Campbell, Duncan, Lt	2447	29 Mar 1792	200
Neal, James A., Pvt	4256	22 Jul 1796	100
Neal, James A., Pvt	3211	22 Jul 1796	100
Crammond, William, Leamy, John, & Holmes, Hugh, Capt	2452	28 Jan 1795	300
Lucas, Nath[anie]l, Capt	2636	28 Feb 1794	300

53 — 30 Jan 1800 — A/1/057

By Whom Registered: Jonas Stanbery
For Whom Registered: Jonas Stanbery
Location: (4000 acres) Mil - 7 2 - 1
Based upon the following Army land warrants:

Issued to	*No.*	*Date*	*Acres*
Hart, Silas, Pvt	9948	10 Jul 1794	100
Thomas, John, Surgeon	2143	28 Dec 1791	400
Yeaty, John, Pvt	8884	12 Nov 1796	100
Allen, Noah, Maj	10	7 Jul 1790	400
Stiver, Michael, Pvt	10369	3 Mar 1794	100
Lilley, Reuben, Pvt	3739	20 Jul 1789	100
Bower, Jacob, Capt	201	22 Feb 1791	300
Dougherty, Hugh, Pvt	12991	2 Sep 1789	100
Bilbury, Wooldrick, Pvt	8100	2 Dec 1791	100
Willis, Isaac, Pvt	8255	14 Apr 1790	100
McGee, Sarah, Pvt	13418	11 Sep 1792	100
McKinley, Alex[ande]r, Pvt	10034	2 Mar 1792	100
Smith, John, Pvt	6757	13 Sep 1790	100
Bryant, Benjamin, Pvt	8141	22 Apr 1790	100
Gould, John, Pvt	3162	26 Nov 1791	100
Brish? [Brisk?] Charles, Pvt	13758	10 Sep 1789	100
Jones, John C., Capt	1161	26 Feb 1794	300
Lacombe, Isabella, Lt	2687	3 Jul 1797	200
de Baufre, James, Pvt	11789	8 Jul 1797	100
Duncan, John, Pvt	13419	24 Jun 1797	100
Woodard, William, Pvt	5684	12 Jun 1797	100
Duncan, John, Pvt	6612	24 Jun 1797	100
Hunt, Alex[ande]r, Pvt	3852	14 May 1794	100
de Baufre, James, Pvt	11087	8 Jul 1797	100
de Baufre, James, Pvt	11166	8 Jul 1797	100
Bell, William, Pvt	7639	15 Sep 1790	100
Crosby, Sampson, Pvt	4170	10 Mar 1795	100
Spaulding, Asa, Pvt	6294	2 Nov 1796	100
Levick, Caleb, Pvt	13395	18 Nov 1791	100

54 — 31 Jan 1800 — A/1/058

By Whom Registered: John Armstrong
For Whom Registered: James Taylor
Location: (4000 acres) Mil - 18 4 - 3
Based upon the following Army land warrants:

Issued to	*No.*	*Date*	*Acres*
Buckner, Elizabeth, LtCol	1066	5 Jul 1799	450
Taylor, James, Capt	2712	17 Jan 1800	300
Taylor, James, Maj	2708	5 Jul 1799	400
Zimmerman, Reuben, Surgeon's Mate	2469	17 Jan 1800	300
Trabue, John, Ens	2221	30 Dec 1796	150
Wright, James, Capt	2429	26 Feb 1793	300
Williams, Lylburne, Capt	2408	24 Feb 1798	300
Ramdell? [Ransdell?] Chilton, Capt	1852	17 Jan 1800	300
Garnet, Henry, Lt	1520	5 Jul 1799	200
Hackley, John, Lt	1077	2 Apr 1790	200
Green, Gabriel, Lt	872	17 Jan 1800	200
Eustace, William, Capt	682	27 Jan 1800	300
Fox, Thomas, Capt	765	17 Jan 1800	300
Blackwell, John, Capt	264	26 Feb 1793	300

55 — 1 Feb 1800 — A/1/058

By Whom Registered: John Rathbone
For Whom Registered: John Rathbone
Location: (4000 acres) Mil - 17 2 - 4
Based upon the following Army land warrants:

Issued to	*No.*	*Date*	*Acres*
Ducas? [Lucas?] Joseph, Pvt	12985	12 Oct 1790	100
Duncost, Joseph, Pvt	12986	12 Oct 1790	100
Duplers? [Duplere?] Henry, Pvt	12988	12 Oct 1790	100
Duncan, John, Pvt	13272	1 May 1797	100
St. Laurent, Etienne, Pvt	13362	12 Oct 1790	100
de Baufre, James, Pvt	13458	9 Jun 1797	100
Mayberry, John, Pvt	13476	29 Apr 1793	100
Nicholson, John, Pvt	13836	7 Apr 1795	100
Ruggles, Nathan[ie]l, Pvt	13913	3 Dec 1796	100
Duncan, John, Pvt	5880	1 May 1797	100
Duncan, John, Pvt	6201	1 May 1797	100
Duncan, John, Pvt	6212	1 May 1797	100
Duncan, John, Pvt	6259	1 May 1797	100
Ruggles, Nath[anie]l, Pvt	6302	3 Dec 1796	100
Rossell, Jeremiah, Pvt	6391	1 Mar 1797	100
Campbell, Andrew, Pvt	6929	22 Dec 1796	100
Darby, William, Drummer	8262	12 Jan 1790	100

55 [continued]

Shaw, Cornelius, Pvt	8703	24 Jun 1797	100
McGuire, Thomas, Sgt	10821	2 Sep 1789	100
Butler, Benj[ami]n, Cpl	12736	9 Jul 1796	100
Lippitt, Waterman, Cpl	12781	16 Oct 1790	100
Coombs, William, Pvt	12943	16 Feb 1797	100
Wheaton, Daniel, Capt	61	16 Jan 1797	300
Drew, Seth, Maj	514	26 Oct 1789	400
Wesson, James, Col	2289	24 Jul 1792	500
Thom, Ch[ristian?][or Christopher?] F? [L?] Pvt	3567	28 Dec 1796	100
Ball, Benjamin, Sgt	3734	25 Feb 1796	100
Duncan, John, Pvt	5408	1 May 1797	100
Duncan, John, Pvt	5480	23 May 1797	100
Ruggles, Nath[anie]l, Pvt	5758	3 Dec 1796	100
Fletcher, John, Pvt	5762	20 Jan 1797	100

56 1 Feb 1800 A/1/059

By Whom Registered: John Rathbone
For Whom Registered: John Rathbone
Location: (4000 acres) Mil - 18 1 - 2
Based upon the following Army land warrants:

Issued to	*No.*	*Date*	*Acres*
Anderson, William, Ens	38	31 Dec 1795	150
Carter, John C., Capt	468	26 Aug 1789	300
de Bert, Claudius, Capt	635	14 Oct 1789	300
Whitcomb, Benj[amin] Ens	1135	27 Aug 1792	150
Learmonth, John, Capt	1289	2 Sep 1789	300
Pierce, John, CaptLt	1653	20 Feb 1790	200
Camp, Robert, Capt	2060	23 Feb 1796	300
Lee, Thomas, Capt	2608	4 Apr 1792	300
Oaksman, Mary, Pvt	3371	3 May 1792	100
Vaughen, Prince, Pvt	3545	31 Dec 1789	100
Tutle, Jonathan, Pvt	3748	15 Nov 1792	100
Lane, William, Pvt	4032	26 Sep 1791	100
McLaughlin, Owen, Pvt	4644	26 Oct 1789	100
Freeman, Plymouth, Pvt	5806	8 May 1793	100
Root, Nicholas, Pvt	5862	15 Sep 1790	100
Whitton, Joseph, Pvt	5887	27 Aug 1796	100
Tourney, Toney, Pvt	6578	20 Sep 1790	100
Slutt, Peter, Pvt	7754	2 Feb 1791	100
Hamilton, James, Pvt	7873	14 Feb 1791	100
Linn, John, Pvt	8129	7 May 1790	100
Linn, John, Pvt	8257	7 May 1790	100
Ludlow, Israel, Pvt	8555	20 Oct 1790	100
Callahan, Patrick, Pvt	9156	11 Mar 1791	100
McCleland, John, Pvt	9206	26 Sep 1791	100
Nicholson, John, Pvt	9938	7 Apr 1795	100
Campbell, Thomas, Pvt	10131	2 Mar 1792	100
Ponsonby, George, Pvt	11562	8 Jan 1796	100
Blakeley, John, Pvt	12302	6 Sep 1796	100

57 1 Feb 1800 A/1/060

By Whom Registered: John Rathbone
For Whom Registered: John Rathbone
Location: (4000 acres) Mil - 18 6 - 3
Based upon the following Army land warrants:

Issued to	*No.*	*Date*	*Acres*
Bryant, Matthew, Pvt	2979	5 Mar 1793	100
Kline, William, Pvt	3190	12 Jun 1792	100
Mice, Magnus, Pvt	3367	5 Jan 1792	100
Blodget, Ezra, Pvt	3778	8 May 1792	100
Blodget, Ezra, Pvt	4637	8 May 1792	100
Mavett? Francis, Pvt	4695	27 Apr 1792	100
Blodget, Ezra, Pvt	4783	8 May 1792	100
Sill, Moses, Pvt	5406	28 Jan 1792	100
Sill, Moses, Pvt	5895	28 Jan 1792	100
Sanford, Zalmon, Pvt	5945	27 Apr 1792	100
Hatch, Moses, Pvt	5963	5 Nov 1795	100
Tobias, Daniel, Pvt	6560	27 Apr 1792	100
Sill, Moses, Pvt	6690	28 Jan 1792	100
Pettit, Jabez, Pvt	7652	24 Sep 1791	100
Grant, George, Pvt	8341	5 Mar 1793	100
Rose, John, Pvt	8674	21 Apr 1790	100
Merkle, Gideon, Pvt	8989	14 Mar 1793	100
Collins, Joseph, Pvt	9153	16 May 1792	100
Leonard, James, Pvt	9605	13 Sep 1789	100
Stout, Philip, Pvt	9665	10 Apr 1793	100
Power, Alexander, Pvt	9827	6 Jun 1792	100
Merkle, Gideon, Pvt	10017	14 Mar 1793	100
Miller, Catherine, Pvt	10038	14 Mar 1793	100
Morgan, Joseph, Pvt	10088	5 Mar 1793	100
Bennett, James, Pvt	10089	23 Jun 1793	100
Neal, James O. [could also be O'Neal, James] Pvt	10172	5 Mar 1793	100
Merkle, Gideon, Pvt	10201	14 Mar 1793	100
Clingman, Jacob, Pvt	10221	19 Apr 1792	100
Sankey, Ezekiel, Pvt	10418	29 Mar 1791	100
Stout, Philip, Pvt	10660	10 Apr 1793	100
Merkle, Gideon, Pvt	11658	14 Mar 1793	100
Stockdell, John, Pvt	12554	4 Jan 1796	100
Ross, Robert, Pvt	12769	24 May 1792	100
Miller, Jacob, Pvt	12790	18 Jun 1792	100
Miller, Jacob, Pvt	13127	16 May 1792	100
Kickbeyer, Adam, Pvt	13186	9 Apr 1793	100
Merles? Clement, Pvt	13456	5 Apr 1793	100
Schriver, Fred[eric]k, Pvt	13751	23 Feb 1792	100
Bamer, Andrew, Pvt	13822	1 Jun 1792	100
Jenkins, Edward, Pvt	14064	1 Mar 1794	100

58 1 Feb 1800 A/1/062

By Whom Registered: John Rathbone
For Whom Registered: John Rathbone
Location: (4000 acres) Mil - 1 7 - 4
Based upon the following Army land warrants:

Issued to	*No.*	*Date*	*Acres*
Fisk, Moses, Surgeon	335	9 Jun 1797	400
Fisbaugh, Simon, Pvt	13325	8 Jul 1791	100
Mundin, John, Pvt	13505	14 Feb 1791	100
Anspach, Peter, Pvt	8712	25 Sep 1789	100
Belknap, Abel, Pvt	8071	21 Aug 1790	100
Goigne, John, Pvt	13130	4 Feb 1790	100
O'Brian, Ann, Pvt	13074	10 Jul 1789	100
Power, Alex[ande]r, Pvt	10450	16 Jan 1793	100
Weekly, Samuel, Pvt	8054	20 Sep 1790	100
Rockwell, John, Pvt	6386	28 Jul 1790	100
Belknap, Abel, Pvt	7700	21 Aug 1790	100
Sunderland, Wallace, Pvt	6667	11 Jan 1797	100
Weeks, James, Pvt	7968	2 Aug 1793	100
Palmer, James, Pvt	3712	3 May 1791	100
Wolcott, Giles, Capt	2278	12 Dec 1797	300
Ten Eyck, Henry, Capt	2173	7 Mar 1792	300
Taylor, Timothy, Capt	2172	21 May 1789	300
Robinson, Elias, Lt	1799	6 Apr 1796	200
Wells, John, & Wells, George, Pvt	5849	6 Apr 1796	100
Brown, Daniel, Pvt	5403	22 Jan 1790	100
Gillegan, Thomas, Pvt	4253	11 Jan 1797	100
Porter, John, Pvt	13614	20 Nov 1789	100
Kerker, John, Pvt	13299	4 Jun 1790	100
Mead, Samuel, Pvt	6172	26 Jun 1790	100
Matthewson, Elisha, Pvt	6138	5 Jan 1792	100
Lothrop, Samuel, Pvt	6080	14 Dec 1793	100
Wells, George, Pvt	6022	15 Aug 1792	100
Gardner, William, Pvt	5859	1 Oct 1789	100

58 [continued]

Issued to	No.	Date	Acres
Murray, John, Pvt	13484	11 Jun 1790	100
Power, Alex[ande]r, Pvt	13865	19 Apr 1791	100

59 1 Feb 1800 A/1/063

By Whom Registered: John Rathbone
For Whom Registered: John Rathbone
Location: (4000 acres)* Mil - 12 2 - 1
Based upon the following Army land warrants:

Issued to	*No.*	*Date*	*Acres*
Eastham, Edward, Pvt	13413	21 Dec 1789	100
Johnson, Eleanor, Pvt	13343	15 May 1792	100
Daugherty, Barney, Pvt	13023	25 Feb 1793	100
Johnson, Benjamin, Pvt	11378	11 Mar 1791	100
Stout, George, Pvt	10794	25 Jan 1793	100
Gross, Christian, Pvt	10519	4 Feb 1796	100
Platt, Richard, Pvt	10488	27 Jul 1789	100
Connelly, Robert, Pvt	10164	8 Mar 1792	100
Connelly, Robert, Pvt	10129	8 Mar 1792	100
Stout, George, Pvt	10036	4 Feb 1793	100
Humphreys, James, Pvt	9985	7 Mar 1793	100
Sheridan, Abraham, Pvt	9943	21 Feb 1793	100
Lamb, Joseph, Pvt	9847	27 Feb 1793	100
Murthwaite, Richard, Pvt	9808	13 Dec 1792	100
Merkle, Gideon, Pvt	9558	21 Feb 1793	100
Merkle, Gideon, Pvt	9557	21 Feb 1793	100
Merkle, Gideon, Pvt	9556	21 Feb 1793	100
Platt, Richard, Pvt	9357	27 Jul 1789	100
Platt, Richard, Pvt	9345	27 Jul 1789	100
Bennett, James, Pvt	9212	28 Jan 1793	100
Carshaw, Abraham, Pvt	9140	17 Jan 1793	100
Bennet, James, Pvt	9085	13 Mar 1793	100
Linn, John, Pvt	8254	7 May 1790	100
Bennedict, Timothy, Pvt	7136	27 Apr 1792	100
Sill, Moses, Pvt	6431	28 Jan 1792	100
Power, Alex[ande]r, Pvt	6359	27 Feb 1793	100
Neal, James A., Pvt	6125	19 Apr 1796	100
Sill, Moses, Pvt	5745	28 Jan 1792	100
Sill, Moses, Pvt	5607	28 Jan 1792	100
Sill, Moses, Pvt	5416	28 Jan 1792	100
Power, Alex[ande]r, Pvt	5005	27 Feb 1793	100
Power, Alex[ande]r, Pvt	4863	27 Feb 1793	100
Ramsay, John, Pvt	4537	22 May 1790	100
Cook, Richard, Pvt	3902	11 Sep 1792	100
Bennet, Terrence, Pvt	3788	28 Jul 1791	100
Neal, James A., Pvt	3308	12 Feb 1796	100
Clingman, Jacob, Lt	2157	4 Jan 1792	200
Manning, Lawrence, Lt	1457	16 Feb 1792	200

*Marginal Notation:

"Location on [above cited tract]		4218.9
Warrants registered [acres]		4000
Reg[ister's] Cert. No. 12 rec'd for [acres]	544.2	
Deducted from that to satisfy this deficiency [acres]	218.9	218.9
		4218.9
Reg[ister's] Cert. No. 36 issued for this residue [acres]	325.3"	

60 1 Feb 1800 A/1/064

By Whom Registered: John Rathbone
For Whom Registered: John Rathbone
Location: (4000 acres) Mil - 18 5 - 2
Based upon the following Army land warrants:

Issued to	*No.*	*Date*	*Acres*
Johnson, Noah, Pvt	7990	17 Apr 1792	100
Blodget, Ezra, Pvt	7844	13 Jan 1792	100
Galloway, Alex[ande]r, Pvt	7325	15 Dec 1790	100
Waldron, Resolve, Pvt	7022	19 Jan 1792	100
Preston, Nathan, Pvt	5181	22 Mar 1796	100
Preston, Nathan, Pvt	3067	22 Mar 1796	100
Talman, Thomas, Lt	2131	14 Feb 1793	200
Greaves, Francis, Lt	2082	13 Dec 1791	200
Patterson, Alex[ande]r Capt	1720	28 Feb 1793	300
Greaves, Francis, Capt	1073	13 Dec 1791	300
Hunt, Ephraim, Lt	924	17 Nov 1789	200
Murray, Reuben, Lt	725	5 Apr 1793	200
Elholm, George C. A., Capt	692	6 Jan 1792	300
Greaves, Francis, Lt	603	13 Dec 1791	200
Keating, John, Pvt	13305	13 May 1791	100
Grimes, Nath[anie]l, Pvt	13160	29 May 1792	100
Preston, Nathan, Pvt	13146	22 Mar 1796	100
Greaves, Francis, Pvt	12556	13 Dec 1791	100
Greaves, Francis, Pvt	11868	13 Dec 1791	100
Williams, Joseph, Pvt	10643	1 Nov 1791	100
Schott, John P., Pvt	10397	21 May 1792	100
Schott, John P., Pvt	9444	21 May 1792	100
Schott, John P., Pvt	9280	21 May 1792	100
Dempsey, Timothy, Pvt	9262	9 Jul 1789	100
Schott, John P., Pvt	8967	21 May 1792	100
Lloyd, William, Pvt	8307	17 Oct 1791	100
White, Lydia, Capt	2556	17 Apr 1790	300

61 1 Feb 1800 A/1/065

By Whom Registered: John Rathbone
For Whom Registered: John Rathbone
Location: (4000 acres) Mil - 11 7 - 3
Based upon the following Army land warrants:

Issued to	*No.*	*Date*	*Acres*
Croft, Henry, Pvt	6995	5 May 1791	100
Van Wagenen, Gerrit, Capt	1974	4 Sep 1790	300
Fisher, Leonard, Pvt	7436	9 Sep 1790	100
Benjamin, Elias, Pvt	7023	9 Jul 1790	100
Scribner, Nath[anie]l, Cpl	7320	9 Jul 1790	100
Benjamin, Elias, Pvt	7681	9 Jul 1790	100
Smith, John, Cpl	7839	24 Sep 1790	100
Cottelle? Philip, Pvt	6987	13 Jul 1790	100
Platt, Richard, Pvt	6735	14 Jul 1790	100
Van Ingen, Dirck, Pvt	7150	14 Jul 1790	100
Fish, Nicholas, Pvt	7665	9 Jul 1790	100
Platt, Richard, Sgt	8039	14 Jul 1790	100
Platt, Richard, Pvt	6897	14 Jul 1790	100
Platt, Richard, Sgt	7750	14 Jul 1790	100
Hamilton, James, Sgt	6780	3 Sep 1790	100
Startwout, Abraham, Capt	2564	13 Jul 1790	300
Curray, Samuel, Pvt	7409	20 Jul 1790	100
Dunscomb, Edmond, Capt	545	22 Jun 1790	300
Addams, Jonas, Lt	33	7 Jul 1790	200
Brewster, Nathan, Capt	826	3 Jul 1790	300
Jackson, Patton, Lt	1145	8 Jul 1790	200
Cumming, William, Pvt	7073	20 Aug 1790	100
Strachan, William, Lt	1987	30 Jul 1790	200
Vosberg, Peter J? Capt	2251	12 Aug 1790	300
Stringer, Samuel, Capt	2365	10 Aug 1790	300

62 1 Feb 1800 A/1/066

By Whom Registered: John Rathbone
For Whom Registered: John Rathbone
Location: (4000 acres) Mil - 19 4 - ?
Based upon the following Army land warrants:

62 [continued]

Issued to	No.	Date	Acres
Greaves, Francis, Pvt	12045	29 May 1792	100
Greaves, Francis, Pvt	11918	29 May 1792	100
Greaves, Francis, Pvt	11915	26 Mar 1792	100
Stringham, Joseph, Pvt	8064	18 Aug 1790	100
Van Courtland, Philip, Pvt	7939	2 Sep 1790	100
McMillen, John, Pvt	7927	29 Jul 1790	100
Rudolph, David, Cpl	7715	29 Jan 1790	100
Mimick? Hendrick, Pvt	7496	3 Sep 1790	100
Kronkhite, Patrick, Pvt	7366	3 Sep 1790	100
Stringham, Joseph, Pvt	7327	18 Aug 1790	100
Henderson, William, Pvt	7311	10 Sep 1790	100
Mapes, James, Pvt	766?	25 Sep 1790	100
McLaughlin, James, Pvt	7098	1 Sep 1790	100
Dobson, John, Pvt	7019	3 Sep 1790	100
Stringham, Joseph, Pvt	6985	18 Aug 1790	100
Craft, Nath[anie]l, Pvt	6932	2 Sep 1790	100
Maxwell, Anth[on]y, Pvt	6813	10 Oct 1791	100
Gilliland, William, Pvt	6764	6 Sep 1791	100
Well,s James, Lt	2314	12 Jan 1792	200
Nicholson, John, Pvt	13487	7 Apr 1795	100
Morris, John, Pvt	13409	27 Sep 1792	100
Lacost, Francis, Pvt	13343	5 Jan 1792	100
Luntz, Alex[ande]r, Pvt	13097	24 May 1791	100
Graves, Francis, Pvt	12557	11 May 1792	100
Graves, Francis, Pvt	12547	29 May 1792	100
Graves, Francis, Pvt	12476	29 May 1792	100
Graves, Francis, Pvt	12409	11 May 1792	100
Graves, Francis, Pvt	12385	26 Mar 1792	100
Graves, Francis, Pvt	12372	11 May 1792	100
Sanford, Peter, Pvt	6264	24 Sep 1790	100
Graves, Francis, Pvt	12369	26 Mar 1792	100
Lamb, Frederick, Pvt	12337	27 Jun 1795	100
Graves, Francis, Pvt	12317	29 May 1792	100
Graves, Francis, Pvt	12278	11 May 1792	100
Graves, Francis, Pvt	12260	12 Apr 1792	100
Graves, Francis, Pvt	12165	26 Mar 1792	100
Graves, Francis, Pvt	12158	12 Apr 1792	100
Graves, Francis, Pvt	12130	26 Mar 1792	100
Graves, Francis, Pvt	12092	12 Apr 1792	100

63 1 Feb 1800 A/1/068

By Whom Registered: Jonas Stanbery
For Whom Registered: Jonas Stanbery
Location: (4000 acres) Mil - 19 3 - 1
Based upon the following Army land warrants:

Issued to	*No.*	*Date*	*Acres*
Newkerk, Charles, Pvt	7356	23 Aug 1790	100
Banks, Justus, Pvt	7312	10 Sep 1790	100
Hanmore, Moses, Pvt	7297	15 Dec 1791	100
Russell, Thomas, Pvt	7216	30 Mar 1793	100
Hoyt, Henry, Pvt	7207	3 Sep 1790	100
Hamilton, James, Pvt	7172	3 Sep 1790	100
Frederick, John, Pvt	7126	3 Sep 1790	100
Gebhard, Johan G., Pvt	6955	9 Sep 1790	100
Suffren, John, Pvt	6784	4 Sep 1790	100
Stephenson, John, Pvt	4993	12 Apr 1792	100
Patch, John, Pvt	4812	26 Aug 1796	100
Peck, John, Pvt	3365	14 Dec 1793	100
Yeomans, Moses, Lt	2574	23 Oct 1790	200
Hale, Mordecai, Surgeon's Mate	2573	23 Oct 1790	300
Williams, Henry A., Lt	2370	11 Feb 1791	200
Woodward, Peter, Lt	2359	23 Oct 1790	200
Throop, John R., Lt	2178	23 Oct 1790	200
McFarran, Thomas, Lt	1405	15 Dec 1790	200
Doyle, Margaret, Lt	170	17 Apr 1795	200
Evitt, Daniel, Pvt	5741	20 Sep 1790	100
Stockdell, John, Pvt	12574	30 Jan 1795	100
Musegenuny, Anth[on]y, Pvt	12787	11 Jan 1796	100
Plomondon, Joseph, Pvt	13590	4 Feb 1790	100
Means, Robert, Pvt	12349	29 May 1792	100
Means, Robert, Pvt	12241	7 Jan 1793	100
Delozear, Asa, Pvt	12080	9 Jul 1794	100
Power, Alex[ande]r, Pvt	9648	21 Jun 1793	100
Child, Evander, Pvt	9593	10 Aug 1792	100
McLure, James, Pvt	8592	9 May 1792	100
Tillotson, Thomas, Pvt	7788	22 Jul 1790	100
Stringer, Samuel, Pvt	7719	25 Aug 1790	100
Norve? [Nowe?] Lewis, Sgt	7541	3 Sep 1790	100

64 1 Feb 1800 A/1/069

By Whom Registered: Jonas Stanbery
For Whom Registered: Jonas Stanbery
Location: (4000 acres) Mil - 20 5 - 1
Based upon the following Army land warrants:

Issued to	*No.*	*Date*	*Acres*
Gorham, Joseph, Pvt	7196	23 Oct 1790	100
Foot, Isaac, Pvt	7142	12 Oct 1789	100
Fenton, Jotham, Pvt	7139	23 Oct 1790	100
Frantz, Conradt, Pvt	7123	15 Dec 1790	100
Scott, Thomas, Pvt	7031	15 Dec 1790	100
Bishop, Nath[anie]l, Pvt	6887	23 Oct 1790	100
Bryan, Elijah, Pvt	5519	9 Apr 1791	100
Brown, Samuel, Pvt	5434	9 Apr 1791	100
Thom, William L., Pvt	3572	11 Sep 1795	100
Woolsey, Melanchton L., Lt	2326	6 Mar 1792	200
Holdridge, Hezekiah, LtCol	947	28 Mar 1797	450
Horton, Elisha, Ens	935	25 Feb 1796	150
Graham, John, Maj	825	4 Jan 1791	400
Fenno, Ephraim, Lt	737	14 May 1794	200
French, Abner, Capt	730	30 Aug 1790	300
Talmadge, James, Pvt	13905	14 Feb 1791	100
Hazard, Richard, Pvt	13226	31 Dec 1789	100
Hole, James, Pvt	13178	27 Jan 1790	100
Greaves, Francis, Pvt	12087	13 Dec 1791	100
Stockdell, John, Pvt	12011	26 Oct 1795	100
Sickles, Jacob, Pvt	8728	25 Feb 1792	100
Stringer, Samuel, Pvt	8034	25 Jan 1791	100
Uthist? John, Pvt	7923	14 Feb 1791	100
Powell, Stephen, Pvt	7587	15 Dec 1790	100
Robertson, Alex[ande]r, Pvt	7528	28 Sep 1790	100
Forst? [Fowt? Font? Towt? Tont?] Robert, Pvt	7449	15 Dec 1790	100
Meyers, Michael, Pvt	7282	9 Oct 1790	100
Bell, William, Pvt	7239	15 Sep 1790	100
Lawrence, Thomas, Pvt	7222	24 Sep 1790	100

65 1 Feb 1800 A/1/070

By Whom Registered: Jonas Stanbery
For Whom Registered: Jonas Stanbery
Location: (4000 acres) Mil - 13 4 - 2
Based upon the following Army land warrants:

Issued to	*No.*	*Date*	*Acres*
Lozier, Hillebrand, Pvt	13392	2 Feb 1790	100
Rogers, Israel, Pvt	7037	25 Jun 1791	100
Ferris, Peter, Pvt	7143	9 Apr 1791	100
Trowbridge, Oliver, Pvt	7213	11 Oct 1790	100
Quinton, David, Pvt	7224	25 Mar 1791	100
Robb, William, Pvt	7254	25 Mar 1791	100
Wadsworth, James, Pvt	7337	9 Apr 1791	100
Magee, Peter, Lt	1395	8 Mar 1794	200

65 [continued]

Issued to	No.	Date	Acres
Vosburgh, Herman, Pvt	7669	27 Jul 1797	100
Peck, John, Pvt	7892	2 Apr 1791	100
Wadsworth, James, Pvt	7895	9 Apr 1791	100
Thompson, Thadeus, Pvt	7896	24 Dec 1790	100
Wadsworth, James, Pvt	8047	9 Apr 1791	100
Bell, Abraham, Pvt	8460	17 Jul 1797	100
Price, John, Pvt	8636	10 Feb 1790	100
Toops? Leonard, Pvt	10486	11 Mar 1791	100
Savage, Edward, Pvt	13289	14 Feb 1791	100
Loshier, Peter, Pvt	13394	10 Apr 1790	100
McClean, Angus, Pvt	13416	20 Aug 1790	100
Denniston, G. T., Lt	547	2 Sep 1790	200
Fowler, Theodonius, Capt	728	9 Jul 1790	300
Platt, Richard, Lt	1266	14 Jul 1790	200
Savage, Joseph, Capt	1928	21 Mar 1791	300
Thompson, Isaiah, CaptLt	2177	14 Jul 1790	200
Platt, Richard, Lt	2186	14 Jul 1790	200
Conklin, Daniel, Pvt	6906	9 Oct 1790	100
Camp, Elisha, Pvt	6923	9 Apr 1791	100
Purdy, Alven, Pvt	7018	6 Jun 1791	100
Childs, Evander, Pvt	7025	3 Jun 1797	100
Fowler, Theodosius, Lt?	6931	9 Jul 1790	200

66 1 Feb 1800 A/1/071

By Whom Registered: Jonas Stanbery

For Whom Registered: Jacob Sebors

Location: (4000 acres) Mil - 17 4 - 4

Based upon the following Army land warrants:

Issued to	*No.*	*Date*	*Acres*
Platt, Richard, Pvt	8247	7 Aug 1789	100
Gladhill, Eli, Pvt	8339	29 Aug 1789	100
Gorden, Bernard, Pvt	8356	16 Mar 1790	100
Job, John, Pvt	8439	29 May 1790	100
Smith, Abel Henry, Pvt	7046	3 May 1793	100
Lewis, Uriah, Pvt	7059	6 Apr 1793	100
Vreedenburgh, William J? Pvt	7091	16 Jul 1790	100
Cumpston, Edward, Pvt	7174	30 Jul 1790	100
Rockefeller, Philip, Pvt	7211	9 Dec 1791	100
Horsford? [Hanford?] Joseph, Pvt	7214	21 May 1791	100
Scribner, Nath[anie]l, Pvt	7339	29 Jul 1790	100
Newkerk, Charles, Pvt	7350	23 Aug 1790	100
Platner, Henry, Pvt	7357	2 Apr 1793	100
Curray, Samuel, Pvt	7471	20 Jul 1790	100
Van Wagenen, Gerrit, Pvt	7475	28 Jul 1790	100
Stout, Philip, Pvt	7518	22 Jul 1793	100
Ogden, David, Pvt	3581	13 Jul 1792	100
Tillotson, Thomas, Pvt	7625	22 Jul 1790	100
Van Norman, Isaac, Pvt	7913	14 Mar 1793	100
Smith, Abel H., Pvt	7918	3 May 1793	100
Van de Burgh, Barth[olomeu]s, Ens?	2259	30 Aug 1790	150
McCrea, Stephen, Physician	2533	15 Dec 1790	450
Gilliland, William, Pvt	5537	8 Feb 1798	100
Gilliland, William, Pvt	5870	9 Dec 1796	100
Moss, Linus, Pvt	6179	24 Sep 1798	100
Moss, Linus, Pvt	6200	24 Sep 1798	100
Tuttle, Enos, Pvt	6579	16 Jan 1797	100
Fowler, Theodosius, Sgt	6759	9 Jul 1790	100
Platt, Richard, Pvt	6886	14 Jul 1790	100
Cumpston, Edward, Pvt	6900	30 Jul 1790	100
Oosterhout, Peter, Pvt	6910	15 Jun 1792	100
Cumpston, Edward, Pvt	6959	30 Jul 1790	100
Platt, Nath[anie]l, Pvt	6967	16 Mar 1792	100
Rogers, Platt, Pvt	8027	24 Sep 1791	100
Rogers, Platt, Pvt	8063	24 Sep 1791	100
Beath, Archib[al]d, Pvt	8153	9 Nov 1791	100

67 1 Feb 1800 A/1/072

By Whom Registered: Jonas Stanbery

For Whom Registered: Jacob Sebors

Location: (4000 Acres) Mil - 11 1 - 3

Based upon the following Army land warrants:

Issued to	*No.*	*Date*	*Acres*
Treat? [Treats?] Malachi, Pvt	2237	29 Sep 1790	450
Deffendorf, Henry, Lt	2614	31 Jul 1793	200
Bacon, Abel, Pvt	3764	13 Feb 1799	100
Dunham, Jeremiah, Pvt	4009	1 Jun 1792	100
Newman, John, Pvt	4751	17 Mar 1792	100
Dunlap, Andrew, Pvt	13016	27 Mar 1793	100
Broome, Samuel, Pvt	13315	11 Nov 1791	100
Copeland, William, Pvt	14041	26 Nov 1792	100
Marselus, Gerrit, Pvt	14070	21 Mar 1794	100
Tupperwine, Christ[ia]n? [or Christopher?] Pvt	14099	30 Jan 1795	100
Roosa, Corn[eliu]s, & Curtenius, Peter, Junior, Lt	166	31 Jan 1791	200
Coventry, John, Surgeon's Mate	505	21 Nov 1793	300
Davis, Puah? Maj	544	3 Jun 1791	400
Elliot, John, Surgeon's Mate	662	14 Aug 1792	300
Keeler, Isaac, Lt	1188	9 May 1789	200
Mooers, Benjamin, Lt	1562	14 Oct 1789	200
McKnight, Charles, Physician	1565	25 Sep 1790	450
Peacock, Hugh, Lt	1688	14 May 1792	200
Ten Broeck, John C., Capt	2184	2 Jun 1792	300

68 1 Feb 1800 A/1/073

By Whom Registered: Jonas Stanbery

For Whom Registered: Jonas Stanbery

Location: (4000 acres)* Mil - 13 2 - 2

Based upon the following Army land warrants:

Issued to	*No.*	*Date*	*Acres*
Rockefeller, Peter, Pvt	3645	28 Jan 1793	100
Walter, Jacob, Pvt	8010	4 Feb 1791	100
Fierd? Joseph C., Pvt	8972	3 Apr 1794	100
Slauch, Bernard, Pvt	9577	12 Jan 1792	100
Burchard, William, Pvt	10697	2 Sep 1789	100
Davis, Henry, Pvt	11050	14 Oct 1795	100
Stalker, William, Pvt	11735	29 Dec 1791	100
Means, Robert, Pvt	11959	7 Jul 1792	100
Greaves, Francis, Pvt	12216	13 Dec 1791	100
Greaves, Francis, Pvt	12368	7 May 1793	100
Means, Robert, Pvt	12404	7 Jul 1792	100
Stockdell, John, Pvt	12516	30 Jan 1795	100
Hughes, James, Pvt	13168	10 Aug 1795	100
Nowill? George, Pvt	13549	11 Apr 1792	100
Orr, Thomas, Pvt	13565	16 Jul 1789	100
Elsworth, Peter, Lt	660	4 Jan 1791	200
Machin, Thomas, Capt	1401	4 Jan 1791	300
Miles, John, Lt	1402	23 Oct 1790	200
Parsons, Charles, Capt	1680	15 Dec 1790	300
Woodruff, Henlock, Surgeon	2363	6 Aug 1790	400
Blodget, Ezra, Pvt	3122	11 May 1792	100
Scott, David, Pvt	3481	29 Sep 1791	100
Muzzy, Amos, Pvt	5400	8 May 1792	100
Acker, Conradt, Pvt	6743	30 Jun 1790	100
Nelson, Abraham, Pvt	7112	1 Oct 1790	100
Hulbert, Aaron, Pvt	7274	10 Dec 1790	100
Osborn, Jeremiah, Pvt	7580	14 May 1790	100
Hunter, Elijah, Pvt	7730	7 Oct 1790	100
Tryon, John, Pvt	7761	15 Dec 1790	100

68 [continued]

Issued to	No.	Date	Acres
Bell, William, Pvt	7854	15**	100
Watkins, Benjamin, Pvt	8009	15 Dec 1790	100

*Marginal notation:

"Location made [as cited above]	5040
Warr. recd. by this State	4000
Since recd.:	
No. 6 Reg[ister's] cert. to Jonas Stanbery, 10 Mar 1800	125.4
1244 Warr. to John Lamont, 12 Apr 1790	300
1345 Warr. to John McCauley, 26 Mar 1792	200
1361 Warr. to John Peck, 19 Apr 1792	200
2590 Warr. to Joseph Stanbery, 8 Aug 1791	150
4455 Warr. to W[illia]m Woodward, 6 Jul 1796	100
	5075.4
Amount of location	5040
	35.4"

**Marginal notation: "No date."

[See also serial entry 271]

69 1 Feb 1800 A/1/074

By Whom Registered: Jonas Stanbery

For Whom Registered: Jonas Stanbery

Location: (4000 acres) Mil - 19 4 - 4

Based upon the following Army land warrants:

Issued to	*No.*	*Date*	*Acres*
Cumpston, Edward, Pvt	6970	30 Jul 1790	100
Cumpston, Edward, Pvt	7057	30 Jul 1790	100
Cumpston, Edward, Pvt	7161	30 Jul 1790	100
Pool, John, Capt	2656	18 Aug 1795	300
Roosevelt, James, Pvt	7235	29 Mar 1791	100
Cumpston, Edward, Pvt	7387	30 Jul 1790	100
Hughes, Peter, Pvt	7450	17 Jun 1790	100
Hathorn, John, Pvt	7597	15 Jul 1790	100
Lilley, Rebuen, Pvt	7941	20 Jul 1789	100
Roosevelt, James, Pvt	7724	29 Mar 1791	100
Boston, John, Pvt	8139	17 Jun 1789	100
Carman, Thomas, Pvt	8222	12 Nov 1796	100
Gallaway, Peter, Pvt	6284	14 Jun 1790	100
Lane, William, Pvt	8223	26 Sep 1791	100
Pope, Joh, Pvt	8404	17 Oct 1789	100
Gallaher, Daniel, Pvt	9473	30 Jan 1792	100
Sheridan, Martin, Pvt	10471	30 Apr 1793	100
Richard, James, Pvt	12462	24 Feb 1794	100
Cumpston, Edward, Pvt	13102	30 Jul 1790	100
Finley, Samuel, Surgeon	715	5 Mar 1790	400
Munson, William, Capt	1564	27 Feb 1797	300
Smith, William, Lt	1956	5 Aug 1789	200
Barton, Simon, Pvt	2976	31 Dec 1789	100
Waterman, Olney, Pvt	3590	17 Oct 1798	100
Alvord, John, Pvt	3611	15 Aug 1796	100
Walker, Peter, Pvt	5319	30 Jul 1790	100
Hooker, James, Pvt	5962	8 Mar*	100
Shelly, Ebenezer, Pvt	6749	20 Sep 1790	100
Glenn, Corn[eliu]s, & Bleecker, Barent, Pvt	6755	24 Aug 1790	100
Cumpston, Edward, Pvt	6832	30 Jul 1790	100
Van Wagenen, Gerrit, Pvt	6852	25 Jul 1790	100
Van Wagenen, Gerrit, Pvt	6965	28 Jul 1790	100

*Marginal notation states that warrant was torn.

70 1 Feb 1800 A/1/075

By Whom Registered: Jonas Stanbery

For Whom Registered: Jonas Stanbery

Location: (4000 acres) Mil - 15 4 - 1

Based upon the following Army land warrants:

Issued to	*No.*	*Date*	*Acres*
Potter, Stephen, Capt	1668	11 Apr 1792	300
Smith, Samuel, Pvt	7878	31 Aug 1790	100
McGregore, James, Pvt	3278	15 Apr 1796	100
Wickham, Stephen, Pvt	7947	5 Jun 1791	100
White, Silvanus, Pvt	7953	25 Jan 1791	100
Vreedenburgh, William J., Pvt	7957	16 Jul 1790	100
Vreedenburgh, William J., Pvt	7958	16 Jul 1790	100
Heller, Jacob, Pvt	8096	20 Dec 1791	100
Newkerk, Charles, Pvt	8061	23 Aug 1790	100
Van Varck, Rachel, Pvt	8815	16 Jul 1789	100
Thomas, William, Pvt	9736	17 Jan 1792	100
McMullen, John, Pvt	9883	9 Jul 1789	100
Gadt, Thomas, Pvt	11210	1 May 1792	100
Williams, James, Pvt	11455	1 Feb 1790	100
Pherson, William, Pvt	11609	22 Mar 1797	100
Castillo, James, Pvt	12059	2 May 1794	100
Duffield, Anthony, Pvt	12096	2 May 1794	100
Haggerty, Patrick, Pvt	12229	2 May 1794	100
Leibeck, Elizabeth, Pvt	13521	5 Mar 1792	100
Geer, Michael, Pvt	4288	30 Dec 1790	100
Ely, William, Pvt	4974	12 Oct 1790	100
Van Wagenen, Gerrit, Pvt	6872	26 Jul 1790	100
Vreedenburgh, William J., Pvt	6883	16 Jul 1790	100
Vreedenburgh, William J., Pvt	6940	16 Jul 1790	100
Talmadge, James, Pvt	7024	14 Feb 1791	100
Rogers, Israel, Pvt	7085	25 Jan 1791	100
Vreedenburgh, W. J., Pvt	7097	16 Jul 1790	100
Vreedenburgh, W. J., Pvt	7209	16 Jul 1790	100
Helme, Anselmus, Pvt	7405	25 Jan 1791	100
Lackey, Hugh, Pvt	7413	30 Aug 1790	100
Vreedenburgh, W. J., Pvt	7458	16 Jul 1790	100
Vreedenburgh, W. J., Pvt	7531	16 Jul 1790	100
Talmadge, James, Pvt	7545	14 Feb 1791	100
Hoffman, Herman, Pvt	7632	3 Feb 1791	100
Stoner, Nicholas, Pvt	7736	3 May 1792	100
Vreedenburgh, W. J., Pvt	7762	16 Jul 1790	100
Glenn, Corn[eliu]s, & Bleecker, Barent, Pvt	7763	24 Aug 1790	100
Titus, Jonathan, Pvt	7872	28 Sep 1790	100

71 3 Feb 1800 A/1/077

By Whom Registered: William Wells

For Whom Registered: William Wells

Location: (4000 acres) Mil - 17 2 - 1

Based upon the following Army land warrants:

Issued to	*No.*	*Date*	*Acres*
Wells, Jemima, Capt	2349	22 Apr 1796	300
Cutler, Ephraim, Pvt	3232	29 Dec 1794	100
Cutler, Ephraim, Pvt	3514	29 Dec 1794	100
Carpenter, William, Pvt	5647	24 Sep 1790	100
Loomis, Dick, Pvt	6088	22 Mar 1798	100
Minor, Elnathan, Pvt	6203	29 Sep 1790	100
Pangbine, Moses, Pvt	6268	18 Jan 1800	100
Judd, William, Pvt	6536	22 Apr 1793	100
Cutler, Ephraim, Pvt	3500	29 Dec 1794	100
Cutler, Menassah, Pvt	3384	16 Mar 1792	100
Benton, Silas, Capt	137	19 Nov 1792	300
Bulkley, Prudence, Capt	138	22 Apr 1796	300
Beers, Nathan, Lt	147	6 Oct 1789	200
Chamberlain, Ephraim, Capt	372	6 Feb 1797	300
Heart, Jonathan, Capt	955	7 Sep 1790	300
Heart, John, Ens	968	22 Aug 1798	150
Higgins, Joseph, Surgeon's Mate	971	13 Dec 1796	300
Judd, William, Capt	1137	1 Jul 1790	300

71 [continued]

Issued to	No.	Date	Acres
Mix, John, Lt	1384	26 Apr 1791	200
Graves, Francis, Ens	1747	26 Mar 1792	150
Williams, Samuel W., Capt	2347	14 May 1796	300

72 3 Feb 1800 A/1/078

By Whom Registered: Matthias Denman
For Whom Registered: Matthias Denman
Location: (4000 acres) Mil - 6 4 - 2
Based upon the following Army land warrants:

Issued to	*No.*	*Date*	*Acres*
Stephenson, John, Pvt	3681	24 Jun 1793	100
Reed, William, Pvt	8666	11 Feb 1791	100
Gilson, Jacob, Pvt	5863	25 Jan 1796	100
Cooper, Samuel L., Lt	358	17 Nov 1789	200
Curtis, Giles, Lt	379	10 Nov 1789	200
Rogers, Sharp, Pvt	6384	10 Jun 1790	100
Fitch, Samuel, Pvt	3905	3 Mar 1797	100
Moers, Benjamin, Pvt	13082	21 Sep 1790	100
Mardin, Edward, Cpl	3321	13 Feb 1790	100
Moers, Benjamin, Pvt	13427	21 Feb 1790	100
Evans, John, Pvt	9358	19 Apr 1796	100
Allen, Jacob, Pvt	3631	26 Nov 1791	100
Raymond, Lemuel? [Samuel?] Pvt	6408	25 Jan 1796	100
Sherran, Francis, Pvt	11008	14 Aug 1795	100
de Baufre, James, Pvt	11416	3 Aug 1797	100
Bound, William, Pvt	8159	7 Feb 1794	100
Rockefeller, Philip, Pvt	8008	9 Dec 1791	100
King, Thomas, Pvt	11411	12 Sep 1792	100
Jenks, Thomas, Pvt	4458	21 Apr 1794	100
Hawkins, Hezekiah, Pvt	3221	28 May 1792	100
Wakelie, Henry, Pvt	6637	21 Mar 1795	100
Townley, Henry, Pvt	11757	19 Aug 1791	100
Cooper, John, Pvt	6941	20 Jul 1791	100
Hogg, Ebenezer, Pvt	9601	17 Jul 1793	100
Handford, Timothy, Pvt	5966	27 Apr 1792	100
Van Wagenen, G. H., Pvt	7837	28 Jul 1790	100
Yairington, Ephraim, Pvt	6720	29 Sep 1790	100
McKnight, Mich[ae]l, Pvt	12401	1 Mar 1793	100
Sherwood, James, Pvt	7752	13 Sep 1791	100
Means, Robert, Pvt	11860	7 Jan 1793	100
Munson, Enias, Pvt	5465	24 Feb 1795	100
Kline, William, Pvt	7099	12 Jun 1792	100
Fitch, Samuel, Pvt	13052	3 Mar 1797	100
Platt, Isaac, Pvt	13616	12 Jul 1792	100
Freeman, Francis, Pvt	11228	26 Nov 1792	100
Ross, Robert, Pvt	9561	17 Jul 1794	100
Prickett, Azariah, Pvt	8651	29 Jul 1794	100
Moers, Benjamin, Pvt	13164	21 Sep 1790	100

73 3 Feb 1800 A/1/079

By Whom Registered: Matthias Denman
For Whom Registered: Matthias Denman
Location: (4000 acres) Mil - 6 5 - 4
Based upon the following Army land warrants:

Issued to	*No.*	*Date*	*Acres*
Diggers, Derbrick? [Dabrick? Derrick?] Pvt	12098	24 Nov 1795	100
Prise, Robert, Pvt	10640	8 Jan 1796	100
Prise, Robert, Pvt	10387	8 Jan 1796	100
Sqirrese? [Sqirrell?] Jacob, Pvt	7760	18 May 1792	100
Huggard, Christian, Pvt	13544	26 Nov 1795	100
Murthwaite, Rich[ar]d, Pvt	9525	19 Aug 1789	100
Quick, Levi, Pvt	12487	24 Nov 1795	100
Hubbard, Christian, Pvt	9663	26 Nov 1795	100
Hubbard, Christian, Pvt	9529	26 Nov 1795	100
Rake, Henry, Pvt	13675	21 Feb 1793	100
Say, John, Pvt	8774	28 Jan 1793	100
Bready, John, Pvt	8128	28 Jan 1793	100
Moore, Henry, Pvt	8578	28 Jan 1793	100
Smith, Samuel, Pvt	7060	31 Aug 1790	100
Blakely, Obed, Pvt	12816	20 Aug 1790	100
Brown, Peter, Pvt	3663	1 Jul 1789	100
Callender, Thomas, Capt	482	12 Aug 1789	300
Kimmey, James, Pvt	10801	2 Sep 1789	100
Layfield, Timothy, Pvt	10811	2 Sep 1789	100
Visbee, Jacob, Pvt	5205	10 Mar 1790	100
Williams, Stacey, Pvt	10587	28 Apr 1791	100
Dyer, Joseph, Pvt	12990	26 Apr 1791	100
Neely, David, Pvt	13545	26 Apr 1791	100
Campbell, John, Pvt	9103	1 Apr 1791	100
Armstrong, Adam, Pvt	6747	26 Jul 1791	100
Cumpston, Edward, Pvt	7702	30 Jul 1790	100
Allison, Joseph, Pvt	7155	9 Sep 1790	100
Williams, James, Pvt	11854	26 Oct 1792	100
Varick, Abraham, Pvt	6869	15 Sep 1790	100
Warren, John, Ens	710	15 Apr 1790	150
Thumb, Mary, Ens	2645	13 Oct 1794	150
Dunlap, Robert, Pvt	7262	11 Aug 1790	100
Alexander, William, Lt	64	10 May 1790	200
Powers, Alex[ande]r, Lt	2592	15 Sep 1791	200
Rockefeller, Philip, Pvt	7382	9 Dec 1791	100

74 3 Feb 1800 A/1/080

By Whom Registered: Matthias Denman
For Whom Registered: Matthias Denman
Location: (4000 acres) Mil - 14 2 - 4
Based upon the following Army land warrants:

Issued to	*No.*	*Date*	*Acres*
Burk, Jonah, Pvt	3780	7 Apr 1790	100
Vreedenburgh, W. J., Pvt	12457	5 May 1790	100
Vickers, Tho[ma]s L., Pvt	8264	29 Sep 1790	100
Vickers, Tho[ma]s L., Pvt	8557	29 Sep 1790	100
Vickers, Tho[ma]s L., Pvt	8358	29 Sep 1790	100
Power, Alex[ande]r, Pvt	5289	27 Feb 1793	100
Taylor, Simeon, Pvt	6557	7 Oct 1789	100
Whitcomb, Benj[amin] Maj	2280	25 Aug 1792	400
Tiff? [Taff?] Major, Pvt	6588	22 Mar 1792	100
Reynolds, James, Pvt	12883	14 Sep 1789	100
Sanford, Peleg, Pvt	3007	24 Feb 1790	100
Holbrook, Nathan, Lt	921	4 Jan 1790	200
Beach, Deborah, Lt	2548	18 Mar 1790	200
Gibbs, Samuel, Lt	822	27 Jul 1789	200
Morrill, Joseph, Pvt?	4019	16 Sep 1791	100
Birch, John, Pvt	6677	23 Jun 1791	100
Waldron, Resolve, Pvt	8292	24 Sep 1791	100
Deming, Andrew, Pvt	4070	31 Oct 1791	100
Gaylord, Ambrose, Pvt	5839	5 Jan 1792	100
Halstead, John, Pvt	5919	27 Jul 1789	100
Jacques, William, Pvt	6023	5 Jan 1792	100
Baldwin, Dan[ie]l, & Co., Pvt	6913	18 Jul 1792	100
Moore, Benj[amin], Pvt	13121	25 Feb 1793	100
Grant, Jessee, Capt	823	18 Feb 1793	300
Quackenbach, John, Pvt	7323	2 Sep 1790	100
Forman, Gabriel, Pvt	13653	19 Apr 1790	100
Warren, John, Pvt	3842	15 Apr 1790	100
Baynton, Abel, Pvt	13664	12 Oct 1790	100
Baynton, Abel, Pvt	5107	12 Oct 1790	100
Baynton, Abel, Pvt	3830	12 Oct 1790	100
Platt, Richard, Pvt	13630	12 Oct 1790	100
Platt, Richard, Pvt	3904	12 Oct 1790	100

75   3 Feb 1800   A/1/081

By Whom Registered: Matthias Denman
For Whom Registered: Matthias Denman
Location: (4000 acres) Mil - 18 3 - 4
Based upon the following Army land warrants:

Issued to	*No.*	*Date*	*Acres*
Williams, Lewis, Pvt	10664	27 Jun 1796	100
Bronson, Isaac, Pvt	4850	19 Apr 1792	100
Osmun, Benjamin, Lt	1611	21 Apr 1790	200
Tice, Elijah, Pvt	8778	26 May 1790	100
Jenkins, James? Pvt	8444	29 Jun 1789	100
Fisher, David, Pvt	8294	26 May 1790	100
Perkins, James, Pvt	7635	14 Feb 1791	100
Van der Werken, James, Pvt	7933	14 Feb 1791	100
Perkins, Joseph, Pvt	7630	14 Feb 1791	100
Zeaster? [Leaster?] Michael, Pvt	8066	14 Feb 1791	100
Tully, Samuel, Pvt	7887	14 Feb 1791	100
Gasper, Peter, Pvt	7188	14 Feb 1791	100
Smith, Samuel, Pvt	6825	18 Jul 1791	100
Means, Robert, Pvt	13966	2 Nov 1792	100
Means, Robert, Pvt	12610	2 Nov 1792	100
Means, Robert, Pvt	13993	2 Nov 1792	100
Means, Robert, Pvt	12641	14 Jul 1792	100
Means, Robert, Pvt	12373	17 May 1792	100
Means, Robert, Pvt	12614	14 Jul 1792	100
Means, Robert, Pvt	12015	14 Jul 1792	100
Larkin, Edward, Pvt	14083	4 Aug 1794	100
de Corey, James, Pvt	10152	7 Aug 1795	100
Chapman, Samuel, Pvt	5636	25 Jun 1793	100
Ely, Gad, Pvt	5748	4 Jan 1791	100
Wright, Alex[ande]r, Pvt	13922	22 Jun 1796	100
Jennings, Monathan, Pvt	6041	5 Mar 1790	100
Drew, Thomas C., Pvt	12739	19 Apr 1796	100
Stevens, James, Pvt	13775	25 Jan 1796	100
Ferguson, Robert, Pvt	12128	15 Dec 1791	100
Talmadge, Benjamin, Pvt	5826	4 Oct 1792	100
Francis, John, Pvt	4142	4 Nov 1794	100
Stillwell, Ezekiel, Pvt	8745	20 Jun 1796	100
Answitz, Appolos, Pvt	5367	5 May 1794	100
Davidson, John, Pvt	4022	14 Apr 1795	100
McNeil, Thomas, Pvt	3335	12 Dec 1795	100
Whiting, Fred[eric]k, Lt	2358	23 Aug 1790	200
Harris, Benjamin, Sgt	4060	16 Oct 1789	100
Selsbury? Jonathan, Pvt	5019	27 Feb 1793	100

76   3 Feb 1800   A/1/083

By Whom Registered: Matthias Denman
For Whom Registered: Matthias Denman
Location: (4000 acres) Mil - 7 6 - 4
Based upon the following Army land warrants:

Issued to	*No.*	*Date*	*Acres*
Hobart, John Slop *et al*, Pvt	12807	15 Sep 1790	100
Platt, Richard, Sgt	10497	7 Aug 1789	100
Southworth, Samuel, Pvt	6515	6 Jan 1792	100
Purdy, Henry, Pvt	11362	22 Dec 1794	100
Crippen, Elisha, Pvt	3841	24 Dec 1791	100
Yarbrough, Edward, Capt	2470	10 May 1790	300
Rose, Alexander, Capt	1863	3 Mar 1791	300
Purdy, Henry, Pvt	11399	18 Dec 1794	100
Purdy, Henry, Pvt	11803	18 Dec 1794	100
Hipple, Henry, Pvt	9737	17 Jun 1794	100
Purdy, Henry, Pvt	11672	18 Dec 1794	100
Purdy, Henry, Pvt	11122	18 Dec 1794	100
Hipple, Henry, Pvt	9962	19 May 1794	100
McCleland, John, Pvt	9539	26 Sep 1791	100
Moore, Benjamin, Pvt	13256	20 Feb 1792	100
Moore, Benjamin, Pvt	13080	14 Aug 1792	100
Moore, Benjamin, Pvt	13192	20 Feb 1792	100
Mooers, Benjamin, Pvt	12763	22 Jan 1790	100
Mooers, Benjamin, Pvt	12765	22 Jan 1790	100
Mooers, Benjamin, Pvt	12799	22 Jan 1790	100
Mooers, Benjamin, Pvt	12797	22 Jan 1790	100
Hoskins, Noah, Pvt	4345	22 Jan 1790	100
Purdy, Henry, Pvt	11446	22 Dec 1794	100
Dicks, George, Pvt	9277	28 Jun 1792	100
Sherrard, Francis, Pvt	11743	28 Jan 1795	100
Sherrard, Francis, Pvt	14092	28 Jan 1795	100
Sherrard, Francis, Pvt	11170	28 Jan 1795	100
Sherrard, Francis, Pvt	14093	28 Jan 1795	100
White, Luther, Pvt	5262	9 Dec 1793	100
Purdy, Henry, Pvt	11473	18 Dec 1793	100
Purdy, Henry, Pvt	11161	18 Dec 1794	100
Purdy, Henry, Pvt	11522	18 Dec 1794	100
Purdy, Henry, Pvt	11624	18 Dec 1794	100
Purdy, Henry, Pvt	11106	18 Dec 1794	100
Bright, Mich[ae]l, Pvt	13067	12 Jan 1792	100
Purdy, Henry, Pvt	11635	18 Dec 1794	100

77   3 Feb 1800   A/1/084

By Whom Registered: Matthias Denman
For Whom Registered: Matthias Denman
Location: (4000 acres) Mil - 13 3 - 2
Based upon the following Army land warrants:

Issued to	*No.*	*Date*	*Acres*
Platt, Henry S., Pvt	8036	12 Oct 1796	100
McCaraher, James, Pvt	13508	9 Jul 1789	100
Owens, Anning? Pvt	7557	7 Oct 1790	100
Cone? William, Pvt	11064	22 Dec 1794	100
Barber, William, Maj	176	19 Aug 1791	400
Price, Thomas, Lt	1732	21 Mar 1792	200
Worsham, Richard, Lt	2655	19 Jun 1795	200
Roase, Jacob, Pvt	7666	8 May 1792	100
Kingsley, Martin, Pvt	12707	11 Apr 1792	100
Riggs, John, Pvt	11627	1 Feb 1790	100
Johnston, Samuel, Pvt	11275	11 Jun 1795	100
Gamble, Jehu, Pvt	12173	24 Jun 1795	100
Sherrard, Francis, Pvt	14120	1 May 1795	100
Bottger, Andrew, Pvt	12766	1 May 1795	100
Ackerman, Andrew, Pvt	12719	20 May 1795	100
Hinds, Leonard, Pvt	3926	28 Apr 1795	100
Bounds, John, Pvt	3708	8 May 1792	100
Bryce, John, Capt	213	9 Jun 1789	300
Whitcomb, Benjamin, Capt	2	27 Aug 1792	300
Peck, Neil? [Heil?] Pvt	4442	13 Jan 1792	100
Blodget, Ezra, Pvt	4386	13 Jan 1792	100
Sill, Moses, Pvt	9282	12 Mar 1792	100
Sill, Moses, Pvt	9538	12 Mar 1792	100
Sill, Moses, Pvt	10605	21 May 1792	100
Sill, Moses, Pvt	5615	12 Mar 1792	100
Sill, Moses, Pvt	9445	14 Mar 1792	100
Sill, Moses, Pvt	9563	21 May 1792	100
Sill, Moses, Pvt	8976	21 May 1792	100
Henry, George, Pvt	9588	29 Jan 1790	100
Hoult, Lewis, Pvt	9609	16 Jul 1789	100
Ballard, Asa, Pvt	7246	22 Oct 1791	100

78   3 Feb 1800   A/1/085

By Whom Registered: Matthias Denman
For Whom Registered: Matthias Denman
Location: (4000 acres) Mil - 17 4 - 1
Based upon the following Army land warrants:

Issued to	*No.*	*Date*	*Acres*
King, Philip, Pvt	7355	4 Aug 1791	100
Hopper, John, Ens	1001	14 Apr 1790	150
Murray, William, Pvt	7488	4 Aug 1791	100
Schoonmaker, Robert, Pvt	7739	20 Jul 1791	100

78 [continued]

Wessells, Hercules, Pvt	8040	26 Jul 1791	100
Hogeboom, Stephen, Pvt	7902	5 May 1791	100
Caldwell, Joseph, Pvt	6979	14 Feb 1791	100
Dean, Steward, Pvt	7583	14 Feb 1791	100
Geers, Benjamin, Pvt	7179	14 Feb 1791	100
Crane, Elisha, Pvt	7203	14 Feb 1791	100
Visscher, Matthew, Pvt	7931	14 Feb 1791	100
Sheldon, James, Pvt	7998	14 Feb 1791	100
Anderson, Samuel, Pvt	6741	14 Feb 1791	100
Blanchard, Ephraim, Pvt	6862	14 Feb 1791	100
Thompson, James, Pvt	7886	14 Feb 1791	100
Thompson, William, Pvt	7182	9 Jun 1791	100
Pixley, David, Pvt	7582	6 Jul 1791	100
English, Samuel, Lt	661	7 Jul 1791	200
Detricks, John, & Detricks, Eliza, Pvt	7407	7 Jul 1791	100
Pinto, Solomon, Ens	1673	3 Jun 1795	150
Hurteigh, John, Pvt	7251	8 Jul 1791	100
Bennett, Joseph, Pvt	6881	26 Apr 1791	100
Denniston, Daniel, Lt	549	22 Jun 1790	200
Ely, William, Pvt	7061	18 Jul 1791	100
O'Bryan, Thomas, Pvt	7569	5 Oct 1790	100
Hudson, Dan[ie]l & Co., Pvt	6824	25 Sep 1790	100
Hudson, Dan[ie]l & Co., Pvt	7326	25 Sep 1790	100
Hudson, Dan[ie]l & Co., Pvt	7255	25 Sep 1790	100
Branson, Isaac, Lt	2150	1 Oct 1792	200
Gilbert, Benjamin, Lt	796	5 Feb 1794	200
Parsons, David, Capt	1667	5 Nov 1795	300
Glascock, Thomas, Lt	877	no date	200

79 3 Feb 1800 A/1/086

By Whom Registered: Matthias Denman
For Whom Registered: Matthias Denman
Location: (4000 acres) Mil - 4 5 - 1
Based upon the following Army land warrants:

Issued to	*No.*	*Date*	*Acres*
de Baufre, James, Pvt	11300	8 Aug 1797	100
de Baufre, James, Pvt	11056	8 Aug 1797	100
Porter, Silas, Pvt	3377	11 Jan 1797	100
Dalton, James, Pvt	8273	9 Feb 1798	100
Wilder, Abel, Pvt	5281	1 Oct 1792	100
Birdsall, Daniel, & Birdsall, William, Pvt	7228	25 Sep 1790	100
Munson, Eneas, Pvt	6296	2 Jan 1796	100
Prentice, Jonas, Pvt	6634	11 Apr 1792	100
Russell, Thomas, Pvt	7871	24 Jun 1793	100
Prentice, Jonas, Pvt	5719	11 Apr 1792	100
Green, Cuff, Pvt	3160	4 May 1791	100
Coe, John D., Pvt	7616	12 Aug 1790	100
Owen, Ebenezer, Pvt	7206	10 Oct 1791	100
Smith, John, Sgt	7765	10 Aug 1790	100
Hayes, William, Pvt	12226	8 May 1794	100
Harris, Benjamin, Pvt	8470	16 Oct 1789	100
Smith, Duncan, Pvt	7791	7 Sep 1790	100
Cobb, Abel	3927	10 Mar 1796	100
Clark, Arthur, Pvt	8180	5 Jan 1790	100
Hazeltine, Thomas, Cpl	3166	13 Feb 1790	100
Kent, Jonas, Pvt	8464	28 Jan 1790	100
Smith, Richard, Pvt	7751	29 Jul 1790	100
Carson, John, Pvt	11040	21 Jan 1794	100
Patterson, Garret, Junior, Pvt	7553	9 Sep 1790	100
Patterson, Garret, Junior, Pvt	7107	9 Sep 1790	100
Trowbridge, Isaac, Pvt	7504	10 Nov 1791	100
Pettee, Timothy, Pvt	7293	23 Feb 1792	100
Brown, John, Pvt	7191	3 Sep 1790	100
Cooper, Samuel, Pvt	7832	1 Sep 1790	100
Graves, Francis, Surgeon	599	31 Jan 1794	400
Darrance, Samuel, Capt	535	5 Mar 1793	300
Means, Robert, Capt	1506	5 Jul 1794	300
Watrous, Abner, Pvt?	6608	26 Feb 1798	100

80 4 Feb 1800 A/1/088

By Whom Registered: Thomas McEwen & Co.
For Whom Registered: James Hamilton
Location: (4000 acres) Mil - 6 6 - 4
Based upon the following Army land warrants:

Issued to	*No.*	*Date*	*Acres*
Armstrong, John, Maj	40	7 Aug 1789	400
Bruce, William, Capt	233	21 Sep 1789	300
Caldwell, Robert, Capt	437	16 Jul 1792	300
Oram, Peter B., Lt	883	21 Jan 1796	200
Jackson, Simon, Capt	1122	21 Mar 1796	300
McClure, James, Capt	1449	20 Aug 1789	300
Merriwether, David, Lt	1511	19 Jun 1795	200
Turner, Marlbry, Ens	1662	23 May 1797	150
Paul, James, Lt	1693	22 Apr 1794	200
Strubin? Philip, Lt	2124	12 Jan 1796	200
Fox, Nathaniel, Capt	2676	21 Jun 1797	300
Neal, James A., Pvt	2990	12 Oct 1795	100
Fitch, Elnathan, Pvt	3713	3 Dec 1799	100
Fuller, John, Pvt	4176	5 Jan 1791	100
Lusk, Stephen, Pvt	7058	12 Feb 1795	100
Shiney, Catharina, Pvt	9659	18 Jan 1791	100
King, Samuel, Pvt	10443	7 May 1794	100
Davis, Henry, Pvt	11146	14 Oct 1795	100
Davis, Henry, Pvt	11389	14 Oct 1795	100
Fricker, George, Pvt	13069	3 Jul 1795	100
Thompson, Moses, Pvt	5154	13 Sep 1792	100
Peck, John, Ens	1239	19 Apr 1792	150

81 4 Feb 1800 A/1/088

By Whom Registered: Charles Jenkins
For Whom Registered: Jonathan Rhea & Erkuries Beatty
Location: (4000 acres) Mil - 14 1 - 2
Based upon the following Army land warrants:

Issued to	*No.*	*Date*	*Acres*
Anderson, James, Lt	68	17 Nov 1791	200
Van Anglen, John, Capt	2511	23 Jul 1789	300
Gray, Jacob, Pvt	8337	19 Mar 1790	100
Stockton, Ebenezer, Lt?	1883	8 Jan 1789	400
Beatty, Reading, Lt?	214	12 Sep 1789	400
Witherspoon, John, Maj	1754	7 May 1789	400
Eaton, Henry, Pvt	9341	20 Jun 1789	100
Cooper, Samuel, Pvt	7960	1 Sep 1790	100
Job, Samuel, Pvt	8449	10 Feb 1792	100
Horan, Moses, Pvt	8389	10 Feb 1792	100
Mott, James, Capt	2523	13 Jul 1797	300
Purdy, Henry, Pvt	10999	18 Jul 1794	100
Cumpston, Edward, Pvt	7796	30 Jul 1790	100
Bellard, Benoni, Pvt	6855	26 Aug 1790	100
Shay, Patrick, Pvt	7766	11 Aug 1790	100
Lusk, Stephen, Pvt	7269	10 Aug 1790	100
Warren, John, Pvt	7322	10 Aug 1790	100
Holmes, John, Capt	995	7 Jul 1789	300
Hostwick, Matthias, Pvt	8372	10 Feb 1792	100
Gavin, John, Pvt	8344	19 Mar 1792	100
Gracey, Matthew, Pvt	8357	10 Feb 1792	100
Giddeman, John, Pvt	8354	10 Feb 1792	100
McMichael, James, Lt	1437	12 Sep 1789	200

82 4 Feb 1800 A/1/089
By Whom Registered: Matthias Denman
For Whom Registered: Matthias Denman
Location: (4000 acres) Mil - 11 2 - 3
Based upon the following Army land warrants:

Issued to	*No.*	*Date*	*Acres*
Van Guilder, Matthew, Pvt	7914	4 Aug 1791	100
Willrey, William, Pvt	8029	4 Aug 1791	100
Willbert, Jacob, Pvt	7942	4 Aug 1791	100
Hart, Ephraim, Pvt	7525	3 Aug 1791	100
Hunt, Thomas, Lt	987	18 Jul 1791	200
Webb, John, Pvt	7962	20 Jun 1791	100
Dermott, Richard, Pvt	7027	26 Jul 1791	100
Adamy, Henry, Pvt	6737	30 Jul 1791	100
Dow, Alex[ande]r, Lt	554	4 Aug 1791	200
Neilion? Andrew, Pvt	10324	4 Mar 1791	100
Letford, Robert, Pvt	9805	10 Mar 1790	100
Willet, Thomas, Pvt	10578	22 Mar 1791	100
Mayberry, Thomas, Pvt	13503	21 Mar 1791	100
Hopper, John G., Pvt	8145	21 Sep 1790	100
McCherney, John, Pvt	9146	3 Nov 1791	100
Ellis, Hannah, Pvt	13960	5 Sep 1791	100
Malony, William, Pvt	9876	9 Feb 1793	100
Leonard, William, Pvt	13959	28 Oct 1791	100
Preston, John, Pvt	10861	2 Sep 1789	100
Garret, Mary, Pvt	13955	5 May 1791	100
Hinman, Samuel, Pvt	5938	27 Nov 1790	100
Blackman, Thomas, Junior? Pvt	8150	1 Sep 1791	100
Spaulding, Asa, Pvt	3997	13 Oct 1791	100
McMonagill, Charles, Pvt	13532	2 Sep 1789	100
Wright, William, Pvt	10905	2 Sep 1789	100
Nick, John, Pvt	4778	28 Oct 1791	100
Glassmire, Jacob G., Pvt	9459	28 Oct 1791	100
Connolly, Patrick, Pvt	10724	2 Sep 1789	100
Bayard, Stephen W., Pvt	7656	14 Feb 1791	100
Callahan, John, Pvt	9095	20 Jun 1789	100
Hefferman, Thomas, Pvt	9647	29 Jun 1791	100
Willing, John C., Pvt	5343	10 Mar 1790	100
Steel? [Heel?] John P., Pvt	10391	20 Jun 1789	100
Blanchfield, James, Pvt	11980	24 Nov 1795	100
Hart, Henry, Pvt	6857	4 Aug 1790	100
Stout, George, Pvt	8011	5 Apr 1793	100
Decker, Christopher, Pvt	7043	25 Jan 1791	100
Scarff, Joseph, Pvt	12593	24 Nov 1795	100

83 4 Feb 1800 A/1/091
By Whom Registered: Thomas McEwen & Co.
For Whom Registered: Nicholas Gilman
Location: (4000 acres) Mil - 7 3 - 1
Based upon the following Army land warrants:

Issued to	*No.*	*Date*	*Acres*
Ladd, Eliphalet, & Cass, T., Pvt	3375	21 Jul 1789	100
Ladd, Eliphalet, & Cass, T., Pvt	3428	21 Jul 1789	100
Ladd, Eliphalet, & Cass, T., Pvt	3432	21 Jul 1789	100
Aiken, Daniel, Pvt	3479	20 Apr 1797	100
Ladd, Eliphalet, & Cass, T., Pvt	3498	21 Jul 1789	100
Hews? [Slews?] Philip, Pvt	3510	3 Jul 1795	100
Ladd, Eliphalet, & Cass, T., Pvt	3555	21 Jul 1789	100
Ladd, Eliphalet, & Cass, T., Pvt	3562	21 Jul 1789	100
Ladd, Eliphalet, & Cass, T., Pvt	3569	21 Jul 1789	100
Ladd, Eliphalet, & Cass, T., Pvt	3573	21 Jul 1789	100
Ladd, Eliphalet, & Cass, T., Pvt	3578	21 Jul 1789	100
Turner, Marlbry, Pvt	3655	23 Mar 1797	100
Bairsto, Moses, Junior, Pvt	3752	14 Jan 1796	100
Cass, Jonathan, Pvt	3802	21 Jul 1789	100
Garrison, William, Pvt	4208	24 Jul 1793	100
Brown, Joseph, Pvt	4247	15 Feb 1797	100
Freeman, John, Pvt	4112	6 Feb 1795	100
Aiken, Daniel, Pvt	4122	14 Apr 1797	100
Brown, Joseph, Pvt	4147	1 Mar 1792	100
Turner, Marlbry, Pvt	4321	23 Mar 1797	100
Wyman, Simeon, Pvt	4322	9 May 1797	100
Blanchard, William, Pvt	4339	23 Feb 1797	100
Turner, Marlbry, Pvt	4353	6 May 1797	100
Cass, Jonathan, Pvt	4368	21 Jul 1789	100
Ladd, Eliphalet, & Cass, T., Pvt	4474	21 Jul 1789	100
Wyman, Simeon, Pvt	4512	8 Apr 1797	100
Hill, Jeremiah, Pvt	4553	9 May 1797	100
Wyman, Simeon, Pvt	4564	9 May 1797	100
Fessenden, Benjamin, Pvt	4925	6 Feb 1797	100
Cass, Jonathan, Pvt	5067	21 Jul 1789	100
Lennox, William, Pvt	5112	22 May 1789	100
Emery, Samuel, Pvt	5495	24 Jun 1793	100
Barton, Jonah, Pvt	6768	9 Mar 1796	100
Addams, John, Pvt	6806	16 Apr 1791	100
Addams, John, Pvt	7774	16 Apr 1791	100
Platt, Richard, Pvt	8148	10 Aug 1789	100
Clark, Ezra, Pvt	8185	8 Oct 1795	100
Foggy, John, Pvt	8384	7 Feb 1792	100
Horneford, Andrew, Pvt	8400	25 Jun 1793	100
Platt, Richard, Pvt	8479	7 Aug 1789	100

84 4 Feb 1800 A/1/092
By Whom Registered: Thomas McEwen & Co.
For Whom Registered: Nicholas Gilman
Location: (4000 acres) Mil - 19 4 - 1
Based upon the following Army land warrants:

Issued to	*No.*	*Date*	*Acres*
Bartlet, Daniel, Surgeon	108	31 Dec 1795	400
Baldwin, Henry, Lt	245	19 Aug 1791	200
Turner, Marlbry, Lt	532	21 Jun 1797	200
Kidd, William, Capt	570	29 Mar 1791	300
Everett, Peletiah, Lt	652	31 Dec 1795	200
Fenner, Robert, Capt	770	28 Jun 1792	300
Moore, George, Lt	1202	19 Mar 1792	200
Lane, Jabez, Capt	1243	14 Dec 1790	300
Crocker, Joseph, Lt	1365	27 Oct 1789	200
Nicholson, John, Lt	1456	7 Apr 1795	200
Nelson, Alexander, Maj	1601	29 Nov 1797	400
Thom, William L., Lt	1626	17 Dec 1795	200
Ladd, Eliphalet, & Cass, T., Capt	1774	21 Jul 1789	300
Summer, Job, Maj	1893	20 Apr 1790	400
Thomas, Edmond, D., Lt	2194	11 Jun 1789	200

85 4 Feb 1800 A/1/093
By Whom Registered: Thomas McEwen & Co.
For Whom Registered: Nicholas Gilman
Location: (4000 acres)* Mil - 12 1 - 1
Based upon the following Army land warrants:

Issued to	*No.*	*Date*	*Acres*
Lepes, John, Pvt	8485	20 Dec 1791	100
King, Samuel, Pvt	9259	28 Jan 1793	100
Stout, Philip, Pvt	9466	22 Jul 1793	100

85 [continued]

Issued to	No.	Date	Acres
de Baufre, James, Pvt	10393	5 Jul 1797	100
Trumheller, Henry, Pvt	10395	6 Aug 1792	100
de Baufre, James, Pvt	10717	26 Jul 1797	100
Sherrard, Francis, Pvt	10927	14 Aug 1795	100
Sherrard, Francis, Pvt	10941	3 Jun 1795	100
Sherrard, Francis, Pvt	10945	14 Aug 1795	100
Sherrard, Francis, Pvt	10956	14 Aug 1795	100
Sherrard, Francis, Pvt	10983	14 Aug 1795	100
Sherrard, Francis, Pvt	10987	14 Aug 1795	100
Sherrard, Francis, Pvt	11032	14 Aug 1795	100
Sherrard, Francis, Pvt	11034	14 Aug 1795	100
Sherrard, Francis, Pvt	11036	14 Aug 1795	100
Sherrard, Francis, Pvt	11046	14 Aug 1795	100
Ponsonby, George, Pvt	11081	8 Jan 1796	100
Ponsonby, George, Pvt	11138	8 Jan 1796	100
Ponsonby, George, Pvt	11223	8 Jan 1796	100
Jarrott, Elisha, Pvt	11306	10 Nov 1797	100
Ponsonby, George, Pvt	11392	8 Jan 1796	100
Ponsonby, George, Pvt	11462	8 Jan 1796	100
Ponsonby, George, Pvt	11573	23 Dec 1795	100
Ponsonby, George, Pvt	11574	8 Jan 1796	100
Ponsonby, George, Pvt	11608	8 Jan 1796	100
de Baufre, James, Pvt	11667	26 Jul 1797	100
Ponsonby, George, Pvt	11764	8 Jan 1796	100
Brown, Edward, Pvt	11979	13 Jul 1795	100
Means, Robert, Pvt	11992	20 Jul 1792	100
Means, Robert, Pvt	12036	14 Jul 1792	100
Means, Robert, Pvt	12181	14 Jul 1792	100
Jordan, Daniel, Pvt	12288	13 Jul 1795	100
Verell, John, Pvt	12231	8 Aug 1796	100
Means, Robert, Pvt	12374	14 Jul 1792	100
Means, Robert, Pvt	12435	14 Jul 1792	100
Smith, Andrew, Pvt	12594	13 Jul 1795	100
Musegenning? Ant[hon]y, Pvt	13044	6 Jul 1791	100
Martin, John, Pvt	13389	15 Nov 1791	100
Aiken, Daniel, Pvt	13410	20 Apr 1797	100
Sherrard, Francis, Pvt	10947	14 Aug 1795	100

*Marginal notation:

"Location made [on Mil - 12 1 - 1] 4220

Warr. recd. [by[this State 4000

Since received:

[No.] 23 Reg[ister's] cert. dated 10 Mar 1800 in favor of Wm. & J. Armstrong 65.7

[No.] 7 Reg[ister's] cert. dated 10 Mar 1800 in favor of Nicholas Gilman 190.3

4256.0

4220

[Overage] 36.0"

[See also serial entry 267]

86 5 Feb 1800 A/1/094

By Whom Registered: James Johnston

For Whom Registered: James Johnston *et al*

Location: (4050 acres) Mil - 11 2 - 4

Based upon the following Army land warrants:

Issued to	*No.*	*Date*	*Acres*
Wayne, Anthony, BrigGen	2379	5 May 1796	850
Latimer, Henry, Physician-Surgeon	1331	6 Jan 1792	450
Robinson, Thomas, LtCol	1819	3 Jul 1789	450
Moore, James, Maj	1419	3 Jun 1790	400
Church, Thomas, Maj	410	11 Mar 1791	400
Finney, Walter, Capt	746	30 Jul 1791	300
Ziegler, David, Capt	2472	17 Oct 1789	300
White, George, Pvt	13933	27 Jun 1792	100
Ennos, Mary, Pvt	9346	25 Mar 1797	100
Spence, David, Pvt	10358	31 Oct 1795	100
Cannon, John, Pvt	8087	26 Feb 1794	100
Murphy, Lawrence, Pvt	13507	24 Feb 1794	100
Kirkpatrick, Francis, Pvt	13209	30 Feb! 1794	100
Kirkpatrick, Francis, Pvt	10635	18 Jan 1794	100
Hart, Silas, Pvt	9094	30 Jun 1794	100
Shindle, Conrad, Pvt	10360	5 Jul 1794	100

87 5 Feb 1800 A/1/095

By Whom Registered: Adam Harbison

For Whom Registered: Adam Harbison

Location: (4000 acres) Mil - 12 2 - 3

Based upon the following Army land warrants:

Issued to	*No.*	*Date*	*Acres*
Bayard, Stephen, LtCol	190	5 Nov 1789	450
Brackenridge, Robert, Lt	273	14 Apr 1790	200
Means, Robert, Lt	280	29 May 1792	200
Brackenridge, Alex[ande]r, Capt	287	14 Apr 1790	300
Thom, William S., Capt	323	24 Jun 1795	300
Campbell, James, Lt	422	29 Jan 1790	200
Thayer, Ebenezer, Ass[istant] Apoth[ecary?]	503	3 May 1793	400
Lusk, William, Capt	1275	16 Jul 1789	300
Posey, Thomas, LtCol	1733	7 Dec 1791	450
Scott, Matthew, Capt	2034	9 Jul 1789	300
McCracken, William, Lt	2625	24 Dec 1792	200
Sawyer, Paul, Pvt	5049	20 Apr 1798	100
Gibb, William, Pvt	9471	9 Jul 1789	100
Stever, Michael, Pvt	9837	10 Mar 1795	100
Power, Alex[ande]r, Pvt	10126	28 Nov 1792	100
Nicholson, John, Pvt	10153	6 Apr 1790	100
Stever, Michael, Pvt	10297	10 Mar 1795	100
Pullen, Sam[ue]l, Pvt	13600	16 Jul 1789	100

88 5 Feb 1800 A/1/095

By Whom Registered: Adam Harbison

For Whom Registered: Adam Harbison

Location: (4000 acres) Mil - 18 6 - 4

Based upon the following Army land warrants:

Issued to	*No.*	*Date*	*Acres*
Harbison, Adam, Pvt	10142	2 Mar 1792	100
Jarrett, Abraham, Pvt	11445	16 Jul 1797	100
Powell, Thomas, Pvt	12482	2 May 1794	100
Jarrett, Abraham, Pvt	11742	17 Jul 1797	100
Jarrett, Abraham, Pvt	11249	17 Jul 1797	100
McKnight, David, Lt	1439	16 Jul 1789	200
Harbison, Adam, Lt!	9524	21 Dec 1791	100
Harbison, Adam, Lt!	9401	26 Jul 1792	100
Harvey, George, Pvt	9543	17 Aug 1789	100
Justice, Jacob, Pvt	9673	6 Apr 1790	100
Harbison, Adam, Pvt	9188	19 Apr 1792	100
Gross, Christian, Pvt	10373	16 Jul 1791	100
Harbison, Adam, Pvt	9788	21 Dec 1791	100
Zane? [Lane?] William, Pvt	10852	13 Jan 1792	100
Zane? [Lane?] William, Pvt	10798	13 Jan 1792	100
Zane? [Lane?] William, Pvt	11441	13 Jan 1792	100
Zane? [Lane?] William, Pvt	10617	13 Jan 1792	100
Higgins, James, Capt	2647	27 Nov 1794	300
Zane? [Lane?] William, Pvt	8699	17 Jan 1792	100
Zane? [Lane?] William, Pvt	12970	19 Jan 1792	100

88 [continued]

Jackson, Mich[ae]l, Lt	1124	9 May 1796	200
Harrison, Elisha, Capt	2632	30 May 1793	300
Magee, William, Pvt	8580	2 Jul 1791	100
Camp, Robert, Capt	1867	14 Dec 1795	300
Lowe, James T., Lt	1297	28 Feb 1795	200
Creamer, Francis, Pvt	9168	5 Sep 1791	100
Finley, Sam[ue]l, Maj	761	5 Nov 1796	400
Zane? [Lane?] William, Maj!	12804	13 Jan 1791	100

89 6 Feb 1800 A/1/097

By Whom Registered: Thomas Worthington
For Whom Registered: Thomas Worthington
Location: (4000 acres) Mil - 17 1 - 4
Based upon the following Army land warrants:

Issued to	*No.*	*Date*	*Acres*
Bedinger, Henry, Capt	267	25 Aug 1789	300
Bedinger, Dan[ie]l, Ens	285	25 Aug 1789	150
Conaway, Joseph, Lt	461	17 Feb 1797	200
Craik, James, Physician-General	502	3 Jun 1789	500
Dark, William, LtCol Com-[manding]	598	25 Aug 1789	500
Grier, Sarah, Surgeon's Mate	897	6 Sep 1791	300
Lawrence, Harrison, Lt	1074	30 Apr 1793	200
Jordan, John, Capt	1165	14 Feb 1791	300
Malary, Philip, Capt	1502	25 Aug 1789	300
McGuire, William, LtCol!	1522	25 Aug 1789	200
North, George, Col	1591	19 Aug 1789	200
Swearingnen* Joseph, Capt	2065	25 Aug 1789	300
Schaffner, Casper, Cornet	2127	27 May 1790	150
Duncan, John, Pvt	4211	27 Nov 1797	100
Woodward, William, Pvt	6380	16 Feb 1797	100
Ervin, James, Pvt	11192	1 Feb 1790	100
Roberts, William, Pvt	11628	1 Feb 1790	100

*So spelled.

90 6 Feb 1800 A/1/098

By Whom Registered: John Warder
For Whom Registered: John Warder
Location: (4000 acres) Mil - 11 2 - 1
Based upon the following Army land warrants:

Issued to	*No.*	*Date*	*Acres*
Smyth, Richard, Lt	767	21 May 1794	200
Cay, David, Lt	1106	4 Jun 1792	200
McClintock, Sarah, Lt	1476	14 May 1791	200
Swartz, Godfried, Lt	2123	23 Jun 1789	200
White, Moses, Capt	2378	22 Nov 1791	300
Taylor, George, Junior, Pvt	8800	16 Jan 1800	100
Arrance, James, Pvt	12734	15 Jan 1793	100
Crouch, Robert, Pvt	12962	18 Jan 1800	100
Hill, George, Pvt	13236	19 Jun 1795	100
Manley, John, Pvt	13525	21 Dec 1799	100
Spot? [Spots?] William, Pvt	13702	8 Mar 1791	100
Nelson, Jemima *et al*, Lt	182	1 Mar 1799	200
Matthews, William, Capt	192	11 Jul 1797	300
Elmer, Ebenezer, Surgeon	663	21 Apr 1790	400
Wilson, William, Capt	2382	26 Aug 1789	300
Harris, Rezina, Capt	2673	22 Oct 1796	300
Dunham, Richard, Pvt	4020	22 Jan 1799	100
Phelps, Silas, Pvt	6321	7 Apr 1796	100
Abbot, Richard, Pvt	8086	10 Aug 1792	100
Stives, William, Pvt	8775	21 Dec 1798	100
Smith, John, Pvt	10401	24 Dec 1796	100
Clarke, David, Pvt	10473	21 Jul 1791	100
Wilrick, Jacob, Pvt	10568	8 Mar 1793	100
Stevenson, Alex[ande]r, Pvt	11717	11 May 1790	100

91 6 Feb 1800 A/1/098

By Whom Registered: Sampson Davis
For Whom Registered: Sampson Davis
Location: (4000 acres) Mil - 13 2 - 1
Based upon the following Army land warrants:

Issued to	*No.*	*Date*	*Acres*
Evans, Thomas, Capt	685	12 Sep 1789	300
Manifold, Peter, Maj	741	21 Mar 1795	400
Graves, Francis, Capt	1737	26 Mar 1792	300
Neal, James A., Pvt	3380	12 Oct 1795	100
Bedinger, Philip, Pvt	6833	4 Jan 1791	100
Crosby, Benjamin, Pvt	6895	13 Sep 1791	100
Cook, George, Pvt	6920	12 Oct 1790	100
Dickerson, David, Pvt	7028	5 Jan 1791	100
Rogers, Israel, Pvt	7045	25 Jan 1791	100
Dorn, John, Pvt	7067	5 Jan 1791	100
Howell, George, Pvt	7223	12 Oct 1790	100
Tremper, Henry, Pvt	7253	11 Oct 1790	100
Harter, Adam, Pvt	7256	5 Jan 1791	100
Loudon? [London?] Samuel, Pvt	7324	4 May 1791	100
Leonard, Robert, Pvt	7404	1 Oct 1791	100
McColm, Samuel, Pvt	7494	5 May 1791	100
Ludlam, Henry, Pvt	7780	26 Apr 1791	100
Tremper, Henry, Pvt	7951	11 Oct 1790	100
Wethereck, Michael, Pvt	7986	5 Jan 1791	100
Shaw, John, Pvt	10385	26 Nov 1795	100
Lecatt, Levin, Pvt	10819	26 May 1790	100
Bigwood, James, Pvt	10975	11 Mar 1791	100
Bias, James, Pvt	10976	11 Jun 1790	100
Gilby, Henry, Pvt	11254	11 Mar 1791	100
Jarrett, Elisha, Pvt	11270	7 Jun 1798	100
Ward, Joshua, Pvt	11538	11 Jan 1796	100
Ryley, Patrick, Pvt	11636	11 Mar 1791	100
Ward, Joshua, Pvt	11656	11 Jan 1796	100
Ward, Joshua, Pvt	11790	11 Jan 1796	100
Smyth, Richard, Pvt	12179	21 May 1794	100
Gregory, John, Pvt	13126	1 Mar 1797	100
Shapard* Sam[ue]l B., Pvt	13979	20 Jun 1798	100
Fleetwood, Abigail, Pvt	14139	15 Oct 1795	100

*So spelled.

92 7 Feb 1800 A/1/099

By Whom Registered: Jonathan Dayton
For Whom Registered: Jonathan Dayton
Location: (4000 acres) Mil - 13 3 - 4
Based upon the following Army land warrants:

Issued to	*No.*	*Date*	*Acres*
Smith, John K., Pvt	4804	23 Feb 1797	100
Maus, Sam[ue]l, Pvt	13591	21 Mar 1792	100
Cole, Isaac, Pvt	12439	14 Aug 1792	100
Holbrook, Abijah, Pvt	11279	22 Mar 1797	100
Holbrook, Abijah, Pvt	11054	22 Mar 1797	100
Holbrook, Abijah, Pvt	11208	22 Mar 1797	100
Holbrook, Abijah, Pvt	13155	22 Mar 1797	100
Holbrook, Abijah, Pvt	11663	22 Mar 1797	100
Holbrook, Abijah, Pvt	11409	22 Mar 1797	100
de Baufre, James, Pvt	11732	31 Mar 1797	100
de Baufre, James, Pvt	11339	31 Mar 1797	100
de Baufre, James, Pvt	10795	31 Mar 1797	100
de Baufre, James, Pvt	10815	31 Mar 1797	100
de Baufre, James, Pvt	10918	31 Mar 1797	100

92 [continued]

Issued to	No.	Date	Acres
de Baufre, James, Pvt	11302	24 Mar 1797	100
de Baufre, James, Pvt	11497	24 Mar 1797	100
de Baufre, James, Pvt	11119	18 Apr 1797	100
de Baufre, James, Pvt	11435	18 Apr 1797	100
de Baufre, James, Pvt	10810	19 Apr 1797	100
Warfield, Walter, Surgeon	2405	27 Apr 1795	400
Ferguson, Robert, Lt	2272	22 Nov 1791	200
Bellows, Samuel, Pvt	5528	24 May 1790	100
Moore, Forbris, Pvt	6226	24 May 1790	100
Munson, Eneas, Pvt	13613	16 Dec 1793	100
Nesbitt, Henry, Pvt	10855	21 Apr 1791	100
Thomas, William, Pvt	12774	5 Dec 1791	100
Means, Robert, Pvt	11923	14 Jul 1792	100
Flowers, Zephon, Pvt	5825	26 Apr 1792	100
Loudon, Stephen, Pvt	12510	21 Jan 1792	100
Clarey, Samuel, Pvt	5657	6 Apr 1795	100
Blake, Reuben, Pvt	5422	23 Aug 1790	100
Peck, Ward, Pvt	6305	24 Jan 1794	100
Morris, John, Junior, Pvt	8579	23 Jan 1792	100
Sheppard, Nathaniel, Pvt	8718	10 Mar 1790	100
Means, Robert, Pvt	12491	7 Jan 1793	100
Means, Robert, Pvt	13964	18 Feb 1793	100

93 7 Feb 1800 A/1/101

By Whom Registered: Jonathan Dayton
For Whom Registered: Jonathan Dayton
Location: (4000 acres) Mil - 20 7 - 4
Based upon the following Army land warrants:

Issued to	*No.*	*Date*	*Acres*
Hulings, John, Maj	1030	8 Mar 1791	400
Clemons, Edward, Pvt	3913	26 Aug 1789	100
Furness, Mary, Pvt	3129	19 Aug 1791	100
King, Daniel, Pvt	3529	21 Feb 1795	100
Kitley? William, Pvt	4518	14 Feb 1795	100
Tuttle, Jon[athan?] Pvt	5247	2 Nov 1791	100
Tuttle, Jon[athan?] Pvt	6307	2 Nov 1791	100
Smith, John, Pvt	6888	13 Sep 1790	100
Battle, James, Pvt	5214	21 Apr 1794	100
Bartholomew, George, Pvt	6839	28 Sep 1790	100
Bartholomew, George, Pvt	7714	28 Sep 1790	100
Maxwell, Anth[on]y, Pvt	6984	10 Oct 1791	100
Maxwell, Anth[on]y, Pvt	7287	10 Oct 1791	100
Veeder, Simon, Pvt	6928	30 Aug 1790	100
Veeder, Simon, Pvt	7636	30 Aug 1790	100
Veeder, Volkert, Pvt	7970	30 Aug 1790	100
McMillen, Charles, Pvt	8525	30 Sep 1791	100
Power, Alex[ande]r, Pvt	9285	30 Apr 1793	100
Platt, Richard, Pvt	9925	10 Aug 1789	100
Faires, John, Pvt	11668	21 Jan 1795	100
Faires, John, Pvt	11766	21 Jan 1795	100
Faires, John, Pvt	10998	21 Jan 1795	100
Purdy, Henry, Pvt	11808	18 Dec 1794	100
Purdy, Henry, Pvt	11568	18 Dec 1794	100
Purdy, Henry, Pvt	11243	18 Dec 1794	100
Purdy, Henry, Pvt	11395	18 Dec 1794	100
Purdy, Henry, Pvt	11728	18 Dec 1794	100
Cook, William, Pvt	12018	29 Aug 1791	100
Means, Robert, Pvt	12005	15 May 1795	100
Spencer, John, Pvt	12519	29 Jun 1793	100
Dowling, Lawrence, Pvt	12992	13 Jul 1791	100
Parker, John, Pvt	10207	10 Mar 1790	100
Fulmer, Casper, Pvt	13060	10 Mar 1791	100
Groves, John, Pvt	13139	3 Mar 1791	100
Bradbury, Dan[ie]l, Pvt	2942	8 Mar 1791	100
Ramsay, John, Pvt	5467	22 May 1790	100
Parker, John, Pvt	8980	10 Mar 1790	100

94 7 Feb 1800 A/1/102

By Whom Registered: Jonathan Dayton
For Whom Registered: Jonathan Dayton
Location: (4000 acres) Mil - 16 1 - 1
Based upon the following Army land warrants:

Issued to	*No.*	*Date*	*Acres*
Humpton, Rich[ar]d, Col	1006	18 Jan 1791	500
Gassaway, John, Capt	853	19 Jun 1789	300
Hoomes, Benj[amin] Capt	2666	24 Mar 1796	300
Clements, Mace, Surgeon	464	29 May 1792	400
Savage, Joseph, Surgeon's Mate	2088	25 Apr 1789	300
Wallace, Will B., Lt	2441	27 Mar 1794	200
Barnaby, John, Lt	2516	27 Mar 1794	200
Brewster, Caleb, CaptLt	172	15 Dec 1790	200
Burnet, Robert R., Lt	173	15 Sep 1790	200
Popham, William, Capt	1765	27 Sep 1790	300
Cropsey, Jasper, Lt	2563	9 Nov 1791	200
Guion? Isaac, Lt	832	18 May 1790	200
Bronson, Isaac, Pvt	6445	11 Mar 1791	100
Bronson, Isaac, Pvt	5699	11 Mar 1791	100
Bronson, Isaac, Pvt	3759	11 Mar 1791	100
Bronson, Isaac, Pvt	6107	11 Mar 1791	100
Bronson, Isaac, Pvt	5674	11 Mar 1791	100
Bronson, Isaac, Pvt	4698	11 Mar 1791	100
McKee, Edith, Pvt	13219	3 Sep 1792	100

95 7 Feb 1800 A/1/103

By Whom Registered: Jonathan Dayton
For Whom Registered: Jonathan Dayton
Location: (4000 acres)* Mil - 12 3 - 4
Based upon the following Army land warrants:

Issued to	*No.*	*Date*	*Acres*
Nicholas, Lewis, Col	1588	27 Feb 1790	500
Pinkerton, John, Capt	1199	24 Jul 1789	300
Thom, Will S., Lt	1624	17 Feb 1797	200
Haskell, Benj[amin] Pvt	4610	8 May 1792	100
Haskell, Benj[amin] Pvt	4791	8 May 1792	100
Ponsonby, George, Pvt	11439	23 Dec 1795	100
Ponsonby, George, Pvt	11420	23 Dec 1795	100
Ponsonby, George, Pvt	11457	23 Dec 1795	100
Ponsonby, George, Pvt	11715	23 Dec 1795	100
Ponsonby, George, Pvt	11644	23 Dec 1795	100
Ponsonby, George, Pvt	11529	23 Dec 1795	100
Ponsonby, George, Pvt	11530	23 Dec 1795	100
Steel, George, Pvt	6217	8 Apr 1797	100
Steel, George, Pvt	6158	8 Apr 1797	100
Dunscomb, Andrew, Pvt	13986	4 Sep 1792	100
Kearns, William, Pvt	13284	27 Jun 1789	100
Knight, Thomas, Pvt	9339	26 Mar 1792	100
Clingman, Jacob, Pvt	12611	22 Oct 1791	100
Clingman, Jacob, Pvt	12387	22 Oct 1791	100
Clingman, Jacob, Pvt	12356	22 Oct 1791	100
Clingman, Jacob, Pvt	11924	5 Oct 1791	100
Clingman, Jacob, Pvt	11925	22 Oct 1791	100
de Baufre, James, Pvt	11222	11 Apr 1797	100
de Baufre, James, Pvt	11725	11 Apr 1797	100
de Baufre, James, Pvt	10716	8 Apr 1797	100
de Baufre, James, Pvt	11250	8 Apr 1797	100
de Baufre, James, Pvt	11424	6 Apr 1797	100
de Baufre, James, Pvt	11805	6 Apr 1797	100
de Baufre, James, Pvt	13802	24 Apr 1797	100
de Baufre, James, Pvt	11809	24 Apr 1797	100
de Baufre, James, Pvt	11010	19 Apr 1797	100
de Baufre, James, Pvt	10996	11 Apr 1797	100
de Baufre, James, Pvt	11796	19 Apr 1797	100

*Marginal notation [continued next page].

95 [continued]
"Location made [as cited above][acres] 4094.2
Warr. recd. [by] this State 4000
Since received:
Warr. No. 2258 dated 18 Jul 1789 in favor of John Van Dyk for 200 acres. 100 recd. to cover this excess. 100 to cover excess on state. No. 235 100
[Total warrants received] 4100
Amount of location 4094.2
[Overage][acres] 5.8"

96 8 Feb 1800 A/1/104
By Whom Registered: John Matthews
For Whom Registered: Alex[ande]r McGlaughlin*
Location: (4050 acres) Mil - 15 7 - 1
Based upon the following Army land warrants:

Issued to	*No.*	*Date*	*Acres*
Smith, Elphalet, Pvt	3698	9 Jul 1789	100
McCormick, John, Pvt	9882	9 Jul 1789	100
Hamilton, Cumbert, Pvt	9541	9 Jul 1789	100
Brown, James, Pvt	8947	16 Jul 1789	100
Morgan, Dan[ie]l, BrigGen	1496	25 Aug 1789	850
Wilfong, David, Pvt	10628	25 Sep 1789	100
Ward, John, Pvt	10656	1 Oct 1789	100
Kelso, John, Pvt	9715	5 Nov 1789	100
Newman, Owen, Sgt	12429	5 Nov 1789	100
Stubbling, Sigismond, Capt	2066	24 Feb 1796	300
Rewick, Owen, Pvt	13693	21 Nov 1797	100
Nevile? [Nevill?] Presley, Capt	1596	24 Feb 1796	300
Butler, Law[rence] Capt	261	22 May 1789	300
Springer, Jacob, Lt	2070	3 Jan 1800	200
Keep, James, Pvt	12297	3 Jul 1795	100
Hugo, Thomas B., Capt	1049	4 Aug 1789	300
Joseph, John Baptiste [& Co?] Col	1334	6 Feb 1795	500
Morrison, James, Pvt	12066	12 May 1792	100
Lodge, Benj[ami]n, Lt	1276	18 Jun 1792	200

97 8 Feb 1800 A/1/105
By Whom Registered: John A. Seitz
For Whom Registered: James Morrison
Location: (4000 acres)* Mil - 2 9 - 3
Based upon the following Army land warrants:

Issued to	*No.*	*Date*	*Acres*
Barret, William, Capt	270	28 May 1789	300
Morrison, James, Lt	601	21 Apr 1796	200
Harrison, Will B., Ens	1091	18 Jun 1793	150
Mansfield, John, Lt	1382	17 May 1790	200
Morrison, James, Ens	1443	5 Nov 1789	150
Shaylor, Joseph, Lt	1960	16 Sep 1789	200
Turberville, Geo[rge] L., Capt	2508	15 Jul 1789	300
Casteel, Samuel, Pvt	9221	20 Aug 1791	100
Henley, Mich[ae]l, Pvt	9442	23 Feb 1792	100
Hoback, Philip, Pvt	9443	23 Feb 1792	100
Girdler, James, Pvt	9508	14 Mar 1799	100
Morrison, James, Pvt	10104	21 Apr 1796	100
Vertner, Dan[ie]l, Pvt	10237	9 May 1797	100
Robinson, Simon, Pvt	10321	6 Oct 1794	100
Vertner, Dan[ie]l, Pvt	10661	9 May 1797	100
Davis, Sam[ue]l, Pvt	11169	27 Aug 1789	100
Bean, John, Pvt	11901	2 Sep 1790	100
Morrison, James, Pvt	11994	21 Apr 1796	100
Vertner, Dan[ie]l, Pvt	12188	9 May 1797	100
Morrison, James, Pvt	12291	12 May 1792	100
Morrison, James, Pvt	12343	12 May 1792	100
Moore, Thomas, Pvt	12348	23 Feb 1792	100
Vertner, Dan[ie]l, Pvt	12377	9 May 1797	100
Vertner, Dan[ie]l, Pvt	12383	9 May 1797	100
Morrison, James, Pvt	12490	12 May 1792	100
Morrison, James, Pvt	12493	12 May 1792	100
Thornton, Pat, Pvt	12599	20 Aug 1791	100
Woods, William, Pvt	12646	20 Aug 1791	100
Morrison, James, Pvt	12650	12 May 1792	100
Morrison, James, Pvt	12655	12 May 1792	100
Foster, Geo[rge], Pvt	13970	19 Jun 1793	100
Harrison, Will B., Pvt	13978	18 Apr 1794	100

*Marginal notation:
"Location made [as cited above][acres] 4353
Warr. recd. [by] this State 4000
No. 97 Reg[ister's] Cert. dated 10 Mar 1800[!] in favor of James Johnston 50
11897 Warr. dated 21 Apr 1796 in favor of James Morrison 100
10469 Warr. ditto ditto 100
10383 Warr. ditto ditto 100
4350
Recd. by the reg[ister] for 3 acres 6 dollars 3
Amount of location 4353"
[See also serial entry 268]

98 8 Feb 1800 A/1/106
By Whom Registered: William McCluney
For Whom Registered: William Aulmon
Location: (4000 acres) Mil - 1 7 - 2
Based upon the following Army land warrants:

Issued to	*No.*	*Date*	*Acres*
Wright, John, Junior, Lt	1369	30 Dec 1796	200
McPherson, Will, Maj	1416	13 May 1789	400
Smith, John K., Capt	1900	24 Apr 1794	300
Stevenson, Stephen, Capt	2013	12 Jan 1791	300
Little, Eleazer, Lt	2561	21 Jun 1790	200
Flick, Martin, Pvt	7125	26 Jul 1796	100
McDade, Will, Pvt	8590	15 Jul 1789	100
Riley, James, Pvt	8675	15 Dec 1792	100
Andrew, John, Pvt	8892	16 Apr 1792	100
Collins, John, Pvt	9125	22 Feb 1792	100
Thompson, Ebenezer, Pvt	10513	26 May 1792	100
Toland, Benj[amin] Pvt	10783	4 Aug 1789	100
Harper, Thomas, Pvt	10788	2 Sep 1789	100
Toland, Benj[amin] Pvt	10893	4 Aug 1789	100
Biswell, John, Pvt	11912	2 May 1794	100
Pigman, Will, Pvt	12455	2 May 1794	100
Fisher, Will, Pvt	12129	2 May 1794	100
Hoggans, Thomas, Pvt	12225	2 May 1794	100
Pope, Thomas, Pvt	12456	2 May 1794	100
Priest, John, Pvt	12481	2 May 1794	100
Robinson, Will, Pvt	12509	2 May 1794	100
Manuel, Peter, Pvt	12862	6 May 1795	100
Hempfield, John, Pvt	13189	27 Aug 1792	100
Oliver, Nicholas, Pvt	13573	10 Sep 1790	100
Shade, Julius, Pvt	13764	19 Nov 1793	100
Strahn, John, Pvt	13801	10 Dec 1791	100
Werble, Henry, Pvt	13897	19 Nov 1793	100
Mason, William, Pvt	13449	19 Jan 1792	100
Means, Robert, Capt	2466	23 Jun 1795	300

99 8 Feb 1800 A/1/107
By Whom Registered: William H. Harrison
For Whom Registered: John C[leves] Symmes
Location: (4000 acres) Mil - 14 5 - 3
Based upon the following Army land warrants:

Issued to	*No.*	*Date*	*Acres*

99 [continued]

Issued to	No.	Date	Acres
Sullivan, Dan[ie]l, Pvt	10427	16 May 1791	100
Courtney, Hannah, Pvt	9164	2 Feb 1791	100
May, Will, Pvt	13445	5 Mar 1791	100
Nagle, Christian, Pvt	10158	11 Apr 1791	100
Welch, Patrick, Pvt	10634	10 May 1791	100
Cooley, James, Pvt	9100	5 May 1791	100
Jones, Robert, Pvt	9675	5 Mar 1791	100
Battersby, John, Pvt	8981	16 May 1791	100
Lord, Jabez, Pvt	6118	23 Aug 1790	100
de Witt, Peter, Pvt	5608	15 Apr 1790	100
Hull, Sam[ue]l, Pvt	5982	23 Aug 1790	100
de Witt, Peter, Pvt	6266	15 Apr 1790	100
Dodge, Israel, Pvt	5713	28 Jan 1790	100
de Witt, Peter, Pvt	6310	15 Apr 1790	100
Squire, Ashur, Pvt	6447	23 Aug 1790	100
Cooke, Miles, Pvt	5628	23 Aug 1790	100
Price, William, Pvt	8655	26 Apr 1791	100
Shrink, Andrew, Pvt	11740	7 Apr 1791	100
Henry, Philip, Pvt	9549	12 Mar 1791	100
Reynolds, James, Pvt	13582	9 Sep 1789	100
Day, John, Pvt	7079	2 Dec 1789	100
Schott, John P., Pvt	6630	12 Mar 1792	100
Watkins, John, Pvt	6625	14 Nov 1791	100
Spaulding, Asa, Pvt	4476	12 Oct 1790	100
Tisdale, Mau[rice?]	5203	14 Mar 1791	100
Thomas, Elijah, Pvt	6542	13 Jul 1792	100
Stewart, John, Pvt	6469	9 Oct 1789	100
Fanning, Thomas, Pvt	5771	2 Jul 1790	100
Vose, Jesse, Pvt	6596	17 May 1790	100
Watson, Guy, Pvt	3600	31 Dec 1789	100
Camp, Elisha, Pvt	6646	17 Nov 1791	100
Watson, Jack, Pvt	3594	31 Dec 1789	100
Wilhelm, Henry, Pvt	10632	5 Mar 1791	100
Hammond, Prince, Pvt	3237	31 Dec 1789	100
Groat, Jonathan, Pvt	5516	5 Dec 1791	100
Mead, Shadwick, Pvt	7283	24 Feb 1791	100
Lawrence, Thomas, Pvt	7521	24 Sep 1790	100
Sherrard, Francis, Pvt	11031	14 Aug 1795	100
Wells, George, Pvt	5886	15 Aug 1792	100
Wechter, Anth[on]y, Pvt	8888	19 Mar 1792	100

100 8 Feb 1800 A/1/108

By Whom Registered: William H. Harrison
For Whom Registered: John C[leves] Symmes
Location: (4000 acres) Mil - 13 1 - 4
Based upon the following Army land warrants:

Issued to	*No.*	*Date*	*Acres*
Duffield, John, Surgeon	528	9 May 1789	400
Pepoon, Silas, Lt	649	12 Apr 1792	200
Frisbie, Thaddeus, Lt	718	11 Oct 1791	200
Stratton, Aaron, Capt	1899	6 Jan 1792	300
Dugan, Ann, Pvt	11253	17 Apr 1792	100
Jones, James, Pvt	8454	19 Jul 1790	100
Polock, Asher, Pvt	3410	4 May 1791	100
Blackwood, John, Pvt	8952	13 Jul 1791	100
Kingsley, Ebenezer, Pvt	3730	22 Oct 1791	100
Rous, Jacob, Pvt	10251	16 Nov 1791	100
Reed, Jesse, Pvt	4954	23 Dec 1791	100
Kean, Mary, Pvt	9725	29 Dec 1791	100
Sylvester, Isaac, Pvt	8740	9 Feb 1793	100
Tuttle, Jon[athan?] Pvt	3681	15 Nov 1792	100
Pepoon, Silas, Pvt	4214	12 Apr 1792	100
Smith, Ichiel, Pvt	6462	6 Apr 1790	100
Giffins, Joshua, Pvt	8363	31 Aug 1791	100
Hutch, John, Pvt	8396	19 Aug 1791	100
Tuttle, Dan[ie]l, Pvt	8790	30 Oct 1789	100
Preston, Joseph, Pvt	10862	2 Sep 1789	100
Birch, James, Pvt	8113	7 Jul 1789	100
Berry, Barth[olomew] Pvt	8940	22 May 1793	100
Purdy, Henry, Pvt	9396	22 Dec 1794	100
Faires, John, Pvt	11069	21 Jan 1795	100
France, Emanuel, Pvt	11848	30 Jan 1794	100
Doolittle, Geo[rge] Pvt	5677	18 Nov 1790	100
Battle, James, Pvt	4829	21 Apr 1794	100
Sherrard, Francis, Pvt	14106	24 Feb 1795	100
Van Duser? [Dusen?] Thomas, Pvt	6602	26 Oct 1789	100
Adams, Levi, Pvt	5392	24 May 1790	100
Childs, Charles, Pvt	5665	28 Jan 1790	100
Coy, Edw[ard] Pvt	5668	23 Aug 1790	100
Woodruff, Baldwin, Pvt	6705	23 Aug 1790	100

101 8 Feb 1800 A/1/109

By Whom Registered: William H. Harrison
For Whom Registered: John C[leves] Symmes
Location: (4000 acres) Mil - 14 3 - 3
Based upon the following Army land warrants:

Issued to	*No.*	*Date*	*Acres*
Mills, George, Pvt	4689	6 May 1793	100
Taylor, Will, Maj	2501	8 Dec 1797	400
Taylor, Lewis, Pvt	5167	16 May 1793	100
Jamison, Rich[ard] Pvt	9656	22 Mar 1794	100
Richmond, Nath[aniel] Pvt	4906	6 May 1793	100
McGaffy, Neal, Lt	1340	5 Apr 1792	200
Green, John M., Lt	788	30 Jun 1790	200
Anspach, -- & Rogers, -- Ens	328	7 Aug 1789	150
Rogers, Joseph, Ens	1801	21 Jul 1789	150
Dodge, Levi, Lt	520	2 May 1789	200
Peirce, Isaac, Lt	2513	20 Feb 1792	200
Fosdick, Joseph, Lt	117	19 Apr 1796	200
Bartlet, Dan[ie]l, Pvt	3881	19 Feb 1796	100
Goddard, Edward, Pvt	5851	7 Mar 1796	100
Surrage, Isaac, Pvt	5114	10 Mar 1794	100
Davenport, James, Pvt	4052	17 Aug 1796	100
Richards, Sam[ue]l, Pvt	4947	17 Aug 1796	100
Wiswall, Dan[ie]l, Pvt	5331	17 Aug 1796	100
Dana, Benj[amin] Pvt	5155	23 May 1797	100
Wyman, Simeon, Pvt	3805	15 Jun 1797	100
Farnum, John, Pvt	3596	12 Mar 1793	100
Ward, Ichabod, Pvt	3268	11 Dec 1793	100
Wyman, Simeon, Pvt	5111	15 Jun 1797	100
Wyman, Simeon, Pvt	4102	15 Jun 1797	100
Fosdick, Joseph, Pvt	3948	3 Aug 1797	100
Wyman, Simeon, Pvt	3624	3 Aug 1797	100
Adlington, James, Pvt	5290	10 Jul 1797	100
Boynton, Able, Pvt	4127	13 Dec 1796	100
Boynton, Able, Pvt	2992	15 Feb 1797	100
Haven, John, Pvt	4329	13 Dec 1796	100
Boynton, Able, Pvt	3784	15 Feb 1797	100

102 8 Feb 1800 A/1/111

By Whom Registered: William H. Harrison
For Whom Registered: John C[leves] Symmes
Location: (4000 acres) Mil - 16 3 - 3
Based upon the following Army land warrants:

Issued to	*No.*	*Date*	*Acres*
Bevins, Henry, Pvt	5499	23 Aug 1790	100
Johnson, Will, Pvt	6035	23 Aug 1790	100
Germain, Henry, Pvt	9710	26 Apr 1791	100
Murrow, Thomas, Pvt	10122	26 Apr 1791	100
McDonald, John, Pvt	10019	26 Apr 1791	100
Rrish* Thomas, Pvt	10293	26 Apr 1791	100
Trowbridge, Isaac, Pvt	13474	7 Sep 1790	100
Cady, Darius, Pvt	3990	28 Jan 1790	100
Rutter, Penelope, Pvt	13849	23 Feb 1791	100
La Rochelle, Mich[ae]l, Pvt	13323	13 May 1790	100

102 [continued]

Issued to	No.	Date	Acres
Lipscomb, James, Pvt	13383	19 Apr 1791	100
Hodge, David, Pvt	5981	9 Oct 1789	100
Tallmadge, Benj[amin] Pvt	6141	7 Oct 1789	100
Lewis, Daniel, Pvt	12305	16 May 1791	100
Lewis, William, Pvt	13957	16 May 1791	100
Nichols, Sam[ue]l, Pvt	6239	9 Apr 1791	100
Morgan, John, Pvt	11542	24 Jan 1791	100
Phrener, Will, Pvt	10198	20 Jul 1789	100
Northrup, Ichabod, Pvt	3368	21 Dec 1789	100
Williss, John, Pvt	14055	17 Dec 1793	100
Marine, Charles, Pvt	10849	14 Dec 1793	100
Boynton, Abel, Pvt	4343	23 Feb 1796	100
Harding, Israel, Pvt	5920	13 Jul 1792	100
James, David, Pvt	8422	12 Jul 1792	100
Phares? [Pharis?] Moses, Pvt	10860	2 Sep 1789	100
Ballard, Asa, Capt	1808	22 Oct 1791	300
Fosdick, Joseph, Lt	1652	19 Apr 1796	200
Robinson, Peter, Capt	1795	14 Sep 1789	300
Hopkins, David, Maj	1087	29 Jul 1790	400
Peckham, Benj[amin] Capt	1628	31 Dec 1789	300

*So spelled.

103 8 Feb 1800 A/1/112

By Whom Registered: William H. Harrison
For Whom Registered: John C[leves] Symmes
Location: (4000 acres) Mil - 18 2 - 1
Based upon the following Army land warrants:

Issued to	*No.*	*Date*	*Acres*
Hubbart, John, Pvt	2959	22 Dec 1795	100
Cleveland, Timothy, Lt	2688	31 Dec 1795	200
Sherrard, Francis, Pvt	14119	1 May 1795	100
Jackson, Will, Pvt	7074	8 Sep 1790	100
Hamilton, James, Pvt	6785	14 Feb 1791	100
Hilty, Conrad, Pvt	7286	15 Sep 1790	100
Fowler, Theodosius, Pvt	6889	9 Jul 1790	100
Lawrence, John, Maj	1389	22 Oct 1790	400
Emery, Samuel, Pvt	4027	17 Jan 1793	100
Roberts, Rich[ar]d B., Capt	1869	20 Apr 1790	300
Stanbury, Jonas, Pvt	8669	20 Mar 1790	100
Denwood, Levin, Surgeon	583	4 Jun 1789	400
Moers, Benj[amin] Pvt	13607	21 Sep 1790	100
Trip, Joshua, Pvt	3534	21 Dec 1789	100
Bryan, Mich[ael] Pvt	13884	5 Mar 1792	100
Murthwaite, Rich[ard] Pvt	10681	19 Aug 1789	100
Jones, Abraham, Pvt	7315	16 Jan 1792	100
Shaw, Arch[ibald] Pvt	8312	29 Dec 1791	100
Wilson, Thom, Pvt	7963	6 Sep 1791	100
Thomas, Will, Pvt	13086	24 Jan 1792	100
Haskell, Benj[amin] Pvt	5092	12 Mar 1792	100
Chandler, Geo[rge] Lt	2432	18 Jul 1791	200
Morey, Pero, Pvt	3351	31 Dec 1789	100
Gardner, Abijah, Pvt	5843	14 Mar 1793	100
Emery, Sam[ue]l, Pvt	4933	14 Jan 1793	100
Quinton, David, Pvt	4969	1 May 1792	100
Brown, Thomas, Pvt	5493	10 Jun 1794	100
Bishop, Nath[aniel] Lt	2659	31 Dec 1795	200
Sherrard, Francis, Pvt	14115	25 Mar 1795	100

104 8 Feb 1800 A/1/113

By Whom Registered: James Parker
For Whom Registered: James Parker
Location: (4000 acres) Mil - 15 5 - 4
Based upon the following Army land warrants:

Issued to	*No.*	*Date*	*Acres*
Belding, Simeon, Lt	142	1 Sep 1789	200
Platt, Richard, Lt	1278	24 Jul 1789	200
Pray, John, Capt	1642	6 Aug 1789	300
Phillips, Jon[athan] Capt	1692	16 Jul 1789	300
Reab? Geo[rge] Lt	1785	20 Apr 1790	200
Reading, Sam[uel] Maj	1813	6 Nov 1789	400
Winton, James, Pvt	3548	9 Sep 1789	100
Lott, Peter, Pvt	4282	19 Aug 1789	100
Hall, Oliver, Pvt	4424	12 Aug 1789	100
Anspach, Peter, Pvt	4563	7 Aug 1789	100
Newman, Thomas, Pvt	4753	14 Aug 1789	100
Aldon, Mason F., Pvt	5356	8 Sep 1790	100
Sebor, James F., Pvt	5374	9 Sep 1790	100
Ryon, James [or John*] Pvt	5435	8 Sep 1790	100
Goldsmith, Will, Pvt	5858	23 Sep 1789	100
Sebor, James F., Pvt	6122	9 Sep 1790	100
Sebor, James F., Pvt	6159	9 Sep 1790	100
Sebor, James F., Pvt	6597	9 Sep 1790	100
Sebor, James F., Pvt	6609	9 Sep 1790	100
Conner, Matthew, Pvt	9139	4 Sep 1789	100
Gray, James, Pvt	9305	26 Aug 1789	100
Platt, Rich[ard] Pvt	9504	27 Jul 1789	100
Platt, Rich[ard] Pvt	9706	27 Jul 1789	100
Platt, Rich[ard] Pvt	9708	27 Jul 1789	100
Platt, Rich[ard] Pvt	10315	27 Jul 1789	100
Spalding, John, Pvt	10350	29 Jul 1790	100
Short, Ann, Pvt	10375	4 Sep 1789	100
Platt, Rich[ard] Pvt	10448	27 Jul 1789	100
Vredenburgh, Will J? Pvt	10771	7 Sep 1789	100
Sebor, James F., Pvt	12751	9 Sep 1790	100

*As per pencilled notation.

105 8 Feb 1800 A/1/114

By Whom Registered: James Parker
For Whom Registered: James Parker
Location: (4000 acres) Mil - 19 3 - 4
Based upon the following Army land warrants:

Issued to	*No.*	*Date*	*Acres*
Mason, Jere[miah?] Capt	699	18 Apr 1796	300
Mason, Jere[miah?] Lt	805	18 Apr 1796	200
Lloyd, Thomas, Lt	816	18 Apr 1796	200
Hamilton, John, Lt	1058	1 Sep 1789	200
Heth, Henry, Capt	1070	29 Aug 1791	300
Mason, Jere[miah?] Lt	1130	18 Apr 1796	200
Allis, William, Lt	1645	13 Oct 1791	200
Spaulding, Simon, Capt	1948	15 Dec 1791	300
Stotsberry, John, Capt	2015	4 Aug 1790	300
Stow, Lazarus, Lt	2036	11 Jun 1792	200
Smith, Jonathan, Lt	2079	7 Oct 1794	200
Mason, Jere[miah?] Col	2243	18 Apr 1796	500
Mason, Jere[miah?] Lt	2330	18 Apr 1796	200
Mason, Jere[miah?] Pvt	3180	28 Jul 1796	100
Bryson, James, Pvt	3763	13 Sep 1796	100
Beard, Moses, Pvt	3970	29 Feb 1792	100
Beard, Moses, Pvt	4671	10 Nov 1792	100
Quinton, David, Pvt	5158	1 May 1792	100
Quinton, David, Pvt	5251	1 May 1792	100
Beard, Moses, Pvt	5316	29 Feb 1792	100

106 8 Feb 1800 A/1/114

By Whom Registered: James Parker
For Whom Registered: James Parker
Location: (4000 acres) Mil - 17 3 - 3
Based upon the following Army land warrants:

Issued to	*No.*	*Date*	*Acres*
Bonet, Joseph, Pvt	5433	13 Feb 1790	100

106 [continued]

Coon, James, Pvt	5591	22 Oct 1792	100
Sebor, James F., Pvt	5594	9 Sep 1790	100
Sebor, James F., Pvt	5686	24 Sep 1790	100
Blanchard, John, Pvt	5780	12 Mar 1792	100
Root, Mich[ae]l, Pvt	6029	15 Sep 1790	100
Butler, Benj[amin] Pvt	6151	9 Nov 1791	100
Sebor, James F., Pvt	6443	9 Sep 1790	100
Bartholomew, G. & Fisher, --, Pvt	6739	28 Sep 1790	100
Bartholomew, G. & Fisher, --, Pvt	6298	28 Sep 1790	100
Bartholomew, G. & Fisher, --, Pvt	7344	29 May 1793	100
Bartholomew, G. & Fisher, --, Pvt	7426	28 Sep 1790	100
Bartholomew, G. & Fisher, --, Pvt	7533	28 Sep 1790	100
Ackley, Bezaliel, Pvt	8075	14 Aug 1789	100
Gray, James, Pvt	8446	26 Aug 1789	100
Moore, William, Pvt	8539	8 May 1794	100
Shuffey, William, Pvt	8748	22 Jul 1789	100
Short, Ann, Pvt	8996	4 Sep 1789	100
Platt, Richard, Pvt	9956	27 Jul 1789	100
Quigley, Sam[ue]l, Pvt	10275	2 Jul 1793	100
Platt, Richard, Pvt	10544	27 Jul 1789	100
Wright, John, Pvt	10939	15 Jan 1793	100
Wright, John, Pvt	11852	12 Sep 1792	100
Purdy, Henry, Pvt	11905	7 Aug 1794	100
Graves, Francis, Pvt	11949	6 Jul 1793	100
Graves, Francis, Pvt	11957	6 Jul 1793	100
Means, Robert, Pvt	12163	7 Jan 1793	100
Greaves, Francis, Pvt	12194	6 Jul 1793	100
Greaves, Francis, Pvt	12199	13 Dec 1791	100
Greaves, Francis, Pvt	12376	9 Dec 1793	100
Greaves, Francis, Pvt	12661	31 Jan 1794	100
Greaves, Francis, Pvt	12687	31 Jan 1794	100
Burke, John, Pvt	12758	17 Aug 1789	100
Ossey, Francis, Pvt	13562	3 Aug 1789	100
Vredenburgh, Will S? Pvt	13744	7 Sep 1789	100
Vredenburgh, Will S? Pvt	13745	7 Sep 1789	100
Sebor, James F., Pvt	13793	7 Sep 1790	100
Anspach, Peter, Pvt	13855	25 Sep 1789	100
Short, Ann, Pvt	13942	4 Sep 1789	100
Groaves, Francis, Pvt	13982	4 Sep 1789	100

107 10 Feb 1800 A/1/116

By Whom Registered: George Taylor, Junior
For Whom Registered: Jonathan Burrall
Location: (4000 acres) Mil - 7 7 - 1
Based upon the following Army land warrants:

Issued to	*No.*	*Date*	*Acres*
Barbee, Thomas, Capt	258	15 Jul 1789	300
Baldwin, Ab[salo]m? Capt	310	8 Aug 1797	300
Donnell, Nath[anie]l, Capt	527	4 Mar 1791	300
Irvine, William, & Irvine, James, Capt	1150	29 Jul 1789	300
Platt, Rich[ard] Lt	1436	27 Jul 1789	200
Baldwin, Ab[salo]m? Lt	1768	8 Aug 1797	200
Rose, John, Lt	1825	18 May 1789	200
Power, Alex[ande]r, Capt	2549	30 Mar 1798	300
Stone, Sam[ue]l, Pvt	3113	5 Apr 1796	100
Stone, Sam[ue]l, Pvt	3179	5 Apr 1796	100
Stone, Sam[ue]l, Pvt	3442	5 Apr 1796	100
Stone, Sam[ue]l, Pvt	3522	5 Apr 1796	100
Stone, Sam[ue]l, Pvt	3756	5 Apr 1796	100
Aiken, Daniel, Pvt	4389	20 Apr 1797	100
Perkins, Theodore, Pvt	4803	15 Mar 1798	100
Harris, Amos, Pvt	5979	20 Apr 1796	100
Wilcox, Samuel, Pvt	6669	1 Jun 1792	100
Russell, Thomas, Pvt	6994	24 Jun 1793	100
Russell, Thomas, Pvt	7012	14 May 1793	100
Russell, Thomas, Pvt	7280	1 Jan 1793	100
Russell, Thomas, Pvt	7341	31 Mar 1793	100
Russell, Thomas, Pvt	7444	14 May 1793	100
Russell, Thomas, Pvt	7677	31 Mar 1793	100
Bell, Abraham, Pvt	8408	19 Jan 1798	100
Patton, Thomas, Pvt	10225	5 Mar 1795	100
Brooks, Charles, Pvt	11891	5 Nov 1789	100
Knight, Eliz[abeth] Pvt	14135	26 Aug 1795	100

108 10 Feb 1800 A/1/117

By Whom Registered: Macan, John G.
For Whom Registered: Macan, John G.,
Location: (4000 acres) Mil - 14 4 - 3
Based upon the following Army land warrants:

Issued to	*No.*	*Date*	*Acres*
Christie, Thomas, Surgeon	466	19 Dec 1793	400
Crittendon, John, Lt	471	19 Apr 1792	200
Emery, Sam[ue]l, Lt	801	10 Mar 1794	200
Nicholson, John, LtCol	1415	7 Apr 1795	450
Roche, Edward, Lt	1835	30 May 1789	200
Van Wagenon, Gerritt, Ens	2125	4 Sep 1790	150
Ten Eyck, Ab[raha]m, Lt	2187	6 Aug 1790	200
Yancey, Layton, Lt	2467	5 Sep 1796	200
Peyton, John, Capt	2479	24 May 1796	300
Love, Will, Lt	2644	21 Jun 1794	200
Blanchard, John, Pvt	4557	8 Aug 1793	100
Ogden, Edward, Pvt	7978	2 Apr 1792	100
Cropsey, Jesper* Pvt	8002	12 Jul 1792	100
Shelfox? [Shilfox?] Jane, Pvt	8388	1 Jan 1793	100
Kirkpatrick, Fran[cis] Pvt	8931	17 Jun 1793	100
Power, Alex[ande]r, Pvt	9176	27 Apr 1793	100
Kirkpatrick, Fran[cis] Pvt	9555	17 Jun 1793	100
Kirkpatrick, Fran[cis] Pvt	9591	24 Jun 1793	100
Hazlehurst, John, Pvt	9637	26 Sep 1791	100
Humphreys, James, Pvt	9755	24 Jun 1793	100
Nicholson, John, Pvt	10189	7 Apr 1795	100
Carlon, William, Pvt	11044	2 Sep 1789	100
Fallin, John, Pvt	11198	11 May 1790	100
Britt, James, Pvt	12754	6 May 1793	100
MacRee, G. T? Pvt	12700	2 Aug 1796	100

*So spelled.

109 10 Feb 1800 A/1/117

By Whom Registered: John Matthews
For Whom Registered: David Townsend, John Warren, William Eustis, & Samuel Adams*
Location: (4000 acres) Mil - 16 1 - 4
Based upon the following Army land warrants:

Issued to	*No.*	*Date*	*Acres*
Prescott, Joseph, Surgeon's Mate	1697	24 Jul 1795	300
Fosdick, Joseph, Capt	1779	2 Nov 1795	300
Bayley, Thomas, Lt	126	16 Apr 1792	200
Emery, Sam[ue]l, Lt	109	2 Jun 1795	200
Hill, Jeremiah, Lt	352	6 Nov 1795	200
Hill, Jeremiah, Lt	922	4 Jan 1794	200
Hill, Jeremiah, Lt	925	6 Nov 1795	200
Hall, William, Lt	1184	11 Oct 1796	200
Hingman, Loring, Pvt	4539	17 Aug 1796	100

109 [continued]

Kessler, John, Pvt	3959	17 Aug 1796	100
Tuttle, Sam[ue]l, Lt	2167	26 Aug 1789	200
Townsend, David, Physician	2236	26 Oct 1789	450
Warren, John, Physician	2457	26 Oct 1789	450
Eustis, Will, Surgeon	690	26 Oct 1789	450
Adams, Sam[uel] Surgeon	69	8 Feb 1800	450

*Marginal notation:
"Congress granted to Nathaniel Sawyer, see his letter [word illegible] Chilicothe 5 Nov 1822."

110 10 Feb 1800 A/1/118

By Whom Registered: John Matthews
For Whom Registered: Edward D. Turner, Oliver Ormsby, & John Matthews
Location: (4000 acres) Mil - 12 6 - 4
Based upon the following Army land warrants:

Issued to	*No.*	*Date*	*Acres*
Kirkpatrick, Ab[raha]m, Capt	1210	5 Nov 1789	300
Bryson, Sam[ue]l, Lt	205	9 Jul 1789	200
Dill, Thomas, Lt	593	24 Dec 1794	200
Kersey, William, Lt	1196	21 Apr 1790	200
Montour, John, Capt	1572	24 Oct 1789	300
Sparks, William, Pvt	5136	26 Jan 1796	100
Crocker, J?, & Crocker, A., Pvt	5263	31 Dec 1795	100
Ruggles, Nath[anie]l, Pvt	5441	15 Apr 1796	100
Ruggles, Nath[anie]l, Pvt	5659	15 Apr 1796	100
Keeler, Hezekiah, Pvt	6061	27 Jan 1796	100
Keeler, Hezekiah, Pvt	6120	27 Jan 1796	100
Russell, Thomas, Pvt	7845	28 Feb 1794	100
Butler, William, Pvt	9041	8 Jan 1795	100
Vinegardner, John, Pvt	10545	27 Sep 1799	100
Bell, John, Pvt	10864	2 Sep 1789	100
Goddard, Sam[ue]l, Pvt	13137	19 Nov 1792	100
Hanna, John, Pvt	13176	22 Nov 1797	100
Jones, John, Pvt	13261	10 Feb 1797	100
Ruggles, Nath[anie]l, Pvt	13877	15 Apr 1796	100
Bowers, John, Pvt	8143	11 Jun 1789	100
Flemming, Jere[miah?] Pvt	8304	14 Aug 1789	100
Scarlett, William, Pvt	10403	17 Aug 1789	100
Wagner, John, Pvt	13895	21 Jan 1793	100
Kelly, Will, Pvt	9738	16 May 1792	100
Bodwin, Henry, Pvt	9029	5 Nov 1789	100
Shea, John, Pvt	12538	2 Apr 1796	100
Graydon, Alex[ander] Capt	2576	5 Jan 1791	300
Phelps, Asahel, Pvt	6349	23 Feb 1799	100
Thom, Will S., Pvt	3210	1 Feb 1799	100
Lee, Andrew, Lt	1330	21 Dec 1789	200

111 10 Feb 1800 A/1/119

By Whom Registered: John Matthews
For Whom Registered: Jesse Hunt & Abijah Hunt *et al**
Location: (4000 acres) Mil - 4 6 - 2
Based upon the following Army land warrants:

Issued to	*No.*	*Date*	*Acres*
Ross, William, Pvt	8676	21 Mar 1795	100
True, Ephraim, Pvt	3280	30 Oct 1789	100
True, Ephraim, Pvt	3112	30 Oct 1789	100
True, Ephraim, Pvt	3499	17 Jun 1793	100
True, Ephraim, Pvt	2911	30 Oct 1789	100
True, Ephraim, Pvt	3016	30 Oct 1789	100
True, Ephraim, Pvt	3530	30 Oct 1789	100
Converse, Thomas, Capt	371	14 Feb 1791	300
Rankins, James, Pvt	8686	14 Jul 1796	100
Wendell, John, Pvt	8000	18 Jun 1792	100
Morris, Lewis, Maj	1390	13 Feb 1796	400
Ball, John, Lt	143	3 Feb 1797	200
Morgan, Lewis, Pvt	13415	3 Mar 1790	100
Holmes, Thomas, Pvt	5953	8 May 1790	100
Percival, Thomas**	5622	26 Jun 1789	100
Percival, James, Pvt	5524	26 Jun 1789	100
Percival, James, Pvt	5500	26 Jun 1789	100
Percival, James, Pvt	13771	26 Jun 1789	100
Hill, Adam, Pvt	9551	15 May 1795	100
Morris, Jona[than] Ford, Maj	2539	16 Oct 1789	400
Pierson, Sam[ue]l, Pvt	8630	7 Jul 1789	100
Crosier, James, Pvt	11073	7 Jul 1789	100
Riblett, Peter, Pvt	10307	26 Aug 1789	100
McGuire, And[rew] Pvt	13510	16 May 1797	100
Clark, John, Capt	419	19 Aug 1789	300
Hunt, Thomas, Capt	912	26 Oct 1789	300
Heaton, John, Pvt	6508	2 Nov 1795	100

*Marginal notation: "The certificate issued to the Secretary of State, signed by the Secretary of the Treasury, & countersigned by the Register was in the following names. Part[?]"
**Entry has additional notation: "Jas. [James?]"

112 10 Feb 1800 A/1/120

By Whom Registered: William McCluney
For Whom Registered: William McCluney
Location: (4000 acres) Mil - 12 6 - 2
Based upon the following Army land warrants:

Issued	*No.*	*Date*	*Acres*
Beall, Will D., Maj	229	2 Mar 1795	400
Graves, Francis, Capt	602	26 Mar 1792	300
Wells, William, Lt	723	24 Dec 1799	200
Scott, John, Lt	2080	18 Apr 1786	200
Scott, Charles, Ens	2083	6 Mar 1797	150
Canfield, Hhaman* Pvt	6593	21 Mar 1791	100
Hunter, Elijah, Pvt	7667	7 Oct 1790	100
Crane, Jonas, Pvt	8537	16 Dec 1799	100
Connor, John, Pvt	9219	5 Nov 1789	100
Phillips, John, Pvt	9383	19 Aug 1789	100
Fisher, James, Pvt	9393	25 Jul 1793	100
Kellar* George, Pvt	9769	16 Aug 1795	100
Repton, William, Pvt	10091	3 Mar 1795	100
McMullen, Dan[iel] Pvt	10093	16 Apr 1790	100
Hubbard, Christian, Pvt	10446	31 Mar 1795	100
Wren, Joseph, Pvt	10631	11 Jul 1791	100
Hurdle, Law[ren]ce, Pvt	11361	1 Feb 1790	100
Johnston, Rob[ert] Physician	1178	15 Oct 1789	450
Thomas, Abishai, Pvt	12053	14 Apr 1795	100
Wiggin, Henry, Pvt	12094	10 Nov 1796	100
Grimes, Nath[anie]l, Pvt	12723	1 Mar 1792	100
Trick, John, Pvt	13257	20 Sep 1792	100
Feger, Conrad, Pvt	13260	19 Apr 1792	100
Karsh, Geo[rge] Pvt	13293	9 May 1795	100
Mullet, Mary, Pvt	13493	8 Dec 1792	100
Peran, Henry, Pvt	13587	7 May 1790	100
Sampson, Etienne, Pvt	13746	12 Oct 1790	100
Feger, Conrad, Pvt	13755	19 Apr 1792	100
Kelly, Timothy, Pvt	13880	12 Nov 1791	100

*So spelled.

113 10 Feb 1800 A/1/122

By Whom Registered: John Stites
For Whom Registered: John Stites
Location: (4000 acres) Mil - 17 2 - 3
Based upon the following Army land warrants:

Issued to	*No.*	*Date*	*Acres*

113 [continued]

Issued to	No.	Date	Acres
Finley, James E. B., Surgeon	714	1 Apr 1790	400
Bicker, Henry, Junior, Capt	194	12 May 1789	300
Mazyck, Stephen, Lt	1546	31 Dec 1796	200
Polhemus, John, Capt	1096	22 Jul 1789	300
Connolly, Rob[ert] Lt	845	5 Mar 1792	200
Pepin, Andrew, Lt	2611	3 Sep 1792	200
Bacot, Peter, Capt	291	31 Dec 1796	300
Delievre? Fran[cis?] Suzor, Surgeon's Mate	2543	8 Jul 1797	300
Theus, Simeon, Capt	2227	31 Dec 1796	300
Stevens, William L., Surgeon's Mate	2119	31 Dec 1796	300
Ramsay, Jos[eph?] H., Surgeon's Mate	1873	31 Dec 1796	300
Wisner, John, Pvt	7360	25 Jan 1791	100
Kellum, Reuben, Pvt	7361	11 Jan 1792	100
Pells, Henry, Pvt	7039	18 Jul 1791	100
Rogers, Ichabod, Pvt	7499	2 Mar 1792	100
Wempell, John, Pvt	7803	24 Mar 1792	100
Thorne, Stephen, Pvt	6956	24 Jan 1792	100
Jayne, Jotham, Pvt	7900	7 Jul 1791	100
Quinton, David, Pvt	7651	1 May 1792	100
Brown, John, Pvt	6850	5 Apr 1792	100

114 10 Feb 1800 A/1/122

By Whom Registered: John Rathbone
For Whom Registered: John Rathbone
Location: (4000 acres) Mil - 15 5 - 1
Based upon the following Army land warrants:

Issued to	*No.*	*Date*	*Acres*
Henderson, William, Capt	1011	15 Oct 1789	300
Munson, Eneas, Surgeon's Mate	1387	30 May 1791	300
Bostwicke, Obadiah, Lt	2524	23 Dec 1799	200
Taylor, And[rew] Pvt	3584	27 Jun 1798	100
Graves, Francis, Pvt	3829	26 Mar 1792	100
Cooke, Lemuel, Pvt	5670	18 Nov 1790	100
Long, Robert, Pvt	6102	15 Nov 1792	100
Spaulding, Asa, Pvt	6246	20 Aug 1796	100
Prout, William, Pvt	6311	9 Mar 1797	100
Cumpston, Edward, Pvt	6729	30 Jul 1790	100
Cumpston, Edward, Pvt	6732	30 Jul 1790	100
Cumpston, Edward, Pvt	6781	30 Jul 1790	100
Cumpston, Edward, Pvt	6841	30 Jul 1790	100
Cumpston, Edward, Pvt	6845	30 Jul 1790	100
Cumpston, Edward, Pvt	6854	30 Jul 1790	100
Wendell, John W., Pvt	6972	30 Jul 1790	100
van Rensselaer, Jer[emiah?] Pvt	7479	6 Aug 1790	100
Cumpston, Edward, Pvt	7594	30 Jul 1790	100
Cumpston, Edward, Pvt	7797	30 Jul 1790	100
Cumpston, Edward, Pvt	7948	30 Jul 1790	100
Cumpston, Edward, Pvt	8004	30 Jul 1790	100
Linwood, John, Pvt	8491	24 Jul 1790	100
Cunias, John, Pvt	9576	2 Oct 1789	100
Nicholson, John, Pvt	10366	7 Apr 1795	100
Wainwright, James, Pvt	10907	2 Sep 1789	100
Purdy, Henry, Pvt	11100	7 Aug 1794	100
Purdy, Henry, Pvt	11145	6 Oct 1794	100
Torresdale? [Forresdale?] Stafford, Pvt	11211	11 May 1790	100
Purdy, Henry, Pvt	11816	6 Oct 1794	100
McIntosh, Alex[ande]r, Pvt	12342	20 Jun 1789	100
Cloud, Joseph, Pvt	12919	12 Oct 1790	100
Delisle, John, Pvt	12983	12 Oct 1790	100
Dupre, John B., Pvt	12984	12 Oct 1790	100
Fisbaugh, Simon, Pvt	13281	8 Jul 1791	100
Welch, William, Pvt	13920	19 Apr 1792	100

115 10 Feb 1800 A/1/124

By Whom Registered: John Rathbone
For Whom Registered: John Rathbone
Location: (4000 acres) Mil - 8 1 - 3
Based upon the following Army land warrants:

Issued to	*No.*	*Date*	*Acres*
Bliss, Joseph, Lt	123	10 Mar 1790	200
Hutton, William, Pvt	3231	31 Dec 1789	100
Hall, London, Pvt	3234	31 Dec 1789	100
Bronson, Isaac, Pvt	4011	19 Apr 1792	100
Reed, Hezekiah, Pvt	4911	14 May 1790	100
Stanford, John, Pvt	5057	2 Apr 1796	100
Bradley, Ichiel, Pvt	5487	7 Oct 1789	100
Beach, Nath[anie]l, Pvt	5511	20 Sep 1790	100
Downs, John, Pvt	5703	20 Sep 1790	100
Fields, Edmond, Pvt	5756	14 May 1790	100
Leinberger, John, Pvt	6033	10 Oct 1791	100
Taylor, John, Pvt	6559	25 Jan 1796	100
Clarke, John, Pvt	6899	5 Sep 1791	100
Gregg, Robert, Pvt	7170	7 Jul 1791	100
Lambert, John, Pvt	7419	6 Sep 1791	100
McCollum, Reuben, Pvt	7515	16 Jul 1790	100
Griggs, William, Pvt	8329	22 Jun 1791	100
Scudder, Ahijah* Pvt	8749	1 Oct 1789	100
Hubbert, Christ[ian?] Pvt	8897	25 Jan 1792	100
Power, Alex[ande]r, Pvt	9122	3 Feb 1794	100
Cunias, John, Pvt	9142	2 Oct 1789	100
Loudon, Stephen, Pvt	9400	26 Jan 1792	100
Freese, Martin, Pvt	9403	13 Jan 1796	100
Klein, John, Pvt	9478	24 Oct 1791	100
Harbeson, Geo[rge] Pvt	9592	26 Sep 1791	100
Loudon, Stephen, Pvt	9753	5 Jan 1792	100
McFatridge, Dan[ie]l Pvt	9914	3 Jun 1791	100
McLean, Jacob, Pvt	9929	5 Jan 1796	100
Phillips, Martin, Pvt	10238	31 Aug 1791	100
Hodge, John, Pvt	10270	23 Jan 1793	100
Sheppard, Sarah, Pvt	10491	19 Jan 1792	100
Drury, William, Pvt	10755	2 Sep 1789	100
Jones, Thomas, Pvt	11400	21 Jan 1792	100
Watson, Thomas, Pvt	11810	21 Jan 1792	100
Cole, Isaac, Pvt	12048	14 Aug 1792	100
Musegenning, Anth[on]y, Pvt	12997	6 Jul 1791	100
Martin, Francis, Pvt	13429	4 Feb 1790	100
Meredith, Sam[uel] Pvt	13539	2 Sep 1789	100
Klein, John, Pvt	13714	21 Oct 1791	100

*So spelled.

116 10 Feb 1800 A/1/125

By Whom Registered: Matthias Denman
For Whom Registered: Matthias Denman
Location: (4000 acres) Mil - 16 4 - 3
Based upon the following Army land warrants:

Issued to	*No.*	*Date*	*Acres*
Furman, Gabriel, Pvt	6861	8 Aug 1791	100
Wilkin, Robert, Capt	2383	3 Mar 1795	300
Cole, Hester, Lt	2610	10 Apr 1792	200
McHaffey, James, Pvt	9952	19 Oct 1789	100
Thomas, Abishai, Pvt	11884	1 Jun 1790	100
Matthews, William, Pvt	11487	25 Jan 1790	100
Flannagen* Dennis, Pvt	11232	9 Nov 1789	100
Platt, Rich[ar]d, Pvt	10648	7 Aug 1789	100
Platt, Rich[ar]d, Pvt	12757	10 Aug 1789	100
Platt, Rich[ar]d, Pvt	10515	10 Aug 1789	100

116 [continued]

	No.	Date	Acres
Moers, Benj[amin] Pvt	13861	22 Jan 1790	100
Purdy, Henry, Pvt	11277	22 Dec 1794	100
Purdy, Henry, Pvt	11775	22 Dec 1794	100
Purdy, Henry, Pvt	11285	22 Dec 1794	100
Purdy, Henry, Pvt	11564	22 Dec 1794	100
Ammends, Peter, Pvt	11871	27 Dec 1794	100
Billip, Henry, Pvt	11971	22 Dec 1794	100
Hart, Henry, Pvt	13483	4 Aug 1790	100
Horton, Christ[opher?] Pvt	5960	2 Sep 1789	100
Walton, Geo[rge] Pvt	10463	24 Sep 1791	100
Farnham, Ebenezer, Pvt	4415	18 Oct 1791	100
Farnham, Ebenezer, Pvt	5577	18 Oct 1791	100
Berry, Mich[ael] Pvt	12834	19 Aug 1791	100
Fox, Peter, Pvt	8301	10 Mar 1790	100
Kesseback, Oswald, Pvt	13308	21 Aug 1791	100
Munday, Thomas, Pvt	9944	6 Sep 1791	100
McGahey, John, Pvt	13485	6 Sep 1791	100
McCleland, John, Pvt	11593	26 Sep 1791	100
McCleland, John, Pvt	9352	26 Sep 1791	100
Peters, Elizabeth, Pvt	10212	23 Mar 1791	100
Bostil, Sarah, Pvt	12825	5 Jan 1791	100
Hollingshead, John, Pvt	8230	28 Dec 1789	100
Hollingshead, John, Pvt	8702	28 Dec 1789	100
Sherrard, Francis, Pvt	14096	28 Jan 1795	100
Sherrard, Francis, Pvt	14097	28 Jan 1795	100
Sherrard, Francis, Pvt	14095	28 Jan 1795	100
Sherrard, Francis, Pvt	14094	28 Jan 1795	100

*So spelled.

117 10 Feb 1800 A/1/126

By Whom Registered: [Benjamin] Morgan* & [Chandler] Price*

For Whom Registered: [Benjamin] Morgan* & [Chandler] Price*

Location: (4000 acres) Mil - 6 5 - 1

Based upon the following Army land warrants:

Issued to	*No.*	*Date*	*Acres*
Zeckler, Mich[ael] Pvt	13938	27 Mar 1792	100
Davidson, James, Surgeon	559	24 Oct 1789	400
Hubley, Bernard, Capt	1027	14 May 1793	300
Boyd, John, Lt	211	28 Feb 1795	200
Boyd, John, Lt	218	28 Feb 1795	200
Boyd, John, Lt	219	28 Feb 1795	200
Phelps, Noah A., Pvt	12731	6 Dec 1799	100
Dana, Benjamin, Pvt	4057	5 Jan 1797	100
Ashford, Street, Pvt	11964	28 Apr 1798	100
Fitzgerald, Tho[mas] Lt	1536	6 Mar 1798	200
Holmes, Gabriel, Pvt	12581	18 May 1797	100
Holmes, Gabriel, Pvt	12699	18 May 1797	100
Holmes, Gabriel, Pvt	12522	13 Dec 1796	100
Holmes, Gabriel, Pvt	12283	18 May 1797	100
Holmes, Gabriel, Lt	1100	7 Feb 1798	200
Holmes, Gabriel, Pvt	12628	13 Dec 1796	100
Nance, Buckner, Pvt	10595	7 Jul 1797	100
Holmes, Gabriel, Pvt	12591	18 May 1797	100
Joslin, Thomas, Pvt	6136	10 Aug 1795	100
Holmes, Gabriel, Pvt	11967	18 May 1797	100
Wheaton, Dan[iel] Pvt	11083	16 Jan 1797	100
Wheaton, Dan[iel] Pvt	9581	16 Jan 1797	100
Moylan, Stephen, Col	1413	7 Sep 1789	500
Morgan, David, Pvt	13265	8 Dec 1799	100
King, John, Pvt	9766	4 Feb 1791	100
McLean, Charles, Pvt	10074	14 Feb 1791	100

*Forename supplied from marginal notation.

118 10 Feb 1800 A/1/127

By Whom Registered: Thomas McEwen & Co.

For Whom Registered: James Hamilton

Location: (4000 acres) Mil - 18 2 - 4

Based upon the following Army land warrants:

Issued to	*No.*	*Date*	*Acres*
Allen, Sam[uel] Pvt	3901	15 Aug 1792	100
Stephenson, John, Pvt	4561	14 Sep 1792	100
Blodget, Ezra, Pvt	5294	11 May 1792	100
Stephenson, John, Pvt	5426	14 Sep 1792	100
Bailey, Theodoris, Pvt	7567	9 May 1796	100
Murphy, Stephen, Pvt	8982	8 Mar 1792	100
Bailey, James, Pvt	8991	7 Sep 1796	100
Iserloan, Casper, Pvt	9000	25 Nov 1793	100
Baker, James, Pvt	9054	21 Dec 1792	100
Manning, Rosanna, Pvt	9286	7 Feb 1792	100
Peters, John, Pvt	9890	24 Oct 1792	100
Nagle, Chris[tia]n, Pvt	10278	2 Mar 1792	100
Taylor, Sam[ue]l, Pvt	10501	12 Oct 1792	100
Molineux, Fred[eric]k, Pvt	10504	27 Oct 1792	100
Lebo, Paul, Pvt	10526	18 Oct 1792	100
Taylor, Geo[rge] Pvt	10530	17 Sep 1792	100
Loudon, Stephen, Pvt	10575	3 Feb 1792	100
Welsh, John, Pvt	10580	12 May 1792	100
Hart, Silas, Pvt	10598	30 Jun 1794	100
Wagoner, Jacob, Pvt	10604	23 May 1797	100
de Baufre, Ja[me]s, Pvt	10817	1 May 1797	100
de Baufre, Ja[me]s, Pvt	10834	12 May 1797	100
de Baufre, Ja[me]s, Pvt	11364	12 May 1797	100
de Baufre, Ja[me]s, Pvt	11418	4 May 1797	100
de Baufre, Ja[me]s, Pvt	11607	12 May 1797	100
de Baufre, Ja[me]s, Pvt	11653	4 May 1797	100
Reynolds, Ja[me]s, Pvt	12019	26 Sep 1792	100
Reynolds, Ja[me]s, Pvt	12153	8 Oct 1792	100
Newton, Tho[ma]s, Pvt	12197	6 Oct 1792	100
Newton, Tho[ma]s, Pvt	12382	6 Oct 1792	100
Newton, Tho[ma]s, Pvt	12454	6 Oct 1792	100
Ross, Rob, Pvt	12906	13 Jul 1792	100
Moore, Ben, Pvt	12911	20 Feb 1792	100
Dixon, Ja[me]s, Pvt	13004	14 Feb 1791	100
Ross, Rob, Pvt	13048	13 Jul 1792	100
Hemphill, Jos[eph?] Pvt	13239	20 Oct 1789	100
Sherridan, Ab[raha]m, Pvt	13307	20 Jul 1792	100
Sherridan, Ab[raha]m, Pvt	13317	20 Jul 1792	100
Moore, Ben, Pvt	13346	20 Feb 1792	100
Moore, Ben, Pvt	13637	20 Feb 1792	100

119 10 Feb 1800 A/1/129

By Whom Registered: Jonathan Dayton

For Whom Registered: Jonathan Dayton

Location: (4000 acres) Mil - 13 1 - 1

Based upon the following Army land warrants:

Issued	*No.*	*Date*	*Acres*
Graves, Francis, Capt	1072	7 May 1793	300
Reynolds, James, Pvt	12122	13 Apr 1791	100
Reynolds, James, Pvt	12148	13 Apr 1791	100
Reynolds, James, Pvt	12258	13 Apr 1791	100
Reynolds, James, Pvt	12264	13 Apr 1791	100
Reynolds, James, Pvt	12608	13 Apr 1791	100
Reynolds, James, Pvt	12133	13 Apr 1791	100
Reynolds, James, Pvt	12575	13 Apr 1791	100
Reynolds, James, Pvt	11930	13 Apr 1791	100
Reynolds, James, Pvt	12147	13 Apr 1791	100
Ballard, Asa, Pvt	6921	22 Oct 1791	100
Morris, Slayton, Pvt	10844	11 Oct 1791	100
Thornton, Daniel, Pvt	6567	3 Feb 1794	100
Fitzbaugh, Simon, Pvt	2982	20 Jul 1791	100
Fitzbaugh, Simon, Pvt	8920	8 Jul 1791	100
Fitzbaugh, Simon, Pvt	9532	8 Jul 1791	100

119 [continued]

Fitzbaugh, Simon, Pvt	9987	8 Jul 1791	100
Means, Rob[ert] Pvt	11869	7 Jan 1791	100
Means, Rob[ert] Pvt	11939	14 Jul 1792	100
Ponsonby, George, Pvt	11075	8 Jan 1796	100
Ponsonby, Geo[rge] Pvt	11558	8 Jan 1796	100
Ponsonby, Geo[rge] Pvt	11821	8 Jan 1796	100
Ponsonby, Geo[rge] Pvt	11415	8 Jan 1796	100
Ponsonby, Geo[rge] Pvt	11349	8 Jan 1796	100
Hetfield, Moses, Pvt	7321	19 Apr 1791	100
Hetfield, Moses, Pvt	7117	19 Apr 1791	100
Hetfield, Moses, Pvt	7972	19 Apr 1791	100
Tillotson, Thomas, Pvt	7257	22 Jul 1799	100
Tillotson, Thomas, Pvt	7805	22 Jul 1799	100
Tillotson, Thomas, Pvt	7967	22 Jul 1799	100
Tillotson, Thomas, Pvt	7359	22 Jul 1799	100
Tillotson, Thomas, Pvt	7694	22 Jul 1799	100
Elwood, Benjamin, Pvt	7592	21 Sep 1790	100
Elwood, Benjamin, Pvt	8017	21 Sep 1790	100
Elwood, Benjamin, Pvt	6736	21 Sep 1790	100
Gross, Johan Dan[ie]l, Rev[erend] Pvt	7416	14 Oct 1790	100
Newton, Thomas C., Pvt	8926	20 May 1793	100
Newton, Thomas C., Pvt	9194	20 May 1793	100

120 10 Feb 1800 A/1/130

By Whom Registered: Jonathan Dayton
For Whom Registered: Jonathan Dayton
Location: (4000 acres) Mil - 18 1 - 1
Based upon the following Army land warrants:

Issued to	*No.*	*Date*	*Acres*
Quinn, Samuel, Lt	1769	29 Jan 1795	200
Rykman, Wilhemus, Lt	1809	12 Oct 1790	200
Pepoon, Silas, Pvt	4463	22 Dec 1791	100
Blodget, Ezra, Pvt	4033	13 Jan 1792	100
Warren, William, Pvt	5428	13 Sep 1791	100
Munson, Eneas, Pvt	5770	21 Mar 1794	100
Muzzy, Amos, Pvt	5808	8 May 1792	100
Munson, Eneas, Pvt	6003	21 Mar 1794	100
Matthews, William, Pvt	6154	21 Aug 1789	100
Row? [Rowland?*] Sherman, Pvt	6381	26 May 1790	100
Draper, Nathaniel, Pvt	6463	26 Mar 1792	100
Thomas, Samuel, Pvt	6573	15 Apr 1790	100
Wheeler, Thomas, Pvt	6644	15 Mar 1790	100
Lawrance, John, Pvt	6724	24 Jul 1790	100
Lawrance, John, Pvt	6738	24 Jul 1790	100
Lawrance, John, Pvt	6765	24 Jul 1790	100
Lawrance, John, Pvt	6801	24 Jul 1790	100
Benedict, Ambrose, Pvt	6814	21 Jun 1791	100
Hobart, John Sloss, Pvt	6816	15 Sep 1790	100
Hobart, John Sloss, Pvt	6867	15 Sep 1790	100
Tillotson, Thomas, Pvt	6842	22 Jul 1790	100
Hart, Silas, Pvt	9303	10 Jun 1794	100
Hart, Silas, Pvt	10210	10 Jun 1794	100
Hart, Silas, Pvt	10396	10 Jun 1794	100
Hart, Silas, Pvt	10402	10 Jun 1794	100
Hart, Silas, Pvt	10610	10 Jun 1794	100
Hart, Silas, Pvt	10032	10 Jun 1794	100
Greaves, Francis, Pvt	12300	13 Dec 1791	100
Clingman, John, Pvt	12323	12 Nov 1791	100
Means, Robert, Pvt	12393	29 May 1792	100
Means, Robert, Pvt	12397	14 Jul 1792	100
Means, Robert, Pvt	12406	14 Jul 1792	100
Means, Robert, Pvt	12443	14 Jul 1792	100
Means, Robert, Pvt	12475	18 Feb 1792	100
Means, Robert, Pvt	12568	18 Feb 1793	100
Means, Robert, Pvt	12606	31 Jan 1799	100
Means, Robert, Pvt	12665	18 Feb 1793	100
Vreedenburgh, W. J., Pvt	12903	24 Sep 1790	100

*Surname has pencilled suffix "-land."

121 10 Feb 1800 A/1/132

By Whom Registered: Thomas Salter
For Whom Registered: Thomas Salter
Location: (4000 acres)* Mil - 12 3 - 1
Based upon the following Army land warrants:

Issued to	*No.*	*Date*	*Acres*
Wyllys, John P., Pvt	5639	18 Oct 1789	100
Walden, John, Pvt	5503	6 May 1793	100
Pollard, Isaac, Pvt	6312	7 Oct 1789	100
Mason, Jeremiah, Pvt	5040	31 Jul 1797	100
Allen, William, Pvt	14086	4 Nov 1794	100
Jones, William, Pvt	11397	3 Feb 1792	100
de Calla, Theodore, Pvt	13011	11 Aug 1795	100
Doty, Isaac, Pvt	8234	11 Aug 1795	100
Barnes, Richard, Pvt	8919	13 Oct 1791	100
McCleland, John, Pvt	13111	24 Sep 1791	100
Satterlee, Elisha, Pvt	6427	5 Jan 1790	100
Purdy, Henry, Pvt	11932	1 Aug 1794	100
Blanchard, John, Pvt	4926	19 Nov 1792	100
McConnell, Matthew, Pvt	10588	29 Jun 1789	100
Coger, Enoch, Pvt	12876	19 Nov 1792	100
Bryan, John, Pvt	9055	12 Jul 1792	100
Smith, Samuel, Pvt	7938	9 Mar 1791	100
Barker, Moses W., Pvt	4768	10 Aug 1790	100
Gibson, Jacob, Capt	858	20 May 1795	300
Talmage, Benjamin, Pvt	6338	5 May 1791	100
Purdy, Henry, Pvt	11458	10 Jul 1794	100
Hopkins, Elisha, Capt	956	9 Aug 1798	300
Cooper, Isaac, Pvt	7001	23 Oct 1790	100
Neider, Ira, & Alen? [Aler?] Alex? Pvt	7571	5 Jan 1791	100
Archer, John, Pvt	7875	29 Sep 1790	100
Rogers, Platt, Pvt	7069	24 Sep 1791	100
Thorn, William, Pvt	7348	7 Feb 1792	100
Gamison, Abraham, Pvt	7202	5 Jan 1791	100
Haburn, William, Pvt	7265	9 Oct 1790	100
Foote, Ebenezer, Pvt	7433	15 Dec 1799	100
Goodwin, Abraham, Fife Major	7144	5 Aug 1790	100
Demott, William, Fifer	7087	14 Aug 1790	100
Cline, William, Pvt	6964	25 Aug 1790	100
Smith, Jeremiah, Pvt	7835	10 Aug 1790	100
Van Ingen, Dirck, Pvt	7731	13 Jul 1790	100
Smith, Samuel, Pvt	6097	9 Mar 1791	100

*Marginal notation:

"Location made [per above citation]	4305
Warr. recd. [by] this State	4000
Since recd.:	
No. 939 Warr. to Abijah Hammond dated 27 Feb 1800[!]	200
No 5546 ditto to Zephaniah Swift dated 27 Mar 1794	100
	4300
10 dollars paid to Register for	5
[Total acres]	4305"

[See also serial entry 276]

122 10 Feb 1800 A/1/133

By Whom Registered: Thomas Salter
For Whom Registered: Thomas Salter
Location: (4000 acres) Mil - 16 6 - 2
Based upon the following Army land warrants:

Issued to	*No.*	*Date*	*Acres*
Grimes, Nathaniel, Pvt	13888	1 Mar 1792	100
Stout, George, Pvt	11659	26 Apr 1792	100
Hyde, William, Pvt	3484	19 Nov 1792	100
Salisbury, Ab[raha]m, Junior, Pvt	7509	10 Aug 1790	100
Coe, Benjamin, Pvt	7728	12 Aug 1790	100
Coe, John D., Pvt	7020	12 Aug 1790	100
Cumpston, Edward, Pvt	7302	13 Jul 1790	100

122 [continued]

Coe, John D., Pvt	7881	12 Aug 1790	100
Cumpston, Edward, Pvt	7313	30 Jul 1790	100
Cumpston, Edward, Pvt	7568	30 Jul 1790	100
Watson, Elkaniah, Pvt	7812	24 Jun 1790	100
Dixon, David, Pvt	5700	28 Feb 1794	100
Thompson, Joseph, Pvt	5156	12 Nov 1789	100
Addoms* John, Pvt	13835	1 Nov 1791	100
Fowler, Theodosius, Pvt	6760	9 Jul 1790	100
Woodruff, Samuel, Hospital Mate	2460	26 Jun 1789	300
Spalding, Asa, Pvt	7675	24 Jun 1794	100
Harding, Oliver, Pvt	7301	31 Jan 1792	100
Fairchild, Pete, Pvt	6664	22 Dec 1791	100
Fairchild, Pete, Pvt	5602	22 Dec 1791	100
Edwards, Richard, Pvt	7013	30 Mar 1791	100
Robinson, John, Pvt	3443	26 Aug 1789	100
Bishop, Benoni, Pvt	2980	10 Oct 1791	100
Bonnell, Samuel, Pvt	8112	23 Apr 1790	100
Arrison, Jeptha, Pvt	8106	27 May 1790	100
Osmoen, Benijah, Pvt	8612	3 Feb 1790	100
Henry, Barzillah, Pvt	5924	21 Dec 1789	100
Arrison, Jeptha, Pvt	8690	27 May 1790	100
Thom, William S., Lt	1775	9 Mar 1797	200
Grove, William B., Capt	1616	31 Dec 1796	300
McKenzie, Murdoch M., Pvt	12602	14 Feb 1797	100
Thom, Chris[topher?] or [Christian?] S., Pvt	3492	10 Mar 1797	100
Thom, Chris[topher?] or [Christian?] S., Pvt	3451	10 Mar 1797	100
McKenzie, Murdoch, Pvt	12055	14 Feb 1797	100
McKenzie, Murdoch, Pvt	12601	14 Feb 1797	100

*So spelled.

123 10 Feb 1800 A/1/134

By Whom Registered: Thomas Salter
For Whom Registered: Thomas Salter
Location: (4000 acres) Mil - 17 5 - 3
Based upon the following Army land warrants:

Issued to	*No.*	*Date*	*Acres*
Rossell* Thomas, Pvt	7241	12 Aug 1790	100
Russell, Eleazor, Pvt	6369	26 Jul 1792	100
Mason, Jeremiah, Pvt	5302	31 Jul 1797	100
Mossman, Matthias, Capt	944	5 Mar 1793	300
Mosely, William, Pvt	6570	15 Aug 1796	100
Fish? [Fisk?] Nicholas, Maj	727	9 Jul 1790	400
Fisk, Moses, Pvt	3423	9 Jun 1797	100
Ovutt? William, Pvt	6255	27 Jun 1789	100
Reed, James R., Maj	1874	3 Jul 1789	400
Davis, Pricilla, Pvt	10607	20 May 1791	100
Coe, Benjamin, Pvt	8059	12 Aug 1790	100
Coe, Samuel, Pvt	7109	12 Aug 1790	100
Gee, Thomas, Pvt	8067	15 Dec 1790	100
Sill, Moses, Pvt	9565	12 Mar 1792	100
Striker, John, CaptLt	2022	19 May 1789	200
Harris, Benjamin, Pvt	8732	16 Oct 1789	100
Sytez, George, Capt	1975	23 Aug 1790	300
Walton, George, Pvt	10756	27 Sep 1791	100
Palmore, Jonathan, Pvt	7584	9 Aug 1798	100
Cook, Joel, Pvt	5550	17 May 1790	100
Lawrence, Thomas, Pvt	7650	24 Sep 1790	100
Pollock, Carlile, Pvt	13621	6 Jul 1791	100
Thompson, William, Pvt	7817	30 Jul 1790	100
Vacher, John [Francis?] Surgeon	2248	8 Jul 1790	400
Newkerk, Charles, Pvt	7113	23 Aug 1790	100
Parker, Edmund, Pvt	7646	23 Oct 1790	100

*So spelled.

124 10 Feb 1800 A/1/135

By Whom Registered: Thomas Salter
For Whom Registered: Thomas Salter
Location: (4000 acres) Mil - 19 6 - 2
Based upon the following Army land warrants:

Issued to	*No.*	*Date*	*Acres*
Root, Nicholas, Pvt	6655	15 Sep 1790	100
Root, Nicholas, Pvt	5721	15 Sep 1790	100
Root, Nicholas, Pvt	5795	15 Sep 1790	100
Fowler, Theodosius, Pvt	7971	9 Jul 1790	100
van Rensselaer, Jerem[iah] Pvt	7802	15 Jul 1790	100
Scribner, Nathaniel, Pvt	7332	9 Jul 1790	100
Shober, Frederick, Pvt	7015	6 Jul 1790	100
Smith, Moses, Pvt	7768	31 Jan 1791	100
St. Clair, William, Pvt	11680	22 Mar 1793	100
Goodrich, William, Pvt	13115	6 Sep 1791	100
McFarlane, John, Pvt	8523	20 Jun 1789	100
Prentice, Jonas, Pvt	6561	11 Apr 1792	100
Wetmore, Victory, Pvt	6308	13 Apr 1791	100
Seward, Jedediah, Pvt	6525	16 Jun 1789	100
Chandler, George, Capt	1525	17 Nov 1791	300
Sherrard, Francis, Pvt	14103	24 Feb 1795	100
Sherrard, Francis, Pvt	14102	24 Feb 1795	100
Prentice, Jonas, Pvt	6018	11 Apr 1792	100
Prentice, Jonas, Pvt	5711	7 Mar 1792	100
Ruttledge, Joshua, Lt	1843	7 Mar 1791	200
Tuttle, Jonathan, Pvt	5618	7 Mar 1792	100
Brickell, Sarah, Pvt	12827	8 Dec 1791	100
Miller, Jacob, Pvt	10384	2 Mar 1792	100
McCleland, John, Pvt	8902	26 Sep 1791	100
Means, Robert, Pvt	12653	14 Jul 1792	100
Means, Robert, Capt	1507	14 Jul 1792	300
Rhea, Jonathan, Pvt	12901	7 Jul 1795	100
Rhea, Jonathan, Lt	1803	15 Jun 1795	200
Olcott, Nathaniel, Capt	101	24 Nov 1795	300
Rockwell, Grove, Pvt	6372	15 Nov 1791	100
Middleton, Christo[pher?] Pvt	6148	15 Nov 1791	100
Stedman, Cato, Pvt	6434	15 Nov 1791	100

125 10 Feb 1800 A/1/136

By Whom Registered: Thomas Salter
For Whom Registered: Thomas Salter
Location: (4000 acres) Mil - 9 2 - 2
Based upon the following Army land warrants:

Issued to	*No.*	*Date*	*Acres*
Thorn, Stephen, Pvt	3525	6 Dec 1791	100
Coe, John D., Pvt	7434	12 Aug 1790	100
Thorn, Stephen, Pvt	13721	24 Jan 1792	100
Thorn, Stephen, Pvt	13701	6 Dec 1791	100
Thorn, Stephen, Pvt	13262	6 Dec 1791	100
Thorn, Stephen, Pvt	13172	6 Dec 1791	100
Thorn, Stephen, Pvt	12927	6 Dec 1791	100
Thorn, Stephen, Pvt	6492	6 Dec 1791	100
Thorn, Stephen, Pvt	5760	6 Dec 1791	100
Thorn, Stephen, Pvt	5423	6 Dec 1791	100
Thorn, Stephen, Pvt	5396	6 Dec 1791	100
Thorn, Stephen, Pvt	4466	6 Dec 1791	100
Thorn, Stephen, Pvt	5362	6 Dec 1792	100
Thorn, Stephen, Pvt	6379	24 Jan 1792	100
Thorn, Stephen, Pvt	6190	12 Apr 1792	100
Thorn, Stephen, Pvt	6457	12 Apr 1792	100
Thorn, Stephen, Pvt	6319	1 Jun 1793	100
Thorn, Stephen, Pvt	6015	12 Apr 1792	100
Thorn, Stephen, Pvt	5828	6 Dec 1791	100
Thorn, Stephen, Pvt	5901	26 Jul 1794	100
Thorn, Stephen, Pvt	6070	12 Apr 1792	100
Thorn, Stephen, Pvt	6333	12 Apr 1792	100

125 [continued]

Thorn, Stephen, Pvt	6704	1 Jun 1793	100
Thorn, Stephen, Pvt	5655	12 Apr 1792	100
Thorn, Stephen, Pvt	5474	24 Jan 1792	100
Thorn, Stephen, Pvt	5572	6 Dec 1791	100
Thorn, Stephen, Pvt	5540	1 Jun 1793	100
Thorn, Stephen, Pvt	5535	6 Dec 1791	100
Thorn, Stephen, Lt	962	24 Jan 1792	200
de Baufre, James, Pvt	11111	26 Jul 1797	100
de Baufre, James, Pvt	11682	4 May 1797	100
de Baufre, James, Pvt	10708	22 Jul 1797	100
de Baufre, James, Pvt	11396	22 Jul 1797	100
de Baufre, James, Pvt	11760	22 Jul 1797	100
de Baufre, James, Pvt	11674	8 Jul 1797	100
de Baufre, James, Pvt	11440	4 May 1797	100
Glenn, C., & Bleecker, B., Pvt	7508	24 Aug 1790	100
Glenn, C., & Bleecker, B., Pvt	7703	24 Aug 1790	100
Glenn, C., & Bleecker, B., Pvt	6860	24 Aug 1790	100

126 — 10 Feb 1800 — A/1/138

By Whom Registered: Thomas Salter
For Whom Registered: Thomas Salter
Location: (4000 acres) Mil - 20 6 - 1
Based upon the following Army land warrants:

Issued to	*No.*	*Date*	*Acres*
Robertson, Alex[ande]r, Pvt	7574	28 Sep 1790	100
Robertson, Alex[ande]r, Pvt	7129	28 Sep 1790	100
Robertson, Alex[ande]r, Pvt	7395	28 Sep 1790	100
Lusk? [Lush?] Stephen, Pvt	6827	10 Aug 1790	100
Lusk? [Lush?] Stephen, Pvt	7814	10 Aug 1790	100
Lusk? [Lush?] Stephen, Pvt	7748	10 Aug 1790	100
Tuttle, Jonathan, Pvt	2999	7 Mar 1792	100
Tuttle, Jonathan, Pvt	5479	7 Mar 1792	100
Tuttle, Jonathan, Pvt	5791	2 Nov 1791	100
Tuttle, Jonathan, Pvt	5853	7 Mar 1792	100
Childs, Evander, Pvt	7370	27 Aug 1792	100
Childs, Evander, Pvt	4606	17 Mar 1795	100
McCleland, John, Lt	2554	12 Oct 1791	200
McCleland, John, Lt	10551	26 Sep 1791	100
Ward, Joshua, Pvt	11299	11 Jan 1796	100
Ward, Joshua, Pvt	11068	11 Jan 1796	100
Ward, Joshua, Pvt	11291	11 Jan 1796	100
Ward, Joshua, Pvt	11153	11 Jan 1796	100
Bartholomew, Geo[rge] & Fisher, J., Pvt	7833	28 Sep 1790	100
Bartholomew, Geo[rge] & Fisher, J., Pvt	7316	28 Sep 1790	100
Bartholomew, Geo[rge] & Fisher, J., Pvt	6740	28 Sep 1790	100
Sherrard, Francis, Pvt	14101	24 Feb 1795	100
Sherrard, Francis, Pvt	14104	24 Feb 1795	100
Sherrard, Francis, Pvt	14105	24 Feb 1790	100
Maxwell, Anthony, Pvt	7538	10 Oct 1791	100
Maxwell, Anthony, Pvt	8045	10 Oct 1791	100
Fisher, Bartholomew, Pvt	7152	10 Jun 1793	100
Means, Robert, Pvt	13981	2 Nov 1792	100
Landee? [Sander?] John, Pvt	3289	13 Jan 1794	100
Prentice, Jonas, Pvt	6477	7 Mar 1792	100
Johnston, Samuel, Pvt	11619	25 Jan 1796	100
Waldron, Resolve, Pvt	7610	24 Sep 1791	100
Glenn, Cornelius, Pvt	7279	12 Aug 1790	100
Chadwick, John, Capt	2585	6 Jul 1792	300
Munson, Eneas, Pvt	6314	16 Dec 1793	100
Fowler, Theodosius, Pvt	7770	9 Jul 1799	100
Brown, Joseph, Pvt	3240	25 May 1795	100

127 — 10 Feb 1800 — A/1/139

By Whom Registered: William Robinson
For Whom Registered: William Robinson
Location: (4000 acres) Mil - 8 1 - 2
Based upon the following Army land warrants:

Issued to	*No.*	*Date*	*Acres*
English, Andrew, Capt	648	11 Aug 1795	300
Hardman, Henry, Maj	1045	11 Jun 1790	400
Ledlie, Andrew, Surgeon	1231	26 Aug 1789	400
Shrawder, Philip, Lt	2029	12 Sep 1789	200
Nicholson, Samuel, Surgeon's Mate	2204	14 Feb 1791	300
Weitzel, Jacob, Lt	2385	24 May 1790	200
Christian, Michael, Pvt	6992	27 Mar 1792	100
Hunt, Ralph, Pvt	8595	28 Oct 1789	100
Wood, Ellis, Pvt	8832	7 Jul 1789	100
Adams, Jonathan, Pvt	8904	28 Jan 1795	100
McKinley, Peter, Pvt	9967	2 Mar 1799	100
Gover, Robert, Lt	1055	4 Oct 1797	200
Tripner, George, Pvt	10507	17 Jul 1793	100
Knowles, Rob[ert] Pvt	10805	26 May 1790	100
Morris, Zadock, Pvt	10846	2 Sep 1789	100
Simpson, William, Pvt	10884	2 Sep 1789	100
Lang, Francis, Pvt	11433	11 Mar 1791	100
Mason, James, Pvt	11472	11 May 1790	100
Purcell, William, Pvt	11598	15 Aug 1795	100
Beatty? [Beatly?] James, Pvt	11960	4 Mar 1796	100
Means, Robert, Pvt	12040	7 Jan 1793	100
Marshall, Richard, Pvt	12367	4 Mar 1796	100
Majorr? [Major?] James, Pvt	12399	4 Mar 1796	100
Stratton, Seth, Pvt	12551	4 Mar 1796	100
Ferree? Joseph, Pvt	13071	23 Feb 1792	100
Roberts, Griffith, Pvt	13671	21 Jun 1797	100
Grimes, Nathaniel, Pvt	13882	1 Mar 1792	100

128 — 10 Feb 1800 — A/1/140

By Whom Registered: Theodorus Bailey
For Whom Registered: Theodorus Bailey
Location: (4000 acres)* Mil - 13 1 - 2
Based upon the following Army land warrants:

Issued to	*No.*	*Date*	*Acres*
Noise, Peter, Pvt	4724	3 Oct 1791	100
Dimmick, Benjamin, Lt	541	4 Sep 1789	200
Butler, Ezekiel, Pvt	5508	11 Dec 1799	100
Bailey, Theodorus, Pvt	6811	22 Mar 1796	100
Payne, Elisha, Pvt	7463	5 Jan 1792	100
Chapman, Rufus, Pvt	3035	16 May 1794	100
Knapp, Andreas, Pvt	3422	9 Mar 1791	100
Knapp, Andreas, Pvt	7088	3 Oct 1791	100
Tomey? [Fomey?] Dennis, Pvt	5794	24 Dec 1796	100
Barrett, Oliver, Lt	80	4 Jun 1793	200
McNamara, Darby? Pvt	11498	5 Sep 1789	100
Means, Robert, Pvt	12208	6 Jul 1793	100
Powers, Alexander? Pvt	13353	2 Dec 1791	100
Means, Robert, Pvt	12577	14 Jul 1792	100
Power, Alexander, Pvt	13147	26 Apr 1791	100
Means, Robert, Pvt	11880	7 Jan 1793	100
Means, Robert, Pvt	12157	11 May 1792	100
Stiver, Michael, Pvt	9009	3 Mar 1794	100

128 [continued]

Connolly, Michael, Pvt	7984	6 Mar 1792	100
Brockway, Gideon, Pvt	4130	16 Mar 1795	100
Murray, Reuben, Pvt	13650	12 Jul 1793	100
Kingsley, Martin, Pvt	4821	11 Apr 1792	100
Norton, Elon, Pvt	6238	24 Dec 1789	100
Day, Ezekiel, Pvt	8427	20 Dec 1792	100
Murray, Reuben, Pvt	5939	12 Jul 1793	100
Johnson, Abraham, Pvt	6032	29 Sep 1790	100
Hebard, Samuel, Pvt	7291	20 Jun 1795	100
Wells, George, Pvt	6356	15 Aug 1792	100
Mullener, Moses, Pvt	7453	17 Nov 1792	100
King, Daniel, Pvt	4932	12 Dec 1792	100
Means, Robert, Pvt	12514	14 Jul 1792	100
Means, Robert, Pvt	13998	7 Jan 1793	100
Means, Robert, Pvt	12207	6 Jul 1793	100
Means, Robert, Pvt	12484	14 Jul 1792	100
Means, Robert, Pvt	12043	12 Apr 1792	100
Means, Robert, Pvt	11889	6 Jul 1793	100
Thoma? [Thomas?] John G., Pvt	13844	4 Mar 1796	100
Culver, Reuben, Pvt	6587	25 Jan 1796	100

*Marginal notation:

"Location made [as cited above][acres] 4920
Amount Warr. [recd. by] this State 4000
Since recd., see same Stat? [not listed!] 1050
5050
4920

Reg[ister's] Cert. dated 14 Feb 1801[!] given to Theo. Bailey for 130"

[See also serial entry 263]

129 10 Feb 1800 A/1/141

By Whom Registered: Theodorus Bailey
For Whom Registered: Theodorus Bailey
Location: (4000 acres) Mil - 13 6 - 3
Based upon the following Army land warrants:

Issued to	*No.*	*Date*	*Acres*
Carter, Benjamin, Capt	480	30 Jul 1792	300
Chase, Reuben, Pvt	3895	2 Apr 1792	100
Daskum, William, Pvt	5712	27 Jun 1789	100
Emerson, Nathaniel, Pvt	5735	22 Oct 1792	100
Bradley, James, Pvt	5404	22 Oct 1792	100
Chapman, Thomas, Pvt	5584	22 Oct 1792	100
McLean, Henry, Pvt	6176	22 Oct 1792	100
Donnells, David, Pvt	5690	22 Oct 1792	100
McLean, Jacob, Pvt	6166	22 Oct 1792	100
Patterson, James, Pvt	7617	9 Oct 1790	100
Stymer? [Stymez?] Rachel, Pvt	7850	12 Oct 1790	100
Weed, Smith, Pvt	6698	27 Jun 1789	100
Ludlam, Henry, Pvt	7225	26 Apr 1791	100
Graham, Lewis, Pvt	8056	11 Oct 1790	100
Brebner, James, Pvt	7252	3 May 1791	100
Brebner, James, Pvt	7544	3 May 1791	100
Tremper, Henry, Pvt	7926	11 Oct 1790	100
Hyser, Hendrick, Pvt	7133	21 Apr 1791	100
King, Daniel, Pvt	4588	12 Jan 1792	100
Caldwell, James, Pvt	7709	19 May 1791	100
Trowbridge, Isaac, Pvt	7432	7 Sep 1790	100
Millard, Elisha, Pvt	7683	5 Jan 1791	100
Archer, John, Pvt	7662	19 May 1791	100
Clark, Ebenezer, Pvt	7351	18 May 1791	100
Halsey, Silas, Pvt	7969	12 Oct 1790	100
Zuntz, Alexander, Pvt	7319	26 Apr 1791	100
Graham, Lewis, Pvt	7317	11 Oct 1790	100
Greene, Benjamin, Pvt	7711	21 Apr 1791	100
Row, Matthias, Pvt	7713	27 May 1791	100
Alexander, Alex[ande]r, Pvt	7187	14 Feb 1791	100
Quinton, David, Pvt	6873	21 Apr 1791	100
Quinton, David, Pvt	7707	21 Apr 1791	100
Quinton, David, Pvt	7520	19 Apr 1791	100
Gale, Sam[ue]l, Pvt	7193	3 May 1791	100
Radelift? [Radclife?] William, Pvt	7566	5 Jan 1791	100
Chandler, John, Pvt	7716	26 Jan 1791	100
Clark, Ebenezer, Pvt	7003	25 Sep 1790	100
Weed, Smith, Pvt	5510	27 Jun 1789	100

130 10 Feb 1800 A/1/143

By Whom Registered: William Steele
For Whom Registered: William Steele
Location: (4000 acres) Mil - 18 4 - 2
Based upon the following Army land warrants:

Issued to	*No.*	*Date*	*Acres*
Sherrard, Francis, Pvt	14100	24 Feb 1795	100
Stockdell, John, Pvt	12101	26 Oct 1795	100
Brooks, Isaac, Pvt	7393	3 Oct 1791	100
Greaves, Francis, Pvt	12370	18 Dec 1791	100
Means, Robert, Pvt	11873	7 Jul 1792	100
Downs, James, Pvt	5704	20 Sep 1790	100
Wofe, Charles, Pvt	6598	9 Apr 1791	100
Benjamins, Aaron, Lt	149	16 May 1796	200
Buxton, James, Capt	98	3 Mar 1797	300
Thoms, Samuel, Capt	2165	12 Apr 1790	300
Fisher, Peter, Pvt	8326	26 Nov 1796	100
Newman, Silas, Pvt	7642	16 Mar 1792	100
Little, Jacob, Pvt	8473	20 Jul 1795	100
Malpus, Ezekiel, Pvt	12424	20 Nov 1794	100
Bremigion, Thomas, Pvt	3787	26 Aug 1796	100
Curl, John, Pvt	12058	7 Oct 1795	100
Means, Robert, Pvt	12668	14 Jul 1792	100
Means, Robert, Pvt	14000	2 Nov 1792	100
Means, Robert, Pvt	12609	7 Jul 1792	100
Means, Robert, Pvt	12347	29 May 1792	100
Christie, James, Pvt	8544	10 Aug 1795	100
Stockdell, John, Pvt	11879	26 Oct 1795	100
Monty, Claude, Pvt	13424	4 Feb 1790	100
Pickering, Joshua, Pvt	3141	26 Aug 1796	100
Means, Robert, Pvt	11864	29 May 1792	100
Holbrook, Abijah, Pvt	6042	25 Jul 1799	100
Pickering, Joshua, Pvt	3357	26 Aug 1796	100
Biddle, Richard, Pvt	10955	22 Mar 1797	100
O'Neal, Henry, Pvt	8606	22 Mar 1797	100
Reed, William, Pvt	10272	3 Feb 1796	100
McCracken, Philip, Pvt	13414	24 Jul 1790	100
Pepoon, Silas, Pvt	5588	14 Dec 1793	100
Bell, Abraham, Pvt	8797	17 Jul 1797	100
Wayman, Jonathan, Pvt	8349	2 Jun 1797	100
Allen, Samuel, Pvt	5393	3 Mar 1797	100

131 10 Feb 1800 A/1/144

By Whom Registered: William Steele
For Whom Registered: William Steele
Location: (4000 acres) Mil - 17 3 - 2
Based upon the following Army land patents:

Issued to	*No.*	*Date*	*Acres*
Ricker, Henry, Pvt	13656	12 Nov 1796	100
Waldon, Resolve, Pvt	6498	19 Jan 1792	100
Brooks, Isaac, Pvt	6766	26 Nov 1791	100
Smith, Eleazer, Pvt	6426	17 Jun 1793	100
Barr, Jacob	13639	15 Sep 1791	100
Ludlam, John, Pvt	7390	14 Apr 1792	100
Hannon, William, Pvt	9623	4 Feb 1791	100
Carty? [M'Carty?] Richard M., Pvt	9984	24 Mar 1792	100
Hunt, Joseph, Pvt	7289	6 Jun 1791	100
Emerson, Joseph, Capt	135	26 Oct 1796	300

131 [continued]

Issued to	No.	Date	Acres
Daskum, John, Pvt	5685	20 Sep 1790	100
Winford, Henry, Pvt	8025	2 Apr 1792	100
Verlie? [Nerlie?] Bernard, Pvt	13853	4 Feb 1790	100
Means, Robert, Pvt	12003	29 May 1792	100
Mundon, John, Pvt	13504	14 Feb 1791	100
Oram, Peter B., Lt	2442	14 Dec 1795	200
Chandler, George, Pvt	4625	17 Nov 1791	100
Russ, Jonathan, Pvt	13648	9 Apr 1791	100
Smith, George, Lt	2572	23 Oct 1790	200
Harvey, Elisha, Lt	992	28 Mar 1791	200
Hardenberg, Abraham, Lt	985	29 Jul 1790	200
Pry, Elizabeth, Capt	1766	24 May 1791	300
Sweet, Caleb, Capt	828	23 Aug 1790	300
Chapel, Isaac, Pvt	3880	22 Aug 1789	100
Holbrook, Abijah, Pvt	5824	25 Jul 1799	100
Holbrook, Abijah, Pvt	4221	25 Jul 1799	100
Brown, McAuley V? Pvt	7250	28 Sep 1790	100
Brown, McAuley V? Pvt	6820	28 Sep 1790	100
Clarke, John, Pvt	7009	15 Mar 1791	100
Harrioh? Israel, Pvt	7292	15 Mar 1791	100

132 10 Feb 1800 A/1/145

By Whom Registered: William Steele
For Whom Registered: William Steele
Location: (4000 acres) Mil - 12 4 - 1
Based upon the following Army land warrants:

Issued to	*No.*	*Date*	*Acres*
Clarke, John, Pvt	8049	15 Mar 1791	100
Mayley, John, Pvt	7176	28 Sep 1790	100
Reynolds, Timothy, Pvt	7685	20 Oct 1790	100
Gilbert, Seth, Pvt	7169	20 Oct 1790	100
Shephard, Jonathan, Pvt	7621	5 Jan 1791	100
Price, Paul, Pvt	6289	30 Oct 1789	100
Heron, Herc ules, Pvt	7306	20 Jul 1790	100
Chadwick, John, Pvt	5413	16 Dec 1793	100
Warren, William, Pvt	7949	13 Sep 1792	100
Gurnee, John J? Pvt	6937	13 Jul 1790	100
Arthur, Joseph, Pvt	7153	2 Aug 1790	100
Glenn, C., & Bleecker, B., Pvt	7910	24 Aug 1790	100
Yeates, Christ[ophe]r, Executor of estate of, Pvt	8033	28 Aug 1790	100
Munson, Eneas, Junior, Pvt	4589	19 Aug 1795	100
Richards, Bradley, Pvt	4884	15 Apr 1796	100
Updike, Caesar, Pvt	3542	31 Dec 1789	100
Lush, Stephen, Pvt	7549	10 Aug 1790	100
Munson, Eneas, Junior, Pvt	5765	7 Sep 1795	100
Ten Eyck, Abraham, Pvt	7465	6 Aug 1790	100
Hathorn, John, Pvt	7598	15 Jul 1790	100
Worthington, Benjamin, Pvt	11817	10 Aug 1790	100
Gehan, Peter, Pvt	9435	10 Jun 1789	100
McConnell, William, Pvt	9989	23 Jun 1789	100
McMahon, Peter, Pvt	10072	8 Jun 1789	100
Means, Robert, Pvt	12320	29 May 1792	100
Harvey? Selby, Col	1093	6 Aug 1789	500
Fowler, Theodosius, Lt	1686	9 Jul 1790	200
Knight, William, Pvt	7346	22 Jun 1790	100
Bronson, Isaac, Pvt	5649	19 Apr 1792	100
Munson, Eneas, Junior, Lt	2353	6 Jul 1795	200
Emery, Samuel, Lt	74	16 Jan 1793	200
Wallis, Joseph, Pvt	6650	20 Jan 1797	100
Gillaspy, Joseph, Pvt	7194	25 Jan 1791	100

133 10 Feb 1800 A/1/147

By Whom Registered: William Steele
For Whom Registered: William Steele
Location: (4000 acres) Mil - 13 2 - 4
Based upon the following Army land warrants:

Issued to	*No.*	*Date*	*Acres*
Reed, James, BrigGen	2540	1 Apr 1790	850
Beard, Moses, Pvt	4815	29 Feb 1792	100
Stockdale, John, Pvt	12472	31 Jan 1794	100
Beard, Moses, Pvt	5076	29 Feb 1792	100
Tuttle, Jonathan, Pvt	13918	15 Nov 1792	100
Peck, John, Ens	933	19 Apr 1792	150
Nicholson, John, Pvt	10312	7 Apr 1795	100
Davis, George, Pvt	8270	9 May 1792	100
Hart, Silas, Pvt	9907	10 Jun 1794	100
Quinton, David, Pvt	4421	1 May 1792	100
Greaves, Francis, Pvt	12089	13 Dec 1791	100
Bollington, John, Pvt	14045	4 Feb 1793	100
Hart, Silas, Pvt	10215	10 Jun 1794	100
Greaves, Francis, Pvt	12553	13 Dec 1791	100
Beard, Moses, Pvt	4983	29 Feb 1792	100
Tuttle, Jonathan, Pvt	13899	15 Nov 1792	100
Smith, --, & Ridgway, --, Capt	2431	27 Aug 1795	300
Mead, Job, Pvt	14036	16 May 1792	100
Purdy, Joseph, Pvt	7410	12 Jul 1792	100
Shuntz, Christian, Pvt	7743	1 Jun 1792	100
Camp, Elisha, Pvt	6817	17 Nov 1791	100
Moore, John, Pvt	7534	7 Jul 1791	100
Love, David, Pvt	7417	1 Nov 1791	100
Colliar, Richard, Pvt	7084	8 Nov 1791	100
Pemberton, Thomas, Pvt	7589	8 Dec 1792	100
Ketchum, Joseph, Pvt	7368	25 Jan 1791	100
Humphrey, James, Pvt	7245	5 Jan 1791	100
Watson, Matthew, Pvt	7511	16 Sep 1791	100
Farnham, Ebenezer, Pvt	6775	18 Nov 1791	100
Boyd, Rob[er]t, Pvt	7983	28 Jul 1791	100

134 10 Feb 1800 A/1/148

By Whom Registered: William Steele
For Whom Registered: William Steel
Location: (4000 acres) Mil - 7 6 - 3
Based upon the following Army land warrants:

Issued to	*No.*	*Date*	*Acres*
Sanford, Peleg, Lt	145	24 Sep 1790	200
Sanford, Peleg, Lt	377	24 Sep 1790	200
Bell, William M., Capt	73	2 Jul 1790	300
Gosselin, Clement, Capt	885	22 Jan 1790	300
Fleming, George, Capt	736	10 May 1790	300
d'Utrich, Lewis, Baron, Capt	636	10 Oct 1789	300
Hughes, Thomas, Capt	903	31 Dec 1789	300
Boyer, Peter, Capt	216	8 Aug 1789	300
Bennet, James, Lt	150	9 Apr 1791	200
Burlingham, Chandler, Lt	86	31 Dec 1789	200
Allison, Robert, Lt	43	6 Apr 1791	200
Beach, Samuel, Lt	79	18 Jun 1791	200
Stevens, John, Capt	1944	18 Jun 1791	300
Richardson, John, Capt	1832	14 Feb 1791	300
Martin, Absalom, Capt	1408	10 Sep 1790	300
Bates, Benoni, Pvt	2971	31 Dec 1789	100

135 10 Feb 1800 A/1/148

By Whom Registered: William Steele
For Whom Registered: William Steele
Location: (4000 acres) Mil - 13 4 - 4
Based upon the following Army land warrants:

Issued to	*No.*	*Date*	*Acres*

135 [continued]

Issued to	No.	Date	Acres
McElhatton, William, Lt	1455	14 Feb 1791	200
Caldwell, James, Lt	1989	15 Sep 1790	200
Anspach, --, & Rogers, --, Lt	1627	7 Aug 1789	200
Hite, George, Lt	1089	6 Mar 1790	200
Sherman, Henry, Lt	1971	31 Dec 1789	200
Anspach, --, & Rogers, --, Lt	1222	7 Aug 1789	200
Morris, Catherine, Lt	1464	16 May 1791	200
McPherson, Murdoch, Lt	1563	22 Jan 1790	200
Johnston, William, Lt	1128	7 Jul 1791	200
Brown, Andrew, Pvt	2963	31 Dec 1789	100
Turner, Peter, Surgeon	2136	31 Dec 1789	400
Reynolds, James, Capt	2366	13 Dec 1790	300
Dow, Alexander, Capt	2553	14 Feb 1791	300
Martin, Moses, Lt	2575	20 Dec 1790	200
White, Henry, Lt	2306	12 Oct 1790	200
White, Francis, Lt	2386	28 Jan 1791	200
Atkinson, Stephen, Pvt	2906	21 Oct 1790	100
Maxwell, Anthony, Pvt	3957	14 Jun 1791	100
Howland, Thomas, Pvt	3226	31 Dec 1789	100
Rhodes, Prime? [Prince?] Pvt	3457	31 Dec 1789	100
Stephens, Timothy, Pvt	3430	24 Dec 1789	100

136 — 10 Feb 1800 — A/1/149

By Whom Registered: William Steele
For Whom Registered: William Steele
Location: (4000 acres) Mil - 18 5 - 4
Based upon the following Army land warrants:

Issued to	*No.*	*Date*	*Acres*
McIntire, Thomas, Capt	2581	28 Feb 1791	300
Knap, David, Pvt	4662	10 Jun 1790	100
Petrie, Edward, Pvt	4864	21 Jun 1791	100
Lee, Mose[s] Pvt	4554	21 Jun 1791	100
McClennan, William, Pvt	4736	8 Oct 1790	100
Segor, Daniel, Pvt	5755	26 Jan 1790	100
Cox, Robert, Pvt	5554	21 Jun 1791	100
Knap, David, Pvt	5729	26 Dec 1789	100
Crouch, Daniel, Pvt	5574	21 Jan 1791	100
Knap, David, Pvt	5447	10 Jun 1790	100
Knap, David, Pvt	5605	10 Jun 1790	100
Knap, David, Pvt	5469	26 Dec 1789	100
Host, Peter, Pvt	5985	31 Dec 1789	100
Bell, William, Pvt	6930	15 Sep 1790	100
Johnson, Israel, Pvt	6007	21 Jun 1791	100
Thorn, Stephen, Pvt	6076	21 Jun 1791	100
Smith, Platt, Pvt	6948	19 May 1790	100
Ellis, Samuel, Pvt	6996	15 Sep 1790	100
Osborn, Jeremiah, Pvt	7372	14 May 1790	100
Knap, David, Pvt	6460	26 Dec 1789	100
Liberty, Cuff, Pvt	6110	15 Sep 1789	100
Rockwell, Nehemiah, Pvt	7201	25 Sep 1790	100
Edwards, Richard, Pvt	7308	30 Mar 1791	100
Edwards, Richard, Pvt	7540	30 Mar 1791	100
Maxwell, Anthony, Pvt	7487	14 Jun 1791	100
Smith, Platt, Pvt	7051	19 May 1790	100
Smith, Platt, Pvt	7460	15 Sep 1790	100
Crane, Ezekiel, Pvt	7441	9 Sep 1790	100
Bell, William, Pvt	7220	9 Sep 1790	100
Bell, William, Pvt	7783	9 Sep 1790	100
Smith, Platt, Pvt	7536	19 May 1790	100
Bell, William, Pvt	7523	15 Sep 1790	100
Curray, Samuel, Pvt	7248	20 Jul 1790	100
Crane, Ezekiel, Pvt	7790	9 Sep 1790	100
Bell, William, Pvt	7062	15 Sep 1790	100
Bell, William, Pvt	7120	15 Sep 1790	100
Bell, William, Pvt	7836	15 Sep 1790	100
Aspel, James, Pvt	7976	15 Dec 1790	100

137 — 10 Feb 1800 — A/1/150

By Whom Registered: Charles Copland
For Whom Registered: Charles Copland
Location: (4000 acres) Mil - 7 2 - 2
Based upon the following Army land warrants:

Issued to	*No.*	*Date*	*Acres*
Copland, Charles, Surgeon	2224	17 Dec 1799	400
Richards, John, Junior, Maj	1850	16 Feb 1798	400
Camp, Rob[er]t, Capt	1167	3 Jul 1799	300
Kendall, Curtis, Capt	1209	26 Jun 1789	300
Marsh, Samuel, Maj	1734	26 Jun 1797	400
Siffin, John, Pvt	8714	31 May 1790	100
Bell, Abraham, Pvt	12868	6 Jun 1799	100
Nichols, Charles, Pvt	12433	15 Feb 1799	100
Wright, John, Pvt	11172	12 Sep 1792	100
Stowell, Israel, Junior, Pvt	5724	13 Jan 1799	100
Stowell, Israel, Junior, Pvt	6511	13 Jan 1799	100
Greaves, Francis, Pvt	12069	14 Jul 1792	100
Stowell, Israel, Junior, Pvt	5498	13 Jan 1799	100
Clayton, Philip, Lt	460	16 Apr 1792	200
Scott, Joseph, Junior, Capt	2062	20 Feb 1799	300
Seayres, John, LtCol	2520	24 Aug 1789	450
Ternant, John, LtCol	2241	26 Nov 1796	450

138 — 10 Feb 1800 — A/1/151

By Whom Registered: Samuel Cobb
For Whom Registered: Samuel Cobb
Location: (4000 acres) Mil - 13 7 - 3
Based upon the following Army land warrants:

Issued to	*No.*	*Date*	*Acres*
Anderson, Joseph J? Capt	36	14 May 1790	300
Costigan, Lewis, Lt	403	12 Feb 1790	200
Jackson, Michael, Col	1121	9 May 1796	500
Condict, Silas, Pvt	8430	23 Dec 1796	100
Miller, John, Pvt	8571	12 Jan 1790	100
Nestor, John, Pvt	8603	6 Mar 1797	100
Smith, States, Pvt	8733	23 Feb 1790	100
Califf? Stephen, Pvt	12955	2 Apr 1790	100
Masters, John, Pvt	8585	30 Dec 1796	100
Simmons, Reuben, Pvt	8726	8 Dec 1789	100
Anspach, --, & Rogers, --, Pvt	3270	7 Aug 1789	100
Sebor, James F., Pvt	3551	9 Sep 1790	100
Maxwell, Anthony, Pvt	3710	10 Oct 1791	100
Sebor, James F., Pvt	4377	9 Sep 1790	100
Taylor, George, Pvt	5766	19 Sep 1789	100
Sanford, Peleg, Pvt	5412	24 Sep 1790	100
Hinds, John, Pvt	8410	-- 1790	100
Logan, William, Pvt	8480	21 Sep 1789	100
McCollum, John, Pvt	8551	30 Sep 1791	100
May, Andrew, Pvt	8553	17 Aug 1789	100
Denman, Matthias, Pvt	8558	11 Aug 1789	100
Denman, Matthias, Pvt	8569	11 Aug 1789	100
Mahoney, James, Pvt	9957	4 Mar 1791	100
Platt, Richard, Pvt	10602	27 Jul 1789	100
Leonard, Zepheniah, Pvt	13328	6 Aug 1789	100
Smith, John, Pvt	13728	25 Mar 1790	100
Tennett, John Peter, Pvt	13817	25 Mar 1790	100
Dallas, A., Dallas, C., Dallas, A., heirs of Dallas, Arch[ibal]d, Capt	2686	24 May 1797	300
Pope, John, Pvt	8382	21 May 1797	100

138 [continued]

Issued to	No.	Date	Acres
Lepetrill? [Lepetrile?] John, Pvt	13372	9 Feb 1793	100
Hays, Mich[ae]l, Pvt	13635	24 May 1797	100

139 10 Feb 1800 A/1/152

By Whom Registered: Jonathan Dayton
For Whom Registered: Jonathan Dayton
Location: (4000 acres) Mil - 18 3 - 2
Based upon the following Army land warrants:

Issued to	*No.*	*Date*	*Acres*
Cunningham, Henry, Lt	384	26 Jul 1790	200
Tallmadge, Benjamin, Pvt	6581	7 Oct 1789	100
Tallmadge, Benjamin, Pvt	5823	7 Oct 1789	100
Tallmadge, Benjamin, Pvt	6045	7 Oct 1789	100
Tallmadge, Benjamin, Pvt	3449	14 May 1790	100
Tallmadge, Benjamin, Pvt	6467	7 Oct 1789	100
Starr, Josiah, Pvt	6051	21 Mar 1791	100
Starr, Josiah, Pvt	5509	21 Mar 1791	100
Starr, Josiah, Pvt	6397	21 Mar 1791	100
Starr, Josiah, Pvt	5687	21 Mar 1791	100
Starr, Josiah, Pvt	5857	21 Mar 1791	100
Starr, Josiah, Pvt	6283	21 Mar 1791	100
Starr, Josiah, Pvt	torn	21 Mar 1791	100
Tillotson, Thomas, Pvt	7831	22 Jul 1790	100
Tillotson, Thomas, Pvt	7985	22 Jul 1790	100
Tillotson, Thomas, Pvt	7994	22 Jul 1790	100
Tillotson, Thomas, Pvt	7403	22 Jul 1790	100
Tillotson, Thomas, Pvt	7397	22 Jul 1790	100
Fosdick, Joseph, Pvt	4068	1 Aug 1796	100
Fosdick, Joseph, Pvt	4434	1 Aug 1796	100
Fosdick, Joseph, Pvt	5077	19 Apr 1796	100
Fosdick, Joseph, Pvt	5117	24 Aug 1796	100
Ponsonby, George, Pvt	11456	8 Jan 1796	100
Ponsonby, George, Pvt	11623	8 Jan 1796	100
Ponsonby, George, Pvt	11246	8 Jan 1796	100
Ponsonby, George, Pvt	11297	8 Jan 1796	100
Ponsonby, George, Pvt	11224	8 Jan 1796	100
Ponsonby, George, Pvt	11632	8 Jan 1796	100
Ponsonby, George, Pvt	11133	8 Jan 1796	100
Ponsonby, George, Pvt	11434	8 Jan 1796	100
Ponsonby, George, Pvt	11156	8 Jan 1796	100
Ponsonby, George, Pvt	11847	8 Jan 1796	100
Ponsonby, George, Pvt	11248	8 Jan 1796	100
Harbrouck, Isaac, Pvt	7167	12 Oct 1790	100
Harbrouck, Isaac, Pvt	7645	12 Oct 1790	100
Norton, George, Sgt	7542	23 Sep 1790	100
Slingerland, R., Slingerland, P., & Slingerland, A., adm[inistrators] of Slingerland, A., Pvt	6840	22 Sep 1790	100
Allison, Rich[ar]d, & Conklin, Dan[ie]l, Pvt	13958	8 Jun 1791	100
Tallmadge, Benjamin, Pvt	6021	14 May 1790	100

140 10 Feb 1800 A/1/154

By Whom Registered: Jonathan Dayton
For Whom Registered: Jonathan Dayton
Location: (4000 acres) Mil - 19 1 - 1
Based upon the following Army land warrants:

Issued to	*No.*	*Date*	*Acres*
Hunter, Robert, Lt	993	29 Sep 1790	200
Platt, Richard, Pvt	13601	10 Aug 1789	100
Platt, Richard, Pvt	13053	10 Aug 1789	100
Platt, Richard, Pvt	13357	10 Aug 1789	100
Platt, Richard, Pvt	12852	7 Aug 1789	100
Platt, Richard, Pvt	12882	10 Aug 1789	100
Platt, Richard, Pvt	12846	10 Aug 1789	100
Platt, Richard, Pvt	12837	14 Dec 1789	100
Platt, Richard, Pvt	10178	7 Aug 1789	100
Platt, Richard, Pvt	10203	7 Aug 1789	100
Platt, Richard, Pvt	9983	7 Aug 1789	100
Platt, Richard, Pvt	9988	7 Aug 1789	100
Platt, Richard, Pvt	10458	7 Aug 1789	100
Platt, Richard, Pvt	10496	7 Aug 1789	100
Platt, Richard, Pvt	10353	7 Aug 1789	100
Platt, Richard, Pvt	13138	10 Aug 1789	100
Platt, Richard, Pvt	13220	14 Dec 1789	100
Platt, Richard, Pvt	13282	10 Aug 1789	100
Platt, Richard, Pvt	13344	7 Aug 1789	100
Platt, Richard, Pvt	13482	14 Jul 1790	100
Platt, Richard, Pvt	13511	14 Dec 1789	100
Platt, Richard, Pvt	13724	10 Aug 1789	100
Platt, Richard, Pvt	13742	10 Aug 1789	100
Platt, Richard, Pvt	13772	10 Aug 1789	100
Platt, Richard, Pvt	13940	10 Aug 1789	100
Hobert, John Sloss, Benson, E., McKesson, J., Howard? E., & Platt, Rich[ar]d, Pvt	7673	15 Sep 1790	100
Fisher, Hannah, Pvt	6756	17 Jun 1791	100
Fisher, Hannah, Pvt	7006	17 Jun 1791	100
Loudon? [London?] Stephen, Pvt	8898	5 Mar 1791	100
Hetfield, Moses, Pvt	7160	19 Apr 1791	100
Faulkner, William, Pvt	6945	24 May 1791	100
Anspach, Peter, Pvt	8486	7 Aug 1789	100
Anspach, --, & Rogers, --, Pvt	3877	7 Aug 1789	100
Anspach, --, & Rogers, --, Pvt	4220	7 Aug 1789	100
Anspach, --, & Rogers, --, Pvt	6269	7 Aug 1789	100
Crane, Elisha, & Don, E., Pvt	7801	14 Feb 1791	100
Folsom, John, Pvt	7227	7 Sep 1790	100
Faulkner, William, Pvt	7786	7 Sep 1790	100
Fowler, Theodosius, Pvt	13213	1 Sep 1790	100

141 10 Feb 1800 A/1/155

By Whom Registered: Jonathan Dayton
For Whom Registered: Jonathan Dayton
Location: (4000 acres) Mil - 15 5 - 2
Based upon the following Army land warrants:

Issued to	*No.*	*Date*	*Acres*
Aorson, Aaron, Capt	32	15 Sep 1790	300
Fitch, Andrew, Capt	721	7 Aug 1789	300
Hobert, J[ohn] Sloss, Benson, E., McKesson, J., & Platt, Rich[ar]d, Pvt	7000	15 Sep 1790	100
Johnston, Joseph, Pvt	7002	26 May 1790	100
Hobart, J[ohn] Sloss, Benson, E., McKesson, J., & Platt, Rich[ar]d, Pvt	7032	15 Sep 1790	100
Thompson, John, Pvt	7071	1 Oct 1791	100
Rogers, Israel, Pvt	7093	25 Jan 1791	100
Hobart, John Sloss, *et al*, Pvt	7101	15 Sep 1790	100
Watson, Elkanah, Pvt	7105	12 Oct 1790	100
Hobart, John Sloss, *et al*, Pvt	7111	15 Sep 1790	100
Tremper, Henry, Pvt	7121	11 Oct 1790	100
Hobart, John Sloss, *et al*, Pvt	7122	15 Sep 1790	100
Fryday, Conradt, Pvt	7124	20 Sep 1790	100

141 [continued]

Gardner, Jesse, Pvt	7164	2 Aug 1790	100
Gee, John, Pvt	7165	8 Jul 1790	100
Hobart, John Sloss, *et al*	7168	15 Sep 1790	100
Hobart, John Sloss, *et al*	7171	15 Sep 1790	100
Hogeboom, Stephen	7180	12 Oct 1790	100
Hobart, John Sloss, *et al*	7192	15 Sep 1790	100
Pollock, Carlile	7197	6 Jul 1791	100
Garrison, Thomas, Pvt	7199	22 May 1789	100
Outhoudt? [Oothoudt?] Abraham	7268	27 Sep 1790	100
Hobart, John Sloss, *et al*	7281	15 Sep 1790	100
Platt, Richard	7296	18 Jul 1791	100
Van Rensselaer, Jeremiah	7330	14 Feb 1791	100
Kenner, Jonathan	7349	23 Oct 1790	100
Hobart, John Sloss, *et al*	7373	15 Sep 1790	100
Pollock, Carlile	7378	6 Jul 1791	100
Ludlam, Daniel, Pvt	7391	28 Apr 1791	100
Hobart, John Sloss, *et al*	7396	15 Sep 1790	100
Hobart, John Sloss, *et al*	7398	15 Sep 1790	100
Prince, John	7401	4 Oct 1790	100
Van Rensselaer, Jeremiah	7411	14 Feb 1791	100
Hobart, John Sloss, *et al*	7424	15 Sep 1790	100
Hobart, John Sloss, *et al*	7425	15 Sep 1790	100
Hobart, John Sloss	7455	15 Sep 1790	100

142 10 Feb 1800 A/1/156

By Whom Registered: Jonathan Dayton
For Whom Registered: Jonathan Dayton
Location: (4000 acres) Mil - 15 4 - 4
Based upon the following Army land warrants:

Issued to	*No.*	*Date*	*Acres*
Clinton, Alexander, Lt	396	15 Sep 1790	200
Cady, Palmer, Lt	494	12 Oct 1790	200
Stanmer, Francis, Lt	989	28 Sep 1790	200
Hobart, John Sloss, *et al*	7459	15 Sep 1790	100
Hogeboome, Stephen	7468	12 Oct 1790	100
Tillotson, Thomas	7469	22 Jul 1790	100
Hobart, John Sloss, *et al*	7486	15 Sep 1790	100
Hobart, John Sloss, *et al*	7495	15 Sep 1790	100
Lawrance, John	7502	24 Jul 1790	100
McLane, John, Sgt	7505	12 Oct 1790	100
Hobart, John Sloss, *et al*	7526	15 Sep 1790	100
Teneyck, Meyndert	7551	4 Oct 1790	100
Oudenkerk, Myndert, Pvt	7575	27 Sep 1790	100
Hobart, John Sloss, *et al*	7579	15 Sep 1790	100
Pullis, John, Pvt	7600	8 Mar 1791	100
Alwater? [Atwater?] Jesse	7612	7 Mar 1792	100
Hobart, John Sloss, *et al*	7620	15 Sep 1790	100
Lawrance, John	7668	24 Jul 1790	100
Russell, William, Pvt	7679	20 Oct 1790	100
Tillotson, Thomas	7689	22 Jul 1790	100
Lawrance, John	7710	24 Jul 1790	100
Ray, Caleb, Pvt	7717	24 Sep 1790	100
McGill, William	7734	25 Sep 1790	100
Hobart, John Sloss, *et al*	7756	15 Sep 1790	100
Hobart, John Sloss, *et al*	7792	15 Sep 1790	100
Salier, Zacheus, Pvt	7804	5 Oct 1790	100
Hobart, John Sloss, *et al*	7830	15 Sep 1790	100
Platt, Richard	7841	18 Jul 1791	100
Sebor, James F.	7898	27 Sep 1790	100
Fowler, Theodosius	7906	9 Jul 1790	100
Moore, Assaph	7917	7 Jul 1791	100
Platt, Richard	7925	18 Jul 1791	100
Elwood, Benjamin	7929	21 Sep 1790	100
Van Ranselear, Henry J.	7943	1 Aug 1791	100
Tillotson, Thomas	7955	22 Jul 1790	100
Seeber? [Leeber?] Conrad	7974	12 Oct 1790	100
Elwood, Benjamin	7975	21 Sep 1790	100

143 11 Feb 1800 A/1/158

By Whom Registered: Jonathan Dayton
For Whom Registered: Jonathan Dayton
Location: (4000 acres) Mil - 16 6 - 3
Based upon the following Army land warrants:

Issued to	*No.*	*Date*	*Acres*
Gilchrist, Robert	2115	29 Apr 1791	400
Smyth, William Pitt, Surgeon's Mate	2116	29 Sep 1790	300
Van Schaaick, Mary	2146	15 Sep 1790	500
Whitlock, Ephraim L., Lt	2377	11 Jun 1789	200
Burnet, Ichabod, Maj	2565	1 Sep 1790	400
Danford, Prince, Pvt	7044	14 Feb 1791	100
Kepp, Amos, Pvt	7354	8 Sep 1792	100
Howell, Hezekiah	7838	25 Jan 1791	100
Dill, Robert	8015	7 Sep 1792	100
Baker, John, Pvt	8094	26 Sep 1789	100
Burrell, Zachariah, Pvt	8109	12 Oct 1790	100
Bowers, James, Pvt	8114	29 Sep 1791	100
Hunt, Josiah	8168	2 Apr 1790	100
Arrison, Jeptha	8233	27 May 1790	100
Donaldson, James, Pvt	8236	24 Nov 1791	100
Hunt, Josiah	8250	22 Jul 1789	100
Jackson, Richard, Sgt	8442	24 Mar 1790	100
Mersereau, Joshua	8443	26 May 1790	100
Miller, Joseph, Pvt	8589	10 Dec 1789	100
Norcross, John	8600	10 Sep 1790	100
Osmun, John, Pvt	8620	26 Jan 1789	100
Peck, David, Pvt	8632	29 Aug 1789	100
Parrot, Adoniram, Pvt	8635	14 Aug 1789	100
Arrison, Jeptha	8697	1 Jan 1800	100
Mersereau, Joshua	8793	26 May 1790	100
Broadwell, Hezekiah	13676	21 Apr 1791	100
Jewell, Mary	13952	2 Oct 1790	100

144 11 Feb 1800 A/1/159

By Whom Registered: Jonathan Dayton
For Whom Registered: Jonathan Dayton
Location: (4000 acres) Mil - 13 3 - 1
Based upon the following Army land warrants:

Issued to	*No.*	*Date*	*Acres*
Finch, Andrew, Capt	729	9 Oct 1790	300
Gansevoort, Peter, Col	824	27 Sep 1790	500
Johnson, John, Capt	1143	29 Sep 1790	300
Lamb, John, Col	1259	20 Aug 1790	500
Sedam? [Ledam?] Cornelius R., Ens	2000	20 Jun 1789	150
Atayalagkroughta, Lewis, LtCol	2600	8 Mar 1792	450
Hobart, John Sloss, *et al*	6909	15 Sep 1790	100
Hobart, John Sloss, *et al*	6918	15 Aug 1790	100
Laurance, John	6922	24 Jul 1790	100
Cowdry, Benjamin, Pvt	6951	7 Sep 1790	100
Clough, Benjamin, Pvt	6961	5 Oct 1790	100
Vreedenburgh, William J.	6963	12 Jan 1791	100
Crouse? Elbert, Pvt	6973	19 May 1791	100
Hobart, John Sloss, *et al*	6976	15 Sep 1790	100
Tillotson, Thomas	6978	22 Jul 1790	100
Pollock, Carlile	6986	6 Jul 1791	100
Lawrance, John	8005	24 Jul 1790	100
Stitchin, And[re]w, & Smith, J.	8041	8 Sep 1790	100
Parcell, Anthony, Pvt	8629	9 May 1792	100

144 [continued]

Stevens, Peter, Pvt	8706	9 May 1792	100
Shoemaker, Jacob	8772	10 May 1793	100
Greaves, Francis	11881	13 Dec 1791	100
Means, Robert	11999	7 Jul 1792	100
Stockdale, John	12044	31 Jan 1794	100

145 — 11 Feb 1800 — A/1/159

By Whom Registered: Jonathan Dayton
For Whom Registered: Jonathan Dayton
Location: (4000 acres) Mil - 19 4 - 2
Based upon the following Army land warrants:

Issued to	*No.*	*Date*	*Acres*
Kip, James H.	1566	28 Jul 1791	300
Neely, Abraham, Capt	1583	13 Sep 1790	300
Stevens, Ebenezer, LtCol	1972	15 Jun 1790	450
Smith, Israel, Capt	1976	5 Jan 1791	300
Swartwout, Bernardus, Ens	1983	7 Jul 1790	150
Van Banshooten, Peter, Lt	2257	22 Sep 1790	200
Allen, Lucretia	2586	20 Jul 1791	300
Pelton, Benjamin, Capt	2587	14 Jul 1791	300
Broome, Samuel	6769	11 Nov 1791	100
Vreedenburgh, William J.	7005	16 Jul 1790	100
Henderson, William	7491	9 Sep 1790	100
Wood, Samuel	7501	4 Sep 1790	100
Prentice, Jonas	7524	13 Sep 1790	100
Space, John, Pvt	7757	15 Sep 1790	100
Thompson, Andrew	7767	2 Sep 1790	100
Henderson, William	7779	10 Sep 1790	100
Curray, Samuel	7928	20 Jul 1790	100
Banks, Justus	7950	10 Sep 1790	100
Mead, Jonathan, Pvt	8068	10 Sep 1790	100
Stock[d]ale, John	12279	11 May 1795	100
Smith, William, Pvt	13769	16 Nov 1791	100
Smith, Heber, Pvt	13792	20 Sep 1790	100
Forrey, Samuel, Sgt	13814	12 Oct 1790	100
Wood, Samuel, Pvt	13927	21 Aug 1790	100
Vreedenburgh, William J.	13928	16 Jul 1790	100

146 — 11 Feb 1800 — A/1/160

By Whom Registered: Jonathan Dayton
For Whom Registered: Jonathan Dayton
Location: (4000 acres) Mil - 20 5 - 4
Based upon the following Army land warrants:

Issued to	*No.*	*Date*	*Acres*
Hobart, John Sloss, *et al*	1144	15 Sep 1790	200
Ledyard, Isaac, Assistant Purveyor	1333	9 Apr 1791	400
Sanford, Peleg	1386	24 Sep 1790	200
Mott, Elizabeth	1400	7 Jul 1791	300
Morris, William W., Lt	1403	13 May 1789	200
McConnell, Matthew	1569	29 Jun 1789	200
McConnell, Matthew	2028	29 Jun 1789	200
McConnell, Matthew	8893	29 Jun 1789	100
McConnell, Matthew	8945	16 Jul 1789	100
McConnell, Matthew	9050	29 Jun 1789	100
McConnell, Matthew	9199	29 Jun 1789	100
McConnell, Matthew	9281	29 Jun 1789	100
McConnell, Matthew	9464	29 Jun 1789	100
McConnell, Matthew	9920	16 Jul 1789	100
McConnell, Matthew	10234	29 Jun 1789	100
McConnell, Matthew	10245	16 Jul 1789	100
McConnell, Matthew	10333	29 Jun 1789	100
McConnell, Matthew	10394	29 Jun 1789	100
McConnell, Matthew	10419	29 Jun 1789	100
McConnell, Matthew	10434	29 Jun 1789	100
McConnell, Matthew	10554	29 Jun 1789	100
McConnell, Matthew	10558	16 Jul 1789	100
McConnell, Matthew	10633	29 Jun 1789	100
McConnell, Matthew	10652	29 Jun 1789	100
McConnell, Matthew	10655	16 Jul 1789	100
McConnell, Matthew	10565	29 Jun 1789	100
McConnell, Matthew	10581	16 Jul 1789	100
McConnell, Matthew	12813	29 Jun 1789	100
McConnell, Matthew	12933	29 Jun 1789	100
McConnell, Matthew	13116	29 Jun 1789	100

147 — 11 Feb 1800 — A/1/161

By Whom Registered: William McCluney
For Whom Registered: William McCluney
Location: (4000 acres) Mil - 4 1 - 2
Based upon the following Army land warrants:

Issued to	*No.*	*Date*	*Acres*
Callander, John, Lt	356	31 Mar 1794	200
Means, Robert	469	6 Jan 1795	200
Means, Robert	677	29 May 1792	300
McFarlane, James, Lt	1428	6 Apr 1790	200
Parker, Daniel	1510	19 Dec 1791	200
Mills, John, Lt	1512	26 Oct 1791	200
Means, Robert	1770	29 May 1792	200
Smith, Nathaniel, Lt	2024	16 Jul 1789	200
Holmes, Gabriel	2096	18 May 1797	200
Means, Robert	2220	31 Jan 1794	200
Oram, Peter B.	2439	14 Dec 1795	200
Barr, Martha	2536	10 Aug 1790	200
Craig, James, Capt	2648	5 Dec 1794	300
Nelson, Joseph	2650	31 Jan 1795	200
Walsh, John, Capt	2668	24 May 1796	300
Brown, John, Pvt	9015	4 Sep 1792	100
Jones, John	9342	10 Mar 1795	100
Keamer, Nicholas, Pvt	9761	7 Apr 1792	100
Moreland, Moses, Pvt	9909	9 May 1795	100
Gillespie, John, Pvt	13122	2 Apr 1792	100
Griffith, Levi, Lt	837	13 Feb 1797	200

148 — 11 Feb 1800 — A/1/162

By Whom Registered: Abijah Hunt
For Whom Registered: John E. Howard
Location: (4000 acres) Mil - 12 6 - 1
Based upon the following Army land warrants:

Issued to	*No.*	*Date*	*Acres*
Sparks, William	1637	16 Apr 1796	400
Rice, Nathan, Maj	1778	26 Oct 1789	400
Ripley, Hezekiah, Lt	1782	18 Jun 1791	200
Friscatt, Lemuel, Maj	2140	28 Sep 1791	400
Winn, Samuel, Lt	2660	5 Jan 1796	200
Sheldon, Job, Pvt	2507	28 May 1792	100
Philips, James	5305	20 Jan 1796	100
Carter, Evan, Pvt	5564	23 Aug 1790	100
Chittendon, Gideon, Pvt	5581	23 Aug 1790	100
Talmadge, Benjamin	5692	5 May 1791	100
Williams, Cornelius	5876	29 Sep 1790	100
Talmadge, Benjamin	5888	5 May 1791	100
Hall, Amos, Pvt	5928	23 Aug 1790	100
Kirkam, William, Drummer	6068	14 Jul 1789	100
Leach, Lewis, Pvt	6082	29 Jun 1791	100
Merriam, Edmund, Pvt	6167	23 Aug 1790	100
Talmadge, Benjamin	6412	5 May 1791	100
Talmadge, Benjamin	6708	5 May 1791	100
Hawkins, David	6919	29 Jun 1792	100
Deeker, Martin, Pvt	7042	25 Jan 1791	100
Seaman, Eliphalet	7205	23 Jul 1792	100
Atwater, Jesse	7634	19 Jul 1792	100
Robinson, Edmond, Pvt	7661	24 Sep 1792	100
Duggan, James	7787	5 Apr 1793	100
Duggan, James	7822	5 Apr 1793	100

148 [continued]

Issued to	No.	Date	Acres
Everitt, Nicholas	8014	23 Feb 1792	100
Silsbee, Benjamin	13581	6 Apr 1796	100
House, Jacob, Pvt	14068	21 Mar 1794	100
House, Christian, Pvt	14069	21 Mar 1794	100

149 11 Feb 1800 A/1/163

By Whom Registered: Jonas Stanbery
For Whom Registered: Jonas Stanbery
Location: (4000 acres) Mil - 12 4 - 3
Based upon the following Army land warrants:

Issued to	*No.*	*Date*	*Acres*
Gates, Horatio, MajGen	863	18 Nov 1790	1100
Quinton, David	3273	25 Mar 1791	100
Quinton, David	3908	25 Mar 1791	100
Quinton, David	4920	25 Mar 1791	100
Carter, Aaron, Pvt	5566	23 Aug 1790	100
Nutmire, Henderick, Pvt	6248	2 Apr 1793	100
Van Wagenen, Garrit H.	6751	26 Jul 1790	100
Vreedenburgh, William J.	6856	16 Jul 1790	100
Cannon, Thomas, Sgt	6962	30 Aug 1790	100
Hardenberg, Abraham	6975	29 Jul 1790	100
Davis, Richard, Pvt	7016	20 Jul 1790	100
Vreedenburgh, William J.	7116	16 Jul 1790	100
Martin, Adam	7178	7 Jul 1791	100
Vreedenburgh, William J.	7181	16 Jul 1790	100
Roosevelt, James	7233	29 Mar 1791	100
Marvin, Elihu	7362	25 Jan 1791	100
Veeder, Simon	7363	30 Aug 1790	100
Rogers, Platt	7427	24 Sep 1791	100
Vreedenburgh, William J.	7466	16 Jul 1790	100
Camp, Elisha	7489	17 Nov 1791	100
Hathorn, John	7503	15 Jul 1790	100
Camp, Elisha	7659	17 Nov 1791	100
Griffin, Peter	7704	28 Jul 1790	100
Lawry, James	7706	20 Aug 1790	100
Waldron, Resolve	7865	30 Jul 1791	100
Wilkelow, John, Pvt	7959	1 Oct 1791	100
Curtis, John, Sgt	8163	18 Jan 1790	100
McCleland, John	9527	6 Jul 1791	100
Quinton, David	13625	25 Mar 1791	100
Stringer, Samuel	14027	5 Oct 1791	100

150 11 Feb 1800 A/1/164

By Whom Registered: Jonas Stanbery
For Whom Registered: Jonas Stanbery
Location: (4000 acres) Mil - 13 1 - 3
Based upon the following Army land warrants:

Issued to	*No.*	*Date*	*Acres*
Bull, William, Capt	160	15 Dec 1790	300
Ryan, Richardson	165	27 May 1793	200
Rosecranse, James, Maj	1806	23 Jul 1790	400
Loree, Ephraim, Surgeon's Mate	2681	25 Mar 1797	300
Beach, Reuben, Pvt	5490	20 Sep 1791	100
Frisby, Reuben, Pvt	5792	23 Aug 1790	100
Goldsmith, Joseph, Pvt	5878	23 Sep 1789	100
Hawkins, Joseph, Pvt	5978	23 Aug 1790	100
Parsons, William Walter	6575	28 Jan 1790	100
Hardenberg, Abraham	6830	29 Jul 1790	100
Vreedenburgh, William J.	6838	16 Jul 1790	100
Broome, Samuel	6988	11 Nov 1791	100
Doty, Isaac, Pvt	7072	25 Apr 1792	100
Vreedenburgh, William J.	7119	16 Jul 1790	100
House, John, Pvt	7273	18 Aug 1790	100
Van Wagenen, Gerrit H.	7278	28 Jul 1790	100
Watkins, John W.	7305	1 Sep 1791	100
Van Wagenen, Gerrit H.	7472	28 Jul 1790	100
Watkins, John W.	7535	1 Sep 1791	100
Vreedenburgh, William J.	7556	16 Jul 1790	100
Wendell, John W.	7595	30 Jul 1790	100
Russell, Ebenezer	7670	7 Jul 1791	100
Roosevelt, James	7708	29 Mar 1791	100
Watkins, John	7732	31 Aug 1791	100
Stout, George	7828	24 May 1793	100
Gurnee, John J.	7852	30 Jul 1790	100
Watkins, John W.	7877	28 Jul 1790	100
Van Wagenen, Gerrit H.	7905	28 Jul 1790	100
Warren, John	7980	1 Jun 1790	100
Van Dyck, Cornelius	8012	28 Dec 1791	100
Stringer, Samuel	8024	25 Aug 1790	100
Quinton, David	13330	25 Mar 1791	100

151 11 Feb 1800 A/1/166

By Whom Registered: John Stites
For Whom Registered: John Stites
Location: (4000 acres) Mil - 15 5 - 3
Based upon the following Army land warrants:

Issued to	*No.*	*Date*	*Acres*
Hubbey, David	7371	2 Apr 1792	100
Childs, Evander	4887	30 Dec 1796	100
Brady, Michael, Pvt	8934	29 Mar 1791	100
Gilbert, Jesse	5867	30 Dec 1790	100
Fox, Andrew	10524	8 Mar 1792	100
Williams, John, Pvt	11827	11 May 1790	100
Melvin, James, Pvt	14143	5 Sep 1796	100
Thom, Christopher S.	3173	28 Dec 1796	100
Shaw, Michael, Pvt	10453	10 Mar 1790	100
Bowen, Sabritt, Pvt	9020	23 Feb 1797	100
Emery, Samuel	4462	31 Dec 1793	100
Bailey, Benjamin	4487	14 Mar 1793	100
Emery, Samuel	3521	8 Nov 1792	100
Emery, Samuel	4684	21 Sep 1792	100
Green, Joshua, Junior	5215	26 Oct 1789	100
Bailey, Benj[amin]	3271	14 Mar 1793	100
Boardman, William, Pvt	3750	1 May 1792	100
Emery, Samuel	3233	26 Jul 1792	100
Winchester, Charles, Pvt	5326	24 Jul 1792	100
Emery, Samuel	4470	16 Jan 1793	100
Emery, Samuel	4173	16 Jan 1793	100
Emery, Samuel	13683	17 Jan 1793	100
Quinton, David	4143	1 May 179?	100
Brown, Joseph	3837	7 Jul 1790	100
Finney, Samuel	3135	8 Aug 1793	100
Emery, Samuel	4720	12 Mar 1793	100
Emery, Samuel	4596	12 Mar 1793	100
Emery, Samuel	3516	8 Nov 1792	100
Emery, Samuel	5151	14 Dec 1793	100
Emery, Samuel	5328	5 Apr 1793	100
Washington, William, LtCol	2421	7 Mar 1798	450
McCalla, Thomas, Surgeon	1448	2 May 1796	400
Schuyler, Dirck, Ens	1984	25 Feb 1792	150

152 11 Feb 1800 A/1/167

By Whom Registered: Jonas Stanbery
For Whom Registered: Joseph Hardy
Location: (4000 acres) Mil - 12 4 - 2
Based upon the following Army land warrants:

Issued to	*No.*	*Date*	*Acres*
Philips, Mills	1988	6 Jun 1791	200
Tiebout, Henry, Capt	2183	22 Jul 1790	300
Van Howenbergh, Rudolphus, Lt	2254	5 May 1791	200
Van Volkenburg, Barth, Lt	2255	19 Aug 1790	200

152 [continued]

Willet, Marinus, LtCol Com-[mandan]t	2362	30 Jul 1790	500
Burnet, John, Lt	2570	12 Oct 1790	200
Tuttle, Jonathan	5039	7 Mar 1792	100
Lowrey, James	6843	20 Aug 1790	100
McKowan, William	6871	18 Jul 1791	100
Chittingdon, Jared	6999	20 Jul 1791	100
Lowry, James	7277	20 Aug 1790	100
Sanger, Jeddediah	7284	18 Jul 1791	100
Van Wagenen, Gerrit	7353	28 Jul 1790	100
Warren, John	7376	10 Aug 1790	100
Van Wagenen, Gerrit H.	7517	28 Jul 1790	100
Warren, John	7631	10 Aug 1790	100
Vreedenburgh, William J.	7848	20 Aug 1790	100
Waggerman, Emaniel* Pvt	7988	18 Aug 1790	100
Lowry, James	8007	20 Aug 1790	100
Walliser, Christian, Pvt	8020	20 Jul 1791	100
Welch, John	8023	2 Jul 1790	100
Chapelone, Peter, Junior, Fifer	12887	7 Aug 1789	100
Whitlock? [Whittock?] James, Pvt	10645	2 Jun 1797	100
Bailey, Benjamin	4749	14 Mar 1793	100
Emery, Samuel	4895	22 Aug 1793	100
Emery, Samuel	5084	14 Dec 1793	100
Leavenworth, Nathan, Surgeon's Mate	2635	19 Jul 1793	300
Munson, Enease* Junior, *et al*	5576	15 May 1795	100

*So spelled.

153 — 11 Feb 1800 — A/1/168

By Whom Registered: Jonas Stanbery
For Whom Registered: John A. Hardenbrook
Location: (4000 acres)* Mil - 7 4 - 4
Based upon the following Army land warrants:

Issued to	*No.*	*Date*	*Acres*
Cortlandt, Philip, Col	388	7 Jul 1790	500
Munson, Eneas, Junior	966	6 Jul 1795	200
Lane, Derrick, Capt	1271	21 Dec 1795	300
Malcome, William, Col	1404	9 Jul 1790	500
Reed, Enoch, Capt	1794	29 May 1789	300
Smith, Pter, Lt	2021	20 Oct 1789	200
Power, Thomas, Pvt	3378	24 Jun 1793	100
York, John, Pvt	3605	24 Jun 1793	100
Emery, Samuel	3765	2 Jun 1795	100
Warren, John	4279	1 Jun 1790	100
Pitkin, Timothy, Junior	5610	30 Nov 1795	100
Dewey, John, Pvt	4012	18 Dec 1789	100
Warren, John	5003	15 Apr 1790	100
Turner, William, Pvt	5126	13 Jul 1792	100
Ross, James	5337	9 Apr 1791	100
Munson, Eneas, Junior	5360	2 Mar 1795	100
Baker, Robert, Pvt	5522	24 Jun 1793	100
Cutler, Joseph	5548	30 Oct 1789	100
Pitkin, Timothy, Junior	5593	30 Nov 1795	100
Gilbert, John, Pvt	5850	26 Apr 1792	100
Meigs, Nathan	6165	14 Jul 1789	100
Pratt, Jasper	6276	27 Jan 1796	100
Curtiss, Abijah	6502	27 Jan 1796	100
Munson, Eneas, Junior	6635	6 Jul 1795	100
Smith, Peter	9548	20 Oct 1789	100
Darrah, William, Pvt	14075	19 Apr 1794	100

*Marginal notation:
"Location made [as cited above] 4045.4
Warr. recd. [by] this State 4000
Since received:
No. 2986 Warr. to Philip Schuyler [dtd] 100
21 Dec 1790 Amount of location 4100"
[See also serial entry 275]

154 — 11 Feb 1800 — A/1/169

By Whom Registered: Jonas Stanbery
For Whom Registered: Joseph Hardy
Location: (4000 acres)* Mil - 13 2 - 3
Based upon the following Army land warrants:

Issued to	*No.*	*Date*	*Acres*
Blanchard, James, Lt	78	30 Jul 1790	200
Bleecker, Leonard, Capt	158	30 Jun 1790	300
Beekman? [Beckman?] Jerrick, Lt	161	2 Oct 1790	200
Godwin, Catelina	829	19 Aug 1790	300
Higbee, Joseph	873	24 Jun 1793	200
Harrison, Dirck, Capt	981	13 Jul 1790	300
Hardey, Joseph	1101	31 Mar 1796	850
Luse, Francis, Ens	1273	9 Dec 1789	150
Moody, Margaret	1399	29 Jul 1790	300
Newkirk, Charles, Lt	1586	23 Jul 1790	200
Pell, P., & Pell, D.	1681	15 Dec 1790	300
Stevens, William, Capt	1973	15 Jul 1790	300
Sweet, Caleb, Surgeon	1985	23 Aug 1790	400

*Marginal notation:
"Location made [as cited above] 4920
Warr. recd. [by] this State 4000
Since received:
No. 14 Reg[ister's] Cert. to J. Hardy,
10 Mar 1800 540
793 Warr. Henry Newman, 13 Sep 1792 300
3863 ditto Abel Crane, 22 Jul 1789 100
4940
Amount of location 4920
20
[See also serial entry 272]

155 — 11 Feb 1800 — A/1/169

By Whom Registered: Jonas Stanbery
For Whom Registered: Benjamin J. Moore
Location: (4000 acres) Mil - 14 7 - 2
Based upon the following Army land warrants:

Issued to	*No.*	*Date*	*Acres*
Smith, --, & Ridgway, --	1752	27 Aug 1795	300
Starr, Thomas, Lt	1957	29 May 1792	200
Young, Guy, Capt	2464	20 Nov 1792	300
Niles, Gaius, Pvt	3358	16 Feb 1795	100
Richards, Joseph Anthony, Pvt	3462	22 Mar 1794	100
Green, Joshua, Junior	4977	26 Oct 1789	100
Briston, Peter, Pvt	5411	2 Apr 1792	100
Barnum, Amos, Pvt	5437	1 Aug 1795	100
Bronson, Isaac	5583	31 Dec 1791	100
Bronson, Isaac	6662	19 Apr 1792	100
Albright, John, Cpl	6722	3 Sep 1790	100
Bartoe, Morris, Pvt	6767	6 Aug 1790	100
Wright, Joseph	6770	26 Aug 1790	100
Rogers, Platt	6797	24 Sep 1791	100
Anderson, Thomas	6969	9 Jun 1790	100
Wright, Joseph	7096	26 Aug 1790	100
Luffren, John	7147	4 Sep 1790	100
Stringham, Joseph	7183	18 Aug 1790	100
Stringham, Joseph	7244	18 Aug 1790	100
Lee, Daniel, Pvt	7414	30 Aug 1790	100
Rogers, Platt	7560	16 Mar 1792	100
Platt, Richard	7588	14 Jul 1790	100
Roosa, Albert	7692	5 Dec 1791	100
Vreedenburgh, William J.	7776	16 Jul 1790	100
Shearman, Peter, Pvt	7807	3 Aug 1790	100
Bogart, Isaac	7834	27 Oct 1791	100
Rogers, Platt	7890	24 Sep 1791	100
Rhea, Jonathan	8200	7 Jul 1795	100
Decorcy, James	9611	7 Aug 1795	100
Decorcy, James	10177	7 Aug 1795	100
Simmons, Isles, Pvt	10424	3 Apr 1798	100

155 [continued]

Means, Robert	12607	20 Jul 1792	100
Hansell, George, Pvt	13211	31 Mar 1794	100
Bronson, Isaac	13475	19 Apr 1792	100
Bronson, Isaac	13856	19 Apr 1792	100

156 11 Feb 1800 A/1/171

By Whom Registered: John G. Macan
For Whom Registered: John G. Macan
Location: (4000 acres) Mil - 17 1 - 3
Based upon the following Army land warrants:

Issued to	*No.*	*Date*	*Acres*
Beall, Lloyd, Capt	234	13 Aug 1796	300
Bowyer, Michael, Capt	288	24 Jun 1796	300
Crawford, Edward, Lt	421	15 Oct 1789	200
Curry, James, Capt	449	28 Jul 1790	300
Rose, Robert, Surgeon	1855	28 May 1789	400
McFarren, Margaret	2640	5 Apr 1794	200
Green, Timothy, Pvt	4232	26 Oct 1789	100
Polk, Job, Pvt	8695	25 Feb 1792	100
Bentley, Henry, Pvt	8925	9 Jul 1789	100
Coffee, John, Pvt	9115	6 Apr 1790	100
Davidson, David, Sgt	9241	9 Jul 1789	100
Farrall, Patrick, Pvt	9369	9 Jul 1789	100
Laughrey, Michael, Pvt	9792	9 Jul 1789	100
Moser, Samuel, Junior	10039	12 Dec 1797	100
Newby, John, Pvt	10162	6 Jul 1798	100
Robinson, James, Sgt	10252	29 Mar 1791	100
Watson, John, Pvt	10552	23 Jan 1796	100
Walters, Christopher, Pvt	10594	9 Jul 1789	100
Walters, John, Pvt	10614	9 Jul 1789	100
Burton, Jacob, Pvt	10706	2 Sep 1789	100
Mason, Thomas, Pvt	10825	19 Apr 1792	100
Murphey, William, Pvt	10839	2 Sep 1789	100
Wharton, Charles, Pvt	10916	2 Sep 1789	100
Reilly, Patrick, Pvt	11649	20 Sep 1799	100
Brooks, Benjamin, Pvt	11892	24 Oct 1789	100
Scott, Levi, Pvt	11722	11 Mar 1791	100
Harrison, William B.	12544	19 Jun 1793	100
Dralle? John, Pvt	12975	25 Aug 1789	100
Burrell, Noah, Pvt	3672	1 Apr 1790	100

157 11 Feb 1800 A/1/172

By Whom Registered: William Edgar, Junior
For Whom Registered: William Edgar, Junior
Location: (4000 acres) Mil - 6 4 - 3
Based upon the following Army land warrants:

Issued to	*No.*	*Date*	*Acres*
Baker, Henry, Lt	239	28 May 1789	200
Greer, Henry, Lt	842	18 May 1791	200
Palmer, Thomas	1701	28 Aug 1792	400
McGregore, James	2324	15 Apr 1796	200
Swartwout, B., Junior	3074	7 Jul 1791	100
Gifford, Jonathan, Pvt	3155	30 May 1791	100
Cannen, Joseph	3245	15 Apr 1796	100
May, Deborah	3369	16 May 1791	100
Neal, James A.	3576	12 Oct 1795	100
Angle, Israel	3725	28 May 1792	100
Coats, Charles, Pvt	3894	24 May 1790	100
Calwell, Medford, Pvt	3943	2 Dec 1789	100
Elliot, Francis, Pvt	4090	24 May 1790	100
Graves, Ebenezer, Pvt	4223	24 May 1790	100
Gay, Jonathan, Cpl	4272	24 May 1790	100
Prescott, Benjamin	4515	24 May 1790	100
Freedom, Ned, Pvt	5766	12 Jul 1792	100
Munson, Eneas, Junior	5869	16 Jan 1796	100
Green, Samuel, Pvt	5884	1 Mar 1796	100
Hubbard, Abijah, Pvt	5986	14 Dec 1792	100
Van Rensselaer, Jeremiah	6734	15 Jul 1790	100
Stowell? [Howell?]* John	7041	19 Jul 1790	100
Dickerson, Abraham, Sgt	7017	17 Jun 1790	100
Watkins, John W.	7135	1 Sep 1791	100
Watson, Elkanah	7285	24 Jun 1790	100
Van Ingen, Dirck	7304	13 Jul 1790	100
Miles, John	7529	16 Jul 1790	100
Linnott? [Sinnott?] Patrick, SgtMaj	7721	15 Jun 1790	100
Weissenfels, Ch[arle]s Fred[ric]k	7901	10 Dec 1789	100
Fordon, James, Pvt	8309	13 May 1791	100
Hart, Patrick, Pvt	8399	25 Mar 1790	100
Powers, George, Pvt	8638	31 Aug 1791	100
Ward, John, Pvt	8834	1 Oct 1789	100
Albert, Jacob, Pvt	8887	14 Jun 1791	100

*Originally entered as Stowell; pencilled notation corrects to Howell.

158 11 Feb 1800 A/1/173

By Whom Registered: William Edgar, Junior
For Whom Registered: William Edgar, Junior
Location: (4000 acres) Mil - 17 6 - 4
Based upon the following Army land warrants:

Issued to	*No.*	*Date*	*Acres*
Ashton, Benjamin, Pvt	8895	14 Feb 1791	100
Purdy, Henry	9467	22 Dec 1794	100
Gray, John, Pvt	9515	22 Dec 1794	100
Purdy, Henry	9544	22 Dec 1794	100
Power, Alexander	9582	15 Jan 1796	100
Purdy, Henry	9598	22 Dec 1794	100
Kelly, John, Pvt	9771	27 Jun 1791	100
Montgomery, James, Pvt	9881	14 Feb 1791	100
Purdy, Henry	9916	22 Dec 1794	100
Purdy, Henry	9933	22 Dec 1794	100
Purdy, Henry	9733	22 Dec 1794	100
Purdy, Henry	9955	22 Dec 1794	100
Faires, John	11305	21 Jan 1795	100
Purdy, Henry	11431	22 Dec 1794	100
Wright, John	11555	24 Dec 1794	100
Wright, Jesse, Pvt	11806	10 Jun 1789	100
Wirey, Michael, Pvt	11812	22 Dec 1794	100
Hailey, John	11845	24 Dec 1794	100
Young, John, Pvt	11855	22 Dec 1794	100
Purdy, Henry	10183	22 Dec 1794	100
Roberts, William, Pvt	10246	20 May 1791	100
Reese, David, Pvt	10254	16 May 1791	100
Purdy, Henry	10298	22 Dec 1794	100
Shehan, Daniel, Pvt	10330	18 Jan 1791	100
Purdy, Henry	10340	22 Dec 1794	100
Platt, Richard	10390	27 Jul 1789	100
Thomas, William, Pvt	10485	1 Jun 1791	100
Templer, Thomas	10510	6 Jun 1791	100
McNeal, James	10536	8 Jan 1793	100
Purdy, Henry	10994	22 Dec 1794	100
Clappard, John, Pvt	12057	7 Oct 1795	100
Reynolds, James	12121	13 Apr 1791	100
Reynolds, James	12275	13 Apr 1791	100
Minton, Ebenezer, Pvt	12361	29 Dec 1794	100
Reynolds, James	12541	13 Apr 1791	100
Reynolds, James	12600	13 Apr 1791	100
Spaulding, Asa	12847	22 Jun 1791	100
Beans? [Beaver?] Frederick, Pvt	12851	14 Feb 1791	100
Power, Alexander	12941	18 May 1791	100
Fox, Andrew, Pvt	13066	30 Mar 1791	100

159 11 Feb 1800 A/1/174

By Whom Registered: William H. Harrison

159 [continued]
For Whom Registered: John C[leves] Symmes
Location: (4000 acres) Mil - 16 4 - 4
Based upon the following Army land warrants:

Issued to	*No.*	*Date*	*Acres*
Wilson, Abraham	392	1 Sep 1790	200
Fisher, Leonard	1587	9 Sep 1790	200
Weatherby, Benjamin, Capt	2374	24 Jul 1790	300
Dexter, Joseph, Pvt	3077	13 Sep 1791	100
Dixon, Robert, Pvt	3079	31 Dec 1789	100
Palmer, James	3676	3 May 1791	100
Smith, Samuel	3729	3 Oct 1791	100
Lyons, Josiah, Pvt	4569	3 Oct 1791	100
Waggs, Elisha, Pvt	3595	31 Dec 1789	100
Quinton, David	3610	25 Mar 1791	100
Rogers, Samuel	4770	23 May 1795	100
Emery, Samuel	4834	29 Nov 1792	100
Emery, Samuel	5239	28 Feb 1794	100
Moore, William	6008	15 Jul 1790	100
Boardman, D., & Boardman, Elijah	6177	21 Mar 1791	100
Fish, Nicholas	6752	27 Aug 1790	100
de Witt, Peter	6885	4 Aug 1790	100
de Witt, Peter	7010	4 Aug 1790	100
Addoms* John	7722	16 Apr 1791	100
Maxwell, Anthony	7070	10 Oct 1791	100
Courtlandt, George	7941	6 Sep 1791	100
Addoms* John	8035	16 Apr 1791	100
Drake, Cornelius, Pvt	8244	5 Apr 1793	100
Walters, Jacob, Pvt	8878	8 Aug 1791	100
Sherrard, Francis	11025	14 Aug 1795	100
Hall, Casa, Pvt	10784	2 Sep 1789	100
Sherrard, Francis	10957	14 Aug 1795	100
Sherrard, Francis	10958	14 Aug 1795	100
Sherrard, Francis	11029	14 Aug 1795	100
Sherrard, Francis	11030	14 Aug 1795	100
Lee, John, Pvt	11459	3 Jun 1795	100
Purdy, Henry	11724	18 Dec 1794	100
Stockdell, John	12016	31 Jan 1794	100
Boyd, William	13206	8 Aug 1791	100
Tuttle, Jonathan	13577	2 Nov 1791	100
Platt, Richard	13597	14 Jul 1790	100

*So spelled.

160 11 Feb 1800 A/1/176
By Whom Registered: William H. Harrison
For Whom Registered: John C[leves] Symmes
Location: (4000 acres) Mil - 16 3 - 1
Based upon the following Army land warrants:

Issued to	*No.*	*Date*	*Acres*
Power, Alexander	749	18 May 1791	300
Hollister, Jesse, Capt	916	30 Sep 1791	300
Orr, John, Lt	1612	28 May 1791	200
Tuttle, Jonathan	4349	2 Nov 1791	100
Tuttle, Jonathan	5443	2 Nov 1791	100
Tuttle, Jonathan	5445	7 Mar 1792	100
Tuttle, Jonathan	5446	2 Nov 1791	100
Tuttle, Jonathan	5491	2 Nov 1791	100
Tuttle, Jonathan	5789	2 Nov 1791	100
Tuttle, Jonathan	5943	2 Nov 1791	100
Tuttle, Jonathan	6332	2 Nov 1791	100
Halsey, Joseph, Junior	6336	30 Sep 1790	100
Tuttle, Jonathan	6488	2 Nov 1791	100
Gilliland, William	6763	6 Sep 1791	100
Burnet, Ebenezer, Pvt	6779	3 Sep 1790	100
Fish, Nicholas	6896	27 Aug 1790	100
Vreedenburgh, W[illiam] J.	7090	26 Aug 1790	100
Fish, Nicholas	7217	27 Aug 1790	100
McMillen, John	7267	29 Jul 1790	100
Bristol, John	7314	25 Sep 1790	100
Kronkhite, John, Pvt	7365	3 Sep 1790	100
McKown, William	7392	26 Aug 1790	100
Marius, Jacob, Pvt	7527	8 Sep 1790	100
Cline, William	7552	25 Aug 1790	100
Rose, Elijah	7559	26 Aug 1790	100
Carr, William	7570	26 Aug 1790	100
Peters, John, Pvt	7618	24 Aug 1790	100
Saffren? [Laffren?] John	7624	4 Aug 1790	100
Simmonds, John, Pvt	7764	6 Aug 1790	100
Suffren? [Luffren?] John	7772	4 Sep 1790	100
Suffren? [Luffren?] John	7810	4 Sep 1790	100
Cline, William	7820	25 Aug 1790	100
Patterson, Garret, *et al*	7880	9 Sep 1790	100
Townsend, Benjamin	7888	26 Aug 1790	100
Halsey, Joseph, Junior	8105	30 Sep 1790	100

161 11 Feb 1800 A/1/177
By Whom Registered: William H. Harrison
For Whom Registered: John C[leves] Symmes
Location: (4000 acres) Mil - 14 2 - 3
Based upon the following Army land warrants:

Issued to	*No.*	*Date*	*Acres*
Appleton, Abraham, Lt	37	20 Jul 1790	200
Scudder, William, Lt	1978	7 Jul 1790	200
Gilbert, Ebenezer, Pvt	5846	15 Feb 1797	100
Waggoner, Michael, Pvt	6707	4 Aug 1796	100
Atkinson, James, Pvt	6750	25 Jan 1791	100
Black, David, Pvt	6804	26 Apr 1796	100
Mitsco, Conrod* Pvt	8576	12 Dec 1791	100
Pearson, Matthew, Pvt	8631	12 Sep 1789	100
Steel, David, Pvt	10425	3 Feb 1794	100
Sherrard, Francis	10943	14 Aug 1795	100
de Baufre, James	11026	2 Jun 1797	100
Ponsonby, George	11074	8 Jan 1796	100
Ward, Joshua	11086	11 Jan 1796	100
Ponsonby, George	11109	8 Jan 1796	100
Ponsonby, George	11165	8 Jan 1796	100
de Baufre, James	11227	8 Jun 1797	100
Davis, Henry	11269	14 Oct 1795	100
de Baufre, James	11292	8 Jun 1797	100
Ward, Joshua	11322	11 Jan 1796	100
Ponsonby, George	11335	8 Jan 1796	100
de Baufre, James	11348	8 Jun 1797	100
Ponsonby, George	11453	8 Jan 1796	100
Ward, Joshua	11685	11 Jan 1796	100
de Baufre, James	11705	4 May 1797	100
de Baufre, James	11856	8 Jun 1797	100
Mansfield, George	12009	26 Nov 1792	100
Sherrard, Francis	14107	24 Feb 1795	100
Sherrard, Francis	14108	24 Feb 1795	100
Sherrard, Francis	14121	1 May 1795	100
Moon, James, Pvt	9950	15 Jan 1796	100
Britton, Joseph, Lt	244	30 Jul 1790	200
Lapsley, Sally Woods	1301	29 Oct 1792	300
Duncan, James, Capt	626	22 Sep 1789	300

*So spelled.

162 11 Feb 1800 A/1/178
By Whom Registered: William H. Harrison
For Whom Registered: John C[leves] Symmes
Location: (4000 acres) Mil - 14 4 - 1
Based upon the following Army land warrants:

Issued to	*No.*	*Date*	*Acres*
Prentice, Jonas	1255	29 Jan 1793	200
Quinton, David	3781	25 Mar 1791	100
Street, Titus	3855	2 Nov 1791	100
Heaton, John	3951	7 Mar 1792	100
Gleason, William, Pvt	4235	6 Jan 1792	100

162 [continued]

Ashley, William	4498	8 Jan 1793	100
Heaton, John	4998	7 Mar 1792	100
Curtiss, Eleasar	5449	20 Sep 1791	100
Street, Titus	5462	2 Nov 1791	100
Street, Titus	5744	2 Nov 1791	100
Street, Titus	5768	2 Nov 1791	100
Parsons, William Wal[te]r	5810	28 Jan 1790	100
Gilbert, Burr, Pvt	5829	26 Apr 1792	100
Street, Titus	5834	2 Nov 1791	100
Heaton, John	5835	2 Nov 1791	100
He-ton, John	5916	2 Nov 1791	100
Morgan, Daniel, Pvt	6142	23 Aug 1790	100
Meeker, Hezekiah, Pvt	6170	6 Sep 1792	100
Roberts, Isaac	6396	23 Aug 1790	100
Street, Titus	6411	2 Nov 1791	100
Street, Titus	6442	2 Nov 1791	100
Parsons W[illia]m Walter	6628	28 Jan 1790	100
Cassedy, Edward, Pvt	7014	30 Aug 1790	100
Cumpston, Edward	7052	20 Jul 1790	100
Maxwell, Cornelius, Sgt	7473	22 Jul 1790	100
Van Shaaick, Mary	7480	9 Sep 1790	100
Cumpston, Edward	7562	30 Jul 1790	100
Bartholomew, G., & Fisher, J.	7572	28 Sep 1790	100
Bartholomew, G., & Fisher, J.	7697	28 Sep 1790	100
Roosevelt, James	7813	29 Mar 1791	100
Thompson, John, Pvt	7885	9 May 1792	100
Veeder, L? & Conyer, P.	8006	30 Aug 1790	100
Cumpston, Edward	8031	30 Jul 1790	100
Sherrard, Francis	10973	14 Aug 1795	100
Purdy, Henry	11103	18 Dec 1794	100
Purdy, Henry	11527	18 Dec 1794	100
Spencer, John	12277	29 Jun 1793	100
Heaton, John	12729	2 Nov 1791	100
Ashley, William	13516	12 Mar 1793	100

163 11 Feb 1800 A/1/179

By Whom Registered: Dudley Woodbridge
For Whom Registered: Dudley Woodbridge, "of Marietta [Ohio]"
Location: (4000 acres) Mil - 8 3 - 1
Based upon the following Army land warrants:

Issued to	*No.*	*Date*	*Acres*
Barrett, James, Lt	163	24 May 1793	200
Woodbridge, Dudley	518	31 Aug 1790	300
Houdin, Michael Gabriel, Capt	917	23 Oct 1790	300
Worthington, Asa	1961	19 Apr 1791	200
Woodbridge, Dudley	4432	31 Aug 1790	100
Woodbridge, Dudley	4767	31 Aug 1790	100
Coney, Michael, Pvt	5646	13 Apr 1791	100
Woodbridge, Dudley	6057	31 Aug 1790	100
Wakeley, Benjamin, Pvt	6695	10 Apr 1791	100
Woodbridge, Dudley	7555	31 Aug 1790	100
Woodbridge, Dudley	8944	31 Aug 1791	100
Woodbridge, Dudley	8968	31 Aug 1790	100
Baker, John, Pvt	9036	6 Jan 1792	100
Conner, John, Pvt	9101	29 Mar 1791	100
Griffith, William, Pvt	9427	8 Apr 1791	100
Iserloan, Jasper	9454	14 Aug 1793	100
Myer, John	9545	2 Dec 1791	100
Harris, George, Pvt	9636	9 Apr 1791	100
Shepperd, Sarah	9679	3 Feb 1792	100
Le Count, John, Pvt	9859	14 Apr 1791	100
Iserloan, Jasper	9999	14 Aug 1793	100
Stevenson, William, Pvt	10442	9 Apr 1791	100
Wiser, Solomon, Pvt	10597	6 Dec 1791	100
Webb, Andrew, Pvt	10625	9 Apr 1791	100
Benson, Elizabeth	10702	19 Apr 1792	100
McCleland, John	10886	6 Dec 1791	100
Flora, Jacob, Pvt	11204	24 Dec 1791	100
Clingman, John	11921	12 Nov 1791	100
La Barbier Duplessis, Peter	12702	12 Jan 1797	100
Cromwell, Hugh, Pvt	12916	19 Apr 1791	100
Kelly, Timothy	13049	12 Nov 1791	100
Heaton, James, Pvt	13183	19 Apr 1791	100
McGlaughlin, Patrick	13602	26 Jul 1791	100
Slevoght, Christian, Pvt	13716	15 Nov 1791	100

164 11 Feb 1800 A/1/181

By Whom Registered: Dudley Woodbridge
For Whom Registered: Dudley Woodbridge "of Marietta, [Ohio]"
Location: (4000 acres) Mil - 16 2 - 3
Based upon the following Army land warrants:

Issued to	*No.*	*Date*	*Acres*
Mills, William, Capt	1357	29 Feb 1792	300
Petigrew, James, Lt	1709	27 Jul 1791	200
Scott, William, Capt	1896	8 May 1792	300
Woodbridge, Dudley	3010	29 Dec 1792	100
McDonald, John, Pvt	4634	2 Apr 1793	100
Parker, James	4844	29 Dec 1792	100
Buell, Joseph	5379	8 Sep 1789	100
Fanning, Frederick Q[uartermaste]r Sgt	5177	21 Aug 1789	100
Freeman, Prince, Pvt	5807	6 May 1791	100
Hallet, Thomas, Pvt	5910	6 May 1791	100
Webster, Zepheniah, Pvt	6712	4 Jun 1793	100
Hill, Obadiah, Pvt	7299	7 Oct 1789	100
Woodbridge, Dudley	7554	11 Aug 1790	100
Cole, Henry	8115	22 Jun 1790	100
Mount, George, Cpl	8518	28 Oct 1791	100
Allen, Samuel, Pvt	8889	14 May 1793	100
Baker, Christian, Pvt	8917	14 May 1793	100
Bennet, James	9197	14 Apr 1793	100
Day, Moses, Pvt	9290	13 May 1793	100
Woodbridge, Dudley	9314	31 Aug 1790	100
Woodbridge, Dudley	9705	31 Aug 1790	100
Woodbridge, Dudley	9817	31 Aug 1790	100
McKimmens, John, Cpl	9879	10 Mar 1790	100
Woodbridge, Dudley	10051	31 Aug 1790	100
Woodbridge, Dudley	10455	31 Aug 1790	100
Loudon, Stephen	10557	6 Jul 1791	100
Finker, Joseph	10566	7 Jul 1792	100
Clingman, John	12104	12 Nov 1791	100
Clingman, John	12215	12 Nov 1791	100
Earnest, Christian, Pvt	13040	20 May 1793	100
Woodbridge, Dudley	13065	31 Aug 1790	100
Kenniston, John, Pvt	13310	25 Jan 1791	100
McCormack, James, Pvt	13399	16 May 1793	100
McCombs, John, Pvt	13494	24 Feb 1791	100
Lybert? [Sybert?] Adam, Pvt	13761	15 Nov 1791	100

165 11 Feb 1800 A/1/182

By Whom Registered: Martin Baum
For Whom Registered: Martin Baum
Location: (4000 acres) Mil - 6 5 - 3
Based upon the following Army land warrants:

Issued to	*No.*	*Date*	*Acres*
Gray, James	9618	26 Aug 1789	100
Mun, Isaac	8229	15 Sep 1790	100
Anderson, Michael, Pvt	12711	12 Apr 1796	100
Mitchell, Richard, Pvt	11520	11 Mar 1791	100

165 [continued]

Walker, John, Pvt	11791	1 Feb 1790	100
Smith, George	6020	29 Sep 1790	100
Smith, Thomas	11738	11 May 1790	100
Mitchell, Aaron, Pvt	11502	11 Mar 1791	100
Neal, Daniel, Pvt	11571	11 Mar 1791	100
Heaton, John	5720	2 Nov 1791	100
Mead, Shadwick	8048	24 Feb 1791	100
Brooks, Isaac	6455	6 Sep 1791	100
Brooks, Isaac	13961	6 Sep 1791	100
Sherrard, Francis	10961	14 Aug 1795	100
Baynton, Abel	4878	12 Oct 1790	100
Pettol? [Pettot?] Enas, Pvt	6313	18 Mar 1790	100
O'Reilly, Martin	7075	16 Nov 1791	100
Johnson, John, Pvt	4456	14 Jul 1796	100
Bissell, Moses	4847	7 May 1792	100
Gent, George, Pvt	4278	29 Jun 1789	100
Drake, Abraham	243	2 Aug 1797	200
Lavoix, Lewis, Pvt	13337	20 Aug 1789	100
Platt, Richard	9775	7 Aug 1789	100
Platt, Richard	13148	7 Aug 1789	100
Mooers, Benjamin	13340	22 Jan 1790	100
Merryman, Josiah, Cpl	6220	11 Jan 1790	100
Ward, Joshua	11807	11 Jan 1796	100
Westerdall, Francis, Pvt	12690	22 Jan 1799	100
Holbrook, Abijah	3539	13 Jan 1800	100
Holbrook, Abijah	3502	13 Jan 1800	100
Holbrook, Abijah	9484	13 Jan 1800	100
Holbrook, Abijah	4882	13 Jan 1800	100
Adams, John, Pvt	10938	11 Mar 1791	100
O'Neal? [Neal?] Ferdinand O., Capt	1617	7 Jul 1797	300
Taylor, Othniel, Capt	2144	4 Dec 1795	300

166 11 Feb 1800 A/1/183

By Whom Registered: Baum, --, & Schenck, --
For Whom Registered: Baum, --, & Schenck, --
Location: (4000 acres) Mil - 4 6 - 3
Based upon the following Army land warrants:

Issued to	*No.*	*Date*	*Acres*
Williams, Otho H., Esq., BrigGen	2401	12 May 1789	850
Evans, Elijah, Capt	673	25 May 1789	300
Rourk, James, Pvt	11634	11 May 1790	100
Moore, William, Pvt	11496	11 May 1790	100
Van Lear, William, Capt	2264	9 Jul 1789	300
Herbert, Stewart, Lt	1021	28 May 1789	200
Pendell? [Pindell?] Richard, Surgeon	1730	25 Sep 1789	400
Mitchell, William, Pvt	14063	11 Feb 1794	100
Evans, Thomas, Pvt	11176	1 Feb 1790	100
Bonham? [Bonharu?] Matakiah, Lt	24	28 May 1789	200
Gorden, John	11768	29 Nov 1790	100
Wilson, Barney	11850	29 Nov 1790	100
Smyth, James, Pvt	11746	11 Jan 1790	100
Smith, William	11736	29 Nov 1790	100
Smith, John	11707	29 Nov 1790	100
Moore, James	11506	29 Nov 1790	100
Jones, John	11375	29 Nov 1790	100
Clerk, Zachariah, Pvt	11102	11 Jun 1790	100
Winaham? [Windham?] George	10934	29 Nov 1790	100
Davis, Rezin, Capt	586	25 Sep 1789	300
Hart, William D.	594	18 Nov 1795	150

167 11 Feb 1800 A/1/184

By Whom Registered: Baum, --, & Shenck, --
For Whom Registered: Samuel B. Vance & Solomon Sibley
Location: (4000 acres) Mil - 8 1 - 1
Based upon the following Army land warrants:

Issued to	*No.*	*Date*	*Acres*
Casgrove, Thomas, Pvt	9145	13 Jul 1789	100
Rigby, Simon	9911	10 Mar 1795	100
Ripely, Mary	9494	17 Jun 1791	100
Witherby, William, Pvt	10667	25 Jun 1794	100
Feger, Conrad	13333	19 Apr 1792	100
Rigby, Simon	10190	31 Mar 1795	100
Rigby, Simon	10026	31 Mar 1795	100
Campbell, William, Pvt	9195	2 Feb 1792	100
Stever, Michael	9479	26 May 1794	100
Schott, John P.	10106	28 Sep 1792	100
Power, Alexander	9986	12 May 1795	100
Hunter, Robert	9266	10 Mar 1795	100
Crawford, Alexander	10287	5 Jan 1792	100
Hubbard, Christian	8773	5 Mar 1793	100
Sheppard, Sarah	9287	29 Dec 1791	100
Merkle, Gideon	10185	25 Jun 1794	100
Merkle, Gideon	10242	12 Feb 1794	100
Dick, Jacob, Pvt	13010	9 Apr 1799	100
Bell, Abraham	13107	27 Apr 1799	100
Bell, Abraham	8502	10 Apr 1799	100
Bell, Abraham	8240	10 Apr 1799	100
Verner, Philip, Pvt	10535	9 Jul 1789	100
Thackston, James, LtCol	2225	15 Nov 1791	500
Savage, John, Capt	2032	18 Apr 1795	300
Cockle, John, Pvt	3986	20 Jun 1789	100
Boon, John, Pvt	9057	20 Jun 1789	100
Doyle, Thomas, Lt	563	7 Jul 1789	200
Cummins, Edward, Pvt	9093	20 Jun 1789	100
McKinney, John, Pvt	10113	2 Apr 1791	100
Forrest, Andrew, Capt	754	16 Mar 1790	300
Beaty, John, Pvt	8961	21 Jan 1793	100

168 11 Feb 1800 A/1/185

By Whom Registered: Samuel Dick
For Whom Registered: Samuel Dick
Location: (4000 acres) Mil - 10 6 - 1
Based upon the following Army land warrants:

Issued to	*No.*	*Date*	*Acres*
Cox, William, Capt	433	26 May 1790	300
Pelham, Charles, Maj	1735	3 Dec 1792	400
Davis, Comfort, Pvt	4100	24 Jul 1789	100
Knapp, Elijah, Pvt	6053	11 Nov 1791	100
Street, Titus	6112	2 Nov 1791	100
Munn, Justice, Pvt	6225	28 Jan 1790	100
Plant, Ethel, Pvt	6340	28 Jan 1790	100
Hobart, John Sloss, *et al*	6728	15 Sep 1790	100
Hobart, John Sloss, *et al*	6789	15 Sep 1790	100
Hobart, John Sloss, *et al*	6809	15 Sep 1790	100
Bracket, Cornelius, Pvt	6890	20 Aug 1790	100
Hobart, John Sloss, *et al*	7379	15 Sep 1790	100
Hobart, John Sloss, *et al*	7412	15 Sep 1790	100
Hobart, John Sloss, *et al*	7558	15 Sep 1790	100
Oliphant, William, Pvt	7573	20 Oct 1790	100
Hobart, John Sloss, *et al*	7585	15 Sep 1790	100
Hobart, John Sloss, *et al*	7605	15 Sep 1790	100
Veeder, F., & Alexander, Alex[ande]r	7629	4 Oct 1790	100
Hobart, John Sloss, *et al*	7672	15 Sep 1790	100
Hobart, John Sloss, *et al*	8055	15 Sep 1790	100
Morse, Philip, Pvt	8520	14 Jul 1796	100
Pruden, Adoniram, Pvt	8637	4 Oct 1790	100
Stevenson, William, Pvt	8721	28 Jul 1791	100
Waggoner, George, Sgt	8826	9 Dec 1789	100
Chilcott, Thomas, Sgt	9193	20 Jun 1789	100
Griffith, John, Pvt	9456	16 May 1791	100

168 [continued]

Issued to	No.	Date	Acres
Sinckle? [Finckle?] Jacob	10329	5 Nov 1791	100
Singleton? [Lingleton?] John, Pvt	10451	19 Mar 1793	100
Mooers, Benjamin	12923	22 Jan 1790	100
Geary, James	13221	19 Apr 1791	100
Mooers, Benjamin	13448	22 Jan 1790	100
Mooers, Benjamin	13467	22 Jan 1790	100
Mooers, Benjamin	13473	22 Jan 1790	100
Spencer, John, Pvt	13790	8 May 1793	100
Wright, John, Pvt	13929	4 Feb 1793	100

169 11 Feb 1800 A/1/186

By Whom Registered: Baum, --, & Schenck, --
For Whom Registered: John N. Cummings, John Burnet, George W. Burnet
Location: (4000 acres)* Mil - 12 2 - 4
Based upon the following Army land warrants:

Issued to	*No.*	*Date*	*Acres*
Reed, George, Pvt	8691	10 Feb 1795	100
Sears, Betsy	8725	17 Jul 1789	100
Wayne, John, Pvt	8830	25 Feb 1796	100
Beach, Stephen, Pvt	8001	19 May 1798	100
Mason, Andrew, Sgt	8512	7 Jul 1789	100
Wolfe, Henry, Pvt	8828	2 Jul 1789	100
Monty, Enfant, Pvt	13433	12 Oct 1790	100
Whitehead, Samuel, Pvt	8852	14 Apr 1792	100
Garlinghouse, Benj[ami]n, Pvt	8331	5 Jan 1792	100
Lasambert, Antoine, Pvt	13338	12 Oct 1790	100
Field, Joseph Coles	5932	3 Apr 1794	100
Libell, Guillaume, Pvt	13341	12 Oct 1790	100
Colly, William, Pvt	3021	15 Oct 1792	100
Fairweather, Samuel, Pvt	5757	20 Sep 1790	100
Boles, John	12977	21 Apr 1791	100
Boles, John	5817	21 Apr 1791	100
Little, Lewis	13944	25 Sep 1789	100
Dean, William, Pvt	9268	19 Apr 1791	100
Potter, Ephraim, Pvt	12483	7 Oct 1795	100
Curwain, Edward, Pvt	6933	1 Jun 1792	100
Johnston, James, Pvt	12271	8 May 1794	100
Peak, Jesse, Pvt	12458	8 May 1794	100
Kuntz, Christian	13278	7 Aug 1789	100
Maxwell, Anthony	5123	10 Oct 1791	100
Maxwell, Anthony	7259	10 Oct 1791	100
Lilley, Reuben	3628	26 Jul 1789	100
Webster, Cyprian, Junior	6133	2 Nov 1791	100
Parkerson, James, Pvt	12461	8 May 1794	100
Dodge, John, Pvt	3080	17 Jun 1793	100
Harris, Henry, Pvt	7303	19 Jun 1790	100
Tuttle, Jonathan	4802	2 Nov 1791	100
Tuttle, Jonathan	12843	2 Nov 1791	100
Smith, Thomas, Pvt	12529	8 May 1794	100
Hite, Julius, Pvt	12223	8 May 1794	100
Munson, Eneas, Junior	6553	24 Feb 1795	100
Munson, Eneas, Junior	6017	15 Dec 1795	100
Munson, Eneas, Junior	6733	15 Dec 1795	100
Means, Robert	11958	23 Jun 1795	100
Burns, Lawrence, Pvt	8950	5 Feb 1800	100
Spering, John, Pvt	10413	14 Aug 1792	100

*Marginal notation:

"Location made [as cited above]	4220
Warrants recd. [by] this State	4000
Ditto since recd. [not listed]	250
	4250"

[See also serial entry 264]

170 11 Feb 1800 A/1/188

By Whom Registered: John Brown
For Whom Registered: John Brown
Location: (4000 acres) Mil - 15 3 - 4
Based upon the following Army land warrants:

Issued to	*No.*	*Date*	*Acres*
Fowler, John	271	24 Jun 1794	200
Pasteurs, Thomas, Lt	1758	3 Mar 1791	200
Tatum, James, Ens	2226	10 Jan 1791	200
Wells, William	2339	14 Apr 1790	400
Thom, William L? [S?]	3025	11 Sep 1795	100
Thom, William L? [S?]	3275	11 Sep 1795	100
Beers, Peleg, Pvt	3698	20 Jun 1789	100
Sebor, James F.	3731	9 Sep 1790	100
Vredenburgh, William J.	5072	7 Sep 1789	100
Van Rensselaer, John	5821	6 Aug 1790	100
Wendell, John W.	6792	30 Jul 1790	100
Hart, Philip	6800	3 Oct 1791	100
Bush, Conradt, Pvt	6870	11 Jul 1791	100
Clark, David, Sgt	6917	28 Sep 1790	100
Countz, Adam, Pvt	6958	12 Oct 1791	100
Deymont, Hanjost, Pvt	7053	18 Nov 1790	100
Belknap, Abel	7063	17 Aug 1790	100
Fryer, Susannah	7140	2 Nov 1791	100
Waldron, Resolve	7550	24 Sep 1791	100
Hudson, Daniel, & Co.	7599	25 Sep 1790	100
Cumpston, Edward	7795	30 Jul 1790	100
Terwilliger, James, Pvt	7862	5 Dec 1791	100
Miller, Burnet	7866	9 Nov 1791	100
Thorp, Thomas, Pvt	7897	27 Oct 1791	100
Pope, John	8510	7 Oct 1789	100
Tharp, Benjamin, Pvt	8785	7 Jul 1789	100
Weston, William, Pvt	8858	30 Jul 1789	100
Stever, Daniel	9979	4 Mar 1794	100
Stever, Michael	10508	4 Mar 1794	100
Means, Robert	12032	14 Jul 1792	100
Means, Robert	12155	14 Jul 1792	100
Means, Robert	12437	14 Jul 1792	100
Devoe, Jeremiah, Pvt	13038	2 Jul 1790	100
Means, Robert	13968	2 Nov 1792	100

171 11 Feb 1800 A/1/189

By Whom Registered: John Brown
For Whom Registered: John Brown
Location: (4000 acres) Mil - 8 1 - 4
Based upon the following Army land warrants:

Issued to	*No.*	*Date*	*Acres*
Darragh, Daniel, Lt	579	21 May 1794	200
Lavering, Joseph, & Lavering, Benjamin	9807	9 Aug 1791	100
Cogan, Richard, Pvt	10733	2 Sep 1789	100
Ward, Joshua	11430	11 Jan 1796	100
Ward, Joshua	11615	11 Jan 1796	100
Richards, Paul, Pvt	11633	4 Jan 1796	100
McCrum, Michael, Pvt	13527	27 Mar 1793	100
Lowell, James, Lt	1308	18 May 1795	200
Craig, Samuel, Capt	411	4 Nov 1789	300
Mix, Peter, Pvt	6214	15 Dec 1789	100
Towbridge, Isaac	6263	26 Dec 1789	100
Mills, John, Pvt	7513	20 Aug 1790	100
Pope, John	8577	9 Sep 1790	100
Pope, John	8803	9 Sep 1790	100
Hiltsdorph? [Hillsdorph?] John, Pvt	9546	7 Jun 1790	100
Tootle, Ann	11708	1 Feb 1790	100
Hawkins, John H., Sgt	13198	2 Jul 1790	100
Ludeman, John, Pvt	13388	11 May 1790	100
Pile, George, Pvt	13598	16 Jul 1790	100
Roads, Joseph	13777	26 Aug 1790	100
McClellan, John, Capt	1420	25 Mar 1796	300
Thomas, Joseph	2908	7 Nov 1796	100
Thomas, Joseph	2909	7 Nov 1796	100

171 [continued]

Thomas, Joseph	4570	7 Nov 1796	100
Hart, Samuel, Lt	967	27 Jun 1789	200
Weed, Thadeus, Capt	2345	27 Jun 1789	300
Brown, William, Sgt	5432	8 Aug 1789	100
Hart, Samuel	5518	27 Jun 1789	100
Hart, Samuel	5952	27 Jun 1789	100
Kellog, Enoch, Pvt	6072	24 Mar 1790	100
Whitney, Ezekiel	6658	27 Jun 1789	100

172 11 Feb 1800 A/1/190

By Whom Registered: Joseph Higbee
For Whom Registered: Joseph Higbee
Location: (4000 acres) Mil - 16 5 - 1
Based upon the following Army land warrants:

Issued to	*No.*	*Date*	*Acres*
Bevier, Philip D., Capt	159	12 Oct 1790	300
Cochran, John, D?Gen	498	11 Aug 1790	850
Hardenbergh, John L., Lt	986	9 Apr 1791	200
Livingston, James, Col	1260	21 Apr 1791	500
Means, Robert	1771	17 May 1792	150
Tunnison, Garret, Surgeon	2193	1 Apr 1791	400
Lozier, Oliver, Pvt	7421	17 Jul 1790	100
Morrill, Isaac, Pvt	7440	9 Apr 1791	100
Morrill, John, Pvt	7445	9 Apr 1791	100
Miller, Elisha, Pvt	7462	20 Oct 1790	100
Davenport, Cornelius	7470	21 Apr 1791	100
Bostwick, Oliver	7561	21 Apr 1791	100
Maley, John	7565	14 Feb 1791	100
Haskin, William	7775	5 May 1791	100
Sunderland, John, Pvt	7842	13 Sep 1791	100
Scofield, Nathaniel, Pvt	7847	21 Apr 1791	100
Broadwell, Hezekiah	7919	21 Apr 1791	100
Rockefeller, Philip	7924	9 Dec 1791	100
Vanamburgh? [Vandenburgh?] Abraham, Pvt	7930	21 Apr 1791	100
Wetherick, George, Pvt	8022	5 Jan 1791	100
Wetherstine, John, Pvt	8026	5 Jan 1791	100
Berwick, William	12848	6 Oct 1794	100

173 11 Feb 1800 A/1/191

By Whom Registered: Joseph Higbee
For Whom Registered: Joseph Higbee
Location: (4000 acres) Mil - 14 4 - 4
Based upon the following Army land warrants:

Issued to	*No.*	*Date*	*Acres*
Bradford, Gamaliel, Col	89	3 Sep 1789	500
Dixon, Sankey? [Lankey?] Lt	567	10 Mar 1790	200
Jones, David	1302	17 Jun 1790	300
Turner, Marlborough	1660	23 Feb 1796	150
Stoy? [Hoy?] John, Lt	2020	10 Mar 1790	200
Webb, George, Capt	2294	22 Dec 1796	300
Fosdick, Joseph	2312	19 Jan 1796	200
Turner, Marlbry	2320	16 Feb 1799	150
Walker, Silas, Lt	2332	19 May 1797	200
Wyman, Simeon	3766	18 Aug 1797	100
Fosdick, Joseph	3789	20 Jan 1796	100
Fosdick, Joseph	3906	20 Jan 1796	100
Turner, Marlbry	4230	8 Apr 1797	100
Fosdick, Joseph	4897	19 Jan 1796	100
Fosdick, Joseph	5006	19 Jan 1796	100
Hathorn, John	6776	25 Jan 1791	100
Chew, Richard, Pvt	8175	26 May 1790	100
Garrison, Silas, Pvt	8335	7 Jul 1789	100
Bymer, George, Pvt	8930	26 Jan 1790	100
Bentley, John, Pvt	8951	10 Mar 1790	100
Blake, Edward, Sgt	8954	10 Mar 1790	100
McGilton? [McGillon?] William, Sgt	10009	10 Mar 1790	100
Neilson, Andrew	10154	7 Sep 1789	100
Rice, Michael, Pvt	10288	10 Mar 1790	100
Tool, Edward, Pvt	10522	10 Mar 1790	100
Leonard, James, Pvt	10809	2 Sep 1789	100
Bryan, Edward, Pvt	12849	7 Sep 1789	100

174 11 Feb 1800 A/1/192

By Whom Registered: Joseph Higbee
For Whom Registered: Joseph Higbee
Location: (4000 acres) Mil - 14 3 - 4
Based upon the following Army land warrants:

Issued to	*No.*	*Date*	*Acres*
Means, Robert	263	5 Feb 1794	300
Means, Robert	764	14 Jul 1792	300
Thom, William L.	1227	11 Sep 1795	450
Muhlenberg, Peter, BrigGen	1495	18 May 1789	850
Overlon, Thomas	2067	30 May 1797	300
Thom William L.	2130	11 Sep 1795	200
Means, Robert	2223	5 Jul 1794	200
Means, Robert	2271	29 May 1792	300
Brown, Austin, Pvt	5424	20 Jun 1795	100
Norton, Abraham, Pvt	6240	14 Jul 1789	100
Conroy, James, Pvt	9170	6 Apr 1790	100
Fagan, Catherine	9379	1 Mar 1792	100
Laveringhouse, Christian, Pvt	9830	13 Oct 1791	100
Richardson, Richard, Pvt	12524	24 Jun 1795	100
Hall, David, Pvt	13161	6 Sep 1792	100
McGlaughlin, Patrick, Pvt	13460	10 Mar 1790	100
Marks, Abisha, Pvt	13477	27 Aug 1792	100
Tomlinson, William, Cpl	13838	10 Mar 1790	100
Sullivan, Murtaugh	14029	21 Jan 1791	100

175 11 Feb 1800 A/1/193

By Whom Registered: Joseph Higbee
For Whom Registered: Joseph Higbee
Location: (4000 acres) Mil - 15 1 - 1
Based upon the following Army land warrants:

Issued to	*No.*	*Date*	*Acres*
Lee, Henry	58	9 Sep 1789	150
Foudey, Douw J., Ens	735	1 Jun 1792	150
Graham, Charles, Capt	827	12 Oct 1790	300
Gildersleeve, Finch, Lt	831	13 Sep 1791	200
Hicks, Benjamin, Capt	982	9 Jun 1791	300
Hallet, Jonathan, Capt	984	20 Oct 1790	300
Hallet, Jonah, Lt	1024	12 Oct 1790	200
Livingston, Abraham, Capt	1262	21 Apr 1791	300
Mott, Ebenezer, Lt	1392	9 Mar 1791	200
Snow, Chloe	1981	16 Apr 1791	200
Wood? [Word?] Daniel, Capt	2373	28 Apr 1791	300
Bogaart, Isaac, Lt	2577	12 Jan 1791	200
Ball, John, Lt	2613	2 Aug 1793	200
Bartholomew, John, Pvt	6771	11 Jul 1791	100
Thompson, William	6774	24 Aug 1791	100
Tremper, Henry	6782	11 Oct 1790	100
Beaver, Edward, Pvt	6884	5 Oct 1790	100
Casey, Robert, Pvt	6957	29 Mar 1792	100
Clark, George, Pvt	7007	21 Apr 1791	100
Davis, Chapman, Pvt	7036	25 May 1791	100
Hathorn, John	7369	21 Feb 1792	100
Kyser, Hendrick	7375	21 Apr 1791	100
Fowler, Theodosius, & Co.	7381	7 Apr 1791	100

176 11 Feb 1800 A/1/194

By Whom Registered: Joseph Higbee
For Whom Registered: Joseph Higbee
Location: (4000 acres) Mil - 5 5 - 1
Based upon the following Army land warrants:

Issued to	*No.*	*Date*	*Acres*
Brown, Joseph	118	24 Feb 1796	200
Bussey, Elijah	125	22 Jan 1799	200
Turner, Ma[r]lborough	129	23 Feb 1796	200
Henley, Samuel, Capt	911	16 Oct 1789	300
Hastings, Joseph, Capt	919	6 Aug 1792	300
Turner, Ma[r]lborough	1375	23 Feb 1796	300
Parker, Benjamin, Lt	1646	9 Jun 1790	200
Turner, Ma[r]lborough	2163	23 Feb 1796	400
Russell, William, Pvt	3445	28 Apr 1794	100
Fitch, Elnathan	3526	14 Jan 1799	100
Thom, Christopher L.	3622	18 Apr 1798	100
Peck, John	3675	22 Feb 1792	100
Brown, Joseph	3773	23 Feb 1796	100
Stow, Edward, Junior	3884	2 Jun 1795	100
Brewer, George, Junior	3981	28 Jul 1795	100
Goff, James, Sgt	4212	23 Feb 1796	100
Pond, John	4225	16 Feb 1799	100
Brown, Joseph	4324	23 Feb 1796	100
Brown, Joseph	4477	23 Feb 1796	100
Brown, Joseph	4517	23 Feb 1796	100
Brown, Joseph	4573	23 Feb 1796	100
Packard, Nehemiah, Pvt	4851	23 Feb 1796	100
Brown, Joseph	4970	23 Feb 1796	100
Jenks, Jonathan	4986	13 Sep 1792	100
Turner, Ma[r]lborough	4988	23 Feb 1796	100
Brewer, George, Junior	4996	28 Jul 1795	100
Stowe? [Howe?] Edward	5293	13 Aug 1795	100

177 11 Feb 1800 A/1/196

By Whom Registered: Joseph Higbee
For Whom Registered: Joseph Higbee
Location: (4000 acres) Mil - 17 4 - 3
Based upon the following Army land warrants:

Issued to	*No.*	*Date*	*Acres*
Crocker, Joseph	45	27 Oct 1789	300
Forbes, Lucy	91	7 Apr 1798	500
Benjamin, Samuel, Lt	112	4 Apr 1796	200
Kleckner, Catherine	429	6 Jun 1795	150
Crocker, Allen	515	10 Jan 1797	400
Duponceau, Peter L., Capt	638	21 Jan 1794	300
Richardson, Abijah, Surgeon	1781	4 Mar 1794	400
Whiting, Daniel, LtCol	2290	7 Sep 1789	450
Kesster, John	2679	27 Feb 1797	200
Wyman, Simeon	3790	18 Aug 1797	100
Fosdick, Joseph	5177	21 Jul 1798	100
Appleton, Nath[anie]l W.	5186	17 May 1792	100
Wyman, Simeon	5234	18 Aug 1797	100
Woods, John	5286	19 May 1797	100
Thornton, Thomas G.	5891	7 Mar 1798	100
Adam, Henry	7184	5 Nov 1791	100
Ellis, Levy	7234	25 Jan 1791	100
McConnally, Hugh, Pvt	7483	9 Apr 1791	100
Gould, Thomas	10901	8 Aug 1797	100
Jarrett, Elisha	11088	22 Dec 1798	100

178 11 Feb 1800 A/1/195

By Whom Registered: William Martin
For Whom Registered: John Bray
Location: (4000 acres) Mil - 9 2 - 4
Based upon the following Army land warrants:

Issued to	*No.*	*Date*	*Acres*
Bentley, William, Capt	266	12 ? 1794	300
Mason, Jeremiah	701	18 Apr 1796	300
Lyman, Elihu, Lt	1246	10 Feb 1792	200
Mason, Jere[miah]	4472	18 Apr 1796	100
Jack, John	4875	3 Apr 1797	100
Job, John, Pvt	8450	17 Apr 1794	100
Power, Alexander	8988	27 Nov 1794	100
Graves, Francis	11937	14 Jul 1792	100
Graves, Francis	11938	14 Jul 1792	100
Means, Robert	12408	14 Jul 1792	100
Means, Robert	12243	14 Jul 1792	100
Stockdale, John	12562	31 Jan 1794	100
Jones, Catherine	12805	12 Mar 1792	100
Kelly, David, Pvt	13287	12 Jul 1792	100
Stout, Philip	13738	7 Jun 1793	100
Jack, John	1356	3 Apr 1797	300
Jack, John	2304	3 Apr 1797	200
Barker, Jonas	4004	18 Apr 1796	100
Jack, John	4617	3 Apr 1797	100
Mason, Jeremiah	4735	18 Apr 1796	100
Jack, John	4945	3 Apr 1797	100
Jack, John	4849	3 Apr 1797	100
Hyde, William	5143	19 Nov 1792	100
Power, Aaron, Pvt	6350	19 Mar 1792	100
Wood, Jacob, Pvt	6611	19 Mar 1792	100
Cumming, William	7004	20 Aug 1790	100
Caldwell, James	7758	15 Sep 1790	100
Caldwell, James	7819	15 Sep 1790	100
McCleland, John	8890	22 Aug 1791	100
Kalley, Eleanor	11333	28 Dec 1791	100
Means, Robert	12384	14 Jul 1792	100
Teague, John, Pvt	12632	7 Oct 1795	100

[See also serial entry 274]

179 11 Feb 1800 A/1/197

By Whom Registered: William Martin
For Whom Registered: John Bray
Location: (4000 acres) Mil - 7 3 - 3
Based upon the following Army land warrants:

Issued to	*No.*	*Date*	*Acres*
King, Daniel	711	12 Dec 1792	150
Reed, John, Lt	1814	21 Apr 1790	200
Lupp, Mary, *et al*	2273	16 Dec 1799	450
Arraby, Jack, Pvt	5381	24 Sep 1789	100
Bebee, Joel, Pvt	5482	26 Oct 1789	100
Caldwell, James	6942	15 Sep 1790	100
Griswold, J., & Starkey, T? [F?]	7806	21 Apr 1791	100
Crawford, John	8074	7 Jul 1790	100
Bagley, Asher, Pvt	8140	5 Apr 1793	100
Crawford, John	8534	7 Jul 1790	100
McDonald, Benjamin, Pvt	8593	20 Feb 1790	100
Holmes, John	8782	6 Jan 1792	100
Young, David, Pvt	8880	5 Jan 1791	100
Gordon, Daniel	9453	19 Apr 1791	100
Power, Alexander	9699	3 Dec 1792	100
Slauch, Bernard	10478	29 Mar 1792	100
Young, Joseph, Pvt	10683	28 Dec 1793	100
Oram, Robert, Sgt	10856	2 Sep 1789	100
Ryan, John, Pvt	10870	2 Sep 1789	100
Crommy, Andrew, Pvt	11107	3 Mar 1792	100
Fields, George, Pvt	11216	3 Feb 1792	100
Marbury, William	11262	14 Jul 1795	100
Marbury, William	11556	14 Jul 1795	100
Wooseley, Thomas, Pvt	12267	8 May 1794	100
Martin, John, Pvt	1239	8 May 1794	100
Payne, Richard, Pvt	12460	8 May 1794	100
Plunket, John, Pvt	12463	8 May 1794	100
Wilkinson, David, Pvt	12663	8 May 1794	100
Whaley, John, Pvt	12664	8 May 1794	100
Williams, William, Pvt	12666	8 May 1794	100

179 [continued]

	No.	Date	Acres
Fancour, John, Pvt	13063	20 Jun 1789	100
Johnson, Samuel, Pvt	13249	28 Mar 1797	100
McAuley, Daniel, Pvt	13466	8 May 1794	100
Mansfield, Daniel, Pvt	13512	17 May 1790	100
Dobbs, Nathaniel, Pvt	14132	7 Aug 1795	100

180 11 Feb 1800 A/1/198

By Whom Registered: John Matthews
For Whom Registered: John Matthews
Location: (4000 acres) Mil - 14 7 - 3
Based upon the following Army land warrants:

Issued to	*No.*	*Date*	*Acres*
Swan, Timothy, Pvt	10465	28 Dec 1793	100
March, Charles, Pvt	13463	29 Mar 1796	100
Farmer, Lewis, LtCol	751	30 Jul 1789	450
Simonds, Jonas, Capt	2026	19 Aug 1789	300
Pugh, Catherine	1718	19 Aug 1789	200
Coltman, Robert, Capt	425	31 Mar 1796	300
Pearson, Anthony	1703	2 Jul 1795	300
Angell, Israel	3220	28 May 1792	100
Angell, Israel	3117	28 May 1792	100
Angell, Israel	12752	28 May 1792	100
Angell, Israel	2962	28 May 1792	100
Angell, Israel	3535	28 May 1792	100
Angell, Israel	3411	28 May 1792	100
Angell, Israel	3230	28 May 1792	100
Hutton, Andrew	10869	2 Sep 1789	100
Eyster, Peter	10064	18 Jan 1800	100
Eyster, Peter	10470	18 Jan 1800	100
Anderson, Richard, Capt	51	11 Jun 1790	300
Crawford, Andrew, Pvt	9196	6 Jun 1792	100
Wuibert? Anthony Felix, LtCol	2461	5 Nov 1789	450
Fullerton, Richard, Lt	747	19 Aug 1789	200
Thom, Christopher L.	13228	18 Apr 1798	100
Bell, Abraham	8416	11 Feb 1800	100

181 11 Feb 1800 A/1/199

By Whom Registered: Baum, --, & Schenck, --
For Whom Registered: Baum, --, & Schenck, --
Location: (4000 acres) Mil - 12 1 - 4
Based upon the following Army land warrants:

Issued to	*No.*	*Date*	*Acres*
Bauman, Sebastian, Maj	168	2 Jul 1790	400
Baldwin, Cornelius, Surgeon	255	25 Aug 1789	400
Waggener, Andrew, Maj	2424	25 Aug 1789	400
Gano, John	387	20 Jul 1790	850
Montfort, Joseph, Capt	1531	6 Aug 1789	300
Platt, John, Lt	1727	30 May 1789	200
Smith, James, Lt	2027	9 Sep 1790	200
McAllister, Richard	2637	14 Mar 1794	200
Thom, Stephen	1918	6 Dec 1791	150
Benedict, George, Pvt	9056	9 Jul 1789	100
Welch, Andrew, Pvt	14084	4 Aug 1794	100
Washunks, Abel, Pvt	6620	13 Jan 1792	100
Beckwith, Timothy, Pvt	5458	15 Nov 1791	100
Rathbon, Asa, Pvt	6402	13 Jan 1792	100
Miller, Edward, Pvt	6191	15 Nov 1791	100
Watson, Seip? [Leip?] Pvt	6657	15 Nov 1791	100
Taylor, Monathan, Pvt	6546	15 Nov 1791	100
Cook, William, Pvt	5578	15 Nov 1791	100

182 11 Feb 1800 A/1/200

By Whom Registered: Baum, --, & Schenck, --
For Whom Registered: Baum, --, & Schenck, --
Location: (4000 acres) Mil - 4 1 - 3
Based upon the following Army land warrants:

Issued to	*No.*	*Date*	*Acres*
Campfield, Jabez, Surgeon	401	3 Sep 1790	400
Barnet, Isaac Cox	177	7 Sep 1789	400
Colfax, William, Capt	378	9 Dec 1796	300
Ward, Bernard, Capt	2481	28 May 1789	300
Morand, Charles, Pvt	13453	12 Oct 1790	100
Kennedy, Dennis, Pvt	9737	20 Jun 1789	100
McFoutcheon, George, Pvt	4668	21 Dec 1790	100
Demmon, John, Pvt	13025	20 Jun 1789	100
Ray, Joseph, Pvt	4894	16 Dec 1791	100
Stevens, Thomas, Pvt	5000	9 Jun 1791	100
Hill, Ichabod, Pvt	4359	5 May 1794	100
Ballard, Bruster, Pvt	3720	26 Oct 1789	100
Provandie, Louis, Pvt	4886	12 Jul 1797	100
Gay, John, Pvt	4246	24 Jul 1792	100
Root, Eleazer, Pvt	4898	21 Nov 1791	100
Hubbard, Abner, Pvt	5927	31 Oct 1791	100
Heath, John, Cpl	13223	7 May 1790	100
McCulloch, Robert, Pvt	6223	31 May 1793	100
Guard, Daniel, Pvt	8340	27 Jan 1797	100
Tamerlane, Thomas, Pvt	12631	25 Aug 1796	100
Lorgain, Francis, Pvt	12336	30 Aug 1796	100
Louis, Samuel, Pvt	6081	31 Oct 1791	100
Ward, Joshua	11147	11 Jan 1796	100
Ward, Joshua	11758	11 Jan 1796	100
Ward, Joshua	11410	11 Jan 1796	100
Iserloan, Casper	9751	11 Jun 1793	100
Iserloan, Casper	13302	11 Jun 1793	100
Hamtramck, John F., Capt	983	4 Aug 1791	300

183 11 Feb 1800 A/1/201

By Whom Registered: Baum, --, & Schenck, --
For Whom Registered: Baum, --, & Schenck, --
Location: (4000 acres) Mil - 5 5 - 4
Based upon the following Army land warrants:

Issued to	*No.*	*Date*	*Acres*
Bell, Abraham	10639	22 Jul 1799	100
Bell, Abraham	10436	19 Sep 1799	100
Bell, Abraham	13191	19 Sep 1799	100
Bell, Abraham	8731	18 Sep 1799	100
Bell, Abraham	9634	19 Sep 1799	100
Bell, Abraham	8688	17 Jul 1797	100
Bell, Abraham	8077	17 Jul 1797	100
Bell, Abraham	10646	9 Jul 1799	100
Bell, Abraham	13452	22 Jul 1799	100
Bell, Abraham	13672	19 Sep 1799	100
Haskell, Benjamin	4167	8 May 1792	100
Nichols, Margaret	8853	25 Feb 1796	100
Broome, Samuel	7987	11 Nov 1791	100
Ogden, Edmund	7108	1 Apr 1792	100
Stow? [How?] Abner	5159	13 Feb 1795	100
Waldron, Resolve	4490	19 Jan 1792	100
Stout, George	8752	21 Feb 1793	100
Bonney, James	8809	26 Jan 1790	100
Dumond, John B.	7991	20 Jul 1790	100
Reiley, Luke	11857	11 Jun 1793	100
Godfrey, John	10024	15 Oct 1791	100
Mifflin, Benjamin	12350	31 Dec 1791	100
Farnham? Ebenezer	8130	18 Oct 1791	100
Means, Robert	12673	14 Jul 1792	100
Lane, William	4449	26 Sep 1791	100
Cumming, John Noble	8660	15 Jun 1795	100
Cumming, John Noble	8854	15 Jun 1795	100
Thompson, William	4658	30 Aug 1792	100
Thompson, William	3801	8 Oct 1792	100
McCleland, John	10192	26 Sep 1791	100

183 [continued]

McCleland, John	9078	2 Apr 1792	100
McCleland, John	12957	26 Sep 1791	100
Iserloan, Casper	13641	11 Jun 1793	100
Iserloan, Casper	9004	29 Aug 1793	100
Iserloan, Casper	9370	29 Aug 1793	100
Iserloan, Casper	9743	14 Aug 1793	100
Iserloan, Casper	10226	14 Aug 1793	100
Iserloan, Casper	9213	14 Aug 1793	100
Iserloan, Casper	9102	14 Aug 1793	100
Iserloan, Casper	13870	3 Aug 1793	100

184 11 Feb 1800 A/1/202

By Whom Registered: William Martin
For Whom Registered: John Bray
Location: (4000 acres) Mil - 14 2 - 2
Based upon the following Army land warrants:

Issued to	*No.*	*Date*	*Acres*
Brownson, Gideon, Maj	72	14 Feb 1793	400
Sawyer, Ephraim, Capt	1930	5 Jul 1797	300
Levensworth, David	2277	29 Jun 1790	500
Washburn, Azel, Surgeon	2279	5 Mar 1798	400
Dubois, Lewis, Col	2643	6 Jun 1794	500
Smith, John	3547	13 Apr 1796	100
Bissell, Moses	3953	17 May 1792	100
Hagaman, John	5082	2 Jul 1793	100
Griggs, Jacob	5383	4 Oct 1796	100
Abbey, Jeduthen, *et al*	5391	9 Feb 1797	100
Bissell, Moses	5819	17 May 1792	100
Cornwell, Thomas P.	5909	3 Mar 1795	100
Fitch, Samuel	5942	3 Mar 1797	100
Prichard, Benjamin, Pvt	6280	17 May 1790	100
Wardwell, Samuel, Pvt	6679	9 Apr 1791	100
Roberts, Joseph	6742	23 Aug 1796	100
Roberts, Joseph	6790	23 Aug 1796	100
Roberts, Joseph	6954	23 Aug 1796	100
Clark, James, Pvt	8178	18 Jul 1789	100
Polston, Robert, Pvt	10194	21 Dec 1790	100
George, Edward, Pvt	12175	15 Oct 1795	100
Means, Robert	13536	15 Nov 1791	100
Noble, Gideon, Pvt	13553	23 Aug 1796	100
Ferrall, Zepheniah, Pvt	14130	13 Oct 1795	100

185 11 Feb 1800 A/1/203

By Whom Registered: William Martin
For Whom Registered: Robinson Thomas
Location: (4000 acres) Mil - 12 3 - 2
Based upon the following Army land warrants:

Issued to	*No.*	*Date*	*Acres*
Forman, Jonathan, LtCol	739	11 Jun 1789	450
Rhea, Jonathan, Lt	1816	11 Jun 1789	200
Stewart, Charles, Ens	2677	1 Mar 1797	150
Courtney, Luke, Pvt	8209	11 Aug 1789	100
Bond, Lewis	8225	16 Oct 1789	100
Linn, John	8256	7 May 1790	100
Eccles, John, Drummer	8288	25 Feb 1790	100
Whitehead, David	8291	4 Sep 1789	100
Smith, Israel	8318	2 Jul 1790	100
Halfpenny, Thomas, Pvt	8338	31 Oct 1789	100
McDonald, John, Pvt	8521	7 Dec 1789	100
Morgan, Charles, Pvt	8538	30 Mar 1790	100
Morrison, James, Pvt	8549	20 Jun 1789	100
Moorehouse, Jacob, Pvt	8575	4 Aug 1791	100
Bray, John	8652	16 Jul 1789	100
Parker, Garshorn, Pvt	8662	11 Sep 1789	100
Ryan, Patrick, Pvt	8698	7 Dec 1789	100
Leighton, John	8727	7 Oct 1790	100
Smith, Israel	8819	2 Jul 1790	100
Williams, John, Pvt	8829	23 Sep 1789	100
Wooley, Jacob, Pvt	8839	25 Sep 1789	100
White, Thomas, Pvt	8845	20 Jun 1789	100
Walker, William, Pvt	8856	12 Sep 1789	100
Whitehead, David	8861	4 Sep 1789	100
Tallmadge, Benjamin	13578	14 May 1790	100
Power, Alexander	2387	19 Aug 1791	200
Wainwright, Francis, Surgeon's Mate	2534	1 Oct 1789	300
Neal, James A.	2994	26 Jan 1796	100
Neal, James A.	3009	26 Jan 1796	100
Neal, James A.	3288	26 Jan 1796	100
Neal, James A.	3568	26 Jan 1796	100
Sherman, Edmond, Pvt	7851	4 Nov 1791	100

186 11 Feb 1800 A/1/204

By Whom Registered: William Martin
For Whom Registered: John Bray
Location: (4000 acres) Mil - 15 1 - 4
Based upon the following Army land warrants:

Issued to	*No.*	*Date*	*Acres*
Alexander, Nathaniel, Capt	23	31 Jan 1794	300
Brevitt, John, Lt	241	16 Oct 1789	200
McConnell, Matthew	259	28 Oct 1789	300
Satterlee, Nathaniel	367	6 Jun 1797	400
Satterlee, Nathaniel	368	6 Jun 1797	400
Frink? [Trink?] Samuel, Ens	712	6 May 1789	150
Lyman, Cornelius, Ens	1238	2 Dec 1789	150
McHenry, Charles, Capt	1460	9 May 1791	300
Wyllys, John Palsgrave, Maj	2336	27 Jul 1789	400
Clarke, Beriah, Pvt	3034	1 Jun 1792	100
Foote, Joseph, Junior, Pvt	4134	28 Mar 1797	100
Feith, John, Pvt	4156	11 Feb 1791	100
Gardner, Thomas, Sgt	4271	24 May 1790	100
Warriner, Aaron, Pvt	4348	24 May 1790	100
Lilly, Reuben, Pvt	4354	20 Jul 1789	100
Smith, Henry, Pvt	5096	18 Jul 1791	100
Bissell, Moses	5521	17 May 1792	100
Neal, James A.	6010	25 Aug 1796	100
Sandford? [Landford?] Benjamin	6019	3 Feb 1794	100
Marsh, Robert, Pvt	6196	6 Jun 1789	100
Russell, William, Pvt	6401	10 Jul 1789	100
Neal, James A.	6470	25 Aug 1796	100
Goodrich, Chauncy	6783	17 May 1796	100

187 11 Feb 1800 A/1/205

By Whom Registered: Thomas Biddle
For Whom Registered: Paul Bentalore? [Bentalon? Bentalow?]
Location: (4000 acres) Mil - 13 8 - 3
Based upon the following Army land warrants:

Issued to	*No.*	*Date*	*Acres*
Broadhead, Daniel, Col	187	15 Feb 1790	500
Bentalow, Paul, Capt	321	8 Jun 1789	300
Piercy, Henry, Lt	1707	7 Jan 1794	200
Philips, John	2394	19 Aug 1789	300
Decker, Jacob	2599	24 Dec 1791	300
Taylor, George, Pvt	5125	10 Aug 1793	100
Hamilton, Thomas, Pvt	8405	5 Nov 1791	100
Merckle, Gideon	9128	13 Dec 1791	100
Graham, John, Pvt	9449	28 Oct 1791	100
Lane, William	9614	20 Dec 1791	100
Merckle, Gideon	9731	13 Dec 1791	100

187 [continued]

Walton? [Wallon?] George	9878	20 Dec 1791	100
Madera, Samuel, Pvt	10240	14 Dec 1791	100
Adams, Bartholomew, Pvt	10693	2 Sep 1789	100
Lane, William	10698	28 Dec 1791	100
Hook, William, Pvt	10789	9 Jul 1799	100
Manship, Henry, Pvt	10847	2 Sep 1789	100
O'Neal? [Neal?] J. O., & O'Neal? [Neal?] E. O.	10858	9 Jul 1799	100
Phelps, Asahel	11136	13 Sep 1799	100
Eales, Emanuel, Pvt	11197	31 Dec 1791	100
Furrover, Edward, Pvt	11229	9 Jul 1799	100
Lane, William	11390	28 Dec 1791	100
Kerrick? [Kewick?] Benjamin H., Pvt	11429	25 Sep 1789	100
Phelps, Assahel	11563	13 Sep 1799	100
Phelps, Assahel	11588	13 Sep 1799	100
Phelps, Assahel	11648	13 Sep 1799	100
de Baufre, James	11679	17 Jun 1799	100
Stokes, Peter, *et al*	11747	9 Jul 1799	100
Lane, William	13318	28 Dec 1791	100

188 11 Feb 1800 A/1/206

By Whom Registered: Thomas Biddle
For Whom Registered: Thomas Biddle
Location: (4000 acres) Mil - 18 3 - 3
Based upon the following Army land warrants:

Issued to	*No.*	*Date*	*Acres*
Bernard, William R.	450	22 Feb 1799	300
Edminston, Samuel, Lt	674	23 Jan 1792	200
Watkins, J., & Bernard, W[illia]m R.	1069	22 Feb 1799	300
Kirkpatrick, David, Lt	1195	30 May 1789	200
Moore, William, Lt	1427	5 Feb 1794	200
Masson, Issacher	1494	8 May 1790	150
Manifold, Peter	1828	17 Jul 1794	200
Tilton, James, Surgeon	2238	30 May 1789	450
Duncan, Thomas, Pvt	7026	7 Jul 1790	100
Williams, Richard, Cpl	8053	19 Jun 1790	100
Hollingshead, John	8366	28 Dec 1789	100
Shepperd, Sarah	10263	9 Feb 1792	100
Shepperd, Sarah	10352	6 Jan 1798	100
Tilton, James	10768	2 Sep 1789	100
Means, Robert	11870	12 Apr 1792	100
Means, Robert	12037	7 Jul 1792	100
Means, Robert	12070	20 Jul 1792	100
Means, Robert	12071	20 Jul 1792	100
Means, Robert	12076	20 Jul 1792	100
Means, Robert	12091	20 Jul 1792	100
Means, Robert	12126	20 Jul 1792	100
Means, Robert	12206	20 Jul 1792	100
Means, Robert	12273	14 Jul 1792	100
Means, Robert	12294	7 Jul 1792	100
Means, Robert	12407	5 Jul 1794	100
Means, Robert	12636	14 Jul 1792	100
Means, Robert	12667	14 Jul 1792	100
Crowley, David, Pvt	12936	4 Sep 1789	100

189 11 Feb 1800 A/1/207

By Whom Registered: Abraham Mosser
For Whom Registered: Abraham Mosser & Thomas Boude
Location: (4000 acres) Mil - 2 10 - 1
Based upon the following Army land warrants:

Issued to	*No.*	*Date*	*Acres*
Miller, Nicholas, Pvt	13470	11 Mar 1791	100
Pole, Henry, Pvt	13592	12 Apr 1790	100
Fayrer, William, Pvt	13104	12 Dec 1797	100
Sloughter, Dedluff, Pvt	13734	28 Jun 1791	100
Waldman, Ludwick, Pvt	10609	1 Apr 1796	100
Hoofman, Christian	12743	2 Jun 1791	100
McLean, James, Pvt	9953	20 Jul 1799	100
Mullen, Patrick, Pvt	9891	2 Jul 1791	100
Desperitt, Henry, Pvt	9328	11 Mar 1791	100
Shroder, Godfried Israel, Sgt	13709	29 Jan 1790	100
Hausman, Mary	9575	31 Jan 1800	100
Burgess, William	9954	16 Dec 1794	100
Morris, John, Surgeon	1568	29 Jan 1790	400
Shellman, Ernest, Pvt	13708	25 Aug 1789	100
Boude, Thomas, Capt	200	24 Feb 1791	300
Boude, Thomas	2580	24 Feb 1791	200
Carbery, Henry, Capt	415	20 Dec 1791	300
Harrison, John, Sgt	13241	19 Mar 1790	100
Jackson, James, Pvt	9677	9 Jul 1789	100
Crawford, Samuel, Pvt	9097	29 Mar 1791	100
Ebert, Henry	13763	7 Jul 1789	100
Dillman, William, Pvt	9264	7 Oct 1791	100
McAlister, John, Pvt	10010	29 Mar 1791	100
Young, Jacob, Pvt	10682	6 Apr 1790	100
Thompson, John, Pvt	10495	9 Jul 1789	100
Grier, John, Pvt	9424	9 Jul 1789	100
Weavor* Jacob, Capt	2381	6 Jul 1791	300
Bevins, Wilder, Lt	204	28 Oct 1791	200
Cawhawk, James, Pvt	9151	30 Jan 1792	100

*So spelled.

190 11 Feb 1800 A/1/208

By Whom Registered: James Parker
For Whom Registered: James Parker
Location: (4000 acres) Mil - 14 5 - 4
Based upon the following Army land warrants:

Issued to	*No.*	*Date*	*Acres*
Bard, John, Capt	311	27 Jul 1795	300
Bard, John	1736	27 Jul 1795	300
Lush, Stephen	2188	10 Aug 1790	200
Wilson, Willis, Lt	2434	28 Jan 1800	200
Boyd? [Boyce?]* William, Lt	2485	3 Feb 1800	200
Breck, John, Pvt	5427	26 Apr 1793	100
Bartholomew, G., & Fisher, J.	6821	28 Sep 1790	100
Lansing, John, Junior	6858	6 Aug 1790	100
Hart, Henry	6863	4 Aug 1790	100
Close, John	6966	11 Aug 1790	100
Hart, Henry	7249	4 Aug 1790	100
Ten Eyck, Abraham	7389	6 Aug 1790	100
Close, John	7641	11 Aug 1790	100
Hart, Henry	7699	4 Aug 1790	100
Smith, Robert, Pvt	7818	10 Aug 1790	100
Conger, Enoch, Junior	8266	25 May 1797	100
Dunham, Nathaniel, Pvt	8274	16 Jul 1789	100
Holmes, William	8364	6 Jun 1797	100
Jones, William, Pvt	8440	30 Jul 1789	100
Perry, Thomas, Pvt	8644	27 Jan 1797	100
Swanley, Isaac, Pvt	8762	6 Jun 1797	100
Wooley, Isaac	8838	15 Sep 1789	100
Hubbert, Christian	10030	9 Apr 1796	100
Graves, Francis	11948	6 Jul 1793	100
Graves, Francis	11950	6 Jul 1793	100
Graves, Francis	11953	6 Jul 1793	100
Graves, Francis	11954	6 Jul 1793	100
Graves, Francis	12327	6 Jul 1793	100
Means, Robert	12436	18 Feb 1793	100
Weimer, Charles, Pvt	13894	29 Nov 1792	100
Graves, Francis	13975	6 Jul 1793	100
Graves, Francis	13990	31 Oct 1792	100
Barton, John, Pvt	14147	7 Mar 1798	100

*Originally entered Boyd; corrected to Boyce.

191 11 Feb 1800 A/1/209

By Whom Registered: James Williams
For Whom Registered: James Williams
Location: (4000 acres) Mil - 12 5 - 3
Based upon the following Army land warrants:

Issued to	*No.*	*Date*	*Acres*
Gassaway, Henry, Lt	859	28 Jul 1790	200
Pearl, James, Capt	1757	1 Jun 1792	300
Stewart, Philip, Lt	2081	16 Feb 1796	200
Whiting, Francis, Lt	2440	25 Aug 1789	200
Blackham, George, Pvt	10946	7 Feb 1790	100
Barton, Joseph, Pvt	10949	7 Feb 1790	100
Barret, Joshua, Sgt	10954	7 Feb 1790	100
Brannan, Laurence, Pvt	10981	28 Apr 1791	100
Berry, Edward, Pvt	11011	5 Sep 1789	100
Carter, William, Pvt	11027	7 Feb 1790	100
Clancy, Michael, Pvt	11048	7 Feb 1790	100
Callahan, Samuel, Pvt	11070	7 Feb 1790	100
Carrol, John, Pvt	11091	1 Feb 1790	100
Champlin, Hugh, Pvt	11114	16 Mar 1793	100
Donoho, Joseph, Pvt	11160	11 Mar 1791	100
Evans, John, Pvt	11194	1 Feb 1790	100
Ferrell, William, Pvt	11226	1 Feb 1790	100
Fisher, Henry, Pvt	11237	1 Feb 1790	100
Gregory, John, Pvt	11247	11 Jun 1790	100
Gainer, Hugh, Pvt	11274	7 Feb 1790	100
Holland, Edward, Pvt	11287	5 Sep 1789	100
Jones, Thomas, Pvt	11374	2 Jun 1794	100
Ireland, John, Pvt	11403	7 Feb 1790	100
Irons, John, Pvt	11407	11 Mar 1791	100
Kelson, George, Pvt	11427	1 Feb 1790	100
Moore, Matthew, Pvt	11489	7 Feb 1790	100
Maxwell, John, Pvt	11519	1 Feb 1790	100
Milstead, John, Pvt	11551	11 Mar 1791	100
Nicholson, Henry, Pvt	11561	7 Feb 1790	100
Purchase, William, Pvt	11595	7 Feb 1790	100
Pennifield, Thomas, Pvt	11600	11 Mar 1791	100
Perry, Thomas, Pvt	11612	11 Mar 1791	100
Prout, John, Pvt	11618	12 Dec 1792	100
Redding, Henry, Pvt	11652	7 Feb 1790	100
Sanders? [Landers?] George, Pvt	11688	7 Feb 1790	100

192 11 Feb 1800 A/1/211

By Whom Registered: James Williams
For Whom Registered: James Williams
Location: (4000 acres) Mil - 15 7 - 2
Based upon the following Army land warrants:

Issued to	*No.*	*Date*	*Acres*
Crawford, Jacob, Lt	440	7 May 1790	200
Fitzhugh, Peregrine, Capt	762	2 Jun 1796	300
Spurrier, Edward, Capt	2042	13 May 1795	300
Waters, Richard, Capt	2409	7 Jun 1790	300
Ahcarn? William, Pvt	10920	7 Feb 1790	100
Alby, John, Pvt	10933	1 Feb 1790	100
Askew, Peregrine, Pvt	10937	1 Feb 1790	100
Boody, John, Pvt	10986	1 Feb 1790	100
Connolly, William, Pvt	11123	1 Feb 1790	100
Cardiff, Thomas, Pvt	11125	7 Feb 1790	100
Downey, John, Pvt	11139	28 Apr 1791	100
Driskell, Jeremiah, Pvt	11142	1 Feb 1790	100
Ennis, Leonard, Pvt	11173	7 Feb 1790	100
Fairbrother, Francis, Pvt	11210	1 Feb 1790	100
Hader, Nehemiah, Pvt	11327	1 Feb 1790	100
Holt, Leonard, Pvt	11328	7 Feb 1790	100
Hawke, Michael, Pvt	11354	7 Feb 1790	100
Higgs, Henry, Pvt	11355	1 Feb 1790	100
Jones, Aaron, Pvt	11391	1 Feb 1790	100
Kelly, James, Pvt	11414	1 Feb 1790	100
Larymore, Thomas, Pvt	11449	1 Feb 1790	100
Marsh? Benjamin, Pvt	11474	1 Feb 1790	100
Murphy, Thomas, Pvt	11486	7 Feb 1790	100
Pearce, Joshua, Pvt	11594	7 Feb 1790	100
Rone? [Rowe?] Paul, Pvt	11645	7 Feb 1790	100
Smith, Elijah, Pvt	11684	7 Feb 1790	100
Shorter, Rodger, Pvt	11711	7 Feb 1790	100
Smallwood, John, Pvt	11713	1 Feb 1790	100
Sharpless, Robert, Pvt	11729	1 Feb 1790	100
Thompson, Jesse, Pvt	11779	1 Feb 1790	100
Wood, Thomas, Sgt	11800	1 Feb 1790	100
Wilson, John, Pvt	11830	1 Feb 1790	100
Mulloy, Martin, Pvt	13462	7 May 1790	100

193 11 Feb 1800 A/1/212

By Whom Registered: James Williams
For Whom Registered: James Williams
Location: (4000 acres) Mil - 13 6 - 2
Based upon the following Army land warrants:

Issued to	*No.*	*Date*	*Acres*
Watkins, Gassaway, Capt	2406	11 May 1790	300
Duvall, Benj[amin] *et al*	2672	11 Apr 1799	200
Lane, William	9099	26 Nov 1791	100
Walton, George	10553	20 Dec 1791	100
Bell, Abraham	10686	7 Jun 1799	100
Lane, William	10873	28 Dec 1791	100
Allen, James, Pvt	10928	7 Feb 1790	100
Tootle? Ann	10932	1 Feb 1790	100
Adams, John, Pvt	10935	9 Feb 1792	100
Tootle, Ann	10940	1 Feb 1790	100
Tootle, Ann	10992	1 Feb 1790	100
Carter, Luke, Pvt	11024	7 Feb 1790	100
Cook, William, Pvt	11055	7 Feb 1790	100
Peacock, Neal, Pvt	11601	7 Feb 1790	100
Farrare, Emanuel, Pvt	11233	7 Feb 1790	100
Harrison, Thomas, Pvt	11288	11 Mar 1791	100
Holland, Isaac, Pvt	11289	7 Feb 1790	100
Hicken, John, Pvt	11295	7 Feb 1790	100
Haslip, Richard B., Pvt	11296	11 Mar 1791	100
Holder, John, Pvt	11336	7 Feb 1790	100
Jackson, James, Pvt	11376	7 Feb 1790	100
Jones, Charles, Pvt	11388	1 Feb 1790	100
Johnson, Benedict, Pvt	11404	1 Feb 1790	100
King, John, Pvt	11423	28 Apr 1791	100
Leister, Joshua, Pvt	11436	5 Sep 1789	100
Lewis, Jonathan, Pvt	11443	7 Feb 1790	100
Mann, Daniel, Pvt	11503	11 Mar 1791	100
Tootle, Ann	11647	1 Feb 1790	100
Redmond, Michael, Pvt	11669	7 Feb 1790	100
Shovel, John, Pvt	11673	1 Feb 1790	100
Summers, Solomon, Pvt	11696	7 Feb 1790	100
Clark, Keziah	11761	5 Sep 1789	100
Tootle, Ann	11770	1 Feb 1790	100
Fernan, Dennis, Pvt	11781	1 Feb 1790	100
Wiley, John, Pvt	11798	7 Feb 1790	100
Felts? [Pelts?] Christopher, Pvt	13088	7 Feb 1790	100
Bell, Abraham	13288	17 Jun 1799	100

194 11 Feb 1800 A/1/213

By Whom Registered: James Williams
For Whom Registered: James Williams
Location: (4000 acres) Mil - 4 5 - 3
Based upon the following Army land warrants:

Issued to	*No.*	*Date*	*Acres*
Ball, Burges, Esq., LtCol	252	28 May 1789	500
Chapman, Henry H., Lt	444	11 Feb 1791	200

194 [continued]

Dyson, Thomas A., Lt	588	21 Sep 1789	200
Duvall? Benjamin, *et al*	590	11 Apr 1799	200
Gunby, John, Col	851	8 Sep 1789	500
Hamilton, Edward, Lt	1054	10 Mar 1790	200
Clark, Keziah	1059	5 Sep 1789	200
Kilty? [Killy?] William, Surgeon	1207	21 Dec 1792	400
Kilty? [Killy?] John, Capt	1212	21 Apr 1796	300
McPherson, Samuel, Capt	1481	16 Mar 1790	300
Mitchell, John, Capt	1484	25 Sep 1789	300
Marbury, Joseph, Capt	1486	10 Mar 1790	300
Somerville, James, Capt	2044	14 Feb 1797	300
Grant, William, Pvt	11286	11 Mar 1791	100

195 11 Feb 1800 A/1/214

By Whom Registered: Waddington, --, & Harwood, --
For Whom Registered: Galbreath, --, & Elmes, --
Location: (4000 acres) Mil - 12 1 - 2
Based upon the following Army land warrants:

Issued to	*No.*	*Date*	*Acres*
Woodson, Tucker M.	2426	9 Mar 1795	300
Bailey, Benjamin	3144	14 Mar 1793	100
Platt, Richard	7821	14 Jul 1790	100
Platt, Richard	8650	7 Aug 1789	100
Platt, Richard	8969	7 Aug 1789	100
Platt, Richard	8970	7 Aug 1789	100
Platt, Richard	9135	7 Aug 1789	100
Doyle, Morris, Pvt	9252	19 Feb 1790	100
Platt, Richard	9386	7 Aug 1789	100
Platt, Richard	9566	7 Aug 1789	100
Platt, Richard	9630	7 Aug 1789	100
Kincaid, Andrew, Pvt	9767	3 Mar 1790	100
McGee, Daniel, Pvt	10081	4 Jan 1789	100
McClelland, John	10156	10 Nov 1791	100
Vredenburgh, William J.	11917	5 May 1790	100
Vredenburgh, William J.	12017	5 May 1790	100
Vredenburgh, William J.	12120	5 May 1790	100
Vredenburgh, William J.	12137	5 May 1790	100
Vredenburgh, William J.	12220	5 May 1790	100
Vredenburgh, William J.	12262	5 May 1790	100
Vredenburgh, William J.	12359	5 May 1790	100
Vredenburgh, William J.	12380	5 May 1790	100
Vredenburgh, William J.	12431	5 May 1790	100
Vredenburgh, William J.	12677	5 May 1790	100
Mooers, Benjamin	12709	22 Jan 1790	100
Mooers, Benjamin	12718	22 Jan 1790	100
Fowler, Theodosius	12841	12 Dec 1789	100
Fowler, Theodosius	12874	12 Dec 1789	100
Mooers, Benjamin	12994	22 Jan 1790	100
Mooers, Benjamin	13336	22 Jan 1790	100
Hobart, John Sloss, *et al*	13370	15 Sep 1790	100
Long, Judith	13380	8 Nov 1791	100
Moore, Thomas, Pvt	13500	10 Mar 1790	100
Pappee, Robert, Cpl	13576	28 Oct 1789	100
Mooers, Benjamin	13610	22 Jan 1790	100
Mooers, Benjamin	13665	22 Jan 1790	100
Fourcout, Francis, Pvt	13826	4 Nov 1789	100
Wolfe, Christian, Pvt	13898	23 Sep 1789	100

196 11 Feb 1800 A/1/215

By Whom Registered: Waddington, --, & Harwood, --
For Whom Registered: Galbreath, --, & Elmes, --
Location: (4000 acres) Mil - 1 7 1 1
Based upon the following Army land warrants:

Issued to	*No.*	*Date*	*Acres*
Taliafero, Benjamin, Capt	2217	14 Nov 1794	300
Grout, Jonathan	3358	16 Feb 1795	100
Stow? [How?] Abner	4841	13 Feb 1795	100
Clark, Martin, Pvt	5463	24 Sep 1790	100
Davis, William	5774	16 May 1794	100
Sebor, James F.	5885	24 Sep 1790	100
Otis, Joseph, Pvt	6256	24 Sep 1790	100
Palmer, Jared, Pvt	6330	24 Sep 1790	100
Wild, Samuel	6480	2 Apr 1793	100
Sperry, Armey, Pvt	6487	24 Sep 1790	100
Thomas, John, Pvt	6571	24 Sep 1790	100
Woolcott, Elijah, Pvt	6693	24 Sep 1790	100
Fado? [Zado?]* Congo, Pvt	6721	24 Sep 1790	100
Akins, James, Pvt	6758	12 Jul 1792	100
Dutcher, Barnard, Pvt	7050	4 Oct 1792	100
Benedict, Timothy	7307	3 Apr 1794	100
Phelps, Israel, Pvt	7622	4 Nov 1791	100
Sebor, James F.	7654	27 Sep 1790	100
Smith, Melanchton	7952	29 Sep 1790	100
Phillips, Jonathan	8224	24 Apr 1792	100
Moore, Benjamin	12764	20 Feb 1792	100
Power, Alexander	10006	13 Jun 1792	100
Dupelle, Antoine, Pvt	13001	12 Oct 1790	100
Fulford, John, Sgt	13095	30 Oct 1789	100
Hubert, Paul, Pvt	13170	12 Oct 1790	100
Hall, Ceasar** Pvt	13231	12 Jul 1792	100
Izabel, Augustine	13254	12 Oct 1790	100
Jelly, Joseph, Pvt	13255	12 Oct 1790	100
Latourneau, Joseph, Pvt	13339	12 Oct 1790	100
Labbe, Joseph, Pvt	13360	12 Oct 1790	100
Lefrais, Peter, Pvt	13361	12 Oct 1790	100
La Croix, Michael, Pvt	13368	12 Oct 1790	100
Ludlow, Stephen, Pvt	13386	22 Jun 1791	100
St. Pierre, John, Pvt	13608	12 Oct 1790	100
Racine, Charles, Pvt	13654	12 Oct 1790	100
Ray, Joseph, Pvt	13666	12 Oct 1790	100
Faddor? [Saddor?]*** Stephen, Pvt	13750	12 Oct 1790	100
Perkins, John, Pvt	14042	19 Dec 1792	100

*Originally registered as Fado; pencilled notation corrects to Zado.

**So spelled.

***Originally registered as Faddor; pencilled correction to Saddor.

197 11 Feb 1800 A/1/217

By Whom Registered: Waddington, --, & Harwood, --
For Whom Registered: Galbreath, --, & Elmes, --
Location: (4000 acres) Mil - 10 2 - 2
Based upon the following Army land warrants:

Issued to	*No.*	*Date*	*Acres*
Ashton, John, Lt	49	24 Aug 1792	200
Bells? [Betts?] Stephen, Capt	139	18 May 1789	300
Day, Asa	326	14 Dec 1793	200
Hicks, Isaac, Capt	1113	12 Mar 1794	300
Lewis, Samuel, Lt	1263	9 Aug 1790	200
Legget, Abraham, Lt	1264	6 Sep 1791	200
Brinkerhoff, John G.	1980	7 Jul 1791	200
Vanderburgh, Henry, Capt	2250	4 Aug 1791	300
Taylor, Amos	2638	14 Mar 1794	200
Fall, Joshua, Pvt	3103	3 Dec 1794	100
Neal, James A.	3174	12 Oct 1795	100
Brooks, Nathan, Pvt	3660	12 Jan 1792	100
Eberhard, John, Pvt	5737	24 Sep 1790	100
Platt, Nathaniel	7377	16 Mar 1792	100
Addoms, Jonas	7481	19 Aug 1791	100
Birdsall, Samuel	7769	12 Dec 1791	100
Cromstock, Stephen	7911	24 Sep 1790	100
Holman, George, Pvt	8379	24 Aug 1793	100
Kirkpatrick, Francis	9098	11 Nov 1794	100

197 [continued]

Merkle, Barnard	10618	31 Oct 1795	100
Ellis, Thomas, Pvt	11183	22 Dec 1791	100
Atkins, Lewis, Pvt	11866	17 Nov 1794	100
Bragg, Benjamin, Pvt	11913	14 Nov 1794	100
Means, Robert	12192	6 Jul 1793	100
Stockdell, John	12503	30 Jan 1795	100
McLaughlin, Owen, Pvt	13439	25 Feb 1792	100
Shett, Lewis	13515	15 Jun 1792	100
Cato, John	14046	30 May 1793	100

198 11 Feb 1800 A/1/218

By Whom Registered: Waddington, --, & Harwood, --
For Whom Registered: Galbreath, --, & Elmes, --
Location: (4000 acres) Mil - 18 2 - 2
Based upon the following Army land warrants:

Issued to	*No.*	*Date*	*Acres*
Dole, James, Lt	542	1 Dec 1789	200
Fergus, James, Surgeon	769	1 Aug 1794	400
Jolly, Charles	1157	12 May 1796	300
Miller, Joseph, Lt	1363	31 Jul 1792	200
Seymour, Horace, Lt	1966	28 Apr 1795	200
Summers, John, Capt	2094	15 Nov 1791	300
Davis, Joseph	2949	31 Mar 1796	100
Davis, Joseph	3017	31 Mar 1796	100
Dewey, Noble	3736	3 Dec 1792	100
Hawes, Pelatiah, Pvt	4369	2 Apr 1792	100
Lee, Edward, Pvt	4567	21 Dec 1792	100
Woodstock, William, Cpl	5339	2 Jun 1790	100
Moorehouse, David, Pvt	6188	20 Sep 1790	100
Davis, Joseph	6267	31 Mar 1796	100
Thompson, Stephen, Pvt	6582	21 Feb 1792	100
Chappel, Elizabeth	6927	25 Sep 1790	100
Prindle, Enos Jones, Pvt	7655	1 Aug 1795	100
Roberts, John, Pvt	8681	22 Aug 1789	100
Stever, Michael	9552	17 Nov 1794	100
Slauch? [Hauch?] Barnard	9692	29 Mar 1792	100
McConnell, Matthew	9975	29 Jun 1789	100
Stever, Michael	10117	4 Nov 1794	100
Shrofe, Adam, Pvt	10444	22 Dec 1791	100
Ward, John, Pvt	10550	3 Feb 1796	100
Purdy, Henry	11575	6 Oct 1794	100
Cusack, Christopher	11596	8 Aug 1794	100
Cusack, Christopher	11771	8 Aug 1794	100
Birdsall, Daniel, & Birdsall, W[illia]m	12946	25 Sep 1790	100
King, Benjamin, Pvt	13291	6 Aug 1792	100
McDonald, Daniel, Pvt	13447	22 Oct 1792	100

199 11 Feb 1800 A/1/219

By Whom Registered: Waddington, --, & Harwood, --
For Whom Registered: Galbreath, --, & Elmes, --
Location: (4000 acres)* Mil - 17 3 - 1
Based upon the following Army land warrants:

Issued to	*No.*	*Date*	*Acres*
Bradley, Philip P., Col	131	14 May 1796	500
Lane, William	834	31 Aug 1792	300
Hull, William, LtCol	909	26 Oct 1789	450
Inskeep, John	1211	18 Jul 1791	200
Phelps, Seth, Capt	1674	5 Jul 1796	300
Haskell, Henry, LtCol	2634	7 Jun 1793	450
Jenks, Jonathan	3197	13 Sep 1792	100
Jenks, Jonathan	3248	13 Sep 1792	100
Beard, Moses	4469	29 Feb 1792	100
Haskell, Benjamin	4754	22 Jun 1792	100
Beard, Moses	5074	29 Feb 1792	100
Beard, Moses	5193	11 May 1792	100
Quinton, David	5252	1 May 1792	100
Stevenson, John	5595	27 Feb 1793	100
Peters, Jonathan, Pvt	6275	21 Aug 1789	100
Beers, Oliver	6878	29 Sep 1790	100
Afflick, Robert	7935	12 Mar 1792	100
Polhemus, John	8069	23 Feb 1791	100
Stout? [Hout?] Philip	9584	24 Jun 1793	100
Campbell, Thomas	10130	2 Mar 1792	100
Paulson, James	12759	11 Jun 1793	100
Fund, Nicholas, Pvt	13081	1 Mar 1792	100
Osborn, Edward	13187	24 Jun 1793	100
Seller? [Selter?] Conrad, Pvt	13759	6 May 1793	100

*Marginal notation: "See vol. 1, page 296, of Patents [Register?]"

200 11 Feb 1800 A/1/219

By Whom Registered: Waddington, --, & Harwood, --
For Whom Registered: Galbreath, --, & Elmes, --
Location: (4000 acres)* Mil - 17 6 - 1
Based upon the following Army land warrants:

Issued to	*No.*	*Date*	*Acres*
Wheeler, John, Pvt	9288	28 Jun 1793	100
Perret, Peter, Capt	1677	8 Jan 1790	300
Means, Robert, Pvt	11877	6 Jul 1793	100
Stout? [Hout?] Philip, Pvt	8995	24 Jun 1793	100
Hailey, John, & Hailey, Eleanor, Pvt	10876	14 Dec 1791	100
Stout? [Hout?] Elisha, Pvt	8707	16 Dec 1791	100
Wheeler, John, Pvt	9578	28 Jun 1793	100
Wheeler, John, Pvt	9293	28 Jun 1793	100
Molineux, Fred[eric]k, Pvt	11523	13 Dec 1792	100
Power, William, Pvt	11007	6 Sep 1792	100
White, James, Pvt	13965	4 Mar 1794	100
Hubbart, Christian, Pvt	10684	10 Jun 1793	100
Kettle, Daniel, Pvt	11426	19 Apr 1793	100
Kirkpatrick, Fran[ci]s, Pvt	10264	27 May 1793	100
Denton, Thomas, Pvt	9165	20 Feb 1794	100
Coon, Henry, Pvt	11590	21 Mar 1794	100
Coram, William, Pvt	12007	4 Mar 1794	100
Power, Alex[ande]r, Pvt	14031	1 Mar 1792	100
Brown, Joseph, Pvt	3794	1 Mar 1792	100
Broadhead, Luke, Capt	222	26 Mar 1793	300
Beal, William, Pvt	11946	14 Nov 1794	100
Rhea, James, Pvt	8295	16 Aug 1792	100
Epperson, Samuel, Pvt	12102	17 N-v 1794	100
Hyde, William, Lt	1579	19 Nov 1792	200
Prior, Abner, Surgeon's Mate	1685	28 Sep 1791	300
Stantford? [Hantford?] John, Capt	1997	22 Jul 1790	300
Hoover, John, Pvt	10361	13 Jan 1792	100
Power, Alex[ande]r, Pvt	9772	2 Mar 1792	100
Power, Alex[ande]r, Pvt	9813	2 Mar 1792	100
Kline, John, Pvt	12808	3 Mar 1794	100
Means, Robert, Pvt	12204	6 Jul 1793	100

*Marginal notation: "See vol. 1, page 300, of Patents [Register?]"

201 11 Feb 1800 A/1/221

By Whom Registered: Waddington, --, & Harwood, --
For Whom Registered: Galbreath, --, & Elmes, --
Location: (4000 acres)* Mil - 11 1 - 2
Based upon the following Army land warrants:

Issued to	*No.*	*Date*	*Acres*
Bruen, Jacobus, LtCol	157	15 Sep 1790	450

201 [continued]

Gansey, John	167	5 Jan 1792	150
Carpenter, Nehemiah, Ens	395	4 Jan 1791	150
Fondey, John, Ens	734	12 Oct 1790	150
Menema, Daniel, Surgeon	1398	6 Jul 1790	400
Gilliland, William, Surgeon	1582	5 Oct 1791	400
Pike, Benjamin, Capt	1640	11 Jun 1790	300
Thomas, Joseph, Capt	2162	26 Mar 1792	300
Tucker, Jonathan, Pvt	3527	4 Oct 1790	100
Tinney? [Finney?] Samuel	4316	8 Aug 1793	100
Emery, Samuel	5488	17 Jan 1793	100
Tuttle, Jonathan	8042	29 Mar 1792	100
Cathcart, Andrew	6169	13 Jan 1796	100
Breadon, John, Pvt	6787	15 Jun 1792	100
Van Benthuysen, Barent	6849	7 Mar 1792	100
Bishop, Levi, Pvt	6876	4 Jan 1791	100
Broome, Samuel	6968	11 Nov 1791	100
Broome, Samuel	6997	11 Nov 1791	100
Broome, Samuel	7177	11 Nov 1791	100
Maxwell, Anthony	7735	10 Oct 1791	100
Maxwell, Anthony	7741	10 Oct 1791	100
Hagaman, John	7755	13 Jun 1792	100
Shultz, Christopher, Pvt	7856	19 Apr 1792	100
Tapan, Daniel, Pvt	7870	23 Aug 1790	100
Kline, William	8065	12 Jun 1792	100

*Marginal notation: "See vol. 1, page 297, of Patents [Register?]"

202 11 Feb 1800 A/1/221

By Whom Registered: Waddington, --, & Harwood, --
For Whom Registered: Galbreath, --, & Elmes, --
Location: (4000 acres)* Mil - 13 4 - 1
Based upon the following Army land warrants:

Issued to	*No.*	*Date*	*Acres*
Moore, Ezekiel	146	9 Jun 1790	200
Blackwell, Joseph, Capt	265	26 Feb 1793	300
Mooers, Benjamin	886	21 Sep 1790	200
Mooers, Benjamin	1767	21 Sep 1790	300
Edis, Peter	2334	26 Sep 1791	200
Beard, Moses	3644	29 Feb 1792	100
Graves, Francis	14060	10 Feb 1794	100
Boughton, John, Pvt	5505	5 Apr 1792	100
Hawley, Abraham, Sgt	5940	15 Mar 1790	100
Root, Nicholas	6659	15 Sep 1790	100
Baldwin, Dan[ie]l, & Shay, P.	6901	18 Jul 1792	100
Knox, George	7338	3 Jan 1792	100
Thompson, John	7671	1 Oct 1791	100
Grace, John, Pvt	9486	27 Oct 1791	100
Hogg, Ebenezer	9603	17 Apr 1793	100
Merkle, Barnard	10008	31 Oct 1795	100
McCleland, John	10405	16 Mar 1793	100
Rowan, John, Sgt	10868	2 Sep 1789	100
Turner, James, Pvt	10888	2 Sep 1789	100
Ackerman, Francis, Pvt	12712	22 Sep 1791	100
Root, Nicholas	12835	15 Sep 1790	100
Moore, Benjamin	12884	20 Feb 1792	100
Moore, Benjamin	12987	20 Feb 1792	100
Camp, Casper	13182	30 Jul 1792	100
Moore, Benjamin	13345	14 Aug 1792	100
Moore, Benjamin	13450	14 Aug 1792	100
Moore, Benjamin	13451	20 Feb 1792	100
Moore, Benjamin	13735	20 Feb 1792	100
Moore, Benjamin	13825	20 Aug 1792	100
Moore, Benjamin	13857	20 Feb 1792	100
Graves, Francis	14024	31 Oct 1792	100
Quinton, David	927	1 May 1792	100

*Only 3900 acres in warrants are listed. It is probable that one of the 100-acre warrants should have been entered as a 200-acre warrant.

203 11 Feb 1800 A/1/223

By Whom Registered: Waddington, --, & Harwood, --
For Whom Registered: Galbreath, -- & Elmes, --
Location: (4000 acres) Mil - 18 4 - 4
Based upon the following Army land warrants:

Issued to	*No.*	*Date*	*Acres*
Moore, Benjamin	782	20 Feb 1792	200
Quinton, David	3699	1 May 1792	100
Quinton, David	3775	1 May 1792	100
Hodgkins, Joseph, Pvt	4426	16 Mar 1792	100
Emery, Samuel	4852	2 Jun 1795	100
Farrar, Peter	4973	1 May 1791	100
Emery, Samuel	5327	2 May 1795	100
Porter, Nathaniel, Pvt	6271	27 Jun 1796	100
Rice, Asa	7530	11 Oct 1790	100
Crosby, Sampson	7876	8 Aug 1793	100
Van Ranselear, Henry J.	7944	1 Aug 1791	100
McLure, Andrew, Pvt	8554	14 Jan 1791	100
Allen, John, Pvt	8913	19 Oct 1789	100
Biddle, John, Pvt	9011	12 Mar 1792	100
Hanlin, Patrick, Pvt	9585	17 Dec 1795	100
Harris, William, Pvt	9596	13 Dec 1791	100
McSwine, George, Pvt	9923	27 Jun 1791	100
Patridge, John, Pvt	10202	9 Jul 1789	100
Slaterback? [Haterback?] Michael, Pvt	10429	26 Feb 1791	100
Sharpe, Sarah	10447	25 Jan 1792	100
Keiner, Jasper	10560	31 Oct 1791	100
Backer? [Barker?]* William, Pvt	10695	2 Sep 1789	100
Cusack, Christopher	11776	8 Aug 1794	100
Means, Robert	11952	7 Jul 1792	100
Graves, Francis	12025	31 Jan 1794	100
Thomas, Abishai	12139	10 Jun 1791	100
Stockdale, John	12576	31 Jan 1794	100
Moore, Benjamin	12796	25 Feb 1793	100
Moore, Benjamin	12798	25 Feb 1793	100
Ten Eyck, Abraham	12821	6 Aug 1790	100
Moore, Benjamin	12878	14 Aug 1792	100
Moore, Benjamin	12924	25 Feb 1793	100
Moore, Benjamin	13083	14 Aug 1792	100
Moore, Benjamin	13131	14 Aug 1792	100
Moore, Benjamin	13251	20 Feb 1792	100
Lord, Jeremiah, Sgt	13385	18 Nov 1789	100
Osborne, Nathaniel, Sgt	13560	15 Mar 1790	100
Moore, Benjamin	13760	14 Aug 1792	100
Sherrard, Francis	14117	14 Apr 1795	100

*Originally regstered as Backer; pencilled correct to Barker.

204 11 Feb 1800 A/1/224

By Whom Registered: Waddington, --, & Harwood, --
For Whom Registered: Galbreath, --, & Elmes, --
Location: (4000 acres) Mil - 17 5 - 1
Based upon the following Army land warrants:

Issued to	*No.*	*Date*	*Acres*
Broome, Samuel	164	11 Nov 1791	200
Harman, Jaques, Ens	969	26 May 1790	150
Hyat[t] Abraham, Lt	988	5 May 1791	200
Vreedenburgh, William J.	991	16 Jul 1790	150
Lansing, Garrett, Ens	1265	22 Jan 1791	150
Lawrance, Jonathan, Lt	1269	2 Jun 1789	200
Morell, Joseph, Ens	1396	15 Sep 1790	150
Trotter, Mathew	2367	2 Aug 1791	200
Thompson, John	2597	28 Nov 1791	300

204 [continued]

Cook, William H.	2598	22 Dec 1791	300
Tewahangarahkaw, Hangere, Capt	2601	8 Mar 1792	300
Wakarantharaw, James, Capt	2602	8 Mar 1792	300
Otaawighton, John, Capt	2603	8 Mar 1792	300
Sogoharasie, John, Lt	2604	8 Mar 1792	200
Kahiktotow, Cornelius, Lt	2605	8 Mar 1792	200
Thaosagwat, Hamjoost, Lt	2606	8 Mar 1792	200
Jenks, Jonathan	4138	13 Sep 1792	100
Pepoon, Silas	4229	6 Jul 1791	100
Boardman, D., & Boardman, Elijah	5603	21 Mar 1791	100
Ransom, George P., Pvt	6366	8 Jul 1790	100
Bashman, Abraham	7633	13 Jun 1792	100

205 11 Feb 1800 A/1/225

By Whom Registered: David Lynn
For Whom Registered: David Lynn
Location: (4000 acres) Mil - 19 2 - 1
Based upon the following Army land warrants:

Issued to	*No.*	*Date*	*Acres*
Lingen, James M., Capt	1294	19 Mar 1792	300
Lamar, William, Capt	1293	11 Feb 1800	300
Smith, John, Capt	2045	26 Jan 1792	300
Blackwell, Thomas, Capt	2493	25 Feb 1793	300
Beatty, Thomas, Lt	246	27 May 1796	200
Nelson, Roger, Lt	1600	23 Dec 1799	200
Glesan? [Glisau?] Thomas, Pvt	11284	18 Dec 1799	100
Loyd, Michael	10997	29 Nov 1790	100
McManus, Thomas	11189	29 Nov 1790	100
Shaw, Bazil	11276	29 Nov 1790	100
Curren, James	11365	29 Nov 1790	100
Thorton, John	11460	29 Nov 1790	100
Moore, James	11581	29 Nov 1790	100
Hall, Frederick	11610	29 Nov 1790	100
Tanner? [Fanner?] John	11723	29 Nov 1790	100
Turner, John, Pvt	11765	11 Jun 1790	100
Bailey, John, Pvt	10979	11 Jun 1790	100
Legg, Edward, Pvt	11469	11 Jun 1790	100
Dixon, William, Pvt	11167	11 Jun 1790	100
Rawdon, Daniel, Pvt	11665	11 Jun 1790	100
Boss, Christian, Pvt	11013	11 Jun 1790	100
Gordon, John, Pvt	11266	11 Jun 1790	100
Conden, Thomas, Pvt	11112	1 Feb 1790	100
Newton, William, Pvt	11559	11 Jun 1790	100
Fowler, Joseph, Pvt	11205	1 Feb 1790	100
McManus, Thomas	11099	29 Nov 1790	100
Blair, John	11531	29 Nov 1790	100
Smith, William, Pvt	13753	11 Jun 1790	100
Boswell, Samuel, Pvt	10959	1 Feb 1790	100
Hall, Frederick	11611	29 Nov 1790	100

206 13 Feb 1800 A/1/226

By Whom Registered: William Steele
For Whom Registered: William Steele
Location: (4000 acres) Mil - 18 3 - 1
Based upon the following Army land warrants:

Issued to	*No.*	*Date*	*Acres*
Platt, Nathaniel	7221	16 Mar 1792	100
Purdy, Henry	11063	6 Oct 1794	100
Bedkin, Elizabeth	319	10 Oct 1789	300
Mifflin, Benjamin	12527	31 Dec 1791	100
Gibson, James, Capt	2552	2 Apr 1791	300
Hubbell, John, Pvt	8380	29 Jan 1794	100
Blanchard, John	4145	12 Mar 1792	100
Hunter, John	7507	2 Jul 1790	100
Hoof, James, Pvt	12177	22 Apr 1794	100
Clews, Thomas, Pvt	12950	31 Oct 1791	100
Pembrook, David, Pvt	7643	27 Oct 1791	100
Purdy, Henry	11767	6 Oct 1794	100
King, Eli, Pvt	6069	30 Mar 1792	100
Sanford, Strong, Sgt	6452	27 Apr 1790	100
Webb, John, Capt	2356	13 Nov 1792	300
Rowlandson, Joseph, Pvt	6398	8 Aug 1791	100
Purdy, Henry	11689	6 Oct 1794	100
Purdy, Henry	10977	6 Oct 1794	100
Hoge, John	9976	23 Jan 1793	100
Purdy, Henry	11799	6 Oct 1794	100
Whitehead, John, Pvt	7982	6 Mar 1792	100
Bolton, Matthew, Pvt	6822	6 Jul 1790	100
Olds, Horace	3433	3 Dec 1796	100
Angell, Israel	3517	28 May 1792	100
Lomas, Jacob, Pvt	7385	8 Sep 1790	100
Van Mater, John, Pvt	8811	5 Dec 1791	100
Veeder, Simon	5100	30 Aug 1790	100
Tucker, Jarvis, Pvt	6589	9 Jan 1794	100
Rochefontaine, Etienne N. M. B., Capt	1875	19 Apr 1793	300
Hatch, Ichabod	4412	12 Dec 1797	100
Sherburne, Benjamin, Lt	1970	14 Nov 1792	200

207 13 Feb 1800 A/1/227

By Whom Registered: Zaccheus Biggs
For Whom Registered: Archibald Woods, William Griffith, Absalom Ridgely, Zaccheus Biggs
Location: (4000 acres) Mil - 12 1 - 3
Based upon the following Army land warrants:

Issued to	*No.*	*Date*	*Acres*
Wood, James, Col	2419	14 Feb 1792	500
New, Anthony	12394	24 Feb 1794	100
Bailey, William, Pvt	11942	16 Apr 1794	100
New, Anthony	12561	24 Feb 1794	100
New, Anthony	12038	24 Feb 1794	100
Denniston, James, Pvt	9324	23 Apr 1793	100
Lackey, Robert, Pvt	9822	16 Jul 1789	100
Wilkinson, William, Pvt	10666	5 Nov 1789	100
Irish, Nathaniel, Capt	2591	30 Aug 1791	300
Richardson, John, Pvt	12495	6 Jun 1797	100
Davidson, John, Maj	582	1 Sep 1789	400
Gillass, Arthur, Pvt	9495	16 Mar 1799	100
Vaughan, John, Sgt	11788	5 Sep 1789	100
Hurd, John	932	26 Oct 1789	150
Richardson, Addison	2698	9 Feb 1798	150
Hall, William	4785	18 Oct 1796	100
Jackson, Daniel	4624	6 Jul 1796	100
Wyman, Simeon	5133	15 Jul 1797	100
Foster, Abraham	3669	23 Dec 1796	100
Jackson, Daniel	5080	6 Jul 1796	100
Wyman, Simeon	5336	15 Jul 1797	100
Coats, John	798	23 Feb 1796	200
Doyle, Henry, Sgt	13005	2 Sep 1789	100
Brady, Samuel, Capt	197	21 Jan 1793	300
Morris, Jonathan, Capt	1483	11 Dec 1795	300

208 14 Feb 1800 A/1/228

By Whom Registered: Benjamin Elliot
For Whom Registered: Benjamin Elliot
Location: (4000 acres) Mil - 12 3 - 3
Based upon the following Army land warrants:

Issued to	*No.*	*Date*	*Acres*
Holliday, John, *et al*	2699	11 Feb 1800	200
McGaw, Robert, Col	1412	16 Jul 1789	500
Derumple, Robert, Pvt	9260	6 Apr 1790	100

208 [continued]

Forbes, James, Pvt	4153	7 Jul 1797	100
Moore, King, Pvt	4734	26 Apr 1798	100
Maynard, Adam	7809	24 Jun 1794	100
Keeler, Thaddeus, Lt	1187	16 Jan 1797	200
Bowen, Barzillia	3115	24 Jun 1794	100
Crosby, Sampson	12756	18 Nov 1794	100
Tryon, William, Pvt	5162	7 Jul 1797	100
Spaulding, Asa	5257	18 Nov 1794	100
Crosby, Sampson	13514	18 Nov 1794	100
Denmark, John, Pvt	9295	9 Jul 1789	100
Finnigan, Christopher, Pvt	9376	6 Apr 1790	100
Henderson, Andrew, Lt	1020	14 Jan 1795	200
Marshall, John, Capt	1422	12 Jan 1791	300
Peck, John	13200	22 Feb 1792	100
Moore, Thomas Lt? Maj	1417	22 May 1789	400
Craig, Thomas, Col	409	27 Feb 1792	500
Febiger, Christian, Esq., Col	760	5 May 1789	500

209 15 Feb 1800 A/1/229

By Whom Registered: William Wells & John Armstrong

For Whom Registered: William Wells & John Armstrong

Location: (4000 acres) Mil - 19 6 - 4

Based upon the following Army land warrants:

Issued to	*No.*	*Date*	*Acres*
Bawyer, Henry, Lt	283	21 Dec 1795	200
Hite, Abraham, Capt	1071	28 Jul 1790	300
Powell, Peyton, Lt	1743	22 Nov 1791	200
Crockett, Joseph, Maj	2509	15 Jul 1789	400
Jouett, John	2510	15 Jul 1789	300
Hoge, John, Lt	2630	23 Apr 1793	200
Taylor, James	2711	17 Jan 1800	200
Case, Ezekiel	5624	4 Sep 1789	100
Case, Ezekiel	5663	4 Sep 1789	100
Case, Ezekiel	5666	4 Sep 1789	100
Case, Ezekiel	5933	4 Sep 1789	100
Case, Ezekiel	5934	4 Sep 1789	100
Case, Ezekiel	6047	4 Sep 1789	100
Case, Ezekiel	6096	4 Sep 1789	100
Robinson, John, Pvt	6361	20 Dec 1791	100
Case, Ezekiel	6422	4 Sep 1789	100
Case, Ezekiel	6569	4 Sep 1789	100
Shaw, Thomas	7336	2 Mar 1792	100
King, Joseph, Pvt	8461	16 Jun 1792	100
Voorhise, John, Pvt	8716	13 Oct 1792	100
Williams, John, Pvt	8841	11 Sep 1792	100
McKelvey, Thomas, Pvt	9932	5 May 1791	100
Taylor, William, *et al*	12074	8 Apr 1796	100
Gorman, John, Pvt	11255	11 May 1790	100
Morris, Isaac, Pvt	12398	15 Jul 1789	100
Taylor, William, *et al*	12492	8 Apr 1796	100
Dunn, James, Pvt	12703	16 Dec 1795	100
Case, Ezekiel	13054	4 Sep 1789	100
Harvey, Matthew, Pvt	13237	9 Apr 1796	100

210 15 Feb 1800 A/1/230

By Whom Registered: William Wells & John Armstrong

For Whom Registered: William Wells & John Armstrong

Location: (4000 acres) Mil - 17 3 - 4

Based upon the following Army land warrants:

Issued to	*No.*	*Date*	*Acres*
Bartholomew, Benjamin, Capt	195	19 Aug 1789	300
Cole, Isaac	478	14 Aug 1792	300
Peters, William, Ens	1683	15 Feb 1796	150
Smith, Samuel, Capt	2006	28 Jan 1800	300
Sample, Robert, Capt	2016	26 Oct 1791	300
Ross, John	2201	30 Mar 1796	200
Ashley, Oliver	2910	5 Apr 1796	100
Ashley, Oliver	3167	5 Apr 1796	100
Ashley, Oliver	3387	5 Apr 1796	100
Ashley, Oliver	3421	5 Apr 1796	100
Ashley, Oliver	3496	5 Apr 1796	100
Ashley, Oliver	3552	5 Apr 1796	100
Ashley, Oliver	4162	5 Apr 1796	100
Ashley, Oliver	4226	5 Apr 1796	100
Ashley, Oliver	4236	5 Apr 1796	100
Rademacker, John, Pvt	4964	15 Nov 1791	100
Ashley, Oliver	5047	5 Apr 1796	100
Ashley, Oliver	5956	5 Apr 1796	100
Keeler, Jeremiah, Pvt	6052	16 Jan 1797	100
Ashley, Oliver	6481	5 Apr 1796	100
Apker, Henry	10540	18 Jan 1797	100
Watrouse, Benjamin, Pvt	6697	10 May 1790	100
Peters, Anthony, Pvt	10216	9 Jul 1789	100
Smith, Nicholas, Pvt	11694	18 Mar 1795	100
Barns, Andrew, Pvt	11928	20 Mar 1797	100
Ashley, Oliver	13163	5 Apr 1796	100
Murray, John, LtCol	1414	5 Apr 1791	450

211 15 Feb 1800 A/1/231

By Whom Registered: William Wells & John Armstrong

For Whom Registered: William Wells & John Armstrong

Location: (4000 acres)* Mil - 16 4 - 2

Based upon the following Army land warrants:

Issued to	*No.*	*Date*	*Acres*
Mouton? [Morton?]** James Lt	1514	26 Apr 1798	200
Smith, Francis, Lt	2074	26 Apr 1798	200
Rhodes, Dick, Pvt	3458	31 Dec 1789	100
Bennet, Ruffus, Pvt	5418	8 Sep 1790	100
Walker, Obadiah	5573	11 Jul 1798	100
Sanford, Peleg	5714	24 Sep 1790	100
Sanford, Peleg	5799	24 Sep 1790	100
Power, Alexander	5950	27 Feb 1793	100
Sebor, James F.	6044	24 Sep 1790	100
Sebor, James F.	6186	24 Sep 1790	100
Sebor, James F.	6270	24 Sep 1790	100
Sebor, James F.	6339	24 Sep 1790	100
Sebor, James F.	6406	24 Sep 1790	100
Walker, Obadiah, Pvt	6631	6 Oct 1797	100
Sebor, James F.	6676	24 Sep 1790	100
Sanford, Peleg	6678	24 Sep 1790	100
Brown, William, Pvt	8136	27 Apr 1798	100
Finley, William, Pvt	8314	5 Aug 1789	100
Vandoren, Hezekiah, Pvt	8810	2 Jan 1790	100
Carnahan, William, Pvt	9133	13 Apr 1791	100
Merkle, Barnard	10069	8 Jan 1796	100
Platt, Richard	10309	27 Jul 1789	100
Gross, Christian	10630	19 Mar 1792	100
Jones, Nelsey, Pvt	11379	18 Jan 1793	100
Barnes, Charles, Pvt	11982	31 Mar 1794	100
Clingman, Jacob	12083	22 Oct 1791	100
Flemister, Lewis, Pvt	12127	19 Mar 1794	100
Gunnill, John, Pvt	12150	27 Mar 1794	100
Haley, George, Pvt	12212	31 Mar 1794	100
Clingman, Jacob	12214	22 Oct 1791	100
Surlock, William, Pvt	12592	31 Mar 1794	100
Gross, Christian	12746	12 Mar 1792	100
Kistwhite, Henry, Pvt	13290	20 Aug 1789	100
Shehee, John, Pvt	13703	2 Dec 1793	100

211 [continued]

Sanford, Peleg	13914	24 Sep 1790	100
White, Charles, Pvt	14015	21 Mar 1794	100
Wright, John	14116***	25 Mar 1795	100
Wright, John	14123	3 Jun 1795	100

*Marginal notation: "See Pat[ent] record Vol. 1, p. 50."

**Originally recorded as Mouton; pencilled correction to Morton.

***Originally entered as 14166; pencilled correction to 14116.

212 15 Feb 1800 A/1/232

By Whom Registered: [William] Wells & [John] Armstrong

For Whom Registered: Lucas Sullivant

Location: (4000 acres) Mil - 14 7 - 1

Based upon the following Army land warrants:

Issued to	*No.*	*Date*	*Acres*
Bowyer, Henry	268	31 Dec 1795	300
Clark, Silas, Capt	336	12 Mar 1790	300
Carrington, Clement, Ens	475	18 Apr 1796	150
Wiggen, Henry	483	10 Nov 1796	200
Hunter, Robert, Ens	907	25 Apr 1791	150
Harrison, John, Lt	1075	10 Feb 1800	200
Wiggen, Henry	1864	10 Nov 1796	300
Smith, William L., Lt	2073	9 May 1796	200
Towles, Oliver, LtCol	2213	7 Dec 1791	450
Weedon, George, BrigGen	2418	3 May 1791	850
Sullivant, Lucas	2433	10 Feb 1800	200
Cole, Benjamin, Pvt	5653	6 May 1794	100
Forbush, William, Pvt	10765	6 Apr 1793	100
Brady, John, Pvt	10978	18 Apr 1794	100
Baptiste, John, Pvt	11944	20 Jan 1796	100
New, Anthony	12311	10 Feb 1796	100
Means, Robert	12670	10 Feb 1800	100
Taylor, William, *et al*	12672	8 Apr 1796	100

213 19 Feb 1800 A/1/233

By Whom Registered: John Wright

For Whom Registered: John Wright

Location: (4000 acres) Mil - 14 7 - 4

Based upon the following Army land warrants:

Issued to	*No.*	*Date*	*Acres*
Shoemaker, Peter, Pvt	13715	31 Dec 1790	100
Poorham, John, Pvt	13606	18 Jul 1795	100
Camp, Robert, Pvt	12021	9 Feb 1796	100
Schott, William P., Pvt	10613	13 Dec 1791	100
Schott, William P., Pvt	10579	13 Dec 1791	100
Stiedelman? [Steidelman?] John, Pvt	10410	1 Mar 1796	100
Christie, James, Pvt	8786	10 Aug 1795	100
Lumley, Samuel, Pvt	8478	22 Jun 1792	100
Russell, Thomas, Pvt	7644	24 Jun 1793	100
Fletcher, Robert, Pvt	2930	8 Feb 1796	100
Granniss, Eneas, Lt	2663	10 Mar 1796	200
Wagnon, John P., Lt	2456	7 Apr 1796	200
Stout? [Hout?] Wessell T., Lt	1997	30 Aug 1790	200
Rice, William, Capt	1821	25 Mar 1790	300
McIntosh, Lachlin, Lt	1657	6 Jun 1796	200
Otto, Marg[are]t? & Otto, John, Physician & Surgeon	1621	18 Oct 1794	450
Wright, John, Capt	1552	14 Apr 1799	300
Wright, John, LtCol	1550	14 Apr 1799	500
Henderson, William, LtCol	1102	23 Jul 1790	450
Denny, Robert, Lt	589	1 Sep 1789	200

214 19 Feb 1800 A/1/234

By Whom Registered: John Coates

For Whom Registered: John Coates

Location: (4000 acres) Mil - 17 1 - 2

Based upon the following Army land warrants:

Issued to	*No.*	*Date*	*Acres*
Coates, John, Lt	22	18 Oct 1796	200
Brooks, John, LtCol Com-[manding]	92	14 Mar 1796	500
Coates, John, Surgeon	107	23 Feb 1796	400
Coates, John, Capt	647	18 Oct 1796	300
Coates, John, Capt	703	18 Oct 1796	300
Francis, Judith, Col	719	8 Jul 1789	500
Coates, John, Lt	795	18 Oct 1796	200
Sanger, Calvin, LtCol	2244	22 Apr 1793	450
Richardson, Addison, Capt	2674	30 Jan 1797	300
Richardson, Addison, LtCol	2695	9 Feb 1798	450
Richardson, Addison, Lt	2696	9 Feb 1798	200
Coates, John, Pvt	3680	18 Oct 1796	100
Coates, John, Pvt	4165	18 Oct 1796	100

215 20 Feb 1800 A/1/234

By Whom Registered: John G. Jackson

For Whom Registered: John G. Jackson

Location: (4000 acres) Mil - 7 2 - 3

Based upon the following Army land warrants:

Issued to	*No.*	*Date*	*Acres*
Higgins, Peter, Lt	1076	5 Apr 1796	200
Strong, Phineas, Pvt	6516	10 Nov 1792	100
Cool, Isaac, Pvt	5611	10 Nov 1792	100
Cool, Hyman, Pvt	5560	10 Nov 1792	100
Thraul, William, Pvt	6572	10 Nov 1792	100
Williams, James, Capt	2427	2 Apr 1790	300
McKim, John, Lt	1169	24 Feb 1797	200
Smith, --, & Ridgway, --, Capt	839	27 Aug 1795	300
Smith, --, & Ridgway, --, Lt	453	27 Aug 1795	200
Wallcut, Benjamin, *et al*, Ens	2335	26 Nov 1798	150
McKensey, Joshua, Pvt	11513	5 Jan 1793	100
Macon, Nath[anie]l, Capt	1534	7 Jan 1797	300
Howell, John, Pvt	12251	21 Apr 1798	100
Creesy, Thomas, & Murfree, Hardy, Pvt	12281	21 Apr 1798	100
Murfree, Hardy, Lt	773	25 Nov 1796	200
Murfree, Hardy, LtCol	1528	6 Aug 1789	450
Miller, Marg[are]t? Capt	2583	16 Apr 1791	300
Carrington, George, Lt	474	21 Jan 1800	200
Mussey, Amos, Pvt	5359	15 Apr 1796	100
Lassell, Othniel, Capt	295	19 Feb 1800	300
Brautigam, Daniel, Pvt	10222	21 Oct 1795	100

216 22 Feb 1800 A/1/235

By Whom Registered: Thomas Parker, Junior

For Whom Registered: George Suckley

Location: (4000 acres) Mil - 9 6 - 1

Based upon the following Army land warrants:

Issued to	*No.*	*Date*	*Acres*
Gilman, Nicholas, Capt	784	14 Aug 1789	300
Gilder, Reuben, Surgeon	849	19 May 1789	400
Stuart, Christ[ophe]r, LtCol	2009	7 Dec 1791	450
Cass, Jonathan, Ens	2319	21 Jul 1789	150
Thom, Chr[istophe]r L? [S?] Pvt	3364	27 May 1797	100
Curtis, Joseph, Pvt	3872	13 Sep 1792	100

216 [continued]

Cushing, Thomas, Pvt	3885	1 Aug 1789	100
Turner, Marlbry, Pvt	3922	6 May 1797	100
Sanger, Calvin, Pvt	3938	7 Jan 1796	100
Foye, Henry, Pvt	3974	4 Nov 1795	100
Newman, Henry, Pvt	3983	10 Sep 1789	100
Peck? [Peek?] John, Pvt	3984	25 Mar 1792	100
Cushing, Thomas, Pvt	3998	1 Aug 1789	100
Newman, Henry, Pvt	4026	13 Sep 1792	100
Perkins, Joseph, Pvt	4064	29 Apr 1794	100
Peck, John, Pvt	4152	22 Feb 1792	100
Blurn? [Blum?] George, Pvt	4182	26 Mar 1792	100
Quinton, David, Pvt	4193	21 Nov 1791	100
Sanger, Calvin, Pvt	4206	11 Feb 1797	100
Blanchard, Augustus, Pvt	4210	13 Dec 1792	100
Peck, John, Pvt	4224	22 Feb 1792	100
Green, John, Pvt	4231	26 Oct 1789	100
Thom, Stephen, Pvt	4371	29 Jun 1792	100
Thom, Stephen, Pvt	5386	29 Jun 1792	100
Thom, Stephen, Pvt	6059	29 Jun 1792	100
Thom, Stephen, Pvt	6257	29 Jun 1792	100
Sanger? [Langer?] Calvin, Pvt	13028	7 Jan 1796	100
Newman, Henry, Pvt	13384	10 Sep 1789	100
Peck, John, Pvt	13617	19 Apr 1792	100
Emery, Samuel, Pvt	13707	9 Jul 1794	100
McCondry, Will, Pvt	14087	4 Nov 1794	100

[See also serial entry 269]

217 24 Feb 1800 A/1/236

By Whom Registered: Zaccheus Biggs
For Whom Registered: Zaccheus Biggs
Location: (4000 acres) Mil - 1 1 - 2
Based upon the following Army land warrants:

Issued to	*No.*	*Date*	*Acres*
Johnston, Andrew, Lt	1152	7 Jul 1789	200
Lyons, Moses, Pvt	9811	30 May 1791	100
Kincaid, John, Pvt	9764	22 Aug 1799	100
Daniel, Andrew, Pvt	10754	2 Sep 1789	100
Smith, Conrad, Pvt	10332	17 Aug 1789	100
Thom, Christopher L? [S?]	3309	27 May 1797	100
Johnston, Andrew	10372	29 Jan 1790	100
Compton, James, Pvt	8193	13 Feb 1800	100
Wordoth? John, Pvt	13931	12 Feb 1800	100
Baldwin, Asa	4233	16 Dec 1793	100
Foster, Dwight	4396	9 Dec 1799	100
Jones, Joseph	3910	14 Feb 1793	100
Foster, Dwight	4572	9 Dec 1799	100
Gale, Enoch	4297	9 Dec 1799	100
Lilley, Reuben, Lt	1235	20 Jul 1789	200
Foster, Dwight	2709	11 Dec 1799	300
Stacey, John, Pvt	5037	12 Aug 1793	100
Cunningham, William, Maj	2664	22 Mar 1796	400
Gibbons, R., & Wills, A. R.	2562	4 Jan 1792	400
Spears, Richard	3170	6 Jan 1797	100
Webster, John B., Lt	2391	12 Sep 1789	200
Ashby, Benjamin, Lt	55	28 Jul 1790	200
Davidson, John	14035	8 May 1792	100
Burns, Harvey, Pvt	12791	24 Mar 1798	100
Hughs, John, Lt	1013	29 Jan 1790	200
Roystan, James, Cpl	11661	5 Sep 1789	100
Ennis, Enoch, Pvt	11180	5 Sep 1789	100

218 24 Feb 1800 A/1/237

By Whom Registered: Zaccheus Biggs
For Whom Registered: Zaccheus Biggs
Location: (4000 acres) Mil - 14 6 - 2
Based upon the following Army land warrants:

Issued to	*No.*	*Date*	*Acres*
Butt, Burduck, Pvt	10974	3 Feb 1796	100
Hazard, Sampson, Pvt	3236	31 Dec 1789	100
Maxwell, Anthony	13594	4 Dec 1790	100
Langworthy, Southcote? Pvt	3295	31 Dec 1789	100
Savoy, Philip, Pvt	11675	11 Mar 1791	100
Shepherd, Abraham, Capt	2529	25 Aug 1789	300
Waters, John	2665	23 Mar 1796	300
Morison, Isaac, Capt	2521	3 Jun 1791	300
Force, Henry, Pvt	13075	3 Jun 1791	100
Ferry, James, Pvt	11753	12 Dec 1792	100
Stanton, William, Pvt	10885	2 Sep 1789	100
Hammond, David, Lt	1007	21 Dec 1790	200
Morgan, Simon, Capt	1500	16 Apr 1794	300
Johnson, James, Pvt	12257	16 Apr 1794	100
Jarrett, Elisha	11526	1 Nov 1797	100
Jarrett, Elisha	11801	1 Nov 1797	100
Gass, Solomon	5365	20 Feb 1790	100
Gass, Solomon	5617	20 Feb 1790	100
Gass, Solomon	6251	20 Feb 1790	100
Gass, Solomon	5840	20 Feb 1790	100
Gass, Solomon	6568	20 Feb 1790	100
Carnahan, James, Capt	417	26 Sep 1792	300
Taylor, Josiah, Pvt	6577	31 Jul 1789	100
Taylor, Noah, Sgt	6550	31 Jul 1789	100
Gilbert, Moses, Sgt	5831	31 Jul 1789	100
McBeath, Alexander	10835	10 Dec 1799	100
McBeath, Alexander	10863	10 Dec 1799	100
McDonald, Archibald, Pvt	9868	6 Sep 1791	100
Stallions, Abraham, Pvt	11719	29 May 1795	100

219 24 Feb 1800 A/1/238

By Whom Registered: Robert Campbell
For Whom Registered: Robert Campbell
Location: (4000 acres) Mil - 19 6 - 1
Based upon the following Army land warrants:

Issued to	*No.*	*Date*	*Acres*
Ford, David, Pvt	10770	26 Jun 1797	100
Craigie, Andrew, Apoth-[ecary]	500	30 Dec 1790	450
Woodward, William	3096	6 Jul 1796	100
Fitch, Samuel	376	3 Mar 1797	300
Wright, Joseph A., Maj	2342	30 Oct 1789	400
Riley, John, Capt	1792	22 Apr 1796	300
Trotter, John, Capt	2149	11 Jul 1797	300
Fowler, Theodosius	169	9 Jul 1790	300
Knapp, Joshua, Ens	1189	25 Jun 1789	150
Conner? [Cannon?]* Joseph	3242	15 Apr 1796	100
Baldwin, Daniel, Capt	2515	30 Jul 1789	300
Emery, Samuel	4039	14 Dec 1793	100
Goodrich, Noah, Pvt	4205	21 Apr 1794	100
Heacock, Esther	5407	9 Oct 1789	100
Clerk, Joseph, Sgt	5621	12 Oct 1790	100
Fields, George, Pvt	5782	14 Feb 1793	100
Sanford, Elihu, Sgt	6483	12 Oct 1789	100
Miller, Samuel	6551	19 Nov 1792	100
Benedict, Timothy	6643	20 Jan 1795	100
Preston, Benjamin, Pvt	7626	5 Jan 1791	100
Stringer, Samuel	7853	25 Aug 1790	100
Cushing? [Cashing?] Thomas	3850	1 Aug 1789	100
Carey, Joseph, Pvt	3870	13 Sep 1792	100

*Originally entered as Conner; pencilled correction to Cannon.

220 24 Feb 1800 A/1/239

By Whom Registered: John Heckewelder
For Whom Registered: Frederick Butler

220 [continued]
Location: (4000 acres) Mil - 8 3 - 4
Based upon the following Army land warrants:

Issued to	*No*	*Date*	*Acres*
Patridge, C., & Patridge, M.	24	12 Dec 1797	500
Turner, Marlbry	88	8 Apr 1797	500
Dennett, John, Capt	510	9 Sep 1789	300
Helm, John, Capt	1035	15 Feb 1790	300
Brown, Joseph	3919	15 Feb 1797	100
Foster, Abraham	4238	23 Dec 1796	100
Holmes, Robert, Pvt	4302	26 Sep 1791	100
Miller, James	4313	27 Jan 1797	100
Hayward, Caleb, Pvt	4314	13 Sep 1792	100
Peck, John	4309	22 Feb 1792	100
Foster, Abraham	4334	23 Dec 1796	100
Stowe? [Howe?] Edward	4363	3 Jul 1795	100
Boynton, Abel	4400	26 Jun 1799	100
Hill, Jeremiah	4404	25 Jun 1794	100
Peck, John	4408	26 Mar 1792	100
Peck, John	4438	22 Feb 1792	100
Sanger? [Langer?] Calvin	4444	7 Jan 1796	100
Peck, John	4461	22 Feb 1792	100
Peck, John	4507	22 Feb 1792	100
Peck, John	4513	26 Mar 1792	100
Sanger? [Langer?] Calvin	4566	7 Jan 1796	100
Emery, Samuel	4650	4 Nov 1794	100
Peck, John	4666	19 Apr 1792	100
Peck, John	4710	22 Feb 1792	100
Emery, Samuel	4723	4 Nov 1794	100
Peck, John	4733	22 Feb 1792	100
Peck, John	4823	22 Feb 1792	100
Sheridan, Thomas	4907	4 Nov 1794	100

221 24 Feb 1800 A/1/240
By Whom Registered: John A. Seitz
For Whom Registered: James Morrison
Location: (4000 acres) Mil - 19 3 - 2
Based upon the following Army land warrants:

Issued to	*No.*	*Date*	*Acres*
Coleman, Whitehead, Capt	467	8 Aug 1792	300
Russell, Elizabeth	1849	19 May 1794	500
Ferry, Nathaniel, Capt	2216	14 Dec 1796	300
Wilmoll? [Wilmott?] Robert, Lt	2415	28 Jan 1800	200
Terrill, Richmond	2627	14 Feb 1793	200
Amberson, Johnson, Pvt	8909	13 Jul 1789	100
Rodermall, Peter	9112	8 Nov 1791	100
Rodermall, Peter	9273	19 Jan 1792	100
Dennis, Michael, Pvt	9321	13 Jul 1789	100
Rodermel, Peter	9348	8 Nov 1791	100
Gladden, John, Pvt	9506	13 Jul 1789	100
Kidder, Benjamin, Pvt	9777	13 Jul 1789	100
Rodermel, Peter	10289	8 Nov 1791	100
Jarrett, Elisha	11315	1 Nov 1797	100
Jones, Jonathan	12135	22 Feb 1799	100
Fenman, Simon, Pvt	13087	13 Jul 1789	100
Bradley, Gee, Capt	293	10 Jan 1791	300
Forrest, Uriah, LtCol	756	13 Sep 1799	450
Means, Robert	867	29 May 1792	450
Ludlam, Henry	7229	26 Apr 1791	100
Johnson, John, Sgt	8434	25 May 1790	100

222 24 Feb 1800 A/1/241
By Whom Registered: Zaccheus Biggs
For Whom Registered: John Bever
Location: (4000 acres) Mil - 3 5 - 2
Based upon the following Army land warrants:

Issued to	*No.*	*Date*	*Acres*
Spencer, Anna	2688	7 Jul 1797	200
Burwell, Nathaniel, Capt	260	13 Feb 1798	300
Peterson, Gabriel, Lt	1712	2 Sep 1790	200
Heth, William, Col	1064	9 Feb 1798	500
Butler, Edward, Lt	208	9 Feb 1798	200
Crawford, John, Lt	423	22 Sep 1791	200
McDonald, Robert, Pvt	9901	15 Jan 1793	100
Nevill, John, Capt[!]	1595	13 Jan 1800	500
Callahan, John, Pvt	9225	5 Nov 1789	100
Young, Joseph, Physician & Surgeon	2471	14 Jul 1790	450
Mourey, Christian, Pvt	10109	5 Nov 1789	100
Smith, John, Pvt	12530	5 Nov 1789	100
Burns, James, Senior, Pvt	9048	5 Nov 1789	100
Adams, Robert, Cpl	8910	5 Nov 1789	100
Hughs, Henry, Ens	1082	24 Sep 1795	150
Madder? Martin, Pvt	12378	5 Nov 1789	100
Evans, Anthony, Fife? Major	9360	5 Nov 1789	100
Hurley, Matthew, Pvt	12187	5 Nov 1789	100
Help, Ludwick, Pvt	9627	5 Nov 1789	100
Young, John, Surgeon's Mate	2567	8 Sep 1790	300

223 25 Feb 1800 A/1/242
By Whom Registered: Robert Campbell
For Whom Registered: Robert Campbell
Location: (4000 acres) Mil - 11 6 - 2
Based upon the following Army land warrants:

Issued to	*No.*	*Date*	*Acres*
Craig, Garard, Pvt	12944	28 Feb 1791	100
Betters, John, Pvt	3826	8 Dec 1791	100
Peck, John	1644	2 Apr 1791	300
Cushing, Thomas	3843	1 Aug 1789	100
Cushing, Thomas	3767	1 Aug 1789	100
Sanger? [Langer?] Calvin	3747	7 Jan 1796	100
Newman, Henry	3685	6 May 1797	100
Newman, Henry	3683	10 Sep 1789	100
Sanger? [Langer?] Calvin	3677	7 Jan 1796	100
Sanger? [Langer?] Calvin	3673	11 Feb 1797	100
Peck, John	3671	22 Feb 1792	100
Cushing, Thomas	3658	1 Aug 1789	100
Finney, Samuel	3601	17 May 1792	100
Peck, John	3472	22 Feb 1792	100
Peck, John	3300	22 Feb 1792	100
Peck, John	3265	19 Apr 1792	100
Peck, John	3192	22 Feb 1792	100
Hodgman, Joseph, Pvt	3172	13 Sep 1792	100
Peck, John	3020	22 Feb 1792	100
Appleton, Francis	2991	18 Dec 1795	100
Brown, Joseph	2987	4 Nov 1795	100
Bryant, Elizabeth	2691	10 Jul 1797	300
Turner, Marlbry	2331	1 Oct 1799	200
Wales, Joseph, Lt	2317	11 Jan 1793	200
Cushing, Thomas	2299	1 Aug 1789	300
Tufts, Francis, Lt	2159	20 Mar 1796	200
Newman, Henry	2154	10 Sep 1789	200
Rouse, Oliver	1780	1 Oct 1799	300

224 25 Feb 1800 A/1/243
By Whom Registered: Martin Baum
For Whom Registered: Martin Baum & Co.
Location: (4000 acres) Mil - 5 6 - 4
Based upon the following Army land warrants:

Issued to	*No.*	*Date*	*Acres*
McCleland, John	2061	22 Aug 1791	300

Issued to	No.	Date	Acres
Cruize, Walter, Capt	432	27 Nov 1794	300
Caldwell, Andrew, Hospital Mate	2506	27 Jun 1789	300
Dietrich, Michael, Hospital Mate	621	9 Oct 1789	300
Lyon, Stephen, Pvt	13349	27 Oct 1792	100
Ridgway, Henry	9167	24 Oct 1792	100
Graves, Francis	11936	14 Jul 1792	100
Ammerman, Dirck	6726	7 Mar 1792	100
Wyshover, Jacob, Pvt	7996	31 Oct 1791	100
McClelland, John	10335	22 Aug 1791	100
Jones, Catharine	12778	12 May 1792	100
Pells, Henry	12779	18 Jul 1791	100
Hubbard, Christian	10520	28 Dec 1793	100
Hubbard, Christian	9498	28 Dec 1793	100
Hubbard, Christian	10452	28 Dec 1793	100
McCleland, John	9375	22 Aug 1791	100
Wilson, Robert	7940	7 Jul 1791	100
Fowler, Joseph, Pvt	8310	26 May 1790	100
Lane, William	10792	28 Dec 1791	100
Jones, Josiah, Pvt	9660	21 Dec 1791	100
Paulier, Clement	13604	1 Feb 1790	100
Sebor, James F.	6030	24 Sep 1790	100
Cayore, Pierre, Pvt	12910	4 Feb 1790	100
Gilbert, George	9432	13 Jun 1792	100
Eversole, Peter, Pvt	9343	21 Feb 1793	100
Porter, Daniel, Pvt	6300	26 May 1790	100
Woolsey, Melancthon L.	12840	12 May 1796	100
Hubbard, Abner, Pvt	4350	14 Feb 1791	100
Means, Robert	12345	14 Jul 1792	100
Mitchell, James, Pvt	10014	29 Aug 1795	100
Pollock, Margaret	10040	16 Jul 1795	100
Bannon, Jeremiah, Pvt	9075	5 Nov 1789	100

<u>225</u> 25 Feb 1800 A/1/244

By Whom Registered: Martin Baum
For Whom Registered: Martin Baum & Co.
Location: (4000 acres) Mil - 12 7 - 1
Based upon the following Army land warrants:

Issued to	*No.*	*Date*	*Acres*
Cushing, Thomas	4006	1 Aug 1789	100
Brown, Joseph	4079	4 Nov 1795	100
Fosdick, Joseph	4098	2 Nov 1795	100
Newman, Henry	4135	10 Sep 1789	100
Brown, Joseph	4184	4 Nov 1795	100
Stowe? [Howe?] Edward	4194	26 Oct 1795	100
Cushing, Thomas	4222	1 Aug 1789	100
Hill, Jeremiah	4289	6 Nov 1795	100
Cushing, Thomas	4306	1 Aug 1789	100
Fosdick, Joseph	4467	2 Nov 1795	100
Inkerston, Robert, Pvt	4494	23 Feb 1796	100
Newman, Henry	4529	10 Sep 1789	100
Newman, Henry	4737	10 Sep 1789	100
Cushing, Thomas	4867	1 Aug 1789	100
Fosdick, Joseph	4871	2 Nov 1795	100
Newman, Henry	4877	10 Sep 1789	100
Cushing, Thomas	4942	1 Aug 1789	100
Hill, Jeremiah	4948	6 Nov 1795	100
Peck, John	5030	19 Apr 1792	100
Newman, Henry	5033	10 Sep 1789	100
Blanchard, Augustus	5055	13 Dec 1792	100
Cushing, Thomas	5103	1 Aug 1789	100
Peck, John	5129	22 Feb 1792	100
Cushing, Thomas	5165	1 Aug 1789	100
Thomas, Caleb, Sgt	5168	13 Dec 1796	100
Nelson, Josiah, Junior	5171	27 Jan 1797	100
Peck, John	5195	9 Jul 1794	100
Waterman, Ephraim, Pvt	5222	13 Sep 1792	100
Sanger? [Langer?] Calvin	5231	7 Jan 1796	100
Seward, Thomas	5245	17 Apr 1792	100
Fosdick, Joseph	5255	2 Nov 1795	100
Deman? [Diman?] Cesar	5271	24 Jan 1797	100
Webb, Benjamin, Pvt	5279	6 Feb 1797	100
Quinton, David	5313	1 May 1792	100
Cushing, Thomas	5746	1 Aug 1789	100
Finch, Isaac, Pvt	5801	19 Jun 1790	100
Peck, John	6098	22 Feb 1792	100
Steel? [Heel?] John	6486	8 Apr 1797	100
Sanger? [Langer?] Calvin	7637	7 Jan 1796	100
Peck, John	12949	22 Feb 1792	100

<u>226</u> 25 Feb 1800 A/1/245

By Whom Registered: William Wells
For Whom Registered: William Wells
Location: (4000 acres) Mil - 19 5 - 1
Based upon the following Army land warrants:

Issued to	*No.*	*Date*	*Acres*
Cogswell, J. Fitch, & Cogswell, M.	350	25 Jan 1799	200
Day, Luke, Capt	517	15 Oct 1789	300
Dagget, Henry, Lt	539	21 Aug 1789	200
Smith, David, Maj	1941	16 Sep 1789	400
Talmadge, Benjamin, Maj	2171	7 Oct 1789	400
Tanner, Ebenezer, Lt	2174	14 Dec 1795	200
Warner, Robert, Maj	2340	8 Apr 1796	400
Walcott, Chloe	2346	23 Feb 1799	300
Tracy, Uriah	3776	19 Feb 1800	100
Hazard, Ebenezer	4642	16 Apr 1793	100
Bacon, Richard, Pvt	5306	22 Feb 1799	100
Allen, John	5778	10 May 1798	100
Talmadge, Benjamin	5779	1 Apr 1795	100
Hitchcock, Jared, Pvt	5903	20 Jun 1795	100
Rice, Joel	5912	29 Mar 1792	100
Tracy, Uriah	5944	7 Jan 1800	100
Hine, Titus, Pvt	5969	29 Mar 1792	100
Rice, Joel	6001	29 Mar 1792	100
Talmadge, Benjamin	6318	14 May 1790	100
Goodwin, Micah	6433	4 Jan 1796	100
Stedman, Levi, Pvt	6514	6 Oct 1792	100
Squire, Asa, Pvt	6522	7 Feb 1800	100
Wainwright, Samuel, Pvt	6700	16 Nov 1789	100
Dorr, Samuel, Pvt	13015	3 Feb 1800	100

<u>227</u> 25 Feb 1800 A/1/246

By Whom Registered: William Wells
For Whom Registered: William Wells
Location: (4000 acres) Mil - 19 3 - 3
Based upon the following Army land warrants:

Issued to	*No.*	*Date*	*Acres*
Collon? [Cotton?] George, Ens	380	15 Feb 1799	150
Hay, Samuel, LtCol	1008	4 Nov 1789	450
Markland, John, Lt	1432	2 Jul 1792	200
Ladd, E., & Cass, J.	3286	21 Jul 1789	100
Murray, Reuben	3326	12 Jul 1793	100
Emery, Samuel	4905	24 Jun 1793	100
Hitchcock, Abel	5955	20 Jun 1795	100
Mix, Amos, Pvt	6189	20 Jun 1795	100
Webster, Chr[istopher] & Webster, George	6851	9 Jul 1790	100
Canfield, Ithamar	6564	21 Mar 1791	100
Coe, John D.	6912	12 Aug 1790	100
Henderson, William	7110	10 Sep 1790	100
Glenn, C., & Bleecker, B.	7134	24 Aug 1790	100
Coe, John D.	7145	12 Aug 1790	100
Cumpston, Edward	7478	30 Jul 1790	100
Watson, Elkanah	7628	24 Jun 1790	100
Platt, Richard	7840	14 Jul 1790	100

227 [continued]

Woodsides, Robert, Pvt	8877	25 Feb 1793	100
Fowler, Theodosius	7904	9 Jul 1796	100
Kirkpatrick, Francis	9402	30 Jul 1793	100
Stever? [Hever?] Michael	10606	16 Mar 1793	100
Purdy, Henry	11065	18 Dec 1794	100
Purdy, Henry	1110	18 Dec 1794	100
Jenkins, Thomas, Pvt	11154	22 Dec 1794	100
Means, Robert	11878	7 Jan 1793	100
Jones, William, Pvt	12287	24 Jan 1795	100
Means, Robert	12400	5 Jul 1794	100
Means, Robert	12438	18 Feb 1793	100
Sudthard, John, Pvt	14124	19 Jun 1795	100
Sherrard, Francis	14098	28 Jan 1795	100
Henry, James	14050	18 Jul 1793	100
Snell, John	12976	13 Jul 1792	100
Young, John, Pvt	12701	22 Jun 1795	100
Thurston, Thomas, Pvt	12633	24 Jun 1795	100
O'Neil, Ferrill	12445	16 Jul 1793	100

228 25 Feb 1800 A/1/248

By Whom Registered: John Brown
For Whom Registered: John Brown & Israel Ludlow
Location: (4000 acres) Mil - 16 5 - 2
Based upon the following Army land warrants:

Issued to	*No.*	*Date*	*Acres*
Anderson, Richard C., LtCol	53	14 Dec 1795	450
Edgard, David, Capt	664	4 Aug 1790	300
Lemin, William	1288	31 Mar 1796	200
McKey, William, Capt	1424	7 Jul 1789	300
Magaw, William, Surgeon	1446	1 Sep 1789	400
Vaughn, Hannah	2268	1 May 1794	450
McMyers, Mary	2505	11 Jun 1789	300
Bridges, John	3471	6 Jul 1792	100
Bridges, John	3687	6 Jul 1792	100
Bridges, John	5190	6 Jul 1792	100
Connally, James, Pvt	5660	11 Dec 1789	100
Edgar, William	8483	12 Feb 1800	100
Lyon, Joseph	8689	20 Apr 1790	100
Gowan, Hugh, Pvt	9463	14 Mar 1791	100
Davis, Henry	11309	14 Oct 1795	100
McDowell, Hugh, Pvt	11549	9 Jul 1794	100
Hartkie, John, Pvt	13156	12 Sep 1789	100
Miller, John, Pvt	13469	24 Jun 1791	100
O'Brian, James, Pvt	13557	3 May 1791	100
Patterson, Jonathan, Pvt	13599	28 Jun 1790	100
Schott, John P.	13652	3 Feb 1792	100
Schultz, Christian, Pvt	13765	27 Jun 1791	100
Frazier, Jeremiah, Pvt	14058	20 Mar 1794	100

229 25 Feb 1800 A/1/248

By Whom Registered: Ebenezer Peirce
For Whom Registered: Ebenezer Peirce
Location: (4050 acres) Mil - 18 4 - 1
Based upon the following Army land warrants:

Issued to	*No.*	*Date*	*Acres*
Paterson, John, BrigGen	1632	22 Jul 1789	850
Thompson, Thaddeus, Surgeon	2141	22 Jul 1789	400
Stone, Enos, Capt	1929	22 Aug 1789	300
Williams, Ebenezer, *et al*	1352	22 Aug 1789	300
Williams, Ebenezer, Lt	2308	22 Aug 1789	200
Benedict, Levi, Pvt	5536	1 Jun 1792	100
Winchell, Benjamin	4801	22 Aug 1789	100
Walker, Robert, Capt	2297	22 Jul 1789	300
Thompson, Thaddeus	1885	22 Jul 1789	300
Saterlee? [Laterlee?] William, Capt	2112	22 Aug 1789	300
Parsons, Charles	2307	22 Jan 1799	200
Eggleston, Azariah, Lt	651	22 Jul 1789	200
Pomeroy, Grove, Pvt	4858	22 Aug 1789	100
Berry, Joseph, Pvt	3704	22 Jul 1789	100
Smith, Ebenezer, Capt	1901	22 Aug 1789	300

230 25 Feb 1800 A/1/249

By Whom Registered: Ebenezer Peirce
For Whom Registered: Ebenezer Peirce
Location: (4000 acres) Mil - 17 4 - 2
Based upon the following Army land warrants:

Issued to	*No.*	*Date*	*Acres*
Marshall, Thomas, Col	1348	21 Jan 1797	500
Holdridge, John, Lt	923	22 Aug 1789	200
Jewett, David, Fifer	4452	22 Jul 1789	100
Sewall, Henry, Capt	1898	26 Jun 1789	300
Rash, Jacob, Pvt	6409	22 Jul 1789	100
Smith, Israel, Pvt	5066	22 Aug 1789	100
Kilburn, Charles, Pvt	4506	22 Aug 1789	100
Woodward, William, Sgt	13876	22 Aug 1789	100
Tiffany, Isaiah, Lt	2175	22 Aug 1789	200
Phipps, Samuel, Pvt	4120	22 Jul 1789	100
Maynard, Peter, Pvt	4683	22 Jul 1789	100
Parker, Abraham, Cpl	6323	22 Jul 1789	100
Barnard, Pharez, Pvt	5478	22 Jul 1789	100
Frisbee, Thaddeus, Sgt	4107	22 Aug 1789	100
Ballantine, Ebenezer, Surgeon's Mate	127	22 Aug 1789	300
Murray, Elijah, Sgt	4627	22 Jul 1789	100
Hawkins, William, Pvt	4338	22 Aug 1789	100
Tilley? Samuel, Sgt	5163	22 Aug 1789	100
Dean, Walter, Capt	519	22 Aug 1789	300
Ashley, Moses	4580	22 Aug 1789	100
Herrick, Zebulon, Pvt	4401	22 Jul 1789	100
Jackson, Nathan, Pvt	4478	22 Jul 1789	100
Ashley, Moses, Maj	11	22 Jul 1789	400
Winchell, Benjamin	4576	22 Aug 1789	100
Winchell, Benjamin	3727	22 Aug 1789	100

231 25 Feb 1800 A/1/250

By Whom Registered: Jonathan Dayton
For Whom Registered: Jonathan Dayton
Location: (4000 acres) Mil - 16 1 - 2
Based upon the following Army land warrants:

Issued to	*No.*	*Date*	*Acres*
McConnell, Matthew	212	16 Jul 1789	200
McConnell, Matthew	8894	29 Jun 1789	100
McConnell, Matthew	8949	16 Jul 1789	100
McConnell, Matthew	8966	15 May 1790	100
McConnell, Matthew	8985	16 Jul 1789	100
McConnell, Matthew	9019	29 Jun 1789	100
McConnell, Matthew	9032	29 Jun 1789	100
McConnell, Matthew	9044	16 Jul 1789	100
McConnell, Matthew	9045	29 Jun 1789	100
McConnell, Matthew	9111	29 Jun 1789	100
McConnell, Matthew	9141	29 Jun 1789	100
McConnell, Matthew	9147	28 Oct 1789	100
McConnell, Matthew	9177	29 Jun 1789	100
McConnell, Matthew	9183	28 Oct 1789	100
McConnell, Matthew	9208	29 Jun 1789	100
McConnell, Matthew	9247	29 Jun 1789	100
McConnell, Matthew	9263	29 Jun 1789	100
McConnell, Matthew	9308	28 Oct 1789	100
McConnell, Matthew	9315	31 Jun 1789	100
McConnell, Matthew	9372	29 Jun 1789	100
McConnell, Matthew	9384	29 Jun 1789	100
McConnell, Matthew	9394	16 Jun 1789	100
McConnell, Matthew	9406	29 Jun 1789	100
McConnell, Matthew	9430	29 Jun 1789	100

231 [continued]

McConnell, Matthew	9505	29 Jun 1789	100
McConnell, Matthew	9533	29 Jun 1789	100
McConnell, Matthew	9542	29 Jun 1789	100
McConnell, Matthew	9583	29 Jun 1789	100
McConnell, Matthew	9723	28 Oct 1789	100
McConnell, Matthew	9784	29 Jun 1789	100
McConnell, Matthew	9791	16 Jul 1789	100
McConnell, Matthew	9798	29 Jun 1789	100
McConnell, Matthew	9814	29 Jun 1789	100
McConnell, Matthew	9924	29 Jun 1789	100
McConnell, Matthew	9927	29 Jun 1789	100
McConnell, Matthew	9990	29 Jun 1789	100
McConnell, Matthew	9992	28 Oct 1789	100
McConnell, Matthew	9997	16 Jul 1789	100
McConnell, Matthew	10084	16 Jul 1789	100

232 25 Feb 1800 A/1/251

By Whom Registered: Jonathan Dayton
For Whom Registered: Jonathan Dayton
Location: (4000 acres) Mil - 17 2 - 2
Based upon the following Army land warrants:

Issued to	*No.*	*Date*	*Acres*
Fullerton, Richard	114	25 Feb 1792	200
Connelly, Robert, Capt	431	13 Dec 1791	300
McConnell, Matthew	1018	28 Oct 1789	200
Janson, Cornelius J., Capt	1142	1 Sep 1791	300
Emerson, Joseph	6803	14 Sep 1792	100
Henderson, William	7726	10 Sep 1790	100
Webb, Samuel B.	7056	2 Aug 1791	100
Broome, Samuel	7131	11 Nov 1791	100
Loder, Daniel, Pvt	7388	26 Aug 1790	100
Broome, Samuel	7827	11 Nov 1791	100
Webb, Samuel B.	8032	2 Aug 1791	100
McConnell, Matthew	10200	29 Jun 1789	100
McConnell, Matthew	10213	28 Oct 1789	100
McConnell, Matthew	10231	29 Jun 1789	100
McConnell, Matthew	10232	28 Oct 1789	100
McConnell, Matthew	10283	29 Jun 1789	100
McConnell, Matthew	10318	29 Jun 1789	100
McConnell, Matthew	10363	28 Oct 1789	100
McConnell, Matthew	10430	29 Jun 1789	100
McConnell, Matthew	10523	29 Jun 1789	100
McConnell, Matthew	10641	16 Jul 1789	100
McConnell, Matthew	12938	29 Jun 1789	100
McConnell, Matthew	12958	29 Jun 1789	100
McConnell, Matthew	13207	4 Aug 1789	100
McConnell, Matthew	13280	16 Jul 1789	100
McConnell, Matthew	13489	29 Jun 1789	100
McConnell, Matthew	13524	29 Jun 1789	100
McConnell, Matthew	13559	28 Oct 1789	100
McConnell, Matthew	13579	29 Jun 1789	100
McConnell, Matthew	13682	29 Jun 1789	100
McConnell, Matthew	13684	29 Jun 1789	100
McConnell, Matthew	13779	16 Jul 1789	100
McConnell, Matthew	13828	16 Jul 1789	100
McConnell, Matthew	13886	29 Jun 1789	100

233 25 Feb 1800 A/1/253

By Whom Registered: Jonathan Dayton
For Whom Registered: Jonathan Dayton
Location: (4000 acres) Mil - 17 5 - 4
Based upon the following Army land warrants:

Issued to	*No.*	*Date*	*Acres*
Curty, Barnaby, Pvt	9090	9 Jul 1789	100
Cooney, James, Pvt	9148	9 Jul 1789	100
Cavenaugh, Barney, Pvt	9226	21 Feb 1791	100
Broom, John	9254	9 Aug 1796	100
Dixon, William, Pvt	9323	9 Jul 1789	100
Howe, William, Cpl	9631	16 Jul 1789	100
Murray, Patrick, Pvt	9971	9 Jul 1789	100
Broom, John	10260	9 Aug 1796	100
Sullivan, Patrick, Pvt	10365	9 Jul 1789	100
Swick? [Smick? Smietz?] Reinard, Pvt	10457	19 Sep 1795	100
Roberts, Henry, Pvt	10874	2 Sep 1789	100
Wright, John	11021	17 Jan 1793	100
Johnston, Samuel	11190	11 Jun 1795	100
Johnston, Samuel	11579	11 Jun 1795	100
Smyth, Richard	11907	21 May 1794	100
Graves, Francis	11947	6 Jul 1793	100
Gamble, Robert, Pvt	12172	24 Jun 1795	100
Jones, Richard, Pvt	12280	17 Oct 1791	100
Graves, Francis	12324	9 Dec 1793	100
Graves, Francis	12328	9 Dec 1793	100
Means, Robert	12392	6 Jan 1795	100
Parker, Elias	12448	21 Oct 1791	100
Parker, Elias	12498	21 Oct 1791	100
Sharp, Benjamin, Pvt	12588	5 Jan 1792	100
Parker, Elias	12674	21 Oct 1791	100
Stockdell, John	12678	30 Jan 1795	100
Kingsley, Martin	12708	11 Apr 1792	100
Kingsley, Martin	12775	11 Apr 1792	100
Edes, James, Pvt	13050	22 Jul 1791	100
Frazier, Ducan, Pvt	13096	5 Jan 1791	100
Pomeroy, Samuel W., & Co.	13437	24 Nov 1791	100
Otto, Thomas, Pvt	13566	20 May 1791	100
Hallet, James	13595	20 Jul 1791	100
Aspel, James	13773	15 Dec 1790	100
Watrous, William, Pvt	13915	25 Sep 1790	100
Graves, Francis	13980	6 Jul 1793	100
Ryland, John, Pvt	13987	17 Oct 1791	100
Graves, Francis	14047	8 May 1793	100
Means, Robert	14091	8 Jan 1795	100
Sherrard, Francis	14109	24 Feb 1795	100

234 25 Feb 1800 A/1/254

By Whom Registered: Jonathan Dayton
For Whom Registered: Jonathan Dayton
Location: (4000 acres)* Mil - 18 1 - 3
Based upon the following Army land warrants:

Issued to	*No.*	*Date*	*Acres*
Dixon, Wayne, Lt	614	22 Nov 1791	200
Kingsley, Martin	1374	11 Apr 1792	300
Neal, James A.	2934	12 Oct 1795	100
Daily, Peter, Pvt	3086	12 Jan 1796	100
Miller, Daniel, Pvt	3342	7 Jun 1790	100
Neal, James A.	3398	12 Oct 1795	100
Answorth, Ephraim	3617	15 Apr 1795	100
Kingsley, Martin	3982	2 Dec 1791	100
Kingsley, Martin	4003	2 Dec 1791	100
Leavitt, David, Pvt	4551	12 Jul 1790	100
Kingsley, Martin	5016	7 Dec 1791	100
Kingsley, Martin	5160	28 Jun 1792	100
White, Nathan	5219	19 Apr 1792	100
Witham, James, Pvt	5227	13 Dec 1792	100
Smith, George	5230	11 Aug 1795	100
Munn, Reuben	5303	13 Apr 1795	100
Kingsley, Martin	5361	11 Apr 1792	100
Brown, Obadiah, Pvt	5415	31 Dec 1796	100
Kingsley, Martin	5697	11 Apr 1792	100
Kingsley, Martin	5852	5 Dec 1791	100
Loshane, Henry, Pvt	6129	31 Jan 1793	100
Winn, John, Pvt	6702	21 May 1794	100
Allen, Almissy, Pvt	6744	25 Sep 1790	100
Brown, Elias, Pvt	6893	21 Apr 1792	100
Fisher, Hannah	8043	17 Jun 1791	100
Wandle, Jacob, Sgt	8016	9 Jun 1790	100

234 [continued]

Milson? [Wilson?] James, Pvt	8524	26 May 1790	100
Easton, Samuel, Pvt	8286	6 Feb 1790	100
Butler, Patrick, Pvt	8955	13 Jun 1795	100
Lakee, William, Pvt	8499	14 Jan 1791	100
Dayton, Elias, & Son	8429	21 Aug 1789	100
Johnston, Windsor, Pvt	8438	21 May 1794	100
Landon, Laban, Pvt	8481	8 Dec 1794	100
White, Jonathan, Pvt	8051	29 Jan 1793	100
Chambers, James, Pvt	8220	6 Aug 1790	100
Stiles? [Hiles?] Job, Pvt	8729	29 Oct 1792	100
Beggs, Thomas, Sgt	8927	16 Jul 1789	100

*Marginal notation: "Patented in volume 1, page 61."

235 25 Feb 1800 A/1/255

By Whom Registered: Jonathan Dayton
For Whom Registered: Jonathan Dayton
Location: (4000 acres)* Mil - 12 5 - 4
Based upon the following Army land warrants:

Issued to	*No.*	*Date*	*Acres*
Conine, Philip, Lt	391	4 Jan 1791	200
De Forest, Samuel, Lt	538	3 Jun 1789	200
Logan, Samuel, Maj	1261	7 Sep 1790	400
Van Wagenen, Gerrit	1391	4 Sep 1790	300
Thompson, Andrew, Lt	2189	2 Sep 1790	200
Dunbar, William, Pvt	7035	1 Oct 1791	100
Rogers, Israel	7081	25 Jan 1791	100
Roe, James	7048	19 Apr 1791	100
Broome, John	7106	9 Aug 1796	100
Ballard, Asa	7146	22 Oct 1791	100
Reed, James	7149	20 Jul 1791	100
Goodwin, George, Pvt	7159	27 Sep 1790	100
Guth, John G.	7173	18 Apr 1791	100
Hawkey, William	7212	29 Apr 1793	100
Folsom, John	7380	7 Sep 1790	100
Connolly, Michael	7394	6 Mar 1792	100
Nugent, Patrick	7422	9 Apr 1791	100
Maxwell, Anthony	7423	14 Jun 1791	100
Van Howenburgh, Rudolphus	7454	5 May 1791	100
Morgan, Joseph, Pvt	7461	20 Oct 1790	100
Yates, Chris[tophe]r, Executors of [estate of]	7548	28 Aug 1790	100
Crane, Ezekiel	7602	9 Sep 1790	100
Hinton, John	7690	15 Sep 1790	100
Ryan, Robert, Pvt	7693	14 Feb 1791	100
Fisher, Hannah	7746	17 Jun 1791	100
Woodhull, Abel	7747	19 Apr 1791	100
Shelly, Cyrus, Pvt	7811	9 Nov 1791	100
Shaw, Michael, Pvt	7859	9 Apr 1791	100
Learman, Peter	7861	18 Jun 1791	100
Thornton, James, Pvt	7883	9 Apr 1791	100
Reed, James	7920	14 Jul 1791	100
de Witt, Moses	7934	9 Apr 1791	100

*Marginal notation:

"Location made [as cited above]	4092.1
Warr. recd. by this State	4000
Since recd.: Warr. No. 2258, dated 18 Jul 1789 in favor of John Van Dyk for 200 acres one half of which recd. to cover this excess, the other [half] to cover excess on loc[ation] made on State. No. 95	100
	4100
Amount of location	4092.1
	7.9"

[See also serial entry 270]

236 25 Feb 1800 A/1/257

By Whom Registered: Jonathan Dayton
For Whom Registered: Jonathan Dayton
Location: (4000 acres) Mil - 17 5 - 2
Based upon the following Army land warrants:

Issued to	*No.*	*Date*	*Acres*
Baker, Jesse, Capt	304	4 Jan 1795	300
Glentworth, James, Lt	836	14 Aug 1789	200
Lee, Henry	1171	9 Sep 1789	200
Kingsley, Martin	1229	28 Jun 1792	300
Nicholson, John	1453	7 Apr 1795	300
Richards, Samuel, Lt	1797	5 Oct 1790	200
Reed, John, Lt	1811	3 Sep 1790	200
Lee, Henry	2064	9 Sep 1789	300
Taulman? [Faulman?] Peter, Capt	2185	26 Aug 1790	300
Nicholson, John	2202	7 Apr 1795	200
Cuyler, Jacob, & Cuyler, L.	2261	21 Dec 1790	200
Waugh, James, Capt	2396	9 Jul 1789	300
Lee, Henry	2443	9 Sep 1789	200
Wright, Jotham, Lt	2558	2 Jan 1790	200
Hassell, John	13465	12 Jun 1795	100
Sherrard, Francis	14110	24 Feb 1795	100
Sherrard, Francis	14111	24 Feb 1795	100
Sherrard, Francis	14112	24 Feb 1795	100
Sherrard, Francis	14113	25 Mar 1795	100
Sherrard, Francis	14114	25 Mar 1795	100

237 25 Feb 1800 A/1/257

By Whom Registered: Theodore Foster
For Whom Registered: Theodore Foster & Co.
Location: (4000 acres) Mil - 17 1 - 1
Based upon the following Army land warrants:

Issued to	*No.*	*Date*	*Acres*
Foster, Theodore	1880	11 Feb 1800	500
Fuller, Sylvester	3344	18 Jan 1797	100
Horsewell, Ephraim, Cpl	3227	15 Jan 1800	100
Briggs, Jonathan, Pvt	2961	11 Feb 1800	100
Clark, John Innes	477	23 Feb 1795	500
Drowne, Philip, Pvt	3083	15 Jan 1800	100
Brown, William L? [F?]	3165	15 Jan 1800	100
Nelson, Nehemiah	3874	20 Dec 1799	100
Nelson, Nehemiah	4030	20 Dec 1799	100
Tabor, Henry, Pvt	3538	4 Nov 1794	100
Bemiss, Jonas, Pvt	3735	14 Feb 1793	100
Cushing, Matthew	14142	19 Mar 1799	100
Procter, Joseph, & Torrey, Melzer	2704	4 Jan 1800	200
Graves, Francis	11876	26 Mar 1792	100
Blackwell, Joseph	14128	8 Aug 1795	100
Ponsonby, George	11631	23 Dec 1795	100
Ponsonby, George	11642	23 Dec 1795	100
Ponsonby, George	11698	23 Dec 1795	100
Stites, John	307	16 May 1796	200
Stites, John	1108	16 May 1796	200
Stites, John	1543	16 May 1796	300
Axtell, Henry, & Axtell, L.	3632	7 Aug 1797	100
Greenman, Jeremiah, Lt	789	9 Mar 1796	200
Rogers, John, Lt	1776	11 Feb 1800	200
Barrows, Peter, Pvt	2955	11 Feb 1800	100

238 25 Feb 1800 A/1/258

By Whom Registered: Theodore Foster
For Whom Registered: Theodore Foster & Co.
Location: (4000 acres) Mil - 14 1 - 4

238 [continued]
Based upon the following Army land warrants:

Issued to	*No.*	*Date*	*Acres*
Foster, Theodore	3128	11 Feb 1800	100
Abbott, Stephen	14	23 Dec 1796	300
Winchester, Jacob B., Pvt	5233	23 Dec 1796	100
Gale, Edmund, Sgt	4213	23 Dec 1796	100
Stoker, Ebenezer, Lt	1909	12 Dec 1799	200
Humphreys, Anna, & Humphreys, John	952	5 Feb 1800	300
Hull, Joseph, Lt	980	24 Feb 1791	200
Stevens, Aaron, Capt	1945	10 Apr 1795	300
Mills, Alexander, Pvt	6195	27 Jun 1789	100
Maltbee, David	6681	18 Jan 1797	100
Brooks, Samuel, Pvt	6892	25 May 1790	100
Hinman, Samuel	5983	30 Jan 1790	100
Davenport, James	5722	24 May 1797	100
Church, Asa, Sgt	3928	28 Jan 1800	100
Wheeler, Adam, Capt	2322	4 Jan 1800	300
Sprague, Obadiah	3509	24 Feb 1800	100
Foster, William, Pvt	3116	24 Feb 1800	100
Creepman, Jonathan	12891	24 Feb 1800	100
Wallen, Jonathan, Capt	2288	24 Feb 1800	300
O'Brian, Abigail	4748	24 Feb 1800	100
Lesure, Gideon, Pvt	4584	24 Feb 1800	100
Humphrey, Tower, Pvt	4362	24 Feb 1800	100
Noble, Isaac, Pvt	4756	24 Feb 1800	100
Tarp, John, in trust for Haydon, Phebe	14156	24 Feb 1800	100
McAfferty, Charles, Pvt	3343	24 Feb 1800	100
Card, Potter, Pvt	3038	24 Feb 1800	100
Moers, Benjamin	3972	21 Sep 1790	100
Sprague, Obadiah	5787	24 Feb 1800	100

239 25 Feb 1800 A/1/259
By Whom Registered: James Johnston
For Whom Registered: James Johnston
Location: (4050 acres) Mil - 14 2 - 1
Based upon the following Army land warrants:

Issued to	*No.*	*Date*	*Acres*
Dehuff, Abraham, Capt	575	13 Jul 1795	300
Shockey, Christian, Sgt	10334	17 Feb 1800	100
Boyer, Michael, Sgt	861	14 Sep 1789	200
Boyer, Michael	237	14 Sep 1789	300
Neal, James A.	5309	26 Jan 1796	100
Stever? [Hever?] Michael	10085	17 Nov 1794	100
Blanchard, John	7539	2 Dec 1791	100
Ladd, Eliphalet, & Cass, J.	3301	21 Jul 1789	100
Roberts, J., & Roberts, Jos[eph?] Junior	14089	13 Sep 1798	100
Richardson, Addison	2697	9 Feb 1798	150
Sullivan, John, Sgt	13778	4 Sep 1789	100
Peek, Benjamin, Pvt	7649	19 Oct 1790	100
Leech, James, Pvt	9851	29 Mar 1791	100
Bremer, Lewis, Pvt	9043	11 Feb 1800	100
McNair, Angus	13563	26 Oct 1789	100
Mills, Isaac, Pvt	13530	5 Mar 1792	100
Wilson, Joseph	8723	26 Nov 1794	100
Jones, Francis, Pvt	9686	7 Sep 1789	100
Begley? [Bigley?] John, Pvt	11976	2 May 1794	100
Cautz? [Cantz?] Mark, Pvt	6971	4 Jan 1791	100
Hamilton, John, Pvt	9587	26 Jan 1795	100
Day, Isaac, Pvt	5716	23 Feb 1797	100
Chapman, Ceasar* Pvt	5565	2 Nov 1791	100
Southworth, Cousland	3049	15 Jan 1793	100
Houghton, Levy	5335	15 Dec 1795	100
Morrill, Amos, Major	1337	11 Feb 1800	400
Oliver, Richard	7100	5 Dec 1791	100
Glenn, C., & Bleecker, B.	13472	24 Aug 1790	100
Linn, John	1320	16 Mar 1792	200
Weidman, John, Lt	2392	13 Jul 1796	200

*So spelled.

240 25 Feb 1800 A/1/260
By Whom Registered: James Johnston
For Whom Registered: Charles C. Pinckney
Location: (4000 acres) Mil - 14 4 - 2
Based upon the following Army land warrants:

Issued to	*No.*	*Date*	*Acres*
Pinckney, Charles C., Col	1759	25 Feb 1800	500
Middleton, John	2705	2 Mar 1799	150
Hamilton, James, Maj	1010	20 Apr 1796	400
Lining, Charles, Capt	1316	15 Jan 1799	300
Marley? [Wharley?]* Felix	2451	1 Mar 1799	300
Pinckney, Thomas, Maj	1760	28 Dec 1798	400
Wharley, Felix	2449	1 Mar 1799	300
Read, William, Physician & Surgeon	1872	25 Feb 1800	450
Wharley, Felix, Capt	2448	11 Dec 1797	300
Flagg, Henry Collins, Surgeon	775	25 Feb 1800	400
Kennedy, James	616	10 May 1796	300
Kennedy, James, Lt	1216	10 May 1796	200

*Originally entered as Marley; pencilled notation shows Wharly in parentheses.

241 25 Feb 1800 A/1/261
By Whom Registered: Elijah Backus
For Whom Registered: Elijah Backus
Location: (4000 acres) Mil - 14 6 - 4
Based upon the following Army land warrants:

Issued to	*No.*	*Date*	*Acres*
Hammond, James, Cpl	11359	5 Sep 1789	100
Coursey, Hampton, Pvt	11053	11 Mar 1791	100
Woodward, Theophilus	3091	10 Oct 1796	100
Harris, Israel	6464	26 May 1798	100
Davis, Isaac	7682	24 Feb 1794	100
Woodward, William	2926	10 Oct 1796	100
Woodward, Theophilus	3425	10 Oct 1796	100
Woodward, Theophilus	5357	17 Feb 1797	100
Woodward, William	4713	7 Jun 1798	100
Harris, Israel	2956	27 Dec 1798	100
Harris, Israel	1946	19 Dec 1799	300
Eno, William, Pvt	5738	13 Mar 1798	100
Anderson, John, Pvt	3634	1 Oct 1791	100
Woodward, William	4083	10 Oct 1796	100
Banks, Zachariah, Pvt	3761	4 Sep 1792	100
Huntington, Jedediah, BrigGen	945	26 Oct 1791	850
Maxwell, Hugh, LtCol	1350	6 Feb 1795	450
Ballard, William H., Maj	94	24 Mar 1792	400
Rann, Solomon, Pvt	5457	16 Apr 1792	100
Kingsley, Martin	5032	2 Dec 1791	100
Day, Elijah, Lt	526	15 Oct 1789	200
Adams, John, Lt	4	23 Jul 1791	200

242 25 Feb 1800 A/1/262
By Whom Registered: William Steele
For Whom Registered: William Steele
Location: (4000 acres)* Mil - 4 5 - 2
Based upon the following Army land warrants:

242 [continued]

Issued to	No.	Date	Acres
Rapalje, Richard	13691	11 Dec 1789	100
Ostrand [blot] Thomas, Lt	2615	6 Dec 1792	200
Blanchard? [Blanckard?] John	3822	2 Dec 1791	100
Pepoon, Silas	6701	6 Jul 1791	100
Prentice, Jonas	1253	7 Jul 1792	300
Anderson, John, Pvt	6754	12 Jul 1792	100
Pepoon, Silas	3609	6 Jul 1791	100
Haskell, Benj[amin]	3700	8 May 1792	100
Quinton, David	4000	14 Mar 1791	100
Cronin, Patrick, Ens	398	1 Sep 1790	150
Prentice, Jonas, Lt	1962	7 Mar 1792	200
Webb, Samuel B., Col	2337	29 Jan 1790	500
Post, Anthony, Capt	2566	7 Sep 1790	300
Gilchrist, Robert	838	16 Sep 1789	200
Giles, Aquilla, Maj	852	22 Sep 1789	400
Johnston, John, Pvt	9667	21 Nov 1791	100
Broome, Samuel	7964	11 Nov 1791	100
Cline, William	2369	25 Aug 1790	150
Strong, Nathan, Capt	1992	6 Mar 1792	300
Lawrance, John	2612	3 Sep 1792	300
Hassell, John	10021	12 Jun 1795	100

*Marginal notation:

"Location made [as cited above]	4076.3
Warr. recd. [by] this State	4000
Since received:	
No. 6130 Warr. to Ephraim Little dated 24 Nov 1789	100
	4100
Amount of location	4076.3
	23.7"

[See also serial entry 277]

243 — 25 Feb 1800 — A/1/262

By Whom Registered: William Steele
For Whom Registered: William Steele
Location: (4000 acres) Mil - 17 6 - 3
Based upon the following Army land warrants:

Issued to	No.	Date	Acres
Crane, Ezekiel	8021	9 Sep 1790	100
Buxton, John, Pvt	8992	13 Dec 1790	100
Meads, James, Pvt	8567	28 Jan 1790	100
Unkey, John, Pvt	10537	13 Feb 1791	100
Bond, Thomas, Pvt	12826	14 Feb 1791	100
Thorn, Stephen, Pvt	13768	21 Jun 1791	100
Hartman, Peter, Pvt	13199	22 Feb 1791	100
Irvin, Wil[liam?] Sgt	8283	12 Mar 1790	100
Haskell, Benjamin	2327	12 Mar 1792	300
Stout, Philip	9123	7 Jun 1793	100
Davis, William, Esq., Col	597	7 May 1789	500
Broome, Samuel	7506	11 Nov 1791	100
Knapp, Caleb, Pvt	7340	10 Oct 1791	100
Loux, Hendrick, Pvt	7418	6 Sep 1791	100
Bartholomew, George	7849	28 Sep 1790	100
Thomas, Henry, Pvt	7869	19 Jul 1790	100
Davis, Daniel, Pvt	14037	1 Jun 1792	100
Howell, David	7591	24 Sep 1790	100
Boyd, Robert	7640	28 Jul 1791	100
Safford? [Lafford?] Samuel, LtCol	1881	14 Feb 1793	450
Huntington, Ebenezer, LtCol	949	13 Oct 1789	450
Benson, Joshua, Capt	106	--	300
Montjoy, John, Capt	2492	26 Feb 1793	300

244 — 25 Feb 1800 — A/1/263

By Whom Registered: John Wells & John Armstrong
For Whom Registered: John Wells & John Armstrong
Location: (4000 acres) Mil - 19 7 - 3
Based upon the following Army land warrants:

Issued to	No.	Date	Acres
Bushnell, David, Capt	141	3 Feb 1800	300
Clift, Lemuel, Capt	373	2 Sep 1790	300
Duff, Thomas	581	2 Sep 1789	300
Donohoe, Thomas, Maj	608	3 May 1796	400
LeRoy, George, Lt	1277	28 May 1790	200
Stout, Abraham, Lt	1995	8 May 1792	200
Sanders? [Landers?] William	2098	22 Nov 1791	200
Mebane, William	2578	21 Feb 1791	500
Ladd, E[liphalet] & Cass, J.	2945	21 Jul 1789	100
Ladd, E[liphalet] & Cass, J.	2988	14 Jan 1790	100
Ladd, E[liphalet] & Cass, J.	3022	14 Jan 1790	100
Ladd, E[liphalet] & Cass, J.	3023	21 Jul 1789	100
Ladd, E[liphalet] & Cass, J.	3069	21 Jul 1789	100
Ladd, E[liphalet] & Cass, J.	3114	21 Jul 1789	100
Ladd, E[liphalet] & Cass, J.	3140	21 Jul 1789	100
Ladd, E[liphalet] & Cass, J.	3189	21 Jul 1789	100
Thom, Chris[tophe]r L? [S?]	3202	27 May 1797	100
Ladd, E[liphalet] & Cass, J.	3261	21 Jul 1789	100
Ladd, E[liphalet] & Cass, J.	3285	21 Jul 1789	100
McGlocklin, John, Pvt	8556	3 Apr 1797	100
Due Hammell, John B., Pvt	9283	28 May 1790	100
Johnston, Joseph, Pvt	9682	19 Feb 1800	100
Knight, Michael, Cpl	9742	20 Jun 1789	100
Childs, George, Cpl	11039	11 May 1790	100

245 — 25 Feb 1800 — A/1/264

By Whom Registered: Thomas Biddle
For Whom Registered: Clement Biddle
Location: (4000 acres) Mil - 12 5 - 2
Based upon the following Army land warrants:

Issued to	No.	Date	Acres
Baily, J., & Cooke, T.	390	8 Sep 1790	400
Eggleston, John, Maj	671	18 Apr 1794	400
Janes, Elijah, Lt	1140	15 Dec 1791	200
Purvis, George, Capt	1726	30 May 1789	300
Singleton, Anthony, Capt	2068	13 Aug 1792	300
White, Nathan	2166	3 Feb 1792	300
Wilson, Simon Wilmer, Capt	2400	2 Sep 1789	300
Wilkinson, Young, Lt	2414	1 Sep 1789	200
White, Nathan	3071	3 Feb 1792	100
White, Nathan	3444	3 Feb 1792	100
White, Nathan	4393	3 Feb 1792	100
White, Nathan	4407	3 Feb 1792	100
Averill, Ephraim, Pvt	5395	16 Jan 1792	100
Morrison, William, Pvt	6229	15 Dec 1791	100
Edgerly, John, Pvt	7104	28 Dec 1791	100
Harris, Benjamin	8827	16 Oct 1789	100
Butler, T? [F?] & Davidson, J.	9084	25 Jan 1793	100
Riglass, Joseph	9190	10 Mar 1795	100
Feagen, James, Pvt	9392	8 Aug 1796	100
Norton, Henry, Pvt	10148	5 Aug 1796	100
Phelon, Peter, Pvt	10195	5 Aug 1796	100

245 [continued]

	No.	Date	Acres
Hull, George, Pvt	10379	5 Aug 1796	100
Handley? [Standley?] Peter, Pvt	10392	2 Sep 1796	100
Ponsonby, George	11421	23 Dec 1795	100

246 — 25 Feb 1800 — A/1/265

By Whom Registered: Philemon Thomas
For Whom Registered: Philemon Thomas
Location: (4000 acres) Mil - 19 2 - 4
Based upon the following Army land warrants:

Issued to	*No.*	*Date*	*Acres*
Bradford, Gamaliel, Lt	119	11 May 1790	200
Eaton, Benjamin	655	22 Apr 1796	200
Emery, Samuel	656	4 Nov 1794	300
Wildreth, William, Lt	930	15 Dec 1796	200
Thomas, Philemon	1526	11 Feb 1800	300
Waddell, Sarah	1602	24 Jan 1797	850
Crossman, George	1678	7 Jun 1794	300
Read, James, Capt	1865	11 Nov 1791	300
Seagres? [Seayres?] Thomas, Ens	2086	18 Sep 1789	150
Thomas, Philemon	8393	11 Feb 1800	100
McConnell, James, Pvt	8514	9 Jul 1789	100
Sherlock, John W., Pvt	8704	18 Jan 1790	100
Lewis, Samuel	9823	16 Jul 1789	100
Thomas, Philemon	9824	11 Feb 1800	100
Sloan, John, Cpl	10406	9 Jul 1789	100
Winters, Timothy	10571	--	100
Thomas, Philemon	10848	11 Feb 1800	100
Hayton? [Stayton? Slayton?]* Joseph, Pvt	10881	5 Jul 1797	100
Thomas, Philemon	11550	11 Feb 1800	100
Thomas, Philemon	13238	11 Feb 1800	100
Williams, John, Pvt	10627	16 Jul 1789	100

*Originally entered as Hayton; pencilled correction to Stayton or Slayton.

247 — 25 Feb 1800 — A/1/266

By Whom Registered: James Johnston
For Whom Registered: James Johnston
Location: (4000 acres) Mil - 16 3 - 2
Based upon the following Army land warrants:

Issued to	*No.*	*Date*	*Acres*
Greene, Catharine	787	22 Dec 1795	1100
Joynes, Leven, LtCol	1163	24 Nov 1792	500
Lawrence, John, Capt	1285	15 Feb 1790	300
Craig, John, Capt	427	30 Jan 1792	300
Graves, Francis	13996	31 Oct 1792	100
Power, Alexander	9810	27 Nov 1794	100
Britton, Mary	11956	16 Mar 1792	100
Howe, Joseph, Sgt	4398	17 Mar 1794	100
Blake, John Willand	3933	9 Dec 1797	100
Smith, Nathan, Pvt	4979	5 Apr 1793	100
Middleton, John, Pvt	10836	13 Sep 1793	100
Power, Alexander	9762	6 Aug 1792	100
Power, Alexander	9297	6 Aug 1792	100
Bond, Abijah	3469	19 Nov 1792	100
West, Thomas, Pvt	10599	6 Apr 1790	100
Lamberton, James	13881	3 Jul 1795	100
Call, Hugh, Pvt	9134	16 Jul 1789	100
Ap[p]leby, Thomas, Pvt	8896	16 Jul 1789	100
Smith, John	13776	6 Dec 1799	100
Hunter, Robert	9192	10 Mar 1795	100
Foster, Abraham	9903	31 Mar 1795	100
Warner, Ludwick, Pvt	10569	8 Aug 1796	100

248 — 25 Feb 1800 — A/1/267

By Whom Registered: Nathan Jones
For Whom Registered: Abraham B. DePeyster of N.Y.
Location: (4000 acres) Mil - 18 6 - 2
Based upon the following Army land warrants:

Issued to	*No.*	*Date*	*Acres*
Neale, James A.	2985	6 Nov 1795	100
Neale, James A.	3058	6 Nov 1795	100
Crosby, Sampson? [Lampson?]	3134	12 Aug 1795	100
Bond, Abijah	3137	19 Nov 1792	100
Neale, James A.	3146	19 Aug 1795	100
Austin, Elijah	4126	21 Feb 1792	100
Walton? [Wallon?] George	4191	1 Nov 1791	100
Hall, Robert, Pvt	4373	21 Apr 1796	100
Knieerbecker, Herman, Pvt	4509	21 Apr 1796	100
Austin, Elijah	4891	21 Feb 1792	100
Haskell, Benjamin	5116	8 May 1792	100
Austin, Elijah	5517	21 Feb 1792	100
Armstrong, William	5769	9 Mar 1796	100
Holmes, Simeon, Pvt	5951	21 Apr 1796	100
Austin, Elijah	6378	21 Feb 1792	100
Tubbs, Martin, Pvt	6534	21 Apr 1796	100
Bright, James, Pvt	6879	26 Nov 1791	100
Cockrem* Thomas, Sgt	6983	24 May 1790	100
Byram, Asa	7264	12 Oct 1790	100
Robert, John	7447	10 Aug 1790	100
Dewitt, John C.	7658	6 Mar 1792	100
Cumpston, Edward	8003	30 Jul 1790	100
Beadue, Elias, Pvt	8122	2 Apr 1796	100
Lane, William	10461	1 Nov 1791	100
Walton, George	10574	1 Nov 1791	100
McClelland, John	10612	4 Nov 1791	100
Lane, William	11321	1 Nov 1791	100
Lane, William	12035	1 Nov 1791	100
Stockdell, John	12235	31 Jan 1794	100
Stockdell, John	12360	31 Jan 1794	100
Stockdell, John	12518	6 Jan 1795	100
Stockdell, John	12566	31 Jan 1794	100
Stockdell, John	12645	31 Jan 1794	100
Crosby, Sampson? [Lampson?]	13268	29 Oct 1794	100
Palmer, Thomas	7891	3 May 1791	100
Ferris, Jacob	7899	9 Apr 1791	100
Cole, Isaac	12285	14 Aug 1792	100
Cole, Isaac	12335	14 Aug 1792	100
Cole, Isaac	12697	14 Aug 1792	100
Wood, Ebenezer, Pvt	13926	15 Sep 1790	100

*So spelled.

249 — 17 Mar 1800 — A/1/268

By Whom Registered: Elijah Backus
For Whom Registered: Elijah Backus
Location: (2511.2 acres) Mil - 13 6 - 4
Based upon the following Army land warrants:

Issued to	*No.*	*Date*	*Acres*
Calderwood, Adam, Capt	2594	20 Oct 1796	300
Pratt, William, Lt	1630	5 Mar 1800	200
Stewart, Walter, Col	2008	19 Aug 1799	500
Mackey, James, Lt	1467	24 Mar 1794	200
Warner, James, Drummer	5237	1 Apr 1790	100
Wheelock, Levi, Pvt	5213	5 Dec 1789	100
Harris, William, Pvt	4403	11 Apr 1792	100
Ebert, Henry, Pvt	12722	7 Jul 1789	100
Backus, Elijah	25*	10 Mar 1800	50
Backus, Elijah	25*	10 Mar 1800	861.2

*Register's certificate.

250 — 25 Apr 1800 — A/1/268

By Whom Registered: John Mathews
For Whom Registered: John Mathews
Location: (3463.8 acres) Mil - 11 7 - 2
Based upon the following Army land warrants:

Issued to	*No.*	*Date*	*Acres*
Holbrook, Abijah, Pvt	4146	15 Apr 1800	100
Holbrook, Abijah, Pvt	3124	30 Nov 1799	100
Holbrook, Abijah, Pvt	4239	30 Nov 1799	100
Holbrook, Abijah	3291	30 Nov 1799	100
Holbrook, Abijah, Pvt	4171	30 Nov 1799	100
Holbrook, Abijah, Pvt	13912	30 Nov 1799	100
Holbrook, Abijah, Pvt	5705	30 Nov 1799	100
Holbrook, Abijah, Pvt	3586	30 Nov 1799	100
Holbrook, Abijah, Pvt	6684	30 Nov 1799	100
Holbrook, Abijah, Pvt	3223	30 Nov 1799	100
Duncan, John, Pvt	12823	29 Nov 1799	100
Merrill, Jane, Pvt	13660	22 Feb 1799	100
Hamtramick, J. T.	22*	10 Mar 1800	1637
Burrall, Jonathan	8*	10 Mar 1800	105.6
Underwood, Robert	5*	10 Mar 1800	521.2

*Register's certificate.

251 — 25 Apr 1800 — A/1/269

By Whom Registered: John Armstrong
For Whom Registered: Jonathan Dayton
Location: (3056.9 acres) Mil - 13 5 - 4
Based upon the following Army land warrants:

Issued to	*No.*	*Date*	*Acres*
Dayton, Jonathan	19*	10 Mar 1800	918.1
Dayton, Jonathan	24*	10 Mar 1800	863.0
Dayton, Jonathan	15*	10 Mar 1800	920.0
Dayton, Jonathan	18*	10 Mar 1800	355.8

*Register's certificate.

252 — 25 Apr 1800 — A/1/269

By Whom Registered: Nathan Jones
For Whom Registered: Cornelia Ryckman
Location: (2300 acres) Mil - 13 5 - 1
Based upon the following Army land warrants:

Issued to	*No.*	*Date*	*Acres*
Bush, William, Lt	298	14 Aug 1792	200
Bell, Robert, Lt	300	14 Aug 1792	200
Janney, Thomas, Lt	1155	25 Jan 1791	200
Jones, Samuel, Capt	1173	14 Aug 1792	300
Ivey, Curtis, Lt	1174	14 Aug 1792	200
Norton, Nathaniel, Capt	1584	17 Sep 1792	300
Seeley, Isaac, Capt	2017	22 Aug 1791	300
Bunt, Lodwick, Pvt	6672	4 May 1791	100
Force, David, Pvt	7130	21 May 1791	100
Fleming, Michael, Pvt	7132	19 May 1791	100
Granger, John, Pvt	7162	14 Feb 1791	100
Luster, John, Pvt	7384	5 Jan 1791	100
Parr, Mathias, Pvt	7590	21 Apr 1791	100

253 — 29 Oct 1801 — A/1/278

By Whom Registered: Thomas McEwen & Co.
For Whom Registered: Zaccheus Biggs & Zaccheus A. Beatty
Location: (4013 acres) Mil - 3 2 3 -
Based upon the following Army land warrants:

Issued to	*No.*	*Date*	*Acres*
Wyley, John, Maj	2291	22 Jul 1789	400
Dorrance, Samuel, Sgt	5539	19 Feb 1799	100
Pierce, Benjamin, Lt	1648	13 Dec 1792	200
Taylor, Joshua, Sgt	6552	24 Jul 1789	100
Potter, Samuel, *et al*, Cpl	8462	22 Oct 1789	100
Potter, Samuel, *et al*, Pvt	8738	22 Oct 1789	100
Bindon, Joseph, Pvt	7309	6 Jun 1791	100
Morton, Silas, Lt	1359	24 Jan 1800	200
Sanford, Samuel, Capt	1947	30 Oct 1789	300
Mooney, Barnet, Sgt	8511	22 Jun 1789	100
Potter, Samuel, *et al*, Pvt	8161	22 Oct 1789	100
Post, John, *et al*, Pvt	8101	15 Sep 1790	100
Millett, Abraham, Pvt	4708	22 Feb 1799	100
Brockaway, Gideon, Sgt	6357	30 Nov 1796	100
Torrey, William, Lt	2234	22 Jan 1790	200
Goodall, Silas, Lt	813	13 May 1796	200
Munson, Eneas, Junior	5902	18 Dec 1795	100
Maxwell, Anthony, Pvt	7663	4 May 1791	100
Cassedy, Michael, Pvt	3860	2 May 1789	100
Thistle, Samuel, Pvt	6545	25 Jun 1789	100
Steele, William	17*	10 Mar 1800	920
Steele, William	13*	10 Mar 1800	193

*Register's certificate.

254 — 26 Dec 1801 — A/1/278

By Whom Registered: [not stated]
For Whom Registered: James Johnson
Location: (4012.2 acres) Mil - 1 2 1 -
Based upon the following Army land warrants:

Issued to	*No.*	*Date*	*Acres*
Brown, Joseph, Surgeon	191	4 Jan 1793	400
Blyth, Joseph, Surgeon	290	20 Oct 1791	400
Williams, Henry, Lt	1687	15 Sep 1790	200
Skolfield, William, Lt	2035	20 Jun 1796	200
Payne, John, Pvt	3319	30 Mar 1798	100
Font, Mathew, Pvt	9412	21 Apr 1800	100
Polley, Uriah, Pvt	6335	18 Jan 1798	100
Moore, James, Pvt	11544	11 Jun 1790	100
Gallup, Oliver, Pvt	5041	30 Dec 1796	100
Morrison, James, Pvt	11997	21 Apr 1796	100
Jones, Joseph, Pvt	8730	7 Aug 1789	100
McDonald, Rebecca, Pvt	10020	15 Mar 1790	100
Duncan, William, Pvt	8421	7 May 1800	100
Swan, Caleb	2*	10 Mar 1800	64
Warder, John	9*	10 Mar 1800	386.6
Johnston, James	10*	10 Mar 1800	456.5
Campbell, Robert	11*	10 Mar 1800	655.1
Mathews, John	32*	30 Apr 1800	200.0
Stark, John	--	4 Aug 1801	50.0
Leonard, Jacob	**	22 Aug 1801	50.0
McEwen, John	--	22 Aug 1801	50.0

*Register's certificate.
**Bears pencilled notation: "1237?"
[See also serial entry 296]

255 — 26 Dec 1801 — A/1/279

By Whom Registered: [James Johnson]
For Whom Registered: James Johnson
Location: (4000 acres) Mil - 7 1 - 4
Based upon the following Army land warrants:

Issued to	*No.*	*Date*	*Acres*
Lilley, Reuben, Sgt	4675	20 Jul 1789	100
Ceasor, James, Pvt	8195	8 Mar 1800	100
Hutt, Preston, Pvt	10786	20 Mar 1800	100
Ceasor, James, Pvt	8198	14 Mar 1800	100
Nagle, Henry, Sgt	10161	2 Jan 1796	100
Armstrong, John, Pvt	10922	11 Mar 1791	100
Cable, Jacob, Pvt	9113	20 Jan 1797	100
Masterson, Philip, Pvt	11548	11 Mar 1791	100
Jackson, John, Pvt	11384	11 Mar 1791	100

255 [continued]

Issued to	No.	Date	Acres
Becket, Humphrey, Pvt	10984	11 Mar 1791	100
Smith, John, Pvt	11678	24 Sep 1789	100
Buxton, Abijah, Pvt	10951	11 Mar 1791	100
Oldwine, Barnard, Pvt	10170	13 Jul 1789	100
McDuffy, Archibald, Pvt	8566	5 Nov 1789	100
Lytle, William, Capt	1312	10 Jun 1791	300
Chambers, Leonard, Pvt	6960	5 Nov 1789	100
Darby, Charles, Fifer	7021	5 Nov 1789	100
Woolford, Thomas, Col	2402	20 Feb 1794	500
Peebles, Seth, Pvt	12334	11 Dec 1797	100
McGloghlin, William, Pvt	11488	24 Sep 1789	100
Holmes, Hardy, Lt	1099	31 May 1796	200
Peebles, Seth, Pvt	12580	13 Feb 1797	100
Edwards, Nathaniel, Lt	659	14 Dec 1792	200
Blodget, Samuel, Lt	76	2 Apr 1800	200
McKillen, Edward, Pvt	10002	29 Mar 1791	100
Liswell, John, Lt	1241	13 Jul 1790	200
Scott, William, Maj	1882	26 Jan 1790	400

256 — 26 Dec 1801 — A/1/280

By Whom Registered: [not stated]
For Whom Registered: Daniel Thompson
Location: (4000 acres) Mil - 10 2 - 10*
Based upon the following Army land warrants:

Issued to	*No.*	*Date*	*Acres*
O'Brien, Ann, Pvt	13658	14 Jun 1791	100
Morgan, Samuel, Pvt	8522	5 May 1791	100
Wadsworth, Peleg, Capt	1232	22 Dec 1798	300
McGlaughlin, Patrick, Pvt	13446	21 Jun 1791	100
Titcomb, Daniel, Pvt	3318	25 Mar 1800	100
Marsh, William, Pvt	4686	15 Nov 1792	100
Fennimore, Samuel, Pvt	9528	19 Dec 1791	100
Fennimore, James, Pvt	8186	31 Oct 1791	100
List, Lewis, Pvt	13326	14 Jul 1789	100
Jones, Asal, Sgt	8415	4 Apr 1798	100
Welch, Anna, Capt	2680	3 Mar 1797	300
Connorey, John, Pvt	12030	20 Nov 1794	100
Douglass, Zebulon, Sgt	4451	21 Jul 1798	100
McGlaughlin, Patrick, Pvt	12773	21 Jun 1791	100
Stanbury, Jonas, Pvt	8682	20 Mar 1790	100
Pree? [Price?]** John, Pvt	10218	2 Sep 1796	100
Collier, Joseph, Lt	420	9 Jul 1789	200
Ennis, William, Lt	646	12 Feb 1799	200
Gamble, James, Lt	841	27 May 1791	200
Black, John, Lt	2101	30 Apr 1792	200
Demond, Peter, Pvt	9309	16 Nov 1791	100
Heath, William, MajGen	908	3 Jul 1789	1100

*Bears additional notation: "No. 1."
**Originally entered as Pree [probably apRee in Welsh]; pencilled correction to Price.

257 — 26 Dec 1801 — A/1/281

By Whom Registered: [not stated]
For Whom Registered: Jonas Stansberry
Location: (4020.6 acres) Mil - 6 1 3 -
Based upon the following Army land warrants:

Issued to	*No.*	*Date*	*Acres*
Heyer, Jacob, Ens	1000	19 Aug 1789	150
Saterlee, James, Fifer	6490	15 May 1790	100
Pope, John, Pvt	8737	17 Oct 1789	100
Weatherhead, Edmund, Pvt	6714	15 May 1790	100
Hance, John, Pvt	8101	15 Dec 1789	100
Hall, Lee, Pvt	6005	16 Mar 1792	100
Rogers, Platt, Pvt	6874	24 Sep 1791	100
Rice, James, Pvt	8677	6 Sep 1791	100
Rockefeller, Peter P., Ens	2190	9 Dec 1791	150
Hoghland, John, Pvt	13240	7 Jun 1790	100
Riker, John B., Surgeon	2528	18 Nov 1791	400
Rogers, Hezekiah, Capt	1793	21 Jul 1789	300
Bemus, Jotham, Cpl	2953	15 Jun 1789	100
Nestel, Godlieb, Pvt	3563	29 Mar 1792	100
Dowlan? [Dorolar?] George, Pvt	7065	10 Sep 1790	100
Rowlee, Samuel, Pvt	4893	6 Mar 1798	100
Stanbery, Jonas, Lt	814	25 Feb 1800	200
Mitchell, Barnabas, Pvt	6206	15 May 1790	100
Heckenwelder, John	1*	10 Mar 1800	180.4
Galbreath, --, & Elmes, --	20*	10 Mar 1800	569.8
Dayton, Jonathan	34*	30 Apr 1800	445.1
Rathbone, John	36*	12 Sep 1801	325.3

*Register's certificate.

258 — 29 Dec 1802 — A/1/285

By Whom Registered: George Jackson
For Whom Registered: George Jackson
Location: (4127.9 acres) Mil - 9 2 1 -
Based upon the following Army land warrants:

Issued to	*No.*	*Date*	*Acres*
Shirts, Peter, Pvt	7798	4 May 1791	100
Malster, Benjamin, Pvt	13537	2 Sep 1789	100
Lazarus, Frederick, Pvt	9832	20 Aug 1795	100
Eastman, Jacob, Pvt	3089	30 Mar 1798	100
Lester, Damaris, *et al*, Lt	1257	23 Apr 1800	200
Phelps, Asahel, Pvt	11298	9 Jul 1800	100
Leland, Joseph, Lt	1236	29 May 1797	200
Phelps, Asahel, Pvt	11494	12 May 1800	100
Gardner, Henry G., Surgeon's Mate	1370	25 Jan 1796	300
Wolcott, Solomon, Pvt	4908	25 Jan 1796	100
Leavitt, Nathaniel, Lt	2689	7 Jul 1797	200
Muse, Walker, Capt	1485	21 Sep 1789	300
Clayes, Peter, Capt	341	25 Jan 1799	300
Freeman, Constant, CaptLt	717	9 Jul 1790	200
Halkerstone, Robert, Lt	1033	21 Sep 1789	200
Ware, Francis M., Lt	2410	21 Sep 1789	200
Stanton, William, Capt	1965	25 Jun 1789	300
Green, Jesse, Lt	1206	31 May 1797	200
Coines, Dominic, Pvt	14051	24 Aug 1793	100
Humphrey, Samuel, Pvt	7238	27 May 1795	100
Henzian? [Hensian?] Joseph, Pvt	9645	14 Mar 1800	100
Phelps, Asahel, Pvt	11272	17 Dec 1799	100
Richmond, Christopher, Capt	1841	1 Sep 1789	300
Skinner, George	26*	10 Mar 1800	50
Mathews, John	33*	30 Apr 1800	77.9

*Register's certificate.

259 — 31 Dec 1802 — A/1/286

By Whom Registered: Jonathan Dayton
For Whom Registered: Jonathan Dayton
Location: (4000 acres) Mil - 2 10 - 4
Based upon the following Army land warrants:

Issued to	*No.*	*Date*	*Acres*
Lewis, Joseph, Pvt	8095	27 Oct 1796	100
Townsend, Kneeland, Pvt	5815	20 Dec 1797	100
Gardner, Henry G., Pvt	6374	23 Jan 1796	100
Sickles, Abraham, Pvt	7794	25 Aug 1790	100
Wolcott, Solomon, Junior, Pvt	4179	8 Jul 1797	100
Wolcott, Solomon, Pvt	6358	21 May 1798	100
Gardner, Henry G., Pvt	3418	23 Jan 1796	100
Bicker, Henry, Col	221	11 May 1789	500

259 [continued]

Issued to	No.	Date	Acres
Stilwell, Elias, Capt	1952	29 Sep 1790	300
Trowbridge, John, Lt	2176	13 Sep 1790	200
Connor, Joseph, Pvt	3523	15 Apr 1796	100
King, Josiah, Pvt	4508	22 Jan 1796	100
Underwood, Robert, Pvt	6555	11 Apr 1792	100
Sill, Elizabeth, *et al*, Capt	1950	15 Dec 1790	300
Sill, Elizabeth, *et al*, Pvt	6898	15 Dec 1790	100
Glenn, Cornelius, Pvt	7272	12 Aug 1790	100
Shenkland, Thomas, Pvt	5307	4 Oct 1790	100
Smith, Samuel, Pvt	14133	11 Aug 1795	100
Welch, Michael, Pvt	8860	30 Mar 1793	100
Sloan, Sturgin, Lt	1916	27 Feb 1795	200
Larned, Simon, Capt	1233	22 Aug 1789	300
Scudder, William, Pvt	13668	30 Aug 1792	100
Croughton, Charles, Lt	282	21 Jun 1796	200
Scott, Thomas P., Lt	1764	28 Jan 1797	200
Beardsley, Abijah, Pvt	5475	2 Jul 1790	100
Campbell, Lewis, Pvt	8232	19 Jun 1789	100

260 — 31 Dec 1802 — A/1/286

By Whom Registered: Jonathan Dayton
For Whom Registered: Joseph Vance
Location: (3900 acres)* Mil - 10 2 4 -
Based upon the following Army land warrants:

Issued to	*No.*	*Date*	*Acres*
Williams, Joshua, Capt	2395	12 Dec 1794	300
Tilden, John B., Lt	2200	10 Oct 1796	200
McChristy, Michael, Pvt	10099	5 Nov 1789	100
Pinkerton, Andrew, Pvt	10239	3 Mar 1794	100
Greaves, Francis, LtCol	2422	13 Dec 1791	450
Patten, Thomas, Capt	2551	31 Oct 1791	300
Green, Stephen, Pvt	13153	15 May 1799	100
Richardson, Ebenezer, Sgt	4899	15 Dec 1796	100
Jones, Samuel, Pvt	4454	14 Dec 1796	100
Sanders, Isaac, Pvt	8816	21 Feb 1793	100
Rollins, Aaron, Pvt	3447	17 Apr 1800	100
Holbrook, Abijah, Sgt	3929	21 May 1800	100
Schrack, David, Capt	2033	23 Nov 1799	300
Wilds, Ebenezer, Lt	2311	23 Aug 1791	200
Crossman, William, Pvt	14148	13 Mar 1798	100
Hughes, Robert, Pvt	4312	15 Mar 1800	100
Loudon, Samuel, Pvt	7329	4 May 1791	100
Duncan, John, Cpl	8083	17 May 1800	100
Tuttle, William, Ens	2195	30 Sep 1789	150
Curtis, Enoch, Pvt	12954	14 Nov 1791	100
Johnston, Samuel, Pvt	11784	11 Jun 1795	100
Painter, George, Pvt	13059	7 Jun 1790	100
Patterson, William, Pvt	7608	3 Jan 1797	100
Camp, Aaron, Pvt	5547	7 Mar 1792	100
Camp, Aaron, Pvt	6185	7 Mar 1792	100
Coggshell, William, Pvt	5485	10 Mar 1796	100
Vandyck, Cornelius, Pvt	6846	18 Apr 1792	100

*Marginal notation:
"Amount of warrants recd. 3900
Amount of location 3850
Reg[ister's] cert[ificate] issued for 50"

261 — 31 Mar 1803 — A/1/288

By Whom Registered: John Davidson
For Whom Registered: John Davidson
Location: (4100 acres) Mil - 12 7 2 -
Based upon the following Army land warrants:

Issued to	*No.*	*Date*	*Acres*
Marshall, John, CaptLt	880	13 Feb 1800	200
Russell, Albert, Lt	1857	18 Jun 1793	200
Heffernan, Hugh, Sgt	9579	20 Jun 1789	100
Canfield, Ithamar, Pvt	13725	15 May 1800	100
Canfield, Ithamar, Pvt	5601	23 Feb 1797	100
Canfield, Ithamar, Pvt	6564	15 May 1800	100
Canfield, Ithamar, Pvt	6593	15 May 1800	100
Starr, Josiah, Pvt	13438	23 Feb 1797	100
Collins, John, Junior, Pvt	12896	2 Sep 1790	100
Scott, Perry, Pvt	13805	2 Sep 1789	100
Kelly, John, Cpl	9719	10 Mar 1790	100
Jackson, Pomp, Pvt	4423	9 Dec 1796	100
Hopkins, Richard, Cpl	4385	15 May 1790	100
Cutter? [Cutler?] Benjamin, Pvt	3935	26 Feb 1799	100
Clark, William, Cpl	9203	10 Mar 1790	100
Hutton, James, Pvt	9572	16 Jul 1789	100
Lynn, John, Pvt	9835	5 Nov 1789	100
Woodman, Joshua, Lt	2313	14 May 1800	200
Goodrick, Solomon P., Pvt	14153	3 Jan 1800	100
Goodrick, Solomon P., Pvt	12331	3 Jan 1800	100
Roiblet, Abraham, Pvt	10305	16 Jul 1789	100
Eagin, John, Fifer	9347	9 Jul 1789	100
Hawkins, David, Pvt	7773	9 Jun 1791	100
Hawkins, David, Pvt	6818	9 Jun 1791	100
James, Elizabeth, Pvt	13259	29 Feb 1792	100
Paine, John, Pvt	3334	22 Feb 1799	100
Bent, Prince, Pvt	2983	4 Nov 1794	100
Bulger, Daniel, Pvt	10985	11 Jun 1790	100
Lovejoy, Ezekiel, Lt	973	18 Jan 1791	200
Goldsborough, William, Lt	860	15 May 1789	200
Barrett, Solomon? [Simon?]* Fifer	14152	28 Jun 1799	100
Spencer, Humphrey, Pvt	11681	9 May 1797	100
Dickerson, Mahlon, Pvt	8420	18 Sep 1799	100
Dickerson, Mahlon, Pvt	8692	3 Jun 1800	100
Ford, Daniel, Pvt	8664	18 Sep 1799	100
Ford, Daniel, Pvt	8290	18 Sep 1799	100

*Originally entered as Solomon; pencilled correction to Simon.

262 — 5 Mar 1805 — A/1/290

By Whom Registered: David Jones
For Whom Registered: David Jones
Location: (4053.2 acres)* Mil - 15 7 3 -
Based upon the following Army land warrants:

Issued to	*No.*	*Date*	*Acres*
Maxim, William, Philip Schroeder? devisee	9908	28 Feb 1797	100
Adams, William, Surgeon	47	24 Oct 1789	400
Ogden, Daniel, Pvt	7563	30 Jul 1792	100
McCoskey, Samuel A., Surgeon	1458	16 Jul 1789	400
Philips, Francis, Pvt	8656	20 Jul 1790	100
Cooper, Spencer, Matross	11985	27 Aug 1800	100
Shirts, Matthias, Pvt	8764	1 Mar 1796	100
Hyatt, John Vance, Lt	1040	30 May 1789	200
Hughes, John, Lt	1016	16 Jul 1789	200
Morgan, Joseph, Sgt	6135	13 Apr 1798	100
Hyatt, Minnah, Pvt, Snow, Elijah, assignee	7243	2 Jan 1796	100
Barrell, William, Pvt	8155	23 Sep 1789	100
Covert, Tunis, Pvt, Heller? [Hiller?] Jacob, assignee	8206	20 Dec 1791	100
Burnsides, John, Pvt	11894	28 May 1791	100
Bull? [Bulls? Butts?] Thomas, Pvt	12801	6 Apr 1790	100
McCoy, Roderick, Cpl	9963	16 Jul 1789	100

262 [continued]

Caldwell, James, Matross	9214	27 Nov 1790	100
Humphrey, John, Lt	1026	19 Aug 1789	200
Humphrey, Jacob, Capt	1012	19 Aug 1789	300
Muller, Jeremiah C., Ens, Radclife, William, Junior, assignee	2667	30 Dec 1796	150
O'Bryan, Philip, Pvt	11582	28 Feb 1791	100
Davis, Sampson	16**	10 Mar 1800	803.2

*Marginal notation:
"Content of [location cited above] 4000.0
Amount of warrants . . . 4053.2
Amount unsatisfied 53.2
For which 53.2 surplus certificate no. 39 was issued.
**Register's certificate.

263 No date A/1/270
By Whom Registered: Theodorus Bailey
For Whom Registered: Theodorus Bailey
Location: (1050 acres) [See serial entry 128]
Based upon the following Army land warrants:

Issued to	*No.*	*Date*	*Acres*
Mathews, Henry, Junior	3350	4 Nov 1794	100
Hopkins, James, Pvt	3225	28 May 1792	100
Davis, Robert, Capt	530	24 Jul 1792	300
Gray, Charles, Pvt	3156	28 May 1792	100
Barney, Jabez, Ens	130	14 Mar 1796	150
Hull, Thomas, Pvt	4761	23 Jan 1799	100
Olney, Stephen, Pvt	3583	24 Dec 1789	100
Hull, Thomas, Pvt	4360	23 Jan 1799	100

264 No date A/1/270
By Whom Registered: Baum, --, & Schenck, --
For Whom Registered: John N. Cummings, John Burnet, & George W. Burnet
Location: (250 acres) [See serial entry 169]
Based upon the following Army land warrants:

Issued to	*No.*	*Date*	*Acres*
Sproule, Moses, Ens	1999	7 Oct 1789	150
Trelegan, John, Pvt	8808	26 Jun 1789	100

265 No date A/1/270
By Whom Registered: William Simmons
For Whom Registered: William Simmons
Location: (250 acres) [See serial entry 31]
Based upon the following Army land warrants:

Issued to	*No.*	*Date*	*Acres*
Brevard, Joseph, Lt	299	12 Jan 1799	200
Johnston, James	*	10 Mar 1800	50

*Register's certificate no. 29.

266 No date A/1/270
By Whom Registered: Martin Baum
For Whom Registered: Martin Baum
Location: (417.8 acres) [See serial entry 38]
Based upon the following Army land warrants:

Issued to	*No.*	*Date*	*Acres*
Newkirk, Charles, Pvt	6903	23 Aug 1790	100
Baum, Martin	*	10 Mar 1800	317.8

*Register's certificate no. 4.

267 No date A/1/270
By Whom Registered: Thomas McEwen & Co.
For Whom Registered: Nicholas Gilman
Location: (256 acres) [See serial entry 85]
Based upon the following Army land warrants:

Issued to	*No.*	*Date*	*Acres*
Wells, William, & Armstrong, J.	*	10 Mar 1800	65.7
Gilman, Nicholas	**	10 Mar 1800	190.3

*Register's certificate no. 23.
**Register's certificate no. 7.

268 No date A/1/270
By Whom Registered: John A. Seitz
For Whom Registered: James Morrison
Location: (350 acres) [See serial entry 97]
Based upon the following Army land warrants:

Issued to	*No.*	*Date*	*Acres*
Johnston, James	*	10 Mar 1800	50
Morrison, James, Pvt	11897	21 Apr 1796	100
Morrison, James, Pvt	10469	21 Apr 1796	100
Morrison, James, Pvt	10383	21 Apr 1796	100

*Register's certificate no. 27.

269 No date A/1/271
By Whom Registered: [Thomas Parker, Junior?]
For Whom Registered: George [Suckley?]
Location: (100 acres) [See serial entry 216]
Based upon the following Army land warrant:

Issued to	*No.*	*Date*	*Acres*
Lewis, Margaret, Pvt	4620	22 Jun 1791	100

270 No date A/1/271
By Whom Registered: Jonathan Dayton
For Whom Registered: Jonathan Dayton
Location: (200 acres) [See serial entry 235]
Based upon the following Army land warrant:

Issued to	*No.*	*Date*	*Acres*
Van Dyk, John, Lt	2258	18 Jul 1789	200

271 No date A/1/271
By Whom Registered: Jonas Stanbery
For Whom Registered: Jonas Stanbery
Location: (1075.4 acres) [See serial entry 68]
Based upon the following Army land warrants:

Issued to	*No.*	*Date*	*Acres*
Stansbery, Jonas	*	10 Mar 1800	125.4
Stanbury, Joseph, Ens	2590	8 Aug 1791	150
Woodward, William, Pvt	4455	6 Jul 1796	100
McCauley, John, Lt	1345	26 Mar 1792	200
Peck, John, Lt	1361	19 Apr 1792	200
Lamont, John, Capt	1244	12 Apr 1790	300

*Register's certificate no. 6.

272 No date A/1/271
By Whom Registered: Jonas Stanbery
For Whom Registered: Joseph Hardy
Location: (940 acres) [See serial entry 154]
Based upon the following Army land warrants:

Issued to	*No.*	*Date*	*Acres*
Hardy, Joseph	*	10 Mar 1800	540

272 [continued]

Newman, Henry, Capt	793	13 Sep 1792	300
Crane, Abel, Pvt	3868	22 Jul 1789	100

*Register's certificate no. 14.

273 No date A/1/271

By Whom Registered: Cairnoen Medowell
For Whom Registered: Cairnoen Medowell
Location: (50 acres) [See serial entry 13]
Based upon the following Army land warrant:

Issued to	*No.*	*Date*	*Acres*
McGlaughlin, Alexander	*	10 Mar 1800	50

*Register's certificate no. 31.

274 No date A/1/271

By Whom Registered: William Martin
For Whom Registered: John Bray
Location: (100 acres) [See serial entry 178]
Based upon the following Army land warrant:

Issued to	*No.*	*Date*	*Acres*
Hunter, William, Pvt	9559	18 Jun 1789	100

275 No date A/1/271

By Whom Registered: Jonas Stanbery
For Whom Registered: John A. Hardenbrook
Location: (100 acres) [See serial entry 153]
Based upon the following Army land warrant:

Issued to	*No.*	*Date*	*Acres*
Schuyler, Philip, Pvt	2986	21 Dec 1790	100

276 No date A/1/271

By Whom Registered: [Thomas Salter]
For Whom Registered: Thomas Salter
Location: (300 acres) [See serial entry 121]
Based upon the following Army land warrants:

Issued to	*No.*	*Date*	*Acres*
Hammond, Abijah, Lt	939	27 Feb 1800	200
Swift, Zepheniah, Pvt	5546	27 Mar 1794	100

277 No date A/1/271

By Whom Registered: William Steele
For Whom Registered: William Steele
Location: (100 acres) [See serial entry 242]
Based upon the following Army land warrant:

Issued to	*No.*	*Date*	*Acres*
Little, Ephraim, Pvt	6130	24 Nov 1789	100

278 No date A/1/282

By Whom Registered: Jacob D. Hart
For Whom Registered: Thomas McKean Thompson
Location: (1100 acres)* [See serial entry 27]
Based upon the following Army land warrants:

Issued to	*No.*	*Date*	*Acres*
Trifts? [Tufts?] Turrell, Pvt	5984	29 Nov 1792	100
Trifts? [Tufts?] Turrell, Pvt	4516	29 Nov 1792	100
Maxwell, William, Sgt	10883	2 Sep 1789	100
Hosmer, Timothy, Surgeon	970	15 Sep 1799	400
McConnell, Mathew, Capt	2121	29 Jun 1789	300
Trifts? [Tufts?] Turrell Pvt	12793	28 Nov 1792	100

*Marginal notation: "These warrants patented to Thomas McKean Thompson in a 5040-acre tract, 3d quarter, 3d township, 13th range, dated 24 Apr 1802. Recorded Volume 1, page 412."

279 No date A/1/272

100-Acre Patents to Enlisted Men Corresponding to Land Certificates: 1 through 29

Name of Patentee *War. No.*	*Date*	*Location*					
Messer, George, Pvt 10100	12 Jan 1791	**Mil**	-	20	5	2	5
Marker, Andrew, Cpl 13519	21 Aug 1789	Mil	-	19	1	2	2
Orr, John, Pvt 8616	22 Jun 1789	Mil	-	19	1	2	1
Millington, Peter, assignee of David French? [Finch?] Sgt 4172	18 Jan 1800	Mil	-	19	2	3	14
Scott, Moses, Pvt 6475	3 Aug 1790	Mil	-	20	7	3	1
Millington, Peter, assignee of Ezra Tryon, Pvt 6574	13 Jan 1800	Mil	-	20	6	3	11
Lipky, Henry, Pvt 9849	11 Nov 1791	Mil	-	20	6	2	13
Woods, William, Pvt 8849	10 Mar 1796	Mil	-	20	6	2	8
Hart, Nicholas, Pvt 9613	21 Apr 1792	Mil	-	10	7	1	10
Carbury, Francis, Pvt 8218	7 Dec 1798	Mil	-	20	4	1	6
Anderson, George, Pvt 8912	9 Jul 1789	Mil	-	20	4	4	6
Stowers, John, Drummer 10404	24 Dec 1790	Mil	-	20	6	3	3
Homes, Thomas, Pvt 3181	24 Apr 1800	Mil	-	19	2	3	15
Rowan, John, Pvt 10292	8 May 1800	Mil	-	15	1	3	33
Ward, John, Cpl 13924	4 Apr 1800	Mil	-	20	4	4	6
Coyle, Mark, Pvt 9169	15 May 1790	Mil	-	1	8	2	30
La Fleche, John, Pvt 13320	11 Feb 1800	Mil	-	1	8	2	31
Terms, Peter, Pvt 13808	22 May 1800	Mil	-	1	8	2	32
Statinger, John, Pvt 10412	7 Jul 1796	Mil	-	13	8	4	20
Collins, Oliver, Cpl 3988	10 Jan 1800	Mil	-	20	4	4	5
McKinley, John, Pvt 9965	10 Mar 1790	Mil	-	10	9	3	34
McKinley, Alexander, Pvt 9977	19 Mar 1790	Mil	-	10	9	3	35
Gwinnup, George, Pvt 8334	17 Nov 1796	Mil	-	20	7	3	2
Hart, Joseph, Pvt 5949	27 Jun 1789	Mil	-	15	2	2	10
Hart, Joel, Pvt 5980	10 May 1798	Mil	-	15	2	2	8
McDonald, William, Pvt 13528	19 Feb 1790	Mil	-	8	5	1	5

279 [continued]
Atkins, David, Pvt
5388 25 Jun 1789 Mil - 13 8 1 10
Chamberlain, Theodore, Pvt
5567 25 Jun 1789 Mil - 13 8 1 7
Doud, Richard, Pvt
5717 25 Jun 1789 Mil - 13 8 1 6
Smith, Nathaniel, assignee of Gibbs, Moore, Pvt
5890 14 Dec 1796 Mil - 14 8 3 35
Stoddard, Simeon C., Pvt
6500 21 Aug 1789 Mil - 14 8 3 12
Peck, John, Pvt
6299 26 Oct 1789 Mil - 14 8 3 5

280 No date A/1/271
100-Acre Patents to Enlisted Men Corresponding to Land Certificates: 30 through 34
Name of Patentee
War. No. Date Location
Lewis, Naboth, Pvt
6128 25 Jun 1789 Mil - 13 8 1 5
Smith, Asaph, Pvt
6512 25 Jun 1789 Mil - 13 8 1 4
Smith, Josiah, Pvt
6520 25 Jun 1789 Mil - 13 8 1 3
Stow, Zaccheus, Pvt
6440 25 Jun 1789 Mil - 13 8 1 2
Treat, John, Pvt
6504 25 Jun 1789 Mil - 13 8 1 1

281 No date A/1/275
100-Acre Patents to Enlisted Men Corresponding to Land Certificates: 35 through 40
Name of Patentee
War. No. Date Location
Shope, William, Sgt
12545 30 Apr 1800 Mil - 16 2 4 32
Edwards, Edmond, Pvt
14077 27 May 1794 Mil - 16 2 4 30
Montgomery, John, Pvt
9978 6 Apr 1790 Mil - 16 2 4 31
Gray, Frazier, Pvt
10775 2 Sep 1789 Mil - 16 2 4 20
Finney, Roger, Pvt
9374 3 Dec 1792 Mil - 16 2 4 15
De Hart, Abraham, Pvt
9245 15 May 1793 Mil - 16 2 4 14

282 No date A/1/276
100-Acre Patents to Enlisted Men Corresponding to Land Certificates: 41 through 46
Name of Patentee
War.No. Date Location
Calhoon, Andrew, Trumpet[er]
12027 2 Mar 1799 Mil - 16 2 4 19
Ruggles, William, Fifer
10250 9 Jul 1789 Mil - 16 2 4 18
Hall, John, Pvt
12198 6 Jan 1791 Mil - 16 3 4 30
Smith, Michael, Pvt
12535 14 Dec 1795 Mil - 16 2 4 29
Lehea, John, Pvt
10807 28 Apr 1800 Mil - 3 5 1 4
Hogins, Benoni, Pvt
5993 6 Nov 1789 Mil - 3 5 1 11

283 No date A/1/282
100-Acre Patents to Enlisted Men Corresponding to Land Certificates: 47 through 49
Name of Patentee
War.No. Date Location

284 No date A/1/276
100-Acre Patents to Enlisted Men Corresponding to Land Certificates: 50 through 52
Name of Patentee
War. No. Date Location
Means, Thomas, Pvt
9922 23 Feb 1797 Mil - 1 8 3 12
Beatty, William, Pvt
9059 31 Mar 1800 Mil - 1 8 3 22
Moore, John, Sgt
11493 1 Feb 1790 Mil - 2 6 3 25

285 No date A/1/284
100-Acre Patents to Enlisted Men Corresponding to Land Certificate: 53
Name of Patentee
War. No. Date Location
Knapp, Jared, Pvt
6054 1 Feb 1797 Mil - 14 8 3 34

286 No date A/1/276
100-Acre Patents to Enlisted Men Corresponding to Land Certificates: 54 through 57
Name of Patentee
War. No. Date Location
Swett, Jonathan, Pvt
5118 10 Oct 1796 Mil - 2 10 2 21
Tinney? [Finney?] John, Pvt
12598 28 Feb 1800 Mil - 1 8 4 33
Rich, Samuel, Pvt
6404 15 Apr 1800 Mil - 2 2 3 29
White, Philip, Pvt
6691 15 Apr 1800 Mil - 2 2 3 37

287 No date A/1/277
100-Acre Patents to Enlisted Men Corresponding to Land Certificates: 58 through 61
Name of Patentee
War. No. Date Location
Beaham, James, Pvt
11895 6 Apr 1790 Mil - 2 2 3 38
Snow, Elizabeth, heir of Thomas Snow, Pvt
14157 7 May 1800 Mil - 2 2 3 36
Smith, Elnathan, Sgt
6518 7 Apr 1790 Mil - 9 1 3 30
Andrews, John? Cpl
5397 10 Dec 1789 Mil - 9 1 3 35

288 No date A/1/278
100-Acre Patents to Enlisted Men Corresponding to Land Certificates: 62 through 64
Name of Patentee

288 [continued]

War. No.	*Date*	*Location*					
Shreve, Godfrey, Pvt							
5015	24 Jun 1795	Mil	-	2	8	4	4
Weaver, John, Pvt							
7973	29 Jun 1790	Mil	-	2	8	4	3
Blundin, William, Drum Major							
12815	20 Jun 1789	Mil	-	9	1	3	29

289 — No date — A/1/282

100-Acre Patents to Enlisted Men Corresponding to Land Certificates: 65 through 77

Name of Patentee							
War. No.	*Date*	*Location*					
Bailey, Ichabod, heirs of							
5459	7 Jan 1800	Mil	-	14	8	3	27
Barnes, Ambrose, Cpl							
5444	7 Jan 1800	Mil	-	14	8	3	20
Hurlbut, Raphael, Pvt							
6004	25 Jun 1789	Mil	-	14	8	3	13
Fifield, John, Pvt							
4195	10 Mar 1800	Mil	-	14	8	3	23
Luce, Jonathan, Pvt							
6123	19 May 1797	Mil	-	2	6	3	17
Guthrie, Joseph, Pvt							
4203	21 Apr 1794	Mil	-	6	6	2	21
Nourse, James, Pvt							
13556	23 Dec 1796	Mil	-	15	2	2	35
Shields, David, Sgt							
5022	18 Dec 1799	Mil	-	15	2	2	36
Coon, Israel, Pvt							
12965	9 Sep 1790	Mil	-	10	3	4	33
Kirkpatrick, James, Pvt							
8466	11 Sep 1792	Mil	-	13	8	4	17
Meeker, Michael, Pvt							
8519	7 Jul 1789	Mil	-	2	6	3	16
Oldwine, Barney, Pvt							
10187	12 Feb 1795	Mil	-	13	8	2	12
Barber, Silas, Sgt							
3827	7 Jun 1790	Mil	-	1	6	2	58

290 — No date — A/1/283

100-Acre Patents to Enlisted Men Corresponding to Land Certificates: 78 through 86

Name of Patentee							
War. No.	*Date*	*Location*					
Painter, George, Sgt							
13634	7 Jun 1790	Mil	-	1	6	2	37
Greaffe, Frederick, Pvt							
13113	12 Jan 1796	Mil	-	1	6	2	17
Solinger, Adam, Pvt							
13726	21 Feb 1792	Mil	-	1	6	2	24
Mitchell, John, Pvt							
4699	21 Aug 1789	Mil	-	1	6	2	27
Krug, Philip, Pvt							
13279	15 Mar 1797	Mil	-	1	6	2	25
Reppert, Jacob, Pvt							
13643	12 Jan 1796	Mil	-	1	6	2	26
Bryan, Charles, Pvt							
9021	23 Dec 1793	Mil	-	1	6	2	16
Horne, Christian, Pvt							
13181	28 Feb 1794	Mil	-	20	6	2	3
Husband, James, Pvt							
10787	2 Sep 1789	Mil	-	20	4	1	5

291 — No date — A/1/285

100-Acre Patents to Enlisted Men Corresponding to Land Certificate: 87

Name of Patentee							
War. No.	*Date*	*Location*					
Benedict, John, administrator of Eleazar Benedict, Pvt							
13947	9 Dec 1789	Mil	-	15	2	2	6

292 — No date — A/1/283

100-Acre Patents to Enlisted Men Corresponding to Land Certificates: 88 through 100

Name of Patentee							
War. No.	*Date*	*Location*					
Coffin, Arthur, Pvt							
11038	11 Mar 1791	Mil	-	16	2	4	33
Crosby, Jesse, Pvt							
12961	16 May 1792	Mil	-	15	2	2	33
Terry, Gamaliel, Pvt							
6549	26 Dec 1798	Mil	-	15	2	2	34
Gass, Henry, Pvt							
9431	6 Apr 1790	Mil	-	3	1	1	6
Williams, John, Pvt							
12647	6 Apr 1790	Mil	-	3	1	1	5
McElroy, John, Fife Major							
9980	9 Jul 1789	Mil	-	3	1	1	12
McCrosson, Patrick, Pvt							
9899	6 Apr 1790	Mil	-	3	1	1	22
Roberts, Patrick, Pvt							
10261	9 Jul 1789	Mil	-	3	1	1	13
Hagan, Peter, Pvt							
13162	9 Jul 1789	Mil	-	3	1	1	21
Conner, Patrick, Drummer							
9158	9 Jul 1789	Mil	-	3	1	1	11
Miller, John, Pvt							
10110	5 Nov 1789	Mil	-	2	2	3	22
Jacobs, David, Pvt							
9676	6 Apr 1790	Mil	-	8	2	3	34
Parker, Wyman, Sgt							
6320	19 Jul 1798	Mil	-	15	1	3	34

293 — No date — A/1/285

100-Acre Patents to Enlisted Men Corresponding to Land Certificates: 101 and 102

Name of Patentee							
War. No.	*Date*	*Location*					
Webb, David, Sgt							
6671	27 Jun 1789	Mil	-	13	8	4	24
Smith, Sarah, heir of Smith, Arthur, Cpl							
14155	17 Jan 1800	Mil	-	2	7	4	6

294 — No date — A/1/287

100-Acre Patents to Enlisted Men Corresponding to Land Certificates: 103 through 107

Name of Patentee							
War. No.	*Date*	*Location*					
Barber, John, Pvt							
14073	3 Apr 1794	Mil	-	2	2	3	21
Greenland, James, Pvt							
9511	24 Mar 1792	Mil	-	2	2	3	30
Knapp, Usal, Sgt							
6066	27 Jun 1789	Mil	-	2	2	3	3-?

294 [continued]

Name	Location				
Basford, Ma--s? [Mairs? Moses?] Pvt					
2946 23 Dec 1799	Mil	- 15	8	5	*
Ribbels, William, Pvt					
8673 2 Jan 1790	Mil	- 14	8	*	*

*Torn.

295 No date A/1/289

100-Acre Patents to Enlisted Men Corresponding to Land Certificates: 108 through 116

Name of Patentee *War. No.* *Date*	*Location*				
Cavenaugh, Garrett, Pvt					
11989 7 Aug 1798	Mil	- 14	8	1	4
Crosby, Nathan, Pvt					
3871 8 May 1790	Mil	- 2	2	3	27
Sanford, Liffe, Pvt					
6453 11 Apr 1796	Mil	- 14	8	3	33
Timmonds, Roberts, Pvt					
10897 2 Sep 1799	Mil	- 2	2	3	34
Kershaw, Mitchell, Sgt					
10803 15 Apr 1799	Mil	- 2	2	3	35
Gibson, James, Sgt					
8346 17 Jun 1789	Mil	- 14	8	3	4
Verrey, Jonathan, Pvt					
13862 5 Oct 1790	Mil	- 3	1	1	26
Beetley, Isaac, Pvt					
3782 16 Aug 1796	Mil	- 3	1	1	15
Smalley, Thomas, Pvt					
7782 24 Mar 1795	Mil	- 3	1	1	14

296 No date A/1/277

*Unidentified Entry**

Name of Warrantee	*No.*	*Date*	*Acres*
McDonald, Rebecca, the legal representative of William McDonald, Pvt	10020	15 Mar 1790	100

*Marginal note: "--? as an original location & included --? location No. 254 for a quarter township." [This may refer to serial entry 254 above.]

297 No date A/1/275

100-Acre Patents to Officers
Land Certificates: 1 through 18

Name of Warrantee *War. No.* *Date*	*Location*				
McHenry, James, Maj					
1480 13 Mar 1800	Mil	- 20	5	2	1
	Mil	- 20	5	2	2
	Mil	- 20	5	2	3
	Mil	- 20	5	2	4
Ragsdale, Drury, Capt					
1854 24 Aug 1789	Mil	- 20	3	1	1
	Mil	- 20	3	1	2
	Mil	- 20	3	1	3
Titcomb, Daniel, son of Benjamin Titcomb, LtCol					
2129 31 Dec 1799	Mil	- 19	2	2	14
	Mil	- 19	2	2	15
	Mil	- 19	2	2	16
	Mil	- 19	2	2	17
Walker, Benjamin, LtCol					
2364 4 Aug 1790	Mil	- 20	4	4	8
	Mil	- 20	4	4	9
	Mil	- 20	4	4	10
	Mil	- 20	4	4	11
Eaton, John, heir of Pinkethman Eaton, Maj					
2713 14 Mar 1800	Mil	- 19	2	3	1
	Mil	- 19	2	3	2
	Mil	- 19	2	3	11
	Mil	- 19	2	3	12
Patton, Robert, Capt					
1706 30 Mar 1792	Mil	- 20	6	3	16
	Mil	- 20	6	3	17
	Mil	- 20	6	3	18
McConnell, Mathew, Capt					
1454 29 Jun 1789	Mil	- 20	7	3	12
	Mil	- 20	7	3	14
	Mil	- 20	7	3	15
Kosciuszko, Thaddeus, Col					
1219 23 Aug 1797	Mil	- 19	2	2	4
	Mil	- 19	2	2	7
	Mil	- 19	2	2	10
	Mil	- 19	2	2	18
	Mil	- 19	2	2	19
Rodgers, John R. B., Surgeon					
1822 7 Sep 1789	Mil	- 19	2	3	4
	Mil	- 19	2	3	5
	Mil	- 19	2	3	6
	Mil	- 19	2	3	13
Butler, Thomas, Capt					
193 16 Jul 1789	Mil	- 20	4	1	14
	Mil	- 20	4	1	17
	Mil	- 20	4	1	18
Harmar, Josiah, LtCol					
1009 17 Oct 1789	Mil	- 20	4	1	11
	Mil	- 20	4	1	12
	Mil	- 20	4	1	13
	Mil	- 20	4	1	9
Butler, Richard, Col					
188 5 May 1789	Mil	- 10	7	1	24
	Mil	- 10	7	1	9
	Mil	- 10	7	1	11
	Mil	- 10	7	1	12
	Mil	- 10	7	1	5
Mathews, George, Col					
1497 7 Aug 1789	Mil	- 20	7	3	11
	Mil	- 20	7	3	13
	Mil	- 20	7	3	8
	Mil	- 20	7	3	9
	Mil	- 20	7	3	7
Briscoe, Reuben, Capt					
2475 26 May 1789	Mil	- 19	2	3	8
	Mil	- 19	2	3	9
	Mil	- 19	2	3	10
Chambers, James, Col					
408 24 Oct 1789	Mil	- 20	6	2	21
	Mil	- 20	6	2	16
	Mil	- 20	6	2	15
	Mil	- 20	6	2	22
	Mil	- 20	6	2	18
McIntosh, Lachlin, BrigGen					
1549 13 Mar 1800	Mil	- 20	6	2	23
	Mil	- 20	6	2	24
	Mil	- 20	6	2	20
	Mil	- 20	6	2	19
	Mil	- 20	6	2	11
	Mil	- 20	6	2	12
	Mil	- 20	6	2	10
	Mil	- 20	6	2	9
McLane, Allen, Capt					
1474 25 Jul 1789	Mil	- 8	2	1	4
	Mil	- 8	2	1	5
	Mil	- 8	2	1	6

297 [continued]
Gregory, Mathew, Lt
819 5 Dec 1799 Mil - 8 2 3 31
Mil - 8 2 3 40

298 No date A/1/274
100-Acre Patents to Officers
Land Certificates: 19 through 39
Name of Warrantee
War. No. Date *Location*

Crogan, William, Maj
448 10 Mar 1799 Mil - 20 4 1 20
Mil - 20 4 1 19
Mil - 20 4 1 15
Mil - 20 4 1 16

Lane, Joseph, Maj
1325 5 Sep 1791 Mil - 8 2 3 30
Mil - 8 2 3 29
Mil - 8 2 3 32
Mil - 8 2 3 39

Leibert, Philip, Capt
1332 28 Dec 1799 Mil - 19 2 2 11
Mil - 19 2 2 12
Mil - 19 2 2 13

Winder, Levin, LtCol
2404 2 Jun 1789 Mil - 19 2 2 5
Mil - 19 2 2 6
Mil - 19 2 2 8
Mil - 19 2 2 9

Hill, Thomas, Maj
1067 24 Aug 1789 Mil - 20 4 4 4
Mil - 20 4 4 7
Mil - 20 4 4 3
Mil - 20 4 4 2

Hungerford, Thomas, Lt
2476 26 May 1789 Mil - 20 4 4 1
Mil - 20 4 4 12

Liddle, James, & George Washington Liddle, heirs of George Liddle, Capt
1317 22 Apr 1800 Mil - 8 2 1 2
Mil - 8 2 1 3
Mil - 8 2 1 10

Clark, Jonathan, LtCol
447 11 Dec 1797 Mil - 20 4 1 3
Mil - 20 4 1 4
Mil - 20 4 1 7
Mil - 20 4 1 8

Henderson, John, administrator of Gustavus H. Henderson, Surgeon
1029 24 May 1791 Mil - 8 2 3 28
Mil - 8 2 3 33
Mil - 8 2 3 38

Handy, George, Capt
1061 1 Mar 1800 Mil - 19 2 2 1
Mil - 19 2 2 2
Mil - 19 2 2 3

Dungan, Thomas, Lt
566 19 Aug 1789 Mil - 20 6 3 1
Mil - 20 6 3 10

Williams, David, Lt
2435 19 Apr 1792 Mil - 19 2 3 3
Mil - 19 2 3 7

Christie, James, Capt
416 6 Sep 1792 Mil - 20 4 1 1
Mil - 20 4 1 2
Mil - 20 4 1 10

Meigs, Return Jon[atha]n, Col
1376 20 May 1791 Mil - 20 6 3 9
Mil - 20 6 3 2
Mil - 20 6 3 12
Mil - 20 6 3 13
Mil - 20 6 3 8

Blount, Reading, Maj
289 21 Dec 1795 Mil - 15 7 4 3
Mil - 15 7 4 4
Mil - 15 7 4 13
Mil - 15 7 4 14

Arrington, Peter, guardian, in trust for Thomas Jones Armstrong, heir of Thomas Armstrong, Capt
62 22 Feb 1798 Mil - 6 6 2 26
Mil - 6 6 2 27
Mil - 6 6 2 28

Gerrard, Charles, Lt
884 1 Jun 1792 Mil - 15 7 4 19
Mil - 15 7 4 20

Sumner, Thomas E., & Jackey S. Blount (late Sumner) heirs of Jethro Sumner, BrigGen
2092 9 Feb 1798 Mil - 15 7 4 1
Marginal notation: Mil - 15 7 4 2
"Register's certificate Mil - 15 7 4 15
given for 50 acres re- Mil - 15 7 4 16
maining unsatisfied." Mil - 15 7 4 17
Mil - 15 7 4 18
Mil - 15 7 4 31
Mil - 15 7 4 32

Fawn, William, Capt
771 8 Feb 1798 Mil - 7 6 1 38
Mil - 7 6 1 39
Mil - 7 6 1 40

Campen, James, Capt
485 18 Apr 1796 Mil - 7 6 1 25
Mil - 7 6 1 26
Mil - 7 6 1 27

Ingles, John, Capt
1172 8 Feb 1790 Mil - 6 6 2 23
Mil - 6 6 2 24
Mil - 6 6 2 25

299 No date A/1/273
100-Acre Patents to Officers
Land Certificates: 40 through 63
Name of Warrantee
War. No. Date *Location*

Fenner, Richard, Lt
772 17 May 1796 Mil - 15 7 4 ?
Mil - 15 7 4 ?

Talbert, Hannah, administratrix of Samuel Talbert, Capt
2199 4 Dec 1792 Mil - 20 6 2 ?
Mil - 20 6 2 ?
Mil - 20 6 2 ?

Claypoole, Abraham G., Capt
414 3 May 1796 Mil - 20 6 3 15
Mil - 20 6 3 14
Mil - 20 6 3 6

Lee, Henry, LtCol
1299 3 Jul 1789 Mil - 19 7 1 8
Mil - 20 7 3 5
Mil - 20 7 3 6
Mil - 20 6 3 7

Jack, William, Capt
1176 17 Feb 1798 Mil - 20 6 2 4

299 [continued]

	Mil	-	20	6	2	5
	Mil	-	20	6	2	6
Bishop, John, Ens						
185 25 Feb 1800	Mil	-	13	8	4	21
Hill, Baylor, Capt						
2716 3 May 1800	Mil	-	7	6	1	1
	Mil	-	7	6	1	16
	Mil	-	7	6	1	17
Tetard? [Fetard?] Benjamin, Surgeon						
2230 20 Aug 1799	Mil	-	1	10	1	27
	Mil	-	1	10	1	28
	Mil	-	1	10	1	37
	Mil	-	1	10	1	38
Cowan, Edward, Lt						
491 20 Aug 1799	Mil	-	1	10	1	21
	Mil	-	1	10	1	22
Ward, John P., Lt						
2453 19 Mar 1800	Mil	-	1	10	1	5
	Mil	-	1	10	1	6
White, Edward, Lt						
2318 18 May 1799	Mil	-	1	10	1	11
	Mil	-	1	10	1	12
Bruff? [Bruffin?] James, Capt						
235 2 Nov 1791	Mil	-	2	10	2	7
	Mil	-	2	10	2	8
	Mil	-	2	10	2	10
Baylies, Hodijah, Maj						
96 16 Feb 1795	Mil	-	6	8	3	19
	Mil	-	6	8	3	20
	Mil	-	6	8	3	33
	Mil	-	6	8	3	34
Blair, Archibald, heir of John Blair, deceased, Lt						
2538 19 Sep 1789	Mil	-	7	6	1	5
	Mil	-	7	6	1	6
Evans, William, Lt						
681 26 Apr 1798	Mil	-	7	6	1	7
	Mil	-	7	6	1	8
Marshall, Dixon, Lt						
1535 3 May 1800	Mil	-	7	8	2	9
	Mil	-	7	8	2	24
Hait? [Hart?] Joseph, LtCol						
946 14 Dec 1789	Mil	-	15	2	2	9
	Mil	-	15	2	2	23
	Mil	-	15	2	2	24
	Mil	-	15	2	2	26
Hait? [Hart?] Samuel, Capt						
953 27 Jun 1789	Mil	-	15	2	2	25
	Mil	-	15	2	2	39
	Mil	-	15	2	2	40
Yates, Jasper, Junior, executor of Stephen Chambers, Capt						
434 12 Sep 1789	Mil	-	3	1	1	24
	Mil	-	3	1	1	25
	Mil	-	3	1	1	40
Darcey, John, Surgeon's Mate						
620 3 Mar 1797	Mil	-	8	5	1	2
	Mil	-	8	5	1	3
	Mil	-	8	5	1	4
Hubbel, Salmon, Lt						
960 16 Jun 1789	Mil	-	15	2	2	37
	Mil	-	15	2	2	38
Reed, Philip, Capt						
1840 3 Mar 1791	Mil	-	13	8	4	1
	Mil	-	13	8	4	2
	Mil	-	13	8	4	3
Rasin, William, Lt						
1844 4 Oct 1800	Mil	-	13	8	4	4
	Mil	-	13	8	4	5
Pratt, John, Lt						
1710 17 Oct 1789	Mil	-	13	8	1	11
	Mil	-	13	8	1	12

300 No date A/1/275

100-Acre Patents to Officers
Land Certificates: 64
Name of Warrantee
War. No. Date *Location*

Butler, Percival, Lt						
203 9 Mar 1791	Mil	-	20	6	3	4
	Mil	-	20	6	3	5

301 No date A/1/276

100-Acre Patents to Officers
Land Certificates: 65 through 78
Name of Warrantee
War. No. Date *Location*

Roxburgh, Alexander, Maj						
1837 10 Jun 1789	Mil	-	6	8	3	21
	Mil	-	6	8	3	22
	Mil	-	6	8	3	31
	Mil	-	6	8	3	32
Green, Moses, executor of John Green, late a Colonel in the Virginia Line						
866 20 Sep 1800	Mil	-	16	3	4	33
	Mil	-	16	3	4	34
	Mil	-	16	3	4	35
	Mil	-	16	3	4	36
	Mil	-	16	3	4	37
Steed, John, Capt						
2654 20 May 1795	Mil	-	16	3	4	38
	Mil	-	16	3	4	39
	Mil	-	16	3	4	40
Everly, Michael, Lt						
667 11 Mar 1791	Mil	-	16	2	4	16
	Mil	-	16	2	4	17
McDowell, William, Lt						
1433 4 May 1791	Mil	-	16	3	4	31
	Mil	-	16	3	4	32
North, William, Capt						
1575 10 Feb 1795	Mil	-	8	5	1	9
	Mil	-	8	5	1	10
	Mil	-	8	5	1	25
Baskerville, Samuel, Lt						
272 9 Apr 1800	Mil	-	8	5	1	26
	Mil	-	8	5	1	40
Cushing, Thomas, Lt						
344 1 Sep 1795	Mil	-	9	7	3	36
	Mil	-	9	7	3	37
Burbeck, Henry, Capt						
122 3 Dec 1789	Mil	-	9	7	3	19
	Mil	-	9	7	3	20
	Mil	-	9	7	3	29
Stark, John, BrigGen						
1879 20 May 1796	Mil	-	3	5	1	21
	Mil	-	3	5	1	22
	Mil	-	3	5	1	27
	Mil	-	3	5	1	28
	Mil	-	3	5	1	29
	Mil	-	3	5	1	30
	Mil	-	3	5	1	31
	Mil	-	3	5	1	32
Perez, Peter, Surgeon						
1717 14 Aug 1789	Mil	-	3	5	1	5
	Mil	-	3	5	1	12

301 [continued]

Name of Warrantee / War. No. / Date	Location					
	Mil	-	3	5	1	13
	Mil	-	3	5	1	20
Stark, John, executor to Archibald Stark, Lt						
1886	Mil	-	3	5	1	14
	Mil	-	3	5	1	19
Knox, William, Lt						
1201 19 Aug 1791	Mil	-	3	5	1	26
	Mil	-	3	5	1	33
Selden, Charles, Lt						
1911 1 Mar 1800	Mil	-	2	7	4	1
	Mil	-	2	7	4	2

302 No date A/1/277

100-Acre Patents to Officers

Land Certificates: 79 through 99

Name of Warrantee / *War. No.* *Date*	*Location*					
Hamilton, John A., Capt						
1047 25 May 1789	Mil	-	2	7	4	12
	Mil	-	2	7	4	13
	Mil	-	2	7	4	24
Buford, Abraham, Col						
251 3 May 1793	Mil	-	1	8	3	17
	Mil	-	1	8	3	18
	Mil	-	1	8	3	19
	Mil	-	1	8	3	20
	Mil	-	1	8	3	21
McDowell, John, Surgeon						
1444 3 Apr 1798	Mil	-	1	8	3	13
	Mil	-	1	8	3	14
	Mil	-	1	8	3	15
	Mil	-	1	8	3	16
McCay, John, Lt						
1491 4 Aug 1789	Mil	-	3	6	4	1
	Mil	-	3	6	4	2
Biggs, Benjamin, Capt						
257 3 Jun 1791	Mil	-	2	6	3	26
	Mil	-	2	6	3	34
	Mil	-	2	6	3	35
Reed, Jacob, Capt						
1810 3 Sep 1790	Mil	-	2	6	3	27
	Mil	-	2	6	3	32
	Mil	-	2	6	3	33
Van Rensselaer, Nicholas, Capt						
2249 30 Aug 1790	Mil	-	2	6	1	10
	Mil	-	2	6	1	13
	Mil	-	2	6	1	14
Leonard, Jacob, Ens						
1237 7 Mar 1798	Mil	-	2	5	2	38
McEven, John, Ens						
1410 9 Oct 1790	Mil	-	3	5	1	2
Maxwell, Anthony, Lt						
1394 2 Aug 1790	Mil	-	3	5	1	10
	Mil	-	3	5	1	7
Markle, Charles, Capt						
2537 4 Mar 1800	Mil	-	3	5	1	15
	Mil	-	3	5	1	18
	Mil	-	3	5	1	23
Cole, Abner, Ens						
382 15 Apr 1800	Mil	-	2	2	3	28
Baltzell, Charles, Capt						
238 4 Mar 1800	Mil	-	2	8	4	8
	Mil	-	2	8	4	9
	Mil	-	2	8	4	10
Tillard, Edward, LtCol						
2207 4 Mar 1800	Mil	-	2	8	4	13
	Mil	-	2	8	4	14
	Mil	-	2	8	4	17
	Mil	-	2	8	4	18
Sillman, Jonathan, Junior, Maj						
2040 31 Mar 1796	Mil	-	2	8	4	6
	Mil	-	2	8	4	7
	Mil	-	2	8	4	15
	Mil	-	2	8	4	16
Beck, John, Lt						
275 3 Jun 1791	Mil	-	1	8	3	1
	Mil	-	1	8	3	2
Peebles, Robert, Lt						
1711 9 Jul 1789	Mil	-	8	2	3	26
	Mil	-	8	2	3	35
McCully, George, Capt						
1426 5 Nov 1789	Mil	-	2	5	2	34
	Mil	-	2	5	2	35
	Mil	-	2	5	2	36
Finley, John, Capt						
745 24 Oct 1789	Mil	-	2	2	3	23
	Mil	-	2	2	3	24
	Mil	-	8	2	3	27
Bradley, Daniel, Lt						
148 13 Mar 1790	Mil	-	9	1	3	31
	Mil	-	9	1	3	32
Pike, William, Lt						
1672 18 Jan 1790	Mil	-	9	1	3	33
	Mil	-	9	1	3	34

303 No date A/1/283

100-Acre Patents to Officers

Land Certificates: 100 through 107

Name of Warrantee / *War. No.* *Date*	*Location*					
Welch, John, Lt						
2287 14 Dec 1796	Mil	-	14	8	3	21
	Mil	-	14	8	3	26
Carr, James, Maj						
324 31 Dec 1799	Mil	-	14	8	3	7
	Mil	-	14	8	3	8
	Mil	-	14	8	3	9
	Mil	-	14	8	3	10
Cogswell, Amos, Capt						
343 31 Dec 1799	Mil	-	14	8	3	6
	Mil	-	14	8	3	11
	Mil	-	14	8	3	22
Turnbull, Charles, Capt						
2203 9 May 1789	Mil	-	2	7	4	3
	Mil	-	2	7	4	11
	Mil	-	2	7	4	14
Chapman, Elijah, Capt						
375 19 May 1797	Mil	-	2	6	3	5
	Mil	-	2	6	3	6
	Mil	-	2	6	3	15
Higgins, William, Lt						
963 17 May 1796	Mil	-	13	8	1	8
	Mil	-	13	8	1	9
Noyes, John, Surgeon						
1580 29 May 1789	Mil	-	13	8	4	25
	Mil	-	13	8	4	16
	Mil	-	13	8	4	15
	Mil	-	13	8	4	6
Cilley, Jonathan, Lt						
327 16 Jan 1800	Mil	-	8	5	1	1
	Mil	-	8	5	1	17

304 No date A/1/284

100-Acre Patents to Officers

Land Certificates: 108 through 118

Name of Warrantee

War. No. *Date* *Location*

304 [continued]

Name of Warrantee / War. No. Date	Location					
Cilley, Jonathan, heir to Joseph Cilley, Col						
322 16 Jun 1800	Mil	-	8	5	1	6
	Mil	-	8	5	1	7
	Mil	-	8	5	1	8
	Mil	-	8	5	1	11
	Mil	-	8	5	1	12
Brownlee, William, Lt						
2609 6 Mar 1795	Mil	-	16	3	4	1
	Mil	-	16	3	4	2
Finley, Joseph L., Capt						
743 6 Apr 1791	Mil	-	16	3	4	15
	Mil	-	16	3	4	16
	Mil	-	16	3	4	17
Pride, Reuben, Lt						
1671 6 Nov 1789	Mil	-	9	1	3	11
	Mil	-	9	1	3	12
Towson, William, Lt						
2210 25 May 1789	Mil	-	9	3	1	21
	Mil	-	9	3	1	22
Cook, Jesse, Capt						
385 23 Apr 1798	Mil	-	6	6	2	13
	Mil	-	6	6	2	14
	Mil	-	6	6	2	20
Carlile, John, Capt						
493 20 Apr 1792	Mil	-	16	2	4	6
	Mil	-	16	2	4	7
	Mil	-	16	2	4	8
Gassaway, Nicholas, Lt						
862 25 Feb 1800	Mil	-	20	6	2	1
	Mil	-	20	6	2	2
Robinson, Andrew, Lt						
1827 4 Jun 1789	Mil	-	9	7	3	30
	Mil	-	9	7	3	35
Johnson, Samuel, Maj						
1141 23 Jul 1789	Mil	-	13	8	2	3
	Mil	-	13	8	2	4
	Mil	-	13	8	2	8
	Mil	-	13	8	2	9
Bull, Aaron, Lt						
151 25 Jun 1789	Mil	-	13	8	2	2
	Mil	-	13	8	2	5

305 No date A/1/282

100-Acre Patents to Officers
Land Certificate: 119

Name of Warrantee / *War. No. Date*	*Location*					
Walmsley, William, Ens						
2355 27 Jun 1789	Mil	-	15	2	2	7
	Mil	-	1	8	2	37W

306 No date A/1/284

100-Acre Patents to Officers
Land Certificates: 120 through 130

Name of Warrantee / *War. No. Date*	*Location*					
Marshall, John, assignee of Benjamin Temple, LtCol						
2214 1 Feb 1800	Mil	-	9	1	3	25
	Mil	-	9	1	3	26
	Mil	-	9	1	3	37
	Mil	-	9	1	3	38
Cogswell, Thomas, Maj						
332 8 Feb 1800	Mil	-	14	8	3	24
	Mil	-	14	8	3	25
	Mil	-	14	8	3	36
	Mil	-	14	8	3	37
Porter, John, assignee of John Medearis, Capt						
2675 16 May 1797	Mil	-	1	1	3	32
[A line is marked through Porter's name.]	Mil	-	1	1	3	33
	Mil	-	1	1	3	34
Rice, Nehemiah, Capt						
1791 18 Jun 1790	Mil	-	13	8	2	1
	Mil	-	13	8	2	6
	Mil	-	13	8	2	7
Weltner, Mary, executrix of the estate of Ludwick Weltner, Col, deceased						
2403 14 Sep 1789	Mil	-	14	8	3	1
	Mil	-	14	8	3	2
	Mil	-	14	8	3	15
	Mil	-	14	8	3	16
	Mil	-	14	8	3	17
Davis, Ebenezer, Lt						
524 11 Oct 1792	Mil	-	15	1	3	35
	Mil	-	15	1	3	36
Gist, John, Capt						
857 16 Dec 1799	Mil	-	13	8	4	9
	Mil	-	13	8	4	10
	Mil	-	13	8	4	11
Hall, David, Col						
1038 2 Sep 1789	Mil	-	13	8	4	7
	Mil	-	13	8	4	8
	Mil	-	13	8	4	12
	Mil	-	13	8	4	13
	Mil	-	13	8	4	14
Gurunke, John Faucheraude, LtCol						
888 25 Mar 1797	Mil	-	13	8	4	18
	Mil	-	13	8	4	19
	Mil	-	13	8	4	22
	Mil	-	13	8	4	23
Burgess, Joshua, Lt						
242 10 May 1800	Mil	-	7	7	2	1
	Mil	-	7	7	2	16
Benson, Perry, Capt						
236 15 May 1789	Mil	-	14	8	3	30
	Mil	-	14	8	3	31
	Mil	-	14	8	3	32

307 No date A/1/289

100-Acre Patents to Officers
Land Certificates: 131 through 144

Name of Warrantee / *War. No. Date*	*Location*					
Reid, George, Col						
1772 15 Jan 1800	Mil	-	15	8	4	3
	Mil	-	15	8	4	4
	Mil	-	15	8	4	5
	Mil	-	15	8	4	9
	Mil	-	15	8	4	10
Williams, Joseph, Capt						
2298 1 Apr 1790	Mil	-	15	8	3	5
	Mil	-	15	8	3	6
	Mil	-	15	8	3	15
Senter, Asa, Capt						
1884 15 Jan 1800	Mil	-	15	8	3	3
	Mil	-	15	8	3	4
	Mil	-	15	8	3	7
Campbell, Donald, Col						
2507 20 Jul 1790	Mil	-	15	8	4	19
	Mil	-	15	8	4	20
	Mil	-	15	8	4	21
	Mil	-	15	8	4	28

307 [continued]

	Mil	-	15	8	4 29
Brooke, Francis, Lt					
281 27 Jun 1797	Mil	-	14	8	1 1
	Mil	-	14	8	1 3
Hawkins, Henry, Lt					
1057 23 May 1797	Mil	-	17	7	4 1
	Mil	-	17	7	4 2
Talley, E., guardian to the heirs of John Andersen, Capt					
54 15 Feb 1799	Mil	-	15	8	4 6
	Mil	-	15	8	4 7
	Mil	-	15	8	4 8
Clarke, Edmund, Lt					
458 14 Apr 1800	Mil	-	18	7	1 6
	Mil	-	18	7	1 18
Parker, Thomas, Capt					
1742 24 May 1793	Mil	-	17	7	4 3
	Mil	-	17	7	4 4
	Mil	-	17	7	4 5
Gray, Sam[ue]l, guardian to the heirs of Eben-[eze]r Gray, LtCol					
812 23 Feb 1798	Mil	-	18	7	1 7
	Mil	-	18	7	1 8
	Mil	-	18	7	1 9
	Mil	-	18	7	1 19
Talbot, Silas, LtCol					
2133 27 Oct 1792	Mil	-	8	2	1 27
	Mil	-	8	2	1 28
	Mil	-	8	2	1 33
	Mil	-	8	2	1 34
Boyd, Thomas, Lt, heirs of					
248 8 Jan 1799	Mil	-	7	7	2 10
	Mil	-	7	7	2 23
Brown, William, Maj					
230 18 May 1799	Mil	-	8	5	1 13
	Mil	-	8	5	1 14
	Mil	-	8	5	1 15
	Mil	-	8	5	1 16
Shick, Frederick, Lt					
2109 20 Aug 1799	Mil	-	7	7	2 21
	Mil	-	7	7	2 22
Halting, Solomon, Lt? or Surgeon?					
-- (50 acres)	Mil	-	1?	8	2 25W

308 No date A/1/290

100-Acre Patents to Officers

Land Certificates: 145 through 148

Name of Warrantee *War. No.* *Date*	*Location*				
Vernon, Frederick, Maj					
2263 29 Dec 1792	Mil	-	2	2	3 25
	Mil	-	2	2	3 26
	Mil	-	2	2	3 39
	Mil	-	2	2	3 40
Le Enfant, Peter C., Capt					
1335 30 Nov 1789	Mil	-	8	2	3 23
	Mil	-	8	2	3 24
	Mil	-	8	2	3 25
Mills, Joseph, Lt					
1343 16 Jan 1800	Mil	-	8	5	1 23
	Mil	-	8	5	1 24
Smith, John,* Capt					
2043 26 May 1798	Mil	-	18	7	1 2
[*Pencilled correction: "Joseph"]	Mil	-	18	7	1 3
	Mil	-	18	7	1 4

309 21 Mar 1804 A/1/291

Registered by: Thomas Worthington [Reg Chl]
Registered for: John Rounsavell
Location: Mil - 8 2 3 14
Based upon the following Army land warrant:

Issued to	*No.*	*Acres*
Rounsavell, John, Pvt	8684	100

310 21 Mar 1804 A/1/291

Registered by: Thomas Worthington [Reg Chl]
Registered for: Robert Smiley
Location: Mil - 8 2 3 17
Based upon the following Army land warrant:

Issued to	*No.*	*Acres*
Smiley, Robert, Pvt	8724	100

311 23 Mar 1804 A/1/291

Registered by: John A. Hanna, Esq.
Registered for: Henry Weaver
Location: Mil - 11 9 4 23
Based upon the following Army land warrant:

Issued to	*No.*	*Acres*
Weaver, Henry, Pvt	10621	100

312 23 Mar 1804 A/1/291

Registered by: [Isaac] Van Horn [Rec Zan]
Registered for: Evan Holt
Location: Mil - 15 7 4 25
Based upon the following Army land warrant:

Issued to	*No.*	*Acres*
Holt, Evan, Pvt	9537	100

(Note: Sent per post to A. Gregg, 3 Jul 1804.)

313 23 Mar 1804 A/1/291

Registered by: [Isaac] Van Horn [Rec Zan]
Registered for: Origen Eaton
Location: Mil - 15 7 4 24
Based upon the following Army land warrant:

Issued to	*No.*	*Acres*
Eaton, Origen, Pvt	4078	100

(Note: Sent per post to Samuel Smith, 30 Jul 1804.)

314 23 Mar 1804 A/1/291

Registered by: [Isaac] Van Horn [Rec Zan]
Registered for: Robert Fowler
Location: Mil - 15 8 4 14
Based upon the following Army land warrant:

Issued to	*No.*	*Acres*
Fowler, Robert	155	100

(Note: Sent by post to Col Armstrong with letter of 30 Jul 1804)

315 23 Mar 1804 A/1/291

Registered by: [Isaac] Van Horn [Rec Zan]
Registered for: Moses Eaton
Location: Mil - 15 8 4 18
Based upon the following Army land warrant:

Issued to	*No.*	*Acres*
Eaton, Moses	156	100

(Note: Sent per post to Col Armstrong with letter of 30 Jul 1804.)

316 27 Mar 1804 A/1/291

Registered by: Thomas Worthington [Reg Chl]

316 [continued]
Registered for: Richard Wells, Assignee
Location: Mil - 8 2 3 9
Mil - 8 2 3 18
Mil - 8 2 3 36
Based upon the following Army land warrant:

Issued to	*No.*	*Acres*
Thomas, Lewis, Capt	113	300

(Note: Delivered to Noah Zane.)

317 27 Mar 1804 A/1/291
Registered by: -- Thomas [Member of Congress?] New York
Registered for: Jacob Spicer
Location: Mil - 11 8 1 19
Based upon the following Army land warrant:

Issued to	*No.*	*Acres*
Spicer, Jacob, Pvt	7759	100

(Note: Delivered to Mr. Thomas.)

318 No date A/1/291
Registered by: Israel Smith, Senator, Ver[mon]t
Registered for: Zaccheus Biggs
Location: Mil - 1 10 1 10
Based upon the following Army land warrant:

Issued to	*No.*	*Acres*
Barnard, Richard, Pvt	3656	100

319 No date A/1/291
Registered by: Not stated
Registered for: Not stated
Location: Mil - 15 2 2 22
Mil - 15 2 2 27
Mil - 15 2 2 28
Based upon the following Army land warrant:

Issued to	*No.*	*Acres*
Comstock, Samuel, Capt	374	300

(Note: Delivered to Mr. Davenport, 20 Jun 1804.)

320 No date A/1/291
Registered by: Zaccheus Biggs
Registered for: Zaccheus Biggs, assignee
Location: Mil - 2 3 4 2
Mil - 2 3 4 1
Based upon the following Army land warrant:

Issued to	*No.*	*Acres*
Pomeroy, Ralph, Lt	100	200

(Note: By request of Z[accheus] B[iggs] sent Pat[ent] by mail to Steubenville, Ohio . . . 30 Jun 1804.)

321 21 Jun 1804 A/1/291
Registered by: [William?] McCluney
Registered for: Hezekiah Morton
Location: Mil - 2 3 4 3
Mil - 2 3 4 20
Mil - 2 3 4 21
Based upon the following Army land warrant:

Issued to	*No.*	*Acres*
Morton, Hezekiah, Capt	69	300

322 No date A/1/291
Registered by: Albert Gallatin, Esq
Registered for: John Riley
Location: Mil - 2 3 4 12
Mil - 2 3 4 11
Mil - 2 3 4 ?
Based upon the following Army land warrant:

Issued to	*No.*	*Acres*
Riley, John, Capt	1820	300

(Note: See letter from the individual dated 6 May 1804.)

323 5 Apr 1804 A/1/291
Registered by: Not stated
Registered for: Gregory Thomas
Location: Mil - 15 2 2 21
Based upon the following Army land warrant:

Issued to	*No.*	*Acres*
Thomas, Gregory, Pvt	6556	100

(Note: Delivered to Mr. Davenport, 22 Dec 1804.)

324 18 May 1804 A/1/291
Registered by: Zaccheus Biggs
Registered for: Zaccheus Biggs, assignee
Location: Mil - 2 3 4 33
Based upon the following Army land warrant:

Issued to	*No.*	*Acres*
Bascom? Samuel, Pvt	90	100

(Note: Delivered by request of Z. Biggs by mail to Steubenville, Ohio.)

325 18 May 1804 A/1/291
Registered by: Zaccheus Biggs
Registered for: Zaccheus Biggs, assignee
Location: Mil - 2 3 4 34
Based upon the following Army land warrant:

Issued to	*No.*	*Acres*
Henderson, William, Pvt	107	100

(Note: Delivered by request of Z. Biggs by post to Steubenville, Ohio.)

326 18 May 1804 A/1/291
Registered by: George Beemer
Registered for: George Beemer, assignee
Location: Mil - 2 3 4 19
Based upon the following Army land warrant:

Issued to	*No.*	*Acres*
Mullin, Anthony, Pvt	11	100

(Note: Sent per post to G. Beemer, 30 Jul 1804.)

327 18 May 1804 A/1/291
Registered by: Not stated
Registered for: John Corbet
Location: Mil - 2 3 4 8
Based upon the following Army land warrant:

Issued to	*No.*	*Acres*
Corbet, John, Pvt	12942	100

(Note: Delivered to Michael Nourse.)

328 24 May 1804 A/1/291
Registered by: Not stated
Registered for: John Coleman
Location: Mil - 2 3 4 7
Based upon the following Army land warrant:

Issued to	*No.*	*Acres*
Coleman, John, Pvt	124	100

(Note: Delivered to Mr. Helms, see Rec[eiver's] certificate to location 144.)

329 15 Apr 1804 A/1/291
Registered by: William Kennedy, Esq
Registered for: John Howard

329 [continued]
Location: Mil - 2 3 4 6
Based upon the following Army land warrant:

Issued to	*No.*	*Acres*
Howard, John, Fife major	4351	100

(Note: Sent per post to Mr. Kennedy, 30 Jul 1804.)

330 21 Mar 1804 A/1/291
Registered by: Thomas Worthington [Reg Chl]
Registered for: Ezekiel Tophand
Location: Mil - 2 3 4 28
Based upon the following Army land warrant:

Issued to	*No.*	*Acres*
Tophand, Ezekiel, Pvt	6538	100

(Note: Sent per post to G. Beemer, 30 Jul 1804.)

331 21 Mar 1804 A/1/291
Registered by: Thomas Worthington [Reg Chl]
Registered for: John Welch
Location: Mil - 2 3 4 29
Based upon the following Army land warrant:

Issued to	*No.*	*Acres*
Welch, John, Pvt	11829	100

(Note: Sent per post to G. Beemer.)

332 9 Jul 1804 A/1/291
Registered by: T[homas] M[cKean] Thompson
Registered for: Edward Armstrong
Location: Mil - 1 8 3 23
Mil - 1 8 3 24
Based upon the following Army land warrant:

Issued to	*No.*	*Acres*
Armstrong, Edward, Lt	35	200

(Note: Delivered patent to W[illia]m Findley, Esq.)

333 10 Jul 1804 A/1/291
Registered by: Joshua Dawson
Registered for: Jesse St. John
Location: Mil - 15 8 4 13
Based upon the following Army land warrant:

Issued to	*No.*	*Acres*
St. John, Jesse, Cpl	6026	100

(Note: . . . Rogers received. . . .)

334 25 Jul 1804 A/1/292
Registered by: Zaccheus Biggs
Registered for: John Sprig Belt
Location: Mil - 2 3 4 35
Mil - 2 3 4 36
Mil - 2 3 4 37
Based upon the following Army land warrant:

Issued to	*No.*	*Acres*
Belt, John Sprig, Capt	232	300

(Note: Delivered certificate 179, M[ichael] Nourse, agent, 6 Dec 1804.)

335 25 Jul 1804 A/1/292
Registered by: Zaccheus Biggs
Registered for: Philip Lackey
Location: Mil - 2 3 4 10
Based upon the following Army land warrant:

Issued to	*No.*	*Acres*
Lackey, Philip, Soldier	9795	100

(Note: Delivered certificate 156 to Mr. M[ichael] Nourse, agent.)

336 25 Jul 1804 A/1/292
Registered by: Zaccheus Biggs
Registered for: Not stated
Location: Not stated
Based upon the following Army land warrant:

Issued to	*No.*	*Acres*
Cary, John D., Lt	445	200

337 25 Jul 1804 A/1/292
Registered by: Zaccheus Biggs
Registered for: James Black
Location: Mil - 1 1 3 25
Based upon the following Army land warrant:

Issued to	*No.*	*Acres*
Devon, Liske? Pvt	160	100

338 25 Jul 1804 A/1/292
Registered by: Zaccheus Biggs
Registered for: Zaccheus Biggs
Location: Mil - 2 3 4 17
Based upon the following Army land warrant:

Issued to	*No.*	*Acres*
Holbrook, Abijah, Pvt	53	100

(Note: Transferred to Mr. Biggs, Michael Nourse, 4 Sep 1804.)

339 25 Jul 1804 A/1/292
Registered by: Zaccheus Biggs
Registered for: Zaccheus Biggs
Location: Mil - 2 3 4 30
Mil - 2 3 4 31
Mil - 2 3 4 32
Based upon the following Army land warrant:

Issued to	*No.*	*Acres*
Shaw, John, Capt	158	300

(Note: Transferred to Mr. Biggs, Michael Nourse, 4 Sep 1804.)

340 25 Jul 1804 A/1/292
Registered by: Zaccheus Biggs
Registered for: Zaccheus Biggs
Location: Mil - 2 3 4 18
Based upon the following Army land warrant:

Issued to	*No.*	*Acres*
Brown, William, Pvt	101	100

(Note: Transferred to Mr. Biggs, Michael Nourse, 4 Sep 1804.)

341 27 Aug 1804 A/1/292
Registered by: Robert Underwood
Registered for: George Cantine
Location: Mil - 8 2 3 13
Based upon the following Army land warrant:

Issued to	*No.*	*Acres*
Cantine, George, Pvt	3980	100

(Note: Delivered to Mr. Underwood.)

342 16 Nov 1804 A/1/292
Registered by: Michael Nourse
Registered for: Michael Nourse
Location: Mil - 3 1 1 2
Based upon the following Army land warrant:

Issued to	*No.*	*Acres*
Corneil? [Coneil?] John, Sgt, heirs of	16	100

(Note: Delivered certificate to M. Nourse.)

343 16 Nov 1804 A/1/292
Registered by: Michael Nourse
Registered for: Michael Nourse
Location: Mil - 3 1 1 3
Based upon the following Army land warrant:
Issued to *No.* *Acres*
Smith, Enoch, Pvt 91 100
(Note: Delivered certificate 158 to M. Nourse.)

344 16 Nov 1804 A/1/292
Registered by: Michael Nourse
Registered for: Michael Nourse
Location: Mil - 3 1 1 1
Based upon the following Army land warrant:
Issued to *No.* *Acres*
Hess, Reuben, Cpl 94 100
(Note: Delivered certificate 159 to M. Nourse.)

345 16 Nov 1804 A/1/292
Registered by: Col [Thomas] Worthington
Registered for: Richard Wells
Location: Mil - 8 2 3 2
Mil - 8 2 3 3
Mil - 8 2 3 4
Mil - 8 2 3 5
Mil - 8 2 3 7
Based upon the following Army land warrant:
Issued to *No.* *Acres*
Lytle, William, LtCol Commanding 84 500
(Note: Delivered patent to Noah Zane.)

346 16 Nov 1804 A/1/292
Registered by: Col [Thomas] Worthington
Registered for: Anthony Sharp
Location: Mil - 10 3 4 24
Mil - 10 3 4 25
Mil - 10 3 4 26
Based upon the following Army land warrant:
Issued to *No.* *Acres*
Sharp, Anthony, Capt 2095 300
(Note: Delivered patent to Col Worthington.)

347 23 Nov 1804 A/1/292
Registered by: Zaccheus Biggs
Registered for: Zaccheus Biggs
Location: Mil - 2 3 4 13
Based upon the following Army land warrant:
Issued to *No.* *Acres*
Selden, Ebenezer, Pvt 17 100
(Note: Delivered certificate to M. Nourse, agent of Z. B[iggs].)

348 26 Nov 1804 A/1/292
Registered by: William Findlay
Registered for: Isaac Miller
Location: Mil - 2 3 4 16
Based upon the following Army land warrants:
Issued to *No.* *Acres*
Miller, Isaac, Soldier 10102 100
(Note: Delivered patent to Mr. Findlay.)

349 26 Nov 1804 A/1/292
Registered by: General Van Cortlandt
Registered for: Mason Wattles
Location: Mil - 11 8 1 3
Mil - 11 8 1 4
Mil - 11 8 1 5
Based upon the following Army land warrant:
Issued to *No.* *Acres*
Wattles, Mason, Capt 2301 300
(Note: Delivered to General Van Cortlandt.)

350 6 Dec 1804 A/1/292
Registered by: Wm? Mott, [Congressman] New Jersey
Registered for: Elizabeth Mannington, heir
Location: Mil - 6 8 3 28
Based upon the following Army land warrant:
Issued to *No.* *Acres*
Ferguson, Jane, administratrix 14032 100
(Note: Delivered to Mr. Mott, 23 Feb 1805.)

351 6 Dec 1804 A/1/292
Registered by: Peter Mills, Marietta [Ohio]
Registered for: Menasseth? [Monapeth?] Sawyer
Location: Mil - 11 9 4 24
Based upon the following Army land warrant:
Issued to *No.* *Acres*
Sawyer, Menasseth? [Monapeth?] Soldier 3497? 100

352 11 Dec 1804 A/1/292
Registered by: William Findley, M.C., Penna.
Registered for: Adam Wallace
Location: Mil - 11 8 1 1
Based upon the following Army land warrant:
Issued to *No.* *Acres*
Cook, John, Soldier 10734 100
(Note: Delivered patent to Mr. Findley, 23 Feb 1805.)

353 11 Dec 1804 A/1/292
Registered by: William Findley, M.C., Penna.
Registered for: Adam Wallace
Location: Mil - 11 8 1 2
Based upon the following Army land warrant:
Issued to *No.* *Acres*
Hoorn, Moses, Soldier 10692 100
(Note: Delivered to Mr. Findley, 23 Feb 1805.)

354 11 Dec 1804 A/1/292
Registered by: Zaccheus Biggs
Registered for: Zaccheus Biggs
Location: Mil - 1 10 1 30
Based upon the following Army land warrant:
Issued to *No.* *Acres*
Chapin, Joel, Soldier 3897 100
(Note: Delivered patent to Michael Nourse.)

355 11 Dec 1804 A/1/292
Registered by: Zaccheus Biggs
Registered for: Zaccheus Biggs
Location: Mil - 1 10 1 29
Based upon the following Army land warrant:
Issued to *No.* *Acres*
Whipple, Joseph, Sgt 6639 100
(Note: Delivered patent to Michael Nourse.)

356 15 Dec 1804 A/1/292
Registered by: Major -- Rogers

356 [continued]
Registered for: Caleb Gibbs
Location: Mil - 16 8 4 4
Mil - 16 8 4 6
Mil - 16 8 4 9
Mil - 16 8 4 10
Based upon the following Army land warrant:

Issued to	*No.*	*Acres*
Gibbs, Caleb, Maj	792	400

(Note: Delivered to Major Rogers.)

357 15 Dec 1804 A/1/292
Registered by: Col [Thomas] Worthington
Registered for: William Foreman, heir at law
Location: Mil - 8 2 3 22
Based upon the following Army land warrant:

Issued to	*No.*	*Acres*
Reid, Philip, Junior? Soldier	11219	100

(Note: Delivered patent to R. Wright, senator from Virginia?)

358 15 Dec 1804 A/1/292
Registered by: General Van Cortlandt
Registered for: Not stated
Location: Not stated
Based upon the following Army land warrant:

Issued to	*No.*	*Acres*
Stewart, William, Lt	2114	200

359 20 Dec 1804 A/1/292
Registered by: Ezekiel King
Registered for: John P. Helfenstein
Location: Mil - 6 7 3 30
Based upon the following Army land warrant:

Issued to	*No.*	*Acres*
Horner, John, Soldier	9571	100

(Note: Delivered certificate to E. King, agent.)

360 20 Dec 1804 A/1/292
Registered by: Richard Gernon, Philadelphia
Registered for: Richard Gernon
Location: Not stated
Based upon the following Army land warrant:

Issued to	*No.*	*Acres*
Sloan, Joseph, Soldier	8821	100

(Note illegible on microfilm.)

361 20 Dec 1804 A/1/292
Registered by: Richard Gernon, Philadelphia
Registered for: Richard Gernon
Location: Mil - 11 8 1 6
Based upon the following Army land warrant:

Issued to	*No.*	*Acres*
Garvin, Henry, Soldier	9434	100

(Note: Date of delivery? 12 Apr 1805.)

362 20 Dec 1804 A/1/292
Registered by: Richard Gernon, Philadelphia
Registered for: Richard Gernon
Location: Mil - 2 6 1 6
Based upon the following Army land warrant:

Issued to	*No.*	*Acres*
Ralston, Andrew, Sgt	10255	100

(Note: Delivered patent to J. Davidson, 1 Feb 1805.)

363 20 Dec 1804 A/1/292
Registered by: Richard Gernon, Philadelphia
Registered for: Richard Gernon
Location: Mil - 11 8 1 7
Mil - 11 8 1 8
Based upon the following Army land warrant:

Issued to	*No.*	*Acres*
Ball, B. W.? Lt	207	200

(Note: Delivered on 12 Apr 1805.)

364 20 Dec 1804 A/1/293
Registered by: Richard Gernon, Philadelphia
Registered for: Richard Gernon
Location: [all 100-acre lots] Mil - 2 6 1 3
Mil - 11 8 1 9
Mil - 2 6 1 4
Mil - 11 8 1 10
Mil - 11 8 1 11
Mil - 11 8 1 22
Mil - 11 8 1 23
Mil - 11 8 1 24?
Mil - 11 8 1 25
Based upon the following Army land warrants:

Issued to	*No.*	*Acres*
Shirtliff, Amasa, Sgt	4966	100
Snow, James, Soldier	4995	100
Hazard, Ebenezer, Soldier	7443	100
Crumm, William, Dragoon	9187	100
Taylor, Richard, Soldier	10896	100
Armstrong, Robert, Soldier	12710	100
Blaney, John, Soldier	12772	100
Leary, Dennis, Cpl	13381	100
Quigley, Edward, Soldier	13638	100

365 24 Dec 1804 A/1/293
Registered by: Zaccheus Biggs
Registered for: Zaccheus Biggs
Location: Mil - 1 10 1 4
Mil - 1 10 1 19
Based upon the following Army land warrant:

Issued to	*No.*	*Acres*
Mason, David, Lt	1366	200

(Note: Delivered certificate to M. Nourse.)

366 28 Dec 1804 A/1/293
Registered by: Benjamin Tallmadge, Esq.
Registered for: Henry Purkett? [Parkett?]
Location: Mil - 8 5 1 36
Based upon the following Army land warrant:

Issued to	*No.*	*Acres*
Parkett? [Purkett?] Henry, Quartermaster Sgt	6344	100

(Note: Delivered to Mr. Tallmadge.)

367 28 Dec 1804 A/1/293
Registered by: Samuel Tenney, Esq., M.C.
Registered for: Abel Chandler
Location: Mil - 11 9 4 13
Based upon the following Army land warrant:

Issued to	*No.*	*Acres*
Chandler, Abel, Pvt	171	100

(Note: Enclosed to Mr. Tenney in letter of 7 Jan 1804 [sic]).

368 4 Jan 1805 A/1/293
Registered by: Sent to Register [of Treasury?]
Registered for: Thomas Schuyler Sill
Location: Mil - 15 7 4 9
Mil - 15 7 4 10
Mil - 15 7 4 23
Based upon the following Army land warrant:
Issued to *No.* *Acres*
Sill, Thomas, Capt 2710 300
(Note: Delivered certificate to M. Nourse.)

369 5 Jan 1805 A/1/293
Registered by: T[homas] Worthington, Esq.
Registered for: Thurston Hillard
Location: Mil - 10 3 4 39
Based upon the following Army land warrant:
Issued to *No.* *Acres*
Hillard, Thurston, Soldier 13201 100
(Note: Sent patent to Noah Zane.)

370 5 Jan 1805 A/1/293
Registered by: [Isaac?] Van Horn, Esq.
Registered for: William Martin
Location: Mil - 16 2 4 35
Based upon the following Army land warrant:
Issued to *No.* *Acres*
Martin, William, Sgt 13397 100
(Note: Delivered to Mr. Van Horne, 16 Jan 1805.)

371 5 Jan 1805 A/1/293
Registered by: John Hoge, Esq.
Registered for: C. Schlokerman? [Schokerman?]
Location: Mil - 1 10 1 39
Based upon the following Army land warrant:
Issued to *No.* *Acres*
Schokerman? [Schlokerman?]
Christopher, Soldier 10433 100
(Note: Delivered to Mr. Hoge, 10 Jan 1805.)

372 5 Jan 1805 A/1/293
Registered by: Hon. Nathaniel Mason? [Macon?]
Registered for: S. Hog, Junior, etc.
Location: Mil - 6 10 4 1
Mil - 6 10 4 2
Mil - 6 10 4 3
Mil - 6 10 4 4
Based upon the following Army land warrant:
Issued to *No.* *Acres*
Hog, Samuel, Junior? &
John Bablis? Hog 104 400
(Note: Delivered to Mr. Mason? [Macon?].)

373 10 Jan 1805 A/1/293
Registered by: Zaccheus Biggs
Registered for: Zaccheus Biggs
Location: Mil - 1 10 1 15
Based upon the following Army land warrant:
Issued to *No.* *Acres*
Grayson? [Prayson?]
Nathaniel 167 100
(Note: Delivered to M[ichael] Nourse.)

374 12 Jan 1805 A/1/293
Registered by: -- Nelson, M.C., Maryland
Registered for: Thomas McMullen, heir
Location: Mil - 5 10 4 7
Based upon the following Army land warrant:
Issued to *No.* *Acres*
McMullen, Mary, adminis-
tratrix of Hugh McMul-
len 11501 100

375 1 Feb 1805 A/1/293
Registered by: John Condit, Esq.
Registered for: Squire Cockrem*
Location: Mil - 6? 2 2 29
Based upon the following Army land warrant:
Issued to *No.* *Acres*
Cockrem* Squire, Pvt 115 100
*So spelled.

376 2 Feb 1805 A/1/293
Registered by: Abijah Holbrook
Registered for: Abijah Holbrook
Location: Mil - 16? 2 4 21
Mil - 16? 2 4 22
Mil - 16? 2 4 23
Mil - 16? 2 4 25
Mil - 16? 2 4 26
Mil - 16? 2 4 27
Mil - 16? 2 4 28
Mil - 16? 2 4 36
Mil - 16? 2 4 37
Mil - 16? 2 4 38
Based upon the following Army land warrants:
Issued to *No.* *Acres*
Holbrook, Abijah, assig-
nee 33 100
Holbrook, Abijah, assig-
nee 34 100
Holbrook, Abijah, assig-
nee 35 100
Holbrook, Abijah, assig-
nee 36 100
Holbrook, Abijah, assig-
nee 37 100
Holbrook, Abijah, assig-
nee 38 100
Holbrook, Abijah, assig-
nee 40 100
Holbrook, Abijah, assig-
nee 41 100
Holbrook, Abijah, assig-
nee 42 100
Holbrook, Abijah, assig-
nee 43 100

377 2 Feb 1805 A/1/294
Registered by: Abijah Holbrook
Registered for: Abijah Holbrook
Location: Mil - 16 2 4 39
Mil - 16 2 4 40
Mil - 16 2 4 11
Mil - 16 2 4 12
Mil - 16 2 4 1
Mil - 16 2 4 2
Mil - 16 2 4 8
Based upon the following Army land warrants:
Issued to *No.* *Acres*
Holbrook, Abijah, assig-
nee 44 100
Holbrook, Abijah, assig-
nee 45 100
Holbrook, Abijah, assig-
nee 46 100

377 [continued]

Holbrook, Abijah, assignee	47	100
Holbrook, Abijah, assignee	48	100
Holbrook, Abijah, assignee	50	100
Holbrook, Abijah, assignee	51	100
Holbrook, Abijah, assignee	52*	100
Holbrook, Abijah, assignee	39*	100
Holbrook, Abijah, assignee	49*	100

*Not located; warrant returned to Mr. Holbrook.

378 8 Feb 1805 A/1/294
Registered by: Eben Elmer
Registered for: Henry Ferver? [Tower?]
Location: Mil - 15 2 2 30
Based upon the following Army land warrant:

Issued to	*No.*	*Acres*
Ferver? [Tower?] Henry, Pvt	128	100

(Note: Delivered patent to Mr. Elmer.)

379 8 Feb 1805 A/1/294
Registered by: Jesse Franklin
Registered for: Samuel McCraw
Location: Mil - 11 8 1 40
Based upon the following Army land warrant:

Issued to	*No.*	*Acres*
McCraw, Samuel, Pvt	73	100

(Note: Delivered to Mr. Franklin.)

380 8 Feb 1805 A/1/294
Registered by: Ezekiel King
Registered for: John P. Helfenstein
Location: Mil - 6 7 3 31
Based upon the following Army land warrant:

Issued to	*No.*	*Acres*
Fellows, Tobias, Pvt	13078	100

(Note: Delivered to Mr. King.)

381 9 Feb 1805 A/1/294
Registered by: Hon. John Earle?
Registered for: Louis P. Martin
Location: Mil - 3 6 4 6
Mil - 3 6 4 7
Mil - 3 6 4 8?
Based upon the following Army land warrant:

Issued to	*No.*	*Acres*
Martin, Louis P., Capt	173	300

(Note: Delivered to Mr. Earle.)

382 11 Feb 1805 A/1/294
Registered by: Hon. W? Chittenden
Registered for: Zaccheus Peaslee
Location: Mil - 8 2 3 20
Mil - 8 2 3 21
Based upon the following Army land warrant:

Issued to	*No.*	*Acres*
Peaslee, Zaccheus, Lt	1763?	200

(Note: Delivered to Mr. Chittenden.)

383 12 Feb 1805 A/1/294
Registered by: Mr. -- Thompkins
Registered for: Jonas Stansbery
Location: Mil - 2 7 4 7
Based upon the following Army land warrant:

Issued to	*No.*	*Acres*
Winans, William, Pvt	6689?	100

384 12 Feb 1805 A/1/294
Registered by: M[ichael] Nourse
Registered for: Zaccheus Biggs
Location: Mil - 1 10 1 18
Based upon the following Army land warrant:

Issued to	*No.*	*Acres*
Sowers? [Lewis?] William, Pvt	[torn]	100

385 15 Feb 1805 A/1/294
Registered by: Jeremiah Morrow, Esq.
Registered for: James Ryan
Location: Mil - 16 2 4 24
Based upon the following Army land warrant:

Issued to	*No.*	*Acres*
Ryan, James, Pvt	[torn]	100

(Note: Delivered to Mr. Morrow.)

386 15 Feb 1805 A/1/294
Registered by: Jeremiah Morrow, Esq.
Registered for: David Gibbons
Location: Mil - 16 2 4 10
Based upon the following Army land warrant:

Issued to	*No.*	*Acres*
Gibbons, David, Pvt	[torn]	100

(Note: Delivered patent to Mr. Morrow.)

387 15 Feb 1805 A/1/294
Registered by: Eben Seavers? [Leavin?] Esq.
Registered for: Eben Seavers? [Leavin?] Esq.
Location: Mil - 11 8 1 12
Mil - 11 8 1 21
Mil - 11 8 1 13
Mil - 11 8 1 14
Mil - 11 8 1 20?
Based upon the following Army land warrants:

Issued to	*No.*	*Acres*
Luther, Peleg, Sgt	77?	100
Barker? [Backer?] Barnabas Sgt	76	100
Sturtevant, Isaac, Lt	4	200
Lee, Edward, Pvt	6	100

388 21 Feb 1805 A/1/294
Registered by: Hon. J. A. Bayard, Esq.
Registered for: James Booth, his executor
Location: Mil - 11 8 1 16
Mil - 11 8 1 15
Based upon the following Army land warrant:

Issued to	*No.*	*Acres*
McWilliam, Stephen, Lt	1473	200

(Note: Delivered to Mr. Bayard.)

389 22 Feb 1805 A/1/294
Registered by: Joseph Copes
Registered for: Mitchell Kershaw

389 [continued]
Location: Mil - 2 2 3 33
Based upon the following Army land warrant:

Issued to	*No.*	*Acres*
Bright, Levi, Soldier	10713	100

(Note: Sent by mail, 27 Apr 1805.)

390 25 Feb 1805 A/1/294
Registered by: Andrew Gregg, Esq.
Registered for: William Early, assignee
Location: Mil - 15 7 4 40
Based upon the following Army land warrant:

Issued to	*No.*	*Acres*
Hairbolt? [Hairbott?] Adam, Soldier	9607	100

(Note: Delivered to Mr. Gregg.)

391 25 Feb 1805 A/1/294
Registered by: Hon. James Holland
Registered for: Alexander Brevard?
Location: Mil - 11 8 1 17
Mil - 11 8 1 18
Mil - 11 8 1 32
Based upon the following Army land warrant:

Issued to	*No.*	*Acres*
Brevard? Alexander, Capt	294	300

(Note: Delivered to Mr. Holland.)

392 25 Feb 1805 A/1/294
Registered by: Robert Underwood
Registered for: George Knorpler?
Location: Mil - 8 2 1 16
Based upon the following Army land warrant:

Issued to	*No.*	*Acres*
Knorpler? George, Soldier	13421	100

(Note: Delivered to Mr. Underwood.)

393 26 Feb 1805 A/1/294
Registered by: John Mathews
Registered for: Robert Parker
Location: Mil - 8 2 1 36
Mil - 8 2 1 37
Based upon the following Army land warrant:

Issued to	*No.*	*Acres*
Parker, Robert, CaptLt	[torn]	200

(Note: Located for the inspection [of] warrantees by J. Mathews who received the certificates; to Secretary of State for the patent of each, 2 Mar 1805.)

394 26 Feb 1805 A/1/294
Registered by: John Mathews
Registered for: William Porter
Location: Mil - 8 2 1 38
Mil - 8 2 1 39
Based upon the following Army land warrant:

Issued to	*No.*	*Acres*
Porter, William, Lt	[torn]	200

(Same note as in serial entry 393.)

395 26 Feb 1805 A/1/295
Registered by: John Mathews
Registered for: William Clark
Location: Mil - 8 2 1 40
Based upon the following Army land warrant:

Issued to	*No.*	*Acres*
Smith, Isaac, Soldier	6441	100

(Same note as in serial entry 393.)

396 26 Feb 1805 A/1/295
Registered by: John Mathews
Registered for: Daniel St. Clair
Location: Mil - 9 1 3 1
Mil - 9 1 3 2
Based upon the following Army land warrant:

Issued to	*No.*	*Acres*
St. Clair, Daniel, Lt	2025	200

(Same note as in serial entry 393.)

397 26 Feb 1805 A/1/295
Registered by: John Mathews
Registered for: John Mercer
Location: Mil - 10 3 4 37
Mil - 10 3 4 38
Mil - 10 3 4 40
Based upon the following Army land warrant:

Issued to	*No.*	*Acres*
Mercer, John, Capt	1411	300

(Same note as in serial entry 393.)

398 26 Feb 1805 A/1/295
Registered by: John Mathews
Registered for: Samuel Montgomery
Location: Mil - 17 7 4 14
Mil - 17 7 4 15
Mil - 17 7 4 16
Mil - 17 7 4 13
Mil - 17 7 4 12
Mil - 17 7 4 11
Based upon the following Army land warrants:

Issued to	*No.*	*Acres*
Montgomery, Samuel, Capt	1425	300
Berry, James, Soldier	8938	100
Winn, John, Soldier	10062	100
Conner, Charles, Soldier	9110	100

(Same note as in serial entry 393.)

399 15 Mar 1805 A/1/295
Registered by: William Blackledge, Esq.
Registered for: William Blackledge
Location: Mil - 17 7 4 37
Mil - 17 7 4 36
Based upon the following Army land warrants:

Issued to	*No.*	*Acres*
Clark, Isaac, Pvt	191	100
Freeman, Samuel, Pvt	190	100

(Same note as in serial entry 393.)

400 1 Mar 1805 A/1/295
Registered by: Col Gaither
Registered for: Henry Gaither
Location: Mil - 17 7 4 20
Mil - 17 7 4 21
Mil - 17 7 4 22
Based upon the following Army land warrant:

Issued to	*No.*	*Acres*
Gaither, Henry, Capt	854	300

401 1 Mar 1805 A/1/295
Registered by: John Matthews
Registered for: William Wells

401 [continued]
Location: Mil - 17 7 1 10E
Based upon the following Army land warrant:

Issued to	*No.*	*Acres*
Walker, Benjamin, LtCol	*	50

*Probably located on Register's certificate.

402 2 Mar 1805 A/1/295
Registered by: Cesar A. Rodney, Esq.
Registered for: Heirs (by name) [not given]
Location: Mil - 15 7 4 7
Based upon the following Army land warrant:

Issued to	*No.*	*Acres*
Cochran, Daniel, Sgt	10736	100

403 4 Mar 1805 A/1/295
Registered by: Joseph Heister, Esq.
Registered for: Stephen Barth
Location: Mil - 15 7 4 5
Based upon the following Army land warrant:

Issued to	*No.*	*Acres*
Barth, Stephen, Dragoon	178	100

(Note: Sent to Mr. Heister.)

404 5 Mar 1805 A/1/295
Registered by: Andrew Gregg, Esq.
Registered for: John Akely
Location: Mil - 15 7 4 6
Based upon the following Army land warrant:

Issued to	*No.*	*Acres*
Akely, John, Dragoon	179	100

(Note: Sent by W. Gregg's order to J. Watson, Mifflintown.)

405 5 Mar 1805 A/1/295
Registered by: William Duane
Registered for: James Donohoo
Location: Mil - 8 2 1 7
Based upon the following Army land warrant:

Issued to	*No.*	*Acres*
Donohoo, James, Pvt	183	100

(Note: Delivered certificate to Mr. Duane.)

406 6 Mar 1805 A/1/295
Registered by: Jeremiah Morrow, Esq.
Registered for: John Inglish
Location: Mil - 16 2 4 9
Based upon the following Army land warrant:

Issued to	*No.*	*Acres*
English [also Inglish] John, Pvt	181	100

(Note: Delivered to M. Nourse for Morrow.)

407 7 Mar 1805 A/1/295
Registered by: Major -- Rogers
Registered for: Sarah Munson [word blotted]
Location: Mil - 8 2 1 18
Mil - 8 2 1 13
Mil - 8 2 1 14
Based upon the following Army land warrant:

Issued to	*No.*	*Acres*
Munson, Theophilus, Capt	185	300

408 7 Mar 1805 A/1/295
Registered by: Mr. Griswold? by C. Nourse
Registered for: Luther Reeves
Location: Mil - 8 2 1 9
Based upon the following Army land warrant:

Issued to	*No.*	*Acres*
Reeves, Luther, Pvt	6388	100

(Note: Delivered to Mr. C. Nourse.)

409 7 Mar 1805 A/1/295
Registered by: Mr. Tallmadge by W? Sheldon
Registered for: Stephen Chapman
Location: Mil - 8 2 3 10
Based upon the following Army land warrant:

Issued to	*No.*	*Acres*
Chapman, Stephen, Cpl	186	100

410 7 Mar 1805 A/1/295
Registered by: Zaccheus Biggs
Registered for: John McCreery? assignee
Location: Mil - 1 10 1 20
Based upon the following Army land warrant:

Issued to	*No.*	*Acres*
McClelland, John, Soldier	10035	100

(Note: Delivered certificate to M. Nourse.)

411 7 Mar 1805 A/1/295
Registered by: Mr. Van Horne
Registered for: Zaccheus Biggs
Location: Mil - 1 10 1 9
Mil - 1 10 1 10
Mil - 1 10 1 23
Mil - 1 10 1 24
Based upon the following Army land warrant:

Issued to	*No.*	*Acres*
Davidson, William, LtCol	607	450

412 7 Mar 1805 A/1/295
Registered by: David Holmes, Esq.
Registered for: Lewis Boyer
Location: Mil - 8 2 1 25
Based upon the following Army land warrant:

Issued to	*No.*	*Acres*
Boyer, Lewis, Dragoon	187	100

(Note: Sent patent to Mr. Holmes, 11 May 1805.)

413 7 Mar 1805 A/1/295
Registered by: John Archer, Esq.
Registered for: Edward Prall? [Pratt?]
Location: Mil - 8 2 3 6
Mil - 8 2 3 15
Mil - 8 2 3 16
Based upon the following Army land warrant:

Issued to	*No.*	*Acres*
Prall? [Pratt?] Edward, Capt	1729	300

(Note: Sent to Mr. Archer per mail, 26 Mar 1805.)

414 11 Mar 1805 A/1/295
Registered by: W. M. Nourse
Registered for: Isaac Prior
Location: Mil - 2 2 3 32
Based upon the following Army land warrant:

Issued to	*No.*	*Acres*
Farrell, William, Soldier	9407	100

(Note: Delivered certificate to W. M. Nourse.)

415 — 12 Mar 1805 — A/1/295

Registered by: George Beymer
Registered for: George Rice
Location: Mil - 2 2 3 5
Mil - 2 2 3 6
Mil - 2 2 3 7
Based upon the following Army land warrant:

Issued to	*No.*	*Acres*
Rice, George, Capt	2498	300

(Note: Sent per post to Mr. Beymer at Zanesville [Ohio] according to his directions.)

416 — 12 Mar 1805 — A/1/295

Registered by: George Beymer
Registered for: John McNair
Location: Mil - 3 1 1 10
Based upon the following Army land warrant

Issued to	*No.*	*Acres*
McNair, John, Soldier	9949	100

(Same footnote as in serial entry 415.)

417 — 15 Mar 1805 — A/1/295

Registered by: William Blackledge, Esq.
Registered for: Heirs of John Patton
Location: Mil - 17 7 4 27
Mil - 17 7 4 28
Mil - 17 7 4 29
Mil - 17 7 4 30
Mil - 17 7 4 31
Based upon the following Army land warrant:

Issued to	*No.*	*Acres*
Patton, John, Col	194	500

(Note: These patents were ordered to be kept until Mr. Blackledge gives orders about them.)

418 — 15 Mar 1805 — A/1/295

Registered by: William Blackledge, Esq.
Registered for: Simon Alderson
Location: Mil - 17 7 4 38
Based upon the following Army land warrant:

Issued to	*No.*	*Acres*
Alderson, Simon, Pvt	192	100

(Same note as in serial entry 417.)

419 — 20 Mar 1805 — A/1/295

Registered by: Hezekiah Rogers
Registered for: Stephen Ambler
Location: Mil - 16 7 2 15
Based upon the following Army land warrant:

Issued to	*No.*	*Acres*
Ambler, Stephen, Pvt	12725	100

420 — 20 Mar 1805 — A/1/295

Registered by: Hezekiah Rogers
Registered for: Peter Ambler
Location: Mil - 16 7 2 16
Based upon the following Army land warrant:

Issued to	*No.*	*Acres*
Ambler, Peter, Pvt	12726	100

(End of Source A)

421 21 Mar 1804 B/1/001
Registered by: Thomas Worthington for Noah Zane
Registered for: John Rounsavell
Location: Mil - 8 2 3 14
Based upon the following Army land warrant:

Issued to	*No.*	*Acres*
Rounsavell, John, Pvt	8684	100

422 21 Mar 1804 B/1/001
Registered by: Thomas Worthington for Noah Zane
Registered for: Robert Smiley
Location: Mil - 8 2 3 17
Based upon the following Army land warrant:

Issued to	*No.*	*Acres*
Smiley, Robert, Pvt	8724	100

423 23 Mar 1804 B/1/001
Registered by: [not stated]
Registered for: Henry Weaver
Location: Mil - 11 9 4 23
Based upon the following Army land warrant:

Issued to	*No.*	*Acres*
Weaver, Henry, Pvt	10621	100

(Note: Patent delivered to John A. Hanna, Esq.)

424 23 Mar 1804 B/1/001
Registered by: -- Vanhorne
Registered for: Evan Holt
Location: Mil - 15 7 4 25
Based upon the following Army land warrant:

Issued to	*No.*	*Acres*
Holt, Evan, Pvt	9537	100

(Note: Sent per post to A. Gregg, letter of 30 Jul 1804.)

425 23 Mar 1804 B/1/001
Registered by: -- Vanhorne
Registered for: Origen Eaton
Location: Mil - 15 7 4 24
Based upon the following Army land warrant:

Issued to	*No.*	*Acres*
Eaton, Origen, Pvt	4078	100

(Note: Sent per post to Samuel Smith, 13 Sep 1804.)

426 23 Mar 1804 B/1/001
Registered by: -- Vanhorne
Registered for: Robert Fowler
Location: Mil - 15 8 4 14
Based upon the following Army land warrant:

Issued to	*No.*	*Acres*
Fowler, Robert, Pvt	155	100

(Note: Sent per post to Col Armstrong, 30 Jul 1804.)

427 23 Mar 1804 B/1/001
Registered by: -- Vanhorne
Registered for: Moses Easton
Location: Mil - 15 8 4 18
Based upon the following Army land warrant:

Issued to	*No.*	*Acres*
Easton, Moses, Pvt	156	100

(Note: Sent per post to Col Armstrong, 30 Jul 1804.)

428 27 Mar 1804 B/1/001
Registered by: Thomas Worthington
Registered for: Richard Wells, assignee
Location: Mil - 8 2 3 9
Mil - 8 2 3 18
Mil - 8 2 3 36
Based upon the following Army land warrant:

Issued to	*No.*	*Acres*
Thomas, Lewis, Capt	113	300

(Note: Delivered patent to Noah Zane.)

429 27 Mar 1804 B/1/001
Registered by: -- Thomas, M.C., New York
Registered for: Jacob Spicer
Location: Mil - 11 8 1 19
Based upon the following Army land warrant:

Issued to	*No.*	*Acres*
Spicer, Jacob, Pvt	7750	100

(Note: Delivered patent to Mr. Thomas, 27 Feb 1805.)

430 Not given B/1/001
Registered by: Israel Smith, Senator, Vermont
Registered for: Zaccheus Biggs
Location: Mil - 1 10 1 10
Based upon the following Army land warrant:

Issued to	*No.*	*Acres*
Barnard, Richard, Pvt	3656	100

431 Not given B/1/001
Registered by: [Not stated]
Registered for: Samuel Comstock
Location: Mil - 15 2 2 22
Mil - 15 2 2 27
Mil - 15 2 2 28
Based upon the following Army land warrant:

Issued to	*No.*	*Acres*
Comstock, Samuel, Capt	374	300

(Note: Delivered to Mr. Davenport, 1 Dec 1804.)

432 Not given B/1/001
Registered by: Zaccheus Biggs
Registered for: Zaccheus Biggs, assignee
Location: Mil - 2 3 4 1
Mil - 2 3 4 2
Based upon the following Army land warrant:

Issued to	*No.*	*Acres*
Pomeroy, Ralph, Lt	100	200

(Note: By request of Z. B[iggs] sent patent per mail to Steubenville, Ohio, 10 Jul 1804.)

433 Not given B/1/001
Registered by: -- McCluney
Registered for: Hezekiah Morton
Location: Mil - 2 3 4 3
Mil - 2 3 4 20
Mil - 2 3 4 21
Based upon the following Army land warrant:

Issued to	*No.*	*Acres*
Morton, Hezekiah, Capt	69	300

434 Not given B/1/001
Registered by: Albert Gallatin, Esq.*
Registered for: John Reily

434 [continued]
Location: Mil - 2 3 4 5
Mil - 2 3 4 11
Mil - 2 3 4 12
Based upon the following Army land warrant:
Issued to *No.* *Acres*
Reily, John, Capt 1820 300
*See letter from individual dated 6 May 1804.
(Note: Delivered to the Register of the Treasury for the Secretary of the Treasury, 30 Jun 1804.)

435 5 Apr 1804 B/1/001
Registered by: [Not stated]
Registered for: Gregory Thomas
Location: Mil - 15 2 2 21
Based upon the following Army land warrant:
Issued to *No.* *Acres*
Thomas, Gregory, Pvt 6556 100
(Note: Delivered patent to Mr. Davenport, 22 Dec 1804.)

436 18 May 1804 B/1/001
Registered by: Zaccheus Biggs
Registered for: Zaccheus Biggs, assignee
Location: Mil - 2 3 4 33
Based upon the following Army land warrant:
Issued to *No.* *Acres*
Bascom, Samuel, Pvt 90 100
(Note: Sent per mail to Z. B[iggs] at Steuben-ville, Ohio.)

437 18 May 1804 B/1/001
Registered by: Zaccheus Biggs
Registered for: Zaccheus Biggs, assignee
Location: Mil - 2 3 4 34
Based upon the following Army land warrant:
Issued to *No.* *Acres*
Henderson, William, Pvt 107 100
(Note: Sent per mail to Z. B[iggs] at Steuben-ville, Ohio.)

438 18 May 1804 B/1/001
Registered by: George Beemer
Registered for: George Beemer, assignee
Location: Mil - 2 3 4 19
Based upon the following Army land warrant:
Issued to *No.* *Acres*
Mullin, Anthony, Pvt 11 100
(Note: Sent per post to G. B[eemer], letter of 30 Jul 1804.)

439 18 May 1804 B/1/001
Registered by: [Not given]
Registered for: John Corbet
Location: Mil - 2 3 4 8
Based upon the following Army land warrant:
Issued to *No.* *Acres*
Corbet, John, Pvt 12942 100
(Note: Patent delivered to Michael Nourse.)

440 24 May 1804 B/1/001
Registered by: [Not given]
Registered for: John Coleman
Location: Mil - 2 3 4 7
Based upon the following Army land warrant:
Issued to *No.* *Acres*
Coleman, John, Pvt 124 100
(Note: Delivered to Mr. Helms; see Rec[eipt?] to Certificate of location 144.)

441 13 Apr 1804 B/1/001
Registered by: William Kennedy, Esq.
Registered for: John Howard
Location: Mil - 2 3 4 6
Based upon the following Army land warrant:
Issued to *No.* *Acres*
Howard, John, Fife Major 4351 100
(Note: Sent per post to Mr. Kennedy, letter of 30 Jul 1804.)

442 21 Mar 1804 B/1/001
Registered by: Thomas Worthington
Registered for: Ezekiel Tophand
Location: Mil - 2 3 4 28
Based upon the following Army land warrant:
Issued to *No.* *Acres*
Tophand, Ezekiel, Pvt 6538 100
(Note: Sent per post to G. Beemer, letter of 30 Jul 1804.)

443 21 Mar 1804 B/1/001
Registered by: Thomas Worthington
Registered for: John Welch
Location: Mil - 2 3 4 29
Based upon the following Army land warrant:
Issued to *No.* *Acres*
Welch, John, Pvt 11829 100
(Note: Sent per post to G. Beemer, letter of 30 Jul 1804.)

444 9 Jul 1804 B/1/001
Registered by: T[homas] M[cKean] Thompson
Registered for: Edward Armstrong
Location: Mil - 1 8 3 23
Mil - 1 8 3 24
Based upon the following Army land warrant:
Issued to *No.* *Acres*
Armstrong, Edward, Lt 35 200
(Note: Delivered patent to W[illiam] Findley, Esq.)

445 10 Jul 1804 B/1/001
Registered by: Joshua Dawson
Registered for: Jesse St. John
Location: Mil - 15 8 4 13
Based upon the following Army land warrant:
Issued to *No.* *Acres*
St. John, Jesse, Cpl 6026 100
(Note: Hez[ekiah?] Rogers received the C[erti-ficate].)

446 25 Jul 1804 B/1/001
Registered by: Zaccheus Biggs
Registered for: John Sprig Bell
Location: Mil - 2 3 4 35
Mil - 2 3 4 36
Mil - 2 3 4 37
Based upon the following Army land warrant:
Issued to *No.* *Acres*
Bell, John Sprig, Capt 232 100
(Note: Delivered certificate to M. Nourse, agent.)

447 25 Jul 1804 B/1/001
Registered by: Zaccheus Biggs
Registered for: Philip Lackey
Location: Mil - 2 3 4 10
Based upon the following Army land warrant:
Issued to *No.* *Acres*
Lackey, Philip, Soldier 9795 100
(Note: Delivered certificate to M. Nourse, agent.)

448 25 Jul 1804 B/1/001
Registered by: [Not given]
Registered for: [Not given]
Location: [Not given]
Based upon the following Army land warrant:
Issued to *No.* *Acres*
Cary, John D., Lt 445 [200]
(Note: "See page 15 [otherwise unidentified].)

449 25 Jul 1804 B/1/001
Registered by: Zaccheus Biggs
Registered for: James Black
Location: Mil - 1 1 3 25
Based upon the following Army land warrant:
Issued to *No.* *Acres*
Devore, Luke, Pvt 160 100

450 25 Jul 1804 B/1/002
Registered by: Zaccheus Biggs
Registered for: Zaccheus Biggs
Location: Mil - 2 3 4 17
Based upon the following Army land warrant:
Issued to *No.* *Acres*
Holbrook, Abijah, Pvt 53 100
(Note: Transmitted to Mr. Biggs.)

451 25 Jul 1804 B/1/002
Registered by: Zaccheus Biggs
Registered for: John Shaw
Location: Mil - 2 3 4 30
Mil - 2 3 4 31
Mil - 2 3 4 32
Based upon the following Army land warrant:
Issued to *No.* *Acres*
Shaw, John, Capt 158 300
(Note: Transmitted to Mr. Biggs.)

452 25 Jul 1804 B/1/002
Registered by: Zaccheus Biggs
Registered for: Zaccheus Biggs
Location: Mil - 2 3 4 18
Based upon the following Army land warrant:
Issued to *No.* *Acres*
Bacon, William, Pvt 101 100
(Note: Transmitted to Mr. Biggs.)

453 27 Aug 1804 B/1/002
Registered by: Robert Underwood
Registered for: George Cantine
Location: Mil - 8 2 3 13
Based upon the following Army land warrant:
Issued to *No.* *Acres*
Cantine, George, Pvt 3980 100
(Note: Delivered certificate to Mr. Underwood.)

454 16 Nov 1804 B/1/002
Registered by: Michael Nourse
Registered for: Michael Nourse
Location: Mil - 3 1 1 2
Based upon the following Army land warrant:
Issued to *No.* *Acres*
Corneil, John, heirs [of]
Sgt 16 100
(Note: Delivered certificate to Mr. Nourse.)

455 16 Nov 1804 B/1/002
Registered by: Michael Nourse
Registered for: Michael Nourse
Location: Mil - 3 1 1 3
Based upon the following Army land warrant:
Issued to *No.* *Acres*
Smith, Enoch, Pvt 91 100
(Note: Delivered certificate to Mr. Nourse.)

456 16 Nov 1804 B/1/002
Registered by: Michael Nourse
Registered for: Michael Nourse
Location: Mil - 3 1 1 1
Based upon the following Army land warrant:
Issued to *No.* *Acres*
Moss, Reuben, Cpl 94 100
(Note: Delivered certificate to Mr. Nourse.)

457 16 Nov 1804 B/1/002
Registered by: Col [Thomas] Worthington
Registered for: Richard Wells
Location: Mil - 8 2 3 2
Mil - 8 2 3 3
Mil - 8 2 3 4
Mil - 8 2 3 5
Mil - 8 2 3 7
Based upon the following Army land warrant:
Issued to *No.* *Acres*
Lytle, William, LtCol
Commanding 84 500
(Note: Delivered patent to Noah Zane.)

458 16 Nov 1804 B/1/002
Registered by: Col [Thomas] Worthington
Registered for: Anthony Sharp
Location: Mil - 10 3 4 24
Mil - 10 3 4 25
Mil - 10 3 4 26
Based upon the following Army land warrant:
Issued to *No.* *Acres*
Sharp, Anthony, Capt 2095 300
(Note: Delivered patent to Col Worthington.)

459 23 Nov 1804 B/1/002
Registered by: Zaccheus Biggs
Registered for: Zaccheus Biggs
Location: Mil - 2 3 4 13
Based upon the following Army land warrant:
Issued to *No.* *Acres*
Selden, Ebenezer, Pvt 17 100
(Note: Delivered certificate to M. Nourse, agent of [Zaccheus] Biggs.)

460 26 Nov 1804 B/1/002
Registered by: William Findley, Esq.
Registered for: Isaac Miller
Location: Mil - 2 3 4 16

460 [continued]
Based upon the following Army land warrant:
Issued to — *No.* — *Acres*
Miller, Isaac, Soldier — 10102 — 100
(Note: Delivered patent to Mr. Findley.)

461 — 26 Nov 1804 — B/1/002
Registered by: General -- Van Cortlandt
Registered for: Mason Wattles
Location: Mil - 11 8 1 3
Mil - 11 8 1 4
Mil - 11 8 1 5
Based upon the following Army land warrant:
Issued to — *No.* — *Acres*
Wattles, Mason, Capt — 2301 — 300
(Note: Delivered patent to General Van Cortlandt.)

462 — 6 Dec 1804 — B/1/002
Registered by: -- Mott, M.C., New Jersey
Registered for: Eliza[beth] Mannington, heiress
Location: Mil - 6 8 3 28
Based upon the following Army land warrant:
Issued to — *No.* — *Acres*
Ferguson, Jane, adm[inistratrix] Soldier — 14032 — 100
(Note: Delivered patent to Mr. Mott.)

463 — -- 1804 — B/1/002
Registered by: Peter Mills, Marietta [Ohio]
Registered for: Menasseh Sawyer
Location: Mil - 11 9 4 24
Based upon the following Army land warrant:
Issued to — *No.* — *Acres*
Sawyer, Menasseh, Soldier — 3497 — 100

464 — 11 Dec 1804 — B/1/002
Registered by: William Findley, M.C., Penna.
Registered for: Adam Wallace
Location: Mil - 11 8 1 1
Based upon the following Army land warrant:
Issued to — *No.* — *Acres*
Cook, John, Soldier — 10734 — 100
(Note: Delivered patent to Mr. Findley.)

465 — 11 Dec 1804 — B/1/002
Registered by: William Findley, M.C., Penna.
Registered for: Adam Wallace
Location: Mil - 11 8 1 2
Based upon the following Army land warrant:
Issued to — *No.* — *Acres*
Alcorn, William, Soldier — 10692 — 100
(Note: Delivered patent to Mr. Findley.)

466 — 11 Dec 1804 — B/1/002
Registered by: Zaccheus Biggs
Registered for: Zaccheus Biggs
Location: Mil - 1 10 1 30
Based upon the following Army land warrant:
Issued to — *No.* — *Acres*
Chapin, Joel, Soldier — 3897 — 100
(Note: Delivered patent to M. Nourse.)

467 — 11 Dec 1804 — B/1/002
Registered by: Zaccheus Biggs
Registered for: Zaccheus Biggs
Location: Mil - 1 10 1 29
Based upon the following Army land warrant:
Issued to — *No.* — *Acres*
Whipple, Joseph, Sgt — 6639 — 100
(Note: Delivered patent to Mr. Nourse.)

468 — 15 Dec 1804 — B/1/002
Registered by: Maj -- Rogers
Registered for: Caleb Gibbs
Location: Mil - 16 8 4 4
Mil - 16 8 4 6
Mil - 16 8 4 9
Mil - 16 8 4 10
Based upon the following Army land warrant:
Issued by — *No.* — *Acres*
Gibbs, Caleb, Maj — 792 — 400
(Note: Delivered patent to Maj Rogers.)

469 — 15 Dec 1804 — B/1/002
Registered by: Col [Thomas] Worthington
Registered for: William Foreman, heir at law
Location: Mil - 8 2 3 22
Based upon the following Army land warrant:
Issued to — *No.* — *Acres*
Reed, Philip [deceased?] Soldier — 11219 — 100
(Note: Delivered patent to R. Wright, Esq., Senator from Maryland.)

470 — Not stated — B/1/002
Registered by: General -- Van Cortlandt
Registered for: [Not stated]
Location: [Not stated]
Based upon the following Army land warrant:
Issued to — *No.* — *Acres*
Stewart, William, Lt — 2114 — [200]

471 — 20 Dec 1804 — B/1/002
Registered by: Ezekiel King
Registered for: John P. Helfenstein
Location: Mil - 6 7 3 30
Based upon the following Army land warrant:
Issued to — *No.* — *Acres*
Horner, John, Soldier — 9571 — 100
(Note: Delivered certificate to E. King, agent.)

472 — 20 Dec 1804 — B/1/002
Registered by: Richard Gernon, Philadelphia
Registered for: [Not stated]
Location: [Not stated]
Based upon the following Army land warrant:
Issued to — *No.* — *Acres*
Sloan, Joseph, Soldier — 8821 — 100
(Note: Returned to Mr. Gernon in letter of 3 Jan 1805.)

473 — 20 Dec 1804 — B/1/002
Registered by: Richard Gernon, Philadelphia
Registered for: Richard Gernon
Location: Mil - 11 8 1 6
Based upon the following Army land warrant:
Issued to — *No.* — *Acres*
Garvin? [Gawin?] Henry, Soldier — 9434 — 100

474 20 Dec 1804 B/1/002
Registered by: Richard Gernon, Philadelphia
Registered for: Richard Gernon
Location: Mil - 2 6 1 6
Based upon the following Army land warrant:

Issued to	*No.*	*Acres*
Ralston, Andrew, Sgt	10255	100

(Note: Delivered patent to J. Davidson.)

475 20 Dec 1804 B/1/002
Registered by: Richard Gernon, Philadelphia
Registered for: Richard Gernon
Location: Mil - 11 8 1 7
Mil - 11 8 1 8
Based upon the following Army land warrant:

Issued to	*No.*	*Acres*
Ball, B. W., Lt	207	200

476 20 Dec 1804 B/1/002
Registered by: Richard Gernon, Philadelphia
Registered for: Richard Gernon
Location: Mil - 2 6 1 3
Based upon the following Army land warrant:

Issued to	*No.*	*Acres*
Shirtliff, Amasa, Sgt	4966	100

(Note: Delivered patent to J. Davidson.)

477 20 Dec 1804 B/1/002
Registered by: Richard Gernon, Philadelphia
Registered for: Richard Gernon
Location: Mil - 11 8 1 9
Based upon the following Army land warrant:

Issued to	*No.*	*Acres*
Snow, James, Soldier	4995	100

478 20 Dec 1804 B/1/002
Registered by: Richard Gernon, Philadelphia
Registered for: Richard Gernon
Location: Mil - 2 6 1 4
Based upon the following Army land warrant:

Issued to	*No.*	*Acres*
Hazard, Ebenezer, Soldier	7443	100

(Note: Delivered patent to J. Davidson.)

479 20 Dec 1804 B/1/003
Registered by: Richard Gernon, Philadelphia
Registered for: Richard Gernon
Location: Mil - 11 8 1 10
Based upon the following Army land warrant:

Issued to	*No.*	*Acres*
Crumm, William, Dragoon	9187	100

(Note: Delivered patent to J. Davidson.)

480 20 Dec 1804 B/1/003
Registered by: Richard Gernon, Philadelphia
Registered for: Richard Gernon
Location: Mil - 11 8 1 11
Based upon the following Army land warrant:

Issued to	*No.*	*Acres*
Taylor, Richard, Soldier	10896	100

(Note: Delivered patent to J. Davidson.)

481 20 Dec 1804 B/1/003
Registered by: Richard Gernon, Philadelphia
Registered for: Richard Gernon
Location: Mil - 11 8 1 22
Based upon the following Army land warrant:

Issued to	*No.*	*Acres*
Armstrong, Robert, Soldier	12710	100

482 20 Dec 1804 B/1/003
Registered by: Richard Gernon, Philadelphia
Registered for: Richard Gernon
Location: Mil - 11 8 1 23
Based upon the following Army land warrant:

Issued to	*No.*	*Acres*
Blaney, John, Soldier	12772	100

(Note: Delivered patent to J. Davidson.)

483 20 Dec 1804 B/1/003
Registered by: Richard Gernon, Philadelphia
Registered for: Richard Gernon
Location: Mil - 11 8 1 24
Based upon the following Army land warrant:

Issued to	*No.*	*Acres*
Leary, Dennis, Cpl	13381	100

(Note: Delivered patent to J. Davidson.)

484 20 Dec 1804 B/1/003
Registered by: Richard Gernon, Philadelphia
Registered for: Richard Gernon
Location: Mil - 11 8 1 25
Based upon the following Army land warrant:

Issued to	*No.*	*Acres*
Quigley, Edward, Soldier	13638	100

485 20 Dec 1804 B/1/003
Registered by: David Jones
Registered for: David Jones
Location: (4000 acres) Mil - 15 7 - 3
(50 acres) Mil - 17 7 1 16W
Based upon the following Army land warrants:

Issued to	*No.*	*Acres*
Morgan, Joseph, Sgt	6135	100
Hughes, John, Lt	1016	200
Hyatt, John Vance, Lt	1040	200
Philips, Francis, Soldier	8656	100
Snow, Elijah, Soldier	7243	100
Shirts, Matthias, Soldier	8764	100
Barrel, William, Soldier	8155	100
Cooper, Spencer, Matross	11985	100
Following are the property of Maj Jacob Humphreys:		
Humphrey, John, Lt	1026	200
Humphrey, Jacob, Capt	1012	300
Caldwell, James, Matross	9214	100
Butts, Thomas, Soldier	12801	100
McCoy, Roderick, Cpl	9963	100
Burnsides, John, Soldier	11894	100
Heller, Jacob, Soldier	8206	100
Following are the property of Enoch Jones:		
McCoskey, Samuel A., Surgeon	1458	400
Ogden, Daniel, Soldier	7563	100
Adams, William, Surgeon	47	400
Shreader, Philip, Soldier	9908	100
Following are property of Simson and Catherine Davis:		

485 [continued]
O'Bryar [O'Bryan?] Philip,
Soldier 11582 100
Radcliff, William, Junior,
Ens 2667 150
Davis, Sampson * 803.2
*Register's certificate no. 16.

486 24 Dec 1804 B/1/004
Registered by: Zaccheus Biggs
Registered for: Zaccheus Biggs
Location: Mil - 1 10 1 4
Mil - 1 10 1 19
Based upon the following Army land warrant:
Issued to *No.* *Acres*
Mason, David, Lt 1366 200
(Note: Delivered certificate to M. Nourse, agent.)

487 28 Dec 1804 B/1/004
Registered by: Benjamin Tallmadge, Esq.
Registered for: Henry Purkett
Location: Mil - 8 5 1 36
Based upon the following Army land warrant:
Issued to *No.* *Acres*
Purkett, Henry, Quarter-
master Sgt 6344 100
(Note: Delivered patent to Mr. Tallmadge.)

488 28 Dec 1804 B/1/004
Registered by: Samuel Tenney, Esq., M.C.
Registered for: Abiel Chandler
Location: Mil - 11 9 4 13
Based upon the following Army land warrant:
Issued to *No.* *Acres*
Chandler, Abiel, Pvt 171 100
(Note: Enclosed to Mr. Tenney in letter of 7 Jan 1804 [sic].)

489 4 Jan 1805 B/1/004
Registered by: Sent to Register
Registered for: Thomas Schuyler Sill
Location: Mil - 15 7 4 9
Mil - 15 7 4 10
Mil - 15 7 4 23
Based upon the following Army land warrant:
Issued to *No.* *Acres*
Sill, Thomas, Capt 2710 300
(Note: Delivered certificate to Mr. Nourse, agent.)

490 5 Jan 1805 B/1/004
Registered by: T[homas] Worthington, Esq.
Registered for: Thurston Hillard
Location: Mil - 10 3 4 39
Based upon the following Army land warrant:
Issued to *No.* *Acres*
Hillard, Thurston, Sol-
dier 13201 100
(Note: Delivered patent to Noah Zane.)

491 5 Jan 1805 B/1/004
Registered by: -- Van Horne, Esq.
Registered for: William Martin
Location: Mil - 16 2 4 35
Based upon the following Army land warrant:
Issued to *No.* *Acres*
Martin, William, Sgt 13397 100
(Note: Delivered to Mr. Van Horne.)

492 5 Jan 1805 B/1/004
Registered by: John Hoge, Esq.
Registered for: C. Schlokerman
Location: Mil - 1 10 1 39
Based upon the following Army land warrant:
Issued to *No.* *Acres*
Schlokerman, Christopher,
Soldier 10433 100
(Note: Delivered to Mr. Hoge.)

493 5 Jan 1805 B/1/004
Registered by: Hon. Nathaniel Mason? [Macon?]
Registered for: S. Hogg, Junior, *et al*
Location: Mil - 6 10 4 1
Mil - 6 10 4 2
Mil - 6 10 4 3
Mil - 6 10 4 4
Based upon the following Army land warrant:
Issued to *No.* *Acres*
Hog[g] Samuel, Junior, &
Hogg, John Bablish?
Senior? Maj 104 400
(Note: Delivered to Mr. Macon?)

494 10 Jan 1805 B/1/004
Registered by: Zaccheus Biggs
Registered for: Zaccheus Biggs
Location: Mil - 1 10 1 15
Based upon the following Army land warrant:
Issued to *No.* *Acres*
Samson, Nathan, Pvt 167 100
(Note: Delivered to Mr. Nourse.)

495 12 Jan 1805 B/1/004
Registered by: -- Nelson, M.C., Maryland
Registered for: Thomas McMullin, heir
Location: Mil - 5 10 4 7
Based upon the following Army land warrant:
Issued to *No.* *Acres*
McMullen? [McMullin?]
Mary, administratrix
of Hugh McMullin, Pvt 11501 100
(Note: Sent by mail directed to Mr. Nelson at Frederickstown [Maryland] by desire.)

496 1 Feb 1805 B/1/004
Registered by: John Condit, Esq.
Registered for: Squire Cockrem
Location: Mil - 15 2 2 29
Based upon the following Army land warrant:
Issued to *No.* *Acres*
Cockrem, Squire, Pvt 115 100
(Note: Delivered patent to Mr. Condit.)

497 2 Feb 1805 B/1/004
Registered by: Abijah Holbrook
Registered for: Abijah Holbrook
Location: Mil - 16 2 4 21
Mil - 16 2 4 22
Mil - 16 2 4 23
Mil - 16 2 4 25
Mil - 16 2 4 26

497 [continued]

Mil	-	16	2	4	27
Mil	-	16	2	4	28
Mil	-	16	2	4	36
Mil	-	16	2	4	37
Mil	-	16	2	4	38
Mil	-	16	2	4	39
Mil	-	16	2	4	40
Mil	-	16	2	4	11
Mil	-	16	2	4	12
Mil	-	16	2	4	1
Mil	-	16	2	4	2
Mil	-	16	2	4	8

Based upon the following Army land warrants:

Issued to	*No.*	*Acres*
Holbrook, Abijah, assignee	33	100
Holbrook, Abijah, assignee	34	100
Holbrook, Abijah, assignee	35	100
Holbrook, Abijah, assignee	36	100
Holbrook, Abijah, assignee	37	100
Holbrook, Abijah, assignee	38	100
Holbrook, Abijah, assignee	40	100
Holbrook, Abijah, assignee	41	100
Holbrook, Abijah, assignee	42	100
Holbrook, Abijah, assignee	43	100
Holbrook, Abijah, assignee	44	100
Holbrook, Abijah, assignee	45	100
Holbrook, Abijah, assignee	46	100
Holbrook, Abijah, assignee	47	100
Holbrook, Abijah, assignee	48	100
Holbrook, Abijah, assignee	50	100
Holbrook, Abijah, assignee	51	100
Holbrook, Abijah, assignee	52*	[100]

*"Received this warrant back [signed] Abijah Holbrook."

498 — 2 Feb 1805 — B/1/005
Registered by: Abijah Holbrook
Registered for: --
Location: --
Based upon the following Army land warrant:

Issued to	*No.*	*Acres*
Wheeler, Benjamin, Cpl	39*	100

*"Received this warrant back [signed] Abijah Holbrook."

499 — 2 Feb 1805 — B/1/005
Registered by: Abijah Holbrook
Registered for: --
Location: --
Based upon the following Army land warrant:

Issued to	*No.*	*Acres*
Spencer, Thomas, Sgt	49*	100

*"Received this warrant back [signed] Abijah Holbrook."

500 — 8 Feb 1805 — B/1/005
Registered by: Ebenezer Elmer
Registered for: Henry Ferver
Location: Mil - 15 2 2 30
Based upon the following Army land warrant:

Issued to	*No.*	*Acres*
Ferver, Henry, Pvt	128	100

(Note: Delivered patent to Mr. Elmer.)

501 — 8 Feb 1805 — B/1/005
Registered by: Jesse Franklin
Registered for: Samuel McCraw
Location: Mil - 11 8 1 40
Based upon the following Army land warrant:

Issued to	*No.*	*Acres*
McCraw, Samuel, Pvt	73	100

(Note: Delivered patent to Mr. Franklin.)

502 — 9 Feb 1805 — B/1/005
Registered by: Ezekiel King
Registered for: John P. Helfenstein
Location: Mil - 6 7 3 31
Based upon the following Army land warrant:

Issued to	*No.*	*Acres*
Fellows, Tobias, Pvt	13078	100

(Note: Delivered patent to Mr. King.)

503 — 9 Feb 1805 — B/1/005
Registered by: Hon. John Earle
Registered for: Louis D. Martin
Location: Mil - 3 6 4 6
Mil - 3 6 4 7
Mil - 3 6 4 8
Based upon the following Army land warrant:

Issued to	*No.*	*Acres*
Martin, Louis D., Capt	173	300

(Note: Delivered patent to Mr. Earle.)

504 — 11 Feb 1805 — B/1/005
Registered by: Hon. M. Chittenden
Registered for: Z[accheus] Peaster
Location: Mil - 8 2 3 20
Mil - 8 2 3 21
Based upon the following Army land warrant:

Issued to	*No.*	*Acres*
Peaster, Zaccheus, Lt	1763	200

(Note: Delivered patent to Mr. Chittenden.)

505 — 12 Feb 1805 — B/1/005
Registered by: -- Tompkins
Registered for: Jonas Stansbery
Location: Mil - 2 7 4 7
Based upon the following Army land warrant:

Issued to	*No.*	*Acres*
Winans, William, Pvt	6689	100

506 — 12 Feb 1805 — B/1/005
Registered by: M[ichael] Nourse
Registered for: Zaccheus Biggs
Location: Mil - 1 10 1 18
Based upon the following Army land warrant:

Issued to	*No.*	*Acres*
Sowers, William, Pvt	6494	100

(Note: To wait Mr. Nourse' direction.)

507 — 15 Feb 1805 — B/1/005
Registered by: Jeremiah Morrow, Esq.
Registered for: James Ryan
Location: Mil - 16 2 4 24
Based upon the following Army land warrant:

Issued to	*No.*	*Acres*
Ryan, James, Pvt	10294	100

(Note: Delivered patent to Mr. Morrow.)

508 — 15 Feb 1805 — B/1/005
Registered by: Jeremiah Morrow, Esq.
Registered for: David Gibbons

508 [continued]
Location: Mil - 16 2 4 10
Based upon the following Army land warrant:
Issued to *No.* *Acres*
Gibbons, David, Pvt 9513 100
(Note: Delivered patent to Mr. Morrow.)

509 16 Feb 1805 B/1/005
Registered by: Ebenezer Seaver, Esq.
Registered for: Ebenezer Seaver
Location: Mil - 11 8 1 12
Based upon the following Army land warrant:
Issued to *No.* *Acres*
Luther, Peleg, Sgt 77 100
(Note: Patent sent to E. Seaver, Esq.)

510 16 Feb 1805 B/1/005
Registered by: Ebenezer Seaver, Esq.
Registered for: Ebenezer Seaver
Location: Mil - 11 8 1 21
Based upon the following Army land warrant:
Issued to *No.* *Acres*
Barker, Barnabas, Sgt 76 100
(Note: Patent sent to Phanuel Bishop, Esq.)

511 16 Feb 1805 B/1/005
Registered by: Ebenezer Seaver, Esq.
Registered for: Isaac Sturtevant
Location: Mil - 11 8 1 13
Mil - 11 8 1 14
Based upon the following Army land warrant:
Issued to *No.* *Acres*
Sturtevant, Isaac, Lt 4 200
(Note: Delivered patent to Mr. Seaver.)

512 16 Feb 1805 B/1/005
Registered by: Ebenezer Seaver, Esq.
Registered for: Edward Lee
Location: Mil - 11 8 1 20
Based upon the following Army land warrant:
Issued to *No.* *Acres*
Lee, Edward, Pvt 6 100
(Note: Delivered patent to Mr. Seaver.)

513 21 Feb 1805 B/1/005
Registered by: Hon. J. A. Bayard, Esq.
Registered for: James Booth, his executor
Location: Mil - 11 8 1 15
Mil - 11 8 1 16
Based upon the following Army land warrant:
Issued to *No.* *Acres*
McWilliam, Stephen, Lt 1473 200
(Note: Delivered patent to Mr. Bayard.)

514 22 Feb 1805 B/1/005
Registered by: Joseph Copes
Registered for: Mitchell Kershaw
Location: Mil - 2 2 3 33
Based upon the following Army land warrant:
Issued to *No.* *Acres*
Bright, Levi, Soldier 10713 100
(Note: Sent per mail, 5 Apr 1805.)

515 25 Feb 1805 B/1/005
Registered by: Andrew Gregg, Esq.
Registered for: William Early, assignee
Location: Mil - 15 7 4 40
Based upon the following Army land warrant:
Issued to *No.* *Acres*
Hairbolt, Adam, Soldier 9607 100
(Note: Delivered patent to Mr. Gregg.)

516 25 Feb 1805 B/1/005
Registered by: Hon. James Holland
Registered for: Alexander Brevard
Location: Mil - 11 8 1 17
Mil - 11 8 1 18
Mil - 11 8 1 32
Based upon the following Army land warrant:
Issued to *No.* *Acres*
Brevard, Alexander, Capt 294 300
(Note: Delivered patent to Mr. Holland.)

517 26 Feb 1805 B/1/005
Registered by: Robert Underwood
Registered for: George Kneopler
Location: Mil - 8 2 1 16
Based upon the following Army land warrant:
Issued to *No.* *Acres*
Kneopler, George, Soldier 13421 100
(Note: Delivered patent to Mr. Underwood.)

518 26 Feb 1805 B/1/005
Registered by: John Mathews
Registered for: Robert Parker
Location: Mil - 8 2 1 36
Mil - 8 2 1 37
Based upon the following Army land warrant:
Issued to *No.* *Acres*
Parker, Robert, CaptLt 1714 200
(Note: Sent certificate to J. Mathews, 2 Mar 1805.)

519 26 Feb 1805 B/1/005
Registered by: John Mathews
Registered for: William Porter
Location: Mil - 8 2 1 38
Mil - 8 2 1 39
Based upon the following Army land warrant:
Issued to *No.* *Acres*
Porter, William, Lt 1745 200
(Note: Sent certificate to J. Mathews, 2 Mar 1805.)

520 26 Feb 1805 B/1/005
Registered by: John Mathews
Registered for: William Clark
Location: Mil - 8 2 1 40
Based upon the following Army land warrant:
Issued to *No.* *Acres*
Smith, Isaac, Soldier 6441 100
(Note: Sent certificate to J. Mathews, 2 Mar 1805.)

521 26 Feb 1805 B/1/005
Registered by: John Mathews
Registered for: Daniel St. Clair
Location: Mil - 9 1 3 1
Mil - 9 1 3 2
Based upon the following Army land warrant:

521 [continued]

Issued to	*No.*	*Acres*
St. Clair, Daniel, Lt	2025	200

(Note: Sent certificate to J. Mathews, 2 Mar 1805.)

522 — 26 Feb 1805 — B/1/005
Registered by: John Mathews
Registered for: John Mercer
Location: Mil - 10 3 4 37
Mil - 10 3 4 38
Mil - 10 3 4 40
Based upon the following Army land warrant:

Issued to	*No.*	*Acres*
Mercer, John, Capt	1411	300

(Note: Sent Certificate to J. Mathews, 2 Mar 1805.)

523 — 26 Feb 1805 — B/1/005
Registered by: John Mathews
Registered for: Samuel Montgomery
Location: Mil - 17 7 4 14
Mil - 17 7 4 15
Mil - 17 7 4 16
Based upon the following Army land warrant:

Issued to	*No.*	*Acres*
Montgomery, Samuel, Capt	1425	300

(Note: Sent certificate to J. Mathews, 2 Mar 1805.)

524 — 26 Feb 1805 — B/1/005
Registered by: John Mathews
Registered for: Samuel Montgomery
Location: Mil - 17 7 4 13
Based upon the following Army land warrant:

Issued to	*No.*	*Acres*
Berry, James, Soldier	8938	100

(Note: Sent certificate to J. Mathews, 2 Mar 1805.)

525 — 26 Feb 1805 — B/1/005
Registered by: John Mathews
Registered for: Samuel Montgomery
Location: Mil - 17 7 4 12
Based upon the following Army land warrant:

Issued to	*No.*	*Acres*
Winn, John, Soldier	10562	100

(Note: Sent certificate to J. Mathews, 2 Mar 1805.)

526 — 26 Feb 1805 — B/1/005
Registered by: John Mathews
Registered for: Samuel Montgomery
Location: Mil - 17 7 4 11
Based upon the following Army land warrant:

Issued to	*No.*	*Acres*
Conner, Charles, Soldier	9110	100

(Note: Sent certificate to J. Mathews, 2 Mar 1805.)

527 — 1 Mar 1805 — B/1/006
Registered by: Col -- Gaither
Registered for: Henry Gaither
Location: Mil - 17 7 4 20
Mil - 17 7 4 21
Mil - 17 7 4 22
Based upon the following Army land warrant:

Issued to	*No.*	*Acres*
Gaither, Henry, Capt	854	300

528 — 1 Mar 1805 — B/1/006
Registered by: John Mathews
Registered for: William Wells
Location: Mil - 17 7 1 16E
Based upon the following surplus certificate:

Issued to	*No.*	*Acres*
Walker, Benjamin, LtCol	--	50

529 — 2 Mar 1805 — B/1/006
Registered by: Caesar A. Rodney, Esq.
Registered for: Heirs by name
Location: Mil - 15 7 4 7
Based upon the following Army land warrant:

Issued to	*No.*	*Acres*
Cochran, Daniel, Sgt	10736	100

530 — 4 Mar 1805 — B/1/006
Registered by: Jos[eph] Heister, Esq.
Registered for: Stephen Barth
Location: Mil - 15 7 4 5
Based upon the following Army land warrant:

Issued to	*No.*	*Acres*
Barth, Stephen, Dragoon	178	100

(Note: Sent to Mr. Hiester, 11 May 1805.)

531 — 5 Mar 1805 — B/1/006
Registered by: Andrew Gregg, Esq.
Registered for: John Akely
Location: Mil - 15 7 4 6
Based upon the following Army land warrant:

Issued to	*No.*	*Acres*
Akely, John, Dragoon	179	100

(Note: Sent according to Mr. Gregg's order to J. Watson, c/o Mifflintown, Penna.)

532 — 5 Mar 1805 — B/1/006
Registered by: William Duane
Registered for: James Donahoo
Location: Mil - 8 2 1 7
Based upon the following Army land warrant:

Issued to	*No.*	*Acres*
Donahoo, James, Pvt	183	100

(Note: Delivered certificate to Mr. Duane.)

533 — 6 Mar 1805 — B/1/006
Registered by: Jeremiah Morrow, Esq.
Registered for: John Inglish*
Location: Mil - 16 2 4 9
Based upon the following Army land warrant:

Issued to	*No.*	*Acres*
English* John, Pvt	181	100

*So spelled.
(Note: Delivered patent to M. Nourse, agent for Mr. Morrow.)

534 — 7 Mar 1805 — B/1/006
Registered by: Maj -- Rogers
Registered for: Sarah Munson, administratrix in trust, etc.
Location: Mil - 8 2 1 8
Mil - 8 2 1 13
Mil - 8 2 1 14

534 [continued]
Based upon the following Army land warrant:

Issued to	*No.*	*Acres*
Munson, Theophilus, Capt	185	300

535 7 Mar 1805 B/1/006
Registered by: -- Griswold by C. Nourse
Registered for: Luther Reeves
Location: Mil - 8 2 1 9
Based upon the following Army land warrant:

Issued to	*No.*	*Acres*
Reeves, Luther, Pvt	6388	100

(Note: Delivered certificate to Mr. Nourse.)

536 7 Mar 1805 B/1/006
Registered by: -- Tallmadge by M. Sheldon
Registered for: Stephen Chapman
Location: Mil - 8 2 3 10
Based upon the following Army land warrant:

Issued to	*No.*	*Acres*
Chapman, Stephen, Cpl	186	100

537 7 Mar 1805 B/1/006
Registered by: Zaccheus Biggs
Registered for: John McCreary, assignee
Location: Mil - 1 10 1 20
Based upon the following Army land warrant :

Issued to	*No.*	*Acres*
McClelland, John, Soldier	10035	100

(Note: Delivered certificate to M. Nourse.)

538 7 Mar 1805 B/1/006
Registered by: -- Vanhorne
Registered for: [not stated]
Location: [not stated]
Based upon the following Army land warrant:

Issued to	*No.*	*Acres*
Davidson, William, LtCol	607	450

539 7 Mar 1805 B/1/006
Registered by: David Holmes, Esq.
Registered for: Lewis Boyer
Location: Mil - 8 2 1 25
Based upon the following Army land warrant:

Issued to	*No.*	*Acres*
Boyer, Lewis, Dragoon	187	100

(Note: Sent patent to Mr. Holmes, 11 May 1805.)

540 7 Mar 1805 B/1/006
Registered by: John Archer, Esq.
Registered for: Edward Prall
Location: Mil - 8 2 3 6
Mil - 8 2 3 15
Mil - 8 2 3 16
Based upon the following Army land warrant:

Issued to	*No.*	*Acres*
Prall, Edward, Capt	1729	300

(Note: Sent to Mr. Archer by mail, 2 Apr 1805.)

541 11 Mar 1805 B/1/006
Registered by: M[ichael] Nourse
Registered for: Isaac Prior
Location: Mil - 2 2 3 32
Based upon the following Army land warrant:

Issued to	*No.*	*Acres*
Farrell, William, Soldier	9407	100

(Note: Delivered certificate to M. Nourse.)

542 12 Mar 1805 B/1/006
Registered by: George Beymer
Registered for: George Rice
Location: Mil - 2 2 3 5
Mil - 2 2 3 6
Mil - 2 2 3 7
Based upon the following Army land warrant:

Issued to	*No.*	*Acres*
Rice, George, Capt	2498	300

(Note: Sent per post to Mr. Beymer at Zanesville [Ohio] . . ., 12 Jul 1805.)

543 12 Mar 1805 B/1/006
Registered by: George Beymer
Registered for: John McNair
Location: Mil - 3 1 1 10
Based upon the following Army land warrant:

Issued to	*No.*	*Acres*
McNair, John, Soldier	9949	100

(Note: Sent per post to Mr. Beymer at Zanesville [Ohio] . . ., 12 Jul 1805.)

544 15 Mar 1805 B/1/006
Registered by: William Blackledge, Esq.
Registered for: Heirs of J. Patten
Location: Mil - 17 7 4 27
Mil - 17 7 4 28
Mil - 17 7 4 29
Mil - 17 7 4 30
Mil - 17 7 4 31
Based upon the following Army land warrant:

Issued to	*No.*	*Acres*
Patten, John, Col	194	500

(Note: Directed to be kept until Mr. Blackledge gives order. . . .)

545 15 Mar 1805 B/1/006
Registered by: William Blackledge, Esq.
Registered for: Simon [or Simeon] Alderson
Location: Mil - 17 7 4 38
Based upon the following Army land warrant:

Issued to	*No.*	*Acres*
Alderson, Simon, Pvt	192	100

(Note: Directed to be kept until Mr. Blackledge gives order. . . .)

546 15 Mar 1805 B/1/006
Registered by: William Blackledge, Esq.
Registered for: W. Blackledge
Location: Mil - 17 7 4 37
Based upon the following Army land warrant:

Issued to	*No.*	*Acres*
Clark, Isaac, Pvt	191	100

(Note: Directed to be kept until Mr. Blackledge gives order. . . .)

547 15 Mar 1805 B/1/006
Registered by: William Blackledge, Esq.
Registered for: W. Blackledge
Location: Mil - 17 7 4 36
Based upon the following Army land warrant:

Issued to	*No.*	*Acres*
Freeman, Samuel, Pvt	190	100

548 20 Mar 1805 B/1/006
Registered by: Hezekiah Rogers
Registered for: Stephen Ambler
Location: Mil - 16 7 2 15
Based upon the following Army land warrant:

Issued to	*No.*	*Acres*
Ambler, Stephen, Pvt	12725	100

549 20 Mar 1805 B/1/006
Registered by: Hezekiah Rogers
Registered for: Peter Ambler
Location: Mil - 16 7 2 16
Based upon the following Army land warrant:

Issued to	*No.*	*Acres*
Ambler, Peter, Pvt	12726	100

550 20 Mar 1805 B/1/006
Registered by: Hezekiah Rogers
Registered for: Squire Ambler
Location: Mil - 16 7 2 17
Based upon the following Army land warrant:

Issued to	*No.*	*Acres*
Ambler, Squire, Pvt	12727	100

551 20 Mar 1805 B/1/006
Registered by: William Kilty? [Hilty?]
Registered for: Benjamin Fickle
Location: Mil - 16 7 2 18
Mil - 16 7 2 19
Based upon the following Army land warrant:

Issued to	*No.*	*Acres*
Fickle, Ben[jami]n, Lt	197	200

(Note: Delivered patent to Mr. Nourse.)

552 20 Mar 1805 B/1/006
Registered by: Hezekiah Rogers
Registered for: Philip Turner
Location: Mil - 16 7 2 31
Mil - 16 7 2 32
Mil - 16 7 2 33
Mil - 16 7 2 34
Mil - 17 7 1 1E
Based upon the following Army land warrant:

Issued to	*No.*	*Acres*
Turner, Philip, Physician	199	450

553 26 Mar 1805 B/1/006
Registered by: Zaccheus Biggs
Registered for: Ambrose Norton
Location: Mil - 1 10 1 25
Based upon the following Army land warrant:

Issued to	*No.*	*Acres*
Norton, Ambrose, Cpl	6237	100

554 26 Mar 1805 B/1/006
Registered by: Zaccheus Biggs
Registered for: Jonathan Goss
Location: Mil - 1 10 1 26
Based upon the following Army land warrant:

Issued to	*No.*	*Acres*
Look? [Lock?] Henry, assignee of Samuel Prince	83	100

555 26 Mar 1805 B/1/007
Registered by: Zaccheus Biggs
Registered for: Charles Morgan
Location: Mil - 2 3 4 15
Based upon the following Army land warrant:

Issued to	*No.*	*Acres*
Morgan, Charles, Soldier	12352	100

556 26 Mar 1805 B/1/007
Registered by: Zaccheus Biggs
Registered for: Daniel Hinds
Location: Mil - 1 10 1 31
Based upon the following Army land warrant:

Issued to	*No.*	*Acres*
Landiss, Roger, Soldier	11432	100

557 26 Mar 1805 B/1/007
Registered by: Zaccheus Biggs
Registered for: Samuel Chappell
Location: Mil - 1 10 1 3
Based upon the following Army land warrant:

Issued to	*No.*	*Acres*
Chappell, Samuel, Soldier	11089	100

558 26 Mar 1805 B/1/007
Registered by: Joseph Nourse
Registered for: John Smith, assignee
Location: Mil - 3 1 1 23
Mil - 3 1 1 27
Mil - 3 1 1 28
Based upon the following Army land warrant:

Issued to	*No.*	*Acres*
Smith, Nathan, Capt	200	300

(Note: Delivered patent to Mr. Nourse for J. Nourse.)

559 27 Mar 1805 B/1/007
Registered by: Hez[ekiah] Rogers
Registered for: Samuel Keeler
Location: Mil - 16 7 2 20
Mil - 16 7 2 29
Mil - 16 7 2 30
Based upon the following Army land warrant:

Issued to	*No.*	*Acres*
Keeler, Samuel, Capt	201	300

560 27 Mar 1805 B/1/007
Registered by: John Barr
Registered for: John Barr
Location: Mil - 1 10 1 36
Based upon the following Army land warrant:

Issued to	*No.*	*Acres*
Barr, John, Soldier	12800	100

561 27 Mar 1805 B/1/007
Registered by: Michael Nourse
Registered for: Zaccheus Biggs
Location: Mil - 1 10 1 7
Mil - 1 10 1 8
Based upon the following Army land warrant:

Issued to	*No.*	*Acres*
Maynard, John, Lt	1360	200

562 28 Mar 1805 B/1/007
Registered by: Charles Kessinger
Registered for: Charles Kessinger

562 [continued]
Location: Mil - 1 10 1 13
Based upon the following Army land warrant:
Issued to *No.* *Acres*
Kessinger, Charles, Soldier 202 100
(Note: Delivered patent to C. Kessinger.)

563 29 Mar 1805 B/1/007
Registered by: John Dundas, Alex[andri]a, [Va.]
Registered for: William Hepburn & John Dundas
Location: Mil - 15 1 3 31
Mil - 15 1 3 32
Based upon the following Army land warrant:
Issued to *No.* *Acres*
Head, Richard, Lt 1119 200
(Note: Sent to John Dundas by mail, 13 May 1805.)

564 1 Apr 1805 B/1/007
Registered by: Michael Nourse
Registered for: [Not stated]
Location: Mil - 1 10 1 40
Based upon the following Army land warrant:
Issued to *No.* *Acres*
Wheeler, Benj[amin] Cpl 39 100

565 1 Apr 1805 B/1/007
Registered by: Michael Nourse
Registered for: [Not stated]
Location: Mil - 1 10 1 16
Based upon the following Army land warrant:
Issued to *No.* *Acres*
Ratton, John, Soldier 52 100

566 1 Apr 1805 B/1/007
Registered by: George Beymer
Registered for: George Beymer
Location: Mil - 2 2 3 15
Mil - 2 2 3 16
Mil - 2 2 3 17
Based upon the following Army land warrant:
Issued to *No.* *Acres*
Walton, William, Capt 2445 300
(Note: Sent to Mr. Beymer per post, 12 Jul 1805. . . .)

567 1 Apr 1805 B/1/007
Registered by: William Bierce
Registered for: William Bierce
Location: Mil - 3 1 1 18
Based upon the following Army land warrant:
Issued to *No.* *Acres*
Bierce, William, Sgt 14154 100
(Note: Sent by mail to W. Bierce, Cornwall, Connecticut, 13 May 1805.)

568 4 Apr 1805 B/1/007
Registered by: John Smith
Registered for: Joseph Strong
Location: Mil - 3 1 1 19
Mil - 3 1 1 20
Mil - 3 1 1 29
Mil - 3 1 1 30
Based upon the following Army land warrant:
Issued to *No.* *Acres*
Rose, John, Surgeon 1804 400

569 4 Apr 1805 B/1/007
Registered by: James Denny, Chillicothe
Registered for: [Not stated]
Location: [Not stated]
Based upon the following Army land warrant:
Issued to *No.* *Acres*
Stack, Richard, Fife Major 10389 100
(Note: Received this warrant for the owner. See letter of 5 Apr 1805. [signed] James Denny.)

570 8 Apr 1805 B/1/007
Registered by: Maj -- Swan
Registered for: Heirs of Chilion Ford
Location: Mil - 2 2 3 18
Mil - 2 2 3 19
Based upon the following Army land warrant:
Issued to *No.* *Acres*
Ford, Chilion, heirs of 203 200
(Note: Gave the patent to Maj Swan.)

571 10 Apr 1805 B/1/007
Registered by: -- Tompkins
Registered for: John Bryant
Location: Mil - 2 2 3 1
Based upon the following Army land warrant:
Issued to *No.* *Acres*
Bryant, John, Soldier 204 100

572 12 Apr 1805 B/1/007
Registered by: -- Pleasonton
Registered for: George McKeehan
Location: Mil - 15 1 3 14
Based upon the following Army land warrant:
Issued to *No.* *Acres*
McDonald, Francis, Soldier, 9928 100

573 12 Apr 1805 B/1/007
Registered by: -- Pleasonton
Registered for: George McKeehan
Location: Mil - 15 1 3 3
Based upon the following Army land warrant:
Issued to *No.* *Acres*
Foster, Moses, Soldier 11209 100
(Note: Gave certificate to Mr. Pleasonton.)

574 12 Apr 1805 B/1/007
Registered by: -- Pleasonton
Registered for: George McKeehan
Location: Mil - 15 1 3 4
Based upon the following Army land warrant:
Issued to *No.* *Acres*
Flannagen, Timo[thy?] Pvt 9388 100
(Note: Gave certificate to Mr. Pleasonton.)

575 15 May 1805 B/1/007
Registered by: George Taylor, Junior
Registered for: Zaccheus Biggs
Location: Mil - 1 10 1 16
Based upon the following Army land warrant:
Issued to *No.* *Acres*
Sloan, Joseph, &?
Walburn, Francis, Soldier 8821 100

576 7 Jun 1805 B/1/007
Registered by: -- Thom, for A. Ellison
Registered for: John Armstrong
Location: Mil - 17 7 4 32
Mil - 17 7 4 33
Mil - 17 7 4 34
Mil - 17 7 4 35
Based upon the following Army land warrant:

Issued to	*No.*	*Acres*
Armstrong, John, LtCol	60	400

(Note: Certificate issued for surplus [50 acres])

577 18 Jun 1805 B/1/007
Registered by: Maj James Taylor
Registered for: Robert Gamble
Location: Mil - 16 3 4 18
Mil - 16 3 4 19
Mil - 16 3 4 20
Based upon the following Army land warrant:

Issued to	*No.*	*Acres*
Gamble, Robert, Capt	869	300

(Note: Delivered to Mr. John Smith, agen for M. Taylor.)

578 18 Jun 1805 B/1/007
Registered by: Maj James Taylor
Registered for: John Hays
Location: Mil - 16 3 4 11
Mil - 16 3 4 12
Mil - 16 3 4 13
Mil - 16 3 4 14
Based upon the following Army land warrant:

Issued to	*No.*	*Acres*
Hays, John, Maj	1068	400

(Note: Delivered to Mr. John Smith, agen for M. Taylor.)

579 18 Jun 1807 B/1/007
Registered by: Maj James Taylor
Registered for: William Robertson
Location: Mil - 16 7 4 16
Mil - 16 7 4 17
Based upon the following Army land warrant:

Issued to	*No.*	*Acres*
Robertson, William, Lt	1860	200

580 18 Jun 1805 B/1/007
Registered by: Maj James Taylor
Registered for: Robert Porterfield
Location: Mil - 16 3 4 21
Mil - 16 3 4 22
Mil - 16 3 4 23
Based upon the following Army land warrant:

Issued to	*No.*	*Acres*
Porterfield, Robert, Capt	1738	300

(Note: Delivered to Mr. [John?] Smith, agent for Major Taylor.)

581 18 Jun 1805 B/1/007
Registered by: Maj James Taylor
Registered for: Robert Kirk
Location: Mil - 16 3 4 7
Mil - 16 3 4 16
Based upon the following Army land warrant:

Issued to	*No.*	*Acres*
Kirk, Robert, Lt	1214	200

582 18 Jun 1805 B/1/007
Registered by: Maj James Taylor
Registered for: David Stephenson
Location: Mil - 16 7 4 1
Mil - 16 7 4 2
Mil - 16 7 4 3
Mil - 16 7 4 4
Based upon the following Army land warrant:

Issued to	*No.*	*Acres*
Stephenson, David, Maj	2057	400

583 18 Jun 1805 B/1/007
Registered by: Maj James Taylor
Registered for: John Steele
Location: Mil - 16 3 4 28
Mil - 16 3 4 29
Based upon the following Army land warrant:

Issued to	*No.*	*Acres*
Steele, John, Lt	2077	200

(Note: Delivered to Mr. [John?] Smith, agent of Major Taylor.)

584 1 Aug 1805 B/1/008
Registered by: Maj -- Swan
Registered for: John Bush, in trust
Location: Mil - 17 7 4 6
Mil - 17 7 4 7
Mil - 17 7 4 8
Mil - 17 7 4 9
Based upon the following Army land warrant:

Issued to	*No.*	*Acres*
Bush, Lewis, heirs of, Maj	210	400

(Note: Delivered patent to Maj Swan.)

585 1 Aug 1805 B/1/008
Registered by: -- Smith, Ohio
Registered for: Heirs, by name
Location: Mil - 15 7 4 8
Based upon the following Army land warrant:

Issued to	*No.*	*Acres*
Chester, John, Pvt	95	100

(Note: Delivered certificate to M. Nourse, agent.)

586 1 Aug 1805 B/1/008
Registered by: -- Smith, Ohio
Registered for: Heirs by name
Location: Mil - 15 7 4 26
Based upon the following Army land warrant:

Issued to	*No.*	*Acres*
Enimerton, James, Sgt	96	100

(Note: Delivered certificate to M. Nourse, agent.)

587 1 Aug 1805 B/1/008
Registered by: -- Smith, Ohio
Registered for: Heir, by name
Location: Mil - 15 7 4 39
Based upon the following Army land warrant:

Issued to	*No.*	*Acres*
Young, Thomas, Pvt	97	100

(Note: Delivered certificate to M. Nourse.)

588 1 Aug 1805 B/1/008
Registered by: -- Smith, Ohio

588 [continued]
Registered for: Heirs, by name
Location: Mil - 15 7 4 27
Based upon the following Army land warrant:
Issued to *No.* *Acres*
Yater, John, Sgt 98 100
(Note: Delivered certificate to M. Nourse, agent.)

589 1 Aug 1805 B/1/008
Registered by: -- Smith, Ohio
Registered for: James Ryan
Location: Mil - 15 7 4 38
Based upon the following Army land warrant:
Issued to *No.* *Acres*
Ryan, James, Pvt 170 100
(Note: Delivered certificate to M. Nourse, agent.)

590 1 Aug 1805 B/1/008
Registered by: Michael Nourse
Registered for: Michael Nourse
Location: Mil - 3 1 1 4
Based upon the following Army land warrant:
Issued to *No.* *Acres*
Burnett, James, Sgt 211 100
(Note: Delivered certificate to M. Nourse, proprietor.)

591 24 Aug 1805 B/1/008
Registered by: Michael Nourse
Registered for: Zaccheus Biggs
Location: Mil - 1 10 1 23
Mil - 1 10 1 9
Mil - 1 10 1 24
Based upon the following Army land warrants:
Issued to *No.* *Acres*
Ratton, John, Soldier 52 100
Waldron, Nath[anie]l, Soldier 209 100
Wheeler, Benj[ami]n, Cpl 39 100

592 12 Sep 1805 B/1/008
Registered by: Samuel Vincent
Registered for: Heirs & devisees
Location: Mil - 2 2 3 8
Mil - 2 2 3 9
Based upon the following Army land warrant:
Issued to *No.* *Acres*
Bickham, John, Lt 188 200

593 3 Oct 1805 B/1/008
Registered by: Michael Nourse
Registered for: William Rickard
Location: Mil - 15 8 3 1
Mil - 15 8 3 2
Based upon the following Army land warrant:
Issued to *No.* *Acres*
Rickard, William, Lt 85 200
(Note: Delivered certificate to M. Nourse, Agent.)

594 16 Oct 1805 B/1/008
Registered by: Samuel Morris
Registered for: Samuel Morris
Location: Mil - 8 2 1 12
Based upon the following Army land warrant:
Issued to *No.* *Acres*
Morris, Samuel, Sgt 214 100
(Note: Delivered certificate to Samuel Morris.)

595 16 Nov 1805 B/1/008
Registered by: M[ichael] Nourse
Registered for: John Russel
Location: Mil - 1 1 3 3
Based upon the following Army land warrant:
Issued to *No.* *Acres*
Crane, Stephen, Soldier 8190 100
(Note: Delivered patent to M. Nourse, agent.)

596 16 Nov 1805 B/1/008
Registered by: M[ichael] Nourse
Registered for: Edward Sanders
Location: Mil - 1 1 3 36
Based upon the following Army land warrant:
Issued to *No.* *Acres*
Perry, William, Soldier 10865 100
(Note: Delivered patent to M. Nourse, agent.)

597 16 Nov 1805 B/1/008
Registered by: M[ichael] Nourse
Registered for: John Rogers
Location: Mil - 1 1 3 20
Based upon the following Army land warrant:
Issued to *No.* *Acres*
Fluheart, Massy, Soldier 13085 100
(Note: Delivered patent to M. Nourse, agent.)

598 19 Dec 1805 B/1/008
Registered by: Jacob Cist
Registered for: George Everley
Location: Mil - 2 7 4 18
Based upon the following Army land warrant:
Issued to *No.* *Acres*
Everley, George, Soldier 9351 100

599 20 Dec 1805 B/1/008
Registered by: Joseph Barker, Esq.
Registered for: Thomas Sproat, assignee
Location: Mil - 8 2 1 26
Based upon the following Army land warrant:
Issued to *No.* *Acres*
Smith, Ebenezer, Soldier 216 100

600 21 Dec 1805 B/1/008
Registered by: Jeremiah Morrow, Esq.
Registered for: John Duncan
Location: Mil - 15 1 3 27
Based upon the following Army land warrant:
Issued to *No.* *Acres*
Berlin, Isaac, Soldier 9027 100
(Note: Sent to Mr. Morrow, 18 Mar 1806

601 21 Dec 1805 B/1/008
Registered by: Jeremiah Morrow, Esq.
Registered for: Stephen Hoggatt
Location: Mil - 15 1 3 28
Based upon the following Army land warrant:
Issued to *No.* *Acres*
Freeman, Nathan, Soldier 121 100
(Note: Sent to Mr. Morrow, 18 Mar 1806.)

602 21 Dec 1805 B/1/008
Registered by: Jeremiah Morrow, Esq.
Registered for: Stephen Hoggatt
Location: Mil - 15 1 3 37
Based upon the following Army land warrant:
Issued to *No.* *Acres*
Dowell, James, Soldier 118 100
(Note: Sent to Mr. Morrow, 18 Mar 1806.)

603 21 Dec 1805 B/1/008
Registered by: Jeremiah Morrow, Esq.
Registered for: Stephen Hoggatt
Location: Mil - 15 1 3 38
Based upon the following Army land warrant:
Issued to *No.* *Acres*
Desearn, Fred[eric]k, Soldier 119 100
(Note: Sent to Mr. Morrow, 18 Mar 1806.)

604 21 Dec 1805 B/1/008
Registered by: Ebenezer Elmer, Esq.
Registered for: Silas Woodruf
Location: Mil - 8 2 1 31
Based upon the following Army land warrant:
Issued to *No.* *Acres*
Levick, Robert, Soldier 129 100

605 27 Dec 1805 B/1/008
Registered by: Jeremiah Morrow, Esq.
Registered for: John Service
Location: Mil - 1 8 3 8
Based upon the following Army land warrant:
Issued to *No.* *Acres*
Service, John, Soldier 10878 100
(Note: Sent to Mr. Morrow, 18 Mar 1806.)

606 27 Dec 1805 B/1/008
Registered by: William Findley, Esq.
Registered for: Thomas Maddin
Location: Mil - 1 8 3 11
Based upon the following Army land warrant:
Issued to *No.* *Acres*
Maddin, Thomas, Soldier 217 100

607 27 Dec 1805 B/1/008
Registered by: Andrew Gregg, Esq.
Registered for: John Balsely
Location: Mil - 1 8 3 9
Based upon the following Army land warrant:
Issued to *No.* *Acres*
Balsely, John, Soldier 8999 100
(Note: Sent [patent?] to Mr. Gregg.)

608 27 Dec 1805 B/1/008
Registered by: Andrew Gregg, Esq.
Registered for: James Boyd
Location: Mil - 1 8 3 7
Based upon the following Army land warrant:
Issued to *No.* *Acres*
Sweeny, Hugh, Soldier 10338 100

609 27 Dec 1805 B/1/008
Registered by: John Dawson, Esq.
Registered for: Anthony de Marcellin
Location: Mil - 1 8 3 5
Mil - 1 8 3 6
Based upon the following Army land warrant:
Issued to *No.* *Acres*
de Marcellin, Anthony, Lt 568 200
(Note: Sent to Mr. Dawson, 18 Mar 1806.)

610 2 Jan 1806 B/1/009
Registered by: John Woodside
Registered for: John Woodside
Location: Mil - 1 1 3 30
Mil - 1 1 3 35
Based upon the following Army land warrant:
Issued to *No.* *Acres*
Woodside, John, Lt 2398 200
(Note: Delivered certificate to Mr. Woodside.)

611 2 Jan 1806 B/1/009
Registered by: Col [Thomas] Worthington
Registered for: John Line, administrator
Location: Mil - 15 8 4 17
Based upon the following Army land warrant:
Issued to *No.* *Acres*
Hensey, William, Soldier 159 100
(Note: Sent [patent?] to Col Worthington, 8 Apr 1806.)

612 9 Jan 1806 B/1/009
Registered by: Zaccheus Biggs
Registered for: William Carter
Location: Mil - 1 1 3 14
Mil - 1 1 3 15
Mil - 1 1 3 16
Based upon the following Army land warrant:
Issued to *No.* *Acres*
Hendry, William, Capt 996 300
(Note: Delivered certificate to Mr. Biggs.)

613 9 Jan 1806 B/1/009
Registered by: Zaccheus Biggs
Registered for: Reuben Field
Location: Mil - 1 1 3 17
Mil - 1 1 3 18
Mil - 1 1 3 19
Based upon the following Army land warrant:
Issued to *No.* *Acres*
Field, Reuben, Capt 763 100
(Note: Delivered certificate to Mr. Biggs.)

614 9 Jan 1806 B/1/009
Registered by: Zaccheus Biggs
Registered for: Thomas Armstrong
Location: Mil - 1 1 3 31
Based upon the following Army land warrant:
Issued to *No.* *Acres*
Bennet, John, Soldier 12855 100
(Note: Delivered certificate to Mr. Biggs.)

615 9 Jan 1806 B/1/009
Registered by: Zaccheus Biggs
Registered for: Zaccheus Biggs
Location: Mil - 1 8 2 25W
Based upon the following surplus certificate:
Issued to *No.* *Acres*
Cole, Abner, Ens -- 50
(Note: Delivered certificate to Mr. Biggs.)

616 9 Jan 1806 B/1/009
Registered by: Zaccheus Biggs
Registered for: Zaccheus Biggs
Location: Mil - 1 8 2 25E
Based upon the following surplus certificate:

Issued to	*No.*	*Acres*
Tillard, Edward, Lt	--	50

(Note: Delivered certificate to Mr. Biggs.)

617 10 Jan 1806 B/1/009
Registered by: Zaccheus Biggs
Registered for: Roger McBride
Location: Mil - 1 1 3 2
Based upon the following Army land warrant:

Issued to	*No.*	*Acres*
McBride, Roger, Pvt	219	100

(Note: Delivered certificate to Mr. Biggs.)

618 10 Jan 1806 B/1/009
Registered by: Zaccheus Biggs
Registered for: John Fling
Location: Mil - 1 1 3 13
Based upon the following Army land warrant:

Issued to	*No.*	*Acres*
Fling, John, SgtMaj	218	100

(Note: Delivered certificate to Mr. Biggs.)

619 10 Jan 1806 B/1/009
Registered by: Zaccheus Biggs
Registered for: James Colter
Location: Mil - 1 8 4 34
Based upon the following Army land warrant:

Issued to	*No.*	*Acres*
Colter, James, Soldier	9118	100

(Note: Delivered certificate to Mr. Biggs.)

620 10 Jan 1806 B/1/009
Registered by: Zaccheus Biggs
Registered for: Joseph Cook
Location: Mil - 1 8 4 35
Based upon the following Army land warrant:

Issued to	*No.*	*Acres*
Shaler, Jacob, Soldier	8734	100

(Note: Delivered certificate to Mr. Biggs.)

621 18 Jan 1806 B/1/009
Registered by: Ebenezer Elmer, Esq.
Registered for: William Collins
Location: Mil - 9 7 3 15
Based upon the following Army land warrant:

Issued to	*No.*	*Acres*
Collins, William, Soldier	172	100

622 18 Jan 1806 B/1/009
Registered by: Ebenezer Williams, Esq.
Registered for: Devisees by will
Location:
Mil - 8 2 1 11
Mil - 8 2 1 18
Mil - 8 2 1 19
Mil - 8 2 1 20
Mil - 8 2 1 21
Mil - 8 2 1 29
Mil - 8 2 1 30
Mil - 8 2 1 32
Mil - 8 2 3 11
Mil - 8 2 3 12
Mil - 8 2 3 19
Based upon the following Army land warrant:

Issued to	*No.*	*Acres*
von Steuben, --, Baron, MajGen	2128	1100

(Note: Sent to Mr. Williams, 27 Mar 1806.)

623 23 Jan 1806 B/1/009
Registered by: M[ichael] Nourse
Registered for: Richard Brookover
Location:
Mil - 9 1 3 5
Mil - 9 1 3 6
Based upon the following Army land warrant:

Issued to	*No.*	*Acres*
Hite, Isaac, Lt	189	100

(Note: Delivered patent to M. Nourse, agent.)

624 23 Jan 1806 B/1/009
Registered by: M[ichael] Nourse
Registered for: Carlos A. Norton
Location:
Mil - 9 1 3 7
Mil - 9 1 3 8
Based upon the following Army land warrant:

Issued to	*No.*	*Acres*
Robinson, Robert, Drummer	133	100
Cowdery, Samuel? Dragoon	132	100

(Note: Delivered [certificate?] to M. Nourse.)

625 27 Jan 1806 B/1/009
Registered by: William Findley, Esq.
Registered for: Jacob Miller
Location:
Mil - 1 1 3 22
Mil - 1 1 3 21
Based upon the following Army land warrant:

Issued to	*No.*	*Acres*
Blake, William, Sgt	222	100
Pinkerton, Andrew, Pvt	223	100

(Note: Sent to Mr. Findley, 18 Mar 1806.)

626 27 Jan 1806 B/1/009
Registered by: William Findley, Esq.
Registered for: Son & widow [names not given]
Location: Mil - 1 1 3 29
Based upon the following Army land warrant:

Issued to	*No.*	*Acres*
O'Harra, Josh[ua?] Pvt	224	100

(Note: Sent to Mr. Findley, 8 Apr 1806.)

627 30 Jan 1806 B/1/009
Registered by: C. J. Nourse
Registered for: Zaccheus Biggs
Location: Mil - 1 1 3 8
Based upon the following Army land warrant:

Issued to	*No.*	*Acres*
Seger, Ebenezer, Sgt	215	100

(Note: Delivered to Mr. Nourse, agent, 8 Apr 1806.)

628 31 Jan 1806 B/1/009
Registered by: John Archer, Esq.
Registered for: Edward Kean
Location: Mil - 8 2 1 35
Based upon the following Army land warrant:

Issued to	*No.*	*Acres*
Kean, Edward, Pvt	225	100

629 31 Jan 1806 B/1/009
Registered by: Zaccheus Biggs, Esq.
Registered for: Joseph? W. Carruthers
Location: Mil - 1 1 3 11
Mil - 1 1 3 12
Based upon the following Army land warrant:
Issued to *No.* *Acres*
Carruthers, John, Lt 406 200
(Note: Sent patent to M. Nourse, agent.)

630 1 Feb 1806 B/1/009
Registered by: James Sloan, Esq.
Registered for: Charles Ellis
Location: Mil - 17 7 4 10
Based upon the following Army land warrant:
Issued to *No.* *Acres*
Blare, William, Drummer 8088 100

631 10 Feb 1806 B/1/009
Registered by: John McWhorter
Registered for: John? [James?] McWhorter
Location: Mil - 15 1 3 25
Based upon the following Army land warrant:
Issued to *No.* *Acres*
McCurdy, Pat[rick?] Soldier 10824 100
(Note: Sent to McWhorter per mail, 3 Apr 1807.)

632 10 Feb 1806 B/1/009
Registered by: Michael Nourse
Registered for: Isaac Northrop
Location: Mil - 9 1 3 3
Based upon the following Army land warrant:
Issued to *No.* *Acres*
Northrop, Isaac, Cpl 6244 100
(Note: Delivered [certificate?] to M. Nourse.)

633 15 Feb 1806 B/1/009
Registered by: [Not given]
Registered for: James Merriwether
Location: Mil - 15 1 3 29
Mil - 15 1 3 30
Based upon the following Army land warrant:
Issued to *No.* *Acres*
Merriwether, James, Lt 1509 100

634 19 Feb 1806 B/1/010
Registered by: Ezra Darby, Esq.
Registered for: John Heckewelder
Location: Mil - 2 7 3 1
Mil - 2 7 3 2
Mil - 2 6 1 2
Based upon the following Army land warrant:
Issued to *No.* *Acres*
Mills, James, Capt 1533 300
(Note: Sent to Mr. Darby, 3 Apr 1806.)

635 19 Feb 1806 B/1/010
Registered by: William Findley, Esq.
Registered for: Alexander McBride
Location: Mil - 1 1 3 28
Based upon the following Army land warrant:
Issued to *No.* *Acres*
Stewart, Hugh, Soldier 10378 100
(Note: Sent to Mr. Findley, 27 Mar 1806.)

636 22 Feb 1806 B/1/010
Registered by: John Dawson, Esq.
Registered for: William O'Callis
Location: Mil - 2 2 3 13
Mil - 2 2 3 14
Based upon the following Army land warrant:
Issued to *No.* *Acres*
O'Callis, William, Lt 2484 200
(Note: Sent to Mr. Dawson, 3 Apr 1806.)

637 27 Feb 1806 B/1/010
Registered by: Col [Thomas] Worthington
Registered for: Samuel Hoey Smith
Location: Mil - 10 3 4 3?
Mil - 10 3 4 23
Mil - 10 3 4 27
Based upon the following Army land warrant:
Issued to *No.* *Acres*
Turner, James, Capt 226 300
(Note: Assigned [to?] S. H. Smith by C[ol?] Worthington.)

638 27 Feb 1806 B/1/010
Registered by: Col [Thomas] Worthington
Registered for: [Not stated]
Location: [Not stated]
Based upon the following Army land warrant:
Issued to *No.* *Acres*
Fossett, James, Soldier 193 100
(Note: Assigned to Jacob Swamley by C[ol?] Worthington.)

639 27 Feb 1806 B/1/010
Registered by: -- McCleery
Registered for: James Bruff
Location: Mil - 2 10 2 6
Based upon the following Army land warrant:
Issued to *No.* *Acres*
Allen, John, Soldier 12724 100

640 27 Feb 1806 B/1/010
Registered by: Jacob Swanley*
Registered for: [Not stated]
Location: [Not stated]
Based upon the following Army land warrant:
Issued to *No.* *Acres*
Gitling, William, Cornet 196 150
*So spelled.

641 27 Feb 1806 B/1/010
Registered by: J. G. Jackson, Esq.
Registered for: [Not stated]
Location: [Not stated]
Based upon the following Army land warrant:
Issued to *No.* *Acres*
Storrs, Justus, Surgeon's Mate 2692 300

642 27 Feb 1806 B/1/010
Registered by: J. G. Jackson, Esq.
Registered for: [Not stated]
Location: [Not stated]
Based upon the following Army land warrant:
Issued to *No.* *Acres*
Brigham, Joel, Sgt. 195 100

643 27 Feb 1806 B/1/010
Registered by: Gen -- Van Cortlandt
Registered for: John Lesuer
Location: Mil - 15 1 3 7
Based upon the following Army land warrant:

Issued to	*No.*	*Acres*
Lesuer, John, Ens	184	100

(Note: Sent to Gen Van Cortlandt, 4 Jun 1806.)

644 24 Dec 1802* B/1/010
Registered by: William McCluney
Registered for: George Beemer
Location: Mil - 2 3 4 22
Based upon the following Army land warrant:

Issued to	*No.*	*Acres*
Sheridan, James, Soldier	13780	100

*Date out of sequence; no explanation given.
(Note: [Certificate] 328 sent per mail to Mr. McCluney, 3 Jun 1806.)

645 24 Dec 1802* B/1/010
Registered by: William McCluney
Registered for: William Helanen
Location: Mil - 2 3 4 27
Based upon the following Army land warrant:

Issued to	*No.*	*Acres*
Stevens, Ira, Soldier	6428	100

*Date out of sequence; no explanation given.
(Note: [Certificate] 329 sent per mail to Mr. McCluney, 3 Jun 1806.)

646 1 Feb 1806* B/1/010
Registered by: M[ichael] Nourse
Registered for: Vincent Redman**
Location: Mil - 6 2 1 6
Mil - 6 2 1 7
Mil - 6 2 1 8
Mil - 6 2 1 11
Based upon the following Army land warrant:

Issued to	*No.*	*Acres*
Belfield, John, Maj	254	400

*Date out of sequence; no explanation given.
**Name striken out; John Belfield written in pencil.
(Note: Delivered to M. Nourse, agent. . . .? a copy of this patent is demanded? by the Loflaw Co? [lawful?]. He has been written for reasons copy sent?)

647 31 Mar 1806 B/1/010
Registered by: John Condit, Esq.
Registered for: [Not given]
Location: [Not given]
Based upon the following Army land warrant:

Issued to	*No.*	*Acres*
Cole, David, Soldier	6915	100

(Note: Warrant returned to the owner in letter of 15 May 1806.)

648 31 Mar 1806 B/1/010
Registered by: John Condit, Esq.
Registered for: [Not stated]
Location: [Not stated]
Based upon the following Army land warrant:

Issued to	*No.*	*Acres*
Brooks, Thomas, Soldier	6795	100

(Note: Warrant returned to the owner in letter of 15 May 1806.)

649 10 Apr 1806 B/1/010
Registered by: Gen -- Smith
Registered for: [See serial entry 673]
Location: [Not stated]
Based upon the following Army land warrant:

Issued to	*No.*	*Acres*
Sears, John, Lt	2049	200

650 14 Apr 1806 B/1/010
Registered by: Col [Thomas] Worthington
Registered for: [Not stated]
Location: [Not stated]
Based upon the following Army land warrant:

Issued to	*No.*	*Acres*
Turner, James, Capt	226	300

(Note: Assigned to S[amuel] H[oey] Smith by C[ol?] Worthington.

651 14 Apr 1806 B/1/010
Registered by: Ebenezer Elmer, Esq.
Registered for: George Holcombe
Location: Mil - 9 7 3 1
Based upon the following Army land warrant:

Issued to	*No.*	*Acres*
Young, Aaron, Soldier	8881	100

(Note: Sent patent to Mr. Elmer.)

652 17 Apr 1806 B/1/010
Registered by: Andrew Gregg, Esq.
Registered for: Widow, in trust
Location: Mil - 17 7 4 18
Based upon the following Army land warrant:

Issued to	*No.*	*Acres*
O'Hara, Francis, Soldier	233	100

(Note: Mr. Gregg received patent from Department of State.)

653 17 Apr 1806 B/1/010
Registered by: Andrew Gregg, Esq.
Registered for: John Gonter
Location: Mil - 17 7 4 17
Based upon the following Army land warrant:

Issued to	*No.*	*Acres*
Gonter, John, Soldier	234	100

(Note: Mr. Gregg received patent from Department of State.)

654 18 Apr 1806 B/1/010
Registered by: Frederick Conrad, Esq.
Registered for: Christopher Bauman, *et al?*
Location: Mil - 17 7 4 39
Based upon the following Army land warrant:

Issued to	*No.*	*Acres*
Bauman, Christopher, Fifer	243	100

(Note: [Certificate] 306 sent to Mr. Conrad, 27 May 1806.)

655 18 Apr 1806 B/1/010
Registered by: Frederick Conrad, Esq.
Registered for: Samuel Filbert
Location: Mil - 17 7 4 19
Based upon the following Army land warrant:

Issued to	*No.*	*Acres*
Effinger, John, Cpl	244	100

(Note: [Certificate 307 sent to Mr. Conrad, 27 May 1806.)

656 18 Apr 1806 B/1/010
Registered by: William Findley, Esq.
Registered for: Godfrey Kerns
Location: Mil - 15 1 3 19
Based upon the following Army land warrants:

Issued to	*No.*	*Acres*
Kerns, Godfrey, Pvt	241	100

(Note: [Certificate] 308 sent to Mr. Findley, 28 May 1806.)

657 18 Apr 1806 B/1/010
Registered by: William Findley, Esq.
Registered for: John McGinnis
Location: Mil - 15 1 3 1
Based upon the following Army land warrant:

Issued to	*No.*	*Acres*
McGinnis, John, Soldier	10053	100

(Note: [Certificate] 309 sent to Mr. Findley, 28 May 1806.)

658 18 Apr 1806 B/1/010
Registered by: William Findley, Esq.
Registered for: Edward McCaley
Location: Mil - 15 1 3 2
Based upon the following Army land warrant:

Issued to	*No.*	*Acres*
McCaley, Edward, Soldier	10101	100

(Note: [Certificate] 310 sent to Mr. Findley, 28 May 1806.)

659 18 Apr 1806 B/1/010
Registered by: William Findley, Esq.
Registered for: John McAllister
Location: Mil - 15 1 3 16
Based upon the following Army land warrant:

Issued to	*No.*	*Acres*
McAllister, John, Soldier	9994	100

(Note: [Certificate] 311 sent to Mr. Findley, 28 May 1806.)

660 18 Apr 1806 B/1/010
Registered by: William Findley, Esq.
Registered for: Martin Yost
Location: Mil - 15 1 3 15
Based upon the following Army land warrant:

Issued to	*No.*	*Acres*
Yost, Martin, Soldier	10677	100

(Note: [Certificate] 312 sent to Mr. Findley, 28 May 1806.)

661 18 Apr 1806 B/1/010
Registered by: William Findley, Esq.
Registered for: William Bryan
Location: Mil - 15 1 3 17
Based upon the following Army land warrant:

Issued to	*No.*	*Acres*
Bryan, William, Soldier	9008	100

(Note: [Certificate] 313 sent to Mr. Findley, 28 May 1806.)

662 18 Apr 1806 B/1/010
Registered by: William Findley, Esq.
Registered for: Mary Doyle
Location: Mil - 15 1 3 18
Based upon the following Army land warrant:

Issued to	*No.*	*Acres*
Kelly, Edward, Soldier	9735	100

(Note: [Certificate] 314 sent to Mr. Findley, 28 May 1806.)

663 18 Apr 1806 B/1/011
Registered by: John Davenport, Esq., for John Cotten Smith, Esq.
Registered for: Ebenezer Foote & Justin Foote
Location: Mil - 18 7 2 7
Based upon the following Army land warrant:

Issued to	*No.*	*Acres*
Whittier, Jacob, Cpl	5338	100

(Note: Delivered certificate to Mr. Coyle, agent for J. C. Smith.)

664 18 Apr 1806 B/1/011
Registered by: John Davenport, Esq., for John Cotten Smith, Esq.
Registered for: Ebenezer Foote & Justin Foote
Location: Mil - 18 7 2 8
Based upon the following Army land warrant:

Issued to	*No.*	*Acres*
Tharp, Peter, Soldier	8780	100

(Note: Delivered certificate to Mr. Coyle, agent for J. C. Smith.)

665 18 Apr 1806 B/1/011
Registered by: John Davenport, Esq., for John Cotten Smith, Esq.
Registered for: David Parsons
Location: Mil - 18 7 2 10
Based upon the following Army land warrant:

Issued to	*No.*	*Acres*
Parsons, David, Soldier	232	100

(Note: Delivered certificate to Mr. Coyle, agent for J. C. Smith.)

666 18 Apr 1806 B/1/011
Registered by: T[homas] Worthington, Esq.
Registered for: [Not stated]
Location: [Not stated]
Based upon the following Army land warrant:

Issued to	*No.*	*Acres*
Turner, Jacob, Capt	226	300

(Note: Recorded in preceding page. Assigned to S[amuel] H[oey] Smith by C[ol?] Worthington. [See serial entry 637 wherein shown as James Turner.])

667 18 Apr 1806 B/1/011
Registered by: Samuel Maday, Esq.
Registered for: [Not stated]
Location: [Not stated]
Based upon the following Army land warrant:

Issued to	*No.*	*Acres*
Bleakney, James, Sgt	240	100

(Note: Mr. Maday withdrew this warrant, to be sent to the owner.)

668 18 Apr 1806 B/1/011
Registered by: R. Whitehill, Esq.
Registered for: Thomas Henderson, *et al?*
Location: Mil - 17 7 2 9
Based upon the following Army land warrant:

Issued to	*No.*	*Acres*
Henderson, Samuel, Soldier	246	100

(Note: Sent to Mr. Whitehill, 5 Jun 1806.)

669 18 Apr 1806 B/1/011
Registered by: R. Whitehill, Esq.
Registered for: John McMullin
Location: Mil - 17 7 2 20
Based upon the following Army land warrant:

Issued to	*No.*	*Acres*
McMullin, John, Soldier	245	100

(Note: Sent to Mr. Whitehill, 5 Jun 1806.)

670 18 Apr 1806 B/1/011
Registered by: Jeremiah Morrow, Esq., for Joseph Vance of Franklinton [Ohio]
Registered for: John Rudduck
Location: Mil - 18 7 2 1
Mil - 18 7 2 2
Based upon the following Army land warrant:

Issued to	*No.*	*Acres*
Griffin, John, Soldier	116	100
York, William, Soldier	120	100

(Note: [Certificates] 315 & 316 sent by mail to Joseph Vance, Franklinton, Ohio, 26 May 1806.)

671 18 Apr 1806 B/1/011
Registered by: Jeremiah Morrow, Esq., for Joseph Vance of Franklinton [Ohio]
Registered for: Elias N. D. Lashmutt
Location: Mil - 15 1 3 39
Based upon the following Army land warrant:

Issued to	*No.*	*Acres*
Hillock, Robert, Soldier	4303	100

(Note: [Certificate] 330 sent by mail to Joseph Vance, Franklinton, Ohio, 26 May 1806.)

672 18 Apr 1806 B/1/011
Registered by: Col [Thomas] Worthington
Registered for: John Kerr
Location: Mil - 19 7 1 7
Based upon the following Army land warrant:

Issued to	*No.*	*Acres*
Hobaugh, Philip, Soldier	212	100

(Note: See letter, 24 Sep 1806.)

673 18 Apr 1806 B/1/011
Registered by: Gen Samuel Smith
Registered for: John Sears
Location: Mil - 18 7 1 20
Mil - 18 7 1 21
Based upon the following Army land warrant:

Issued to	*No.*	*Acres*
Sears, John, Lt	2049	200

(Note: [Certificate] 226 sent to Gen Smith, 3 Jun 1806.)
[See also serial entry 649.]

674 18 Apr 1806 B/1/011
Registered by: -- Rhea of Pennsylvania
Registered for: John Nulton
Location: Mil - 17 7 4 23
Based upon the following Army land warrant:

Issued to	*No.*	*Acres*
Nulton, John, Soldier	249	100

(Note: Sent to Mr. Rhea per mail, 30 May 1806.)

675 18 Apr 1806 B/1/011
Registered by: -- Rhea of Pennsylvania
Registered for: Jonathan Trickle
Location: Mil - 17 7 4 24
Based upon the following Army land warrant:

Issued to	*No.*	*Acres*
Trickle, Jonathan, Gunner	250	100

(Note: Sent to Mr. Rhea, per mail, 30 May 1806.)

676 18 Apr 1806 B/1/011
Registered by: J. G. Jackson, Esq.
Registered for: [Not stated]
Location: [Not stated]
Based upon the following Army land warrant:

Issued to	*No.*	*Acres*
Barron, Benj[amin]	67	100

677 21 Apr 1806 B/1/011
Registered by: William Findley, Esq.
Registered for: David Davis
Location: Mil - 15 1 3 20
Based upon the following Army land warrant:

Issued to	*No.*	*Acres*
Davis, David, Soldier	252	100

(Note: [Certificate] 319 sent to Mr. Findley, 4 Jun 1806.)

678 22 Apr 1806 B/1/011
Registered by: R. Whitehill, Esq.
Registered for: Mary Barkley
Location: Mil - 17 7 2 21
Based upon the following Army land warrant:

Issued to	*No.*	*Acres*
Barkley, Mary	255	100

(Note: Sent to Mr. Whitehill, 5 May 1806.)

679 24 Apr 1806 B/1/011
Registered by: J. J. Moore for J. Nourse
Registered for: Zachariah Roswell
Location: Mil - 8 2 1 17
Based upon the following Army land warrant:

Issued to	*No.*	*Acres*
Roswell, Zachariah, Sgt	256	100

(Note: Sent to Mr. Broom, 26 May 1806.)

680 24 Apr 1806 B/1/011
Registered by: J. J. Moore for J. Nourse
Registered for: Henry Hilger
Location: Mil - 2 2 3 2
Based upon the following Army land warrant:

Issued to	*No.*	*Acres*
Hilger, Henry, Cpl	257	100

(Note: [Certificate] 332 sent to H. Hilger, 7 Jun 1806.)

681 28 Apr 1806 B/1/011
Registered by: Capt -- Davidson
Registered for: [Not shown]
Location: Mil - 2 7 4 25*
Based upon the following Army land warrant:

Issued to	*No.*	*Acres*
Bogart, James N., Soldier	13953	100

(Note: Capt Davidson withdrew the warrant, 11 Jun 1806.)
*So shown.

682 30 Apr 1806 B/1/011
Registered by: -- Laub? [Lamb?]
Registered for: John Andrew
Location: Mil - 2 10 2 4
Based upon the following Army land warrant:

Issued to	*No.*	*Acres*
Andrew, John, Soldier	258	100

(Note: [Certificate] 327 given to Mr. Laub.)

683 30 Apr 1806 B/1/011
Registered by: Daniel Brent
Registered for: Michael Nourse (Daniel Brent)
Location: Mil - 15 8 4 22
Mil - 15 8 4 23
Mil - 15 8 4 27
Based upon the following Army land warrant:

Issued to	*No.*	*Acres*
Rovely, Francis? Capt	261	300

(Note: Gave certificate to Mr. Nourse.)

684 2 May 1806 B/1/011
Registered by: Mary Conner
Registered for: Mary [Conner] the widow
Location: Mil - 15 1 3 26
Based upon the following Army land warrant:

Issued to	*No.*	*Acres*
Conner, Michael, Soldier	268	100

(Note :Gave patent to the widow.)

685 14 May 1806 B/1/011
Registered by: Michael Nourse
Registered for: John Buchanan
Location: Mil - 7 6 1 29
Mil - 7 6 1 30
Mil - 7 6 1 31
Based upon the following Army land warrant:

Issued to	*No.*	*Acres*
Buchanan, John, Capt	271	300

(Note: Delivered patent to M. Nourse, 26 May 1806.)

686 14 May 1806 B/1/011
Registered by: Michael Nourse
Registered for: Hugh Milling
Location: Mil - 7 6 1 32
Mil - 7 6 1 33
Mil - 7 6 1 34
Based upon the following Army land warrant:

Issued to	*No.*	*Acres*
Milling, Hugh, Capt	272	300

(Note: Delivered patent to M. Nourse, 26 May 1806.)

687 14 May 1806 B/1/011
Registered by: Michael Nourse
Registered for: Henry Moore
Location: Mil - 7 6 1 35
Mil - 7 6 1 36
Based upon the following Army land warrant:

Issued to	*No.*	*Acres*
Moore, Henry, Lt	273	200

(Note: Delivered patent to M. Nourse, 26 May 1806.)

688 28 May 1806 B/1/011
Registered by: -- Pleasonton
Registered for: Sarah Donovan
Location: Mil - 8 2 1 24
Based upon the following Army land warrant:

Issued to	*No.*	*Acres*
Donovan, Sarah	260	100

(Note: Sent certificate to Mr. Pleasonton.)

689 28 May 1806 B/1/011
Registered by: John Shorb [Short?]
Registered for: Nicholas Jacoby
Location: Mil - 2 2 3 10
Based upon the following Army land warrant:

Issued to	*No.*	*Acres*
Jacoby, Nicholas, Soldier	278	100

(Note: Gave the patent certificate to John Shorb, same day.)

690 11 Jun 1806 B/1/012
Registered by: Capt -- Davidson
Registered for: Jonas Stanbery
Location: Mil - 2 7 4 25
Mil - 2 7 4 26
Based upon the following Army land warrant:

Issued to	*No.*	*Acres*
Meeker, Uzal, Lt	1409	200

691 19 Jun 1806 B/1/012
Registered by: Charles Plumline
Registered for: Charles Plumline
Location: Mil - 2 3 4 23
Based upon the following Army land warrant:

Issued to	*No.*	*Acres*
Plumline, Charles, Soldier	279	100

692 19 Jun 1806 B/1/012
Registered by: Joel Barlow, Esq.
Registered for: Joel Barlow, Esq.
Location: Mil - 15 7 4 28
Mil - 15 7 4 33
Mil - 15 7 4 34
Mil - 15 7 4 35
Mil - 15 7 4 36
Mil - 15 7 4 37
Based upon the following Army land warrants:

Issued to	*No.*	*Acres*
Case, Richard, Soldier	264	100
Mygatt, Elisha, Soldier	265	100
Weaver, Samuel, Soldier	266	100
Abbe, Eleazer, Soldier	267	100
Meara, Patrick, Soldier	269	100
Hurleroy, John, Soldier	270	100

(Note: Delivered patents to Mr. Barlow, 7 Mar 1807.)

693 1 Jul 1806 B/1/012
Registered by: William Wedderburn
Registered for: William Wedderburn
Location: Mil - 3 10 2 4
Based upon the following Army land warrant:

Issued to	*No.*	*Acres*
Read, Henry, Soldier	169	100

(Note: Delivered patent certificate to William Wedderburn.)

694 17 Jul 1806 B/1/012
Registered by: Benjamin Brown
Registered for: Benjamin Brown
Location: Mil - 3 10 2 5
Based upon the following Army land warrant:
Issued to *No.* *Acres*
Scott, Alexander, Soldier 168 100
(Note: Patent sent to post office Alexandria [Virginia?] by his direction, 7 Aug 1806.)

695 4 Aug 1806 B/1/012
Registered by: Hon. Gen -- Sumter
Registered for: Thomas Worthington
Location: Mil - 16 8 4 5
Based upon the following Army land warrant:
Issued to *No.* *Acres*
Buckley, Michael, Soldier 176 100

696 21 Aug 1806 B/1/012
Registered by: John Laub
Registered for: Heirs, by name
Location: Mil - 2 10 2 19
Based upon the following Army land warrant:
Issued to *No.* *Acres*
Hathaway, Shadrach, Soldier 154 100

697 30 Aug 1806 B/1/012
Registered by: Michael Nourse
Registered for: Isaac Van Horne
Location: Mil - 8 4 3 3
Mil - 8 4 3 4
Mil - 8 4 3 5
Mil - 8 4 3 6
Based upon the following Army land warrant:
Issued to *No.* *Acres*
Davidson, William, LtCol 607 450
(Note: Sent patent and surplus certificate in letter of 26 Sep 1806. Surplus certificate for 50 acres not at present location.)

698 1 Sep 1806 B/1/012
Registered by: Capt -- Davidson
Registered for: Nicholas Bogart
Location: Mil - 2 7 4 23
Based upon the following Army land warrant:
Issued to *No.* *Acres*
Bogart, Nicholas, Soldier 13953 100

699 1 Sep 1806 B/1/012
Registered by: Capt -- Davidson
Registered for: [Not stated]
Location: Mil - 2 7 3 7
Mil - 2 7 3 11
Mil - 2 7 3 12
Mil - 2 7 3 18
Based upon the following Army land warrant:
Issued to *No.* *Acres*
Grier, James, Maj 833 400

700 -- Sep 1806 B/1/012
Registered by: [Not stated]
Registered for: John Kerr
Location: Mil - 19 7 1 7
Based upon the following Army land warrant:
Issued to *No.* *Acres*
Hobaugh, Philip, Soldier 212 100
(Note: Sent in pursuance of Mr. Kerr's letter of 1 Sep 1806 on the 24th of same month.)

701 29 Sep 1806 B/1/012
Registered by: John Craig
Registered for: John Craig
Location: Mil - 17 7 4 26
Based upon the following Army land warrant:
Issued to *No.* *Acres*
Craig, John 286 100
(Note: Delivered patent certificate to John Craig.)

702 8 Oct 1806 B/1/012
Registered by: Col [Thomas] Worthington
Registered for: [Not stated]
Location: Mil - 10 7 1 2
Mil - 10 7 1 3
Mil - 10 7 1 4
Based upon the following Army land warrant:
Issued to *No.* *Acres*
Barker, Samuel, Capt 220 300
(Note: Assigned by Col Worthington to S[amuel] H[oey] Smith; gave the patent to M[ichael] Nourse, his agent.)

703 23 Oct 1806 B/1/012
Registered by: George Ziegler
Registered for: Catharine [Rhesnick?] heiress
Location: [Not stated]
Based upon the following Army land warrant:
Issued to *No.* *Acres*
Rhesnick, Christian, Surgeon's Mate 282 300

704 14 Nov 1806 B/1/012
Registered by: M[ichael] Nourse
Registered for: M[ichael] Nourse
Location: Mil - 10 3 4 34
Mil - 10 3 4 35
Based upon the following Army land warrants:
Issued to *No.* *Acres*
Fisher, Schuyler, Pvt 140 100
Kennedy, Thomas, Pvt 291 100
(Note: Delivered certificates to Mr. Nourse.)

705 26 Nov 1806 B/1/012
Registered by: M[ichael] Nourse
Registered for: Zaccheus A. Beatty
Location: Mil - 2 10 2 1
Based upon the following Army land warrant:
Issued to *No.* *Acres*
McClure, John, Sgt 10094 100
(Note: [Certificate] given to M. Nourse, 9 Jan 1807; patent delivered to him, 27 Jan 1807.)

706 11 Dec 1806 B/1/012
Registered by: Maj James Taylor
Registered for: James Taylor
Location: Mil - 16 3 4 6
Mil - 16 3 4 25
Mil - 16 3 4 26
Mil - 16 3 4 27
Mil - 16 3 4 8
Mil - 16 3 4 9

706 [continued]

Mil - 16 3 4 24
Mil - 16 3 4 3
Mil - 16 3 4 4
Mil - 16 3 4 5

Based upon the following Army land warrants:

Issued to	*No.*	*Acres*
Reed, Zachariah, Pvt	182	100
Martin, Thomas, Capt	236	300
Knight, John, Surgeon's Mate	238	300
Overton, John, Capt	1615	300

707 15 Dec 1806 B/1/012
Registered by: Henry Shettar
Registered for: Catharine Shettar
Location: Mil - 1 8 3 10
Based upon the following Army land warrant:

Issued to	*No.*	*Acres*
McCurdy, Moses, Soldier	283	100

708 15 Dec 1806 B/1/012
Registered by: Henry Shettar
Registered for: Casper Greeger
Location: Mil - 1 8 4 32
Based upon the following Army land warrant:

Issued to	*No.*	*Acres*
Nicholson, William, Soldier	10145	100

709 16 Dec 1806 B/1/012
Registered by: RegTreas
Registered for: Angus McKeever
Location: Mil - 1 8 4 16
Based upon the following Army land warrant:

Issued to	*No.*	*Acres*
McKeever, Angus, Soldier	299	100

(Note: Sent patent to William Davison, Winchester, Virginia, 29 Dec 1806.)

710 17 Dec 1806 B/1/013
Registered by: Montgomery Montour*
Registered for: Montgomery Montour
Location: Mil - 16 7 2 36
Mil - 16 7 2 37
Mil - 16 7 2 38
Based upon the following Army land warrant:

Issued to	*No.*	*Acres*
Montour, John, Capt	301	300

*In parentheses: "An Indian." [It is not certain that note pertains to Montour or Col Hamilton in following serial entry.]

711 31 Dec 1806 B/1/013
Registered by: Col -- Hamilton*
Registered for: Thomas Liggit
Location: Mil - 1 8 4 17
Based upon the following Army land warrant:

Issued to	*No.*	*Acres*
Liggit, Thomas, Soldier	303	100

*In parentheses: "An Indian." [It is not certain that this note pertains to Hamilton or to Montgomery Montour, previous serial entry.] Department of State 9 Jan 1807; sent to Col Hamilton, 17 Jan 1807.

712 5 Jan 1807 B/1/013
Registered by: Robert Whitehill, Esq.
Registered for: Elizabeth [Hummiston?] heiress
Location: Mil - 10 3 4 36
Based upon the following Army land warrant:

Issued to	*No.*	*Acres*
Hummiston, Daniel, Cpl	305	100

(Note: Sent to Mr. Whitehill, 27 Feb 1807.)

713 10 Jan 1805 B/1/013
Registered by: Gurdon L? Mumford, Esq.
Registered for: Zepheniah Brown
Location: Mil - 15 7 4 11
Mil - 15 7 4 21
Mil - 15 7 4 22
Based upon the following Army land warrant:

Issued to	*No.*	*Acres*
Brown, Zepheniah, Capt	85	300

(Note: Sent patent to Mr. Mumford, 27 Feb 1807.)

714 12 Jan 1807 B/1/013
Registered by: John Rea, Esq.
Registered for: Fred[eric]k Hentze
Location: Mil - 15 2 2 11
Based upon the following Army land warrant:

Issued to	*No.*	*Acres*
Hentze, Frederick, Soldier	307	100

(Note: By direction of Mr. Rea, sent patent to Jacob Bonnett, Esq., at Bedford, Pennsylvania, 6 Apr 1808.)

715 12 Jan 1807 B/1/013
Registered by: John Rea, Esq.
Registered for: Chris[topher] Hite
Location: Mil - 15 2 2 12
Based upon the following Army land warrant:

Issued to	*No.*	*Acres*
Hile? [Hite?] Christopher, Soldier	308	100

(Note: By direction of Mr. Rea, sent patent to Jacob Bonnett, Esq., at Bedford, Pennsylvania, 6 Apr 1808.)

716 13 Jan 1807 B/1/013
Registered by: -- Pleasonton
Registered for: Heirs of John Young, assignee
Location: Mil - 1 10 1 40
Based upon the following Army land warrant:

Issued to	*No.*	*Acres*
Clemens, John, Soldier	312	100

717 20 Jan 1807 B/1/013
Registered by: William Findley, Esq.
Registered for: James O'Kain
Location: Mil - 15 8 3 18
Based upon the following Army land warrant:

Issued to	*No.*	*Acres*
O'Kain, James, Soldier	319	100

(Note: Sent patent to Mr. Findley, 28 Jan 1808.)

718 20 Jan 1807 B/1/013
Registered by: William Findley, Esq.
Registered for: Ann Hunter
Location: Mil - 15 8 3 19
Mil - 15 8 3 20

718 [continued]
Based upon the following Army land warrant:

Issued to	*No.*	*Acres*
Sloan, David, Lt	320	200

(Note: Sent patent to Mr. Findley, 28 Jan 1808.)

719 29 Jan 1807 B/1/013
Registered by: Ezra Darby, Esq.
Registered for: [Not given]
Location: [Not given]
Based upon the following Army land warrant:

Issued to	*No.*	*Acres*
Gillet, John	5830	100

(Note: Returned this warrant to Mr. Darby, 25 Feb 1807.)

720 7 Feb 1807 B/1/013
Registered by: Col [Thomas] Worthington for Noah Zane
Registered for: Samuel Y. Keene
Location: Mil - 5 3 3 13
Mil - 5 3 3 16
Mil - 5 3 3 33
Based upon the following Army land warrant:

Issued to	*No.*	*Acres*
Keene, Sam[uel] Y., Surgeon's Mate	213	300

(Note: Sent to Noah Zane in letter of 9 Mar 1808.)

721 14 Feb 1807 B/1/013
Registered by: John Dawson, Esq.
Registered for: Churchill Jones
Location: Mil - 9 1 3 23
Mil - 9 1 3 24
Mil - 9 1 3 39
Based upon the following Army land warrant:

Issued to	*No.*	*Acres*
Jones, Churchill, Capt	304	300

(Note: Sent to Mr. Dawson, 3 Mar 1807.)

722 21 Feb 1807 B/1/013
Registered by: Frederick Conrad, Esq.
Registered for: Heirs, by name
Location: Mil - 8 2 1 15
Based upon the following Army land warrant:

Issued to	*No.*	*Acres*
Levering, Abel, *et al*, Pvt	325	100

(Note: Sent patent to Mr. Conrad, 27 Feb 1807.)

723 23 Feb 1807 B/1/013
Registered by: Andrew Gregg, Esq.
Registered for: Alexander Parker
Location: Mil - 5 3 3 34
Mil - 5 3 3 35
Mil - 5 3 3 36
Based upon the following Army land warrant:

Issued to	*No.*	*Acres*
Parker, Alexander, Capt	1705	300

(Note: Sent patent to Mr. Gregg, 3 Mar 1807.)

724 26 Feb 1807 B/1/013
Registered by: Hon. M? Milledge
Registered for: John Milton
Location: Mil - 16 7 4 33
Mil - 16 7 4 34
Mil - 16 7 4 35
Based upon the following Army land warrant:

Issued to	*No.*	*Acres*
Milton, John, Capt	323	300

(Note: Delivered certificate to Mr. Pleasonton for Mr. Milledge, 5 Mar 1807. Afterwards sent patent per mail, 11 Apr 1807.)

725 28 Feb 1804 B/1/013
Registered by: Samuel Hoy Smith
Registered for: [Not given]
Location: [Not given]
Based upon the following Army land warrant:

Issued to	*No.*	*Acres*
Meriwether, David, Ens	331	[150]

(Note: For? Mr. M. Nourse requested & has received this warrant.)

726 2 Mar 1807 B/1/013
Registered by: William Findley, Esq.
Registered for: James Brady, assignee
Location: Mil - 15 8 3 11
Based upon the following Army land warrant:

Issued to	*No.*	*Acres*
Bodle, Abraham, Soldier	291	100

(Note: Sent patent to Mr. Findley, 28 Jan 1808.)

727 2 Mar 1807 B/1/013
Registered by: J. A. Bayard, Esq.
Registered for: Ann Garnet
Location: Mil - 15 1 3 8
Mil - 15 1 3 9
Based upon the following Army land warrant:

Issued to	*No.*	*Acres*
Garnet, Benj[amin] Lt	328	200

(Note: Gave the patent to Edward Tiffin, Esq.)

728 3 Mar 1807 B/1/013
Registered by: Nathan Williams, Esq.
Registered for: [Not stated]
Location: [Not stated]
Based upon the following Army land warrant:

Issued to	*No.*	*Acres*
Cook, William, Soldier	5558	100

(Note: To await the decision of J. G. Jackson, Esq.)

729 3 Mar 1807 B/1/013
Registered by: John Archer, Esq.
Registered for: Patrick Doran
Location: Mil - 15 7 4 12
Based upon the following Army land warrant:

Issued to	*No.*	*Acres*
Doran, Patrick, Sgt	11158	100

(Note: Sent to Mr. Archer per mail, 3 Apr 1807.)

730 3 Mar 1807 B/1/013
Registered by: Daniel Reintzell, Esq.
Registered for: Kennedy Robinson
Location: Mil - 15 1 3 24
Based upon the following Army land warrant:

Issued to	*No.*	*Acres*
Antrim, John, Soldier	12704	100

(Note: Sent to Mr. Reintzell per post, 3 Apr 1807.)

731 30 Mar 1807 B/1/013

Registered by: John Fowler
Registered for: Walker Baylor
Location: Mil - 18 7 1 5
Mil - 18 7 1 15
Mil - 18 7 1 17
Mil - 16 8 4 3
Mil - 17 7 2 15

Based upon the following Army land warrant:

Issued to	*No.*	*Acres*
Baylor, Walker, Col	114	500

(Note: Sent the patent to Col Worthington, 12 Nov? 1808.)

732 11 Apr 1807 B/1/013

Registered by: Peter Manifold
Registered for: Peter Manifold, assignee
Location: [Not stated]

Based upon the following Army land warrant:

Issued to	*No.*	*Acres*
Irwine, Matthew	342	?

(Note: Warrant withdrawn.)

733 11 Apr 1807 B/1/013

Registered by: Col [Thomas] Worthington
Registered for: [Not stated]
Location : [Not stated]

Based upon the following Army land warrant:

Issued to	*No.*	*Acres*
Hiett, Jacob	117	?

(Note: Hon. Edward Tiffin withdrew this warrant by desire of Col Worthington, 12 Nov 1808.)

734 13 Apr 1807 B/1/013

Registered by: Capt -- Davidson
Registered for: Jonas Stanbery
Location: Mil - 3 10 1 21
Mil - 3 10 2 1
Mil - 3 10 2 2

Based upon the following Army land warrant:

Issued to	*No.*	*Acres*
Barnard, John, Capt	133	300

(Note: Capt Davidson received patent.)

735 27 Apr 1807 B/1/013

Registered by: Francis Johnson
Registered for: Francis Johnson
Location: Mil - 10 3 4 28

Based upon the following Army land warrant:

Issued to	*No.*	*Acres*
Johnson, Francis, Pvt	346	100

(Note: The warrantee took the patent from the Department of State.)

736 4 May 1807 B/1/013

Registered by: Capt -- Davidson
Registered for: Jonas Stanbery
Location: Mil - 3 10 1 19?
Mil - 3 10 1 14
Mil - 3 10 1 20
Mil - 3 10 1 13

Based upon the following Army land warrants:

Issued to	*No.*	*Acres*
Fitch, Elnathan, Lt	29	200
Farmer, Aaron, Pvt	318	100
Gillet, John, Pvt	5830	100

(Note: Delivered patents to Capt Davidson.)

737 10 Jun 1807 B/1/014

Registered by: -- Laub
Registered for: John Melone
Location: Mil - 2 10 2 17

Based upon the following Army land warrant:

Issued to	*No.*	*Acres*
Melone, John, Pvt	353	100

(Note: Gave the certificate to Mr. Laub.)

738 22 Jul 1807 B/1/014

Registered by: Jonathan Goss
Registered for: Jonathan Goss
Location: Mil - 3 10 1 22

Based upon the following Army land warrant:

Issued to	*No.*	*Acres*
Wood, Joseph, Pvt	12649	100

(Note: Gave certificate to Jonathan Goss.)

739 22 Jul 1807 B/1/014

Registered by: M[ichael] Nourse
Registered for: Toppan Webster
Location: Mil - 3 10 2 3

Based upon the following Army land warrant:

Issued to	*No.*	*Acres*
Snailbaker, Daniel, Pvt	310	100

(Note: Gave certificate to Mr. Nourse.)

740 25 Jul 1807 B/1/014

Registered by: Capt -- Davidson
Registered for: Jonas Stanbery
Location: Mil - 3 10 1 18
Mil - 3 10 1 19

Based upon the following Army land warrant:

Issued to	*No.*	*Acres*
Blackleach, John, Lt	156	200

(Note: Delivered to Capt Davidson.)

741 28 Jul 1807 B/1/014

Registered by: M[ichael] Nourse
Registered for: Toppan Webster
Location: Mil - 3 10 1 23
Mil - 3 10 1 24

Based upon the following Army land warrants:

Issued to	*No.*	*Acres*
Jess, Samuel, Pvt	309	100
Waltman, Michael, Pvt	11811	100

(Note: Delivered to M. Nourse.)

742 7 Aug 1807 B/1/014

Registered by: Capt -- Davidson
Registered for: Jonas Stanbery
Location: Mil - 3 10 1 14

Based upon the following Army land warrant:

Issued to	*No.*	*Acres*
Scudder, David, Pvt	298	100

(Note: Gave patent to Capt Davidson.)

743 24 Sep 1807 B/1/014

Registered by: Gen -- Smith, Virg[inia]
Registered for: W. Ball
Location: Mil - 3 10 2 6

Based upon the following Army land warrant:

Issued to	*No.*	*Acres*
Ball, William, Sgt	357	100

(Note: Sent patent to Gen Smith in letter of 2 Oct 1807.)

744 27 Oct 1807 B/1/014
Registered by: Zaccheus Biggs, Esq.
Registered for: Zaccheus Biggs
Location: Mil - 1 1 3 37
Based upon the following Army land warrant:

Issued to	*No.*	*Acres*
Woodward, Joshua, Pvt	150	100

(Note: Gave patent to Mr. Biggs.)

745 31 Oct 1807 B/1/014
Registered by: Andrew Gregg, Esq.
Registered for: Daniel Salday
Location: Mil - 16 7 2 25
Based upon the following Army land warrant:

Issued to	*No.*	*Acres*
Salday, Daniel, Pvt	10423	100

(Note: Sent to Mr. Gregg in Senate.)

746 31 Oct 1807 B/1/014
Registered by: Andrew Gregg, Esq.
Registered for: Christian Miller
Location: Mil - 16 7 2 40
Based upon the following Army land warrant:

Issued to	*No.*	*Acres*
Miller, Christian, Pvt	364	100

(Note: Sent to Mr. Gregg in Senate.)

747 13 Nov 1807 B/1/014
Registered by: A[lbert] Gallatin, Esq.
Registered for: Ebenezer Blackshire
Location: Mil - 1 1 3 7
Based upon the following Army land warrant:

Issued to	*No.*	*Acres*
Blackshire, Ebenezer, Pvt	349	100

(Note: Gave patent to A. Gallatin, Secretary of Treasury.)

748 13 Nov 1807 B/1/014
Registered by: Capt James Taylor
Registered for: Martin Chandler
Location: Mil - 16 7 4 39
Based upon the following Army land warrant:

Issued to	*No.*	*Acres*
Chandler, Martin, Pvt	347*	100

*Pencilled: 8214.

749 13 Nov 1807 B/1/014
Registered by: Capt James Taylor
Registered for: James Taylor
Location: Mil - 16 7 4 30
Mil - 16 7 4 31
Mil - 16 7 4 32
Mil - 15 1 3 5
Mil - 15 1 3 6
Based upon the following Army land warrants:

Issued to	*No.*	*Acres*
Sayers, Rob[ert] Capt	351	300
Pearson, Thomas, Lt	352	200

750 30 Nov 1807 B/1/014
Registered by: Michael Nourse
Registered for: Zaccheus A. Beatty
Location: Mil - 4 4 3 7
Mil - 4 4 3 23
Mil - 4 4 3 24
Based upon the following Army land warrant:

Issued to	*No.*	*Acres*
Pemberton, Thomas, Capt	1751	100

(Note: Delivered to M. Nourse.)

751 1 Dec 1807 B/1/014
Registered by: Michael Nourse
Registered for: Argilaas* Doan
Location: Mil - 15 8 4 2
Based upon the following Army land warrant:

Issued to	*No.*	*Acres*
Adams, Joshua, Pvt	247	100

*So spelled.
(Note: Delivered to M. Nourse.)

752 1 Dec 1807 B/1/014
Registered by: Michael Nourse
Registered for: Coonrad Goodner
Location: Mil - 15 8 4 7*
Based upon the following Army land warrant:

Issued to	*No.*	*Acres*
Slape, Thomas, Pvt	14079	100

*Pencilled notation: Mil - 13 8 2 10 & Mil - 15 8 4 26.

753 1 Dec 1807 B/1/014
Registered by: Michael Nourse
Registered for: Robert Means
Location: Mil - 15 8 4 24
Mil - 15 8 4 25
Based upon the following Army land warrant:

Issued to	*No.*	*Acres*
Starke, Richard, Lt	295	200

(Note: Delivered to M. Nourse.)

754 1 Dec 1807 B/1/014
Registered by: Michael Nourse
Registered for: Michael Nourse
Location: Mil - 15 8 4 11
Mil - 15 8 4 12
Mil - 15 8 4 15
Mil - 15 8 4 16
Based upon the following Army land warrant:

Issued to	*No.*	*Acres*
Irvine, Matthew, Surgeon	342	400

(Note: Delivered to M. Nourse.)

755 1 Dec 1807 B/1/014
Registered by: Michael Nourse
Registered for: Robert Means
Location: Mil - 8 2 3 37
Mil - 10 3 4 21
Based upon the following Army land warrant:

Issued to	*No.*	*Acres*
Walker, David, Junior, Lt	345	200

(Note: Gave patent to M. Nourse, agent.)

756 1 Dec 1807 B/1/014
Registered by: Michael Nourse
Registered for: Samuel Hoey Smith
Location: Mil - 10 3 4 9
Mil - 10 3 4 23
Mil - 10 3 4 27
Based upon the following Army land warrant:

Issued to	*No.*	*Acres*
Turner, Jacob, Capt	226	300

757 — 1 Dec 1807 — B/1/014
Registered by: Michael Nourse
Registered for: Robert Means
Location: Mil - 10 3 4 7
Mil - 10 3 4 8
Mil - 10 3 4 10
Mil - 10 3 4 22
Mil - 10 3 4 29
Based upon the following Army land warrants:

Issued to	*No.*	*Acres*
Minor, Peter, Capt	344	300
Dix, Thomas, Lt	254	200

(Note: Gave patents to M. Nourse.)

758 — 1 Dec 1807 — B/1/014
Registered by: -- Laub
Registered for: Joel Gaylor
Location: Mil - 2 10 2 2
Based upon the following Army land warrant:

Issued to	*No.*	*Acres*
Gaylord, Joel, Pvt	374	100

(Note: Gave patent to Mr. Laub.)

759 — 1 Dec 1807 — B/1/014
Registered by: for Col [Thomas] Worthington
Registered for: Samuel McFarland
Location: Mil - 18 7 1 16
Based upon the following Army land warrant:

Issued to	*No.*	*Acres*
Brown, Edward, Matross	379	100

(Note: Gave patent to E[dward] Tiffin, Esq.)

760 — 3 Jan 1808 — B/1/014
Registered by: John Rathbone
Registered for: John Rathbone
Location: Mil - 18 7 1 10
Mil - 18 7 1 11
Based upon the following Army land warrant:

Issued to	*No.*	*Acres*
Allyn, Robert, Lt	29	200

(Note: Sent patent in letter of 1 Apr 1808.)

761 — 5 Jan 1808 — B/1/014
Registered by: Edward Tiffin, Esq.
Registered for: David Curson
Location: Mil - 13 8 4 26
Based upon the following Army land warrant:

Issued to	*No.*	*Acres*
McMahon, Andrew, Sgt	12340	100

(Note: Sent patent to Mr. Tiffin at the Senate, 2 Feb 1808.)

762 — 8 Jan 1808 — B/1/014
Registered by: Edward Tiffin, Esq.
Registered for: Nathaniel Darby
Location: Mil - 16 8 4 1
Mil - 16 8 4 2
Based upon the following land warrant:

Issued to	*No.*	*Acres*
Darby, Nathaniel, Lt	605	200

(Note: Sent patent to Mr. Tiffin at the Senate, 2 Feb 1808.)

763 — 18 Jan 1808 — B/1/015
Registered by: Maj James Taylor
Registered for: William Edmonds, in trust
Location: Mil - 15 1 3 11
Mil - 15 1 3 12
Based upon the following Army land warrant:

Issued to	*No.*	*Acres*
Green, Robert, Lt	365	200

(Note: Gave patent to Maj [Hezekiah?] Rogers, as directed by Mr. Taylor.)

764 — 18 Jan 1808 — B/1/015
Registered by: Maj James Taylor
Registered for: Richard Apperson
Location: Mil - 15 2 2 1
Mil - 15 2 2 2
Mil - 15 2 2 15
Based upon the following Army land warrant:

Issued to	*No.*	*Acres*
Apperson, Rich[ar]d, Capt	386	300

(Note: Gave patent to Maj [Hezekiah?] Rogers, as directed by Mr. Taylor.)

765 — 18 Jan 1808 — B/1/015
Registered by: Maj James Taylor
Registered for: James Taylor
Location: Mil - 15 2 2 16
Mil - 15 2 2 17
Based upon the following Army land warrant:

Issued to	*No.*	*Acres*
Futt? [Tutt?] Charles, Lt	384	200

(Note: Gave patent to Maj [Hezekiah?] Rogers, as directed by Mr. Taylor.)

766 — 18 Jan 1808 — B/1/015
Registered by: William Findley, Esq.
Registered for: James Brady
Location: Mil - 15 8 3 17
Mil - 15 8 3 9
Based upon the following Army land warrants:

Issued to	*No.*	*Acres*
Pearson, George, Soldier	388	100
Hays, William, Soldier	389	100

(Note: Sent patent to Mr. Findley, 28 Jan 1808.)

767 — 18 Jan 1808 — B/1/015
Registered by: Capt -- Davidson
Registered for: Jonas Stanbery
Location: [Not stated*]
Based upon the following Army land warrant:

Issued to	*No.*	*Acres*
Gardner, Henry G., assignee of William Cummins, Soldier	13	100

*Pencilled notation: Mil - 2 7 4? 27.

768 — 26 Jan 1808 — B/1/015
Registered by: Maj James Taylor
Registered for: Hezekiah Rogers
Location: Mil - 15 2 2 18
Based upon the following Army land warrant:

Issued to	*No.*	*Acres*
Marston, James, Pvt	391	100

(Note: Gave certificate to Maj Rogers.)

769 — 1 Feb 1808 — B/1/015
Registered by: Michael Nourse

769 [continued]
Registered for: [Not stated]
Location: [Not stated]
Based upon the following Army land warrant:

Issued to	*No.*	*Acres*
Cobbs, Samuel, Lt	355	[200]

770 1 Feb 1808 B/1/015
Registered by: -- Cist
Registered for: Abraham Romish
Location: Mil - 1 6 2 5
Based upon the following Army land warrant:

Issued to	*No.*	*Acres*
Manning, Andrew, Pvt	72	100

(Note: Gave patent to Mr. Cist.)

771 21 Feb 1808 B/1/015
Registered by: Ebenezer Seaver, Esq.
Registered for: Isaac Vanhorne
Location: Mil - 7 4 2 40
Based upon the following Army land warrant:

Issued to	*No.*	*Acres*
Tompkins, James, Pvt	3537	100

(Note: Sent patent to Mr. Vanhorne, 29 Mar 1808.)

772 21 Feb 1808 B/1/015
Registered by: Nehemiah Knight, Esq.
Registered for: Isaac Vanhorne
Location: Mil - 7 4 2 39
Based upon the following Army land warrant:

Issued to	*No.*	*Acres*
Stanton, Joseph, Pvt	380	100

(Note: Sent patent to Mr. Vanhorne, 29 Mar 1808.)

773 26 Feb 1808 B/1/015
Registered by: [John?] Mathews
Registered for: D. Humphreys
Location: Mil - 7 9 2 25
Mil - 7 9 2 37
Mil - 7 9 2 38
Mil - 7 9 2 39
Mil - 1 8 2 29W
Based upon the following Army land warrant:

Issued to	*No.*	*Acres*
Humphreys, David, LtCol	948	450

(Note: Gave certificate to Maj [Hezekiah?] Rogers.)

774 4 Mar 1808 B/1/015
Registered by: -- Smoot
Registered for: John Wilder
Location: Mil - 17 7 2 22
Mil - 17 7 2 23
Mil - 17 7 2 30
Mil - 17 7 2 31
Based upon the following Army land warrant:

Issued to	*No.*	*Acres*
Call, William, Maj	354	400

775 5 Mar 1808 B/1/015
Registered by: -- Gregg
Registered for: Francis Leland
Location: Mil - 7 4 2 38
Based upon the following Army land warrant:

Issued to	*No.*	*Acres*
Leland, Francis, Pvt	397	100

(Note: Sent patent to Mr. Gregg, 8 Mar 1808.)

776 12 Mar 1808 B/1/015
Registered by: Hon. Edward Tiffin
Registered for: Peter Mills
Location: Mil - 19 7 1 3
Mil - 19 7 1 4
Mil - 19 7 1 5
Mil - 19 7 1 6
Based upon the following Army land warrant:

Issued to	*No.*	*Acres*
Hastings, Walter, Surgeon	936	400

(Note: Sent patent to Mr. Tiffin.)

777 12 Mar 1808 B/1/015
Registered by: Hon. Edward Tiffin
Registered for: Peter Mills
Location: Mil - 19 7 1 1
Mil - 15 8 3 10
Based upon the following Army land warrant:

Issued to	*No.*	*Acres*
Moor, William, Lt	1367	200

(Note: Located; but warrant returned to Mr. Mills for the producing [of a] proper assignment [by?] J. Moore.)

778 26 Mar 1808 B/1/015
Registered by: Thomas Kenan, Esq.
Registered for: John Hewell, the Sen[ior]
Location: Mil - 3 10 1 16
Mil - 3 10 1 17
Based upon the following Army land warrant:

Issued to	*No.*	*Acres*
Hewell, John, Lt	227	200

(Note: Sent patent to Mr. Kenan, 6 Apr 1808.)

779 29 Mar 1808 B/1/015
Registered by: Jeremiah Morrow, Esq.
Registered for: David Parkhill
Location: Mil - 3 10 1 15
Based upon the following Army land warrant:

Issued to	*No.*	*Acres*
Caswell, Job, Pvt	368	100

(Note: Sent patent to Mr. Morrow [6 Apr 1808].)

780 12 Apr 1808 B/1/015
Registered by: William Findley, Esq.
Registered for: James Brady
Location: Mil - 15 8 3 12
Based upon the following Army land warrant:

Issued to	*No.*	*Acres*
Brady, James, Pvt	407	100

(Note: Sent to Mr. Findley, 16 Apr 1808. J. G? Moore.)

781 12 Apr 1808 B/1/015
Registered by: Michael Nourse
Registered for: Z[accheus] A. Beatty
Location: Mil - 4 4 3 9
Based upon the following Army land warrant:

Issued to	*No.*	*Acres*
Layland, William, Pvt	381	100

(Note: Sent patent to M. Nourse.)

782 15 Apr 1808 B/1/015
Registered by: Hon. P. Goodwyn
Registered for: John Baird
Location: Mil - 17 7 2 6
Mil - 17 7 2 5
Mil - 17 7 2 4
Mil - 17 7 2 3
Based upon the following Army land warrant:

Issued to	*No.*	*Acres*
Middleton, Basil, Surgeon	358	450

(Note: Issued [surplus] certificate for 50 acres.)

783 18 Apr 1808 B/1/015
Registered by: RegTreas
Registered for: Isaac Vanhorne
Location: Mil - 8 5 1 21
Mil - 8 5 1 22
Based upon the following Army land warrants:

Issued to	*No.*	*Acres*
Hall, Samuel, Pvt	385	100
Frazer, Charles, Pvt	403	100

(Note: Patent sent to Mr. Vanhorne, 2 Aug 1808.)

784 18 Apr 1808 B/1/015
Registered by: Jonas Stanbery
Registered for: Jonas Stanbery
Location: Mil - 3 10 1 9
Mil - 3 10 1 12
Based upon the following Army land warrant:

Issued to	*No.*	*Acres*
Honeyman, William, Lt	285	200

(Note: Gave patent to Capt Davidson, his agent.)

785 21 Apr 1808 B/1/015
Registered by: Peter Mills
Registered for: Peter Mills
Location: Mil - 9 7 3 16
Mil - 9 7 3 39
Mil - 9 7 3 40
Based upon the following Army land warrant:

Issued to	*No.*	*Acres*
Frotheringham, Ben[jamin] Capt	716	300

786 21 Apr 1808 B/1/015
Registered by: Maj [Hezekiah?] Rogers for Col Taylor
Registered for: [Not stated]
Location: Mil - 15 2 2 3
Mil - 15 2 2 4
Mil - 15 2 2 13
Mil - 15 2 2 14
Based upon the following Army land warrant:

Issued to	*No.*	*Acres*
Fleming, John, Maj	409	400

787 21 Apr 1808 B/1/015
Registered by: J. G. Jackson, Esq.
Registered for: [Not stated]
Location: [Not stated]
Based upon the following Army land warrant:

Issued to	*No.*	*Acres*
Stockman, Arshual, Pvt	398	100

788 21 Apr 1808 B/1/015
Registered by: J. G. Jackson, Esq.
Registered for: George Jackson
Location: Mil - 8 4 3 7*
Based upon the following Army land warrant:

Issued to	*No.*	*Acres*
Ransom, Samuel, Capt	408	[300]

*Apparently only 100 acres patented, even though captaincy worth 300 acres.
(Note: Sent [to] Hon. Mr. Jackson, 9 Mar 1816.)

789 21 Apr 1808 B/1/015
Registered by: J. G. Jackson, Esq.
Registered for: George Humphries
Location: Mil - 7 4 2 16
Based upon the following Army land warrant:

Issued to	*No.*	*Acres*
Lilley, Benj[amin] Sgt	322	100

(Note: Patent to J. G. Jackson, Esq.)

790 27 Apr 1808 B/1/016
Registered by: M[ichael] Nourse
Registered for: Adam Hoops
Location: Mil - 3 10 2 7
Mil - 3 10 2 8
Mil - 3 10 2 9
Based upon the following Army land warrant:

Issued to	*No.*	*Acres*
Hoops, Adam, Capt	350	300

(Note: Mr. Nourse received the patent.)

791 3 May 1808 B/1/016
Registered by: M[ichael] Nourse
Registered for: Robert Means
Location: Mil - 10 7 1 25
Based upon the following Army land warrant:

Issued to	*No.*	*Acres*
Gleason, Patrick, Pvt	293	100

(Note: Gave certificate 401 to Mr. Nourse.)

792 3 May 1808 B/1/016
Registered by: M[ichael] Nourse
Registered for: John Slauter
Location: Mil - 10 7 1 14
Based upon the following Army land warrant:

Issued to	*No.*	*Acres*
Waddle, William, Pvt	7997	100

(Note: Gave certificate 397 to Mr. Nourse.)

793 3 May 1808 B/1/016
Registered by: M[ichael] Nourse
Registered for: Azor Sturdavant
Location: Mil - 10 7 1 15
Based upon the following Army land warrant:

Issued to	*No.*	*Acres*
Halsted, Richard, Pvt	205	100

(Note: Gave certificate 398 to Mr. Nourse.)

794 3 May 1808 B/1/016
Registered by: M[ichael] Nourse
Registered for: John Coulter
Location: Mil - 8 9 1 2
Based upon the following Army land warrant:

Issued to	*No.*	*Acres*
Coulter, John, Pvt	274	100

(Note: Gave certificate 399 to Mr. Nourse.)

795 | 3 May 1808 | B/1/016
Registered by: M[ichael] Nourse
Registered for: Eleanor Cookerly
Location: Mil - 8 9 1 16
Mil - 8 9 1 17
Mil - 8 9 1 18
Based upon the following Army land warrant:

Issued to	*No.*	*Acres*
Rice, Benjamin, Capt	341	300

(Note: Gave certificate 283 to Mr. Nourse.)

796 | 3 May 1808 | B/1/016
Registered by: M[ichael] Nourse
Registered for: Joseph S. Smith
Location: Mil - 10 7 1 23
Based upon the following Army land warrant:

Issued to	*No.*	*Acres*
Smith, Joseph S., Cornet	2126	150

(Note: Gave certificate to Mr. Nourse.)

797 | 3 May 1808 | B/1/016
Registered by: M[ichael] Nourse
Registered for: John D. Cary
Location: Mil - 8 9 1 14
Mil - 8 9 1 15
Based upon the following Army land warrant:

Issued to	*No.*	*Acres*
Cary, John D., Lt	445	200

(Note: Gave certificate to Mr. Nourse.)

798 | 3 May 1808 | B/1/016
Registered by: Maj H[ezekiah?] Rogers
Registered for: H[ezekiah?] Rogers
Location: Mil - 15 2 2 18
Based upon the following Army land warrant:

Issued to	*No.*	*Acres*
Marston, James, Pvt	391	100

(Note: Gave certificate to Maj Rogers.)

799 | 3 May 1808 | B/1/016
Registered by: Maj H[ezekiah?] Rogers
Registered for: The executors
Location: [Not stated]
Based upon the following Army land warrant:

Issued to	*No.*	*Acres*
Gadsden, Thomas, Capt	288	[300]

(Note: Received this warrant for the owners. [signed] John Williams.)

800 | 11 May 1808 | B/1/016
Registered by: Peter Mills
Registered for: Peter Mills
Location: Mil - 7 7 2 2
Based upon the following Army land warrant:

Issued to	*No.*	*Acres*
Campbell, Arch[ibal]d, Lt	421	100

(Note: This warrant was issued by the Secretary of War for one-half the Lieutenant's claim, to one heir; another warrant is to issue to the other heir.)

801 | 23 May 1808 | B/1/016
Registered by: -- Morrow, Agent
Registered for: Isaac Vanhorne
Location: [Not stated]
Based upon the following Army land warrants:

Issued to	*No.*	*Acres*
Hall, Samuel, Pvt	385	100
Frazer, Charles, Pvt	403	100

802 | 1 Jun 1808 | B/1/016
Registered by: Matthew Bleakley
Registered for: Matthew Bleakley
Location: Mil - 3 5 1 6
Based upon the following Army land warrant:

Issued to	*No.*	*Acres*
Longdon, John, Sgt	423	100

(Note: The owner received the patent certificate.)

803 | 1 Jun 1808 | B/1/016
Registered by: M[ichael] Nourse
Registered for: Zaccheus A. Beatty
Location: Mil - 4 4 3 12
Mil - 4 4 3 21
Mil - 4 4 3 25
Based upon the following Army land warrant:

Issued to	*No.*	*Acres*
Jackson, Jeremiah, Capt	1149	300

804 | 30 Jun 1808 | B/1/016
Registered by: M[ichael] Nourse
Registered for: Abraham Mosser
Location: Mil - 2 10 2 3
Based upon the following Army land warrant:

Issued to	*No.*	*Acres*
Harris, John, Soldier	9564	100

(Note: Patent sent to Ab[raham] Mosser per mail, 9 Nov 1808.)

805 | -- Jun? 1808 | B/1/016
Registered by: -- Forrest
Registered for: Richard Sparrow
Location: [Not stated]
Based upon the following Army land warrant:

Issued to	*No.*	*Acres*
Sparrow, Richard, Soldier	12534	100

806 | -- Jun? 1808 | B/1/016
Registered by: -- Forrest
Registered for: John Donaldson
Location: [Not stated]
Based upon the following Army land warrant:

Issued to	*No.*	*Acres*
Donaldson, John, Soldier	8238	100

807 | 1 Aug 1808 | B/1/016
Registered by: M[ichael] Nourse
Registered for: Elijah Ransom
Location: Mil - 8 9 1 25
Mil - 8 9 1 26
Based upon the following Army land warrant:

Issued to	*No.*	*Acres*
Ransom, Elijah, Lt	1798	200

(Note: Delivered patent to Mr. Nourse, agent.)

808 | 15 Aug 1808 | B/1/016
Registered by: Ab[raha]m Bradley
Registered for: Benj[amin] Carpenter
Location: Mil - 15 1 3 23
Mil - 15 1 3 10

808 [continued]
Based upon the following Army land warrants:

Issued to	*No.*	*Acres*
Cuyzer, Fred[eric]k, Pvt	289	100
Perkins, Aaron, Pvt	277	100

809 15 Aug 1808 B/1/016
Registered by: Ab[raha]m Bradley
Registered for: James Carpenter
Location: Mil - 15 1 3 22
Based upon the following Army land warrant:

Issued to	*No.*	*Acres*
Gaylord, Ambrose, Pvt	290	100

810 -- Nov 1807* B/1/016
Registered by: Col James Taylor
Registered for: Weaver, --, & Taylor, --
Location: Mil - 16 7 4 36
Mil - 16 7 4 37
Mil - 16 7 4 38
Based upon the following Army land warrant:

Issued to	*No.*	*Acres*
McConnell, Robert, Capt	276	300

*Date out of sequence in source ledger.
(Note: Certificate 253; Weaver 2/3, Taylor 1/3.)

811 5 Sep 1808 B/1/016
Registered by: Isaac Vanhorne, Esq.
Registered for: Isaac Vanhorne
Location: Mil - 8 4 3 8
Mil - 6 5? 3 6
Mil - 6 5? 3 7
Mil - 6 5? 3 15
Based upon the following Army land warrant:

Issued to	*No.*	*Acres*
Boyle, Thomas H., Maj	338	400

812 8 Sep 1808 B/1/016
Registered by: M[ichael] Nourse
Registered for: Zaccheus A. Beatty
Location: Mil - 4 4 3 5
Mil - 4 4 3 26
Based upon the following Army land warrants:

Issued to	*No.*	*Acres*
Pollard, James, Pvt	148	100
Harris, John, Bombardier	9628	100

(Note: Delivered certificate to Mr. Nourse.)

813 27 Sep 1808 B/1/016
Registered by: Thomas M. Thompson
Registered for: Thomas M. Thompson
Location: Mil - 8 9 2 7
Mil - 8 9 1 30
Mil - 8 9 1 31
Based upon the following Army land warrants:

Issued to	*No.*	*Acres*
Greenewalt, Abraham, Soldier	426	100
Young, Marcus, Lt	428	200

(Note: Patent sent to Mr. Thompson, 16 Mar 1811.)

814 30 Sep 1808 B/1/016
Registered by: Phineas Bradley, Esq.
Registered for: Jacob Cist
Location: [Not stated]
Based upon the following Army land warrant:

Issued to	*No.*	*Acres*
Tubbs, Samuel, Pvt	378	100

815 12 Nov 1808 B/1/017
Registered by: John Smilie, Esq.
Registered for: Peter Gary
Location: Mil - 6 6 2 22
Based upon the following Army land warrant:

Issued to	*No.*	*Acres*
Gary, Peter, Sgt	361	100

(Note: Sent patent to Mr. Smilie, 30 Nov 1808.)

816 12 Nov 1808 B/1/017
Registered by: Edward Tiffin, Esq.
Registered for: John Lamme
Location: Mil - 16 8 4 7
Based upon the following Army land warrant:

Issued to	*No.*	*Acres*
Shotte? [Sholte?] Richard, Soldier	10336	100

(Note: Sent to Mr. Tiffin, 30? Nov 1808.)

817 21 Nov 1808 B/1/017
Registered by: Daniel Montgomery
Registered for: [Not stated]
Location: [Not stated]
Based upon the following Army land warrant:

Issued to	*No.*	*Acres*
Kurtz, Michael, Pvt	375	100

818 28 Nov 1808 B/1/017
Registered by: M[ichael] Nourse
Registered for: Zaccheus A. Beatty
Location: Mil - 3 1 1 36
Mil - 3 1 1 37
Based upon the following Army land warrants:

Issued to	*No.*	*Acres*
Wyman, Asa Miller, Pvt	396	100
Wyman, John, Pvt	395	100

819 -- Nov 1808 B/1/017
Registered by: Daniel Montgomery, Esq.
Registered for: Legal heirs, by name
Location: Mil - 11 9 4 25
Mil - 11 9 4 26
Mil - 11 9 4 27
Mil - 11 9 4 28
Based upon the following Army land warrant:

Issued to	*No.*	*Acres*
Anderson, Arch[ibal]d, Maj	390	400

(Note: Sent to Mr. Montgomery, 30 Nov 1808.)

820 20 Dec 1808 B/1/017
Registered by: -- Tannehill, Esq.
Registered for: George Morris
Location: Mil - 15 2 2 5
Based upon the following Army land warrant:

Issued to	*No.*	*Acres*
Morris, George, Fifer	330	100

821 20 Dec 1808 B/1/017
Registered by: Edward Tiffin, Esq.
Registered for: David Parkhill
Location: Mil - 2 10 2 1

821 [continued]
Based upon the following Army land warrant:
Issued to *No.* *Acres*
Smith, Samuel, Pvt 117 100
(Note: Gave the patent to Edward Tiffin, Esq.)

822 29 Dec 1808 B/1/017
Registered by: Maj [Hezekiah?] Rogers
Registered for: Bryan Rossetter
Location: Mil - 15 2 2 19
Based upon the following Army land warrant:
Issued to *No.* *Acres*
Rossetter, Bryan, Sgt 435 100
(Note: Maj Rogers received patent.)

823 31 Dec 1808 B/1/017
Registered by: Nicholas Cusick
Registered for: Nicholas Cusick
Location: Mil - 15 2 2 31
Mil - 15 2 2 32
Based upon the following Army land warrant:
Issued to *No.* *Acres*
Cusick, Nicholas, Lt 439 200
(Note: The Indian received the patent.)

824 31 Dec 1808 B/1/017
Registered by: Nathan Wilson, Esq.
Registered for: Joseph Gambel
Location: Mil - 15 2 2 20
Based upon the following Army land warrant:
Issued to *No.* *Acres*
Gambel, Joseph, Soldier 335 100
(Note: Sent to Mr. Wilson, 17 Jan 1809.)

825 16 Jan 1809 B/1/017
Registered by: William Findley, Esq.
Registered for: Alexander Gray
Location: Mil - 3 1 1 33
Based upon the following Army land warrant:
Issued to *No.* *Acres*
Gray, Alex[ande]r, Sol-
dier 425 100
(Note: Patent delivered to Mr. Findley.)

826 16 Jan 1809 B/1/017
Registered by: William Findley, Esq.
Registered for: James Brady
Location: Mil - 15 8 3 8
Based upon the following Army land warrant:
Issued to *No.* *Acres*
Hare, Michael, Soldier 441 100
(Note: Mr. James McClary received patent.)

827 16 Jan 1809 B/1/017
Registered by: William Findley, Esq.
Registered for: Mary, widow of heir
Location: Mil - 15 8 3 13
Based upon the following Army land warrant:
Issued to *No.* *Acres*
Martin, George, Soldier 442 100
(Note: Mr. James McClary received patent.)

828 16 Jan 1809 B/1/017
Registered by: M[ichael] Nourse
Registered for: Zaccheus A. Beatty
Location: Mil - 3 1 1 34
Mil - 3 1 1 35
Based upon the following Army land warrant:
Issued to *No.* *Acres*
Williams, David, Lt 235 200

829 17 Feb 1809 B/1/017
Registered by: Daniel Montgomery, Esq.
Registered for: Simon Herold
Location: Mil - 2 7 4 28
Based upon the following Army land warrant:
Issued to *No.* *Acres*
Kurtz, Michael, Soldier 375 100
(Note: Gave patent to Daniel Montgomery.)

830 17 Feb 1809 B/1/017
Registered by: M[ichael] Nourse
Registered for: James Barnett
Location: Mil - 8 9 3 7
Mil - 8 9 3 8
Based upon the following Army land warrant:
Issued to *No.* *Acres*
Barnett, James, Lt 424 200
(Note: Gave patent to Mr. Nourse.)

831 17 Feb 1809 B/1/017
Registered by: M[ichael] Nourse
Registered for: Abraham Cazier
Location: Mil - 1 10 1 34
Based upon the following Army land warrant:
Issued to *No.* *Acres*
Goss, Jonathan, Soldier 347 100

832 20 Feb 1809 B/1/017
Registered by: Henry Gaither, Esq.
Registered for: Jesse Suit
Location: Mil - 6 8 3 5
Based upon the following Army land warrant:
Issued to *No.* *Acres*
Suit, Jesse, Sgt 11695 100
(Note: Patent delivered to Col Gaither.)

833 20 Feb 1809 B/1/017
Registered by: Henry Gaither, Esq.
Registered for: John Smith
Location: Mil - 6 8 3 16
Based upon the following Army land warrant:
Issued to *No.* *Acres*
Smith, John, Soldier 11699 100
(Note: Patent delivered to Col Gaither.)

834 25 Feb 1809 B/1/017
Registered by: J. G. Jackson, Esq.
Registered for: George W. Humphreys
Location: Mil - 7 4 2 17
Based upon the following Army land warrant:
Issued to *No.* *Acres*
Dayley, Robert, Matross 440 100

835 3 Mar 1809 B/1/017
Registered by: Capt -- Davidson
Registered for: Towl? -- & Stow, --
Location: Mil - 3 8 4 1
Based upon the following Army land warrants:
Issued to *No.* *Acres*

835 [continued]
Kneeland, Seth, Soldier 13300 100
Moody, George, Soldier 4645 100
Butler, John, Soldier 12755 100
Pears, John, Soldier 7606 100
(Note: [Excepting for the first listed above,] received these warrants [signed] John Davidson.)

836 7 Mar 1809 B/1/017
Registered by: Hon. Philip Read
Registered for: Rebecca Hawkins, heiress
Location: Mil - 9 7 3 18
Based upon the following Army land warrant:
Issued to *No.* *Acres*
Shepherd, James, Soldier 11693 100
(Note: Patent delivered to Mr. Read.)

837 13 Mar 1809 B/1/017
Registered by: Joseph Vance
Registered for: John? Parker, in trust for heirs
Location: Mil - 15 1 3 40
Based upon the following Army land warrant:
Issued to *No.* *Acres*
Parker, Timothy, Pvt 259 100

838 14 Mar 1809 B/1/017
Registered by: -- Simmons
Registered for: John Bantham
Location: Mil - 11 6 1 39
Based upon the following Army land warrant:
Issued to *No.* *Acres*
Bantham, John, Soldier 434 100

839 24 Apr 1809 B/1/017
Registered by: M[ichael] Nourse
Registered for: Z[accheus] A. Beatty
Location: Mil - 3 1 1 38
Based upon the following Army land warrant:
Issued to *No.* *Acres*
Bruff, William, Sgt 433 100

840 1 May 1809 B/1/018
Registered by: George Kneopler
Registered for: Peter Lisk
Location: Mil - 8 2 3 1
Based upon the following Army land warrant:
Issued to *No.* *Acres*
Lisk, Peter, Soldier 458 100
(Note: Sent patent per mail to G. Kneopler.)

841 27 May 1809 B/1/018
Registered by: Maj -- Swan
Registered for: John Shadley
Location: Mil - 11 9 4 5
Based upon the following Army land warrant:
Issued to *No.* *Acres*
Barr, John, Soldier 284 100
(Note: Gave patent to Maj Swan.)

842 31 May 1809 B/1/018
Registered by: Jeremiah Morrow, Esq.
Registered for : David Parkhill
Location: Mil - 3 10 1 7
Based upon the following Army land warrant:
Issued to *No.* *Acres*
Bunkam? [Bunham?] Asahel, Soldier 447 100

843 3 Jun 1809 B/1/018
Registered by: John Davenport, Esq.
Registered for: [Not stated]
Location: [Not stated]
Based upon the following Army land warrant:
Issued to *No.* *Acres*
Scoffield, Seely, Soldier 6489 100
(Note: Mr. Davenport withdrew this warrant on 10 Apr 1812 [signed] J. J. Moore.)

844 16 Jun 1809 B/1/018
Registered by: Maj [Hezekiah?] Rogers
Registered for: John Morriss
Location: Mil - 11 9 4 3
Mil - 11 9 4 4
Based upon the following Army land warrant:
Issued to *No.* *Acres*
Coverly, Thomas, Lt 406 200

845 4 Nov 1809 B/1/018
Registered by: M[ichael] Nourse
Registered for: Thomas [McKean?] Thompson
Location: Mil - 1 1 3 38
Based upon the following Army land warrant:
Issued to *No.* *Acres*
Maxwell, James, Soldier 10098 100
(Note: Mr. M. Nourse received patent.)

846 7 Nov 1809 B/1/018
Registered by: Peter Mills
Registered for: Baum, --, & Perry, --, in trust
Location: Mil - 1 1 3 6
Mil - 1 1 3 39
Mil - 1 1 3 40
Based upon the following Army land warrant:
Issued to *No.* *Acres*
Mayberry, Beriah, administrator of James Smith, Capt 2046 300
(Note: Received patents [signed] Peter Mills.)

847 14 Nov 1809 B/1/018
Registered by: M[ichael] Nourse
Registered for: [Not stated]
Location: [Not stated]
Based upon the following Army land warrant:
Issued to *No.* *Acres*
Brann, Andrew 207 ?

848 4 Dec 1809 B/1/018
Registered by: Joseph Vance
Registered for: Daniel McCoy
Location: Mil - 17 7 2 7
Mil - 17 7 2 8
Based upon the following Army land warrant:
Issued to *No.* *Acres*
McCay, Daniel, Lt 229 200
(Note: Sent patent to Mr. Vance, 10 Jan 1811.)

849 4 Dec 1809 B/1/018
Registered by: Joseph Vance

849 [continued]
Registered for: [Not stated]
Location: [Not stated]
Based upon the following Army land warrant:

Issued to	*No.*	*Acres*
Flanders, John, Pvt	449	100

850 18 Dec 1809 B/1/018
Registered by: Bohn, --, & Slingluff, --
Registered for: Bohn, --, & Slingluff, --
Location: Mil - 3 8 4 2
Based upon the following Army land warrant:

Issued to	*No.*	*Acres*
Hoogland, William, Pvt	9619	100

(Note: Mr. M. Nourse received patent.)

851 18 Dec 1809 B/1/018
Registered by: M[ichael] Nourse
Registered for: Humphrey Fullerton
Location: Mil - 20 7 3 3
Mil - 20 7 3 4
Mil - 19 7 2 2
Based upon the following Army land warrant:

Issued to	*No.*	*Acres*
Craine, James, Capt	444	300

(Note: Mr. M. Nourse received patent.)

852 3 Jan 1810 B/1/018
Registered by: Samuel Alward
Registered fot: John Vermilyea
Location: Mil - 11 6 1 32
Based upon the following Army land warrant:

Issued to	*No.*	*Acres*
Vermilyea, John, Matross	228	100

(Note : Samuel Alward received patent [witnessed] John Gardiner.)

853 3 Jan 1810 B/1/018
Registered by: Samuel Alward
Registered for: John Matthews
Location: Mil - 11 6 1 33
Based upon the following Army land warrant:

Issued to	*No.*	*Acres*
Matthews, John, Sgt	321	100

(Note: Samuel Alward received patent [witnessed] John Gardiner.)

854 3 Jan 1810 B/1/018
Registered by: Samuel Alward
Registered for: Samuel Alward
Location: Mil - 11 6 1 25
Mil - 11 6 1 26
Mil - 11 6 1 27
Based upon the following Army land warrant:

Issued to	*No.*	*Acres*
Brownfield, Robert, Surgeon's Mate	306	300

(Note: Samuel Alward received patent [witnessed] John Gardiner.)

855 9 Jan 1810 B/1/018
Registered by: Ret[urn] J. Meigs, Esq.
Registered for: Tagert, --; McLaughlin, --; Gray, --; & Taylor, --
Location: Mil - 6 10 3 2
Mil - 6 10 3 3
Mil - 6 10 3 4
Based upon the following Army land warrant:

Issued to	*No.*	*Acres*
Booker, Samuel, Capt	315	300

(Note: Sent patent 27 Jan 1810 to R. J. Meigs. See letter book.)

856 16 Jan 1810 B/1/018
Registered by: John Graham, Esq.
Registered for: [Not stated]
Location: [Not stated]
Based upon the following Army land warrants:

Issued to	*No.*	*Acres*
Andrews, Ephraim, Pvt	415	100
Donaldson, John, Pvt	8238	100
Sparrow, Richard, Pvt	12534	100

(Note: Received 20 Mar 1810 Ephraim Andrews warrants? 415, 8238, 12534 [signed] Nathaniel Frye. Returned by Mr. Frye, 8 May 1810, J. Gardiner.)

857 18 Jan 1810 B/1/018
Registered by: M[ichael] Nourse
Registered for: Joshua Danforth
Location: Mil - 17 7 2 1
Mil - 17 7 2 2
Based upon the following Army land warrant:

Issued to	*No.*	*Acres*
Danforth, Joshua, Lt	174	200

(Note: Gave certificate to Mr. Nourse.)

858 18 Jan 1810 B/1/018
Registered by: M[ichael] Nourse
Registered for: Heirs at law
Location : Mil - 17 7 2 12
Mil - 17 7 2 13
Mil - 17 7 2 14
Based upon the following Army land warrant:

Issued to	*No.*	*Acres*
Ells? [Ellis?] Edward, Capt	102	300

(Note: Gave certificate to Mr. Nourse.)

859 20 Jan 1810 B/1/018
Registered by: M[ichael] Nourse
Registered for: Zaccheus A. Beatty
Location: Mil - 4 4 3 15
Mil - 4 4 3 18
Based upon the following Army land warrant:

Issued to	*No.*	*Acres*
Long, Reuben, Lt	480	200

(Note: Gave patent to M. Nourse, 21 Jul 1812.)

860 -- Jan 1810 B/1/018
Registered by: M[ichael] Nourse
Registered for: Daniel Call, in trust
Location: Mil - 6 10 4 9
Mil - 6 10 4 7
Mil - 6 10 4 8
Based upon the following Army land warrants:

Issued to	*No.*	*Acres*
Foster, Cosby, Pvt	292	100
Cobbs, Samuel, Lt	355	200

(Note: Gave certificate to M. Nourse.)

861 20 Jan 1810 B/1/018
Registered by: William Whann, Esq.
Registered for: Jonas Stanbery

861 [continued]
Location: Mil - 7 7 2 7
Mil - 7 7 2 8
Mil - 7 7 2 6
Mil - 11 6 1 24
Based upon the following Army land warrants:

Issued to	*No.*	*Acres*
Jones, Albrigton, Lt	359	200
Anthony, Jack, Pvt	297	100
Bell, Abraham, assignee of Alex[ander] McCalla, Pvt	475	100

(Note: Sent the patent to Mr. Whann by Mr. Pickford, 22 Feb 1810 [signed] J. J. Moore.)

862 25 Jan 1810 B/1/019
Registered by: Hon. Samuel Shaw
Registered for: Stephen Thorn
Location: Mil - 2 5 2 25
Mil - 2 10 2 15
Mil - 3 7 1 7
Mil - 3 7 1 10
Mil - 2 7 4 15
Mil - 2 7 4 8
Mil - 2 7 4 9
Mil - 3 8 4 5
Mil - 3 8 4 6
Mil - 3 8 4 4
Mil - 1 6 2 14
Based upon the following Army land warrants:

Issued to	*No.*	*Acres*
Platt, Richard, Maj	348	400
Egbert, Jacob, Surgeon's Mate	691	300
Brewster, James, Lt	171	200
Hull, Samuel, Soldier	14146	100
Denniston, Mathew, Soldier	4066	100

(Note: Sent patents to Mr. Shaw, 22 Feb 1810.)

863 26 Jan 1810 B/1/019
Registered by: Henry Southard, Esq.
Registered for: Doty, --, & Southard, --
Location: Mil - 15 8 4 1
Based upon the following Army land warrant:

Issued to	*No.*	*Acres*
Wood, Isaac, Soldier	221	100

(Note: Sent patent to Mr. Southard, 22 Feb 1810.)

864 31 Jan 1810 B/1/019
Registered by: Samuel Alward
Registered for: Samuel Alward
Location: Mil - 11 6 1 30
Based upon the following Army land warrant:

Issued to	*No.*	*Acres*
Watson, Thomas W., Dragoon	476	100

(Note: Sent patent to Samuel Alward, 22 Feb 1810.)

865 31 Jan 1810 B/1/019
Registered by: Capt -- Davidson
Registered for: Jonas Stanbery
Location: Mil - 3 7 1 1
Mil - 3 7 1 2
Mil - 3 7 1 8
Based upon the following Army land warrants:

Issued to	*No.*	*Acres*
Epes, William, CaptLt	360	200
Martin, William, Soldier	6222	100

(Note: Gave patent to Capt Davidson, 28 Feb 1810.)

866 20 Mar 1810 B/1/019
Registered by: Nath[anie]l Frye, Esq.
Registered for: J. N. Cummins
Location: Mil - 6 10 3 5
Based upon the following Army land warrant:

Issued to	*No.*	*Acres*
Pinkney, William, Pvt	473	100

(Note: Patent delivered to Nathaniel Frye.)

867 20 Mar 1810 B/1/019
Registered by: M[ichael] Nourse
Registered for: Henry Massie
Location: Mil - 4 10 3 2
Mil - 4 10 3 3
Mil - 4 10 3 14
Based upon the following Army land warrant:

Issued to	*No.*	*Acres*
Beall, Robert, heirs of, Capt	431	300

(Note: Gave certificate to Mr. Nourse.)

868 20 Mar 1810 B/1/019
Registered by: M[ichael] Nourse
Registered for: Jesse McKay, assignee
Location: Mil - 6 10 4 17
Mil - 6 10 4 18
Mil - 6 10 4 19
Based upon the following Army land warrant:

Issued to	*No.*	*Acres*
Fauntleroy, Griffin, heir of, Capt	2694	300

869 20 Mar 1810 B/1/019
Registered by: M[ichael] Nourse
Registered for: James Morrison
Location: Mil - 4 10 3 5
Based upon the following Army land warrant:

Issued to	*No.*	*Acres*
Brann, Joseph, Cpl	208	100

(Note: Gave certificate to Mr. Nourse.)

870 20 Mar 1810 B/1/019
Registered by: M[ichael] Nourse
Registered for: Henry Wallace
Location: Mil - 4 10 3 4
Based upon the following Army land warrant:

Issued to	*No.*	*Acres*
Crowder, John, Pvt	280	100

(Note: Gave certificate to Mr. Nourse.)

871 20 Mar 1810 B/1/019
Registered by: G. S. Mumford, Esq.
Registered for: Evander Childs
Location: Mil - 11 6 1 22
Mil - 11 6 1 23
Based upon the following Army land warrants:

Issued to	*No.*	*Acres*
Bell, Abraham, assignee of Ichabod Coe, Fifer	474	100
Richards, Samuel, Sgt	14151	100

(Note: Sent patent to Mr. Mumford, 31 Mar 1810.)

872 22 Mar 1810 B/1/019
Registered by: Col James Taylor
Registered for: James Taylor
Location: Mil - 16 7 4 8
Based upon the following Army land warrant:

Issued to	*No.*	*Acres*
Sawyer, James, Cpl	387	100

873 22 Mar 1810 B/1/019
Registered by: Col James Taylor
Registered for: Nathaniel Beall?
Location: Mil - 15 1 3 21
Based upon the following Army land warrant:

Issued to	*No.*	*Acres*
Beall, Nathaniel, Pvt	493	100

874 22 Mar 1810 B/1/019
Registered by: Col James Taylor
Registered for: Richard Taylor
Location: Mil - 16 6 1 7
Mil - 16 6 1 8
Mil - 16 6 1 9
Mil - 16 6 1 10
Based upon the following Army land warrant:

Issued to	*No.*	*Acres*
Taylor, Richard, LtCol	494	450

(Note: Issued surplus certificate for 50 acres. Patented 27 Aug 1824.)

875 22 Mar 1810 B/1/019
Registered by: Col James Taylor
Registered for: --? Moore, in trust
Location: Mil - 16 7 4 40
Based upon the following Army land warrant:

Issued to	*No.*	*Acres*
Moore, Zedekiah, Ens	1493	150

(Note: Issued surplus certificate for 50 acres. 15 May 1810 delivered patents for 100 and 50 acres to Col Taylor.)

876 22 Mar 1810 B/1/019
Registered by: Joseph Ogle
Registered for: Joseph Ogle
Location: Mil - 7 4 2 18
Based upon the following Army land warrant:

Issued to	*No.*	*Acres*
Parks, Solomon, Pvt	412	100

(Note: Sent patent to Mr. Ogle by mail, 7 Apr 1810.)

877 24 Mar 1810 B/1/019
Registered by: G. S. Mumford, Esq.
Registered for: Jedediah Waterman
Location: Mil - 11 6 1 9
Mil - 17 7 1 24E
Based upon the following Army land warrant:

Issued to	*No.*	*Acres*
Waterman, Jedediah, Ens	2321	150

(Note: Sent patents to Mr. Mumford, 7 Apr 1810.)

878 26 Mar 1810 B/1/019
Registered by: M[ichael] Nourse
Registered for: Zaccheus A. Beatty
Location: Mil - 1 1 3 24
Based upon the following Army land warrant:

Issued to	*No.*	*Acres*
Nunley, John, Sgt	1	100

(Note: Delivered patent to M. Nourse.)

879 28 Mar 1810 B/1/019
Registered by: Moses Rawlins
Registered for: Moses Rawlins
Location: Mil - 16 7 4 25
Based upon the following Army land warrant:

Issued to	*No.*	*Acres*
Rawlins, Moses, Pvt	499	100

(Note: He received treasury certificate.)

880 28 Mar 1810 B/1/019
Registered by: G. S. Mumford, Esq.
Registered for: Samuel Decker
Location: Mil - 16 7 4 26
Based upon the following Army land warrant:

Issued to	*No.*	*Acres*
Decker, Samuel, Pvt	490	100

(Note: Sent patent to Mr. Mumford, 11 Apr 1810.)

881 2 Apr 1810 B/1/019
Registered by: Hon. John Condit
Registered for: Heirs at law
Location: Mil - 16 6 1 6
Based upon the following Army land warrant:

Issued to	*No.*	*Acres*
Lewis, Benjamin, Pvt	483	100

(Note: Sent patent to Mr. Condit, 7 Apr 1810.)

882 5 Apr 1810 B/1/019
Registered by: Hon. James Breckenridge
Registered for: Stephen R. Price
Location: Mil - 18 7 1 1
Based upon the following Army land warrant:

Issued to	*No.*	*Acres*
Price, Stephen R., Sgt	451	100

(Note: Sent patent to Mr. Breckenridge by Mr. Herty, 15 Apr 1810.)

883 5 Apr 1810 B/1/019
Registered by: -- Jenkins
Registered for: Thomas? M. Thompson
Location: Mil - 8 9 2 8
Based upon the following Army land warrant:

Issued to	*No.*	*Acres*
Burns, John, Pvt	496	100

(Note: Mr. Jenkins withdrew the warrant. Mr. Thompson sent it back [to General Land Office]. It was located [as per above]. Patent sent to Mr. Thompson, 16 --? 1811?)

884 18 Apr 1810 B/1/020
Registered by: Peter Mills
Registered for: Israel Loomis
Location: Mil - 8 9 2 24
Based upon the following Army land warrant:

Issued to	*No.*	*Acres*
Loomis, Israel, Sgt	4615	100

885 19 Apr 1810 B/1/020
Registered by: Hon. Philip Read
Registered for: Heirs, by name
Location: Mil - 9 7 3 14
Based upon the following Army land warrant:

885 [continued]

Issued to	No.	Acres
Smith, Daniel, Pvt	513	100

(Note: Sent patent to Mr. Read, 22 Jan 1811.)

886 20 Apr 1810 B/1/020
Registered by: Hon. G. S. Mumford
Registered for: Isaac G. Graham
Location: Mil - 11 6 1 10
Mil - 11 6 1 11
Mil - 11 6 1 12
Based upon the following Army land warrant:

Issued to	No.	Acres
Graham, Isaac G., Surgeon's Mate	807	300

(Note: Sent to Mr. Mumford, 30 Apr 1810.)

887 20 Apr 1810 B/1/020
Registered by: Michael Nourse
Registered for: Daniel Call, in trust
Location: Mil - 6 10 4 12
Mil - 6 10 4 13
Based upon the following Army land warrants:

Issued to	No.	Acres
Annis, Levi, Pvt	411	100
Richardson, Daniel	414	100

888 -- Apr 1810 B/1/020
Registered by: James Taylor
Registered for: Oldham, --, & Taylor, --
Location: Mil - 16 7 4 13
Mil - 16 7 4 14
Mil - 16 7 4 15
Based upon the following Army land warrant:

Issued to	No.	Acres
Oldham, Conway, Capt	503	300

(Note: 15 May 1810, delivered patent to Col Taylor.)

889 28 Apr 1810 B/1/020
Registered by: D. L? [or S.] Garland
Registered for: Bartlett Hawkins
Location: Mil - 8 9 2 16
Based upon the following Army land warrant:

Issued to	No.	Acres
Hawkins, Bartlett, Dragoon	515	100

(Note: 2 May 1810 delivered [to] D. L? Garland, Esq.)

890 17 May 1810 B/1/020
Registered by: Michael Nourse
Registered for: Charles Woodson
Location: Mil - 16 8 4 8
Mil - 16 8 4 12
Based upon the following Army land warrant:

Issued to	No.	Acres
Caule, John, Lt	367	200

891 22 Jun 1810 B/1/020
Registered by: Bohn, --, & Slingluff, --
Registered for: Bohn, --, & Slingluff, --
Location: Mil - 3 8 4 13
Based upon the following Army land warrant:

Issued to	No.	Acres
Tucker, Zadoc, Pvt	468	100

(Note: Received these patents [signed] Christian Deardorff.)

892 22 Jun 1810 B/1/020
Registered by: Bohn, --, & Slingluff, --
Registered for: Isaac Vanbibber
Location: Mil - 3 8 4 14
Based upon the following Army land warrant:

Issued to	No.	Acres
Landes, David, Pvt	460	100

(Note: Received these patents [signed] Christian Deardorff.)

893 22 Jun 1810 B/1/020
Registered by: Bohn, --, & Slingluff, --
Registered for: Andrew Cole
Location: Mil - 1 8 4 15
Based upon the following Army land warrant:

Issued to	No.	Acres
Cole, Andrew, Pvt	8171	100

(Note: Received this patent [signed] Christian Deardorff.)

894 26 Jun 1810 B/1/020
Registered by: Nathaniel Frye, Esq.
Registered for: Moses Willcox? [Wilhof?] & Aaron Willcox? [Wilhof?]
Location: Mil - 6 10 3 10
Based upon the following Army land warrant:

Issued to	No.	Acres
Wheedon, Rufus, Soldier	6605	100

895 26 Jun 1810 B/1/020
Registered by: Nathaniel Frye, Esq.
Registered for: Linus Parmellee, in trust
Location: Mil - 6 10 3 9
Based upon the following Army land warrant:

Issued to	No.	Acres
Parmellee, Luther, Artificer	337	100

896 6 Jul 1810 B/1/020
Registered by: Col James Taylor
Registered for: [Not stated]
Location: [Not stated]
Based upon the following Army land warrant:

Issued to	No.	Acres
Moore, Zechariah, Sgt	517	100

(Pencilled notation: Mil - 11? 1 4 40 . . . ? awaiting further direction.)

897 6 Jul 1810 B/1/020
Registered by: Col James Taylor
Registered for: [Not stated]
Location: [Not stated]
Based upon the following Army land warrant:

Issued to	No.	Acres
Pierce, William, Capt	518	[300]

(Note: Pat[ented] 27 Aug 1824. [It is uncertain that the note pertains to this warrant.])

898 26 Jul 1810 B/1/020
Registered by: -- Dunn
Registered for: Daniel Call, in trust
Location: Mil - 6 10 4 16
Mil - 6 10 4 6
Based upon the following Army land warrants:

Issued to	No.	Acres
Rawleigh, William, Pvt	413	100
Metcalf, Walter, Pvt	410	100

898 [continued
(Note: Mr. William Dunn received certificate.)

899 19 Sep 1810 B/1/020
Registered by: M[ichael] Nourse
Registered for: M[ichael] Nourse
Location: Mil - 15 8 4 26
Mil - 2 10 2 13
Mil - 2 10 2 16
Based upon the following Army land warrants:

Issued to	*No.*	*Acres*
McMullen, John, Pvt	18	100
Lane, William, Cpl	21	100
Nickerson, Edward, Sgt	22	100

900 25 Sep 1810 B/1/020
Registered by: Joseph Vance
Registered for: William Dennison
Location: Mil - 6 2 1 33
Mil - 6 2 1 37
Based upon the following Army land warrant:

Issued to	*No.*	*Acres*
Avery, Thomas, Lt	313	200

(Note: Sent patent to Mr. Vance, 10 Jan 1811.)

901 25 Sep 1810 B/1/020
Registered by: Joseph Vance
Registered for: James Swinorton*
Location: [Not stated]
Based upon the following Army land warrant:

Issued to	*No.*	*Acres*
Griswold, Samuel, Pvt	336	100

*So spelled.

902 25 Sep 1810 B/1/020
Registered by: Joseph Vance
Registered for: Thomas Swan
Location: Mil - 16 7 2 35
Based upon the following Army land warrant:

Issued to	*No.*	*Acres*
Herrington, Jacob, Pvt	438	100

(Note: Sent patent to Mr. Vance, 10 Jan 1811.)

903 22 Oct 1810 B/1/020
Registered by: John Cox Stockton
Registered for: John Cox Stockton
Location: Mil - 5 3 3 17
Based upon the following Army land warrant:

Issued to	*No.*	*Acres*
Mitchel, Thomas, Fifer	462	100

(Note: Sent to Mr. Stockton, 16 Mar 1811.)

904 24 Oct 1810 B/1/020
Registered by: John Smith
Registered for: Samuel Way
Location: Mil - 6 2 1 20
Based upon the following Army land warrant:

Issued to	*No.*	*Acres*
Way, Samuel, Pvt	401	100

(Note: Gave certificate to Mr. Smith, 22 Jan 1811. J. J. Moore.)

905 24 Oct 1810 B/1/020
Registered by: John Smith
Registered for: Benjamin Frazer
Location: Mil - 6 2 1 21
Based upon the following Army land warrant:

Issued to	*No.*	*Acres*
Frazer, Benj[ami]n, Pvt	402	100

(Note: Gave certificate to Mr. Smith, 22 Jan 1811. J. J. Moore.)

906 24 Oct 1810 B/1/020
Registered by: John Smith
Registered for: Jacob Crevester
Location: Mil - 6 2 1 22
Based upon the following Army land warrant:

Issued to	*No.*	*Acres*
Crevester, Jacob, Pvt	454	100

(Note: Gave certificate to Mr. Smith, 22 Jan 1811. J. J. Moore.)

907 24 Oct 1810 B/1/020
Registered by: John Smith
Registered for: Moses Beeman
Location: Mil - 6 2 1 27
Based upon the following Army land warrant:

Issued to	*No.*	*Acres*
Beeman, Moses, Pvt	455	100

(Note: Gave certificate to Mr. Smith, 22 Jan 1811. J. J. Moore.)

908 28? Oct 1810 B/1/020
Registered by: Joseph Stokely
Registered for: Joseph Stokely
Location: Mil - 2 2 3 3
Mil - 2 2 3 4
Based upon the following Army land warrant:

Issued to	*No.*	*Acres*
Finley, Andrew, Lt	528	200

(Note: Patent receipted for [in] Certificate Book. . . .?)

909 25 Oct 1810 B/1/021
Registered by: Joseph Stokely
Registered for: Joseph Stokely
Location: Mil - 2 2 3 11
Mil - 2 2 3 12
Mil - 2 2 3 7
Based upon the following Army land warrant:

Issued to	*No.*	*Acres*
Chilton, John, Capt	519	300

(Note: Patent receipted for in Certificate Book (No. 324).)

910 11 Dec 1810 B/1/021
Registered by: Peter Mills, Esq.
Registered for: Peter Mills
Location: Mil - 16 6 6 1
Mil - 16 6 6 2
Mil - 7 4 2 4
Mil - 7 4 2 19
Mil - 7 4 2 32
Based upon the following Army land warrant:

Issued to	*No.*	*Acres*
Crane, John, Col	330	500

(Note: Patent sent to Mr. Mills, 16 Mar 1811.)

911 15 Dec 1810 B/1/021
Registered by: Christian Deardorff
Registered for: Slingluff, --, & Fahnestock, --

911 [continued]
Location: Mil - 3 8 4 20
Mil - 3 8 4 16
Mil - 3 8 4 21
Based upon the following Army land warrants:

Issued to	*No.*	*Acres*
Larkin, Covel, Pvt	28	100
Leech, Ebenezer, Cpl	24	100
Sheffield, Charles, Pvt	19	100

(Note: Receipts in Certificate Book.)

912 15 Dec 1810 B/1/021
Registered by: Christian Deardorf
Registered for: Slingluff, --, & Bohn, --
Location: Mil - 3 8 4 3
Mil - 5 9 3 1
Based upon the following Army land warrants:

Issued to	*No.*	*Acres*
Curtis, Jonah, Sgt	25	100
Rogers, John, Sgt	26	100

(Note: Receipts in Certificate Book.)

913 15 Dec 1810 B/1/021
Registered by: Christian Deardorf
Registered for: Bohn, --, & Slingluff, --
Location: Mil - 3 7 1 9
Mil - 3 7 1 19
Mil - 3 7 1 20
Mil - 3 7 1 21
Mil - 5 9 3 6
Mil - 5 9 3 7
Mil - 5 9 3 10
Mil - 5 9 3 11
Based upon the following Army land warrants:

Issued to	*No.*	*Acres*
Snead, Smith, Maj	2056	400
Gilchrist, George, Maj	868	400

(Note: Receipts in Certificate Book.)

914 20 Dec 1810 B/1/021
Registered by: John Davidson
Registered for: Nathan Reed
Location: Mil - 16 8 4 11
Mil - 16 8 4 13
Mil - 16 8 4 14
Based upon the following Army land warrant:

Issued to	*No.*	*Acres*
Reed, Nathan, Capt	522	300

(Note: Capt Davidson received patent.)

915 29 Dec 1810 B/1/021
Registered by: Jona[tha]n Robinson, Sena[to]r
Registered for: Nathaniel Bates
Location: Mil - 3 8 4 19
Based upon the following Army land warrant:

Issued to	*No.*	*Acres*
Bates, Nath[anie]l, Pvt	479	100

(Note: Sent patent 22 Jan 1811 to Mr. Robinson.)

916 29 Dec 1810 B/1/021
Registered by: Joseph Vance, Franklinton [Ohio]
Registered for: [Not stated]
Location: [Not stated]
Based upon the following Army land warrant:

Issued to	*No.*	*Acres*
Mallary, Amos, Soldier	6163	100

917 29 Dec 1810 B/1/021
Registered by: Charles Roberts, Zanesville [Ohio]
Registered for: Artemis Swetland
Location: Mil - 16 6 1 16
Based upon the following Army land warrant:

Issued to	*No.*	*Acres*
Swetland, Luke, Pvt	477	100

(Note: Patent sent to Mr. Stockton, 16 Mar 1811.)

918 29 Dec 1810 B/1/021
Registered by: Charles Roberts, Zanesville [Ohio]
Registered for: Jared Baldwin
Location: Mil - 7 4 2 3
Mil - 7 4 2 20
Mil - 7 4 2 24
Based upon the following Army land warrants:

Issued to	*No.*	*Acres*
Brooks, Thomas, Pvt	30	100
Middleton, Peter, Pvt	31	100
Bostwick, Eben[eze]r, Sgt	32	100

919 31 Jan 1811 B/1/021
Registered by: Peter Mills, Esq.
Registered for: Alexander P[arker] heir
Location: Mil - 7 4 2 21
Mil - 7 4 2 22
Mil - 7 4 2 23
Mil - 7 4 2 31
Mil - 7 4 2 33
Based upon the following Army land warrant:

Issued to	*No.*	*Acres*
Parker, Richard, Col	525	500

(Note: Sent patent to Mr. Mills, 16 Mar 1811.)

920 12 Feb 1811 B/1/021
Registered by: Gen [Thomas] Worthington
Registered for: Amos Stackhouse
Location: Mil - 4 4 3 14
Based upon the following Army land warrant:

Issued to	*No.*	*Acres*
Stackhouse, Amos, Pvt	509	100

(Note: To Department of State, 15 Feb 1811; sent T. Worthington, 21 Feb 1811.)

921 14 Feb 1811 B/1/021
Registered by: W. Helms
Registered for: -- Lin, in trust for the heirs of Dr. Andrew Linn
Location: Mil - 16 7 4 12
Based upon the following Army land warrant:

Issued to	*No.*	*Acres*
Kemble, Nathan, Pvt	536	100

(Note: Sent to Hon. Mr. Helms, 21 Feb 1811.)

922 14 Feb 1811 B/1/021
Registered by: W. Helms
Registered for: John Harding
Location: Mil - 16 7 4 11
Based upon the following Army land warrant:

Issued to	*No.*	*Acres*
Harding, John, Pvt	534	100

(Note: Sent to Hon. Mr. Helms, 21 Feb 1811.)

923 2 Mar 1811 B/1/021
Registered by: Hon. James Cochran
Registered for: Abner Quarles

923 [continued]
Location: Mil - 11 6 1 34
Based upon the following Army land warrant:

Issued to	*No.*	*Acres*
Quarles, Abner, Pvt	548	100

(Note: Sent 2 Mar 1811.)

924 2 Mar 1811 B/1/021
Registered by: Hon. Uri Tracy
Registered for: Hezekiah Tracy
Location: Mil - 11 6 1 37
Mil - 11 6 1 38
Based upon the following Army land warrant:

Issued to	*No.*	*Acres*
Tracy, Hezekiah, Lt	547	200

(Note: 2 Mar [1811] sent Mr. Simmons, Esq., John Moore, per messenger.)

925 2 Mar 1811 B/1/021
Registered by: Hon. D. L? [or S.] Garland
Registered for: Benjamin Hawkins
Location: Mil - 8 9 2 25
Based upon the following Army land warrant:

Issued to	*No.*	*Acres*
Hawkins, Benj[amin] Pvt	552	100

(Note: Sent to Hon David L? Garland, New Glasgow, Amherst County, Virginia, 4 Mar 1811.)

926 9 Mar 1811 B/1/021
Registered by: Hon. Samuel Smith
Registered for: Fielding Barrain? [Barram?]
Location: Mil - 19 7 1 2
Based upon the following Army land warrant:

Issued to	*No.*	*Acres*
Barrain? [Barram?] Fielding, Sgt	551	100

(Note: Patent delivered to Mr. Smith.)

927 15 Mar 1811 B/1/021
Registered by: Ez[ekie]l King for James Riddle
Registered for: [Not stated]
Location: [Not stated]
Based upon the following Army land warrant:

Issued to	*No.*	*Acres*
Mulveny, John, Soldier	10031	100

928 15 Mar 1811 B/1/021
Registered by: Thomas M. Thompson
Registered for: Thomas M. Thompson
Location: Mil - 8 9 2 3
Mil - 8 9 2 4
Mil - 8 9 2 5
Based upon the following Army land warrant:

Issued to	*No.*	*Acres*
Steele, John, Capt	396	300

(Note: Patent sent to Mr. Thompson, 16 Mar 1811.)

929 18 Mar 1811 B/1/021
Registered by: Francis Granger
Registered for: Roger E. Hills
Location: Mil - 8 9 3 6
Mil - 8 9 3 10
Based upon the following Army land warrants:

Issued to	*No.*	*Acres*
Cobb, John, Cpl	537	100
Sawyer, M--h? Sgt	538	100

(Note: Received patent 13 Jan 1812 [signed] T. Granger.)

930 26 Mar 1811 B/1/022
Registered by: -- Johns
Registered for: Abraham Jones
Location: Mil - 7 4 2 34
Based upon the following Army land warrant:

Issued to	*No.*	*Acres*
Moore, John, Soldier	11518	100

(Note: Mr. Johns received patent from Department of State.)

931 5 Apr 1811 B/1/022
Registered by: John F. Mansfield, Esq.
Registered for: William Harris
Location: Mil - 11 6 1 35
Based upon the following Army land warrant:

Issued to	*No.*	*Acres*
Binns, Thomas, Pvt	466	100

(Note: Sent patent to Mr. Mansfield at Cincinnati, 14 Apr 1811.)

932 13 May 1811 B/1/022
Registered by: Chauncy Laurance
Registered for: Rachel Poor
Location: Mil - 16 8 3 3
Mil - 16 8 3 4
Mil - 16 8 3 5
Based upon the following Army land warrant:

Issued to	*No.*	*Acres*
Hutchens, Nath[anie]l, Capt	531	300

(Note: Receipted in Certificate Book.)

933 13 May 1811 B/1/022
Registered by: Chauncy Laurance
Registered for: David Jewett Poor
Location: Mil - 16 7 4 24
Mil - 16 8 3 2
Mil - 16 6 1 3
Based upon the following Army land warrants:

Issued to	*No.*	*Acres*
Clark, David, Pvt	527	100
Fuller, Barzillai, Cpl	529	100
Fuller, Robert, Pvt	530	100

(Note: Receipted in Certificate Book.)

934 1 Jun 1811 B/1/022
Registered by: Charles Bohn
Registered for: Bohn, --, & Slingluff, --
Location: Mil - 3 8 4 31
Based upon the following Army land warrant:

Issued to	*No.*	*Acres*
Lane, Isaac, Pvt	20	100

(Note: Patent sent to Mr. Charles Bohn, Baltimore [Maryland] 7 Aug 1811.)

935 1 Jun 1811 B/1/022
Registered by: Charles Bohn
Registered for: Christian Deardoff
Location: Mil - 3 8 4 18
Based upon the following Army land warrant:

Issued to	*No.*	*Acres*
Willcox, Josiah, Cpl	27	100

(Note: Patent sent to Mr. Charles Bohn, Baltimore [Maryland] 7 Aug 1811.)

936 — 1 Jun 1811 — B/1/022
Registered by: Charles Bohn
Registered for: Bohn, --, & Slingluff, --
Location: Mil - 3 8 4 7
Based upon the following Army land warrant:

Issued to	*No.*	*Acres*
Hopkins, T. F., Pvt	302	100

(Note: Patent sent to Mr. Charles Bohn, Baltimore [Maryland] 7 Aug 1811.)

937 — 17 Jun 1811 — B/1/022
Registered by: Stephen Barlow
Registered for: Ephraim Estep
Location: Mil - 8 9 2 9
Based upon the following Army land warrant:

Issued to	*No.*	*Acres*
Hain, John, Pvt	487	100

(Note: Mr. Barlow received patent.)

938 — 22 Jun 1811 — B/1/022
Registered by: Michael Nourse
Registered for: Perry Evans
Location: Mil - 5 10 4 26
Based upon the following Army land warrant:

Issued to	*No.*	*Acres*
Evans, Perry, Sgt	417	100

(Note: Error corrected: [cites] vol. 3, p. 108 [not otherwise identified].)

939 — 22 Jul 1811 — B/1/022
Registered by: Michael Nourse
Registered for: Samuel Currey
Location: Mil - 10 9 1 2
Based upon the following Army land warrant:

Issued to	*No.*	*Acres*
Currey, Samuel, assignee of John Butler, Soldier	12755	100

940 — 22 Jul 1811 — B/1/022
Registered by: Michael Nourse
Registered for: James Morrison
Location: Mil - 5 10 3 9
Based upon the following Army land warrant:

Issued to	*No.*	*Acres*
Brann, Andrew, Soldier	207	100

941 — 22 Jul 1811 — B/1/022
Registered by: Michael Nourse
Registered for: Samuel H[oey] Smith
Location: Mil - 7 9 2 16
Mil - 7 9 2 18
Mil - 7 9 2 29
Based upon the following Army land warrant:

Issued to	*No.*	*Acres*
Garland, Peter, Capt	524	100

942 — 11 Nov 1811 — B/1/022
Registered by: Charles Roberts
Registered for: Nathan Roberts
Location: Mil - 5 3 3 21
Based upon the following Army land warrant:

Issued to	*No.*	*Acres*
George, William A., Sgt	484	100

(Note: Patent issued 8 Jul 1812. Sent to Mr. Charles Roberts 21 Jul 1812. See his letter of 29 Oct 1811.)

943 — 11 Nov 1811 — B/1/022
Registered by: Charles Roberts
Registered for: Meshick Walker
Location: Mil - 5 3 3 18
Based upon the following Army land warrant:

Issued to	*No.*	*Acres*
Walker, Meshick, Cpl	362	100

(Note: Sent to him, 27 Jan 1812.)

944 — 16 Nov 1811 — B/1/022
Registered by: Michael Nourse
Registered for: Jesse McKinsey
Location: Mil - 4 10 3 1
Based upon the following Army land warrant:

Issued to	*No.*	*Acres*
McKinsey, Jesse, Soldier	11512	100

(Note: Receipted for in Certificate Book.)

945 — 25 Nov 1811 — B/1/022
Registered by: Hon. Jere[mia]h Morrow
Registered for: Samuel Scholl
Location: Mil - 3 8 4 15
Based upon the following Army land warrant:

Issued to	*No.*	*Acres*
Bellows, Elihu, Dragoon	488	100

946 — 25 Nov 1811 — B/1/022
Registered by: Hon. Jere[mia]h Morrow
Registered for: James Parkhill
Location: Mil - 4 10 3 18
Based upon the following Army land warrant:

Issued to	*No.*	*Acres*
Powers, Simeon, Soldier	489	100

947 — 25 Nov 1811 — B/1/022
Registered by: John Bush, Esq.
Registered for: John Bush, Esq.
Location: Mil - 16 6 1 30
Mil - 16 6 1 31
Mil - 16 6 1 32
Based upon the following Army land warrant:

Issued to	*No.*	*Acres*
Bush, John, Capt	196	300

(Note: Receipted for in Certificate Book.)

948 — 2 Dec 1811 — B/1/022
Registered by: Michael Nourse
Registered for: David Cole
Location: Mil - 14 8 1 2
Based upon the following Army land warrant:

Issued to	*No.*	*Acres*
Cole, David, Soldier	6915	100

(Note: Receipted for in Certificate Book.)

949 — 10 Dec 1811 — B/1/022
Registered by: W. Smoot
Registered for: John Wilder
Location: Mil - 17 7 2 16
Mil - 17 7 2 17
Based upon the following Army land warrant:

Issued to	*No.*	*Acres*
King, Elisha, Lt	324	200

(Note: Gave patent to Mr. Smoot, 17 Jul 1812.)

950 -- Dec 1811 B/1/022
Registered by: M[ichael] Nourse
Registered for: James Morrison
Location: Mil - 10 3 4 1
Mil - 10 7 1 26
Mil - 10 7 1 39
Mil - 10 7 1 40
Based upon the following Army land warrants:

Issued to	*No.*	*Acres*
Tennell, George, Sgt	206	100
Willmot [Mott?] William,* Capt	281	300

*Pencilled interlineation: William Mo--?
(Note: M. Nourse received patent certificates.)

951 -- Dec 1811 B/1/022
Registered by: Hon. Jere[mia]h Morrow
Registered for: Obadiah Wells
Location: Mil - 7 4 2 15
Based upon the following Army land warrant:

Issued to	*No.*	*Acres*
Stafford, Thomas, Soldier	469	100

(Note: Sent to Mr. Morrow, 10 Mar 1810 [sic].)

952 1 Feb 1812 B/1/022
Registered by: Hon. -- Jennings
Registered for: Aaron Keeler
Location: Mil - 8 9 7 27
Based upon the following Army land warrant:

Issued to	*No.*	*Acres*
Keeler, Aaron, Ens	1191	150

(Note: [Fifty] acres certificated. To Department of State, 6 Feb; to Mr. Jennings 12 Feb 1812.)

953 1 Feb 1812 B/1/022
Registered by: Hon. -- Jennings
Registered for: William Leggins
Location: Mil - 1 10 1 14
Based upon the following Army land warrant:

Issued to	*No.*	*Acres*
Leggins, William, Soldier	501	100

954 1 Feb 1812 B/1/022
Registered by: Hon. -- Condit
Registered for: J. B. Day
Location: Mil - 15 8 3 14
Based upon the following Army land warrant:

Issued to	*No.*	*Acres*
Day, J. B., assignee of Henry Rick, Soldier	275	100

(Note: To Department of State, 6 Feb; patent to Mr. Condit, 12 Feb 1812.)

955 1 Feb 1812 B/1/022
Registered by: Hon. -- Condit
Registered for: Eli Hull
Location: Mil - 15 8 3 16
Based upon the following Army land warrant:

Issued to	*No.*	*Acres*
Hull, Eli, Soldier	5935	100

(Note: To Department of State, 6 Feb; patent to Mr. Condit, 12 Feb 1812.)

956 1 Feb 1812 B/1/022
Registered by: Hon. [Jeremiah?] Morrow
Registered for: Eli Baldwin
Location: Mil - 4 10 1 5
Based upon the following Army land warrant:

Issued to	*No.*	*Acres*
Baldwin, Eli, assignee of the heirs of Reuben Carter	571	100

(Note: Sent patent to Mr. Morrison, . . .? 1812.)

957 15 Feb 1812 B/1/023
Registered by: -- Campbell, Senator [from] Ohio
Registered for: Henry Bedinger
Location: Mil - 7 9 2 30
Based upon the following Army land warrant:

Issued to	*No.*	*Acres*
Imhoff, Fred, Soldier	492	100

(Note: Sent to Dr. Campbell, 27 Feb 1812.)

958 17 Feb 1812 B/1/023
Registered by: William Simmons
Registered for: Allen Neilson
Location: Mil - 11 6 1 36
Based upon the following Army land warrant:

Issued to	*No.*	*Acres*
Neilson, Allen, Soldier	7547	100

(Note: Patent issued, 22 Feb 1812.)

959 13 Feb 1812 B/1/023
Registered by: -- Vance
Registered for: John? R. Stokes
Location: Mil - 16 6 1 33
Mil - 16 6 1 34
Mil - 16 6 1 35
Based upon the following Army land warrant:

Issued to	*No.*	*Acres*
Stokes, John, Capt	526	300

(Note: The warrants are entered some pages back. Patent issued, 25 Feb 1812.)

960 13 Feb 1812 B/1/023
Registered by: -- Vance
Registered for: Reuben Carpenter
Location: Mil - 16 6 1 37
Based upon the following Army land warrant:

Issued to	*No.*	*Acres*
Flanders, Jacob, Soldier	449	100

(Note: The warrants are entered some pages back. Patent issued, 25 Feb 1812.)

961 13 Feb 1812 B/1/023
Registered by: -- Vance
Registered for: James Swenorton
Location: Mil - 16 6 1 38
Based upon the following Army land warrant:

Issued to	*No.*	*Acres*
Griswold, Samuel, Soldier	336	100

(Note: The warrants are entered some pages back. Patent issued, 25 Feb 1812.)

962 13 Feb 1812 B/1/023
Registered by: -- Vance
Registered for: Jacob Poe
Location: Mil - 17 7 1 7W
Mil - 16 6 1 15
Based upon the following Authorizations:

962 [continued]

Issued to	*No.*	*Acres*
Baylis, N. J., Ens	26*	50
Baylis, N. J., Ens	491**	100

*Register's certificate.
**Army land warrant.
(Note: The warrants are entered some pages back. Patent issued, 25 Feb 1812.)

963 22 Feb 1812 B/1/023
Registered by: -- Sheldon
Registered for: Noah Linsley,
Location: Mil - 5 3? 3 1
Mil - 5 3? 3 2
Mil - 5 3? 3 3
Mil - 5 3? 3 15
Based upon the following Army land warrant:

Issued to	*No.*	*Acres*
Falkner, Ralph, Maj	514	400

(Note: Mr. Sheldon received patent.)

964 22 Feb 1812 B/1/023
Registered by: M[ichael] Nourse
Registered for: Slingluff, --, & Fahnestock, D.
Location: Mil - 3 8 4 28
Mil - 3 7 1 6
Mil - 3 7 1 30
Based upon the following Army land warrant:

Issued to	*No.*	*Acres*
Maynard, Jonathan, Capt	1351	300

(Note: Gave patent to Mr. Nourse, 21 Mar 1812; [latter two patents] to Mr. Roberts, 23 Mar 1812.)

965 22 Feb 1812 B/1/023
Registered by: Jon[atha]n Roberts
Registered for: Matthew Knox
Location: Mil - 3 7 1 4
Mil - 3 7 1 5
Based upon the following Army land warrant:

Issued to	*No.*	*Acres*
Knox, Matthew, Lt	508	200

(Note: Sent to Mr. Roberts, 23 Mar 1812.)

966 11 Mar 1812 B/1/023
Registered by: M[ichael] Nourse
Registered for: Lloyd Talbott
Location: Mil - 5 3 3 4
Based upon the following Army land warrant:

Issued to	*No.*	*Acres*
Bennet, Fred[eric]k, Soldier	10963	100

(Note: Gave this patent to M. N[ourse] 21 Mar 1812.)

967 24 Mar 1812 B/1/023
Registered by: Hon. Dr. -- Mitchell
Registered for: Garret Sickles
Location: Mil - 11 6 1 21
Based upon the following Army land warrant:

Issued to	*No.*	*Acres*
[Not stated]	452	100

(Note: Patent issued by General Land Office, 9 Jul 1812 & sent to Mr. Sickles, 17 Jul 1812.)

968 10 Apr 1812 B/1/023
Registered by: Hon. Asa Fitch
Registered for: Sally Ann Faulkner
Location: Mil - 2 10 2 12
Mil - 2 10 2 18
Based upon the following Army land warrant:

Issued to	*No.*	*Acres*
Drake, Joshua, Lt	579	200

(Note: To Hon. Mr. Fitch, 15 Apr 1812.)

969 14 Apr 1812 B/1/023
Registered by: Nath[anie]l Frye, Esq.
Registered for: Jacob Swiger & Jacob Rolf
Location: Mil - 6 2 1 38
Based upon the following Army land warrant:

Issued to	*No.*	*Acres*
Smith, Weeden, Pvt	523	100

(Note: Department of State, 20 Apr 1812; sent patent to Mr. Frye, 29 Jul 1812.)

970 14 Apr 1812 B/1/023
Registered by: Nath[anie]l Frye, Esq.
Registered for: Jonas Roupe
Location: Mil - 5 3 3 5
Based upon the following Army land warrant:

Issued to	*No.*	*Acres*
McCann, Daniel, Pvt	9959	100

(Note: Department of State, 20 Apr 1812; sent patent to Mr. Frye, 29 Jul 1812.)

971 14 Apr 1812 B/1/023
Registered by: Nath[anie]l Frye, Esq.
Registered for: Daniel Welker
Location: Mil - 5 3 3 7
Based upon the following Army land warrant:

Issued to	*No.*	*Acres*
Welker, Daniel, Pvt	450	100

(Note: Department of State, 20 Apr 1812; sent patent to Mr. Frye, 29 Jul 1812.)

972 14 Apr 1812 B/1/023
Registered by: Nath[anie]l Frye, Esq.
Registered for: John Putnam
Location: Mil - 5 3 3 8
Based upon the following Army land warrant:

Issued to	*No.*	*Acres*
Hull, Zephaniah, Pvt	521	100

(Note: Department of State, 20 Apr 1812; sent patent to Mr. Frye, 29 Jul 1812.)

973 15 Apr 1812 B/1/023
Registered by: Hon. John Davenport
Registered for: Seely Scoffield
Location: Mil - 5 3 3 12
Based upon the following Army land warrant:

Issued to	*No.*	*Acres*
Scoffield, Seely, Pvt	6489	100

(Note: Issued 24 Mar 1813, see letter to him of this day. Sent to John Matthew [Mathews?].)

974 20 May 1812 B/1/023
Registered by: Joseph Vance of Franklinton, Ohio
Registered for: Andrew Wallace
Location: [Not stated]
Based upon the following Army land warrant:

Issued to	*No.*	*Acres*
Wallace, Andrew, Capt	543	[300]

975 23 May 1812 B/1/023
Registered by: Hon. Gen. [Thomas?] Worthington
Registered for: [Not stated]
Location: [Not stated]
Based upon the following Army land warrant:

Issued to	*No.*	*Acres*
Foster, John Hardin, Ens	589	150

976 11 Jun 1812 B/1/023
Registered by: Michael Nourse
Registered for: Samuel H[oey] Smith
Location: Mil - 7 9 2 34
Mil - 7 9 2 36
Based upon the following Army land warrant:

Issued to	*No.*	*Acres*
Pears, John, Soldier	7606	100
Moody, George, Soldier	4645	100

(Note: Gave patent to M. Nourse, 21 Jul 1812.)

977 15 Jun 1812 B/1/023
Registered by: Michael Nourse
Registered for: Slingluff, --, & Fahnestock, --
Location: Mil - 1 8 3 3
Mil - 3 8 4 24
Based upon the following Army land warrant:

Issued to	*No.*	*Acres*
Gadsden, Thomas, Capt	470	300

[Entry incomplete; see serial entry 980 below.]

978 23 Jun 1812 B/1/023
Registered by: R. Johns
Registered for: Dennis? Lackland
Location: Mil - 4 10 3 15
Based upon the following Army land warrant:

Issued to	*No.*	*Acres*
Denoon, John, Soldier	11135	100

(Note: Patented 2 Jul 1812. Sent patent to Mr. Johns, 20 Jul 1812.)

979 8 Jul 1812 B/1/023
Registered by: Charles Roberts
Registered for: Elias? Green
Location: Mil - 5 3 3 27
Mil - 5 3 3 28
Based upon the following Army land warrant:

Issued to	*No.*	*Acres*
Brown, David, Pvt	461	100
Cary, John, Pvt	598	100

(Note: Patent sent to Mr. Roberts, 21 Jul 1812.)

980 8 Jul 1812 B/1/023
Registered by: Michael Nourse
Registered for: Slingluff, --, & Fahnestock, D.
Location: Mil - 1 8 3 3
Mil - 3 8 4 24
Mil - 3 8 4 29
Mil - 3 8 4 30
Based upon the following Army land warrants:

Issued to	*No.*	*Acres*
Gadsden, Thomas, Capt	470	300
Turner, Elisha, Pvt	445	100

(Note: Patents delivered to Mr. Nourse.)

981 20 Jul 1812 B/1/023
Registered by: Michael Nourse
Registered for: --? Akin & Huff, Phillip
Location: Mil - 1 1 3 10
Based upon the following Army land warrant:

Issued to	*No.*	*Acres*
McCurdy, James, Pvt	9877	100

(Note: Gave the patent to Mr. Nourse, 21 Jul 1812.)

982 -- Jul 1812 B/1/024
Registered by: Charles Roberts, Zanesville, Ohio
Registered for: Abner Wade
Location: Mil - 6 2 1 3
Mil - 6 2 1 4
Mil - 6 2 1 5
Based upon the following Army land warrant:

Issued to	*No.*	*Acres*
Durkee, Robert, Capt	432	300

(Note: Sent patent to Mr. Roberts, 21 Jul 1812.)

983 27 Jul 1812 B/1/024
Registered by: Joseph Copp
Registered for: Joseph Copp
Location: Mil - 3 8 4 33
Based upon the following Army land warrant:

Issued to	*No.*	*Acres*
Copp, Joseph, Drum Major	569	100

(Note: Sent patent to Mr. Copp, 29 Jul 1812.)

984 10 Aug 1812 B/1/024
Registered by: G. Bumford
Registered for: Philip Price
Location: Mil - 11 6 1 28
Mil - 11 6 1 29
Based upon the following Army land warrant:

Issued to	*No.*	*Acres*
Price, Philip, [Lt?]	1654	200

(Note: 10 Aug 1812 sent to G. Bumford. [This entire entry is a pencilled interlineation in the source register, apparently made at a later date.])

985 2 Oct 1812 B/1/024
Registered by: William James
Registered for: Casper Shee
Location: Mil - 6 10 4 10
Based upon the following Army land warrant:

Issued to	*No.*	*Acres*
Shee, Casper, Pvt	10440	100

986 2 Oct 1812 B/1/024
Registered by: William James
Registered for: Francis Smith
Location: Mil - 6 10 4 14
Based upon the following Army land warrant:

Issued to	*No.*	*Acres*
Smith, Francis, Pvt	10388	100

987 2 Oct 1812 B/1/024
Registered by: William James
Registered for: Thomas Horsefield
Location: Mil - 6 10 4 15
Based upon the following Army land warrant:

Issued to	*No.*	*Acres*
Horsefield, Thomas, Pvt	12180	100

988 16 Nov 1812 B/1/024

988 [continued]
Registered by: By letter of John Jonas
Registered for: John Jonas
Location: Mil - 11 6 1 16
Mil - 11 6 1 40
Based upon the following Army land warrants:

Issued to	*No.*	*Acres*
Gilman, Joseph, Sgt	596	100
Jonas, John, Pvt	593	100

(Note: Issued 16 Nov. Sent by Mr. Tiffin to J. Jonas.)

989 20 Nov 1812 B/1/024
Registered by: Benjamin Chesney, alias Chesnut
Registered for: Benjamin Chesney
Location: Mil - 11 6 1 17
Based upon the following Army land warrant:

Issued to	*No.*	*Acres*
Chesney, alias Chesnut, Benjamin, Pvt	598	100

(Note: 20 Nov delivered patent to B. Chesney, per receipt in vol. 3, p. 154 [not otherwise identified].)

990 25 Nov 1812 B/1/024
Registered by: Jacob Shetter? [Shelter? Shetler?]
Registered for: Michael Shetter?
Location: Mil - 2 8 4 20
Based upon the following Army land warrant:

Issued to	*No.*	*Acres*
Roybecker? John, Pvt	400	100

(Note: 25 Nov delivered patent to Jacob Shetler? per receipt, vol. 3, p. 155 [not otherwise identified].)

991 29 Nov 1812 B/1/024
Registered by: Hon. Col -- Stewart
Registered for: William Halinsdoff
Location: Mil - 11 6 1 1
Based upon the following Army land warrant:

Issued to	*No.*	*Acres*
Halinsdoff, William, Pvt	599	100

(Note: 29 Nov sent to Col Stewart.)

992 8 Dec 1812 B/1/024
Registered by: Edward Tiffin, Esq.
Registered for: Jesse Slingluff
Location: Mil - 3 10 2 10
Based upon the following Army land warrant:

Issued to	*No.*	*Acres*
Hoffman, George, Pvt	13180	100

(Note: 8 Dec patent delivered to E. Tiffin, Esq.)

993 8 Dec 1812 B/1/024
Registered by: Edward Tiffin, Esq.
Registered for: Fahnestock, --, & Slingluff, J.
Location: Mil - 1 8 4 36
Mil - 4 10 1 2
Mil - 1 8 4 4
Mil - 1 8 4 3
Based upon the following Army land warrants:

Issued to	*No.*	*Acres*
Hollis, Samuel, Pvt	584	100
Drew, Samuel, Cpl	582	100
Lawrance, Daniel, Sgt	585	100
Howard, Thomas, Pvt	583	100

994 8 Dec 1812 B/1/024
Registered by: William Simmon, Esq.
Registered for: J[ohn?] Woodruff
Location: Mil - 11 6 1 15
Based upon the following Army land warrant:

Issued to	*No.*	*Acres*
Woodruff, J[ohn?] Pvt	600	100

(Note: 8 Dec sent W. Simmons (by his messenger) Received patent for J. Woodruff.)

995 10 Dec 1812 B/1/024
Registered by: J. L. Lawrence
Registered for: Lewis Wartman? [Wortman?]
Location: Mil - 11 6 1 2
Based upon the following Army land warrant:

Issued to	*No.*	*Acres*
Freedon, Dick, Pvt	590	100

(Note: 10 Dec received patent for L. Wartman [signed] J. L. Lawrence.)

996 16 Dec 1812 B/1/024
Registered by: Hon. William Jennings
Registered for: Zaccheus Biggs
Location: Mil - 1 8 2 3E*
Based upon the following Army land warrant:

Issued to	*No.*	*Acres*
Smith, Jos[eph] Tim[othy?] Cornet	22	[150]

*50-acre lot.
(Note: Delivered patent to Mr. Jennings.)

997 23 Dec 1812 B/1/024
Registered by: William Thornton
Registered for: William Thornton
Location: Mil - 11 6 1 18
Based upon the following Army land warrant:

Issued to	*No.*	*Acres*
Thornton, William, Pvt	602	100

(Note: 23 Dec delivered patent to William Thornton.)

998 29 Dec 1812 B/1/024
Registered by: Thomas L. Birch
Registered for: John Johnson
Location: Mil - 4 10 3 16
Based upon the following Army land warrant:

Issued to	*No.*	*Acres*
Murphy, John, Pvt	564	100

(Note: 29 Dec delivered patent to Mr. Birch.)

999 29 Dec 1812 B/1/024
Registered by: Thomas L. Birch
Registered for: Legal heirs of Francis Miller
Location: Mil - 4 10 3 6
Based upon the following Army land warrant:

Issued to	*No.*	*Acres*
Miller, Francis, deceased, Sgt	603	100

(Note: 29 Dec delivered patent to Mr. Birch.)

1000 29 Dec 1812 B/1/024
Registered by: Nathan Hambrick*
Registered for: Heirs of David Hambric*
Location: Mil - 11 6 1 14
Based upon the following Army land warrant:

1000 [continued]
Issued to — *No.* — *Acres*
Hambric? [Hambrie?]
David, heirs of, Pvt 604 100
*So spelled.
(Note: 29 Dec delivered patent to N. Hambric.*)

1001 20 Jan 1813 B/1/024
Registered by: Henry Northup
Registered for: Henry Northup
Location: Mil - 5 3 3 31
Based upon the following Army land warrant:
Issued to — *No.* — *Acres*
Minsell? [Hinsell?]
Frederick, Pvt 544 100
(Note: 21 Jan 1813 delivered patent to patentee same day.)

1002 23 Jan 1813 B/1/024
Registered by: Hon. Mr. -- Little
Registered for: Slingluff, --, & Fahnestock, --
Location: Mil - 4 10 1 3
Based upon the following Army land warrant:
Issued to — *No.* — *Acres*
Richmond, Benjamin, Ens 596 100 of 150
(Note: Sent to Hon. Mr. Little, 25 Jan 1813.)

1003 23 Jan 1813 B/1/024
Registered by: Hon. Mr. -- Little
Registered for: Christian Deardorff
Location: Mil - 1 8 2 7W*
Based upon the following Army land warrant:
Issued to — *No.* — *Acres*
Richmond, Benjamin, Ens 596 [150]
*50-acre lot.
(Note: Sent to Hon. Mr. Little, 25 Jan 1813.)

1004 17 Dec 1812* B/1/024
Registered by: John Kerr
Registered for: Joseph Kerr
Location: Mil - 17 7 4 25
Based upon the following Army land warrant:
Issued to — *No.* — *Acres*
Wilson, David, heir at law of M. Wilson, Pvt 482 100
*Per letter of [this date].
(Note: Sent to John Kerr, 26 Jan 1813.)

1005 17 Dec 1812* B/1/024
Registered by: John Kerr
Registered for: John Kerr
Location: Mil - 17 7 1 4W**
Based upon the following Army land warrant:
Issued to — *No.* — *Acres*
Foster, Hardin, Ens 589 [150]
*Per letter of [this date].
**50-acre lot.
(Note: Sent to John Kerr, 26 Jan 1813.)

1006 4 Feb 1813 B/1/024
Registered by: Mr. -- Johnes [also Johns]
Registered for: Joseph Cross
Location: Mil - 16 6 1 4
Mil - 16 6 1 5
Based upon the following Army land warrant:
Issued to — *No.* — *Acres*
Cross, Joseph, Lt 311 200
(Note: 4 Feb delivered to Mr. Johns, per receipt received.)

1007 26 Feb 1813 B/1/024
Registered by: Nathaniel Frye, Junior
Registered for: John Wilkins
Location: Mil - 10 1 2 36
Based upon the following Army land warrant:
Issued to — *No.* — *Acres*
Caldwell, Thomas, Pvt 9131 100
(Note: 27 Feb sent to Mr. Frye, per letter of this date.)

1008 3 Mar 1813 B/1/025
Registered by: F. Tschiffely, by request of William Simmons, Esq.
Registered for: George Hill
Location: Mil - 11 6 1 13
Based upon the following Army land warrant:
Issued to — *No.* — *Acres*
Hill, George, Pvt 614 100
(Note: Sent to Mr. Simmons, per receipt in Record Book.)

1009 8 Mar 1813 B/1/025
Registered by: Michael Nourse
Registered for: Henry Northup
Location: Mil - 5 3 3 6
Mil - 5 3 3 11
Mil - 5 3 3 30
Based upon the following Army land warrant:
Issued to — *No.* — *Acres*
Smith, Alex[ande]r, Surgeon's Mate 2052 300
(Note: Delivered to H. Northup, per receipt.)

1010 1 Jun 1813 B/1/025
Registered by: Peter Mills
Registered for: Heirs of Edward Antill [Antell?]
Location: Mil - 16 7 2 26
Mil - 16 7 2 27
Mil - 16 7 2 28
Mil - 16 7 2 39
Mil - 17 7 1 38E*
Based upon the following Army land warrant:
Issued to — *No.* — *Acres*
Antell? [Antill?] Edward, LtCol 67 450
*50-acre lot.
(Note: Delivered to Mr. Mills, 28 Jun [1813].)

1011 8 Jun 1813 B/1/025
Registered by: Michael Nourse
Registered for: Henry Northup
Location: Mil - 5 3 3 29
Based upon the following Army land warrant:
Issued to — *No.* — *Acres*
Francis, Alexander, Pvt 11206 100
(Note: Delivered to Michael Nourse.)

1012 10 Jun 1813 B/1/025
Registered by: Hon. William Findley
Registered for: James Brady
Location: Mil - 15 1 3 21
Based upon the following Army land warrant:

1012 [continued]

Issued to | *No.* | *Acres*
Heny, David, Pvt 427 100
(Note: Delivered to E. Tiffin, Esq. [pencilled notation: "Error"].)

1013 24 Jun 1813 B/1/025
Registered by: Reasin Beall
Registered for: Joseph H. Larwill? [Sarwill?]
Location: Mil - 7 9 2 7
Mil - 7 9 2 8
Based upon the following Army land warrant:
Issued to *No.* *Acres*
McPherson, Mark, Lt 481 200
(Note: Delivered to Reasin Beall.)

1014 10 Jul 1813 B/1/025
Registered by: Mr. L? [S?] Farrow
Registered for: John Rochell? [Rockell?]
Location: Mil - 6 2 1 9
Mil - 6 2 1 10
Mil - 6 2 1 23
Based upon the following Army land warrant:
Issued to *No.* *Acres*
Rochell? [Rockell?] John, Capt 2700 100
(Note: Delivered to Mr. Farrow, per receipt.)

1015 27 Jun 1813 B/1/025
Registered by: Hon. Mr. -- Lacock
Registered for: M. Brannon's heirs
Location: Mil - 5 3 3 32
Based upon the following Army land warrant:
Issued to *No.* *Acres*
Brannon, Michael, Pvt 9072 100
(Note: Sent to Mr. Lacock, per letter of 28 Jul 1813.)

1016 27 Jul 1813 B/1/025
Registered by: Hon. Mr. -- Lacock
Registered for: John Lawrence
Location: Mil - 16 8 3 1
Based upon the following Army land warrant:
Issued to *No.* *Acres*
McEllery, Hugh, Pvt 393 100
(Note: Sent to Mr. Lacock, per letter of 28 Jul 1813.)

1017 13 Aug 1813 B/1/025
Registered by: Michael Nourse
Registered for: Shroyer, --, & Benter, --
Location: Mil - 5 3 3 14
Based upon the following Army land warrant:
Issued to *No.* *Acres*
Dyce, alias Dins, George, Pvt 618 100
(Note: 1 Sep delivered to Mr. Nourse.)

1018 11 Jan 1814 B/1/025
Registered by: Hon. William Piper
Registered for: McGlaughlin, --, & Smith, --
Location: Mil - 14 8 3 18
Based upon the following Army land warrant:
Issued to *No.* *Acres*
McGlaughlin, Charles, Pvt 472 100
(Note: Sent to Hon. William Piper.)

1019 13 Jan 1814 B/1/025
Registered by: Christian Deardorff
Registered for: Bohn, --, & Slingluff, --
Location: Mil - 5 10 4 15
Mil - 2 8 4 *
Based upon the following Army land warrant:
Issued to *No.* *Acres*
Jenkins, John, Lt 448 200
*. . . plot not numbered, containing 44.75 acres.
(Note: Delivered to Mr. Deardorff.)

1020 31 Jan 1814 B/1/025
Registered by: Michael Nourse
Registered for: William Robinson, Junior
Location: Mil - 10 1 2 11
Mil - 10 1 2 12
Based upon the following Army land warrant:
Issued to *No.* *Acres*
Holt, James, Lt 453 200
(Note: Delivered to Mr. Nourse.)

1021 3 Feb 1814 B/1/025
Registered by: Hon. Reasin Beall
Registered for: Samuel H. Smith
Location: Mil - 7 9 2 35
Based upon the following Army land warrant:
Issued to *No.* *Acres*
Jackson, Joseph, Pvt 550 100
(Note: Sent to Hon. M. R. Beall.)

1022 28 Feb 1814 B/1/025
Registered by: Hezekiah Carr
Registered for: Hezekiah Carr
Location: Mil - 6 2 1 35
Based upon the following Army land warrant:
Issued to *No.* *Acres*
Carr, Hezekiah, Drummer 563 100
(Note: Delivered to H. Carr.)

1023 29 Mar 1814 B/1/025
Registered by: John Gardiner
Registered for: Heirs or representatives of G. Mariner
Location: Mil - 1 1 3 1
Based upon the following Army land warrant:
Issued to *No.* *Acres*
Mariner, Gilbert, Pvt 10828 100
(Note: Delivered to Mr. Tiffin, Esq.)

1024 6 Apr 1814 B/1/025
Registered by: John Gardiner
Registered for: Samuel H. Smith
Location: Mil - 7 9 2 27
Based upon the following Army land warrant:
Issued to *No.* *Acres*
Brooks, Thomas, Pvt 6795 100
(Note: Sent Hon. R. Beall.)

1025 11 Apr 1814 B/1/025
Registered by: John Gardiner
Registered for: Ephraim Thayer
Location: Mil - 6 2 1 36
Mil - 6 2 1 39
Based upon the following Army land warrant:
Issued to *No.* *Acres*

1025 [continued]
Thayer, Barth[olome]w, Lt 601 200
(Note: Sent by mail to the patentee.)

1026 27 Apr 1814 B/1/025
Registered by: William Marsh
Registered for: William Marsh
Location: Mil - 8 9 3 23
Based upon the following Army land warrant:
Issued to *No.* *Acres*
Stewart, Charles, Pvt 457 100
(Note: Delivered to patentee, per receipt.)

1027 6 Jun 1814 B/1/025
Registered by: Christian Deardorff
Registered for: David Foreman
Location: Mil - 1 8 4 26
Based upon the following Army land warrant:
Issued to *No.* *Acres*
Bowan, Henry, Cpl 10867 100
(Note: Delivered to Mr. Deardorff, per receipt.)

1028 6 Jun 1814 B/1/025
Registered by: I? C. Gist
Registered for: Heirs or representatives of M. Gist, deceased
Location: Mil - 11 8 1 28
Mil - 11 8 1 29
Mil - 11 8 1 30
Mil - 11 8 1 36
Mil - 11 8 1 37
Mil - 11 9 4 1
Mil - 11 9 4 2
Mil - 11 9 4 12
Mil - 1 8 2 2E*
Based upon the following Army land warrant:
Issued to *No.* *Acres*
Gist, Mordecai, BrigGen 850** 850
*50-acre lot.
**So shown, but could be in error because it is the same as the acreage.
(Note: Sent to Independent Gist, Esq., Emmitsburg, Frederick County, Maryland.)

1029 24 Jun 1814 B/1/025
Registered by: Edward Tiffin, Esq.
Registered for: J. G. Jackson
Location: Mil - 8 4 3 26
Mil - 8 4 3 36
Based upon the following Army land warrant:
Issued to *No.* *Acres*
Ransom, Samuel, Capt* 408 200
*So shown; however, a captaincy would have entitled him to 300 acres, rather than the 200 located above.
(Note: Sent to J. G. Jackson.)

1030 8 Aug 1814 B/1/025
Registered by: John Gardiner*
Registered for: John Babcock *et al*
Location: Mil - 7 9 2 13
Based upon the following Army land warrant:
Issued to *No.* *Acres*
Gardner* Sharper, Pvt 619 100
*So spelled.
(Note: Sent to patentee, 8 Aug 1814.)

1031 17 Aug 1814 B/1/025
Registered by: Michael Nourse
Registered for: Samuel H. Smith
Location: Mil - 10 9 1 1
Based upon the following Army land warrant:
Issued to *No.* *Acres*
Bennet, Henry, Pvt 6836 100
(Note: Delivered to Michael Nourse.)

1032 18 Aug 1814 B/1/025
Registered by: Michael Nourse
Registered for: James Alexander
Location: Mil - 6 2 1 34
Based upon the following Army land warrant:
Issued to *No.* *Acres*
Mee, Thomas, Pvt 164 100
(Note: Delivered to Michael Nourse.)

1033 18 Aug 1814 B/1/025
Registered by: Michael Nourse
Registered for: James Miller
Location: Mil - 5 3 3 22
Based upon the following Army land warrant:
Issued to *No.* *Acres*
Dancy? [Deney?] Bazel,
Pvt 161 100
(Note: Delivered to Michael Nourse.)

1034 18 Aug 1814 B/1/026
Registered by: Michael Nourse
Registered for: James Miller
Location: Mil - 5 3 3 19
Based upon the following Army land warrant:
Issued to *No.* *Acres*
Boice, George, Pvt 163 100
(Note: Delivered to Michael Nourse.)

1035* -- Sep 1814 B/1/026
Registered by: Tim[oth]y Risley
Registered for: Tim[oth]y Risley
Location: Mil - 15 2 2 26
Based upon the following Army land warrant:
Issued to *No.* *Acres*
Sherewood? [Sherwood?]
Zach[ariah] Pvt 467 100
*This entire entry crossed out in source register.

1036* -- Sep 1814 B/1/026
Registered by: Benjamin Hough
Registered for: William Wickersham
Location: Mil - 13 8 2 13
Based upon the following Army land warrant:
Issued to *No.* *Acres*
Unthank, --, assignee of
Quillan, --, Pvt 392 100
(Note: Sent by mail same day.)
*This entire entry crossed out in source register.

1037 10 Oct 1814 B/1/026
Registered by: Michael Nourse
Registered for: Henry Northup
Location: Mil - 7 4 2 2
Based upon the following Army land warrant:

1037 [continued]

Issued to	*No.*	*Acres*
Shovel, James, deceased, Pvt	636	100

(Note: Delivered to Michael Nourse.)

1038 10 Oct 1814 B/1/026
Registered by: William B. Randolph
Registered for: Henry Northup
Location: Mil - 6 2 1 40
Based upon the following Army land warrant:

Issued to	*No.*	*Acres*
McGee, James, Pvt	10840	100

(Note: Delivered to Michael Nourse.)

1039 16 Oct 1814 B/1/026
Registered by: John Gardiner
Registered for: John Vain? [Pain?]
Location: Mil - 16 6 1 17
Mil - 16 6 1 18
Based upon the following Army land warrants:

Issued to	*No.*	*Acres*
Callin, Phineas, Pvt	545	100
Hoyl? [Floyd?] Jared, Pvt	5991	100

(Note: 28 Nov 1814 sent to B[enjamin] Hough.)

1040 16 Oct 1814 B/1/026
Registered by: Hon. James Kilbourn
Registered for: James Holmes
Location: Mil - 10 1 2 30
Based upon the following Army land warrant:

Issued to	*No.*	*Acres*
Jenkins, Enoch, Pvt	332	100

(Note: Delivered to Mr. J. Kilbourn.)

1041 22 Dec 1814 B/1/026
Registered by: Hon. James Kilbourn
Registered for: William Stanbery
Location: Mil - 10 1 2 26
Mil - 10 1 2 29
Mil - 10 1 2 37
Based upon the following Army land warrant:

Issued to	*No.*	*Acres*
Dobson, Henry, Capt	592	300

(Note: Delivered to Mr. J. Kilbourn.)

1042 31 Dec 1814 B/1/026
Registered by: Michael Nourse
Registered for: James Miller
Location: Mil - 6 2 1 28
Based upon the following Army land warrant:

Issued to	*No.*	*Acres*
McAway, Christ[ophe]r, Pvt	162	100

(Note: Delivered to Michael Nourse.)

1043 31 Dec 1814 B/1/026
Registered by: Michael Nourse
Registered for: James Alexander
Location: Mil - 5 3 3 20
Based upon the following Army land warrant:

Issued to	*No.*	*Acres*
Jones, Philip, Pvt	165	100

(Note: Delivered to Michael Nourse.)

1044 23 Jan 1815 B/1/026
Registered by: And[rew] Ellison
Registered for: Isaac Edginton
Location: Mil - 6 10 4 20
Based upon the following Army land warrant:

Issued to	*No.*	*Acres*
Edginton, Isaac, Pvt	11998	100

(Note: Delivered to And[rew] Ellison, 26 Jan.)

1045 23 Jan 1815 B/1/026
Registered by: And[rew] Ellison
Registered for: Robert Blair
Location: Mil - 16 7 2 4
Based upon the following Army land warrant:

Issued to	*No.*	*Acres*
Cottle, Jedediah, Pvt	500	100

(Note: Delivered to Joseph Vance.)

1046 23 Jan 1815 B/1/026
Registered by: And[rew] Ellison
Registered for: Michael Baker
Location: Mil - 16 7 2 3
Based upon the following Army land warrant:

Issued to	*No.*	*Acres*
Baker, Michael, Pvt	616	100

(Note: Delivered to Joseph Vance.)

1047 26 Jan 1815 B/1/026
Registered by: Hon. Mr. -- Creighton, Junior
Registered for: William Sheppard
Location: Mil - 10 1 2 39
Based upon the following Army land warrant:

Issued to	*No.*	*Acres*
Sheppard, William, Pvt	566	100

(Note: Sent to Hon. Mr. Creighton.)

1048 26 Jan 1815 B/1/026
Registered by: Hon. Mr. -- Creighton, Junior
Registered for: George Adams
Location: Mil - 10 1 2 38
Based upon the following Army land warrant:

Issued to	*No.*	*Acres*
Adams, George, Drummer	8911	100

(Note: Sent to Hon. Mr. Creighton.)

1049 6 Feb 1815 B/1/026
Registered by: Joseph Vance
Registered for: John Ruff
Location: Mil - 16 7 2 1
Mil - 16 7 2 2
Mil - 16 7 2 14
Mil - 16 7 2 5
Mil - 16 7 2 6
Mil - 16 7 2 7
Based upon the following Army land warrants:

Issued to	*No.*	*Acres*
Wallace, Andrew, Capt	543	300
Wallace, Adam, Capt	542	300

(Note: Sent to John Ruff by mail, 28 Mar 1815.)

1050 6 Feb 1815 B/1/026
Registered by: Joseph Vance
Registered for: John Halfpenny
Location: Mil - 16 7 2 8
Based upon the following Army land warrant:

1050 [continued]

Issued to	*No.*	*Acres*
Halfpenny, John, Pvt	633	100

(Note: Sent Hon. William Creighton, Junior.)

1051* 6 Feb 1815 B/1/026
Registered by: Joseph Vance
Registered for: John Burgess
Location: Mil - 16 6 1 39
Based upon the following Army land warrant:

Issued to	*No.*	*Acres*
Brabston, William, Pvt	180	100

(Note: "No? patent issued, see . . .? [Mil - 18 7 2 13].)
*This entire entry crossed out in source register.

1052 8 Feb 1815 B/1/026
Registered by: Joseph Vance
Registered for: George Volts? [Votts?]
Location: Mil - 10 1 2 1
Mil - 10 1 2 2
Mil - 10 1 2 3
Based upon the following Army land warrant:

Issued to	*No.*	*Acres*
Volts? [Votts?] Joseph, Capt	612	300

(Note: Sent to Hon. W. Creighton, Junior.)

1053 15 Feb 1815 B/1/026
Registered by: Hon. E. Goldsborough
Registered for: Edward Neil Cox
Location: Mil - 8 5 1 30
Mil - 8 5 1 31
Mil - 8 5 1 35
Based upon the following Army land warrant:

Issued to	*No.*	*Acres*
Cox, Daniel V? [or P?] Capt	532	300

(Note: Sent to Hon. E. Goldsborough.)

1054 28 Feb 1815 B/1/026
Registered by: John Coyle
Registered for: William Smith
Location: Mil - 17 7 1 2E*
Based upon the following Army land warrant:

Issued to	*No.*	*Acres*
Hait, Joseph [Lt?]Col	946**	[450]

*50-acre lot.
**Part thereof.
(Note: Delivered to Mr. John Coyle.)

1055 25 Mar 1815 B/1/026
Registered by: Abraham Shane
Registered for: C[hristian] Deardorff & A. Shane
Location: Mil - 1 8 4 18
Based upon the following Army land warrant:

Issued to	*No.*	*Acres*
Macmihin, Susanna, heir[ess] of J. Macmihin, Pvt	370	100

(Note: Delivered to A. Shane.)

1056 7 Apr 1815 B/1/026
Registered by: F. D. Tschiffely
Registered for: Henry Entrol
Location: Mil - 1 1 3 26
Based upon the following Army land warrant:

Issued to	*No.*	*Acres*
Entrol, Henry, Pvt	4096	100

(Note: Sent to Charles Roberts, Zanesville [Ohio].)

1057 14 Apr 1815 B/1/026
Registered by: Michael Nourse
Registered for: Zaccheus A. Beatty
Location: Mil - 3 1 1 16
Mil - 4 4 3 4
Based upon the following Army land warrant:

Issued to	*No.*	*Acres*
Tatum, Henry, Lt	316	200

(Note: Delivered to Michael Nourse.)

1058 13 May 1815 B/1/026
Registered by: Horace Avery
Registered for: Miles Avery
Location: Mil - 6 6 2 4
Based upon the following Army land warrant:

Issued to	*No.*	*Acres*
Avery, Miles, Pvt	5353	100

1059 13 Jun 1815 B/1/026
Registered by: John Gardiner
Registered for: Joseph Fox
Location: Mil - 6 2 1 16
Mil - 6 2 1 17
Mil - 6 2 1 32
Based upon the following Army land warrant:

Issued to	*No.*	*Acres*
Fox, Joseph, Capt	700	300

(Note: Sent to Charles Roberts, Zanesville [Ohio].)

1060 21 Jul 1815 B/1/026
Registered by: John Gardiner
Registered for: James Williams
Location: Mil - 10 1 2 7
Mil - 10 1 2 18
Based upon the following Army land warrant:

Issued to	*No.*	*Acres*
Stoddart, William T., Lt	2051	200

(Note: Sent to J. Williams, Annapolis? [Maryland].)

1061 21 Jul 1815 B/1/027
Registered by: Michael Nourse
Registered for: James Stanbery
Location: Mil - 10 1 2 25
Mil - 10 1 2 28
Mil - 10 1 2 31
Based upon the following Army land warrant:

Issued to	*No.*	*Acres*
McGregor, John, Capt	1377	300

(Note: Delivered to Michael Nourse.)

1062 21 Jul 1815 B/1/027
Registered by: Michael Nourse
Registered for: Jacob Lent
Location: Mil - 10 1 2 40
Based upon the following Army land warrant:

Issued to	*No.*	*Acres*
Lent, Jacob, Pvt	630	100

(Note: Delivered to Michael Nourse.)

1063 21 Jul 1815 B/1/027
Registered by: Michael Nourse
Registered for: Isaac Jackson
Location: Mil - 10 1 2 35
Based upon the following Army land warrant:

Issued to	*No.*	*Acres*
Jackson, Isaac, Pvt	549	100

(Note: Delivered to Michael Nourse.)

1064 21 Jul 1815 B/1/027
Registered by: Michael Nourse
Registered for: Truman Skeel
Location: Mil - 10 1 2 16
Based upon the following Army land warrant:

Issued to	*No.*	*Acres*
Norton, Rufus, Pvt	6236	100

(Note: Delivered to Michael Nourse.)

1065 2 Sep 1815 B/1/027
Registered by: Michael Nourse
Registered for: Henry Northup*
Location: Mil - 6 2 1 26
Mil - 6 2 1 29
Mil - 8 4 3 34
Mil - 8 4 3 37
Based upon the following Army land warrant:

Issued to	*No.*	*Acres*
Doherty, George, Maj	343	400

*The name Caleb Harvey is crossed out and corrected to the above.

1066 28 Oct 1815 B/1/027
Registered by: Barnabas Kobler
Registered for: James Nowell
Location: Mil - 1 10 1 2
Based upon the following Army land warrant:

Issued to	*No.*	*Acres*
Nowell, James, Pvt	643	100

(Note: Delivered to Mr. Kobler.)

1067 28 Oct 1815 B/1/027
Registered by: Barnabas Kobler
Registered for: Barnabas Eopler
Location: Mil - 1 10 1 1
Based upon the following Army land warrant:

Issued to	*No.*	*Acres*
Eopler, Barnabas, Pvt	628	100

(Note: Delivered to Mr. Kobler.)

1068 21 Dec 1815 B/1/027
Registered by: John Gardiner
Registered for: Abr[aham] Shane
Location: Mil - 1 8 4 29
Mil - 3 10 2 11
Mil - 3 10 2 12
Based upon the following Army land warrant:

Issued to	*No.*	*Acres*
Thornton, Presley, Capt	553	300

(Note: Sent to R. J. Meigs, Esq.)

1069 16 Jan 1816 B/1/027
Registered by: Josiah Meigs
Registered for: Joseph Bruner
Location: Mil - 6 2 1 13
Based upon the following Army land warrant:

Issued to	*No.*	*Acres*
Bartlett, John, Sgt	520	100

(Note: Sent to C[harles] Roberts, Zanesville [Ohio].)

1070 26 Jan 1816 B/1/027
Registered by: Michael Nourse
Registered for: Christian Deardorff
Location: Mil - 1 10 1 33
Based upon the following Army land warrant:

Issued to	*No.*	*Acres*
Taylor, John, Pvt	533	100

(Note: Sent to Michael Nourse.)

1071 26 Jan 1816 B/1/027
Registered by: Michael Nourse
Registered for: Daniel Johnson, a black man
Location: Mil - 8 4 3 28
Based upon the following Army land warrant:

Issued to	*No.*	*Acres*
McCrea, Philip, Pvt	329	100

(Note: Sent to Michael Nourse.)

1072 12 Feb 1816 B/1/027
Registered by: Hon. Gen Roberts
Registered for: John Metz
Location: Mil - 8 4 3 33
Based upon the following Army land warrant:

Issued to	*No.*	*Acres*
Metz, John, Pvt	9870	100

(Note: Sent to Hon. Mr. Roberts.)

1073 4 Mar 1816 B/1/027
Registered by: Hon -- Creighton
Registered for: Anna? Marie Bowie Chew
Location: Mil - 16 6 1 21
Mil - 16 6 1 26
Mil - 16 6 1 27
Mil - 16 6 1 28
Based upon the following Army land warrant:

Issued to	*No.*	*Acres*
Brooks, Benjamin, Maj	228	400

(Note: Sent to Hon. Mr. Creighton.)

1074 19 Mar 1816 B/1/027
Registered by: Michael Nourse
Registered for: Hamlet Paterson
Location: Mil - 10 7 1 28
Based upon the following Army land warrant:

Issued to	*No.*	*Acres*
Smith, Richard, Sgt	570	100

(Note: Sent to Michael Nourse.)

1075 19 Mar 1816 B/1/027
Registered by: Michael Nourse
Registered for: Charles McKee
Location: Mil - 10 7 1 27
Based upon the following Army land warrant:

Issued to	*No.*	*Acres*
Adee, Aner* Pvt	5389	100

*So spelled.

1076 4 Apr 1816 B/1/027
Registered by: J. G? Jackson
Registered for George Jackson

1076 [continued]
Location: Mil - 8 4 3 38
Mil - 4 10 3 9
Mil - 6 6 2 1
Based upon the following Army land warrant:
Issued to *No.* *Acres*
Gale, John, Capt 422 300
(Note: Sent to Hon. Mr. Jackson.)

1077 12 Apr 1816 B/1/027
Registered by: Michael Nourse
Registered for: William Stanberry
Location: Mil - 5 9 3 33
Based upon the following Army land warrant:
Issued to *No.* *Acres*
Miller, Christian, Pvt 10007 100
(Note: Sent to Michael Nourse.)

1078 6 May 1816 B/1/027
Registered by: F. D. Tschiffely
Registered for: Abr[aha]m Shane
Location: Mil - 5 9 3 40
Based upon the following Army land warrant:
Issued to *No.* *Acres*
Goldsborough, Charles, Pvt 647 100
(Note: Sent to Michael Nourse.)

1079 14 May 1816 B/1/027
Registered by: F. D. Tschiffely
Registered for: James McMannamay
Location: Mil - 9 7 3 9
Based upon the following Army land warrant:
Issued to *No.* *Acres*
Rodes, Jacob, Pvt 510 100
(Note: Sent to Michael Nourse.)

1080 4 Jun 1816 B/1/027
Registered by: John Gardiner
Registered for: Ransom Clark
Location: Mil - 16 6 1 22
Based upon the following Army land warrant:
Issued to *No.* *Acres*
Peters, Philip, Pvt 8626 100
(Note: Sent to Ransom Clark.)

1081 27 Jun 1816 B/1/027
Registered by: W. H. Beard
Registered for: Charles Williams
Location: Mil - 5 9 3 23
Based upon the following Army land warrant:
Issued to *No.* *Acres*
Young, Henry, Pvt 635 100
(Note: Delivered to W. H. Beard.)

1082 2 Sep 1816 B/1/027
Registered by: John Gardiner
Registered for: Heirs of E. Leavenworth
Location: Mil - 11 8 1 31
Mil - 11 8 1 33
Mil - 11 8 1 34
Mil - 11 8 1 35
Based upon the following Army land warrant:
Issued to *No.* *Acres*
Leavenworth, Eli, Maj 641 400
(Note: Sent to J. Jeffords & J. M. Vandenburgh.)

1083 21 Sep 1816 B/1/027
Registered by: David Ott
Registered for: Heirs at law of William Beatty
Location: Mil - 3 10 2 14
Mil - 3 10 2 15
Mil - 3 10 2 16
Based upon the following Army land warrant:
Issued to *No.* *Acres*
Beatty, William, Capt 644 300
(Note: Delivered to David Ott, Esq.)

1084 27 Sep 1816 B/1/027
Registered by: Michael Nourse
Registered for: A[braham] Shane & H[enry] Northup
Location: Mil - 3 10 2 13
Mil - 5 9 3 25
Mil - 5 9 3 29*
Mil - 5 10 3 17
Mil - 5 10 3 18
Mil - 5 10 3 19
Mil - 5 10 3 21
Mil - 5 10 3 22
Mil - 6 2 1 2
Mil - 6 2 1 14
Mil - 6 2 1 30
Based upon the following Army land warrant:
Issued to *No.* *Acres*
Smallwood, William, heirs
at law of, MajGen 656 1100
*Marginal notation states: "Should be 39."
(Note: Delivered to Michael Nourse.)

1085 14 Oct 1816 B/1/028
Registered by: Abraham Shane
Registered for: H. Northup & A. Shane
Location: Mil - 6 6 2 2
Mil - 1 8 2 24W*
Based upon the following Army land warrant:
Issued to *No.* *Acres*
Floyd, Ebenezer, Ens 709 150
*50-acre lot.
(Note: Delivered to A[braham] Shane.)

1086 27 Oct 1816 B/1/028
Registered by: F. D. Tschiffely
Registered for: H. Northup & A. Shane
Location: Mil - 5 10 3 28
Based upon the following Army land warrant:
Issued to *No.* *Acres*
Ingle, William, Pvt 11381 100
(Note: Delivered to Michael Nourse.)

1087 18 Nov 1816 B/1/028
Registered by: Nath[anie]l Cutting
Registered for: Walter Jones, in trust for Anne & Angelique Cutting
Location: Mil - 5 10 3 3
Mil - 5 10 3 4
Mil - 5 10 3 5
Mil - 5 10 3 8
Based upon the following Army land warrant:
Issued to *No.* *Acres*
Cutting, John B., Apothecary 650 450
(Note: Delivered to Nathaniel Cutting.)

1088 29 Nov 1816 B/1/028
Registered by: James Nourse
Registered for: [H.] Northup & [A.] Shane
Location: Mil - 5 9 3 26
Based upon the following Army land warrant:

Issued to	*No.*	*Acres*
Harman* Edward, Pvt	11311	100

*So spelled; see following serial entry.
(Note: Delivered to James Nourse.)

1089 29 Nov 1816 B/1/028
Registered by: James Nourse
Registered for: [A.] Shane & [H.] Northup
Location: Mil - 5 9 3 22
Based upon the following Army land warrant:

Issued to	*No.*	*Acres*
Harmar* Lazarus, Pvt	11353	100

*So spelled; see preceding serial entry.
(Note: Delivered to James Nourse.)

1090 3 Dec 1816 B/1/028
Registered by: Hon. Daniel Cady
Registered for: John Bateman
Location: Mil - 10 1 2 14
Mil - 10 1 2 15
Based upon the following Army land warrant:

Issued to	*No.*	*Acres*
Bateman, John, Lt	2626	200

(Note: Sent to Hon. Daniel Cady.)

1091 19 Dec 1816 B/1/028
Registered by: Nath[anie]l Cutting
Registered for: Benj[amin] Hough
Location: Mil - 5 9 3 19
Based upon the following Army land warrant:

Issued to	*No.*	*Acres*
Green, Robert, Dragoon	640	100

(Note: Delivered to Nathaniel Cutting.)

1092 24 Dec 1816 B/1/028
Registered by: Hon. -- Birdsall
Registered for: Sylvester Miner
Location: Mil - 5 9 3 17
Based upon the following Army land warrant:

Issued to	*No.*	*Acres*
Miner, Sylvester, Pvt	652	100

(Note: Sent to Hon. Mr. Birdsall.)

1093 28 Dec 1816 B/1/028
Registered by: Samuel D. Ingham
Registered for: James Kirk
Location: Mil - 5 9 3 32
Based upon the following Army land warrant:

Issued to	*No.*	*Acres*
Kirk, James, Pvt	9732	100

(Note: Sent to Hon. Mr. Ingham.)

1094 8 Jan 1817 B/1/028
Registered by: F. D. Tschiffely
Registered for: Henry Northorp*
Location: Mil - 6 10 4 5
Based upon the following Army land warrant:

Issued to	*No.*	*Acres*
Gross, Elisha, Sgt	177	100

(Note: Sent to Michael Nourse.)

1095 16 Jan 1817 B/1/028
Registered by: John Coates
Registered for: John Coates
Location: Mil - 2 5 3 36
Mil - 8 4 3 14
Based upon the following Army land warrants:

Issued to	*No.*	*Acres*
Hill, John, Pvt	663	100
Fleming, James, Sgt	664	100

(Note: Delivered to John Coates.)

1096 16 Jan 1817 B/1/028
Registered by: John Coates
Registered for: Peter McNamar
Location: Mil - 8 5 1 34
Based upon the following Army land warrant:

Issued to	*No.*	*Acres*
McNamar, Peter, Cpl	661	100

(Note: Delivered to John Coates.)

1097 23 Jan 1817 B/1/028
Registered by: F. D. Tschiffely
Registered for: A[braham] Shane
Location: Mil - 5 10 3 13
Based upon the following Army land warrant:

Issued to	*No.*	*Acres*
Ford, Sanbun* Pvt	498	100

*So spelled.

1098 23 Jan 1817 B/1/028
Registered by: F. D. Tschiffely
Registered for: M[ichae]l? Lwovoland?
Location: Mil - 5 9 3 24
Based upon the following Army land warrant:

Issued by	*No.*	*Acres*
Sullivan, William, Pvt	10887	100

(Note: Delivered to Michael Nourse.)

1099 23 Jan 1817 B/1/028
Registered by: F. D. Tschiffely
Registered for: H[enr]y Northorp*
Location: Mil - 5 9 3 21
Based upon the following Army land warrant:

Issued to	*No.*	*Acres*
Phillips, John, Sgt	4889	100

*So spelled.

1100 30 Jan 1817 B/1/028
Registered by: Peter Little
Registered for: James Starr
Location: Mil - 5 9 3 2
Based upon the following Army land warrant:

Issued to	*No.*	*Acres*
Starr, James, Cpl	586	100

(Note: Sent to Hon. P. Little.)

1101 7 Feb 1817 B/1/028
Registered by: Hon. B. Tallmadge
Registered for: Solomon Doud
Location: Mil - 5 9 3 34
Based upon the following Army land warrant:

Issued to	*No.*	*Acres*
Doud, Solomon, Pvt	419	100

(Note: [Delivered?] to B. Tallmadge.)

1102 20 Feb 1817 B/1/028
Registered by: W. H. Beard
Registered for: Henry Laffer
Location: Mil - 1 10 1 35
Based upon the following Army land warrant:

Issued to	*No.*	*Acres*
Sellick, Benj[amin] Cpl	436	100

(Note: Sent to Hon. Mr. Sampson.)

1103 26 Feb 1817 B/1/028
Registered by: John R. Nourse
Registered for: [A.] Shane & [H.] Northorp
Location: Mil - 5 10 3 24
Mil - 5 10 3 25
Mil - 6 8 2 1
Mil - 6 8 3 10
Based upon the following Army land warrants:

Issued to	*No.*	*Acres*
Reeves, Enos, Lt	1823	200
Hanson, Samuel, Lt	1050	200

(Note: Sent to Hon. J. C. Spencer [signed?] J. J? Moore.)

1104 1 Mar 1817 B/1/028
Registered by: Hon. P. Little
Registered for: Owen Allen
Location: Mil - 5 9 3 15
Based upon the following Army land warrant:

Issued to	*No.*	*Acres*
Mayhew, William, Sgt	611	100

(Note: Sent to Hon. P. Little.)

1105 1 Mar 1817 B/1/028
Registered by: Hon. P. Little
Registered for: Peter Little
Location: Mil - 5 9 3 3
Based upon the following Army land warrant:

Issued to	*No.*	*Acres*
Sewall, James, Pvt	554	100

(Note: Sent to Hon. P. Little.)

1106 1 Mar 1817 B/1/028
Registered by: F. D. Tschiffely
Registered for: Heirs of T. H. Luckett
Location: Mil - 5 10 3 14
Mil - 5 10 3 15
Mil - 5 9 3 12
Mil - 5 9 3 16
Based upon the following Army land warrant:

Issued to	*No.*	*Acres*
Luckett, T. H., heirs of, Maj	653	400

(Note: Sent to C. Wallace, 28 Mar 1817.)

1107 11 Apr 1817 B/1/028
Registered by: F. D. Tschiffely
Registered for: Peter Himes
Location: Mil - 2 10 2 11
Based upon the following Army land warrant:

Issued to	*No.*	*Acres*
Steel, Robert, Drum Maj	654	100

(Note: Sent to Michael Nourse.)

1108 7 May 1817 B/1/028
Registered by: F. D. Tschiffely
Registered for: Henry Northorp
Location: Mil - 5 3 3 23
Based upon the following Army land warrant:

Issued to	*No.*	*Acres*
Johnson, Ebenezer, Pvt	658	100

(Note: Sent to Michael Nourse.)

1109 7 May 1817 B/1/028
Registered by: M[ichael] Nourse
Registered for: [H.] Northorp & [A.] Shane
Location: Mil - 5 9 3 20
Mil - 5 9 3 30
Mil - 5 9 3 31
Based upon the following Army land warrant:

Issued to	*No.*	*Acres*
Jones, Daniel, Capt	506	300

(Note: Sent to Michael Nourse.)

1110 11 Jun 1817 B/1/028
Registered by: Abr[aham] Beadley? [Readley?] Junior
Registered for: Abr[aham] Beadley? [Readley?] Junior
Location: Mil - 6 2 1 15
Based upon the following Army land warrant:

Issued to	*No.*	*Acres*
Shanks, John, Pvt	262	100

(Note: Sent to Mr. Beadley?)

1111 12 Jun 1817 B/1/029
Registered by: F. D. Tschiffely
Registered for: Frederick Crary
Location: Mil - 5 7 1 7
Mil - 5 7 1 8
Based upon the following Army land warrants:

Issued to	*No.*	*Acres*
Cozzens, Richard, Pvt	3045	100
Champlin, York, Pvt	3046	100

(Note: Sent to A. Shane, New Philadelphia [Tuscarawas County, Ohio].)

1112 18 Jun 1817 B/1/029
Registered by: D. Parker
Registered for: Frederick Granger
Location: Mil - 5 7 1 9
Based upon the following Army land warrant:

Issued to	*No.*	*Acres*
Granger, Frederick, Musician	7	100

(Note: Sent to D. Parker.)

1113 10 Jul 1817 B/1/029
Registered by: F. D. Tschiffely
Registered for: [H.] Northorp & [A.] Shane
Location: Mil - 6 10 3 1
Mil - 6 10 4 11
Based upon the following Army land warrant:

Issued to	*No.*	*Acres*
Barnum, Eli, Lt	144	200

(Note: Sent to Michael Nourse.)

1114 10 Jul 1817 B/1/029
Registered by: F. D. Tschiffely
Registered for: John Benfer
Location: Mil - 3 7 1 38
Mil - 3 7 1 39
Based upon the following Army land warrants:

1114 [continued]

Issued to	*No.*	*Acres*
Bailey, Eph[raim?] Pvt	485	100
Blackmore, T? Pvt	591	100

(Note: Sent to Michael Nourse.)

1115 10 Jul 1817 B/1/029
Registered by: F. D. Tschiffely
Registered for: Jos[eph] Haviland
Location: Mil - 8 9 3 1
Mil - 8 9 3 2*
Based upon the following Army land warrants:

Issued to	*No.*	*Acres*
Allyn, John, Pvt	567	100
Smith, Joel, Ens	198	150*

*Since an Ens was due 150 acres, the patentee is due an additional 50 acres, not assigned above.
(Note: Sent to Michael Nourse.)

1116 17 Jul 1817 B/1/029
Registered by: Col Jos[eph] Watson
Registered for: Elizab[eth] Wilson
Location: Mil - 2 5 3 36
Based upon the following Army land warrant:

Issued to	*No.*	*Acres*
Besterfield, And[rew] Pvt	624	100

(Note: Delivered to Col Watson.)

1117 30 Jul 1817 B/1/029
Registered by: Michael Nourse
Registered for: [H.] Northorp & [A.] Shane
Location: Mil - 7 10 4 2
Mil - 2 10 2 28
Based upon the following Army land warrant:

Issued to	*No.*	*Acres*
Harrison, William, Lt	507	200

(Note: Sent to Michael Nourse.)

1118 4 Oct 1817 B/1/029
Registered by: F. D. Tschiffely
Registered for: Henry Northorp
Location: Mil - 8 4 3 27
Mil - 6 2 1 1
Based upon the following Army land warrants:

Issued to	*No.*	*Acres*
Keeler, Thomas, Pvt	639	100
Hill, William, Pvt	673	100

(Note: Sent to Michael Nourse.)

1119* 4 Nov 1817 B/1/029
Registered by: John M. Moore
Registered for: Pain, --, & Arnold, --
Location: Mil - 11 8 1 33
Based upon the following Army land warrant:

Issued to	*No.*	*Acres*
Clinton, Thomas, Fifer	632	100

(Note: Delivered to John M. Moore.)
*This entire serial entry cancelled in source register.

1120 10 Nov 1817 B/1/029
Registered by: F. D. Tschiffely
Registered for: John McAllister
Location: Mil - 18 7 2 9
Based upon the following Army land warrant:

Issued to	*No.*	*Acres*
Haslet, Henley, Pvt	575	100

(Note: Sent to Michael Nourse.)

1121 6 Dec 1817 B/1/029
Registered by: Hon. -- Sampson
Registered for: Heirs of N. Winslow
Location: Mil - 16 7 2 10
Mil - 16 7 2 11
Mil - 16 7 2 12
Mil - 16 7 2 13
Based upon the following Army land warrant:

Issued to	*No.*	*Acres*
Winslow, Nath[anie]l, Maj	446	400

(Note: Delivered to Mr. Sampson.)

1122 6 Dec 1817 B/1/029
Registered by: F. D. Tschiffely
Registered for: Benj[amin] Gleason
Location: Mil - 10 7 1 20
Based upon the following Army land warrant:

Issued to	*No.*	*Acres*
Gleason, Benj[amin] Pvt	642	100

(Note: Sent to Hon. Mr. Richards.)

1123 10 Dec 1817 B/1/029
Registered by: Michael Nourse
Registered for: [A.] Shane & [H.] Northorp
Location: Mil - 5 9 3 13
Mil - 5 9 3 14
Based upon the following Army land warrant:

Issued to	*No.*	*Acres*
Moxley, R., heirs of, Lt	597	200

(Note: Sent to Michael Nourse.)

1124 10 Dec 1817 B/1/029
Registered by: Michael Nourse
Registered for: Henry Northorp
Location: Mil - 6 6 2 3
Based upon the following Army land warrant:

Issued to	*No.*	*Acres*
Nourse [Michael?] assignee of -- Peak, Sgt	672	100

(Note: Sent to Michael Nourse.)

1125 -- Dec? 1817 B/1/029
Registered by: [illegible]
Registered for: Valentine Kain
Location: Mil - 5 9 3 27
Based upon the following Army land warrant:

Issued to	*No.*	*Acres*
Bradley, James, Pvt	595	100

(Note: Sent to Michael Nourse.)

1126 20 Dec 1817 B/1/029
Registered by: W. H. Sampson
Registered for: Canada Asher
Location: Mil - 16 7 2 21
Based upon the following Army land warrant:

Issued to	*No.*	*Acres*
Asher, Canada, Pvt	676	100

(Note: Sent to Hon. Mr. Sampson.)

1127 20 Dec 1817 B/1/029
Registered by: Josiah? Meigs

1127 [continued]
Registered for: Samuel Wiley
Location: Mil - 6 6 2 10
Based upon the following Army land warrant:

Issued to	*No.*	*Acres*
Wiley, Samuel, Pvt	646	100

(Note: Sent to Hon. J. C. Spencer.)

1128 1 --? 1818 B/1/029
Registered by: Hon. Robert Moore
Registered for: Charles Martin
Location: Mil - 16 6 1 11
Mil - 16 6 1 12
Based upon the following Army land warrant:

Issued to	*No.*	*Acres*
Martin, Charles, Quarter? [or Baggage?] Master	670	100

(Note: Sent to Hon. Robert Moore.)

1129 9 --? 1818 B/1/029
Registered by: John Gardiner
Registered for: Heirs of T. Hall
Location: Mil - 5 9 3 36
Based upon the following Army land warrant:

Issued to	*No.*	*Acres*
Hall, Thomas, Cpl	5931	100

(Note: Sent to Hon. Mr. Daggett.)

1130 13 --? 1818 B/1/029
Registered by: W. H. Beard
Registered for: William Cazeir
Location: Mil - 5 9 3 37
Based upon the following Army land warrant:

Issued to	*No.*	*Acres*
Gilbert, Thomas, Fifer	651	100

(Note: Delivered to W. H. Beard.)

1131 19 --? 1818 B/1/029
Registered by: J. Prall
Registered for: David Hains
Location: Mil - 11 6 1 8
Mil - 11 6 1 7
Based upon the following Army land warrant:

Issued to	*No.*	*Acres*
Scholfield, Jos[eph], heirs of, Pvt	609	100
Thorn, D., heirs of, Matross	638	100

(Note: Delivered to J. Prall.)

1132* 10 Mar 1818 B/1/029
Registered by: John Underwood
Registered for: Jonas Stansbery
Location: Mil - 11 9 3 2
Mil - 11 9 3 3
Based upon the following Army land warrant:

Issued to	*No.*	*Acres*
Bell, Henry, Lt	623	200

(Note: Delivered to J. Underwood.)
*This entire serial entry is crossed out in source register.

1133 10 Mar 1818 B/1/029
Registered by: John Underwood
Registered for: Jonas Stansbery
Location: Mil - 11 9 3 6
Mil - 11 9 3 7
Based upon the following Army land warrants:

Issued to	*No.*	*Acres*
Augin? Isaac, Drummer	677	100
Henwood, Robert, Pvt	674	100

(Note: Delivered to J. Underwood.

1134 10 Mar 1818 B/1/030
Registered by: John Underwood
Registered for: Jonas Stanbery
Location: Mil - 11 9 3 2
Mil - 11 9 3 3
Based upon the following Army land warrant:

Issued to	*No.*	*Acres*
Blake, Edward, Lt	680	200

(Note: Delivered to John Underwood.)

1135 16 Mar 1818 B/1/030
Registered by: Hon. C. Storer
Registered for: Ebenezer Storer
Location: Mil - 10 3 4 31
Mil - 10 3 4 32
Based upon the following Army land warrant:

Issued to	*No.*	*Acres*
Storer, Ebenezer, Lt	1906	200

(Note: Delivered to Hon. Mr. Storer.)

1136 16 Mar 1818 B/1/030
Registered by: Michael Nourse
Registered for: Henry Northorp?*
Location: Mil - 6 2 1 31
Based upon the following Army land warrant:

Issued to	*No.*	*Acres*
Whiting, Stephen, Pvt	679	100

(Note: Delivered to Michael Nourse.)
*"Heirs of S. Whiting" crossed out on source register.

1137 16 Mar 1818 B/1/030
Registered by: William Patten
Registered for: William Patten
Location: Mil - 10 9 3 23
Mil - 10 9 3 24
Mil - 10 9 3 33
Based upon the following Army land warrant:

Issued to	*No.*	*Acres*
Gunn, James, Capt	659	300

(Note: Sent him by mail.)

1138 31 Mar 1818 B/1/030
Registered by: Hon. Levi Barber
Registered for: William Taylor
Location: Mil - 11 9 3 4
Mil - 11 9 3 5
Based upon the following Army land warrant:

Issued to	*No.*	*Acres*
Taylor, William, Lt	2152	200

(Note: Sent to Hon. Levi Barber.)

1139 3 Apr 1818 B/1/030
Registered by: F. D. Tschiffely
Registered for: John Val[entine?] Shuler
Location: Mil - 10 1 2 4
Based upon the following Army land warrant:

1139 [continued]

Issued to	*No.*	*Acres*
Dobson, Thomas, Pvt	631	100

(Note: Delivered to Michael Nourse.)

1140 14 Apr 1818 B/1/030
Registered by: W. B. Beall
Registered for: S. B. Beall
Location: Mil - 11 6 1 4
Mil - 11 6 1 5
Based upon the following Army land warrant:

Issued to	*No.*	*Acres*
Beall, S. B., Lt	690	200

(Note: Delivered to W. B. Beall.)

1141 14 Apr 1818 B/1/030
Registered by: Hon. Mr. -- Moseley
Registered for: Heirs of Ezra Selden
Location: Mil - 11 9 3 1
Mil - 11 9 3 8
Mil - 11 9 3 9
Based upon the following Army land warrant:

Issued to	*No.*	*Acres*
Selden, Ezra, heirs of, Capt	687	300

(Note: Sent to Hon. Mr. Moseley.)

1142 14 Apr 1818 B/1/030
Registered by: Hon. Mr. -- Moseley
Registered for: Samuel Prentice
Location: Mil - 11 9 3 16
Based upon the following Army land warrant:

Issued to	*No.*	*Acres*
Fargo, William, Pvt	5754	100

(Note: Sent to Hon. Mr. Moseley.)

1143 16 Apr 1818 B/1/030
Registered by: James Nourse
Registered for: Henry Northorp
Location: Mil - 6 6 2 15
Based upon the following Army land warrant:

Issued to	*No.*	*Acres*
Adkins, Isaiah, Cpl	649	100

(Note: Delivered to James Nourse.)

1144 23 Apr 1818 B/1/030
Registered by: John Guthrie
Registered for: John Guthrie
Location: Mil - 11 9 3 12
Based upon the following Army land warrant:

Issued to	*No.*	*Acres*
Guthrie, John, Pvt	691	100

(Note: Delivered to John Guthrie.)

1145 27 Apr 1818 B/1/030
Registered by: F. D. Tschiffely
Registered for: David Marshall
Location: Mil - 11 9 3 14
Mil - 11 9 3 15
Based upon the following Army land warrant:

Issued to	*No.*	*Acres*
Marshall, David, Lt	1440	200

(Note: Sent to William Anderson.)

1146 6 May 1818 B/1/030
Registered by: Philip Richerick
Registered for: Philip Richerick
Location: Mil - 7 4 2 37
Based upon the following Army land warrant:

Issued to	*No.*	*Acres*
Richerick, Philip, Pvt	592	100

(Note: Delivered to himself.)

1147 25 Jun 1818 B/1/030
Registered by: Thomas Elrod (Ohio)
Registered for: John Wilson, assignee
Location: Mil - 17 7 2 25
Based upon the following Army land warrant:

Issued to	*No.*	*Acres*
Helm, *alias* Ellem, Leonard, Pvt	573	100

(Note: Sent by mail.)

1148 25 Jun 1818 B/1/030
Registered by: Thomas Elrod (Ohio)
Registered for: Legal representative of Philip King
Location: Mil - 17 7 2 26
Based upon the following Army land warrant:

Issued to	*No.*	*Acres*
Briant, William, Pvt	416	100

(Note: Sent by mail.)

1149 11 Jul 1818 B/1/030
Registered by: John Underwood
Registered for: Jacob Phifer
Location: Mil - 11 9 4 18
Mil - 11 9 4 19
Mil - 11 9 4 15
Mil - 11 9 4 14
Based upon the following Army land warrant:

Issued to	*No.*	*Acres*
Burrows, John, heirs of, Maj	610	400

(Note: Delivered to J. Underwood.)

1150 13 Jul 1818 B/1/030
Registered by: F. D. Tschiffely
Registered for: William Johnston
Location: Mil - 12 9 4 14
Mil - 12 9 4 13
Mil - 12 9 4 12
Based upon the following Army land warrants:

Issued to	*No.*	*Acres*
Osborne, Samuel, Pvt	12442	100
Paul, Edward, Pvt	12450	100
Finnigan, P., Pvt	555	100

(Note: Sent by mail to S. H. Smith, 21 Jul 1818.)

1151 13 Jul 1818 B/1/030
Registered by: F. D. Tschiffely
Registered for: A. Stevens & heirs of Ebenezer Stevens
Location: Mil - 12 9 4 11
Mil - 17 7 1 23W*
Based upon the following Army land warrant:

Issued to	*No.*	*Acres*
Stevens, A., & heirs of Eben[ezer] Stevens, Ens	625	150

*50-acre lot.
(Note: Sent by mail to S. H. Smith, 21 Jul 1818.)

1152 22 Jul 1818 B/1/030
Registered by: F. D. Tschiffely
Registered for: Alexander Hedges
Location: Mil - 12 9 4 1
Mil - 12 9 4 2
Mil - 12 9 4 6
Mil - 12 9 4 7
Based upon the following Army land warrant:

Issued to	*No.*	*Acres*
Motte, William, heir of Charles Motte, Maj	629	400

(Note: Sent to Mr. Bullard.)

1153* 28 Jul 1818 B/1/030
Registered by: Joseph Stokely
Registered for: Joseph Stokely
Location: Mil - 6 6 2 2
Based upon the following Army land warrant:

Issued to	*No.*	*Acres*
Granland, J., Pvt	689	100

(Note: Delivered to himself.)
*This entire serial entry is crossed out in source register.

1154 28 Jul 1818 B/1/030
Registered by: John N. Feerer*
Registered for: Joshua Shule?
Location: Mil - 11 9 4 6
Based upon the following Army land warrant:

Issued to	*No.*	*Acres*
Robins, John, Pvt	11638	100

(Note: Delivered to J. N. Feehrer.*)
*So spelled.

1155 20 Aug 1818 B/1/030
Registered by: F. D. Tschiffely
Registered for: Henry Northup
Location: Mil - 5 3 3 10
Mil - 5 7 1 6
Mil - 5 10 3 11
Mil - 5 10 3 12
Based upon the following Army land warrants:

Issued to	*No.*	*Acres*
Willington, J., Pvt	5232	100
McKinley, A., Pvt	692	100
Hammond, John, Pvt	693	100
White, John, heirs at law of, Pvt	429	100

(Note: Sent to Michael Nourse & H? N? Sampson.)

1156 2 Sep 1818 B/1/030
Registered by: F. D. Tschiffely
Registered for: Heirs of B. Sergeants
Location: Mil - 6 6 2 30
Based upon the following Army land warrant:

Issued to	*No.*	*Acres*
Sergeants, Barnard, heirs at law of, Pvt	694	100

(Note: Sent . . . Mr. Hogg.)

1157 18 Oct 1818 B/1/030
Registered by: F. D. Tschiffely
Registered for: Henry Northup
Location: Mil - 5 10 3 26
Based upon the following Army land warrant:

Issued to	*No.*	*Acres*
Middlebrook, John, Pvt	565	100

1158 29 Oct 1818 B/1/031
Registered by: Michael Nourse
Registered for: Henry Northup
Location: Mil - 6 2 1 25
Mil - 6 8 3 8
Mil - 5 10 3 27
Based upon the following Army land warrant:

Issued to	*No.*	*Acres*
Melven, George, Capt	175	300

(Note: Sent to Michael Nourse.)

1159 29 Oct 1818 B/1/031
Registered by: F. D. Tschiffely
Registered for: Heirs of J. Gardner
Location: Mil - 16 6 1 19
Mil - 16 6 1 20
Based upon the following Army land warrant:

Issued to	*No.*	*Acres*
Gardner, James, CaptLt	668	200

(Note: Sent to E. Lovett, Albany.)

1160 29 Oct 1818 B/1/031
Registered by: F. D. Tschiffely
Registered for: Henry Northup
Location: Mil - 7 10 4 4
Mil - 7 10 4 3
Mil - 6 6 2 12
Based upon the following Army land warrants:

Issued to	*No.*	*Acres*
Ramsdell, James, Pvt	626	100
Satterlee, James, Fifer	405	100
Terrant, Henry, Pvt	675	100

(Note: Sent to H. Northup.)

1161 12 Nov 1818 B/1/031
Registered by: F. D. Tschiffely
Registered for: Amos Skeel
Location: Mil - 12 9 3 6
Based upon the following Army land warrant:

Issued to	*No.*	*Acres*
Skeel, William, Sgt	666	100

1162 12 Nov 1818 B/1/031
Registered by: F. D. Tschiffely
Registered for: James Riggs
Location: Mil - 12 9 3 7
Based upon the following Army land warrant:

Issued to	*No.*	*Acres*
Riggs, James, Pvt	657	100

(Note: Sent to S. H. Smith, Clinton, Knox County, Ohio.)

1163 12 Nov 1818* B/1/031
Registered by: F. D. Tschiffely
Registered for: Heirs of [G.] Lightheiser
Location: Mil - 6 7 3 3*
Based upon the following Army land warrant:

Issued to	*No.*	*Acres*
Lightheiser [Lichtheiser] George, Pvt	314	100

(Note: Sent to Catherine Lightheiser.)
*Notation states patent reissued 26 Nov 1831. Apparently, the original tract citation was erroneously shown as [Mil - 7 6 3 3].

1164 16 Nov 1818 B/1/031
Registered by: F. D. Tschiffely
Registered for: Jonas Stanbery
Location: Mil - 5 9 3 35
Based upon the following Army land warrant:

Issued to	*No.*	*Acres*
Macomber, John, Pvt	3340	100

(Note: Delivered to Seth Hyatt.)

1165 16 Nov 1818 B/1/031
Registered by: F. D. Tschiffely
Registered for: A. Shane?
Location: Mil - 5 10 3 20
Based upon the following Army land warrant:

Issued to	*No.*	*Acres*
Hunt, David, Pvt	296	100

(Note: Delivered to A. Shane.)

1166 16 Nov 1818 B/1/031
Registered by: Luther Paul
Registered for: Luther Paul
Location: Mil - 6 6 2 29
Based upon the following Army land warrant:

Issued to	*No.*	*Acres*
Withington, Elijah, Pvt	678	100

(Note: To patentee.)

1167 20 Nov 1818 B/1/031
Registered by: F. D. Tschiffely
Registered for: Abel Wyman
Location: Mil - 5 10 3 23
Based upon the following Army land warrant:

Issued to	*No.*	*Acres*
Wyman, Abel, assignee of John Bradford, Pvt	4949	100

(Note: Sent to S. Blagge, Boston.)

1168* 18 Dec 1818 B/1/031
Registered by: S. Hyatt
Registered for: Jonas Stanberry
Location: Mil - 11 9 3 2
Mil - 11 9 3 3
Based upon the following Army land warrant:

Issued to	*No.*	*Acres*
Bell, H., Lt	623	100

(Note: Delivered to S. Hyatt.)
*This entire serial entry crossed ou in source register.

1169 19 Dec 1818 B/1/031
Registered by: Hon. Z. Sampson
Registered for: P. Winsor
Location: Mil - 11 6 1 6
Based upon the following Army land warrant:

Issued to	*No.*	*Acres*
Winsor, Peter, Pvt	721	100

(Note: Sent to Hon. Mr. Sampson.)

1170 19 Dec 1818 B/1/031
Registered by: Hon. Z. Sampson
Registered for: J. Seaver
Location: Mil - 1 8 3 4
Mil - 1 8 2 23W*
Based upon the following Army land warrant:

Issued to	*No.*	*Acres*
Seaver, James, Ens	717	150

*50-acre lot.

1171 1 Jan 1819 B/1/031
Registered by: F. D. Tschiffely
Registered for: H. Northup
Location: Mil - 6 2 1 18
Mil - 8 9 2 2
Mil - 8 5 1 33
Mil - 7 9 2 22
Mil - 7 9 2 24
Based upon the following Army land warrant:

Issued to	*No.*	*Acres*
Young, Anne, heiress of John Durkee, Col	580	500

(Note: Sent to H. Northup.)

1172 16 Jan 1819 B/1/031
Registered by: F. D. Tschiffely
Registered for: William Halbert
Location: Mil - 10 9 3 31
Based upon the following Army land warrant:

Issued to	*No.*	*Acres*
Halbert, William, Pvt	607	100

(Note: Sent to Hon. R. L? [or S?] Garnett.)

1173 18 Jan 1819 B/1/031
Registered by: Hon. P. Beecher
Registered for: M. Merrill
Location: Mil - 7 10 4 1
Based upon the following Army land warrant:

Issued to	*No.*	*Acres*
Merrill, Mead *alias* M., Pvt	665	100

(Note: Sent to Hon. P. Beecher.)

1174 18 Jan 1819 B/1/031
Registered by: Hon. P. Beecher
Registered for: Lawton? Hayes
Location: Mil - 16 7 2 22
Based upon the following Army land warrant:

Issued to	*No.*	*Acres*
Allen, Edward, Pvt	682	100

(Note: Sent to Hon. P. Beecher.)

1175 25 Jan 1819 B/1/031
Registered by: Hon. John R. Drake
Registered for: William Stewart
Location: Mil - 10 9 3 29
Mil - 10 9 3 30
Based upon the following Army land warrant:

Issued to	*No.*	*Acres*
Stewart, William, Lt	2114	200

(Note: Sent to Hon. Mr. Drake.)

1176 27 Jan 1819 B/1/031
Registered by: F. D. Tschiffely
Registered for: T. Elwell
Location: Mil - 12 9 3 1
Based upon the following Army land warrant:

Issued to	*No.*	*Acres*
Elwell, Thomas, Matross	695	100

(Note: Sent to himself.)

1177 27 Jan 1819 B/1/031
Registered by: Josiah Meigs
Registered for: R. Williams
Location: Mil - 12 9 3 3
Based upon the following Army land warrant:
Issued to *No.* *Acres*

1177 [continued]
Williams, Richard, Pvt 724 100
(Note: Sent to Hon. C. Tompkins.)

1178 8 Feb 1819 B/1/031
Registered by: F. D. Tschiffely
Registered for: B. Thayer
Location: Mil - 6 6 2 17
Based upon the following Army land warrant:
Issued to *No.* *Acres*
Greenland, James, Pvt 689 100
(Note: Sent to Hon. Mr. Herricks.)

1179 20 Feb 1819 B/1/031
Registered by: Hon. P. Beecher
Registered for: A. Reckless
Location: Mil - 7 10 4 5
Mil - 7 10 4 7
Based upon the following Army land warrant:
Issued to *No.* *Acres*
Reckless, Anthony, Lt 1818 200
(Note: Sent to Hon. P. Beecher.)

1180 23 Feb 1819 B/1/031
Registered by: Hon. Z. Sampson
Registered for: Heirs of J. Allen
Location: Mil - 16 7 4 21
Mil - 16 7 4 22
Mil - 16 7 4 23
Based upon the following Army land warrant:
Issued to *No.* *Acres*
Allen, Jacob, heirs of,
Capt 752 300
(Note: Sent to Hon. Z. Sampson.)

1181 26 Feb 1819 B/1/031
Registered by: F. D. Tschiffely
Registered for: Stephen Sprague
Location: Mil - 16 6 1 14
Based upon the following Army land warrant:
Issued to *No.* *Acres*
Sprague, S., assignee? of
R. Smith, Pvt 645 100
(Note: Sent him.)

1182 2 Sep 1819 B/1/031
Registered by: Hon. Samuel Hogg
Registered for: James Winchester
Location: Mil - 12 9 4 5
Mil - 12 9 4 8
Mil - 12 9 4 9
Based upon the following Army land warrant:
Issued to *No.* *Acres*
Winchester, James, Capt 2407 300
(Note: Sent to Hon. Mr. Hogg.)

1183 3 Mar 1819 B/1/032
Registered by: Seth Hyatt
Registered for: Jonas Stanberry
Location: Mil - 6 6 2 11
Mil - 6 7 3 34
Mil - 5 9 3 9
Based upon the following Army land warrant:
Issued to *No.* *Acres*
Bailey, Mountjoy, Capt 685 300
(Note: Delivered to Seth Hyatt.)

1184 4 Mar 1819 B/1/032
Registered by: Hon. J. R. Drake
Registered for: A. Parker
Location: Mil - 2 10 2 29
Based upon the following Army land warrant:
Issued to *No.* *Acres*
Parker, Amasa, Pvt 768 100
(Note: Sent to Hon. Mr. Drake.)

1185 8 Mar 1819 B/1/032
Registered by: F. D. Tschiffely
Registered for: Henry Newman
Location: Mil - 2 10 2 34
Based upon the following Army land warrant:
Issued to *No.* *Acres*
Blinn, George, Pvt 2968 100
(Note: Sent to W. H. Freeman, S[eal?] Harbour.)

1186 13 Apr 1819 B/1/032
Registered by: F. D. Tschiffely
Registered for: Henry Northup
Location: Mil - 6 7 3 12
Mil - 7 9 2 21
Mil - 7 9 2 23
Based upon the following Army land warrant:
Issued to *No.* *Acres*
Wyman, Dean, Pvt 728 100
Mitchall, Samuel, Pvt 729 100
Prentiss, Val[entine?]
Pvt 749 100

1187 6 May 1819 B/1/032
Registered by: R. J. Meigs, Junior
Registered for: Joseph Haviland
Location: Mil - 1 8 2 22W*
Based upon the following Army land warrant:
Issued to *No.* *Acres*
Smith, Joel, Ens 198 150*
(Note: Delivered to R. J. Meigs, Esq.)
*50-acre lot of 150 acres due an Ens.

1188 22 May 1819 B/1/032
Registered by: N. B. Van Zandt
Registered for: Henry Northup
Location: Mil - 8 9 1 29
Based upon the following Army land warrant:
Issued to *No.* *Acres*
Joy, David, Pvt 696 100
(Note: Delivered to N. B. Van Zandt.)

1189 25 May 1819 B/1/032
Registered by: F. D. Tschiffely
Registered for: Daniel Galpin
Location: Mil - 6 7 3 5
Based upon the following Army land warrant:
Issued to *No.* *Acres*
Galpin, Daniel, Pvt 253 100

1190 27 May 1819 B/1/032
Registered by: N. B. Van Zandt
Registered for: H. Northup
Location: Mil - 6 6 2 19
Based upon the following Army land warrant:
Issued to *No.* *Acres*
Manning, William T., Sgt 785 100

1191 24 Jun 1819 B/1/032
Registered by: John Underwood
Registered for: Jonas Stanberry
Location: Mil - 5 10 3 10
Mil - 6 7 3 4
Based upon the following Army land warrant:

Issued to	*No.*	*Acres*
Bell, Henry, Lt	623	200

1192 10 Jul 1819 B/1/032
Registered by: F. D. Tschiffely
Registered for: J. J. Melius
Location: Mil - 6 7 3 1
Based upon the following Army land warrant:

Issued to	*No.*	*Acres*
Rose, Elijah, Sgt	4929	100

(Note: Sent to R. Nichols, New York.)

1193 10 Jul 1819 B/1/032
Registered by: F. D. Tschiffely
Registered for: H. Northup
Location: Mil - 6 6 2 16
Based upon the following Army land warrant:

Issued to	*No.*	*Acres*
Tuttle, William, Pvt	697	100

1194 13 Jul 1819 B/1/032
Registered by: F. D. Tschiffely
Registered for: Jonas Stanberry
Location: Mil - 8 4 3 24
Mil - 8 4 3 23
Based upon the following Army land warrant:

Issued to	*No.*	*Acres*
Treal? [Treat?] Samuel, Pvt	794	100
Lavering, Isaac, Pvt	793	100

1195 14 Jul 1819 B/1/032
Registered by: Nicholas Van Zandt
Registered for: Henry Northup
Location: Mil - 6 7 3 10
Mil - 6 7 3 2
Mil - 6 7 3 6
Mil - 6 7 3 13
Mil - 6 7 3 11
Mil - 6 7 3 23
Based upon the following Army land warrants:

Issued to	*No.*	*Acres*
Brockins, Artemus, Pvt	698	100
Swell, S., Pvt	801	100
Grant, Daniel, Pvt	807	100
Mathews, E., Sgt	700	100
Dill, Lemuel, Drummer	699	100
Brackett, William, Pvt	708	100

1196 5 Aug 1819 B/1/032
Registered by: F. D. Tschiffely
Registered for: Jonas Stanberry
Location: Mil - 6 7 3 7
Mil - 6 7 3 8
Mil - 6 7 3 25
Mil - 5 10 3 2
Mil - 5 10 3 7
Mil - 5 10 3 16
Based upon the following Army land warrants:

Issued to	*No.*	*Acres*
Newall, Calvin, Pvt	688	100
Wait, Jeduthan, Pvt	762	100
Baker, Samuel, Pvt	713	100
Boothe, William, Matross	712	100
Hall, James, CaptLt	5	200

1197 13 Sep 1819 B/1/032
Registered by: F. D. Tschiffely
Registered for: William Salsbury
Location: Mil - 6 7 3 29
Based upon the following Army land warrant:

Issued to	*No.*	*Acres*
Salsbury, William, Pvt	456	100

1198 21 Sep 1819 B/1/032
Registered by: F. D. Tschiffely
Registered for: Henry Northup
Location: Mil - 6 6 2 18
Mil - 7 9 2 11
Based upon the following Army land warrant:

Issued to	*No.*	*Acres*
Archer, P. F., Lt	300	200

1199 22 Sep 1819 B/1/033
Registered by: N[ichola]s Van Zandt
Registered for: Ira Fish
Location: Mil - 7 9 2 9
Mil - 7 9 2 10
Mil - 5 9 3 26
Mil - 5 9 3 28
Mil - 5 9 3 29
Mil - 6 6 2 32
Mil - 6 6 2 33
Based upon the following Army land warrants:

Issued to	*No.*	*Acres*
Wentworth, Phineas, Pvt	774	100
Wooster, James, Pvt	775	100
Young, Joseph, Pvt	776	100
Medah, Stephen, Pvt	772	100
Randall, Edward, Pvt	773	100
Brown, Benj[amin] Pvt	770	100
Fall, George, Pvt	771	100

1200 21 Oct 1819 B/1/033
Registered by: F. D. Tschiffely
Registered for: Henry Northup
Location: Mil - 7 9 2 28
Mil - 7 9 2 17
Based upon the following Army land warrants:

Issued to	*No.*	*Acres*
Saraway, P., Pvt	809	100
Denning, J., Sgt	745	100

1201 26 Oct 1819 B/1/033
Registered by: F. D. Tschiffely
Registered for: Jonas Stanberry
Location: Mil - 6 7 3 9
Mil - 5 9 3 18
Mil - 6 7 3 27
Mil - 6 7 3 26
Based upon the following Army land warrants:

Issued to	*No.*	*Acres*
Kenniston, J., Pvt	784	100
Durant, E., Pvt	787	100
Boomer, E., Pvt	792	100
Chapman, John, Pvt	791	100

1202 15 Nov 1819 B/1/033
Registered by: F. D. Tschiffely
Registered for: -- Swyier? & [Jonas?] Stanberry
Location: Mil - 7 6 1 2
Mil - 7 6 1 3
Based upon the following Army land warrants:

Issued to	*No.*	*Acres*
Walden, John, Pvt	778	100
Story, John, Pvt	780	100

1203 7 Dec 1819 B/1/033
Registered by: F. D. Tschiffely
Registered for: Henry Northup
Location: Mil - 6 7 3 24
Mil - 6 8 2 18
Mil - 6 8 2 17
Mil - 6 8 2 19
Mil - 6 8 3 11
Based upon the following Army land warrants:

Issued to	*No.*	*Acres*
House, Henry, Pvt	7242	100
Tufts, William, Pvt	799? [749?]	100
Shelton, C., heir of, Capt	740	300

1204 11 Dec 1819 B/1/033
Registered by: Hon. John Linn
Registered for: J? L. Ayres
Location: Mil - 6 8 3 30
Based upon the following Army land warrant:

Issued to	*No.*	*Acres*
Daily, Solomon, Pvt	3087	100

1205 15 Dec 1819 B/1/033
Registered by: F. D. Tschiffely
Registered for: Henry Northup
Location: Mil - 7 9 2 1
Based upon the following Army land warrant:

Issued to	*No.*	*Acres*
Andrus, Elisha, Pvt	587	100

1206 15 Dec 1819 B/1/033
Registered by: F. D. Tschiffely
Registered for: -- Swyier? & [Jonas?] Stanberry
Location: Mil - 7 6 1 12
Based upon the following Army land warrant:

Issued to	*No.*	*Acres*
Casey, John, Pvt	779	100

1207 27 Dec 1819 B/1/033
Registered by: Hon. S. C. Crafts
Registered for: Benjamin Durkee
Location: Mil - 8 9 1 9
Mil - 8 9 1 10
Mil - 8 9 1 32
Based upon the following Army land warrant:

Issued to	*No.*	*Acres*
Durkee, Benjamin, Capt	420	300

(Note: Sent to Hon. S. C. Crafts.)

1208 4 Jan 1820 B/1/033
Registered by: Hon. P. Beecher
Registered for: John Jenness
Location: Mil - 7 9 2 12
Based upon the following Army land warrant:

Issued to	*No.*	*Acres*
Jenness, John, Pvt	758	100

1209 4 Jan 1820 B/1/033
Registered by: Hon. P. Beecher
Registered for: Zebedee Cook, Junior
Location: Mil - 6 8 2 21
Mil - 6 8 2 20
Mil - 6 8 2 30
Mil - 6 8 2 31
Mil - 6 8 2 32
Based upon the following Army land warrants:

Issued to	*No.*	*Acres*
Cottle, R., Sgt	572	100
Fisk, Joseph, Surgeon	686	400

(Note: Sent to Hon. P. Beecher.)

1210 25 Jan 1820 B/1/033
Registered by: F. D. Tschiffely
Registered for: Samuel H. Smith
Location: Mil - 7 9 2 3
Based upon the following Army land warrant:

Issued to	*No.*	*Acres*
Martin, David, Pvt	6228	100

1211 4 Feb 1820 B/1/033
Registered by: Josiah Meigs, Esq.
Registered for: Heirs of R. Finlay
Location: Mil - 11 6 1 3
Based upon the following Army land warrant:

Issued to	*No.*	*Acres*
Finlay, R., Pvt	8299	100

(Note: Sent to Hon. J. J. Wilson.)

1212 4 Feb 1820 B/1/033
Registered by: F. D. Tschiffely
Registered for: Paul Ferson
Location: Mil - 4 10 3 37
Mil - 4 10 3 38
Based upon the following Army land warrants:

Issued to	*No.*	*Acres*
Rogers, William, Pvt	746	100
George, Michael, Pvt	777	100

(Note: Sent to Henry Northup.)

1213 4 Feb 1820 B/1/034
Registered by: F. D. Tschiffely
Registered for: Paul Ferson
Location: Mil - 5 10 4 5
Mil - 5 10 4 6
Based upon the following Army land warrants:

Issued to	*No.*	*Acres*
Storey, Mary, daughter of Parker Storey, Pvt	761	100
Norwood, Nathan, Pvt	814	100

1214 4 Feb 1820 B/1/034
Registered by: F. D. Tschiffely
Registered for: Philip Baker
Location: Mil - 5 10 4 24
Based upon the following Army land warrant:

Issued to	*No.*	*Acres*
Sadler, John, Pvt	747	100

(Note: Sent to Mr. Northup.)

1215 7 Feb 1820 B/1/034
Registered by: [Nicholas B.?] Van Zandt & -- Rockwell
Registered for: Henry Northup

1215 [continued]

Location: Mil - 7 9 2 20
Mil - 5 9 3 4
Mil - 7 9 2 19
Mil - 6 8 3 26
Mil - 6 8 3 24
Mil - 6 8 3 17
Mil - 6 8 3 12
Mil - 6 8 3 13
Mil - 6 8 3 25
Mil - 6 8 3 24

Based upon the following Army land warrants:

Issued to	*No.*	*Acres*
Vose, --, assignee of John Rankins, Pvt	804	100
Vose, --, assignee of A. Bennett, Pvt	803	100
Vose, --, assignee of J. Rollings, Pvt	805	100
Vose, --, assignee of G. Webber, Pvt	806	100
Nevins, D., heirs of, Sgt	824	100
Hall, John, heirs of, Pvt	821	100
Holmes, Z., Pvt	816	100
Cobb, M., Sgt	812	100
McAlpin, G., heirs of, Pvt	825	100
Colby, D., heir of, Pvt	730	100

1216 8 Feb 1820 B/1/034

Registered by: F. D. Tschiffely
Registered for: Heirs of E. Bliss
Location: Mil - 8 9 2 14

Based upon the following Army land warrant:

Issued to	*No.*	*Acres*
Bliss, E., Sgt	574	100

(Note: Sent to Hon. S. C. Crofts.)

1217 8 Feb 1820 B/1/034

Registered by: F. D. Tschiffely
Registered for: D. Marsh
Location: Mil - 8 9 2 13

Based upon the following Army land warrant:

Issued to	*No.*	*Acres*
Marsh, Daniel, Pvt	739	100

(Note: Sent to Hon. S. C. Crofts.)

1218 16 Feb 1820 B/1/034

Registered by: Hon. William McCoy
Registered for: Jesse Slingluff
Location: Mil - 3 7 1 11

Based upon the following Army land warrant:

Issued to	*No.*	*Acres*
Winter, Joseph, Pvt	783	100

1219 23 Feb 1820 B/1/034

Registered by: Hon. P. Beecher
Registered for: N. Eastman
Location: Mil - 6 8 2 14
Mil - 6 8 2 15

Based upon the following Army land warrant:

Issued to	*No.*	*Acres*
Morrow, Joshua, Lt	756	200

(Note: Sent to Hon. P. Beecher.)

1220 23 Feb 1820 B/1/034

Registered by: Hon. P. Beecher
Registered for: Jonas? Umberhooker
Location: Mil - 6 8 2 2?

Based upon the following Army land warrant:

Issued to	*No.*	*Acres*
Cline, George, Pvt	12880	100

(Note: Sent to Hon. P. Beecher.)

1221 23 Feb 1820 B/1/034

Registered by: Hon. P. Beecher
Registered for: Anthony Boucher
Location: Mil - 7 9 2 14

Based upon the following Army land warrant:

Issued to	*No.*	*Acres*
Stack, Richard, Fife Maj	10389	100

(Note: Sent to Hon. P. Beecher.)

1222 25 Feb 1820 B/1/034

Registered by: Hon. S. Gross
Registered for: James Simers
Location: Mil - 7 9 2 15

Based upon the following Army land warrant:

Issued to	*No.*	*Acres*
Simers, John, Pvt	10380	100

(Note: Sent to Hon. S. Gross.)

1223 3 Mar 1820 B/1/034

Registered by: F. D. Tschiffely
Registered for: Jonas Stanberry
Location: Mil - 6 7 3 16
Mil - 6 7 3 28

Based upon the following Army land warrants:

Issued to	*No.*	*Acres*
Desilvia, William, heir of, Pvt	817	100
Higgins, Benjamin, Pvt	767	100

(Note: Sent to Jonas Stanberry.)

1224 11 Mar 1820 B/1/034

Registered by: Hon. Nath[anie]l Silsbee
Registered for: Heirs of John Glover
Location: Mil - 6 7 3 17
Mil - 6 7 3 18
Mil - 6 7 3 19
Mil - 6 7 3 20
Mil - 6 7 3 21
Mil - 6 7 3 22
Mil - 7 7 2 4
Mil - 7 7 2 5
Mil - 1 8 2 23E*

Based upon the following Army land warrant:

Issued to	*No.*	*Acres*
Glover, John, dec[eased] BrigGen	763	850

*50-acre lot.
(Note: Sent to Hon. N. Silsbee.)

1225 11 Mar 1820 B/1/034

Registered by: Cadwallader Wallace
Registered for: Residuary legatees of A. Gordon
Location: Mil - 16 8 3 6*
Mil - 6 8 2 22

Based upon the following Army land warrant:

Issued to	*No.*	*Acres*
Gordon, Amb[rose?] Lt	539	200

(Note: Sent to C. Wallace.)
*Originally shown as Mil - 16 7 3 6.

1226 3 Apr 1820 B/1/034
Registered by: Hon. James Wallace
Registered for: Michael Waltz
Location: Mil - 5 10 4 22
Based upon the following Army land warrant:

Issued to	*No.*	*Acres*
Waltz, Michael, Pvt	876	100

(Note: Sent to Hon. J. Wallace.)

1227 17 Apr 1820 B/1/034
Registered by: F. D. Tschiffely
Registered for: C[hristian] Deardorff
Location: Mil - 3 7 1 27
Based upon the following Army land warrant:

Issued to	*No.*	*Acres*
Waterburg, E., administrator of Charles Perkins, Pvt	340	100

(Note: Sent to Michael Nourse.)

1228 3 May 1820 B/1/034
Registered by: F. D. Tschiffely
Registered for: George? Fricks
Location: Mil - 6 8 3 9
Based upon the following Army land warrant:

Issued to	*No.*	*Acres*
Glenn, Hugh, heir of, Pvt	634	100

(Note: [Delivered? to] Hon. David Merchand.)

1229 16 May 1820 B/1/035
Registered by: Nicholas B. Van Zandt & F. D. Tschiffely
Registered for: Henry Northup
Location: Mil - 6 7 3 33
Mil - 6 8 3 18
Mil - 7 4 2 30
Mil - 6 8 3 4
Based upon the following Army land warrants:

Issued to	*No.*	*Acres*
Seaver, T., heirs of, Pvt	818	100
Phinney, John, Pvt	808	100
Mann, H. V., heir of E. Blake, Pvt	786	100
Tucker, John, Sgt	893	100

1230 23 Jun 1820 B/1/035
Registered by: F. D. Tschiffely
Registered for: John M. Haupt
Location: Mil - 6 8 3 27
Based upon the following Army land warrant:

Issued to	*No.*	*Acres*
Haupt, John M., Pvt	869	100

1231 30 Jun 1820 B/1/035
Registered by: F. D. Tschiffely
Registered for: Jacob Shottler
Location: Mil - 1 8 4 1
Based upon the following Army land warrant:

Issued to	*No.*	*Acres*
Shottler, Jacob, assignee of J. W. Taylor, Pvt	904	100

(Note: Sent to G. Y. Lansing.)

1232 10 Jul 1820 B/1/035
Registered by: F. D. Tschiffely
Registered for: Daniel Moss
Location: Mil - 16 6 1 13
Based upon the following Army land warrant:

Issued to	*No.*	*Acres*
Moss, Daniel, Pvt	810	100

1233 22 Aug 1820 B/1/035
Registered by: F. D. Tschiffely
Registered for: Henry Northup
Location: Mil - 7 4 2 14
Based upon the following Army land warrant:

Issued to	*No.*	*Acres*
Ellis, J. R., assignee of E. Mitchell, Pvt*	829	100

*It is not clear whether Ellis or Mitchell is the Revolutionary War veteran.

1234 30 Aug 1820 B/1/035
Registered by: F. D. Tschiffely
Registered for: Heirs of D. Breaty
Location: Mil - 12 9 3 5
Based upon the following Army land warrant:

Issued to	*No.*	*Acres*
Breaty, D., heirs of, Pvt	880	100

1235 8 Sep 1820 B/1/035
Registered by: F. D. Tschiffely
Registered for: Heirs of P. Scaus
Location: Mil - 5 10 4 19
Based upon the following Army land warrant:

Issued to	*No.*	*Acres*
Scaus, P., heirs of, Pvt	989? [or 909?]	100

(Note: Sent to H. Northup same day.)

1236* 21 Sep 1820 B/1/035
Registered by: Nich[ola]s Van Zandt
Registered for: Job Ripple
Location: Mil - 6 8 3 19
Based upon the following Army land warrant:

Issued to	*No.*	*Acres*
Ripple, Job, Pvt	920	100

*This entire serial entry crossed out in source register; see serial entry 1240 below.

1237 28 Sep 1820 B/1/035
Registered by: F. D. Tschiffely
Registered for: Jonas Stanberry
Location: Mil - 6 8 3 2
Based upon the following Army land warrant:

Issued to	*No.*	*Acres*
Withers, W. R., Ens	760	100*

*Portion of 150 acres due an Ens; see serial entry 1246 for remainder.

1238 6 Oct 1820 B/1/035
Registered by: F. D. Tschiffely
Registered for: Heirs of A. Woodworth
Location: Mil - 7 9 2 32
Based upon the following Army land warrant:

Issued to	*No.*	*Acres*
Woodworth, Asa, heirs at law of, Pvt	830	100

(Note: Sent to James Woodworth.)

1239 9 Oct 1820 B/1/035

1239 [continued]
Registered by: F. D. Tschiffely
Registered for: Jonas Herrick, *et al*
Location: Mil - 6 8 3 29
Based upon the following Army land warrant:

Issued to	*No.*	*Acres*
Herrick, Jonas, Sgt	855	100

1240* 13 Oct 1820 B/1/035
Registered by: Nich[ola]s Van Zandt
Registered for: Job Ripple
Location: Mil - 6 8 3 23
Based upon the following Army land warrant:

Issued to	*No.*	*Acres*
Ripple, Job, Pvt	920	100

*See also serial entry 1236 above.

1241 4 Nov 1820 B/1/035
Registered by: Hon. L. Sawyer
Registered for: Lemuel Sawyer
Location: Mil - 3 8 4 8
Based upon the following Army land warrant:

Issued to	*No.*	*Acres*
Fennder, D., heirs of, Pvt	151	100

1242 7 Dec 1820 B/1/035
Registered by: Abraham Shane
Registered for: Abraham Shane
Location: Mil - 1 8 2 7E*
Based upon the following Army land warrant:

Issued to	*No.*	*Acres*
Scott, John, Ens	819	150*

(Note: Handed J. Gardiner, Esq.)
*50-acre lot; portion of 150 acres due an Ens.

1243 7 Dec 1820 B/1/035
Registered by: F. D. Tschiffely
Registered for: H[enry] Northup
Location: Mil - 8 9 3 3
Based upon the following Army land warrant:

Issued to	*No.*	*Acres*
Reynolds, T., heirs of, Pvt	813	100

1244 11 Dec 1820 B/1/035
Registered by: W. H. Beard
Registered for: J[onas] Stanberry
Location: Mil - 9 9 4 10
Based upon the following Army land warrant:

Issued to	*No.*	*Acres*
Chase, Robert, Pvt	798	100

1245 7 Feb 1821 B/1/035
Registered by: F. D. Tschiffely
Registered for: Seth Gansey
Location: Mil - 6 8 2 13
Based upon the following Army land warrant:

Issued to	*No.*	*Acres*
Gansey, Seth, Pvt	897	100

(Note: Sent to Hon. Mr. Mallary.)

1246 15 Feb 1821 B/1/035
Registered by: F. D. Tschiffely
Registered for: Jonas Stanberry
Location: Mil - 1 8 2 11W*
Based upon the following Army land warrant:

Issued to	*No.*	*Acres*
Withers, W. R., Ens	760	150*

*50-acre lot of 150 acres due an Ens; see also serial entry 1237 above.

1247 17 Feb 1821 B/1/035
Registered by: William H. Brown
Registered for: Barbara Engle
Location: Mil - 3 10 1 1
Based upon the following Army land warrant:

Issued to	*No.*	*Acres*
Engle, B[arbara] heir[ess] of J. Laib, Pvt	949	100

1248 19 Feb 1821 B/1/035
Registered by: J[osiah] Meigs, Esq.
Registered for: D. Kenniston
Location: Mil - 3 10 1 5
Based upon the following Army land warrant:

Issued to	*No.*	*Acres*
Kenniston, D., Pvt	903	100

1249 22 Feb 1821 B/1/035
Registered by: William Eisenbeck
Registered for: Henry Rise
Location: Mil - 3 10 1 2
Based upon the following Army land warrant:

Issued to	*No.*	*Acres*
Rise, Henry, Pvt	928	100

(Note: Delivered to William Eisenbeck.)

1250 30 Apr 1821 B/1/035
Registered by: Nich[ola]s B. Van Zandt
Registered for: Jesse Ward
Location: Mil - 4 10 3 27
Based upon the following Army land warrant:

Issued to	*No.*	*Acres*
Hossam, *alias* Horsum, Ebenezer, Pvt	886	100

1251 8 May 1821 B/1/035
Registered by: Alexander Holmes
Registered for: Heirs of Robert Howe
Location: Mil - 2 5 3 3
Mil - 2 5 3 6
Mil - 2 5 3 7
Mil - 2 5 3 14
Mil - 2 5 3 19
Mil - 2 5 3 21
Mil - 2 5 3 22
Mil - 2 5 3 24
Mil - 2 5 3 25
Mil - 2 5 3 31
Mil - 2 5 3 32
Based upon the following Army land warrant:

Issued to	*No.*	*Acres*
Howe, Robert, heirs of, MajGen	856	1100

1252 8 May 1821 B/1/035
Registered by: Alexander Holmes
Registered for: Harmony Cornwale [Cornwall?]
Location: Mil - 2 5 2 31
Based upon the following Army land warrant:

1252 [continued]

Issued to	*No.*	*Acres*
Cornwale [Cornwall?] Harmony, Pvt	917	100

1253 8 May 1821 B/1/035
Registered by: Alexander Holmes
Registered for: Alexander Holmes
Location: Mil - 2 5 3 10
Mil - 2 5 3 23
Based upon the following Army land warrant:

Issued to	*No.*	*Acres*
Callahan, David, Pvt	964	100
English, James, Pvt	965	100

1254 14 May 1821 B/1/036
Registered by: N. B. Van Zandt
Registered for: Henry Northup
Location: Mil - 8 9 2 12
Based upon the following Army land warrant:

Issued to	*No.*	*Acres*
Gray, Timothy, E[xecutor?] & H[eir?] of B. G[ray?] Pvt	800	100

1255 15 May 1821 B/1/036
Registered by: N. B. Van Zandt
Registered for: Mordecai Moore
Location: Mil - 5 10 4 21
Mil - 5 10 4 20
Mil - 5 10 4 34
Mil - 5 10 4 33
Based upon the following Army land warrants:

Issued to	*No.*	*Acres*
Wales, Timothy, Pvt	923	100
Lemon, John, Pvt	950	100
Kenniston, Joseph E., father & heir at law of Job Kenniston, Pvt	737	100
Whitcomb, Nathaniel, Pvt	822	100

1256 28 May 1821 B/1/036
Registered by: N. B. Van Zandt
Registered for: Benjamin Hostutler*
Location: Mil - 5 10 4 16
Based upon the following Army land warrant:

Issued to	*No.*	*Acres*
Patterson, Samuel, & the other heir of S. Patterson, Pvt	859	100

*So spelled.

1257 29 May 1821 B/1/036
Registered by: A. Boden
Registered for: Eliza[beth] Smith
Location: Mil - 4 10 3 8
Based upon the following Army land warrant:

Issued to	*No.*	*Acres*
Dailey, Joseph, Pvt	900	100

(Note: Sent to A. Boden.)

1258 4 Jun 1821 B/1/036
Registered by: N. B. Van Zandt
Registered for: Alexander Crab
Location: Mil - 4 10 3 31
Mil - 4 10 3 32
Based upon the following Army land warrants:

Issued to	*No.*	*Acres*
McCormick, Hugh, Pvt	846	100
Moore, Susanna, heir[ess] of Elkins Moore, Pvt	731	100

1259 1 Jul 1821 B/1/036
Registered by: N. B. Van Zandt
Registered for: Abraham Shane
Location: Mil - 5 7 1 23
Mil - 5 7 1 24
Mil - 5 10 4 3
Mil - 5 10 4 17
Mil - 4 10 3 39
Based upon the following Army land warrants:

Issued to	*No.*	*Acres*
Johnson, Eleanor, heir[ess] at law of Jacob Rowe, Pvt	930	100
Jotham, Lurany? [Surany?] sister & heir[ess2 at law of Joel Sugarmug, Pvt	985	100
Lincoln, Rufus, Capt	990	300

1260 19 Jul 1821 B/1/036
Registered by: Jonas Stanbery
Registered for: Jonas Stanbery
Location: Mil - 8 9 1 28
Based upon the following Army land warrant:

Issued to	*No.*	*Acres*
Crawley, James, Pvt	834	100

1261 16 Jul 1821 B/1/036
Registered by: Calvin Gardner
Registered for: Calvin Gardner, son, & other heirs of I. Gardner
Location: Mil - 5 10 4 4
Based upon the following Army land warrant:

Issued to	*No.*	*Acres*
Gardner, Isaac, Pvt	986	100

(Note: Sent to L. Blagge, Boston.)

1262 16 Jul 1821 B/1/036
Registered by: Philander Chase
Registered for: Sarah Russele
Location: Mil - 8 9 2 17
Mil - 8 9 2 18
Based upon the following Army land warrant:

Issued to	*No.*	*Acres*
Russele, Cornelius, Lt	248	200

1263 21 Jun 1821* B/1/036
Registered by: Michael Nourse
Registered for: Joseph Selden
Location: Mil - 8 9 1 6
Based upon the following Army land warrant:

Issued to	*No.*	*Acres*
Phelps, David, Musician	6325	100

*Out of chronological sequence.

1264 21 Aug 1821 B/1/036
Registered by: Z[accheus] A. Beatty
Registered for: Robert Nicholson
Location: Mil - 3 1 1 39
Based upon the following Army land warrant:

1264 [continued]

Issued to	*No.*	*Acres*
Conneley, Hugh, Pvt	827	100

1265 25 Sep 1821 B/1/036
Registered by: A[braham] Shane
Registered for: Lucinda? Skinner & the other heirs
Location: Mil - 5 10 4 35
Based upon the following Army land warrant:

Issued to	*No.*	*Acres*
Skinner, Timothy, Pvt	946	100

(Note: Sent to her at Zanesville.)

1266 2 Oct 1821 B/1/036
Registered by: A. Holmes
Registered for: Peter Ollom
Location: Mil - 10 1 2 18
Based upon the following Army land warrant:

Issued to	*No.*	*Acres*
Williams, Jeremiah, Pvt	875	100

(Note: Sent to A. Holmes, Newark.)

1267 -- May 1821* B/1/036
Registered by: Joseph Watson
Registered for: Henry Northup
Location: Mil - 7 4 2 1
Based upon the following Army land warrant:

Issued to	*No.*	*Acres*
Lock, Elijah, & the other heirs of Moser Lock, Pvt	736	100

*Out of chronological sequence.

1268 18 Jun 1821 B/1/036
Registered by: Walter Dun
Registered for: Abraham Shane
Location: Mil - 5 7 1 27
Based upon the following Army land warrant:

Issued to	*No.*	*Acres*
Hilliard, Joseph, Pvt	933	100

(Note: Delivered to N. B. Van Zandt.)

1269 6 Dec 1821 B/1/036
Registered by: Winslow? Lewis
Registered for: Caleb Lincoln
Location: Mil - 5 10 4 2
Based upon the following Army land warrant:

Issued to	*No.*	*Acres*
Lincoln, Caleb, Pvt	963	100

1270 10 Dec 1821 B/1/036
Registered by: Col -- Chambers, H[ouse] of Repre-[sentatives]
Registered for: James Pierce, Junior
Location: Mil - 8 4 3 13
Based upon the following Army land warrant:

Issued to	*No.*	*Acres*
Battersly, Robert* Pvt	956	100

*Interlineation: Reuben Whitcomb.

1271 7 Dec 1821 B/1/036
Registered by: Hon. James Pleasant, [U.S.] Senate
Registered for: Cary Drew, *et al*
Location: Mil - 2 10 2 24
Mil - 2 10 2 25
Based upon the following Army land warrant:

Issued to	*No.*	*Acres*
Drew, Cary, & the other heirs of John Drew, Lt	981	200

1272 3 Dec 1821 B/1/036
Registered by: Hon. Lewis Williams
Registered for: John Campbell
Location: Mil - 5 10 4 13
Mil - 5 10 4 14
Based upon the following Army land warrant:

Issued to	*No.*	*Acres*
Campbell, James, Lt	487	200

1273 20 Dec 1821 B/1/036
Registered by: J. F. Johnson
Registered for: Heirs of James Armstrong
Location: Mil - 5 10 4 9
Mil - 5 10 4 10
Mil - 5 10 4 11
Mil - 5 10 4 12
Mil - 5 10 4 18
Based upon the following Army land warrant:

Issued to	*No.*	*Acres*
Armstrong, James, heirs of, Col	594	500

(Note: Sent to R. M. Johnson, [U.S.] Senate.

1274 -- Nov 1821* B/1/036
Registered by: Abraham Shane
Registered for: Christian Deardorff
Location: Mil - 4 10 3 26
Mil - 4 10 3 28
Mil - 4 10 3 33
Based upon the following Army land warrant:

Issued to	*No.*	*Acres*
Wade, Abner, Capt	797	300

*Out of chronological sequence.

1275 7 Dec 1820** B/1/036
Registered by: Abraham Shane
Registered for: Abraham Shane
Location: Mil - 4 10 2 1*
Based upon the following Army land warrant:

Issued to	*No.*	*Acres*
Scott, John, Ens	819	150*

(Note: Sent to A. Shane, Baltimore.)
*100 acres of 150 acres due an Ens. A note indicates that Shane had previously been assigned a 50-acre lot pertaining to this warrant.
**Out of chronological sequence.

1276 B/1/036
Registered by: S. Blagge
Registered for: John Bailey
Location: Mil - 4 10 3 29
Based upon the following Army land warrant:

Issued to	*No.*	*Acres*
Bailey, John, Pvt	744	100

(Note: Sent to S. Blagge, Boston.)

1277 22 Dec 1821 B/1/037
Registered by: Hon. S. S. Southard
Registered for: Abbygail Hepburn
Location: Mil - 4 10 3 34
Based upon the following Army land warrant:

Issued to	*No.*	*Acres*
Hepburn, Peter, Pvt	14043	100

1278 15 Jan 1822 B/1/037
Registered by: A. Holmes
Registered for: Alex[ander] Holmes
Location: Mil - 10 1 2 22
Based upon the following Army land warrant:

Issued to	*No.*	*Acres*
Orme, Charles, Pvt	896	100

(Note: [To] A. Holmes, Newark, same day.)

1279 15 Jan 1822 B/1/037
Registered by: Henry Northup
Registered for: Henry Northup
Location: Mil - 5 3 3 38
Mil - 7 9 2 4
Mil - 6 8 2 16
Based upon the following Army land warrants:

Issued to	*No.*	*Acres*
Mitchell, Joseph, Pvt	853	100
Mitchell, Martin, Pvt	852	100
Casey, Joshua, Pvt	845	100

1280 16 Jan 1822 B/1/037
Registered by: N. B. Van Zandt
Registered for: Samuel Woodin
Location: Mil - 7 9 2 5
Based upon the following Army land warrant:

Issued to	*No.*	*Acres*
Woodin, Samuel, Pvt	10911	100

(Note: [To] Hon. J. R. Poinsett.)

1281 12 Feb 1822 B/1/037
Registered by: N. Bullock
Registered for: Samuel J? Mathewson & Nathaniel Bullock
Location: Mil - 7 9 2 2
Based upon the following Army land warrant:

Issued to	*No.*	*Acres*
Hanly, *alias* Handy, Russell, Pvt	753	100

(Note: [To] N. Bullock, Bristol, R. I? [or B?])

1282 1 Feb 1822 B/1/037
Registered by: Joseph Watson
Registered for: Alexander Holmes
Location: Mil - 10 1 2 27
Mil - 2 5 2 30
Based upon the following Army land warrant:

Issued to	*No.*	*Acres*
White, Elijah, Pvt	142	100
Stepenson [Stephenson?] Daniel, Pvt	139	100

(Note: [To] Alex[ander] Holmes at Newark.)

1283 12 Mar 1822 B/1/037
Registered by: Hon. J. Crudup
Registered for: Jonathan Sneed & other heirs
Location: Mil - 4 10 3 20
Mil - 4 10 3 13
Based upon the following Army land warrant:

Issued to	*No.*	*Acres*
Parker, Cader, Lt	1028	200

(Note: [To] H. G. Burton, House of Representatives. [pencilled notation:] North Carolina.)

1284 25 Mar 1822 B/1/037
Registered by: Henry Northup
Registered for: Wooster James
Location: Mil - 10 1 2 21
Based upon the following Army land warrant:

Issued to	*No.*	*Acres*
Guile? Asa, Pvt	984	100

1285 25? Mar 1822 B/1/037
Registered by: Isaac Purdy
Registered for: Isaac Purdy
Location: Mil - 7 7 2 11
Based upon the following Army land warrant:

Issued to	*No.*	*Acres*
Arnold, Monathan, Pvt	887	100

(Note: Sent to him at Millersburg, Ohio.)

1286 12 Apr 1822 B/1/037
Registered by: Nathan M. Whittemore
Registered for: Nathan M. Whittemore & the other heirs of P. Whittemore
Location: Mil - 10 1 2 34
Based upon the following Army land warrant:

Issued to	*No.*	*Acres*
Whittemore, Paul, Pvt	1013	100

(Note: Sent to him at Cincinnati.)

1287 15 Apr 1822 B/1/037
Registered by: N. B. Van Zandt
Registered for: Joseph Troyer
Location: Mil - 5 10 3 1
Based upon the following Army land warrant:

Issued to	*No.*	*Acres*
Britton, John, Pvt	999	100

1288 -- Mar 1822* B/1/037
Registered by: N. B. Van Zandt
Registered for: Michael Hosack
Location: Mil - 4 10 3 19
Mil - 4 10 3 21
Based upon the following Army land warrants:

Issued to	*No.*	*Acres*
Davis, John, Drummer?	702	100
Pollard, Barton, Pvt	703	100

*Out of chronological sequence.

1289 15 Apr 1822 B/1/037
Registered by: Hon. David Chambers
Registered for: Erastus S. S. Rouse
Location: Mil - 5 3 3 9
Based upon the following Army land warrant:

Issued to	*No.*	*Acres*
Adams, Samuel, Pvt	955	100

1290 26 Apr 1822 B/1/037
Registered by: George Plumer
Registered for: James Brady
Location: Mil - 1 10 1 17
Mil - 5 10? 4 31*
Mil - 1 10 1 32
Based upon the following Army land warrants:

Issued to	*No.*	*Acres*
Harwood, Thomas, Pvt	861	100
Barclay, John, Lt	1041**	200

*Could also read Mil - 5 11 4 31.
**"In lieu? of No. 577."

1291 — 1 May 1822 — B/1/037
Registered by: James L? [or S?] Smith
Registered for: James L? [or S?] Smith
Location: Mil - 3 7 1 24
Mil - 3 7 1 25
Mil - 3 7 1 40
Based upon the following Army land warrant:

Issued to	*No.*	*Acres*
Child, Francis, Capt	383	300

(Note: Sent to him same day, Hillsborough, N.C.)

1292 — 18 May 1822 — B/1/037
Registered by: Jeremiah Causden
Registered for: Hezekiah Ford
Location: Mil - 3 10 1 3
Mil - 3 10 1 4
Based upon the following Army land warrant:

Issued to	*No.*	*Acres*
Ford, Hezekiah, Lt	758	200

(Note: To Hon. J. Causden in Elkton.)

1293 — 21 May 1822 — B/1/037
Registered by: M. Petry, Consul of France
Registered for: Heirs of Baron -- de Kalb
Location: Mil - 4 10 1 1
Mil - 4 10 1 4
Mil - 4 10 1 6
Mil - 4 10 1 7
Mil - 4 10 1 8
Mil - 4 10 1 9
Mil - 4 10 1 10
Mil - 4 10 3 25
Mil - 4 10 3 30
Mil - 4 10 3 35
Mil - 4 10 3 36
Based upon the following Army land warrant:

Issued to	*No.*	*Acres*
de Kalb, -- Baron, MajGen	1002	1100

1294 — 11 Jun 1822 — B/1/037
Registered by: N. B. Van Zandt
Registered for: Abraham Shane
Location: Mil - 6 10 3 8
Mil - 5 10 4 8
Based upon the following Army land warrants:

Issued to	*No.*	*Acres*
Rockwood? [Rackwood?] Ebenezer, Pvt	927	100
Vose, Jesse, Pvt	706	100

1295 — 11 Jun 1822 — B/1/037
Registered by: M. Petry [Consul of France]
Registered for: John Baptiste Viscount de Lomague
Location: Mil - 8 9 2 19
Mil - 8 9 2 20
Mil - 8 9 2 21
Mil - 8 9 2 22
Based upon the following Army land warrant:

Issued to	*No.*	*Acres*
de Lomague, John Baptiste Viscount, Maj	1003	400

1296 — 12 Jul 1822 — B/1/037
Registered by: Mathew Organ
Registered for: Mathew? Organ, son, & the other heirs of John Organ
Location: Mil - 2 5 3 9
Based upon the following Army land warrant:

Issued to	*No.*	*Acres*
Organ, John, Pvt	1029	100

(Note: [To] Mathew Organ, Washington, Pennsylvania.)

1297 — 7 Aug 1822 — B/1/037
Registered by: S. Blagge
Registered for: --? Hartwell:
Location: Mil - 10 3 4 11
Based upon the following Army land warrant:

Issued to	*No.*	*Acres*
Brooks, Nehemiah, Pvt	982	100

1298 — 29 --? 1822 — B/1/037
Registered by: Alexander Maker
Registered for: Alexander Maker
Location: Mil - 11 6 1 19
Based upon the following Army land warrant:

Issued to	*No.*	*Acres*
Jaquish, John, Pvt	931	100

(Note: [Sent] to him at Mount Vernon, Knox County, Ohio.)

1299 — 12 Feb 1822 — B/1/038
Registered by: Joseph Watson
Registered for: Alexander Holmes
Location: Mil - 9 7 3 8
Based upon the following Army land warrant:

Issued to	*No.*	*Acres*
McElroy, William, Pvt	137	100

(Note: To A. Holmes, Newark [Ohio].)

1300 — -- Sep 1822 — B/1/038
Registered by: C. Lofland
Registered for: Mordecai Myers
Location: Mil - 12 9 4 4
Based upon the following Army land warrant:

Issued to	*No.*	*Acres*
Tool [O'Tool?] Patrick, Pvt	1038	100

(Note: To M. Myers & Co., New York.)

1301 — 12 Dec 1822 — B/1/038
Registered by: D. Chambers
Registered for: Jonas Stanberry
Location: Mil - 9 9 4 37
Based upon the following Army land warrant:

Issued to	*No.*	*Acres*
Nevite? [Nevin? Nevill?] John, Pvt	1035	100

1302 — 11 Jan 1823 — B/1/038
Registered by: Samuel? Campbell
Registered for: Thomas Newell
Location: Mil - 5 10 4 28
Based upon the following Army land warrant:

Issued to	*No.*	*Acres*
Newell, Thomas, Pvt	147	100

(Note: To Hon. S. Campbell, H[ouse] of R[epresentatives] same day.)

1303 — 17 Jan 1823 — B/1/038
Registered by: David Chambers
Registered for: Henry Northup

1303 [continued]
Location: Mil - 7 9 2 6
Based upon the following Army land warrant:

Issued to	*No.*	*Acres*
Turner, Abiel, Pvt	978	100

1304 17 Jan 1823 B/1/038
Registered by: Alexander Holmes
Registered for: George Chadwell
Location: Mil - 2 5 2 21
Based upon the following Army land warrant:

Issued to	*No.*	*Acres*
Blood, Ephraim, Pvt	966	100

(Note: To A. Holmes, Newark, Ohio.)

1305 20 Jan 1822* B/1/038
Registered by: D. Chambers
Registered for: David Chambers
Location: Mil - 10 1 2 19
Based upon the following Army land warrant:

Issued to	*No.*	*Acres*
Grover, Jacob, Pvt	748	100

(Note: To him, H[ouse] of R[epresentatives].)
*Not in chronological sequence.

1306 -- Jan 1823 B/1/038
Registered by: N. B. Van Zandt
Registered for: A[braham] Shane
Location: Mil - 3 10 1 25?
Mil - 8 7 3 2
Mil - 8 7 3 3
Mil - 9 9 4 36
Mil - 2 7 4 19
Mil - 2 5 2 10
Mil - 5 10 4 27
Based upon the following Army land warrants:

Issued to	*No.*	*Acres*
Duntlin, Nathan, Pvt	888	100
Fitzpatrick, James, Pvt	937	100
Reiley, John, Pvt	993	100
Wickham, Isaac, Pvt	906	100
Harley, Benjamin, Pvt	991	100
Satherwhite, John L, Pvt	1010	100
Fuller, Joseph	905	100

(Note: Sent to him, 27 Jan [1823] Dover, Ohio.)

1307 4 Feb 1823 B/1/038
Registered by: William Rhodes
Registered for: William Rhodes
Location: Mil - 8 9 2 11
Based upon the following Army land warrant:

Issued to	*No.*	*Acres*
Rhodes, William, Pvt	1026	100

(Note: [Sent] to him, Urbana, Ohio.)

1308 4 Feb 1823 B/1/038
Registered by: Joseph Watson
Registered for: David Chambers
Location: Mil - 9 9 2 2
Based upon the following Army land warrant:

Issued to	*No.*	*Acres*
Conant, Solomon, Pvt	942	100

(Note: [Sent] to him, H[ouse] of R[epresentatives].)

1309 22 Feb 1823 B/1/038
Registered by: D. Chambers
Registered for: Abr[aham] Shane
Location: Mil - 9 9 2 3
Based upon the following Army land warrant:

Issued to	*No.*	*Acres*
Benedict, Daniel, Pvt	714	100

(Note: [Delivered] to him, H[ouse] of R[epresentatives].)

1310 22 Feb 1823 B/1/038
Registered by: C. Lofland
Registered for: Mordecai Myers
Location: Mil - 8 9 2 10
Based upon the following Army land warrant:

Issued to	*No.*	*Acres*
Kelly, Edward, Pvt	1009	100

(Note: Sent to him at New York.)

1311 14 Jan 1823* B/1/038
Registered by: J? Sloan
Registered for: Alonson? Drury
Location: Mil - 5 9 3 8
Mil - 5 9 3 38
Based upon the following Army land warrants:

Issued to	*No.*	*Acres*
Peirce, Abel, Pvt	683	100
Barr, Alex[ander], Pvt	684	100

(Note: Sent to Hon. J. Sloan, H[ouse] of R[epresentatives].)
*Not in chronological sequence.

1312 27 Feb 1823 B/1/038
Registered by: R. Saunders
Registered for: Reuben Benson
Location: Mil - 16 7 2 24
Based upon the following Army land warrant:

Issued to	*No.*	*Acres*
Benson, Reuben, Pvt	1045	100

(Note: To Hon. R. Saunders, H[ouse] of R[epresentatives].)

1313 27 Feb 1823 B/1/038
Registered by: R. Saunders
Registered for: Sally Thomas and the other heirs of L. Thomas
Location: Mil - 15 7 2 9
Based upon the following Army land warrant:

Issued to	*No.*	*Acres*
Thomas, Sally, daughter, and the other heirs of L. Thomas, Pvt	1011	100

(Note: To Hon R. Saunders, H[ouse] of R[epresentatives].)

1314 28 Feb 1823 B/1/038
Registered by: Hon. C. Borland, Junior
Registered for: John Brasbridge
Location: Mil - 8 9 1 23
Based upon the following Army land warrant:

Issued to	*No.*	*Acres*
Brasbridge, John, Pvt	1067	100

1315 1 Mar 1823 B/1/038
Registered by: William Smith
Registered for: Martin Delaney
Location: Mil - 5 10 4 23

1315 [continued]
Based upon the following Army land warrant:

Issued to	*No.*	*Acres*
Delaney, Martin, Pvt	1056	100

1316 2 Apr 1823 B/1/038
Registered by: D. Chambers
Registered for: Jonas Stanberry
Location: Mil - 6 8 2 3
Mil - 6 8 2 23
Based upon the following Army land warrant:

Issued to	*No.*	*Acres*
Stetson, Thomas, Lt	995	100

(Note: To J. Stanberry, Putnam.)

1317 1 Mar 1823* B/1/038
Registered by: D. Chambers
Registered for: Henry Northup
Location: Mil - 8 5 1 32
Based upon the following Army land warrant:

Issued to	*No.*	*Acres*
Hunt, William, Pvt	913	100

(Note: To Thomas B. Northup at Zanesville.)

1318 1 Mar 1823 B/1/038
Registered by: P. Shaeffer
Registered for: Jonas Stanberry
Location: Mil - 11 9 4 20
Based upon the following Army land warrant:

Issued to	*No.*	*Acres*
Herring, H. G., Junior? Pvt	833	100

(Note: To J. Stanberry . . . Zanesville.)

1319 10 May 1823 B/1/038
Registered by: D. D. Tompkins
Registered for: Amos Thorp
Location: Mil - 12 9 4 10
Based upon the following Army land warrant:

Issued to	*No.*	*Acres*
Thorp, Amos, Pvt	382	100

1320 23 Jun 1823 B/1/038
Registered by: J. Watson & -- Chambers
Registered for: Henry Northup
Location: Mil - 5 3 3 37
Based upon the following Army land warrant:

Issued to	*No.*	*Acres*
Lemon, John, Fifer	149	100

1321 27 Jun 1823 B/1/039
Registered by: Henry Northup
Registered for: Elijah Graves
Location: Mil - 7 4 2 12
Based upon the following Army land warrant:

Issued to	*No.*	*Acres*
Bowdler, Samuel, Pvt	871	100

(Note: [Sent] to Thomas J. Northup, Zanesville.)

1322 27 Jun 1823 B/1/039
Registered by: Henry Northup
Registered for: Michael Miller
Location: Mil - 7 6 1 4
Based upon the following Army land warrant:

Issued to	*No.*	*Acres*
Hall? [Hale?] Job, Pvt	782	100

(Note: [Sent] to Thomas J. Northup, Zanesville.)

1323 27 Jun 1823 B/1/039
Registered by: Henry Northup
Registered for: Samuel Morrison
Location: Mil - 7 7 2 37
Based upon the following Army land warrant:

Issued to	*No.*	*Acres*
Holden, Joseph, Pvt	877	100

(Note: [Sent] to Thomas J. Northup, Zanesville.)

1324 27 Jun 1823 B/1/039
Registered by: Henry Northup
Registered for: George Hite
Location: Mil - 7 10 3 1
Based upon the following Army land warrant:

Issued to	*No.*	*Acres*
Brown, Jacob, Pvt	707	100

(Note: [Sent] to Thomas J. Northup, Zanesville.)

1325 5 Jul 1823 B/1/039
Registered by: Erastus Root
Registered for: Matthew Marvin
Location: Mil - 9 9 1 11
Based upon the following Army land warrant:

Issued to	*No.*	*Acres*
Marvin, Matthew, Sgt	1061	100

(Note: [Sent] to E. Root, Delhi, New York.)

1326 10 Aug 1823 B/1/039
Registered by: Andrew Sherer
Registered for: Andrew Sherer
Location: Mil - 7 6 1 23
Based upon the following Army land warrant:

Issued to	*No.*	*Acres*
Huston, Philip, Pvt	857	100

(Note: [Sent] to him at Claysville, Washington, County, Pennsylvania.)

1327 19 Aug 1823 B/1/039
Registered by: Alexander Holmes
Registered for: Alexander Holmes
Location: Mil - 11 6 1 20
Mil - 11 6 1 31
Mil - 2 5 3 30
Based upon the following Army land warrant:

Issued to	*No.*	*Acres*
Davis, George W., and the other heir of James Davis, Capt	1051	300

(Note: [Sent] to him at Newark [Ohio].)

1328 1 Oct 1823 B/1/039
Registered by: Alexander Holmes
Registered for: Alexander Holmes
Location: Mil - 11 9 4 8
Based upon the following Army land warrant:

Issued to	*No.*	*Acres*
Bloon* Solomon, Pvt	908	100

(Note: Sent to A. Holmes, Newark, Ohio.)
*So spelled.

1329 1 Oct 1823 B/1/039
Registered by: Thomas Carter

1329 [continued]
Registered for: Alexander Holmes
Location: Mil - 11 9 4 16
Based upon the following Army land warrant:

Issued to	*No.*	*Acres*
Harrington, Samuel, Pvt	953	100

(Note: Sent to A. Holmes, Newark, Ohio.)

1330 1 Oct 1823 B/1/039
Registered by: Alexander Holmes
Registered for: Alexander Holmes
Location: Mil - 11 9 4 17
Based upon the following Army land warrant:

Issued to	*No.*	*Acres*
Clark, James, Pvt	898	100

(Note: Sent to A. Holmes, Newark, Ohio.)

1331 -- Aug 1822* B/1/039
Registered by: Archibald Davis
Registered for: [Heirs?] of A. Stewart
Location: Mil - 9 9 2 5
Mil - 9 9 2 6
Mil - 9 9 2 9
Mil - 9 9 4 40
Based upon the following Army land warrant:

Issued to	*No.*	*Acres*
Stewart, Alexander, Surgeon	2010	400

(Note: Retained in office.)
*Not in chronlogical sequence.

1332 -- Nov 1822 B/1/039
Registered by: Richard Galegher
Registered for: Richard Galegher
Location: Mil - 6 8 2 4
Based upon the following Army land warrant:

Issued to	*No.*	*Acres*
Freeman, John, Pvt	939	100

(Note: Sent to him at Zanesville.)

1333 3 Feb 1824 B/1/039
Registered by: Joseph Watson
Registered for: Charles Korns
Location: Mil - 8 9 1 1
Based upon the following Army land warrant:

Issued to	*No.*	*Acres*
Chandler, Moses, Pvt	769	100

(Note: Sent to him care of Peter Casey, Millersburg, Coshocton? [now Holmes] County, Ohio.)

1334 3 Feb 1824 B/1/039
Registered by: Joseph Watson
Registered for: [Not stated]
Location: Mil - 8 7 3 13
Mil - 8 7 3 4
Mil - 8 7 3 12
Based upon the following Army land warrants:

Issued to	*No.*	*Acres*
Kent, John, Pvt	701	100
McDaniel, Mary, *et al*, Pvt	1049	100
Tinum, Hezekiah, Pvt	954	100

(Note: Sent to H. Northup at Zanesville.)

1335 3 Feb 1824 B/1/039
Registered by: Joseph Watson
Registered for: William Griffith
Location: Mil - 8 7 3 5
Based upon the following Army land warrant:

Issued to	*No.*	*Acres*
Snell, Asa, Pvt	907	100

(Note: Sent to H. Northup at Zanesville.)

1336 3 Feb 1824 B/1/039
Registered by: Joseph Watson
Registered for: Henry Northup
Location: Mil - 6 6 2 9
Mil - 8 4 3 35
Based upon the following Army land warrants:

Issued to	*No.*	*Acres*
Welch, Lemuel, Pvt	989	100
Woodward, Benjamin, Pvt	843	100

(Note: Sent to H. Northup at Zanesville.)

1337 17 Feb 1824 B/1/039
Registered by: David Chambers
Registered for: Jonas Stanberry
Location: Mil - 9 9 1 2
Mil - 10 1 2 20
Based upon the following Army land warrants:

Issued to	*No.*	*Acres*
Downing, James, Pvt	715	100
Melvin, John, Pvt	899	100

(Note: [Sent] to him at Zanesville.)

1338 17 Feb 1824 B/1/039
Registered by: David Chambers
Registered for: David Chambers
Location: Mil - 4 10 3 23
Based upon the following Army land warrant:

Issued to	*No.*	*Acres*
Colby, Joseph, Pvt	735	100

(Note: To Hon. B. Ruggles [U.S.] Senate.)

1339 20 Feb 1824 B/1/039
Registered by: John C. Wright
Registered for: John C. Wright
Location: Mil - 5 10 3 6
Based upon the following Army land warrant:

Issued to	*No.*	*Acres*
Clark, Asa, Pvt	892	100

(Note: Sent to Hon. John C. Wright, H[ouse] of R[epresentatives].)

1340 20 Feb 1824 B/1/039
Registered by: John C. Wright
Registered for: Isaac? Thomas
Location: Mil - 5 10 4 32
Based upon the following Army land warrant:

Issued to	*No.*	*Acres*
Parsons, Ebenezer, Pvt	832	100

(Note: Sent to Hon. John C. Wright, H[ouse] of R[epresentatives].)

1341 2 Mar 1824 B/1/039
Registered by: Hon. Charles A. Forte
Registered for: Hannah Edwards & the other heirs of Fred[eric]k Parker
Location: Mil - 7 7 2 38
Based upon the following Army land warrant:

Issued to	*No.*	*Acres*
Edwards, Hannah, & the other heirs of Fred[erick] Parker, Pvt	755	100

1341 [continued]
Note: [Delivered] to Hon. Chas. A. Forte, H[ouse] of R[epresentatives].

1342 4 Mar 1824 B/1/039
Registered by: John C. Wright
Registered for: John C. Wright
Location: Mil - 2 10 2 31
Mil - 5 7 1 1
Mil - 5 7 1 2
Mil - 3 7 1 22
Mil - 4 10 3 7
Based upon the following Army land warrants:

Issued to	*No.*	*Acres*
Bracket, Charles, Pvt	962	100
Jenifer, Walter H., s[on?] & the other h[eirs?] of D. Jenifer, Doctor*	1082	450

*See also serial entry 1370 below.

1343 26 Mar 1824 B/1/040
Registered by: John C. Wright
Registered for: Henry? Crabbs
Location: Mil - 5 7 1 22
Based upon the following Army land warrant:

Issued to	*No.*	*Acres*
Derrick, James, Pvt	766	100

(Note: To Hon. J. C. Wright, H[ouse] of R[epresentatives].)

1344 2 Apr 1824 B/1/040
Registered by: John C. Wright
Registered for: David? Seldenright
Location: Mil - 4 10 3 17
Based upon the following Army land warrant:

Issued to	*No.*	*Acres*
Leach, Sally, Pvt	914	100

(Note: To Hon. J. C. Wright, H[ouse] of R[epresentatives].)

1345 2 Apr 1824 B/1/040
Registered by: John C. Wright
Registered for: Jacob? Smith
Location: Mil - 3 8 4 25
Based upon the following Army land warrant:

Issued to	*No.*	*Acres*
Patterson, Samuel, Pvt	858	100

(Note: To Hon. J. C. Wright, H[ouse] of R[epresentatives].)

1346 5 Apr 1824 B/1/040
Registered by: Jonas Stanberry
Registered for: Jonas Stanberry
Location: Mil - 10 7 1 33
Mil - 11 9 4 7
Mil - 11 9 4 21
Mil - 11 8 1 26
Mil - 7 6 1 20
Based upon the following Army land warrants:

Issued to	*No.*	*Acres*
Ebett, William, Pvt	842	100
McCann, John, Lt	883	200
Jewell, John, Pvt	704	100
Brittan, William, Pvt	838	100

(Note: Sent to him at Zanesville.)

1347 13 Apr 1824 B/1/040
Registered by: N. Beasley
Registered for: Edward Stein
Location: Mil - 7 10 4 8
Based upon the following Army land warrant:

Issued to	*No.*	*Acres*
Stein, Edward, Pvt	1007	100

(Note: Sent to N. Beasley, Decatur, Ohio.)

1348 13 Apr 1824 B/1/040
Registered by: J. Stanberry
Registered for: Jonas Stanberry
Location: Mil - 7 6 1 22
Based upon the following Army land warrant:

Issued to	*No.*	*Acres*
Hodgkins, Timothy, Pvt	1033	100

(Note: Sent to him at Zanesville.)

1349 29 Apr 1824 B/1/040
Registered by: Hon. Justin Divinell
Registered for: Ezekiel Merrett
Location: Mil - 8 9 3 4
Based upon the following Army land warrant:

Issued to	*No.*	*Acres*
Merrett, Ezekiel, Pvt	826	100

(Note: Sent to Hon. Justin Divinell same day.)

1350 11 May 1824 B/1/040
Registered by: James Hamilton
Registered for: Eliab Kingman
Location: Mil - 7 10 4 6
Based upon the following Army land warrant:

Issued to	*No.*	*Acres*
Kingman, Eliab, Pvt	4544	100

(Note: Sent to Hon. James Hamilton, H[ouse] of R[epresentatives].)

1351 12 May 1824 B/1/040
Registered by: John Rhea
Registered for: Thomas Brabson
Location: Mil - 11 8 1 27
Mil - 12 9 3 2
Mil - 12 9 3 4
Based upon the following Army land warrant:

Issued to	*No.*	*Acres*
Ballard, Kader, Capt	292	100

(Note: To Hon. John Blair, H[ouse] of R[epresentatives].)

1352 21 May 1824 B/1/040
Registered by: John Taliaferro
Registered for: Martha C. Taylor & [other heirs?] of J. McAdam
Location: Mil - 2 10 2 26
Mil - 2 10 2 27
Mil - 2 10 2 30
Based upon the following Army land warrant:

Issued to	*No.*	*Acres*
McAdam, John, Capt	1088	300

(Note: To Hon. J. Taliaferro, Fred[erick]sburg, Virginia.)

1353 21 May 1824 B/1/040
Registered by: William Smith

1353 [continued]
Registered for: Thomas Butt [*et al?*]
Location: Mil - 2 10 2 23
Mil - 2 10 2 32
Based upon the following Army land warrant:

Issued to	*No.*	*Acres*
Butt, Edward, Pvt	1072	100
Butt, Zach[ariah?] Pvt	1073	100

(Note: To William Smith, Lewisburg, Greenbrier County, Virginia.)

1354 24 May 1824 B/1/040
Registered by: E. Litchfield
Registered for: Hannah Lantford? [Santford?]
Location: Mil - 12 9 4 3
Mil - 11 9 4 9
Mil - 11 9 4 10
Based upon the following Army land warrant:

Issued to	*No.*	*Acres*
Lantford? [Santford?] John, Capt	1083	300

(Note: To E. Litchfield, H[ouse] of R[epresentatives].)

1355 21 May 1824 B/1/040
Registered by: Hon. John C. Wright
Registered for: John C. Wright
Location: Mil - 4 10 3 10
Based upon the following Army land warrant:

Issued to	*No.*	*Acres*
Mitchell, Timothy, Pvt	848	100

1356 21 May 1824 B/1/040
Registered by: John Coventry
Registered for: Michael Woolford
Location: Mil - 1 6 2 21
Based upon the following Army land warrant:

Issued to	*No.*	*Acres*
Woolford, Michael, Pvt	648	100

(Note: Sent to Hon. John C. Wright.)

1357 21 May 1824 B/1/040
Registered by: William Finch
Registered for: William P. Finch
Location: Mil - 11 9 3 13
Based upon the following Army land warrant:

Issued to	*No.*	*Acres*
Brown, Samuel, Pvt	938	100

(Note: Sent to him at Grenville [Greenville?] W[estchester?] County, New York.)

1358 27 May 1824 B/1/040
Registered by: John Lawson
Registered for: John Lawson
Location: Mil - 16 6 1 23
Based upon the following Army land warrant:

Issued to	*No.*	*Acres*
Lake, Ruben, Pvt	546	100

(Note: [Sent] to him at Delaware, Ohio.)

1359 27 May 1824 B/1/040
Registered by: John C. Wright
Registered for: John C. Wright
Location: Mil - 5 7 1 5
Mil - 3 10 1 8
Mil - 5 7 1 12
Mil - 5 7 1 3
Based upon the following Army land warrants:

Issued to	*No.*	*Acres*
Hazleton, Prina? [Prince?] Pvt	922	100
Buker? [Bicker?] Windsor, Pvt	926	100
Curtis, D., Pvt	929	100
Conn, William, Pvt	1070	100

(Note: [Sent] to him at Steubenville.)

1360 1 Jun 1824 B/1/040
Registered by: P. Beecher
Registered for: Jonas Stanberry
Location: Mil - 7 6 1 24
Based upon the following Army land warrant:

Issued to	*No.*	*Acres*
Clark, Moses, Pvt	725	100

(Note [Sent] to him at Zanesville.)

1361 14 Jun 1824 B/1/040
Registered by: J. Watson
Registered for: David Clancy
Location: Mil - 7 9 2 33
Based upon the following Army land warrant:

Issued to	*No.*	*Acres*
Langworthy, William, Pvt	1052	100

(Note: [Sent] to P. Casey, Millersburg, Ohio.)

1362 18 Jun 1824 B/1/040
Registered by: J. Watson
Registered for: Tyler? Hughes
Location: Mil - 8 9 1 19
Based upon the following Army land warrant:

Issued to	*No.*	*Acres*
Morrill, John, Pvt	879	100

(Note: [Sent] to P. Casey, Millersburg, Ohio.)

1363 28 Jul 1824 B/1/041
Registered by: Joseph Watson
Registered for: Joseph Watson
Location: Mil - 20 6 3 19*
Based upon the following Army land warrant:

Issued to	*No.*	*Acres*
Jones, Walter, as trustee [warrantee's name not given], Surgeon	650	450

*Fraction. This may be only a 50-acre lot. The remaining 400 acres of 450 acres due a Surgeon are not listed here, although there is an illegible note regarding this remainder.

1364 27 Aug 1824 B/1/041
Registered by: James Taylor
Registered for: James Taylor
Location: Mil - 16 6 1 7
Mil - 16 6 1 8
Mil - 16 6 1 9
Mil - 16 6 1 10
Mil - 17 7 1 15E*
Mil - 16 6 1 24
Mil - 16 6 1 25
Mil - 16 6 1 40
Mil - 16 7 4 28
Mil - 16 7 4 29
Based upon the following Army land warrants:

Issued to	*No.*	*Acres*
Taylor, Richard, LtCol	494	450
Pierce, William L., Capt	518	300

1364 [continued]
Eastin, Philip, Lt 621 200
(Note: Sent to him at Newport, B? Y? [R? I? or N? Y?].)
*50-acre lot.

1365 27 Aug 1824 B/1/041
Registered by: James Taylor
Registered for: [N?] Beall & James Taylor
Location: Mil - 16 7 4 20
Based upon the following Army land warrant:

Issued to	*No.*	*Acres*
Beall, Nathaniel, Pvt	493	100

(Note: Sent to him at Newport, B? Y? [R? I? or N? Y?].) [Might also read Newport, Kentucky.]

1366 -- Feb 1822* B/1/041
Registered by: D. Chambers
Registered for: Jonas Stanberry
Location: Mil - 6 8 2 2
Mil - 6 8 2 33
Based upon the following Army land warrant:

Issued to	*No.*	*Acres*
Webster, D., Lt	1005	100

(Note: Sent to him at Zanesville.)
Pencilled interlineation: "See folio 38 this book."
*Not in chronological sequence.

1367 -- Feb 1824 B/1/041
Registered by: P. Beecher
Registered for: Jonas Stanberry
Location: Mil - 6 6 2 34
Based upon the following Army land warrant:

Issued to	*No.*	*Acres*
Polden, George, Pvt	839	100

(Note: Sent to him at Zanesville.)

1368 24 Aug 1824 B/1/041
Registered by: John C. Wright
Registered for: John C. Wright
Location: Mil - 4 10 3 40
Mil - 6 10 4 21
Mil - 8 5 1 41
Mil - 5 7 1 13
Based upon the following Army land warrant:

Issued to	*No.*	*Acres*
Marrs? [Mans?] John N., Surgeon	1063	400

(Note:Sent to him at Steubenville, 20 Sep 1824.)

1369 27 Sep 1824 B/1/041
Registered by: Jonas Stanberry
Registered for: Jonas Stanberry
Location: Mil - 10 7 1 32
Mil - 20 3 1 4
Based upon the following Army land warrants:

Issued to	*No.*	*Acres*
Sheppard, Stephen, Pvt	1018	100
Marshall, Richard, Pvt	961	100

(Note: [Sent] to him at Zanesville.)

1370 27 Sep 1824 B/1/041
Registered by: John C. Wright
Registered for: John C. Wright
Location: Mil - 6 10 3 12
Mil - 1 6 2 10
Mil - 1 6 2 12
Mil - 1 6 2 19
Mil - 1 6 2 9
Mil - 3 10 2 17
Based upon the following Army land warrants:

Issued to	*No.*	*Acres*
Jenifer, W. H., etc.*	1082	[100]
Harrison, Penelope, Capt	1047	300
Wells, Nathaniel, Pvt	1032	100
Wells, John, Pvt	796	100

(Note: Sent to him in Steubenville.)
*See serial entry 1342 above.

1371 13 Oct 1824 B/1/041
Registered by: Charles Williams
Registered for: Charles Williams
Location: Mil - 6 8 3 35
Based upon the following Army land warrant:

Issued to	*No.*	*Acres*
Riley, Christopher, Pvt	1075	100

(Note: Sent to Mr. W. Verry? Washington City.)

1372 21 Oct 1824 B/1/041
Registered by: Jonas Stanberry
Registered for: Jonas Stanberry
Location: Mil - 7 6 4 21
Based upon the following Army land warrant:

Issued to	*No.*	*Acres*
Thorpe, Thomas, Pvt	1008	100

1373 24 Nov 1824 B/1/041
Registered by: William Curtis
Registered for: Andrew Griswold
Location: Mil - 10 7 1 34
Mil - 10 7 1 35
Based upon the following Army land warrant:

Issued to	*No.*	*Acres*
Griswold, Andrew, Lt	1068	200

(Note: Sent to William Curtis, Mount Vernon, Ohio.)

1374 17 Jan 1825 B/1/041
Registered by: Duncan McArthur
Registered for: Charles Lofland
Location: Mil - 19 2 2 20
Based upon the following Army land warrant:

Issued to	*No.*	*Acres*
McGahey, William, Pvt	1004	100

(Note: Sent to G. McArthur, H[ouse] of R[epresentatives].)

1375 31 Jan 1825 B/1/041
Registered by: James E. Smith
Registered for: James E. Smith
Location: Mil - 7 9 2 31
Based upon the following Army land warrant:

Issued to	*No.*	*Acres*
Cross, Daniel, Pvt	1014	100

(Note: Returned in K? Desk? Sent to him at Philadelphia, 11 Apr.)

1376 31 Jan 1825 B/1/041
Registered by: H. L. Martindale
Registered for: Heirs of Joshua Dinsdell
Location: Mil - 7 7 2 28

1376 [continued]
Based upon the following Army land warrant:
Issued to | *No.* | *Acres*
Dinsdell, Joshua, heirs of, Pvt | 711 | 100

1377 31 Jan 1825 B/1/041
Registered by: H. L. Martindale
Registered for: Heirs of William Wentworth
Location: Mil - 7 7 2 27
Based upon the following Army land warrant:
Issued to | *No.* | *Acres*
Wentworth, William, heirs of, Pvt | 788 | 100

1378 31 Jan 1825 B/1/041
Registered by: Joseph Burt
Registered for: Heirs of Benjamin Everett
Location: Mil - 2 7 4 4
Based upon the following Army land warrant:
Issued to | *No.* | *Acres*
Everett, Benj[amin] heirs of, Pvt | 1031 | 100
(Note: Sent to Joseph Burt, Moscow, Livingston? County, New York.)

1379 31 Jan 1825 B/1/041
Registered by: Jonas Stanberry
Registered for: Jonas Stanberry
Location: Mil - 10 1 2 32
Mil - 7 6 1 19
Mil - 10 1 2 23
Based upon the following Army land warrants:
Issued to | *No.* | *Acres*
Goldsbury, Mark, Pvt | 1084 | 100
Chapman, Bethia, Pvt | 1060 | 100
Maker, Borden, Pvt | 1058 | 100
(Note: Sent to him at Zanesville.)

1380 21 Mar 1825 B/1/042
Registered by: John C. Wright
Registered for: John? Gladden
Location: Mil - 2 10 2 35
Mil - 4 10 2 3
Based upon the following Army land warrant:
Issued to | *No.* | *Acres*
Turner, Vienna P? [Lt?] | 1059 | 200
(Note: Sent same day to Hon. J. C. Wright, Steubenville [Ohio].)

1381 21 Mar 1825 B/1/042
Registered by: Joseph Watson
Registered for: Heirs of A. Read
Location: Mil - 6 8 2 6
Mil - 6 8 2 7
Based upon the following Army land warrant:
Issued to | *No.* | *Acres*
Read, Thomas, & the other heir of A. Read, Lt | 1090 | 200
(Note: Sent to A. L. Mountain, Pittsburgh, Pennsylvania.)

1382 6 Apr 1825 B/1/042
Registered by: P. Beecher
Registered for: Jonas Stanberry
Location: Mil - 8 4 3 25
Based upon the following Army land warrant:
Issued to | *No.* | *Acres*
Faunce? Elizabeth, & the other heir of J? Lylwith? [Sylwith?] Pvt | 885 | 100
(Note: Sent to him at Zanesville.)

1383 5 May 1825 B/1/042
Registered by: Alex[ander] Holmes
Registered for: Alex[ander] Holmes
Location: Mil - 10 1 2 33
Mil - 2 5 2 39
Based upon the following Army land warrants:
Issued to | *No.* | *Acres*
Getchell, Seth, Pvt | 844 | 100
Ellis, Robert, Pvt | 720 | 100
(Note: To him at Newark, Ohio.)

1384 1 Jun 1825 B/1/042
Registered by: Alex[ander] Holmes
Registered for: Heirs of Nathan Smith
Location: Mil - 2 6 3 4
Mil - 2 5 2 18
Mil - 2 5 2 16
Based upon the following Army land warrant:
Issued to | *No.* | *Acres*
Smith, William C., *et al*, [heirs of Nathan Smith] Surgeon's Mate | 1069 | 300
(Note: Sent to A. Holmes at Newark [Ohio].)

1385 1 Jun 1825 B/1/042
Registered by: Alex[ander] Holmes
Registered for: Heirs of M. Kirtland
Location: Mil - 2 5 2 37
Mil - 2 5 3 33
Mil - 2 5 3 34
Based upon the following Army land warrant:
Issued to | *No.* | *Acres*
Kirtland, Martin, & other [heirs of M. Kirtland] Surgeon's Mate | 1085 | 300
(Note: Sent to A. Holmes at Newark [Ohio].)

1386 1 Jun 1825 B/1/042
Registered by: Jonas Stanberry
Registered for: Jonas Stanberry
Location: Mil - 8 4 3 16
Based upon the following Army land warrant:
Issued to | *No.* | *Acres*
Low? Peter, assignee [veteran's name not given] Pvt | 8568 | 100
(Note: Sent to him at Zanesville.)

1387 1 Jun 1825 B/1/042
Registered by: J. B. Moore
Registered for: Samuel Schoolcraft
Location: Mil - 10 1 2 10
Based upon the following Army land warrant:
Issued to | *No.* | *Acres*
Schoolcraft, Samuel, Pvt | 1108 | 100
(Note: Sent to J. B. Moore . . . Renselarsville? A? County, New York.)

1388 7 Jul 1825 B/1/042

1388 [continued]
Registered by: Alexander Holmes
Registered for: Alexander Holmes
Location: Mil - 2 5 3 37
Based upon the following Army land warrant:

Issued to	*No.*	*Acres*
Adams, Sarah, sister? [& heiress of veteran whose name is not given] Pvt	901	100

(Note: Sent to him . . . at Newark, Ohio.)

Note: Sent to Hon. J. Sloan at Wooster.)

1389 1 Jul 1825* B/1/042
Registered by: H. Northup
Registered for: Thomas J. Northup
Location: Mil - 8 7 3 14
Mil - 8 9 2 1
Based upon the following Army land warrant:

Issued to	*No.*	*Acres*
Worthington, Eliz[abeth] R., h[eiress?] of L. N. Ricketts? Lt	1124	200

(Note: Delivered to H. Northup.)
*Not in chronological sequence.

1390 26 Apr 1825* B/1/042
Registered by: Parker Williams
Registered for: Levi Long
Location: Mil - 2 7 4 10
Based upon the following Army land warrant:

Issued to	*No.*	*Acres*
Long, Levi, Pvt	924	100

(Note: Sent to Parker Williams, New Philadelphia? Ohio.)
*Not in chronological sequence.

1391 18 Aug 1825 B/1/042
Registered by: Joseph Watson
Registered for: John C. Wright
Location: Mil - 5 7 1 4
Mil - 1 6 2 7
Based upon the following Army land warrants:

Issued to	*No.*	*Acres*
Stoker, William, & the other heirs of [veteran's name not given] Musician?	734	100
Murdock, William, heirs of, Cornet	263	100

1392 18 Aug 1825 B/1/042
Registered by: A. Shaw
Registered for: Peter Housman
Location: Mil - 1 6 2 13
Based upon the following Army land warrant:

Issued to	*No.*	*Acres*
Hall, Nicholas, Pvt	1015	100

(Note: Sent to A. Shaw, New Philadelphia? [Ohio])

1393 1 Sep 1825 B/1/042
Registered by: Joseph Kidder
Registered for: Samuel Farmer *et al*
Location: Mil - 1 8 4 31
Based upon the following Army land warrant:

Issued to	*No.*	*Acres*
Farmer, William, heirs of, Pvt	789	100

(Note: Sent to Hon. J. Sloan at Wooster.)

1394 12 Jul 1825* B/1/042
Registered by: Josiah Ewing
Registered for: Grey Owen['s] daughter
Location: Mil - 11 9 4 22
Based upon the following Army land warrant:

Issued to	*No.*	*Acres*
Owen, Nancy, daughter [& heiress of?] Grey? Owen, Pvt	977	100

(Note: Sent to J. Ewing . . . Zanesville.)
*Not in chronological sequence.

1395 27 Sep 1825 B/1/042
Registered by: Jonas Stanberry
Registered for: Jonas Stanberry
Location: Mil - 10 3 4 16
Based upon the following Army land warrant:

Issued to	*No.*	*Acres*
Lott? Peter, assignee [veteran's nate not given] Pvt	8135	100

(Note: Sent to him . . . at Zanesville.)

1396 27 Sep 1825 B/1/042
Registered by: Daniel Bird
Registered for: Daniel Bird
Location: Mil - 1 1 3 27
Based upon the following Army land warrant:

Issued to	*No.*	*Acres*
Bird, Edmund, Pvt	983	100

(Note: [Sent] to him at Boston.)

1397 4 Oct 1825 B/1/042
Registered by: A. Holmes
Registered for: Abraham Bell
Location: Mil - 10 3 4 6
Mil - 10 3 4 2
Mil - 10 3 4 15
Based upon the following Army land warrants:

Issued to	*No.*	*Acres*
Bell, Abraham, Pvt	971	100
Bell, Abraham, Pvt	969	100
Bell, Abraham, Pvt	972	100

(Note: Sent to J. W. Salter? Elizabeth Town, New Jersey.)

1398 4 Oct 1825 B/1/042
Registered by: A. Holmes
Registered for: Isaac Dyer
Location: Mil - 7 4 2 25
Based upon the following Army land warrant:

Issued to	*No.*	*Acres*
Dyer, Isaac, Pvt	399	100

(Note: Sent to Mr. Holmes, Newark [Ohio].)

1399 4 Oct 1825 B/1/042
Registered by: A. Holmes
Registered for: G. Moore & R. Morrow*
Location: Mil - 7 4 2 8
Based upon the following Army land warrant:

Issued to	*No.*	*Acres*
Moore, G., & Morrow, R., Pvt	718	100

(Note: Sent to Mr. Holmes, Newark [Ohio].)
*See also serial entry 1406 below.

1400 4 Oct 1825 B/1/042
Registered by: S. H. Smith
Registered for: [John?] E. Darby & the other heirs of E. Darby
Location: Mil - 9 9 4 20
Mil - 9 9 1 3
Based upon the following Army land warrant:
Issued to *No.* *Acres*
Darby, Ephraim, heirs of, Lt 608 200

1401 4 Oct 1825 B/1/042
Registered by: S. H. Smith
Registered for: Elias Darby, Junior
Location: Mil - 8 9 3 25
Based upon the following Army land warrant:
Issued to *No.* *Acres*
Darby, John E., Pvt 605 100
(Note: Delivered to Mr. Bartley, 11 Jan 1825.)

1402 4 Oct 1825 B/1/042
Registered by: S. H. Smith
Registered for: [Thomas?] Jefferson Darby
Location: Mil - 9 9 1 6
Based upon the following Army land warrant:
Issued to *No.* *Acres*
Chapman, Elias, Pvt 627 100
(Note: Delivered to Mr. Bartley, 11 Jan 1825.)

1403 3 Nov 1825 B/1/043
Registered by: Joseph Watson
Registered for: Henry Fiss
Location: Mil - 2 5 3 4
Mil - 2 5 3 5
Based upon the following Army land warrant:
Issued to *No.* *Acres*
Fiss, Henry, Lt 1134 200

1404 3 Nov 1825 B/1/043
Registered by: Joseph Watson
Registered for: William? McKissac
Location: Mil - 2 5 3 1
Mil - 2 5 3 16
Mil - 2 5 3 17
Based upon the following Army land warrant:
Issued to *No.* *Acres*
McKissac, William, Capt 1137 300

1405 3 Nov 1825 B/1/043
Registered by: Joseph Watson
Registered for: George Ord *et al*
Location: Mil - 2 5 3 18
Mil - 2 5 3 13
Based upon the following Army land warrant:
Issued to *No.* *Acres*
Ord, George, *et al* 1140 [or 1040] 200

1406 3 Nov 1825 B/1/043
Registered by: A. Holmes
Registered for: John Moore & Rebecca Morrow*
Location: Mil - 10 3 4 20
Based upon the following Army land warrant:
Issued to *No.* *Acres*
Moore, John, & Rebecca Morrow, heirs of Jesse Moore, Pvt 719 100
(Note: Sent same day to A. Holmes, Newark, Ohio.)
*See also serial entry 1399 above.

1407 3 Nov 1825 B/1/043
Registered by: Cadwallader Wallace
Registered for: Joseph Carter
Location: Mil - 2 7 4 16
Based upon the following Army land warrant:
Issued to *No.* *Acres*
Carter, Joseph, Pvt 1094 100
(Note: Sent to Wallace at Chillicothe.)

1408 15 Nov 1825 B/1/043
Registered by: Henry? G. Northup
Registered for: Thomas J. Northup
Location: Mil - 7 4 2 35
Mil - 8 9 1 34
Based upon the following Army land warrant:
Issued to *No.* *Acres*
Onion, Julich? Lt 1128 200
(Note: Delivered to Henry Northup & sent to T. J. [Northup?] at Zanesville.)

1409 29 Nov 1825 B/1/043
Registered by: Joseph Watson
Registered for: Thomas J. Northup
Location: Mil - 8 9 1 24
Based upon the following Army land warrant:
Issued to *No.* *Acres*
Towle, William, Pvt 836 100
(Note: Delivered to Henry Northup & sent to T. J. [Northup?] at Zanesville.)

1410 31 Dec 1825 B/1/043
Registered by: Joseph Watson
Registered for: Richard Skinner *et al*
Location: Mil - 7 4 2 7
Mil - 7 4 2 11
Mil - 7 4 2 27
Mil - 8 4 3 17
Based upon the following Army land warrant:
Issued to *No.* *Acres*
Skinner, Richard, *et al*, Surgeon 1131 400
(Note: Sent to Thomas J. Northup, Zanesville.)

1411 31 Dec 1825 B/1/043
Registered by: H. Northup
Registered for: James M. Pike
Location: Mil - 7 6 1 18
Based upon the following Army land warrant:
Issued to *No.* *Acres*
Edwards, John, Pvt 882 100
(Note: Sent patent to him at Lexington, Kentucky.)

1412 31 Dec 1825 B/1/043
Registered by: Joseph Watson
Registered for: Heirs of Isaac Rawlings [&] Thomas J. Northup
Location: Mil - 3 6 4 9
Mil - 3 6 4 10
Based upon the following Army land warrant:
Issued to *No.* *Acres*
King? [Hug?] Sarah, & the other heirs of Isaac Rawlings, Lt 1130 100
(Note: Sent to [T. Northup] at Zanesville.)

1413* 3 Jan 1826 B/1/043
Registered by: John C. Wright
Registered for: [John?] H. Cummins
Location: Mil - 3 7 1 23
Based upon the following Army land warrant:

Issued to	*No.*	*Acres*
Leonard, Cuff, Pvt	1044	100

*This entire serial entry crossed out in source register but repeated on following page thereof.

1414 3 Jan 1826 B/1/044
Registered by: John C. Wright
Registered for: [John?] C. Cummins
Location: Mil - 3 7 1 23
Based upon the following Army land warrant:

Issued to	*No.*	*Acres*
Leonard, Cuff, Pvt	1044	100

(Note: Sent to J. C. Wright.)

1415 1 Sep 1821* B/1/044
Registered by: J. W. Campbell
Registered for: Garnett? King
Location: Mil - 7 4 2 9
Based upon the following Army land warrant:

Issued to	*No.*	*Acres*
Humphries, Joseph, Pvt	935	100

(Note: 23 Jan 1826 sent to J. W. Campbell, House of Representatives.)
*Not in chronological sequence.

1416 2 Feb 1826 B/1/044
Registered by: P. Adams
Registered for: Jonas Stanberry
Location: Mil - 7 4 2 26
Mil - 7 6 1 14
Based upon the following Army land warrant:

Issued to	*No.*	*Acres*
Guyger, George, Lt	1135	200

(Note: Sent to [him] at Zanesville.)

1417 2 Feb 1826 B/1/044
Registered by: A. Holmes
Registered for: Abraham Bell
Location: Mil - 7 4 2 28
Mil - 7 4 2 29
Based upon the following Army land warrants:

Issued to	*No.*	*Acres*
Bell, Abraham, Pvt	974	100
Bell, Abraham, Pvt	975	100

(Note: Sent same day to Th[eodo]r? Salter, Elizabeth Town, New Jersey.)

1418 6 Feb 1826 B/1/044
Registered by: Samuel Smith
Registered for: Samuel Smith
Location: Mil - 1 1 3 4
Based upon the following Army land warrant:

Issued to	*No.*	*Acres*
Martin, James, Pvt	1016	100

(Note: Sent to him at Union Town, Pennsylvania.)

1419 8 Feb 1826 B/1/044
Registered by: Thomas Kennedy
Registered for: Thomas Kennedy
Location: Mil - 1 6 2 35
Based upon the following Army land warrant:

Issued to	*No.*	*Acres*
Bower, William, Pvt	958	100

1420 15 Feb 1826 B/1/044
Registered by: Jonas Stanberry
Registered for: Jonas Stanberry
Location: Mil - 7 4 2 10
Mil - 7 4 2 13
Based upon the following Army land warrants:

Issued to	*No.*	*Acres*
Martin, Nathaniel, Pvt	757	100
Putney, Joseph, Pvt	873	100

(Note: Sent to him at Zanesville.)

1421 15 Feb 1826 B/1/044
Registered by: John Blair
Registered for: Jacob Achor
Location: Mil - 2 5 3 35
Based upon the following Army land warrant:

Issued to	*No.*	*Acres*
Achor, Jacob, Pvt	1146	100

(Note: Sent to Hon. J. Blair, H[ouse] of R[epresentatives].)

1422 1 Mar 1826 B/1/044
Registered by: Samuel Smith
Registered for: Hannah Barnes
Location: Mil - 1 1 3 5
Based upon the following Army land warrant:

Issued to	*No.*	*Acres*
Barnes, Hannah, Pvt	1048	100

(Note: Sent to S. Smith, Union Town [Pennsylvania].)

1423 1 Mar 1826 B/1/044
Registered by: B. F. Hopkins
Registered for: Benjamin F. Hopkins
Location: Mil - 7 7 2 25
Mil - 7 7 2 26?
Based upon the following Army land warrant:

Issued to	*No.*	*Acres*
Hopkins, Benjamin F., Adjutant?	1039	200

(Note: Sent same day. See letter on Rec?)

1424 24 Mar 1826 B/1/044
Registered by: Nathaniel Leeman
Registered for: Nathaniel Leeman & heirs?
Location: Mil - 15 8 3 22
Mil - 17 7 1 3W*
Based upon the following Army land warrant:

Issued to	*No.*	*Acres*
Leeman, N., & other [heirs] of S. Leeman, Ens	815	150

(Note: Sent to him at New Ipswich.)
*50-acre lot.

1425 1 Apr 1826 B/1/044
Registered by: Joseph Watson
Registered for: -- Patton *et al*
Location: Mil - 2 5 3 20
Mil - 2 3 4 9
Mil - 3 5 1 3
Based upon the following Army land warrant:

Issued to	*No.*	*Acres*
Davis, Joseph, Capt	1168	300

(Note: Sent to H. Northup at Harrisburg.)

1426 — 1 Apr 1826 — B/1/044
Registered by: Jonas Stanberry
Registered for: Jonas Stanberry
Location: Mil - 7 6 1 28
Mil - 7 6 1 11
Mil - 9 7 3 34
Based upon the following Army land warrants:

Issued to	*No.*	*Acres*
Haven, James, Pvt	92	100
Clark, Paul, Pvt	941	100
Parmeter? Abraham, Pvt	1071	100

(Note: Sent to him at Zanesville.)

1427 — 11 Apr 1826 — B/1/044
Registered by: G. Kremer?
Registered for: Elizabeth Easterly
Location: Mil - 1 6 2 36
Based upon the following Army land warrant:

Issued to	*No.*	*Acres*
Johnston, George, Pvt	8441	100

(Note: Sent to Mr. Kremer? H[ouse] of R[epresentatives].)

1428 — 2 May 1825 — B/1/044
Registered by: J. C. Wright
Registered for: P? Hubley, daughter, & other heirs of Adam Hubley
Location: Mil - 1 6 2 4
Mil - 1 6 2 28
Mil - 1 6 2 31
Mil - 1 6 2 30
Mil - 1 6 2 34
Based upon the following Army land warrant:

Issued to	*No.*	*Acres*
Hubley, Adam, heirs of, Col	1151	500

1429 — 17 May 1825 — B/1/044
Registered by: Allen Cook
Registered for: Allen Cook
Location: Mil - 10 7 1 1
Based upon the following Army land warrant:

Issued to	*No.*	*Acres*
Cook, William, Pvt	5558	100

(Note: Sent to Mr. Hugenins, H[ouse] of R[epresentatives].)

1430 — 24 May 1826 — B/1/044
Registered by: J. Watson
Registered for: --? Rudolph *et al?*
Location: Mil - 1 1 3 9
Mil - 1 1 3 23
Based upon the following Army land warrant:

Issued to	*No.*	*Acres*
Rudolph, John, nephew? [& heir of unnamed veteran] Lt	1183	200

(Note: Sent to John Haga, Mercer, Mercer County, Pennsylvania.)

1431 — 4 Jun 1826 — B/1/044
Registered by: W. C. Rives
Registered for: Edmond Davis
Location: Mil - 3 8 4 17
Based upon the following Army land warrant:

Issued to	*No.*	*Acres*
Davis, Edmond, Pvt	944	100

(Note: Sent to Hon. Rives, Castle Hill? Lindsay's Store? Alb[emarle County] Virginia.)

1432 — 16 Aug 1826 — B/1/044
Registered by: P. Carland
Registered for: [Heirs of?] L. Cooper
Location: Mil - 10 3 4 12
Mil - 10 3 4 13
Mil - 10 3 4 30
Based upon the following Army land warrant:

Issued to	*No.*	*Acres*
Cooper, L., Heirs of, Capt	1111	300

(Note: Sent 4 Sep [1826] to P. Carland at Newark [Ohio?].)

1433 — 4 Oct 1825* — B/1/045
Registered by: Alex[ander] Holmes
Registered for: Abraham Bell
Location: Mil - 2 5 1 6
Based upon the following Army land warrant:

Issued to	*No.*	*Acres*
Bell, Abraham, assignee, Pvt	973	100

(Note: Sent to him at Thomas Salter['s] Elizabeth City, New Jersey.)
*Not in chronological sequence.

1434 — in the year 1825 — B/1/045
Registered by: Richard Gallegher
Registered for: Heirs of Jacob French & Alex[ander] Holmes
Location: Mil - 2 5 3 38
Based upon the following Army land warrant:

Issued to	*No.*	*Acres*
French, Jacob, heirs of, Pvt	957	100

(Note: Sent to A. Holmes, Newark, Ohio, 21 Jun 1826.)

1435 — in the year 1825 — B/1/045
Registered by: Alex[ander] Holmes
Registered for: Heirs of Thomas Moore & Alexander Holmes
Location: Mil - 2 5 1 33
Mil - 2 5 3 2
Mil - 2 5 3 11
Mil - 2 5 3 15
Based upon the following Army land warrant:

Issued to	*No.*	*Acres*
Moore, Thomas, heirs of, Maj	1081	400

(Note: Sent to A. Holmes, Newark, Ohio, 21 Jun 1826.)

1436 — -- May 1826 — B/1/045
Registered by: Alex[ander] Holmes
Registered for: Robert Porterfield
Location: Mil - 2 5 1 22
Mil - 2 5 1 34
Mil - 2 5 1 35
Mil - 2 5 3 8
Mil - 1 8 2 29E*
Based upon the following Army land warrant:

Issued to	*No.*	*Acres*
Porterfield, Charles, LtCol	1145	450

(Note: Sent to W. Kinney, Junior, Staunton,

1436 [continued]
Aug[usta?] County, Virginia.)
*50-acre lot.

1437 — 21 Oct 1826 — B/1/045
Registered by: Ambrose Hitchcock
Registered for: Ambrose Hitchcock, assignee?
Location: Mil - 7 7 2 12
Based upon the following Army land warrant:

Issued to	*No.*	*Acres*
Hitchcock, Ambrose, Pvt	1185	100

(Note: Sent to A. Hitchcock, care of William Battell, Torrington?)

1438 — 1 Nov 1826 — B/1/045
Registered by: John C. Wright
Registered for: Jacob Strohl
Location: Mil - 5 7 1 33
Based upon the following Army land warrant:

Issued to	*No.*	*Acres*
Strohl, Jacob, Pvt	1178	100

(Note: Sent to Mr. Wright, Steubenville.)

1439 — 1 Nov 1826 — B/1/045
Registered by: John C. Wright
Registered for: [Lydia?] M. Reynolds, heir[ess] of Capt Reynolds
Location: Mil - 5 7 1 31
Mil - 5 7 1 34
Mil - 1 8 4 2
Based upon the following Army land warrant:

Issued to	*No.*	*Acres*
Reynolds, Lydia Moore, heir[ess] of J. Reynolds, Capt	1148	300

(Note: Sent to Mr. Wright, Steubenville.)

1440 — 1 Nov 1826 — B/1/045
Registered by: Catharine Ziegler
Registered for: Catharine Ziegler
Location: Mil - 2 7 3 17
Mil - 2 7 3 20
Mil - 2 7 3 29
Based upon the following Army land warrant:

Issued to	*No.*	*Acres*
Rheinick, Christia[n] Surgeon's Mate	282	300

(Note: Delivered to F. Ziegler.)

1441 — -- Oct 1826* — B/1/045
Registered by: Michael Nourse
Registered for: Charles? Hanna, Junior, & James Hanna
Location: Mil - 3 1 1 31
Mil - 3 1 1 32
Based upon the following Army land warrant:

Issued to	*No.*	*Acres*
Crossly, Jesse, heirs of, Lt	1184	200

(Note: Delivered to Mr. Nourse.)
*Not in chronological sequence.

1442 — 28 Nov 1826 — B/1/045
Registered by: N. Rhodes
Registered for: N. Rhodes
Location: Mil - 2 7 4 17
Based upon the following Army land warrant:

Issued to	*No.*	*Acres*
Rhodes, Nicholas, Pvt	1169	100

(Note: Sent to him at Columbus.)

1443 — 18 Dec 1826 — B/1/045
Registered by: A. Holmes
Registered for: Seth Leavitt *et al*
Location: Mil - 2 5 1 31
Based upon the following Army land warrant:

Issued to	*No.*	*Acres*
Leavitt, Seth, *et al*, assignees? of Th[eodo]re Geralds, Pvt	1034	100

(Note: Sent to A. Beldin, Granville, Hamden County, Massachusetts.)

1444 — 2 Jan 1827 — B/1/045
Registered by: John Warner
Registered for: John Warner
Location: Mil - 2 5 1 3
Based upon the following Army land warrant:

Issued to	*No.*	*Acres*
Warner, John, Pvt	1181	100

(Note: Sent to M. B. Lawrie, Pittsburg[h].)

1445 — 20 Feb 1827 — B/1/045
Registered by: Cadwallader Wallace
Registered for: Elizabeth Radford & William J. Mosely
Location: Mil - 17 7 2 24
Mil - 17 7 2 27
Mil - 17 7 2 28
Mil - 17 7 2 29
Based upon the following Army land warrant:

Issued to	*No.*	*Acres*
Radford, Elizabeth, & William J. Mosely, children of M? Mosely, Maj	1189	400

(Note: [Sent] to C. Wallace, Chillicothe.)

1446 — 20 Feb 1827 — B/1/045
Registered by: [not stated]
Registered for: Frances? E. Henderson
Location: Mil - 2 7 4 21
Mil - 2 7 4 22
Mil - 2 7 4 30
Mil - 2 7 3 30
Mil - 1 8 2 8W*
Based upon the following Army land warrant:

Issued to	*No.*	*Acres*
Henderson, Frances? E., heir[ess?] of -- Lauring? LtCol	781	450

(Note: Delivered to W? Henderson.)
*50-acre lot.

1447 — 20 Feb 1827 — B/1/045
Registered by: John C. Wright
Registered for: John C. Wright
Location: Mil - 1 6 2 33
Mil - 2 7 3 24
Based upon the following Army land warrants:

Issued to	*No.*	*Acres*
Dillard, Nancy, heir[ess] of L. Harlow, Pvt	840	100
Howland, Fortune, Pvt	849	100

(Note: Sent to him, House of Representatives.)

1448 28 Mar 1827 B/1/045
Registered by: A. W. Paine
Registered for: [Heir?] of J. Dockum
Location: Mil - 2 5 3 41
Based upon the following Army land warrant:
Issued to *No.* *Acres*
Dockum, James, Pvt 968 100
(Note: Sent to A. W. Paine, Boston.)

1449 11 May 1827 B/1/045
Registered by: M[ichael] Nourse
Registered for: [Zaccheus?] A. Beatty
Location: Mil - 4 4 3 20
Mil - 3 1 1 17
Based upon the following Army land warrant:
Issued to *No.* *Acres*
Houston, John, Lt 1217 200
(Note: Delivered to Mr. Nourse.)

1450 15 May 1827 B/1/046
Registered by: Peter Casey
Registered for: William? L. Hopkins *et al*
Location: Mil - 9 9 1 5
Mil - 9 9 1 7
Mil - 8 9 3 11
Based upon the following Army land warrant:
Issued to *No.* *Acres*
Hopkins, D., heirs of,
Capt 1190 300
(Note: Sent to P. Casey, Millersburg, Ohio.)

1451 15 May 1827 B/1/046
Registered by: Jonas Stanberry
Registered for: Jonas Stanberry
Location: Mil - 9 9 4 15
Based upon the following Army land warrant:
Issued to *No.* *Acres*
Craig, Thomas, Pvt 1187 100
(Note: Sent to him at Zanesville.)

1452 25 May 1827 B/1/046
Registered by: John Smith
Registered for: John Smith
Location: Mil - 10 9 3 28
Based upon the following Army land warrant:
Issued to *No.* *Acres*
Smith, Willam, Drummer 1119 100
(Note: Sent to him at Annapolis.)

1453 20 Jun 1825* B/1/046
Registered by: J. C. Wright
Registered for: Aaron Hale, a colored man**
Location: Mil - 5 7 1 16
Mil - 5 7 1 17
Based upon the following Army land warrant:
Issued to *No.* *Acres*
Hale, Aaron, Lt 1203 200
(Note: Sent to him at Greenfield, Saratoga County, New York.)
*Not in chronological sequence.
**It is not clear that this description pertains to Hale or to the John Smith in the previous serial entry.

1454 25 Jun 1827 B/1/046
Registered by: Joel Hall? [Hale?]
Registered for: Samuel Handy
Location: Mil - 9 9 4 39
Based upon the following Army land warrant:
Issued to *No.* *Acres*
Handy, Samuel, Pvt 5498 100
(Note: Sent to Joel Hall?[Hale] at Berlin, Holmes County, Ohio.)

1455 25 Jun 1827 B/1/046
Registered by: Joel Hall? [Hale?]
Registered for: Phileom Hall? [Hale?]
Location: Mil - 9 9 1 18
Mil - 8 9 3 9
Based upon the following Army land warrant:
Issued to *No.* *Acres*
Hall? [Hale?] Philemon,
Lt 961 200
(Note: Sent to Joel Hall? [Hale?] at Berlin, Holmes County, Ohio.)

1456 25 Jun 1827 B/1/046
Registered by: Jonas Stanberry
Registered for: Heirs of Job Vernon & Jonas Stanberry
Location: Mil - 10 1 2 17
Mil - 7 4 2 36
Mil - 9 9 4 11
Based upon the following Army land warrant:
Issued to *No.* *Acres*
Vernon, Job, heir of,
Capt 1066 300
(Note: Sent to Stanberry at Zanesville.)

1457 25 Jun 1827 B/1/046
Registered by: William Morton
Registered for: Elizabeth Waring
Location: Mil - 3 8 4 32
Mil - 3 8 4 34
Based upon the following Army land warrant:
Issued to *No.* *Acres*
Waring, Elizabeth, heir[ess]
of B. Waring, Lt 1020 200
(Note: Delivered to Mr. Morton, Auditor's? Office.)

1458 25 Jun 1827 B/1/046
Registered by: E. Reynolds
Registered for: Samuel? Frothingham
Location: Mil - 2 7 3 10
Mil - 2 7 3 19
Based upon the following Army land warrant:
Issued to *No.* *Acres*
Frothingham, E., heir of,
Lt 1229 200

1459 1? Aug 1827 B/1/046
Registered by: A. Shane
Registered for: H? McClelland
Location: Mil - 1 6 2 2
Based upon the following Army land warrant:
Issued to *No.* *Acres*
McClelland, H., Pvt 1116 100

1460 1? Aug 1827 B/1/046
Registered by: F. Wright
Registered for: Francis Wright *et al*

1460 [continued]
Location: Mil - 8 4 3 18
Based upon the following Army land warrant:

Issued to	*No.*	*Acres*
Wright, Francis, *et al*, Pvt	1118	100

(Note: [Sent] to him at Baltimore.)

1461 — 1? Aug 1827 — B/1/046
Registered by: Eliza[beth] Spinolla
Registered for: Eliza[beth] Spinolla
Location: Mil - 2 6 3 30
Mil - 2 6 3 31
Based upon the following Army land warrant:

Issued to	*No.*	*Acres*
Spinolla, Eliza[beth] d[aughter?] of -- Phelan, Lt	1121	200

(Note: [Sent] to her at New York.)

1462 — 1? Aug 1827 — B/1/046
Registered by: John Newell, T[reasur]y Office
Registered for: --? L. Habersham & Marina? Elliott
Location: Mil - 2 7 4 5
Mil - 2 7 4 20
Mil - 2 7 4 29
Based upon the following Army land warrant:

Issued to	*No.*	*Acres*
Elliott, B., heirs of, Capt	1213	300

(Note: Delivered to Mr. Newell at the T[reasury] Office.)

1463 — 1? Aug 1827 — B/1/046
Registered by: John Newell, T[reasur]y Office
Registered for: Joseph? C. Habersham, son, & the other heirs of J. Habersham
Location: Mil - 2 7 3 3
Mil - 2 7 3 6
Mil - 2 7 3 13
Mil - 2 7 3 16
Based upon the following Army land warrant:

Issued to	*No.*	*Acres*
Habersham, John, heirs of, Maj	1226	400

(Note: Delivered to Mr. Newell at the T[reasur]y Office.)

1464 — 1? Aug 1827 — B/1/046
Registered by: James Taylor
Registered for: Griffin Taylor
Location: Mil - 16 6 1 29
Mil - 16 6 1 36
Based upon the following Army land warrant:

Issued to	*No.*	*Acres*
Taylor, Griffin, Lt	505	200

(Note: Sent to James Taylor, Newport, Kentucky.)

1465 — 1? Aug 1827 — B/1/046
Registered by: James Taylor
Registered for: James Taylor
Location: Mil - 16 7 4 5
Mil - 16 7 4 6
Mil - 16 7 4 7
Mil - 19 1 2 3
Based upon the following Army land warrants:

Issued to	*No.*	*Acres*
Muir, Francis, Capt	237	300
Robinson, Zachariah, Pvt	1055	100

(Note: Sent to James Taylor, Newport, Kentucky.)

1466 — -- Sep 1827 — B/1/046
Registered by: Thomas M. Bayley
Registered for: Thomas M. Bayley
Location: Mil - 5 7 1 40
Mil - 5 7 1 25
Based upon the following Army land warrants:

Issued to	*No.*	*Acres*
Bayley, Thomas M., Pvt	1253	100
Bayley, Thomas M., Pvt	1254	100

(Note: Sent to him . . . Accomac Courthouse, Virginia.)

1467 — -- Sep 1827 — B/1/046
Registered by: Job Caswell
Registered for: Job Caswell
Location: Mil - 2 5 2 20
Based upon the following Army land warrant:

Issued to	*No.*	*Acres*
Caswell, Job, Fifer	369	100

(Note: Sent to Thomas Bailey, his agent, B[altimore?].)

1468 — 20 Nov 1827 — B/1/046
Registered by: Amos Hale
Registered for: Rachel Lawler? & the other heir of Stephen Hale
Location: Mil - 9 9 4 21
Mil - 9 9 4 33
Mil - 9 9 4 35
Based upon the following Army land warrant:

Issued to	*No.*	*Acres*
Hale, Stephen, Capt	1193	300

(Note: Sent to him at Bloomfield, New York.)

1469 — 3 Dec 1827 — B/1/046
Registered by: D. Woodcock
Registered for: Abraham Losey
Location: Mil - 9 7 3 13
Based upon the following Army land warrant:

Issued to	*No.*	*Acres*
Losey, Abraham, Pvt	1186	100

(Note: Sent to Hon. D. Woodcock, H[ouse] of R[epresentatives].)

1470 — -- Dec 1827 — B/1/047
Registered by: Joseph Watson
Registered for: Maria McIntosh
Location: Mil - 7 4 2 5
Mil - 7 4 2 6
Based upon the following Army land warrant:

Issued to	*No.*	*Acres*
McIntosh, Maria, daughter of P? Hillary, Lt	1243	200

1471 — -- Dec 1827 — B/1/047
Registered by: Thomas M. Bayley
Registered for: Thomas M. Bayley
Location: Mil - 3 8 4 11
Mil - 3 8 4 12
Mil - 7 7 2 14
Based upon the following Army land warrants:
Issued to — *No.* — *Acres*

1471 [continued]
Bayley, Thomas M., assignee of -- O'Neil? Lt 1251 200
Bayley, Thomas M., assignee of Z. Bailey, Pvt 1252 100
(Note: Sent to him at Accomac C[ourt] H[ouse] [Virginia].)

1472 9 Feb 1828 B/1/047
Registered by: Noah Agard
Registered for: Levina? Agard & the other h[eirs?] of James Jones
Location: Mil - 2 7 3 21
Based upon the following Army land warrant:
Issued to *No.* *Acres*
Jones, James, heirs of, Pvt 1141 100
(Note: Sent to N. Agard, Catharine, New York.)

1473 9 Feb 1828 B/1/047
Registered by: Hon. Samuel McKean
Registered for: F? D. French *et al*
Location: Mil - 5 10 4 1
Based upon the following Army land warrant:
Issued to *No.* *Acres*
French, William, heir of, Pvt 1200 100
(Note: Sent to Mr. McKean, H[ouse] of R[epresentatives].)

1474 10 Feb 1828 B/1/047
Registered by: Joel Yancy
Registered for: George Pierce
Location: Mil - 1 6 2 15
Based upon the following Army land warrant:
Issued to *No.* *Acres*
Pierce, George, Pvt 1176 100
(Note: Sent to Hon. J. Yancy, H[ouse] of R[epresentatives].)

1475 10 Feb 1828 B/1/047
Registered by: P. Sprague
Registered for: John Blackeney
Location: Mil - 17 7 4 40
Based upon the following Army land warrant:
Issued to *No.* *Acres*
Blackeney, John, Pvt 8936 100
(Note: Sent to P. Sprague at Delaware, Ohio.)

1476 21 Mar 1828 B/1/047
Registered by: John C. Wright
Registered for: Thomas Joyes
Location: Mil - 2 7 3 35
Based upon the following Army land warrant:
Issued to *No.* *Acres*
Gillaham, Clemens, Pvt 1027 100
(Note: [Delivered] to Mr. Wright, H[ouse] of R[epresentatives].)

1477 2 Apr 1828 B/1/047
Registered by: George McDuffie
Registered for: Richard Pollard, son, & the other heirs at law of Richard Pollard, deceased
Location: Mil - 10 9 3 25
Mil - 10 9 3 26
Mil - 10 9 3 32
Based upon the following Army land warrant:
Issued to *No.* *Acres*
Pollard, Richard, son, & the other heirs at law of Richard Pollard, deceased, Capt 1282 300
(Note: [Sent to] Hon. G. McDuffie same day.)

1478 2 Apr 1828 B/1/047
Registered by: J. Strong
Registered for: Heirs of Thomas Parkman
Location: Mil - 2 6 1 15
Based upon the following Army land warrant:
Issued to *No.* *Acres*
Parkman, Thomas, heirs of, Pvt 870 100
(Note: [Delivered] to Hon. M. Strong same day.)

1479 12 Apr 1828 B/1/047
Registered by: J. Watson
Registered for: Heirs of David Morgan & C--? Northup
Location: Mil - 7 7 2 39
Mil - 7 7 2 40
Based upon the following Army land warrant:
Issued to *No.* *Acres*
Morgan, David, heirs of, Lt 1191 200
(Note: Sent to C. Northup.)

1480 17 Apr 1828 B/1/047
Registered by: William Marks [U.S.] Senate
Registered for: Martin Carringer
Location: Mil - 6 8 3 3
Based upon the following Army land warrant:
Issued to *No.* *Acres*
Carringer, Martin, Pvt 1259 100

1481 24 Apr 1828 B/1/047
Registered by: Thomas Elliott
Registered for: Thomas Elliott
Location: Mil - 2 5 3 12
Based upon the following Army land warrant:
Issued to *No.* *Acres*
Elliott, Thomas, Pvt 1300 100
(Note: Sent to him at Baltimore.)

1482 24 Apr 1828 B/1/047
Registered by: Jonas Stanberry
Registered for: Jonas Stanberry
Location: Mil - 7 7 2 3
Based upon the following Army land warrant:
Issued to *No.* *Acres*
Whaley, Edward, Pvt 1162 100
(Note: Sent to him at Zanesville.)

1483 24 Apr 1828 B/1/047
Registered by: Benjamin Dana
Registered for: Benjamin Dana
Location: Mil - 2 5 1 2
Mil - 2 5 1 16
Based upon the following Army land warrant:
Issued to *No.* *Acres*
Dana, Benjamin, Lt 523 200
(Note: Sent to him at Boston.)

1484 24 Apr 1828 B/1/047
Registered by: William McLean
Registered for: Anthony Geohagan
Location: Mil - 4 10 3 12
Based upon the following Army land warrant:

Issued to	*No.*	*Acres*
Geohagan, Anthony, Pvt	1269	100

(Note: Sent to William McLean, H[ouse] of R[epresentatives].)

1485 24 Apr 1828 B/1/047
Registered by: J. K. Skinner
Registered for: J. K. Skinner
Location: Mil - 2 7 3 5
Based upon the following Army land warrant:

Issued to	*No.*	*Acres*
Howe, Simon, Pvt	1204	100

(Note: Sent to him at Hannover, York County, Pennsylvania.)

1486 24 Apr 1828 B/1/047
Registered by: John Blair & Wal---?
Registered for: John Rock
Location: Mil - 2 6 1 11
Based upon the following Army land warrant:

Issued to	*No.*	*Acres*
Rock, John, Pvt	1112	100

(Note: [Sent] to Hon. J. Blair same day.)

1487 9 Jun 1828 B/1/047
Registered by: B. P. Johnson
Registered for: Israel B. Spencer
Location: Mil - 2 5 1 4
Based upon the following Army land warrant:

Issued to	*No.*	*Acres*
Spencer, Israel B., Pvt	3482	100

(Note: Sent to B. P. Johnson, Rome, New York.)

1488 6 May 1828* B/1/047
Registered by: James Patrick
Registered for: Jacob? Howe
Location: Mil - 2 7 3 15
Based upon the following Army land warrant:

Issued to	*No.*	*Acres*
Ryan, William, Pvt	1120	100

(Note: [Sent] to James Patrick, New Philadelphia? Ohio.)
*Not in chronological sequence.

1489 15 Jul 1828 B/1/047
Registered by: Major Hook
Registered for: Christopher Taylor
Location: Mil - 2 7 3 25
Mil - 2 7 3 26
Mil - 2 7 3 34
Based upon the following Army land warrant:

Issued to	*No.*	*Acres*
Taylor, Christopher, Surgeon's Mate	1335	300

(Note: Sent to Dr. Snyder at Reisterstown, Maryland.)

1490 15 Jul 1828 B/1/048
Registered by: Hon. A. Ward
Registered for: David Lands? [Sands?]
Location: Mil - 5 7 1 26
Based upon the following Army land warrant:

Issued to	*No.*	*Acres*
Piper, Simon, Pvt	1330	100

(Note: Sent to Hon. A. Ward, Mt. Pleasant, W[est] Chester, New York.)

1491 11 Jul 1828 B/1/048
Registered by: Isaac Widdows
Registered for: Abraham Widdows
Location: Mil - 7 6 1 37
Based upon the following Army land warrant:

Issued to	*No.*	*Acres*
Widdows, Abraham, Pvt	1093	100

(Note: Sent to him, I. Widdows, Waynesburg, F? [or T?] County, Pennsylvania.)

1492 9 Sep 1828 B/1/048
Registered by: D. Corey
Registered for: Sarah Harman, daughter, & the other heirs at [law] of William Brown
Location: Mil - 3 7 1 18
Based upon the following Army land warrant:

Issued to	*No.*	*Acres*
Harman, Sarah [daughter] [& other] heirs of William Brown, Pvt	1332	100

(Note: [Sent] to D. Corey at York, Pennsylvania.)

1493 18 Sep 1828 B/1/048
Registered by: Joseph Watson
Registered for: [Joseph] Watson & the heirs of Benjamin Ford
Location: Mil - 1 8 2 6W*
Based upon the following Army land warrant:

Issued to	*No.*	*Acres*
Ford, Benjamin, heirs of Chs? Ale:? Lt Col	1133	450*

(Note: Delivered to Mr. Watson.)
*50-acre lot. An additional note says 400 acres patented to G. Burk-, 9 Jun 1835.

1494 18 Sep 1828 B/1/048
Registered by: Joseph Watson
Registered for: Joseph Watson & part of John Johnson's heirs
Location: Mil - 6 2 1 24
Based upon the following Army land warrant:

Issued to	*No.*	*Acres*
Johnson, John, heirs of, Pvt	802	100

(Note: Delivered to J. Watson.)

1495 7 Oct 1828 B/1/048
Registered by: J. Stanberry
Registered for: Jonas Stanberry
Location: Mil - 8 7 3 6
Based upon the following Army land warrant:

Issued to	*No.*	*Acres*
Durrington, William, Pvt	1091	100

(Note: Sent to him at Zanesville.)

1496 28 Oct 1828 B/1/048
Registered by: Joseph Horner
Registered for: John Harrell
Location: Mil - 2 5 1 15
Based upon the following Army land warrant:

Issued to *No.* *Acres*

1496 [continued]
Harrell, John, Pvt 1316 100
(Note: [Sent] to J. Horner at Warrentown, same date.)

1497 12 Nov 1828 B/1/048
Registered by: Thomas J. Humphrey
Registered for: William Humphrey
Location: Mil - 9 9 4 30
Mil - 9 9 4 31
Mil - 9 9 2 7
Based upon the following Army land warrant:

Issued to	*No.*	*Acres*
Humphrey, William, Capt	1306	300

1498 12 Nov 1828 B/1/048
Registered by: Josiah K. Skinner
Registered for: Josiah K. Skinner & the heirs of John Findlay
Location: Mil - 2 7 3 14
Based upon the following Army land warrant:

Issued to	*No.*	*Acres*
Findlay, John, heirs of, Pvt	979	100

(Note: Sent to Skinner at Lockport, New York.)

1499 5 Dec 1828 B/1/048
Registered by: David Woodcock
Registered for: George McKenzie
Location: Mil - 5 7 1 10
Based upon the following Army land warrant:

Issued to	*No.*	*Acres*
McKenzie, George, Pvt	1418	100

(Note: Sent to Hon. D. Woodcock, H[ouse] of [Representatives].)

1500 12 Dec 1828 B/1/048
Registered by: Leroy Jordan
Registered for: Leroy Jordan
Location: Mil - 1 6 2 6
Based upon the following Army land warrant:

Issued to	*No.*	*Acres*
Chapman, Thomas, Pvt	1358	100

(Note: Sent to him at Chambliss? Store? Virginia.)

1501 12 Dec 1828 B/1/048
Registered by: N. H. Claiborne
Registered for: Jason? [Anderson?] Thomson
Location: Mil - 2 5 1 5
Based upon the following Army land warrant:

Issued to	*No.*	*Acres*
Clark, John, Pvt	1336	100

(Note: Sent to Claiborne at H[ouse] of R[epresentatives].)

1502 17 Dec 1828 B/1/048
Registered by: Thomas Carberry
Registered for: Clement Sewall
Location: Mil - 10 7 1 13
Mil - 17 7 1 24W*
Based upon the following Army land warrant:

Issued to	*No.*	*Acres*
Sewall, Clement, Ens	1444	150

(Note: Delivered to T. Carberry.)
*50-acre lot.

1503 29 Dec 1828 B/1/048
Registered by: John Delany
Registered for: John Delany
Location: Mil - 1 8 4 14
Based upon the following Army land warrant:

Issued to	*No.*	*Acres*
Delany, John, Pvt	1343	100

(Note: Sent to Leesburg, Virginia.)

1504 2 Jan 1829 B/1/048
Registered by: Nath[anie]l Chapman
Registered for: Nath[anie]l Chapman
Location: Mil - 7 7 2 18
Based upon the following Army land warrant:

Issued to	*No.*	*Acres*
Taylor, James, Pvt	1420	100

(Note: Sent to him at Chillicothe.)

1505 10 Jan 1829 B/1/048
Registered by: N. H. Claiborne
Registered for: --?* Jordan & the other heirs of Peter Berry
Location: Mil - 9 7 3 21
Based upon the following Army land warrant:

Issued to	*No.*	*Acres*
Berry, Thomas** son, & the other heirs of Peter Berry, Pvt	1422	100

(Note: Sent to Mr. Claiborne, H[ouse] of R[epresentatives].)
*Forename obscured in microfilm; National Archives may be able to read the source register.
**The name Thomas Berry is crossed out on source register.

1506 10 Jan 1829 B/1/048
Registered by: N. H. Claiborne
Registered for: Anderson? Thomson
Location: Mil - 4 10 3 11
Based upon the following Army land warrant:

Issued to	*No.*	*Acres*
Coulter, Samuel, Pvt	1357	100

(Note: Sent to Mr. Claiborne, H[ouse] of R[epresentatives].)

1507 10 Jan 1829 B/1/048
Registered by: N. H. Claiborne
Registered for: Anderson? Thomson & to the heirs of Th[eodo]r? Hill
Location: Mil - 4 10 3 22
Based upon the following Army land warrant:

Issued to	*No.*	*Acres*
Hill, James, brother, & the other heirs of Th[eodo]r? Hill, Pvt	1429	100

(Note: Sent to Mr. Claiborne, H[ouse] of R[epresentatives].)

1508 20 Jan 1829 B/1/048
Registered by: Edward Randolph
Registered for: [Jack?] B. F. Edmund, son, & the other heirs of Thomas Edmund
Location: Mil - 10 3 4 14
Mil - 10 3 4 18
Mil - 10 3 4 19
Based upon the following Army land warrant:

1508 [continued]

Issued to	*No.*	*Acres*
Edmund, Jack B. F., son, & the other heirs of Thomas Edmund, Capt	997	300

(Note: Sent to E. Randolph, Hopkinsville? Kentucky.)

1509 27 Jan 1829 B/1/049
Registered by: William Stanberry
Registered for: Jonas Stanberry
Location: Mil - 9 7 3 6
Based upon the following Army land warrant:

Issued to	*No.*	*Acres*
Uncas, John, Pvt	1288	100

(Note: Sent same day to Hon. -- Stanberry, H[ouse] of R[epresentatives].)

1510 4 Feb 1829 B/1/049
Registered by: David Woodcock
Registered for: Aaron Day & Ruth Curtiss
Location: Mil - 10 1 2 5
Mil - 10 1 2 6
Based upon the following Army land warrant:

Issued to	*No.*	*Acres*
Day, Aaron, heirs of, Lt	1454	200

1511 4 Feb 1829 B/1/049
Registered by: Nath[anie]l Chapman
Registered for: Nath[anie]l Chapman
Location: Mil - 10 1 2 24
Based upon the following Army land warrant:

Issued to	*No.*	*Acres*
Green? John, heirs of, Pvt	1435	100

(Note: Sent to him at Chillicothe.)

1512 2 Mar 1829 B/1/049
Registered by: Joseph Watson
Registered for: --? P. Watson & to the heirs of Francis Lovejoy
Location: Mil - 7 6 1 13
Based upon the following Army land warrant:

Issued to	*No.*	*Acres*
Lovejoy, Daniel, & the other heirs of Francis Lovejoy, Pvt	976 [or 975]	100

(Note: Sent to Columbus same day.)

1513 2 Mar 1829 B/1/049
Registered by: Joseph Watson
Registered for: Sally? Byram
Location: Mil - 6 8 3 1
Based upon the following Army land warrant:

Issued to	*No.*	*Acres*
Byram, Robert, Pvt	916	100

1514 2 Mar 1829 B/1/049
Registered by: Joseph Watson
Registered for: [John?] P. Watson & the other heirs of Abiel Stevens
Location: Mil - 6 8 2 5
Based upon the following Army land warrant:

Issued to	*No.*	*Acres*
Stevens, Abiel, Pvt	820	100

1515 11 Mar 1829 B/1/049
Registered by: Joseph Watson
Registered for: Joseph Wheat
Location: Mil - 10 7 1 6
Based upon the following Army land warrant:

Issued to	*No.*	*Acres*
Wheat, Joseph, Pvt	1417	100

(Note: Delivered to Col Watson.)

1516 11 Mar 1829 B/1/049
Registered by: Jesse B. Thomas
Registered for: George Hunter
Location: Mil - 10 7 1 8
Based upon the following Army land warrant:

Issued to	*No.*	*Acres*
Jones, Robert, Pvt	1109	100

(Note: Sent to J. B. Thomas, Mount Vernon, Ohio.)

1517 11 Mar 1829 B/1/049
Registered by: Anth[ony] Evans
Registered for: Daniel Lea
Location: Mil - 2 5 1 40
Based upon the following Army land warrant:

Issued to	*No.*	*Acres*
McGears? Abitha, h[eiress] of John Williams, Pvt	1363	100

(Note: Sent to A. Evans at Lancaster, Fairfield County, Ohio.)

1518 11 Mar 1829 B/1/049
Registered by: Anth[ony] Evans
Registered for: Anth[ony] Evans
Location: Mil - 8 7 3 7
Mil - 8 7 3 10
Mil - 8 7 3 11
Based upon the following Army land warrant:

Issued to	*No.*	*Acres*
Hawkins, William L? [or S?] son of M. Hawkins, Capt	1449	300

(Note: Sent to A. Evans at Lancaster, Fairfield County, Ohio.)

1519 11 Mar 1829 B/1/049
Registered by: Maitland, Kennedy, & Maitland
Registered for: Stephen Thorn(e)
Location: Mil - 2 5 1 9
Mil - 2 5 1 8
Mil - 2 5 1 26
Mil - 2 5 1 41
Mil - 2 5 1 25
Based upon the following Army land warrants:

Issued to	*No.*	*Acres*
Thorn(e) Stephen, assignee of William Forrest, Pvt	4144	100
Thorn(e) Stephen, assignee of G. Cornish, Pvt	3845	100
Thorn(e) Stephen, assignee of R. Stevens, Pvt	3466	100
Thorn(e) Stephen, assignee of H. Myers, Pvt	7500	100
Thorn(e) Stephen, assignee of A. Granda? Pvt	4273	100

(Note: Sent to Messrs. Maitland, Kennedy, & Maitland, New York.)

1520 19 Mar 1829 B/1/049
Registered by: William Stanberry
Registered for: Jonas Stanberry
Location: Mil - 9 9 4 25
Mil - 9 7 3 10
Based upon the following Army land warrants:

Issued to	*No.*	*Acres*
Willis, James, Pvt	951	100
Palmer, Jenkins, Pvt	1439	100

(Note: Sent to him at Zanesville.)

1521 2 Apr 1829 B/1/049
Registered by: William Y. Purviance
Registered for: Susanna Gwynn & the other heirs of John Gwynn
Location: Mil - 2 5 2 11
Based upon the following Army land warrant:

Issued to	*No.*	*Acres*
Gwynn, Susanna, & the other heirs of John Gwynn, Pvt	1494	100

(Note: To Purviance at Baltimore.)

1522 6 Apr 1829 B/1/050
Registered by: Isaac Norris
Registered for: John Simler
Location: Mil - 9 9 1 8
Based upon the following Army land warrant:

Issued to	*No.*	*Acres*
Simler, John, Pvt	1403	100

(Note: To Isaac Norris, Philadelphia.)

1523 16 Apr 1829 B/1/050
Registered by: Floet? Smith
Registered for: James J. Gough
Location: Mil - 10 7 1 21
Based upon the following Army land warrant:

Issued to	*No.*	*Acres*
McGhee, William, Pvt	1355	100

(Note: Sent to F. Smith, Chaptico, Maryland.)

1524 9 May 1827* B/1/050
Registered by: S. H. Smith
Registered for: S. H. Smith
Location: Mil - 8 9 3 5
Based upon the following Army land warrant:

Issued to	*No.*	*Acres*
Barnum, Ebenezer, Pvt	1074	100

(Note: Sent to him 12 Apr 1829.)
*Not in chronological sequence.)

1525 18 Jul 1825* B/1/050
Registered by: S. Quimby
Registered for: John Sarville
Location: Mil - 5 9 3 5
Based upon the following Army land warrant:

Issued to	*No.*	*Acres*
Parsons, Osborn, Pvt	1089	100

(Note: Sent to S. Quimby, Wooster.)
*Not in chronological sequence.

1526 -- Apr 1829 B/1/050
Registered by: Charles Whitely
Registered for: Charles Whitely
Location: Mil - 2 5 1 7
Mil - 2 5 1 21
Based upon the following Army land warrants:

Issued to	*No.*	*Acres*
Ramsy? James* Pvt	1473	100
Overline, William, Pvt	1466	100

*Originally shown as James & John Ramsy, but John's name is stricken out.

1527 -- Apr 1829 B/1/050
Registered by: Paten Morris
Registered for: Paten Morris
Location: Mil - 2 5 1 12
Based upon the following Army land warrant:

Issued to	*No.*	*Acres*
Bigbie, William, Pvt	1457	100

(Note: Sent to him at Chillicothe.)

1528 4 May 1829 B/1/050
Registered by: P. W. Homrighaus
Registered for: P. W. Homrighaus
Location: Mil - 3 7 1 12
Based upon the following Army land warrant:

Issued to	*No.*	*Acres*
Baumgartner, Leon[ar]d, Pvt	1305	100

(Note: Sent same day to York [Pennsylvania?].)

1529 4 May 1829 B/1/050
Registered by: Charles Whitely
Registered for: Charles Whitely
Location: Mil - 2 5 1 20
Mil - 2 5 1 10
Mil - 2 5 1 11
Based upon the following Army land warrants:

Issued to	*No.*	*Acres*
Boyd, Alex[ande]r, Pvt	1470	100
Rice, George, Pvt	1471	100
Rice, Basdel, Pvt	1472	100

(Note: Sent to C. Whitely at Chillicothe.)

1530 4 May 1829 B/1/050
Registered by: Charles Whitely
Registered for: Catherine? Pollard *et al*
Location: Mil - 2 5 1 30
Based upon the following Army land warrant:

Issued to	*No.*	*Acres*
Nichols, John, Pvt	1474	100

(Note: Sent to C. Whitely, Chillicothe.)

1531 4 May 1829 B/1/050
Registered by: James T. Aidy
Registered for: James T. Aidy
Location: Mil - 2 5 1 14
Based upon the following Army land warrant:

Issued to	*No.*	*Acres*
Colter, John, Pvt	1467	100

(Note: Sent to C. Whitely, Chillicothe.)

1532 11 May 1829 B/1/050
Registered by: Charles Whitely
Registered for: Charles Whitely & to the heirs at law of James Ball
Location: Mil - 2 5 1 17
Mil - 2 5 1 19
Based upon the following Army land warrant:

Issued to	*No.*	*Acres*
Ball, William, son, & the other heirs at law of		

1532 [continued]
James Bell, Lt 1464 200
(Note: Sent to him at Chillicothe.)

1533 12 May 1829 B/1/050
Registered by: E. F. Eastman
Registered for: Martha Eastman & Mary? M. Eastman
Location: Mil - 9 7 3 22
Mil - 9 7 3 27
Based upon the following Army land warrant:
Issued to *No.* *Acres*
Eastman, Martha, & the other heirs at law of David Miller, Lt 1328 200
(Note: Sent to him at Maint? Paint? Creek P[ost] Office.)

1534 12 May 1829 B/1/050
Registered by: James Wright
Registered for: James Wright & to the other heirs at law of William Hudson
Location: Mil - 2 5 1 23
Mil - 2 5 1 24
Based upon the following Army land warrant:
Issued to *No.* *Acres*
Jordan, Mary Ann, & the other heirs at law of William Hudson, Pvt 1346 100
(Note: Sent to him at Chambless St[ore?] Virginia.)

1535 12 May 1829 B/1/050
Registered by: James Wright
Registered for: James Wright & to the other heirs at law of Jesse Farmer
Location: Mil - 2 5 1 27
Based upon the following Army land warrant:
Issued to *No.* *Acres*
Farmer, John, & the other heirs of Jesse Farmer, Pvt 1349 100
(Note: Sent to him at Chambless St[ore?] Virginia.)

1536 14 May 1829 B/1/050
Registered by: W. Y. Purviance
Registered for: Heirs of R. Burke
Location: Mil - 3 5 1 1
Based upon the following Army land warrant:
Issued to *No.* *Acres*
Burke, Richard, heirs of, Pvt 1507 100
(Note: Sent to Purviance at Baltimore.)

1537 14 May 1829 B/1/050
Registered by: Benjamin G. Green
Registered for: Benjamin G. Green & the other heirs of Ebenezer Green
Location: Mil - 9 9 4 16
Mil - 9 9 4 22
Mil - 9 9 4 23
Based upon the following Army land warrant:
Issued to *No.* *Acres*
Green, Ebenezer, heirs of, Capt 1324 300
(Note: Sent to him at Lyme, New Hampshire.)

1538 14 May 1829 B/1/050
Registered by: Joseph Watson
Registered for: Joseph Watson
Location: Mil - 2 3 4 38
Based upon the following Army land warrant:
Issued to *No.* *Acres*
Compton, Edmond, Lt* 1266 100*
(Note: To Z[accheus A.] Beatty, Cambridge, Ohio.)
*A lieutenant was entitled to 200 acres; no explanation given regarding remaining 100 acres not granted herein.

1539 3 Jun 1829 B/1/050
Registered by: Peter Johnson
Registered for: Peter Johnson
Location: Mil - 2 5 1 18
Based upon the following Army land warrant:
Issued to *No.* *Acres*
Cunningham, James, Pvt 1409 100
(Note: Sent to him at Chambless St[ore?] Virginia.)

1540 3 Jun 1829 B/1/050
Registered by: Charles Whitely
Registered for: Charles Whitely & to the heirs of William Craig
Location: Mil - 2 5 2 8
Based upon the following Army land warrant:
Issued to *No.* *Acres*
Carnes, Sally, & the other heirs of William Craig, Pvt 1345 100
(Note: Sent to him at Chillicothe.)

1541 3 Jun 1829 B/1/050
Registered by: Charles Whitely
Registered for: Charles Whitely & to the heirs of John Johnson
Location: Mil - 2 5 1 32
Based upon the following Army land warrant:
Issued to *No.* *Acres*
Johnson, William, & the other heirs of John Johnson, Pvt 1362 100
(Note: Sent to him at Chillicothe.)

1542 -- May 1829 B/1/051
Registered by: Charles Whitely
Registered for: Charles Whitely & to the heirs at law of Michael Murphy
Location: Mil - 2 5 2 1
Based upon the following Army land warrant:
Issued to *No.* *Acres*
Murphy, John, & the other heirs at law of Michael Murphy, Pvt 1425 100
(Note: Sent to C. Whitely at Chillicothe.)

1543 -- May 1829 B/1/051
Registered by: Charles Whitely
Registered for: Charles Whitely & to the heirs at law of William Martin
Location: Mil - 2 5 2 2
Based upon the following Army land warrant:
Issued to *No.* *Acres*
Martin, Samuel, & the other heirs of William Martin,

1543 [continued]
Pvt 1463 100
(Note: Sent to C. Whitely at Chillicothe.)

1544 -- May 1829 B/1/051
Registered by: Joseph Watson
Registered for: Joseph Watson
Location: Mil - 4 10 3 24
Based upon the following Army land warrant:
Issued to *No.* *Acres*
Compton, Edmond, Lt 1266 100
(Note: Sent to him at Cambridge, Ohio.)

1545 -- May 1829 B/1/051
Registered by: Joseph Watson
Registered for: Eve Searfoss? & Mary Homel & the other heirs of Nich[olas?] Miller, Capt
Location: Mil - 1 6 2 3
Mil - 1 6 2 20
Mil - 1 6 2 29
Based upon the following Army land warrant:
Issued to *No.* *Acres*
Searfoss? Eve, & Mary Homel & the other heirs of Nich-[olas?] Miller, Capt 1136 300
(Note: Delivered to his office on P[ennsylvani]a Avenue [Washington, D.C.?].)

1546 -- May 1829 B/1/051
Registered by: Joseph Watson
Registered for: Christiana Seth & the other heirs of John Duguid, Lt
Location: Mil - 2 8 4 1
Mil - 2 8 4 19
Based upon the following Army land warrant:
Issued to *No.* *Acres*
Seth, Christiana, & the other heirs of John Duguid, Lt 1159 200
(Note: Delivered to his office on P[ennsylvani]a Avenue [Washington, D.C.?].)

1547 12 Jun 1829 B/1/051
Registered by: David Corey
Registered for: David Corey*
Location: Mil - 5? 7 1 26**
Mil - 5? 7 2 6**
Based upon the following Army land warrants:
Issued to *No.* *Acres*
Steagel, Susannah, & the other heirs of Conrad Steagel, Pvt 1301 100
Warner, Michael, Pvt 1279 100
(Note: Sent to him at York, Pennsylvania.)
*Interlineation: See vol. 4, pp. 438, 439.
**Could read Mil - 3 7 1 26 and
Mil - 3 7 2 6.

1548 12 Jun 1829 B/1/051
Registered by: John Frew
Registered for: John? Jones*
Location: Mil - 5 7 1 39
Based upon the following Army land warrant:
Issued to *No.* *Acres*
Wood, Elizabeth, daughter & heir[ess] of John Phil-lips, Pvt 1434 100
(Note: To John Frew at Chillicothe.)
*Interlineation: See vol. 4, p. 440.

1549 19 Jun 1829 B/1/051
Registered by: Charles Whitely
Registered for: Charles Whitely & to the heirs of Jacob Hutts
Location: Mil - 2 5 2 19
Based upon the following Army land warrant:
Issued to *No.* *Acres*
Hutts, Jacob, heirs of, Pvt 1347 100
(Note: Sent to C. Whitely at Chillicothe.)

1550 19 Jun 1829 B/1/051
Registered by: Charles Whitely
Registered for: Charles Whitely & to the heirs of Matthew Craig
Location: Mil - 2 5 1 13
Based upon the following Army land warrant:
Issued to *No.* *Acres*
Craig, Matthew, heirs of, Pvt 1360 100
(Note: Sent to C. Whitely at Chillicothe.)

1551 23 Jun 1829 B/1/051
Registered by: William Stanberry
Registered for: Jonas Stanberry
Location: Mil - 8 9 3 22
Based upon the following Army land warrant:
Issued to *No.* *Acres*
Bowen, William, son & heir of Michael Bowen, Pvt 1264 100
(Note: Sent to him at Zanesville.)

1552 30 Jun 1829 B/1/051
Registered by: Capt -- Stevens of the Navy
Registered for: Stephen Rainey
Location: Mil - 10 3 4 3
Mil - 10 3 4 4
Mil - 10 3 4 5
Mil - 10 3 4 17
Mil - 3 6 4 11
Based upon the following Army land warrant:
Issued to *No.* *Acres*
Rainey, Stephen, Hospital Surgeon 1374 450
(Note: Delivered to Capt Stevens.)

1553 11 Jul 1829 B/1/051
Registered by: William Stanberry
Registered for: Jonas Stanberry
Location: Mil - 10 7 1 22
Based upon the following Army land warrant:
Issued to *No.* *Acres*
Georgia, Simon, Pvt 1289 100
(Note: Sent to him at Zanesville.)

1554 11 Jul 1829 B/1/051
Registered by: Charles Whitely
Registered for: Charles Whitely & to the [heirs] of John Biggs
Location: Mil - 2 5 2 13
Based upon the following Army land warrant:
Issued to *No.* *Acres*
Biggs, John, Pvt 1421 100

1554 [continued]
(Note: Sent to C. Whitely, Liberty, Bedford County, Pennsylvania.)

1555 11 Jul 1829 B/1/051
Registered by: Charles Whitely
Registered for: Charles Whitely & to the [heirs] of James Craig
Location: Mil - 2 5 2 3
Based upon the following Army land warrant:

Issued to	*No.*	*Acres*
Craig, James, Pvt	1359	100

(Note: Sent to C. Whitely, Liberty, Bedford County, Pennsylvania.)

1556 11 Jul 1829 B/1/051
Registered by: James Johnston
Registered for: James Johnston
Location: Mil - 2 5 1 39
Based upon the following Army land warrant:

Issued to	*No.*	*Acres*
Fanner? [Farmer?] Nathan, Pvt	1348	100

1557 18 Jul 1829 B/1/052
Registered by: Z. Morrison
Registered for: Zach[ariah?] Morrison
Location: Mil - 5 7 1 29
Mil - 5 7 1 35
Mil - 5 7 1 36
Based upon the following Army land warrant:

Issued to	*No.*	*Acres*
Harris, John, heirs of, Capt	1428	300

(Note: Sent to him at Coshocton.)

1558 18 Jul 1829 B/1/052
Registered by: Dav[id] Easton
Registered for: Sarah Easton, heiress of John Jordan
Location: Mil - 16 7 2 23
Mil - 17 7 2 32*
Based upon the following Army land warrant:

Issued to	*No.*	*Acres*
Easton, Sarah, heir[ess] of John Jordan, Cornet	1510	150

(Note: Delivered to him.)
*Fraction; [50-acre lot?].

1559 14 Jun 1829 B/1/052
Registered by: Charles Whitely
Registered for: Jeremiah Allen & the other heir of William Allen
Location: Mil - 2 5 2 4
Based upon the following Army land warrant:

Issued to	*No.*	*Acres*
Allen, Jeremiah, & the other heir of William Allen, Pvt	1356	100

(Note: Sent to Charles Whitely at Liberty, Bedford County, Virginia [!].)

1560 14 Jun 1829 B/1/052
Registered by: Charles Whitely
Registered for: Samuel English & the other heirs of Charles English
Location: Mil - 2 5 2 24
Based upon the following Army land warrant:

Issued to	*No.*	*Acres*
English, Samuel, & the other heirs of Charles English, Pvt	1379	100

(Note: Sent to Charles Whitely, Liberty, Bedford County, Virginia [!].)

1561 -- Jan 1829* B/1/052
Registered by: J. C. Wright
Registered for: Jacob? Blickendorfer
Location: Mil - 3 7 1 15
Mil - 3 7 2 7
Mil - 5 7 1 30
Based upon the following Army land warrant:

Issued to	*No.*	*Acres*
Walker, Catharina D? heir[ess] of James? Walker, Pvt	1218	100

(Note: Sent to him at Canal Dover.)
*Not in chronological sequence.

1562 -- Jan 1829 B/1/052
Registered by: Peter Casey
Registered for: Chaney? Clow
Location: Mil - 8 9 3 16
Based upon the following Army land warrant:

Issued to	*No.*	*Acres*
Battles, John, & the other heir of J. Battles, Capt	1222	300*

(Note: Sent to P. Casey, Millersburg, Ohio.)
*The claim of a captaincy was 300 acres; there is no explanation of the 200 acres not granted herewith.

1563 1 Oct 1829 B/1/052
Registered by: John Stiles
Registered for: John Stiles & the other heirs of Robert Stiles
Location: Mil - 2 5 2 15
Based upon the following Army land warrant:

Issued to	*No.*	*Acres*
Stiles, John, & the other heirs of Robert Stiles, Capt*	1368	300

(Note: Sent to J. Stiles, Liberty, Virginia.)
*A captaincy indicated in source ledger but may be in error, as only 100 acres granted herewith.

1564 13 Oct 1829 B/1/052
Registered by: J. Philbrick
Registered for: --?* Eaton
Location: Mil - 11 8 1 39
Based upon the following Army land warrant:

Issued to	*No.*	*Acres*
Eaton, Jonath[an] Pvt?	1334	100

(Note: Sent to Philbrick at Seabrook.)
*Forename obscured on microfilm, but National Archives may be able to read from source register.

1565 23 Oct 1829 B/1/052
Registered by: J. K. Douglass
Registered for: Mary? Douglass & the heirs of James Martin
Location: Mil - 3 7 2 39
Mil - 3 7 2 40

1565 [continued]
Mil - 2 7 3 22
Mil - 2 7 3 23
Based upon the following Army land warrant:
Issued to *No.* *Acres*
Martin, James, heirs of, Surgeon 1524 400
(Note: Sent to J. K. Douglass at Camden, South Carolina.)

1566 27 Oct 1829 B/1/052
Registered by: A. Shane
Registered for: --?* Barton
Location: Mil - 3 8 4 22
Mil - 3 8 4 27
Based upon the following Army land warrant:
Issued to *No.* *Acres*
Price, William, Lt 1440 200
(Note: Sent to him at Canal Dover.)
*Forename obscured on microfilm, but National Archives may be able to read from source register.

1567 27 Oct 1829 B/1/052
Registered by: Sylvester Gilbert
Registered for: --?* * Mary Rolo
Location: Mil - 7 7 2 33
Based upon the following Army land warrant:
Issued to *No.* *Acres*
Rolo, Z., heirs of, Pvt 1448 100
(Note: Sent to S. Gilbert, Hebron, Connecticut?)
*A forename obscured on microfilm, but National Archives may be able to read from source register.

1568 31 Oct 1829 B/1/052
Registered by: James Colvin
Registered for: James Colvin & to the heir of George Freeborn
Location: Mil - 3 8 4 35
Based upon the following Army land warrant:
Issued to *No.* *Acres*
Freeborn, George, heirs of, Pvt 1402 100
(Note: Sent to Colvin at Columbia, Pennsylvania.)

1569 11 Nov 1829 B/1/052
Registered by: Mr. -- Hodgson
Registered for: Isaac Morris, brother, & the other heirs of Benjamin Morris
Location: Mil - 2 3 4 24
Based upon the following Army land warrant:
Issued to *No.* *Acres*
Morris, Benjamin, heirs of, Cornet 1568 150
(Note: Sent to Isaac Morris, East Bethlehem, Washington County, Pennsylvania.)

1570 15 Nov 1829 B/1/052
Registered by: Mr. -- Hodgson
Registered for: Robert McFarlane
Location: Mil - 2 3 4 39
Mil - 2 3 4 40
Based upon the following Army land warrant:
Issued to *No.* *Acres*
McFarlane, Robert, assignee of Andrew McFarlane, Lt 1569 200
(Note: Sent to Elizabeth Town, Allegheny County, Pennsylvania.)

1571 24 Nov 1829 B/1/052
Registered by: Leroy Jordan
Registered for: Leroy Jordan
Location: Mil - 2 5 2 23
Based upon the following Army land warrant:
Issued to *No.* *Acres*
Davis, William, Pvt 1536 100
(Note: Sent to him at Chillicothe.)

1572 24 Nov 1829 B/1/052
Registered by: Leroy Jordan
Registered for: Leroy? Jordan & to the heirs of Rush Hudson
Location: Mil - 2 5 2 29
Based upon the following Army land warrant:
Issued to *No.* *Acres*
Mountcastle, Lucy, & the other heirs of Rush Hudson, Pvt 1432 100
(Note: Sent to him at Chillicothe.)

1573 24 Nov 1829 B/1/053
Registered by: James Wright
Registered for: Leroy Jordan & to the heirs of James Thomas
Location: Mil - 2 5 1 36
Based upon the following Army land warrant:
Issued to *No.* *Acres*
Thomas, James [Junior] & the other heirs of James Thomas [Senior] Pvt 1433 100
(Note: Sent to [Jordan] at Chillicothe.)

1574 24 Nov 1829 B/1/053
Registered by: James Wright
Registered for: Leroy Jordan & to the heirs of Patrick Murphy
Location: Mil - 2 5 1 37
Based upon the following Army land warrant:
Issued to *No.* *Acres*
Murphy, John, nephew, & the other heirs of Patrick Murphy, Pvt 1430 100
(Note: Sent to [Jordan] at Chillicothe.)

1575 24 Nov 1829 B/1/053
Registered by: James Wright
Registered for: Leroy Jordan & to the heirs of John Brown
Location: Mil - 2 5 2 5
Based upon the following Army land warrant:
Issued to *No.* *Acres*
Brown, Jennings, brother, & the other heirs of John Brown, Pvt 1367 100
(Note: Sent to [Jordan] at Chillicothe.)

1576 24 Nov 1829 B/1/053
Registered by: James Wright
Registered for: Leroy Jordan & to the heirs of James Fitzgerald
Location: Mil - 2 5 2 14
Based upon the following Army land warrant:

1576 [continued]

Issued to	*No.*	*Acres*
Fitzgerald, Elijah, son, & the other heirs of James Fitzgerald, Pvt	1436	100

(Note: Sent to [Jordan] at Chillicothe.)

1577 2 Dec 1829 B/1/053

Registered by: John Gilmore
Registered for: James Burnside
Location: Mil - 11 8 1 38
Based upon the following Army land warrant:

Issued to	*No.*	*Acres*
Burnside, James, Pvt	9047	100

(Note: Sent to Hon. J. Gilmore, H[ouse] of R[epresentatives].)

1578 9 Dec 1829 B/1/053

Registered by: S. H. Smith
Registered for: Elizabeth Wells & the other heirs of Edward Dyer
Location: Mil - 8 9 2 6
Mil - 8 9 2 15
Mil - 9 9 1 1
Based upon the following Army land warrant:

Issued to	*No.*	*Acres*
Wells, Elizabeth, the late E Dyer, & the other heirs of Edward Dyer, Capt	620	300

(Note: Sent to S. H. Smith, Vinia, Huron? County, Ohio.)

1579 9 Dec 1829 B/1/053

Registered by: Absalom Bud
Registered for: Ethan? Wakefield, grandson, & the other heirs of Samuel Chapin
Location: Mil - 8 9 3 18
Mil - 8 9 3 19
Based upon the following Army land warrant:

Issued to	*No.*	*Acres*
Chapin, Samuel, heirs of, Lt	1556	200

(Note: Sent to A. Bud, Black Rock.)

1580 19 Dec 1829 B/1/053

Registered by: Dr. -- Goodenow
Registered for: [Abraham?] Shane
Location: Mil - 5 7 1 38
Based upon the following Army land warrant:

Issued to	*No.*	*Acres*
Davis, Thomas, Pvt	1453	100

(Note: To Goodenow, H[ouse] of R[epresentatives].)

1581 21 Dec 1829 B/1/053

Registered by: J. A. King
Registered for: Frederick Shliker
Location: Mil - 3 7 1 13
Based upon the following Army land warrant:

Issued to	*No.*	*Acres*
Shliker, Frederick, Pvt	1372	100

(Note: To Hon. J. A. King, H[ouse] of R[epresentatives].)

1582 21 Dec 1829 B/1/053

Registered by: W. Silliman
Registered for: --?* L. Brown
Location: Mil - 10 7 1 7
Based upon the following Army land warrant:

Issued to	*No.*	*Acres*
Ball, Abr[aham] assignee of John Lane, Pvt	1062	100

(Note: Sent to him at Mt. Vernon, Ohio.)
*Forename obscured on microfilm, but National Archives may be able to read it from source register.

1583 31 Dec 1829 B/1/053

Registered by: Joseph Watson
Registered for: Peter Mills
Location: Mil - 8 2 1 1*
Based upon the following Army land warrant:

Issued to	*No.*	*Acres*
Priestly, John, Capt*	1139	300

(Note: Sent to Zanesville, Ohio. [A note to the effect that patent was delivered to Mr. Underwood is stricken out.])
*Two hundred acres (of 300 acres due a captaincy) was patented in October 1813.

1584 31 Dec 1829 B/1/053

Registered by: Joel Davis
Registered for: --?* Webb & to the other heirs of James Weare
Location: Mil - 2 5 2 27
Based upon the following Army land warrant:

Issued to	*No.*	*Acres*
Weare, George, son, & the other heir of James Weare, Pvt	1437	100

(Note: Sent to Webb at Cadwallader Post Office, Ohio.)
*Forename obscured on microfilm, but National Archives may be able to read it from source register.

1585 29 Dec 1829 B/1/054

Registered by: Hon. J. Holmes
Registered for: Theodore Linsett
Location: Mil - 1 8 4 40
Based upon the following Army land warrant:

Issued to	*No.*	*Acres*
Linsett, Theodore, Pvt	1296	100

(Note: To Hon. J. Holmes, [U.S.] Senate.)

1586 29 Dec 1829 B/1/054

Registered by: Charles Whitely
Registered for: Charles Whitely & to the heirs of James McIntire
Location: Mil - 2 6 3 7
Based upon the following Army land warrant:

Issued to	*No.*	*Acres*
McIntire, James [Junior?] & the other heirs of James McIntire, Pvt	1431	100

(Note: Sent to Charles Whitely . . . Cadwallader Post Office, Ohio.)

1587 15 Jan 1830 B/1/054

Registered by: William Dwight
Registered for: William Perry
Location: Mil - 1 8 4 30
Mil - 1 8 2 6E*
Based upon the following Army land warrant:

1587 [continued]

Issued to	*No.*	*Acres*
Perry, William [Junior?] son of William Perry, deceased, Cornet	1588	150

(Note: Sent to Hon. W. Dwight, H[ouse] of R[epresentatives].)
*50-acre lot.

1588 1 Feb 1830 B/1/054
Registered by: Jonathan Andrews
Registered for: Jonathan Andrews
Location: Mil - 2 6 3 20
Based upon the following Army land warrant:

Issued to	*No.*	*Acres*
Murray, Daniel, Pvt	1575	100

(Note: Sent to A. Randal . . . Cadwallader Post Office, Ohio.)

1589 29 Jan 1830 B/1/054
Registered by: D. Adams
Registered for: Mordecai Myers
Location: Mil - 2 6 1 12
Based upon the following Army land warrant:

Issued to	*No.*	*Acres*
Bishop, Levi, Pvt	1342	100

(Note: Sent to M. Myers, New York.)

1590 3 Feb 1830 B/1/054
Registered by: George Handy
Registered for: Andrew Murray
Location: Mil - 2 6 3 24
Based upon the following Army land warrant:

Issued to	*No.*	*Acres*
Hunter, Benjamin, Pvt	1375	100

(Note: Sent to G. Handy, Philadelphia.)

1591 23 Feb 1830 B/1/054
Registered by: Jonas Stanberry
Registered for: Jonas Stanberry
Location: Mil - 1 8 2 5E*
Based upon the following Army land warrant:

Issued to	*No.*	*Acres*
Porter, Moses, Ens	934	150

(Note: Sent to J. Stanberry, Zanesville.)
*50-acre lot (of 150 acres due an Ensign).

1592 24 Feb 1830 B/1/054
Registered by: James Patrick
Registered for: George Becker
Location: Mil - 3 7 1 35*
Based upon the following Army land warrant:

Issued to	*No.*	*Acres*
Broadhead, Daniel, Lt*	1095	200

*One hundred acres of 200 acres due a Lieutenant.

1593 22 Feb 1830 B/1/054
Registered by: William Stanberry
Registered for: Jonas Stanberry
Location: Mil - 9 9 2 1
Based upon the following Army land warrant:

Issued to	*No.*	*Acres*
Taylor, Elijah, Pvt	1485	100

(Note: Sent to J. Stanberry, Zanesville.)

1594 5 Mar 1830 B/1/054
Registered by: William Marks
Registered for: William Diehl, son, & the other heirs at law of William Diehl, *alias* Deal
Location: Mil - 2 6 3 14
Based upon the following Army land warrant:

Issued to	*No.*	*Acres*
Crawford, Patrick, Pvt	1596	100

(Note: Sent to Mr. Marks, [U.S.] Senate.)

1595 2 Mar 1830 B/1/054
Registered by: Huldah M. Humphreys
Registered for: Huldah M. Humphreys & Ruama? Whalin
Location: Mil - 3 8 4 10
Based upon the following Army land warrant:

Issued to	*No.*	*Acres*
Humphreys, Israel? [Jovael?] Pvt	1600	100

(Note: Delivered to Huldah.)

1596 11 Mar 1830 B/1/054
Registered by: Dr. -- Goodenow
Registered for: Francis Gernant
Location: Mil - 3 7 2 11
Based upon the following Army land warrant:

Issued to	*No.*	*Acres*
Mack, Richard, Pvt	1447	100

(Note: Sent to Dr. Goodenow in Congress.)

1597 12 Mar 1830 B/1/054
Registered by: William Creighton
Registered for: --?* T. Fulton
Location: Mil - 3 7 1 14
Based upon the following Army land warrant:

Issued to	*No.*	*Acres*
Hearney, David, Pvt	1152	100

(Note: Delivered to Mr. Creighton.)
*Forename obscured on microfilm, but National Archives may be able to read from source register.

1598 16 Mar 1830 B/1/054
Registered by: Townsend Ross
Registered for: Stephen Price
Location: Mil - 7 7 2 13
Based upon the following Army land warrant:

Issued to	*No.*	*Acres*
Price, Stephen, Pvt	1557	100

(Note: Sent to T. Ross, Homer, New York.)

1599 16 Mar 1830 B/1/054
Registered by: Charles Handly
Registered for: Hezekiah Hobby, son & devisee, & the other heirs of Thomas Hobby
Location: Mil - 1 8 4 13
Mil - 1 8 4 14
Mil - 1 8 4 20
Mil - 1 8 4 21
Mil - 1 8 2 4E*
Based upon the following Army land warrant:

Issued to	*No.*	*Acres*
Hobby, Hezekiah, son & devisee, & the other heirs of Thomas Hobby [Lt?] Col	1543	450

(Note: Sent to C. Handly, Stamford? Connecticut?)

1600 13 Apr 1830 B/1/055
Registered by: Joseph Watson
Registered for: Lewis Hart
Location: Mil - 6 8 2 26
Based upon the following Army land warrant:

Issued to	*No.*	*Acres*
Hart, Lewis, Pvt	497	100

(Note: Sent to M[ordecai] Myers & Co., New York.)

1601 13 Apr 1830 B/1/055
Registered by: D. Adams
Registered for: George Blaney & to the heirs of Caleb Thomas
Location: Mil - 9 9 4 3
Based upon the following Army land warrant:

Issued to	*No.*	*Acres*
Thomas, William, son, & the other heirs of Caleb Thomas, Pvt	1274	100

(Note: Sent to M[ordecai] Myers & Co., New York.)

1602 16 Apr 1830 B/1/055
Registered by: Joseph Watson
Registered for: John Morris Foght
Location: Mil - 8 7 3 16
Mil - 8 7 3 17
Based upon the following Army land warrant:

Issued to	*No.*	*Acres*
Foght, John Morris, Lt	1491	200

(Note: Sent to him at New York.)

1603 16 Apr 1830 B/1/055
Registered by: Joseph Watson
Registered for: John Head
Location: Mil - 8 7 3 32
Based upon the following Army land warrant:

Issued to	*No.*	*Acres*
Head, John, Pvt	1384	100

(Note: Delivered to J. Watson.)

1604 16 Apr 1830 B/1/055
Registered by: Joseph Watson
Registered for: James Neal
Location: Mil - 3 7 2 8
Based upon the following Army land warrant:

Issued to	*No.*	*Acres*
Neal, James, Pvt	1406	100

(Note: Delivered to J. Watson.)

1605 16 Apr 1830 B/1/055
Registered by: Joseph Watson
Registered for: John Weaver
Location: Mil - 3 7 2 23
Based upon the following Army land warrant:

Issued to	*No.*	*Acres*
Weaver, John, Pvt	1391	100

(Note: Delivered to J. Watson.)

1606 16 Apr 1830 B/1/055
Registered by: Joseph Watson
Registered for: John Hughes
Location: Mil - 2 5 2 26
Based upon the following Army land warrant:

Issued to	*No.*	*Acres*
Hughes, John, Pvt	1390	100

(Note: Delivered to J. Watson.)

1607 22 Apr 1830 B/1/055
Registered by: Joseph Watson
Registered for: John Townsend
Location: Mil - 10 9 3 21
Based upon the following Army land warrant:

Issued to	*No.*	*Acres*
Townsend, John, Pvt	1490	100

(Note: Delivered to Col Watson.)

1608 21 Apr 1830 B/1/055
Registered by: Joseph Watson
Registered for: Robert Dickerson
Location: Mil - 10 9 1 3
Based upon the following Army land warrant:

Issued to	*No.*	*Acres*
Dickerson, Robert, Pvt	1385	100

(Note: Delivered to Col Watson.)

1609 22 Apr 1830 B/1/055
Registered by: Joseph Watson
Registered for: Nathaniel Mallory
Location: Mil - 10 9 3 22
Based upon the following Army land warrant:

Issued to	*No.*	*Acres*
Mallory, Nathaniel, Pvt	1389	100

(Note: Delivered to Col Watson.)

1610 23 Jan 1829* B/1/055
Registered by: Jonas Stanberry
Registered for: Jonas Stanberry
Location: Mil - 9 9 4 27
Based upon the following Army land warrant:

Issued to	*No.*	*Acres*
Porter, Moses, Ens	934	150

(Note: Sent to J. Stanberry, 15 May 1830.)
*Not in chronological sequence.

1611 10 May 1830 B/1/055
Registered by: H. Muhlenberg
Registered for: D[anie]l? Koch & the other heir of Adam Koch
Location: Mil - 10 9 3 27
Based upon the following Army land warrant:

Issued to	*No.*	*Acres*
Koch, Adam, heirs of, Pvt	1618	100

(Note: Sent to Muhlenberg, H[ouse] of R[epresentatives].)

1612 15 May 1830 B/1/055
Registered by: H. Y? Asbury
Registered for: Matthew Brothers
Location: Mil - 11 9 4 11
Based upon the following Army land warrant:

Issued to	*No.*	*Acres*
Brother(s), Matthew, Pvt	9073	100

(Note: Sent to H. Asbury, Lexington, Kentucky.)

1613 24 May 1830 B/1/055
Registered by: A. Shane
Registered for: Henry? Knestrick
Location: Mil - 8 9 3 15
Based upon the following Army land warrant:

Issued to	*No.*	*Acres*
Pond, P., Pvt	881	100

(Note: Sent to A. Shane, Canal Dover.)

1614 — 24 May 1830 — B/1/055

Registered by: J. Thompson
Registered for: James Fegnis
Location: Mil - 1 8 4 5
Based upon the following Army land warrant:

Issued to	*No.*	*Acres*
Fegnis? James, Pvt	1602	100

(Note: To J. Thompson, H[ouse] of R[epresentatives].)

1615 — 9 Jun 1830 — B/1/055

Registered by: Isaac Morris
Registered for: Isaac Morris, brother, & the other heirs of Benjamin Morris
Location: Mil - 1 8 2 26E*
Based upon the following Army land warrant:

Issued to	*No.*	*Acres*
Morris, Benjamin, Ens	1568	150

(Note: Sent to him at East Bethlehem, Pennsylvania.)
*50-acre lot of 150 acres due an Ensign.

1616 — 9 Jun 1830 — B/1/055

Registered by: John Frew
Registered for: John Frew
Location: Mil - 5 7 1 18
Based upon the following Army land warrant:

Issued to	*No.*	*Acres*
Harman, George, Pvt	1361	100

(Note: Sent to him at Coshocton.)

1617 — 28 Sep 1830 — B/1/055

Registered by: Ira T. Neal
Registered for: Susan Stoddard & Lanea? Clark, heir[esses] of B. Clark
Location: Mil - 8 7 3 15
Based upon the following Army land warrant:

Issued to	*No.*	*Acres*
Stoddard, Susan, & Lanea? Clark, heir[esses] of B. Clark, Pvt	1451	100

(Note: [Sent] to I. T. Neal, Waterbury, Connecticut?)

1618 — -- 1827 — B/1/055

Registered by: J. Watson
Registered for: [Heir] of James McFadon
Location: Mil - 7 6 1 9
Mil - 7 6 1 10
Based upon the following Army land warrant:

Issued to	*No.*	*Acres*
McFadon, James, heir of, Lt	1079	200

(Note: Sent to V. Maxey, solicitor.)
*Not in chronological sequence.

1619 — 18-22 Nov 1830 — B/1/056

Army land warrants converted to scrip:

Warrant holder	*War. no.*	*scrip issued to*	*Acres*
Smith, Ebenezer, Capt	1057	William Stanberry	300
John, Violet, Soldier Virginia Line	1387	Robert Lucas	100
Young, Joseph, Pvt	1479	Jonas Stanberry	100
Jacobs, George, Lt	1450	Jonas Stanberry	200
Clark, George, Lt	1484	Jonas Stanberry	200
Handley, George, Capt	1255	Jonas Stanberry	300
Nestler, John, Soldier	1542	Jonas Stanberry	100
Burke, William, Pvt	1353	Joseph Watson	100
Emerson, John, Lt	1611	Joseph Watson	200
Mosby, William, Pvt	1612	Joseph Watson	100
Hamilton, John, Pvt	1613	Joseph Watson	100
Tharp, Perry, Pvt	1477	Joseph Watson	100
Jones, Thomas, Pvt	1648	Thomas Jones	100
Basey, William, Sgt	1650	William Basey	100
Hayden, Jeremiah, Pvt	1617	Jeremiah Hayden	100
Wiley, Aldrick, Lt	1673	Sarah Chamberlain	200
Parrott, Joseph, Lt	1578	Joseph Watson	200
Hackney, John, Pvt	1516	Joseph Watson	100
Jones, James Morris, Lt	1242	Joseph Watson	200
Boyles, David, Pvt	1456	Joseph Watson	100
Rankin, Robert, Lt	1380	Joseph Watson	200
White, Robert, Capt	1679*	Joseph Watson	300
Fosbrook, John, Pvt	1676	John Fosbrook	100
Baker, Edmund, Pvt	750	Mary Baker, heir	100
Veroney, Joseph, Pvt	1327	Daniel D. --?[1]	100
Mayhew, James, Pvt	872	William W. --?[1]	100
Snyder, Philip, Ens	1142	George C. Snyder	150
Shaffner, George, Maj	2120	Mary Shaffner & other heirs	400
Wright, Nathan, Lt	1220	John Wright *et al*	200

*Interlineation: 1678.
1. Surname obscured on microfilm, but National Archives may be able to read from source register.

1620 — 22-27 Nov 1830 — B/1/057

Army land warrants converted to scrip:

Warrant holder	*War. no.*	*Scrip issued to*	*Acres*
Wall, Edward, Pvt	1644	Edward Wall	100
Bowers, James, Pvt	1643	James Bowers	100
Slaughter, Philip, Capt	1653	Philip Slaughter	300
Boswell, William, Soldier	1527	Peter Mills	100
Martin, Ichabod, Pvt	1514	Peter Mills	100
Watcher, Nicholas, Pvt	1671	Nicholas Watcher	100
Wilson, John, Lt	1626	Frances J. Hickman, heir[ess]	200
Hanley, James, Soldier	7226	Ransom --?[1]	100
Spires, Richard, Pvt	1672	Richard Spires	100
Cyrus, Bartholomew, Pvt	1475	Bartholomew Cyrus	100
Thompson, William, Pvt	1610	Allen --?[1]	100
Jacob, John J., Lt	1405	John J. Jacob	200
Minor, Thomas, Capt	1678	Thomas Minor	300
Nicholas, John, Capt	1386	Jonas Stanberry	300
Sommers, Simon, Lt	1480	James N. Taylor	200
Gibbon, James, Capt	1538	James Gibbon	300
Ross, Valentine, Pvt	1623	Valentine Ross	100
McManis, Christ[oph]r, Pvt	1589	Christopher Morris	100
Lawson, Benjamin, Lt	1225	Fabius Lawson, heir, etc.	200
Frost, George P., Capt	1616	George P. Frost	300
Butler, John, Pvt	1505	Allen Latham?	100
Robinson, Levi, Pvt	1291	Levi Robinson	100
Whalen, Joseph, Pvt	1553	William B. Huff?[1]	100
Freeman, Joseph, Pvt	1540	William B. Huff?[1]	100
Curtis, Zachariah, Pvt	1544	William B. Huff?[1]	100
Ward, Jabez, Pvt	1303	Robert --?[1]	100
Smith, William, Drummer	1630	William Smith	100

1620 [continued]

Warrant holder	War. no.	Scrip issued to	Acres
Sestre? [Lestre?] Francis, Pvt	1551	Samuel Lee?[1]	100
Justin, Charles, Pvt	1172	Samuel Lee?[1]	100

1. Surname obscured on microfilm, but National Archives may be able to read from source register.

1621 29 Nov 1830 - 17 Feb 1831 B/1/058

Army land warrants converted to scrip:

Warrant holder	*War. no.*	*Scrip issued to*	*Acres*
Van Huff, John, Pvt	1656	John Van Huff	100
Parker, Nathan, Pvt	1661	Nathan Parker	100
Farley, Jonathan, Pvt	1668	Jonathan Farley	100
Utter, Solomon, Pvt	1651	Solomon Utter	100
Rhodes, John, Pvt	1669	John Rhodes	100
Hillary, Rignal, Lt[1]	1659	Elizabeth McGruder	200
Bowman, Abraham, Col	1566	John[2] & George H. Bowman	500
Slatker? Peter, Soldier	1381	Mahlon Mason?	100
Ward, Stephen, Pvt	1399	William Stanberry	100
Foster, William, Pvt	1552	William Stanberry	100
Cornwall, Richard, Pvt	1586	William Stanberry	100
Young, William, Pvt	1398	William Stanberry	100
Norgan[3] John, Pvt	1397	William Stanberry	100
Bottom, John, Pvt	1396	William Stanberry	100
Kirtland, Gideon, Pvt	1304	William Stanberry	100
Black, Joseph, Pvt	1395	William Stanberry	100
Poor, D. J., Sgt	560	James Holmes	100
Rucker, Israel, Sgt	890	Israel Rucker	100
Lewis, Chancy, Cornet	1278	Jonas Stanberry	100
Luckett, David [Lt?]	1086	--?[2] Luckett & the other heirs at law	200
Foster, William, Matross	1462	Ebenezer Smith?[4]	100
Johnston, Peter, Pvt	1263	Charles C. --?[4]	100
Davidson, Barabas, Pvt	1680	John Davidson	100
Russell, Asher, Pvt	1195	Peter Mills	100
Dennis, Daniel, Lt	1682	Elizabeth Griffith?[4]	200
Broadhed, Daniel, Lt	1095	--? --?[4]	100*
Smith, John David? Soldier	1427	William B. Huff?[4]	100
Lucas, Samuel, Pvt	1539	Cad Lucas?[4]	100
Bryant, *alias* Bryan, [not given] Pvt	1605	Cad Lucas?[4]	100

1. Warrant presented by Cadwallader Wallace.
2. Forename obscured on microfilm, but National Archives may be able to read from source register.
3. So spelled.
4. Surname obscured on microfilm, but National Archives may be able to read from source register.

*Originally 200 acres, but corrected to 100. Was Broadhed a Lieutenant?

1622 17-21 Feb 1831 B/1/059

Army land warrants converted to scrip:

Warrant holder	*War. no.*	*Scrip issued to*	*Acres*
Welden, Jere or Jeremiah, Soldier	1521	Cadwallader Wallace	100
Smith, John, Pvt	1563	Cadwallader Wallace	100
Heath, William, Pvt	1709	William Heath	100
Hood, George, Pvt	1487	Allen Latham	100
Sears, Elnathan, Pvt	1614	Jonas Stanberry	100
Cook, William, Pvt	1415	Jonas Stanberry	100
Wilson, John, Soldier	1525	Lewis Wakely	100
Robertson, John, Pvt	1565	Lewis Wakely	100
Chadwick, Thomas, Soldier	1547	Lewis Wakely	100
Gillen, Thomas, Pvt	1597	Lewis Wakely	100
Wakely, Abel, Pvt	1337	Lewis Wakely	100
Carr, William, Pvt	910	Leonard Jarvis	100
Wright, Joel, Pvt	1499	Joseph Watson	100
Stevens, John, Pvt	1443	Joseph Watson	100
Thompson, William, Pvt[1]	1530	Charles C. Gilbert	100
Patterson, John, Capt	1587	Mary Thomas?[2,3]	300
Thompson, Barnaby, *alias* Barnato, Pvt	1698	Barnaby Thompson[4]	100
Lawson, John, Pvt	1697	John Lawson[4]	100
Fleece, John, Pvt	1696	John Fleece[4]	100
Slade, Stephen, Lt	1632	Mary D. --?[2] & Margaret P. Worthington[4]	200
Paine, Edward, Pvt	1307	Mary --?[2, 5]	100
Dorothy, Charles, Pvt	1344	Joseph Duncan	100
Merrill, Caleb, Pvt	1633	Caleb Merrill[6]	100
Baldwin, Zachariah, Soldier	1693	Emeline Ferguson?[7]	100
Harrison, R. H. [Lt?] Col	1700	Sarah Hanson?[2] & Dorothy Storer[8]	450
Laurence, John, Pvt	1493	John Laurence[9]	100
Carter, Nicholas, Pvt	1704	Nicholas Carter[10]	100
Rucker, Elliot, Lt	1702	Elliot Rucker[11]	200
Gibbs, Churchill, Lt	1694	Churchill Gibbs[12]	200

1. This case suspended.
2. Surname obscured on microfilm, but National Archives may be able to read from source register.
3. Presented by J. W. Taylor.
4. Presented by Hon. J. W. Kincaid.
5. Presented by D. Pearce.
6. Presented by Earll Jones.
7. Presented by Hon. -- Verplanck.
8. Presented by Isaac Hanson.
9. Presented by Wilson Lumpkin.
10. Presented by C. A. Unckliffe?
11. Presented by Col R. M. Johnson.
12. Presented by Col -- Gibbs.

1623 21 Feb - 3 Mar 1831 B/1/060

Army land warrants converted to scrip:

Warrant holder	*War. no.*	*Scrip issued to*	*Acres*
Rucker, Angus, Capt	1695	Angus Rucker[1]	300
Vawter, William, Lt	1699	W. Vawter, E. Vawter, G. Vawter[2]	200
Hopkins, Wright, Capt	1115	John Stephens[3]	300
Meckle, Reuben, Pvt	1639	Reuben Meckle[4]	100
Bedell, David, Pvt	1634	David Bedell[5]	100
Dixon, William, Pvt	1147	William Dixon	100
Bragdon, Samuel, Lt	1670	Samuel Bragdon	200
Coomer, William, Pvt	1622	Polly Coomer	100
Willard, William, Pvt	1710	William Willard	100
Fernald, Tobias [Lt?] Col	847	Albert G. Lane *et al*	450
Maxwell, James, Capt	1501	James Maxwell	300
Earlywine, Daniel, Pvt	1649	Phebe Ritchie?[6] *et al*	100

1623 [continued]

Warrant holder	War. no.	Scrip issued to	Acres
Robertson, James, Pvt	1573	Sally Robertson	100
Carter, John, Pvt	1545	John Carter	100
Bennett, William, Pvt	1590	John Bennett	100
Wright? [Wight?] Asahel, Sgt	1509	Frederick Swinehart	100
Irvin, James, Lt	1099	James Irvin	200
Tillotson, Thomas, Surgeon	2239	Thomas Tillotson	400*
Tillotson, Thomas, Surgeon	2239	Joseph Watson	50*
Cheever, Abijah, Surgeon's Mate	1512	John Varnum? [Parnum?]	300
Hancock, Bennet, Pvt	1629	Bennet Hancock[7]	100
Fitzgibbon, James, Pvt	1591	Eleanor Breck?[6]	100
Mote, Edgerton, Pvt	1619	Joseph Watson	100
Fowler, Joseph, Pvt	1370	Thomas Hambrick?[6]	100
Holloway, James, Lt	1715	Fletcher?[8] Ruskin *et al*	200
Sommerville, John, Pvt	1714	John Sommerville	100
Alden, Judah, Capt	1716	Jerab? Alden	300
Malory, Archibald, Pvt	1707	Henry Northup	100
Fitzgerald, --, Pvt	1338	-- Fitzgerald	100

1. Presented by Mr. -- Gibbs.
2. Presented by Col -- Johnson.
3. Presented by Gen -- Robinson.
4. Presented by -- Irvin.
5. Presented by Hon. -- Carson.
6. Surname obscured on microfilm, but National Archives may be able to read from source register.
7. Presented by Mr. -- Reives.
8. Forename obscured on microfilm, but National Archives may be able to read from source register.

*Total grant was 450 acres for a Surgeon with the corresponding scrip issued to two persons.

1624 — 18 Mar - 24 Jun 1831 — B/1/061

Army land warrants converted to scrip:

Warrant holder	*War. no.*	*Scrip issued to*	*Acres*
Dumas, Peter, Pvt	1617	Jasper Dumas?[1] *et al*	100
Gunnels, William, Soldier	12149	Thomas J. Northup	100
Atkinson, Theodore, Pvt	1706	Theodore Atkinson	100
McDuff, Danie[l?] Capt	1620	David? McDuff[2]	300
Sill, Henry, assignee of W. Love, [Pvt?]	1550	Henry Sill[3]	100
Boyles, Charles, Pvt	1455	Joseph Watson	100
Tucker, George, Pvt	1571	Mary Barnes *et al*	100
Batterson, Joseph, Pvt	1404	Joseph Batterson	100
Hill, Philip, Lt	1051	Joseph Watson	100
Cogswell, William, Hospital Mate	1273	Joseph Duncan	300
Fitzsimmons, Thomas? Pvt	1635	Thomas? Fitzsimmons	100
Brownson, Abr[aham] Soldier	1720	Abr[aham] Brownson	100
Brock, Uriah, Pvt	1722	Uriah Brock	100
Brown, Barron, Pvt	1154	Raisa R. Baldwin	100
Hill, Thomas, Pvt	1283	I. S. Johnson	100
Call, John, Pvt	1727	Isaiah Call & S. C[all?]	100
Mills, Walter, Pvt	1728	Walter F? Mills & John [Mills?]	100
Miller, John, Pvt	1621	J? Miller & R. Miller	100
Stone, Ezekiel, Pvt	1677	Ezekiel Stone	100
Scutliff, Benjamin, Lt	1681	George Scutliff	200
Maxfield, Joseph, Pvt	1645	Joseph Maxfield	100
Collins, Daniel, Pvt	1646	Michael? Collins	100
Grown, Ebenezer? Pvt	1426	Samuel? Lee	100
Stevens, Tim[oth]y, Pvt	1286	Samuel? Lee	100
Smith, James, Lt	459	--?[4] Smith *et al*	200
Todd, John, Pvt	1532	Lewis Wakeley	100
Warren, William, Pvt	1554	Lewis Wakeley	100
Brewer, Henry, Pvt	1631	-- Brewer & -- Davis, *et al*	100

1. Surname obscured on microfilm, but National Archives may be able to read from source register.
2. According to marginal note: "This warrant has been located in the Huntsville [Alabama] District by authority of an Act of Congress 2 & 24 Apr 1830? [1831?]."
3. Sent to him at Burlington, New York.
4. Forename obscured on microfilm, but National Archives may be able to read from source register.

1625 — 24 Jun 1831 — B/1/061

Registered by: William Davis
Registered for: William Davis
Location: Mil - 3 8 4 9
Based upon the following Army land warrant:

Issued to	*No.*	*Acres*
Davis, William, Pvt	1459	100

(Note: Sent to him at Beaver, Pennsylvania.)

1626 — 24 Jun - 18 Aug 1831 — B/1/062

Army land warrants converted to scrip:

Warrant holder	*War. no.*	*Scrip issued to*	*Acres*
Springer, Jacob, Pvt	1392	--?[1] Vance & William Browning	100
Brittan, Jeremiah Sgt	1729	Jeremiah Brittan	100
Carter, Benjamin, Sgt	1730	Benjamin Carter	100
Ward, Samuel, LtCol	317	Temple Cutler	450
Johnston, James, Pvt	1719	Mary Johnston	100
Van Guilder, Isaac, Pvt	1658	Isaac Van Guilder	100
Warner, Jacob, Pvt	1642	Jacob Warner	100
Burk, Silas, Pvt	1721	Silas Burk	100
Forbes, John, Pvt	1298	Mary Blinn	100
Woolworth, Ebenezer, Pvt	1023	Boswell White	100
Allen, John, Pvt	1708	John Allen	100
Goatley, John, Pvt	1438	Clad[iu?]s Northup	100
Newman, John, Pvt	1638	John, Solomon, Polly, & Betsy Newman	100
Ames, Jotham, Lt	1410	Joseph Watson	200
Sloulter? Andrew, Pvt	1522	Wm. B. Nicholls	100
King, James, Soldier	1546	Wm. B. Nicholls	100
Livingston, H. B., Lt	1117	H. B. Livingston	200
Austin, Joshua, Pvt	878	Wm. B. Nicholls	100
Potter, Samuel, Pvt	7606	Sarah Craig *et al*	100
Barsith? John, Pvt	1660	John Barsith?	100
Scott, John, Pvt	1489	Peter Mills	100
Long, William, Pvt	1734	William Long	100

1626 [continued]

Hamilton, Reuben, Pvt	1742	Joseph Watson	100
Barlow, John, Pvt	1416	Wm. L. Nicholls	100
Wilkinson, David, Pvt	1685	Allen?[1] Wilkinson *et al*	100
Whitaker, Samuel? Pvt	1732	Jeremiah?[1] Whitaker	100

1. Forename obscured on microfilm, but National Archives may be able to read from source register.

1627 — 18 Aug 1831 — B/1/062

Registered by: Joseph Watson
Registered for: William? J. Northup
Location: Mil - 6 8 2 34
Based upon the following Army land warrant:

Issued to	*No.*	*Acres*
Smith, Christian, Pvt	1122	100

(Note: Sent to him at Zanesville.)

1628 — 18 Aug 1831 — B/1/062

Registered by: David Corey
Registered for: David Corey & the other heirs of Matthias Mayer
Location: Mil - 3 7 1 28
Based upon the following Army land warrant:

Issued to	*No.*	*Acres*
Murphy, Margarett, & to the other heirs of Matthias Mayer, Pvt	1407	100

(Note: Delivered to D. Corey.)

1629 — No dates [ca. 1831] — B/1/063

Army land warrants converted to scrip:

Warrant holder	*War. no.*	*Scrip issued to*	*Acres*
Stoddard, Samuel, Pvt	1724	Sarah Packard	100
Easton, Julian, Pvt	1209	Lewis Wakeley	100
Whitty, John, Pvt	1452	Peter Mills	100
McDowell, John, Lt	1749	John McDowell	200
Campbell, William, Pvt	1754	William Campbell	100
Pender, Thomas, Pvt	1753	Thomas Pender	100
Shed, Sam[ue]l? [or Saul?] Pvt	561	-- Poor & -- Kidd	100
Smith, John, Pvt	1523	Peter Mills	100
McNair, Arch[ibal]d, Sgt	1640	Archibald McNair	100
Martin, John, Soldier	1736	Ann Martin	100
Waples, Samuel, Lt	1733	Samuel Waples	200
Firman, Nathan, Pvt	1684	Nathan Firman	100
Trowbridge, Isaac, Pvt	1743	Jasper Trowbridge *et al*	100
Smith, Amos, Pvt	1598	Lewis Wakeley	100
Wear, Cornelius, Pvt	1641	Cornelius Wear	100
Walker, Peter, Pvt	1483	Joseph Willis	100
Denniston, James, Pvt	1558	Wm. L. Nicholls	100
Crosby, Ebenezer, Surgeon	1759	Wm. B. Crosby	400
Godwin, David, Musician	1593	David Godwin	100
Lynn, William, Lt	1763	David Lynn *et al*	200
Richardson, Samuel, Soldier	1764	Joseph Watson	100
Beebe, Asahel, Pvt	1751	Asahel Beebe	100
Wrightman, George, Soldier	1561	George Wrightman	100
Champlin, Newport, Soldier	1768	Prince? Champlin	100
Foster, Peter, Lt	1770	Peter Foster	200
Thomas, John, Capt	1769	John Thomas	300

1630 — No dates [ca. 1831-1832] — B/1/064

Army land warrants converted to scrip:

Warrant holder	*War. no.*	*Scrip issued to*	*Acres*
Triplett, George, Lt	1766	George Triplett	200
Lemmon, Francis, Pvt	1757	Samuel Lemmon	100
Goodrich, John, Pvt	1607	Lewis Wakeley	100
Sowers, Michael, Pvt	1461	Michael Sowers	100
Lee, William, Pvt	1745	William Lee	100
Bawcult, or Bawcolt, William, Pvt	1364	Daniel Taggart	100
Vanorman [Van Norman?] James, Pvt	1689	Elizabeth Ayres	100
Moyer, Jacob, Pvt	1654	Samuel Moyer[1]	100
Brannon, John, Pvt	1741	John Brannon	100
Ogden, Barney, Lt	1773	Ann Francis Price	200
Mead, Uriah, Soldier	1775	Uriah Mead	100
Triplett, Thomas, Senior, Capt	1777	Joseph Watson	300
Biggs, John, Matross	1767	John Biggs	100
McBane, Daniel, Soldier	1541	Joseph Watson	100
Lord, Simeon, *alias* Simon, Capt	894	Joseph Watson	300
Brown, Joseph, Soldier	1780	Catherine Williamson	100
Pierce, John, Soldier	1750	Richard Pierce	100
Mason, Nath[aniel or Nathan] Pvt	1758	Nathaniel? Mason	100
Lockner, Henry, Pvt	1531	Wm. L. Nicholls	100
Cork, Jacob, Pvt	1781	Joseph Watson	100
Mather, Timothy, Surgeon	1711	--?[2] Painter & E. Phelps	400
Claridge, Levin, Soldier	1779	Henry Claridge	100
Somersett, Thomas, Pvt	1171	William W. Irvin	100
Cummings, John, Pvt	960	Samuel H. Smith[3]	100
Davidson, Joseph A., Capt	1249	Edward Smith	300
Smith, John, Soldier	1776	Call?[2] Smith	100
Parkinson, Richard, Pvt	1782	Richard Parkinson	100
Fancher, Isaac, Pvt	1786	Isaac Fancher	100

1. Marginal notation: "Application no. 463."
2. Forename obscured on microfilm, but National Archives may be able to read from source register.
3. Illegible notation.

1631 — 29 Nov 1831 — B/1/064

Registered by: [Not stated]
Registered for: --?* Gardner, assignee
Location: Mil - 6 7 3 3
Based upon the following Army land warrant:

Issued to	*No.*	*Acres*
Lighthiser [Lichtheiser] George, heirs of, Pvt	314	100

*Forename obscured on microfilm, but National Archives may be able to read from source register.

1632 — No dates [ca. 1832] — B/1/065

Army land warrants converted to scrip:

Warrant holder	*War. no.*	*Scrip issued to*	*Acres*

1632 [continued]

Patchen, Azor, Soldier	1378	Azor Patchen	100
Rathburn, Solomon, Pvt	1445	Peter Mills	100
Wallace, John, Pvt	1784	Joseph Watson	100
White, Ephraim, Pvt	1765	Ephraim White	100
Scoomaker, Daniel, Pvt	1783	Rush Perry	100
Wilson, Hosea, Pvt	1793	Baths[heb]a? Caswell	100
Clifton, George, Pvt	1794	George Clifton	100
Lowe, Phelp, Maj	1797	Eliza B. Roberts	400
Briley, John, Pvt	1790	John Briley	100
Wishart, Thomas, Lt	1795	Sidney Wishart, *et al*	200
Flourney, Josiah, Lt	1597	Josiah Flourney	200
McLain, Laughlin, Soldier	12346	William Sherrard, *et al*	100
Ring, Jonathan, Senior, Pvt	850	John Ring, Junior	100
Meech, Thomas, Pvt	1712	Jacob Meech	100
Chadwick, James, Pvt	1458	Cath[erin]a? Skinner	100
Estell, William, Pvt	1798	William Estell	100
Roberts, John, Maj	1718	John Roberts	400
Murphey, James, Pvt	1377	James M. Bell	100
Humphreys, George, Pvt	1401	--?[1] Humphreys	100
Brooks, Joshua, Pvt	1787	Joshua Brooks	100
Bloom, Albert, Soldier	1788	William B. Goff	100
Edwards, William, Pvt	1756	Charles? M. Edwards & El[izabeth?] Edwards	100
Sawyer, John, Soldier	1771	--?[1] Harrison, *et al*	100
Dennis, William, Pvt	1782	William Dennis	100
Jackson, William, Pvt	1791	William Jackson	100
Bradwell, Nat[haniel? or Nathan?] Lt	1211	Joseph Watson	200
Coleman, Jacob, Lt	1206	Mary Coleman	200
Smith, Charles, Trump[eter?]	1520	Charles Smith	100
Hall, Richard, Soldier	1801	Richard Hall	100

1. Forename obscured on microfilm, but National Archives may be able to read from source register.

1633 No dates [ca. 1832] B/1/066

Army land warrants converted to scrip:

Warrant holder	*War. no.*	*Scrip issued to*	*Acres*
Harleston, Isaac, Maj	1800	James? Corbett, *et al*	400
Johnston, John [Pvt]	1735	Milly Johnston	100
Cochran, John, Pvt	1796	John Cochran	100
Cason, Jesse, Pvt	915	Joshua Cason	100
Williams, Daniel, Capt	1624	James Williams	300
Clendenon, John, Lt	1803	Ann Martin, *et al*	200
Shaw, Aaron, Pvt	1262	Aaron Shaw	100
Utter, Gilbert, Pvt	1579	William Utter, *et al*	100
Beeting? [Buting?] Conrad, Pvt	1268	Wm. L. Nicholls, assignee	100
Blair, John, Lt	1809	John Blair's devisees	200
Gray, William, Lt	1486	John Gray, *et al*	200
Sabins? [Sabin?] Samuel, Pvt	994	Matt St. C. Clark	100
Mills, Peter, Pvt	851	Eleazar Robinson	100
Palmour, George, Pvt	1755	Mary Palmour & Jacob? Palmour	100
Pillbury [or Pilsbury] Daniel, Capt	1807	James?[1] Pilsbury, *et al*	300
Eagles, Michael, Pvt	1805	George Gibson	100
Noys [or Noyes] Wadleigh, Pvt	1808	Moses? Noyes *et al*	200
Wade, Edward, Pvt	1812	Richard?[1] Wade	100
McGee, James, Pvt	1382	David Cory	100
Moore, John, Pvt	1813	Henry Moore	100
Houston, Elijah, Soldier	1814	Eliza[beth] Marvel	100
Brown, Windsor, Capt	1816	Henry?[1] E. King	300
Huger, Benjamin, Maj	1817	--?[1] Huger & Mary Rutledge	400
Ruggles, Joseph, Pvt	1819	Joseph Ruggles	100
Frickett? [Jackett?] E., Pvt	1560	Matt?[1] St. C. Clark	100
Smith, Massey Arra? Pvt	1820	Massey Arra Smith	100
Wallace, Ebenezer, Pvt	1815	Ebenezer Wallace	100

1. Forename obscured on microfilm, but National Archives may be able to read from source register.

1634 -- 1826 B/1/066

Registered by: Joseph Watson
Registered for: David W. Kennedy
Location: Mil - 1 6 2 11
Based upon the following Army land warrant:

Issued to	*No.*	*Acres*
Broadstreet, Mason, Pvt	998	100

(Note: Delivered to Jane? Kennedy, 29 Feb 1832.)

1635 1 May 1832 B/1/066

Registered by: Joseph Watson
Registered for: William Geiger
Location: Mil - 5 10 4 25
Based upon the following Army land warrant:

Issued to	*No.*	*Acres*
Gordon, Eliph[alet?] Pvt	1054	100

(Illegible note.)

1636 No dates [ca. 1832] B/1/067

Army land warrants converted to scrip:

Warrant holder	*War. no.*	*Scrip issued to*	*Acres*
Kingsman, Edward, Ens	1824	Edward Kingsman	150
Tucker, Joseph, Pvt	1107	Chauncey G. Moore	100
Case, Saba A., Pvt	1826	Saba A. Case[1]	100
Schenck, Ralph, Pvt	1615	David Crawford	100
Wooster, Moses, Pvt	1806	Dorcaster Wooster, *et al*	100
Garden, Alex[ander] Lt	1825	Lester?[2] Garden	200
Roux, Albert, Capt	1818	Lewis Roux	300
McCown? [McCorin?] John, Capt	1822	Martha Smith *et al*	300
Scooler, William, Pvt	1827	William Scooler	100
Lansdale [or Landsdale] Thomas, Maj	1227	Cornelia?[2] Landsdale, *et al*	400
Doubleday, Benjamin, Pvt	1829	Mary Doubleday	100
Aldridge, John, Pvt	1831	John Aldridge	100

1636 [continued]

Axson, Samuel J., Surgeon's Mate[3]	1250	--?[2] Axson, *et al*	300
Axson, Samuel J., Surgeon	1830	--?[2] Axson, *et al*	100
Taylor, John, Lt	1828	John M. Taylor, Administrator	200
Slurnan, John, Capt	1799	Mary?[2] Bennett, *et al*	300
Knox, James, Maj	1832	--?[2] Crittenden, *et al*	400
Patton, Robert, Capt	1833	Robert Patton	300
Pholon, Edward, Lt	1076	Joseph Watson	200
Pholon, Patrick, Lt	1077	Joseph Watson	200
Vose, Thomas, Capt	723	James?[2] P. Vose, *et al*	300
Wetheral(1), James, Ens	1835	James Wetherall	150
Ames, Elisha, Pvt	1293	Lewis Wakeley	100
Gudgeon, Robert, Pvt	741	Matt?[2] St. C. Clark	100
Corey, Gideon, Pvt	1837	John Corey	100
Reynolds, John, Pvt	1838	John Reynolds	100
Beal, Zac[ariah? or Zaccheus?] Capt	1839	--?[2] Beal, *et al*	300
Spencer, Robert, Lt	1840	--?[2] Chatwood	200
de Saussure? Lewis, Lt	1585	--?[2] Hale	200

1. Marginal notation: "Application no. 616."
2. Forename obscured on microfilm, but National Archives may be able to read from source register.
3. Apparently first classified as a Surgeon's Mate and given a 300-acre grant, then reclassified as a Surgeon and given an extra 100 acres.

1637 No dates [ca. 1832] B/1/068

Army land warrants converted to scrip:

Warrant holder	*War. no.*	*Scrip issued to*	*Acres*
Trumbull, John, Pvt	1125	Joseph Watson	100
Richardson, Robert, Pvt	1725	--?* Taylor *et al*	100
Hubner, Frederick, Pvt	1319	--?* Hollyworth? *et al*	100
Kemper, Jacob, Lt	1329	--?* Kemper, *et al*	200
Balitz, George, Pvt	1843	William Balitz	100
Armstead, Thomas, Capt	1846	Catherine Pierce	300
Partridge, A., Pvt	1746	Fanny Carpenter	100
Somers, George, Pvt	1844	Jacob Somers	100
Williams, Joseph, Pvt	1841	Joseph Williams	100
Jones, Samuel, Pvt	1848	Samuel Jones	100
Hawkins, Moses, Capt	1847	William S. Hawkins	300
Ewell, Charles, Capt	1850	Heirs of [Charles Ewell]	300
Shopp, Peter, Pvt	1210	Lewis Wakeley	100
Smith, E. M., Lt	1180	--?* Smith, *et al*	200
Elliott, George? Pvt	1153	George Elliott	100
Lawrence? Nathan, Capt	1851	--?* V. Lawrence	300
Gregg, John, Lt	1322	Dimas Adams	200
Kirkham, Ben[jamin] Pvt	6071	--?* F. Jacobs	100
Cobb, Jere[miah?] Pvt	326	--?* Rounseville	100
Wilbur, W., Soldier	1853	J? C. Wilbur, *et al*	100
Day, Aaron, Lt	1849	--?* B. Lefever, *et al*	200
Root, David, Pvt	1810	Daniel? Root	100
Hatch, J., Pvt	1394	George?* Hale	100
Jenks, Anthony, Pvt	1845	Anthony Jenks	100
Newan, N., Pvt	1662	Katerina?* Moyer	100
Russell, John, Lt	1856	--?* B. Russell, *et al*	200
Gillen, Hugh, Pvt	1852	Hanna?* Crissey	100
Jenks, John, Drummer	1821	John Jenks	100
Shute, John, Pvt	1564	--?* Buckingham & Co.	100

*Forename obscured on microfilm, but National Archives may be able to read from source register.

1638 No dates [ca. 1832-1833] B/1/069

Army land warrants converted to scrip:

Warrant holder	*War. no.*	*Scrip issued to*	*Acres*
Decker, Michael, Pvt	1572	Joseph Watson	100
Banger? Walter [Pvt]	1599	Joseph Watson	100
Hewett, Caleb [Pvt]	1280	Joseph Watson	100
Busk? [Bush?] George, Capt	1744	Thomas Cull?*	300
Lawrence, Frank? Capt	1858	Margaret Roseman?*	300
Warren, Samuel, Capt	1859	Samuel Warren	300
Macomber, John, Pvt	1400	Philo Hale	100
Hubbell? Seth, Pvt	1500	Philo Hale	100
Robinson, Win, Pvt	1309	H. R. Verseilles?*	100
Goodrich, Daniel, Pvt	1548	Philo Hale	100
Blackwell, William, Pvt [Capt?]	1861	Elizabeth Scott	300
Lewis, John, Capt	1864	W. L. Lewis, *et al*	300
Bogart, N., Surgeon's Mate	1157	Philo Hale	300
Tomlinson, David, Ens	1314	Philo Hale	150
Ball, John, Lt	1197	Demas Adams	200
Munroe, John, Pvt	1219	Demas Adams	100
Clark, Joel, Pvt	1515	Philo Hale	100
Thornton, John, Lt	1870	Isaac Winston?*	200
Purshall, James, Sgt	1690	James Purshall	100
Miller, Jason? Lt	1871	Abijah Parsons	200
Gist, Nathaniel, Col	1874	Henry --?*	500
Broadus, William, Lt	1875	William Pitser?*	200
Tyler, Amos, Soldier	1371	Orne Fowler?*	100
Jones, James, Pvt	1876	James Jones	100
Young, Robert, Lt	1860	Thomas Long?*	200
Cobea, John, Capt	1224	Townsend Wilkenson?*	300
Ennis, John, Pvt	1867	John E. --?*	100
Walker, Peter, Soldier	5321	Peter Walker *et al*	100

*Surname obscured on microfilm, but National Archives may be able to read from source register.

1639 -- 1828 B/1/069

Registered by: Henry Sill
Registered for: Henry Sill
Location: Mil - 9 9 4 6
Based upon the following Army land warrant:

Issued to	*No.*	*Acres*
Basy? [Rasy?] Stephen [or Stephen, Ray] assignee of Henry Sill* [Pvt]	1518	100

(Note: Sent to him at Burlington, 15 Jan 1832?)
*This appears to be in error; it is more likely that Stephen Basy? was the original warrantee & Henry Sill was the assignee.

1640 No dates [ca. 1832-1833] B/1/070

Army land warrants converted to scrip:

Warrant holder	*War. no.*	*Scrip issued to*	*Acres*
Ramsey, James, Pvt	1503	James Ramsey	100
Avery, Simeon, Lt	1143	G. Huntington	200
Wigglesworth? William, Lt	1465	G. Huntington	200
Spencer, David, Lt	334	G. Huntington	200
Leason? Job, Pvt	1272	G. Huntington	100
Rider, Asa, Pvt	1878	Asa Rider	100
Bemas? [Bemis?] John, Pvt	1481	L. John Phelps	100
Brumigan? D., Pvt	1786	George Malcomb	100
Burnley, Garland, Capt	1885	G. B. Taylor	300
Knolton? Thomas, LtCol	1140	G. Huntington	450
McQueen, J? [or I?] Sgt	1883	G. Huntington	100
Aldrich? [Aldrick?] Gustavus, Pvt	1882	Nathan Aldrick?	100
Harrison, A., Pvt	1884	Charles Booth	100
Moser, George, Pvt	1877	Esther Moser	100
Eddy, Ebenezer, Pvt	1022	Ebenezer Eddy	100
Porter, Thalia, Lt	1887	Thalia Porter	200
Williams, Thomas, Pvt	1275	Philo Hale	100
Ward, John, Pvt	1737	John Ward	100
Brown, William, Pvt	1881	C. Washington? *et al*	100
Wardroff [*also* Wardroof] H., Cpl	1892	Harding Wardroof	100
Jones, Ab[raha]m, Pvt	1893	--?* Jones	100
Williams, Nathan, Lt	1666	--?* Banfield, *et al*	200
Bishop, John, Lt	1667	John Bishop	200
Lewis, John, Capt**	1864	William L. Lewis	266
		--?* C. Stanley	34
Wales, Ebenezer, Lt	1895	John Simmons	200
Slaughter, William, Lt	1899	--?* B. Brasdel?	200
Whittaker, Ephraim, Capt	1902	Ephraim Whittaker	300
Gorham, John, Pvt	1905	John Gorham	100

*Name obscured, but National Archives may be able to read from source register.

**A 300-acre grant split between two scrip holders.

1641 No dates [ca. 1832-1833] B/1/071

Army land warrants converted to scrip:

Warrant holder	*War. no.*	*Scrip issued to*	*Acres*
Davenport, Thomas, Capt	1904	Thomas Davenport	300
Whitwell, Samuel, Surgeon	1778	Samuel Whitwell, *et al*	400
Mosler, John, Lt	1177	Charles Mosler	200
Fay [or Facy?] Joseph Ens	902	Joseph L. Fay	150
Cowell, John, Surgeon	1907	--?* Cowell	300
Campbell, William, Capt	1903	Esau? Campbell	300
Pritchard, Thomas, Capt	987	Lucy?* Pritchard, *et al*	300
Neil, Daniel, Capt	1804	Maria Mallam Brooks	300
Smith, Robert? [Hobert?] Pvt	1906	Levi Smith, *et al*	100
Tasker, Richard, Pvt	1113	James Wilson	100
Hyde, Udney? LtCol	1258	--?* Ann Hyde	450
Miller, William, Pvt	1896	Warren Miller	100
Barney, Nathaniel, Pvt	1888	Enoch Barney, *et al*	100
Porter, Ephraim, Pvt	1866	--?* Hitchcock	100
Clinton, Joseph, Pvt[1]	1086	--?* Clinton, *et al*	100
Clinton, Joseph, Pvt[1]	1813	--?* Clinton, *et al*	100
Vickey, John, Pvt	1879	John Vickey	100
Albie [or Albee] John, or Eleazar, Pvt	1762	John Albee, *et al*	100
Paal? [Paul?] Hugh, Pvt	1897	Catherine Shepper?	100
Brooks, David, Lt	1909	David Brooks	200
Taylor, Thornton, Ens	1901	Bradford?* Taylor	150
Grayson, William, Col	1366	--?* Washington	500
Jones? James, Pvt	1894	George Freeman	100
Roberts, Edward, Pvt	1911	Elizabeth Walker	100
Jackson, Peter, Pvt	1900	--?* Jackson	100
Bumpus, Asa, Pvt	912	Philo Hale	100
Dinsmore, Thomas, Pvt	1910	Thomas Dinsmore	100
Hart, F. A., Pvt	1912	F. A. Hart	100
Guthree, Christian, Pvt	1915	--?* Guthree, *et al*	100
Castle, James, Pvt	1508	James Castle	100

1. No explanation given for this duplication. There is, however, a marginal notation: "Application . . .? 1843."

*Name obscured on microfilm, but National Archives may be able to read from source register.

1642 17 Oct 1832 B/1/072

Registered by: Joseph Watson

Registered for: --?* Hall & other heirs

Location:

Mil	-	10	7	1	18
Mil	-	1	6	2	23

Based upon the following Army land warrant:

Issued to	*No.*	*Acres*
Hall, Talmage, Lt	1232	200

*Forename obscured on microfilm, but National Archives may be able to read from source register.

1643 17 Oct 1832 B/1/072

Registered by: Joseph Watson

Registered for: Joseph Watson

Location:

Mil	-	8	7	3	1
Mil	-	5	3	3	40
Mil	-	1	6	2	22
Mil	-	8	9	2	26
Mil	-	6	6	2	31
Mil	-	3	10	1	6
Mil	-	5	3	3	39
Mil	-	9	7	3	7
Mil	-	8	4	5	15

Based upon the following Army land warrants:*

Issued to	*No.*	*Acres*
Marshall, Benjamin, Lt	1163	200
Priestly, John, Capt*	1139	300
Walcut, Benjamin, Capt	2328	300
Brooke, Edmund, Lt	1097	200

*On the basis of the above-listed warrants, Watson would have been entitled to 1000 acres, rather than the 900 acres patented above. It may be that Priestly is incorrectly listed as a Captain, rather than a Lieutenant.

1644 10 Jul 1832 B/1/072
Registered by: Representatives of Thomas Fosdick
Registered for: Legal representatives [of Thomas Fosdick]
Location: Mil - 2 7 3 4
Based upon the following Army land warrant:

Issued to	*No.*	*Acres*
Fosdick, Thomas W., Ens	1239	150

1645 17 Oct 1832 B/1/072
Registered by: Joseph Watson
Registered for: Joseph Watson
Location: Mil - 9 9 1 4
Mil - 3 10 1 26
Based upon the following Army land warrants:

Issued to	*No.*	*Acres*
Eastman, Zachariah, Cpl	733	100
White, James, Pvt	1126	100

1646 17 Oct 1832 B/1/072
Registered by: Joseph Watson
Registered for: --?* Cork & other heirs
Location: Mil - 4 4 3 13
Based upon the following Army land warrant:

Issued to	*No.*	*Acres*
Cork, John, Pvt	1078	100

*Forename obscured on microfilm, but National Archives may be able to read from source register.

1647 17 Oct 1832 B/1/072
Registered by: Joseph Watson
Registered for: Joseph Watson
Location: Mil - 8 9 3 23
Mil - 8 9 3 24
Based upon the following Army land warrants:

Issued to	*No.*	*Acres*
Smart, Nath[aniel] Pvt	732	100
Flowers, Thomas, Pvt	1201	100

1648 17 Oct 1832 B/1/072
Registered by: Joseph Watson
Registered for: Nathaniel? B. Haswell
Location: Mil - 2 7 3 9
Based upon the following Army land warrant:

Issued to	*No.*	*Acres*
Hadlock, Samuel, Pvt	860	100

1649 17 Oct 1832 B/1/072
Registered by: Joseph Watson
Registered for: --?* Hudson & Co.
Location: Mil - 7 6 1 15
Mil - 5 3 3 26
Mil - 9 9 4 7
Based upon the following Army land warrants:

Issued to	*No.*	*Acres*
Brown, Joseph, Pvt	6807	100
Peak, William, Cpl	7604	100
Burnett, John, Soldier	6794	100

1650 14 Feb 1833 B/1/072
Registered by: Joseph Watson
Registered for: David Howell, *et al*
Location: Mil - 5 3 3 25
Based upon the following Army land warrant:

Issued to	*No.*	*Acres*
Howell, David, Soldier	7477	100

1651 10 Jul 1833 B/1/072
Registered by: Ichabod Rollins, *et al*
Registered for: Ichabod Rollins, *et al*
Location: Mil - 6 8 2 12
Mil - 6 8 2 11
Mil - 6 8 2 24
Mil - 6 8 2 10
Mil - 6 8 2 8
Mil - 6 8 2 9
Based upon the following Army land warrants:

Issued to	*No.*	*Acres*
Clement, Aaron, Pvt	868	100
Lord, William, Pvt	866	100
Grant, Edward, Pvt	867	100
Dudley, Tineworthy, Pvt	863	100
Marden, James, Pvt	864	100
Bickford, Aaron, Pvt	865	100

1652 10 Jul 1833 B/1/072
Registered by: James J. van Vorst
Registered for: James J. van Vorst
Location: Mil - 1 6 2 1
Based upon the following Army land warrant:

Issued to	*No.*	*Acres*
van Vorst, James J., Pvt	1526	100

1653 10 Jul 1833 B/1/072
Registered by: John Burgess
Registered for: John Burgess
Location: Mil - 18 7 2 13
Based upon the following Army land warrant:

Issued to	*No.*	*Acres*
Bradston, William, Pvt	180	100

1654 10 Jul 1833 B/1/072
Registered by: Joseph Vana
Registered for: Joseph Vana
Location: Mil - 18 7 2 14
Based upon the following Army land warrant:

Issued to	*No.*	*Acres*
Malary, Amos, Pvt	6163? [or 6161?]	100

1655 10 Jul 1833 B/1/072
Registered by: Henry Sill
Registered for: Henry Sill
Location: Mil - 9 9 4 19
Mil - 9 9 4 24
Mil - 9 9 4 32
Mil - 9 9 1 17*
Based upon the following Army land warrants:

Issued to	*No.*	*Acres*
Frink, Thomas, Pvt	1506	100
Foot, Ichiel, Pvt	1540	100
Howell, Nicholas, Pvt	1517	100
Bates, Samuel, Pvt*	1534*	100*

*Stricken out in source register.

1656 24 Feb 1833 B/1/073
Registered by: John Boyle
Registered for: Heirs of Thomas Warman
Location: Mil - 10 7 1 29
Mil - 10 7 1 30
Mil - 10 7 1 31
Based upon the following Army land warrant:

1656 [continued]

Issued to	*No.*	*Acres*
Warman, Thomas, heirs of, Capt	1789	300

(Note: Sent to Hal? [Hon?] A. Wickliff.)

1657 14 Feb 1833 B/1/073
Registered by: John Boyle
Registered for: Heirs of Josiah Marks
Location: Mil - 10 7 1 36
Mil - 10 7 1 37
Mil - 10 7 1 38
Based upon the following Army land warrant:

Issued to	*No.*	*Acres*
Marks, Josiah, heirs of, Capt	1655	300

1658 10 Jul 1832 B/1/073
Registered by: Henry Sill
Registered for: Henry Sill
Location: Mil - 9 9 4 40
Mil - 8 9 3 33
Based upon the following Army land warrants:

Issued to	*No.*	*Acres*
Beebe, Peter, Pvt	1365	100
Warren, John, Pvt	1341	100

1659 10 Jul 1832 B/1/073
Registered by: Abraham Shane, *et al*
Registered for: Abraham Shane, *et al*
Location: Mil - 18 7 2 15
Based upon the following Army land warrant:

Issued to	*No.*	*Acres*
Barkley, James, Pvt	14144	100

1660 10 Jul 1832 B/1/073
Registered by: John Mulveny
Registered for: John Mulveny
Location: Mil - 18 7 2 16
Based upon the following Army land warrant:

Issued to	*No.*	*Acres*
Mulveny, John, Pvt	10031	100

1661 14 Feb 1833 B/1/073
Registered by: Abraham Overholt
Registered for: Abraham Overholt
Location: Mil - 3 8 4 40
Based upon the following Army land warrant:

Issued to	*No.*	*Acres*
Fox, Nath[anie]l, Pvt	1555	100

1662* 3 Apr 1833 B/1/073
Registered by: Allen Latham
Registered for: W? J. Blood?
Location: Mil - 10 9 1 4
Based upon the following Army land warrant:

Issued to	*No.*	*Acres*
Jeffs, Thomas, Cpl	862	100

*This entire entry stricken out in source register. See serial entry 1676 hereinafter.

1663* 17 Oct 1833? B/1/073
Registered by: Joseph Watson
Registered for: Joseph Watson
Location: Mil - 8 9 3 24
Based upon the following Army land warrant:

Issued to	*No.*	*Acres*
Flowers, Thomas, Pvt	1201	100

*This entire entry stricken out in source register; but see serial entry 1647 above.

1664 9 Apr 1833 B/1/073
Registered by: Joseph Watson
Registered for: Joseph Gorman
Location: Mil - 1 6 2 8
Mil - 1 8 2 36E*
Based upon the following Army land warrant:

Issued to	*No.*	*Acres*
Gorman, Joseph, Ens	1244	150

(Note: Patent sent to J. Kinney, Belvidere, New Jersey.)
*50-acre lot.

1665 9 Apr 1833 B/1/073
Registered by: Joseph Watson
Registered for: Heirs of Caleb Parry
Location: Mil - 1 8 2 7W*
Based upon the following Army land warrant:

Issued to	*No.*	*Acres*
Parry, Caleb, heirs of, LtCol	1857	450*

*50-acre lot of 450 acres due a LtCol.

1666 9 Apr 1833 B/1/073
Registered by: Joseph Watson
Registered for: Susannah S. Keen
Location: Mil - 1 6 2 18*
Based upon the following Army land warrant:

Issued to	*No.*	*Acres*
Keen, Lawrence, Capt	1235	300*

*100 acres of 300 acres due a Capt.

1667 9 Apr 1833 B/1/073
Registered by: Joseph Watson?
Registered for: Heirs of James Houston
Location: Mil - 1 8 2 36W*
Based upon the following Army land warrant:

Issued to	*No.*	*Acres*
Houston, James, [LtCol]	1231	450*

*50-acre lot of 450 acres due a LtCol.

1668 10 Jul 1832 B/1/073
Registered by: Henry Sill
Registered for: Henry Sill, assignee
Location: Mil - 9 9 1 17
Based upon the following Army land warrant:

Issued to	*No.*	*Acres*
Bates, Samuel? heirs of, Soldier	1534	100

1669** 17 Oct 1832 B/1/073
Registered by: J[oseph?] W[atson?]
Registered for: John Hall, *et al*
Location: Mil - 1 6 2 23*
Based upon the following Army land warrant:

Issued to	*No.*	*Acres*
Hall, T., Lt	1232	200*

*100 acres of 200 acres due a Lt.
**This entire entry stricken out of source register.

1670 — 22 May 1833 — B/1/073

Registered by: J[oseph?] W[atson?]
Registered for: R? V? Enos
Location: Mil - 6 8 2 28
Based upon the following Army land warrant:

Issued to	*No.*	*Acres*
Cobb, John, Pvt	1529	100

1671 — 1 May 1833 — B/1/073

Registered by: J[oseph?] W[atson?]
Registered for: J[oseph?] Watson
Location: Mil - 2 11 3? 2
Based upon the following Army land warrant:

Issued to	*No.*	*Acres*
Mindock? William, Ens	263	100

1672 — 10 Apr 1833 — B/1/073

Registered by: J. Taylor
Registered for: J? Taylor & Z. Moore
Location: Mil - 16 7 4 10
Based upon the following Army land warrant:

Issued to	*No.*	*Acres*
Moore, Zach[ariah] Pvt	517	100

(Note: Delivered to James Taylor.)

1673 — 10 Apr 1833 — B/1/073

Registered by: J. Taylor
Registered for: Heirs of [H. Irvin]
Location: Mil - 16 7? 4 9
Mil - 16 7? 4 18
Mil - 16 7? 4 19
Mil - 16 7? 4 27
Mil - 17 7 1 38W*
Based upon the following Army land warrant:

Issued to	*No.*	*Acres*
Irvin, H., LtCol	504	450

*50-acre lot.

1674 — 1 Jun 1833 — B/1/073

Registered by: Alex[ander] Lockheart
Registered for: Alex[ander] Lockheart
Location: Mil - 8 9 3 14
Based upon the following Army land warrant:

Issued to	*No.*	*Acres*
Moore, John, Pvt	726	100

1675 — 1 Jun 1833 — B/1/073

Registered by: James Taylor
Registered for: James Taylor
Location: Mil - 15 8 4 30
Mil - 16 8 3 7
Mil - 18 7 1 24
Based upon the following Army land warrant:

Issued to	*No.*	*Acres*
Fountly? Henry, heirs of, Capt	1087	300

1676 — No dates [ca. 1833] — B/1/074

Army land warrants converted to scrip:

Warrant holder	*War. no.*	*Scrip issued to*	*Acres*
Richardson, Nath[aniel] Pvt	1916	--?* Richardson	100
Tuttle, Aaron, Pvt	1496	Philo Hale	100
McKenny, Andrew, Pvt	967	--?* McKenny	100
Barnes, James, Pvt	1323	Philo Hale	100
van Vorst, Christian, Pvt	1921	--? Vanderhyden, *et al*	100
Vickers, John, Pvt	1918	John Vickers	100
Merriweather, Thomas, Maj[1]	1920	--?* L. Hawkins	300
Pierce, Ag? Drummer	1919	John? Hilton	100
Etter, John, Dragoon?	1502	John Etter	100
Yarborough, Charles, Lt	1923	John Adair	200
Swift, Isaac, Soldier	1926	Hannah Cowett?	100
Tobias, Job, Cpl[2]	1927	Joseph? Tobias	100
Tobias, Job, Cpl[2]	1928	Joseph? Tobias	100
Keeler? James, Soldier	1929	Patience? Allen	100
Sears, Peter, Lt	1930	Polly?* Litchfield	200
Hemptin? [Kemptin?] Oliver, Pvt	884	Philo Hale	100
Gracey, John, Pvt	1925	John Gracey	100
Jackson, Samuel, Pvt	1167	Freeman Jackson	100
Holmes, Sylvester, Sgt	795	Israel?* Holmes, *et al*	100
Staynor, Roger, Capt	1245	Nathan?* Staynor	300
McIntyre, Henry, Pvt	1880	--?* Tracey	100
Brown, Peter, Pvt	1686	--?* S. Brown	100
Jeffs, Thomas, Cpl	862	--?* J. Blood	100
Chadwick, John, Soldier	1855	Catherine McCarty	100
Withers, James, Lt	1938	James Withers	200
Grymes, George [Pvt]	1939	--?* Hodgkins, *et al*	100
Grooms, Levi, Lt	1937	--?* Grooms, *et al*	200
Paulett, Richard, Lt	1940	Richard Paulett	200
White, John, Pvt	1933	James White	100

1. A Major was entitled to 400 acres. No explanation as to why only 300 acres was granted above.
2. No explanation of duplication given.
*Name obscured on microfilm, but National Archives may be able to read from source register.

1677 — No dates [ca. 1833] — B/1/075

Army land warrants converted to scrip:

Warrant holder	*War. no.*	*Scrip issued to*	*Acres*
Penny, Simon, Soldier	1941	--?* Pocknett	100
Austin, John, Lt	1943	--?* Austin, *et al*	200
Vaughn, John, Pvt	1946	John Vaughn	100
Walker, Peter, Pvt	5321	Heirs of [Peter] Walker	100
Rider, Asa, Pvt	1878	Asa Rider	100
Hempton, Oliver, Pvt[1]	884	Philo Hale	100
Welch, Daniel, Pvt	919	Martha Nevery?	100
Kelley [or Kelly] William, Pvt	1947	Daniel Kelly, *et al*	100
Filgham, Tench, LtCol	1158	--?* T. Goldsborough	450
Hudson, Rush, Pvt	1948	Rush Hudson	100
Skindler, John, Pvt	1000	Mary McConnell	100
Morgan, William, Pvt	1944	William Morgan	100
Allen, David, Surgeon?	1609	Demas Allen	300
Smith, Godfrey, Pvt	1006	Peter Mills	100
Truman, Samuel, Cpl	1413	Nathan Allen, Junior	100
Berdeon? [Berdeen?] Timothy, Pvt	1953	Timothy Berdeon?	100
Pinner, John, Pvt	1952	John Pinner	100
Danon? [Danow?] Benjamin, Pvt	1945	Benjamin Danon?	100
Tatum, Zac[hariah]Ens	1955	Henry W. Tatum	150

1677 [continued]

Warrant holder	War. no.	Scrip issued to	Acres
King, John, Pvt	1951	Hugh King, *et al*	100
Stark, Caleb, Lt	1351	Caleb Stark	200
Gutzinger, John? Pvt	1962	George Gutzinger	100
Gorman, Josiah, Pvt	1965	Josiah Gorman	100
Fontain, William, LtCol	1949	Sarah?* F. Ross, *et al*	450
Grant, or Grandt, George, Pvt	1228	George Skinner	100
Ingles, William, Pvt	1957	William Ingles [or Ingless]	100
Coger, Joseph, Pvt	1889	--?* Coger, *et al*	100
Timmons, Josh[ua?] Pvt	1966	Paul?* Timmons	100
Powell, Eleven, Pvt	1935	Eleven Powell	100

1. Duplicates serial entry 1676 above.
*Forename obscured on microfilm, but National Archives may be able to read from source register.

1678 No dates [ca. 1833] B/1/076

Army land warrants converted to scrip:

Warrant holder	*War. no.*	*Scrip issued to*	*Acres*
Smith, David, Pvt	841	Wm. L. Nicholls	100
Lunt, Job, Pvt	1964	Mary Libby, *et al*	100
McLean, Enoch, Pvt	1970	--?* McLean, *et al*	100
Haggerry [or Haggary] Cornel, Pvt	1971	John Haggary	100
Simmons, William, Pvt	1972	Sarah Taylor, *et al*	100
Keller, Conrad, Pvt	1969	Israel Keller	100
Foster, Jonathan, Pvt	1973	T. Buck, *et al*	100
Fayssour [or Fossin] Peter, Surgeon	1976	Martha Fossin, *et al*	450
Decker, Adam, Pvt	1862	--?* Decker, *et al*	100
Buchannon, John, Lt	1959	John Smith	200
Johnson, James, Pvt	1963	James Johnson	100
Burton, James, Capt	1924	Elizabeth Burton	300
Richardson, Daniel, Pvt	1863	Daniel Richardson	100
Hutton, James, Pvt	1974	--?* Hutton, *et al*	100
Thompson, John, Pvt	1975	Margaret Weston	100
Jones, Peter, Lt	1980	--?* Jones, *et al*	200
Doggett, Richard, Capt	1983	--?* Doggett	300
Waterfield, John, Pvt	1978	--?* White, *et al*	100
Freeman, Doss, Pvt	1981	--?* Freeman, *et al*	100
Oaks, John, Drummer	1982	Anna Green	100
Bunner, Rudolph, Lt	1984	Charles F. Bunner	200
Curtis, Chaney, Pvt	1986	--?* Curtis, *et al*	100
Gibson, George, Col	1985	--?* Gibson, *et al*	500
Ortan, William, Pvt	1987	--?* Eastin? *et al*	100
Benny, Barnabas, Hospital Surgeon	1989	--?* Benny, *et al*	450
Potter, Samuel, Sgt	1990	Samuel Potter	100
Hathaway, John, Soldier	1931	--?* Fisher, *et al*	100
Dran? [Doan?] Benjamin, Soldier	1988	Hannah?* Pettingill	100
Nicho? Jeremiah, Pvt	1991	Mary Burr, *et al*	100

*Forename obscured on microfilm, but National Archives may be able to read from source register.

1679 No dates [ca. 1834] B/1/077

Army land warrants converted to scrip:

Warrant holder	*War. no.*	*Scrip issued to*	*Acres*
Hiemer, Daniel, Pvt	1991	Daniel Hiemer, *et al*	100
Welch, Ebenezer [Pvt?] Cont[inental] Line	1196	Jacques?* D. S. Hines	100
Van Horne? [Herne?] David, Capt	2260	Henry Northup	300
Jackson, William, Pvt	1036	--?* Chapman	100
De Masters, Edward, Cpl	1995	--?* De Masters	100
Thurmond, William, Sgt	1996	--?* Jones, *et al*	100
Conner, John, Pvt	1977	Abigail?* Withers	100
Turner, Jonathan, Capt	478	Wm. S. Nichol[l]s	300
Darragh, Charles, Lt	1997	--?* Hall, *et al*	200
Bowser, James, Pvt	2001	--?* Bowser, *et al*	100
Ford, Lot? Soldier	2002	Lot? Ford	100
Culver, Stephen, Soldier	2003	Mabel?* Roach, *et al*	100
Culver, Levin, Soldier	2004	Mabel?* Roach, *et al*	100
Drummond, Peter, Lt	1994	--?* Drummond, *et al*	200
Armstrong, Jesse, Matross	2000	--?* Armstrong	100
Taylor, Obadiah, Pvt	1476	Obadiah Taylor	100
King, Josiah, Soldier	1992	Josiah King, *et al*	100
Waller, Nelson, Pvt	1958	--?* McIlvain	100
Milleway, Isaac, Soldier	1998	--?* Milleway	100
Shaddick? William, Pvt	502	--?* Shaddick, *et al*	100
Kellow? William, Sgt	1934	--?* A. Bean, *et al*	100
Ashe, Samuel, Lt	1233	--?* Osborne, *et al*	200
Hoth? Silas, Lt	1774	Linda? Clark, *et al*	200
Chapman, Samuel, Pvt	1954	--?* Buckingham, *et al*	100
Norman, Mingo? Pvt	1687	--?* Norman, *et al*	100
Gordon, Joseph, Cpl	2009	Joseph Gordon	100
Ellis, David, Pvt	2010	--?* Millaway	100
Whiteman, John, Pvt	2011	--?* Whiteman, *et al*	100
Brown, Joshua, Pvt	2012	--?* Brown, *et al*	100

*Forename obscured on microfilm, but National Archives may be able to read from source register.

1680 No dates [ca. 1834] B/1/078

Army land warrants converted to scrip:

Warrant holder	*War. no.*	*Scrip issued to*	*Acres*
Lawrence, William, Pvt	1968	William Lawrence	100
Sherwood, Lemuel, Pvt	1739	--?* Clarke	100
Cook, Paul, Pvt	2016	Paul Cook	100
Geyer, John, Pvt	2013	John Geyer	100
Frazier, John, Lt	2015	John?* L. Frazier, *et al*	200
Skinner, Henry, Pvt	2014	Henry Skinner	100
Mosher, John, Lt	1177	--?* Mosher, *et al*	200
Connelly, William, Soldier	1967	--?* Connelly, *et al*	100
Dougherty, James, Pvt	1202	Abraham Hall	100
Clarkson, Matthew, Maj	2019	--?* Clarkson, *et al*	400
Ewer, Prince, Soldier	2008	Abigail?* Meade, *et al*	100
Slaughter, William, Ens	1836	William Slaughter	150

1680 [continued]

Warrant holder	War. no.	Scrip issued to	Acres
Loar, *alias* Laws, Henry, Pvt	1393	Henry Loar, *alias* Laws	100
McWilliams? [Williams?] James M? Pvt	2022	James McWilliams? [M. Williams?]	100
Blackmore, John, Master? L--?	1100	Mary Sweet	100
Cartwright, Thomas, Capt	2021	--?* Cartwright, *et al*	300
Henderson, David, Pvt	2023	David Henderson	100
Lashbrook? William, Soldier	1376	William S. Ely	100
Ferris, Peter, Pvt	1331	--?* De Ferris	100
Erwin, Peter, Pvt	2028	--?* Kress, *et al*	100
McCabe, John, Pvt	2027	Arthur? McCabe	100
Dodd, Eli, Pvt	2026	--?* Wilbank	100
Greeley, Richard, Cpl	2029	--?* Hilly Welsh	100
Mitchell, Nathaniel, Maj	1868	--?* Mitchell, *et al*[1]	200
		--?* M. King[1]	200
Flanders, Jacob, Pvt	2030	Jacob Flanders	100
Gordon, John, Pvt	2031	Mary?* Heart	100
Means, Hugh, Ens	2032	Hugh Means	150
Clark, John, Officer[2]	3	Mary?* Clark, *et al*	850

1. The 400 acres due a Major has been equally divided between two scrip holders.
2. Marginal notation: "Special." No further explanation is given for this large grant.
*Forename obscured on microfilm, but National Archives may be able to read from source register.

1681 No dates [ca. 1834] B/1/079

Army land warrants converted to scrip:

Warrant holder	*War. no.*	*Scrip issued to*	*Acres*
Eason, Peter, Pvt	1340	--?* Thayer, *et al*	100
Gifford, Ichabod, Pvt	2017	William?* Gifford, *et al*	100
Shaw, Samuel, Capt	3006	--?* G. Shaw, *et al*	300
Phillips, James, Pvt	2025	--?* Phillips	100
Fopless, John, Pvt	2024	John Fopless, *et al*	100
Raderback, Peter, Pvt	2035	Peter Raderback	100
Cleaveland, Aquilla, Soldier	2036	--?* Cleaveland	100
Littlepage, John, Pvt	2037	James Eppes, *et al*	100
Finley, John H., Lt	2038	John Finley, *et al*	200
Curle, Richard, Drummer	2040	Richardson Curle, *et al*	100
Curle, Jacob, Pvt	2041	Richardson Curle, *et al*	100
Kingsbury, John, Capt	1208	--?* Freeman, *et al*	300
Ake, William, Pvt	2043	Thomas Ake, *et al*	100
Davis, Van, Pvt	2044	Nancy Rose	100
Richardson, John, Pvt	1574	--?* James	100
Smith, Joseph, Lt	1001	--?* Clark, *et al*	200
Eshom, John, Sgt	2033	--?* Eshom	100
Rothmaklee [Rothmakler] Erasmus, Ens	2034	Thomas? B. Rothmaklee, *et al*	150
Young, Christian, Pvt	1811	Jacob Young	100
Ball, Joshua, Pvt	1320	--?* D. Stevenson, assignee	100
Slouter, Jacob, Pvt	1064	Abner?* Armstrong	100
Quick, Jacob, Pvt	1065	Abner?* Armstrong	100
Bradford, Charles, Lt	2055	--?* H. Finley, *et al*	200
Morgan, John, Ens	2049	--?* Morgan, *et al*	150
Newfoelle? [Newfeld?] William, Surgeon	2056	Eliza Holmes, *et al*	400
Threadgill, Thomas, Capt	2054	--?* Threadgill	300
Barkus, John, Pvt	2050	--?* Barkus, *et al*	100
Klinger, Philip, Pvt	2051	Michael? Klinger, *et al*	100
Roberts, Cyrus, Capt	2053	Catherine? Covington, *et al*	300

*Forename obscured on microfilm, but National Archives may be able to read from source register.

1682 No dates [ca. 1834] B/1/080

Army land warrants converted to scrip:

Warrant holder	*War. no.*	*Scrip issued to*	*Acres*
Webb, John, Lt	2052	Mary E. Deshields, *et al*	200
King, Joseph, Drummer	2046	Cavin?* King	100
Hall, John, Pvt	1492	Philo Hale	100
Manning, Samuel, Junior, Pvt	1050	--?* Manning	100
Nelson, Henry, Lt	2057	Mary Nelson, *et al*	200
Cann, Augustine, Pvt	2059	Mary Johnson, *et al*	100
Sullivan, Perry, Pvt	2058	Rebecca Sullivan	100
Dixon, Joseph, Matross	1103	Joseph Dixon	100
Richey, John, Pvt	2061	Joseph Richey, *et al*	100
Johnson, Peter, Pvt	2042	Peter Johnson	100
Moseley, Benjamin, Lt	1932	Mary Watkins, *et al*	200
Meade, Everard, Capt	2063	Abijah?* Meade, *et al*	300
Rosgrove, *alias* Roscrow, Henry, Soldier	2064	Henry Rosgrove	100
Winder, Levin, LtCol	2404	L. Winder, *et al*	450
Simlock, James, Lt	2041	John Simlock, *et al*	200
Lloyd, Edward, Lt	2007	--?* A. Bailey	200
Wilson, Barney, Pvt	2067	Betsy Reed, *et al*	100
Brown, Bazil, Pvt	2068	Bazil Brown, *et al*	100
Campbell, George, Surgeon	2062	William Campbell, *et al*	450
Burnhart, Daniel, Pvt	2066	Daniel Burnhart	100
Murphy, Richard, Pvt	2065	--?* Murphy, *et al*	100
Miller, Samuel, [Capt?]	1104	Samuel Miller	300
Ames, Ephraim, Pvt	2069	--?* Ames	100
Redman? Michael, Soldier	2070	Mary Kateman?	100
Fisher, Thomas, Pvt	2071	--?* W. Fisher, *et al*	100
Shreeve, William, Pvt	2074	William Shreeve	100
Boyce, Jonathan, Pvt	2072	Elly?* Wood, *et al*	100
Andrew, Joseph, Lt**	2073	John?* Andrew	200

*Forename obscured on microfilm, but National Archives may be able to read from source register.
**This warrant issued in lieu of no. 2559, old series, according to marginal notation.

1683 No dates [ca. 1835] B/1/081

Army land warrants converted to scrip:

Warrant holder	*War. no.*	*Scrip issued to*	*Acres*
Clark, Thomas, Pvt	2047	--?* Clark, *et al*	100
Massey, John, Cornet	2076	Robert?* Massey, *et al*	100
Davis, Daniel, Pvt	1199	--?* E. Pettit	100
Cooper, Ephraim, Pvt	1165	Daniel C. Goth?	100
Hanson, William, Pvt	1446	--?* A. Blake	100
Parry, Caleb, Lt	1857	John?* J. Perry, *et al*	200
Stuart, John, Soldier	2081	Esau?* Watson	100
Nicholls, Samuel, Pvt	2078	Nathaniel Nicholls	100
Nicholls, Nehemiah, Pvt	2079	Nathaniel Nicholls	100
Walker, William, Soldier	2080	Henry?* Walker	100
Ryall, *alias* Royal, William, Pvt	2082	William Ryall	100
Miller, William, Capt	2088	Elizabeth Ege	300
Polan, *or* Poland, John, Pvt	2084	[illegible]	100
Pherson, *or* Fearson, Joseph, Pvt	2089	Samuel?* S. Fearson	100
Williams, Benjamin, Pvt	2083	Benjamin Williams	100
Maginnis, Daniel, Soldier	1834	Daniel Maginnis	100
Wilson, Barnaby, Soldier	11819	Thomas Thornburg	100
Hancock, Elisha, Pvt	1760	--?* Hancock, *et al*	100
Hills, Ebenezer, Pvt	1691	Ebenezer Hills	100
McFarland, Moses, Capt	1854**	Osgood Page, *et al*	300
Fox, Allyn, Pvt	1315	Allen S. Wares	100
Timberlake, Joseph, Pvt	2119	Joseph Timberlake	100
McBride, Robert, Lt	1701	Robert McBride, *et al*	200
Archer, Joseph, Lt	2120	William L. Archer, *et al*	200
Thomas, Joseph, Lt	1318	Lovey? Sanborn, *et al*	200
Carso, Robert, Pvt	2127	Nancy Nason	100

*Forename obscured on microfilm, but National Archives may be able to read from source register.

**Could read 11854.

1684 9 Sep 1828 B/1/081

Registered by: Joseph Watson

Registered for: --?* Burke, *et al*

Location:

Mil	-	2	5	1	1
Mil	-	2	5	3	26
Mil	-	2	5	3	39
Mil	-	5	3	3	24

Based upon the following Army land warrant:

Issued to	*No.*	*Acres*
Ford, Benjamin, heirs of, [Lt]Col	1133	450

(Note: Delivered 9 Jun 1835 to G. Burke. Fifty acres patented to J[oseph] W[atson] 18 Sep 1828.

*Forename obscured on microfilm, but National Archives may be able to read from source register.

1685 No dates [ca. 1835] B/1/082

Army land warrants converted to scrip:

Warrant holder	*War. no.*	*Scrip issued to*	*Acres*
Campbell, Robert, Musician	947	Enis Beckwith	100
Blowers, Ephraim, Pvt	1956	Ephraim Blowers	100
Taylor, John, Pvt	1740	Morrison Taylor	100
Rogers, John, Pvt	2075	Hannah Daniel, *et al*	100
Charity, Charles, Pvt	2085	Charles Charity	100
Harrington, William, Pvt	2095	Levin Harrington	100
Putnam, John, Pvt	1570	John Pearsons	100
Mills, Samuel, Pvt	2020	Samuel Mills	100
Dove, Thomas, Pvt	2090	Thomas Dove	100
Bickford, Benjamin, Sgt	742	Elizabeth Allen	100
Grateclass, Gilbert, Cpl	8330	Gilbert Grateclass	100
Garvin, Bartholomew, Pvt	1652	Elenor Garvin, *et al*	100
Johnstone, William, Pvt	2086	Ann Brown	100
Wright, John G., Surgeon's Mate	2005	Susannah Wright	300
Davidson, David, Matross	1417	Willie Roberts	100
Smoot, William, Lt	1234	John M. Walker	200
Shoup, Lewis, *alias* Ludwig, Pvt	2149	Lewis Shoup	100
Floyd, Perry, Pvt	2087	Isaac Floyd, *et al*	100
Frost, Nathaniel, Sgt	727	Sarah Frost, *et al*	100
Shelley? [Shelby?] Samuel, Pvt	1339	Nathan Rathbun	100
Torrey, Joseph, Maj	2153	John Torrey, *et al*	400
Burns, James, Soldier	1663	James Burns, *et al*	100
Alexander, Abraham, Pvt	2039	Abraham Alexander	100
Morgan, M., Lt	1170	Edwin A. Hollingshead	200
Alexander, Solomon, Pvt	1914	Solomon Alexander	100
Glencer, John, Pvt	2094	John Glencer	100
Townsend, William, Pvt	2116	Lucy Ann Townsend	100
Weeks, Micajah, Pvt	1592	Isaac Brainard	100
McCoy, William, Pvt	2093	Catherine Passman, *et al*	100

1686 No dates [ca. 1835] B/1/083

Army land warrants converted to scrip:

Warrant holder	*War. no.*	*Scrip issued to*	*Acres*
Holt, John H., Capt	2121	Elizabeth H. Balfour, *et al*	300
Hewitt, James, Pvt	2125	Eleanor Hewitt	100
Jones, Phillip, Lt	2123	Courtland Freeland, *et al*	200
Canady, John, Pvt	2091	George Canady	100
Elbert, Samuel, Col	1230	Sarah Elbert	500
Warner, Zachariah, Pvt	2060	Peter Warner, *et al*	100
McCawley, James, Pvt	1752	Daniel McCawley, *et al*	100
Tripner, George, Pvt	2115	George Tripner	100
Shelcut, Ezekiel, Pvt	1261	Alexander Stewart	100
Frierson, John, Lt	2096	John J. Frierson	200
McGee, Levin, Pvt	2130	John McGee, *et al*	100
Watts, Francis, Pvt	2114	John Watts, *et al*	100
Fenton, John, Pvt	1627	John Fenton	100
Lyford, Thomas, Lt	1913	Fifield Lyford, *et al*	200

1686 [continued]

Lyon, Asa, Lt	1869	Jabez Lyon, *et al*	200
Cuthbert, Alexander, Capt	2142	Alfred Cuthbert	300
Bird, Andrew, Pvt	2134	Andrew Bird	100
Settlemyer, Godfrey, Soldier	2133	Godfrey Settlemyer	100
Jackson, John, Fifer	2106	J. W. Odenheimer	100
Mitchell, James, Capt	2105	James M. Love, *et al*	300
Eichotts, John, Soldier	2108	Jacob Eichotts, *et al*	100
McKinley, Robert, Pvt	2107	James McKinley	100
Swan, Joshua, Pvt	2109	Christine Swan, *et al*	100
Kelly, Patrick, Pvt	2110	James Kelly	100
McNees? John, Pvt	2147	Nancy Hill, *et al*	100
Beeman, Jabez, Fifer	2118	Seth Bliss	100
Harper, James, Lt	2148	Robert M. Harper	200
Root, Elihu, Ens	1723	William Clark	150
Bartlet, Jonathan, Pvt	1017	Leonard Jarvis	100

1687 No dates [ca. 1835] B/1/084

Army land warrants converted to scrip:

Warrant holder	*War. no.*	*Scrip issued to*	*Acres*
Wilbour, Asa, Drummer	166	Sarah L. Gudgeon	100
Clark, James, Lt	2045	Jonas Clark, *et al*	200
Jacobs, Henry, Pvt	2124	John Jacobs	100
Washington, George A., Lt	2146	George F. Washington, *et al*	200
Edwards, Charles, Pvt	1297	William Edwards, *et al*	100
Bateman, Nathan, Soldier	2132	Rebecca Greaves	100
Hoffman, Henry, Pvt	2135	Henry Hoffman	100
Hoffler, William, Capt	2162	Sarah Higgenbotham	300
Bracco, Bennet, Capt	2167	Bennet Bracco	300
Dodge, Francis, Pvt	1042	Chester Parker	100
Elbert, John L., Apothecary	2157	John L. Elbert, *et al*	150
Rose, Enoch, Pvt	1198	Philo Hale	100
Brown, William, Lt	2139	Mary Judd, *et al*	200
Chillson, John, Pvt	1908	Eliza Ann Willson, *et al*	100
Rundle, John, Pvt	2170	Mary Morgan	100
Simmons, Samuel, Pvt	2155	Samuel Simmons	100
Talbot, David, Pvt	2122	David T. Warren	100
Barnes, Ceasar** Pvt	2102	John Barnes, *et al*	100
Mitchell, Elisha, Pvt	572*	Mary Mitchell	100
Harrington, Asa, Sgt	751	Charles Gibson	100
Ford, John, Lt	2143	Mary Ellis	200
Allison, John, LtCol	2159	Rebecca Allison	450
Webster, Thomas, Pvt	2180	Thomas Webster	100
Kinkaid, John, Soldier	2144	George W. Kinkaid	100
Van Ingen, Dirk, Sgt	2181	Abraham van Ingen	100
Jackson, Thomas, Capt	2141	Thomas Jackson, *et al*	300
Snyder, George C., Pvt	2145	Polly Lenhan, *et al*	100
Tanner, Quain, Pvt	1636	Quain Tanner	100
Stanley? Jacob, Soldier	13784	William Davidson	100

*Could also read 512.
**So spelled.

1688 No dates [ca. 1835] B/1/085

Army land warrants converted to scrip:

Warrant holder	*War. no.*	*Scrip issued to*	*Acres*
Morrison, Larkin, Soldier	13498	William Davidson	100
Johnston, Joseph, Sgt	13263	William Davidson	100
Mullen, William, Soldier	9874	William Davidson	100
Doran, James, Soldier	9276	William Davidson	100
Hangard, Gabriel, Soldier	13215	William Davidson	100
Leonard, Richard, Soldier	9806	William Davidson	100
Kelly, Thomas, Soldier	9756	William Davidson	100
Grace, George, Soldier	9482	William Davidson	100
Grace, Aron, Soldier	9483	William Davidson	100
Tayler, John, Pvt	1740	Morrison Taylor, *et al*	100
Day, Joseph, Capt	2175	Eliza L. Morrell, *et al*	300
Bailey, Henry, Pvt	1594	Phebe Bailey, *et al*	100
Quarles, Moses, Pvt	2164	John L. Quarles, *et al*	100
Price, Isaac, Pvt	2172	Isaac Price	100
Drake, Joshua, Lt	553	Henry Northup	200
Jenkins, John, Pvt	2174	John Jenkins	100
Haden, Anthony, Pvt	2158	John Hade, *et al*	100
McCartney, Peter, Pvt	2184	Catherine Mount, *et al*	100
Tiffany, Walter, Soldier	2169	Sarah Cushick, *et al*	100
Dean, John, Soldier	2186	Thomas Dean	100
Minter? [Winter?] Barker, Pvt	2187	Richard Sherwood, *et al*	100
White, Peter, Pvt	2136	William White, *et al*	100
Lines, Francis, Sgt	2185	Mary Schoonmacker	100
Truman, Alexander, Capt	2156	Alexander M. Truman	150*
		William B. Truman, *et al*	150*
Hodges, William, Pvt	2188	John B. Hodges, *et al*	100
Lakeman, Thomas, Sgt	2100	Lydia Ann Lakeman	100
Durgin, Henry, Pvt	2103	Nancy Neal	100
Derrick, Thomas, Pvt	2183	Rachel Johnson, *et al*	100

*The 300 acres due a Captain have been equally divided between two sets of heirs.

1689 No dates [ca. 1835] B/1/086

Army land warrants converted to scrip:

Warrant holder	*War. no.*	*Scrip issued to*	*Acres*
Bacon, Henry, Soldier	2138	Henry Bacon	100
Warmack, William, Pvt	2140	William Warmack	100
Van Court, John, Lt	669	John Hitchcock	200
Stocking, Eber, Sgt	581	Daniel L? [or S?] Stocking	100
Billings, Robert, Soldier	2104	Jesse Billings, *et al*	100
Allen, Jacob, Pvt	1865	Garret Allen, *et al*	100

1689 [continued]

Warrant holder	War. no.	Scrip issued to	Acres
Perry John, Cornet	1692	Charles M. Perry, *et al*	100
Tufts, Samuel, 1st Regt. Mas. Q.[1]	988	Mary Tufts, *et al*	100
Horn, Jacob, Soldier	1898	Jacob Horn, Junior	100
Ronnay? [Ronndy?] Luke, Ens	2189	Mary Goodridge	150
Brownson, Nathan, Deputy Purveyor	2154	Mrs. Eliza[beth?] Jones	400
Allen, Ethan, Col	1601*	Ethan A. Allen	208.4*
		Lucy C. Hitchcock	145.6*
Hyrne, Edmund M., Maj	1478	Richard B. Baker, *et al*	400
Hollis, Barnabas, Soldier	2192	Barnabas Hollis	100
Bliss, Elijah, Sgt	2193	Elijah Bliss	100
Miller, John, Pvt	2126	Peter L. Miller	100
Lindsey, David, Drummer	854	Sarah Belden	100
Carpenter, Robert, Cpl	1354	James Parramore, assignee	100
Thompson, Thomas, Lt	1482	John Thompson, *et al*	200
Baker, Richard B., Capt	1221	Richard B. Baker, *et al*	300
King, Joshia [Josiah?] Soldier	1992	[see below[2]]	
Burns, James, Soldier	1663	Samuel Burns, *et al*	37.5
		James Burns, *et al*	62.5
Blatchford, John, Pvt	2166	John C. Blatchford	100
Ainger? Jesse, Pvt	1260	Daniel Stevens & James A. Stevens, assignees	100
Wills, Abraham, Pvt	2176	Abraham Wills	100

*Warrant number may read 1001. Scrip assigned above does not add up to 500 acres due a Colonel. No other scrip certificate found for remaining 146 acres due his heirs.

1. This enlisted man's rating is not otherwise defined.
2. Scrip assigned as follows:

Josiah King, *et al*	70.75 acres
Maria King, *et al*	14.15
Calvin King, *et al*	14.15
	99.05 acres

This does not add up to the 100 acres due a soldier. No explanation given.

1690 No dates [ca. 1835] B/1/087

Army land warrants converted to scrip:

Warrant holder	*War. no.*	*Scrip issued to*	*Acres*
Lincoln, Elijah, Pvt	2077	C. C. Hayward, assignee	100
Hill, William, Sgt	2182	John Hill, *et al*	100
Evans, George, Lt	2197	George Evans	200
Taylor, John, Pvt	1740	William Taylor, *et al*	60*
		Elizabeth Taylor	20*
		John M. Taylor, *et al*	20*
Crandall, Hosea, Pvt	1308	Hosea Crandall	100
Frost, Nathaniel, Sgt	2198	Mary Twombly	100
Marion, Francis, LtCol [commanding[1]]	2199	Louisa C. Marion	500
Campbell, Robert, Musician	947	Emily Beckwith, *et al*	100
Jeffries, John, Pvt	2191	James Jeffries, *et al*	100
Williams, William, Capt	2202	William W. Williams	300
Jenkins, Samuel, Pvt	2203	Thomas R. Jenkins	100
Madison, William, Lt	2205	William Madison	200
Russell, Charles, Lt	2151	Elgin Russell, *et al*	200
Fishburn, Benjamin, Capt	2206	Elizabeth Fishburn	300
Wright, John G., Surgeon's Mate	2005	Susanna Wright & H. B. [Wright?]	200*
		Groesbeck Wright	100*
Lynn, Michael, Pvt	2207	Roberts Lynn	100
Harris, Robert, Surgeon's Mate	1173	Joshua F. Cox	300
Welch, William, Pvt	2190	Robert Welch	100
Armor, James, Lt	1383	William Manahan	200
Conner, William, Pvt	2209	Marmaduke W. Conner	100
Haynie, Ezekiel, Surgeon	743	Henrietta B. Haynie	400
Meakins, Bennett, Pvt	2210	Joseph L? [or S?] Meakins	100
Townsend, William, Pvt	2116	Lucy Ann Townsend	100
Shields, James, Pvt	2211	James Shields	100
Allison, John, Pvt	1657	Sarah Brooks	100
White, William, Lt	2213	Richard B. White, *et al*	200

*Scrip divided among several sets of heirs.

1. The legal claim of a Lieutenant Colonel was for 450 acres, but, if commanding, was raised to 500 acres.

1691 Various dates B/1/088

List of caveats on file in the office of the Register of the Treasury relative to military land warrants:

Warrantee	*War. no.*	*Comment*
Sankey, Ezekiel	10418	[Before Mar 1796]: Fraudulently taken from the War Office by a forged instrument of writing.
Dougherty, James	9257	[Before Mar 1796]: Fraudulently taken from the War Office by a forged power of attorney to William Lane.
Buchanan, Alexander, assignee of Capt James Cornaghan & Conrad Cook	417	11 Mar 1796: Lost out of his [Buchanan's] pocket at Pittsburgh, November 1795.
Buchanan, Alexander, assignee of Capt James Cornaghan & Conrad Cook	12892	11 Mar 1796: Lost out of his [Buchanan's] pocket at Pittsburgh, November 1795.
Benson, Perry	236	21 Mar 1796: Lost in 1794.
Stuart, Benjamin	11724	3 May 1796: Issued to Henry Purdy on a forged power of attorney.

1691 [continued]

Sweeny, Daniel, assignee of Benjamin Beaver	9000	6 May 1796: Sweeny alleges that it was issued to Casper Iserloan on a fraudulent conveyance.
Taylor, Griffin, assignee of William Eskridge	679	27 May 1796: Warrant lost.
Doyle, James	11140	24 Jul 1796: Alleges to have been wrongfully issued to George Ponsonby.
Cloutier, Charles	12911	30 Jul 1796: Issued to Benjamin Moore? on a fraudulent conveyance.
Redman, John	13694	9 Aug 1796: Fraudulently obtained from the War Office by a person under the same name.
Chartier, Joseph	12909	18 Aug 1796: Issued to Benjamin Moore on a fraudulent conveyance.
Hoos? [Hous?] Hendric	4343	6 Jan 1797: Issued to Benjamin Moore on a fraudulent conveyance.
Lyon, Thomas	1222	3 Feb 1797: Issued to Anspach & Rogers on a false power of attorney.
[von] Steuben, Baron [Frederick]	2128	6 Feb 1797: Warrant lost or mislaid. Warrant has since been produced and located by Steuben's legatees.
Hilger, Henry	13187	29 Dec 1798: Issued to Edward Osborn on a false assignment. Note: This caveat seems to be ill-founded; the warrant against which it points, No. 13187, being to Andrew Hilger. Warrant has since been granted.
Fitch, Samuel, assignee of Azel Washburn	2279 5942	25 Apr 1799: The warrants lost.
Richard, Joseph A.	3462	-- Oct 1799: Lost his certificate (warrant).
Finney, William, caveats *vs* [Hugh Haney]	9525	2 Jan 1800: Issued in the name of Hugh Haney[1]
Alden, Judah	3912 12*	2 Jan 1800: Lost in the streets of Boston.
Gadsden, Thomas, Capt	288	22 Sep 1809: Lost; another (No. 47) . . .? issued instead [for] 300 acres.
Wright, John G., Surgeon's Mate	Unknown	11 Oct 1810: Put in hands of Aaron Burr by the widow of the warrantee.
Caswell, Job, Junior	369	24 May 1819: Illegally obtained. See John Coates' letter of 15 May 1819.
Moore, James	667	-- 1819?: Lost. Caveat verbally by Hon. T. Patterson M[ember of] C[ongress].
[Name not given][2]	1164	7 Dec 1826: [Caveat?] by Hon. John Woodrof? Ohio.
Chadwick, --	716	-- Feb 1828: Illegally written? See special? Act of Congress, 2 Mar 1839.

1. Surname obscured on microfilm, but National Archives may be able to read from source register.
2. This entire entry corssed out on source register.
*Warrant number crossed out on source register.

1692 No dates B/1/[089]

Informal pencilled notes:

Warrant holder	*War. no.*	*Comment*
[Name not given]	933?	Samuel Brown caveat against issu[ance] of warrant [additional remarks partially illegible--perhaps a lost assignment].
[Name not given]	465	No patent to issue on presentation of this warrant, as warrant 491 issued in lieu thereof.
[Name not given]	1160	Caveat against this warrant by the Secretary of War in his letter.
Stanbury, Jonas, assignee of J. Bradly	5486	Has been patented to Jonas Stanbury, assignee of J. Bradly in the year 1808 but has been omitted entirely in this book [source register].
Flower, Thomas	8801?	[Caveat?] in the name of Thomas Flower by Hon. Mr. Jennings, 14 Jan 1828.

1693 No dates [after 1835] B/1/090

Army land warrants converted to scrip:

Warrant holder	*War. no.*	*Scrip issued to*	*Acres*
Stevenson, William, [Lt]	2212	Francis S. Mallary	200
Ham, John, Soldier	2214	Hannah Garland, *et al*	100
Lucas, John, Capt	2215	Margaret Lucas, *et al*	300
Hopkins, David, Capt	2216	Sarah Hopkins, executrix	300
Curtis, Nathan, Pvt	2150	Nathan Curtis, *et al*	100
Ross, Benjamin, Pvt	1606	Eli Tainter, assignee	100
Pirsley, *alias* Pursley, Peter [Pvt]	2218	James Chadowick, *et al*	100

1693 [continued]

Warrant holder	War. no.	Scrip issued to	Acres
Alexander, Solomon, [Pvt]	1914	James Alexander & Edward Alexander	100
Hockaday, Phillip, [Lt]	2217	Cynthia Williams, *et al*	200
Wood, Gerrard [Capt]	2160	Mary Crain *et al*	233.3*
		Robert J. Young & A. Young	66.7*
Lightfoot, Phillip, [Lt]	2220	Phillip Lightfoot	200
Smith, Larkin [Capt]	2221	John Hill Smith, *et al*	300
Root, Elihu	2225	William Clark, *et al*	50
Marston, John [Lt]	2223	Sarah M. Bolling, *et al*	200
Dun, Isaac Budd, [Capt]	2224	Abby Dun	300
Hemingway, James, [Pvt]	2222	Elizabeth Cox, *et al*	100
Van Campen, Moses, [Lt]	2219	Moses Van Campen	200
Sweet, Mary, sister of John Bl[ake?]-more [Blackmore?][1] [Pvt]	1100	Jeremiah B. Whiting, assignee	100
Dye, Jonathan [Lt]	2226	Sarah E. Davis	200
Priest, John [Pvt]	2227	Hannah Cummings	100
Underwood, S. [Pvt]	1223	Thomas A. Dugdale, assignee	100
Porter, Asa [Pvt]	2098	Elisha Porter	100
Gustin, Jesse [Pvt]	2229	Sarah Powell	100
Stewart, Charles [Capt]	2228	John W. Peterson, *et al*	300
Walker, John [Pvt]	2230	William Walker, *et al*	100
Doud, Solomon [Pvt]	5694**	Henry Northup, assignee	100
Morfit, Henry [Lt]	2232	Henry M. Morfit	200
Stockbridge, John, [Pvt]	2233	John Stockbridge, *et al*	100
Ramsey, Alex[ande]r, [Lt]	1333	Charles J. Nourse, assignee	200

1. Name obscured on microfilm, but National Archives may be able to read from source register.
*Warrant for 300 acres divided among several scrip holders.
**Warrant 419 has previously been issued in lieu of 5694 and patented for same claim.

1694 No dates [after 1835] B/1/091

Army land warrants converted to scrip:

Warrant holder	*War. no.*	*Scrip issued to*	*Acres*
Russwurm, William, [Lt]	2234	John S. Russwurm	200
McCarroll, John [Pvt]	2195	Jacob McCarroll	100
Davis, Ellen, daughter [of unnamed veteran] [Pvt]	2235	Ellen Davis	100
Thompson, C., *et al* [heirs? of unnamed veteran] [Lt]	1310	Cassandra Thompson	100*
		Mary Wagner	100*
Campbell, Julia, *et al* [heirs? of unnamed veteran] [Pvt]	2196	Julia Campbell, *et al*	100
Hucorn, Eliza, *et al* [heirs? of unnamed veteran] [Pvt]	2201	Eliza Hucorn, *et al*	100
Billings, Mary [heiress? of unnamed veteran] [Lt]	2237	Mary Billings	200
Lakin, Mary [heiress? of unnamed veteran] [Pvt]	2238	Mary Lakin	100
Wharry, Daniel, brother [of unnamed veteran] [Capt]	2239	Daniel Wharry	300
Spitfathom, John [Ens]	2240	John Spitfathom	150
Williams, Lucy, daughter of [unnamed veteran] [Capt]	2161	C. H. Williams, assignee	300
Kerr, Andrew, son [of unnamed veteran] [Pvt]	660	Joseph Stokely, assignee	100
Rogers, Andrew [heir? of unnamed veteran] [Pvt]	2165	Henry Morten, assignee	100
Babcock, Polly [heiress of unnamed veteran] [Pvt]	2242	Polly Babcock, *et al*	100
Peyton, Valentine S. [heir? of unnamed veteran] [Capt]	2241	Valentine S. Peyton, *et al*	225*
		Francis Rector, *et al*	75*

*Value of warrant divided between two scrip holders.

(End of source B)

1695 — 12 Mar 1800 — C/-/001

Quarter Townships:

Patentee	*Acres*	*Location*
Biggs, Zaccheus	4000.0	Mil - 1 1 - 2
Johnson, James	4000.0	Mil - 1 2 - 1
Galbreath, --, & Elmes, --	4000.0	Mil - 1 7 - 1
Aulman, William	4000.0	Mil - 1 7 - 2
Heckewelder, John	3923.0	Mil - 1 7 - 3
Rathbone? [Rathborne?] John	4000.0	Mil - 1 7 - 4
Haga, Godfrey	4000.0	Mil - 1 10 - 3
Morgan, David	4000.0	Mil - 2 1 - 3
Haga, Godfrey	3662.9	Mil - 2 6 - 2
Haga, Godfrey	3694.7	Mil - 2 8 - 1
Heckewelder, John	3819.9	Mil - 2 8 - 2
Morrison, James	4353.8	Mil - 2 9 - 3
Rich, J. C., *et al*	4000.0	Mil - 2 9 - 4
Mosser, --, & Boude, --	4000.0	Mil - 2 10 - 1
Dayton, Jonathan	4000.0	Mil - 2 10 - 4
Biggs, Zaccheus, & Beatty, Zaccheus	4000.0	Mil - 3 2 - 3
Cheney, William M.	4000.0	Mil - 3 2 - 4
Beaver? John	3999.8	Mil - 3 5 - 2
McCluney, W[illia]m	4000.5	Mil - 4 1 - 2
Cumming, John N.	4000.0	Mil - 4 1 - 3
Denman, Matthias	4000.0	Mil - 4 5 - 1
Steele, William	4076.3	Mil - 4 5 - 2
Williams, James	4000.0	Mil - 4 5 - 3
Hunt, Jesse, & Hunt, Abijah	4000.0	Mil - 4 6 - 2
Baum, --, & Schenck, --	4013.6	Mil - 4 6 - 3
Higbee, Joseph	4000.7	Mil - 5 5 - 1
Swan, Caleb	3936.7	Mil - 5 5 - 2
Cumming, John N.	4000.0	Mil - 5 5 - 4
Lynn, David	3998.0	Mil - 5 6 - 1

1696 — 12 Mar 1800 — C/-/002

Quarter Townships:

Patentee	*Acres*	*Location*
Baum, Martin, & Co	4000.0	Mil - 5 6 - 4
Stanberry, Jonas	4000.0	Mil - 6 1 - 3
Denman, Matthias	4000.0	Mil - 6 4 - 2
Edgar, William, Junior	4000.0	Mil - 6 4 - 3
Morgan, --, & Price, --	4000.0	Mil - 6 5 - 1
Backus, Elijah	3138.8	Mil - 6 5 - 2
Baum, Martin	3682.2	Mil - 6 5 - 3
Denman, Matthias	4000.0	Mil - 6 5 - 4
Underwood, Robert	3478.8	Mil - 6 6 - 3
Hamilton, James	4000.0	Mil - 6 6 - 4
Underwood, Robert	4000.0	Mil - 7 1 - 2
Underwood, Robert	3817.0	Mil - 7 1 - 3
Johnston, James	4000.0	Mil - 7 1 - 4
Stanberry, Jonas	3874.6	Mil - 7 2 - 1
Copeland, Charles	4000.0	Mil - 7 2 - 2
Jackson, John G.	4000.0	Mil - 7 2 - 3
Gilman, Nich[ola]s	3809.7	Mil - 7 3 - 1
Cass, Jonathan	4000.0	Mil - 7 3 - 2
Bray, John	4000.0	Mil - 7 3 - 3
Hardenbrook, J. A.	4045.4	Mil - 7 4 - 4
Skinner, George	4000.0	Mil - 7 6 - 2
Steele, William	4000.0	Mil - 7 6 - 3
Denman, Matthias	4000.0	Mil - 7 6 - 4
Burrall? [Bunall?] Jonathan	3894.4	Mil - 7 7 - 1
Vance, --, & Sibley, --	4000.0	Mil - 8 1 - 1
Robinson, William	4013.7	Mil - 8 1 - 2
Rathbone? [Rathborne?] John	4000.0	Mil - 8 1 - 3
Brown, John	3643.3	Mil - 8 1 - 4
Woodbridge, Dudley	4000.0	Mil - 8 3 - 1
Boller, F.	3995.8	Mil - 8 3 - 4
Medowell, Cairnoan	4000.0	Mil - 8 6 - 3
Simmons, William	4237.2	Mil - 8 6 - 4
Jackson, G.	4120.0	Mil - 9 2 - 1
Salter, Thomas	4000.0	Mil - 9 2 - 2

1697 — 12 Mar 1800 — C/-/003

Quarter Townships:

Patentee	*Acres*	*Location*
Terrill, John	4000.0	Mil - 9 2 - 3
Bray, John	4038.0	Mil - 9 2 - 4
Luckley, George	4080.3	Mil - 9 6 - 1
Taylor, James, & Gillespey, --, & Henry? --	4000.0	Mil - 9 6 - 2
Medowell, Cairnoan	4050.8	Mil - 9 6 - 3
Thompson, Daniel	3962.0	Mil - 10 2 - 1
Galbreath, --, & Elmes, --	4000.0	Mil - 10 2 - 2
Dayton, Jonathan	3850.0	Mil - 10 2 - 4
Dick, Samuel	4000.0	Mil - 10 6 - 1
Galbreath, --, & Ives, --	4000.0	Mil - 11 1 - 2
Sebor? [Lebor?] Jacob	4000.0	Mil - 11 1 - 3
Warder, John	3613.4	Mil - 11 2 - 1
Wilkins, John, Junior	4000.0	Mil - 11 2 - 2
Denman, Matthias	4000.0	Mil - 11 2 - 3
Johnson, James	3543.4	Mil - 11 2 - 4
Baldwin, Jesse	4000.0	Mil - 11 5 - 1
Campbell, Robert	3344.9	Mil - 11 6 - 2
Rhea, --, & Barton, --	4000.0	Mil - 11 7 - 1
Matthews [Mathews?] John	3185.9	Mil - 11 7 - 2
Rathborne [Rathbone?] John	3455.3	Mil - 11 7 - 3
Turner, Edward D.	4000.0	Mil - 11 7 - 4
Gilman, Nicholas	4220.0	Mil - 12 1 - 1
Galbreath, --, & Elmes, --	4000.0	Mil - 12 1 - 2
Woods, Arch[ibal]d; Griffith, William; Ridgelay, Abs[alom?]; Biggs, Z[accheus?]	4000.0	Mil - 12 1 - 3
Baum, --, & Schenck, --	4000.0	Mil - 12 1 - 4
Rathborne [Rathbone?] John	4218.9	Mil - 12 2 - 1
Jackson, G.	4000.0	Mil - 12 2 - 2
Harberson [Harbison?] Adam	4000.0	Mil - 12 2 - 3
Cumming, John N., & Bevinet? [Bennet?] John G. W.	4220.0	Mil - 12 2 - 4
Salter, Thomas	4305.0	Mil - 12 3 - 1
Robinson, Thomas	4000.0	Mil - 12 3 - 2
Elliott, Benjamin	4000.0	Mil - 12 3 - 3
Dayton, Jonathan	4094.2	Mil - 12 3 - 4
Steele, William	3807.0	Mil - 12 4 - 1

1698 — 12 Mar 1800 — C/-/004

Quarter Townships:

Patentee	*Acres*		*Location*				
Hardy, Joseph	3460.0	Mil	-	12	4	-	2
Stanberry, Jonas	4000.0	Mil	-	12	4	-	3
Asheton, Joseph	4000.0	Mil	-	12	5	-	1
Biddle, Clement	3978.3	Mil	-	12	5	-	2
Williams, James	4000.0	Mil	-	12	5	-	3
Dayton, Jonathan	4092.1	Mil	-	12	5	-	4
Howard, John C.	4000.0	Mil	-	12	6	-	1
McCluney, William	3989.1	Mil	-	12	6	-	2
Baum, Martin	4381.1	Mil	-	12	6	-	3
Turner, --, Ormsby, --, & Matthews, --	4000.0	Mil	-	12	6	-	4
Baum, Martin, & Co	4000.0	Mil	-	12	7	-	1
Davidson, John	4095.0	Mil	-	12	7	-	2
Howard, John E.	4000.0	Mil	-	12	7	-	4
Dayton, Jonathan	3080.0	Mil	-	13	1	-	1
Bailey, Theo[dorus]	4920.0	Mil	-	13	1	-	2
Stanberry, Jonas	4000.0	Mil	-	13	1	-	3
Symmes, John C[leves]	4000.0	Mil	-	13	1	-	4
Davis, Sampson	3196.8	Mil	-	13	2	-	1
Stanberry, Jonas	5040.0	Mil	-	13	2	-	2
Hardy, Joseph	4920.0	Mil	-	13	2	-	3
Steele, William	3080.0	Mil	-	13	2	-	4
Dayton, Jonathan	3644.2	Mil	-	13	3	-	1
Denman, Matthias	4000.0	Mil	-	13	3	-	2
Thompson, Thomas McKean	5040.0	Mil	-	13	3	-	3
Dayton, Jonathan	3081.9	Mil	-	13	3	-	4
Galbreath, --, & Noyes, --	3430.2	Mil	-	13	4	-	1
Stanberry, Jonas	4000.0	Mil	-	13	4	-	2
Baldwin, Abraham	4000.0	Mil	-	13	4	-	3
Steele, William	3882.1	Mil	-	13	4	-	4
Ryckman, Cornelia	2263.2	Mil	-	13	5	-	1
Baldwin, Abraham	4000.0	Mil	-	13	5	-	3
Dayton, Jonathan	2611.8	Mil	-	13	5	-	4
Hamtramick, J. F.	2363.0	Mil	-	13	6	-	1
Williams, James	4000.0	Mil	-	13	6	-	2

1699 — 12 Mar 1800 — C/-/005

Quarter Townships

Patentee	*Acres*		*Location*				
Bayley, Theodore	4000.0	Mil	-	13	6	-	3
Backus, Elijah	2472.0	Mil	-	13	6	-	4
Armstrong, John	4000.0	Mil	-	13	7	-	2
Cobb, Lemuel	4000.0	Mil	-	13	7	-	3
Bentalon, Paul	4000.0	Mil	-	13	8	-	3
Backus, Elijah	4000.0	Mil	-	14	1	-	1
Rhea, --, & Beatty, --	4000.0	Mil	-	14	1	-	2
Wilkins, John	4000.0	Mil	-	14	1	-	3
Foster, Theodore, & Co.	4000.0	Mil	-	14	1	-	4
Johnston, James	4000.0	Mil	-	14	2	-	1
Bray, John	4000.0	Mil	-	14	2	-	2
Symmes, John C[leves]	4000.0	Mil	-	14	2	-	3
Denman, Matthias	4000.0	Mil	-	14	2	-	4
Johnston, James	4000.0	Mil	-	14	3	-	1
Symmes, John C[leves]	4000.0	Mil	-	14	3	-	3
Higbee, Joseph	4000.0	Mil	-	14	3	-	4
Symmes, John C[leves]	4000.0	Mil	-	14	4	-	1
Pinckney, Charles C.	4000.0	Mil	-	14	4	-	2
Macan, John G.	4000.0	Mil	-	14	4	-	3
Higbee, Joseph	4000.0	Mil	-	14	4	-	4
Symmes, John C[leves]	4000.0	Mil	-	14	5	-	3
Parker, James	4000.0	Mil	-	14	5	-	4
Craig, Isaac	4000.0	Mil	-	14	6	-	1
Biggs, Zacch[eus]	4000.0	Mil	-	14	6	-	2
Backus, Elijah	4000.0	Mil	-	14	6	-	3
Backus, Elijah	4000.0	Mil	-	14	6	-	4
Sullivan, Lucus*	4000.0	Mil	-	14	7	-	1
Moore, Benjamin J.	4000.0	Mil	-	14	7	-	2
M-thews, John	4000.0	Mil	-	14	7	-	3
Wright, John	4000.0	Mil	-	14	7	-	4
Higbee, Joseph	4000.0	Mil	-	15	1	-	1
Bray, John	4000.0	Mil	-	15	1	-	4
Marsh, Daniel	4000.0	Mil	-	15	2	-	1
Matthews? [Mathews?] John & Co.	4000.0	Mil	-	15	3	-	1

*So spelled.

1700 — 12 Mar 1800 — C/-/006

Quarter Townships:

Patentee	*Acres*		*Location*				
Brown, John	4000.0	Mil	-	15	3	-	4
Stanberry, Jonas	4000.0	Mil	-	15	4	-	1
Dayton, Jonathan	4000.0	Mil	-	15	4	-	4
Rathborne [Rathbone?] John	4000.0	Mil	-	15	5	-	1
Dayton, Jonathan	4000.0	Mil	-	15	5	-	2
Stites, John	4000.0	Mil	-	15	5	-	3
Parker, James	4000.0	Mil	-	15	5	-	4
McLaughlin, Alexander	4000.0	Mil	-	15	7	-	1
Williams, James	4000.0	Mil	-	15	7	-	2
Dayton, Jonathan	4000.0	Mil	-	16	1	-	1
Dayton, Jonathan	4000.0	Mil	-	16	1	-	2
Hand, Edward	4000.0	Mil	-	16	1	-	3
Warren, Townsend, *et al*	4000.0	Mil	-	16	1	-	4
Woodbridge, Dudley	4000.0	Mil	-	16	2	-	3
Symmes, John C[leves]	4000.0	Mil	-	16	3	-	1
Johnston, James	4000.0	Mil	-	16	3	-	2
Symmes, John C[leves]	4000.0	Mil	-	16	3	-	3
Wells, --, & Armstrong, --	4000.0	Mil	-	16	4	-	2
Denman, Matthias	4000.0	Mil	-	16	4	-	3
Symmes, John C[leves]	4000.0	Mil	-	16	4	-	4
Higbee, Joseph	4000.0	Mil	-	16	5	-	1
Brown, --, & Ludlow, --	4000.0	Mil	-	16	5	-	2
Porter, Robert	4000.0	Mil	-	16	5	-	3
Holmes, --, & Rainey, --	4000.0	Mil	-	16	5	-	4
Salter, Thomas	4000.0	Mil	-	16	6	-	2
Dayton, Jonathan	4000.0	Mil	-	16	6	-	3
Foster, Theodore, & Co.	4000.0	Mil	-	17	1	-	1
Coates, John	4000.0	Mil	-	17	1	-	2
Macan, John G.	4000.0	Mil	-	17	1	-	3
Worthington, Thomas	4000.0	Mil	-	17	1	-	4
Wells, William	4000.0	Mil	-	17	2	-	1
Dayton, Jonathan	4000.0	Mil	-	17	2	-	2
Stites, John	4000.0	Mil	-	17	2	-	3
Rathborn [Rathbone?] John	4000.0	Mil	-	17	2	-	4

1701 12 Mar 1800 C/-/007

Quarter Townships:

Patentee	*Acres*	*Location*
Galbreath, --, & Elmes, --	4000.0	Mil - 17 3 - 1
Steele, William	4000.0	Mil - 17 3 - 2
Parker, James	4000.0	Mil - 17 3 - 3
Wells, --, & Armstrong, --	4000.0	Mil - 17 3 - 4
Denman, Matthias	4000.0	Mil - 17 4 - 1
Pierce, Ebenezer	4000.0	Mil - 17 4 - 2
Higbee, Joseph	4000.0	Mil - 17 4 - 3
Sebor, Jacob	4000.0	Mil - 17 4 - 4
Galbreath, --, & Elmes, --	4000.0	Mil - 17 5 - 1
Dayton, Jonathan	4000.0	Mil - 17 5 - 2
Salter, Thomas	4000.0	Mil - 17 5 - 3
Dayton, Jonathan	4000.0	Mil - 17 5 - 4
Galbreath, --, & Elmes, --	4000.0	Mil - 17 6 - 1
Steele, William	4000.0	Mil - 17 6 - 3
Edgar, William, Junior	4000.0	Mil - 17 6 - 4
Dayton, Jonathan	4000.0	Mil - 18 1 - 1
Rathborne [Rathbone?] John	4000.0	Mil - 18 1 - 2
Dayton, Jonathan	4000.0	Mil - 18 1 - 3
Stephenson, George	4000.0	Mil - 18 1 - 4
Symmes, John C[leves]	4000.0	Mil - 18 2 - 1
Galbreath, --, & Ives, --	4000.0	Mil - 18 2 - 2
Dunlap, John	4000.0	Mil - 18 2 - 3
Hamilton, James	4000.0	Mil - 18 2 - 4
Steele, William	4000.0	Mil - 18 3 - 1
Dayton, Jonathan	4000.0	Mil - 18 3 - 2
Biddle, Thomas	4000.0	Mil - 18 3 - 3
Denman, Matthias	4000.0	Mil - 18 3 - 4
Pierce, Ebenezer	4000.0	Mil - 18 4 - 1
Steele, William	4000.0	Mil - 18 4 - 2
Taylor, James	4000.0	Mil - 18 4 - 3
Galbreath, --, & Elmes, --	4000.0	Mil - 18 4 - 4
Rathborne [Rathbone?] John	4000.0	Mil - 18 5 - 2
Baldwin, Abraham	4000.0	Mil - 18 5 - 3
Steele, William	4000.0	Mil - 18 5 - 4

1702 12 Mar 1800 C/-/008

Quarter Townships:

Patentee	*Acres*	*Location*
de Peyster, Abraham B.	4000.0	Mil - 18 6 - 2
Rathborne [Rathbone?] John	4000.0	Mil - 18 6 - 3
Harbison, Adam	4000.0	Mil - 18 6 - 4
Dayton, Jonathan	4000.0	Mil - 19 1 - 1
Backus, Elijah	2979.6	Mil - 19 1 - 4
Lynn, David	4000.0	Mil - 19 2 - 1
Thomas, Philemon	4000.0	Mil - 19 2 - 4
Stanberry, Jonas	4000.0	Mil - 19 3 - 1
Morrison, James	3909.0	Mil - 19 3 - 2
Wells, William	3185.0	Mil - 19 3 - 3
Parker, James	4000.0	Mil - 19 3 - 4
Gilman, Nicholas	4000.0	Mil - 19 4 - 1
Dayton, Jonathan	4000.0	Mil - 19 4 - 2
Rathborne [Rathbone?] John	4000.0	Mil - 19 4 - 3
Stanberry, Jonas	4000.0	Mil - 19 4 - 4
Wells, William	4000.0	Mil - 19 5 - 1
Porter, Andrew	4000.0	Mil - 19 5 - 2
Taylor, James	4000.0	Mil - 19 5 - 3
Baldwin, Abraham	4000.0	Mil - 19 5 - 4
Campbell, Robert	4000.0	Mil - 19 6 - 1
Salter, Thomas	4000.0	Mil - 19 6 - 2
Wells, --, & Armstrong, --	4000.0	Mil - 19 6 - 4
Wells, --, & Armstrong, --	3934.5	Mil - 19 7 - 3
Stanberry, Jonas	3986.0	Mil - 20 5 - 1
Dayton, Jonathan	3255.2	Mil - 20 5 - 4
Salter, Thomas	4000.0	Mil - 20 6 - 1
Jones, Samuel	4000.0	Mil - 20 6 - 4
Dayton, Jonathan	3137.0	Mil - 20 7 - 4

1703 Various C/-/010

100-Acre Lots:

Patentee & Location Date	*Location*
Vacant	Mil - 1 1 3 1
McBride, Roger, 10 Jan 1805	Mil - 1 1 3 2
Crane, Stephen, assignee of (John Russell), 16 Nov 1805	Mil - 1 1 3 3
Vacant	Mil - 1 1 3 4
Vacant	Mil - 1 1 3 5
Baum, Martin, & Perry, S., in trust for the heirs of J. Smith, deceased, 23 Feb 1810	Mil - 1 1 3 6
Blackshire, Ebenezer, 23 Mar 1808	Mil - 1 1 3 7
Seger? [Leger?] Ebenezer, assignee of (Zaccheus Biggs), 30 Jan 1806	Mil - 1 1 3 8
Vacant	Mil - 1 1 3 9
Asken, --, & Huff, --, 1812	Mil - 1 1 3 10
Caruthers, John, heirs of, 31 Jan 1806	Mil - 1 1 3 11
Caruthers, John, heirs of, 31 Jan 1806	Mil - 1 1 3 12
Fling, John, 10 Jan 1806	Mil - 1 1 3 13
Hendry, Samuel, assignee of (William Carter) 9 Jan 1806	Mil - 1 1 3 14
Hendry, Samuel, assignee of (William Carter) 9 Jan 1806	Mil - 1 1 3 15
Hendry, Samuel, assignee of (William Carter) 9 Jan 1806	Mil - 1 1 3 16
Fields, Reuben, 9 Jan 1806	Mil - 1 1 3 17
Fields, Reuben, 9 Jan 1806	Mil - 1 1 3 18
Fields, Reuben, 9 Jan 1806	Mil - 1 1 3 19
Fleeheart? Massey, assignee of (John Rogers) 16 Nov 1805	Mil - 1 1 3 20
Pinkerton, Andrew, assignee of (Jacob Miller) 15 Feb 1806	Mil - 1 1 3 21
Blake, William, assignee of (Jacob Miller) 15 Feb 1806	Mil - 1 1 3 22
Vacant	Mil - 1 1 3 23
Beatty, Zaccheus A., 5 Apr 1810	Mil - 1 1 3 24

1703 [continued]

Patentee & Location Date						
Devore, Luke, assignee of (John Black) 16 Nov 1805	Mil	-	1	1	3	25
Vacant	Mil	-	1	1	3	26
Vacant	Mil	-	1	1	3	27
Stewart, Hu[gh?] assignee of (Alexander McBride) 26 Feb 1806	Mil	-	1	1	3	28
O'Hara, Jos[eph?] heirs of, 15 Feb 1806	Mil	-	1	1	3	29
Woodside, John, 3 Jan 1806	Mil	-	1	1	3	30

1704 Various C/-/011

100-Acres Lots:

Patentee & Location Date	*Location*					
Bennet, John, assignee of (not stated) 9 Jan 1806	Mil	-	1	1	3	31
Medearis, John, 12 May 1802	Mil	-	1	1	3	32
Medearis, John, 12 May 1802	Mil	-	1	1	3	33
Medearis, John, 12 May 1802	Mil	-	1	1	3	34
Woodside, John, 3 Jan 1806	Mil	-	1	1	3	35
Perry, William, 16 Nov 1805	Mil	-	1	1	3	36
Biggs, Zaccheus, 27 Oct 1807	Mil	-	1	1	3	37
Maxwell, James, assignee of (not stated) 15 Dec 1809	Mil	-	1	1	3	38
Baum, Martin, & Perry, S., in trust for the heirs of James Smith, deceased, 23 Feb 1810	Mil	-	1	1	3	39
Baum, Martin, & Perry, S., in trust for the heirs of James Smith, deceased, 23 Jan 1810	Mil	-	1	1	3	40
Halinsdoff, William, 1812	Mil	-	1	6	2	1
Vacant	Mil	-	1	6	2	2
Vacant	Mil	-	1	6	2	3
Vacant	Mil	-	1	6	2	4
Rosnick? [Bosnick? Romick?] Abraham, 18 Feb 1808	Mil	-	1	6	2	5
Vacant	Mil	-	1	6	2	6
Vacant	Mil	-	1	6	2	7
Vacant	Mil	-	1	6	2	8
Vacant	Mil	-	1	6	2	9
Vacant	Mil	-	1	6	2	10
Vacant	Mil	-	1	6	2	11
Vacant	Mil	-	1	6	2	12
Vacant	Mil	-	1	6	2	13
Thorn, Stephen, 30 Jan 1810	Mil	-	1	6	2	14
Vacant	Mil	-	1	6	2	15
Bryon, Charles, 31 Dec 1801	Mil	-	1	6	2	16
Greaffe, Fred[eric]k, 31 Dec 1801	Mil	-	1	6	2	17
Vacant	Mil	-	1	6	2	18
Vacant	Mil	-	1	6	2	19
Vacant	Mil	-	1	6	2	20
Vacant	Mil	-	1	6	2	21
Vacant	Mil	-	1	6	2	22
Vacant	Mil	-	1	6	2	23
Solinger, Adam, 31 Dec 1801	Mil	-	1	6	2	24

1705 Various C/-/012

100-Acre Lots:

Patentee & Location Date	*Location*					
Krugg, Philip, 31 Dec 1801	Mil	-	1	6	2	25
Reppert? [Ruppert?] Jacob, 31 Dec 1801	Mil	-	1	6	2	26
Mitchell, John, 31 Dec 1801	Mil	-	1	6	2	27
Vacant	Mil	-	1	6	2	28
Vacant	Mil	-	1	6	2	29
Vacant	Mil	-	1	6	2	30
Vacant	Mil	-	1	6	2	31
Vacant	Mil	-	1	6	2	32
Vacant	Mil	-	1	6	2	33
Vacant	Mil	-	1	6	2	34
Vacant	Mil	-	1	6	2	35
Vacant	Mil	-	1	6	2	36
Painter, George, 31 Dec 1801	Mil	-	1	6	2	37
Barber, Silas, 31 Dec 1801	Mil	-	1	6	2	38
Vacant [50-acre lot]	Mil	-	1	8	2	1E
Vacant [50-acre lot]	Mil	-	1	8	2	1W
Vacant [50-acre lot]	Mil	-	1	8	2	2W
Biggs, Zaccheus, 1812 [50-acre lot]	Mil	-	1	8	2	3E
Vacant [50-acre lot]	Mil	-	1	8	2	3W
Vacant [50-acre lot]	Mil	-	1	8	2	4E
Vacant [50-acre lot]	Mil	-	1	8	2	4W
Vacant [50-acre lot]	Mil	-	1	8	2	5E
Vacant [50-acre lot]	Mil	-	1	8	2	5W
Vacant [50-acre lot]	Mil	-	1	8	2	6E
Vacant [50-acre lot]	Mil	-	1	8	2	6W
Vacant [50-acre lot]	Mil	-	1	8	2	7E
Vacant [50-acre lot]	Mil	-	1	8	2	7W
Vacant [50-acre lot]	Mil	-	1	8	2	8E
Vacant [50-acre lot]	Mil	-	1	8	2	8W
Vacant [50-acre lot]	Mil	-	1	8	2	9E
Vacant [50-acre lot]	Mil	-	1	8	2	9W
Vacant [50-acre lot]	Mil	-	1	8	2	10E
Vacant [50-acre lot]	Mil	-	1	8	2	10W
Vacant [50-acre lot]	Mil	-	1	8	2	11E

1706 Various C/-/013

50-Acre lots:

Patentee & Location Date	*Location*					
Vacant	Mil	-	1	8	2	11W
Vacant	Mil	-	1	8	2	12E
Vacant	Mil	-	1	8	2	12W
Vacant	Mil	-	1	8	2	13E
Vacant	Mil	-	1	8	2	13W
Vacant	Mil	-	1	8	2	14E
Vacant	Mil	-	1	8	2	14W
Vacant	Mil	-	1	8	2	15E
Vacant	Mil	-	1	8	2	15W
Vacant	Mil	-	1	8	2	16E
Vacant	Mil	-	1	8	2	16W
Vacant	Mil	-	1	8	2	17E
Deardoff, Christian, 1812	Mil	-	1	8	2	17W
Vacant	Mil	-	1	8	2	18E
Vacant	Mil	-	1	8	2	18W
Vacant	Mil	-	1	8	2	19E

1706 [continued]

Vacant	Mil	-	1	8	2	19W
Vacant	Mil	-	1	8	2	20E
Vacant	Mil	-	1	8	2	20W
Vacant	Mil	-	1	8	2	21E
Vacant	Mil	-	1	8	2	21W
Vacant	Mil	-	1	8	2	22E
Vacant	Mil	-	1	8	2	22W
Vacant	Mil	-	1	8	2	23E
Vacant	Mil	-	1	8	2	23W
Heckewelder, John, 13 Mar 1807	Mil	-	1	8	2	24E
Vacant	Mil	-	1	8	2	24W
Biggs, Zaccheus, 9 Jan 1806	Mil	-	1	8	2	25E
Biggs, Zaccheus, 9 Jan 1806	Mil	-	1	8	2	25W
Vacant	Mil	-	1	8	2	26E
Vacant	Mil	-	1	8	2	26W
Vacant	Mil	-	1	8	2	27E
Vacant	Mil	-	1	8	2	27W
Vacant	Mil	-	1	8	2	28E
Vacant	Mil	-	1	8	2	28W

1707 Various C/-/014

50-Acre & 100-Acre Lots: Patentee & Location Date — *Location*

Vacant	Mil	-	1	8	2	29E
Humphries, David, 1 Mar 1808	Mil	-	1	8	2	29W
Coyle, Mark, 24 May 1800	Mil	-	1	8	2	30
La Fleche, John, 24 May 1800	Mil	-	1	8	2	31
Terms? Peter, 24 May 1800	Mil	-	1	8	2	32
Vance, Joseph, 31 Dec 1802	Mil	-	1	8	2	33E
Thompson, Thomas McKean, 13 Nov 1802	Mil	-	1	8	2	33W
Barber, George C., & Chetwood, Mary, 19 Jan 1804	Mil	-	1	8	2	34E
Sumner, T. E., & Blount, J. L., 12 Mar 1803	Mil	-	1	8	2	34W
Edminston, Samuel, 30 Aug 1803	Mil	-	1	8	2	35E
Halling, Solomon, 14 Jun 1803	Mil	-	1	8	2	35W
Vacant	Mil	-	1	8	2	36E
Vacant	Mil	-	1	8	2	36W
Faucher, John, & Grimke, --, 12 Aug 1802	Mil	-	1	8	2	37E
Walmsley, William, 4 Aug 1802	Mil	-	1	8	2	37W
Beck, John, 17 Sep 1801	Mil	-	1	8	3	1
Beck, John, 17 Sep 1801	Mil	-	1	8	3	2
Slingluff, --, & Fenestock [Fahnestock] --, 1812	Mil	-	1	8	3	3
Vacant	Mil	-	1	8	3	4
de Marellin, Anthony, 23 Dec 1805	Mil	-	1	8	3	5
de Marellin, Anthony, 23 Dec 1805	Mil	-	1	8	3	6
Sweeny, Hu[gh?] assignee of (James Boyd)	Mil	-	1	8	3	7
Service, John, 7 Jan 1806	Mil	-	1	8	3	8
Balsely, John, 7 Jan 1806	Mil	-	1	8	3	9
Shettar? [Shellar?] Catherine, 15 Dec 1806	Mil	-	1	8	3	10
Madden, Thomas, 28 Dec 1805	Mil	-	1	8	3	11
Means, Thomas, 4 Aug 1801	Mil	-	1	8	3	12
McDowell, John, 4 Aug 1801	Mil	-	1	8	3	13
McDowell, John, 4 Aug 1801	Mil	-	1	8	3	14
McDowell, John, 4 Aug 1801	Mil	-	1	8	3	15
McDowell, John, 4 Aug 1801	Mil	-	1	8	3	16
Buford, Abraham, 4 Aug 1801	Mil	-	1	8	3	17
Buford, Abraham, 4 Aug 1801	Mil	-	1	8	3	18
Buford, Abraham, 4 Aug 1801	Mil	-	1	8	3	19
Buford, Abraham, 4 Aug 1801	Mil	-	1	8	3	20
Buford, Abraham, 4 Aug 1801	Mil	-	1	8	3	21

1708 Various C/-/015

100-Acre Lots: Patentee & Location Date — *Location*

Beatty, William, 8 Aug 1801	Mil	-	1	8	3	22
Armstrong, Edward, 18 Dec 1804	Mil	-	1	8	3	23
Armstrong, Edward, 18 Dec 1804	Mil	-	1	8	3	24
Vacant	Mil	-	1	8	4	1
Vacant	Mil	-	1	8	4	2
Vacant	Mil	-	1	8	4	3
Slingluff, --, & Fenestock [Fahnestock] --, 1812	Mil	-	1	8	4	4
Vacant	Mil	-	1	8	4	5
Vacant	Mil	-	1	8	4	6
Vacant	Mil	-	1	8	4	7
Vacant	Mil	-	1	8	4	8
Vacant	Mil	-	1	8	4	9
Vacant	Mil	-	1	8	4	10
Vacant	Mil	-	1	8	4	11
Vacant	Mil	-	1	8	4	12
Vacant	Mil	-	1	8	4	13
Vacant	Mil	-	1	8	4	14
Cole, Andrew, 22 Jun 1810	Mil	-	1	8	4	15
McBeever? Angus, 17 Dec 1806	Mil	-	1	8	4	16
Ligget, Thomas, 8 Jan 1807	Mil	-	1	8	4	17
Vacant	Mil	-	1	8	4	18
Vacant	Mil	-	1	8	4	19
Vacant	Mil	-	1	8	4	20
Vacant	Mil	-	1	8	4	21
Vacant	Mil	-	1	8	4	22
Vacant	Mil	-	1	8	4	23
Slingluff, --, & Fenestock [Fahnestock] --, 1812	Mil	-	1	8	4	24
Vacant	Mil	-	1	8	4	25
Vacant	Mil	-	1	8	4	26
Vacant	Mil	-	1	8	4	27
Vacant	Mil	-	1	8	4	28
Vacant	Mil	-	1	8	4	29
Vacant	Mil	-	1	8	4	30
Vacant	Mil	-	1	8	4	31

1709 Various C/-/016

100-Acre Lots:

Patentee & Location Date	*Location*					
Greeger, Casher, 15 Dec 1806	Mil	-	1	8	4	32
Twinney, John, 17 Sep 1801	Mil	-	1	8	4	33
Cotter, James, 11 Jan 1806	Mil	-	1	8	4	34
Shafer, Jacob, assignee of (Joseph Cook) 11 Jan 1806	Mil	-	1	8	4	35
Shafer, Jacob, assignee of (Joseph Cook) 11 Jan 1806	Mil	-	1	8	4	36
Vacant	Mil	-	1	8	4	37
Vacant	Mil	-	1	8	4	38
Vacant	Mil	-	1	8	4	39
Vacant	Mil	-	1	8	4	40
Vacant	Mil	-	1	10	1	1
Vacant	Mil	-	1	10	1	2
Chappell, Samuel, 7 Jan 1805	Mil	-	1	10	1	3
Mason, David, assignee of (Zaccheus Biggs) 24 Dec 1804	Mil	-	1	10	1	4
Ward, John P., 4 Aug 1800	Mil	-	1	10	1	5
Ward, John P., 4 Aug 1800	Mil	-	1	10	1	6
Maynard, John, assignee of (Zaccheus Biggs) 24 Aug 1805	Mil	-	1	10	1	7
Maynard, John, assignee of (Zaccheus Biggs) 24 Aug 1805	Mil	-	1	10	1	8
Waldron, Nath[anie]l, assignee of (Zaccheus Biggs) 24 Aug 1805	Mil	-	1	10	1	9
Bernard, Richard, assignee of (Zaccheus Biggs) 24 Aug 1805	Mil	-	1	10	1	10
White, Edward, 4 Aug 1800	Mil	-	1	10	1	11
White, Edward, 4 Aug 1800	Mil	-	1	10	1	12
Kessinger, Charles, 7 May 1805	Mil	-	1	10	1	13
Siggins? [Liggins?] William, 1812	Mil	-	1	10	1	14
Lawson, Nathan, assignee of (Zaccheus Biggs) 14 Jan 1805	Mil	-	1	10	1	15
Walburn, Thomas, assignee of (Zaccheus Biggs) 24 Aug 1805	Mil	-	1	10	1	16
Vacant	Mil	-	1	10	1	17
Sowers? [Lowers?] William, assignee of (Zaccheus Biggs) 8 Mar 1805	Mil	-	1	10	1	18
Mason, David, assignee of (Zaccheus Biggs)	Mil	-	1	10	1	19
McClelland, John, assignee of (John McCreary) 8 Mar 1805	Mil	-	1	10	1	20
Cowan, Edward, 4 Aug 1800	Mil	-	1	10	1	21
Cowan, Edward, 4 Aug 1800	Mil	-	1	10	1	22
Ralton, John, assignee of (Zaccheus Biggs) 24 Aug 1805	Mil	-	1	10	1	23
Wheeler, Benjamin, assignee of (Zaccheus Biggs) 24 Aug 1805	Mil	-	1	10	1	24
Norton, Amb., 7 May 1805	Mil	-	1	10	1	25

1710 Various C/-/017

100-Acre Lots:

Patentee & Location Date	*Location*					
Prince, Samuel, assignee of (John Gloss? [Glass?]) 7 May 1805	Mil	-	1	10	1	26
Fetard? [Felard?] Benjamin, 4 Aug 1800	Mil	-	1	10	1	27
Fetard? [Felard?] Benjamin, 4 Aug 1800	Mil	-	1	10	1	28
Whipple, Joseph, assignee of (Zaccheus Biggs) 17 Dec 1804	Mil	-	1	10	1	29
Chapin, Joel, assignee of (Zaccheus Biggs) 17 Dec 1804	Mil	-	1	10	1	30
Londess, Roger, assignee of (Daniel Hinds) 7 May 1805	Mil	-	1	10	1	31
Vacant	Mil	-	1	10	1	32
Vacant	Mil	-	1	10	1	33
Brown, James, Junior, assignee of (Abraham Cazier? [Lazier?]) 20 Feb 1809	Mil	-	1	10	1	34
Vacant	Mil	-	1	10	1	35
Barr, John, 7 May 1805	Mil	-	1	10	1	36
Fetard? [Felard?] Benjamin, 4 Aug 1800	Mil	-	1	10	1	37
Fetard? [Felard?] Benjamin, 4 Aug 1800	Mil	-	1	10	1	38
Schlokerman, Christ[ophe]r, 7 Jan 1805	Mil	-	1	10	1	39
Young, John, heirs of, 14 Jan 1807	Mil	-	1	10	1	40
Bryant, John, 10 Apr 1805	Mil	-	2	2	3	1
Hilger, Henry, 26 May 1806	Mil	-	2	2	3	2
Stokely, Joseph, 26 Oct 1810	Mil	-	2	2	3	3
Stokely, Joseph, 26 Oct 1810	Mil	-	2	2	3	4
Rice, George, 8 Apr 1805	Mil	-	2	2	3	5
Rice, George, 8 Apr 1805	Mil	-	2	2	3	6
Rice, George, 8 Apr 1805	Mil	-	2	2	3	7
Vacant	Mil	-	2	2	3	8
Bickham, John, 12 Sep 1805	Mil	-	2	2	3	9
Jackoby [Jacobi] Nicholas, 30 May 1806	Mil	-	2	2	3	10
Stokely, Joseph, 16 Nov 1810	Mil	-	2	2	3	11
Stokely, Joseph, 16 Nov 1810	Mil	-	2	2	3	12
Callis, William, 24 Feb 1806	Mil	-	2	2	3	13
Callis, William, 24 Feb 1806	Mil	-	2	2	3	14
Walton, William, assignee of (George Beymer)	Mil	-	2	2	3	15
Walton, William, assignee of (George Beymer) 8 Apr 1805	Mil	-	2	2	3	16
Walton, William, assignee of (George Beymer) 8 Apr 1805	Mil	-	2	2	3	17
Thompson, Thomas, heirs of the deviser of, 10 Apr 1805	Mil	-	2	2	3	18
Thompson, Thomas, heirs of the deviser of, 10 Apr 1805	Mil	-	2	2	3	19

1711 Various C/-/018

100-Acre Lots:

Patentee & Location Date	*Location*					
Rich, Nathaniel [assignee of?] (William Talbert?) 8 Mar 1804	Mil	-	2	2	3	20
Barber, John, 12 Mar 1803	Mil	-	2	2	3	21
Miller, John, 25 May 1802	Mil	-	2	2	3	22
Finley, John, 21 Sep 1801	Mil	-	2	2	3	23
Finley, John, 21 Sep 1801	Mil	-	2	2	3	24
Vernon, Frederick, 30 Dec 1802	Mil	-	2	2	3	25
Vernon, Frederick, 30 Dec 1802	Mil	-	2	2	3	26
Crosby, Nathan, 12 Mar 1803	Mil	-	2	2	3	27
Cole, Abner, 17 Sep 1801	Mil	-	2	2	3	28
Rich, Samuel, 17 Dec 1801	Mil	-	2	2	3	29
Greenland, James, 24 Dec 1802	Mil	-	2	2	3	30
Knapp, Uzal, 24 Dec 1802	Mil	-	2	2	3	31
Farrall, William, assignee of (John? Price)	Mil	-	2	2	3	32
Bright, Levi, assignee of (Mitchell Kershaw?) 22 Feb 1805	Mil	-	2	2	3	33
Timmons, Robert, 31 Dec 1802	Mil	-	2	2	3	34
Kershaw, Mitchell, 31 Dec 1802	Mil	-	2	2	3	35
Snow, Thomas, heirs of, 18 Sep 1801	Mil	-	2	2	3	36
White, Philip, 17 Sep 1801	Mil	-	2	2	3	37
Beaham, James 18 Sep 1801	Mil	-	2	2	3	38
Vernon? [Vornan] Frederick, 30 Dec 1802	Mil	-	2	2	3	39
Vernon? [Vornan] Frederick, 30 Dec 1802	Mil	-	2	2	3	40
Pomney? [Tomney?] Ralph, assignee of (Zaccheus Biggs) 18 May 1804	Mil	-	2	3	4	1
Pomney? [Tomney?] Ralph, assignee of (Zaccheus Biggs) 18 May 1804	Mil	-	2	3	4	2
Norton, Hezekiah, 24 May 1804	Mil	-	2	3	4	3
Frazier, Charles, 18 Feb 1804	Mil	-	2	3	4	4
Reilly, John, 1 Jun 1804	Mil	-	2	3	4	5
Howard, John, 24 May 1804	Mil	-	2	3	4	6
Coleman, John, 24 May 1804	Mil	-	2	3	4	7
Carbett, John, 22 May 1804	Mil	-	2	3	4	8
Vacant	Mil	-	2	3	4	9
Lockey, Philip, 7 Nov 1804	Mil	-	2	3	4	10
Reilly, John, 1 Jun 1804	Mil	-	2	3	4	11
Reilly, John, 1 Jun 1804	Mil	-	2	3	4	12
Gill, Jos[eph? or Josiah?] assignee of (Zaccheus Biggs) 24 Nov 1804	Mil	-	2	3	4	13
Wentworth, Levi, 18 Feb 1804	Mil	-	2	3	4	14

1712 Various C/-/019

100-Acre Lots:

Patentee & Location Date	*Location*					
Morgan, Charles, 7 May 1805	Mil	-	2	3	4	15
Miller, Isaac, 26 Nov 1804	Mil	-	2	3	4	16
Spence, Daniel, assignee of (Zaccheus Biggs) 31 Jul 1804	Mil	-	2	3	4	17
Bacon, William, assignee of (Zaccheus Biggs) 31 Jul 1804	Mil	-	2	3	4	18
Mullin, Anthony, assignee of (George Beemer) 22 May 1804	Mil	-	2	3	4	19
Morton, Hezekiah, 24 May 1804	Mil	-	2	3	4	20
Morton, Hezekiah, 24 May 1804	Mil	-	2	3	4	21
Sheriden, James, assignee of (George Beemer) 1 May 1806	Mil	-	2	3	4	22
Plumline, Charles, 19 Jun 1806	Mil	-	2	3	4	23
Vacant	Mil	-	2	3	4	24
Vacant	Mil	-	2	3	4	25
Vacant	Mil	-	2	3	4	26
Steavens, Ira? assignee of (William --?) 1 May 1806	Mil	-	2	3	4	27
Tophand, Ezekiel, 26 May 1804	Mil	-	2	3	4	28
Welsh, John, 26 May 1804	Mil	-	2	3	4	29
Shaw, Sylvanus, assignee of the heir of (Isaac? Metzger?) 31 Jul 1804	Mil	-	2	3	4	30
Shaw, Sylvanus, assignee of the heir of (Isaac? Metzger) 31 Jul 1804	Mil	-	2	3	4	31
Shaw, Sylvanus, assignee of the heir of (Isaac? Metzger?) 31 Jul 1804	Mil	-	2	3	4	32
Bacomb, Samuel, assignee of (Zaccheus Biggs) 18 May 1804	Mil	-	2	3	4	33
Henderson, William, assignee of (Zaccheus Biggs)	Mil	-	2	3	4	34
Belt, John Sprigg, 6 Dec 1804	Mil	-	2	3	4	35
Belt, John Sprigg, 6 Dec 1804	Mil	-	2	3	4	36
Belt, John Sprigg, 6 Dec 1804	Mil	-	2	3	4	37
Vacant	Mil	-	2	3	4	38
Vacant	Mil	-	2	3	4	39
Vacant	Mil	-	2	3	4	40

1713 Various C/-/ *

100-Acre Lots:

Patentee & Location Date	*Location*					
Vacant	Mil	-	2	5	1	1
Vacant	Mil	-	2	5	1	2
Vacant	Mil	-	2	5	1	3
Vacant	Mil	-	2	5	1	4
Vacant	Mil	-	2	5	1	5
Vacant	Mil	-	2	5	1	6
Vacant	Mil	-	2	5	1	7
Vacant	Mil	-	2	5	1	8
Vacant	Mil	-	2	5	1	9
Vacant	Mil	-	2	5	1	10
Vacant	Mil	-	2	5	1	11
Vacant	Mil	-	2	5	1	12

1713 [continued]

Vacant	Mil	-	2	5	1	13
Vacant	Mil	-	2	5	1	14
Vacant	Mil	-	2	5	1	15
Vacant	Mil	-	2	5	1	16
Vacant	Mil	-	2	5	1	17
Vacant	Mil	-	2	5	1	18
Vacant	Mil	-	2	5	1	19
Vacant	Mil	-	2	5	1	20
Vacant	Mil	-	2	5	1	21
Vacant	Mil	-	2	5	1	22
Vacant	Mil	-	2	5	1	23
Vacant	Mil	-	2	5	1	24
Vacant	Mil	-	2	5	1	25
Vacant	Mil	-	2	5	1	26
Vacant	Mil	-	2	5	1	27
Vacant	Mil	-	2	5	1	28
Vacant	Mil	-	2	5	1	29
Vacant	Mil	-	2	5	1	30
Vacant	Mil	-	2	5	1	31
Vacant	Mil	-	2	5	1	32
Vacant	Mil	-	2	5	1	33
Vacant	Mil	-	2	5	1	34
Vacant	Mil	-	2	5	1	35
Vacant	Mil	-	2	5	1	36
Vacant	Mil	-	2	5	1	37
Vacant	Mil	-	2	5	1	38
Vacant	Mil	-	2	5	1	39
Vacant	Mil	-	2	5	1	40
Vacant	Mil	-	2	5	1	41

*This township has been placed in sequence; it will be found on the last page of source.

1714 None C/-/019

100-Acre Lots:
Patentee & Location Date — *Location*

Vacant	Mil	-	2	5	2	1
Vacant	Mil	-	2	5	2	2
Vacant	Mil	-	2	5	2	3
Vacant	Mil	-	2	5	2	4
Vacant	Mil	-	2	5	2	5
Vacant	Mil	-	2	5	2	6
Vacant	Mil	-	2	5	2	7
Vacant	Mil	-	2	5	2	8

1715 Various C/-/020

100-Acre Lots:
Patentee & Location Date — *Location*

Vacant	Mil	-	2	5	2	9
Vacant	Mil	-	2	5	2	10
Vacant	Mil	-	2	5	2	11
Vacant	Mil	-	2	5	2	12
Vacant	Mil	-	2	5	2	13
Vacant	Mil	-	2	5	2	14
Vacant	Mil	-	2	5	2	15
Vacant	Mil	-	2	5	2	16
Vacant	Mil	-	2	5	2	17
Vacant	Mil	-	2	5	2	18
Vacant	Mil	-	2	5	2	19
Vacant	Mil	-	2	5	2	20
Vacant	Mil	-	2	5	2	21
Vacant	Mil	-	2	5	2	22
Vacant	Mil	-	2	5	2	23
Vacant	Mil	-	2	5	2	24
Thorn, Stephen, 30 Jan 1810	Mil	-	2	5	2	25
Vacant	Mil	-	2	5	2	26
Vacant	Mil	-	2	5	2	27
Vacant	Mil	-	2	5	2	28
Vacant	Mil	-	2	5	2	29
Vacant	Mil	-	2	5	2	30
Vacant	Mil	-	2	5	2	31
Vacant	Mil	-	2	5	2	32
Vacant	Mil	-	2	5	2	33
McCully, George, 21 Sep 1801	Mil	-	2	5	2	34
McCully, George, 21 Sep 1801	Mil	-	2	5	2	35
McCully, George, 21 Sep 1801	Mil	-	2	5	2	36
Vacant	Mil	-	2	5	2	37
Leonard, Jacob, 22 Aug 1801	Mil	-	2	5	2	38
Vacant	Mil	-	2	5	2	39
Vacant	Mil	-	2	5	3	1
Vacant	Mil	-	2	5	3	2
Vacant	Mil	-	2	5	3	3
Vacant	Mil	-	2	5	3	4

1716 None C/-/021

100-Acre Lots:
Patentee & Location Date — *Location*

Vacant	Mil	-	2	5	3	5
Vacant	Mil	-	2	5	3	6
Vacant	Mil	-	2	5	3	7
Vacant	Mil	-	2	5	3	8
Vacant	Mil	-	2	5	3	9
Vacant	Mil	-	2	5	3	10
Vacant	Mil	-	2	5	3	11
Vacant	Mil	-	2	5	3	12
Vacant	Mil	-	2	5	3	13
Vacant	Mil	-	2	5	3	14
Vacant	Mil	-	2	5	3	15
Vacant	Mil	-	2	5	3	16
Vacant	Mil	-	2	5	3	17
Vacant	Mil	-	2	5	3	18
Vacant	Mil	-	2	5	3	19
Vacant	Mil	-	2	5	3	20
Vacant	Mil	-	2	5	3	21
Vacant	Mil	-	2	5	3	22
Vacant	Mil	-	2	5	3	23
Vacant	Mil	-	2	5	3	24
Vacant	Mil	-	2	5	3	25
Vacant	Mil	-	2	5	3	26
Vacant	Mil	-	2	5	3	27
Vacant	Mil	-	2	5	3	28
Vacant	Mil	-	2	5	3	29
Vacant	Mil	-	2	5	3	30
Vacant	Mil	-	2	5	3	31
Vacant	Mil	-	2	5	3	32
Vacant	Mil	-	2	5	3	33
Vacant	Mil	-	2	5	3	34
Vacant	Mil	-	2	5	3	35
Vacant	Mil	-	2	5	3	36*
Vacant	Mil	-	2	5	3	37
Vacant	Mil	-	2	5	3	38
Vacant	Mil	-	2	5	3	39
Vacant	Mil	-	2	5	3	40

*Pencilled note: "Forks of road to Cadiz & Morristown."

1717 Various C/-/022

100-Acre Lots:
Patentee & Location Date — *Location*

1717 [continued]

Vacant	Mil	-	2	5	3	41
Vacant	Mil	-	2	6	1	1
Mills, James, assignee of (John Heckewelder?) 24 Feb 1806	Mil	-	2	6	1	2
Shirtliffe, Amasa, assignee of the heirs of (Richard Gernon?) 2 Jan 1805	Mil	-	2	6	1	3
Morrison, David, assignee of the heirs of (Richard Gernon) 2 Jan 1805	Mil	-	2	6	1	4
Vacant	Mil	-	2	6	1	5
Ralston, Andrew, assignee of (Richard Gernon) 2 Jan 1805	Mil	-	2	6	1	6
Rouse? Thomas, 31 Oct 1803	Mil	-	2	6	1	7
Rouse? Thomas, 31 Oct 1803	Mil	-	2	6	1	8
Rouse, Thomas [pencilled]	Mil	-	2	6	1	9
van Ranselaar, N., 22 Aug 1801	Mil	-	2	6	1	10
Vacant	Mil	-	2	6	1	11
Vacant	Mil	-	2	6	1	12
van Ranselaar, N., 22 Aug 1801	Mil	-	2	6	1	13
van Ranselaar, N., 22 Aug 1801	Mil	-	2	6	1	14
Vacant	Mil	-	2	6	1	15
Vacant	Mil	-	2	6	3	1
Vacant	Mil	-	2	6	3	2
Vacant	Mil	-	2	6	3	3
Vacant	Mil	-	2	6	3	4
Chapman, Elijah, 29 Dec 1801	Mil	-	2	6	3	5
Chapman, Elijah, 29 Dec 1801	Mil	-	2	6	3	6
Vacant	Mil	-	2	6	3	7
Vacant	Mil	-	2	6	3	8
Vacant	Mil	-	2	6	3	9
Vacant	Mil	-	2	6	3	10
Vacant	Mil	-	2	6	3	11
Vacant	Mil	-	2	6	3	12
Vacant	Mil	-	2	6	3	13
Vacant	Mil	-	2	6	3	14
Chapman, Elijah, 29 Dec 1801	Mil	-	2	6	3	15
Meecher, M., 31 Dec 1801	Mil	-	2	6	3	16
Luce, Jonathan, 29 Dec 1801	Mil	-	2	6	3	17
Vacant	Mil	-	2	6	3	18
Vacant	Mil	-	2	6	3	19

1718 Various C/-/023

100-Acre Lots:

Patentee & Location Date	*Location*					
Vacant	Mil	-	2	6	3	20
Vacant	Mil	-	2	6	3	21
Vacant	Mil	-	2	6	3	22
Vacant	Mil	-	2	6	3	23
Vacant	Mil	-	2	6	3	24
Moore, John, 17 Aug 1801	Mil	-	2	6	3	25
Biggs, Ben, 17 Aug 1801	Mil	-	2	6	3	26
Reed, Jacob, 22 Aug 1801	Mil	-	2	6	3	27
Vacant	Mil	-	2	6	3	28
Vacant	Mil	-	2	6	3	29
Vacant	Mil	-	2	6	3	30
Vacant	Mil	-	2	6	3	31
Reed, Jacob, 22 Aug 1801	Mil	-	2	6	3	32
Reed, Jacob, 22 Aug 1801	Mil	-	2	6	3	33
Biggs, Ben, 17 Aug 1801	Mil	-	2	6	3	34
Biggs, Ben, 17 Aug 1801	Mil	-	2	6	3	35
Mills, James, assignee of the heirs of (John Heckewelder) 24 Feb 1806	Mil	-	2	7	3	1
Mills, James, assignee of the heirs of (John Heckewelder) 24 Feb 1806	Mil	-	2	7	3	2
Vacant	Mil	-	2	7	3	3
Vacant	Mil	-	2	7	3	4
Vacant	Mil	-	2	7	3	5
Vacant	Mil	-	2	7	3	6
Stanberry, Jonas, 30 Sep 1806	Mil	-	2	7	3	7
Cummins, William, assignee of (John Heckewelder) 27 Feb 1809	Mil	-	2	7	3	8
Vacant	Mil	-	2	7	3	9
Vacant	Mil	-	2	7	3	10
Stanberry, Jonas, 30 Sep 1806	Mil	-	2	7	3	11
Stanberry, Jonas, 30 Sep 1806	Mil	-	2	7	3	12
Vacant	Mil	-	2	7	3	13
Vacant	Mil	-	2	7	3	14
Vacant	Mil	-	2	7	3	15
Vacant	Mil	-	2	7	3	16
Vacant	Mil	-	2	7	3	17
Stanberry, Jonas, 30 Sep 1806	Mil	-	2	7	3	18

1719 Various C/-/024

100-Acre Lots:

Patentee & Location Date	*Location*					
Vacant	Mil	-	2	7	3	19
Vacant	Mil	-	2	7	3	20
Vacant	Mil	-	2	7	3	21
Vacant	Mil	-	2	7	3	22
Vacant	Mil	-	2	7	3	23
Vacant	Mil	-	2	7	3	24
Vacant	Mil	-	2	7	3	25
Vacant	Mil	-	2	7	3	26
Vacant	Mil	-	2	7	3	27
Vacant	Mil	-	2	7	3	28
Vacant	Mil	-	2	7	3	29
Vacant	Mil	-	2	7	3	30
Vacant	Mil	-	2	7	3	31
Vacant	Mil	-	2	7	3	32
Vacant	Mil	-	2	7	3	33
Vacant	Mil	-	2	7	3	34
Vacant	Mil	-	2	7	3	35
Vacant	Mil	-	2	7	3	36
Vacant	Mil	-	2	7	3	37
Vacant	Mil	-	2	7	3	38
Vacant	Mil	-	2	7	3	39
Selden, Charles, 3 Aug 1801	Mil	-	2	7	4	1
Selden, Charles, 3 Aug 1801	Mil	-	2	7	4	2
Trumbull, Charles, 29 Dec 1801	Mil	-	2	7	4	3
Vacant	Mil	-	2	7	4	4
Vacant	Mil	-	2	7	4	5
Smith, Arthur, heir of, 16 Nov 1802	Mil	-	2	7	4	6
Winans, William, assignee of (Jonas Stanberry) 18 Feb 1805	Mil	-	2	7	4	7

1719 [continued]

Thorne, Stephen, 30 Jan 1810	Mil	-	2	7	4	8
Thorne, Stephen, 30 Jan 1810	Mil	-	2	7	4	9
Vacant	Mil	-	2	7	4	10
Trumbull, Charles, 29 Dec 1801	Mil	-	2	7	4	11
Hamilton, John A., 3 Aug 1801	Mil	-	2	7	4	12
Hamilton, John A., 3 Aug 1801	Mil	-	2	7	4	13
Trumbull, Charles, 29 Dec 1801	Mil	-	2	7	4	14

1720 Various C/-/025

100-Acre Lots:

Patentee & Location Date	*Location*					
Thorn[e] Stephen, 30 Jan 1810	Mil	-	2	7	4	15
Vacant	Mil	-	2	7	4	16
Vacant	Mil	-	2	7	4	17
Everly, George, 19 Dec 1805	Mil	-	2	7	4	18
Vacant	Mil	-	2	7	4	19
Vacant	Mil	-	2	7	4	20
Vacant	Mil	-	2	7	4	21
Vacant	Mil	-	2	7	4	22
Bogart, Nicholas, -- Sep 1806	Mil	-	2	7	4	23
Hamilton, John A., 3 Aug 1801	Mil	-	2	7	4	24
Stanberry, Jonas, 2 Jul 1806	Mil	-	2	7	4	25
Stanberry, Jonas, 2 Jul 1806	Mil	-	2	7	4	26
Stanberry, Jonas, 1 Apr 1808	Mil	-	2	7	4	27
Kurtz, Michael, assignee of [assignee's name is illegible] 13 Feb 1809	Mil	-	2	7	4	28
Vacant	Mil	-	2	7	4	29
Vacant	Mil	-	2	7	4	30
Vacant	Mil	-	2	8	4	1
Tubbs? Samuel, assignee of [assignee's name is illegible] 1 Oct 1808	Mil	-	2	8	4	2
Weaver, John, 27 Oct 1801	Mil	-	2	8	4	3
Shreve, Godfrey, 27 Oct 1801	Mil	-	2	8	4	4
Gawley? [Gaisley?] John, assignee of [assignee's name is illegible] 16 Nov 1803	Mil	-	2	8	4	5
Stillman, Jon[athan? or Jonah?] Junior, 17 Sep 1801	Mil	-	2	8	4	6
Stillman, Jon[athan? or Jonah?] Junior, 17 Sep 1801	Mil	-	2	8	4	7
Baltzell, Charles, 17 Sep 1801	Mil	-	2	8	4	8
Baltzell, Charles, 17 Sep 1801	Mil	-	2	8	4	9
Baltzell, Charles, 17 Sep 1801	Mil	-	2	8	4	10
Heckewelder, John, 7 Mar 1808	Mil	-	2	8	4	11
Heckewelder, John, 7 Mar 1808	Mil	-	2	8	4	12
Tellard, Edward, 17 Sep 1801	Mil	-	2	8	4	13
Tellard, Edward, 17 Sep 1801	Mil	-	2	8	4	14
Stillman, Jon[athan? or Jonah?] 17 Sep 1801	Mil	-	2	8	4	15
Stillman, Jon[athan? or Jonah?] 17 Sep 1801	Mil	-	2	8	4	16
Tellard? [Tillard?] Edward, 17 Sep 1801	Mil	-	2	8	4	17
Tellard? [Tillard?] Edward, 17 Sep 1801	Mil	-	2	8	4	18
Bohn, --, & Slingluff, --, 13 Jan 1814	Mil	-	2	8	4	19*

*Comprises 44.8 acres only.

1721 Various C/-/026

100-Acre Lots:

Patentee & Location Date	*Location*					
Shetlar? [Shetter?] Michael, 1812	Mil	-	2	8	4	20
Parkhill, David, 6 Dec 1808	Mil	-	2	10	2	1
Gaylord, Joel, 17 Dec 1807	Mil	-	2	10	2	2
Hains, John, assignee of (--? Mosser) 30 Jun 1808	Mil	-	2	10	2	3
Andrew, John, 1 May 1806	Mil	-	2	10	2	4
Schuster, Martin, 22 Jul 1803	Mil	-	2	10	2	5
Allen, John, assignee of (James Bruffe) 27 Feb 1806	Mil	-	2	10	2	6
Bruffe, James, 5 Sep 1800	Mil	-	2	10	2	7
Bruffe, James, 5 Sep 1800	Mil	-	2	10	2	8
Barber, Fran[ci]s, heirs of, 19 Jan 1804	Mil	-	2	10	2	9
Bruff, James, 5 Sep 1800	Mil	-	2	10	2	10
Vacant [pencilled notation: Tuckerman's? R(eserve?)]	Mil	-	2	10	2	11
Falkner [Faulkner] Sally, 1812	Mil	-	2	10	2	12
Nourse, Michael, 21 Sep 1810	Mil	-	2	10	2	13
Clark, Nath[aniel? or Nathan?] assignee of (--? Mosser) 19 Oct 1808	Mil	-	2	10	2	14
Thorn[e] Stephen, 30 Jan 1810	Mil	-	2	10	2	15
Nourse, Michael, 21 Sep 1810	Mil	-	2	10	2	16
Melone [Malone] John, 10 Jun 1807	Mil	-	2	10	2	17
Faulkner, Sally, 1812	Mil	-	2	10	2	18
Hathaway, Shadrach, heirs of, 21 Aug 1806	Mil	-	2	10	2	19
Barber, Fran[ci]s, 19 Jan 1804	Mil	-	2	10	2	20
Sweet, Jonathan, 4 Sep 1801	Mil	-	2	10	2	21
Barber, Francis, heirs of, 19 Jan 1804	Mil	-	2	10	2	22
Barber, Francis, heirs of, 19 Jan 1804	Mil	-	2	10	2	23
Vacant	Mil	-	2	10	2	24

1721 [continued]

Patentee & Location Date			Location			
Vacant	Mil	-	2	10	2	25
Vacant	Mil	-	2	10	2	26
Vacant	Mil	-	2	10	2	27
Vacant	Mil	-	2	10	2	28
Vacant	Mil	-	2	10	2	29
Vacant	Mil	-	2	10	2	30
Vacant	Mil	-	2	10	2	31
Vacant	Mil	-	2	10	2	32
Vacant	Mil	-	2	10	2	33

1722 Various C/-/027

100-Acre Lots:

Patentee & Location Date			*Location*			
Vacant	Mil	-	2	10	2	34
Vacant	Mil	-	2	10	2	35
Beatty, Zaccheus A., 1 Jan 1807	Mil	-	2	11	4	1
Moss, Reuben, assignee of (Michael? Nourse) 16 Nov 1804	Mil	-	3	1	1	1
Corneil? [Carneil?] John, heirs of, 16 Nov 1804	Mil	-	3	1	1	2
Smith, Enoch, heirs of (Pencilled: Michael Nourse) 16 Nov 1804	Mil	-	3	1	1	3
Burnette? [Burnelle?] Thomas, assignee of the heirs of (Michael Nourse) 15 Aug 1805	Mil	-	3	1	1	4
Williams, John, 25 May 1802	Mil	-	3	1	1	5
Gass, Henry, 25 May 1802	Mil	-	3	1	1	6
Stokely, Joseph, 16 Nov 1810	Mil	-	3	1	1	7
Vacant	Mil	-	3	1	1	8
Vacant	Mil	-	3	1	1	9
McNair, John, 8 Apr 1805	Mil	-	3	1	1	10
Cannor, Pk [Patrick?] 25 May 1802	Mil	-	3	1	1	11
McElroy, John, 25 May 1802	Mil	-	3	1	1	12
Roberts, Pat[ric]k, 25 May 1802	Mil	-	3	1	1	13
Smalley, Thomas, 31 Mar 1803	Mil	-	3	1	1	14
Beetley, Isaac, 31 Mar 1803	Mil	-	3	1	1	15
Vacant	Mil	-	3	1	1	16
Vacant	Mil	-	3	1	1	17
Bierce, William, 8 Apr 1805	Mil	-	3	1	1	18
Rose, John, assignee of the devisees of (Joseph Strong) 4 Apr 1805	Mil	-	3	1	1	19
Rose, John, assignee of the devisees of (Joseph Strong) 4 Apr 1805	Mil	-	3	1	1	20
Hagan, Peter, 25 May 1802	Mil	-	3	1	1	21
McCrosson, Patrick, 25 May 1802	Mil	-	3	1	1	22
Smith, Nath[an] assignee of the heirs of (John? Smith?) 27 Mar 1805	Mil	-	3	1	1	23
Chambers, Stephen, executors of, 23 Jan 1801	Mil	-	3	1	1	24
Chambers, Stephen, executors of, 23 Jan 1801	Mil	-	3	1	1	25
Verry, Jonathan, 31 Mar 1803	Mil	-	3	1	1	26
Smith, Nathan, assignee of the heir of (John Smith) 27 Mar 1805	Mil	-	3	1	1	27
Smith, Nathan, assignee of the heir of (John Smith) 27 Mar 1805	Mil	-	3	1	1	28
Rose, John, assignee of the devisee of (Joseph Strong) 4 Apr 1805	Mil	-	3	1	1	29
Rose, John, assignee of the devisee of (Joseph Strong) 4 Apr 1805	Mil	-	3	1	1	30
Vacant	Mil	-	3	1	1	31

1723 Various C/-/028

100-Acre Lots:

Patentee & Location Date			*Location*			
Vacant	Mil	-	3	1	1	32
Gray, Alexander, 17 Jan 1809	Mil	-	3	1	1	33
William, David, assignee of (Zaccheus A. Beatty) 17 Jan 1809	Mil	-	3	1	1	34
William, David, assignee of (Zaccheus A. Beatty) 17 Jan 1809	Mil	-	3	1	1	35
Miller, Asa, assignee of (Zaccheus A. Beatty) 28 Nov 1808	Mil	-	3	1	1	36
Wyman, Joshua, assignee of (Zaccheus A. Beatty) 28 Nov 1808	Mil	-	3	1	1	37
Buff, William, assignee of (Zaccheus A. Beatty) 10 Aug 1809	Mil	-	3	1	1	38
Vacant	Mil	-	3	1	1	39
Chambers, Stever, executors of, 23 Jan 1801	Mil	-	3	1	1	40
Vacant	Mil	-	3	5	1	1
McEven, John, 22 Aug 1801	Mil	-	3	5	1	2
Vacant	Mil	-	3	5	1	3
Lehea? [Schea?] John, 3 Aug 1801	Mil	-	3	5	1	4
Perez, Peter, 3 Aug 1801	Mil	-	3	5	1	5
Blakely, Matthew, 1 Jun 1808	Mil	-	3	5	1	6
Maxwell, Anthony, 22 Aug 1801	Mil	-	3	5	1	7
Vacant	Mil	-	3	5	1	8
Vacant	Mil	-	3	5	1	9
Maxwell, Anthony, 22 Aug 1801	Mil	-	3	5	1	10
Hegins, Benoni, 3 Aug 1801	Mil	-	3	5	1	11
Perez, Peter, 3 Aug 1801	Mil	-	3	5	1	12
Perez, Peter, 3 Aug 1801	Mil	-	3	5	1	13
Stark, Arch[ibal]d, 3 Aug 1801	Mil	-	3	5	1	14
Marckle, Charles, 7 Sep 1801	Mil	-	3	5	1	15
Vacant	Mil	-	3	5	1	16
Vacant	Mil	-	3	5	1	17
Marckle, Charles, 7 Sep 1801	Mil	-	3	5	1	18
Starke, Arch[ibal]d, 3 Aug 1801	Mil	-	3	5	1	19
Perez, Peter, 3 Aug 1801	Mil	-	3	5	1	20
Stark, John, 3 Aug 1801	Mil	-	3	5	1	21
Stark, John, 3 Aug 1801	Mil	-	3	5	1	22

1723 [continued]

Marckle, Charles, 7 Sep 1801	Mil	-	3	5	1	23
Vacant	Mil	-	3	5	1	24
Vacant	Mil	-	3	5	1	25

1724 Various C/-/029

100-Acre Lots:

Patentee & Location Date	*Location*					
Knox, William, 3 Aug 1801	Mil	-	3	5	1	26
Stark, John, 3 Aug 1801	Mil	-	3	5	1	27
Stark, John, 3 Aug 1801	Mil	-	3	5	1	28
Stark, John, 3 Aug 1801	Mil	-	3	5	1	29
Stark, John, 3 Aug 1801	Mil	-	3	5	1	30
Stark, John, 3 Aug 1801	Mil	-	3	5	1	31
Stark, John, 3 Aug 1801	Mil	-	3	5	1	32
Knox, William, 3 Aug 1801	Mil	-	3	5	1	33
Vacant	Mil	-	3	5	1	34
McCay, John, 4 Aug 1801	Mil	-	3	6	4	1
McCay, John, 4 Aug 1801	Mil	-	3	6	4	2
Farrar, Field, heir of, 24 Oct 1803	Mil	-	3	6	4	3
Farrar, Field, [heir of?] 24 Oct 1803	Mil	-	3	6	4	4
Farrar, Field, [heir of?] 24 Oct 1803	Mil	-	3	6	4	5
Martin, Louis D., 9 Feb 1805	Mil	-	3	6	4	6
Martin, Louis D., 9 Feb 1805	Mil	-	3	6	4	7
Martin, Louis D., 9 Feb 1805	Mil	-	3	6	4	8
Vacant	Mil	-	3	6	4	9
Vacant	Mil	-	3	6	4	10
Stanberry, Jonas, 2 Feb 1810	Mil	-	3	7	1	1
Stanberry, Jonas, 2 Feb 1810	Mil	-	3	7	1	2
Vacant	Mil	-	3	7	1	3
Knox, Mathew*	Mil	-	3	7	1	4
Knox, Mathew	Mil	-	3	7	1	5
Vacant	Mil	-	3	7	1	6
Thorn[e] Stephen, 30 Jan 1810	Mil	-	3	7	1	7
Stanberry, Jonas, 2 Feb 1810	Mil	-	3	7	1	8
Bohn, --, & Slingluff, --, 15 Dec 1810	Mil	-	3	7	1	9
Thorn[e] Stephen, 30 Jan 1810	Mil	-	3	7	1	10
Vacant	Mil	-	3	7	1	11
Vacant	Mil	-	3	7	1	12
Vacant	Mil	-	3	7	1	13
Vacant	Mil	-	3	7	1	14
Vacant	Mil	-	3	7	1	15
Vacant	Mil	-	3	7	1	16

*Location may not have been assigned to Knox.

1725 Various C/-/030

100-Acre Lots:

Patentee & Location Date	*Location*					
Vacant	Mil	-	3	7	1	17
Vacant	Mil	-	3	7	1	18
Bohn, --, & Slingluff, --, 15 Dec 1810	Mil	-	3	7	1	19
Bohn, --, & Slingluff, --, 15 Dec 1810	Mil	-	3	7	1	20
Bohn, --, & Slingluff, --, 15 Dec 1810	Mil	-	3	7	1	21
Vacant	Mil	-	3	7	1	22
Vacant	Mil	-	3	7	1	23
Vacant	Mil	-	3	7	1	24
Vacant	Mil	-	3	7	1	25
Vacant	Mil	-	3	7	1	26
Vacant	Mil	-	3	7	1	27
Vacant	Mil	-	3	7	1	28
Vacant	Mil	-	3	7	1	29
Vacant	Mil	-	3	7	1	30
Vacant	Mil	-	3	7	1	31
Vacant	Mil	-	3	7	1	32
Vacant	Mil	-	3	7	1	33
Vacant	Mil	-	3	7	1	34
Vacant	Mil	-	3	7	1	35
Vacant	Mil	-	3	7	1	36
Vacant	Mil	-	3	7	1	37
Vacant	Mil	-	3	7	1	38
Vacant	Mil	-	3	7	1	39
Vacant	Mil	-	3	7	1	40
Vacant	Mil	-	3	7	2	1
Vacant	Mil	-	3	7	2	2
Vacant	Mil	-	3	7	2	3
Vacant	Mil	-	3	7	2	4
Vacant	Mil	-	3	7	2	5
Vacant	Mil	-	3	7	2	6
Vacant	Mil	-	3	7	2	7
Vacant	Mil	-	3	7	2	8
Vacant	Mil	-	3	7	2	9
Vacant	Mil	-	3	7	2	10
Vacant	Mil	-	3	7	2	11
Vacant	Mil	-	3	7	2	12
Vacant	Mil	-	3	7	2	13

1726 Various C/-/031

100-Acre Lots:

Patentee & Location Date	*Location*					
Vacant	Mil	-	3	7	2	14
Vacant	Mil	-	3	7	2	15
Vacant	Mil	-	3	7	2	16
Vacant	Mil	-	3	7	2	17
Vacant	Mil	-	3	7	2	18
Vacant	Mil	-	3	7	2	19
Vacant	Mil	-	3	7	2	20
Vacant	Mil	-	3	7	2	21
Vacant	Mil	-	3	7	2	22
Vacant	Mil	-	3	7	2	23
Vacant	Mil	-	3	7	2	24
Vacant	Mil	-	3	7	2	25
Vacant	Mil	-	3	7	2	26
Vacant	Mil	-	3	7	2	27
Vacant	Mil	-	3	7	2	28
Vacant	Mil	-	3	7	2	29
Vacant	Mil	-	3	7	2	30
Vacant	Mil	-	3	7	2	31
Vacant	Mil	-	3	7	2	32
Vacant	Mil	-	3	7	2	33
Vacant	Mil	-	3	7	2	34
Vacant	Mil	-	3	7	2	35
Vacant	Mil	-	3	7	2	36
Vacant	Mil	-	3	7	2	37
Vacant	Mil	-	3	7	2	38
Vacant	Mil	-	3	7	2	39
Vacant	Mil	-	3	7	2	40
Kneeland, Seth, assignee of [assignee's name illegible] 10 Apr 1809	Mil	-	3	8	4	1
Hoogland, William, assignee of (Bohn, --, &						

1726 [continued]

Slingluff, --) 18 Dec 1809	Mil	-	3	8	4	2
Bohn, E., & Slingluff, J., 15 Dec 1810	Mil	-	3	8	4	3
Thorn[e] Stephen, 2 Feb 1810	Mil	-	3	8	4	4
Thorn[e] Stephen, 30 Jan 1810	Mil	-	3	8	4	5
Thorn[e] Stephen, 30 Jan 1810	Mil	-	3	8	4	6
Bohn, E., & Slingluff, J., 1 Jun 1811	Mil	-	3	8	4	7
Bohn, E., & Slingluff, J., 1 Jun 1811	Mil	-	3	8	4	8

1727 Various C/-/032

100-Acre Lots:

Patentee & Location Date			*Location*			
Vacant	Mil	-	3	8	4	9
Vacant	Mil	-	3	8	4	10
Vacant	Mil	-	3	8	4	11
Vacant	Mil	-	3	8	4	12
Bohn, --, & Slingluff, --, 22 Jun 1810	Mil	-	3	8	4	13
van Bibber, Isaac, 22 Jun 1810	Mil	-	3	8	4	14
Sholl, Samuel, assignee, 25 Nov 1811	Mil	-	3	8	4	15
Slingluff, --, & Fahne-stock, --, 15 Dec 1810	Mil	-	3	8	4	16
Vacant	Mil	-	3	8	4	17
Deardoff, Christian, assignee, 1 Jun 1811	Mil	-	3	8	4	18
Bates, Edward, & Bates, Nathaniel, 29 Dec 1810	Mil	-	3	8	4	19
Slingluff, --, & Fahne-stock, --, 15 Dec 1810	Mil	-	3	8	4	20
Slingluff, --, & Fahne-stock, --, 15 Dec 1810	Mil	-	3	8	4	21
Vacant	Mil	-	3	8	4	22
Vacant	Mil	-	3	8	4	23
Slingluff, --, & Fene-stock [Fahnestock] --, 1812	Mil	-	3	8	4	24
Vacant	Mil	-	3	8	4	25
Vacant	Mil	-	3	8	4	26
Vacant	Mil	-	3	8	4	27
Slingluff, --, & Fene-stock [Fahnestock] --, 1812?	Mil	-	3	8	4	28
Bohn, E., & Slingluff, J., assignees, 1 Jun 1811	Mil	-	3	8	4	29
Bohn, E., & Slingluff, J., assignees, 1 Jun 1811	Mil	-	3	8	4	30
Bohn, E., & Slingluff, J., assignees, 1 Jun 1811	Mil	-	3	8	4	31
Vacant	Mil	-	3	8	4	32
Capp? [Copp?] Joseph, 1812	Mil	-	3	8	4	33
Vacant	Mil	-	3	8	4	34
Vacant	Mil	-	3	8	4	35
Vacant	Mil	-	3	8	4	36
Vacant	Mil	-	3	8	4	37
Vacant	Mil	-	3	8	4	38
Vacant	Mil	-	3	8	4	39
Vacant	Mil	-	3	8	4	40
Vacant	Mil	-	3	10	1	1
Vacant	Mil	-	3	10	1	2
Vacant	Mil	-	3	10	1	3
Vacant	Mil	-	3	10	1	4

1728 Various C/-/033

100-Acre Lots:

Patentee & Location Date			*Location*			
Vacant	Mil	-	3	10	1	5
Vacant	Mil	-	3	10	1	6
Burham, Asahel, assignee of, 31 May 1809	Mil	-	3	10	1	7
Vacant	Mil	-	3	10	1	8
Stanberry, Jonas, 23 Dec 1807	Mil	-	3	10	1	9
Stanberry, Jonas, 23 Dec 1807	Mil	-	3	10	1	10
Stanberry, Jonas, 4 May 1807	Mil	-	3	10	1	11
Stanberry, Jonas, 23 Dec 1807	Mil	-	3	10	1	12
Stanberry, Jonas, 29 May 1807	Mil	-	3	10	1	13
Stanboury, Jonas, 7 Aug 1807	Mil	-	3	10	1	14
Parkhill, David, 29 Mar 1808	Mil	-	3	10	1	15
Herdill? [Hordill?] John, 29 Mar 1808	Mil	-	3	10	1	16
Herdill? [Hordill?] John, 29 Mar 1808	Mil	-	3	10	1	17
Stanberry, Jonas, 4 Aug 1807	Mil	-	3	10	1	18
Stanberry, Jonas, 4 Aug 1807	Mil	-	3	10	1	19
Stanberry, Jonas, 29 May 1807	Mil	-	3	10	1	20
Stanberry, Jonas, 13 Apr 1807	Mil	-	3	10	1	21
Goss, Jonathan, 21 Jul 1807	Mil	-	3	10	1	22
Webster, Topphan, 3 Aug 1807	Mil	-	3	10	1	23
Webster, Topphan, 3 Aug 1807	Mil	-	3	10	1	24
Vacant*	Mil	-	3	10	1	25
Stanberry, Jonas, 13 Apr 1807	Mil	-	3	10	2	1
Stanberry, Jonas, 13 Apr 1807	Mil	-	3	10	2	2
Webster, Topphan, 3 Aug 1807	Mil	-	3	10	2	3
Reid, Henry, assignee of (--? Wedderburn?) 1 Jul 1806	Mil	-	3	10	2	4
Scott, Alen, assignee of, (John? Brown) 17 Jul 1806	Mil	-	3	10	2	5
Ball, William, 24 Sep 1807	Mil	-	3	10	2	6
Hoops, Adam, 3 May 1808	Mil	-	3	10	2	7
Hoops, Adam, 3 May 1808	Mil	-	3	10	2	8
Hoops, Adam, 3 May 1808	Mil	-	3	10	2	9
Slingluff, Jesse, 1812	Mil	-	3	10	2	10
Vacant	Mil	-	3	10	2	11
Vacant	Mil	-	3	10	2	12
Vacant	Mil	-	3	10	2	13
Vacant	Mil	-	3	10	2	14

*Pencilled notation: "Sugar l[oaf?] brushy prairie;" also sketched plat of hill.

1729 Various C/-/034

100-Acre Lots:

Patentee & Location Date	*Location*

1729 [continued]

Vacant	Mil	-	3	10	2	15*
Vacant	Mil	-	3	10	2	16
Vacant	Mil	-	3	10	2	17
Vacant	Mil	-	4	4	3	1
Vacant	Mil	-	4	4	3	2
Vacant	Mil	-	4	4	3	3
Vacant	Mil	-	4	4	3	4
Pollard, James, assignee of (Zaccheus A. Beatty) 26 Sep 1808	Mil	-	4	4	3	5
Beatty, Zaccheus A., 26 Apr 1808	Mil	-	4	4	3	6
Beatty, Zaccheus A., 30 Nov 1807	Mil	-	4	4	3	7
Vacant	Mil	-	4	4	3	8
Beatty, Zaccheus A., 15 Apr 1808	Mil	-	4	4	3	9
Beatty, Zaccheus A., 26 Apr 1808	Mil	-	4	4	3	10
Beatty, Zaccheus A., 26 Apr 1808	Mil	-	4	4	3	11
Beatty, Zaccheus A., 2 Jun 1808	Mil	-	4	4	3	12
Vacant	Mil	-	4	4	3	13
Stockhouse, Amos, 12 Feb 1811	Mil	-	4	4	3	14
Vacant	Mil	-	4	4	3	15
Vacant	Mil	-	4	4	3	16
Vacant	Mil	-	4	4	3	17
Vacant	Mil	-	4	4	3	18
Vacant	Mil	-	4	4	3	19
Vacant	Mil	-	4	4	3	20
Beatty, Zaccheus A., 2 Jun 1808	Mil	-	4	4	3	21
Beatty, Zaccheus A., 26 Apr 1808	Mil	-	4	4	3	22
Beatty, Zaccheus A., 30 Nov 1807	Mil	-	4	4	3	23
Beatty, Zaccheus A., 30 Nov 1807	Mil	-	4	4	3	24
Beatty, Zaccheus A., 2 Jun 1808	Mil	-	4	4	3	25
Hains, John, assignee of (Zaccheus A. Beatty) 27 Sep 1808	Mil	-	4	4	3	26
Vacant	Mil	-	4	4	3	27
Vacant	Mil	-	4	4	3	28
Vacant	Mil	-	4	4	3	29
Vacant	Mil	-	4	4	3	30
Vacant	Mil	-	4	4	3	31
Vacant	Mil	-	4	4	3	32

*Marginal notation: Sketched plat showing hill.

1730 Various C/-/035

100-Acre Lots:

Patentee & Location Date	*Location*					
Vacant	Mil	-	4	4	3	33
Vacant	Mil	-	4	4	3	34
Vacant	Mil	-	4	4	3	35
Vacant	Mil	-	4	4	3	36
Vacant	Mil	-	4	4	3	37
Vacant	Mil	-	4	4	3	38
Vacant	Mil	-	4	4	3	39
Vacant	Mil	-	4	4	3	40
Vacant	Mil	-	4	10	1	1
Slingluff, --, & Fenestock [Fahnestock] --, 1812	Mil	-	4	10	1	2
Slingluff, --, & Fenestock [Fahnestock] --, 1812	Mil	-	4	10	1	3
Vacant	Mil	-	4	10	1	4
Baldwin, Eli, 1812	Mil	-	4	10	1	5
Vacant	Mil	-	4	10	1	6
Vacant	Mil	-	4	10	1	7
Vacant	Mil	-	4	10	1	8
Vacant	Mil	-	4	10	1	9
Vacant	Mil	-	4	10	1	10
Vacant	Mil	-	4	10	2	1*
Reid, Thomas, assignee of (Daniel Foster?) 28 Oct 1803	Mil	-	4	10	2	2*
McKinsey, Jesse, 19 Mar 1811	Mil	-	4	10	3	1
Massie, Henry, 26 Mar 1810	Mil	-	4	10	3	2
Massie, Henry, 26 Mar 1810	Mil	-	4	10	3	3
Wallace, Henry, 26 Mar 1810	Mil	-	4	10	3	4
Morrison, James, 26 Mar 1810	Mil	-	4	10	3	5
Miller, James, heirs of	Mil	-	4	10	3	6
Vacant	Mil	-	4	10	3	7
Vacant	Mil	-	4	10	3	8
Vacant	Mil	-	4	10	3	9
Vacant	Mil	-	4	10	3	10
Vacant	Mil	-	4	10	3	11
Vacant	Mil	-	4	10	3	12
Vacant	Mil	-	4	10	3	13
Massie, Henry, 26 Mar 1810	Mil	-	4	10	3	14
Lackland, Dennis, 1812	Mil	-	4	10	3	15
Johnston, John, 1812	Mil	-	4	10	3	16
Vacant	Mil	-	4	10	3	17

*These locations appear out of sequence on page 36 of the source document.

1731 Various C/-/036

100-Acre Lots:

Patentee & Location Date	*Location*					
Parkhill, James, assignee	Mil	-	4	10	3	18
Vacant	Mil	-	4	10	3	19
Vacant	Mil	-	4	10	3	20
Vacant	Mil	-	4	10	3	21
Vacant	Mil	-	4	10	3	22
Vacant	Mil	-	4	10	3	23
Vacant	Mil	-	4	10	3	24
Vacant	Mil	-	4	10	3	25
Vacant	Mil	-	4	10	3	26
Vacant	Mil	-	4	10	3	27
Vacant	Mil	-	4	10	3	28
Vacant	Mil	-	4	10	3	29
Vacant	Mil	-	4	10	3	30
Vacant	Mil	-	4	10	3	31
Vacant	Mil	-	4	10	3	32
Vacant	Mil	-	4	10	3	33
Vacant	Mil	-	4	10	3	34
Vacant	Mil	-	4	10	3	35
Vacant	Mil	-	4	10	3	36
Vacant	Mil	-	4	10	3	37
Vacant	Mil	-	4	10	3	38
Vacant	Mil	-	4	10	3	39
Vacant	Mil	-	5	3	3	1
Vacant	Mil	-	5	3	3	2
Vacant	Mil	-	5	3	3	3
Talbot, Lloyd, 1812	Mil	-	5	3	3	4

1731 [continued]

Roupe? [Rouse?] Jonas, 1812	Mil	-	5	3	3	5
Northup* Henry, 8 Mar 1813	Mil	-	5	3	3	6
Weeker? [Meeker?] Daniel, 181	Mil	-	5	3	3	7
Putnam, John, 1812	Mil	-	5	3	3	8
Vacant	Mil	-	5	3	3	9
Vacant	Mil	-	5	3	3	10
Northup* Henry, 8 Mar 1813	Mil	-	5	3	3	11
Vacant	Mil	-	5	3	3	12

*So spelled.

1732 Various C/-/037

100-Acre Lots:

Patentee & Location Date	*Location*					
Keen, Samuel Y., 26 Feb 1808	Mil	-	5	3	3	13
Benter, --, & Soyer, --, 13 Aug 1813	Mil	-	5	3	3	14
Vacant	Mil	-	5	3	3	15
Keen, Samuel Y., 26 Feb 1808	Mil	-	5	3	3	16
Stockton, John Cox, 21 Nov 1810	Mil	-	5	3	3	17
Walker, Meshech, 13 Nov 1811	Mil	-	5	3	3	18
Vacant	Mil	-	5	3	3	19
Vacant	Mil	-	5	3	3	20
Vacant	Mil	-	5	3	3	21
Vacant	Mil	-	5	3	3	22
Vacant	Mil	-	5	3	3	23
Vacant	Mil	-	5	3	3	24
Vacant	Mil	-	5	3	3	25
Vacant	Mil	-	5	3	3	26
Green, Elias, 1812	Mil	-	5	3	3	27
Green, Elias, 1812	Mil	-	5	3	3	28
Northup* Henry, 8 Jun 1813	Mil	-	5	3	3	29
Northup* Henry, 8 Mar 1813	Mil	-	5	3	3	30
Northup* Henry, 13 Jan 1813	Mil	-	5	3	3	31
Brannon, Michael, heirs, 27 Jul 1813	Mil	-	5	3	3	32
Keen, Samuel Y., 26 Feb 1808	Mil	-	5	3	3	33
Paker* Alex[ander] 26 Feb 1807	Mil	-	5	3	3	34
Paker* Alex[ander] 26 Feb 1807	Mil	-	5	3	3	35
Paker* Alex[ander] 26 Feb 1807	Mil	-	5	3	3	36
Vacant	Mil	-	5	3	3	37
Vacant	Mil	-	5	3	3	38
Vacant	Mil	-	5	3	3	39
Vacant	Mil	-	5	3	3	40
Vacant	Mil	-	5	7	1	1
Vacant	Mil	-	5	7	1	2
Vacant	Mil	-	5	7	1	3
Vacant	Mil	-	5	7	1	4
Vacant	Mil	-	5	7	1	5
Vacant	Mil	-	5	7	1	6
Vacant	Mil	-	5	7	1	7

*So spelled.

1733 Various C/-/038

100-Acre Lots

Patentee & Location Date	*Location*					
Vacant	Mil	-	5	7	1	8
Vacant	Mil	-	5	7	1	9
Vacant	Mil	-	5	7	1	10
Vacant	Mil	-	5	7	1	11
Vacant	Mil	-	5	7	1	12
Vacant	Mil	-	5	7	1	13
Vacant	Mil	-	5	7	1	14
Vacant	Mil	-	5	7	1	15
Vacant	Mil	-	5	7	1	16
Vacant	Mil	-	5	7	1	17
Vacant	Mil	-	5	7	1	18
Vacant	Mil	-	5	7	1	19
Vacant	Mil	-	5	7	1	20
Vacant	Mil	-	5	7	1	21
Vacant	Mil	-	5	7	1	22
Vacant	Mil	-	5	7	1	23
Vacant	Mil	-	5	7	1	24
Vacant	Mil	-	5	7	1	25
Vacant	Mil	-	5	7	1	26
Vacant	Mil	-	5	7	1	27
Vacant	Mil	-	5	7	1	28
Vacant	Mil	-	5	7	1	29
Vacant	Mil	-	5	7	1	30
Vacant	Mil	-	5	7	1	31
Vacant	Mil	-	5	7	1	32
Vacant	Mil	-	5	7	1	33
Vacant	Mil	-	5	7	1	34
Vacant	Mil	-	5	7	1	35
Vacant	Mil	-	5	7	1	36
Vacant	Mil	-	5	7	1	37
Vacant	Mil	-	5	7	1	38
Vacant	Mil	-	5	7	1	39
Vacant	Mil	-	5	7	1	40
Bohn, E., & Slingluff, J., 25 Dec 1810	Mil	-	5	9	3	1
Vacant	Mil	-	5	9	3	2

1734 Various C/-/039

100-Acre Lots:

Patentee & Location Date	*Location*					
Vacant	Mil	-	5	9	3	3
Vacant	Mil	-	5	9	3	4
Vacant	Mil	-	5	9	3	5
Bohn, --, & Slingluff, --, 25 Dec 1810	Mil	-	5	9	3	6
Bohn, --, & Slingluff, --, 25 Dec 1810	Mil	-	5	9	3	7
Vacant	Mil	-	5	9	3	8
Vacant	Mil	-	5	9	3	9
Bohn, --, & Slingluff, --, 15 Dec 1810	Mil	-	5	9	3	10
Bohn, --, & Slingluff, --, 15 Dec 1810	Mil	-	5	9	3	11
Vacant	Mil	-	5	9	3	12
Vacant	Mil	-	5	9	3	13
Vacant	Mil	-	5	9	3	14
Vacant	Mil	-	5	9	3	15
Vacant	Mil	-	5	9	3	16
Vacant	Mil	-	5	9	3	17
Vacant	Mil	-	5	9	3	18
Vacant	Mil	-	5	9	3	19
Vacant	Mil	-	5	9	3	20
Vacant	Mil	-	5	9	3	21
Vacant	Mil	-	5	9	3	22
Vacant	Mil	-	5	9	3	23
Vacant	Mil	-	5	9	3	24
Vacant	Mil	-	5	9	3	25
Vacant	Mil	-	5	9	3	26
Vacant	Mil	-	5	9	3	27

1734 [continued]

Vacant	Mil	-	5	9	3	28
Vacant	Mil	-	5	9	3	29
Vacant	Mil	-	5	9	3	30
Vacant	Mil	-	5	9	3	31
Vacant	Mil	-	5	9	3	32
Vacant	Mil	-	5	9	3	33
Vacant	Mil	-	5	9	3	34
Vacant	Mil	-	5	9	3	35
Vacant	Mil	-	5	9	3	36
Vacant	Mil	-	5	9	3	37

1735 Various C/-/040

100-Acre Lots:

Patentee & Location Date	*Location*					
Vacant	Mil	-	5	9	3	38
Vacant	Mil	-	5	9	3	39
Vacant	Mil	-	5	9	3	40
Vacant	Mil	-	5	10	3	1
Vacant	Mil	-	5	10	3	2
Vacant	Mil	-	5	10	3	3
Vacant	Mil	-	5	10	3	4
Vacant	Mil	-	5	10	3	5
Vacant	Mil	-	5	10	3	6
Vacant	Mil	-	5	10	3	7
Vacant	Mil	-	5	10	3	8
Morrison, James, assignee, 22 Jul 1811	Mil	-	5	10	3	9
Vacant	Mil	-	5	10	3	10
Vacant	Mil	-	5	10	3	11
Vacant	Mil	-	5	10	3	12
Vacant	Mil	-	5	10	3	13
Vacant	Mil	-	5	10	3	14
Vacant	Mil	-	5	10	3	15
Vacant	Mil	-	5	10	3	16
Vacant	Mil	-	5	10	3	17
Vacant	Mil	-	5	10	3	18
Vacant	Mil	-	5	10	3	19
Vacant	Mil	-	5	10	3	20
Vacant	Mil	-	5	10	3	21
Vacant	Mil	-	5	10	3	22
Vacant	Mil	-	5	10	3	23
Vacant	Mil	-	5	10	3	24
Vacant	Mil	-	5	10	3	25
Vacant	Mil	-	5	10	3	26
Vacant	Mil	-	5	10	3	27
Vacant	Mil	-	5	10	3	28
Vacant	Mil	-	5	10	4	1
Vacant	Mil	-	5	10	4	2

1736 Various C/-/041

100-Acre Lots:

Patentee & Location Date	*Location*					
Vacant	Mil	-	5	10	4	3
Vacant	Mil	-	5	10	4	4
Vacant	Mil	-	5	10	4	5
Vacant	Mil	-	5	10	4	6
McMullen, Hugh, heir of, 18 Feb 1805	Mil	-	5	10	4	7
Vacant	Mil	-	5	10	4	8
Vacant	Mil	-	5	10	4	9
Vacant	Mil	-	5	10	4	10
Vacant	Mil	-	5	10	4	11
Vacant	Mil	-	5	10	4	12
Vacant	Mil	-	5	10	4	13
Vacant	Mil	-	5	10	4	14
Bohn, --, & Slingluff, --, 14 Jan 1814	Mil	-	5	10	4	15
Vacant	Mil	-	5	10	4	16
Vacant	Mil	-	5	10	4	17
Vacant	Mil	-	5	10	4	18
Vacant	Mil	-	5	10	4	19
Vacant	Mil	-	5	10	4	20
Vacant	Mil	-	5	10	4	21*
Vacant	Mil	-	5	10	4	22
Delany, Martin, 1 Mar 1813	Mil	-	5	10	4	23
Vacant	Mil	-	5	10	4	24
Vacant	Mil	-	5	10	4	25
Evans, Perry, 22 Jul 1811	Mil	-	5	10	4	26
Vacant	Mil	-	5	10	4	27
Vacant	Mil	-	5	10	4	28
Vacant	Mil	-	5	10	4	29
Vacant	Mil	-	5	10	4	30
Vacant	Mil	-	5	10	4	31
Vacant	Mil	-	5	10	4	32
Vacant	Mil	-	5	10	4	33
Vacant	Mil	-	5	10	4	34
Vacant	Mil	-	5	10	4	35
Vacant	Mil	-	6	2	1	1
Vacant	Mil	-	6	2	1	2
Wade, Abner, 1812	Mil	-	6	2	1	3

*This lot not listed on source register. Mistakenly omitted?

1737 Various C/-/042

100-Acre Lots:

Patentee & Location Date	*Location*					
Wade, Abner, 1812	Mil	-	6	2	1	4
Wade, Abner, 1812	Mil	-	6	2	1	5
Belfield, John, heir of, 24 Feb 1806	Mil	-	6	2	1	6
Belfield, John, heir of, 24 Feb 1806	Mil	-	6	2	1	7
Belfield, John, heir of, 24 Feb 1806	Mil	-	6	2	1	8
Rockell, John, 10 Jul 1813	Mil	-	6	2	1	9
Rockell, John, 10 Jul 1813	Mil	-	6	2	1	10
Belfield, John, heir of, 24 Feb 1806	Mil	-	6	2	1	11
Vacant	Mil	-	6	2	1	12
Vacant	Mil	-	6	2	1	13
Vacant	Mil	-	6	2	1	14
Vacant	Mil	-	6	2	1	15
Vacant	Mil	-	6	2	1	16
Vacant	Mil	-	6	2	1	17
Vacant	Mil	-	6	2	1	18
Vacant	Mil	-	6	2	1	19
Way, Samuel, 21 Nov 1810	Mil	-	6	2	1	20
Frazer, Benjamin, 21 Nov 1810	Mil	-	6	2	1	21
Crevester, Jacob, 21 Nov 1810	Mil	-	6	2	1	22
Rockell, Jacob, 10 Jul 1813	Mil	-	6	2	1	23
Vacant	Mil	-	6	2	1	24
Vacant	Mil	-	6	2	1	25
Vacant	Mil	-	6	2	1	26
Beeman, Moses, 21 Nov 1810	Mil	-	6	2	1	27
Vacant	Mil	-	6	2	1	28
Vacant	Mil	-	6	2	1	29
Vacant	Mil	-	6	2	1	30

1737 [continued]

Vacant	Mil	-	6	2	1	31
Vacant	Mil	-	6	2	1	32
Dennison, William, 25 Sep 1810	Mil	-	6	2	1	33
Vacant	Mil	-	6	2	1	34
Carr, Hezekiel, 28 Feb 1813	Mil	-	6	2	1	35
Vacant	Mil	-	6	2	1	36
Dennison, William, 25 Sep 1810	Mil	-	6	2	1	37
Swiger, --, & Root? [Roof?] --, 1812	Mil	-	6	2	1	38

1738 Various C/-/043

100-Acre Lots:

Patentee & Location Date	*Location*					
Vacant	Mil	-	6	2	1	39
Vacant	Mil	-	6	2	1	40
Vacant	Mil	-	6	6	2	1
Vacant	Mil	-	6	6	2	2
Vacant	Mil	-	6	6	2	3
Vacant	Mil	-	6	6	2	4
Stors, Justis, assignee of [assignee's name illegible] 1 Dec 1808	Mil	-	6	6	2	5
Stors, Justis, assignee of [assignee's name illegible] 1 Dec 1808	Mil	-	6	6	2	6
Stors, Justis, assignee of [assignee's name illegible] 1 Dec 1808	Mil	-	6	6	2	7
Bigelow, Moses, 1 Dec 1808	Mil	-	6	6	2	8
Vacant	Mil	-	6	6	2	9
Vacant	Mil	-	6	6	2	10
Vacant	Mil	-	6	6	2	11
Vacant	Mil	-	6	6	2	12
Cook, Jesse, 29 Dec 1801	Mil	-	6	6	2	13
Cook, Jesse, 29 Dec 1801	Mil	-	6	6	2	14
Vacant	Mil	-	6	6	2	15
Vacant	Mil	-	6	6	2	16
Vacant	Mil	-	6	6	2	17
Vacant	Mil	-	6	6	2	18
Vacant	Mil	-	6	6	2	19
Cook, Jesse, 29 Dec 1801	Mil	-	6	6	2	20
Gutherie, Joseph, 28 Apr 1802	Mil	-	6	6	2	21
Gray, Peter, 12 Nov 1808	Mil	-	6	6	2	22
Ingles, John, 29 Apr 1800	Mil	-	6	6	2	23
Ingles, John, 29 Apr 1800	Mil	-	6	6	2	24
Ingles, John, 29 Apr 1800	Mil	-	6	6	2	25
Armstrong, Thomas, 29 Apr 1800	Mil	-	6	6	2	26
Armstrong, Thomas, 29 Apr 1800	Mil	-	6	6	2	27
Armstrong, Thomas, 29 Apr 1800	Mil	-	6	6	2	28
Vacant	Mil	-	6	6	2	29
Vacant	Mil	-	6	6	2	30
Vacant	Mil	-	6	6	2	31
Vacant	Mil	-	6	6	2	32
Vacant	Mil	-	6	6	2	33

1739 Various C/-/044

100-Acre Lots:

Patentee & Location Date	*Location*					
Vacant	Mil	-	6	7	3	1
Vacant	Mil	-	6	7	3	2
Vacant	Mil	-	6	7	3	3
Vacant	Mil	-	6	7	3	4
Vacant	Mil	-	6	7	3	5
Vacant	Mil	-	6	7	3	6
Vacant	Mil	-	6	7	3	7
Vacant	Mil	-	6	7	3	8
Vacant	Mil	-	6	7	3	9
Vacant	Mil	-	6	7	3	10
Vacant	Mil	-	6	7	3	11
Vacant	Mil	-	6	7	3	12
Vacant	Mil	-	6	7	3	13
Clagett, Horatio, 14 Jun 1803	Mil	-	6	7	3	14
Clagett, Horatio, 14 Jun 1803	Mil	-	6	7	3	15
Vacant	Mil	-	6	7	3	16
Vacant	Mil	-	6	7	3	17
Vacant	Mil	-	6	7	3	18
Vacant	Mil	-	6	7	3	19
Vacant	Mil	-	6	7	3	20
Vacant	Mil	-	6	7	3	21
Vacant	Mil	-	6	7	3	22
Vacant	Mil	-	6	7	3	23
Vacant	Mil	-	6	7	3	24
Vacant	Mil	-	6	7	3	25
Vacant	Mil	-	6	7	3	26
Vacant	Mil	-	6	7	3	27
Vacant	Mil	-	6	7	3	28
Vacant	Mil	-	6	7	3	29
Horner, John, assignee of (K? P. Helfenstine) 20 Dec 1804	Mil	-	6	7	3	30
Fellows, Tobias, assignee of, 8 Feb 1805	Mil	-	6	7	3	31
Clagett, Horatio, 14 Jun 1803	Mil	-	6	7	3	32
Vacant	Mil	-	6	7	3	33
Vacant	Mil	-	6	7	3	34

1740 -- C/-/045

100-Acre Lots:

Patentee & Location Date	*Location*					
Vacant	Mil	-	6	8	2	1
Vacant	Mil	-	6	8	2	2
Vacant	Mil	-	6	8	2	3
Vacant	Mil	-	6	8	2	4
Vacant	Mil	-	6	8	2	5
Vacant	Mil	-	6	8	2	6
Vacant	Mil	-	6	8	2	7
Vacant	Mil	-	6	8	2	8
Vacant	Mil	-	6	8	2	9
Vacant	Mil	-	6	8	2	10
Vacant	Mil	-	6	8	2	11
Vacant	Mil	-	6	8	2	12
Vacant	Mil	-	6	8	2	13
Vacant	Mil	-	6	8	2	14
Vacant	Mil	-	6	8	2	15
Vacant	Mil	-	6	8	2	16
Vacant	Mil	-	6	8	2	17
Vacant	Mil	-	6	8	2	18
Vacant	Mil	-	6	8	2	19
Vacant	Mil	-	6	8	2	20
Guthrie, Joseph, 21 Dec 1801*	Mil	-	6	8	2	21
Vacant	Mil	-	6	8	2	22
Vacant	Mil	-	6	8	2	23
Vacant	Mil	-	6	8	2	24

1740 [continued]

Vacant	Mil	-	6	8	2	25
Vacant	Mil	-	6	8	2	26
Vacant	Mil	-	6	8	2	27
Vacant	Mil	-	6	8	2	28
Vacant	Mil	-	6	8	2	29
Vacant	Mil	-	6	8	2	30
Vacant	Mil	-	6	8	2	31
Vacant	Mil	-	6	8	2	32
Vacant	Mil	-	6	8	2	33
Vacant	Mil	-	6	8	3	1
Vacant	Mil	-	6	8	3	2

*Marginal notation: Error, see Mil 6 6 2 21.

1741 Various C/-/046

100-Acre Lots:

Patentee & Location Date	*Location*					
Vacant	Mil	-	6	8	3	3
Vacant	Mil	-	6	8	3	4
Vacant	Mil	-	6	8	3	5
Boyle, Thomas H., assignee of (Isaac Vanhorne) 6 Apr 1809	Mil	-	6	8	3	6
Boyle, Thomas H., assignee of (Isaac Vanhorne) 6 Apr 1809	Mil	-	6	8	3	7
Vacant	Mil	-	6	8	3	8
Vacant	Mil	-	6	8	3	9
Vacant	Mil	-	6	8	3	10
Vacant	Mil	-	6	8	3	11
Vacant	Mil	-	6	8	3	12
Vacant	Mil	-	6	8	3	13
Vacant	Mil	-	6	8	3	14
Boyle, Thomas H., assignee of (Isaac Vanhorne) 6 Apr 1809	Mil	-	6	8	3	15
Vacant	Mil	-	6	8	3	16
Vacant	Mil	-	6	8	3	17
Vacant	Mil	-	6	8	3	18
Baylies, Hodijah, 15 Sep 1800	Mil	-	6	8	3	19
Baylies, Hodijah, 15 Sep 1800	Mil	-	6	8	3	20
Boxburgh, Alex[ander] 12 May 1801	Mil	-	6	8	3	21
Boxburgh, Alex[ander] 12 May 1801	Mil	-	6	8	3	22
Vacant	Mil	-	6	8	3	23
Vacant	Mil	-	6	8	3	24
Vacant	Mil	-	6	8	3	25
Vacant	Mil	-	6	8	3	26
Vacant	Mil	-	6	8	3	27
Ferguson, John, heirs of, 29 Dec 1804	Mil	-	6	8	3	28
Vacant	Mil	-	6	8	3	29
Vacant	Mil	-	6	8	3	30
Boxburgh, Alexander, 12 May 1801	Mil	-	6	8	3	31
Boxburgh, Alexander, 12 May 1801	Mil	-	6	8	3	32
Baylies, Hodijah, 16 Sep 1800	Mil	-	6	8	3	33
Baylies, Hodijah, 16 Sep 1800	Mil	-	6	8	3	34
Vacant	Mil	-	6	10	3	1
Booker, Samuel, assignee of (--? Taylor) 9 Jan 1810	Mil	-	6	10	3	2
Booker, Samuel, assignee of (--? Taylor)	Mil	-	6	10	3	3
Booker, Samuel, assignee of (--? Taylor) 9 Jan 1800	Mil	-	6	10	3	4

1742 Various C/-/047

100-Acre Lots:

Patentee & Location Date	*Location*					
Thorn, Stephen, 21 May 1810	Mil	-	6	10	3	5
Andrews, Ephraim [assignee of?](John D. Fieldston?) 20 Mar 1810	Mil	-	6	10	3	6*
Cumming, J? [or I?] N., 20 Mar 1810	Mil	-	6	10	3	7
Vacant	Mil	-	6	10	3	8
Parmelle, Luther, administrator of the heirs of, 26 Jun 1810	Mil	-	6	10	3	9
Wilcox, Moses, & Wilcox, Aaron, 26 Jun 1810	Mil	-	6	10	3	10
Sparrow, Richard, 20 Mar 1810	Mil	-	6	10	3	11
Hogg, Thomas, heirs of, 7 Jan 1805	Mil	-	6	10	4	1
Hogg, Thomas, heirs of, 7 Jan 1805	Mil	-	6	10	4	2
Hogg, Thomas, heirs of, 7 Jan 1805	Mil	-	6	10	4	3
Hogg, Thomas, heirs of, 7 Jan 1805	Mil	-	6	10	4	4
Vacant	Mil	-	6	10	4	5
Call, Daniel, 27 Jul 1810	Mil	-	6	10	4	6
Call, Daniel, executor of R. Mean's last will, 26 Mar 1810	Mil	-	6	10	4	7
Call, Daniel, executor of R. Mean's last will, 26 Mar 1810	Mil	-	6	10	4	8
Call, D[aniel] executor of R. Mean's last will, 26 Mar 1810	Mil	-	6	10	4	9
Shee? [Shea?] Caspar, 1812	Mil	-	6	10	4	10
Vacant	Mil	-	6	10	4	11
Call, Daniel, 20 Apr 1810	Mil	-	6	10	4	12
Call, Daniel, 20 Apr 1810	Mil	-	6	10	4	13
Smith, Francis, 1812	Mil	-	6	10	4	14
Horsefield, Thomas, 1812	Mil	-	6	10	4	15
Call, Daniel, 27 Jul 1810	Mil	-	6	10	4	16
McKay, Jesse, 21 Aug 1810	Mil	-	6	10	4	17
McKay, Jesse, 21 Aug 1810	Mil	-	6	10	4	18
McKay, Jesse, 21 Aug 1810	Mil	-	6	10	4	19
Edginton, Isaac	Mil	-	6	10	4	20
Vacant	Mil	-	7	4	2	1
Vacant	Mil	-	7	4	2	2
Baldwin, Jared, 11 Jan 1811	Mil	-	7	4	2	3
Mills, Peter, 20 Dec 1810	Mil	-	7	4	2	4
Vacant	Mil	-	7	4	2	5
Vacant	Mil	-	7	4	2	6
Vacant	Mil	-	7	4	2	7
Vacant	Mil	-	7	4	2	8
Vacant	Mil	-	7	4	2	9

*Marginal notation: "double location."

1743 Various C/-/048

100-Acre Lots:

Patentee & Location Date *Location*

1743 [continued]

Vacant	Mil	-	7	4	2	10
Vacant	Mil	-	7	4	2	11
Vacant	Mil	-	7	4	2	12
Vacant	Mil	-	7	4	2	13
Vacant	Mil	-	7	4	2	14
Wells, Obadiah, assignee, 2 Jan 1812	Mil	-	7	4	2	15
Libbey, Benj[amin] assignee of [assignee's name not given] 26 Dec 1808	Mil	-	7	4	2	16
Dayley, Robert, assignee of [assignee's name not given] 27 Feb 1809	Mil	-	7	4	2	17
Ogle, James, 24 Mar 1810	Mil	-	7	4	2	18
Mills, Peter, 20 Dec 1810	Mil	-	7	4	2	19
Baldwin, Jared, 11 Jan 1811	Mil	-	7	4	2	20
Parker, Alexander, heir of Loresto? Richard Parker, 12 Mar 1811	Mil	-	7	4	2	21
Parker, Alexander, heir of Loresto? Richard Parker, 12 Mar 1811	Mil	-	7	4	2	22
Parker, Alexander, heir of Loresto? Richard Parker, 12 Mar 1811	Mil	-	7	4	2	23
Baldwin, Jared, 11 Jan 1811	Mil	-	7	4	2	24
Vacant	Mil	-	7	4	2	25
Vacant	Mil	-	7	4	2	26
Vacant	Mil	-	7	4	2	27
Vacant	Mil	-	7	4	2	28
Vacant	Mil	-	7	4	2	29
Vacant	Mil	-	7	4	2	30
Parker, Alexander, heir [of Loresto? Richard Parker] 12 Mar 1811	Mil	-	7	4	2	31
Mills, Peter, 20 Dec 1810	Mil	-	7	4	2	32
Parker, Alexander, heir [of Loresto? Richard Parker] 12 Mar 1811	Mil	-	7	4	2	33
Jones, Alexander, assignee [warrantee's name not given] 27 Mar 1811	Mil	-	7	4	2	34
Vacant	Mil	-	7	4	2	35
Vacant	Mil	-	7	4	2	36
Vacant	Mil	-	7	4	2	37
Leland, Francis, 7 Mar 1808	Mil	-	7	4	2	38
Vanhorne, Isaac, 14 Mar 1808	Mil	-	7	4	2	39
Vanhorne, Isaac, 14 Mar 1808	Mil	-	7	4	2	40
Hill, Baylor, 6 May 1800	Mil	-	7	6	1	1
Vacant	Mil	-	7	6	1	2
Vacant	Mil	-	7	6	1	3
Vacant	Mil	-	7	6	1	4

1744 Various C/-/049

100-Acre Lots: Patentee & Location Date	*Location*					
Blair, John, heirs of, 15 Dec 1800	Mil	-	7	6	1	5
Blair, John, heirs of, 15 Dec 1800	Mil	-	7	6	1	6
Evans, William, 15 Dec 1800	Mil	-	7	6	1	7
Evans, William, 15 Dec 1800	Mil	-	7	6	1	8
Vacant	Mil	-	7	6	1	9
Vacant	Mil	-	7	6	1	10
Vacant	Mil	-	7	6	1	11
Vacant	Mil	-	7	6	1	12
Vacant	Mil	-	7	6	1	13
Vacant	Mil	-	7	6	1	14
Vacant	Mil	-	7	6	1	15
Hill, Baylor, 6 May 1800	Mil	-	7	6	1	16
Hill, Baylor, 6 May 1800	Mil	-	7	6	1	17
Vacant	Mil	-	7	6	1	18
Vacant	Mil	-	7	6	1	19
Vacant	Mil	-	7	6	1	20
Vacant	Mil	-	7	6	1	21
Vacant	Mil	-	7	6	1	22
Vacant	Mil	-	7	6	1	23
Vacant	Mil	-	7	6	1	24
Camjrin? James, 29 Apr 1800	Mil	-	7	6	1	25
Camjrin? James, 29 Apr 1800	Mil	-	7	6	1	26
Camjrin? James, 29 Apr 1800	Mil	-	7	6	1	27
Vacant	Mil	-	7	6	1	28
Buchanan, John, 10 May 1806	Mil	-	7	6	1	29
Buchanan, John, 10 May 1806	Mil	-	7	6	1	30
Buchanan, John, 10 May 1806	Mil	-	7	6	1	31
Milling, Hugh, 10 May 1806	Mil	-	7	6	1	32
Milling, Hugh, 10 May 1806	Mil	-	7	6	1	33
Milling, Hugh, 10 May 1806	Mil	-	7	6	1	34
Moore, Henry, 10 May 1806	Mil	-	7	6	1	35
Moore, Henry, 10 May 1806	Mil	-	7	6	1	36
Vacant	Mil	-	7	6	1	37
Fawn? [Town?] William, 29 Apr 1810	Mil	-	7	6	1	38
Fawn? [Town?] William, 29 Apr 1810	Mil	-	7	6	1	39
Fawn? [Town?] William, 29 Apr 1810	Mil	-	7	6	1	40

1745 Various C/-/050

100-Acre Lots: Patentee & Location Date	*Location*					
Burgess, Joshua, 2 Nov 1802	Mil	-	7	7	2	1
Mills, Peter, 11 May 1808	Mil	-	7	7	2	2
Vacant	Mil	-	7	7	2	3
Vacant	Mil	-	7	7	2	4
Vacant	Mil	-	7	7	2	5
Stanberry, Jonas, 30 Jan 1810	Mil	-	7	7	2	6
Stanberry, Jonas, 30 Jan 1810	Mil	-	7	7	2	7
Stanberry, Jonas, 30 Jan 1810	Mil	-	7	7	2	8
Marshall, Dixon, 10 Jan 1801	Mil	-	7	7	2	9
Boyd, Thomas, heirs of, 28 Dec 1802	Mil	-	7	7	2	10
Vacant	Mil	-	7	7	2	11
Vacant	Mil	-	7	7	2	12
Vacant	Mil	-	7	7	2	13

1745 [continued]

Vacant	Mil	-	7	7	2	14
Stoddart, Nathan, assignee of the heirs of (N. A. Stoddart) 24 Dec 1803	Mil	-	7	7	2	15
Burgess, Joshua, 2 Nov 1802	Mil	-	7	7	2	16
Vacant	Mil	-	7	7	2	17
Vacant	Mil	-	7	7	2	18
Stoddart, Nathan, assignee of the heirs of (N. A. Stoddart) 24 Dec 1803	Mil	-	7	7	2	19
Stoddart, Nathan, assignee of the heirs of (N. A., Stoddart) 24 Dec 1803	Mil	-	7	7	2	20
Shick? [Shirk?] Frederick, 28 Dec 1802	Mil	-	7	7	2	21
Shick? [Shirk?] Frederick, 28 Dec 1802	Mil	-	7	7	2	22
Boyd, Thomas, heirs of, 28 Dec 1802	Mil	-	7	7	2	23
Marshall, Dixon, 10 Jan 1801	Mil	-	7	7	2	24
Vacant	Mil	-	7	7	2	25
Vacant	Mil	-	7	7	2	26
Vacant	Mil	-	7	7	2	27
Vacant	Mil	-	7	7	2	28
Vacant	Mil	-	7	7	2	29
Vacant	Mil	-	7	7	2	30
Vacant	Mil	-	7	7	2	31
Vacant	Mil	-	7	7	2	32
Vacant	Mil	-	7	7	2	33
Vacant	Mil	-	7	7	2	34
Vacant	Mil	-	7	7	2	35

1746 Various C/-/051

100-Acre Lots: Patentee & Location Date	*Location*					
Vacant	Mil	-	7	7	2	36
Vacant	Mil	-	7	7	2	37
Vacant	Mil	-	7	7	2	38
Vacant	Mil	-	7	7	2	39
Vacant	Mil	-	7	7	2	40
Vacant	Mil	-	7	9	2	1
Vacant	Mil	-	7	9	2	2
Vacant	Mil	-	7	9	2	3
Vacant	Mil	-	7	9	2	4
Vacant	Mil	-	7	9	2	5
Vacant	Mil	-	7	9	2	6
Sarwell? Joseph H., 24 Jun 1813	Mil	-	7	9	2	7
Sarwell? Joseph H., 24 Jun 1813	Mil	-	7	9	2	8
Vacant	Mil	-	7	9	2	9
Vacant	Mil	-	7	9	2	10
Vacant	Mil	-	7	9	2	11
Vacant	Mil	-	7	9	2	12
Vacant	Mil	-	7	9	2	13
Vacant	Mil	-	7	9	2	14
Vacant	Mil	-	7	9	2	15
Smith, Samuel H., assignee, 22 Jul 1811	Mil	-	7	9	2	16
Vacant	Mil	-	7	9	2	17
Smith, Samuel H., assignee, 22 Jul 1811	Mil	-	7	9	2	18
Vacant	Mil	-	7	9	2	19
Vacant	Mil	-	7	9	2	20
Vacant	Mil	-	7	9	2	21
Vacant	Mil	-	7	9	2	22
Vacant	Mil	-	7	9	2	23
Vacant	Mil	-	7	9	2	24
Humphries, David, 7 Mar 1808	Mil	-	7	9	2	25
Vacant	Mil	-	7	9	2	26
Vacant	Mil	-	7	9	2	27
Vacant	Mil	-	7	9	2	28
Smith, Samuel H., 22 Jul 1811	Mil	-	7	9	2	29

1747 Various C/-/052

100-Acre Lots: Patentee & Location Date	*Location*					
Bedinger, Henry, 1812	Mil	-	7	9	2	30
Vacant	Mil	-	7	9	2	31
Vacant	Mil	-	7	9	2	32
Vacant	Mil	-	7	9	2	33
Smith, Samuel H., 1812	Mil	-	7	9	2	34
Smith, Samuel H., 3 Feb 1814	Mil	-	7	9	2	35
Smith, Samuel H., 1812	Mil	-	7	9	2	36
Humphries, David, 7 Mar 1808	Mil	-	7	9	2	37
Humphries, David, 7 Mar 1808	Mil	-	7	9	2	38
Humphries, David, 7 Mar 1808	Mil	-	7	9	2	39
Vacant	Mil	-	7	10	3	1
Vacant	Mil	-	7	10	4	1
Vacant	Mil	-	7	10	4	2
Vacant	Mil	-	7	10	4	3
Vacant	Mil	-	7	10	4	4
Vacant	Mil	-	7	10	4	5
Vacant	Mil	-	7	10	4	6
Vacant	Mil	-	7	10	4	7
Vacant	Mil	-	7	10	4	8
Vacant	Mil	-	8	2	1	1
Liddell, James, heirs of, 23 Apr 1800	Mil	-	8	2	1	2
Liddell, James, heirs of, 23 Apr 1800	Mil	-	8	2	1	3
McLane, Allen, 23 Apr 1800	Mil	-	8	2	1	4
McLane, Allen, 23 Apr 1800	Mil	-	8	2	1	5
McLane, Allen, 23 Apr 1800	Mil	-	8	2	1	6
Donahoe, James, 5 Mar 1805	Mil	-	8	2	1	7
Munsons, Theop[hilu]s? heirs of, 7 Mar 1805	Mil	-	8	2	1	8
Reeves, Luther, 7 Mar 1805	Mil	-	8	2	1	9
Liddell, James, heirs of, 23 Apr 1800	Mil	-	8	2	1	10
von Steuben, Baron --, devisees of, 18 Jan 1806	Mil	-	8	2	1	11
Morris, Samuel, 16 Oct 1804	Mil	-	8	2	1	12
Munsons, Theop[hilu]s? heirs of, 7 Mar 1805	Mil	-	8	2	1	13
Munsons, Theop[hilu]s? heirs of, 7 Mar 1805	Mil	-	8	2	1	14
Levering, Abel, & Tyson, Eliza, 21 Feb 1807	Mil	-	8	2	1	15
Misener, Godfrey, assignee of (George Knopiler?) 27 Feb 1805	Mil	-	8	2	1	16

<u>1748</u> Various C/-/053

100-Acre Lots:

Patentee & Location Date	*Location*					
Rosell? [Rossell?] Zachariah, 24 Apr 1806	Mil	-	8	2	1	17
von Steuben, Baron --, devisees of, 18 Jan 1806	Mil	-	8	2	1	18
von Steuben, Baron --, devisees of, 18 Jan 1806	Mil	-	8	2	1	19
von Steuben, Baron --, devisees of, 18 Jan 1806	Mil	-	8	2	1	20
von Steuben, Baron -- devisees of, 18 Jan 1806	Mil	-	8	2	1	21
Peters, Pomp, assignee of 27 Dec 1803	Mil	-	8	2	1	22
Wallingford, Cato, assignee of, 24 Dec 1803	Mil	-	8	2	1	23
Donovan, Tim, administrator of, 29 May 1806	Mil	-	8	2	1	24
Boyer, Lewis, 8 Mar 1805	Mil	-	8	2	1	25
Smith, Ebenezer, assignee of (N? C? Sproat) 20 Dec 1805	Mil	-	8	2	1	26
Talbot, Silas, 24 Dec 1802	Mil	-	8	2	1	27
Talbot, Silas, 24 Dec 1802	Mil	-	8	2	1	28
von Steuben, Baron --, devisees of, 18 Jan 1806	Mil	-	8	2	1	29
von Steuben, Baron --, devisees of, 18 Jan 1806	Mil	-	8	2	1	30
Levick, Robert, assignee of, 23 Dec 1805	Mil	-	8	2	1	31
von Steuben, Baron --, devisees of, 18 Jan 1806	Mil	-	8	2	1	32
Talbot, Silas, 24 Dec 1802	Mil	-	8	2	1	33
Talbot, Silas, 24 Dec 1802	Mil	-	8	2	1	34
Kean, Edward, 31 Jan 1806	Mil	-	8	2	1	35
Parker, Robert, 27 Feb 1805	Mil	-	8	2	1	36
Parker, Robert, 27 Feb 1805	Mil	-	8	2	1	37
Porter, William, 27 Feb 1805	Mil	-	8	2	1	38
Porter, William, 27 Feb 1805	Mil	-	8	2	1	39
Smith, Isaac, assignee of, 27 Feb 1805	Mil	-	8	2	1	40
Lisk, Peter, 2 May 1809	Mil	-	8	2	3	1
Lytle, Arch[ibal]d, assignee of the heirs of (R? Wells) 16 Nov 1804	Mil	-	8	2	3	2
Lytle, Arch[ibal]d, assignee of the heirs of (R? Wells) 16 Nov 1804	Mil	-	8	2	3	3
Lytle, Arch[ibal]d, assignee of the heirs of (R? Wells) 16 Nov 1804	Mil	-	8	2	3	4
Lytle, Arch[ibal]d, assignee of the heirs of (R? Wells) 16 Nov 1804	Mil	-	8	2	3	5
Prall, Edward, 8 Mar 1805	Mil	-	8	2	3	6
Lytle, Arch[ibal]d, assignee of the heirs of (Richard? Wells) 16 Nov 1804	Mil	-	8	2	3	7
Craft, Joseph, assignee of the heir of (Abijah Holbrook) 30 Mar 1805	Mil	-	8	2	3	8
Thomas, Lewis, assignee of the heir of (Richard Wells) 30 Mar 1805	Mil	-	8	2	3	9
Chapman, Stephen, 7 Mar 1805	Mil	-	8	2	3	10

<u>1749</u> Various C/-/054

100-Acre Lots:

Patentee & Location Date	*Location*					
von Steuben, Baron --, devisees of, 18 Jan 1806	Mil	-	8	2	3	11
von Steuben, Baron --, devisees of, 18 Jan 1806	Mil	-	8	2	3	12
Cantine, George, 24 Oct 1804	Mil	-	8	2	3	13
Rounsavell, John, 27 Nov 1804	Mil	-	8	2	3	14
Prall, Edward, 8 Mar 1805	Mil	-	8	2	3	15
Prall, Edward, 8 Mar 1805	Mil	-	8	2	3	16
Smiley, Robert, 22 Nov 1804	Mil	-	8	2	3	17
Thomas, Lewis, assignee of (Richard? Wells) 16 Nov 1804	Mil	-	8	2	3	18
von Steuben, Baron -- devisees of, 18 Jan 1806	Mil	-	8	2	3	19
Peaster, Zacheus, 11 Feb 1805	Mil	-	8	2	3	20
Peaster, Zacheus, 11 Feb 1805	Mil	-	8	2	3	21
Foreman, William, heir of, 11 Dec 1804	Mil	-	8	2	3	22
L'Enfant, Peter C., 31 Dec 1802	Mil	-	8	2	3	23
L'Enfant, Peter C., 31 Dec 1802	Mil	-	8	2	3	24
L'Enfant, Peter C., 31 Dec 1802	Mil	-	8	2	3	25
Peebles, Robert, 18 Sep 1801	Mil	-	8	2	3	26
Finley, John, 21 Sep 1801	Mil	-	8	2	3	27
Henderson, G? H., heirs of, 23 Apr 1800	Mil	-	8	2	3	28
Lane, Joseph, 23 Apr 1800	Mil	-	8	2	3	29
Lane, Joseph, 23 Apr 1800	Mil	-	8	2	3	30
Gregory, Matthew, 23 Apr 1800	Mil	-	8	2	3	31
Lane, Joseph, 23 Apr 1800	Mil	-	8	2	3	32
Henderson, G. H., heirs of, 23 Apr 1800	Mil	-	8	2	3	33
Jacobs, David, 25 May 1802	Mil	-	8	2	3	34
Peebles, Robert, 18 Sep 1801	Mil	-	8	2	3	35
Thomas, Lewis, assignee of (Richard Wells) 16 Nov 1804	Mil	-	8	2	3	36
Means, Robert, 5 Dec 1807	Mil	-	8	2	3	37
Henderson, G. K., heirs of, 23 Apr 1800	Mil	-	8	2	3	38
Lane, Joseph, 23 Apr 1800	Mil	-	8	2	3	39
Gregory, Mathew, 23 Apr 1800	Mil	-	8	2	3	40

1749 [continued]

Holden, Daniel, 7 Nov 1803	Mil -	8	4	3	1
Murphy, James, heirs of, 23 Dec 1803	Mil -	8	4	3	2
Vanhorne, Isaac, 30 Aug 1806	Mil -	8	4	3	3
Vanhorne, Isaac, 30 Aug 1806	Mil -	8	4	3	4
Vanhorne, Isaac, 30 Aug 1806	Mil -	8	4	3	5

1750 Various C/-/055

100-Acre Lots:

Patentee & Location Date	*Location*				
Vanhorne, Isaac, 30 Aug 1806	Mil -	8	4	3	6
Ransom, Samuel, assignee of, 10 Dec 1808	Mil -	8	4	3	7
Boyle, Thomas H., assignee of, 6 Apr 1809	Mil -	8	4	3	8
Beers, James, assignee of (Samuel Dorance?) 1 Dec 1803	Mil -	8	4	3	9
Leach, James, 2 Dec 1803	Mil -	8	4	3	10
Taborn, Joel, assignee of (William B. Chatham?) 16 Nov 1803	Mil -	8	4	3	11
Allyn, Timothy, 6 Dec 1803	Mil -	8	4	3	12
Vacant	Mil -	8	4	3	13
Vacant	Mil -	8	4	3	14
Vacant	Mil -	8	4	3	15
Vacant	Mil -	8	4	3	16
Vacant	Mil -	8	4	3	17
Vacant	Mil -	8	4	3	18
Allyn, Timothy, 6 Dec 1803	Mil -	8	4	3	19
Means, James, 7 Nov 1803	Mil -	8	4	3	20
Means, James, 7 Nov 1803	Mil -	8	4	3	21
Allyn, Timothy, 6 Dec 1803	Mil -	8	4	3	22
Vacant	Mil -	8	4	3	23
Vacant	Mil -	8	4	3	24
Vacant	Mil -	8	4	3	25
Vacant	Mil -	8	4	3	26
Vacant	Mil -	8	4	3	27
Vacant	Mil -	8	4	3	28
Weare, Richard, heir of, 26 Nov 1803	Mil -	8	4	3	29
Means, James, 7 Nov 1803	Mil -	8	4	3	30
Bass, Samuel, devisees of, 24 Nov 1803	Mil -	8	4	3	31
Weare, Richard, heir of, 26 Nov 1803	Mil -	8	4	3	32
Vacant	Mil -	8	4	3	33
Vacant	Mil -	8	4	3	34
Vacant	Mil -	8	4	3	35
Vacant	Mil -	8	4	3	36
Vacant	Mil -	8	4	3	37
Vacant	Mil -	8	4	3	38
Weare, Richard, heir of, 26 Nov 1803	Mil -	8	4	3	39
Andrews, Josiah, 24 Nov 1803	Mil -	8	4	3	40

1751 Various C/-/056

100-Acre Lots:

Patentee & Location Date	*Location*				
Cilley, Jonathan, 29 Dec 1801	Mil -	8	5	1	1
Daney? [Darcey?] John, 30 Jan 1801	Mil -	8	5	1	2
Daney? [Darcey?] John, 30 Jan 1801	Mil -	8	5	1	3
Daney? [Darcey?] John, 30 Jan 1801	Mil -	8	5	1	4
McDonald, William, 23 Feb 1801	Mil -	8	5	1	5
Cilley, Jonathan, heirs of, 29 Dec 1801	Mil -	8	5	1	6
Cilley, Jonathan, heirs of, 29 Dec 1801	Mil -	8	5	1	7
Cilley, Jonathan, heirs of, 29 Dec 1801	Mil -	8	5	1	8
North, William, 7 Jul 1801	Mil -	8	5	1	9
North, William, 7 Jul 1801	Mil -	8	5	1	10
Cilley, Jonathan, 29 Dec 1801	Mil -	8	5	1	11
Cilley, Jonathan, 29 Dec 1801	Mil -	8	5	1	12
Brown, William, 28 Dec 1802	Mil -	8	5	1	13
Brown, William, 28 Dec 1802	Mil -	8	5	1	14
Brown, William, 28 Dec 1802	Mil -	8	5	1	15
Brown, William, 28 Dec 1802	Mil -	8	5	1	16
Cilley, Monathan, 29 Dec 1801	Mil -	8	5	1	17
Vacant	Mil -	8	5	1	18
Vacant	Mil -	8	5	1	19
Vacant	Mil -	8	5	1	20
Vacant	Mil -	8	5	1	21
Vacant	Mil -	8	5	1	22
Mills, Joseph, 12 Mar 1803	Mil -	8	5	1	23
Mills, Joseph, 12 Mar 1803	Mil -	8	5	1	24
North, William, 7 Jul 1801	Mil -	8	5	1	25
Baskerville, Samuel, 16 Jul 1801	Mil -	8	5	1	26
Maben, James, heirs of, 14 Jun 1803	Mil -	8	5	1	27
Maben, James, heirs of, 14 Jun 1803	Mil -	8	5	1	28
Mosby, Littleberry, Junior, 3 Oct 1803	Mil -	8	5	1	29
Vacant	Mil -	8	5	1	30
Vacant	Mil -	8	5	1	31
Vacant	Mil -	8	5	1	32
Vacant	Mil -	8	5	1	33
Vacant	Mil -	8	5	1	34
Vacant	Mil -	8	5	1	35
Purkett, Henry, 28 Dec 1804	Mil -	8	5	1	36

1752 Various C/-/057

100-Acre Lots:

Patentee & Location Date	*Location*				
Mosby, Littleberry, Junior, 3 Oct 1803	Mil -	8	5	1	37
Mosby, Littleberry, Junior, 3 Oct 1803	Mil -	8	5	1	38
Maben, James, heirs of, 14 Jun 1803	Mil -	8	5	1	39

1752

Patentee & Location Date						
Baskerville, Samuel, 16 Jul 1801	Mil	-	8	5	1	40
Vacant	Mil	-	8	7	3	1
Vacant	Mil	-	8	7	3	2
Vacant	Mil	-	8	7	3	3
Vacant	Mil	-	8	7	3	4
Vacant	Mil	-	8	7	3	5
Vacant	Mil	-	8	7	3	6
Vacant	Mil	-	8	7	3	7
Vacant	Mil	-	8	7	3	8
Vacant	Mil	-	8	7	3	9
Vacant	Mil	-	8	7	3	10
Vacant	Mil	-	8	7	3	11
Vacant	Mil	-	8	7	3	12
Vacant	Mil	-	8	7	3	13
Vacant	Mil	-	8	7	3	14
Vacant	Mil	-	8	7	3	15
Vacant	Mil	-	8	7	3	16
Vacant	Mil	-	8	7	3	17
Vacant	Mil	-	8	7	3	18
Vacant	Mil	-	8	7	3	19
Vacant	Mil	-	8	7	3	20
Vacant	Mil	-	8	7	3	21
Vacant	Mil	-	8	7	3	22
Vacant	Mil	-	8	7	3	23
Vacant	Mil	-	8	7	3	24
Vacant	Mil	-	8	7	3	25
Vacant	Mil	-	8	7	3	26
Vacant	Mil	-	8	7	3	27
Vacant	Mil	-	8	7	3	28
Vacant	Mil	-	8	7	3	29
Vacant	Mil	-	8	7	3	30
Vacant	Mil	-	8	7	3	31

1753 Various C/-/058

100-Acre Lots: Patentee & Location Date — *Location*

Patentee & Location Date	Location					
Vacant	Mil	-	8	7	3	32
Vacant	Mil	-	8	7	3	33
Vacant	Mil	-	8	7	3	34
Vacant	Mil	-	8	7	3	35
Vacant	Mil	-	8	7	3	36
Vacant	Mil	-	8	7	3	37
Vacant	Mil	-	8	7	3	38
Vacant	Mil	-	8	7	3	39
Vacant	Mil	-	8	7	3	40
Vacant	Mil	-	8	9	1	1
Bavington? [Barington?] John, 3 May 1808	Mil	-	8	9	1	2
Knight, Jonathan, 7 Jul 1803	Mil	-	8	9	1	3
Knight, Jonathan, 7 Jul 1803	Mil	-	8	9	1	4
Knight, Jonathan, 7 Jul 1803	Mil	-	8	9	1	5
Vacant	Mil	-	8	9	1	6
Booker, Lewis, 14 Jun 1803	Mil	-	8	9	1	7
Booker, Lewis, 14 Jun 1803	Mil	-	8	9	1	8
Vacant	Mil	-	8	9	1	9
Vacant	Mil	-	8	9	1	10
Berry, William, 2 Jun 1808	Mil	-	8	9	1	11
Berry, William, 2 Jun 1808	Mil	-	8	9	1	12
Berry, William, 2 Jun 1808	Mil	-	8	9	1	13
Cary, John D., 3 May 1808	Mil	-	8	9	1	14
Cary, John D., 3 May 1808	Mil	-	8	9	1	15
Cookerly, Eleanor, 3 May 1808	Mil	-	8	9	1	16
Cookerly, Eleanor, 3 May 1808	Mil	-	8	9	1	17
Cookerly, Eleanor, 3 May 1808	Mil	-	8	9	1	18
Vacant	Mil	-	8	9	1	19
Dustin, Moses, executor of, 14 Jun 1803	Mil	-	8	9	1	20
Owens, Joseph, 14 Jun 1803	Mil	-	8	9	1	21
Dustin, Moses, executor of, 14 Jun 1803	Mil	-	8	9	1	22
Dustin, Moses, executor of, 14 Jun 1803	Mil	-	8	9	1	23
Vacant	Mil	-	8	9	1	24
Ransom, Elijah, 17 Aug 1808	Mil	-	8	9	1	25
Ransom, Elijah, 17 Aug 1808	Mil	-	8	9	1	26

1754 Various C/-/059

100-Acre Lots: Patentee & Location Date — *Location*

Patentee & Location Date	Location					
Keeler, Aaron, 1812	Mil	-	8	9	1	27
Vacant	Mil	-	8	9	1	28
Vacant	Mil	-	8	9	1	29
Young, Moses, assignee of, 10 Oct 1808	Mil	-	8	9	1	30
Young, Moses, assignee of, 10 Oct 1808	Mil	-	8	9	1	31
Vacant	Mil	-	8	9	1	32
Vacant	Mil	-	8	9	1	33
Vacant	Mil	-	8	9	2	1
Vacant	Mil	-	8	9	2	2
Thompson, Thomas M., assignee of John Steel, 11 Mar 1811	Mil	-	8	9	2	3
Thompson, Thomas M., assignee of John Steel, 11 Mar 1811	Mil	-	8	9	2	4
Thompson, Thomas M., assignee of John Steel, 11 Mar 1811	Mil	-	8	9	2	5
Vacant	Mil	-	8	9	2	6
Thompson, Thomas M., assignee [of John Steel?] 11 Mar 1811	Mil	-	8	9	2	7
Thompson, Thomas M., assignee [of John Steel?] 11 Mar 1811	Mil	-	8	9	2	8
Estep, Ephraim, assignee, 17 Mar 1811	Mil	-	8	9	2	9
Vacant	Mil	-	8	9	2	10
Vacant	Mil	-	8	9	2	11
Vacant	Mil	-	8	9	2	12
Vacant	Mil	-	8	9	2	13
Vacant	Mil	-	8	9	2	14
Vacant	Mil	-	8	9	2	15
Haws, Bartlett, heirs, 28 Apr 1811	Mil	-	8	9	2	16
Vacant	Mil	-	8	9	2	17
Vacant	Mil	-	8	9	2	18
Vacant	Mil	-	8	9	2	19
Vacant	Mil	-	8	9	2	20
Vacant	Mil	-	8	9	2	21
Vacant	Mil	-	8	9	2	22
Vacant	Mil	-	8	9	2	23
Loomis, Israel, 28 Apr 1810	Mil	-	8	9	2	24
Hawkins, Benjamin, 2 Mar 1811	Mil	-	8	9	2	25
Vacant	Mil	-	8	9	3	1
Vacant	Mil	-	8	9	3	2

1754 [continued]

Vacant	Mil	-	8	9	3	3

1755 Various C/-/060

100-Acre Lots:

Patentee & Location Date	*Location*					
Vacant	Mil	-	8	9	3	4
Vacant	Mil	-	8	9	3	5
Hills, Roger E[nos] 18 Mar 1811	Mil	-	8	9	3	6
Barnett, James, 13 Feb 1809	Mil	-	8	9	3	7
Barnett, James, 13 Feb 1809	Mil	-	8	9	3	8
Vacant	Mil	-	8	9	3	9
Hills, Roger Enos, 18 Mar 1811	Mil	-	8	9	3	10
Vacant	Mil	-	8	9	3	11
Vacant	Mil	-	8	9	3	12
Vacant	Mil	-	8	9	3	13
Vacant	Mil	-	8	9	3	14
Vacant	Mil	-	8	9	3	15
Vacant	Mil	-	8	9	3	16
Vacant	Mil	-	8	9	3	17
Vacant	Mil	-	8	9	3	18
Vacant	Mil	-	8	9	3	19
Vacant	Mil	-	8	9	3	20
Vacant	Mil	-	8	9	3	21
Vacant	Mil	-	8	9	3	22
Vacant	Mil	-	8	9	3	23
Vacant	Mil	-	8	9	3	24
Vacant	Mil	-	8	9	3	25
Vacant	Mil	-	8	9	3	26
Vacant	Mil	-	8	9	3	27
Vacant	Mil	-	8	9	3	28
Vacant	Mil	-	8	9	3	29
Vacant	Mil	-	8	9	3	30
Vacant	Mil	-	8	9	3	31
Vacant	Mil	-	8	9	3	32
Vacant	Mil	-	8	9	3	33
Vacant	Mil	-	8	9	3	34
Vacant	Mil	-	8	9	3	35
Vacant	Mil	-	8	9	3	36
Vacant	Mil	-	8	9	3	37
Vacant	Mil	-	8	9	3	38
Vacant	Mil	-	8	9	3	39
Vacant	Mil	-	8	9	3	40

1756 Various C/-/061

100-Acre Lots:

Patentee & Location Date	*Location*					
St. Clair, Daniel, 27 Feb 1805	Mil	-	9	1	3	1
St. Clair, Daniel, 27 Feb 1805	Mil	-	9	1	3	2
Northrop, Isaac, 11 Feb 1806	Mil	-	9	1	3	3
Swoomley, Jacob, 24 Jan 1811	Mil	-	9	1	3	4
Hite, Isaac, assignee of, (Richard? Brookover?) 28 Jan 1806	Mil	-	9	1	3	5
Hite, Isaac, assignee of, (Richard? Brookover?) 28 Jan 1806	Mil	-	9	1	3	6
Robinson, Robert, assignee of (Caleb? Norton) 28 Jan 1806	Mil	-	9	1	3	7
Cowdry, Samuel, assignee of (Caleb? Norton) 28 Jan 1806	Mil	-	9	1	3	8
Wickham, John, heir of, 21 Feb 1804	Mil	-	9	1	3	9
Wickham, John, heir of, 21 Feb 1804	Mil	-	9	1	3	10
Pride, Reuben, 29 Dec 1801	Mil	-	9	1	3	11
Pride, Reuben, 29 Dec 1801	Mil	-	9	1	3	12
Gray, Peter, 21 Feb 1804	Mil	-	9	1	3	13
Gray, Peter, 21 Feb 1804	Mil	-	9	1	3	14
Gray, Peter, 21 Feb 1804	Mil	-	9	1	3	15
Mintham, William, heirs of, 27 Feb 1804	Mil	-	9	1	3	16
Kennedy, Andrew, 18 Feb 1804	Mil	-	9	1	3	17
Belding, Moses, assignee of (C? M? Goldsberry) 14 Feb 1804	Mil	-	9	1	3	18
Belding, Moses, assignee of (C? M? Goldsberry) 14 Feb 1804	Mil	-	9	1	3	19
Biggs, Arnold, assignee of (P. Fearing) 8 Feb 1804	Mil	-	9	1	3	20
Tawson, William, 29 Dec 1801	Mil	-	9	1	3	21
Tawson, William, 29 Dec 1801	Mil	-	9	1	3	22
Jones, Churchill, 24 Apr 1807	Mil	-	9	1	3	23
Jones, Churchill, 24 Apr 1807	Mil	-	9	1	3	24
Temple, Benjamin, 31 Dec 1801	Mil	-	9	1	3	25
Temple, Benjamin, 31 Dec 1801	Mil	-	9	1	3	26
Parker, John, 14 Jan 1804	Mil	-	9	1	3	27
Spring, Simeon, 2 Jan 1804	Mil	-	9	1	3	28
Blundin, William, 27 Oct 1801	Mil	-	9	1	3	29
Smith, Elnathan, 21 Oct 1801	Mil	-	9	1	3	30
Bradley, Daniel, 21 Oct 1801	Mil	-	9	1	3	31
Bradley, Daniel, 21 Oct 1801	Mil	-	9	1	3	32
Pike, William, 21 Oct 1801	Mil	-	9	1	3	33
Pike William, 21 Oct 1801	Mil	-	9	1	3	34
Andrews, John, 21 Oct 1801	Mil	-	9	1	3	35

1757 Various C/-/062

100-Acre Lots:

Patentee & Location Date	*Location*					
Spring, Simeon, 2 Jan 1804	Mil	-	9	1	3	36
Temple, Benjamin, 31 Dec 1801	Mil	-	9	1	3	37

1757 [continued]

Patentee & Location Date	Location					
Temple, Benjamin, 31 Dec 1801	Mil	-	9	1	3	38
Jones, Churchill, 24 Apr 1807	Mil	-	9	1	3	39
Swoomley, Jacob, 24 Jan 1811	Mil	-	9	1	3	40
Young, Aaron, assignee of (George Holcomb) 17 Apr 1806	Mil	-	9	7	3	1
Vacant	Mil	-	9	7	3	2
Vacant	Mil	-	9	7	3	3
Vacant	Mil	-	9	7	3	4
Vacant	Mil	-	9	7	3	5
Vacant	Mil	-	9	7	3	6
Vacant	Mil	-	9	7	3	7
Vacant	Mil	-	9	7	3	8
Vacant	Mil	-	9	7	3	9
Vacant	Mil	-	9	7	3	10
Vacant	Mil	-	9	7	3	11
Vacant	Mil	-	9	7	3	12
Vacant	Mil	-	9	7	3	13
Smith, Daniel, heirs of, 22 Jun 1810	Mil	-	9	7	3	14
Collins, William, 20 Jan 1806	Mil	-	9	7	3	15
Mills, Peter, 11 May 1808	Mil	-	9	7	3	16
Kennard, John [Junior] son & heir of John Kennard [Senior] 22 Jun 1809	Mil	-	9	7	3	17
Hawkins, Rebecca, heiress of James Shepherd, 7 Mar 1809	Mil	-	9	7	3	18
Burbeck, Henry, 27 Jul 1801	Mil	-	9	7	3	19
Burbeck, Henry, 27 Jul 1801	Mil	-	9	7	3	20
Vacant	Mil	-	9	7	3	21
Vacant	Mil	-	9	7	3	22
Vacant	Mil	-	9	7	3	23
Vacant	Mil	-	9	7	3	24
Vacant	Mil	-	9	7	3	25
Scoone, William; Scoone, George; & Scoone, Henrietta; heirs of George Scoone, 22 Jun 1809	Mil	-	9	7	3	26
Vacant	Mil	-	9	7	3	27
Barron, Benjamin, assignee of (J? G. Jackson) 19 Aug 1808	Mil	-	9	7	3	28
Burbeck, Henry, 27 Jul 1801	Mil	-	9	7	3	29
Robinson, Adrus? [Andrew?] 31 Dec 1801	Mil	-	9	7	3	30

1758 Various C/-/063

100-Acre Lots:

Patentee & Location Date	*Location*					
Vacant	Mil	-	9	7	3	31
Vacant	Mil	-	9	7	3	32
Vacant	Mil	-	9	7	3	33
Vacant	Mil	-	9	7	3	34
Robinson, Andrew, 31 Dec 1801	Mil	-	9	7	3	35
Cushing, Thomas, 27 Jul 1801	Mil	-	9	7	3	36
Cushing, Thomas, 27 Jul 1801	Mil	-	9	7	3	37
Brigham, Joel, assignee of, 19 Aug 1808	Mil	-	9	7	3	38
Mills, Peter, 11 May 1808	Mil	-	9	7	3	39
Mills, Peter, 11 May 1808	Mil	-	9	7	3	40
Vacant	Mil	-	9	9	1	1*
Vacant	Mil	-	9	9	1	2
Vacant	Mil	-	9	9	1	3
Vacant	Mil	-	9	9	1	4
Vacant	Mil	-	9	9	1	5
Vacant	Mil	-	9	9	1	6
Vacant	Mil	-	9	9	1	7
Vacant	Mil	-	9	9	1	8
Vacant	Mil	-	9	9	1	9
Vacant	Mil	-	9	9	1	10
Vacant	Mil	-	9	9	1	11
Vacant	Mil	-	9	9	1	12
Vacant	Mil	-	9	9	1	13
Vacant	Mil	-	9	9	1	14
Vacant	Mil	-	9	9	1	15
Vacant	Mil	-	9	9	1	16
Vacant	Mil	-	9	9	1	17
Vacant	Mil	-	9	9	1	18
Vacant	Mil	-	9	9	1	19
Vacant	Mil	-	9	9	2	1
Vacant	Mil	-	9	9	2	2
Vacant	Mil	-	9	9	2	3
Vacant	Mil	-	9	9	2	4
Vacant	Mil	-	9	9	2	5
Vacant	Mil	-	9	9	2	6
Vacant	Mil	-	9	9	2	7

*Not listed in source register.

1759 None C/-/064

100-Acre Lots:

Patentee & Location Date	*Location*					
Vacant	Mil	-	9	9	2	8
Vacant	Mil	-	9	9	2	9
Vacant	Mil	-	9	9	2	10
Vacant	Mil	-	9	9	2	11
Vacant	Mil	-	9	9	4	1
Vacant	Mil	-	9	9	4	2
Vacant	Mil	-	9	9	4	3
Vacant	Mil	-	9	9	4	4
Vacant	Mil	-	9	9	4	5
Vacant	Mil	-	9	9	4	6
Vacant	Mil	-	9	9	4	7
Vacant	Mil	-	9	9	4	8
Vacant	Mil	-	9	9	4	9
Vacant	Mil	-	9	9	4	10
Vacant	Mil	-	9	9	4	11
Vacant	Mil	-	9	9	4	12
Vacant	Mil	-	9	9	4	13
Vacant	Mil	-	9	9	4	14
Vacant	Mil	-	9	9	4	15
Vacant	Mil	-	9	9	4	16
Vacant	Mil	-	9	9	4	17
Vacant	Mil	-	9	9	4	18
Vacant	Mil	-	9	9	4	19
Vacant	Mil	-	9	9	4	20
Vacant	Mil	-	9	9	4	21
Vacant	Mil	-	9	9	4	22
Vacant	Mil	-	9	9	4	23
Vacant	Mil	-	9	9	4	24
Vacant	Mil	-	9	9	4	25
Vacant	Mil	-	9	9	4	26
Vacant	Mil	-	9	9	4	27
Vacant	Mil	-	9	9	4	28
Vacant	Mil	-	9	9	4	29
Vacant	Mil	-	9	9	4	30

1759 [continued]

Patentee & Location Date	Location					
Vacant	Mil	-	9	9	4	31
Vacant	Mil	-	9	9	4	32

1760 Various C/-/065

100-Acre Lots:

Patentee & Location Date	*Location*					
Vacant	Mil	-	9	9	4	33
Vacant	Mil	-	9	9	4	34
Vacant	Mil	-	9	9	4	35
Vacant	Mil	-	9	9	4	36
Vacant	Mil	-	9	9	4	37
Vacant	Mil	-	9	9	4	38
Vacant	Mil	-	9	9	4	39
Vacant	Mil	-	9	9	4	40
Vacant	Mil	-	9	9	4	41
Vacant	Mil	-	9	9	4	42
Vacant	Mil	-	9	9	4	43
Vacant	Mil	-	9	9	4	44
Vacant	Mil	-	10	1	2	1
Vacant	Mil	-	10	1	2	2
Vacant	Mil	-	10	1	2	3
Vacant	Mil	-	10	1	2	4
Vacant	Mil	-	10	1	2	5
Vacant	Mil	-	10	1	2	6
Vacant	Mil	-	10	1	2	7
Vacant	Mil	-	10	1	2	8
Vacant	Mil	-	10	1	2	9
Vacant	Mil	-	10	1	2	10
Robinson, William, 31 Jan 1814	Mil	-	10	1	2	11
Robinson, William, 31 Jan 1814	Mil	-	10	1	2	12
Vacant	Mil	-	10	1	2	13
Vacant	Mil	-	10	1	2	14
Vacant	Mil	-	10	1	2	15
Vacant	Mil	-	10	1	2	16
Vacant	Mil	-	10	1	2	17
Vacant	Mil	-	10	1	2	18
Vacant	Mil	-	10	1	2	19
Vacant	Mil	-	10	1	2	20
Vacant	Mil	-	10	1	2	21
Vacant	Mil	-	10	1	2	22
Vacant	Mil	-	10	1	2	23

1761 Various C/-/066

100-Acre Lots:

Patentee & Location Date	*Location*					
Vacant	Mil	-	10	1	2	24
Vacant	Mil	-	10	1	2	25
Vacant	Mil	-	10	1	2	26
Vacant	Mil	-	10	1	2	27
Vacant	Mil	-	10	1	2	28
Vacant	Mil	-	10	1	2	29
Vacant	Mil	-	10	1	2	30
Vacant	Mil	-	10	1	2	31
Vacant	Mil	-	10	1	2	32
Vacant	Mil	-	10	1	2	33
Vacant	Mil	-	10	1	2	34
Vacant	Mil	-	10	1	2	35
Wickens, John, 26 Feb 1813	Mil	-	10	1	2	36
Vacant	Mil	-	10	1	2	37
Vacant	Mil	-	10	1	2	38
Vacant	Mil	-	10	1	2	39
Vacant	Mil	-	10	1	2	40
Morrison, James, 30 Dec 1811	Mil	-	10	3	4	1
Vacant	Mil	-	10	3	4	2
Vacant	Mil	-	10	3	4	3
Vacant	Mil	-	10	3	4	4
Vacant	Mil	-	10	3	4	5
Vacant	Mil	-	10	3	4	6
Means, Robert, 5 Dec 1807	Mil	-	10	3	4	7
Means, Robert, 5 Dec 1807	Mil	-	10	3	4	8
Smith, Samuel Hoey, 5 Dec 1807	Mil	-	10	3	4	9
Means, Robert, 5 Dec 1807	Mil	-	10	3	4	10
Vacant	Mil	-	10	3	4	11
Vacant	Mil	-	10	3	4	12
Vacant	Mil	-	10	3	4	13
Vacant	Mil	-	10	3	4	14
Vacant	Mil	-	10	3	4	15
Vacant	Mil	-	10	3	4	16
Vacant	Mil	-	10	3	4	17
Vacant	Mil	-	10	3	4	18
Vacant	Mil	-	10	3	4	19

1762 Various C/-/067

100-Acre Lots:

Patentee & Location Date	*Location*					
Vacant	Mil	-	10	3	4	20
Means, Robert, 5 Dec 1807	Mil	-	10	3	4	21
Means, Robert, 5 Dec 1807	Mil	-	10	3	4	22
Smith, Samuel H., 5 Dec 1807	Mil	-	10	3	4	23
Sharpe, Anthony, 20 Nov 1804	Mil	-	10	3	4	24
Sharpe, Anthony, 20 Nov 1804	Mil	-	10	3	4	25
Sharpe, Anthony, 20 Nov 1804	Mil	-	10	3	4	26
Smith, Samuel H., 5 Dec 1807	Mil	-	10	3	4	27
Johnson, Francis, 27 Apr 1807	Mil	-	10	3	4	28
Means, Robert, 5 Dec 1807	Mil	-	10	3	4	29
Vacant	Mil	-	10	3	4	30
Vacant	Mil	-	10	3	4	31
Vacant	Mil	-	10	3	4	32
Coon, Israel, 31 Dec 1801	Mil	-	10	3	4	33
Nourse, Michael, 24 Feb 1807	Mil	-	10	3	4	34
Nourse, Michael, 24 Feb 1807	Mil	-	10	3	4	35
Mayer, Elizabeth, 21 Feb 1807	Mil	-	10	3	4	36
Mercer, John, 27 Feb 1805	Mil	-	10	3	4	37
Mercer, John, 27 Feb 1805	Mil	-	10	3	4	38
Hillard, Thurston, 7 Jan 1805	Mil	-	10	3	4	39
Mercer, John, 27 Feb 1805	Mil	-	10	3	4	40
Vacant	Mil	-	10	7	1	1
Hoey? [Hocy?] Samuel, 30 Mar 1808	Mil	-	10	7	1	2
Hoey? [Hocy?] Samuel, 30 Mar 1808	Mil	-	10	7	1	3
Hoey? [Hocy?] Samuel, 30 Mar 1808	Mil	-	10	7	1	4
Butler, Richard, 23 Apr 1800	Mil	-	10	7	1	5

1762 [continued]

Vacant	Mil	-	10	7	1	6
Vacant	Mil	-	10	7	1	7
Vacant	Mil	-	10	7	1	8
Butler, Richard, 23 Apr 1800	Mil	-	10	7	1	9
Hart, Nicholas, 23 Apr 1800	Mil	-	10	7	1	10
Butler, Richard, 23 Apr 1800	Mil	-	10	7	1	11
Butler, Richard, 23 Apr 1800	Mil	-	10	7	1	12
Vacant	Mil	-	10	7	1	13
Slaughter, John, 3 May 1808	Mil	-	10	7	1	14

1763 Various C/-/068

100-Acre Lots:

Patentee & Location Date	*Location*					
Sturdavant, Azor, 3 May 1808	Mil	-	10	7	1	15
Vacant	Mil	-	10	7	1	16
Vacant	Mil	-	10	7	1	17
Vacant	Mil	-	10	7	1	18
Vacant	Mil	-	10	7	1	19
Vacant	Mil	-	10	7	1	20
Vacant	Mil	-	10	7	1	21
Vacant	Mil	-	10	7	1	22
Smith, Joseph S., 3 May 1808	Mil	-	10	7	1	23
Butler, Richard, 23 Apr 1800	Mil	-	10	7	1	24
Means, Robert, 3 May 1808	Mil	-	10	7	1	25
Vacant	Mil	-	10	7	1	26
Vacant	Mil	-	10	7	1	27
Vacant	Mil	-	10	7	1	28
Morrison, James, 30 Dec 1811	Mil	-	10	7	1	29
Vacant	Mil	-	10	7	1	30
Vacant	Mil	-	10	7	1	31
Vacant	Mil	-	10	7	1	32
Vacant	Mil	-	10	7	1	33
Vacant	Mil	-	10	7	1	34
Vacant	Mil	-	10	7	1	35
Vacant	Mil	-	10	7	1	36
Vacant	Mil	-	10	7	1	37
Vacant	Mil	-	10	7	1	38
Morrison, James, 30 Dec 1811	Mil	-	10	7	1	39
Morrison, James, 30 Dec 1811	Mil	-	10	7	1	40
Vacant	Mil	-	10	9	1	1
Smith, Samuel H., assignee, 22 Jul 1811	Mil	-	10	9	1	2
Vacant	Mil	-	10	9	1	3
Vacant	Mil	-	10	9	3	1
Vacant	Mil	-	10	9	3	2
Vacant	Mil	-	10	9	3	3
Vacant	Mil	-	10	9	3	4
Vacant	Mil	-	10	9	3	5
Vacant	Mil	-	10	9	3	6
Vacant	Mil	-	10	9	3	7

1764 Various C/-/069

100-Acre Lots:

Patentee & Location Date	*Location*					
Vacant	Mil	-	10	9	3	8
Vacant	Mil	-	10	9	3	9
Vacant	Mil	-	10	9	3	10
Vacant	Mil	-	10	9	3	11
Vacant	Mil	-	10	9	3	12
Vacant	Mil	-	10	9	3	13
Vacant	Mil	-	10	9	3	14
Vacant	Mil	-	10	9	3	15
Vacant	Mil	-	10	9	3	16
Vacant	Mil	-	10	9	3	17
Vacant	Mil	-	10	9	3	18
Vacant	Mil	-	10	9	3	19
Vacant	Mil	-	10	9	3	20
Vacant	Mil	-	10	9	3	21
Vacant	Mil	-	10	9	3	22
Vacant	Mil	-	10	9	3	23
Vacant	Mil	-	10	9	3	24
Vacant	Mil	-	10	9	3	25
Vacant	Mil	-	10	9	3	26
Vacant	Mil	-	10	9	3	27
Vacant	Mil	-	10	9	3	28
Vacant	Mil	-	10	9	3	29
Vacant	Mil	-	10	9	3	30
Vacant	Mil	-	10	9	3	31
Vacant	Mil	-	10	9	3	32
Vacant	Mil	-	10	9	3	33
McKinley, John, 7 Aug 1800	Mil	-	10	9	3	34
McKinley, Alex[ander] 7 Aug 1800	Mil	-	10	9	3	35
Vacant	Mil	-	11	6	1	1
Hartman, Lewis, 1812	Mil	-	11	6	1	2
Vacant	Mil	-	11	6	1	3
Vacant	Mil	-	11	6	1	4
Vacant	Mil	-	11	6	1	5
Vacant	Mil	-	11	6	1	6

1765 Various C/-/070

100-Acre Lots:

Patentee & Location Date	*Location*					
Vacant	Mil	-	11	6	1	7
Vacant	Mil	-	11	6	1	8
Vacant	Mil	-	11	6	1	9
Graham, Isaac G., 20 Apr 1810	Mil	-	11	6	1	10
Graham, Isaac G., 20 Apr 1810	Mil	-	11	6	1	11
Graham, Isaac G., 20 Apr 1810	Mil	-	11	6	1	12
Hill, George, 3 Mar 1813	Mil	-	11	6	1	13
Hambrie? David, heirs of, 1812	Mil	-	11	6	1	14
Woodruff, John, 1812	Mil	-	11	6	1	15
Jonas, John, 1812	Mil	-	11	6	1	16
Chesney, Benjamin, 1812	Mil	-	11	6	1	17
Thornton, Abraham, 1812	Mil	-	11	6	1	18
Vacant	Mil	-	11	6	1	19
Vacant	Mil	-	11	6	1	20
Sickles, Garrett, 1812	Mil	-	11	6	1	21
Childs, Evander, 21 Mar 1810	Mil	-	11	6	1	22
Childs, Evander, 21 Mar 1810	Mil	-	11	6	1	23
Stansberry, Jonas, 30 Jan 1810	Mil	-	11	6	1	24
Brownfield, Robert, assignee of, 3 Jan 1810	Mil	-	11	6	1	25
Brownfield, Robert, assignee of, 3 Jan 1810	Mil	-	11	6	1	26

1765 [continued]

Patentee & Location Date	Location				
Brownfield, Robert, assignee of, 3 Jan 1810	Mil	- 11	6	1	27
Vacant	Mil	- 11	6	1	28
Vacant	Mil	- 11	6	1	29
Alward, Samuel, Junior, 2 Feb 1810	Mil	- 11	6	1	30
Vacant	Mil	- 11	6	1	31
Vermilyea, John, 3 Jan 1810	Mil	- 11	6	1	32
Matthews, John, 3 Jan 1810	Mil	- 11	6	1	33
Quarles, Abner, 2 Mar 1817	Mil	- 11	6	1	34
Vacant	Mil	- 11	6	1	35
Vacant	Mil	- 11	6	1	36
Tracy, Hezekiah, 2 Mar 1811	Mil	- 11	6	1	37
Tracy, Hezekiah, 2 Mar 1811	Mil	- 11	6	1	38
Bantham? [Bautham?] John, 14 Mar 1809	Mil	- 11	6	1	39
Jonas, John, 1812	Mil	- 11	6	1	40

1766 Various C/-/071

100-Acre Lots:

Patentee & Location Date	*Location*				
Cook, John, assignee of, (Adam Wallace) 9 Feb 1805	Mil	- 11	8	1	1
Alcorn, William, assignee of (Adam Wallace) 9 Feb 1805	Mil	- 11	8	1	2
Wattles, Mason, 24 Jan 1805	Mil	- 11	8	1	3
Wattles, Mason, 24 Jan 1805	Mil	- 11	8	1	4
Wattles, Mason, 24 Jan 1805	Mil	- 11	8	1	5
Garvin? [Gawin?] Henry, assignee of (Richard Gernon) 18 Feb 1805	Mil	- 11	8	1	6
Ball, B. W., assignee of, (Richard Gernon) 19 Feb 1805	Mil	- 11	8	1	7
Ball, B. W., assignee of, (Richard Gernon) 19 Feb 1805	Mil	- 11	8	1	8
Snows, James, assignee of, (Richard Gernon) 18 Feb 1805	Mil	- 11	8	1	9
Crumm, William, assignee of (Richard Gernon) 18 Feb 1805	Mil	- 11	8	1	10
Taylor, Richard, assignee of (Richard Gernon) 18 Feb 1805	Mil	- 11	8	1	11
Luther, Peleg, assignee of the heirs of, (Eben-[ezer] Seaver) 16 Feb 1805	Mil	- 11	8	1	12
Sturtevant, Isaac, 16 Feb 1805	Mil	- 11	8	1	13
Sturtevant, Isaac, 16 Feb 1805	Mil	- 11	8	1	14
McWilliam, Stephen, executor of, 25 Feb 1805	Mil	- 11	8	1	15
McWilliam, Stephen, executor of, 25 Feb 1805	Mil	- 11	8	1	16
Brevard, Alex[ander] 26 Feb 1805	Mil	- 11	8	1	17
Brevard, Alex[ander] 26 Feb 1805	Mil	- 11	8	1	18
Spicer, Jacob, 23 Feb 1805	Mil	- 11	8	1	19
Lee, Edward, 16 Feb 1805	Mil	- 11	8	1	20
Barker, Barnabas, 16 Feb 1805	Mil	- 11	8	1	21
Armstrong, Robert, assignee of (Richard Gernon) 18 Feb 1805	Mil	- 11	8	1	22
Blaney, John, assignee of (Richard Gernon) 18 Feb 1805	Mil	- 11	8	1	23
Leary, Dennis, assignee of (Richard Gernon) 18 Feb 1805	Mil	- 11	8	1	24
Quigley, Edward, assignee of (Richard Gernon) 19 Feb 1805	Mil	- 11	8	1	25
Vacant	Mil	- 11	8	1	26
Vacant	Mil	- 11	8	1	27
Vacant	Mil	- 11	8	1	28
Vacant	Mil	- 11	8	1	29
Vacant	Mil	- 11	8	1	30
Vacant	Mil	- 11	8	1	31
Brevard, Alexander, 26 Feb 1805	Mil	- 11	8	1	32
Vacant	Mil	- 11	8	1	33
Vacant	Mil	- 11	8	1	34
Vacant	Mil	- 11	8	1	35
Vacant	Mil	- 11	8	1	36

1767 Various C/-/072

100-Acre Lots:

Patentee & Location Date	*Location*				
Vacant	Mil	- 11	8	1	37
Vacant	Mil	- 11	8	1	38
Vacant	Mil	- 11	8	1	39
McCraw, Francis, assignee of (Samuel McCraw?) 18 Feb 1805	Mil	- 11	8	1	40
Vacant	Mil	- 11	9	3	1
Vacant	Mil	- 11	9	3	2
Vacant	Mil	- 11	9	3	3
Vacant	Mil	- 11	9	3	4
Barr, John, assignee of (John Shadley) 27 May 1809	Mil	- 11	9	3	5
Vacant	Mil	- 11	9	3	6
Vacant	Mil	- 11	9	3	7
Vacant	Mil	- 11	9	3	8
Vacant	Mil	- 11	9	3	9
Vacant	Mil	- 11	9	3	10
Vacant	Mil	- 11	9	3	11
Vacant	Mil	- 11	9	3	12
Vacant	Mil	- 11	9	3	13
Vacant	Mil	- 11	9	3	14
Vacant	Mil	- 11	9	3	15
Vacant	Mil	- 11	9	3	16
Vacant	Mil	- 11	9	4	1
Vacant	Mil	- 11	9	4	2
Coverly, Thomas, assignee of (John Morris) 16 Jun 1809	Mil	- 11	9	4	3
Coverly, Thomas, assignee of (John Morris) 16 Jun 1809	Mil	- 11	9	4	4
Vacant	Mil	- 11	9	4	5
Vacant	Mil	- 11	9	4	6

1767 [continued]

Vacant	Mil	-	11	9	4	7
Vacant	Mil	-	11	9	4	8
Vacant	Mil	-	11	9	4	9
Vacant	Mil	-	11	9	4	10
Vacant	Mil	-	11	9	4	11
Vacant	Mil	-	11	9	4	12
Chandler, Abriel, 28 Dec 1804	Mil	-	11	9	4	13
Vacant	Mil	-	11	9	4	14
Vacant	Mil	-	11	9	4	15
Vacant	Mil	-	11	9	4	16

1768 Various C/-/073

100-Acre Lots:
Patentee &
Location Date

	Location					
Vacant	Mil	-	11	9	4	17
Vacant	Mil	-	11	9	4	18
Vacant	Mil	-	11	9	4	19
Vacant	Mil	-	11	9	4	20
Vacant	Mil	-	11	9	4	21
Vacant	Mil	-	11	9	4	22
Weaver, Henry, 28 Dec 1804	Mil	-	11	9	4	23
Sawyer, Menassatt, 28 Dec 1804	Mil	-	11	9	4	24
Mooney? [Maury? Mary?] Eleanor Woodside, 14 Nov 1808	Mil	-	11	9	4	25
Kendrick, Montgomery, & Kendrick, Mary, heirs of Anderson, Arch[ibal]d, 14 Nov 1808	Mil	-	11	9	4	26
Kendrick, Montgomery, & Kendrick, Mary, heirs of Anderson, Arch[ibal]d, 14 Nov 1808	Mil	-	11	9	4	27
Kendrick, Montgomery, & Kendrick, Mary, heirs of Anderson, Arch[ibal]d, 14 Nov 1808	Mil	-	11	9	4	28
Vacant	Mil	-	12	9	3	1
Vacant	Mil	-	12	9	3	2
Vacant	Mil	-	12	9	3	3
Vacant	Mil	-	12	9	3	4
Vacant	Mil	-	12	9	3	5
Vacant	Mil	-	12	9	3	6
Vacant	Mil	-	12	9	3	7
Vacant	Mil	-	12	9	4	1
Vacant	Mil	-	12	9	4	2
Vacant	Mil	-	12	9	4	3
Vacant	Mil	-	12	9	4	4
Vacant	Mil	-	12	9	4	5
Vacant	Mil	-	12	9	4	6
Vacant	Mil	-	12	9	4	7
Vacant	Mil	-	12	9	4	8
Vacant	Mil	-	12	9	4	9
Vacant	Mil	-	12	9	4	10
Vacant	Mil	-	12	9	4	11
Vacant	Mil	-	12	9	4	12
Vacant	Mil	-	12	9	4	13
Vacant	Mil	-	12	9	4	14
Treat, John, 26 Feb 1801	Mil	-	13	8	1	1
Stow, Zacheus, 26 Feb 1801	Mil	-	13	8	1	2
Smith, Josiah, 26 Feb 1801	Mil	-	13	8	1	3
Smith, Asaph, 26 Feb 1801	Mil	-	13	8	1	4
Lewis, Naboth, 26 Feb 1801	Mil	-	13	8	1	5
Danel, R[ichar]d, 26 Feb 1801	Mil	-	13	8	1	6
Chamberlain, Theodore, 26 Feb 1801	Mil	-	13	8	1	7
Higgins, William, 29 Dec 1801	Mil	-	13	8	1	8
Higgins, William, 29 Dec 1801	Mil	-	13	8	1	9
Atkins, David, 26 Feb 1801	Mil	-	13	8	1	10
Pratt, John, 26 Feb 1801	Mil	-	13	8	1	11
Pratt, John, 26 Feb 1801	Mil	-	13	8	1	12
Rice, Nehemiah, 25 May 1802	Mil	-	13	8	2	1
Bull, Aaron, 31 Dec 1805	Mil	-	13	8	2	2
Johnston, Samuel, 31 Dec 1801	Mil	-	13	8	2	3
Johnston, Samuel, 31 Dec 1801	Mil	-	13	8	2	4
Bull, Aaron, 31 Dec 1805	Mil	-	13	8	2	5
Rice, Nehemiah, 25 May 1802	Mil	-	13	8	2	6
Rice, Nehemiah, 25 May 1802	Mil	-	13	8	2	7
Johnston, Samuel, 31 Dec 1801	Mil	-	13	8	2	8
Johnston, Samuel, 31 Dec 1801	Mil	-	13	8	2	9
Goodner, Coonrod, 1 Dec 1807	Mil	-	13	8	2	10
Hills, Benony, 20 Feb 1807	Mil	-	13	8	2	11
Oldwine, Barney, 31 Dec 1801	Mil	-	13	8	2	12
Vacant	Mil	-	13	8	2	13
Reed, Philip, 26 Feb 1801	Mil	-	13	8	4	1
Reed, Philip, 26 Feb 1801	Mil	-	13	8	4	2
Reed, Philip, 26 Feb 1801	Mil	-	13	8	4	3
Raisin, William, 26 Feb 1801	Mil	-	13	8	4	4
Raisin, William, 26 Feb 1801	Mil	-	13	8	4	5
Noyes, John, 29 Dec 1801	Mil	-	13	8	4	6
Hall, David, 9 Aug 1802	Mil	-	13	8	4	7
Hall, David, 9 Aug 1802	Mil	-	13	8	4	8
Gist, John, 24 Jun 1802	Mil	-	13	8	4	9
Gist, John, 24 Jun 1802	Mil	-	13	8	4	10
Gist, John, 24 Jun 1802	Mil	-	13	8	4	11
Hall, David, 9 Aug 1802	Mil	-	13	8	4	12
Hall, David, 9 Aug 1802	Mil	-	13	8	4	13

1769 Various C/-/074

100-Acre Lots:
Patentee &
Location Date

1770 Various C/-/075

100-Acre Lots:
Patentee &
Location Date

	Location					
Hall, David, 9 Aug 1802	Mil	-	13	8	4	14
Hall, David, 9 Aug 1802	Mil	-	13	8	4	15
Noyes, John, 29 Dec 1801	Mil	-	13	8	4	16
Kirkpatrick, James, 31 Dec 1801	Mil	-	13	8	4	17
Grimke, John F., 12 Aug 1802	Mil	-	13	8	4	18

1770 [continued]

Grimke, John F., 12 Aug 1802	Mil	-	13	8	4	19
Statinger, John, 24 May 1800	Mil	-	13	8	4	20
Bishop, John, 10 May 1800	Mil	-	13	8	4	21
Grimke, John F., 12 Aug 1802	Mil	-	13	8	4	22
Grimke, John F., 12 Aug 1802	Mil	-	13	8	4	23
Webb, David, 30 Sep 1802	Mil	-	13	8	4	24
Noyes, John, 29 Dec 1801	Mil	-	13	8	4	25
Curson, David, 13 Jan 1808	Mil	-	13	8	4	26
Brooke, Francis, 24 Dec 1802	Mil	-	14	8	1	1
Cole, David, 2 Dec 1811	Mil	-	14	8	1	2
Brooke, Francis, 24 Dec 1802	Mil	-	14	8	1	3
Kavenaugh, Garrett, 24 Dec 1802	Mil	-	14	8	1	4
Waltner? [Wattner?] Lud-[wic]k, heirs of, 25 May 1802	Mil	-	14	8	3	1
Waltner? [Wattner?] Lud-[wic]k, heirs of, 25 May 1802	Mil	-	14	8	3	2
Segond, James Chevalier de, 19 Sep 1803	Mil	-	14	8	3	3
Gibson? [Gilson?] James, 13 Mar 1803	Mil	-	14	8	3	4
Peck, John, 29 Dec 1801	Mil	-	14	8	3	5
Cogswell, Amos, 29 Dec 1801	Mil	-	14	8	3	6
Carr, James, 29 Dec 1801	Mil	-	14	8	3	7
Carr, James, 29 Dec 1801	Mil	-	14	8	3	8
Carr, James, 29 Dec 1801	Mil	-	14	8	3	9
Carr, James, 29 Dec 1801	Mil	-	14	8	3	10
Cogswell, Amos, 29 Dec 1801	Mil	-	14	8	3	11
Stoddert, Simon C., 29 Dec 1801	Mil	-	14	8	3	12
Hurlbut, Raphael, 29 Dec 1801	Mil	-	14	8	3	13
Segond, James Chevalier de, 19 Sep 1803	Mil	-	14	8	3	14
Waltner? [Wattner?] Lud-[wic]k, heirs of, 25 May 1802	Mil	-	14	8	3	15
Waltner? [Wattner?] Lud-[wic]k, heirs of, 25 May 1802	Mil	-	14	8	3	16
Waltern? [Wattner?] Lud-[wic]k, heirs of, 25 May 1802	Mil	-	14	8	3	17

1771 Various C/-/076

100-Acre Lots: Patentee & Location Date	*Location*					
McLaughlin, --, & Smith, --, 11 Jan 1814	Mil	-	14	8	3	18
Segond, James Chevalier de, 19 Sep 1803	Mil	-	14	8	3	19
Barnes, Ambrose, 29 Dec 1801	Mil	-	14	8	3	20
Welsh, John, 29 Dec 1801	Mil	-	14	8	3	21
Cogswell, Amas,* 29 Dec 1801	Mil	-	14	8	3	22
Fifield, John, 29 Sep 1801	Mil	-	14	8	3	23
Cogswell, Thomas, 31 Dec 1801	Mil	-	14	8	3	24
Cogswell, Thomas, 31 Dec 1801	Mil	-	14	8	3	25
Welsh, John, 29 Dec 1801	Mil	-	14	8	3	26
Bailey, Ichabod, heirs of, 29 Dec 1801	Mil	-	14	8	3	27
Bailey, Ichabod, heirs of, 29 Dec 1801	Mil	-	14	8	3	28
Ribbets, William, 24 Dec 1802	Mil	-	14	8	3	29
Benson, Pery,* 9 Dec 1802	Mil	-	14	8	3	30
Benson, Pery,* 9 Dec 1802	Mil	-	14	8	3	31
Benson, Pery,* 9 Dec 1802	Mil	-	14	8	3	32
Sandford, Liffe, 26 Dec 1802	Mil	-	14	8	3	33
Knapp, Jared, 29 Dec 1801	Mil	-	14	8	3	34
Gibbs, Moore, 29 Dec 1801	Mil	-	14	8	3	35
Cogswell, Thomas, 31 Dec 1801	Mil	-	14	8	3	36
Cogswell, Thomas, 31 Dec 1801	Mil	-	14	8	3	37
McGinnis? [Ginnis?] John, 19 Apr 1806	Mil	-	15	1	3	1
McCaley, Edward, 19 Apr 1806	Mil	-	15	1	3	2
Foster, Moses, assignee of (G. McKeenhan) 13 Apr 1805	Mil	-	15	1	3	3
Flangen [Flanagen?] Timothy, assignee of (G. McKeehan) 13 Apr 1805	Mil	-	15	1	3	4
Taylor, James, 25 Nov 1807	Mil	-	15	1	3	5
Taylor, James, 25 Nov 1807	Mil	-	15	1	3	6
Lesuer, John, 22 Apr 1806	Mil	-	15	1	3	7
Garnett, Ann, 16 Feb 1808	Mil	-	15	1	3	8
Garnett, Ann, 16 Feb 1808	Mil	-	15	1	3	9
Perkins, Aaron, assignee of (B. Carpenter) 6 Apr 1809	Mil	-	15	1	3	10
Edmunds, William, in trust for Green, S., & Green, R., 19 Jan 1808	Mil	-	15	1	3	11
Edmunds, William, in trust for Green, S., & Green, R., 19 Jan 1808	Mil	-	15	1	3	12
Taylor, James, 10 Apr 1810	Mil	-	15	1	3	13
McDonald, Francis, assignee of (G. McKeehan) 13 Apr 1805	Mil	-	15	1	3	14
Yest [Yost?] Martin, 19 Apr 1806	Mil	-	15	1	3	15

*So spelled.

1772 Various C/-/077

100-Acre Lots: Patentee & Location Date	*Location*					
McAllister, John, 19 Apr 1806	Mil	-	15	1	3	16
Bryan, William, 19 Apr 1806	Mil	-	15	1	3	17
Kellev, Ed[ward] assignee of (Mary? Doyle?) 19 Apr 1806	Mil	-	15	1	3	18

<u>1772</u> [continued]

Kerns, Godfrey, 19 Apr 1806	Mil	-	15	1	3	19
Davis, David, 22 Apr 1806	Mil	-	15	1	3	20
Brady, James, 10 Jun 1813	Mil	-	15	1	3	21
Gaylord, Ambrose, assignee of (assignee's name illegible) 6 Apr 1809	Mil	-	15	1	3	22
Cuyzer, Frederick, assignee of (assignee's name illegible) 6 Apr 1809	Mil	-	15	1	3	23
Robinson, Kennedy, 17 Mar 1807	Mil	-	15	1	3	24
McWhorter, John, 17 Mar 1807	Mil	-	15	1	3	25
Conner? [McConner?] M., heirs of, 3 May 1806	Mil	-	15	1	3	26
Berlin, Isaac, assignee of (John Duncan) 28 Dec 1805	Mil	-	15	1	3	27
Freeman, Nathan, assignee of (assignee's name illegible) 23 Dec 1805	Mil	-	15	1	3	28
Merriwether, James, 15 Feb 1806	Mil	-	15	1	3	29
Merriwether, James, 15 Feb 1806	Mil	-	15	1	3	30
Head, Richard, assignee of (assignee's name illegible) 2 Apr 1805	Mil	-	15	1	3	31
Head, Richard, assignee of (assignee's name illegible) 2 Apr 1805	Mil	-	15	1	3	32
Rowan, John, 14 May 1800	Mil	-	15	1	3	33
Parker, Wyman, 25 May 1802	Mil	-	15	1	3	34
Davis, Ebenezer, 25 May 1802	Mil	-	15	1	3	35
Davis, Ebenezer, 25 May 1802	Mil	-	15	1	3	36
Dowell, James, assignee of (assignee's name illegible) 23 Dec 1805	Mil	-	15	1	3	37
Desearn, Frederick, assignee of (assignee's name illegible) 23 Dec 1805	Mil	-	15	1	3	38
Hillcock, Robert, assignee of (assignee's name illegible) 1 May 1806	Mil	-	15	1	3	39
Parker, John, in trust for heirs of Timothy Parker, 6 Apr 1809	Mil	-	15	1	3	40
Apperson, R[ichar]d, & Taylor, James, 19 Jun 1808	Mil	-	15	2	2	1
Apperson, R[ichar]d, & Taylor, James, 19 Jun 1808	Mil	-	15	2	2	2
Ellis, Mary, & Lewis, Sus[ann]a, heirs of J? Fleming & James Taylor, 25 Aug 1808*	Mil	-	15	2	2	3
Ellis, Mary, & Lewis, Sus[ann]a, heirs of J? Fleming & James Taylor, 25 Aug 1808*	Mil	-	15	2	2	4
Morriss, George, 20 Dec 1808	Mil	-	15	2	2	5
Benedict, Ebenezer, 31 Dec 1801	Mil	-	15	2	2	6
Walmsley, William, 31 Dec 1801	Mil	-	15	2	2	7
Hait? [Hart?] Joel, 10 Jan 1801	Mil	-	15	2	2	8
Hait? [Hart?] Joseph, 10 Jan 1801	Mil	-	15	2	2	9
Hait? [Hart?] Joseph, 10 Jan 1801	Mil	-	15	2	2	10

*These entries do not appear to be correct. It seems more likely that Fleming and Taylor are the assignees, rather than the **devisors**.

<u>1773</u> Various C/-/078

100-Acre Lots:

Patentee & Location Date	*Location*					
Hentze, Frederick, 25 Mar 1808	Mil	-	15	2	2	11
Hite, Christopher, 25 Mar 1808	Mil	-	15	2	2	12
Ellis, Mary, & Lewis, Sus[ann]a, heirs of J? Fleming & James Taylor, 25 Aug 1808*	Mil	-	15	2	2	13
Ellis, Mary, & Lewis, Sus[ann]a, heirs of J? Fleming & James Taylor, 25 Aug 1808*	Mil	-	15	2	2	14
Apperson, R., & Taylor, James, 19 Jan 1808	Mil	-	15	2	2	15
Taylor, James, 19 Jan 1808	Mil	-	15	2	2	16
Taylor, James, 19 Jan 1808	Mil	-	15	2	2	17
Vacant	Mil	-	15	2	2	18
Rossetter, Bryan, 29 Dec 1808	Mil	-	15	2	2	19
Gambell, Joseph, 6 Jan 1809	Mil	-	15	2	2	20
Thomas, Gregory, 7 Apr 1804	Mil	-	15	2	2	21
Comstock, Samuel, 7 Apr 1804	Mil	-	15	2	2	22
Hait, Joseph, 10 Jan 1801	Mil	-	15	2	2	23
Hait, Joseph, 10 Jan 1801	Mil	-	15	2	2	24
Hait, Samuel, 10 Jan 1801	Mil	-	15	2	2	25
Hait, Joseph, 10 Jan 1801	Mil	-	15	2	2	26
Comstock, Samuel, 7 Apr 1804	Mil	-	15	2	2	27
Comstock, Samuel, 7 Apr 1804	Mil	-	15	2	2	28
Cockren, Squire, 1 Feb 1805	Mil	-	15	2	2	29
Ferver, Henry, 8 Feb 1805	Mil	-	15	2	2	30
Curich, Nich[ola]s, 31 Dec 1808	Mil	-	15	2	2	31
Curich, Nich[ola]s, 31 Dec 1808	Mil	-	15	2	2	32
Crosby, Jesse, 12 May 1802	Mil	-	15	2	2	33
Terry, Gamaliel, 12 May 1802	Mil	-	15	2	2	34
Nourse, James, 31 Dec 1801	Mil	-	15	2	2	35
Shields, David, 31 Dec 1801	Mil	-	15	2	2	36
Hubbell, Salmon, 30 Jan 1801	Mil	-	15	2	2	37
Hubbell, Salmon, 30 Jan 1801	Mil	-	15	2	2	38
Hait? [Hart?] Samuel, 10 Jan 1801	Mil	-	15	2	2	39

1773 [continued]

Hait? [Hart?] Samuel, 10 Jan 1801	Mil	-	15	2	2	40
Jones, David, 5 Mar 1805	Mil	-	15	7	3	1
Jones, David, 5 Mar 1805	Mil	-	15	7	3	2
Jones, David, 5 Mar 1805	Mil	-	15	7	3	3
Jones, David, 5 Mar 1805	Mil	-	15	7	3	4
Jones, David, 5 Mar 1805	Mil	-	15	7	3	5

*These entries do not appear to be correct. It seems more likely that Fleming and Taylor are the assignees, rather than the devisors.

1774 Various C/-/079

100-Acre Lots:

Patentee & Location Date	*Location*					
Jones, David, 5 Mar 1805	Mil	-	15	7	3	6
Jones, David, 5 Mar 1805	Mil	-	15	7	3	7
Jones, David, 5 Mar 1805	Mil	-	15	7	3	8
Jones, David, 5 Mar 1805	Mil	-	15	7	3	9
Jones, David, 5 Mar 1805	Mil	-	15	7	3	10
Jones, David, 5 Mar 1805	Mil	-	15	7	3	11
Jones, David, 5 Mar 1805	Mil	-	15	7	3	12
Jones, David, 5 Mar 1805	Mil	-	15	7	3	13
Jones, David, 5 Mar 1805	Mil	-	15	7	3	14
Jones, David, 5 Mar 1805	Mil	-	15	7	3	15
Jones, David, 5 Mar 1805	Mil	-	15	7	3	16
Jones, David, 5 Mar 1805	Mil	-	15	7	3	17
Jones, David, 5 Mar 1805	Mil	-	15	7	3	18
Jones, David, 5 Mar 1805	Mil	-	15	7	3	19
Jones, David, 5 Mar 1805	Mil	-	15	7	3	20
Jones, David, 5 Mar 1805	Mil	-	15	7	3	21
Jones, David, 5 Mar 1805	Mil	-	15	7	3	22
Jones, David, 5 Mar 1805	Mil	-	15	7	3	23
Jones, David, 5 Mar 1805	Mil	-	15	7	3	24
Jones, David, 5 Mar 1805	Mil	-	15	7	3	25
Jones, David, 5 Mar 1805	Mil	-	15	7	3	26
Jones, David, 5 Mar 1805	Mil	-	15	7	3	27
Jones, David, 5 Mar 1805	Mil	-	15	7	3	28
Jones, David, 5 Mar 1805	Mil	-	15	7	3	29
Jones, David, 5 Mar 1805	Mil	-	15	7	3	30
Jones, David, 5 Mar 1805	Mil	-	15	7	3	31
Jones, David, 5 Mar 1805	Mil	-	15	7	3	32
Jones, David, 5 Mar 1805	Mil	-	15	7	3	33
Jones, David, 5 Mar 1805	Mil	-	15	7	3	34
Jones, David, 5 Mar 1805	Mil	-	15	7	3	35
Jones, David, 5 Mar 1805	Mil	-	15	7	3	36
Jones, David, 5 Mar 1805	Mil	-	15	7	3	37
Jones, David, 5 Mar 1805	Mil	-	15	7	3	38
Jones, David, 5 Mar 1805	Mil	-	15	7	3	39
Jones, David, 5 Mar 1805	Mil	-	15	7	3	40
Sumner, Jethro, heirs of, 29 Apr 1800	Mil	-	15	7	4	1

1775 Various C/-/080

100-Acre Lots:

Patentee & Location Date	*Location*					
Sumner, Jethro, heirs of, 29 Apr 1800	Mil	-	15	7	4	2
Blount, Reading, 29 Apr 1805	Mil	-	15	7	4	3
Blount, Reading, 29 Apr 1805	Mil	-	15	7	4	4
Barth, Stephen, 5 Mar 1805	Mil	-	15	7	4	5
Ashely, John, 5 Mar 1805	Mil	-	15	7	4	6
Cochran, Daniel, heirs of, 5 Mar 1805	Mil	-	15	7	4	7
Chester, John, heiress of, 8 Aug 1805	Mil	-	15	7	4	8
Sell, Thomas, heir of, 4 Jan 1805	Mil	-	15	7	4	9
Sell, Thomas, heir of, 4 Jan 1805	Mil	-	15	7	4	10
Brown, Zephania, 21 Feb 1807	Mil	-	15	7	4	11
Doran, Patrick, 11 Mar 1807	Mil	-	15	7	4	12
Blount, Reading, 29 Apr 1806	Mil	-	15	7	4	13
Blount, Reading, 29 Apr 1806	Mil	-	15	7	4	14
Sumner, Jethro, heiress of, 29 Apr 1800	Mil	-	15	7	4	15
Sumner, Jethro, heiress of, 29 Apr 1800	Mil	-	15	7	4	16
Sumner, Jethro, heiress of, 29 Apr 1800	Mil	-	15	7	4	17
Sumner, Jethro, heiress of, 29 Apr 1800	Mil	-	15	7	4	18
Gerard, Charles, 29 Apr 1800	Mil	-	15	7	4	19
Gerard, Charles, 29 Apr 1800	Mil	-	15	7	4	20
Brown, Zephania, 21 Feb 1807*	Mil	-	15	7	4	21
Brown, Zephania, 21 Feb 1807*	Mil	-	15	7	4	22
Sill, Thomas, heir of, 4 Jan 1805	Mil	-	15	7	4	23
Eaton, Origen, 20 Jun 1804	Mil	-	15	7	4	24
Holt, Evan, 28 Jun 1804	Mil	-	15	7	4	25
Emmerson, James, heiress of, 8 Aug 1805	Mil	-	15	7	4	26
Yates, John, heir of, 3 Oct 1805	Mil	-	15	7	4	27
Case, Richard, assignee of (Joel Barlow) 27 Jun 1806	Mil	-	15	7	4	28
Fenner, Richard, 29 Apr 1800	Mil	-	15	7	4	29
Fenner, Richard, 29 Apr 1800	Mil	-	15	7	4	30
Sumner, Jethro, heiress of, 29 Apr 1800	Mil	-	15	7	4	31
Sumner, Jethro, heiress of, 29 Apr 1800	Mil	-	15	7	4	32
Mygatt, Elisha, assignee of (Joel Barlow) 27 Jun 1806	Mil	-	15	7	4	33
Weaver, Samuel, assignee of (Joel Barlow) 27 Jun 1806	Mil	-	15	7	4	34
Abbe, Eleazer, assignee of (Joel Barlow) 27 Jun 1806	Mil	-	15	7	4	35
Meara, Patrick, 27 Jun 1806	Mil	-	15	7	4	36
Hurleray, John, assignee of (Joel Barlow) 27 Jun 1806	Mil	-	15	7	4	37

*Pencilled notation states that lot is vacant.

1776 Various C/-/081

100-Acre Lots:

Patentee & Location Date *Location*

1776 [continued]

Ryan, James, 3 Oct 1805	Mil	-	15	7	4	38
Young, Thomas, heir of, 8 Aug 1805	Mil	-	15	7	4	39
Hairlot, Adam, assignee of (William Earley) 26 Feb 1805	Mil	-	15	7	4	40
Rickard, William, 5 Oct 1805	Mil	-	15	8	3	1
Rickard, William, 5 Oct 1805	Mil	-	15	8	3	2
Senter, Asa, 24 Dec 1802	Mil	-	15	8	3	3
Senter, Asa, 24 Dec 1802	Mil	-	15	8	3	4
Williams, Joseph, 24 Dec 1802	Mil	-	15	8	3	5
Williams, Joseph, 24 Dec 1802	Mil	-	15	8	3	6
Senter, Asa, 24 Dec 1802	Mil	-	15	8	3	7
Brady, James, assignee, 11 Mar 1811	Mil	-	15	8	3	8
Brady, James, assignee, 11 Mar 1811	Mil	-	15	8	3	9
Vacant	Mil	-	15	8	3	10
Brady, James, 18 Jan 1808	Mil	-	15	8	3	11
Brady, James, 12 Apr 1808	Mil	-	15	8	3	12
Martin, Mary, widow, 11 Mar 1811	Mil	-	15	8	3	13
Day, J. B., 1812	Mil	-	15	8	3	14
Williams, Joseph, 24 Dec 1802	Mil	-	15	8	3	15
Hull, Eli, 1812	Mil	-	15	8	3	16
Brady, James, 18 Jan 1808	Mil	-	15	8	3	17
Kaine, James O., 18 Jan 1808	Mil	-	15	8	3	18
Hunter, Ann, 18 Jan 1808	Mil	-	15	8	3	19
Hunter, Ann, 18 Jan 1808	Mil	-	15	8	3	20
Bassford, Moses, 24 Dec 1802	Mil	-	15	8	3	21
Vacant	Mil	-	15	8	3	22
Doty, Daniel, & Southard, Isaac, 30 Jan 1810	Mil	-	15	8	4	1
Dean, Orgilass, 1 Dec 1807	Mil	-	15	8	4	2
Reid, George, 24 Dec 1802	Mil	-	15	8	4	3
Reid, George, 24 Dec 1802	Mil	-	15	8	4	4
Reid, George, 24 Dec 1802	Mil	-	15	8	4	5
Anderson, John, heirs of, 24 Dec 1802	Mil	-	15	8	4	6
Anderson, John, heirs of, 24 Dec 1802	Mil	-	15	8	4	7
Anderson, John, heirs of, 24 Dec 1802	Mil	-	15	8	4	8
Reid, George, 24 Dec 1802	Mil	-	15	8	4	9
Reid, George, 24 Dec 1802	Mil	-	15	8	4	10

1777 Various C/-/082

100-Acre Lots:

Patentee & Location Date	*Location*					
Nourse, Michael, 1 Dec 1807	Mil	-	15	8	4	11
Nourse, Michael, 1 Dec 1807	Mil	-	15	8	4	12
St. John, Jesse, 11 Jul 1804	Mil	-	15	8	4	13
Fowler, Robert, 20 Jun 1804	Mil	-	15	8	4	14
Nourse, Michael, 1 Dec 1807	Mil	-	15	8	4	15
Nourse, Michael, 1 Dec 1804	Mil	-	15	8	4	16
Hennesey, William, administrator of, 28 Dec 1805	Mil	-	15	8	4	17
Easton, Moses, 20 Jun 1804	Mil	-	15	8	4	18
Campbell, Donald, 24 Dec 1802	Mil	-	15	8	4	19
Campbell, Donald, 24 Dec 1802	Mil	-	15	8	4	20
Campbell, Donald, 24 Dec 1802	Mil	-	15	8	4	21
Revelly, Francis, heirs of, 1 Dec 1807	Mil	-	15	8	4	22
Revelly, Francis, heirs of, 1 Dec 1807	Mil	-	15	8	4	23
Means, Robert, 1 Dec 1807	Mil	-	15	8	4	24
Means, Robert, 1 Dec 1807	Mil	-	15	8	4	25
Nourse, Michael, 21 Sep 1810	Mil	-	15	8	4	26
Revelly, F[rancis] heirs of, 1 Dec 1807	Mil	-	15	8	4	27
Campbell, Donald, 24 Dec 1802	Mil	-	15	8	4	28
Campbell, Donald, 24 Dec 1802	Mil	-	15	8	4	29
Litchfield, James, assignee of (Abijah Holbrook) 30 Mar 1805	Mil	-	16	2	4	1
Cooley, Samuel, assignee of (Abijah Holbrook) 30 Mar 1805	Mil	-	16	2	4	2
Selin? Anthony, heirs of, 13 Feb 1804	Mil	-	16	2	4	3
Selin? Anthony, heirs of, 13 Feb 1804	Mil	-	16	2	4	4
Selin? Anthony, heirs of, 13 Feb 1804	Mil	-	16	2	4	5
Carlisle, John, 31 Dec 1801	Mil	-	16	2	4	6
Carlisle, John, 31 Dec 1801	Mil	-	16	2	4	7
Carlisle, John, 31 Dec 1801	Mil	-	16	2	4	8
Inglish, John, 6 Mar 1805	Mil	-	16	2	4	9
Gibbons, David, 15 Feb 1805	Mil	-	16	2	4	10
Scott, Ethiel, assignee of (Abijah Holbrook) 30 Mar 1805	Mil	-	16	2	4	11
Potter, Daniel, assignee of (Abijah Holbrook) 30 Mar 1805	Mil	-	16	2	4	12
Demoss, John, 9 Aug 1803	Mil	-	16	2	4	13
Deheart, Ab[raha?]m [or Absalom?] 24 Jun 1801	Mil	-	16	2	4	14
Finney, Roger, 24 Jun 1801	Mil	-	16	2	4	15
Everley, Michael, 24 Jun 1801	Mil	-	16	2	4	16
Everley, Michael, 24 Jun 1801	Mil	-	16	2	4	17

1778 Various C/-/083

100-Acre Lots:

Patentee & Location Date	*Location*					
Ruggles, William, 24 Jun 1801	Mil	-	16	2	4	18
Calhoon, Andrew, 24 Jun 1801	Mil	-	16	2	4	19

1778 [continued]

Patentee & Location Date			Location			
Gray, Frazer, 24 Jun 1801	Mil	-	16	2	4	20
Duly [Duty? Dooley?] Moses, assignee of (Abijah Holbrook) 30 Mar 1805	Mil	-	16	2	4	21
Hubbart, James? [Joseph?] assignee of (Abijah Holbrook) 30 Mar 1805	Mil	-	16	2	4	22
Rogers, John, assignee of (Abijah Holbrook) 30 Mar 1805	Mil	-	16	2	4	23
Ryan, James, 15 Feb 1805	Mil	-	16	2	4	24
Runnells, Moses, assignee of (Abijah Holbrook) 30 Mar 1805	Mil	-	16	2	4	25
McGaffey, Andrew, assignee of (Abijah Holbrook) 30 Mar 1805	Mil	-	16	2	4	26
Barron, Jonathan, assignee of (Abijah Holbrook) 30 Mar 1805	Mil	-	16	2	4	27
Bishop, Thalmeno? assignee of (Abijah Holbrook) 30 Mar 1805	Mil	-	16	2	4	28
Smith, Michael, 24 Jun 1801	Mil	-	16	2	4	29
Edwards, Edmund, 24 Jun 1801	Mil	-	16	2	4	30
Montgomery, John, 24 Jun 1801	Mil	-	16	2	4	31
Shope, William, 6 Mar 1801	Mil	-	16	2	4	32
Coffin, Arthur, 25 May 1801	Mil	-	16	2	4	33
Campbell, Daniel, assignee of (assignee's name illegible) 9 Mar 1804	Mil	-	16	2	4	34
Martin, William, 8 Jan 1805	Mil	-	16	2	4	35
Collins, Samuel, assignee of (Abijah Holbrook) 30 Mar 1805	Mil	-	16	2	4	36
Lee, Abner, assignee of (Abijah Holbrook) 30 Mar 1805	Mil	-	16	2	4	37
Mansfield, Charles, assignee of (Abijah Holbrook) 30 Mar 1805	Mil	-	16	2	4	38
Meigs, Simeon, assignee of (Abijah Holbrook) 30 Mar 1805	Mil	-	16	2	4	39
Potter, Shelden, assignee of (Abijah Holbrook) 30 Mar 1805	Mil	-	16	2	4	40
Brownlee, William, 29 Dec 1801	Mil	-	16	3	4	1
Brownlee, William, 29 Dec 1801	Mil	-	16	3	4	2
Overton, John, & Taylor, James, 11 Dec 1806	Mil	-	16	3	4	3
Overton, John, & Taylor, James, 11 Dec 1806	Mil	-	16	3	4	4
Overton, John, & Taylor, James, 11 Dec 1806	Mil	-	16	3	4	5
Reed, Zach[ari]a, assignee of (James Taylor) 11 Dec 1806	Mil	-	16	3	4	6
Taylor, James, & Kirk, Robert, 11 Dec 1806	Mil	-	16	3	4	7
Taylor, James, 11 Dec 1806	Mil	-	16	3	4	8
Taylor, James, 11 Dec 1806	Mil	-	16	3	4	9
Taylor, James, & Kirk, Robert, 11 Dec 1806	Mil	-	16	3	4	10
Hays, John, 11 Dec 1806	Mil	-	16	3	4	11
Hays, John, 11 Dec 1806	Mil	-	16	3	4	12

1779 Various C/-/084

100-Acre Lots:

Patentee & Location Date			*Location*			
Hays, John, 11 Dec 1806	Mil	-	16	3	4	13
Hays, John, 11 Dec 1806	Mil	-	16	3	4	14
Finley, Joseph L., 29 Dec 1801	Mil	-	16	3	4	15
Finley, Joseph L., 29 Dec 1801	Mil	-	16	3	4	16
Finley, Joseph L., 29 Dec 1801	Mil	-	16	3	4	17
Gamble, Robert, 11 Dec 1806	Mil	-	16	3	4	18
Gamble, Robert, 11 Dec 1806	Mil	-	16	3	4	19
Gamble, Robert, 11 Dec 1806	Mil	-	16	3	4	20
Porterfield? [Poterfield?] Robert, 11 Dec 1806	Mil	-	16	3	4	21
Porterfield? [Poterfield?] Robert, 11 Dec 1806	Mil	-	16	3	4	22
Porterfield? [Poterfield?] Robert, 11 Dec 1806	Mil	-	16	3	4	23
Taylor, James, 11 Dec 1806	Mil	-	16	3	4	24
Taylor, James, 11 Dec 1806	Mil	-	16	3	4	25
Taylor, James, 11 Dec 1806	Mil	-	16	3	4	26
Taylor, James, 11 Dec 1806	Mil	-	16	3	4	27
Steele, John, 11 Dec 1806	Mil	-	16	3	4	28
Steele, John, 11 Dec 1806	Mil	-	16	3	4	29
Hall, John, 24 Jun 1801	Mil	-	16	3	4	30
McDowell, William, 24 Jun 1801	Mil	-	16	3	4	31
McDowell, William, 24 Jun 1801	Mil	-	16	3	4	32
Green, John, 24 Jun 1801	Mil	-	16	3	4	33
Green, John, 24 Jun 1801	Mil	-	16	3	4	34
Green, John, 24 Jun 1801	Mil	-	16	3	4	35
Green, John, 24 Jun 1801	Mil	-	16	3	4	36
Green, John, 24 Jun 1801	Mil	-	16	3	4	37
Steele, John, 24 Jun 1801	Mil	-	16	3	4	38
Steele, John, 24 Jun 1801	Mil	-	16	3	4	39
Steele, John, 24 Jun 1801	Mil	-	16	3	4	40
Mills, Peter, 20 Dec 1810	Mil	-	16	6	1	1
Mills, Peter, 20 Dec 1810	Mil	-	16	6	1	2
Poor, David Jowett, assigner, 13 May 1811	Mil	-	16	6	1	3
Cross, Joseph, 1812	Mil	-	16	6	1	4
Cross, Joseph, 1812	Mil	-	16	6	1	5
Lewis, Benjamin, heirs of, 2 Apr 1810	Mil	-	16	6	1	6
Vacant	Mil	-	16	6	1	7
Vacant	Mil	-	16	6	1	8

1780 Various C/-/085

100-Acre Lots:

Patentee & Location Date			*Location*			
Vacant	Mil	-	16	6	1	9
Vacant	Mil	-	16	6	1	10
Vacant	Mil	-	16	6	1	11

1780 [continued]

Patentee & Location Date	Location					
Vacant	Mil	-	16	6	1	12
Vacant	Mil	-	16	6	1	13
Vacant	Mil	-	16	6	1	14
Poe, Jacob, 1812	Mil	-	16	6	1	15
Swetland, Artemus, 11 Jan 1810	Mil	-	16	6	1	16
Vacant	Mil	-	16	6	1	17
Vacant	Mil	-	16	6	1	18
Vacant	Mil	-	16	6	1	19
Vacant	Mil	-	16	6	1	20
Vacant	Mil	-	16	6	1	21
Vacant	Mil	-	16	6	1	22
Vacant	Mil	-	16	6	1	23
Vacant	Mil	-	16	6	1	24
Vacant	Mil	-	16	6	1	25
Vacant	Mil	-	16	6	1	26
Vacant	Mil	-	16	6	1	27
Vacant	Mil	-	16	6	1	28
Vacant	Mil	-	16	6	1	29
Bush, John, 25 Nov 1811	Mil	-	16	6	1	30
Bush, John, 25 Nov 1811	Mil	-	16	6	1	31
Bush, John, 25 Nov 1811	Mil	-	16	6	1	32
Stokes, John R., 1812	Mil	-	16	6	1	33
Stokes, John R., 1812	Mil	-	16	6	1	34
Stokes, John R., 1812	Mil	-	16	6	1	35
Vacant	Mil	-	16	6	1	36
Carpenter, Reuben, 1812	Mil	-	16	6	1	37
Sweneton, James, 1812	Mil	-	16	6	1	38
Vacant	Mil	-	16	6	1	39
Vacant	Mil	-	16	6	1	40
Vacant	Mil	-	16	7	2	1
Vacant	Mil	-	16	7	2	2
Vacant	Mil	-	16	7	2	3

1781 Various C/-/086

100-Acre Lots:

Patentee & Location Date	*Location*					
Vacant	Mil	-	16	7	2	4
Vacant	Mil	-	16	7	2	5
Vacant	Mil	-	16	7	2	6
Vacant	Mil	-	16	7	2	7
Vacant	Mil	-	16	7	2	8
Vacant	Mil	-	16	7	2	9
Vacant	Mil	-	16	7	2	10
Vacant	Mil	-	16	7	2	11
Vacant	Mil	-	16	7	2	12
Vacant	Mil	-	16	7	2	13
Vacant	Mil	-	16	7	2	14
Ambler, Stephen, 20 Mar 1805	Mil	-	16	7	2	15
Ambler, Peter, 20 Mar 1805	Mil	-	16	7	2	16
Amberl, Squire, 20 Mar 1805	Mil	-	16	7	2	17
Fichle, Benjamin, 20 Mar 1805	Mil	-	16	7	2	18
Fichle, Benjamin, 20 Mar 1805	Mil	-	16	7	2	19
Keeler, Samuel, 27 Mar 1805	Mil	-	16	7	2	20
Vacant	Mil	-	16	7	2	21*
Vacant	Mil	-	16	7	2	22
Vacant	Mil	-	16	7	2	23
Vacant	Mil	-	16	7	2	24
Salday? Daniel, 28 Nov 1805	Mil	-	16	7	2	25
Antell, Edward, heirs of, 1 Jun 1813	Mil	-	16	7	2	26
Antell, Edward, heirs of, 1 Jun 1813	Mil	-	16	7	2	27
Antell, Edward, heirs of, 1 Jun 1813	Mil	-	16	7	2	28
Keeler, Samuel, 27 Mar 1805	Mil	-	16	7	2	29
Keeler, Samuel, 27 Mar 1805	Mil	-	16	7	2	30
Turner, Philip, 20 Mar 1805	Mil	-	16	7	2	31
Turner, Philip, 20 Mar 1805	Mil	-	16	7	2	32
Turner, Philip, 20 Mar 1805	Mil	-	16	7	2	33
Turner, Philip, 20 Mar 1805	Mil	-	16	7	2	34
Swan, Thomas, 25 Sep 1810	Mil	-	16	7	2	35
Montour, Montgomery, 18 Dec 1806	Mil	-	16	7	2	36
Montour, Montgomery, 18 Dec 1806	Mil	-	16	7	2	37
Montour, Montgomery, 18 Dec 1806	Mil	-	16	7	2	38
Antill, Edward, heirs of, 1 Jun 1813	Mil	-	16	7	2	39
Miller, Christian, 28 Nov 1807	Mil	-	16	7	2	40

*This lot not listed in source register.

1782 Various C/-/087

100-Acre Lots:

Patentee & Location Date	*Location*					
Stephenson, David, & Taylor, James, 25 Nov 1807	Mil	-	16	7	4	1
Stephenson, David, & Taylor, James, 25 Nov 1807	Mil	-	16	7	4	2
Stephenson, David, & Taylor, James, 25 Nov 1807	Mil	-	16	7	4	3
Stephenson, David, & Taylor, James, 25 Nov 1807	Mil	-	16	7	4	4
Vacant	Mil	-	16	7	4	5
Vacant	Mil	-	16	7	4	6
Vacant	Mil	-	16	7	4	7
Taylor, James, 15 May 1810	Mil	-	16	7	4	8
Vacant	Mil	-	16	7	4	9
Vacant	Mil	-	16	7	4	10
Harding, John, 14 Feb 1811	Mil	-	16	7	4	11
Lynn, Robert, 14 Feb 1811	Mil	-	16	7	4	12
Oldham, Samuel, 23 Apr 1810	Mil	-	16	7	4	13
Oldham, Samuel, 23 Apr 1810	Mil	-	16	7	4	14
Oldham, Samuel, 23 Apr 1810	Mil	-	16	7	4	15
Robertson, William, & Taylor, James, 25 Nov 1807	Mil	-	16	7	4	16
Robertson, William, & Taylor, James, 25 Nov 1807	Mil	-	16	7	4	17
Vacant	Mil	-	16	7	4	18
Vacant	Mil	-	16	7	4	19
Vacant	Mil	-	16	7	4	20
Vacant	Mil	-	16	7	4	21

1782 [continued]

Vacant	Mil	-	16	7	4	22
Vacant	Mil	-	16	7	4	23
Poor, David S., assignee, 13 May 1811	Mil	-	16	7	4	24
Rawlinger, Moses, 28 Mar 1810	Mil	-	16	7	4	25
Decker, Samuel, 29 Mar 1810	Mil	-	16	7	4	26
Vacant	Mil	-	16	7	4	27
Vacant	Mil	-	16	7	4	28
Vacant	Mil	-	16	7	4	29
Taylor, James, 25 Nov 1807	Mil	-	16	7	4	30
Taylor, James, 25 Nov 1807	Mil	-	16	7	4	31
Taylor, James, 25 Nov 1807	Mil	-	16	7	4	32
Hilton? [Milton?] John, 2 Mar 1807	Mil	-	16	7	4	33
Hilton? [Milton?] John, 2 Mar 1807	Mil	-	16	7	4	34
Hilton? [Milton?] John, 2 Mar 1807	Mil	-	16	7	4	35

1783 Various C/-/088

100-Acre Lots:

Patentee & Location Date	*Location*					
McConnell, Robert, assignees of (assignees' names illegible) 23 Aug 1808	Mil	-	16	7	4	36
McConnell, Robert, assignees of (assignees' names illegible) 23 Aug 1808	Mil	-	16	7	4	37
McConnell, Robert, assignees of (assignees' names illegible) 23 Aug 1808	Mil	-	16	7	4	38
Chandler, Martin, 25 Nov 1807	Mil	-	16	7	4	39
Moore, George, 9 Apr 1810	Mil	-	16	7	4	40
Laurence, John, 27 Jul 1813	Mil	-	16	8	3	1
Poor, David J? assignee, 13 May 1811	Mil	-	16	8	3	2
Poor, Rachel, heir[ess] 13 May 1813	Mil	-	16	8	3	3
Poor, Rachel, heir[ess] 13 May 1813	Mil	-	16	8	3	4
Poor, Rachel, heir[ess] 13 May 1813	Mil	-	16	8	3	5
Vacant	Mil	-	16	8	3	6
Vacant	Mil	-	16	8	3	7
Darby? [Darly?] Nathaniel, 8 Jan 1808	Mil	-	16	8	4	1
Darby? [Darly?] Nathaniel, 8 Jan 1808	Mil	-	16	8	4	2
Baylor, George, assignee of (Walker? Baylor) 16 Jan 1809	Mil	-	16	8	4	3
Gibbs, Caleb, 18 Dec 1804	Mil	-	16	8	4	4
Worthington, Thomas, -- Jun 1809	Mil	-	16	8	4	5
Gibbs, Caleb, 18 Dec 1804	Mil	-	16	8	4	6
Shotte, Richard, assignee of (John Lamme?) 16 Nov 1808	Mil	-	16	8	4	7
Woodsen, Charles, 26 May 1800	Mil	-	16	8	4	8
Gibbs, Caleb, 18 Dec 1804	Mil	-	16	8	4	9
Gibbs, Caleb, 18 Dec 1804	Mil	-	16	8	4	10
Reed, Nathan, 22 Dec 1810	Mil	-	16	8	4	11
Woodsen, Charles, 26 May 1810	Mil	-	16	8	4	12
Reed, Nathan, 22 Dec 1810	Mil	-	16	8	4	13
Reed, Nathan, 22 Dec 1810	Mil	-	16	8	4	14
Kerr, John, [1812]	Mil	-	17	7	1	1E*
Lesuer, John, 22 Apr 1806	Mil	-	17	7	1	1W*
Vacant	Mil	-	17	7	1	2E*
Vacant	Mil	-	17	7	1	2W*
Vacant	Mil	-	17	7	1	3E*
Vacant	Mil	-	17	7	1	3W*
Armstrong, John, 5 Nov 1805	Mil	-	17	7	1	4E*
Kerr, John, 1812	Mil	-	17	7	1	4W*
Vacant	Mil	-	17	7	1	5E*

*50-acre lot.

1784 Various C/-/089

50-Acre Lots:

Patentee & Location Date	*Location*					
Vacant	Mil	-	17	7	1	5W
Vacant	Mil	-	17	7	1	6E
Vacant	Mil	-	17	7	1	6W
Vacant	Mil	-	17	7	1	7E
Poe, Jacob, 1812	Mil	-	17	7	1	7W
Hanner, Josiah, 24 Dec 1802	Mil	-	17	7	1	8E
Clark, Jonathan, 24 Dec 1802	Mil	-	17	7	1	8W
Gray, Ebenezer, Gray, Charlotte, & Gray, Samuel, 24 Dec 1802	Mil	-	17	7	1	9E
Talbot, Silas, 24 Dec 1802	Mil	-	17	7	1	9W
Vacant	Mil	-	17	7	1	10E
Vacant	Mil	-	17	7	1	10W
Vacant	Mil	-	17	7	1	11E
Vacant	Mil	-	17	7	1	11W
Vacant	Mil	-	17	7	1	12E
Vacant	Mil	-	17	7	1	12W
Vacant	Mil	-	17	7	1	13E
Vacant	Mil	-	17	7	1	13W
Vacant	Mil	-	17	7	1	14E
Vacant	Mil	-	17	7	1	14W
Vacant	Mil	-	17	7	1	15E
Vacant	Mil	-	17	7	1	15W
Wells, William, 1 Mar 1805	Mil	-	17	7	1	16E
Jones, David, 1 Mar 1803	Mil	-	17	7	1	16W
Vacant	Mil	-	17	7	1	17E
Vacant	Mil	-	17	7	1	17W
Vacant	Mil	-	17	7	1	18E
Vacant	Mil	-	17	7	1	18W
Vacant	Mil	-	17	7	1	19E
Vacant	Mil	-	17	7	1	19W
Vacant	Mil	-	17	7	1	20E
Vacant	Mil	-	17	7	1	20W
Vacant	Mil	-	17	7	1	21E
Vacant	Mil	-	17	7	1	21W
Vacant	Mil	-	17	7	1	22E
Vacant	Mil	-	17	7	1	22W

1785 Various C/-/090

50-Acre Lots:

Patentee & Location Date *Location*

1785 [continued]

Vacant	Mil	-	17	7	1	23E
Vacant	Mil	-	17	7	1	23W
Vacant	Mil	-	17	7	1	24E
Kerr, Joseph, 1812	Mil	-	17	7	1	24W
Kerr, Joseph, 1812	Mil	-	17	7	1	25E
Vacant	Mil	-	17	7	1	25W
Vacant	Mil	-	17	7	1	26E
Vacant	Mil	-	17	7	1	26W
Vacant	Mil	-	17	7	1	27E
Vacant	Mil	-	17	7	1	27W
Vacant	Mil	-	17	7	1	28E
Vacant	Mil	-	17	7	1	28W
Vacant	Mil	-	17	7	1	29E
Vacant	Mil	-	17	7	1	29W
Vacant	Mil	-	17	7	1	30E
Vacant	Mil	-	17	7	1	30W
Vacant	Mil	-	17	7	1	31E
Vacant	Mil	-	17	7	1	31W
Vacant	Mil	-	17	7	1	32E
Vacant	Mil	-	17	7	1	32W
Vacant	Mil	-	17	7	1	33E
Vacant	Mil	-	17	7	1	33W
Vacant	Mil	-	17	7	1	34E
Vacant	Mil	-	17	7	1	34W
Vacant	Mil	-	17	7	1	35E
Vacant	Mil	-	17	7	1	35W
Vacant	Mil	-	17	7	1	36E
Baird, John, 21 Apr 1808	Mil	-	17	7	1	36W
Vacant	Mil	-	17	7	1	37E
Vacant	Mil	-	17	7	1	37W
Northup, Henry, 8 Jun 1813	Mil	-	17	7	1	38E
Vacant	Mil	-	17	7	1	38W
Danforth, Joshua, 18 Jan 1810	Mil	-	17	7	2	1*
Danforth, Joshua, 18 Jan 1810	Mil	-	17	7	2	2*
Baird, John, 15 Apr 1808	Mil	-	17	7	2	3*
Baird, John, 15 Apr 1808	Mil	-	17	7	2	4*
Baird, John, 15 Apr 1808	Mil	-	17	7	2	5*

*100-acre lot.

1786 Various C/-/091

100-Acre Lots:

Patentee & Location Date	*Location*					
Baird, John, 15 Apr 1808	Mil	-	17	7	2	6
McCay, Daniel, 4 Dec 1809	Mil	-	17	7	2	7
McCay, Daniel, 4 Dec 1809	Mil	-	17	7	2	8
Henderson, Thomas, heirs of, 22 Apr 1806	Mil	-	17	7	2	9
Wilder, John, 28 Mar 1808	Mil	-	17	7	2	10
Wilder, John, 28 Mar 1808	Mil	-	17	7	2	11
Ells, Edward, heirs of, 18 Jan 1810	Mil	-	17	7	2	12
Ells, Edward, heirs of, 18 Jan 1810	Mil	-	17	7	2	13
Ells, Edward, heirs of, 18 Jan 1810	Mil	-	17	7	2	14
Baylor, George, assignee of (Walter? Baylor) 16 Jun 1809	Mil	-	17	7	2	15
Wilder, John, assignee	Mil	-	17	7	2	16
Wilder, John, assignee	Mil	-	17	7	2	17
Wilder, John, assignee	Mil	-	17	7	2	18
Wilder, John, assignee	Mil	-	17	7	2	19
McCullam, John, 22 Apr 1806	Mil	-	17	7	2	20
Chambers, James? [Joseph?] heir of, 22 Apr 1806	Mil	-	17	7	2	21
Wilder, John, 28 Mar 1805	Mil	-	17	7	2	22
Wilder, John, 28 Mar 1805	Mil	-	17	7	2	23
Vacant	Mil	-	17	7	2	24
Vacant	Mil	-	17	7	2	25
Vacant	Mil	-	17	7	2	26
Vacant	Mil	-	17	7	2	27
Vacant	Mil	-	17	7	2	28
Vacant	Mil	-	17	7	2	29
Wilder, John, 7 Mar 1808	Mil	-	17	7	2	30
Wilder, John, 7 Mar 1808	Mil	-	17	7	2	31
Hawkins, Henry, 29 Dec 1802	Mil	-	17	7	4	1
Hawkins, Henry, 29 Dec 1802	Mil	-	17	7	4	2
Parker, Thomas, 24 Dec 1802	Mil	-	17	7	4	3
Parker, Thomas, 24 Dec 1802	Mil	-	17	7	4	4
Parker, Thomas, 24 Dec 1802	Mil	-	17	7	4	5
Bush, Lewis, heirs of, 2 Aug 1805	Mil	-	17	7	4	6
Bush, Lewis, heirs of, 2 Aug 1805	Mil	-	17	7	4	7
Bush, Lewis, heirs of, 2 Aug 1805	Mil	-	17	7	4	8
Bush, Lewis, heirs of, 2 Aug 1805	Mil	-	17	7	4	9

1787 Various C/-/092

100-Acre Lots:

Patentee & Location Date	*Location*					
Blair, William, assignee of (assignee's name illegible) 3 Feb 1806	Mil	-	17	7	4	10
Conner, Charles, assignee of (--? Young?) 27 Feb 1805	Mil	-	17	7	4	11
Winn, John, assignee of (--? Young?) 27 Feb 1805	Mil	-	17	7	4	12
Berry, James, assignee of (--? Young?) 27 Feb 1805	Mil	-	17	7	4	13
Montgomery, Samuel, 27 Feb 1805	Mil	-	17	7	4	14
Montgomery, Samuel, 27 Feb 1805	Mil	-	17	7	4	15
Montgomery, Samuel, 27 Feb 1805	Mil	-	17	7	4	16
Gonter, John, 17 Apr 1805	Mil	-	17	7	4	17
O'Hara, Francis, heirs of, 17 Apr 1805	Mil	-	17	7	4	18
Effinger, John, assignee of (J. G. Filbert) 19 Apr 1806	Mil	-	17	7	4	19
Gaither, Henry, 11 Mar 1805	Mil	-	17	7	4	20
Gaither, Henry, 11 Mar 1805	Mil	-	17	7	4	21
Gaither, Henry, 11 Mar 1805	Mil	-	17	7	4	22
Nutton? [Nulton?] John, 21 Apr 1806	Mil	-	17	7	4	23
Friehle? [Frickle?] Jonathan, 21 Apr 1806	Mil	-	17	7	4	24
Kerr, Joseph, 1812	Mil	-	17	7	4	25
Craig, John, 29 Sep 1806	Mil	-	17	7	4	26
Patton, John, heirs of, 15 Mar 1805	Mil	-	17	7	4	27

1787 [continued]

Patentee & Location Date	Location					
Patton, John, heirs of, 15 Mar 1805	Mil	-	17	7	4	28
Patton, John, heirs of, 15 Mar 1805	Mil	-	17	7	4	29
Patton, John, heirs of, 15 Mar 1805	Mil	-	17	7	4	30
Patton, John, heirs of, 15 Mar 1805	Mil	-	17	7	4	31
Armstrong, John, 7 Aug 1805	Mil	-	17	7	4	32
Armstrong, John, 7 Aug 1805	Mil	-	17	7	4	33
Armstrong, John, 7 Aug 1805	Mil	-	17	7	4	34
Armstrong, John, 7 Aug 1805	Mil	-	17	7	4	35
Freeman, Samuel, assignee of (--? Blackledge?) 15 Mar 1805	Mil	-	17	7	4	36
Clarke, Isaac, assignee of (--? Blackledge?) 15 Mar 1805	Mil	-	17	7	4	37
Alderson, Simon, 15 Mar 1805	Mil	-	17	7	4	38
Bauman, Frederick, devisees of, 19 Apr 1805	Mil	-	17	7	4	39
Vacant	Mil	-	17	7	4	40
Price, Stephen R., 5 Apr 1810	Mil	-	18	7	1	1
Smith, John, 25 Mar 1803	Mil	-	18	7	1	2
Smith, John, 25 Mar 1803	Mil	-	18	7	1	3
Smith, John, 25 Mar 1803	Mil	-	18	7	1	4
Baylor, George, assignee of (Walter? Baylor) 16 Jun 1809	Mil	-	18	7	1	5
Clarke, Edward, 24 Dec 1802	Mil	-	18	7	1	6

1788 Various C/-/093

100-Acre lots:

Patentee & Location Date	*Location*					
Gray, Ebenezer, heirs of, 24 Dec 1802	Mil	-	18	7	1	7
Gray, Ebenezer, heirs of, 24 Dec 1802	Mil	-	18	7	1	8
Gray, Ebenezer, heirs of, 24 Dec 1802	Mil	-	18	7	1	9
Rathbone, John, 21 Mar 1808	Mil	-	18	7	1	10
Rathbone, John, 21 Mar 1808	Mil	-	18	7	1	11
Smith, Thomas, assignee of (Thomas Boyce?) 8 Jul 1803	Mil	-	18	7	1	12
Smith, Thomas, assignee of (Thomas Boyce?) 8 Jul 1803	Mil	-	18	7	1	13
Baylor, George, assignee of (--? Baylor) 16 Jun 1809	Mil	-	18	7	1	14
Brown, Edward, 16 May 1808	Mil	-	18	7	1	15
Baylor, George, assignee of (--? Taylor)	Mil	-	18	7	1	16
Clake [Clarke?] Edmund, 24 Dec 1802	Mil	-	18	7	1	17
Gray, Ebenezer, heirs of, 24 Dec 1802	Mil	-	18	7	1	18
Sears, John, 19 Apr 1806	Mil	-	18	7	1	19
Sears, John, 19 Apr 1806	Mil	-	18	7	1	20
Sears, John, 19 Apr 1806	Mil	-	18	7	1	21
Edminston, Samuel, 30 Apr 1803	Mil	-	18	7	1	22
Edminston, Samuel, 30 Apr 1803	Mil	-	18	7	1	23
Griffin, John, assignee of (name of assignee illegible) 19 Apr 1806	Mil	-	18	7	2	1
York, William, assignee of (name of assignee illegible) 19 Apr 1806	Mil	-	18	7	2	2
Edmiston, Samuel, 30 Aug 1803	Mil	-	18	7	2	3
Edmiston, Samuel, 30 Aug 1803	Mil	-	18	7	2	4
Halling, Solomon, 14 Jun 1803	Mil	-	18	7	2	5
Halling, Solomon, 14 Jun 1803	Mil	-	18	7	2	6
Whittier, Jacob, assignee of (--? J. Foote) 29 Apr 1806	Mil	-	18	7	2	7
Tharp, Pr., assignee of (--? J. Foote) 29 Apr 1806	Mil	-	18	7	2	8
McAlister, John, 10 Nov 1817	Mil	-	18	7	2	9
Parsons, David, 29 Apr 1806	Mil	-	18	7	2	10
Halling, Solomon, 14 Jun 1803	Mil	-	18	7	2	11
Halling, Solomon, 14 Jun 1803	Mil	-	18	7	2	12
Vacant	Mil	-	18	7	2	13
Vacant	Mil	-	18	7	2	14
Vacant	Mil	-	18	7	2	15
Vacant	Mil	-	18	7	2	16
Orr, John, 23 Apr 1800	Mil	-	19	1	2	1
Marker, Andrew, 23 Apr 1800	Mil	-	19	1	2	2

1789 Various C/-/094

100-Acre Lots:

Patentee & Location Date	*Location*					
Handy, George, 23 Apr 1800	Mil	-	19	2	2	1
Handy, George, 23 Apr 1800	Mil	-	19	2	2	2
Handy, George, 23 Apr 1800	Mil	-	19	2	2	3
Kosciusko, T., 23 Apr 1800	Mil	-	19	2	2	4
Winder, Levin, 23 Apr 1800	Mil	-	19	2	2	5
Winder, Levin, 23 Apr 1800	Mil	-	19	2	2	6
Kosciusko, T., 23 Apr 1800	Mil	-	19	2	2	7
Winder, Levin, 23 Apr 1800	Mil	-	19	2	2	8
Winder, Levin, 23 Apr 1800	Mil	-	19	2	2	9
Kosciusko, T., 23 Apr 1800	Mil	-	19	2	2	10
Leibert, Philip, 23 Apr 1800	Mil	-	19	2	2	11
Leibert, Philip, 23 Apr 1800	Mil	-	19	2	2	12

1789 [continued]

Patentee & Location Date						
Leibert, Philip, 23 Apr 1800	Mil	-	19	2	2	13
Titcomb, Benjamin, 23 Aug 1800	Mil	-	19	2	2	14
Titcomb, Benjamin, 23 Aug 1800	Mil	-	19	2	2	15
Titcomb, Benjamin, 23 Aug 1800	Mil	-	19	2	2	16
Titcomb, Benjamin, 23 Aug 1800	Mil	-	19	2	2	17
Kosciusko, T., 23 Aug 1800	Mil	-	19	2	2	18
Kosciusko, T., 23 Aug 1800	Mil	-	19	2	2	19
Eaton, John, heir to P[inkerton] Eaton, 23 Aug 1800	Mil	-	19	2	3	1
Eaton, John, heir to P[inkerton] Eaton, 23 Aug 1800	Mil	-	19	2	3	2
Williams, David, 23 Aug 1800	Mil	-	19	2	3	3
Rodgers, J. R. B., 23 Aug 1800	Mil	-	19	2	3	4
Rodgers, J. R. B., 23 Aug 1800	Mil	-	19	2	3	5
Rodgers, J. R. B., 23 Aug 1800	Mil	-	19	2	3	6
Williams, Daniel, 23 Aug 1800	Mil	-	19	2	3	7
Priscoe, Reuben, 23 Aug 1800	Mil	-	19	2	3	8
Priscoe, Reuben, 23 Aug 1800	Mil	-	19	2	3	9
Priscoe, Reuben, 23 Aug 1800	Mil	-	19	2	3	10
Eaton, John, heir to Pinkerton Eaton, 23 Aug 1800	Mil	-	19	2	3	11
Eaton, John, heir to Pinkerton Eaton, 23 Aug 1800	Mil	-	19	2	3	12
Rodgers, J. R. B., 23 Aug 1800	Mil	-	19	2	3	13
French, David, 23 Aug 1800	Mil	-	19	2	3	14
Homes, Thomas, 3 May 1800	Mil	-	19	2	3	15
Vacant	Mil	-	19	7	1	1
Barram, Fielding, 11 Mar 1811	Mil	-	19	7	1	2

1790 Various C/-/095

100-Acre Lots:

Patentee & Location Date	*Location*					
Mills, Peter, 21 Mar 1808	Mil	-	19	1	1	3
Mills, Peter, 21 Mar 1808	Mil	-	19	1	1	4
Mills, Peter, 21 Mar 1808	Mil	-	19	1	1	5
Mills, Peter, 21 Mar 1808	Mil	-	19	1	1	6
Hobaugh, Bishop, assignee of (John Kerr) 12 Sep 1806	Mil	-	19	1	1	7
Lee, Henry, 3 May 1800	Mil	-	19	1	1	8
Vacant	Mil	-	19	7	2	1
Crain, James, assignee of (assignee's name illegible) 18 Dec 1809	Mil	-	19	7	2	2
Ragsdale, Drury, 23 Apr 1800	Mil	-	20	3	1	1
Ragsdale, Drury, 23 Apr 1800	Mil	-	20	3	1	2
Ragsdale, Drury, 23 Apr 1800	Mil	-	20	3	1	3
Christie, James, heirs of, 23 Apr 1800	Mil	-	20	4	1	1
Christie, James, heirs of, 23 Apr 1800	Mil	-	20	4	1	2
Clarke, Jonathan, 23 Apr 1800	Mil	-	20	4	1	3
Clarke, Jonathan, 23 Apr 1800	Mil	-	20	4	1	4
Husbands, James, 31 Dec 1801	Mil	-	20	4	1	5
Carbury, Francis, 29 Apr 1800	Mil	-	20	4	1	6
Clark, Jonathan, 23 Apr 1800	Mil	-	20	4	1	7
Clark, Jonathan, 23 Apr 1800	Mil	-	20	4	1	8
Harmer, Josiah, 23 Apr 1800	Mil	-	20	4	1	9
Christie, James, heirs of, 23 Apr 1800	Mil	-	20	4	1	10
Harmer, Josiah, 23 Apr 1800	Mil	-	20	4	1	11
Harmer, Josiah, 23 Apr 1800	Mil	-	20	4	1	12
Harmer, Josiah, 23 Apr 1800	Mil	-	20	4	1	13
Butler, Thomas, 23 Apr 1800	Mil	-	20	4	1	14
Croghan, William, 23 Apr 1800	Mil	-	20	4	1	15
Croghan, William, 23 Apr 1800	Mil	-	20	4	1	16
Butler, Thomas, 23 Apr 1800	Mil	-	20	4	1	17
Butler, Thomas, 23 Apr 1800	Mil	-	20	4	1	18
Croghan, William, 23 Apr 1800	Mil	-	20	4	1	19
Croghan, William, 23 Apr 1800	Mil	-	20	4	1	20
Hungerford, Thomas, 23 Apr 1800	Mil	-	20	4	4	1
Hill, Thomas, 23 Apr 1800	Mil	-	20	4	4	2
Hill, Thomas, 23 Apr 1800	Mil	-	20	4	4	3
Hill, Thomas, 23 Apr 1800	Mil	-	20	4	4	4

1791 Various C/-/096

100-Acre Lots:

Patentee & Location Date	*Location*					
Collins, Oliver, 4 Aug 1800	Mil	-	20	4	4	5
Anderson, George, 29 Apr 1800	Mil	-	20	4	4	6
Hill, Thomas, 23 Apr 1800	Mil	-	20	4	4	7
Walker, Benjamin, 23 Apr 1800	Mil	-	20	4	4	8
Walker, Benjamin, 23 Apr 1800	Mil	-	20	4	4	9
Walker, Benjamin, 23 Apr 1800	Mil	-	20	4	4	10
Walker, Benjamin, 23 Apr 1800	Mil	-	20	4	4	11
Hungerford, Thomas, 23 Apr 1800	Mil	-	20	4	4	12
McHenry, James, 23 Apr 1800	Mil	-	20	5	2	1
McHenry, James, 23 Apr 1800	Mil	-	20	5	2	2

1791 [continued]

Patentee & Location Date	Location					
McHenry, James, 23 Apr 1800	Mil	-	20	5	2	3
McHenry, James, 23 Apr 1800	Mil	-	20	5	2	4
Vacant	Mil	-	20	5	2	5
Gassaway, Nicholas, 31 Dec 1801	Mil	-	20	6	2	1
Gassaway, Nicholas, 31 Dec 1801	Mil	-	20	6	2	2
Herne, Christian, 31 Dec 1801	Mil	-	20	6	2	3
Jackson, William, 5 May 1800	Mil	-	20	6	2	4
Jackson, William, 5 May 1800	Mil	-	20	6	2	5
Jackson, William, 5 May 1800	Mil	-	20	6	2	6
Tolbert? [Talbert?] Samuel, heirs of, 30 Apr 1800	Mil	-	20	6	2	7
Woods, William, 23 Apr 1800	Mil	-	20	6	2	8
McIntosh, Lachlin, 23 Apr 1800	Mil	-	20	6	2	9
McIntosh, Lachlin, 23 Apr 1800	Mil	-	20	6	2	10
McIntosh, Lachlin, 23 Apr 1800	Mil	-	20	6	2	11
McIntosh, Lachlin, 23 Apr 1800	Mil	-	20	6	2	12
Lipkey, Henry, 23 Apr 1800	Mil	-	20	6	2	13
Talbert, Samuel, heirs of, 30 Apr 1800	Mil	-	20	6	2	14
Chambers, James, 23 Apr 1800	Mil	-	20	6	2	15
Chambers, James, 23 Apr 1800	Mil	-	20	6	2	16
Talbert, Samuel, heirs of, 30 Apr 1800	Mil	-	20	6	2	17
Chambers, James, 23 Apr 1800	Mil	-	20	6	2	18
McIntosh, Lachlin, 23 Apr 1800	Mil	-	20	6	2	19
McIntosh, Lachlin, 23 Apr 1800	Mil	-	20	6	2	20
Chambers, James, 23 Apr 1800	Mil	-	20	6	2	21
Chambers, James, 23 Apr 1800	Mil	-	20	6	2	22
McIntosh, Lachlin, 23 Apr 1800	Mil	-	20	6	2	23
McIntosh, Lachlin, 23 Apr 1800	Mil	-	20	6	2	24

1792 Various C/-/097

100-Acre Lots:

Patentee & Location Date	*Location*					
Dungan, Thomas, 23 Apr 1800	Mil	-	20	6	3	1
Meigs, Return J., 23 Apr 1800	Mil	-	20	6	3	2
Stowens? [Howens?] John, 23 Apr 1800	Mil	-	20	6	3	3
Brothers? Percival, 21 Mar 1801	Mil	-	20	6	3	4
Brothers? Percival, 21 Mar 1801	Mil	-	20	6	3	5
Claypool, Ab[raha]m, 2 May 1800	Mil	-	20	6	3	6
Lee, Henry, 3 May 1800	Mil	-	20	6	3	7
Meigs, Return J., 23 Apr 1800	Mil	-	20	6	3	8
Meigs, Return J., 23 Apr 1800	Mil	-	20	6	3	9
Dungan, Thomas, 23 Apr 1800	Mil	-	20	6	3	10
Tyron, Ezra, 23 Apr 1800	Mil	-	20	6	3	11
Meigs, Return J., 23 Apr 1800	Mil	-	20	6	3	12
Meigs, Return J., 23 Apr 1800	Mil	-	20	6	3	13
Claypool, Ab[raha]m G., 2 May 1800	Mil	-	20	6	3	14
Claypool, Ab[raha]m G., 2 May 1800	Mil	-	20	6	3	15
Patton, Robert, 23 Apr 1800	Mil	-	20	6	3	16
Patton, Robert, 23 Apr 1800	Mil	-	20	6	3	17
Patton, Robert, 23 Apr 1800	Mil	-	20	6	3	18
Scott, Moses, 23 Apr 1800	Mil	-	20	7	3	1
Gwinap, George, 8 Dec 1800	Mil	-	20	7	3	2
Craine, James, assignee of (assignee's name illegible) 18 Dec 1809	Mil	-	20	7	3	3
Craine, James, assignee of (assignee's name illegible) 18 Dec 1809	Mil	-	20	7	3	4
Lee, Henry, 3 May 1800	Mil	-	20	7	3	5
Lee, Henry, 3 May 1800	Mil	-	20	7	3	6
Matthews, George, 23 Apr 1800	Mil	-	20	7	3	7
Matthews, George, 23 Apr 1800	Mil	-	20	7	3	8
Matthews, George, 23 Apr 1800	Mil	-	20	7	3	9
Lee, Henry, 3 May 1800	Mil	-	20	7	3	10
Matthews, George, 3 May 1800	Mil	-	20	7	3	11
McConnell, Matthew, 23 Apr 1800	Mil	-	20	7	3	12
Matthews, George, 23 Apr 1800	Mil	-	20	7	3	13
McConnell, Matthew, 23 Apr 1800	Mil	-	20	7	3	14
McConnell, Matthew, 23 Apr 1800	Mil	-	20	7	3	15

(End of source C)

NAME INDEX

Abbe, Eleazer, 692, 1775
Abbey, Jeduthen, 184
Abbot, Richard, 90
Abbott, Joel, 32
Abbott, Reuben, 49
Abbott, Stephen, 238
Achor, Jacob, 1421
Acker, Conradt, 68
Ackerman, Andrew, 77
Ackerman, Francis, 202
Ackley, Bezaliel, 106
Adair, John, 1676
Adam, Henry, 177
Adams, Bartholomew, 187
Adams, Dimas, 1637, 1638
Adams, D., 1589, 1601
Adams, George, 1048
Adams, John, 165, 193, 241
Adams, Jonathan, 127
Adams, Joshua, 751
Adams, Levi, 100
Adams, P., 1416
Adams, Robert, 222
Adams, Samuel, 109, 1289
Adams, Sarah, 1388
Adams, William, 262, 485
Adamy, Henry, 82
Addams, John, 83
Addams, Jonas, 61
Addison, Alexander, 49
Addoms, John, 122, 159
Addoms, Jonas, 197
Adee, Aner, 1075
Adkins, Isaiah, 1143
Adkins, Jabez, 40
Adlington, James, 101
Afflick, Robert, 199
Agard, Levia, 1472
Agard, Noah, 1472
Ahcarn (Ahearn) William, 192
Aidy, James T., 1531
Ainger, Jesse, 1689
Ake, Thomas, 1681
Ake, William, 1681
Akely, John, 404, 531
Aiken, Daniel, 83, 85, 107
Akin, --, 981
Akins, James, 196
Albee, Eleazer, 1641
Albee, John, 1641
Albert, Jacob, 157
Albertson, William, 29
Albie, Eleazer, 1641
Albie, John, 1641
Albright, John, 155
Alby, John, 192
Alcorn, William, 465, 1766
Alden, Jerab, 1623
Alden, Judah, 1623, 1691
Alderson, Simon, 418, 545, 1787
Aldon, Mason F., 104
Aldrich, Gustavus, 1640
Aldrick, Nathan, 1640
Aldridge, John, 1636
Alen, Alex, 121
Alexander, Abraham, 1685
Alexander, Alexander, 129, 168
Alexander, Edward, 1693
Alexander, James, 1032, 1043, 1693
Alexander, Nathaniel, 35, 186
Alexander, Samuel, 51
Alexander, Solomon, 1685, 1693
Alexander, William, 6, 73
Alix, Rufus, 25
Allen, Almissy, 234
Allen, David, 1677
Allen, Demas, 1677
Allen, Edward, 1174
Allen, Elizabeth, 1685
Allen, Ethan, 1689
Allen, Ethan A., 1689
Allen, Garret, 1689
Allen, Jacob, 72, 1180, 1689
Allen, James, 193
Allen, Jeremiah, 1559
Allen, John, 203, 226, 639, 1626, 1721
Allen, Lucretia, 145
Allen, Nathan, Junior, 1677
Allen, Nathaniel C., 32
Allen, Noah, 53
Allen, Owen, 1104
Allen, Patience, 1676
Allen, Samuel, 31, 52, 118, 130, 164
Allen, William, 121, 1559
Allis, William, 105
Allison, John, 1687, 1690

Ashford, Street, 117
Ashley, Moses, 230
Ashley, Oliver, 210
Ashley, William, 162
Ashton, Benjamin, 158
Ashton, John, 197
Ashton, Joseph, 24
Ashur, Gad, 41
Asken, --, & Huff, --, 1703
Askew, Peregrine, 192
Aspel, James, 136, 233
Atayalagkroughta, Lewis, 144
Atkins, David, 279, 1769
Atkins, Josiah, 41
Atkins, Lewis, 197
Atkinson, James, 161
Atkinson, Samuel, 8
Atkinson, Stephen, 135
Atkinson, Theodore, 1624
Atwater, Jesse, 148
Atwater, *see also* Alwater
Augin, Isaac, 1133
Aulman, William, 1695
Aulmon, William, 98
Austin, Elijah, 248
Austin, Holmes, 38
Austin, John, 1677
Austin, Joshua, 1626
Austin, --, 1677
Averill, Ephraim, 245
Avery, Horace, 1058
Avery, Miles, 1058
Avery, Simeon, 1640
Avery, Thomas, 900
Axson, Samuel J., 1636
Axson, --, 1636
Axtell, Henry, 237
Axtell, L., 237
Aymand, John, 25
Ayres, Elizabeth, 1630
Ayres, J. L., 1204

Babcock, John, 1030
Babcock, Polly, 1694
Babcock, Primus, 4
Backer, William, 203
Backus, Elijah, 1, 2, 3, 4, 241, 249, 1696, 1699, 1702
Bacomb, Samuel, 1712
Bacon, Abel, 67
Bacon, George, 31
Bacon, Henry, 1689
Bacon, Richard, 226
Bacon, William, 452, 1712
Bacot, Peter, 113
Baer, George, Junior, 47
Bagley, Asher, 179
Bailey, Benjamin, 151, 152, 195
Bailey, Ephraim, 1114
Bailey, Henry, 1688
Bailey, Ichabod, 289, 1771
Bailey, James, 118
Bailey, John, 205, 1276
Bailey, Louden, 40
Bailey, Mountjoy, 1183
Bailey, Phebe, 1688
Bailey, Theodoris, 118, 128, 129, 263, 1698
Bailey, Thomas, 1467
Bailey, William, 207
Bailey, Z., 1471
Bailey, -- A., 1682
Baily, J., & Cooke, T., 245
Baird, John, 782, 1785, 1786
Bairsto, Moses, Junior, 83
Baker, Christian, 164
Baker, Edmund, 1619
Baker, Henry, 157
Baker, James, 118
Baker, Jesse, 236
Baker, John, 143, 163, 1046, 1619
Baker, Philip, 1214
Baker, Richard B., 1689
Baker, Robert, 153
Baker, Samuel, 1196
Baldwin, Abraham, 23, 25, 26, 35, 1698, 1701, 1702
Baldwin, Absalom, 107
Baldwin, Asa, 217
Baldwin, Caleb, 13
Baldwin, Cornelius, 181
Baldwin, Daniel, 74, 202, 219
Baldwin, Eli, 956, 1730
Baldwin, Henry, 84
Baldwin, Jared, 918, 1742, 1743
Baldwin, Jesse, 34, 1697
Baldwin, Raisa R., 1624
Baldwin, Zachariah, 1622

Baldwine, Waterman, 43
Balfour, Elizabeth H., 1686
Balitz, George, 1637
Balitz, William, 1637
Ball, Abraham, 2, 5, 1582
Ball, Benjamin, 55
Ball, Burges, 194
Ball, B. W., 363, 475, 1766
Ball, James, 1532
Ball, John, 111, 175, 1638
Ball, Joshua, 1681
Ball, William, 743, 1532, 1728
Ballantine, Ebenezer, 230
Ballard, Asa, 77, 102, 119, 235
Ballard, Bruster, 182
Ballard, Kader, 1351
Ballard, William H., 241
Ballard, *see also* Bellard
Balsely, John, 607, 1707
Baltzell, Charles, 302, 1720
Bamer, Andrew, 57
Banfield, --, 1640
Banger, Walter, 1638
Banghman, George, 43
Banks, Justus, 63, 145
Banks, Zachariah, 241
Bankson, John, 42
Bannister, Seth, 2
Bannon, Jeremiah, 224
van Banshooten, Peter, 145
Bantham, John, 838, 1765
Baptiste, John, 212
Barbee, Thomas, 107
Barber, Francis, 1721
Barber, George C., 1707
Barber, James Noyes, 28
Barber, John, 294, 1711
Barber, Levi, 1138
Barber, Silas, 289, 1705
Barber, William, 77
La Barbier-Duplessis, Peter, 163
Barclay, John, 1290
Bard, John, 190
Barington, John, 1753
Barker, Barnabas, 387, 510, 1766
Barker, Ephraim, 1
Barker, Jonas, 178
Barker, Joseph, 599
Barker, Moses W., 1, 121
Barker, Samuel, 702
Barker, William, 203
Barkley, James, 1659
Barkley, Mary, 678
Barkus, John, 1681
Barkus, --, 1681
Barlow, Joel, 692, 1775
Barlow, John, 1626
Barlow, Stephen, 937
Barnaby, John, 94
Barnard, John, 734
Barnard, Pharez, 230
Barnard, Richard, 318, 430
Barnes, Ambrose, 289, 1771
Barnes, Ceasar, 1687
Barnes, Charles, 211
Barnes, Hannah, 1422
Barnes, James, 1676
Barnes, John, 1687
Barnes, Mary, 1624
Barnes, Richard, 121
Barnet, Isaac Cox, 182
Barnett, James, 830, 1755
Barney, Enoch, 1641
Barney, Jabez, 263
Barney, Nathaniel, 1641
Barns, Andrew, 210
Barnum, Amos, 155
Barnum, Ebenezer, 1524
Barnum, Eli, 1113
Barr, Alexander, 1311
Barr, Jacob, 131
Barr, John, 560, 841, 1710, 1767
Barr, Martha, 147
Barrain, Fielding, 926
Barram, Fielding, 926, 1789
Barrel(l), William, 262, 485
Barret, Joshua, 191
Barret, William, 97
Barrett, James, 163
Barrett, Oliver, 128
Barrett, Solomon (*or* Simon), 261
Barron, Benjamin, 676, 1757
Barron, Jonathan, 1778
Barrows, Peter, 237
Barsith, John, 1626
Barstow, *see* Bairsto

Barth, Stephen, 403, 530, 1775
Bartholomew, Benjamin, 210
Bartholomew, George, 93, 243
Bartholomew, G., & Fisher, J., 106, 126, 162, 190
Bartholomew, John, 175
Bartle, George, 11
Bartlet, Daniel, 84, 101
Bartlet, Jonathan, 1686
Bartlett, John, 1069
Bartley, --, 1401, 1402
Bartoe, Morris, 155
Barton, John, 190
Barton, Jonah, 83
Barton, Joseph, 191
Barton, Simon, 69
Barton, William, 5
Barton, --, 1566
Barton, --, & Rhea, --, 1697
Bascom, Samuel, 324, 436
Basey, William, 1619
Basey, *see also* Basy
Basford, Mo[se]s, 294
Bashman, Abraham, 204
Baskerville, Samuel, 301, 1751, 1752
Bass, Samuel, 30, 1750
Bassford, Moses, 1776
Basy, Stephen, 1639
Basy, *see also* Basey
Bateman, John, 1090
Bateman, Nathan, 1687
Bates, Benoni, 134
Bates, Edward, 1727
Bates, Nathaniel, 915, 1727
Bates, Samuel, 1655, 1668
Battell, William, 1437
Batten, John, 11
Battersby, John, 99
Battersly, Robert, 1270
Batterson, Joseph, 1624
Battle, James, 93, 100
Battles, John, 1562
Battles, J., 1562
Bauer, *see* Bower, Bowers
de Baufre, James, 2, 14, 28, 29, 31, 41, 45, 53, 55, 72, 79, 85, 92, 95, 118, 125, 161, 187
Baughman, George, 43
Baughman, *see also* Banghman
Baum, Martin, 34, 38, 165, 166, 167, 169, 181, 182, 183, 224, 225, 266, 1696, 1698
Baum, Martin, & Company, 224, 225, 1696, 1698
Baum, --, & Perry, --, 846, 1703, 1704
Baum, --, & Schenck, --, 34, 264, 1695, 1697
Bauman, Christopher, 654
Bauman, Frederick, 1787
Bauman, Sebastian, 181
Baumgartner, Leonard, 1528
Bautham, John, 1765
Bautham, *see also* Bantham
Bawcolt, William, 1630
Bawcult, William, 1630
Bawyer, Henry, 209
Baxter, William, 50
Bayard, J. A., 388, 513, 727
Bayard, Stephen, 87
Bayard, Stephen W., 82
Bayer, *see* Baer
Bayley, Theodore, 1699
Bayley, Thomas, 109
Bayley, Thomas M., 1466, 1471
Baylies, Hodijah, 299, 1741
Baylis, N. J., 962
Baylor, George, 1783, 1786, 1787, 1788
Baylor, Walker, 731, 1783, 1786
Baylor, Walter, 1787
Baylor, --, 1788
Baynton, Abel, 74, 165
Beach, Deborah, 74
Beach, Nathaniel, 115
Beach, Reuben, 150
Beach, Samuel, 134
Beach, Stephen, 169
Beadley, Abraham, Junior, 1110
Beadue, Elias, 248
Beagley, James, 14
Beaham, James, 287, 1711
Beal, William, 200
Beal, Zaccheus, 1636
Beal, Zachariah, 1636
Beal, --, 1636
Beale, Reasin, *see* Beall
Beall, Lloyd, 156
Beall, Nathaniel, 873, 1365
Beall, N., 1365
Beall, Reasin (Representative; Ohio) 1013, 1021, 1024

Benedict, Timothy, 18, 33, 196, 219
Benfer, John, 1114
Benjamin, Elias, 61
Benjamin, Samuel, 177
Benjamins, Aaron, 130
Bennedict, Timothy, 59
Bennet, Frederick, 966
Bennet, Henry, 1031
Bennet, James, 25, 59, 134, 164
Bennet, John, 614, 1704
Bennet, John G. W., 1697
Bennet, Ruffus, 211
Bennet, Terrence, 59
Bennett, A., 1215
Bennett, Caleb P., 27
Bennett, James, 57, 59
Bennett, John, 9, 1623
Bennett, Joseph, 78
Bennett, Mary, 1636
Bennett, William, 1623
de Benneville, Daniel, 37
Benny, Barnabas, 1678
Benny, --, 1678
Benson, Elizabeth, 163
Benson, E., 140, 141
Benson, Joshua, 243
Benson, Perry, 306, 1691, 1771
Benson, Reuben, 1312
Bent, Prince, 261
Bentalon, Paul, 187, 1699
Bentalore, Paul, 187, 1699
Bentalow, Paul, 187, 1699
Benter, --, & Shroyer, --, 1017
Benter, --, & Soyer, --, 1732
van Benthuysen, Barent, 201
Bentley, Henry, 156
Bentley, John, 173
Bentley, William, 178
Benton, Elijah, 8
Benton, Silas, 71
Berdeen (Berdeon) Timothy, 1677
Berdue, *see* Beadue
Berlin, Isaac, 600, 1772
Bernard, Richard, 1709
Bernard, William R., 42, 188
Bernhart, *see* Burnhart
Berry, Bartholomew, 100
Berry, Edward, 191
Berry, James, 398, 524, 1787
Berry, Joseph, 229
Berry, Michael, 116
Berry, Peter, 1505
Berry, Thomas, 1505
Berry, William, 1753
de Bert, Claudius, 56
Berwick, William, 172
Besterfield, Andrew, 1116
Betters, John, 223
Betts, David, 41
Betts, Stephen, 197
Bever, John, 222
Bevier, Philip D., 172
Bevinet, John G. W., 1697
Bevins, Henry, 102
Bevins, Wilder, 189
Beyer, *see* Baer
Beymer, George, 415, 416, 542, 543, 566, 1710
Beymer, *see also* Beemer, Bymer
Bias, James, 91
van Bibber, Isaac, 892, 1727
Bicker, Henry, 259
Bicker, Henry, Junior, 113
Bicker, Windsor, 1359
Bickford, Aaron, 1651
Bickford, Benjamin, 1685
Bickham, John, 592, 1710
Biddle, Clement, 245, 1698
Biddle, John, 203
Biddle, Richard, 130
Biddle, Thomas, 187, 188, 245, 1701
Bierce, William, 567, 1722
Bigbie, William, 1527
Bigelow, Moses, 1738
Biggs, Arnold, 1756
Biggs, Benjamin, 302, 1718
Biggs, John, 1554, 1630
Biggs, Zaccheus, 207, 217, 218, 222, 253, 318, 320, 324, 325, 334, 335, 336, 337, 338, 339, 340, 347, 354, 355, 365, 373, 384, 410, 411, 430, 432, 436, 437, 446, 447, 449, 450, 451, 452, 459, 466, 467, 486, 494, 506, 537, 553, 554, 555, 556, 557, 561, 575, 591, 612, 613, 614, 615, 616, 617, 618, 619, 620, 627, 629, 744, 996, 1695, 1697, 1699, 1703, 1704, 1705, 1706, 1709, 1710, 1711, 1712

Blood, -- J., 1676
Bloom, Albert, 1632
Bloon, Solomon, 1328
Bount, Jackey S., 298
Blount, J. L., 1707
Blount, Reading, 298, 1775
Blowers, Ephraim, 1685
Blum, George, 216
Blundin, William, 288, 1756
Blurn, George, 216
Blyth, Joseph, 254
Boardman, D., 159, 204
Boardman, Elijah, 159, 204
Boardman, William, 151
Boden, A., 1257
Bodle, Abraham, 726
Bodwin, Henry, 110
Boehmer, *see* Bamer, Beemer, Beymer, Bymer
Boettger, *see* Bottger
Bogaart, Isaac, 175
Bogart, Isaac, 155
Bogart, James N., 681
Bogart, Nicholas, 698, 1720
Bogart, N., 1638
Bohn, Charles, 934, 935, 936
Bohn, C., & Slingluff, J., 850, 891, 892, 893, 912, 913, 934, 936, 1019, 1720, 1724, 1725, 1726, 1727, 1733, 1734, 1736
Boice, George, 1034
Boice, *see also* Boyce
Boles, John, 169
Boller, F., 1696
Bolling, Sarah M., 1693
Bollington, John, 133
Bolton, Joseph, 23
Bolton, Matthew, 206
Bond, Abijah, 247, 248
Bond, Lewis, 185
Bond, Thomas, 243
Bonet, Joseph, 106
Bonham, Matakiah, 166
Bonharu, Matakiah, 166
Bonnell, Samuel, 122
Bonnett, Jacob, 714
Bonney, James, 183
Boody, John, 192
Booker, Lewis, 1753
Booker, Samuel, 855, 1741
Bookman, *see* Buckman
Boomer, E., 1201
Boon, John, 167
Booth, Charles, 1640
Booth, James, 388, 513
Boothe, William, 1196
Borland, C., 1314
Bosnick, Abraham, 1704
Boss, Christian, 47, 205
Bostil, Sarah, 116
Bostman, Frederick, 29
Boston, John, 69
Bostwick, Ebenezer, 918
Bostwick, Oliver, 172
Bostwicke, Obadiah, 114
Boswell, Samuel, 205
Boswell, William, 1, 1620
Bottger, Andrew, 77
Bottom, John, 1621
Botton, Joseph, 23
Boucher, Anthony, 1221
Boude, Thomas, 189
Boude, --, & Mosser, --, 1695
Boughton, John, 202
Bound, William, 72
Bounds, John, 77
Bowan, Henry, 1027
Bowdler, Samuel, 1321
Bowen, Barzillia, 208
Bowen, Michael, 1551
Bowen, Sabritt, 151
Bowen, Thomas Bartholomew, 3
Bowen, William, 1551
Bower, Jacob, 53
Bower, William, 1419
Bowers, Ephraim, 1
Bowers, George, 24
Bowers, James, 143, 1620
Bowers, Joab, 21
Bowers, John, 110
Bowie, *see* Anna Marie Bowie Chew
Bowman, Abraham, 1621
Bowman, George H., 1621
Bowman, John, 1621
Bowser, James, 1679
Bowser, --, 1679
Bowyer, Henry, 212
Bowyer, Michael, 156

Boxburgh, Alexander, 1741
Boyce, George, 1034
Boyce, Jonathan, 1682
Boyce, Thomas, 1788
Boyce, William, 190
Boyce, *see also* Boice
Boyd, Alexander, 1529
Boyd, James, 608, 1707
Boyd, John, 117
Boyd, Robert, 133, 243
Boyd, Thomas, 25, 307, 1745
Boyd, William, 159, 190
Boyer, Lewis, 412, 539, 1748
Boyer, Michael, 239
Boyer, Peter, 134
Boyer, *see also* Bawyer
Boyle, John, 1656, 1657
Boyle, Thomas H., 811, 1741, 1750
Boyles, Charles, 1624
Boyles, David, 1619
Boynton, Able, 101, 102, 220
Boynton, *see also* Baynton
Bowles, Ralph H., 26
Brabson, Thomas, 1351
Brabston, William, 1051
Bracco, Bennet, 1687
Brackenridge, Alexander, 87
Brackenridge, Robert, 87
Brackenridge, *see also* Breckenridge
Bracket, Charles, 1342
Bracket, Cornelius, 168
Bracket, Hezekiah, 29
Brackett, William, 1195
Bradbury, Daniel, 93
Bradford, Charles, 1681
Bradford, Gamaliel, 173, 246
Bradford, John, 1167
Bradford, Robert, 35
Bradford, William, Junior, 37
Bradley, Abraham, 808, 809
Bradley, Daniel, 302, 1756
Bradley, Gee, 221
Bradley, Ichiel, 115
Bradley, James, 129, 1125
Bradley, Philip P., 199
Bradley, Phineas, 814
Bradly, J., 1692
Bradston, William, 1653
Bradwell, Nathan, 1632
Bradwell, Nathaniel, 1632
Brady, James, 726, 766, 780, 826, 1012, 1290, 1772, 1776
Brady, John, 212
Brady, Michael, 151
Brady, Samuel, 207
Bragdon, Samuel, 1623
Bragg, Benjamin, 197
Brainard, Isaac, 1685
Brainard, Othniel, 21
Bramin, Silas, 4
Branhom, William, 6
Brankom, *see* Branhom
Brann, Andrew, 847, 940
Brann, Joseph, 869
Brannan, Lawrence, 47, 191
Brannon, John, 1630
Brannon, Michael, 1015, 1732
Branson, Isaac, 78
Brasbridge, John, 1314
Brasdel, -- B., 1640
Brautigam, Daniel, 215
Bray, John, 178, 179, 184, 185, 186, 274, 1696, 1697, 1699
Breadon, John, 201
Bready, John, 73
Breaty, D., 1234
Brebner, James, 129
Breck, Eleanor, 1623
Breck, John, 190
Breckenridge, James (Representative; Virginia) 882
Breckenridge, *see also* Brackenridge
Breese, Timothy, 49
Bremer, Lewis, 239
Bremigion, Thomas, 130
Brent, Daniel, 683
Brevard, Alexander, 391, 516, 1766
Brevard, Joseph, 31, 265
Brevitt, John, 186
Brewer, George, Junior, 176
Brewer, Henry, 1624
Brewer, Paul, 41
Brewer, --, 1624
Brewster, Caleb, 94
Brewster, James, 862
Brewster, John, 38
Brewster, Nathan, 61

Brownson, Gideon, 184
Brownson, Nathan, 1689
Bruce, William, 80
Bruen, Jacobus, 201
Bruff, James, 299, 639, 1721
Bruff, William, 47, 839
Bruffe, James, 1720, 1721
Bruffin, James, 299
Brumigan, D., 1640
Bruner, Joseph, 1069
Bryan, Charles, 290
Bryan, Edward, 173
Bryan, Elijah, 64
Bryan, James, 1621
Bryan, John, 121
Bryan, Michael, 103
Bryan, William, 661, 1772
Bryan, *see also* O'Bryan
Bryant, Benjamin, 53
Bryant, Elizabeth, 223
Bryant, James, 1621
Bryant, John, 571, 1710
Bryant, Matthew, 57
Bryce, John, 77
Bryon, Charles, 1704
Bryson, James, 105
Bryson, Samuel, 110
Buchanan, Alexander, 1691
Buchanan, James, 11
Buchanan, John, 685, 1744
Buchannon, John, 1678
Buck, Joseph, 6
Buck, T., 1678
Buckingham, --, 1679
Buckingham, --, & Company, 1637
Buckley, Mary, 28
Buckley, Michael, 695
Buckman, Benjamin, 8
Buckner, Elizabeth, 54
Bud, Absalom, 1579
Budd, Samuel, 11
Buell, Joseph, 164
Buff, William, 1723
Buford, Abraham, 302, 1707
Buker, Windsor, 1359
Bulger, Daniel, 47, 261
Bulkley, Prudence, 71
Bull, Aaron, 304, 1769
Bull, Thomas, 262
Bull, William, 150
Bullard, Asa, 33
Bullard, --, 1152
Bullock, Nathaniel, 1281
Bumford, G., 984
Bumpus, Asa, 1641
Bunall, Jonathan, 1696
Bunkam, Asahel, 842
Bunner, Charles F., 1678
Bunner, Rudolph, 1678
Bunt, Lodwick, 252
Burbeck, Henry, 301, 1757
Burchard, William, 68
Burgess, John, 1051, 1653
Burgess, Joshua, 306, 1745
Burgess, William, 189
van de Burgh, Bartholomeus, 66
van den Burgh, Abraham, 172
Burham, Asahel, 1728
Burk, Jonah, 74
Burk, Silas, 1626
Burke, G., 1493, 1684
Burke, John, 106
Burke, Richard, 1536
Burke, William, 1619
Burlingham, Chandler, 134
Burnet, Ebenezer, 160
Burnet, George W., 169, 264
Burnet, Ichabod, 143
Burnet, John, 152, 169, 264
Burnet, Robert R., 94
Burnett, James, 590
Burnett, John, 1649
Burnette, Thomas, 1722
Burnhart, Daniel, 1682
Burnley, Garland, 1640
Burns, Harvey, 217
Burns, James, 1685, 1689
Burns, James, Senior, 222
Burns, James, Junior, 1689
Burns, John, 883
Burns, Lawrence, 169
Burns, Samuel, 1689
Burnside, James, 1577
Burnsides, John, 262, 485
Burr, Aaron, 1691
Burr, Calvin, 22

Burr, Elijah, 22
Burr, Mary, 1678
Burrall, Jonathan, 107, 250, 1696
Burrell, Noah, 156
Burrell, Zachariah, 143
Burrowes, Eden, 11
Burrows, John, 14, 1149
Burt, Joseph, 1378
Burton, Elizabeth, 1678
Burton, H. G. (Representative; North Carolina) 1283
Burton, Jacob, 156
Burton, James, 1678
Burwell, Nathaniel, 222
Bush, Charles, 36
Bush, Conradt, 170
Bush, George, 1638
Bush, John, 584, 947, 1780
Bush, Lewis, 584, 1786
Bush, William, 252
Bushnell, David, 244
Busk, George, 1638
Bussey, Elijah, 176
Buting, Conrad, 1633
Butler, Benjamin, 55, 106
Butler, Edward, 222
Butler, Ezekiel, 128
Butler, Frederick, 220
Butler, John, 835, 939, 1620
Butler, Lawrence, 96
Butler, Patrick, 234
Butler, Percival, 300
Butler, Richard, 297, 1762, 1763
Butler, Thomas, 297, 1790
Butler, T. (*or* F.) 245
Butler, William, 24, 110
Butler, Zebulon, 34
Butt, Burduck, 218
Butt, Edward, 1353
Butt, Thomas, 47, 1353
Butt, Zachariah, 1353
Butts, Thomas, 262, 485
Buxton, Abijah, 255
Buxton, James, 130
Buxton, John, 243
Byerly, Frederick, 24
Bymer, George, 173
Bymer, *see also* Beemer, Beymer
Byram, Asa, 248
Byram, Robert, 1513
Byram, Sally, 1513

Cabell, Samuel J., 39
Cable, Jacob, 255
Cady, Daniel, 1090
Cady, Darius, 102
Cady, Palmer, 142
Cady, Samuel, 4
Cahill, John, 44
Cain, *see* Kain
Calderwood, Adam, 249
Caldwell, Andrew, 224
Caldwell, James, 129, 135, 178, 179, 262, 485
Caldwell, Joseph, 78
Caldwell, Robert, 80
Caldwell, Thomas, 1007
Calhoon, Andrew, 282, 1778
Califf, Stephen, 138
Call, Daniel, 860, 887, 898, 1742
Call, Hugh, 247
Call, Isaiah, 1624
Call, John, 1624
Call, S., 1624
Call, William, 774
de Calla, Theodore, 121
Callahan, David, 1253
Callahan, John, 82, 222
Callahan, Patrick, 56
Callahan, Samuel, 191
Callander, John, 147
Callender, Thomas, 73
Calley, *see* Kalley
Callin, Phineas, 1039
Callis, William, 1710
Calwell, Medford, 157
Camjrin, James, 1744
Camp, Aaron, 260
Camp, Casper, 202
Camp, Elisha, 65, 99, 133, 149
Camp, Robert, 12, 56, 88, 137, 213
Campbell, Alexander (Senator; Ohio) 957
Campbell, Andrew, 55
Campbell, Archibald, 7, 800
Campbell, Collin, 47
Campbell, Daniel, 1778
Campbell, Donald, 307, 1777

Campbell, Duncan, 52
Campbell, Esau, 1641
Campbell, George, 1682
Campbell, James, 27, 87, 1272
Campbell, John, 21, 50, 73
Campbell, Julia, 1694
Campbell, J. J. Richard, 21
Campbell, J. W. (Representative; Ohio) 1415
Campbell, Lewis, 259
Campbell, Robert, 44, 219, 223, 254, 1685, 1690, 1697, 1702
Campbell, Samuel (Representative; New York) 1302
Campbell, Thomas, 7, 48, 56, 199
Campbell, William, 167, 1629, 1641, 1682
Campen, James, 298
van Campen, Moses, 1693
Campfield, Jabez, 182
Campfield, Naptali, 6
Canady, George, 1686
Canady, John, 1686
Canfield, Hhaman, 112
Canfield, Ithamar, 227, 261
Cann, Augustine, 1682
Cannen, Joseph, 157
Cannon, John, 6, 9, 86
Cannon, Joseph, 219
Cannon, Thomas, 149
Cannor, Patrick, 1722
Cantine, George, 341, 453, 1749
Cantz, Mark, 239
Capp, Joseph, 1727
Carbery, Henry, 189
Carberry, Thomas, 1502
Carbett, John, 1711
Carbury, Francis, 279, 1790
Card, Potter, 238
Cardiff, Thomas, 192
Carey, Joseph, 219
Carey, Lewis, 37
Carigan, John, 17
Carland, P., 1432
Carlile, John, 304
Carlisle, John, 1777
Carlon, William 108
Carman, Thomas, 69
Carmine, *see* Carnine
Carnahan, James, 218
Carnahan, William, 211
Carneil, John, 1722
Carner, Abraham, 6
Carnes, Sally, 1540
Carnine, Jeremiah, 11
Carpenter, Benjamin, 808
Carpenter, B., 1771
Carpenter, Fanny, 1637
Carpenter, James, 809
Carpenter, Nehemiah, 201
Carpenter, Reuben, 960, 1780
Carpenter, Robert, 1689
Carpenter, William, 71
Carr, Hezekiah, 1022, 1737
Carr, James, 303, 1770
Carr, Matthew, 26
Carr, William, 160, 1622
Carringer, Martin, 1480
Carrington, Clement, 212
Carrington, George, 215
Carrol, John, 191
Carruthers, Joseph W., 629
Carshaw, Abraham, 59
Carso, Robert, 1683
Carson, John, 79
Carson, Samuel, 49
Carson, Thomas, 25
Carson, --, 1623
Carter, Aaron, 149
Carter, Benjamin, 129, 1626
Carter, Evan, 148
Carter, John, 1623
Carter, John C., 56
Carter, Joseph, 1407
Carter, Luke, 193
Carter, Nicholas, 1622
Carter, Peter, 37
Carter, Reuben, 956
Carter, Thomas, 1329
Carter, William, 191, 612, 1703
Cartwright, Thomas, 1680
Cartwright, --, 1680
Carty, Isaac, 4
Carty, Richard M., 131
Caruthers, John, 1703
Cary, John, 979
Cary, John D., 336, 448, 797, 1753
Case, Benjamin, 25
Case, Ezekiel, 209

Case, Richard, 692, 1775
Case, Saba A., 1636
Casey, John, 1206
Casey, Joshua, 1279
Casey, Peter, 1333, 1361, 1362, 1450, 1562
Casey, Robert, 175
Casgrove, Thomas, 167
Cashing, Thomas, 219
Cason, Jesse, 1633
Cason, Joshua, 1633
Cass, Jonathan, 8, 37, 83, 216, 1696
Cass, J., 227, 239, 244
Cass, T., 83, 84
Cassaday, William, 44
Cassedy, Edward, 162
Cassedy, Michael, 253
Casteel, Samuel, 97
Castillo, James, 70
Castle, James, 1641
Caswell, Bathsheba, 1632
Caswell, Job, 779, 1467, 1691
Cathcart, Andrew, 201
Catlin, Alexander, 25
Catlin, Putnam, 40
Cato, John, 197
Caule, John, 890
Causden, Jeremiah, 1292
Cautz, Mark, 239
Cavenaugh, Barney, 233
Cavenaugh, Garrett, 295
Cavennaugh, John, 7
Cawhawk, James, 189
Cay, David, 50, 52, 90
Cayore, Pierre, 224
Cazeir, William, 1130
Cazier, Abraham, 831, 1710
Ceasor, James, 255
Chadowick, James, 1693
Chadsey, Timothy, Junior, 4
Chadwell, George, 1304
Chadwick, James, 1632
Chadwick, John, 126, 132, 1676
Chadwick, Thomas, 1622
Chadwick, --, 1691
Chadwick, *see also* Chadowick
Challand, William, 9
Chamberlain, Ephraim, 71
Chamberlain, Sarah, 1619
Chamberlain, Theodore, 279, 1769
Chambers, David (Representative; Ohio) 1270, 1289, 1301, 1303, 1305, 1308, 1309, 1316, 1317, 1320, 1337, 1338, 1366
Chambers, James, 234, 297, 1786, 1791
Chambers, Joseph, 1786
Chambers, Leonard, 255
Chambers, Stephen, 299, 1722, 1723
Champlin, Hugh, 191
Champlin, Nathan, 1
Champlin, Newport, 1629
Champlin, Prince, 1629
Champlin, York, 1111
Champney, Nathan, 17
Chandler, Abel, 367, 488, 1767
Chandler, George, 103, 124, 131
Chandler, John, 129
Chandler, Martin, 748, 1783
Chandler, Moses, 1333
Chapel, Isaac, 131
Chapel, *see also* Chappell, Chapple
Chapelone, Peter, Junior, 152
Chapin, Joel, 354, 466, 1710
Chapin, Samuel, 1579
Chapman, Bethia, 1379
Chapman, Ceasar, 239
Chapman, Elias, 1402
Chapman, Elijah, 303, 1717
Chapman, Henry H., 194
Chapman, John, 1201
Chapman, Nathaniel, 1504, 1511
Chapman, Rufus, 128
Chapman, Samuel, 75, 1679
Chapman, Stephen, 409, 536, 1748
Chapman, Thomas, 14, 129, 1500
Chapman, --, 1679
Chappel, Elizabeth, 198
Chappel, Roswell, 1
Chappell, Samuel, 557, 1709
Chapple, Curtis, 8
Chaps, John, 34
Charity, Charles, 1685
Chartier, Joseph, 1691
Chase, Philander, 1262
Chase, Reuben, 129
Chase, Robert, 1244
Chatham, William B., 1750
Chatland, William, 9

Chatwood, --, 1636
Cheever, Abijah, 1623
Cheney, William M., 1695
Chesney, Benjamin, 989, 1765
Chesnut, Benjamin, 989
Chester, Edward, 9
Chester, John, 585, 1775
Chetwood, Mary, 1707
Chew, Anna Marie Bowie, 1073
Chew, Richard, 173
Chilcott, Thomas, 168
Childs, Charles, 100
Child(s), Evander, 63, 65, 126, 151, 871, 1765
Child(s), Francis, 1291
Childs, George, 244
Chillson, John, 1687
Chilton, John, 909
Chittenden, Martin, 504
Chittenden, W., 382
Chittendon, Gideon, 148
Chittingdon, Jared, 152
Christian, Michael, 127
Christie, James, 43, 51, 52, 130, 213, 298, 1790
Christie, John, 35
Christie, Thomas, 108
Church, Asa, 238
Church, Thomas, 86
Cilley, Jonathan, 303, 304, 1751
Cilley, Joseph, 304
Cist, Jacob, 598, 814
Cist, --, 770
Clagett, Horatio, 1739
Claiborne, N. H. (Representative; Virginia) 1501, 1505, 1506, 1507
Claiborne, Richard, 15
Clairey, Daniel, 48
Clake, Edmund, 1788
Clancy, David, 1361
Clancy, John, 47
Clancy, Michael, 191
Clappard, John, 158
Clarey, Samuel, 92
Claridge, Henry, 1630
Claridge, Levin, 1630
Clark, Arthur, 79
Clark, Asa, 1339
Clark, Augustus, 4
Clark, B., 1617
Clark, David, 170, 933
Clark, Ebenezer, 129
Clark, Ezra, 83
Clark, George, 175, 1619
Clark, Isaac, 399, 546
Clark, James, 184, 1330, 1687
Clark, Joel, 1638
Clark, John, 14, 111, 1501, 1680
Clark, John Innes, 237
Clark, Jonas, 1687
Clark, Jonathan, 298, 1784, 1790
Clark, Keziah, 193, 194
Clark, Lanea, 1617
Clark, Linda, 1679
Clark, Martin, 196
Clark, Mary, 1680
Clark, Matt St. C., 1633, 1636
Clark, Moses, 1360
Clark, Nathaniel, 1721
Clark, Paul, 1426
Clark, Ransom, 1080
Clark, Silas, 212
Clark, Thomas, 1683
Clark, William, 5, 261, 395, 520, 1686, 1693
Clark, --, 1681, 1683
Clark, *see also* Clerk
Clarke, Benjamin, 27
Clarke, Beriah, 186
Clarke, David, 90
Clarke, Edmund, 307, 1787
Clarke, Edward, 1787
Clarke, Isaac, 1787
Clarke, John, 115, 131, 132
Clarke, Jonathan, 1790
Clarke, Oliver, 16
Clarke, --, 1680
Clarkson, Matthew, 1680
Clarkson, --, 1680
Clay, Matthew, 26
Clayes, Peter, 258
Claypoole, Abraham G., 299, 1792
Clayton, Philip, 137
Cleary, William, 28
Cleaveland, Aquilla, 1681
Cleaveland, --, 1681
Clemens, Edward, 93
Clemens, John, 716
Clement, Aaron, 1651

de Corey, James, 75
Corey, John, 1636
Cork, Jacob, 1630
Cork, John, 1646
Cork, --, 1646
Cornaghan, James, 1691
Corneil, John, 342, 454, 1722
Cornish, G., 1519
Cornwale, Harmony, 1252
Cornwall, Richard, 1621
Cornwell, Thomas P., 184
Cornwell, William, 36
Cortlandt, Philip, 153
van Cortlandt, Philip (General, Representative; New York) 349, 358, 461, 470, 643
van Cortlandt, *see also* van Courtlandt
Cost, *see* Lacost
Costigan, Lewis, 138
Cottelle, Philip, 61
Cotter, James, 1709
Cottle, Jedediah, 1045
Cottle, R., 1209
Cotter, Edward, 39
Cotton, George, 227
Cotton, Thaddeus, 21
Coulter, Andrew, 44
Coulter, John, 794
Coulter, Samuel, 1506
le Count, John, 163
Countz, Adam, 170
Coursey, Hampton, 241
van Court, John, 1689
van Courtland, Philip, 62
Courtlandt, George, 159
van Courtlandt, *see also* van Cortlandt
Courtney, Hannah, 99
Courtney, Luke, 185
Coventry, John, 67, 1356
Coverly, Thomas, 844, 1767
Covert, Tunis, 262
Covington, Catherine, 1681
Cowan, Edward, 299, 1709
Cowdery (Cowdry) Samuel, 624, 1756
Cowdry, Benjamin, 144
Cowell, John, 1641
Cowell, --, 1641
Cowett, Hannah, 1676
Cox, Daniel V., 1053
Cox, Edward Neil, 1053
Cox, Elizabeth, 1693
Cox, Joshua F., 1690
Cox, Robert, 136
Cox, William, 168
Coy, Edward, 100
Coyle, John, 1054
Coyle, Mark, 279, 1707
Coyle, --, 663, 664, 665
Cozzens, Richard, 1111
Crab, Alexander, 1258
Crabbs, Henry, 1343
Craddock, Robert, 8
Crafordly, William, 37
Craft, Joseph, 1748
Craft, Nathaniel, 62
Crafts, Samuel Chandler (Representative, Senator; Vermont) 1207, 1208, 1216, 1217
Cragan, Dennis, 9
Craig, David, 7
Craig, Garard, 223
Craig, Isaac, 20, 1699
Craig, James, 147, 1555
Craig, John, 247, 701, 1787
Craig, Matthew, 1550
Craig, Samuel, 171
Craig, Sarah, 1626
Craig, Thomas, 208, 1451
Craig, William, 1540
Craigie, Andrew, 219
Craik, James, 89
Crain, Mary, 1693
Craine, James, 851, 1790, 1792
Crammond, William, 52
Crandall, Hosea, 1690
Crane, Abel, 154, 272
Crane, Elisha, 78
Crane, Elisha, & Don, E., 140
Crane, Ezekiel, 136, 235, 243
Crane, John, 910
Crane, Jonas, 112
Crane, Stephen, 595, 1703
Crary, Frederick, 1111
Crawford, Alexander, 167
Crawford, Andrew, 180
Crawford, Charles, 27
Crawford, David, 1636
Crawford, Edward, 156

Curtis, Enoch, 260
Curtis, Giles, 72
Curtis, John, 149
Curtis, Jonah, 912
Curtis, Joseph, 216
Curtis, Marmaduke, 12
Curtis, Nathan, 1693
Curtis, William, 1373
Curtis, Zachariah, 1620
Curtis, --, 1678
Curtiss, Abijah, 153
Curtiss, Eleasar, 162
Curtiss, Ruth, 1510
Curty, Barnaby, 233
Curwain, Edward, 169
Cusack, Christopher, 33, 198, 203
Cushick, Sarah, 1688
Cushing, Elmer, 51
Cushing, Matthew, 237
Cushing, Thomas, 216, 219, 223, 225, 301, 1758
Cusick, Nicholas, 823
Cusick, *see also* Cushick
Cuthbert, Alexander, 1686
Cuthbert, Alfred, 1686
Cutler, Benjamin, 261
Cutler, Ephraim, 71
Cutler, Joseph, 153
Cutler, Menassah, 71
Cutler, Temple, 1626
Cutter, Benjamin, 261
Cutting, Angelique, 1087
Cutting, Anne, 1087
Cutting, John B., 1087
Cutting, Nathaniel, 1087, 1091
Cuyler, Jacob, 236
Cuyler, L., 236
Cuyzer, Frederick, 808, 1772
Cyphers, Andrew, 22
Cyrus, Bartholomew, 1620

Dade, William, 19
Dagget, Henry, 226
Daggett, David (Senator; Connecticut) 1129
Dailey, Joseph, 1257
Daily, Peter, 234
Daily, Solomon, 1204
Dale, *see* Dayle
Dallas, Archibald, 138
Dallas, A., 138
Dallas, C., 138
Dalton, James, 79
Dana, Benjamin, 30, 32, 37, 101, 117, 1483
Dancy, Bazel, 1033
Danel, Richard, 1769
Daney, John, 1751
Danford, Joshua, 37
Danford, Prince, 143
Danforth, Joshua, 857, 1785
Daniel, Andrew, 217
Daniel, Hannah, 1685
Danon, Benjamin, 1677
Danow, Benjamin, 1677
Darby, Charles, 255
Darby, Elias, 1401
Darby, Ephraim, 1400
Darby, Ezra, 634, 719
Darby, John E., 1400, 1401
Darby, Nathaniel, 762, 1783
Darby, Thomas Jefferson, 1402
Darby, William, 55
Darcey, John, 299, 1751
Dark, William, 89
Darly, Nathaniel, 1783
Darragh, Charles, 1679
Darragh, Daniel, 171
Darrah, William, 153
Darrance, Samuel, 79
Daskum, John, 131
Daskum, William, 129
Daugherty, Barney, 59
Davenport, Cornelius, 172
Davenport, James, 101, 238
Davenport, John (Representative; Ohio) 663, 664, 665, 843, 973
Davenport, Thomas, 1641
Davenport, --, 319, 323, 431, 435
Daves, John, 22
Davidson, Barabas, 1621
Davidson, David, 156, 1685
Davidson, James, 117
Davidson, John, 75, 207, 217, 261, 835, 914, 1621, 1698
Davidson, Joseph A., 1630
Davidson, J., 245, 362, 364, 474, 476, 478, 479, 480, 482, 483

Elsworth, Peter, 68
Elwell, Thomas, 1176
Elwood, Benjamin, 119, 142
Ely, Gad, 75
Ely, William, 38, 70, 78
Ely, William S., 1680
Emerson, John, 1619
Emerson, Joseph, 131, 232
Emerson, Nathaniel, 129
Emerson, *see also* Emmerson
Emery, Samuel, 13, 33, 48, 83, 103, 108, 109, 132, 151, 152, 153, 159, 201, 203, 216, 219, 220, 227, 246
Emes, Worsley, 16
Emmerson, James, 1775
l'Enfant, *see* L'Enfant
Engle, Barbara, 1247
Engle, B., 1247
English, Andrew, 127
English, Charles, 1560
English, James, 1253
English, John, 406, 533
English, Samuel, 78, 1560
Enimerton, James, 586
Ennis, Enoch, 217
Ennis, John, 1638
Ennis, Leonard, 192
Ennis, William, 256
Ennos, Mary, 86
Eno, William, 241
Enos, R. V., 1670
Entrol, Henry, 1056
Eopler, Barnabas, 1067
Epes, William, 865
Epperson, Samuel, 200
Eppes, James, 1681
Ervin, James, 89
Erwin, Peter, 1680
Eshom, John, 1681
Eshom, --, 1681
Eskridge, William, 1691
Esperance, Joseph L., 13
Estell, William, 1632
Estep, Ephraim, 937, 1754
Etter, John, 1676
Eustace, William, 54
Eustis, Will, 109
Eustis, William, 109
Evans, Anthony, 222, 1517
Evans, Elijah, 166
Evans, George, 1690
Evans, Jenkin, 49
Evans, John, 72, 191
Evans, Perry, 938, 1736
Evans, Thomas, 91, 166
Evans, William, 299, 1744
Everett, Benjamin, 1378
Everett, Peletiah, 84
Everitt, Nicholas, 148
Everley (Everly) George, 598, 1720
Everley (Everly) Michael, 301, 1777
Eversole, Peter, 224
Evitt, Daniel, 63
Ewell, Charles, 1637
Ewer, Prince, 1680
Ewing, Josiah, 1394
ten Eyck, *see* Ten Eyck
Eyster, Peter, 180

Facy, *see* Fay
Faddor, Stephen, 196
Fado, Congo, 196
Fagan, Catherine, 174
Fahnestock, D., & Slingluff, J., 911, 964, 977, 980, 993, 1002, 1707, 1708, 1727, 1730
Fairbrother, Francis, 192
Fairchild, Pete, 122
Fairer, *see* Fayrer
Faires, John, 93, 100, 158
Fairlie, James, 35
Fairweather, Samuel, 169
Falkner, Ralph, 963
Fall, George, 1199
Fall, Joshua, 197
Fallin, John, 108
Fancher, Isaac, 1630
Fancour, John, 179
Fanner, John, 205
Fanner, Nathan, 1556
Fannier, John, 47
Fanning, Frederick, 164
Fanning, Thomas, 99
Fargo, William, 1142
Farley, Jonathan, 1621
Farley, *see also* Fairlie

Flick, Martin, 98
Fling, John, 618, 1703
Flora, Jacob, 163
Flourney, Josiah, 1632
Flower, Thomas, 1692
Flowers, Thomas, 1647, 1663
Flowers, Zephon, 92
Floyd, Ebenezer, 1085
Floyd, Isaac, 1685
Floyd, Jared, 1039
Floyd, Perry, 1685
Fluhart, Stephen, 28
Fluheart, Massy, 597
Fluheart, *see also* Fleeheart
Foggy, John, 83
Foght, John Morris, 1602
Folsom, John, 140, 235
Fomey, Dennis, 128
Fondey, John, 201
Font, Mathew, 254
Font, Robert, 64
Font, *see also* Fowt
Fontain, William, 1677
Foot, Ichiel, 1655
Foot, Isaac, 64
Foote, Charles A. (Representative; New York) 1341
Foote, Ebenezer, 38, 121, 663, 664
Foote, Joseph, Junior, 186
Foote, Justin, 663, 664
Foote, -- J., 1788
Footman, Peter, 40
Fopless, John, 27, 1681
Forbes, James, 208
Forbes, John, 1626
Forbes, Lucy, 177
Forbush, William, 212
Force, David, 252
Force, Henry, 218
Ford, Benjamin, 1493, 1684
Ford, Chilion, 570
Ford, Daniel, 261
Ford, David, 219, 261
Ford, Hezekiah, 1292
Ford, John, 1687
Ford, Lot, 1679
Ford, Mahlon, 40
Ford, Martin, 41
Ford, Sanbun, 1097
Ford, *see also* Fierd
Forde, Standish, 50
Fordon, James, 157
Foreman, David, 1027
Foreman, William, 357, 469, 1749
de Forest, Samuel, 235
Forman, Gabriel, 74
Forman, Jonathan, 185
Forresdale, Stafford, 114
Forrest, Andrew, 167
Forrest, Uriah, 221
Forrest, William, 1519
Forrest, --, 805, 806
Forrey, Samuel, 145
Forst, Robert, 64
Forst, *see also* Fowt
Fosbrook, John, 1619
Fosdick, Joseph, 37, 101, 102, 109, 139, 173, 177, 225
Fosdick, Thomas W., 1644
Fossett, James, 638
Fossin, Martha, 1678
Fossin, Peter, 1678
Foster, Abraham, 30, 207, 220, 247
Foster, Alexander, 41
Foster, Cosby, 860
Foster, Daniel, 1730
Foster, Dwight, 217
Foster, Hardin, 1005
Foster, Hardin, *same as* John Hardin Foster
Foster, George, 97
Foster, John, 4
Foster, John Hardin, 975
Foster, Jonathan, 1678
Foster, Moses, 573, 1771
Foster, Peter, 1629
Foster, Theodore, 237, 238
Foster, Theodore, & Company, 237, 238, 1699, 1700
Foster, William, 238, 1621
Foudey, Douw J., 175
Fountly, Henry, 1675
Fourcout, Francis, 195
Fowler, Edward, 4
Fowler, John, 170, 731
Fowler, Joseph, 205, 224, 1623
Fowler, Orne, 1638
Fowler, Robert, 314, 426, 1777
Fowler, Theodonius, 65

Geer, Michael, 70
Geers, Benjamin, 78
Gehan, Peter, 132
Geiger, William, 1635
Gent, George, 165
Geohagan, Anthony, 1484
George, Edward, 184
George, Michael, 1212
George, William A., 942
Georgia, Simon, 1553
Geralds, Theodore, 1443
Gerard, Charles, 1775
Germain, Henry, 102
German, William, 16
Gernant, Francis, 1596
Gernan, Richard, 360, 361, 362, 363, 364, 472, 473, 474, 475, 476, 477, 478, 479, 480, 481, 482, 483, 484, 1717, 1766
Gerrard, Charles, 298
Getchell, Seth, 1383
Geyer, John, 1680
Gibb, William, 87
Gibbon, James, 1620
Gibbons, David, 386, 508, 1777
Gibbons, James, 39, 44
Gibbons, R., 217
Gibbs, Caleb, 356, 468, 1783
Gibbs, Churchill, 1622
Gibbs, Moore, 283, 1771
Gibbs, Samuel, 36, 74
Gibbs, --, 1622, 1623
Gibson, Charles, 1687
Gibson, George, 1633, 1678
Gibson, Jacob, 121
Gibson, James, 206, 295, 1770
Gibson, John, 30
Gibson, John, Junior, 39
Gibson, Thomas, 27
Gibson, --, 1678
Giddeman, John, 81
Giffins, Joshua, 100
Gifford, Ichabod, 1681
Gifford, Jonathan, 157
Gifford, William, 1681
Gilbert, Benjamin, 78
Gilbert, Burr, 162
Gilbert, Charles C., 1622
Gilbert, Ebenezer, 161
Gilbert, George, 224
Gilbert, Jesse, 151
Gilbert, John, 153
Gilbert, Moses, 218
Gilbert, Seth, 132
Gilbert, Sylvester, 1567
Gilbert, Thomas, 1130
Gilby, Henry, 91
Gilchrist, George, 913
Gilchrist, Robert, 143, 242
Gilder, Reuben, 216
Gildersleeve, Finch, 175
Giles, Aquilla, 242
Gill, Joseph, 1711
Gill, Josiah, 1711
Gillaham, Clemens, 1476
Gillaspy, George, 29
Gillaspy, Joseph, 132
Gillaspy, --, & Strong, --, 29
Gillass, Arthur, 207
Gillegan, Thomas, 58
Gillen, Hugh, 1637
Gillen, Thomas, 1622
Gillespie, John, 147
Gillespy, --, & Henry, --, 1697
Gillet, John, 719, 736
Gilliland, William, 62, 66, 160, 201
Gilman, Benjamin Ives, 3
Gilman, Joseph, 988
Gilman, Nicholas, 83, 84, 85, 216, 267, 1696, 1697, 1702
Gilmore, John (Representative; Pennsylvania) 1577
Gilson, Jacob, 72
Gilson, James, 1770
Ginnis, John, 1771
Girdler, James, 97
Gist, Independent, 1028
Gist, I. C., 1028
Gist, John, 306, 1769
Gist, Mordecai, 1028
Gist, Nathaniel, 1638
Gitling, William, 640
Gladden, John, 221, 1380
Gladhill, Eli, 66
Glascock, Thomas, 78
Glasser, Silas, 48
Glassmire, Jacob G., 82
Gleason, Benjamin, 1122

Hall, Lee, 257
Hall, London (Loudon) 115
Hall, Nicholas, 1392
Hall, Oliver, 104
Hall, Philemon, 1455
Hall, Richard, 1632
Hall, Robert, 248
Hall, Samuel, 783, 801
Hall, Talmage, 1642, 1669
Hall, Thomas, 1129
Hall, William, 1, 109, 207
Hall, --, 1642, 1679
Hallet, James, 233
Hallet, Jonah, 175
Hallet, Jonathan, 175
Hallet, Thomas, 164
Halling, Solomon, 1707, 1788
Halsey, Joseph, Junior, 160
Halsey, Luther, 16
Halsey, Silas, 129
Halstead, John, 74
Halsted, Richard, 793
Halting, Solomon, 307
Halting, *see also* Halling
Ham, John, 1693
Hambric, David, 1000, 1765
Hambrick, Nathan, 1000
Hambrick, Thomas, 1623
Hambrie, David, 1000, 1765
Hamilton, Cumbert, 96
Hamilton, Edward, 194
Hamilton, George, 2
Hamilton, James, 56, 61, 63, 80, 103, 118, 240, 1696, 1701
Hamilton, James (Representative; South Carolina) 1350
Hamilton, John, 105, 239, 1619
Hamilton, John A., 302, 1719, 1720
Hamilton, Reuben, 1626
Hamilton, Thomas, 187
Hamilton, --, 710, 711
du Hammell, *see* Due Hammell
Hammond, Abijah, 121, 276
Hammond, David, 218
Hammond, James, 241
Hammond, John, 1155
Hammond, Prince, 99
Hamtramick (Hamtramck) John F., 32, 182, 1698
Hamtramick, J. T., 250
Hance, John, 257
Hancock, Bennet, 1623
Hancock, Elisha, 1683
Hancock, Stephen, 14
Hancock, --, 1683
Hand, Edward, 22, 1700
Handford, Timothy, 72
Handley, George, 1619
Handley, Peter, 245
Handly, Charles, 1599
Handy, George, 298, 1590, 1789
Handy, Russell, 1281
Handy, Samuel, 1454
Haney, Hugh, 1691
Hanford, Joseph, 66
Hangard, Gabriel, 1688
Hanley, James, 1620
Hanlin, Patrick, 203
Hanly, Russell, 1281
Hanmore, Moses, 63
Hanna, Charles, Junior, 1441
Hanna, James, 1441
Hanna, John, 6, 110
Hanna, John A., 311, 423
Hanner, Josiah, 1784
Hannon, William, 131
Hansell, George, 155
Hanson, Isaac, 1622
Hanson, John, 27
Hanson, Samuel, 1103
Hanson, Sarah, 1622
Hanson, William, 1683
Hantford, John, 200
Harberson, Adam, 1697
Harbeson, George, 115
Harbison, Adam, 87, 88, 1697, 1702
Harbrouck, Isaac, 139
Hardenberg, Abraham, 131, 149, 150
Hardenbergh, John L., 172
Hardenbrook, John A., 153, 275
Hardenbrook, J. A., 1696
Hardey, Joseph, 154
Harding, Israel, 102
Harding, John, 922, 1782
Harding, Oliver, 122
Hardman, Henry, 127
Hardry, Elias, 47

Haupt, John M., 1230
Haus, *see* House
Hausman, Mary, 189
Haven, James, 1426
Haven, John, 101
Haviland, Joseph, 1115, 1187
Hawes, Pelatiah, 198
Hawke, Michael, 192
Hawkey, William, 235
Hawkins, Bartlett, 889
Hawkins, Benjamin, 925, 1754
Hawkins, David, 148, 261
Hawkins, Henry, 307, 1786
Hawkins, Hezekiah, 72
Hawkins, John H., 171
Hawkins, Joseph, 150
Hawkins, Moses, 1637
Hawkins, M., 1518
Hawkins, Rebecca, 836, 1757
Hawkins, William, 230
Hawkins, William L. (*or* S.) 1518
Hawkins, William S., 1637
Hawkins, -- L., 1676
Hawley, Abraham, 202
Hawley, Nathan, 25
Haws, Bartlett, 1754
Hay, Samuel, 227
Hayden, Jeremiah, 1619
Haydon, Phebe, 238
Hayes, Lawton, 1174
Hayes, William, 79
Haynie, Ezekiel, 1690
Haynie, Henrietta B., 1690
Hays, John, 578, 1778, 1779
Hays, Michael, 138
Hays, Robert, 50
Hays, William, 766
Hayton, Joseph, 246
Hayward, Caleb, 220
Hayward, C. C., 1690
Hazard, Ebenezer, 226, 364, 478
Hazard, Richard, 64
Hazard, Sampson, 218
Hazeltine, Thomas, 79
Hazen, Moses, 21
Hazlehurst, John, 108
Hazleton, Prince, 1359
Heacock, Esther, 219
Head, John, 1603
Head, Richard, 563, 1772
Heard, John, 16
Hearney, David, 1597
Heart, John, 71
Heart, Jonathan, 71
Heart, Mary, 1680
Heart, *see also* Hart
Heath, John, 182
Heath, William, 256, 1622
Heaton, James, 163
Heaton, John, 111, 162, 165
Hebard, Samuel, 128
Heckewelder, John, 9, 10, 220, 257, 634, 1695, 1706, 1717, 1718, 1720
Hedges, Alexander, 1152
Hedley, Moses, 14
Heel, John, 225
Heel, John P., 82
von Heer, Bartholomew, 17
Hefferman, Thomas, 82
Heffernan, Hugh, 261
Hegins, Benoni, 1723
Heil, *see* Hile
Heiner, Jasper, 11
Heiser, *see* Hyser
Heister, Joseph, 403
Heit, *see* Hite
Helanen, William, 645
Helfenstein, John P., 359, 380, 471, 502
Heller, Jacob, 70, 262, 485
Helm, John, 220
Helm, Leonard, 1147
Helme, Anselmus, 70
Helms, William (Representative; New Jersey) 921, 922
Helms, --, 328, 440
Help, Ludwick, 222
Hemingway, James, 1693
Hemingway, *see also* Homingway
Hempfield, John, 98
Hemphill, Joseph, 118
Hemptin, Oliver, 1676, 1677
Henderson, Andrew, 208
Henderson, David, 1680
Henderson, Frances E., 1446
Henderson, Gustavus H., 298
Henderson, G. H., 1749

Hulbert, Aaron, 68
Hulet, John, 14
Hulings, John, 93
Hull, David, 41
Hull, Eli, 955, 1776
Hull, George, 245
Hull, Jeremiah, 4
Hull, Joseph, 238
Hull, Samuel, 99, 862
Hull, Thomas, 263
Hull, William 199
Hull, Zephaniah, 972
Humes, *see also* Hoomes
Hummiston, Daniel, 712
Hummiston, Elizabeth, 712
Humphrey, Jacob, 262, 485
Humphrey, James, 133
Humphrey, John, 262, 485
Humphrey, Samuel, 258
Humphrey, Thomas J., 1497
Humphrey, Tower, 238
Humphrey, William, 1497
Humphreys, Anna, 238
Humphreys, Ashton, 51
Humphreys, David, 773
Humphreys, George, 1632
Humphreys, George W., 834
Humphreys, Huldah M., 1595
Humphreys, Israel, 1595
Humphreys, Jacob, 485
Humphreys, James, 59, 108
Humphreys, John, 238
Humphreys, Jovael, 1595
Humphreys, --, 1632
Humphries, David, 1707, 1746, 1747
Humphries, George, 789
Humphries, Joseph, 1415
Humphrys, James, 23
Humpton, Richard, 94
Hungerford, Thomas, 298, 1790, 1791
Hunt, Abijah, 111, 148, 1695
Hunt, Alexander, 53
Hunt, David, 1165
Hunt, Ephraim, 60
Hunt, Jesse, 111, 1695
Hunt, Joseph, 131
Hunt, Josiah, 143
Hunt, Ralph, 127
Hunt, Thomas, 82, 111
Hunt, William, 1317
Hunter, Ann, 718, 1776
Hunter, Benjamin, 1590
Hunter, Elijah, 68, 112
Hunter, George, 1516
Hunter, John, 206
Hunter, Robert, 8, 140, 167, 212, 247
Hunter, William, 274
Huntington, Ebenezer, 243
Huntington, G., 1640
Huntington, Jedediah, 241
Hurd, John, 207
Hurdle, Lawrence, 112
Hurlbut, Raphael, 289, 1770
Hurleray, John, 1775
Hurleroy, John, 692
Hurley, Matthew, 222
Hurteigh, John, 78
Husband(s) James, 290, 1790
Huston, Philip, 1326
Hutch, John, 100
Hutchens, Nathaniel, 932
Hutchins, John, 12, 51
Hutt, Preston, 255
Hutton, Andrew, 180
Hutton, James, 261, 1678
Hutton, William, 115
Hutton, --, 1678
Hutts, Jacob, 1549
Hyat(t) Abraham, 204
Hyatt, John Vance, 262, 485
Hyatt, Minnah, 262
Hyatt, Seth, 1164, 1168, 1183
Hyde, Azel, 36
Hyde, Udney, 1641
Hyde, William, 122, 178, 200
Hyde, -- Ann, 1641
Hyrne, Edmund M., 1689
Hyser, Hendrick, 129

Imhoff, Fred, 957
van Ingen, Abraham, 1687
Van Ingen, Dirck, 61, 121, 157, 1687
Ingham, Samuel D., 1093
Ingle, William, 1086
Ingles, John, 298, 1738

Jones, Joseph, 217, 254
Jones, Josiah, 224
Jones, Nathan, 248, 252
Jones, Nelsey, 211
Jones, Peter, 1678
Jones, Philip, 1043
Jones, Phillip, 1686
Jones, Richard, 233
Jones, Robert, 99, 1516
Jones, Samuel, 28, 252, 260, 1637, 1702
Jones, Thomas, 115, 191, 1619
Jones, Walter, 1087, 1363
Jones, William, 9, 121, 190, 227
Jones, --, 1640, 1678, 1679
Jordan, Daniel, 85
Jordan, John, 89, 1558
Jordan, Leroy, 1500, 1571, 1572, 1573, 1574, 1575, 1576
Jordan, Mary Ann, 1534
Jordan, --, 1505
Joseph, John Baptiste, 96
Joslin, Thomas, 117
Jotham, Lurany, 1259
Jouett, John, 209
Joy, David, 1188
Joyes, Thomas, 1476
Joynes, Leven, 247
Judd, Mary, 1687
Judd, William, 71
June, Abraham, 35
Jung, *see* Young
Justice, Jacob, 88
Justice, James, 43
Justice, Jesse, 28
Justin, Charles, 1620

Kahiktotow, Cornelius, 204
Kain, Manus, 51
Kain, Valentine, 1125
Kaine, James O., 1776
Kaiser, *see* Ceasor, Kyser
de Kalb, -- Baron, 1293
Kalley, Eleanor, 178
Kane, *see* Kain
Kantner, John, 43
Karsh, George, 112
Kateman, Mary, 1682
Kavenaugh, Garrett, 1770
Kay, *see* Cay
Keamer, Nicholas, 147
Kean, Edward, 628, 1748
Kean, John, 51
Kean, Mary, 100
Kearns, William, 95
Kearsey, John, 40
Keating, John, 60
Keeler, Aaron, 952, 1754
Keeler, Frederick, 26
Keeler, Hezekiah, 110
Keeler, Isaac, 67
Keeler, James, 1676
Keeler, Jeremiah, 210
Keeler, Samuel, 559, 1781
Keeler, Thomas, 1118
Keeler, Thaddeus, 208
Keen, Hannah, 52
Keen, Lawrence, 1666
Keen, Samuel Y., 1732
Keen, Susannah S., 1666
Keene, Samuel Y., 720
Keenon, John, 51
Keenon, *see also* Kenan
Keep, James, 96
Keiner, Jasper, 203
Keiser, *see* Ceasor, Kyser
Keith, Japheth, 17
Kellar, George, 112
Keller, Conrad, 1678
Keller, Israel, 1678
Kelley, Edward, 1772
Kelley, William, 1677
Kellog, Enoch, 171
Kellog, Josiah, 40
Kellog, Solomon, 40
Kellog, William, 40
Kellow, William, 1679
Kellum, Reuben, 113
Kelly, David, 178, 1677
Kelly, Edward, 21, 662, 1310
Kelly, Henry, 43
Kelly, James, 192, 1686
Kelly, John, 158, 261
Kelly, Patrick, 1686
Kelly, Thomas, 1688
Kelly, Timothy, 36, 112, 163

McClerron, Thomas, 49
McClintock, Sarah, 90
McCluney, William, 49, 98, 112, 147, 644, 645, 1695, 1698
McCluney, --, 321, 433
McClure, James, 80
McClure, John, 705
McClure, *see also* McLure
McColgen, John, 17
McCollum, John, 138
McCollum, Reuben, 115
McColm, Samuel, 91
McCombs, John, 164
McCondry, Will, 216
McConnally, Hugh, 177
McConnell, James, 246
McConnell, Mary, 1677
McConnell, Matthew, 10, 11, 17, 33, 121, 146, 186, 198, 231, 232, 278, 297, 1792
McConnell, Robert, 810, 1783
McConnell, William, 132
McConner, M., 1772
McCorin, John, 1636
McCormack, James, 164
McCormick, Hugh, 1258
McCormick, John, 96
McCortley, Michael, 18
McCoskey, Samuel A., 262, 485
McCowan, *see* McKowan
McCown, John, 1636
McCoy, Roderick, 262, 485
McCoy, Samuel, 17
McCoy, William, 1685
McCoy, William (Representative; Virginia) 1218
McCracken, Philip, 130
McCracken, William, 87
McCraw, Francis, 1767
McCraw, Samuel, 379, 501, 1767
McCraw, *see also* Magraw
McCrea, Philip, 1071
McCrea, Stephen, 66
McCreary, John, 537, 1709
McCreery, John, 410
McCrosson, Patrick, 292, 1722
McCrum, Michael, 171
McCullam, John, 1786
McCulloch, Robert, 182
McCully, George, 302, 1715
McCurdy, James, 981
McCurdy, Moses, 707
McCurdy, Patrick, 631
McCurdy, William, 49
McDade, Will, 98
McDaniel, Mary, 1334
McDonald, Archibald, 25, 218
McDonald, Benjamin, 179
McDonald, Charles, 41
McDonald, Daniel, 198
McDonald, Francis, 572, 1771
McDonald, Godfrey, 51
McDonald, James, 23
McDonald, John, 102, 164, 185
McDonald, Rebecca, 254, 296
McDonald, Robert, 222
McDonald, William, 24, 279, 296, 1751
McDowell, Hugh, 228
McDowell, John, 302, 1629, 1707
McDowell, Thomas, 51
McDowell, William, 301, 1779
McDo--od, John, 18
McDuff, Daniel, 1624
McDuff, David, 1624
McDuffie, George (Representative, Senator; South Carolina) 1477
McDuffy, Archibald, 255
McElhatton, William, 135
McEllery, Hugh, 1016
McElready, Hugh, 3
McElroy, John, 292, 1722
McElroy, William, 1299
McEuen (McEven, McEwen) John, 254, 302, 1723
McEvoy, Michael, 25
McEwen, James, 37
McEwen, John, *see also* McEuen
McEwen, Thomas, & Company, 22, 80, 83, 84, 85, 118, 253, 267
McFadon, James, 1618
McFarland, Andrew, 1570
McFarland, Moses, 1683
McFarland, Samuel, 759
McFarlane, Andrew, 1570
McFarlane, James, 147
McFarlane, John, 124
McFarlane, Robert, 1570
McFarran, Thomas, 63
McFarren, Margaret, 156

McFatridge, Daniel, 115
McFoutcheon, George, 182
McGaffey, Andrew, 1778
McGaffy, Neal, 101
McGahey, John, 116
McGahey, William, 1374
McGauhy, Will, 27
McGaw, Robert, 208
McGears, Agitha, 1517
McGee, Daniel, 195
McGee, James, 1038, 1633
McGee, John, 1686
McGee, Levin, 1686
McGee, Sarah, 53
McGee, *see also* Magee
McGhee, William, 1523
McGill, William, 142
McGillon, William, 173
McGilton, William, 173
McGinnis, John, 657, 1771
McGinnis, *see also* Maginnis
McGlaughlin, Alexander, 13, 96, 273
McGlaughlin, Charles, 1018
McGlaughlin, Patrick, 4, 163, 174, 256
McGlaughlin, --, & Smith, --, 1018
McGlocklin, John, 244
McGloghlin, William, 255
McGonnigle, John, 4
McGraw, *see McCraw, Magraw*
McGregor, David, 37
McGregor, John, 1061
McGregore, James, 70, 157
McGruder, Elizabeth, 1621
McGuire, Andrew, 111
McGuire, Thomas, 30, 55
McGuire, William, 89
McHaffey, James, 116
McHenry, Charles, 186
McHenry, James, 297, 1791
Machin, Thomas, 68
McIlvain, --, 1679
McIlvaine, Thomas, 49
McIntire, James, Senior, 1586
McIntire, James, Junior, 1586
McIntire, Thomas, 136
McIntosh, Alexander, 114
McIntosh, Lachlin, 213, 297, 1791
McIntosh, Maria, 1470
McIntyre, Henry, 1676
Mack, Richard, 1596
McKay, Jesse, 868, 1742
McKean, Samuel (Representative, Senator; Pennsylvania) 1473
McKee, Charles, 1075
McKee, Edith, 94
McKeehan, George, 572, 573, 574
McKeehan, G., 1771
McKeever, Angus, 709
McKelvey, Thomas, 209
McKennan, Will, 27
McKenny, Andrew, 1676
McKenny, --, 1676
McKensey, Joshua, 215
McKenzie, Alexander, 23
McKenzie, George, 1499
McKenzie, Murdoch, 122
McKesson, J., 140, 141
Mackey, James, 249
McKey, William, 228
McKillen, Edward, 255
McKim, John, 215
McKimmens, John, 164
McKinley, Alexander, 53, 279, 1764
McKinley, A., 1155
McKinley, James, 1686
McKinley, John, 279, 1764
McKinley, Peter, 127
McKinley, Robert, 1686
McKinney, John, 50, 167
McKinney, Peter, 24
McKinsey, Jesse, 944, 1730
McKinsey, Moses, 47
McKissac, William, 1404
McKnight, Charles, 67
McKnight, David, 88
McKnight, Michael, 72
McKowan, William, 152
McKown, William, 160
McLachlin, Colin, 7
McLain, Laughlin, 1632
McLane, Allen, 297, 1747
McLane, John, 142
McLaughlin, Alexander, 1700
McLaughlin, Hugh, 23
McLaughlin, James, 62
McLaughlin, Owen, 56, 197

Mason, Nathaniel, 372, 493, 1630
Mason, Thomas, 42, 156
Mason, William, 98
Massey, John, 1683
Massey, Robert, 1683
Massie, Henry, 867, 1730
Masson, Issacher, 188
de Masters, Edward, 1679
Masters, John, 138
de Masters, --, 1679
Masterson, Philip, 255
van Mater, John, 206
Mathers, Timothy, 1630
Mathews, E., 1195
Mathews, George, 297
Mathews, Henry, Junior, 263
Mathews, John, 250, 254, 258, 393, 394, 395, 396, 397, 398, 401, 518, 519, 520, 521, 522, 523, 524, 525, 526, 528, 973, 1697, 1699
Mathews, John, *see also* Matthews
Mathews, --, 773
Mathewson, Samuel J., 1281
Matthews, George, 35, 1792
Matthews, James, 11
Matthews, John, 96, 109, 110, 111, 180, 401, 853, 973, 1697, 1765
Matthews, John, & Company, 21, 1699
Matthews, John, *see also* Mathews
Matthews, William, 90, 116, 120
Matthews, --, Turner, --, & Ormsby, --, 1698
Matthewson, Elisha, 58
Maurey, *see also* Mourey
Maury, Eleanor Woodside, 1768
Maus, Samuel, 23, 92
Mauser, *see* Mouser
Mavett, Francis, 57
Maxey, V., 1618
Maxfield, Joseph, 1624
Maxim, William, 262
Maxwell, Anthony, 48, 62, 93, 126, 135, 136, 138, 159, 169, 201, 218, 235, 253, 302, 1723
Maxwell, Cornelius, 162
Maxwell, Hugh, 241
Maxwell, James, 845, 1623, 1704
Maxwell, John, 191
Maxwell, William, 278
May, Andrew, 138
May, Deborah, 157
May, John, 37
May, Will, 99
Mayberry, Beriah, 846
Mayberry, John, 55
Mayberry, Richard, 37
Mayberry, Thomas, 82
Mayer, Elizabeth, 1762
Mayer, Matthias, 1628
Mayhew, James, 1619
Mayhew, William, 1104
Mayley, John, 132
Maynard, Adam, 208
Maynard, John, 561, 1709
Maynard, Jonathan, 964
Maynard, Peter, 230
Mazyck, Stephen, 113
Mead, Job, 133
Mead, Jonathan, 145
Mead, Samuel, 58
Mead, Shadrach, 13
Mead, Shadwick, 99, 100
Mead, Uriah, 1630
Meade, Abigail, 1680
Meade, Abijah, 1682
Meade, Everard, 1682
Meads, James, 243
Meakins, Bennett, 1690
Meakins, Joseph L., 1690
Means, Hugh, 1680
Means, James, 1750
Means, Richard, 2
Means, Robert, 2, 7, 23, 25, 28, 29, 33, 34, 36, 48, 63, 68, 72, 75, 79, 85, 87, 92, 93, 98, 106, 119, 120, 124, 126, 127, 128, 130, 131, 132, 144, 147, 155, 169, 170, 172, 174, 178, 183, 184, 188, 190, 197, 200, 203, 212, 221, 224, 227, 233, 753, 755, 757, 791, 1742, 1749, 1761, 1762, 1763, 1777
Means, Thomas, 284, 1707
Meara, Patrick, 692, 1775
Mebane, William, 244
Meckle, Reuben, 1623
Medah, Stephen, 1199
Medearis, John, 306, 1704
Medowell, Cairnoan, 13, 14, 273, 1696, 1697
Mee, Thomas, 1032
Meech, Jacob, 1632

Moore, Joseph, 43
Moore, J., 777
Moore, J. B., 1387
Moore, J. G., 780
Moore, J. J., 679, 680, 843, 861, 904, 924, 1103
Moore, King, 208
Moore, Matthew, 191
Moore, Mordecai, 1255
Moore, Robert (Representative; Pennsylvania) 1128
Moore, Susanna, 1258
Moore, Thomas, 97, 195, 208, 1435
Moore, William, 106, 159, 166, 188
Moore, Zechariah, 896, 1672
Moore, Zedekiah, 875
Moore, --, 875
Moorehouse, David, 198
Moorehouse, Jacob, 185
Moores, Benjamin, 33
Moores, Benjamin, *see also* Moers, Mooers, Moore
Morand, Charles, 182
Moreland, Moses, 147
Morell, Joseph, 204
Morey, Jonathan, 39
Morey, Pero, 103
Morfit, Henry, 1693
Morfit, Henry M., 1693
Morgan, Benjamin, 18, 117
Morgan, Charles, 185, 555, 1712
Morgan, Daniel, 96, 162
Morgan, David, 18, 117, 1479, 1695
Morgan, John, 102, 1681
Morgan, Joseph, 57, 235, 262, 485
Morgan, Lewis, 111
Morgan, Mary, 1687
Morgan, M., 1685
Morgan, Samuel, 256
Morgan, Simon, 218
Morgan, William, 1677
Morgan, --, 1681
Morgan, --, & Price, --, 1696
Morison, Isaac, 218
Morrell, Eliza L., 1688
Morrill, Amos, 239
Morrill, Isaac, 172
Morrill, John, 172, 1362
Morrill, Joseph, 74
Morris, Benjamin, 1569, 1615
Morris, Catherine, 135
Morris, Christopher, 1620
Morris, David, 24
Morris, George, 820
Morris, Isaac, 209, 1569, 1615
Morris, John, 62, 189, 1767
Morris, John, Junior, 92
Morris, Jonathan, 207
Morris, Jonathan Ford, 111
Morris, Lewis, 111
Morris, Paten, 1527
Morris, Samuel, 594, 1747
Morris, Slayton, 119
Morris, William W., 146
Morris, Zadock, 127
Morrison, David, 1717
Morrison, James, 96, 97, 185, 221, 254, 268, 869, 940, 950, 1695, 1702, 1730, 1735, 1761, 1763
Morrison, Larkin, 1688
Morrison, Samuel, 1323
Morrison, William, 245
Morrison, Zachariah, 1557
Morriss, George, 1772
Morriss, John, 844
Morrow, Jeremiah (Representative, Senator; Ohio) 385, 386, 406, 507, 508, 533, 600, 601, 602, 603, 605, 670, 671, 779, 842, 945, 946, 951, 956
Morrow, Joshua, 1219
Morrow, Rebecca, 1406
Morrow, R., 1399, 1406
Morrow, --, 801
Morse, Philip, 168
Morten, Henry, 1694
Morton, Hezekiah, 321, 433, 1712
Morton, James, 211
Morton, Silas, 253
Morton, William, 1457
Mosby, Littleberry, Junior, 1751, 1752
Mosby, William, 1619
Moseley, Benjamin, 1682
Moseley, --, 1141, 1142
Mosely, M., 1445
Mosely, William, 123
Mosely, William J., 1445
Moser, Esther, 1640
Moser, George, 1640
Moser, Samuel, Junior, 156

Myers, H., 1519
Myers, Mordecai, & Company, 1300, 1310, 1589, 1600, 1601
Mygatt, Elisha, 692, 1775

Nace, George, 40
Nagle, Christian, 99, 118
Nagle, Henry, 255
Nance, Buckner, 117
Nason, Nancy, 1683
Neal, Daniel, 165
Neal, E. O., 187
Neal, Ferdinand O., 165
Neal, Ira T., 1617
Neal, James, 1604
Neal, James A., 13, 38, 48, 52, 59, 80, 91, 157, 185, 186, 197, 234, 239
Neal, James A., *see also* Neale
Neal, James I., 2
Neal, James O., 57
Neal, J. O., 187
Neal, Nancy, 1688
Neal, *see also* O'Neal
Neale, James A., 248
Neale, James A., *see also* Neal
Needer, Simon, 33
Neely, Abraham, 145
Neely, David, 73
Neider, Ira, 121
Neil, Daniel, 1641
Neil, Thomas, 5
Neilion, Andrew, 82
Neilson, Allen, 958
Neilson, Andrew, 173
Nelson, Abraham, 68
Nelson, Alexander, 84
Nelson, Henry, 1682
Nelson, Jemima, 90
Nelson, Joseph, 147
Nelson, Josiah, Junior, 225
Nelson, Mary, 1682
Nelson, Nehemiah, 237
Nelson, Roger, 205
Nelson, --, 374, 495
Nerlie, Bernard, 131
Nesbitt, Henry, 92
van Ness, Cornelius, 15
Nestel, Godlieb, 257
Nestler, John, 1619
Nestor, John, 138
Neufeld, *see* Newfoelle
Nevery, Martha, 1677
Nevile (Nevill) Presley, 96
Nevill, John, 222, 1301
Nevill, *see also* Nowill
Nevin, John, 1301
Nevins, D., 1215
Nevite (Nevin, Nevill) John, 1301
New, Anthony, 207, 212
Newall, Calvin, 1196
Newan, N., 1637
Newby, John, 156
Newell, John, 1462, 1463
Newell, Thomas, 1302
Newfeld, William, 1681
Newfoelle (Newfeld) William, 1681
Newhall, Ezra, 30
Newkerk, Charles, 63, 66, 70, 123
Newkirk, Charles, 23, 38, 154, 266
Newman, Betsy, 1626
Newman, Henry, 154, 216, 223, 225, 272, 1185
Newman, John, 67, 1626
Newman, John, Junior, 1626
Newman, Owen, 96
Newman, Polly, 1626
Newman, Silas, 130
Newman, Solomon, 1626
Newman, Thomas, 104
Newton, Moses, 9
Newton, Thomas, 118
Newton, Thomas C., 119
Newton, William, 205
Niblet, William, 49
Nice, John, 3
Nicho, Jeremiah, 1678
Nicholas, John, 1620
Nicholas, Lewis, 95
Nicholls, Nathaniel, 1683
Nicholls, Nehemiah, 1683
Nicholls, Samuel, 1683
Nicholls, William B., 1626, 1629, 1630, 1633, 1678
Nicholls, William L., 1678
Nicholls, William S., 1679
Nichols, Charles, 137
Nichols, John, 1530

Nourse, Michael [continued] 1441, 1449, 1721, 1722, 1762, 1777
Nourse, W. M., 414
Nourse, --, 1124
Nowe, Lewis, 63
Nowell, James, 1066
Nowill, George, 68
Noyes, John, 303, 1769, 1770
Noyes, Jonathan, 1
Noyes, Moses, 1633
Noyes, Wadleigh, 1633
Noyes, --, & Galbreath, --, 1698
Noys, Wadleigh, 1633
Noys, *see also* Noise
Nugent, Patrick, 235
Nulton, John, 674, 1787
Nunley, John, 878
Nutmire, Henderick, 149
Nutton, 1787

Oakly, John, 25, 38
Oaks, John, 1678
Oaksman, Mary, 56
O'Brian, Abigail, 238
O'Brian, Ann, 58
O'Brian, James 228
O'Brien, Ann, 256
O'Bryan, Philip, 262, 485
O'Bryan, Thomas, 78
O'Bryan, William, 39
O'Callis, William, 636
Ochsman, *see* Oaksman
Odenheimer, J. W., 1686
O'Flaherty, John, 23
Ogden, Barney, 1630
Ogden, Daniel, 262, 485
Ogden, David, 66
Ogden, Edmund, 183
Ogden, Edward, 108
Ogen, Thomas, 37
Ogle, James, 1743
Ogle, Joseph, 876
O'Hara, Francis, 652, 1787
O'Hara (O'Harra) Joseph (*or* Joshua) 626, 1703
O'Kain, James, 717
Olcott, Nathaniel, 124
Oldham, Conway, 888
Oldham, Samuel, 1782
Olds, Horace, 49, 206
Oldwine, Barnard (*or* Barney) 255, 289, 1769
Oliphant, William, 168
Oliver, Nicholas, 98
Oliver, Richard, 239
Ollom, Peter, 1266
Olney, Stephen, 263
Olrie, Loran, 2
O'Neal, E. O., 187
O'Neal, James, 57
O'Neal, Ferdinand O., 165
O'Neal, Henry, 130
O'Neal, J. O., 187
O'Neal, *see also* Neal, Neale
O'Neil, Ferrill, 227
O'Neil, --, 1471
Onion, Julich, 1408
Onions, John, 9
Oosterhout, Peter, 66
Oothoudt, Abraham, 141
Oram, Peter B., 80, 131, 147
Oram, Robert, 179
Orcutt, Seth, 17
Ord, George, 1405
O'Reilly, Martin, 165
Organ, John, 15, 1296
Organ, Matthew, 16, 1296
Orme, Charles, 1278
Ormsby, Oliver, 110
Ormsby, --, Turner, --, & Matthews, --, 1698
Orr, John, 40, 160, 279, 1788
Orr, Thomas, 68
Ortan, William, 1678
Osborn, Edward, 199, 1691
Osborn, Jeremiah, 68, 136
Osborne, Nathaniel, 203
Osborne, Samuel, 1150
Osborne, --, 1679
Osmoen, Benijah, 122
Osmun, Benjamin, 75
Osmun, John, 143
Ossey, Francis, 106
Ostrand, Thomas, 242
Otaawighton, John, 204
Otis, Joseph, 196
O'Tool, Patrick, 1300
Ott, David, 1083

Quay, Lebb, 1
Quick, Jacob, 1681
Quick, Levi, 73
Quigley, Edward, 364, 484, 1766
Quigley, Samuel, 106
Quillan, --, 1036
Quimby, S., 1525
Quinn, Samuel, 120
Quinton, David, 31, 65, 103, 105, 113, 129, 133, 149, 150, 151, 159, 162, 199, 202, 203, 216, 225, 242

Racine, Charles, 196
Rackwood, Ebenezer, 1294
Radclife, William, 129
Radclife, William, Junior, 262
Radcliff, William, Junior, 485
Radelift, William, 129
Rademacker, John, 210
Raderback, Peter, 1681
Radford, Elizabeth, 1445
Ragsdale, Drury, 297, 1790
Rainey, Robert, 46
Rainey, Stephen, 1552
Rainey, --, & Holmes, --, 1700
Raisin, William, 1769
Rake, Henry, 73
Ralston, Andrew, 362, 474, 1717
Ralton, John, 1709
Ramdell, Chilton, 54
Ramdell, *see also* Ramsdell, Ransdell
Ramsay, John, 59, 93
Ramsay, Joseph H., 113
Ramsay, Nathaniel, 42
Ramsdell, James, 1160
Ramsdell, *see also* Ramdell, Ransdell
Ramsey, Alexander, 1693
Ramsey, Henry, 49
Ramsey, James, 1640
Ramsy, James, 1526
Ramsy, John, 1526
Randal, A., 1588
Randall, Edward, 1199
Randolph, Edward, 1508
Randolph, William B., 1038
Rankin, Robert, 1619
Rankins, James, 111
Rankins, John, 1215
Rann, Solomon, 241
Ransdell, Chilton, 54
Ransdell, *see also* Ramdell, Ramsdell
van Ranselaar, N., 1717
van Ranselear, Henry J., 142, 203
van Ranselear, *see also* van Rensselaer
Ransom, Elijah, 807, 1753
Ransom, George P., 204
Ransom, Samuel, 788, 1029, 1750
Rapalje, Richard, 242
Rarity, John, 14
Rash, Jacob, 230
Rasin, William, 299
Rasster, Godfrey J., 38
Rasy, Stephen, 1639
Rathbon, Asa, 181
Rathbone, John, 55, 56, 57, 58, 59, 60, 61, 62, 114, 115, 257, 760, 1695, 1696, 1697, 1700, 1701, 1702, 1788
Rathbun, Nathan, 1685
Rathbun, Solomon, 1632
Ratton, John, 565, 591
Rawdon, Daniel, 205
Rawleigh, William, 898
Rawlinger, Moses, 1782
Rawlings, Aaron, 34
Rawlings, Isaac, 1412
Rawlingson, David, 36
Rawlins, Moses, 879
Ray, Caleb, 142
Ray, Joseph, 182, 196
Ray, Stephen, 1639
Raymond, Lemuel, 72
Rea, *see* Rhea
Reab, George, 104
Read, A., 1381
Read, Charles, 43
Read, Henry, 693
Read, Philip, 836, 885
Read, Thomas, 16, 1381
Read, William, 240
Reading, Samuel, 104
Readley, Abraham, Junior, 1110
Reasoner, John, 18
Reckless, Anthony, 1179
Rector, Francis, 1694
Redding, Henry, 191

Sell, Thomas, 1775
Sell, *see also* Sill
Seller, Conrad, 199
Sellers, Jacob, 46
Sellick, Benjamin, 1102
Selsbury, Jonathan, 75
Seltenreich, *see* Seldenright
Selter, Conrad, 199
Senter, Asa, 307, 1776
Sergeants, Bernard, 1156
Service, John, 605, 1707
Sestre, Francis, 1620
Seth, Christiana, 1546
Settlemyer, Godfrey, 1686
Sewall, Clement, 1502
Sewall, Henry, 230
Sewall, James, 1105
Seward, Jedediah, 124
Seward, Thomas, 225
Seymour, Horace, 198
van Shaaick, Mary, 162
van Shaaick, *see also* van Schaaick
Shaddick, William, 1679
Shaddick, --, 1679
Shade, Julius, 98
Shadley, John, 841, 1767
Shaeffer, P., 1318
Shafer, Jacob, 1709
Shaffner, George, 1619
Shaffner, Mary, 1619
Shaler, Jacob, 620
Shane, Abraham, 1055, 1068, 1078, 1084, 1085, 1086, 1097, 1111, 1165, 1242, 1259, 1265, 1268, 1274, 1275, 1294, 1306, 1309, 1459, 1566, 1580, 1613, 1659
Shane, Abraham, & Northup, Henry, 1085, 1086, 1088, 1089, 1103, 1109, 1113, 1117, 1123
Shanks, John, 1110
Shapard, Samuel B., 91
Sharp(e) Anthony, 346, 458, 1762
Sharp, Benjamin, 233
Sharpe, Sarah, 203
Sharpe, Thomas, 11
Sharpless, Robert, 192
Shaw, Aaron, 1633
Shaw, Archibald, 103
Shaw, A., 1392
Shaw, Bazil, 47, 205
Shaw, Cornelius, 55
Shaw, John, 29, 91, 339, 451
Shaw, Michael, 151, 235
Shaw, Samuel, 862, 1681
Shaw, Sylvanus, 1712
Shaw, Thomas, 209
Shaw, -- G., 1681
Shay, Patrick, 81
Shay, P., 202
Shaylor, Joseph, 97
Shea, Casper, 1742
Shea, John, 110, 1723
Shearman, Peter, 155
Shed, Samuel (*or* Saul) 1629
Shee, Casper, 985, 1742
Sheffield, Charles, 911
Shehan, Daniel, 158
Shehee, John, 211
Shelby, Samuel, 1685
Shelcut, Ezekiel, 1686
Sheldon, James, 78
Sheldon, Job, 148
Sheldon, M., 536
Sheldon, W., 409
Sheldon, --, 963
Shelfox, Jane, 108
Shellar, *see* Shettar
Shelley, Samuel, 1685
Shellman, Ernest, 189
Shelly, Cyrus, 235
Shelly, Ebenezer, 69
Shelter, Jacob, 990
Shelton, C., 1203
Shenkland, Thomas, 259
Shepard, *see* Shapard
Shephard, Jonathan, 132
Shepherd, Abraham, 218
Shepherd, James, 836, 1757
Shepherd, Sarah, 11
Shepherd, Sarah, *see also* Sheppard, Shepperd
Sheppard, Nathaniel, 92
Sheppard, Sarah, 115, 167
Sheppard, Stephen, 1369
Sheppard, William, 1047
Sheppard, *see also* Shapard
Shepper, Catherine, 1641
Shepperd, Sarah, 11, 163, 188
Shepperd, Sarah, *see also* Shepherd, Sheppard

Silsbee, Nathaniel (Representative, Senator; Massachusetts) 1224
de Silvia, *see* Desilvia
Simers, James, 1222
Simers, John, 1222
Simler, John, 1522
Simlock, James, 1682
Simlock, John, 1682
Simmonds, John, 160
Simmonds, *see also* Simonds
Simmons, Isles, 155
Simmons, John, 1640
Simmons, Reuben, 138
Simmons, Samuel, 1687
Simmons, William, 30, 31, 265, 958, 994, 1008, 1678, 1696
Simmons, --, 838, 924
Simonds, Jonas, 180
Simonds, *see also* Simmonds
Simpson, John, 5, 12
Simpson, William, 127
Sinckle, Jacob, 168
Singleton, Anthony, 245
Singleton, John, 168
Sinnott, Patrick, 157
Sizer, Daniel, 21
Skeel, Amos, 1161
Skeel, Truman, 1064
Skeel, William, 1161
Skerritt, Clement, 42
Skindler, John, 1677
Skinner, Catherine, 1632
Skinner, George, 17, 258, 1677, 1696
Skinner, Henry, 1680
Skinner, Josiah K., 1498
Skinner, J. K., 1485
Skinner, Lucinda, 1265
Skinner, Richard, 1410
Skinner, Timothy, 1265
Skinner, William, 39
Skolfield, William, 254
Skolfield, *see also* Scholfield
Slade, Stephen, 1622
Slape, Thomas, 752
Slaterback, Michael, 203
Slatker, Peter, 1621
Slauch, Bernard, 68, 179, 198
Slaughter, John, 1762
Slaughter, Philip, 1620
Slaughter, William, 1640, 1680
Slauter, John, 792
Slayton, Joseph, 246
Slevoght, Christian, 163
Slews, Philip, 83
Slingerland, A., 139
Slingerland, P., 139
Slingerland, R., 139
Slingluff, Jesse, 992, 1218, 1728
Slingluff, J., & Bohn, C., 850, 891, 892, 893, 912, 913, 934, 936, 1019, 1720, 1724, 1725, 1726, 1727, 1733, 1734, 1736
Slingluff, J., & Fahnestock, D., 911, 964, 977, 980, 993, 1002, 1707, 1708, 1727, 1730
Sloan, David, 718
Sloan, Hugh, 13
Sloan, James, 630
Sloan, James (Representative; New Jersey) 1311, 1393
Sloan, John, 246
Sloan, Joseph, 360, 472, 575
Sloan, Sturgin, 259
Sloughter, Dedluff, 189
Sloulter, Andrew, 1626
Slouter, Jacob, 1681
Slurnan, John, 1636
Slutt, Peter, 56
Smalley, Thomas, 295, 1722
Smallwood, John, 192
Smallwood, William, 1084
Smart, Nathaniel, 1647
Smick, Reinard, 233
Smietz, Reinard, 233
Smiley, Robert, 310, 422, 1749
Smilie, John (Representative; Pennsylvania) 815
Smith, Abel Henry, 66
Smith, Alexander, 1009
Smith, Amos, 1629
Smith, Andrew, 85
Smith, Arthur, 293, 1719
Smith, Asaph, 280, 1769
Smith, Ballard, 41
Smith, Call, 1630
Smith, Charles, 1632
Smith, Charlotte, 11
Smith, Christian, 1627
Smith, Conrad, 217

Smith, Daniel, 885, 1757
Smith, David, 226, 1678
Smith, Duncan, 79
Smith, Ebenezer, 229, 599, 1619, 1621, 1748
Smith, Edward, 1630
Smith, Eleazer, 131
Smith, Elijah, 192
Smith, Eliphalet, 96
Smith, Elizabeth, 1257
Smith, Elnathan, 287, 1756
Smith, Enoch, 343, 455, 1722
Smith, E. M., 1637
Smith, Floet, 1523
Smith, Francis, 211, 986, 1742
Smith, George, 131, 165, 234
Smith, Godfrey, 1677
Smith. Heber, 145
Smith, Henry, 186
Smith, Hobert, 1641
Smith, Ichiel, 100
Smith, Isaac, 395, 520, 1748
Smith, Isaiah, 2
Smith, Israel, 145, 185, 230
Smith, Israel (Senator; Vermont) 318, 430
Smith, Jacob, 1345
Smith, James, 38, 47, 181, 846, 1624, 1703, 1704
Smith, James E., 1375
Smith, James L. (*or* S.) 1291
Smith, Jeremiah, 121
Smith, Joel, 1115, 1187
Smith, John, 6, 18, 46, 47, 53, 61, 79, 90, 93, 138, 166, 184, 205, 222, 247, 255, 308, 558, 568, 577, 578, 580, 583, 833, 904, 905, 906, 907, 1452, 1622, 1629, 1630, 1678, 1722, 1787
Smith, John Cotten, 663, 664, 665
Smith, John David, 1621
Smith, John Hill, 1693
Smith, John K., 92, 98
Smith, Jonathan, 105
Smith, Joseph, 28, 308, 1681
Smith, Joseph S., 796, 1763
Smith, Joseph Timothy, 996
Smith, Josiah, 280, 1769
Smith, J., 144
Smith, Larkin, 1693
Smith, Levi, 1641
Smith, Martha, 1636
Smith, Martin, 27
Smith, Massey Arra, 1633
Smith, Melanchton, 196
Smith, Michael, 282, 1778
Smith, Moses, 124
Smith, Nathan, 247, 558, 1384, 1722
Smith, Nathaniel, 147, 283
Smith, Nicholas, 210
Smith, Peter, 153
Smith, Platt, 34, 136
Smith, Richard, 2, 79, 1074
Smith, Robert, 190, 1641
Smith, R., 1181
Smith, Samuel, 70, 73, 75, 121, 159, 210, 259, 313, 425, 673, 821, 1418, 1422
Smith, Samuel Hoey, 637, 650, 666, 673, 725, 756, 926, 941, 976, 1021, 1024, 1031, 1150, 1151, 1162, 1210, 1400, 1401, 1402, 1524, 1578, 1630, 1746, 1747, 1761, 1762 1763
Smith, Sarah, 293
Smith, States, 138
Smith, Thomas, 24, 165, 1788
Smith, Weeden, 969
Smith, Whitfield, 34
Smith, William, 69, 145, 166, 205, 1054, 1315, 1353, 1452, 1620
Smith, William C., 1384
Smith, William L., 15, 212
Smith, --, 585, 586, 587, 588, 589, 649, 706, 743, 1624, 1637
Smith, --, & McGlaughlin, --, 1018, 1771
Smith, --, & Ridgway, --, 133, 155, 215
Smoot, William, 1685
Smoot, W., 949
Smoot, --, 774
Smyth, James, 166
Smyth, Richard, 23, 90, 91, 233
Smyth, William Pitt, 143
Snailbaker, Daniel, 739
Snead, Smith, 913
Sneed, Jonathan, 1283
Snell, Asa, 1335
Snell, John, 13, 23, 227
Snider, Peter, 23
Snow, Chloe, 175
Snow, Elijah, 262, 485
Snow, Elizabeth, 287

Snow(s) James, 364, 477, 1766
Snow, Thomas, 287, 1711
Snyder, George C., 1619, 1687
Snyder, Philip, 1619
Snyder, --, 1489
Sogoharasie, John, 204
Solinger, Adam, 290, 1704
Somers, George, 1637
Somers, Jacob, 1637
Somersett, Thomas, 1630
Somerville, James, 194
Sommers, Simon, 1620
Sommerville, John, 1623
Soper, Richard, 41
Sork, Valentine, 44
Southard, Henry (Representative; New Jersey) 863
Southard, Isaac, 1776
Southard, Samuel L. (Senator; New Jersey) 1277
Southworth, Cousland, 239
Southworth, Samuel, 76
Sowers, Michael, 1630
Sowers, William, 384, 506, 1709
Soyer, --, & Benter, --, 1017, 1732
Space, John, 145
Spalding, Asa, 122
Spalding, Asa, *see also* Spaulding
Spalding, John, 104
Sparks, William, 110, 148
Sparrow, Richard, 805, 856, 1742
Spaulding, Asa, 53, 82, 99, 114, 158, 208
Spaulding, Asa, *see also* Spalding
Spaulding, Simon, 105
Spear, Edward, 44
Spears, Richard, 217
Spence, Daniel, 1712
Spence, David, 86
Spencer, Anna, 222
Spencer, David, 1640
Spencer, Humphrey, 11681
Spencer, Israel B., 1487
Spencer, John, 93, 162, 168
Spencer, John Canfield (Representative; New York) 1103, 1127
Spencer, Robert, 1636
Spencer, Thomas, 377, 499
Spering, John, 169
Sperry, Armey, 196
Spicer, Jacob, 317, 429, 1766
Spinolla, Elizabeth, 1461
Spires, Richard, 1620
Spitfathom, John, 1694
Spot, William, 90
Sprague, Abel, 39
Sprague, Obadiah, 238
Sprague, P., 1475
Sprague, Stephen, 1181
Sprague, S., 1181
Spring, Simeon, 1756, 1757
Springer, Abraham, 17
Springer, Jacob, 96, 1626
Springer, Sylvester, 3
Sproat, N. C., 1748
Sproat, Thomas, 599
Sproat, William, 45
Sproul, Elizabeth, 5
Sproul, Oliver, 5
Sproule, Moses, 264
Spurrier, Edward, 192
Sqirrese (Sqirrell?) Jacob, 73
Squire, Asa, 226
Squire, Ashur, 99
Stacey, John, 217
Stack, Richard, 569, 1221
Stackhouse, Amos, 920
Stafford, Thomas, 951
Stake, *see* Hake
Stalker, William, 68
Stallions, Abraham, 218
Stanbery (Stanberry, Stanboury, Stanbury) Jonas, 53, 63, 64, 65, 66, 67, 68, 69, 70, 103, 149, 150, 152, 153, 154, 155, 256, 257, 271, 272, 275, 383, 505, 690, 734, 736, 740, 742, 767, 784, 861, 865, 1041, 1061, 1077, 1132, 1133, 1134, 1164, 1168, 1183, 1191, 1194, 1196, 1201, 1202, 1206, 1223, 1237, 1244, 1246, 1260, 1301, 1316, 1318, 1337, 1346, 1348, 1360, 1366, 1367, 1369, 1372, 1379, 1382, 1386, 1395, 1416, 1420, 1426, 1451, 1456, 1482, 1495, 1509, 1520, 1551, 1553, 1591, 1593, 1610, 1619, 1620, 1621, 1622, 1692, 1696, 1698, 1700, 1702, 1718, 1720, 1724, 1728, 1745, 1765
Stanbery (Stanberry) William (Representative; Ohio) 1509, 1520, 1551, 1553, 1593, 1619, 1621
Stanberry, --, & Swyier, --, 1202, 1206
Stanbury, *see* Stanbery, Stansbery

Stiles, John, 1563
Stiles, Robert, 1563
Stillman, Jonah, 1720
Stillman, Jonathan, 1720
Stillwell, Ezekiel, 75
Stilwell, Elias, 259
Stitchin, Andrew, 144
Stites, John, 113, 151, 237, 1700
Stiver, Michael, 53, 128
Stiver, *see also* Stever
Stives, William, 90
Stockbridge, John, 1693
Stockdale, John, 23, 29, 133, 144, 145, 178, 203
Stockdell, John, 12, 13, 26, 57, 63, 64, 68, 130, 159, 197, 233, 248
Stockhouse, Amos, 1729
Stocking, Daniel L., 1689
Stocking, Eber, 1689
Stockman, Arshual, 787
Stockton, Ebenezer, 81
Stockton, John Cox, 903, 1732
Stockwell, Levi, 48
Stoddard, Samuel, 1629
Stoddard, Simeon C., 283
Stoddard, Susan, 1617
Stoddart, Nathan, 1745
Stoddart, N. A., 1745
Stoddart, William T., 1060
Stoddert, Simon C., 1770
Stokely, Joseph, 908, 909, 1153, 1694, 1710, 1722
Stoker, Ebenezer, 238
Stoker, William, 1391
Stokes, John, 959
Stokes, John R., 959, 1780
Stokes, Peter, 187
Stone, Enos, 229
Stone, Ezekiel, 1624
Stone, Samuel, 107
Stoner, Nicholas, 70
Storer, Clement (Representative, Senator; New Hampshire) 1135
Storer, Dorothy, 1622
Storer, Ebenezer, 1135
Storey, Mary, 1213
Storey, Parker, 1213
Storrs, Justus, 641
Stors, Justis, 1738
Story, John, 1202
Stotsberry, John, 105
Stout, Abraham, 244
Stout, Elisha, 200
Stout, George, 59, 82, 122, 150, 183
Stout, Philip, 57, 66, 85, 178, 199, 200, 243
Stout, Wessell T., 213
Stow, Abner, 183, 196
Stow, Edward, Junior, 176
Stow, Lazarus, 105
Stow, Zaccheus, 280, 1768
Stow, --, 835
Stowe, Edward, 176, 220, 225
Stowell, Israel, Junior, 137
Stowell, John, 157
Stowens, John, 1792
Stowers, John, 279
Stoy, John, 6, 173
Strachan, William, 61
Strahn, John, 98
Stratton, Aaron, 100
Stratton, Annanias, 10
Stratton, Seth, 127
Straughan, *see* Strahn
Street, Titus, 162, 168
Striker, John, 123
Stringer, Conrad, 17
Stringer, Samuel, 61, 63, 64, 149, 150, 219
Stringham, Joseph, 62, 155
Strohl, Jacob, 1438
Strong, David, 40
Strong, James (Representative; New York) 1478
Strong, Joseph, 568, 1722
Strong, Nathan, 242
Strong, Phineas, 215
Strubin, Philip, 80
Stuart, Benjamin, 1691
Stuart, Christopher, 216
Stuart, John, 1683
Stubbling, Sigismond, 96
Stubbs, Robert, 24
Sturdavant, Azor, 793, 1763
Sturtevant, Isaac, 387, 511, 1766
Stymer, Rachel, 129
Suckley, George, 216, 269
Sudthard, John, 227
Suffren, John, 63, 160
Suffren, *see also* Saffren
Sugarmug, Joel, 1259

Talman, Thomas, 60
Tamerlane, Thomas, 182
Tannehill, Adamson (Representative; Pennsylvania) 15, 820
Tannehill, Josiah, 15
Tanner, Ebenezer, 226
Tanner, John, 205
Tanner, Quain, 1687
Tapan, Daniel, 201
Tarbell, Nathan, 14
Tarp, John, 238
Tasker, Richard, 1641
Tate, Eleanor, 25
Tatum, Henry, 1057
Tatum, Henry W., 1677
Tatum, James, 170
Tatum, Zachariah, 1677
Taulman, Peter, 236
Tawson, William, 1756
Tawson, *see also* Towson
Tayler, John, 1688
Taylor, Amos, 197
Taylor, Andrew, 114
Taylor, Bradford, 1641
Taylor, Christopher, 1489
Taylor, Elijah, 1593
Taylor, Elizabeth, 1690
Taylor, George, 118, 138, 187
Taylor, George, Junior, 2, 90, 107, 575
Taylor, Griffin, 1464, 1691
Taylor, G. B., 1640
Taylor, James, 19, 29, 54, 209, 577, 578, 579, 580, 581, 582, 583, 706, 748, 749, 763, 764, 765, 768, 786, 810, 872, 873, 874, 875, 888, 896, 897, 1364, 1365, 1464, 1465, 1504, 1672, 1673, 1675, 1701, 1702, 1771, 1772, 1773, 1778, 1779, 1782
Taylor, James N., 1620
Taylor, James, & Gillespey & Henry, 1697
Taylor, John, 115, 1070, 1636, 1685, 1690
Taylor, John M., 1636, 1690
Taylor, J. W., 1622
Taylor, Jonathan, 181
Taylor, Josiah, 218
Taylor, Joshua, 253
Taylor, J. W., 1231
Taylor, Lewis, 101
Taylor, Martha C., 1352
Taylor, Morrison, 1685, 1688
Taylor, Noah, 218
Taylor, Obadiah, 1679
Taylor, Othniel, 165
Taylor, Richard, 364, 480, 874, 1364, 1766
Taylor, Samuel, 118
Taylor, Sarah, 1678
Taylor, Simeon, 74
Taylor, Susannah, 10
Taylor, Timothy, 58
Taylor, Will, 101
Taylor, William, 209, 212, 1138, 1690
Taylor, Thornton, 1641
Taylor, --, 855, 1637, 1741, 1788
Teague, John, 178
Teazor, Aaron, 51
Tellard, Edward, 1720
Temple, Benjamin, 306, 1756, 1757
Templer, Thomas, 158
Ten Broeck, John C., 67
Ten Eyck, Abraham, 132, 190, 203
Ten Eyck, Absalom, 108
Ten Eyck, Henry, 58
Teneyck, Meyndert, 142
Tennant, William, 35
Tennell, George, 950
Tennell, John, 36
Tennell, Patrick, 40
Tennett, John Peter, 138
Tenney, Samuel (Representative; New Hampshire) 30, 367, 488
Tenny, Samuel, 30
Terms, Peter, 279, 1707
Ternant, John, 137
Terrant, Henry, 1160
Terrell, John, 36
Terrill, John, 1697
Terrill, Richmond, 221
Terry, Gamaliel, 292, 1773
Terwilliger, James, 170
Tetard, Benjamin, 299
Tewahangarahkaw, Hangere, 204
Thackston, James, 167
Thaosagwat, Hamjoost, 204
Tharp, Benjamin, 170
Tharp, Perry, 1619
Tharp, Peter, 664, 1788
Thayer, Bartholomew, 1025

Wrightington, Robert, 52
Wrightman, George, 1629
Wuibert, Anthony Felix, 180
Wyley, John, 253
Wyllys, John P., 121, 186
Wyllys, Samuel, 14
Wyman, Abel, 1167
Wyman, Asa, 818
Wyman, Dean, 1186
Wyman, John, 818
Wyman, Joshua, 1723
Wyman, Simeon, 83, 101, 173, 177, 207
Wynn, Webster, 38
Wyshover, Jacob, 224

Yairington, Ephraim, 72
Yancey, Layton, 108
Yancy, Joel (Representative; Kentucky) 1474
Yarborough, Charles, 1676
Yarbrough, Edward, 76
Yater, John, 588
Yates, Christopher, 23, 25, 235
Yates, Jasper, Junior, 299
Yates, John, 1775
Yates, Tellis, 25
Yeates, Christopher, 132
Yeaty, John, 53
Yeomans, Moses, 63
Yest, Martin, 1771
Yoder, William, 4
York, John, 153
York, William, 670, 1788
Yost, John, 29
Yost, Martin, 660, 1771
Young, Aaron, 651, 1757
Young, Anne, 1171
Young, A., 1693
Young, Christian, 1681
Young, David, 179
Young, Davis, 49
Young, Guy, 155
Young, Henry, 1081
Young, Jacob, 189, 1681
Young, John, 7, 158, 222, 227, 1710
Young, Joseph, 179, 222, 1199, 1619
Young, Marcus, 813
Young, Moses, 1754
Young, Robert, 1638
Young, Robert J., 1693
Young, Thomas, 587, 1776
Young, William, 1621
Young, --, 1787

Zado, Congo, 196
van Zandt, Nicholas B., 1188, 1190, 1195, 1199, 1236, 1240, 1250, 1254, 1255, 1256, 1258, 1259, 1268, 1280, 1287, 1288, 1294, 1306
van Zandt, N. B., & Rockwell, --, 1215
van Zandt, N. B., & Tschiffely, F. D., 1229
Zane, Noah, 316, 345, 369, 421, 422, 428, 457, 490, 720
Zane, William, 88
Zeaster, Michael, 75
Zeckler, Michael, 117
Zerban, Wendell, 36
Ziegler, Catharine, 1440
Ziegler, David, 86
Ziegler, F., 1440
Ziegler, George, 703
Zimmerman, Reuben, 54
Zuntz, Alexander, 129

TRACT INDEX

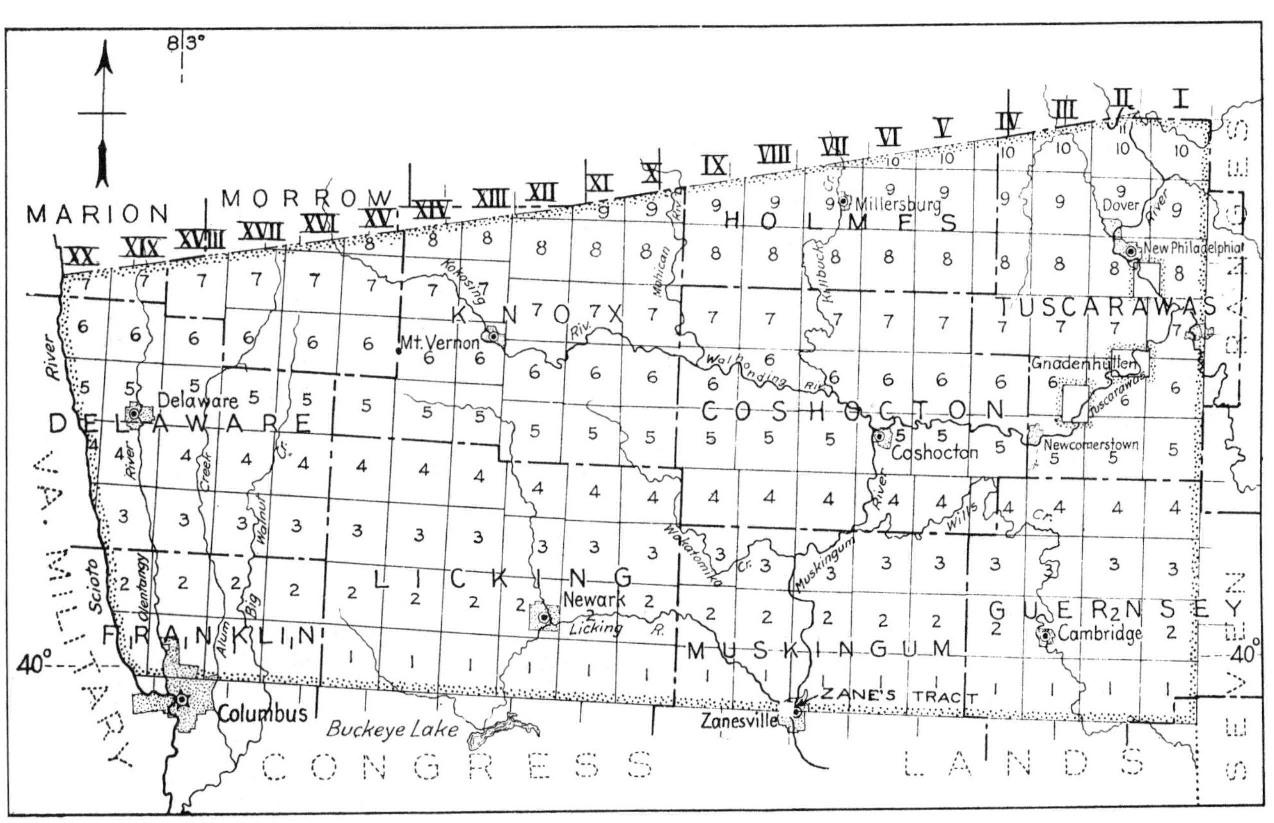

United States Military District, subdivided into 5-mile townships.

Range numbers in roman
Township numbers in arabic
Present county boundaries in broken lines
Present county seats marked by circled dot

UNITED STATES MILITARY DISTRICT OF OHIO

Mil * 1 1 - 2 (*4000-acre tract) 217, 1695
Mil - 1 1 3 1 1023, 1703
Mil - 1 1 3 2 617, 1703
Mil - 1 1 3 3 595, 1703
Mil - 1 1 3 4 1418, 1703
Mil - 1 1 3 5 1422, 1703
Mil - 1 1 3 6 846, 1703
Mil - 1 1 3 7 747, 1703
Mil - 1 1 3 8 627, 1703
Mil - 1 1 3 9 1430, 1703
Mil - 1 1 3 10 981, 1703
Mil - 1 1 3 11 629, 1703
Mil - 1 1 3 12 629, 1703
Mil - 1 1 3 13 618, 1703
Mil - 1 1 3 14 612, 1703
Mil - 1 1 3 15 612, 1703
Mil - 1 1 3 16 612, 1703
Mil - 1 1 3 17 613, 1703
Mil - 1 1 3 18 613, 1703
Mil - 1 1 3 19 613, 1703
Mil - 1 1 3 20 597, 1703
Mil - 1 1 3 21 625, 1703
Mil - 1 1 3 22 625, 1703
Mil - 1 1 3 23 1430, 1703
Mil - 1 1 3 24 878, 1703
Mil - 1 1 3 25 337, 449, 1703
Mil - 1 1 3 26 1056, 1703
Mil - 1 1 3 27 1396, 1703
Mil - 1 1 3 28 635, 1703
Mil - 1 1 3 29 626, 1703
Mil - 1 1 3 30 610, 1703
Mil - 1 1 3 31 614, 1704
Mil - 1 1 3 32 306, 1704
Mil - 1 1 3 33 306, 1704
Mil - 1 1 3 34 306, 1704
Mil - 1 1 3 35 610, 1704
Mil - 1 1 3 36 596, 1704
Mil - 1 1 3 37 744, 1704
Mil - 1 1 3 38 845, 1704
Mil - 1 1 3 39 846, 1704
Mil - 1 1 3 40 846, 1704
Mil * 1 2 1 - (*4000-acre tract) 254, 1695
Mil - 1 6 2 1 1652, 1704
Mil - 1 6 2 2 1459, 1704
Mil - 1 6 2 3 1545, 1704
Mil - 1 6 2 4 1428, 1704
Mil - 1 6 2 5 770, 1704
Mil - 1 6 2 6 1500, 1704
Mil - 1 6 2 7 1391, 1704
Mil - 1 6 2 8 1664, 1704
Mil - 1 6 2 9 1370, 1704
Mil - 1 6 2 10 1370, 1704
Mil - 1 6 2 11 1634, 1704
Mil - 1 6 2 12 1370, 1704
Mil - 1 6 2 13 1392, 1704
Mil - 1 6 2 14 862, 1704
Mil - 1 6 2 15 1474, 1704
Mil - 1 6 2 16 290, 1704
Mil - 1 6 2 17 290, 1704
Mil - 1 6 2 18 1666, 1704
Mil - 1 6 2 19 1370, 1704
Mil - 1 6 2 20 1545, 1704
Mil - 1 6 2 21 1356, 1704
Mil - 1 6 2 22 1643, 1704
Mil - 1 6 2 23 1642, 1669, 1704
Mil - 1 6 2 24 290, 1704
Mil - 1 6 2 25 290, 1705
Mil - 1 6 2 26 290, 1705
Mil - 1 6 2 27 290, 1705
Mil - 1 6 2 28 1428, 1705
Mil - 1 6 2 29 1545, 1705
Mil - 1 6 2 30 1428, 1705
Mil - 1 6 2 31 1428, 1705
Mil - 1 6 2 32 1705
Mil - 1 6 2 33 1447, 1705
Mil - 1 6 2 34 1428, 1705
Mil - 1 6 2 35 1419, 1705
Mil - 1 6 2 36 1427, 1705
Mil - 1 6 2 37 290, 1705
Mil - 1 6 2 38 [58] 289, 1705
Mil * 1 7 - 1 (*4000-acre tract) 196, 1695
Mil * 1 7 - 2 (*4000-acre tract) 98, 1695
Mil * 1 7 - 3 (*4000-acre tract) 10, 1695
Mil * 1 7 - 4 (*4000-acre tract) 58, 1695
Mil - 1 8 2 1E 1705
Mil - 1 8 2 1W 1705
Mil - 1 8 2 2E 1028, 1705
Mil - 1 8 2 2W 1705
Mil - 1 8 2 3E 996, 1705
Mil - 1 8 2 3W 1705

Tract	Pages
Mil - 1 8 2 4E	1599, 1705
Mil - 1 8 2 4W	1705
Mil - 1 8 2 5E	1591, 1705
Mil - 1 8 2 5W	1705
Mil - 1 8 2 6E	1587, 1705
Mil - 1 8 2 6W	1493, 1705
Mil - 1 8 2 7E	1242, 1705
Mil - 1 8 2 7W	1003, 1665, 1705
Mil - 1 8 2 8E	1705
Mil - 1 8 2 8W	1446, 1705
Mil - 1 8 2 9E	1705
Mil - 1 8 2 9W	1705
Mil - 1 8 2 10E	1705
Mil - 1 8 2 10W	1705
Mil - 1 8 2 11E	1705
Mil - 1 8 2 11W	1246, 1706
Mil - 1 8 2 12E	1706
Mil - 1 8 2 12W	1706
Mil - 1 8 2 13E	1706
Mil - 1 8 2 13W	1706
Mil - 1 8 2 14E	1706
Mil - 1 8 2 14W	1706
Mil - 1 8 2 15E	1706
Mil - 1 8 2 15W	1706
Mil - 1 8 2 16E	1706
Mil - 1 8 2 16W	1706
Mil - 1 8 2 17E	1706
Mil - 1 8 2 17W	1706
Mil - 1 8 2 18E	1706
Mil - 1 8 2 18W	1706
Mil - 1 8 2 19E	1706
Mil - 1 8 2 19W	1706
Mil - 1 8 2 20E	1706
Mil - 1 8 2 20W	1706
Mil - 1 8 2 21E	1706
Mil - 1 8 2 21W	1706
Mil - 1 8 2 22E	1706
Mil - 1 8 2 22W	1187, 1706
Mil - 1 8 2 23E	1224, 1706
Mil - 1 8 2 23W	1170, 1706
Mil - 1 8 2 24E	1706
Mil - 1 8 2 24W	1085, 1706
Mil - 1 8 2 25E	616, 1706
Mil - 1 8 2 25W	307, 615, 1706
Mil - 1 8 2 26E	1615, 1706
Mil - 1 8 2 26W	1706
Mil - 1 8 2 27E	1706
Mil - 1 8 2 27W	1706
Mil - 1 8 2 28E	1706
Mil - 1 8 2 28W	1706
Mil - 1 8 2 29E	1436, 1707
Mil - 1 8 2 29W	773, 1707
Mil - 1 8 2 30	279, 1707
Mil - 1 8 2 31	279, 1707
Mil - 1 8 2 32	279, 1707
Mil - 1 8 2 33E	1707
Mil - 1 8 2 33W	1707
Mil - 1 8 2 34E	1707
Mil - 1 8 2 34W	1707
Mil - 1 8 2 35E	1707
Mil - 1 8 2 35W	1707
Mil - 1 8 2 36E	1664, 1707
Mil - 1 8 2 36W	1667, 1707
Mil - 1 8 2 37E	1707
Mil - 1 8 2 37W	305, 1707
Mil - 1 8 3 1	302, 1707
Mil - 1 8 3 2	302, 1707
Mil - 1 8 3 3	977, 980, 1707
Mil - 1 8 3 4	1170, 1707
Mil - 1 8 3 5	609, 1707
Mil - 1 8 3 6	609, 1707
Mil - 1 8 3 7	608, 1707
Mil - 1 8 3 8	605, 1707
Mil - 1 8 3 9	607, 1707
Mil - 1 8 3 10	707, 1707
Mil - 1 8 3 11	606, 1707
Mil - 1 8 3 12	284, 1707
Mil - 1 8 3 13	302, 1707
Mil - 1 8 3 14	302, 1707
Mil - 1 8 3 15	302, 1707
Mil - 1 8 3 16	302, 1707
Mil - 1 8 3 17	302, 1707
Mil - 1 8 3 18	302, 1707
Mil - 1 8 3 19	302, 1707
Mil - 1 8 3 20	302, 1707
Mil - 1 8 3 21	302, 1707
Mil - 1 8 3 22	284, 1708
Mil - 1 8 3 23	332, 444, 1708
Mil - 1 8 3 24	332, 444, 1708
Mil - 1 8 4 1	1231, 1708
Mil - 1 8 4 2	1439, 1708
Mil - 1 8 4 3	993, 1708
Mil - 1 8 4 4	993, 1708
Mil - 1 8 4 5	1614, 1708
Mil - 1 8 4 6	1708
Mil - 1 8 4 7	1708

Mil	-	1	8	4	8	1708
Mil	-	1	8	4	9	1708
Mil	-	1	8	4	10	1708
Mil	-	1	8	4	11	1708
Mil	-	1	8	4	12	1708
Mil	-	1	8	4	13	1599, 1708
Mil	-	1	8	4	14	1503, 1599, 1708
Mil	-	1	8	4	15	893, 1708
Mil	-	1	8	4	16	709, 1708
Mil	-	1	8	4	17	711, 1708
Mil	-	1	8	4	18	1055, 1708
Mil	-	1	8	4	19	1708
Mil	-	1	8	4	20	1599, 1708
Mil	-	1	8	4	21	1599, 1708
Mil	-	1	8	4	22	1708
Mil	-	1	8	4	23	1708
Mil	-	1	8	4	24	1708
Mil	-	1	8	4	25	1708
Mil	-	1	8	4	26	1027, 1708
Mil	-	1	8	4	27	1708
Mil	-	1	8	4	28	1708
Mil	-	1	8	4	29	1068, 1708
Mil	-	1	8	4	30	1587, 1708
Mil	-	1	8	4	31	1393, 1708
Mil	-	1	8	4	32	708, 1709
Mil	-	1	8	4	33	286, 1709
Mil	-	1	8	4	34	619, 1709
Mil	-	1	8	4	35	620, 1709
Mil	-	1	8	4	36	993, 1709
Mil	-	1	8	4	37	1709
Mil	-	1	8	4	38	1709
Mil	-	1	8	4	39	1709
Mil	-	1	8	4	40	1585, 1709
Mil	*	1	10	-	3	(*4000-acre tract) 8, 1695
Mil	-	1	10	1	1	1067, 1709
Mil	-	1	10	1	2	1066, 1709
Mil	-	1	10	1	3	557, 1709
Mil	-	1	10	1	4	365, 486, 1709
Mil	-	1	10	1	5	299, 1709
Mil	-	1	10	1	6	299, 1709
Mil	-	1	10	1	7	561, 1709
Mil	-	1	10	1	8	561, 1709
Mil	-	1	10	1	9	411, 591, 1709
Mil	-	1	10	1	10	318, 411, 430, 1709
Mil	-	1	10	1	11	299, 1709
Mil	-	1	10	1	12	299, 1709
Mil	-	1	10	1	13	562, 1709
Mil	-	1	10	1	14	953, 1709
Mil	-	1	10	1	15	373, 494, 1709
Mil	-	1	10	1	16	565, 575, 1709
Mil	-	1	10	1	17	1290, 1709
Mil	-	1	10	1	18	384, 506, 1709
Mil	-	1	10	1	19	365, 486, 1709
Mil	-	1	10	1	20	410, 537, 1709
Mil	-	1	10	1	21	299, 1709
Mil	-	1	10	1	22	299, 1709
Mil	-	1	10	1	23	411, 591, 1709
Mil	-	1	10	1	24	411, 591, 1709
Mil	-	1	10	1	25	553, 1709
Mil	-	1	10	1	26	554, 1710
Mil	-	1	10	1	27	299, 1710
Mil	-	1	10	1	28	299, 1710
Mil	-	1	10	1	29	355, 467, 1710
Mil	-	1	10	1	30	354, 466, 1710
Mil	-	1	10	1	31	556, 1710
Mil	-	1	10	1	32	1290, 1710
Mil	-	1	10	1	33	1070, 1710
Mil	-	1	10	1	34	831, 1710
Mil	-	1	10	1	35	1102, 1710
Mil	-	1	10	1	36	560, 1710
Mil	-	1	10	1	37	299, 1710
Mil	-	1	10	1	38	299, 1710
Mil	-	1	10	1	39	371, 492, 1710
Mil	-	1	10	1	40	564, 716, 1710
Mil	*	2	1	-	3	(*4000-acre tract)18, 1695
Mil	-	2	2	3	1	571, 1710
Mil	-	2	2	3	2	680, 1710
Mil	-	2	2	3	3	908, 1710
Mil	-	2	2	3	4	908, 1710
Mil	-	2	2	3	5	415, 542, 1710
Mil	-	2	2	3	6	415, 542, 1710
Mil	-	2	2	3	7	415, 542, 909, 1710
Mil	-	2	2	3	8	592, 1710
Mil	-	2	2	3	9	592, 1710
Mil	-	2	2	3	10	689, 1710
Mil	-	2	2	3	11	909, 1710
Mil	-	2	2	3	12	909, 1710
Mil	-	2	2	3	13	636, 1710
Mil	-	2	2	3	14	636, 1710
Mil	-	2	2	3	15	566, 1710
Mil	-	2	2	3	16	566, 1710
Mil	-	2	2	3	17	566, 1710
Mil	-	2	2	3	18	570, 1710
Mil	-	2	2	3	19	570, 1710
Mil	-	2	2	3	20	1711

Mil	-	2	5	1	36	1573, 1713
Mil	-	2	5	1	37	1574, 1713
Mil	-	2	5	1	38	1713
Mil	-	2	5	1	39	1556, 1713
Mil	-	2	5	1	40	1517, 1713
Mil	-	2	5	1	41	1519, 1713
Mil	-	2	5	2	1	1542, 1714
Mil	-	2	5	2	2	1543, 1714
Mil	-	2	5	2	3	1555, 1714
Mil	-	2	5	2	4	1559, 1714
Mil	-	2	5	2	5	1575, 1714
Mil	-	2	5	2	6	1714
Mil	-	2	5	2	7	1714
Mil	-	2	5	2	8	1540, 1714
Mil	-	2	5	2	9	1715
Mil	-	2	5	2	10	1306, 1715
Mil	-	2	5	2	11	1521, 1715
Mil	-	2	5	2	12	1715
Mil	-	2	5	2	13	1554, 1715
Mil	-	2	5	2	14	1576, 1715
Mil	-	2	5	2	15	1563, 1715
Mil	-	2	5	2	16	1384, 1715
Mil	-	2	5	2	17	1715
Mil	-	2	5	2	18	1384, 1715
Mil	-	2	5	2	19	1549, 1715
Mil	-	2	5	2	20	1467, 1715
Mil	-	2	5	2	21	1304, 1715
Mil	-	2	5	2	22	1715
Mil	-	2	5	2	23	1571, 1715
Mil	-	2	5	2	24	1560, 1715
Mil	-	2	5	2	25	862, 1715
Mil	-	2	5	2	26	1606, 1715
Mil	-	2	5	2	27	1584, 1715
Mil	-	2	5	2	28	1715
Mil	-	2	5	2	29	1572, 1715
Mil	-	2	5	2	30	1282, 1715
Mil	-	2	5	2	31	1252, 1715
Mil	-	2	5	2	32	1715
Mil	-	2	5	2	33	1715
Mil	-	2	5	2	34	302, 1715
Mil	-	2	5	2	35	1715
Mil	-	2	5	2	36	302, 1715
Mil	-	2	5	2	37	1385, 1715
Mil	-	2	5	2	38	302, 1715
Mil	-	2	5	2	39	1383, 1715
Mil	-	2	5	3	1	1404, 1715
Mil	-	2	5	3	2	1435, 1715
Mil	-	2	5	3	3	1251, 1715
Mil	-	2	5	3	4	1403, 1715
Mil	-	2	5	3	5	1403, 1716
Mil	-	2	5	3	6	1251, 1716
Mil	-	2	5	3	7	1251, 1716
Mil	-	2	5	3	8	1436, 1716
Mil	-	2	5	3	9	1296, 1716
Mil	-	2	5	3	10	1253, 1716
Mil	-	2	5	3	11	1435, 1716
Mil	-	2	5	3	12	1481, 1716
Mil	-	2	5	3	13	1405, 1716
Mil	-	2	5	3	14	1251, 1716
Mil	-	2	5	3	15	1435, 1716
Mil	-	2	5	3	16	1404, 1716
Mil	-	2	5	3	17	1404, 1716
Mil	-	2	5	3	18	1405, 1716
Mil	-	2	5	3	19	1251, 1716
Mil	-	2	5	3	20	1425, 1716
Mil	-	2	5	3	21	1251, 1716
Mil	-	2	5	3	22	1251, 1716
Mil	-	2	5	3	23	1253, 1716
Mil	-	2	5	3	24	1251, 1716
Mil	-	2	5	3	25	1251, 1716
Mil	-	2	5	3	26	1684, 1716
Mil	-	2	5	3	27	1716
Mil	-	2	5	3	28	1716
Mil	-	2	5	3	29	1716
Mil	-	2	5	3	30	1327, 1716
Mil	-	2	5	3	31	1251, 1716
Mil	-	2	5	3	32	1251, 1716
Mil	-	2	5	3	33	1385, 1716
Mil	-	2	5	3	34	1385, 1716
Mil	-	2	5	3	35	1421, 1716
Mil	-	2	5	3	36	1095, 1116, 1716
Mil	-	2	5	3	37	1388, 1716
Mil	-	2	5	3	38	1434, 1716
Mil	-	2	5	3	39	1684, 1716
Mil	-	2	5	3	40	1716
Mil	-	2	5	3	41	1448, 1717
Mil	*	2	6	-	2	(*4000-acre tract) 7, 1695
Mil	-	2	6	1	1	1717
Mil	-	2	6	1	2	634, 1717
Mil	-	2	6	1	3	364, 476, 1717
Mil	-	2	6	1	4	364, 478, 1717
Mil	-	2	6	1	5	1717
Mil	-	2	6	1	6	362, 474, 1717
Mil	-	2	6	1	7	1717
Mil	-	2	6	1	8	1717
Mil	-	2	6	1	9	1717

Mil	-	2	6	1	10	302, 1717
Mil	-	2	6	1	11	1486, 1717
Mil	-	2	6	1	12	1589, 1717
Mil	-	2	6	1	13	302, 1717
Mil	-	2	6	1	14	302, 1717
Mil	-	2	6	1	15	1478, 1717
Mil	-	2	6	3	1	1717
Mil	-	2	6	3	2	1717
Mil	-	2	6	3	3	1717
Mil	-	2	6	3	4	1384, 1717
Mil	-	2	6	3	5	303, 1717
Mil	-	2	6	3	6	303, 1717
Mil	-	2	6	3	7	1586, 1717
Mil	-	2	6	3	8	1717
Mil	-	2	6	3	9	1717
Mil	-	2	6	3	10	1717
Mil	-	2	6	3	11	1717
Mil	-	2	6	3	12	1717
Mil	-	2	6	3	13	1717
Mil	-	2	6	3	14	1594, 1717
Mil	-	2	6	3	15	303, 1717
Mil	-	2	6	3	16	289, 1717
Mil	-	2	6	3	17	289, 1717
Mil	-	2	6	3	18	1717
Mil	-	2	6	3	19	1717
Mil	-	2	6	3	20	1588, 1718
Mil	-	2	6	3	21	1718
Mil	-	2	6	3	22	1718
Mil	-	2	6	3	23	1718
Mil	-	2	6	3	24	1590, 1718
Mil	-	2	6	3	25	284, 1718
Mil	-	2	6	3	26	302, 1718
Mil	-	2	6	3	27	302, 1718
Mil	-	2	6	3	28	1718
Mil	-	2	6	3	29	1718
Mil	-	2	6	3	30	1461, 1718
Mil	-	2	6	3	31	1461, 1718
Mil	-	2	6	3	32	302, 1718
Mil	-	2	6	3	33	302, 1718
Mil	-	2	6	3	34	302, 1718
Mil	-	2	6	3	35	302, 1718
Mil	-	2	7	3	1	634, 1718
Mil	-	2	7	3	2	634, 1718
Mil	-	2	7	3	3	1463, 1718
Mil	-	2	7	3	4	1644, 1718
Mil	-	2	7	3	5	1485, 1718
Mil	-	2	7	3	6	1463, 1718
Mil	-	2	7	3	7	699, 1718
Mil	-	2	7	3	8	1718
Mil	-	2	7	3	9	1648, 1718
Mil	-	2	7	3	10	1458, 1718
Mil	-	2	7	3	11	699, 1718
Mil	-	2	7	3	12	699, 1718
Mil	-	2	7	3	13	1463, 1718
Mil	-	2	7	3	14	1498, 1718
Mil	-	2	7	3	15	1488, 1718
Mil	-	2	7	3	16	1463, 1718
Mil	-	2	7	3	17	1440, 1718
Mil	-	2	7	3	18	699, 1718
Mil	-	2	7	3	19	1458, 1719
Mil	-	2	7	3	20	1440, 1719
Mil	-	2	7	3	21	1472, 1719
Mil	-	2	7	3	22	1565, 1719
Mil	-	2	7	3	23	1565, 1719
Mil	-	2	7	3	24	1447, 1719
Mil	-	2	7	3	25	1489, 1719
Mil	-	2	7	3	26	1489, 1719
Mil	-	2	7	3	27	1719
Mil	-	2	7	3	28	1719
Mil	-	2	7	3	29	1440, 1719
Mil	-	2	7	3	30	1446, 1719
Mil	-	2	7	3	31	1719
Mil	-	2	7	3	32	1719
Mil	-	2	7	3	33	1719
Mil	-	2	7	3	34	1489, 1719
Mil	-	2	7	3	35	1476, 1719
Mil	-	2	7	3	36	1719
Mil	-	2	7	3	37	1719
Mil	-	2	7	3	38	1719
Mil	-	2	7	3	39	1719
Mil	-	2	7	4	1	301, 1719
Mil	-	2	7	4	2	301, 1719
Mil	-	2	7	4	3	303, 1719
Mil	-	2	7	4	4	1378, 1719
Mil	-	2	7	4	5	1462, 1719
Mil	-	2	7	4	6	293, 1719
Mil	-	2	7	4	7	383, 505, 1719
Mil	-	2	7	4	8	862, 1719
Mil	-	2	7	4	9	862, 1719
Mil	-	2	7	4	10	1390, 1719
Mil	-	2	7	4	11	303, 1719
Mil	-	2	7	4	12	302, 1719
Mil	-	2	7	4	13	302, 1719
Mil	-	2	7	4	14	303, 1719
Mil	-	2	7	4	15	862, 1720
Mil	-	2	7	4	16	1407, 1720

Mil - 2 7 4 17 1442, 1720
Mil - 2 7 4 18 598, 1720
Mil - 2 7 4 19 1306, 1720
Mil - 2 7 4 20 1462, 1720
Mil - 2 7 4 21 1446, 1720
Mil - 2 7 4 22 1446, 1720
Mil - 2 7 4 23 698, 1720
Mil - 2 7 4 24 302, 1720
Mil - 2 7 4 25 681, 690, 1720
Mil - 2 7 4 26 690, 1720
Mil - 2 7 4 27 767, 1720
Mil - 2 7 4 28 829, 1720
Mil - 2 7 4 29 1462, 1720
Mil - 2 7 4 30 1446, 1720
Mil * 2 8 - 1 (*4000-acre tract) 6, 1695
Mil * 2 8 - 2 (*4000-acre tract) 9, 1695
Mil - 2 8 4 - 1019
Mil - 2 8 4 1 1546, 1720
Mil - 2 8 4 2 1720
Mil - 2 8 4 3 288, 1720
Mil - 2 8 4 4 288, 1720
Mil - 2 8 4 5 1720
Mil - 2 8 4 6 302, 1720
Mil - 2 8 4 7 302, 1720
Mil - 2 8 4 8 302, 1720
Mil - 2 8 4 9 302, 1720
Mil - 2 8 4 10 302, 1720
Mil - 2 8 4 11 1720
Mil - 2 8 4 12 1720
Mil - 2 8 4 13 302, 1720
Mil - 2 8 4 14 302, 1720
Mil - 2 8 4 15 302, 1720
Mil - 2 8 4 16 302, 1720
Mil - 2 8 4 17 302, 1720
Mil - 2 8 4 18 302, 1720
Mil - 2 8 4 19 1546, 1720
Mil - 2 8 4 20 990, 1721
Mil * 2 9 - 3 (*4000-acre tract)97, 1695
Mil * 2 9 - 4 (*4000-acre tract)11, 1695
Mil * 2 10 - 1 (*4000-acre tract) 189, 1695
Mil * 2 10 - 4 (*4000-acre tract) 259, 1695
Mil - 2 10 2 1 705, 821, 1721
Mil - 2 10 2 2 758, 1721
Mil - 2 10 2 3 804, 1721
Mil - 2 10 2 4 682, 1721
Mil - 2 10 2 5 1721
Mil - 2 10 2 6 639, 1721
Mil - 2 10 2 7 299, 1721
Mil - 2 10 2 8 299, 1721
Mil - 2 10 2 9 1721
Mil - 2 10 2 10 299, 1721
Mil - 2 10 2 11 1107, 1721
Mil - 2 10 2 12 968, 1721
Mil - 2 10 2 13 899, 1721
Mil - 2 10 2 14 1721
Mil - 2 10 2 15 862, 1721
Mil - 2 10 2 16 899, 1721
Mil - 2 10 2 17 737, 1721
Mil - 2 10 2 18 968, 1721
Mil - 2 10 2 19 696, 1721
Mil - 2 10 2 20 1721
Mil - 2 10 2 21 286, 1721
Mil - 2 10 2 22 1721
Mil - 2 10 2 23 1353, 1721
Mil - 2 10 2 24 1271, 1721
Mil - 2 10 2 25 1271, 1721
Mil - 2 10 2 26 1352, 1721
Mil - 2 10 2 27 1352, 1721
Mil - 2 10 2 28 1117, 1720
Mil - 2 10 2 29 1184, 1721
Mil - 2 10 2 30 1352, 1721
Mil - 2 10 2 31 1342, 1721
Mil - 2 10 2 32 1353, 1721
Mil - 2 10 2 33 1721
Mil - 2 10 2 34 1185, 1722
Mil - 2 10 2 35 1380, 1722
Mil - 2 11 3 2 1671
Mil - 2 11 4 1 1722
Mil - 3 1 1 1 344, 456, 1722
Mil - 3 1 1 2 342, 454, 1722
Mil - 3 1 1 3 343, 455, 1722
Mil - 3 1 1 4 590, 1722
Mil - 3 1 1 5 292, 1722
Mil - 3 1 1 6 292, 1722
Mil - 3 1 1 7 1722
Mil - 3 1 1 8 1722
Mil - 3 1 1 9 1722
Mil - 3 1 1 10 416, 543, 1722
Mil - 3 1 1 11 292, 1722
Mil - 3 1 1 12 292, 1722
Mil - 3 1 1 13 292, 1722
Mil - 3 1 1 14 295, 1722
Mil - 3 1 1 15 295, 1722
Mil - 3 1 1 16 1057, 1722
Mil - 3 1 1 17 1449, 1722

Mil	-	3	1	1	18	567, 1722
Mil	-	3	1	1	19	568, 1722
Mil	-	3	1	1	20	568, 1722
Mil	-	3	1	1	21	292, 1722
Mil	-	3	1	1	22	292, 1722
Mil	-	3	1	1	23	558, 1722
Mil	-	3	1	1	24	299, 1722
Mil	-	3	1	1	25	299, 1722
Mil	-	3	1	1	26	295, 1722
Mil	-	3	1	1	27	558, 1722
Mil	-	3	1	1	28	558, 1722
Mil	-	3	1	1	29	568, 1722
Mil	-	3	1	1	30	568, 1722
Mil	-	3	1	1	31	1441, 1722
Mil	-	3	1	1	32	1441, 1723
Mil	-	3	1	1	33	825, 1723
Mil	-	3	1	1	34	828, 1723
Mil	-	3	1	1	35	828, 1723
Mil	-	3	1	1	36	818, 1723
Mil	-	3	1	1	37	818, 1723
Mil	-	3	1	1	38	839, 1723
Mil	-	3	1	1	39	1264, 1723
Mil	-	3	1	1	40	299, 1723
Mil	*	3	2	3	-	(*4000-acre tract) 253, 1695
Mil	*	3	2	-	4	(*4000-acre tract)49, 1695
Mil	*	3	5	-	2	(*4000-acre tract) 222, 1695
Mil	-	3	5	1	1	1536, 1723
Mil	-	3	5	1	2	302, 1723
Mil	-	3	5	1	3	1425, 1723
Mil	-	3	5	1	4	282, 1723
Mil	-	3	5	1	5	301, 1723
Mil	-	3	5	1	6	802, 1723
Mil	-	3	5	1	7	302, 1723
Mil	-	3	5	1	8	1723
Mil	-	3	5	1	9	1723
Mil	-	3	5	1	10	302, 1723
Mil	-	3	5	1	11	282, 1723
Mil	-	3	5	1	12	301, 1723
Mil	-	3	5	1	13	301, 1723
Mil	-	3	5	1	14	301, 1723
Mil	-	3	5	1	15	302, 1723
Mil	-	3	5	1	16	1723
Mil	-	3	5	1	17	1723
Mil	-	3	5	1	18	302, 1723
Mil	-	3	5	1	19	301, 1723
Mil	-	3	5	1	20	301, 1723
Mil	-	3	5	1	21	301, 1723
Mil	-	3	5	1	22	301, 1723
Mil	-	3	5	1	23	302, 1723
Mil	-	3	5	1	24	1723
Mil	-	3	5	1	25	1723
Mil	-	3	5	1	26	301, 1724
Mil	-	3	5	1	27	301, 1724
Mil	-	3	5	1	28	301, 1724
Mil	-	3	5	1	29	301, 1724
Mil	-	3	5	1	30	301, 1724
Mil	-	3	5	1	31	301, 1724
Mil	-	3	5	1	32	301, 1724
Mil	-	3	5	1	33	301, 1724
Mil	-	3	5	1	34	1724
Mil	-	3	6	4	1	302, 1724
Mil	-	3	6	4	2	302, 1724
Mil	-	3	6	4	3	1724
Mil	-	3	6	4	4	1724
Mil	-	3	6	4	5	1724
Mil	-	3	6	4	6	381, 503, 1724
Mil	-	3	6	4	7	381, 503, 1724
Mil	-	3	6	4	8	381, 503, 1724
Mil	-	3	6	4	9	1412, 1724
Mil	-	3	6	4	10	1412, 1724
Mil	-	3	6	4	11	1552
Mil	-	3	7	1	1	865, 1724
Mil	-	3	7	1	2	865, 1724
Mil	-	3	7	1	3	1724
Mil	-	3	7	1	4	965, 1724
Mil	-	3	7	1	5	965, 1724
Mil	-	3	7	1	6	964, 1724
Mil	-	3	7	1	7	862, 1724
Mil	-	3	7	1	8	865, 1724
Mil	-	3	7	1	9	913, 1724
Mil	-	3	7	1	10	862, 1724
Mil	-	3	7	1	11	1218, 1724
Mil	-	3	7	1	12	1528, 1724
Mil	-	3	7	1	13	1581, 1724
Mil	-	3	7	1	14	1597, 1724
Mil	-	3	7	1	15	1561, 1724
Mil	-	3	7	1	16	1724
Mil	-	3	7	1	17	1725
Mil	-	3	7	1	18	1492, 1725
Mil	-	3	7	1	19	913, 1725
Mil	-	3	7	1	20	913, 1725
Mil	-	3	7	1	21	913, 1725
Mil	-	3	7	1	22	1342, 1725
Mil	-	3	7	1	23	1413, 1414, 1725
Mil	-	3	7	1	24	1291, 1725

Mil - 3 7 1 25 1291, 1725
Mil - 3 7 1 26 1547, 1725
Mil - 3 7 1 27 1227, 1725
Mil - 3 7 1 28 1628, 1725
Mil - 3 7 1 29 1725
Mil - 3 7 1 30 964, 1725
Mil - 3 7 1 31 1725
Mil - 3 7 1 32 1725
Mil - 3 7 1 33 1725
Mil - 3 7 1 34 1725
Mil - 3 7 1 35 1592, 1725
Mil - 3 7 1 36 1725
Mil - 3 7 1 37 1725
Mil - 3 7 1 38 1114, 1725
Mil - 3 7 1 39 1114, 1725
Mil - 3 7 1 40 1291, 1725
Mil - 3 7 2 1 1725
Mil - 3 7 2 2 1725
Mil - 3 7 2 3 1725
Mil - 3 7 2 4 1725
Mil - 3 7 2 5 1725
Mil - 3 7 2 6 1547, 1725
Mil - 3 7 2 7 1561, 1725
Mil - 3 7 2 8 1604, 1725
Mil - 3 7 2 9 1725
Mil - 3 7 2 10 1725
Mil - 3 7 2 11 1596, 1725
Mil - 3 7 2 12 1725
Mil - 3 7 2 13 1725
Mil - 3 7 2 14 1726
Mil - 3 7 2 15 1726
Mil - 3 7 2 16 1726
Mil - 3 7 2 17 1726
Mil - 3 7 2 18 1726
Mil - 3 7 2 19 1726
Mil - 3 7 2 20 1726
Mil - 3 7 2 21 1726
Mil - 3 7 2 22 1726
Mil - 3 7 2 23 1605, 1726
Mil - 3 7 2 24 1726
Mil - 3 7 2 25 1726
Mil - 3 7 2 26 1726
Mil - 3 7 2 27 1726
Mil - 3 7 2 28 1726
Mil - 3 7 2 29 1726
Mil - 3 7 2 30 1726
Mil - 3 7 2 31 1726
Mil - 3 7 2 32 1726
Mil - 3 7 2 33 1726
Mil - 3 7 2 34 1726
Mil - 3 7 2 35 1726
Mil - 3 7 2 36 1726
Mil - 3 7 2 37 1726
Mil - 3 7 2 38 1726
Mil - 3 7 2 39 1565, 1726
Mil - 3 7 2 40 1565, 1726
Mil - 3 8 4 1 835, 1726
Mil - 3 8 4 2 850, 1726
Mil - 3 8 4 3 912, 1726
Mil - 3 8 4 4 862, 1726
Mil - 3 8 4 5 862, 1726
Mil - 3 8 4 6 862, 1726
Mil - 3 8 4 7 936, 1726
Mil - 3 8 4 8 1241, 1726
Mil - 3 8 4 9 1625, 1727
Mil - 3 8 4 10 1595, 1727
Mil - 3 8 4 11 1471, 1727
Mil - 3 8 4 12 1471, 1727
Mil - 3 8 4 13 891, 1727
Mil - 3 8 4 14 892, 1727
Mil - 3 8 4 15 945, 1727
Mil - 3 8 4 16 911, 1727
Mil - 3 8 4 17 1431, 1727
Mil - 3 8 4 18 935, 1727
Mil - 3 8 4 19 915, 1727
Mil - 3 8 4 20 911, 1727
Mil - 3 8 4 21 911, 1727
Mil - 3 8 4 22 1566, 1727
Mil - 3 8 4 23 1727
Mil - 3 8 4 24 977, 980, 1727
Mil - 3 8 4 25 1345, 1727
Mil - 3 8 4 26 1727
Mil - 3 8 4 27 1566, 1727
Mil - 3 8 4 28 964, 1727
Mil - 3 8 4 29 980, 1727
Mil - 3 8 4 30 980, 1727
Mil - 3 8 4 31 934, 1727
Mil - 3 8 4 32 1457, 1727
Mil - 3 8 4 33 983, 1727
Mil - 3 8 4 34 1457, 1727
Mil - 3 8 4 35 1568, 1727
Mil - 3 8 4 36 1727
Mil - 3 8 4 37 1727
Mil - 3 8 4 38 1727
Mil - 3 8 4 39 1727
Mil - 3 8 4 40 1661, 1727

Mil	-	3	10	1	1	1247, 1727
Mil	-	3	10	1	2	1249, 1727
Mil	-	3	10	1	3	1292, 1727
Mil	-	3	10	1	4	1292, 1727
Mil	-	3	10	1	5	1248, 1728
Mil	-	3	10	1	6	1643, 1728
Mil	-	3	10	1	7	842, 1728
Mil	-	3	10	1	8	1359, 1728
Mil	-	3	10	1	9	784, 1728
Mil	-	3	10	1	10	1728
Mil	-	3	10	1	11	1728
Mil	-	3	10	1	12	784, 1728
Mil	-	3	10	1	13	736, 1728
Mil	-	3	10	1	14	736, 742, 1728
Mil	-	3	10	1	15	779, 1728
Mil	-	3	10	1	16	778, 1728
Mil	-	3	10	1	17	1728
Mil	-	3	10	1	18	740, 1728
Mil	-	3	10	1	19	736, 740, 1728
Mil	-	3	10	1	20	736, 1728
Mil	-	3	10	1	21	734, 1728
Mil	-	3	10	1	22	738, 1728
Mil	-	3	10	1	23	741, 1728
Mil	-	3	10	1	24	741, 1728
Mil	-	3	10	1	25	1306, 1728
Mil	-	3	10	1	26	1645
Mil	-	3	10	2	1	734, 1728
Mil	-	3	10	2	2	734, 1728
Mil	-	3	10	2	3	739, 1728
Mil	-	3	10	2	4	693, 1728
Mil	-	3	10	2	5	694, 1728
Mil	-	3	10	2	6	743, 1728
Mil	-	3	10	2	7	790, 1728
Mil	-	3	10	2	8	790, 1728
Mil	-	3	10	2	9	790, 1728
Mil	-	3	10	2	10	992, 1728
Mil	-	3	10	2	11	1068, 1728
Mil	-	3	10	2	12	1068, 1728
Mil	-	3	10	2	13	1084, 1728
Mil	-	3	10	2	14	1083, 1728
Mil	-	3	10	2	15	1083, 1729
Mil	-	3	10	2	16	1083, 1729
Mil	-	3	10	2	17	1370, 1729
Mil	*	4	1	-	2	(*4000-acre tract) 147, 1695
Mil	*	4	1	-	3	(*4000-acre tract) 182, 1695
Mil	-	4	4	3	1	1729
Mil	-	4	4	3	2	1729
Mil	-	4	4	3	3	1729
Mil	-	4	4	3	4	1057, 1729
Mil	-	4	4	3	5	812, 1729
Mil	-	4	4	3	6	1729
Mil	-	4	4	3	7	750, 1729
Mil	-	4	4	3	8	1729
Mil	-	4	4	3	9	781, 1729
Mil	-	4	4	3	10	1729
Mil	-	4	4	3	11	1729
Mil	-	4	4	3	12	803, 1729
Mil	-	4	4	3	13	1646, 1729
Mil	-	4	4	3	14	920, 1729
Mil	-	4	4	3	15	859, 1729
Mil	-	4	4	3	16	1729
Mil	-	4	4	3	17	1729
Mil	-	4	4	3	18	859, 1729
Mil	-	4	4	3	19	1729
Mil	-	4	4	3	20	1449, 1729
Mil	-	4	4	3	21	803, 1729
Mil	-	4	4	3	22	1729
Mil	-	4	4	3	23	750, 1729
Mil	-	4	4	3	24	750, 1729
Mil	-	4	4	3	25	803, 1729
Mil	-	4	4	3	26	812, 1729
Mil	-	4	4	3	27	1729
Mil	-	4	4	3	28	1729
Mil	-	4	4	3	29	1729
Mil	-	4	4	3	30	1729
Mil	-	4	4	3	31	1729
Mil	-	4	4	3	32	1729
Mil	-	4	4	3	33	1730
Mil	-	4	4	3	34	1730
Mil	-	4	4	3	35	1730
Mil	-	4	4	3	36	1730
Mil	-	4	4	3	37	1730
Mil	-	4	4	3	38	1730
Mil	-	4	4	3	39	1730
Mil	-	4	4	3	40	1730
Mil	*	4	5	-	1	(*4000-acre tract)79, 1695
Mil	*	4	5	-	2	(*4000-acre tract) 242, 1695
Mil	*	4	5	-	3	(*4000-acre tract) 194, 1695
Mil	*	4	6	-	2	(*4000-acre tract) 111, 1695
Mil	*	4	6	-	3	(*4000-acre tract) 166, 1695
Mil	-	4	10	1	1	1293, 1730
Mil	-	4	10	1	2	993, 1730

Mil - 4 10 1 3 1002, 1730
Mil - 4 10 1 4 1293, 1730
Mil - 4 10 1 5 956, 1730
Mil - 4 10 1 6 1293, 1730
Mil - 4 10 1 7 1293, 1730
Mil - 4 10 1 8 1293, 1730
Mil - 4 10 1 9 1293, 1730
Mil - 4 10 1 10 1293, 1730
Mil - 4 10 2 1 1275, 1730
Mil - 4 10 2 2 1730
Mil - 4 10 2 3 1380
Mil - 4 10 3 1 944, 1730
Mil - 4 10 3 2 867, 1730
Mil - 4 10 3 3 867, 1730
Mil - 4 10 3 4 870, 1730
Mil - 4 10 3 5 869, 1730
Mil - 4 10 3 6 999, 1730
Mil - 4 10 3 7 1342, 1730
Mil - 4 10 3 8 1257, 1730
Mil - 4 10 3 9 1076, 1730
Mil - 4 10 3 10 1355, 1730
Mil - 4 10 3 11 1506, 1730
Mil - 4 10 3 12 1484, 1730
Mil - 4 10 3 13 1283, 1730
Mil - 4 10 3 14 867, 1730
Mil - 4 10 3 15 978, 1730
Mil - 4 10 3 16 998, 1730
Mil - 4 10 3 17 1344, 1730
Mil - 4 10 3 18 946, 1731
Mil - 4 10 3 19 1288, 1731
Mil - 4 10 3 20 1283, 1731
Mil - 4 10 3 21 1288, 1731
Mil - 4 10 3 22 1507, 1731
Mil - 4 10 3 23 1338, 1731
Mil - 4 10 3 24 1544, 1731
Mil - 4 10 3 25 1293, 1731
Mil - 4 10 3 26 1274, 1731
Mil - 4 10 3 27 1250, 1731
Mil - 4 10 3 28 1274, 1731
Mil - 4 10 3 29 1276, 1731
Mil - 4 10 3 30 1293, 1731
Mil - 4 10 3 31 1258, 1731
Mil - 4 10 3 32 1258, 1731
Mil - 4 10 3 33 1274, 1731
Mil - 4 10 3 34 1277, 1731
Mil - 4 10 3 35 1293, 1731
Mil - 4 10 3 36 1293, 1731
Mil - 4 10 3 37 1212, 1731
Mil - 4 10 3 38 1212, 1731
Mil - 4 10 3 39 1259, 1731
Mil - 4 10 3 40 1368
Mil - 5 3 3 1 963, 1731
Mil - 5 3 3 2 963, 1731
Mil - 5 3 3 3 963, 1731
Mil - 5 3 3 3 1731
Mil - 5 3 3 4 966, 1731
Mil - 5 3 3 5 970, 1731
Mil - 5 3 3 6 1009, 1731
Mil - 5 3 3 7 971, 1731
Mil - 5 3 3 8 972, 1731
Mil - 5 3 3 9 1289, 1731
Mil - 5 3 3 10 1155, 1731
Mil - 5 3 3 11 1009, 1731
Mil - 5 3 3 12 973, 1731
Mil - 5 3 3 13 720, 1732
Mil - 5 3 3 14 1017, 1732
Mil - 5 3 3 15 963, 1732
Mil - 5 3 3 16 720, 1732
Mil - 5 3 3 17 903, 1732
Mil - 5 3 3 18 943, 1732
Mil - 5 3 3 19 1034, 1732
Mil - 5 3 3 20 1732
Mil - 5 3 3 21 942, 1732
Mil - 5 3 3 22 1033, 1732
Mil - 5 3 3 23 1108, 1732
Mil - 5 3 3 24 1684, 1732
Mil - 5 3 3 25 1650, 1732
Mil - 5 3 3 26 1649, 1732
Mil - 5 3 3 27 979, 1732
Mil - 5 3 3 28 979, 1732
Mil - 5 3 3 29 1011, 1732
Mil - 5 3 3 30 1009, 1732
Mil - 5 3 3 31 1001, 1732
Mil - 5 3 3 32 1015, 1732
Mil - 5 3 3 33 720, 1732
Mil - 5 3 3 34 723, 1732
Mil - 5 3 3 35 723, 1732
Mil - 5 3 3 36 723, 1732
Mil - 5 3 3 37 1320, 1732
Mil - 5 3 3 38 1279, 1732
Mil - 5 3 3 39 1643, 1732
Mil - 5 3 3 40 1643, 1732
Mil * 5 5 - 1 (*4000-acre tract) 176, 1695
Mil * 5 5 - 2 (*4000-acre tract)40, 1695
Mil * 5 5 - 4 (*4000-acre tract) 183, 1695

Mil	*	5	6	-	1 (*4000-acre tract)	47, 1695
Mil	*	5	6	-	4 (*4000-acre tract)	224, 1696
Mil	-	5	7	1	1	1342, 1732
Mil	-	5	7	1	2	1342, 1732
Mil	-	5	7	1	3	1359, 1732
Mil	-	5	7	1	4	1391, 1732
Mil	-	5	7	1	5	1359, 1732
Mil	-	5	7	1	6	1155, 1732
Mil	-	5	7	1	7	1111, 1732
Mil	-	5	7	1	8	1111, 1733
Mil	-	5	7	1	9	1112, 1733
Mil	-	5	7	1	10	1499, 1733
Mil	-	5	7	1	11	1733
Mil	-	5	7	1	12	1359, 1733
Mil	-	5	7	1	13	1368, 1733
Mil	-	5	7	1	14	1733
Mil	-	5	7	1	15	1733
Mil	-	5	7	1	16	1453, 1733
Mil	-	5	7	1	17	1453, 1733
Mil	-	5	7	1	18	1616, 1733
Mil	-	5	7	1	19	1733
Mil	-	5	7	1	20	1733
Mil	-	5	7	1	21	1733
Mil	-	5	7	1	22	1343, 1733
Mil	-	5	7	1	23	1259, 1733
Mil	-	5	7	1	24	1259, 1733
Mil	-	5	7	1	25	1466, 1733
Mil	-	5	7	1	26	1490, 1547, 1733
Mil	-	5	7	1	27	1268, 1733
Mil	-	5	7	1	28	1733
Mil	-	5	7	1	29	1557, 1733
Mil	-	5	7	1	30	1561, 1733
Mil	-	5	7	1	31	1439, 1733
Mil	-	5	7	1	32	1733
Mil	-	5	7	1	33	1438, 1733
Mil	-	5	7	1	34	1439, 1733
Mil	-	5	7	1	35	1557, 1733
Mil	-	5	7	1	36	1557, 1733
Mil	-	5	7	1	37	1733
Mil	-	5	7	1	38	1580, 1733
Mil	-	5	7	1	39	1548, 1733
Mil	-	5	7	1	40	1466, 1733
Mil	-	5	7	2	6	1547
Mil	-	5	9	3	1	912, 1733
Mil	-	5	9	3	2	1100, 1733
Mil	-	5	9	3	3	1105, 1734
Mil	-	5	9	3	4	1215, 1734
Mil	-	5	9	3	5	1525, 1734
Mil	-	5	9	3	6	913, 1734
Mil	-	5	9	3	7	913, 1734
Mil	-	5	9	3	8	1311, 1734
Mil	-	5	9	3	9	1183, 1734
Mil	-	5	9	3	10	913, 1734
Mil	-	5	9	3	11	913, 1734
Mil	-	5	9	3	12	1106, 1734
Mil	-	5	9	3	13	1123, 1734
Mil	-	5	9	3	14	1123, 1734
Mil	-	5	9	3	15	1104, 1734
Mil	-	5	9	3	16	1106, 1734
Mil	-	5	9	3	17	1092, 1734
Mil	-	5	9	3	18	1201, 1734
Mil	-	5	9	3	19	1091, 1734
Mil	-	5	9	3	20	1109, 1734
Mil	-	5	9	3	21	1099, 1734
Mil	-	5	9	3	22	1089, 1734
Mil	-	5	9	3	23	1081, 1734
Mil	-	5	9	3	24	1098, 1734
Mil	-	5	9	3	25	1084, 1734
Mil	-	5	9	3	26	1088, 1199, 1734
Mil	-	5	9	3	27	1125, 1734
Mil	-	5	9	3	28	1199, 1734
Mil	-	5	9	3	29	1084, 1199, 1734
Mil	-	5	9	3	30	1109, 1734
Mil	-	5	9	3	31	1109, 1734
Mil	-	5	9	3	32	1093, 1734
Mil	-	5	9	3	33	1077, 1734
Mil	-	5	9	3	34	1101, 1734
Mil	-	5	9	3	35	1164, 1734
Mil	-	5	9	3	36	1129, 1734
Mil	-	5	9	3	37	1130, 1734
Mil	-	5	9	3	38	1311, 1735
Mil	-	5	9	3	39	1084, 1735
Mil	-	5	9	3	40	1078, 1735
Mil	-	5	10	3	1	1287, 1735
Mil	-	5	10	3	2	1196, 1735
Mil	-	5	10	3	3	1087, 1735
Mil	-	5	10	3	4	1087, 1735
Mil	-	5	10	3	5	1087, 1735
Mil	-	5	10	3	6	1339, 1735
Mil	-	5	10	3	7	1196, 1735
Mil	-	5	10	3	8	1087, 1735
Mil	-	5	10	3	9	940, 1735
Mil	-	5	10	3	10	1191, 1735
Mil	-	5	10	3	11	1155, 1735
Mil	-	5	10	3	12	1155, 1735

Mil	-	5	10	3	13	1097, 1735
Mil	-	5	10	3	14	1106, 1735
Mil	-	5	10	3	15	1106, 1735
Mil	-	5	10	3	16	1196, 1735
Mil	-	5	10	3	17	1084, 1735
Mil	-	5	10	3	18	1084, 1735
Mil	-	5	10	3	19	1084, 1735
Mil	-	5	10	3	20	1165, 1735
Mil	-	5	10	3	21	1084, 1735
Mil	-	5	10	3	22	1084, 1735
Mil	-	5	10	3	23	1167, 1735
Mil	-	5	10	3	24	1103, 1735
Mil	-	5	10	3	25	1103, 1735
Mil	-	5	10	3	26	1157, 1735
Mil	-	5	10	3	27	1158, 1735
Mil	-	5	10	3	28	1086, 1735
Mil	-	5	10	4	1	1473, 1735
Mil	-	5	10	4	2	1269, 1735
Mil	-	5	10	4	3	1259, 1736
Mil	-	5	10	4	4	1261, 1736
Mil	-	5	10	4	5	1213, 1736
Mil	-	5	10	4	6	1213, 1736
Mil	-	5	10	4	7	374, 495, 1736
Mil	-	5	10	4	8	1294, 1736
Mil	-	5	10	4	9	1273, 1736
Mil	-	5	10	4	10	1273, 1736
Mil	-	5	10	4	11	1273, 1736
Mil	-	5	10	4	12	1273, 1736
Mil	-	5	10	4	13	1272, 1736
Mil	-	5	10	4	14	1272, 1736
Mil	-	5	10	4	15	1019, 1736
Mil	-	5	10	4	16	1256, 1736
Mil	-	5	10	4	17	1259, 1736
Mil	-	5	10	4	18	1273, 1736
Mil	-	5	10	4	19	1235, 1736
Mil	-	5	10	4	20	1255, 1736
Mil	-	5	10	4	21	1255, 1736
Mil	-	5	10	4	22	1226, 1736
Mil	-	5	10	4	23	1315, 1736
Mil	-	5	10	4	24	1214, 1736
Mil	-	5	10	4	25	1635, 1736
Mil	-	5	10	4	26	938, 1736
Mil	-	5	10	4	27	1306, 1736
Mil	-	5	10	4	28	1302, 1736
Mil	-	5	10	4	29	1736
Mil	-	5	10	4	30	1736
Mil	-	5	10	4	31	1290, 1736
Mil	-	5	10	4	32	1340, 1736
Mil	-	5	10	4	33	1255, 1736
Mil	-	5	10	4	34	1255, 1736
Mil	-	5	10	4	35	1265, 1736
Mil	-	5	11	4	31	1290
Mil	*	6	1	3	-	(*4000-acre tract) 257, 1696
Mil	-	6	2	1	1	1118, 1736
Mil	-	6	2	1	2	1084, 1736
Mil	-	6	2	1	3	982, 1736
Mil	-	6	2	1	4	982, 1737
Mil	-	6	2	1	5	982, 1737
Mil	-	6	2	1	6	646, 1737
Mil	-	6	2	1	7	646, 1737
Mil	-	6	2	1	8	646, 1737
Mil	-	6	2	1	9	1014, 1737
Mil	-	6	2	1	10	1014, 1737
Mil	-	6	2	1	11	646, 1737
Mil	-	6	2	1	12	1737
Mil	-	6	2	1	13	1069, 1737
Mil	-	6	2	1	14	1084, 1737
Mil	-	6	2	1	15	1110, 1737
Mil	-	6	2	1	16	1059, 1737
Mil	-	6	2	1	17	1059, 1737
Mil	-	6	2	1	18	1171, 1737
Mil	-	6	2	1	19	1737
Mil	-	6	2	1	20	904, 1737
Mil	-	6	2	1	21	905, 1737
Mil	-	6	2	1	22	906, 1737
Mil	-	6	2	1	23	1014, 1737
Mil	-	6	2	1	24	1494, 1737
Mil	-	6	2	1	25	1158, 1737
Mil	-	6	2	1	26	1065, 1737
Mil	-	6	2	1	27	907, 1737
Mil	-	6	2	1	28	1737
Mil	-	6	2	1	29	1065, 1737
Mil	-	6	2	1	30	1084, 1737
Mil	-	6	2	1	31	1136, 1737
Mil	-	6	2	1	32	1059, 1737
Mil	-	6	2	1	33	900, 1737
Mil	-	6	2	1	34	1032, 1737
Mil	-	6	2	1	35	1022, 1737
Mil	-	6	2	1	36	1025, 1737
Mil	-	6	2	1	37	900, 1737
Mil	-	6	2	1	38	969, 1737
Mil	-	6	2	1	39	1025, 1738
Mil	-	6	2	1	40	1038, 1738
Mil	-	6	2	2	29	375
Mil	*	6	4	-	2	(*4000-acre tract)72, 1696

Mil	*	6	4	-	3	(*4000-acre tract)	157, 1696
Mil	*	6	5	-	1	(*4000-acre tract)	117, 1696
Mil	*	6	5	-	2	(*4000-acre tract)	1, 1696
Mil	*	6	5	-	3	(*4000-acre tract)	165, 1696
Mil	*	6	5	-	4	(*4000-acre tract)	73, 1696
Mil	-	6	5	3	6		811
Mil	-	6	5	3	7		811
Mil	-	6	5	3	15		811
Mil	*	6	6	-	3	(*4000-acre tract)	51, 1696
Mil	*	6	6	-	4	(*4000-acre tract)	80, 1696
Mil	-	6	6	2	1		1076, 1738
Mil	-	6	6	2	2		1085, 1153, 1738
Mil	-	6	6	2	3		1124, 1738
Mil	-	6	6	2	4		1058, 1738
Mil	-	6	6	2	5		1738
Mil	-	6	6	2	6		1738
Mil	-	6	6	2	7		1738
Mil	-	6	6	2	8		1738
Mil	-	6	6	2	9		1336, 1738
Mil	-	6	6	2	10		1127, 1738
Mil	-	6	6	2	11		1183, 1738
Mil	-	6	6	2	12		1160, 1738
Mil	-	6	6	2	13		304, 1738
Mil	-	6	6	2	14		304, 1738
Mil	-	6	6	2	15		1143, 1738
Mil	-	6	6	2	16		1193, 1738
Mil	-	6	6	2	17		1178, 1738
Mil	-	6	6	2	18		1198, 1738
Mil	-	6	6	2	19		1190, 1738
Mil	-	6	6	2	20		304, 1738
Mil	-	6	6	2	21		289, 1738
Mil	-	6	6	2	22		815, 1738
Mil	-	6	6	2	23		298, 1738
Mil	-	6	6	2	24		298, 1738
Mil	-	6	6	2	25		298, 1738
Mil	-	6	6	2	26		298, 1738
Mil	-	6	6	2	27		298, 1738
Mil	-	6	6	2	28		298, 1738
Mil	-	6	6	2	29		1166, 1738
Mil	-	6	6	2	30		1156, 1738
Mil	-	6	6	2	31		1643, 1738
Mil	-	6	6	2	32		1199, 1738
Mil	-	6	6	2	33		1199, 1738
Mil	-	6	6	2	34		1367
Mil	-	6	7	3	1		1192, 1739
Mil	-	6	7	3	2		1195, 1739
Mil	-	6	7	3	3		1163, 1631, 1739
Mil	-	6	7	3	4		1191, 1739
Mil	-	6	7	3	5		1189, 1739
Mil	-	6	7	3	6		1195, 1739
Mil	-	6	7	3	7		1196, 1739
Mil	-	6	7	3	8		1196, 1739
Mil	-	6	7	3	9		1201, 1739
Mil	-	6	7	3	10		1195, 1739
Mil	-	6	7	3	11		1195, 1739
Mil	-	6	7	3	12		1186, 1739
Mil	-	6	7	3	13		1195, 1739
Mil	-	6	7	3	14		1739
Mil	-	6	7	3	15		1739
Mil	-	6	7	3	16		1223, 1739
Mil	-	6	7	3	17		1224, 1739
Mil	-	6	7	3	18		1224, 1739
Mil	-	6	7	3	19		1224, 1739
Mil	-	6	7	3	20		1224, 1739
Mil	-	6	7	3	21		1224, 1739
Mil	-	6	7	3	22		1224, 1739
Mil	-	6	7	3	23		1195, 1739
Mil	-	6	7	3	24		1203, 1739
Mil	-	6	7	3	25		1196, 1739
Mil	-	6	7	3	26		1201, 1739
Mil	-	6	7	3	27		1201, 1739
Mil	-	6	7	3	28		1223, 1739
Mil	-	6	7	3	29		1197, 1739
Mil	-	6	7	3	30		359, 471, 1739
Mil	-	6	7	3	31		380, 502, 1739
Mil	-	6	7	3	32		1739
Mil	-	6	7	3	33		1229, 1739
Mil	-	6	7	3	34		1184, 1739
Mil	-	6	8	2	1		1740
Mil	-	6	8	2	2		1220, 1366, 1740
Mil	-	6	8	2	3		1316, 1740
Mil	-	6	8	2	4		1332, 1740
Mil	-	6	8	2	5		1514, 1740
Mil	-	6	8	2	6		1381, 1740
Mil	-	6	8	2	7		1381, 1740
Mil	-	6	8	2	8		1651, 1740
Mil	-	6	8	2	9		1651, 1740
Mil	-	6	8	2	10		1651, 1740
Mil	-	6	8	2	11		1651, 1740
Mil	-	6	8	2	12		1651, 1740
Mil	-	6	8	2	13		1245, 1740
Mil	-	6	8	2	14		1219, 1740

Mil	-	6	8	2	15	1219, 1740
Mil	-	6	8	2	16	1279, 1740
Mil	-	6	8	2	17	1203, 1740
Mil	-	6	8	2	18	1203, 1740
Mil	-	6	8	2	19	1203, 1740
Mil	-	6	8	2	20	1209, 1740
Mil	-	6	8	2	21	1209, 1740
Mil	-	6	8	2	22	1225, 1740
Mil	-	6	8	2	23	1316, 1740
Mil	-	6	8	2	24	1651, 1740
Mil	-	6	8	2	26	1600, 1740
Mil	-	6	8	2	27	1740
Mil	-	6	8	2	28	1670, 1740
Mil	-	6	8	2	29	1740
Mil	-	6	8	2	30	1209, 1740
Mil	-	6	8	2	31	1209, 1740
Mil	-	6	8	2	32	1209, 1740
Mil	-	6	8	2	33	1366, 1740
Mil	-	6	8	3	1	1513, 1740
Mil	-	6	8	3	2	1237, 1740
Mil	-	6	8	3	3	1480, 1741
Mil	-	6	8	3	4	1229, 1741
Mil	-	6	8	3	5	832, 1741
Mil	-	6	8	3	6	1741
Mil	-	6	8	3	7	1741
Mil	-	6	8	3	8	1158, 1741
Mil	-	6	8	3	9	1228, 1741
Mil	-	6	8	3	10	1741
Mil	-	6	8	3	11	1203, 1741
Mil	-	6	8	3	12	1215, 1741
Mil	-	6	8	3	13	1215, 1741
Mil	-	6	8	3	14	1741
Mil	-	6	8	3	15	1741
Mil	-	6	8	3	16	833, 1741
Mil	-	6	8	3	17	1215, 1741
Mil	-	6	8	3	18	1229, 1741
Mil	-	6	8	3	19	299, 1236, 1741
Mil	-	6	8	3	20	299, 1741
Mil	-	6	8	3	21	301, 1741
Mil	-	6	8	3	22	301, 1741
Mil	-	6	8	3	23	1240, 1741
Mil	-	6	8	3	24	1215, 1741
Mil	-	6	8	3	25	1215, 1741
Mil	-	6	8	3	26	1215, 1741
Mil	-	6	8	3	27	1230, 1741
Mil	-	6	8	3	28	350, 462, 1741
Mil	-	6	8	3	29	1239, 1741
Mil	-	6	8	3	30	1204, 1741
Mil	-	6	8	3	31	301, 1741
Mil	-	6	8	3	32	301, 1741
Mil	-	6	8	3	33	299, 1741
Mil	-	6	8	3	34	299, 1741
Mil	-	6	8	3	35	1371
Mil	-	6	10	3	1	1113, 1741
Mil	-	6	10	3	2	855, 1741
Mil	-	6	10	3	3	855, 1741
Mil	-	6	10	3	4	855, 1741
Mil	-	6	10	3	5	866, 1742
Mil	-	6	10	3	6	1742
Mil	-	6	10	3	7	1742
Mil	-	6	10	3	8	1294, 1742
Mil	-	6	10	3	9	895, 1742
Mil	-	6	10	3	10	894, 1742
Mil	-	6	10	3	11	1742
Mil	-	6	10	3	12	1370
Mil	-	6	10	4	1	372, 493, 1742
Mil	-	6	10	4	2	372, 493, 1742
Mil	-	6	10	4	3	372, 493, 1742
Mil	-	6	10	4	4	372, 493, 1742
Mil	-	6	10	4	5	1094, 1742
Mil	-	6	10	4	6	898, 1742
Mil	-	6	10	4	7	860, 1742
Mil	-	6	10	4	8	860, 1742
Mil	-	6	10	4	9	860, 1742
Mil	-	6	10	4	10	985, 1742
Mil	-	6	10	4	11	1113, 1742
Mil	-	6	10	4	12	887, 1742
Mil	-	6	10	4	13	887, 1742
Mil	-	6	10	4	14	986, 1742
Mil	-	6	10	4	15	987, 1742
Mil	-	6	10	4	16	898, 1742
Mil	-	6	10	4	17	868, 1742
Mil	-	6	10	4	18	868, 1742
Mil	-	6	10	4	19	868, 1742
Mil	-	6	10	4	20	1044, 1742
Mil	-	6	10	4	21	1368
Mil	*	7	1	-	2	(*4000-acre tract)52, 1696
Mil	*	7	1	-	3	(*4000-acre tract)50, 1696
Mil	*	7	1	-	4	(*4000-acre tract) 255, 1696
Mil	*	7	2	-	1	(*4000-acre tract)53, 1696
Mil	*	7	2	-	2	(*4000-acre tract) 137, 1696
Mil	*	7	2	-	3	(*4000-acre tract) 215, 1696
Mil	*	7	3	-	1	(*4000-acre tract)83, 1696
Mil	*	7	3	-	2	(*4000-acre tract)37, 1696

Mil	*	7	3	-	3 (*4000-acre tract)	179, 1696
Mil	*	7	4	-	4 (*4000-acre tract)	153, 1696
Mil	-	7	4	2	1	1267, 1742
Mil	-	7	4	2	2	1037, 1742
Mil	-	7	4	2	3	918, 1742
Mil	-	7	4	2	4	910, 1742
Mil	-	7	4	2	5	1470, 1742
Mil	-	7	4	2	6	1470, 1742
Mil	-	7	4	2	7	1410, 1742
Mil	-	7	4	2	8	1399, 1742
Mil	-	7	4	2	9	1415, 1742
Mil	-	7	4	2	10	1420, 1743
Mil	-	7	4	2	11	1410, 1743
Mil	-	7	4	2	12	1321, 1743
Mil	-	7	4	2	13	1420, 1743
Mil	-	7	4	2	14	1233, 1743
Mil	-	7	4	2	15	951, 1743
Mil	-	7	4	2	16	1743
Mil	-	7	4	2	17	834, 1743
Mil	-	7	4	2	18	876, 1743
Mil	-	7	4	2	19	910, 1743
Mil	-	7	4	2	20	918, 1743
Mil	-	7	4	2	21	919, 1743
Mil	-	7	4	2	22	919, 1743
Mil	-	7	4	2	23	919, 1743
Mil	-	7	4	2	24	918, 1743
Mil	-	7	4	2	25	1398, 1743
Mil	-	7	4	2	26	1416, 1743
Mil	-	7	4	2	27	1410, 1743
Mil	-	7	4	2	28	1417, 1743
Mil	-	7	4	2	29	1417, 1743
Mil	-	7	4	2	30	1229, 1743
Mil	-	7	4	2	31	919, 1743
Mil	-	7	4	2	32	910, 1743
Mil	-	7	4	2	33	919, 1743
Mil	-	7	4	2	34	930, 1743
Mil	-	7	4	2	35	1408, 1743
Mil	-	7	4	2	36	1456, 1743
Mil	-	7	4	2	37	1146, 1743
Mil	-	7	4	2	38	775, 1743
Mil	-	7	4	2	39	772, 1743
Mil	-	7	4	2	40	771, 1743
Mil	*	7	6	-	2 (*4000-acre tract)	17, 1696
Mil	*	7	6	-	3 (*4000-acre tract)	134, 1696
Mil	*	7	6	-	4 (*4000-acre tract)	76, 1696
Mil	-	7	6	1	1	299, 1743
Mil	-	7	6	1	2	1202, 1743
Mil	-	7	6	1	3	1202, 1743
Mil	-	7	6	1	4	1322, 1743
Mil	-	7	6	1	5	299, 1744
Mil	-	7	6	1	6	299, 1744
Mil	-	7	6	1	7	299, 1744
Mil	-	7	6	1	8	299, 1744
Mil	-	7	6	1	9	1618, 1744
Mil	-	7	6	1	10	1618, 1744
Mil	-	7	6	1	11	1426, 1744
Mil	-	7	6	1	12	1206, 1744
Mil	-	7	6	1	13	1512, 1744
Mil	-	7	6	1	14	1416, 1744
Mil	-	7	6	1	15	1649, 1744
Mil	-	7	6	1	16	299, 1744
Mil	-	7	6	1	17	299, 1744
Mil	-	7	6	1	18	1411, 1744
Mil	-	7	6	1	19	1379, 1744
Mil	-	7	6	1	20	1346, 1744
Mil	-	7	6	1	21	1744
Mil	-	7	6	1	22	1348, 1744
Mil	-	7	6	1	23	1326, 1744
Mil	-	7	6	1	24	1360, 1744
Mil	-	7	6	1	25	298, 1744
Mil	-	7	6	1	26	298, 1744
Mil	-	7	6	1	27	298, 1744
Mil	-	7	6	1	28	1426, 1744
Mil	-	7	6	1	29	685, 1744
Mil	-	7	6	1	30	685, 1744
Mil	-	7	6	1	31	685, 1744
Mil	-	7	6	1	32	686, 1744
Mil	-	7	6	1	33	686, 1744
Mil	-	7	6	1	34	686, 1744
Mil	-	7	6	1	35	687, 1744
Mil	-	7	6	1	36	687, 1744
Mil	-	7	6	1	37	1491, 1744
Mil	-	7	6	1	38	298, 1744
Mil	-	7	6	1	39	298, 1744
Mil	-	7	6	1	40	298, 1744
Mil	-	7	6	3	3	1163
Mil	-	7	6	4	21	1372
Mil	*	7	7	-	1 (*4000-acre tract)	107, 1696
Mil	-	7	7	2	1	306, 1745
Mil	-	7	7	2	2	800, 1745
Mil	-	7	7	2	3	1482, 1745
Mil	-	7	7	2	4	1224, 1745
Mil	-	7	7	2	5	1224, 1745

Mil	-	7	7	2	6	861, 1745
Mil	-	7	7	2	7	861, 1745
Mil	-	7	7	2	8	861, 1745
Mil	-	7	7	2	9	1745
Mil	-	7	7	2	10	307, 1745
Mil	-	7	7	2	11	1285, 1745
Mil	-	7	7	2	12	1437, 1745
Mil	-	7	7	2	13	1598, 1745
Mil	-	7	7	2	14	1471, 1745
Mil	-	7	7	2	15	1745
Mil	-	7	7	2	16	306, 1745
Mil	-	7	7	2	17	1745
Mil	-	7	7	2	18	1504, 1745
Mil	-	7	7	2	19	1745
Mil	-	7	7	2	20	1745
Mil	-	7	7	2	21	307, 1745
Mil	-	7	7	2	22	307, 1745
Mil	-	7	7	2	23	307, 1745
Mil	-	7	7	2	24	1745
Mil	-	7	7	2	25	1423, 1745
Mil	-	7	7	2	26	1423, 1745
Mil	-	7	7	2	27	1377, 1745
Mil	-	7	7	2	28	1376, 1745
Mil	-	7	7	2	29	1745
Mil	-	7	7	2	30	1745
Mil	-	7	7	2	31	1745
Mil	-	7	7	2	32	1745
Mil	-	7	7	2	33	1567, 1745
Mil	-	7	7	2	34	1745
Mil	-	7	7	2	35	1745
Mil	-	7	7	2	36	1746
Mil	-	7	7	2	37	1323, 1746
Mil	-	7	7	2	38	1341, 1746
Mil	-	7	7	2	39	1479, 1746
Mil	-	7	7	2	40	1479, 1746
Mil	-	7	8	2	9	299
Mil	-	7	8	2	24	299
Mil	-	7	9	2	1	1205, 1746
Mil	-	7	9	2	2	1281, 1746
Mil	-	7	9	2	3	1210, 1746
Mil	-	7	9	2	4	1279, 1746
Mil	-	7	9	2	5	1280, 1746
Mil	-	7	9	2	6	1303, 1746
Mil	-	7	9	2	7	1013, 1746
Mil	-	7	9	2	8	1013, 1746
Mil	-	7	9	2	9	1199, 1746
Mil	-	7	9	2	10	1199, 1746
Mil	-	7	9	2	11	1198, 1746
Mil	-	7	9	2	12	1208, 1746
Mil	-	7	9	2	13	1030, 1746
Mil	-	7	9	2	14	1221, 1746
Mil	-	7	9	2	15	1222, 1746
Mil	-	7	9	2	16	941, 1746
Mil	-	7	9	2	17	1200, 1746
Mil	-	7	9	2	18	941, 1746
Mil	-	7	9	2	19	1215, 1746
Mil	-	7	9	2	20	1215, 1746
Mil	-	7	9	2	21	1186, 1746
Mil	-	7	9	2	22	1171, 1746
Mil	-	7	9	2	23	1186, 1746
Mil	-	7	9	2	24	1171, 1746
Mil	-	7	9	2	25	773, 1746
Mil	-	7	9	2	26	1746
Mil	-	7	9	2	27	1024, 1746
Mil	-	7	9	2	28	1200, 1746
Mil	-	7	9	2	29	941, 1746
Mil	-	7	9	2	30	957, 1747
Mil	-	7	9	2	31	1375, 1747
Mil	-	7	9	2	32	1238, 1747
Mil	-	7	9	2	33	1361, 1747
Mil	-	7	9	2	34	976, 1747
Mil	-	7	9	2	35	1021, 1747
Mil	-	7	9	2	36	976, 1747
Mil	-	7	9	2	37	773, 1747
Mil	-	7	9	2	38	773, 1747
Mil	-	7	9	2	39	773, 1747
Mil	-	7	10	3	1	1324, 1747
Mil	-	7	10	4	1	1173, 1747
Mil	-	7	10	4	2	1117, 1747
Mil	-	7	10	4	3	1160, 1747
Mil	-	7	10	4	4	1160, 1747
Mil	-	7	10	4	5	1179, 1747
Mil	-	7	10	4	6	1350, 1747
Mil	-	7	10	4	7	1179, 1747
Mil	-	7	10	4	8	1347, 1747
Mil	*	8	1	-	1 (*4000-acre tract)	167, 1696
Mil	*	8	1	-	2 (*4000-acre tract)	127, 1696
Mil	*	8	1	-	3 (*4000-acre tract)	115, 1696
Mil	*	8	1	-	4 (*4000-acre tract)	171, 1696
Mil	-	8	2	1	1	1583, 1747
Mil	-	8	2	1	2	298, 1747
Mil	-	8	2	1	3	298, 1747
Mil	-	8	2	1	4	297, 1747

Mil	-	8	4	3	18	1460, 1750
Mil	-	8	4	3	19	1750
Mil	-	8	4	3	20	1750
Mil	-	8	4	3	21	1750
Mil	-	8	4	3	22	1750
Mil	-	8	4	3	23	1194, 1750
Mil	-	8	4	3	24	1194, 1750
Mil	-	8	4	3	25	1382, 1750
Mil	-	8	4	3	26	1029, 1750
Mil	-	8	4	3	27	1118, 1750
Mil	-	8	4	3	28	1071, 1750
Mil	-	8	4	3	29	1750
Mil	-	8	4	3	30	1750
Mil	-	8	4	3	31	1750
Mil	-	8	4	3	32	1750
Mil	-	8	4	3	33	1072, 1750
Mil	-	8	4	3	34	1065, 1750
Mil	-	8	4	3	35	1336, 1750
Mil	-	8	4	3	36	1029, 1750
Mil	-	8	4	3	37	1065, 1750
Mil	-	8	4	3	38	1076, 1750
Mil	-	8	4	3	39	1750
Mil	-	8	4	3	40	1750
Mil	-	8	4	5	15	1644
Mil	-	8	5	1	1	303, 1751
Mil	-	8	5	1	2	299, 1751
Mil	-	8	5	1	3	299, 1751
Mil	-	8	5	1	4	299, 1751
Mil	-	8	5	1	5	279, 1751
Mil	-	8	5	1	6	304, 1751
Mil	-	8	5	1	7	304, 1751
Mil	-	8	5	1	8	304, 1751
Mil	-	8	5	1	9	301, 1751
Mil	-	8	5	1	10	301, 1751
Mil	-	8	5	1	11	304, 1751
Mil	-	8	5	1	12	304, 1751
Mil	-	8	5	1	13	307, 1751
Mil	-	8	5	1	14	307, 1751
Mil	-	8	5	1	15	307, 1751
Mil	-	8	5	1	16	307, 1751
Mil	-	8	5	1	17	303, 1751
Mil	-	8	5	1	18	1751
Mil	-	8	5	1	19	1751
Mil	-	8	5	1	20	1751
Mil	-	8	5	1	21	783, 1751
Mil	-	8	5	1	22	783, 1751
Mil	-	8	5	1	23	308, 1751
Mil	-	8	5	1	24	308, 1751
Mil	-	8	5	1	25	301, 1751
Mil	-	8	5	1	26	301, 1751
Mil	-	8	5	1	27	1751
Mil	-	8	5	1	28	1751
Mil	-	8	5	1	29	1751
Mil	-	8	5	1	30	1053, 1751
Mil	-	8	5	1	31	1053, 1751
Mil	-	8	5	1	32	1317, 1751
Mil	-	8	5	1	33	1171, 1751
Mil	-	8	5	1	34	1096, 1751
Mil	-	8	5	1	35	1053, 1751
Mil	-	8	5	1	36	366, 487, 1751
Mil	-	8	5	1	37	1752
Mil	-	8	5	1	38	1752
Mil	-	8	5	1	39	1752
Mil	-	8	5	1	40	301, 1752
Mil	-	8	5	1	41	1368
Mil	*	8	6	-	3	(*4000-acre tract)14, 1696
Mil	*	8	6	-	4	(*4000-acre tract)31, 1696
Mil	-	8	7	3	1	1643, 1752
Mil	-	8	7	3	2	1306, 1752
Mil	-	8	7	3	3	1306, 1752
Mil	-	8	7	3	4	1334, 1752
Mil	-	8	7	3	5	1335, 1752
Mil	-	8	7	3	6	1495, 1752
Mil	-	8	7	3	7	1518, 1752
Mil	-	8	7	3	8	1752
Mil	-	8	7	3	9	1752
Mil	-	8	7	3	10	1518, 1752
Mil	-	8	7	3	11	1518, 1752
Mil	-	8	7	3	12	1334, 1752
Mil	-	8	7	3	13	1334, 1752
Mil	-	8	7	3	14	1389, 1752
Mil	-	8	7	3	15	1617, 1752
Mil	-	8	7	3	16	1602, 1752
Mil	-	8	7	3	17	1602, 1752
Mil	-	8	7	3	18	1752
Mil	-	8	7	3	19	1752
Mil	-	8	7	3	20	1752
Mil	-	8	7	3	21	1752
Mil	-	8	7	3	22	1752
Mil	-	8	7	3	23	1752
Mil	-	8	7	3	24	1752
Mil	-	8	7	3	25	1752
Mil	-	8	7	3	26	1752
Mil	-	8	7	3	27	1752
Mil	-	8	7	3	28	1752
Mil	-	8	7	3	29	1752

Tract						Entries
Mil	-	8	7	3	30	1752
Mil	-	8	7	3	31	1752
Mil	-	8	7	3	32	1603, 1753
Mil	-	8	7	3	33	1753
Mil	-	8	7	3	34	1753
Mil	-	8	7	3	35	1753
Mil	-	8	7	3	36	1753
Mil	-	8	7	3	37	1753
Mil	-	8	7	3	38	1753
Mil	-	8	7	3	39	1753
Mil	-	8	7	3	40	1753
Mil	-	8	9	1	1	1333, 1753
Mil	-	8	9	1	2	794, 1753
Mil	-	8	9	1	3	1753
Mil	-	8	9	1	4	1753
Mil	-	8	9	1	5	1753
Mil	-	8	9	1	6	1263, 1753
Mil	-	8	9	1	7	1753
Mil	-	8	9	1	8	1753
Mil	-	8	9	1	9	1207, 1753
Mil	-	8	9	1	10	1207, 1753
Mil	-	8	9	1	11	1753
Mil	-	8	9	1	12	1753
Mil	-	8	9	1	13	1753
Mil	-	8	9	1	14	797, 1753
Mil	-	8	9	1	15	797, 1753
Mil	-	8	9	1	16	795, 1753
Mil	-	8	9	1	17	795, 1753
Mil	-	8	9	1	18	795, 1753
Mil	-	8	9	1	19	1362, 1753
Mil	-	8	9	1	20	1753
Mil	-	8	9	1	21	1753
Mil	-	8	9	1	22	1753
Mil	-	8	9	1	23	1314, 1753
Mil	-	8	9	1	24	1409, 1753
Mil	-	8	9	1	25	807, 1753
Mil	-	8	9	1	26	807, 1753
Mil	-	8	9	1	27	1754
Mil	-	8	9	1	28	1260, 1754
Mil	-	8	9	1	29	1188, 1754
Mil	-	8	9	1	30	813, 1754
Mil	-	8	9	1	31	813, 1754
Mil	-	8	9	1	32	1207, 1754
Mil	-	8	9	1	33	1754
Mil	-	8	9	1	34	1408, 1754
Mil	-	8	9	2	1	1389, 1754
Mil	-	8	9	2	2	1171, 1754
Mil	-	8	9	2	3	928, 1754
Mil	-	8	9	2	4	928, 1754
Mil	-	8	9	2	5	928, 1754
Mil	-	8	9	2	6	1578, 1754
Mil	-	8	9	2	7	813, 1754
Mil	-	8	9	2	8	883, 1754
Mil	-	8	9	2	9	937, 1754
Mil	-	8	9	2	10	1310, 1754
Mil	-	8	9	2	11	1307, 1754
Mil	-	8	9	2	12	1254, 1754
Mil	-	8	9	2	13	1217, 1754
Mil	-	8	9	2	14	1216, 1754
Mil	-	8	9	2	15	1578, 1754
Mil	-	8	9	2	16	889, 1754
Mil	-	8	9	2	17	1262, 1754
Mil	-	8	9	2	18	1262, 1754
Mil	-	8	9	2	19	1295, 1754
Mil	-	8	9	2	20	1295, 1754
Mil	-	8	9	2	21	1754
Mil	-	8	9	2	22	1295, 1754
Mil	-	8	9	2	23	1754
Mil	-	8	9	2	24	884, 1754
Mil	-	8	9	2	25	925, 1754
Mil	-	8	9	2	26	1643
Mil	-	8	9	3	1	1115, 1754
Mil	-	8	9	3	2	1115, 1754
Mil	-	8	9	3	3	1243, 1754
Mil	-	8	9	3	4	1349, 1755
Mil	-	8	9	3	5	1524, 1755
Mil	-	8	9	3	6	929, 1755
Mil	-	8	9	3	7	830, 1755
Mil	-	8	9	3	8	830, 1755
Mil	-	8	9	3	9	1455, 1755
Mil	-	8	9	3	10	929, 1755
Mil	-	8	9	3	11	1450, 1755
Mil	-	8	9	3	12	1755
Mil	-	8	9	3	13	1755
Mil	-	8	9	3	14	1674, 1755
Mil	-	8	9	3	15	1613, 1755
Mil	-	8	9	3	16	1562, 1755
Mil	-	8	9	3	17	1755
Mil	-	8	9	3	18	1579, 1755
Mil	-	8	9	3	19	1579, 1755
Mil	-	8	9	3	20	1755
Mil	-	8	9	3	21	1755
Mil	-	8	9	3	22	1551, 1755
Mil	-	8	9	3	23	1026, 1647, 1755
Mil	-	8	9	3	24	1647, 1663, 1755
Mil	-	8	9	3	25	1401, 1755

Mil - 8 9 3 26 1755
Mil - 8 9 3 27 1755
Mil - 8 9 3 28 1755
Mil - 8 9 3 29 1755
Mil - 8 9 3 30 1755
Mil - 8 9 3 31 1755
Mil - 8 9 3 32 1755
Mil - 8 9 3 33 1658, 1755
Mil - 8 9 3 34 1755
Mil - 8 9 3 35 1755
Mil - 8 9 3 36 1755
Mil - 8 9 3 37 1755
Mil - 8 9 3 38 1755
Mil - 8 9 3 39 1755
Mil - 8 9 3 40 1755
Mil - 8 9 7 27 952
Mil - 9 1 3 1 396, 521, 1756
Mil - 9 1 3 2 396, 521, 1756
Mil - 9 1 3 3 632, 1756
Mil - 9 1 3 4 1756
Mil - 9 1 3 5 623, 1756
Mil - 9 1 3 6 623, 1756
Mil - 9 1 3 7 624, 1756
Mil - 9 1 3 8 624, 1756
Mil - 9 1 3 9 1756
Mil - 9 1 3 10 1756
Mil - 9 1 3 11 304, 1756
Mil - 9 1 3 12 304, 1756
Mil - 9 1 3 13 1756
Mil - 9 1 3 14 1756
Mil - 9 1 3 15 1756
Mil - 9 1 3 16 1756
Mil - 9 1 3 17 1756
Mil - 9 1 3 18 1756
Mil - 9 1 3 19 1756
Mil - 9 1 3 20 1756
Mil - 9 1 3 21 1756
Mil - 9 1 3 22 1756
Mil - 9 1 3 23 721, 1756
Mil - 9 1 3 24 721, 1756
Mil - 9 1 3 25 306, 1756
Mil - 9 1 3 26 306, 1756
Mil - 9 1 3 27 1756
Mil - 9 1 3 28 1756
Mil - 9 1 3 29 288, 1756
Mil - 9 1 3 30 287, 1756
Mil - 9 1 3 31 302, 1756
Mil - 9 1 3 32 302, 1756
Mil - 9 1 3 33 302, 1756
Mil - 9 1 3 34 302, 1756
Mil - 9 1 3 35 287, 1756
Mil - 9 1 3 36 1757
Mil - 9 1 3 37 306, 1757
Mil - 9 1 3 38 306, 1757
Mil - 9 1 3 39 721, 1757
Mil - 9 1 3 40 1757
Mil * 9 2 1 - (*4000-acre tract) 258, 1696
Mil * 9 2 - 2 (*4000-acre tract) 125, 1696
Mil * 9 2 - 3 (*4000-acre tract)36, 1697
Mil * 9 2 - 4 (*4000-acre tract) 178, 1697
Mil - 9 3 1 21 304
Mil - 9 3 1 22 304
Mil * 9 6 - 1 (*4000-acre tract) 216, 1697
Mil * 9 6 - 2 (*4000-acre tract)29, 1697
Mil * 9 6 - 3 (*4000-acre tract)13, 1697
Mil - 9 7 3 1 651, 1757
Mil - 9 7 3 2 1757
Mil - 9 7 3 3 1757
Mil - 9 7 3 4 1757
Mil - 9 7 3 5 1757
Mil - 9 7 3 6 1509, 1757
Mil - 9 7 3 7 1643, 1757
Mil - 9 7 3 8 1299, 1757
Mil - 9 7 3 9 1079, 1757
Mil - 9 7 3 10 1520, 1757
Mil - 9 7 3 11 1757
Mil - 9 7 3 12 1757
Mil - 9 7 3 13 1469, 1757
Mil - 9 7 3 14 885, 1757
Mil - 9 7 3 15 621, 1757
Mil - 9 7 3 16 785, 1757
Mil - 9 7 3 17 1757
Mil - 9 7 3 18 836, 1757
Mil - 9 7 3 19 301, 1757
Mil - 9 7 3 20 301, 1757
Mil - 9 7 3 21 1505, 1757
Mil - 9 7 3 22 1533, 1757
Mil - 9 7 3 23 1757
Mil - 9 7 3 24 1757
Mil - 9 7 3 25 1757
Mil - 9 7 3 26 1757
Mil - 9 7 3 27 1533, 1757
Mil - 9 7 3 28 1757

Mil	-	9	7	3	29	301, 1757
Mil	-	9	7	3	30	304, 1757
Mil	-	9	7	3	31	1758
Mil	-	9	7	3	32	1758
Mil	-	9	7	3	33	1758
Mil	-	9	7	3	34	1426, 1758
Mil	-	9	7	3	35	304, 1758
Mil	-	9	7	3	36	301, 1758
Mil	-	9	7	3	37	301, 1758
Mil	-	9	7	3	38	1758
Mil	-	9	7	3	39	785, 1758
Mil	-	9	7	3	40	785, 1758
Mil	-	9	9	1	1	1578, 1758
Mil	-	9	9	1	2	1337, 1758
Mil	-	9	9	1	3	1400, 1758
Mil	-	9	9	1	4	1645, 1758
Mil	-	9	9	1	5	1450, 1758
Mil	-	9	9	1	6	1402, 1758
Mil	-	9	9	1	7	1450, 1758
Mil	-	9	9	1	8	1522, 1758
Mil	-	9	9	1	9	1758
Mil	-	9	9	1	10	1758
Mil	-	9	9	1	11	1325, 1758
Mil	-	9	9	1	12	1758
Mil	-	9	9	1	13	1758
Mil	-	9	9	1	14	1758
Mil	-	9	9	1	15	1758
Mil	-	9	9	1	16	1758
Mil	-	9	9	1	17	1655, 1668, 1758
Mil	-	9	9	1	18	1455, 1758
Mil	-	9	9	1	19	1758
Mil	-	9	9	2	1	1593, 1758
Mil	-	9	9	2	2	1308, 1758
Mil	-	9	9	2	3	1309, 1758
Mil	-	9	9	2	4	1758
Mil	-	9	9	2	5	1331, 1758
Mil	-	9	9	2	6	1331, 1758
Mil	-	9	9	2	7	1497, 1758
Mil	-	9	9	2	8	1759
Mil	-	9	9	2	9	1331, 1759
Mil	-	9	9	2	10	1759
Mil	-	9	9	2	11	1759
Mil	-	9	9	4	1	1759
Mil	-	9	9	4	2	1759
Mil	-	9	9	4	3	1759
Mil	-	9	9	4	4	1759
Mil	-	9	9	4	5	1759
Mil	-	9	9	4	6	1639, 1759
Mil	-	9	9	4	7	1649, 1759
Mil	-	9	9	4	8	1759
Mil	-	9	9	4	9	1759
Mil	-	9	9	4	10	1244, 1759
Mil	-	9	9	4	11	1456, 1759
Mil	-	9	9	4	12	1759
Mil	-	9	9	4	13	1759
Mil	-	9	9	4	14	1759
Mil	-	9	9	4	15	1451, 1759
Mil	-	9	9	4	16	1537, 1759
Mil	-	9	9	4	17	1759
Mil	-	9	9	4	18	1759
Mil	-	9	9	4	19	1655, 1759
Mil	-	9	9	4	20	1400, 1759
Mil	-	9	9	4	21	1468, 1759
Mil	-	9	9	4	22	1537, 1759
Mil	-	9	9	4	23	1537, 1759
Mil	-	9	9	4	24	1655, 1759
Mil	-	9	9	4	25	1520, 1759
Mil	-	9	9	4	26	1759
Mil	-	9	9	4	27	1610, 1759
Mil	-	9	9	4	28	1759
Mil	-	9	9	4	29	1759
Mil	-	9	9	4	30	1497, 1759
Mil	-	9	9	4	31	1497, 1759
Mil	-	9	9	4	32	1655, 1759
Mil	-	9	9	4	33	1468, 1760
Mil	-	9	9	4	34	1760
Mil	-	9	9	4	35	1468, 1760
Mil	-	9	9	4	36	1306, 1760
Mil	-	9	9	4	37	1301, 1760
Mil	-	9	9	4	38	1760
Mil	-	9	9	4	39	1454, 1760
Mil	-	9	9	4	40	1331, 1658, 1760
Mil	-	9	9	4	41	1760
Mil	-	9	9	4	42	1760
Mil	-	9	9	4	43	1760
Mil	-	9	9	4	44	1760
Mil	-	10	1	2	1	1052, 1760
Mil	-	10	1	2	2	1052, 1760
Mil	-	10	1	2	3	1052, 1760
Mil	-	10	1	2	4	1139, 1760
Mil	-	10	1	2	5	1510, 1760
Mil	-	10	1	2	6	1510, 1760
Mil	-	10	1	2	7	1060, 1760
Mil	-	10	1	2	8	1760
Mil	-	10	1	2	9	1760
Mil	-	10	1	2	10	1387, 1760

Mil	-	10	1	2	11		1020, 1760
Mil	-	10	1	2	12		1020, 1760
Mil	-	10	1	2	13		1760
Mil	-	10	1	2	14		1090, 1760
Mil	-	10	1	2	15		1090, 1760
Mil	-	10	1	2	16		1064, 1760
Mil	-	10	1	2	17		1456, 1760
Mil	-	10	1	2	18		1060, 1266, 1760
Mil	-	10	1	2	19		1305, 1760
Mil	-	10	1	2	20		1337, 1760
Mil	-	10	1	2	21		1284, 1760
Mil	-	10	1	2	22		1278, 1760
Mil	-	10	1	2	23		1379, 1760
Mil	-	10	1	2	24		1511, 1761
Mil	-	10	1	2	25		1061, 1761
Mil	-	10	1	2	26		1041, 1761
Mil	-	10	1	2	27		1282, 1761
Mil	-	10	1	2	28		1061, 1761
Mil	-	10	1	2	29		1041, 1761
Mil	-	10	1	2	30		1040, 1761
Mil	-	10	1	2	31		1061, 1761
Mil	-	10	1	2	32		1379, 1761
Mil	-	10	1	2	33		1383, 1761
Mil	-	10	1	2	34		1286, 1761
Mil	-	10	1	2	35		1063, 1761
Mil	-	10	1	2	36		1007, 1761
Mil	-	10	1	2	37		1041, 1761
Mil	-	10	1	2	38		1048, 1761
Mil	-	10	1	2	39		1047, 1761
Mil	-	10	1	2	40		1062, 1761
Mil	*	10	2	-	1	(*4000-acre tract)	256, 1697
Mil	*	10	2	-	2	(*4000-acre tract)	197, 1697
Mil	*	10	2	-	4	(*4000-acre tract)	260, 1697
Mil	-	10	3	4	1		950, 1761
Mil	-	10	3	4	2		1397, 1761
Mil	-	10	3	4	3		637, 1552, 1761
Mil	-	10	3	4	4		1552, 1761
Mil	-	10	3	4	5		1552, 1761
Mil	-	10	3	4	6		1397, 1761
Mil	-	10	3	4	7		757, 1761
Mil	-	10	3	4	8		757, 1761
Mil	-	10	3	4	9		756, 1761
Mil	-	10	3	4	10		757, 1761
Mil	-	10	3	4	11		1297, 1761
Mil	-	10	3	4	12		1432, 1761
Mil	-	10	3	4	13		1432, 1761
Mil	-	10	3	4	14		1508, 1761
Mil	-	10	3	4	15		1397, 1761
Mil	-	10	3	4	16		1395, 1761
Mil	-	10	3	4	17		1552, 1761
Mil	-	10	3	4	18		1508, 1761
Mil	-	10	3	4	19		1508, 1761
Mil	-	10	3	4	20		1406, 1762
Mil	-	10	3	4	21		755, 1762
Mil	-	10	3	4	22		758, 1762
Mil	-	10	3	4	23		637, 756, 1762
Mil	-	10	3	4	24		346, 458, 1762
Mil	-	10	3	4	25		346, 458, 1762
Mil	-	10	3	4	26		346, 458, 1762
Mil	-	10	3	4	27		637, 756, 1762
Mil	-	10	3	4	28		735, 1762
Mil	-	10	3	4	29		757, 1762
Mil	-	10	3	4	30		1432, 1762
Mil	-	10	3	4	31		1135, 1762
Mil	-	10	3	4	32		1135, 1762
Mil	-	10	3	4	33		289, 1762
Mil	-	10	3	4	34		704, 1762
Mil	-	10	3	4	35		704, 1762
Mil	-	10	3	4	36		712, 1762
Mil	-	10	3	4	37		397, 522, 1762
Mil	-	10	3	4	38		397, 522, 1762
Mil	-	10	3	4	39		369, 490, 1762
Mil	-	10	3	4	40		397, 522, 1762
Mil	*	10	6	-	1	(*4000-acre tract)	168, 1697
Mil	-	10	7	1	1		1429, 1762
Mil	-	10	7	1	2		702, 1762
Mil	-	10	7	1	3		702, 1762
Mil	-	10	7	1	4		702, 1762
Mil	-	10	7	1	5		297, 1762
Mil	-	10	7	1	6		1515, 1762
Mil	-	10	7	1	7		1582, 1762
Mil	-	10	7	1	8		1516, 1762
Mil	-	10	7	1	9		297, 1762
Mil	-	10	7	1	10		279, 1762
Mil	-	10	7	1	11		297, 1762
Mil	-	10	7	1	12		297, 1762
Mil	-	10	7	1	13		1502, 1762
Mil	-	10	7	1	14		792, 1762
Mil	-	10	7	1	15		793, 1763
Mil	-	10	7	1	16		1763
Mil	-	10	7	1	17		1763
Mil	-	10	7	1	18		1642, 1763
Mil	-	10	7	1	19		1763

Mil	-	10	7	1	20		1122, 1763
Mil	-	10	7	1	21		1523, 1763
Mil	-	10	7	1	22		1553, 1763
Mil	-	10	7	1	23		796, 1763
Mil	-	10	7	1	24		297, 1763
Mil	-	10	7	1	25		791, 1763
Mil	-	10	7	1	26		950, 1763
Mil	-	10	7	1	27		1075, 1763
Mil	-	10	7	1	28		1074, 1763
Mil	-	10	7	1	29		1656, 1763
Mil	-	10	7	1	30		1656, 1763
Mil	-	10	7	1	31		1656, 1763
Mil	-	10	7	1	32		1369, 1763
Mil	-	10	7	1	33		1346, 1763
Mil	-	10	7	1	34		1373, 1763
Mil	-	10	7	1	35		1373, 1763
Mil	-	10	7	1	36		1657, 1763
Mil	-	10	7	1	37		1657, 1763
Mil	-	10	7	1	38		1657, 1763
Mil	-	10	7	1	39		950, 1763
Mil	-	10	7	1	40		950, 1763
Mil	-	10	9	1	1		1031, 1763
Mil	-	10	9	1	2		939, 1763
Mil	-	10	9	1	3		1608, 1763
Mil	-	10	9	1	4		1662
Mil	-	10	9	3	1		1763
Mil	-	10	9	3	2		1763
Mil	-	10	9	3	3		1763
Mil	-	10	9	3	4		1763
Mil	-	10	9	3	5		1763
Mil	-	10	9	3	6		1763
Mil	-	10	9	3	7		1763
Mil	-	10	9	3	8		1764
Mil	-	10	9	3	9		1764
Mil	-	10	9	3	10		1764
Mil	-	10	9	3	11		1764
Mil	-	10	9	3	12		1764
Mil	-	10	9	3	13		1764
Mil	-	10	9	3	14		1764
Mil	-	10	9	3	15		1764
Mil	-	10	9	3	16		1764
Mil	-	10	9	3	17		1764
Mil	-	10	9	3	18		1764
Mil	-	10	9	3	19		1764
Mil	-	10	9	3	20		1764
Mil	-	10	9	3	21		1607, 1764
Mil	-	10	9	3	22		1609, 1764
Mil	-	10	9	3	23		1137, 1764
Mil	-	10	9	3	24		1137, 1764
Mil	-	10	9	3	25		1477, 1764
Mil	-	10	9	3	26		1477, 1764
Mil	-	10	9	3	27		1611, 1764
Mil	-	10	9	3	28		1452, 1764
Mil	-	10	9	3	29		1175, 1764
Mil	-	10	9	3	30		1175, 1764
Mil	-	10	9	3	31		1172, 1764
Mil	-	10	9	3	32		1477, 1764
Mil	-	10	9	3	33		1137, 1764
Mil	-	10	9	3	34		279, 1764
Mil	-	10	9	3	35		279, 1764
Mil	*	11	1	-	2	(*4000-acre tract)	201, 1697
Mil	*	11	1	-	3	(*4000-acre tract)	67, 1697
Mil	-	11	1	4	40		896
Mil	*	11	2	-	1	(*4000-acre tract)	90, 1697
Mil	*	11	2	-	2	(*4000-acre tract)	15, 1697
Mil	*	11	2	-	3	(*4000-acre tract)	82, 1697
Mil	*	11	2	-	4	(*4000-acre tract)	86, 1697
Mil	*	11	5	-	1	(*4000-acre tract)	34, 1697
Mil	*	11	6	-	2	(*4000-acre tract)	223, 1697
Mil	-	11	6	1	1		991, 1764
Mil	-	11	6	1	2		995, 1764
Mil	-	11	6	1	3		1211, 1764
Mil	-	11	6	1	4		1140, 1764
Mil	-	11	6	1	5		1140, 1764
Mil	-	11	6	1	6		1169, 1764
Mil	-	11	6	1	7		1131, 1765
Mil	-	11	6	1	8		1131, 1765
Mil	-	11	6	1	9		877, 1765
Mil	-	11	6	1	10		886, 1765
Mil	-	11	6	1	11		886, 1765
Mil	-	11	6	1	12		886, 1765
Mil	-	11	6	1	13		1008, 1765
Mil	-	11	6	1	14		1000, 1765
Mil	-	11	6	1	15		994, 1765
Mil	-	11	6	1	16		988, 1765
Mil	-	11	6	1	17		989, 1765
Mil	-	11	6	1	18		997, 1765
Mil	-	11	6	1	19		1298, 1765
Mil	-	11	6	1	20		1327, 1765
Mil	-	11	6	1	21		967, 1765
Mil	-	11	6	1	22		871, 1765
Mil	-	11	6	1	23		871, 1765
Mil	-	11	6	1	24		861, 1765
Mil	-	11	6	1	25		854, 1765
Mil	-	11	6	1	26		854, 1765

Mil	-	11	9	4	22		1394, 1768
Mil	-	11	9	4	23		311, 423, 1768
Mil	-	11	9	4	24		351, 463, 1768
Mil	-	11	9	4	25		819, 1768
Mil	-	11	9	4	26		819, 1768
Mil	-	11	9	4	27		819, 1768
Mil	-	11	9	4	28		819, 1768
Mil	*	12	1	-	1	(*4000-acre tract)	85, 1697
Mil	*	12	1	-	2	(*4000-acre tract)	195, 1697
Mil	*	12	1	-	3	(*4000-acre tract)	207, 1697
Mil	*	12	1	-	4	(*4000-acre tract)	181, 1697
Mil	*	12	2	-	1	(*4000-acre tract)	59, 1697
Mil	*	12	2	-	2	(*4000-acre tract)	41, 1697
Mil	*	12	2	-	3	(*4000-acre tract)	87, 1697
Mil	*	12	2	-	4	(*4000-acre tract)	169, 1697
Mil	*	12	3	-	1	(*4000-acre tract)	121, 1697
Mil	*	12	3	-	2	(*4000-acre tract)	185, 1697
Mil	*	12	3	-	3	(*4000-acre tract)	208, 1697
Mil	*	12	3	-	4	(*4000-acre tract)	95, 1697
Mil	*	12	4	-	1	(*4000-acre tract)	132, 1697
Mil	*	12	4	-	2	(*4000-acre tract)	152, 1698
Mil	*	12	4	-	3	(*4000-acre tract)	149, 1698
Mil	*	12	5	-	1	(*4000-acre tract)	24, 1698
Mil	*	12	5	-	2	(*4000-acre tract)	245, 1698
Mil	*	12	5	-	3	(*4000-acre tract)	191, 1698
Mil	*	12	5	-	4	(*4000-acre tract)	235, 1698
Mil	*	12	6	-	1	(*4000-acre tract)	148, 1698
Mil	*	12	6	-	2	(*4000-acre tract)	112, 1698
Mil	*	12	6	-	3	(*4000-acre tract)	38, 1698
Mil	*	12	6	-	4	(*4000-acre tract)	110, 1698
Mil	*	12	7	-	1	(*4000-acre tract)	225, 1698
Mil	*	12	7	2	-	(*4000-acre tract)	261, 1698
Mil	*	12	7	-	4	(*4000-acre tract)	42, 1698
Mil	-	12	9	3	1		1176, 1768
Mil	-	12	9	3	2		1351, 1768
Mil	-	12	9	3	3		1177, 1768
Mil	-	12	9	3	4		1351, 1768
Mil	-	12	9	3	5		1234, 1768
Mil	-	12	9	3	6		1161, 1768
Mil	-	12	9	3	7		1162, 1768
Mil	-	12	9	4	1		1152, 1768
Mil	-	12	9	4	2		1152, 1768
Mil	-	12	9	4	3		1354, 1768
Mil	-	12	9	4	4		1300, 1768
Mil	-	12	9	4	5		1182, 1768
Mil	-	12	9	4	6		1152, 1768
Mil	-	12	9	4	7		1152, 1768
Mil	-	12	9	4	8		1182, 1768
Mil	-	12	9	4	9		1182, 1768
Mil	-	12	9	4	10		1319, 1768
Mil	-	12	9	4	11		1151, 1768
Mil	-	12	9	4	12		1150, 1768
Mil	-	12	9	4	13		1150, 1768
Mil	-	12	9	4	14		1150, 1768
Mil	*	13	1	-	1	(*4000-acre tract)	119, 1698
Mil	*	13	1	-	2	(*4000-acre tract)	128, 1698
Mil	*	13	1	-	3	(*4000-acre tract)	150, 1698
Mil	*	13	1	-	4	(*4000-acre tract)	100, 1698
Mil	*	13	2	-	1	(*4000-acre tract)	91, 1698
Mil	*	13	2	-	2	(*4000-acre tract)	68, 1698
Mil	*	13	2	-	3	(*4000-acre tract)	154, 1698
Mil	*	13	2	-	4	(*4000-acre tract)	133, 1698
Mil	*	13	3	-	1	(*4000-acre tract)	144, 1698
Mil	*	13	3	-	2	(*4000-acre tract)	77, 1698
Mil	*	13	3	-	3	(*4000-acre tract)	27, 1698
Mil	*	13	3	-	4	(*4000-acre tract)	92, 1698
Mil	*	13	4	-	1	(*4000-acre tract)	202, 1698
Mil	*	13	4	-	2	(*4000-acre tract)	65, 1698
Mil	*	13	4	-	3	(*4000-acre tract)	25, 1698
Mil	*	13	4	-	4	(*4000-acre tract)	135, 1698
Mil	*	13	5	-	1	(*4000-acre tract)	252, 1698
Mil	*	13	5	-	3	(*4000-acre tract)	26, 1698
Mil	*	13	5	-	4	(*4000-acre tract)	251, 1698
Mil	*	13	6	-	1	(*4000-acre tract)	32, 1698
Mil	*	13	6	-	2	(*4000-acre tract)	193, 1698
Mil	*	13	6	-	3	(*4000-acre tract)	129, 1699

Mil	-	14	8	1	3	307, 1770
Mil	-	14	8	1	4	295, 1770
Mil	-	14	8	3	1	306, 1770
Mil	-	14	8	3	2	306, 1770
Mil	-	14	8	3	3	1770
Mil	-	14	8	3	4	295, 1770
Mil	-	14	8	3	5	283, 1770
Mil	-	14	8	3	6	303, 1770
Mil	-	14	8	3	7	303, 1770
Mil	-	14	8	3	8	303, 1770
Mil	-	14	8	3	9	303, 1770
Mil	-	14	8	3	10	303, 1770
Mil	-	14	8	3	11	303, 1770
Mil	-	14	8	3	12	283, 1770
Mil	-	14	8	3	13	289, 1770
Mil	-	14	8	3	14	1770
Mil	-	14	8	3	15	306, 1770
Mil	-	14	8	3	16	306, 1770
Mil	-	14	8	3	17	306, 1770
Mil	-	14	8	3	18	1018, 1771
Mil	-	14	8	3	19	1771
Mil	-	14	8	3	20	289, 1771
Mil	-	14	8	3	21	303, 1771
Mil	-	14	8	3	22	303, 1771
Mil	-	14	8	3	23	289, 1771
Mil	-	14	8	3	24	306, 1771
Mil	-	14	8	3	25	306, 1771
Mil	-	14	8	3	26	303, 1771
Mil	-	14	8	3	27	289, 1771
Mil	-	14	8	3	28	1771
Mil	-	14	8	3	29	1771
Mil	-	14	8	3	30	306, 1771
Mil	-	14	8	3	31	306, 1771
Mil	-	14	8	3	32	306, 1771
Mil	-	14	8	3	33	295, 1771
Mil	-	14	8	3	34	285, 1771
Mil	-	14	8	3	35	283, 1771
Mil	-	14	8	3	36	306, 1771
Mil	-	14	8	3	37	306, 1771
Mil	*	15	1	-	1	(*4000-acre tract) 175, 1699
Mil	*	15	1	-	4	(*4000-acre tract) 186, 1699
Mil	-	15	1	3	1	657, 1771
Mil	-	15	1	3	2	658, 1771
Mil	-	15	1	3	3	573, 1771
Mil	-	15	1	3	4	574, 1771
Mil	-	15	1	3	5	749, 1771
Mil	-	15	1	3	6	749, 1771
Mil	-	15	1	3	7	643, 1771
Mil	-	15	1	3	8	727, 1771
Mil	-	15	1	3	9	727, 1771
Mil	-	15	1	3	10	808, 1771
Mil	-	15	1	3	11	763, 1771
Mil	-	15	1	3	12	763, 1771
Mil	-	15	1	3	13	1771
Mil	-	15	1	3	14	572, 1771
Mil	-	15	1	3	15	660, 1771
Mil	-	15	1	3	16	659, 1772
Mil	-	15	1	3	17	661, 1772
Mil	-	15	1	3	18	662, 1772
Mil	-	15	1	3	19	656, 1772
Mil	-	15	1	3	20	677, 1772
Mil	-	15	1	3	21	873, 1012, 1772
Mil	-	15	1	3	22	809, 1772
Mil	-	15	1	3	23	808, 1772
Mil	-	15	1	3	24	730, 1772
Mil	-	15	1	3	25	631, 1772
Mil	-	15	1	3	26	684, 1772
Mil	-	15	1	3	27	600, 1772
Mil	-	15	1	3	28	601, 1772
Mil	-	15	1	3	29	633, 1772
Mil	-	15	1	3	30	633, 1772
Mil	-	15	1	3	31	563, 1772
Mil	-	15	1	3	32	563, 1772
Mil	-	15	1	3	33	279, 1772
Mil	-	15	1	3	34	292, 1772
Mil	-	15	1	3	35	306, 1772
Mil	-	15	1	3	36	306, 1772
Mil	-	15	1	3	37	602, 1772
Mil	-	15	1	3	38	603, 1772
Mil	-	15	1	3	39	671, 1772
Mil	-	15	1	3	40	837, 1772
Mil	*	15	2	-	1	(*4000-acre tract)33, 1699
Mil	-	15	2	2	1	764, 1772
Mil	-	15	2	2	2	764, 1772
Mil	-	15	2	2	3	786, 1772
Mil	-	15	2	2	4	786, 1772
Mil	-	15	2	2	5	820, 1772
Mil	-	15	2	2	6	291, 1772
Mil	-	15	2	2	7	305, 1772
Mil	-	15	2	2	8	279, 1772
Mil	-	15	2	2	9	299, 1772
Mil	-	15	2	2	10	279, 1772
Mil	-	15	2	2	11	714, 1773
Mil	-	15	2	2	12	715, 1773
Mil	-	15	2	2	13	786, 1773

Mil	-	15	8	3	12		780, 1776
Mil	-	15	8	3	13		827, 1776
Mil	-	15	8	3	14		954, 1776
Mil	-	15	8	3	15		307, 1776
Mil	-	15	8	3	16		955, 1776
Mil	-	15	8	3	17		766, 1776
Mil	-	15	8	3	18		717, 1776
Mil	-	15	8	3	19		718, 1776
Mil	-	15	8	3	20		718, 1776
Mil	-	15	8	3	21		1776
Mil	-	15	8	3	22		1424, 1776
Mil	-	15	8	4	1		863, 1776
Mil	-	15	8	4	2		751, 1776
Mil	-	15	8	4	3		307, 1776
Mil	-	15	8	4	4		307, 1776
Mil	-	15	8	4	5		307, 1776
Mil	-	15	8	4	6		307, 1776
Mil	-	15	8	4	7		307, 752, 1776
Mil	-	15	8	4	8		307, 1776
Mil	-	15	8	4	9		307, 1776
Mil	-	15	8	4	10		307, 1776
Mil	-	15	8	4	11		754, 1777
Mil	-	15	8	4	12		754, 1777
Mil	-	15	8	4	13		333, 445, 1777
Mil	-	15	8	4	14		314, 426, 1777
Mil	-	15	8	4	15		754, 1777
Mil	-	15	8	4	16		754, 1777
Mil	-	15	8	4	17		611, 1777
Mil	-	15	8	4	18		315, 427, 1777
Mil	-	15	8	4	19		307, 1777
Mil	-	15	8	4	20		307, 1777
Mil	-	15	8	4	21		307, 1777
Mil	-	15	8	4	22		683, 1777
Mil	-	15	8	4	23		683, 1777
Mil	-	15	8	4	24		753, 1777
Mil	-	15	8	4	25		753, 1777
Mil	-	15	8	4	26		752, 899, 1777
Mil	-	15	8	4	27		683, 1777
Mil	-	15	8	4	28		307, 1777
Mil	-	15	8	4	29		307, 1777
Mil	-	15	8	4	30		1675
Mil	-	15	8	5	*	(*torn)	294
Mil	*	16	1	-	1	(*4000-acre tract)	94, 1700
Mil	*	16	1	-	2	(*4000-acre tract)	231, 1700
Mil	*	16	1	-	3	(*4000-acre tract)	22, 1700
Mil	*	16	1	-	4	(*4000-acre tract)	109, 1700
Mil	*	16	2	-	3	(*4000-acre tract)	164, 1700

Mil	-	16	2	4	1		377, 497, 1777
Mil	-	16	2	4	2		377, 497, 1777
Mil	-	16	2	4	3		1777
Mil	-	16	2	4	4		1777
Mil	-	16	2	4	5		1777
Mil	-	16	2	4	6		304, 1777
Mil	-	16	2	4	7		304, 1777
Mil	-	16	2	4	8		304, 377, 497, 1777
Mil	-	16	2	4	9		406, 533, 1777
Mil	-	16	2	4	10		386, 508, 1777
Mil	-	16	2	4	11		377, 497, 1777
Mil	-	16	2	4	12		377, 497, 1777
Mil	-	16	2	4	13		1777
Mil	-	16	2	4	14		281, 1777
Mil	-	16	2	4	15		281, 1777
Mil	-	16	2	4	16		301, 1777
Mil	-	16	2	4	17		301, 1777
Mil	-	16	2	4	18		282, 1778
Mil	-	16	2	4	19		282, 1778
Mil	-	16	2	4	20		281, 1778
Mil	-	16	2	4	21		376, 497, 1778
Mil	-	16	2	4	22		376, 497, 1778
Mil	-	16	2	4	23		376, 497, 1778
Mil	-	16	2	4	24		385, 507, 1778
Mil	-	16	2	4	25		376, 497, 1778
Mil	-	16	2	4	26		376, 497, 1778
Mil	-	16	2	4	27		376, 497, 1778
Mil	-	16	2	4	28		376, 497, 1778
Mil	-	16	2	4	29		282, 1778
Mil	-	16	2	4	30		281, 1778
Mil	-	16	2	4	31		281, 1778
Mil	-	16	2	4	32		281, 1778
Mil	-	16	2	4	33		292, 1778
Mil	-	16	2	4	34		1778
Mil	-	16	2	4	35		370, 491, 1778
Mil	-	16	2	4	36		376, 497, 1778
Mil	-	16	2	4	37		376, 497, 1778
Mil	-	16	2	4	38		376, 497, 1778
Mil	-	16	2	4	39		377, 497, 1778
Mil	-	16	2	4	40		377, 497, 1778
Mil	*	16	3	-	1	(*4000-acre tract)	160, 1700
Mil	*	16	3	-	2	(*4000-acre tract)	247, 1700
Mil	*	16	3	-	3	(*4000-acre tract)	102, 1700
Mil	-	16	3	4	1		304, 1778
Mil	-	16	3	4	2		304, 1778
Mil	-	16	3	4	3		706, 1778

Mil	-	16	3	4	4	706, 1778
Mil	-	16	3	4	5	706, 1778
Mil	-	16	3	4	6	706, 1778
Mil	-	16	3	4	7	581, 1778
Mil	-	16	3	4	8	706, 1778
Mil	-	16	3	4	9	706, 1778
Mil	-	16	3	4	10	1778
Mil	-	16	3	4	11	578, 1778
Mil	-	16	3	4	12	578, 1778
Mil	-	16	3	4	13	578, 1779
Mil	-	16	3	4	14	578, 1779
Mil	-	16	3	4	15	304, 1779
Mil	-	16	3	4	16	304, 581, 1779
Mil	-	16	3	4	17	304, 1779
Mil	-	16	3	4	18	577, 1779
Mil	-	16	3	4	19	577, 1779
Mil	-	16	3	4	20	577, 1779
Mil	-	16	3	4	21	580, 1779
Mil	-	16	3	4	22	580, 1779
Mil	-	16	3	4	23	580, 1779
Mil	-	16	3	4	24	706, 1779
Mil	-	16	3	4	25	706, 1779
Mil	-	16	3	4	26	706, 1779
Mil	-	16	3	4	27	706, 1779
Mil	-	16	3	4	28	583, 1779
Mil	-	16	3	4	29	583, 1779
Mil	-	16	3	4	30	282, 1779
Mil	-	16	3	4	31	301, 1779
Mil	-	16	3	4	32	301, 1779
Mil	-	16	3	4	33	301, 1779
Mil	-	16	3	4	34	301, 1779
Mil	-	16	3	4	35	301, 1779
Mil	-	16	3	4	36	301, 1779
Mil	-	16	3	4	37	301, 1779
Mil	-	16	3	4	38	301, 1779
Mil	-	16	3	4	39	301, 1779
Mil	-	16	3	4	40	301, 1779
Mil	*	16	4	-	2 (*4000-acre tract)	211, 1700
Mil	*	16	4	-	3 (*4000-acre tract)	116, 1700
Mil	*	16	4	-	4 (*4000-acre tract)	159, 1700
Mil	*	16	5	-	1 (*4000-acre tract)	172, 1700
Mil	*	16	5	-	2 (*4000-acre tract)	228, 1700
Mil	*	16	5	-	3 (*4000-acre tract)	45, 1700
Mil	*	16	5	-	4 (*4000-acre tract)	46, 1700
Mil	*	16	6	-	2 (*4000-acre tract)	122, 1700
Mil	*	16	6	-	3 (*4000-acre tract)	143, 1700
Mil	-	16	6	1	1	1779
Mil	-	16	6	1	2	1779
Mil	-	16	6	1	3	933, 1779
Mil	-	16	6	1	4	1006, 1779
Mil	-	16	6	1	5	1006, 1779
Mil	-	16	6	1	6	881, 1779
Mil	-	16	6	1	7	874, 1364, 1779
Mil	-	16	6	1	8	874, 1364, 1779
Mil	-	16	6	1	9	874, 1364, 1780
Mil	-	16	6	1	10	874, 1364, 1780
Mil	-	16	6	1	11	1128, 1780
Mil	-	16	6	1	12	1128, 1780
Mil	-	16	6	1	13	1232, 1780
Mil	-	16	6	1	14	1181, 1780
Mil	-	16	6	1	15	963, 1780
Mil	-	16	6	1	16	917, 1780
Mil	-	16	6	1	17	1039, 1780
Mil	-	16	6	1	18	1039, 1780
Mil	-	16	6	1	19	1159, 1780
Mil	-	16	6	1	20	1159, 1780
Mil	-	16	6	1	21	1073, 1780
Mil	-	16	6	1	22	1080, 1780
Mil	-	16	6	1	23	1358, 1780
Mil	-	16	6	1	24	1364, 1780
Mil	-	16	6	1	25	1364, 1780
Mil	-	16	6	1	26	1073, 1780
Mil	-	16	6	1	27	1073, 1780
Mil	-	16	6	1	28	1073, 1780
Mil	-	16	6	1	29	1464, 1780
Mil	-	16	6	1	30	947, 1780
Mil	-	16	6	1	31	947, 1780
Mil	-	16	6	1	32	947, 1780
Mil	-	16	6	1	33	959, 1780
Mil	-	16	6	1	34	959, 1780
Mil	-	16	6	1	35	959, 1780
Mil	-	16	6	1	36	1464, 1780
Mil	-	16	6	1	37	960, 1780
Mil	-	16	6	1	38	961, 1780
Mil	-	16	6	1	39	1051, 1780
Mil	-	16	6	1	40	1364, 1780
Mil	-	16	6	6	1	910
Mil	-	16	6	6	2	910
Mil	-	16	7	2	1	1049, 1780
Mil	-	16	7	2	2	1049, 1780
Mil	-	16	7	2	3	1047, 1780
Mil	-	16	7	2	4	1045, 1781

Mil	-	16	7	2	5	1049, 1781	Mil	-	16	7	4	12	921, 1782
Mil	-	16	7	2	6	1049, 1781	Mil	-	16	7	4	13	888, 1782
Mil	-	16	7	2	7	1049, 1781	Mil	-	16	7	4	14	888, 1782
Mil	-	16	7	2	8	1050, 1781	Mil	-	16	7	4	15	888, 1782
Mil	-	16	7	2	9	1781	Mil	-	16	7	4	16	579, 1782
Mil	-	16	7	2	10	1121, 1781	Mil	-	16	7	4	17	579, 1782
Mil	-	16	7	2	11	1121, 1781	Mil	-	16	7	4	18	1673, 1782
Mil	-	16	7	2	12	1121, 1781	Mil	-	16	7	4	19	1673, 1782
Mil	-	16	7	2	13	1121, 1781	Mil	-	16	7	4	20	1365, 1782
Mil	-	16	7	2	14	1049, 1781	Mil	-	16	7	4	21	1180, 1782
Mil	-	16	7	2	15	419, 548, 1781	Mil	-	16	7	4	22	1180, 1782
Mil	-	16	7	2	16	420, 549, 1781	Mil	-	16	7	4	23	1180, 1782
Mil	-	16	7	2	17	550, 1781	Mil	-	16	7	4	24	933, 1782
Mil	-	16	7	2	18	551, 1781	Mil	-	16	7	4	25	879, 1782
Mil	-	16	7	2	19	551, 1781	Mil	-	16	7	4	26	880, 1782
Mil	-	16	7	2	20	559, 1781	Mil	-	16	7	4	27	1673, 1782
Mil	-	16	7	2	21	1126, 1781	Mil	-	16	7	4	28	1364, 1782
Mil	-	16	7	2	22	1174, 1781	Mil	-	16	7	4	29	1364, 1782
Mil	-	16	7	2	23	1558, 1781	Mil	-	16	7	4	30	749, 1782
Mil	-	16	7	2	24	1312, 1781	Mil	-	16	7	4	31	749, 1782
Mil	-	16	7	2	25	745, 1781	Mil	-	16	7	4	32	749, 1782
Mil	-	16	7	2	26	1010, 1781	Mil	-	16	7	4	33	724, 1782
Mil	-	16	7	2	27	1010, 1781	Mil	-	16	7	4	34	724, 1782
Mil	-	16	7	2	28	1010, 1781	Mil	-	16	7	4	35	724, 1782
Mil	-	16	7	2	29	559, 1781	Mil	-	16	7	4	36	810, 1783
Mil	-	16	7	2	30	559, 1781	Mil	-	16	7	4	37	810, 1783
Mil	-	16	7	2	31	552, 1781	Mil	-	16	7	4	38	810, 1783
Mil	-	16	7	2	32	552, 1781	Mil	-	16	7	4	39	748, 1783
Mil	-	16	7	2	33	552, 1781	Mil	-	16	7	4	40	875, 1783
Mil	-	16	7	2	34	552, 1781	Mil	-	16	8	3	1	1016, 1783
Mil	-	16	7	2	35	902, 1781	Mil	-	16	8	3	2	933, 1783
Mil	-	16	7	2	36	710, 1781	Mil	-	16	8	3	3	932, 1783
Mil	-	16	7	2	37	710, 1781	Mil	-	16	8	3	4	932, 1783
Mil	-	16	7	2	38	710, 1781	Mil	-	16	8	3	5	932, 1783
Mil	-	16	7	2	39	1781	Mil	-	16	8	3	6	1225, 1783
Mil	-	16	7	2	40	746, 1781	Mil	-	16	8	3	7	1675, 1783
Mil	-	16	7	3	6	1225	Mil	-	16	8	4	1	762, 1783
Mil	-	16	7	4	1	582, 1782	Mil	-	16	8	4	2	762, 1783
Mil	-	16	7	4	2	582, 1782	Mil	-	16	8	4	3	731, 1783
Mil	-	16	7	4	3	582, 1782	Mil	-	16	8	4	4	356, 468, 1783
Mil	-	16	7	4	4	582, 1782	Mil	-	16	8	4	5	695, 1783
Mil	-	16	7	4	5	1465, 1782	Mil	-	16	8	4	6	356, 468, 1783
Mil	-	16	7	4	6	1465, 1782	Mil	-	16	8	4	7	816, 1783
Mil	-	16	7	4	7	1465, 1782	Mil	-	16	8	4	8	890, 1783
Mil	-	16	7	4	8	872, 1782	Mil	-	16	8	4	9	356, 468, 1783
Mil	-	16	7	4	9	1673, 1782	Mil	-	16	8	4	10	356, 468, 1783
Mil	-	16	7	4	10	1672, 1782	Mil	-	16	8	4	11	914, 1783
Mil	-	16	7	4	11	922, 1782	Mil	-	16	8	4	12	1783

Mil	-	16	8	4	13	914, 1783
Mil	-	16	8	4	14	914, 1783
Mil	*	17	1	-	1 (*4000-acre tract)	237, 1700
Mil	*	17	1	-	2 (*4000-acre tract)	214, 1700
Mil	*	17	1	-	3 (*4000-acre tract)	156, 1700
Mil	*	17	1	-	4 (*4000-acre tract)	89, 1700
Mil	*	17	2	-	1 (*4000-acre tract)	71, 1700
Mil	*	17	2	-	2 (*4000-acre tract)	232, 1700
Mil	*	17	2	-	3 (*4000-acre tract)	113, 1700
Mil	*	17	2	-	4 (*4000-acre tract)	55, 1700
Mil	*	17	3	-	1 (*4000-acre tract)	199, 1700
Mil	*	17	3	-	2 (*4000-acre tract)	131, 1701
Mil	*	17	3	-	3 (*4000-acre tract)	106, 1701
Mil	*	17	3	-	4 (*4000-acre tract)	210, 1701
Mil	*	17	4	-	1 (*4000-acre tract)	78, 1701
Mil	*	17	4	-	2 (*4000-acre tract)	230, 1701
Mil	*	17	4	-	3 (*4000-acre tract)	177, 1701
Mil	*	17	4	-	4 (*4000-acre tract)	66, 1701
Mil	*	17	5	-	1 (*4000-acre tract)	204, 1701
Mil	*	17	5	-	2 (*4000-acre tract)	236, 1701
Mil	*	17	5	-	3 (*4000-acre tract)	123, 1701
Mil	*	17	5	-	4 (*4000-acre tract)	233, 1701
Mil	*	17	6	-	1 (*4000-acre tract)	200, 1701
Mil	*	17	6	-	3 (*4000-acre tract)	243, 1701
Mil	*	17	6	-	4 (*4000-acre tract)	158, 1701
Mil	-	17	7	1	1E	552, 1783
Mil	-	17	7	1	1W	1783
Mil	-	17	7	1	2E	1054, 1783
Mil	-	17	7	1	2W	1783
Mil	-	17	7	1	3E	1783
Mil	-	17	7	1	3W	1424, 1783
Mil	-	17	7	1	4E	1783
Mil	-	17	7	1	4W	1005, 1783
Mil	-	17	7	1	5E	1783
Mil	-	17	7	1	5W	1784
Mil	-	17	7	1	6E	1784
Mil	-	17	7	1	6W	1784
Mil	-	17	7	1	7E	1784
Mil	-	17	7	1	7W	962, 1784
Mil	-	17	7	1	8E	1784
Mil	-	17	7	1	8W	1784
Mil	-	17	7	1	9E	1784
Mil	-	17	7	1	9W	1784
Mil	-	17	7	1	10E	401, 1784
Mil	-	17	7	1	10W	1784
Mil	-	17	7	1	11E	1784
Mil	-	17	7	1	11W	1784
Mil	-	17	7	1	12E	1784
Mil	-	17	7	1	12W	1784
Mil	-	17	7	1	13E	1784
Mil	-	17	7	1	13W	1784
Mil	-	17	7	1	14E	1784
Mil	-	17	7	1	14W	1784
Mil	-	17	7	1	15E	1364, 1784
Mil	-	17	7	1	15W	1784
Mil	-	17	7	1	16E	528, 1784
Mil	-	17	7	1	16W	485, 1784
Mil	-	17	7	1	17E	1784
Mil	-	17	7	1	17W	1784
Mil	-	17	7	1	18E	1784
Mil	-	17	7	1	18W	1784
Mil	-	17	7	1	19E	1784
Mil	-	17	7	1	19W	1784
Mil	-	17	7	1	20E	1784
Mil	-	17	7	1	20W	1784
Mil	-	17	7	1	21E	1784
Mil	-	17	7	1	21W	1784
Mil	-	17	7	1	22E	1784
Mil	-	17	7	1	22W	1784
Mil	-	17	7	1	23E	1785
Mil	-	17	7	1	23W	1151, 1785
Mil	-	17	7	1	24E	877, 1785
Mil	-	17	7	1	24W	1502, 1785
Mil	-	17	7	1	25E	1785
Mil	-	17	7	1	25W	1785
Mil	-	17	7	1	26E	1785
Mil	-	17	7	1	26W	1785
Mil	-	17	7	1	27E	1785
Mil	-	17	7	1	27W	1785
Mil	-	17	7	1	28E	1785
Mil	-	17	7	1	28W	1785
Mil	-	17	7	1	29E	1785
Mil	-	17	7	1	29W	1785
Mil	-	17	7	1	30E	1785

Mil	-	17	7	1	30W	1785
Mil	-	17	7	1	31E	1785
Mil	-	17	7	1	31W	1785
Mil	-	17	7	1	32E	1785
Mil	-	17	7	1	32W	1785
Mil	-	17	7	1	33E	1785
Mil	-	17	7	1	33W	1785
Mil	-	17	7	1	34E	1785
Mil	-	17	7	1	34W	1785
Mil	-	17	7	1	35E	1785
Mil	-	17	7	1	35W	1785
Mil	-	17	7	1	36E	1785
Mil	-	17	7	1	36W	1785
Mil	-	17	7	1	37E	1785
Mil	-	17	7	1	37W	1785
Mil	-	17	7	1	38E	1010, 1785
Mil	-	17	7	1	38W	1673, 1785
Mil	-	17	7	1	39	1010
Mil	-	17	7	2	1	857, 1785
Mil	-	17	7	2	2	857, 1785
Mil	-	17	7	2	3	782, 1785
Mil	-	17	7	2	4	782, 1785
Mil	-	17	7	2	5	782, 1785
Mil	-	17	7	2	6	782, 1786
Mil	-	17	7	2	7	848, 1786
Mil	-	17	7	2	8	848, 1786
Mil	-	17	7	2	9	668, 1786
Mil	-	17	7	2	10	1786
Mil	-	17	7	2	11	1786
Mil	-	17	7	2	12	858, 1786
Mil	-	17	7	2	13	858, 1786
Mil	-	17	7	2	14	858, 1786
Mil	-	17	7	2	15	731, 1786
Mil	-	17	7	2	16	949, 1786
Mil	-	17	7	2	17	949, 1786
Mil	-	17	7	2	18	1786
Mil	-	17	7	2	19	1786
Mil	-	17	7	2	20	669, 1786
Mil	-	17	7	2	21	678, 1786
Mil	-	17	7	2	22	774, 1786
Mil	-	17	7	2	23	774, 1786
Mil	-	17	7	2	24	1445, 1786
Mil	-	17	7	2	25	1147, 1786
Mil	-	17	7	2	26	1148, 1786
Mil	-	17	7	2	27	1445, 1786
Mil	-	17	7	2	28	1445, 1786
Mil	-	17	7	2	29	1445, 1786
Mil	-	17	7	2	30	774, 1786

Mil	-	17	7	2	31	774, 1786
Mil	-	17	7	2	32	1558
Mil	-	17	7	4	1	307, 1786
Mil	-	17	7	4	2	307, 1786
Mil	-	17	7	4	3	307, 1786
Mil	-	17	7	4	4	307, 1786
Mil	-	17	7	4	5	307, 1786
Mil	-	17	7	4	6	584, 1786
Mil	-	17	7	4	7	584, 1786
Mil	-	17	7	4	8	584, 1786
Mil	-	17	7	4	9	584, 1786
Mil	-	17	7	4	10	630, 1787
Mil	-	17	7	4	11	398, 526, 1787
Mil	-	17	7	4	12	398, 525, 1787
Mil	-	17	7	4	13	398, 524, 1787
Mil	-	17	7	4	14	398, 523, 1787
Mil	-	17	7	4	15	523, 1787
Mil	-	17	7	4	16	523, 1787
Mil	-	17	7	4	17	653, 1787
Mil	-	17	7	4	18	652, 1787
Mil	-	17	7	4	19	655, 1787
Mil	-	17	7	4	20	400, 527, 1787
Mil	-	17	7	4	21	400, 527, 1787
Mil	-	17	7	4	22	400, 527, 1787
Mil	-	17	7	4	23	674, 1787
Mil	-	17	7	4	24	675, 1787
Mil	-	17	7	4	25	1004, 1787
Mil	-	17	7	4	26	701, 1787
Mil	-	17	7	4	27	417, 544, 1787
Mil	-	17	7	4	28	417, 544, 1787
Mil	-	17	7	4	29	417, 544, 1787
Mil	-	17	7	4	30	417, 544, 1787
Mil	-	17	7	4	31	417, 544, 1787
Mil	-	17	7	4	32	576, 1787
Mil	-	17	7	4	33	576, 1787
Mil	-	17	7	4	34	576, 1787
Mil	-	17	7	4	35	576, 1787
Mil	-	17	7	4	36	399, 547, 1787
Mil	-	17	7	4	37	399, 546, 1787
Mil	-	17	7	4	38	418, 545, 1787
Mil	-	17	7	4	39	654, 1787
Mil	-	17	7	4	40	1475, 1787
Mil	*	18	1	-	1 (*4000-acre tract)	120, 1701
Mil	*	18	1	-	2 (*4000-acre tract)	56, 1701
Mil	*	18	1	-	3 (*4000-acre tract)	234, 1701
Mil	*	18	1	-	4 (*4000-acre tract)	12, 1701
Mil	*	18	2	-	1 (*4000-acre tract)	103, 1701

Mil	*	18	2	-	2	(*4000-acre tract)	198, 1701
Mil	*	18	2	-	3	(*4000-acre tract)	48, 1701
Mil	*	18	2	-	4	(*4000-acre tract)	118, 1701
Mil	*	18	3	-	1	(*4000-acre tract)	206, 1701
Mil	*	18	3	-	2	(*4000-acre tract)	139, 1701
Mil	*	18	3	-	3	(*4000-acre tract)	188, 1701
Mil	*	18	3	-	4	(*4000-acre tract)	75, 1701
Mil	*	18	4	-	1	(*4000-acre tract)	229, 1701
Mil	*	18	4	-	2	(*4000-acre tract)	130, 1701
Mil	*	18	4	-	3	(*4000-acre tract)	54, 1701
Mil	*	18	4	-	4	(*4000-acre tract)	203, 1701
Mil	*	18	5	-	2	(*4000-acre tract)	60, 1701
Mil	*	18	5	-	3	(*4000-acre tract)	23, 1701
Mil	*	18	5	-	4	(*4000-acre tract)	136, 1701
Mil	*	18	6	-	2	(*4000-acre tract)	248, 1702
Mil	*	18	6	-	3	(*4000-acre tract)	57, 1702
Mil	*	18	6	-	4	(*4000-acre tract)	88, 1702
Mil	-	18	7	1	1		882, 1787
Mil	-	18	7	1	2		308, 1787
Mil	-	18	7	1	3		308, 1787
Mil	-	18	7	1	4		308, 1787
Mil	-	18	7	1	5		731, 1787
Mil	-	18	7	1	6		307, 1787
Mil	-	18	7	1	7		307, 1788
Mil	-	18	7	1	8		307, 1788
Mil	-	18	7	1	9		307, 1788
Mil	-	18	7	1	10		760, 1788
Mil	-	18	7	1	11		760, 1788
Mil	-	18	7	1	12		1788
Mil	-	18	7	1	13		1788
Mil	-	18	7	1	14		1788
Mil	-	18	7	1	15		731, 1788
Mil	-	18	7	1	16		759, 1788
Mil	-	18	7	1	17		731, 1788
Mil	-	18	7	1	18		307, 1788
Mil	-	18	7	1	19		307, 1788
Mil	-	18	7	1	20		673, 1788
Mil	-	18	7	1	21		673, 1788
Mil	-	18	7	1	22		1788
Mil	-	18	7	1	23		1788
Mil	-	18	7	1	24		1675
Mil	-	18	7	2	1		670, 1788
Mil	-	18	7	2	2		670, 1788
Mil	-	18	7	2	3		1788
Mil	-	18	7	2	4		1788
Mil	-	18	7	2	5		1788
Mil	-	18	7	2	6		1788
Mil	-	18	7	2	7		663, 1788
Mil	-	18	7	2	8		664, 1788
Mil	-	18	7	2	9		1120, 1788
Mil	-	18	7	2	10		665, 1788
Mil	-	18	7	2	11		1788
Mil	-	18	7	2	12		1788
Mil	-	18	7	2	13		1051, 1653, 1788
Mil	-	18	7	2	14		1654, 1788
Mil	-	18	7	2	15		1659, 1788
Mil	-	18	7	2	16		1660, 1788
Mil	*	19	1	-	1	(*4000-acre tract)	140, 1702
Mil	*	19	1	-	4	(*4000-acre tract)	3, 1702
Mil	-	19	1	2	1		279, 1788
Mil	-	19	1	2	2		279, 1788
Mil	-	19	1	2	3		1465
Mil	*	19	2	-	1	(*4000-acre tract)	205, 1702
Mil	*	19	2	-	4	(*4000-acre tract)	246, 1702
Mil	-	19	2	2	1		298, 1789
Mil	-	19	2	2	2		298, 1789
Mil	-	19	2	2	3		298, 1789
Mil	-	19	2	2	4		297, 1789
Mil	-	19	2	2	5		298, 1789
Mil	-	19	2	2	6		298, 1789
Mil	-	19	2	2	7		297, 1789
Mil	-	19	2	2	8		298, 1789
Mil	-	19	2	2	9		298, 1789
Mil	-	19	2	2	10		297, 1789
Mil	-	19	2	2	11		298, 1789
Mil	-	19	2	2	12		298, 1789
Mil	-	19	2	2	13		298, 1789
Mil	-	19	2	2	14		297, 1789
Mil	-	19	2	2	15		297, 1789
Mil	-	19	2	2	16		297, 1789
Mil	-	19	2	2	17		297, 1789
Mil	-	19	2	2	18		297, 1789
Mil	-	19	2	2	19		297, 1789
Mil	-	19	2	2	20		1374
Mil	-	19	2	3	1		297, 1789
Mil	-	19	2	3	2		297, 1789
Mil	-	19	2	3	3		298, 1789

Mil	-	19	2	3	4		297, 1789
Mil	-	19	2	3	5		297, 1789
Mil	-	19	2	3	6		297, 1789
Mil	-	19	2	3	7		298, 1789
Mil	-	19	2	3	8		297, 1789
Mil	-	19	2	3	9		297, 1789
Mil	-	19	2	3	10		297, 1789
Mil	-	19	2	3	11		297, 1789
Mil	-	19	2	3	12		297, 1789
Mil	-	19	2	3	13		297, 1789
Mil	-	19	2	3	14		279, 1789
Mil	-	19	2	3	15		279, 1789
Mil	*	19	3	-	1	(*4000-acre tract)	63, 1702
Mil	*	19	3	-	2	(*4000-acre tract)	221, 1702
Mil	*	19	3	-	3	(*4000-acre tract)	227, 1702
Mil	*	19	3	-	4	(*4000-acre tract)	105, 1702
Mil	*	19	4	-	1	(*4000-acre tract)	84, 1702
Mil	*	19	4	-	2	(*4000-acre tract)	145, 1702
Mil	*	19	4	-	3	(*4000-acre tract)	62, 1702
Mil	*	19	4	-	4	(*4000-acre tract)	69, 1702
Mil	*	19	5	-	1	(*4000-acre tract)	226, 1702
Mil	*	19	5	-	2	(*4000-acre tract)	43, 1702
Mil	*	19	5	-	3	(*4000-acre tract)	19, 1702
Mil	*	19	5	-	4	(*4000-acre tract)	35, 1702
Mil	*	19	6	-	1	(*4000-acre tract)	219, 1702
Mil	*	19	6	-	2	(*4000-acre tract)	124, 1702
Mil	*	19	6	-	4	(*4000-acre tract)	209, 1702
Mil	*	19	7	-	3	(*4000-acre tract)	244, 1702
Mil	-	19	7	1	1		777, 1789
Mil	-	19	7	1	2		926, 1789
Mil	-	19	7	1	3		776, 1790
Mil	-	19	7	1	4		776, 1790
Mil	-	19	7	1	5		776, 1790
Mil	-	19	7	1	6		776, 1790
Mil	-	19	7	1	7		672, 700, 1790
Mil	-	19	7	1	8		299, 1790
Mil	-	19	7	2	1		1790
Mil	-	19	7	2	2		851, 1790
Mil	-	20	3	1	1		297, 1790
Mil	-	20	3	1	2		297, 1790
Mil	-	20	3	1	3		297, 1790
Mil	-	20	3	1	4		1369
Mil	-	20	4	1	1		298, 1790
Mil	-	20	4	1	2		298, 1790
Mil	-	20	4	1	3		298, 1790
Mil	-	20	4	1	4		298, 1790
Mil	-	20	4	1	5		290, 1790
Mil	-	20	4	1	6		279, 1790
Mil	-	20	4	1	7		298, 1790
Mil	-	20	4	1	8		298, 1790
Mil	-	20	4	1	9		297, 1790
Mil	-	20	4	1	10		298, 1790
Mil	-	20	4	1	11		297, 1790
Mil	-	20	4	1	12		297, 1790
Mil	-	20	4	1	13		297, 1790
Mil	-	20	4	1	14		297, 1790
Mil	-	20	4	1	15		298, 1790
Mil	-	20	4	1	16		298, 1790
Mil	-	20	4	1	17		297, 1790
Mil	-	20	4	1	18		297, 1790
Mil	-	20	4	1	19		298, 1790
Mil	-	20	4	1	20		298, 1790
Mil	-	20	4	4	1		298, 1790
Mil	-	20	4	4	2		298, 1790
Mil	-	20	4	4	3		298, 1790
Mil	-	20	4	4	4		298, 1790
Mil	-	20	4	4	5		279, 1791
Mil	-	20	4	4	6		279, 1791
Mil	-	20	4	4	7		298, 1791
Mil	-	20	4	4	8		297, 1791
Mil	-	20	4	4	9		297, 1791
Mil	-	20	4	4	10		297, 1791
Mil	-	20	4	4	11		297, 1791
Mil	-	20	4	4	12		298, 1791
Mil	*	20	5	-	1	(*4000-acre tract)	64, 1702
Mil	*	20	5	-	4	(*4000-acre tract)	146, 1702
Mil	-	20	5	2	1		297, 1791
Mil	-	20	5	2	2		297, 1791
Mil	-	20	5	2	3		297, 1791
Mil	-	20	5	2	4		297, 1791
Mil	-	20	5	2	5		279, 1791
Mil	*	20	6	-	1	(*4000-acre tract)	126, 1702
Mil	*	20	6	-	4	(*4000-acre tract)	28, 1702
Mil	-	20	6	2	*	(*torn)	299
Mil	-	20	6	2	1		304, 1791
Mil	-	20	6	2	2		304, 1791
Mil	-	20	6	2	3		290, 1791
Mil	-	20	6	2	4		299, 1791
Mil	-	20	6	2	5		299, 1791